HEALTH PSYCHOLOGY
A Biopsychosocial Approach

FIFTH EDITION

Richard O. Straub
University of Michigan, Dearborn

worth publishers
Macmillan Learning

New York

Vice President, Social Sciences: Charles Linsmeier
Senior Associate Editor: Sarah Berger
Development Editor: Jim Strandberg
Editorial Assistant: Melissa Rostek
Senior Marketing Manager: Katherine Nurre
Marketing Assistant: Morgan Ratner
Executive Media Editor: Noel Hohnstine
Media Editor: Stefani Wallace
Media Editorial Assistant: Nik Toner
Media Producer: Joseph Tomasso
Director, Content Management Enhancement: Tracey Kuehn
Managing Editor, Sciences and Social Sciences: Lisa Kinne
Senior Project Editor: Jane O'Neill
Production Supervisor: Robert Cherry
Senior Photo Editor: Christine Buese
Photo Researcher: Teri Stratford
Director of Design, Content Management: Diana Blume
Cover Designer: Blake Logan
Interior Designer: Patrice Sheridan
Art Manager: Matthew McAdams
Composition: codeMantra U.S. LLC
Printing and Binding: LSC Communications
Cover: © Design Pics Inc./Alamy Stock Photo

Library of Congress Control Number: 2016955197

ISBN-13: 978-1-319-01586-2
ISBN-10: 1-319-01586-7

Printed in the United States of America

Second printing

Worth Publishers
One New York Plaza
Suite 4500
New York, NY 10004-1562
www.macmillanlearning.com

For Pam ... still the one

Bill McNeece

About the Author

Richard O. Straub is professor of psychology and founding director of the graduate program in health psychology at the University of Michigan, Dearborn. After receiving his Ph.D. in experimental psychology from Columbia University and serving as a National Institute of Mental Health Fellow at the University of California, Irvine, Dr. Straub joined the University of Michigan faculty in 1979. Since then, he has focused on research in health psychology, especially mind–body issues in stress, cardiovascular reactivity, and the effects of exercise on physical and psychological health. His research has been published in such journals as *Health Psychology,* the *Journal of Applied Social Psychology,* and the *Journal of the Experimental Analysis of Behavior.*

A recipient of the University of Michigan's Distinguished Teaching award and the Alumni Society's Faculty Member of the Year award, Dr. Straub is extensively involved in undergraduate and graduate medical education. In addition to serving on the board of directors of the Southeast Michigan Center for Medical Education and lecturing regularly at area teaching hospitals, he has created an online learning management system for medical residency programs and authored a series of Web-based modules for teaching core competencies in behavioral medicine.

Dr. Straub's interest in enhancing student learning is reflected further in the study guides, instructor's manuals, and critical thinking materials that he has developed to accompany several leading psychology texts by other authors.

The author's professional devotion to health psychology dovetails with his personal devotion to fitness and good health. Dr. Straub has completed hundreds of road races and marathons (including multiple Boston Marathons, Ironman triathlons, and the 2010 Ironman-Hawaii World Championship) and is a nationally ranked, USAT All-American triathlete. With this text, Dr. Straub combines his teaching vocation with a true passion for health psychology.

Brief Contents

Contents

***

Epilogue: Health Psychology Today and
Tomorrow 468

Preface

Not so long ago, health and psychology were separate disciplines, each aware of the other but unable to connect in any meaningful way. Then, in 1978, the field of *health psychology* was born, and it has grown explosively since then. Now, nearly four decades since it emerged as a specific focus of study, an overwhelming and growing body of evidence continues to demonstrate that good health is more than just a physiological state. From the earliest research linking Type A behavior to increased risk for cardiovascular disease, to the most current discoveries regarding psychosocial influences on gene expression and the inflammatory processes involved in cardiovascular disease, cancer, and other chronic diseases, health psychology already has accomplished much.

More important than individual research findings has been the ongoing refinement of the *biopsychosocial model* as an interdisciplinary template for the study of health issues. Increasingly, researchers are able to pinpoint the physiological mechanisms by which anger, loneliness, and other psychosocial factors adversely affect health, and by which optimism, social connectedness, and a strong sense of self-empowerment exert their beneficial effects.

Experiencing these exciting and productive early years of health psychology inspired me to write this text—to share with aspiring students this vitally important field. My goals in this text have been to present current, relevant, well-supported summaries of the main ideas of the field and to model a scientific way of thinking about those ideas in the process. Understanding human behavior and teaching students are my two professional passions, and nowhere have these passions come together more directly for me than in writing this text about how psychology and health are interconnected.

What's New in the Fifth Edition?

In this thoroughly revised fifth edition, my aim continues to be to present the science of health psychology clearly, accurately, and in an accessible voice that helps students make meaningful connections with their own lives. Yet I've introduced a number of significant changes:

- Over 300 new research citations that provide a complete and up-to-date picture of the field

- Significant streamlining to emphasize the most important topics and make room for cutting-edge research in health psychology

- A broader, global, evidence-based perspective that incorporates information from the World Bank, Institute for Health Metrics and Evaluation, and World Health Organization

- Timely new discussion of research ethics and scientific misconduct in Chapter 2, covering informed consent, debriefing, and the need for reproducibility of results in research

- Expanded coverage of minority stress in Chapter 5, including a full-page table on microaggressions experienced frequently by people of color, and the discussion of stress issues related to the LGBT community

- New section added on electronic cigarettes and health concerns associated with "vaping" in Chapter 9

- New material on the resurgence of marijuana in Chapter 9, including growing support for legalization for both medical and recreational use, and long-term impacts on health and brain functions

- Significantly expanded coverage of communicable and noncommunicable diseases, now in its own section in Chapter 12. Topics in this new section include the epidemiological transition, antimicrobial resistance, and emerging infectious diseases such as the Zika virus.

- New *Diversity and Healthy Living* feature box in Chapter 4 on the Stress of Emerging Adulthood

- Significant expansion in coverage of sleep in Chapter 7, including a new subsection on Sleep Loss and Sleep Disorders and discussion of the mounting evidence regarding the health effects of poor sleep

- An updated Epilogue discussing health psychology's current status and most significant future challenges. The Epilogue, which was placed online in the last edition, is placed back in the actual textbook in this fifth edition.

- New coverage of the ongoing implementation and success of the Affordable Health Care Act, including cross-cultural comparisons of how other countries address the basic human right of health care

- Expanded coverage of positive psychology, mindfulness, cognitive behavioral interventions, and more

Trademark Features of This Text

In an effort to communicate the excitement and value of the field, I have maintained my focus on ensuring that students understand—rather than just memorize—the concepts that make up health psychology. I have retained the following key features:

- **Biopsychosocial approach.** The book follows the biopsychosocial model as the basic organizing template. Throughout, I have strived to convey how the components of this model interact dynamically in influencing the well-being of the *whole* person. Each chapter dealing with a specific health problem—on cardiovascular disease and diabetes, cancer, and substance use/abuse, for example—presents a critical analysis of what we know to be the underlying biological, psychological, and social factors in the onset of the health problem, as well as how these factors affect the course of the disease and the outcome. My commitment to this interdisciplinary *systems* perspective on behavior stems from my eclectic graduate training (some would say, inability to make up my mind as to which career path I would follow!) as a student of learning theorist Herbert Terrace, physiological psychologist Richard Thompson, and social psychologist (and health psychology pioneer) Stanley Schachter.

- **Up-to-date coverage.** Few psychological disciplines generate more research each year—and from such a wide variety of related fields—than does health psychology. I have retained the field's classic studies and concepts, but I have also presented the most important recent developments. More than 25 percent of the references in this fifth edition are from research published since 2012. Across the chapters, health statistics have been updated with the most recent demographic and prevalence information available.

- **Fully integrated gender and cultural diversity coverage.** One of my major goals has been to promote understanding of and respect for differences among groups of people and how these differences affect health and illness. This effort extends beyond merely cataloging ethnic, cultural, and gender differences in disease, health beliefs, and behaviors. I have made an in-depth effort to stimulate students' critical thinking regarding the origins of these differences. For example, many differences in health-related behaviors are the product of restrictive social stereotypes and norms, economic forces, and other overarching ecological processes. Whenever possible, the text digs deeply into diversity issues by considering the origins of these behaviors and their implications for health-promoting treatments and interventions. Examples of this integrated coverage are provided in Tables 1, 3, and 4 on pages xvi–xviii. The *Diversity and Healthy Living* **boxes** found throughout the text expand the integrated coverage of gender and multicultural issues by highlighting specific health issues. For example, students will explore why hypertension is so prevalent among African-Americans, and cultural differences in adapting to type 2 diabetes interventions.

- **The life-course perspective.** In integrated coverage throughout the text, students will learn about the special needs and health challenges of people in every season of life. As with gender and diversity, my approach is to teach students to think critically about aging and health. Increasingly, researchers are realizing that much of what was once considered normal aging is actually disease. Many older people who have made healthy lifestyle choices are "rewriting the book" on successful aging. The choices people make as children and adolescents may determine their fates in later years. Table 2 on page xvii outlines examples of coverage of life-span issues.

- **Coverage of complementary and alternative medicine.** According to a recent *Journal of the American Medical Association* report, 4 out of 10 Americans use acupuncture, massage therapy, naturopathy, or some other form of nontraditional medicine. Chapter 15 carefully explores the validity of these high-interest, alternative interventions.

In addition, the fifth edition retains these effective pedagogy and features:

- *Your Health Assets* boxes that give students self-testing opportunities to connect the material to their own experiences. The fifth edition includes two new *Your Health Assets* boxes: One is a self-test on What Is Your Risk of Developing Skin Cancer? and the other is on Health Literacy (the ability to read a nutritional label on a pint of ice cream).

- *Interpreting Data* boxes that help students become more comfortable with the crucial quantitative component of research in a health psychology context.

- End-of-chapter *Weigh In on Health* features that emphasize critical thinking to help students assess their understanding of material and to make meaningful connections between the course and their own life experiences.

- **Helpful study aids.** This text is designed to bring health psychology alive and reinforce learning at every step. Its clean, student-friendly visual appeal is enhanced by numerous clear graphs of research findings, useful and interesting photos, and compelling artwork that illustrates anatomical structures as well as important concepts and processes. In addition, each chapter includes the following learning aids:

a. An engaging **case study** or **vignette** at the beginning of each chapter connects the world of health psychology to some concrete experience and weaves a thread of human interest throughout the chapter. All of these describe real situations. For example, Chapter 11 describes my own family's life-changing battle against the cancer that threatened my young son's life.

b. All important **terms,** which are boldfaced in the body of the text, are defined concisely and clearly in the margins to enhance students' study efforts. All **key terms** and **concepts to remember** are listed, with their page numbers, at the end of each chapter.

c. **End-of-chapter summaries** distill the important points, concepts, theories, and terms discussed in the chapters.

The Multimedia Supplements Package

As an instructor and supplements author, I know firsthand the importance to a textbook of a good, comprehensive teaching package. Fortunately, Worth Publishers has a well-deserved reputation for producing the best psychology supplements around, for both faculty and students. The supplements package includes several valuable components, described next.

Instructor's Resource Manual
The digital *Instructor's Resource Manual* accompanying *Health Psychology*, Fifth Edition, features chapter-by-chapter previews and lectures, learning objectives, suggestions for planning and teaching health psychology, ideas for projects, and more. They are available for download at: www.macmillanlearning .com/psychology

Downloadable Computerized Test Bank in Diploma
The comprehensive *Test Bank,* based on my classroom experience and testing, contains well over 1000 multiple-choice and short-answer essay questions, each keyed to the American Psychological Association's goals for the undergraduate psychology major and Bloom's Taxonomy. The questions include a wide variety of applied, conceptual, and factual questions, and each item is keyed to the topic and page in the text on which the answer can be found. They are available for download at: www.macmillanlearning.com/psychology

Illustration and Lecture Slides
The Lecture Slides to accompany *Health Psychology*, Fifth Edition, focus on key terms and themes from the text and feature tables, graphs, and figures.

The Illustration Slides include all the illustrations, photos, and tables featured in the text. All slides can be used as they are or customized to fit course needs. They are available for download at: www.macmillanlearning.com/ psychology

LaunchPad Solo for *Health Psychology*

The LaunchPad Solo for *Health Psychology* offers a variety of simulations, tutorials, and study aids organized by chapter, including the following:

- **Online quizzing** This helpful feature offers multiple-choice quizzes tied to each of the book's chapters.

- *Check Your Health* These inherently interesting, automatically tallying self-assessments allow students to examine their own health beliefs and behaviors. For example, students will learn about their stress-management styles, their ability to control anger, potential high-risk health behaviors, and cognitive restructuring of headache pain. Each exercise also gives specific tips that encourage students to manage their own health more actively.

- **Critical thinking exercises** The text has two major goals: (1) to help students acquire a thorough understanding of health psychology's knowledge base and (2) to help students learn to think like health psychologists. The second goal—learning to think like psychologists—involves critical thinking. To support this goal directly, the LaunchPad Solo for *Health Psychology* includes a complete exercise for each chapter designed to stimulate students' critical-thinking skills. These skills include asking questions, observing carefully, seeing connections among ideas, and analyzing arguments and the evidence on which they are based.

Table 1 Coverage of Culture and Multicultural Experience

Coverage of culture and multicultural experiences can be found on the following pages:

Acculturation p. 236

African-American adolescents and personal control, p. 126

African-Americans and hypertension, pp. 40–41, 290–291

Alcohol use, p. 225

Antismoking campaigns, p. 268

Body mass and hypertension among African-Americans, p. 333

Cancer

    and age, p. 320

    and diet, pp. 323–324

    screening interventions, p. 333

    survival rates, p. 332

Cardiovascular disease

    racial and ethnic differences in, pp. 289–290

Childbirth pain, pp. 420–421

Death rates among racial/ethnic groups, pp. 4, 17

Diabetes, pp. 304, 306–307

Eating disorders, pp. 235–236

Food deserts, pp. 225–226

Health care use, pp. 381–382, 388–390

Health insurance, pp. 153–155

Health system barriers, pp. 153–155, 388–390

HIV

    counseling and education, p. 366

    intervention, pp. 364, 369–370

    transmission and AIDS, p. 357–358

Immigrants, p. 18

LGBT issues, pp. 89–90, 120–122, 354–355

Microaggressions, p. 120–121

Obesity, pp. 223–226

Optimism and Hispanic-Americans, p. 125

Pain, pp. 420–421

Personal control, p. 129

Smoking cessation programs, p. 269

Sociocultural perspective in health psychology, pp. 17–18

Socioeconomic status

    and cancer, p. 320

    and cardiovascular disease, pp. 298–290

    and health care providers, pp. 390–391

    and health care use, pp. 381–382

    and obesity, pp. 381–382

    and patient communication problems, pp. 390–391

    and provider communication problems, pp. 388–390

Substance abuse, pp. 254–255

Tobacco use, pp. 263–264

Table 2 Coverage of Life-Span Issues

Life-span issues are discussed on the following pages:

Adolescence and
  exercise, p. 184
  hypertension, p. 291
  perceived vulnerability to
  risky behaviors, p. 148
  tobacco use, pp. 264–265
Age differences in sick
  role-behavior, pp. 379–380
Ageism and compliance, p. 380
Age-pain relationship, p. 417
Age-related conditions and
  cortisol, p. 99
Alcohol, pp. 150, 254
Asthma and childhood, p. 68
Cancer
  and age, p. 320
  and children, pp. 320, 341

Children coping with pain and
  medical procedures, p. 423
Cigarette advertising and
  children, pp. 264–265
Cigarette antismoking campaign
  and children, p. 267
Community and wellness,
  pp. 154, 156
Diabetes and age, pp. 304–305
Eating disorders, demographics
  and genders, p. 223
    treatment of, pp. 237–340
HIV/AIDS and age-appropriate
  counseling, pp. 365–367
Life-course perspective,
  pp. 13–14
Longevity and lifestyle, p. 152

Obesity–health relationship
  and age, p. 220
  and gender, pp. 219–221
Optimism and children, p. 125
Reactivity and hypertension in
  children, p. 110
Research methods, pp. 36–37
Resilience in children, p. 123
Seeking health services,
  pp. 379–380
Shaping pain behavior in
  children, p. 423
Sleep and health, pp. 186–187
Smoking and aging, p. 264
Stress and social support,
  pp. 130–131
Workplace, pp. 160–162

Table 3 Coverage of the Psychology of Women and Men

Coverage of the psychology of women and men can be found on the following pages:

AIDS and HIV
  and psychosocial barriers to
  intervention, pp. 370–371
  and transmission,
  pp. 356–357
Alcohol
  and behavior and personality
  traits, pp. 21–22
  dating behavior, p. 257
  gender and drinking contexts,
  pp. 254–255
Cancer, p. 319
Cardiovascular disease,
  p. 289
Coping styles, pp. 117, 119
Gender, stress, and taste,
  p. 223

Gender and obesity,
  pp. 219–220, 224–225
Gender and use of health
  services, pp. 380–381
Gender bias in medicine,
  pp. 18–22
Gender perspective, pp. 18–22
Hostility and anger, p. 294
Male-pattern and female-pattern
  obesity, p. 219
Pain, pp. 417–419
Reactivity and hypertension in
  men, p. 110
Reproductive system,
  pp. 76–79
Role overload and conflict,
  pp. 92–93

Sexism in health care,
  pp. 19–20, 390
Sexually transmitted infections,
  pp. 358–359
Sexual practices, p. 367
Sick role behavior, pp. 379–381
Smoking cessation programs,
  pp. 270, 273
Social support and effects on
  PSA, pp. 131–132
Stress response, pp. 96,
  98–99, 117
Substance abuse, pp. 254–255
Use of health care services,
  pp. 380–381

Table 4 Coverage of Women's Health

Coverage of women's health can be found on the following pages:

AIDS, pp. 356–357

Alcohol and pregnancy, p. 256

Body image and the media, pp. 236–237

Body image dissatisfaction, pp. 234–237

Breast cancer
  and relationship to alcohol, p. 323
  coping with, p. 336
  and diet, pp. 323–324
  and emotional disclosure, pp. 342–343
  and ethnic differences, p. 320

and exercise, p. 325

and heredity, pp. 325–326

and Nurses' Health Study, p. 324

and obesity, p. 325

and social support, pp. 340–341

Caregiving role and stress, pp. 95–96

Eating disorders, pp. 232–240
  treatment of, pp. 237–240

Employment and health, pp. 90–95

Fertilization, pp. 77–78

HIV transmission
  with breast feeding, p. 357
  during pregnancy, p. 358

Lung cancer, pp. 319, 322

Medical treatment, in comparison to males, pp. 18–22

Reactivity with bullying, p. 110

Self-efficacy and high-risk sexual behaviors, pp. 366–368, 369–370

Smoking and miscarriage, p. 263

Table 5 Coverage of Positive Health Psychology

Coverage of positive health psychology can be found on the following pages:

Alcohol abuse prevention programs, pp. 261–262

Behavioral control, pp. 396–398

Cancer-fighting foods, p. 324

Daily uplifts and stress, p. 87

Education programs, pp. 261–262, 267–268, 366–367

Explanatory style, pp. 123–126

Family therapy, p. 238

Health behaviors, pp. 145–150

Health psychology interventions, defined, pp. 23–24

Heart and healthy diets, pp. 293, 302

Hospitalization, increasing perceived control prior to, pp. 393–394

Hostility and anger, control of, pp. 303–304

Hypertension, control of, pp. 301–302

Nutrition, pp. 208–213

Optimism
  and coping with cancer, p. 336
  and immune system health, pp. 124–126

Personal control and self-efficacy, pp. 126–127

Reducing cholesterol, p. 302

Relaxation, pp. 135–136

Resilience, pp. 122–123

Self-efficacy beliefs in safer sex behaviors, pp. 366–368, 369–370

Self-regulation, pp. 127–130

Smoking
  and effects of, pp. 263–264
  inoculation programs, pp. 268–269

Social support
  and cancer, pp. 340–341
  and cardiovascular disease, p. 298
  and health and mortality, pp. 130–133
  and physiology, pp. 130–133

Work site wellness programs, pp. 161–162

- **Interactive flashcards** Students can use these flashcards for tutoring on all chapter and text terminology, and then to quiz themselves on those terms.
- **PsychSim: Interactive Exercises for Psychology** Key modules from these series (by Thomas Ludwig, a psychology professor at Hope College) allow students to explore research topics, participate in experiments and simulations, and apply health psychology to real-world issues.
- *Health Psychology* **video activities** consist of a collection of video clips spanning the topics in the book.

LaunchPad Solo for *Health Psychology* is available without charge when packaged with this fifth edition of *Health Psychology*, using ISBN 1-319-11584-5. Alternatively, LaunchPad Solo for *Health Psychology* can be previewed and purchased at: launchpadworks.com.

Acknowledgments

Although as the author, my name is on the cover of this book, I certainly did not write the book alone. Writing a textbook is a complex task involving the collaborative efforts of a large number of very talented people.

Many of my colleagues played a role in helping me develop this text over the years. I am indebted to the dozens of academic reviewers who read part or all of this book, providing constructive criticism, suggestions, or just an encouraging word. Their input made this a much better book, and I hope they forgive me for the few suggestions not followed.

I begin by thanking the following reviewers for their excellent advice and encouraging words in the creation of this thoroughly revised **fifth edition** and its multimedia supplements:

Anthony Austin
*University of Arkansas
at Pine Bluff*

Donald DeLorey
University of West Florida

Marc Dingman
*Pennsylvania State
University*

Deborah Flynn
Canadore College

Tawanda Greer
*University of South
Carolina—Columbia*

Erin Merz
*California State University—
Dominiguez Hills*

Jeremy Moss
Swedish Institute

Erin O'Hea
Stonehill College

Kari-Lyn Sakuma
Oregon State University

Brian M. Saltsman
Allegheny College

Barbara Stetson
University of Louisville

Kevin Thompson
University of South Florida

Michelle Williams
Holyoke Community College

I thank the following reviewers for their excellent advice and consultation during the **first, second, third,** and **fourth edition** process:

Christine Abbott
Johnson County Community College

David Abwender
State University of New York at Brockport

Christopher Agnew
Purdue University

Jean Ayers
Towson University

Justin Bailey
Limestone College

Mary Jill Blackwell
DePaul University

Joy Berrenberg
University of Colorado

Amy Badura Brack
Creighton University

Pamela Brouillard
Texas A&M—Corpus Christi

Marion Cohn
Ohio Dominican University

Karen J. Coleman
University of Texas at El Paso

Mark E. Christians
Dordt College

Dale V. Doty
Monroe Community College

Dennis G. Fisher
California State University Long Beach

Deborah Flynn
Nipissing University

Phyllis R. Freeman
State University of New York at New Paltz

Tim Freson
Washington State University

Eliot Friedman
Williams College

Sharon Gillespie
Andrews University

Arthur J. Gonchar
University of La Verne

Bonnie A. Gray
Scottsdale Community College

Linda R. Guthrie
Tennessee State University

Carol A. Hayes
Delta State University

Donna Henderson-King
Grand Valley State University

Rob Hoff
Mercyhurst University

April Kindrick
South Puget Sound Community College

Marc Kiviniemi
University of Nebraska—Lincoln

Robin Kowalski
Western Carolina University

Kristi Lane
Winona State University

Sherri B. Lantinga
Dordt College

Sheryl Leytham
Grand View University

Mee-Gaik Lim
Southeastern Oklahoma State University

Robyn Long
Baker University

Linda Luecken
Arizona State University

Angelina Mackewn
University of Tennessee at Martin

Jon Macy
Indiana University

Dr. J. Davis Mannino
Santa Rosa Junior College

Charlotte Markey
Rutgers University

Leslie Martin
La Sierra University

Cathleen McGreal
Michigan State University

Julie Ann McIntyre
Russell Sage College

Matthias R. Mehl
University of Arizona

Katie Mosack
University of Wisconsin—Milwaukee

James P. Motiff
Hope College

David Nelson
Sam Houston State University

Virginia Norris
South Dakota State University

John Pilosi
Pennsylvania State University

Amy Posey
Benedictine College

Mary Pritchard
Boise State University

Kathleen M. Schiaffino
Fordham University

Elisabeth Sherwin
University of Arkansas at Little Rock

Eve Sledjeski
Kent State University

Margaret K. Snooks
University of Houston—Clear Lake

Rebecca Spencer
University of Massachusetts Amherst

Peter Spiegel
California State University, San Bernardino

Amy Starosta
University at Albany, State University of New York

Alexandra Stillman
Saint Paul College

Gabriele B. Sweidel
Kutztown University of Pennsylvania

Richard J. Tafalla
University of Wisconsin—Stout

Christy Teranishi
Texas A&M International University

Benjamin Toll
Yale School of Medicine

Diane C. Tucker
University of Alabama at Birmingham

Rebecca Warner
University of New Hampshire

Eric P. Wiertelak
Macalester College

Nancy L. Worsham
Gonzaga University

David M. Young
Indiana University—Purdue University at Fort Wayne

Diane Zelman
California School of Professional Psychology

At Worth Publishers—a company that lets nothing stand in the way of producing the finest textbooks possible—a number of people played key roles. Chief among these are Vice President of Content Management Catherine Woods, whose initial interest, vision, and unflagging support gave me the push needed to start the project and sustained me throughout; Senior Associate Editor Sarah Berger, whose wonderful hands-on approach and attention to detail were key factors in building our new team and the conceptualization and execution of this edition; Director of Content Management Enhancement Tracey Kuehn, Managing Editor Lisa Kinne, Senior Project Editor Jane O'Neill, Production Supervisor Bob Cherry, Copyeditor Sharon Kraus, and Proofreader Andrew Roney, who worked wonders throughout production to keep us on course; Art Manager Matthew McAdams, Senior Design Manager Blake Logan, and Interior Designer Patrice Sheridan, whose creative vision resulted in the distinctive design and beautiful art program that exceeded my expectations; Editorial Assistant Melissa Rostek, who meticulously prepared manuscript for production and commissioned reviews and surveys to inform the revision; Executive Marketing Manager Katherine Nurre, who has enthusiastically championed

Health Psychology since its second edition and Senior Photo Editor Christine Buese and Photo Researcher Teri Stratford, who researched the photos that helped give the book its tremendous visual appeal. Finally, no one deserves more credit than Development Editor Jim Strandberg. Jim's skillful editing, encouragement, and as-needed prodding brought out the best in me. His influence can be found on virtually every page.

As ever, my heartfelt thanks go to Pam, for her unwavering confidence and support; to Jeremy, Rebecca, and Melissa, for helping me keep things in perspective; and to the many students who studied health psychology with me and assisted in the class testing of this book. They are a constant reminder of the enormous privilege and responsibilities I have as a teacher; it is for them that I have done my best to bring the field of health psychology alive in this text.

To those of you who are about to teach using this book, I sincerely hope that you will share your experiences with me. Drop me a line and let me know what works, what doesn't, and how you would do it differently. This input will be vital in determining the book's success and in shaping its future.

Richard O. Straub
University of Michigan, Dearborn
Dearborn, MI 48128
rostraub@umich.edu

PART 1 | Foundations of Health Psychology

CHAPTER 1

Introducing Health Psychology

Calaimage/Getty Images

Caroline Flynn stepped aboard a 32-ton steamer on what must have been an uncertain morning in the early 1880s. Bound for the United States, she began her journey of hope in Liverpool, England, in a desperate attempt to escape the economic distress and religious persecution that she and her family suffered in Ireland. The country's troubles had begun decades earlier with "an Gorta Mór" (the Great Hunger), a famine caused by the potato fungus that destroyed the primary—and often only—food of most Irish families.

Caroline's journey was hardly unique. Between 1861 and 1926, four million Irish left the country for similar reasons, and young people like Caroline were brought up for "export" overseas. After a harrowing five- to six-week voyage across the Atlantic, crowded with other emigrants into a steerage compartment that was rarely cleaned, they endured the humiliating processing of immigrants in lower Manhattan. Many of those who were sick or without financial means or sponsors were forced to return to their homeland.

As Caroline doggedly made her way in her adopted country, first north to upstate New York and then west to Chicago, she found that things were better, but life was still hard. Doctors were expensive (and few in number), and she always had to guard against drinking impure water, eating contaminated foods, or becoming infected with typhoid fever, diphtheria, or one of the many other diseases that were prevalent in those days. Despite her vigilance, her survival (and later that of her husband and newborn baby) remained uncertain. Life expectancy was less than 50 years, and one of every six babies died before his or her first birthday. "It would keep you poor, just burying your children," wrote one Irishwoman to her family back home (Miller & Miller, 2001). Equally troubling was the attitude of many native-born Americans, who viewed the Irish as inferior, violent, and drunken. Most of the new immigrants toiled as laborers in the lowest-paid and most dangerous occupations, and they were banished to ghettolike "Paddy" towns that sprang up on the outskirts of cities such as New York and Chicago.

More than a century later, I smile as my mother recounts the saga of my great-grandmother's emigration to the United States. Her grandmother lived a long, productive life and left a legacy of optimism and "indomitable Irishy" that fortified her against the hardships in her life—and carried down through the generations. "How different things are now," I think as our phone call ends, "but how much of Caroline's spirit is still alive in my own children!"

Things are very different now. Advances in hygiene, public health measures, and microbiology have virtually eradicated the infectious diseases that Caroline feared most. Women born in the United States today enjoy a life expectancy of over 81 years, and men on average reach the age of 76. This gift of time has helped us realize that health is much more than freedom from illness. More than ever before, we can get beyond survival mode and work to attain lifelong vitality by modifying our diets, exercising regularly, and remaining socially connected and emotionally centered.

About 12 million immigrants to the United States would pass through lower Manhattan including the author's great grandmother.

M y great-grandmother's story makes clear that many factors interact in determining health. This is a fundamental theme of **health psychology,** a subfield of psychology that applies psychological principles and research to the enhancement of health and the treatment and prevention of illness. Its concerns include social conditions (such as the availability of health care and support from family and friends), biological factors (such as family longevity and inherited vulnerabilities to certain diseases), and even personality traits (such as optimism).

The word *health* comes to us from an old German word that is represented, in English, by the words *hale* and *whole,* both of which refer to a state of "soundness of body." Linguists note that these words derive from the medieval battlefield, where loss of *haleness,* or health, was usually the result of grave bodily injury. Today, we are more likely to think of health as the absence of disease rather than as the absence of a debilitating battlefield injury. Because this definition focuses only on the absence of a negative state, however, it is incomplete. Although it is true that healthy people are free of disease, complete health involves much more. A person may be free of disease but still not enjoy a vigorous, satisfying life. **Health** involves physical as well as psychological and social well-being.

We are fortunate to live in a time when most of the world's citizens have the promise of a longer and better life than their great-grandparents, with far less disability and disease than ever before. However, these health benefits are not universally enjoyed. Consider:

- The number of years a person born today can expect to live differs substantially from country to country, ranging from about 79 to 81 years in high-income countries such as the United States and Canada to well under 50 years in very poor countries such as Sierra Leone and Chad (World Bank, 2015).

- In general, people who live in cities and are members of ethnic majorities enjoy better health than those who live in rural areas and are members of disadvantaged minority groups (Gwatkin and others, 2007).

health psychology The application of psychological principles and research to the enhancement of health and the prevention and treatment of illness.

The health of women is inextricably linked to their status in society. It benefits from equality and suffers from discrimination.

—**World Health Organization**

health A state of complete physical, mental, and social well-being.

Bettmann/Getty Images

health disparities Preventable differences in the burden of disease, injury, violence, or opportunities to achieve optimal health that are experienced by socially disadvantaged populations.

- Women continue to face a number of unique challenges to their health, as do lesbian, gay, bisexual, and transgender people (LGBT) and other marginalized people (Logie, James, Wangari, and Loutfy, 2012).

- At every age, these and other **health disparities** abound. Among American men and women, those of European ancestry have a longer life expectancy than African-Americans, but both groups have shorter life expectancies than people in Japan, Canada, Australia, the United Kingdom, Italy, France, and many other countries (Kochanek, Murphy, & Xu, 2015). It is estimated that nearly 1 million deaths each year in the United States (among all age groups) are preventable (see Table 1.1).

- Beginning in middle age, women have higher disease and disability rates than men (U.S. Census Bureau, 2012).

- Despite having the world's most expensive health care system, the United States ranks worst among 11 wealthy nations as measured by such factors as life expectancy, efficiency, and accessibility to quality health care by all individuals (Commonwealth Fund, 2014).

Data related to health disparities can be found through the WHO (http://www.who.int/research/en/), which documents disparities across and within countries. For the United States, the Kaiser Family Foundation (www.kff.org) provides monthly updates on health disparities and maintains an interactive Web site (www.statehealthfacts.org) with data on ethnic and racial differences on a state-by-state basis.

These statistics reveal some of the challenges in the quest for global wellness. Health professionals are working to reduce the 30-year discrepancy in life expectancy between developed and developing countries, to help adolescents make a safe, healthy transition to adulthood, and to achieve a deeper understanding of the relationships among gender, ethnicity, sociocultural status, and health.

In the United States, the Department of Health and Human Services report, *Healthy People 2020,* identifies specific actions and targets for improving access to health services, eliminating health disparities, reducing chronic diseases such as cancer and diabetes, improving health in people of all ages, preventing injuries and violence, and taking steps in 32 other areas (see Table 1.2). Specifically, the overarching goals are to:

- attain high-quality, longer lives free of preventable disease, disability, injury, and premature death.

- achieve health equity, eliminate disparities, and improve the health of all groups.

- create social and physical environments that promote good health for all.

- promote quality of life, healthy development, and healthy behaviors across all life stages.

Patient Protection and Affordable Care Act (PPACA) A federal law aimed at reducing the number of people in the United States who do not have health insurance, as well as lowering the costs of health care.

To help the nation meet these goals, on March 23, 2010, President Barack Obama signed the **Patient Protection and Affordable Care Act (PPACA),** the most significant overhaul of the U.S. health care system in nearly 50 years. The primary goals of the law

TABLE 1.1

Preventable Injury and Death

- Control of underage and excess use of alcohol could prevent 100,000 deaths from automobile accidents and other alcohol-related injuries.
- Elimination of public possession of firearms could prevent 35,000 deaths.
- Elimination of all forms of tobacco use could prevent 400,000 deaths from cancer, stroke, and heart disease.
- Better nutrition and exercise programs could prevent 300,000 deaths from heart disease, diabetes, cancer, and stroke.
- A reduction in risky sexual behaviors could prevent 30,000 deaths from sexually transmitted diseases.
- Full access to immunizations for infectious diseases could prevent 100,000 deaths.

Source: U.S. Department of Health and Human Services, *Healthy People 2020.* Retrieved August 31, 2014, from www.healthypeople.gov.

TABLE 1.2

Select Topic Area Goals and Targets of Healthy People 2020

Adolescent Health

- Increase the proportion of adolescents who have had a wellness checkup in the past 12 months (target: 75.6 percent)
- Reduce the proportion of adolescents who have been offered, sold, or given an illegal drug on school property (target: 20.4 percent)

Physical Activity

- Increase the proportion of adults who engage in aerobic physical activity of at least moderate intensity for at least 150 minutes/week, or 75 minutes/week of vigorous intensity, or an equivalent combination
- Increase the proportion of the nation's public and private schools that require daily physical education for all students

Nutrition and Weight Status

- Increase the proportion of schools that do not sell or offer calorically sweetened beverages to students (target: 21.3 percent)
- Increase the proportion of adults who are at a healthy weight (target: 33.9 percent)

Injury and Violence Prevention

- Reduce unintentional injury deaths (target: 36.0 deaths per 100,000 population)
- Reduce motor vehicle crash–related deaths (target: 12.4 deaths per 100,000 population)

Sleep Health

- Increase the proportion of adults who get sufficient sleep (target: 70.9 percent)
- Reduce the rate of vehicular crashes per 100 million miles traveled that are due to drowsy driving (target: 2.1 vehicular crashes per 100 million miles traveled)

Information from http://healthypeople.gov/2020/topicsobjectives2020/pdfs/HP2020objectives.pdf.

are to decrease the number of people who do not have health insurance and to lower the costs of health care. Other reforms are aimed at improving health care outcomes and streamlining the delivery of health care. In addition, under PPACA, insurers are required to cover certain types of preventive care at no cost to the consumer, including blood pressure and cholesterol tests, mammograms, colonoscopies, and screenings for osteoporosis.

With the foregoing background material kept in mind, this chapter introduces the field of health psychology, which plays an increasingly important role in meeting the world's health challenges. Consider a few of the more specific questions that health psychologists seek to answer: How do your attitudes, beliefs, self-confidence, and personality affect your physiology and your overall health? Why are so many people turning to acupuncture, yoga, herbal supplements (plus other forms of alternative medicine), as well as do-it-yourself preventive care? Do these interventions really work? Why do so many people ignore unquestionably sound advice for improving their health, such as quitting smoking, moderating food intake, and exercising more? Why are certain health problems more likely to occur among people of a particular age, gender, or ethnic group? Why is being poor, uneducated, or lonely a potentially serious threat to your health? Conversely, why do those who are relatively affluent, well educated, and socially active enjoy better health?

Health psychology is the science that seeks to answer these and many other questions about how our wellness interacts with how we think, feel, and act. We begin by taking a closer look at the concept of health and how it has changed over the course of history. Next, we'll examine the biopsychosocial and systems theory perspectives on health. Finally, we'll take a look at the training needed to become a health psychologist and what you can do with that training.

Health and Illness: Lessons from the Past

Although all human civilizations have been affected by disease, each one has understood and treated it differently (Figure 1.1).

From Ancient Times Through the Renaissance

Our efforts at healing can be traced back 20,000 years. A cave painting in southern France, for example, which is believed to be 17,000 years old, depicts an Ice Age shaman wearing the animal mask of an ancient witch doctor. In religions based on a belief in good and evil spirits, only a shaman (priest or medicine man) can influence these spirits.

For preindustrial men and women, confronted with the often-hostile forces of their environment, survival was based on constant vigilance against these mysterious forces of evil. When a person became sick, there was no obvious physical reason for it. Rather, the stricken individual's condition was misattributed to weakness in the face of a stronger force, bewitchment, or possession by an evil spirit.

During this period of time, sick people were often treated with rituals of sorcery, exorcism, or even a primitive form of surgery called *trephination*. Archaeologists have unearthed prehistoric human skulls containing irregularly shaped holes that were apparently drilled by early healers to allow disease-causing demons to leave patients' bodies. Historical records indicate that trephination was practiced in Europe, Egypt, India, and Central and South America.

Ancient healers did search for a more rational understanding of how the human body functioned. Given the importance of the Nile River, it is not surprising that Egyptian healers drew parallels with how its channels were used to irrigate farmers' fields. The *Nile Theory* reflects their belief that the body had similar channels carrying air, water, and blood, and that people became sick when blockages occurred.

In Greece, the philosopher and physician Hippocrates (460–377 B.C.E.) also rebelled against the ancient focus on mysticism and superstition. Hippocrates, who is often called the "father of Western medicine," was the first to argue that disease is a natural phenomenon and that the causes of disease (and therefore their treatment and prevention) are knowable and worthy of serious study. In this way, he built the earliest foundation for a scientific approach to healing. Historically, physicians took the Hippocratic Oath, with which they swore to practice medicine ethically. Over the centuries, the oath has been rewritten to suit the values of various cultures that were influenced by Greek medicine.

Hippocrates proposed the first rational explanation of why people get sick. According to his **humoral theory,** a healthy body and mind resulted from equilibrium among four bodily fluids called *humors*: blood, yellow bile, black bile, and phlegm. To maintain a proper balance, a person had to follow a healthy lifestyle that included exercise, sufficient rest, a good diet, and the avoidance of excesses. When the humors were out of balance, however, both body and mind were affected in predictable ways, depending on which of the four humors was in excess. Those suffering from headaches and anxiety, for example,

. . . I will prevent disease whenever I can, for prevention is preferable to cure.

I will remember that I remain a member of society, with special obligations to all my fellow human beings, those sound of mind and body as well as the infirm.

If I do not violate this oath, may I enjoy life and art, respected while I live and remembered with affection thereafter. May I always act so as to preserve the finest traditions of my calling and may I long experience the joy of healing those who seek my help.

—Written in 1964 by Louis Lasagna, Academic Dean of the School of Medicine at Tufts University, this is the modern version of the Hippocratic Oath used in many medical schools today.

humoral theory A concept of health proposed by Hippocrates that considered wellness a state of perfect equilibrium among four basic body fluids, called *humors*. Sickness was believed to be the result of disturbances in the balance of humors.

FIGURE 1.1

A Timeline of Historical and Cultural Variations in Illness and Healing From the ancient use of trephination to remove evil spirits to the current use of noninvasive brain scans to diagnose disease, the treatment of health problems has seen major advances over the centuries. A collection of treatments across the ages is shown (from left to right): trephination (on an ancient Peruvian skull); acupuncture from China; early surgery in seventeenth-century Europe; and vaccination by the district vaccinator in nineteenth-century London.

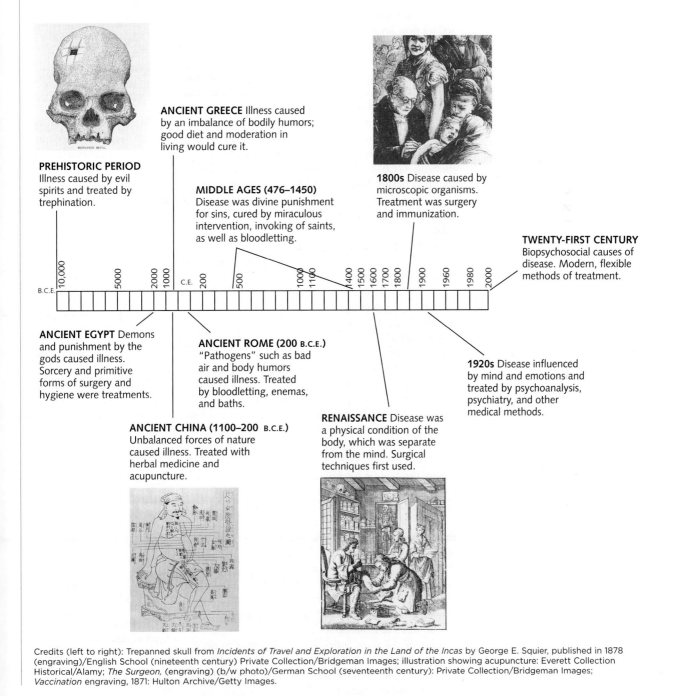

ANCIENT GREECE Illness caused by an imbalance of bodily humors; good diet and moderation in living would cure it.

PREHISTORIC PERIOD Illness caused by evil spirits and treated by trephination.

MIDDLE AGES (476–1450) Disease was divine punishment for sins, cured by miraculous intervention, invoking of saints, as well as bloodletting.

1800s Disease caused by microscopic organisms. Treatment was surgery and immunization.

TWENTY-FIRST CENTURY Biopsychosocial causes of disease. Modern, flexible methods of treatment.

B.C.E. 10,000 5000 2000 1000 C.E. 200 500 1000 1100 1400 1500 1600 1700 1800 1900 1960 1980 2000

ANCIENT EGYPT Demons and punishment by the gods caused illness. Sorcery and primitive forms of surgery and hygiene were treatments.

ANCIENT ROME (200 B.C.E.) "Pathogens" such as bad air and body humors caused illness. Treated by bloodletting, enemas, and baths.

1920s Disease influenced by mind and emotions and treated by psychoanalysis, psychiatry, and other medical methods.

ANCIENT CHINA (1100–200 B.C.E.) Unbalanced forces of nature caused illness. Treated with herbal medicine and acupuncture.

RENAISSANCE Disease was a physical condition of the body, which was separate from the mind. Surgical techniques first used.

Credits (left to right): Trepanned skull from *Incidents of Travel and Exploration in the Land of the Incas* by George E. Squier, published in 1878 (engraving)/English School (nineteenth century) Private Collection/Bridgeman Images; illustration showing acupuncture: Everett Collection Historical/Alamy; *The Surgeon,* (engraving) (b/w photo)/German School (seventeenth century): Private Collection/Bridgeman Images; *Vaccination* engraving, 1871: Hulton Archive/Getty Images.

might have been considered choleric, with an excess of yellow bile and a fiery temperament. They might have been treated with bloodletting (opening a vein to remove blood), liquid diets, enemas, and cooling baths.

Although humoral theory was discarded as advances were made in anatomy, physiology, and microbiology, the notion of personality traits being linked with body fluids still persists in the folk and alternative medicines of many cultures, including those of traditional Eastern and Native American cultures. Moreover, as we'll see in the next chapter, we now know that many diseases involve an imbalance (of sorts) among the brain's neurotransmitters, so Hippocrates was not too far off. Hippocrates was also interested in patients' emotions and thoughts regarding their health and treatment, and thus he called attention to the psychological aspects of health and illness. "It is better to know the patient who has the disease," Hippocrates said, "than it is to know the disease which the patient has" (quoted in Wesley, 2003).

At the same time that Western medicine was emerging, different traditions of healing were developing in other cultures. For example, more than 2,000 years ago, the Chinese developed an integrated system of healing, which we know today as *traditional Oriental medicine (TOM)*. TOM is founded on the principle that internal harmony is essential for good health. Fundamental to this harmony is the concept of *qi* (sometimes spelled *chi*), a vital energy or life force that ebbs and flows with changes in each person's mental, physical, and emotional well-being. Acupuncture, herbal therapy, tai chi, meditation, and other interventions are said to restore health by correcting blockages and imbalances in *qi.*

Ayurveda is the oldest-known medical system in the world, having originated in India around the sixth century B.C.E., coinciding roughly with the lifetime of the Buddha. The word *ayurveda* comes from the Sanskrit roots *ayuh,* which means "longevity," and *veda,* meaning "knowledge." Widely practiced in India, ayurveda is based on the belief that the human body represents the entire universe in a microcosm and that the key to health is maintaining a balance between the microcosmic body and the macrocosmic world. The key to this relationship is held in the balance of three bodily humors, or *doshas: vata, pitta,* and *kapha,* or, collectively, the *tridosha.* We'll explore the history, traditions, and effectiveness of these and other non-Western forms of medicine in Chapter 15.

The fall of the Roman Empire in the fifth century C.E. ushered in the Middle Ages (476–1450), an era between ancient and modern times characterized by a return to supernatural explanations of health and disease in Europe. Religious interpretations colored medieval scientists' ideas about health and disease. Illness was viewed as God's punishment for evildoing, and **epidemic** or **pandemic diseases,** such as the two great outbursts of *plague* (a bacterial disease carried by rats and other rodents) that occurred during the Middle Ages, were believed to be a sign of God's wrath. Medical "treatment" in this era often involved attempts to force evil spirits out of the body. There were few scientific advances in European medicine during these thousand years.

In the late fourteenth century, a new age—the Renaissance—was born. Beginning with the reemergence of scientific inquiry, this period saw the revitalization of anatomical study and medical practice. The taboo on human dissection was lifted sufficiently that the Flemish anatomist and artist Andreas Vesalius (1514–1564) was able to publish an authoritative, seven-volume study of the internal organs, musculature, and skeletal system of the human body. The son of a druggist, Vesalius was fascinated by nature, especially the anatomy of humans and animals. In the pursuit of knowledge, no stray dog, cat, or mouse was safe from his scalpel.

One of the most influential Renaissance thinkers was the French philosopher and mathematician René Descartes (1596–1650), whose first innovation was the concept of the human body as a machine. He described all the basic reflexes of the body, constructing elaborate mechanical models to demonstrate his principles. He believed that disease occurred when the machine broke down, and the physician's task was to repair the machine.

epidemic Literally, *among the people*; an epidemic disease is one that spreads rapidly among many individuals in a community at the same time.

pandemic A pandemic disease is one that affects people over a large geographical area, such as multiple continents or worldwide.

The Middle Ages began with an outbreak of plague that originated in Egypt in 540 C.E. and quickly spread throughout the Roman Empire, killing as many as 10,000 people a day. So great in number were the corpses that gravediggers could not keep up. The solution was to load ships with the dead, row them out to sea, and abandon them.

Descartes is best known for his beliefs that the mind and body are autonomous processes that interact minimally, and that each is subject to different laws of causality. This viewpoint, which is called *mind–body dualism* (or *Cartesian dualism*), is based on the doctrine that humans have two natures, mental and physical. Descartes and other great thinkers of the Renaissance, in an effort to break with the mysticism and superstitions of the past, vigorously rejected the notion that the mind influences the body. Although this viewpoint ushered in a new age of medical research based on confidence in science and rational thinking, it created a lasting bias in Western medicine against the importance of psychological processes in health. As we'll see, this bias has been rapidly unraveling since the 1970s.

From Post-Renaissance Rationality through the Nineteenth Century

Following the Renaissance, physicians were expected to focus exclusively on the biological causes of disease. English physician William Harvey (1578–1657) offered the first detailed description of the circulation of blood, and he also noted that emotions were often associated with how the heart functioned. Physician and Quaker preacher John Fothergill (1656–1745) was noteworthy for being the first to identify diseases that affect the nerves and also for emphasizing the importance of practicing temperance and self-control in maintaining health. Surgeon John Hunter (1728–1793), one of the most distinguished scientists of his day, was an early advocate of careful observation and the importance of applying the scientific method in medicine. Although a ground lens had been used for magnification in ancient times, the first practical microscopes were developed in this era. This made it possible to view blood cells and the structure of skeletal muscles.

Once individual cells became visible, the stage was set for the *germ theory* of disease—the idea that bacteria, viruses, and other microorganisms that invade body cells cause them to malfunction. The germ theory forms the theoretical foundation of modern medicine and was followed by rapid advances in medical knowledge and procedures.

In 1846, William Morton (1819–1868), an American dentist, introduced the gas ether as an anesthetic. This great advance made it possible to operate on patients, who experienced no pain during procedures and thus remained completely relaxed. The German physicist Wilhelm Roentgen (1845–1943) discovered x-rays 50 years later, and, for the first time, physicians were able to directly observe internal organs in a living person. Before the end of the nineteenth century, researchers had identified the microorganisms that caused malaria, pneumonia, diphtheria, syphilis, typhoid, and other diseases that my great-grandmother's generation feared. Armed with this information, medicine began to bring under control diseases that had plagued the world since antiquity.

Musculature Structure of a Man (b/w neg & print)/Vesalius, Andreas (1514-64)/R.C.S. SCUOLA SPA/Fratelli Fabbri, Milan, Italy/Bridgeman Images

First Anatomical Drawings By the sixteenth century, the taboo on human dissection had been lifted long enough that the Flemish anatomist and artist Andreas Vesalius (1514–1564) was able to publish a complete study of the internal organs, musculature, and skeletal system of the human body.

The Twentieth Century and the Dawn of a New Era

As the field of medicine continued to advance during the early part of the twentieth century, it looked more and more to physiology and anatomy, rather than to the study of thoughts and emotions, in its search for a deeper understanding of health and illness. Thus was born the **biomedical model** of health, which maintains that illness always has a biological cause. This model first became widely accepted during the nineteenth century and continues to represent the dominant view in medicine today.

The biomedical model assumes that disease is the result of a **pathogen**—a virus, bacterium, or some other microorganism that invades the body. The model makes no

biomedical model The dominant view of twentieth-century medicine that maintains that illness always has a physical cause.

pathogen A virus, bacterium, or some other microorganism that causes a particular disease.

Bettmann/Getty Images

Louis Pasteur in His Laboratory Pasteur's meticulous work in isolating bacteria in the laboratory, then showing that life can come only from existing life, paved the way for germ-free surgical procedures.

psychosomatic medicine
A branch of psychiatry that developed in the 1900s and focused on the diagnosis and treatment of certain diseases believed to be caused by emotional conflicts.

provision for psychological, social, or behavioral variables in illness. In this sense, the biomedical model embraces *reductionism,* the view that complex phenomena (such as health and disease) derive ultimately from a single primary factor. Second, the biomedical model is based on the Cartesian doctrine of *mind–body dualism* that, as we have seen, considers the mind and the body as separate and autonomous entities that interact minimally. Finally, according to the biomedical model, health is nothing more than the absence of disease. Accordingly, those who work from this perspective focus on investigating the causes of physical illnesses rather than on those factors that promote physical, psychological, and social vitality.

Psychosomatic Medicine

The biomedical model advanced health care significantly through its focus on pathogens. However, it was unable to explain disorders that had no observable physical cause, such as those uncovered by Sigmund Freud (1856–1939), who was initially trained as a physician. Freud's patients exhibited symptoms such as loss of speech, deafness, and even paralysis. Freud believed these maladies were caused by unconscious emotional conflicts that had been "converted" into a physical form. Freud labeled such illnesses *conversion disorders,* and the medical community was forced to accept a new category of disease.

In the 1940s, Franz Alexander advanced the idea that an individual's psychological conflicts could cause specific diseases. When physicians could find no infectious agent or other direct cause for rheumatoid arthritis, Alexander became intrigued by the possibility that psychological factors might be involved. According to his *nuclear conflict* model, each physical disease is the outcome of a fundamental, or nuclear, psychological conflict (Alexander, 1950). For example, individuals with a "rheumatoid personality," who tended to repress anger and were unable to express emotion, were believed to be prone to developing arthritis. Alexander helped establish **psychosomatic medicine,** a subfield of psychiatry named from the root words *psyche,* which means "mind," and *soma,* which means "body." Psychosomatic medicine is concerned with the diagnosis and treatment of physical diseases thought to be caused by faulty processes within the mind.

Psychosomatic medicine was intriguing and seemed to explain the unexplainable. However, it had several weaknesses that ultimately caused it to fall out of favor. Most significantly, psychosomatic medicine was grounded in Freudian theory. As Freud's emphasis on unconscious, irrational urges in personality formation lost popularity, the field of psychosomatic medicine faltered. Psychosomatic medicine, like the biomedical model, was also based on reductionism—in this case, the outmoded idea that a single psychological problem or personality flaw is sufficient to trigger disease. We now know that disease, like good health, is based on the combined interaction of multiple factors, including heredity and environment, as well as the individual's psychological makeup.

Although Freud's theories and psychosomatic medicine were flawed, they laid the groundwork for a renewed appreciation of the connections between medicine and psychology. This was the start of the contemporary trend toward viewing illness and health as *multifactorial.* That is, many diseases are caused by the interaction of several factors, rather than by a single, invading bacterial or viral agent. Among these are *host factors* (such as genetic vulnerability or resiliency), *environmental factors* (such as exposure to pollutants and hazardous chemicals), *behavioral factors* (such as diet, exercise, and smoking), and *psychological factors* (such as optimism and overall "hardiness").

TABLE 1.3

Twentieth-Century Trends That Shaped Health Psychology

Trend	Result
Increased life expectancy	Recognize the need to take better care of ourselves to promote vitality through a longer life
Rise of lifestyle disorders (for example, cancer, stroke, and heart disease)	Educate people to avoid the behaviors that contribute to these diseases (for example, smoking and eating a high-fat diet)
Rising health care costs	Focus efforts on ways to prevent disease and maintain good health to avoid these costs
Rethinking the biomedical model	Develop a more comprehensive model of health and disease—the biopsychosocial approach

Health Psychology Emerges

In 1973, the American Psychological Association (APA) appointed a task force to explore psychology's role in medicine, and in 1978, the APA created the division of health psychology (Division 38). Four years later, the first volume of its official journal, *Health Psychology,* was published. In this issue, Joseph Matarazzo (1982), the first president of the division, laid down the four goals of the new field:

- *To study scientifically the causes or origins of specific diseases,* that is, their **etiology.** Health psychologists are primarily interested in the psychological, behavioral, and social origins of disease. They investigate why people engage in *health-compromising behaviors,* such as smoking or unsafe sex.

- *To promote health.* Health psychologists consider ways to get people to engage in *health-enhancing behaviors* such as exercising regularly and eating nutritious foods.

- *To prevent and treat illness.* Health psychologists design programs to help people stop smoking, lose weight, manage stress, and minimize other risk factors for poor health. They also assist those who are already ill in their efforts to adjust to their illnesses or comply with difficult treatment regimens.

- *To promote public health policy and the improvement of the health care system.* Health psychologists are very active in all facets of health education and consult frequently with government leaders who formulate public policy in an effort to improve the delivery of health care to all people.

As noted in Table 1.3, a number of twentieth-century trends helped shape the new field of health psychology, pushing it toward the broader biopsychosocial perspective, which is the focus of this text.

etiology The scientific study of the causes or origins of specific diseases.

Biopsychosocial Perspective

As history tells us, looking at just one causative factor paints an incomplete picture of a person's health or illness. Health psychologists therefore work from a **biopsychosocial perspective.** As depicted in Figure 1.2, this perspective recognizes that *bio*logical, *psycho*logical, and *sociocultural* forces act together to determine an individual's health and vulnerability to disease; that is, health and disease must be explained in terms of multiple contexts.

biopsychosocial perspective The viewpoint that health and other behaviors are determined by the interaction of biological mechanisms, psychological processes, and social influences.

FIGURE 1.2

The Biopsychosocial Model
According to the biopsychosocial perspective, all health behaviors are best explained in terms of three contexts: biological processes, psychological processes, and social influences. This diagram illustrates how these three processes could promote symptoms of anxiety.

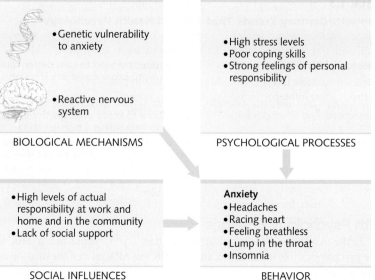

- Genetic vulnerability to anxiety

- Reactive nervous system

BIOLOGICAL MECHANISMS

- High stress levels
- Poor coping skills
- Strong feelings of personal responsibility

PSYCHOLOGICAL PROCESSES

- High levels of actual responsibility at work and home and in the community
- Lack of social support

SOCIAL INFLUENCES

Anxiety
- Headaches
- Racing heart
- Feeling breathless
- Lump in the throat
- Insomnia

BEHAVIOR

The Biological Context

All behaviors, including states of health and illness, occur in a biological context. Every thought, mood, and urge is a biological event made possible because of the characteristic anatomical structure and biological function of a person's body. Health psychology draws attention to those aspects of our bodies that influence health and disease: our genetic makeup and our nervous, immune, and endocrine systems (see Chapter 3).

Our genetic makeup has much to do with how healthy we live and what diseases we get. For example, a person can inherit the genetic component of a disease that has multiple causes, such as breast cancer. As another example, the tendency to abuse alcohol has long been known to run in some families (see Chapter 9). One reason is that alcohol dependency is at least partly genetic, although it does not seem to be linked to a single, specific gene. Instead, some people may inherit a greater sensitivity to alcohol's physical effects, experiencing intoxication as pleasurable and the aftermath of a hangover as minor. Such people may be more likely to drink, especially in certain psychological and social contexts. The complete set of genetic instructions that make a living organism is called its *genome*. Rapid advances in the new field of **genomics** (the study of genomes) reflect the increasing scientific evidence supporting the benefits of using genetic tests and family history to improve health. As evidence mounts, these benefits have been incorporated as new target areas that appear in *Healthy People 2020*.

genomics The study of the structure, function, and mapping of the genetic material of organisms.

The Evolutionary Perspective

A key element of the biological context is our species' evolutionary history, and an *evolutionary perspective* guides the work of many health psychologists. Our characteristic human traits and behaviors exist as they do because they helped our distant ancestors survive long enough to reproduce and send their genes into the future. For example, natural selection has favored the tendency of people to become hungry in the presence of a mouthwatering aroma (see Chapter 8). This sensitivity to food-related cues makes evolutionary sense in that eating is necessary for survival—particularly in the distant past when food supplies were unpredictable and it was advantageous to have a healthy appetite when food was available.

At the same time, biology and behavior constantly interact. For example, some individuals are more vulnerable to stress-related illnesses because they angrily react to daily hassles and other environmental "triggers" (see Chapter 4). Among men, these triggers are correlated with aggressive reaction related to increased amounts of the hormone testosterone. This relationship, however, is reciprocal: Angry outbursts can also lead to elevated testosterone levels. One of the tasks of health psychology is to explain how (and why) this mutual influence between biology and behavior occurs.

It is also important to recognize that biology and behavior do not occur in a vacuum. At first, the remarkable success of the Human Genome Project in mapping all the genes that make up a person seemed to suggest that genes might determine everything; that every aspect of you, including your health, will become whatever you are biologically destined to be. We now know otherwise. It is true that genes influence all traits, both psychological and physical. But even identical twins, who share identical genes, do *not* have identical traits. Increasingly, we're learning that most important traits are **epigenetic.** Epigenetic effects occur throughout our lifetimes. Some "epi-" influences impede our chances for optimal health (for example, environmental toxins, child abuse, and poverty), and some improve them (for example, nourishing food, safe places to grow up, and education). One example of this type of gene–environment interaction comes from research on the *MAOA* gene, which codes for an enzyme that affects key neurotransmitters in the brain. Boys who inherit one variation of the gene and girls who inherit a different variation of the same gene are more likely to engage in high-risk delinquent behavior as adolescents, but only if they were exposed to the "epi-" effect of maltreatment as children (Aslund and others, 2011). The variations in question are *gene promoters,* regions of DNA that regulate the expression of that gene.

As another example, consider *DNA methylation,* a biochemical process that occurs in cells and is essential to the healthy functioning of nearly every body system. Occurring billions of times each second, methylation helps regulate the expression of genes that repair DNA, keep inflammation in check, and promote healthy blood vessels. A breakdown in methylation may promote the development of cancer, diabetes, and cardiovascular disease, and it may even accelerate aging (Alashwal, Dosunmu, & Zawia, 2012). The degree of methylation changes over the life span and is also influenced by "epi-" effects such as diet, tobacco use, and exposure to environmental toxins (Davis & Uthus, 2004).

These examples of epigenetic research demonstrate that *gene–environment* effects are always important. Some genes are *expressed* and affect our health, while some genes are *silenced* and remain unnoticed from one generation to the next unless circumstances, such as the quality of nurturing during childhood, change (Riddihough & Zahn, 2010; Skipper, 2011).

epigenetic The effects of environmental forces on how genes are expressed.

The roots of the word are revealing: epi *means "around" or "near."* Epigenetic, *therefore, calls attention to environmental factors near and around genes that affect their expression.*

Life-Course Perspective

Within the biological context, the *life-course perspective* in health psychology focuses on important age-related aspects of health and illness. This perspective would consider, for example, how a pregnant woman's malnutrition, smoking, or use of psychoactive drugs would affect her child's lifelong development.

The life-course perspective also considers the leading causes of death in terms of the age groups affected. In high-income countries such as the United States and Canada, the top three leading causes of death are stroke, heart disease, and lung cancer (Institute for Health Metrics and Evaluation, 2013b). However, the profile of leading causes of death varies by age group. The chronic diseases that are the leading causes of death in the overall population are more likely to affect middle-aged and elderly adults. Young people between the ages of 1 and 24 years old are much more likely to die from external causes that include accidents, homicide, and suicide, followed by cancer and heart disease (see Figure 1.3).

FIGURE 1.3

The Leading Causes of Death in the United States by Age Group The five leading causes of death in young people include external causes (accidents, homicide, and suicide), followed by cancer and heart disease. This pattern of external causes accounting for more deaths than chronic conditions changes as people get older. In older age groups, chronic conditions account for more deaths than do external causes. For example, accidents account for more than one-third of all deaths among persons aged 1–24 years. Accidental deaths are rarer in older age groups and do not even rank as one of the five leading causes of death in people 65 years and older.

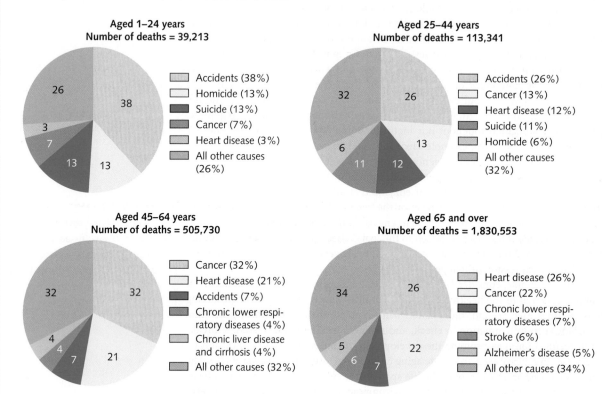

Data from Murphy, S.L., Kochanek, K.D., Xu, J.Q., & Heron. M. (2015). Deaths: Final data for 2012. *National Vital Statistics Reports, 63*(9). Hyattsville, MD: National Center for Health Statistics.

The Psychological Context

The central message of health psychology is, of course, that health and illness are subject to psychological influences. Our personal health practices and behaviors are key determinants of our health. These, in turn, are strongly influenced by our beliefs and attitudes. Our diet, sexual activity, and use of tobacco and other drugs may contribute to the development of heart disease, sexually transmitted infections, cancer, and other unhealthy conditions.

A key factor in how well a person copes with a stressful life experience is how the event is appraised or interpreted (see Chapter 5). Events that are appraised as overwhelming, pervasive, and beyond our control take a much greater toll on us physically and psychologically than do events that are appraised as minor challenges that are temporary and surmountable. Indeed, some evidence suggests that, whether a stressful event is actually experienced or merely imagined, the body's stress response is nearly the same. Health psychologists think that some people may be more susceptible to certain health problems because they replay stressful events over and over again in their minds, which may be functionally equivalent to repeatedly encountering the actual event. The field of *positive psychology* has given rise to many studies of the importance of **subjective well-being**—our

subjective well-being The cognitive and emotional evaluations of a person's life.

TABLE 1.4
Testing Yourself: Subjective Well-Being

The WHO-5 Well-Being Index (WHO-5) is a self-report mood questionnaire developed by the World Health Organization's Collaborating Center in Mental Health.

For each statement, please indicate which is closest to how you have been feeling over the last two weeks. For example, if you have felt cheerful and in good spirits more than half of the time during the last two weeks, put a tick in the box with the number 3 in the upper-right corner.

Over the last two weeks	All of the time	Most of the time	More than half of the time	Less than half of the time	Some of the time	At no time
1. I have felt cheerful and in good spirits	5	4	3	2	1	0
2. I have felt calm and relaxed	5	4	3	2	1	0
3. I have felt active and vigorous	5	4	3	2	1	0
4. I woke up feeling fresh and rested	5	4	3	2	1	0
5. My daily life has been filled with things that interest me	5	4	3	2	1	0

The raw score is calculated by totaling the figures of the five answers. The raw score ranges from 0 to 25, 0 representing worst possible and 25 representing best possible quality of life. A score below 13 indicates poor subjective well-being and may be an indication for additional testing for depression.

Source: Bech, P. (2004). Measuring the dimensions of psychological general well-being by the WHO-5. *Quality of Life Newsletter, 32*, 15–16.

feelings of happiness and sense of satisfaction with life (see Table 1.4). Throughout this book, we will examine the health implications of thinking, perception, motivation, emotion, learning, attention, memory, and other topics of central importance to psychology.

Psychological factors also play an important role in the treatment and management of chronic conditions. The effectiveness of all health care interventions—including medication and surgery, as well as acupuncture and other alternative treatments—is powerfully influenced by a patient's attitude. A patient who believes a drug or other treatment will only cause miserable side effects may experience considerable tension, which can actually worsen his or her physical response to the treatment. This reaction can set up a vicious cycle in which escalating anxiety before treatment is followed by progressively worse physical reactions as the treatment regimen proceeds. On the other hand, a patient who is confident that a treatment will be effective may actually experience a greater therapeutic response to that treatment.

Psychological interventions can help patients learn to manage their tension, thereby lessening negative reactions to treatment. Patients who are more relaxed are usually better able, and more motivated, to follow their doctor's instructions. Psychological interventions can also assist patients in managing the everyday stresses of life, which seem to exert a cumulative effect on the immune system. Negative life events such as bereavement, divorce, job loss, or relocation have been linked to decreased immune functioning and increased susceptibility to illness. By teaching patients more effective ways of managing unavoidable stress, health psychologists may help patients' immune systems combat disease.

The field of *positive psychology* has given rise to many studies of the importance of our feelings of well-being and sense of satisfaction with life.

Brand X Pictures/Getty Images

The Social Context

Turn-of-the-century Irish immigrants like my great-grandmother surmounted poverty and prejudice in the United States by establishing Irish-American associations that strongly reflected an ethic of family and communal support. "Each for himself, but all

birth cohort A group of people who, because they were born at about the same time, experience similar historical and social conditions.

for one another," wrote recent immigrant Patrick O'Callaghan to his sister back home (Miller & Miller, 2001), as he described this system of patronage. In placing health behavior in its social context, health psychologists consider the ways in which we think about, influence, and relate to one another and to our environments. Your gender, for example, entails a particular, socially prescribed role that represents your sense of being a woman or a man. In addition, you are a member of a particular family, community, and nation; you also have a certain racial, cultural, and ethnic identity, and you live within a specific socioeconomic class. You are influenced by the same historical and social factors as others in your **birth cohort**—a group of people born within a few years of each other.

Each of these elements of your unique social context affects your experiences and influences your beliefs and behaviors—including those related to health. For example, those who lived 100 years ago were more likely to die from *communicable diseases* that we in developed countries today consider preventable, such as tuberculosis and diphtheria (Table 1.5), and infant mortality in the United States has dropped significantly (Figure 1.4). These are *acute disorders* that are caused by infection and spread from person to person. Now, however, slowly developing *chronic illnesses*, such as heart disease and cancer, are the main causes of death and disability. Many are *noncommunicable diseases* that are not spread by infection and that people live with and manage with the help of health care providers, for years. The greatest burden of disease is predominantly noncommunicable in all parts of the world except sub-Saharan Africa (where communicable diseases remain the leading causes of death).

Consider the social context in which a chronic disease such as cancer occurs. A spouse, significant other, or close friend provides an important source of social support for many cancer patients. Women and men who feel socially connected to a network of caring friends are less likely to die of all types of cancer than are their socially isolated counterparts (see Chapter 11). Feeling supported by others may serve as a buffer that mitigates the output of stress hormones and keeps the body's immune defenses strong during traumatic situations. It may also promote better health habits, regular checkups, and early screening of worrisome symptoms—all of which may improve a cancer victim's odds of survival.

TABLE 1.5

Leading Causes of Death in the United States, 1900 and 2013

1900	Percent	2013*	Percent of All Deaths
Pneumonia	11.8	Heart disease	23.5
Tuberculosis	11.3	Cancer	22.5
Diarrhea and enteritis	8.3	Chronic lower respiratory disease	5.7
Heart disease	5.2	Accidents	5.0
Liver disease	5.2	Cerebrovascular disease	5.0
Accidents	4.2	Alzheimer's disease	3.3
Cancer	3.7	Diabetes	2.9
Senility	2.9	Influenza and pneumonia	2.2
Diphtheria	2.3	Kidney disease	1.8

*Note that the leading causes of death in 2013 were not new diseases; they were present in earlier times, but fewer people died from them, or they were called something else.

Data from Kochanek, K.D., Murphy, S.L., Xu, J., & Arias, E. (2014). Mortality in the United States, 2013. *NCHS data brief, no. 178.* Hyattsville, MD: National Center for Health Statistics.

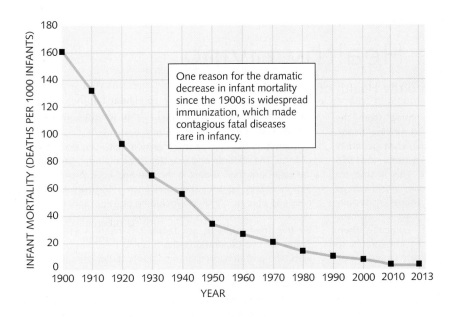

One reason for the dramatic decrease in infant mortality since the 1900s is widespread immunization, which made contagious fatal diseases rare in infancy.

(Graph: Y-axis: INFANT MORTALITY (DEATHS PER 1000 INFANTS) from 0 to 180; X-axis: YEAR from 1900 to 2013)

FIGURE 1.4

Infant Mortality in the United States Less than a century ago, 15 percent of babies born in the United States died before their first birthday. For those who survived, life expectancy was only slightly more than 50 years. With improved health care, today more than 99 percent of newborn babies survive to at least 1 year of age.

Data from *Historical Statistics of the United States: Colonial Times to 1970*, by U.S. Bureau of the Census, 1975, Washington, DC: U.S. Government Printing Office, p. 60; Matthews, T.J., MacDorman, M.F., & Thoma, M.E. (2015). Infant mortality statistics from the 2013 period linked birth/infant death data set. *National Vital Statistics Reports, 64(9).* Hyattsville, MD: National Center for Health Statistics.

Sociocultural Perspective

Within the social context, the *sociocultural perspective* considers how social and cultural factors contribute to health and disease. When psychologists use the term *culture,* they refer to the enduring behaviors, values, and customs that a group of people have developed over the years and transmitted from one generation to the next. Within a culture, there may be two or more *ethnic groups*—large groups of people who tend to have similar values and experiences because they share certain characteristics.

In multiethnic cultures such as those of the United States and most large nations, wide disparities still exist between the life expectancy and health status of ethnic minority groups and the majority population. These disparities were even greater among previous cohorts, such as the ethnic groups of my great-grandmother and others who emigrated to America. Some of these differences undoubtedly reflect variation in *socioeconomic status (SES),* which is a measure of several variables, including income, education, and occupation. For example, the highest rates of chronic disease occur among people who are at the lowest SES levels. Evidence also suggests that bias, prejudice, and stereotyping on the part of health care providers may be factors. Minorities tend to receive lower-quality health care than whites do, even when insurance status, income, age, and severity of conditions are comparable (AHRQ, 2012).

Sociocultural forces also play an important role in the variation in health-related beliefs and behaviors. For example, traditional Native American health care practices are *holistic* (see Chapter 15) and do not distinguish separate models for mental and physical illnesses. As another example, Christian Scientists traditionally reject the use of medicine in their belief that sick people can be cured only through prayer. And Judaic law prescribes that God gives health, and it is the responsibility of each individual to protect it.

In general, health psychologists working from the sociocultural perspective have found wide discrepancies not only among ethnic groups, but also within these groups. Latinos in the United States, for example, are far from homogeneous. The three major nationality groups—Mexicans,

Feeling supported by others may serve as a buffer that mitigates the effects of stress. Here, a cohort of adults supports one another while studying English as a second language.

Getty Images News./Getty Images

Diversity and Healthy Living

The Immigrant Paradox: SES and the Health of Immigrants

A dramatic example of research stemming from the sociocultural perspective concerns the surprising health of Latinos in the United States considering their generally lower incomes and education levels. In general, low SES correlates with poorer health outcomes. This is true for low birth weight, the rate of which increases worldwide as income falls. Immigrants to the United States, especially those from Spanish-speaking countries, have an average lower SES than native-born Americans. Logically, then, researchers would expect babies born to immigrants to weigh less than those born to native-born women. But, paradoxically, babies born to U.S. immigrants are healthier in every way, including birth weight, than babies of the same ethnicity whose mothers, like their babies, were born in the United States. This surprising finding, which was first documented among Mexican-Americans and is also true for U.S. immigrants from other Spanish-speaking countries, from the Caribbean, and from parts of Eastern Europe, continues after birth.

Throughout childhood, children born to low-SES immigrants seem to do better in health and cognition than native-born children of the same ethnicity and income (García Coll & Marks, 2012). Remarkably, the **immigrant paradox** (also called the *Hispanic paradox* or *Latino paradox*) is found throughout the life span. Although Latinos in the United States generally have lower SES, are less likely to have health insurance, use health care less often, and receive less in the way of high-level care when they are sick,

they appear to have lower rates of heart disease, cancer, and stroke—the biggest killers of Americans.

Carry this out a generation or two, however, and things change. The children and grandchildren of immigrants typically surpass their elders in income and education, but as SES increases, so does the prevalence of virtually every illness and chronic condition, including obesity, diabetes, cardiovascular disease, and cancer (Garcia Coll & Marks, 2012). By the time an immigrant family has been in the United States for two generations, the "playing field" has been leveled: The grandchildren of immigrants die at the same rate as those of native-born Americans (Barger & Gallo, 2008).

Even within the life span of a single person, the immigrant paradox can be observed. Adults who immigrated to the United States within the past year are one-tenth as likely to be obese as are their counterparts who arrived as children and who have lived in this country for 15 years or more (Roshania, Narayan, & Oza-Frank, 2008). Similar disparities exist for diabetes, cardiovascular disease, and many other chronic conditions.

One possible explanation for the immigrant paradox, called the *healthy migrant effect*, is that people who choose to leave their native country are healthier to begin with, despite being poor. Although it may be true that some people do not emigrate because they are too sick to make what is often a hazardous journey, this effect is not sufficient to explain the immigrant health advantage (Garcia Coll & Marks, 2012). The immigrant paradox remains a rather remarkable mystery.

immigrant paradox The finding that, although low socioeconomic status usually predicts poor health, this is not true for some ethnic groups, such as Hispanics, in the United States.

Puerto Ricans, and Cubans—differ in education, income, overall health, and risk of disease and death (Angel, Angel, & Hill, 2008). Socioeconomic, religious, and other cultural patterns also may explain why variations in health are apparent not just among ethnic groups, but also from region to region, state to state, and even from one neighborhood to another. For example, out of every 1,000 live births, the number of infants who die before reaching their first birthday is greater in Mississippi (9.38) and Delaware (8.71) than in Alaska (3.75) and Iowa (4.74) (Kochanek, Murphy, & Xu, 2015). In terms of your overall health, the way you age seems to depend on where you live.

Gender Perspective

Also within the social context, the *gender perspective* in health psychology focuses on the study of gender-specific health behaviors, problems, and barriers to health care. With the exceptions of reproductive-system problems and undernourishment, men are more vulnerable than women to nearly every other health problem. Although biology certainly plays a part in gender differences in health, masculinity norms have also been implicated (Gough, 2013). Compared to women, men are more likely to:

- make unhealthy food choices,
- be overweight,
- exceed guidelines for alcohol consumption and engage in binge drinking,
- ignore illness symptoms and avoid seeing doctors,
- engage in risky competitive sports where there is a higher rate of injury, and
- be at greater risk for nearly all the major diseases that affect both sexes.

The idea that masculinity is bad for men's health is a strong theme in health psychology. The effect is cumulative, and by age 80, women outnumber men 2 to 1.

As another example of research guided by the gender perspective, consider that the medical profession has a long history of treating men and women differently. For example, research studies have shown that women treated for heart disease are more likely to be misdiagnosed (Chiaramonte & Friend, 2006); they are less likely than men to receive counseling about the heart-healthy benefits of exercise, nutrition, and weight reduction (Stewart and others, 2004) or to receive and use prescription drugs for the treatment of their heart disease (Vittinghoff and others, 2003). In a classic study, 700 physicians were asked to prescribe treatment for eight heart patients with identical symptoms (Schulman and others, 1999). The "patients" were actors who differed only in gender, race, and reported age (55 or 70). Although diagnosis is a judgment call, most cardiac specialists would agree that diagnostic catheterization is the appropriate treatment for the symptoms

Sociocultural Bias in Diagnosis Physicians were told that these supposed "heart patients" were identical in occupation, symptoms, and every other respect except age, race, and gender. Although catheterization was the appropriate treatment for the described symptoms, the physicians were more likely to recommend it for the younger, white, male patients than for the older, female, or black patients.

Source: Schulman, K.A., and others. (1999). The effect of race and sex on physicians' recommendations for cardiac catheterization. *New England Journal of Medicine, 340,* 618–625.

described by each hypothetical patient. However, the actual recommendations revealed a small, but nevertheless significant, antifemale and anti-African-American bias. For the younger, white, and male patients, catheterization was recommended 90, 91, and 91 percent of the time, respectively; for the older, female, and African-American patients, 86, 85, and 85 percent of the time, respectively.

Problems such as these, and the underrepresentation of women as participants in medical research trials, have led to the criticism of gender bias in health research and care. In response, the National Institutes of Health (NIH) issued detailed guidelines on the inclusion of women and minority groups in medical research (USDHHS, 2001). In addition, in 1991 the NIH launched the Women's Health Initiative (WHI), a long-term study of more than 161,000 postmenopausal women focusing on the determinants and prevention of disability and death in older women. Among the targets of investigation in this sweeping study were osteoporosis, breast cancer, and coronary heart disease. The clinical trials that formed the basis of the WHI tested the effects of hormone therapy, diet modification, and calcium and vitamin D supplements on heart disease, bone fractures, and breast cancer (WHI, 2010).

Despite the significance of such sociocultural and gender influences, remember that it would be a mistake to focus exclusively on this, or any one context, in isolation. Health behavior is not an automatic consequence of a given social, cultural, or gender context. For example, although as a group cancer patients who are married tend to survive longer than unmarried persons, marriages that are unhappy and destructive offer no benefit in this regard and may even be linked to poorer health outcomes.

Biopsychosocial "Systems"

ecological-systems approach The viewpoint that nature is best understood as a hierarchy of systems, in which each system is simultaneously composed of smaller subsystems and larger, interrelated systems.

As these examples indicate, the biopsychosocial perspective emphasizes the mutual influences among the biological, psychological, and social contexts of health. More broadly, it is also based on an **ecological-systems approach.** Applied to health, this approach is based on the idea that our well-being is best understood as a hierarchy of systems in which each system is simultaneously composed of smaller subsystems and part of larger, more encompassing systems (Kazak, Bosch, & Klonoff, 2012) (Figure 1.5).

One way to understand the relationship among systems is to envision a target with a bull's eye at the center and concentric rings radiating out from it. In this model, the individual is at the center. Now consider each of us as a system made up of interacting systems such as the endocrine system, the cardiovascular system, the nervous system, and the immune system. (Also keep in mind that, within each of our biological systems, there are smaller subsystems consisting of tissues, nerve fibers, fluids, cells, and genetic material.) If you move out from the individual at the center and into the radiating outer rings, you can see larger systems that interact with us—and these rings include our families, our schools and workplaces, our neighborhoods, our communities, our societies, and our cultures.

Applied to health, the model emphasizes a crucial point: A system at any given level is affected by and affects systems at other levels. For example, a weakened immune system affects specific organs in a person's body, which affect the person's overall biological health, which in turn might affect the person's relationships with his or her family and friends. Conceptualizing health and disease according to a systems approach allows us to understand the whole person more fully. Recognizing the importance of this approach, a growing number of health psychologists are investigating *biopsychosocial health* as a specific outcome measure in their research (Ferris, Kline, & Bourdage, 2012).

Applying the Biopsychosocial Model

To get a better feeling for the usefulness of biopsychosocial explanations of healthy behaviors, consider the example of *alcohol abuse,* which is a maladaptive drinking pattern in which at least one of the following occurs: recurrent drinking despite its

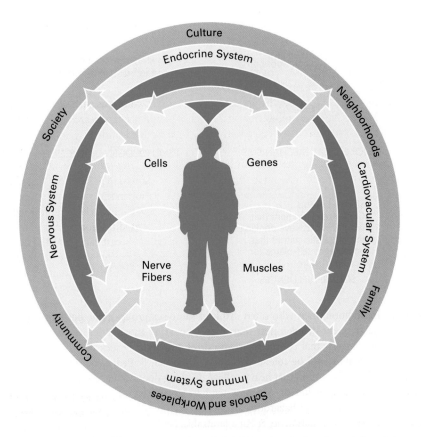

FIGURE 1.5
Ecological-Systems Approach and Health The systems potentially influencing an individual's headache, shortness of breath, sleeplessness, racing heart, and other symptoms of anxiety include the body's internal biological systems (immune, endocrine, cardiovascular, and nervous), as well as an individual's family, neighborhood, and culture.

interference with role obligations; continued drinking despite legal, social, or interpersonal problems related to its use; and recurrent drinking in situations in which intoxication is dangerous. Like most disordered behavior, alcohol abuse is best explained in terms of several mechanisms that include both genetic and environmental components (Ball, 2008) (Figure 1.6). Research studies of families, identical and fraternal twins, and adopted children clearly demonstrate that people (especially men) who have a biological relative who was alcohol dependent are significantly more likely to abuse alcohol themselves (National Institute on Alcohol Abuse and Alcoholism (NIAAA), 2010). In fact, for males, alcoholism in a first-degree relative is the single best predictor of alcoholism (Plomin, DeFries, McClearn, & McGuffin, 2001). In addition, people who inherit a gene variant that results in a deficiency of a key enzyme for metabolizing alcohol are more sensitive to alcohol's effects and far less likely to become problem drinkers (Zakhari, 2006).

On the psychological side, although researchers no longer attempt to identify a single "alcoholic personality," they do focus on specific personality traits and behaviors that are linked with alcohol dependence and abuse. One such trait is poor *self-regulation,* characterized by an inability to exercise control over drinking (Hustad, Carey, Carey, & Maisto, 2009). Another is *negative emotionality,* marked by irritability and agitation. Along with several others, these traits comprise the *alcohol dependency syndrome* that is the basis for a diagnosis of alcohol abuse (Li, Hewitt, & Grant, 2007).

On the social side, alcohol abuse sometimes stems from a history of drinking to cope with life events or overwhelming social demands. Peer pressure, difficult home and work environments, and tension reduction also may contribute to problem drinking. And more generally, as many college students know, certain social contexts promote heavy drinking. Research studies have shown that college students who prefer large social contexts involving both men and women tend to be heavier drinkers than those who prefer smaller mixed-sex

FIGURE 1.6

A Biopsychosocial Model of Alcohol Abuse Alcohol abuse is best understood as occurring in three contexts: biological, psychological, and social.

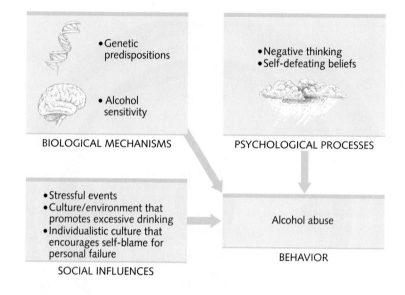

contexts. In addition, men who often drink in same-sex groups (whether large or small) report more frequent drunkenness than men who drink more often in small mixed-sex groups. This suggests that college men who drink heavily may seek out social contexts in which this behavior will be tolerated (LaBrie, Hummer, & Pedersen, 2007). Fortunately, researchers have also found that heavy college drinking does not necessarily predict similar postcollege drinking behavior. Students tend to stop heavy drinking sooner than non-students—*maturing out* of hazardous alcohol use before it becomes a long-term problem (NIAAA, 2006; White, Labouvie, & Papadaratsakis, 2005).

Frequently Asked Questions about a Health Psychology Career

We have seen how views regarding the nature of illness and health have changed over the course of history, examined trends that helped shape the new field of health psychology, and discussed the various theoretical perspectives from which health psychologists work. But you may still have questions about the profession of health psychology. Here are answers to some of the most frequently asked questions.

What Do Health Psychologists Do?

Like all psychologists, health psychologists may serve as *teachers, research scientists,* and/or *clinicians.* As teachers, health psychologists train students in health-related fields such as psychology, physical therapy, and medicine. By understanding the biopsychosocial processes that contribute to certain illnesses, health care professionals can have a clearer understanding of how to prevent them.

As research scientists, they identify the biopsychosocial processes that contribute to health and illness, investigate issues concerning why people do not engage in healthful practices, and evaluate the effectiveness of specific therapeutic interventions. Because

Your Health Assets

College Does a Mind and Body Good

Depending on what your day has been like, it may be difficult for you to believe that attending college is most likely good for your health. To be sure, college can add additional sources of possible stress. Your hectic schedule may include squeezing in an online course between jobs or after putting children to bed at night, leaving you in a sleep-deprived state, with little time for exercising and maintaining a healthy diet. Some group settings on campus may also promote high-risk activities such as binge drinking, violence, and dangerous sexual behaviors. Despite these potential barriers to a healthy lifestyle, women and men who have attended college are healthier than those who have not. Worldwide, college students report fewer symptoms of poor health and lower levels of stress than do nonstudents (Grzywacz, Almeida, Neupert, & Ettner, 2004). Those who graduate from college have lower death rates from all causes, including accidents, infectious diseases, and chronic illness, and they live about 10 years longer than those without a high school diploma (National Center for Health Statistics, 2012).

What factors might explain why higher education is a valuable health asset? One is the impact of college on cognition. According to one classic study (Perry, 1999), thinking advances through nine levels of increasing complexity over a typical four-year college experience. A first-year student may think in simple, dualistic terms (yes/no, right/wrong) on many issues. Over the next three years of college, thinking typically becomes broader and increasingly recognizes the validity of multiple perspectives on issues. Intelligent, educated people thus are more likely to develop higher **health literacy** and become better informed consumers of information, doing their own research and becoming more knowledgeable and empowered when it comes to their health.

A second factor in the college-health relationship is higher income. College students, especially those who graduate, generally find better jobs and have greater average incomes than those who do not (Batty and others, 2008). This gives them greater access to health care and the sometime costly choices of a healthy lifestyle that includes nutritious food, flexible work and leisure time, and safe places to exercise. According to U.S. census data, averaged over a lifetime, a college degree adds about $20,000 per year to a worker's salary.

A third factor is healthier lifestyle. Higher education is associated with better health habits, including avoiding tobacco, eating nutritious food, and exercising regularly. This may partly explain why among U.S. adults, the rate of obesity is 9 percent for those with a college degree, compared to 30 percent for those without (National Center for Health Statistics, 2012).

Throughout the world, the leaders of many nations have accepted the idea that increasing the number of students enrolled in college is an effective way to promote health and increase productivity. This has resulted in **massification** the idea that higher education benefits everyone (that is, the masses) (Altbach, 2010). As a college student, you have an opportunity to acquire many assets that may be reflected in a long, healthy life—including higher income potential, greater health literacy, a social context in which you are surrounded by like-minded, health-conscious friends, and good lifestyle habits.

---

the biopsychosocial model was first developed to explain health problems, until recently the majority of this research has focused on diseases and health-compromising behaviors. Historically, if you weren't a patient, you were considered healthy. However, as part of the positive psychology movement, an increasing amount of research centers on **positive health,** the scientific study of *health assets* that produce longer life and optimal human functioning (APA, 2010). The premise of this movement is simple but critical: The absence of disease and distress is *not* the same thing as health and happiness. The scope of this research—covering assets as diverse as optimism and happiness, psychological hardiness, and the traits of people who live to a ripe old age—shows clearly that the biopsychosocial model guides much of it (see "Your Health Assets").

Clinical health psychologists, who generally focus on treating individuals, are licensed for independent practice in areas such as clinical and counseling psychology. As clinicians, they use the full range of diagnostic assessment, education, and therapeutic techniques in psychology to promote health and assist the physically ill. Interventions are

positive health The scientific study of health assets, which are factors that produce longer life, reduce illness, and increase overall well-being.

health literacy The ability to understand health information and use it to make good decisions about one's health.

massification The transformation of a product or service that was once only available to the wealthy such that it becomes accessible to everyone. Applied to education and health, it is the idea that college can benefit everyone.

not limited to those who are already suffering from a health problem. Healthy or at-risk individuals may be taught preventive healthy behaviors.

Community health psychologists center their work on the health of a community as a whole. They investigate the prevalence of diseases in specific geographical regions and the various factors that might cause them. More broadly, *public health psychologists* investigate the impact of public health programs. They might work to change government health policies to reduce health disparities in low-income and other marginalized groups. They also help organize public health campaigns to prevent the spread of infection, reduce violence, and in other ways promote wellness.

Occupational health psychologists are concerned with the health of people in the workplace. They might work with a business to change workplace policies or counsel individual employees to improve their subjective well-being.

Where Do Health Psychologists Work?

Traditionally, many psychologists accepted teaching or research positions at universities and four-year colleges. Employment opportunities for health psychologists with applied or research skills also include working in government agencies that conduct research, such as the National Institutes of Health (NIH) and the Centers for Disease Control and Prevention (CDC).

In clinics and hospitals, the work of health psychologists falls into several categories. One type of service involves teaching health care providers, conducting research, and becoming involved in policy development. Another type of service involves helping patients cope with illness and the anxiety associated with surgery and other medical interventions. Other clinical health psychologists may administer psychological or neuropsychological tests, or they may intervene to promote patients' adherence to complicated medical regimens. In this capacity, clinical health psychologists often work on interdisciplinary hospital teams. As part of a new model of *integrated care,* these teams improve medical treatment outcomes, lower costs, and offer a successful model for future health care systems (Novotney, 2010a).

In addition, medical residency programs in the United States now have a clear mandate to improve physician training in areas such as sensitivity and responsiveness to patients' culture, age, gender, and disabilities. Increasingly, health psychologists are helping physicians become better listeners and communicators. As we'll see, this mandate stems from mounting evidence that this type of care results in better health outcomes and helps control health care costs (Novotney, 2010a).

Health psychologists may also be found working in health maintenance organizations (HMOs), medical schools, pain and rehabilitation clinics, and private practice (Figure 1.7). A growing number of health psychologists can be found in the workplace, including corporations, nonprofit organizations, and government sectors, where they advise employers and workers on a variety of health-related issues, such as helping employees lose weight and learn adaptive ways of managing stress.

How Do I Become a Health Psychologist?

Preparing for a career in health psychology usually requires an advanced degree in any of a number of different educational programs. Some students enroll in medical or nursing school and eventually become nurses or doctors. Others train for one of the allied health professions, such as nutrition, physical therapy, social work, occupational therapy, or public health. An increasing number of interested undergraduates continue on to graduate

FIGURE 1.7

Where Do Health Psychologists Work? Besides colleges, universities, and hospitals, health psychologists work in a variety of venues, including corporations, HMOs, medical schools, pain and rehabilitation clinics, and independent practices.

Data from *2009 Doctoral Psychology Workforce Fast Facts.* Washington, DC: American Psychological Association.

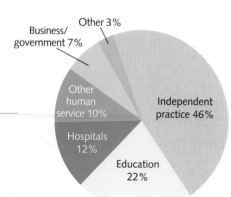

Other 3%
Business/government 7%
Other human service 10%
Hospitals 12%
Education 22%
Independent practice 46%

Those who pursue graduate training in health psychology are more likely to understand the biopsychosocial benefits of participating in a vigorous group activity, such as a martial arts and boxing class.

The Image Bank/Getty Images

school in psychology and acquire research, teaching, and intervention skills. Those who ultimately hope to provide direct services to patients typically take their training in clinical or counseling psychology programs.

Most health psychologists eventually obtain a doctoral degree (Ph.D. or Psy.D.) in psychology. To earn a Ph.D. in psychology, students complete a four- to six-year program, at the end of which they conduct an original research project. Psy.D. programs generally provide slightly more clinical experience and clinical courses, but less research training and experience, than Ph.D. programs.

Graduate training in health psychology is generally based on a curriculum that covers the three basic domains of the biopsychosocial model. Training in the biological domain includes courses in neuropsychology, anatomy, physiology, and psychopharmacology. Training in the psychological domain includes courses in each of the major subfields (biological, developmental, personality, and so on) and theoretical perspectives (social-cultural, cognitive, behavior, neuroscience, and so on). And training in the social domain includes courses on group processes and ways in which the various groups (family, ethnic, and so on) influence their members' health. Some health psychologists also complete specialized training in medical subspecialties such as neurology, immunology, and epidemiology.

Weigh In on Health

Respond to each question below based on what you learned in the chapter. (**Tip:** Use the items in "Summing Up" to take into account related biological, psychological, and social concerns.)

1. Considering how views of health have changed over time, what would be a good description of health for an individual today? How do gender, culture, and the practice of health influence your description?

2. How does the overall health of your school population benefit when different contexts, systems, models, and theories about health are taken into consideration?

3. Your friend Tran is thinking about pursuing a career in health psychology. What general advice would you give him, and how would you suggest he choose a specific career in the field?

Summing Up

1. Health is a state of complete physical, mental, and social well-being. The goals of health psychology are to promote health; prevent and treat illness; investigate the role of biological, behavioral, and social factors in disease; and evaluate and improve the formulation of health policy and the delivery of health care to all people.

2. Although many of the world's citizens have the promise of a longer and better life than their ancestors, these health benefits are not universally enjoyed. Health disparities such as ethnic and socioeconomic group differences in the rates of disease occur in every nation.

Health and Illness: Lessons from the Past

3. In the earliest-known cultures, illness was believed to result from mystical forces and evil spirits that invaded the body. Hippocrates developed the first rational approach to the study of health and disease. Non-Western forms of healing, including TOM and ayurveda, developed simultaneously.

4. In Europe during the Middle Ages, scientific studies of the body (especially dissection) were forbidden, and ideas about health and disease took on religious overtones. Illness was viewed as punishment for evildoing, and treatment frequently involved what amounted to physical torture.

5. French philosopher René Descartes advanced his theory of mind–body dualism—the belief that the mind and body are autonomous processes, each subject to different laws of causality. Descartes's influence ushered in an era of medical research based on the scientific study of the body. This research gave rise to the anatomical, cellular, and germ theories of disease.

6. The dominant view in modern medicine is the biomedical model, which assumes that disease is the result of a virus, bacterium, or some other pathogen invading the body. Because it makes no provision for psychological, social, or behavioral factors in illness, the model embraces both reductionism and mind–body dualism.

7. Sigmund Freud and Franz Alexander promoted the idea that specific diseases could be caused by unconscious conflicts. These views were expanded into the field of psychosomatic medicine, which is concerned with the treatment and diagnosis of disorders caused by faulty processes within the mind. Psychosomatic medicine fell out of favor because it was grounded in psychoanalytic theory and predicated on the outmoded idea that a single problem is sufficient to trigger disease.

Biopsychosocial Perspective

8. Health psychologists approach the study of health and illness from several overlapping perspectives. The life-course perspective in health psychology focuses attention on how aspects of health and illness vary with age, as well as how birth cohort experiences (such as shifts in public health policy) influence health.

9. The sociocultural perspective calls attention to how social and cultural factors, such as ethnic variations in dietary practice and beliefs about the causes of illness, affect health.

10. The gender perspective calls attention to male–female differences in the risk of specific diseases and conditions, as well as in various health-enhancing and health-compromising behaviors.

11. The biopsychosocial perspective in effect combines these perspectives, recognizing that biological, psychological, and social forces act together to determine an individual's health and vulnerability to disease.

12. Biology and behavior do not occur in a vacuum. The new field of epigenetics focuses on environmental factors near and around genes that affect their expression.

13. A key element of the biological context is our species' evolutionary history, and an evolutionary perspective guides the work of many health psychologists

14. According to the ecological-systems model, health is best understood as a hierarchy of systems in which each system is simultaneously composed of smaller subsystems and part of larger, more encompassing systems.

Frequently Asked Questions about a Health Psychology Career

15. Health psychologists are engaged in three primary activities: teaching, research, and clinical intervention. Health psychologists work in a variety of settings, including hospitals, universities and medical schools, health maintenance organizations, rehabilitation clinics, private practice, and, increasingly, the workplace.

16. A growing body of research in health psychology focuses on positive health, the scientific study of health assets that produce longer life and optimal human-functioning.

17. Preparing for a career in health psychology usually requires a doctoral degree. Some students enter health psychology from the fields of medicine, nursing, or one of the allied health professions. An increasing number enroll in graduate programs in health psychology.

Key Terms and Concepts to Remember

health psychology, p. 3
health, p. 3
health disparities, p. 4
Patient Protection and Affordable
  Care Act (PPACA), p. 4
humoral theory, p. 6
epidemic, p. 8
pandemic, p. 8

biomedical model, p. 9
pathogen, p. 9
psychosomatic medicine, p. 10
etiology, p. 11
biopsychosocial perspective,
  p. 11
genomics, p. 12
epigenetic, p. 13

subjective well-being, p. 14
birth cohort, p. 16
immigrant paradox, p. 18
ecological-systems approach, p. 20
positive health, p. 23
health literacy, p. 23
massification, p. 23

 LaunchPad
macmillan learning

To accompany your textbook, you have access to a number of online resources,
including quizzes for every chapter of the book, flashcards, critical thinking exercises,
videos, and *Check Your Health* inventories. To access these resources, please visit the
Straub *Health Psychology* LaunchPad solo at: **launchpadworks.com**

CHAPTER 2

Research in Health Psychology

iStock/Getty Images

Darryl Andrew Kile, the 33-year-old pitching ace for the St. Louis Cardinals, died of coronary disease on June 22, 2002. As news of his sudden death spread, the collective reaction was disbelief. How could an elite athlete die suddenly at such a young age? Kile's death was (wrongly) taken by many as proof that exercise offered no protection against cardiovascular disease. After several weeks of public speculation about drug use or other causes, the coroner attributed Kile's death to a massive heart attack caused by a strong family history of heart disease (his father died of a heart attack at age 44) and 90 percent blockage in two coronary arteries.

About two decades earlier, the world had similarly been shocked by the sudden death of another high-profile athlete— 52-year-old running guru Jim Fixx, who helped launch the running boom in the United States. As with Kile, Fixx's sudden death while running was, regrettably, taken by many as proof that exercise has no real impact on preventing cardiovascular disease. However, this quick explanation was wrong, too. For most of his life, Fixx was overweight and consumed a high-fat, high-cholesterol diet. In addition, he had been a chain smoker, smoking three to four packs of cigarettes a day, and a workaholic, working 16 hours or more each day and getting only a few hours of sleep each night. Fixx was also at high risk of heart disease because his father had died from a heart attack at the young age of 43 years.

Fixx ignored early warning symptoms as well. His fiancée said that he complained of chest tightness during exercise and traveled to Vermont to see whether the fresh air there would alleviate his symptoms, which he believed to be due to allergies. The change of air did not help, and Fixx died while running on his first day in Vermont.

Fixx's autopsy showed severe coronary artery disease, with near-total blockage of one coronary artery and 80 percent blockage of another. There was also evidence of a recent heart attack. On the day Fixx died, more than 1000 other American men and women succumbed to heart attacks. There is overwhelming evidence that heart attacks occur most commonly in males who have high blood pressure, smoke heavily, have high cholesterol levels, and maintain a sedentary lifestyle. Fixx's midlife change to a healthy lifestyle may very well be what allowed him to outlive his father by nine years.

Beware of the trap of believing easy, untested explanations for the causes of diseases or seemingly unexpected physiological events. Medical researchers and health psychologists investigate such cases, comparing situations and considering all relevant factors. Researchers must adopt a formal, systematic approach that has a proven ability to find reliable explanations. This approach is called the scientific method. In this chapter, we will consider how the scientific method is applied to answer questions about health psychology.

Critical Thinking and Evidence-Based Medicine

Health psychology touches on some of the most intriguing, personal, and practical issues of life. Does my family history place me at risk of developing prostate cancer? Which of my lifestyle choices are healthy and which are unhealthy? Why can't I quit smoking? Every day, we seem to be bombarded with new, "definitive" answers to these and countless other vital health questions. Sorting things out can be difficult. Consider, for example, the never-ending controversy surrounding coffee. Almost every day, a study comes out showing that daily (caffeinated) coffee consumption decreases the risk of Alzheimer's disease. Or heart disease. Or Type 2 diabetes. Coffee drinkers rejoice and order a celebratory latte. Then another study is released showing that drinking coffee every day increases gastrointestinal problems, or anemia, or depression. So, is caffeine safe? What are you to believe?

To make good decisions, health psychologists, students, physicians—indeed every one of us—need a "lens" through which to view the information we are bombarded with every day. **Evidence-based medicine** is an approach to health care intended to optimize decision making in treating patients by integrating the best research evidence with clinical expertise and patient values (Sackett, Straus, Richardson, Rosenberg, & Haynes, 2000). This means that all medical interventions are first subjected to rigorous testing and evaluation of their *efficacy* before they are adopted as a *standard of care.*

At the heart of evidence-based medicine is a skeptical attitude that encourages health care providers to evaluate evidence and scrutinize conclusions. This attitude is called *critical thinking,* and it involves a questioning approach to all information and arguments. Whether listening to the evening news report, reading a journal article, or pondering a friend's position, critical thinkers ask questions. How did she arrive at that conclusion? What evidence forms the basis for this person's conclusions? Is there an ulterior motive? Can the results of a particular study be explained in another way? Until you know the answers to these and other questions, you should be cautious—indeed, downright skeptical—of all persuasive arguments, including health reports that appear in the media. Learning which questions to ask will make you a much more informed consumer of health information.

evidence-based medicine The use of current best evidence in making decisions about the care of individual patients or the delivery of health services.

The Dangers of "Unscientific" Thinking

In our quest for greater understanding of healthy behavior, we draw on the available information to formulate *cause-and-effect relationships* about our own and other people's behaviors. If this information derives solely from our personal experiences, beliefs, and attitudes, then we may be like the quick-reacting reporters who tried to make sense of the deaths of Darryl Kile and Jim Fixx—making snap judgments with little attention to accuracy. It is dangerous to base our explanations on hearsay, conjecture, anecdotal evidence, or unverified sources of information. For example, upon seeing a lean, statuesque female gymnast or dancer, we may admire what we believe to be her healthy eating and exercise habits, wishing that we too could possess such willpower and well-being. But we may be shocked to learn that she is actually anorexic and suffering from a stress fracture related to poor diet and excessive, exercise-induced skeletal trauma.

Examples of faulty reasoning unfortunately abound in all fields of science. In the early twentieth century, for example, thousands of Americans died from *pellagra*, a disease marked by dermatitis (skin sores), gastrointestinal disorders, and memory loss. Because the homes of many pellagra sufferers had unsanitary means of sewage removal, many health experts believed that the disease was carried by a microorganism and transmitted through direct contact with infected human excrement. Although hygienic plumbing was certainly a laudable goal, when it came to pinpointing the cause of pellagra, the "experts" fell into a faulty reasoning trap—failing to consider alternative explanations for their observations. This type of leaping to unwarranted (untested) conclusions is an example of **confirmation bias,** which explains why two people can look at the same situation (or data) and draw radically different conclusions.

confirmation bias A form of faulty reasoning in which our expectations prevent us from seeing alternative explanations for our observations.

Fortunately, U.S. Surgeon General Joseph Goldberger's keener powers of observation allowed him to see that many pellagra victims also were malnourished. To pinpoint the cause of the disease, in 1914 Goldberger conducted a simple, if distasteful, empirical test: He mixed small amounts of the feces and urine from two pellagra patients with a few pinches of flour and rolled the mixture into little dough balls, which he, his wife, and several assistants ate! When none of them came down with the disease, Goldberger then fed a group of Mississippi prisoners a diet deficient in niacin and protein (a deficiency that he suspected caused the disease), while another group was fed the normal, more balanced prison diet. Confirming Goldberger's hypothesis, the former group developed symptoms of pellagra within months, while the latter remained disease-free (Stanovich & West, 1998). As this example illustrates, seeking information that confirms preexisting beliefs causes researchers to overlook alternative explanations of observed phenomena.

All cultures develop incorrect beliefs about human behavior. Some people believe the myths that couples who adopt a child are later more likely to conceive a child of their own, or that more babies are born when the moon is full. Be on guard for examples of unscientific psychology in your own thinking.

Health Psychology Research Methods

ealth psychologists use various research methods in their search to learn how psychological factors affect health. The method used depends in large measure on what questions the researcher is seeking to answer. To answer questions regarding how people cope with medical procedures or cancer, for example, a psychologist might observe or ask questions of a large sample of cancer patients. On the other hand, researchers investigating whether lifestyle factors contribute to the onset of cancer might conduct laboratory studies under controlled conditions.

There are two major categories of research methods in psychology—descriptive and experimental (Table 2.1). Health psychologists also borrow methods from the field of **epidemiology,** which seeks to determine the frequency, distribution, and causes of a particular disease or other health outcome in a population. This section describes the research methods employed by psychologists and the tools they use to gather, summarize, and explain their data. Later in this chapter, I will focus on the research methods of epidemiologists.

epidemiology The scientific study of the frequency, distribution, and causes of a particular disease or other health outcome in a population.

Descriptive Studies

Think about how a health psychologist might set about answering the following three questions: What are the psychological and physiological health outcomes for victims of a grave national crisis, such as catastrophic Superstorm Sandy, which made landfall along the New Jersey coastline in October 2012, or the 2015–2016 European refugee crisis? How can hospital staff reduce the anxiety of family members waiting for a loved one to come out of surgery? Does binge drinking occur more often among certain types of college students? Clearly, the answers to each of these important questions will not be found in a research laboratory. Instead, researchers look for answers about the behavior of an individual or a group of people as it occurs in the home, at work, or wherever people spend their time. In such a study, called a **descriptive study,** the researcher observes and records the participants' behavior in a natural setting, often forming hunches that are subjected later to more systematic study. Several types of descriptive studies are commonly used: case studies, interviews, surveys, focus groups, and observational studies.

descriptive study A research method in which researchers observe and record participants' behaviors, often forming hypotheses that are later tested more systematically; includes case studies, interviews and surveys, focus groups, and observational studies.

A case study is a descriptive study in which one person is studied in depth in the hope of revealing general principles. Although case studies are useful in suggesting hypotheses for further study, they do have one serious disadvantage: Any given person may be atypical, limiting the "generalizability" of the results.

Clinical health psychologists use the face-to-face interview as a start for developing a supportive working relationship with a patient. Clinicians also often use surveys for diagnostic assessment as a first step in developing intervention programs. For example,

TABLE 2.1

Comparing Research Methods

Research Method	Research Setting	Data Collection Method	Strengths	Weaknesses
Descriptive studies	Field or laboratory	Case studies, surveys and interviews, focus groups, naturalistic observation	In-depth information about one person; often leads to new hypotheses; detects naturally occurring relationships among variables	No direct control over variables; subject to bias of observer; single cases may be misleading; cannot determine causality; correlation may mask extraneous variables
Experimental studies	Usually laboratory	Statistical comparison of experimental and control groups	High degree of control over independent and dependent variables; random assignment eliminates preexisting differences among groups	Artificiality of laboratory may limit the generalizability of results; certain variables cannot be investigated for practical or ethical reasons
Epidemiological studies	Usually conducted in the field	Statistical comparisons between groups exposed to different risk factors	Useful in determining disease etiology, easy to replicate, good generalizability	Some variables must be controlled by selection rather than by direct manipulation; time-consuming; expensive
Meta-analysis	No new data are collected	Statistical combination of the results of many studies	Helps make sense of conflicting reports, replicable	Potential bias due to selection of studies included

FIGURE 2.1

Did You Have Sexual Intercourse before Age 13? Survey responses from the 2014 Youth Risk Behavior Surveillance survey of high school students throughout the United States reveal that about twice as many ninth-grade girls and boys say they had sex before age 13, compared to twelfth-grade students.

Data from MMWR (June 13, 2014). Youth Risk Behavior Surveillance, United States, 2013. *Morbidity and Mortality Weekly Report.* Centers for Disease Control and Prevention, Table 63. http://www.cdc.gov/mmwr/pdf/ss/ss6304.pdf

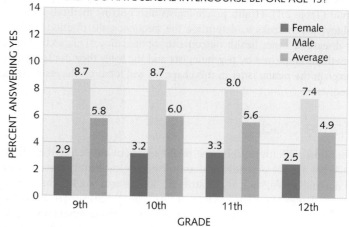

DID YOU HAVE SEXUAL INTERCOURSE BEFORE AGE 13?

Legend: Female, Male, Average

9th: 2.9, 8.7, 5.8
10th: 3.2, 8.7, 6.0
11th: 3.3, 8.0, 5.6
12th: 2.5, 7.4, 4.9

X-axis: GRADE
Y-axis: PERCENT ANSWERING YES

observational study A nonexperimental research method in which a researcher observes and records the behavior of a research participant.

chronic-pain patients may be asked to complete a questionnaire related to their problem that sheds light on the effectiveness of previous treatments and the impact of their condition on their daily functioning. *Focus groups*, in which a small number of participants gather to discuss a specified topic or issue, are also gaining popularity in health and medical research (Wong, 2008).

Survey and interview responses may change with the sequence and wording of the questions. For instance, "global warming" and "climate change" are two ways of wording the same phenomenon, yet survey respondents are more likely to say they believe in climate change than in global warming (McCright & Dunlap, 2011). This is one reason why two surveys that seem to focus on the same issue may reach opposite conclusions.

Another limitation of survey and interview data is that respondents sometimes answer questions in ways that they would like to be perceived or that they believe the investigator expects. For instance, every two years since 1991, a representative sample of all high school students in the United States has been surveyed regarding six categories of health-risk behaviors. The most recent Youth Risk Behavior Surveillance (YRBS) survey included 15,503 students from all 50 states and from schools large and small, public and private (MMWR, June 13, 2014). Among many other topics, students are asked whether they had sexual intercourse before age 13. Every year, compared to the responses of boys who are high school seniors, about twice as many ninth-grade boys say they had sexual intercourse before age 13 (see Figure 2.1). Why might this be? Have students simply forgotten by the time they reach twelfth grade? Are ninth-graders more likely to lie?

Observational Studies

In **observational studies,** the researcher observes participants' behavior and records relevant data. For example, a researcher interested in the physiological effects of everyday hassles might have participants wear a heart-rate monitor while commuting to and from school or work in rush-hour traffic.

Focus groups, such as this one, are increasingly being used in health research.

The Image Bank/Getty Images

Observational studies may be structured or unstructured. Those studies that feature structured observations often take place in the laboratory and involve tasks such as role-playing or responding to a very cold stimulus. In unstructured observations, referred to as naturalistic observation, the researcher attempts to be as unobtrusive as possible in observing and recording the participants' behaviors. For example, a health psychologist might observe family members visiting a parent in a nursing home to gain insight into how people cope with watching a parent decline. These observations may be audiotaped or videotaped and then quantified through rating methods or frequency scores.

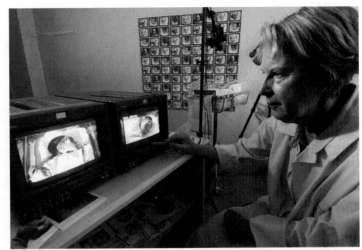

Correlation

Descriptive studies often reveal information about two variables that may be related, such as caffeine consumption and high blood pressure, or hypertension. To determine the extent of a suspected relationship between two variables, psychologists often calculate the **correlation coefficient**.

Suppose, for example, that you are interested in the relationship between body weight and blood pressure. Perhaps you are testing your theory that a lean build lowers a person's risk of cardiovascular disease by reducing hypertension, a documented risk factor. To test your theory with an experiment would require manipulating the body-weight variable and then recording blood pressure. Although measuring blood pressure is certainly possible, manipulating body weight would be unethical. So, instead, you calculate a correlation coefficient. Richard Cooper, Charles Rotimi, and Ryk Ward (1999) did just that, measuring body mass index, or BMI (a measure of a person's weight-to-height ratio), and prevalence of hypertension in a large sample of participants of African descent from several countries. Figure 2.2 displays a **scatterplot** of the results of their study. Each point on the graph represents two numbers for a sample of participants from one country: average BMI and prevalence of hypertension. Notice that the relationship between the two variables appears to be both fairly strong (the points fall roughly along a straight line) and positive (the points sweep upward from the lower left to the upper right). So, body mass and hypertension tend to increase together.

In an observational study, the researcher observes participants' behavior and records relevant data, such as the facial expressions this newborn makes while sleeping.

correlation coefficient A statistical measure of the strength and direction of the relationship between two variables, and thus of how well one predicts the other.

scatterplot A graphed cluster of data points, each of which represents the values of two variables in a descriptive study.

FIGURE 2.2

The Relationship between Body Mass Index and Hypertension in People of African Descent Body mass index (BMI) measures a person's weight-to-height ratio; BMIs over 25 are generally considered a sign of being overweight. In a study comparing key locations in the westward African migration, researchers found that as BMI increased, so did the prevalence of hypertension. The scatterplot reveals a strong positive correlation between BMI and hypertension. The solid line confirms this, showing an upward slope and fairly tight clustering of the data points.

Data from Cooper, R. S., Rotimi, C. N., & Ward, R. (1999). The puzzle of hypertension in African-Americans. *Scientific American, 280*(2), 59.

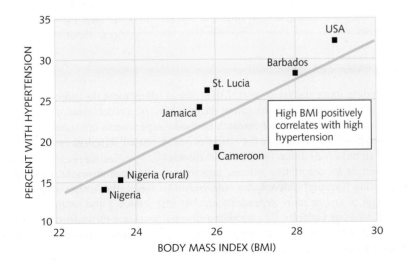

High BMI positively correlates with high hypertension

Interpreting Data...

Association versus Causation

Statistical literacy is the ability to read and interpret statistics in graphs, tables, surveys, and research studies, and to think critically about arguments that use statistics as evidence (Schield, 2010). It focuses on the skills of understanding what is being asserted in a research report, asking good questions, and evaluating evidence.

A common error in reasoning about the results of research is mistaking statements of association for statements of causation. Consider three claims from a hypothetical observational study of body weight and height:

1. People who weigh more tend to be taller (than people who weigh less).
2. Weight is positively associated with height.
3. If you gain weight, you can expect to get taller.

Statement 1 is clearly an example of an association between the variables weight and height. Statement 2 may be misinterpreted as implying causation; that is, changes in weight are mistakenly viewed *as a physical change within one participant in the study*. Statement 3, which is obviously false, is an example of an implied causal relationship.

In this example, it is easy to see that the truth of statement 2 doesn't mean that statement 3 is also true. A common mistake, however, is to conclude that if statement 3 is false, then statement 2 also must be false.

Let's look at another example.

1. Teenagers who play violent video games are more likely to engage in antisocial behavior.
2. Violent video game playing is positively associated with antisocial behavior.
3. If juveniles played fewer violent video games, they would exhibit less antisocial behavior.

In this context, it is more likely that a person will conclude that if statement 2 is true, then statement 3 also must be true. To be statistically literate, one must understand that the difference between the two statements is the difference between association and causation. If the results of an observational study demonstrate that statement number 2 is true, this finding is *evidence* for the possible truth of statement 3.

---

statistical literacy The ability to read and interpret statistics and to think critically about arguments that use statistics as evidence.

It is tempting to draw cause-and-effect conclusions from the Cooper, Rotimi, and Ward study results. However, even when two variables are strongly correlated, one does not necessarily cause the other. Maybe high blood pressure and a high BMI are both caused by a third factor, such as not enough exercise. Correlations do not rule out the possible contributions of other variables. Even if two variables *are* causally related, correlations do not pinpoint directionality—in this case, whether a high BMI elevates blood pressure or vice versa (see Interpreting Data: Association versus Causation).

Despite certain limitations noted in this section, the use of descriptive studies—including case studies, interviews, surveys, observational studies, and focus groups—are often an important first step in research. In health psychology, correlations identify relationships, often among several variables, that later may be studied more closely with experiments.

Experimental Studies

Although descriptive studies are useful, they cannot tell us about the causes of the behaviors that we observe. To pinpoint causal relationships, researchers conduct experiments. Considered the pinnacle of the research methods, experiments are commonly used in health psychology to investigate the effects of health-related behaviors (such as exercise, diet, and so on) on an illness (such as heart disease).

In contrast to descriptive studies, experiments test hypotheses by systematically manipulating (varying) one or more *independent variables* (the "causes") while looking for changes in one or more *dependent variables* (the "effects") and *controlling* (holding constant) all other variables. By controlling all variables except the independent variable, the researcher ensures that any change in the dependent variable is *caused* by the independent variable rather than by another extraneous variable.

FIGURE 2.3

Psychological Research Methods A psychologist interested in studying the relationship between exercise and depression might follow these steps:

1. Using observation, surveys, interviews, and case study results, determine that there is a *negative correlation* between the amount of exercise and depression levels. Higher exercise levels predict lower levels of depression.

2. Use an *experiment* to test the *hypothesis* that exercising more will lower depression levels in mildly depressed individuals.
   Independent variable: exercise
   Dependent variable: depression levels

| Administer surveys to volunteer participants that assess depression levels. | → | Randomly assign the mildly depressed participants to either the experimental or the control conditions for 10 weeks. | → | A. Experimental condition: Exercise aerobically for 20 minutes, three times per week. |
| | | | | B. Control condition: No aerobic exercise. |

3. Readminister surveys that assess depression levels. Compare depression levels before and after for each participant, and calculate any differences between the experimental and control conditions.

A growing body of research evidence demonstrates that symptoms of depression often improve with exercise (Harvard Medical School, 2010).

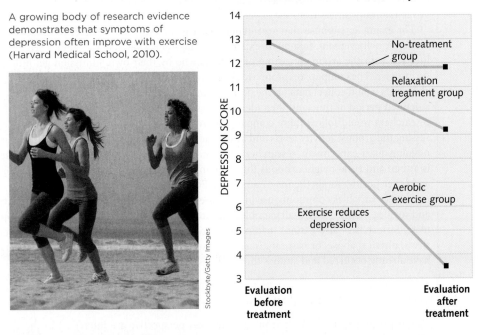

McCann & Holmes (1984) Study Results

DEPRESSION SCORE

No-treatment group

Relaxation treatment group

Aerobic exercise group

Exercise reduces depression

Evaluation before treatment — Evaluation after treatment

Stockbyte/Getty Images

Typically, the researcher randomly assigns a sample of participants to two or more study groups and administers the condition or treatment of interest (the independent variable) to one group, the *experimental group,* and a different or no treatment to the other group, the *control group.* For example, one experimental study examined the impact of an SMS-texting and gaming intervention to encourage physical activity (Thorsteinsen, Vittersø, & Svendsen, 2014). The participants were healthy adults recruited through ads in local newspapers. Researchers *randomly assigned* participants to the intervention or to a control group for comparison. Participants in the intervention group received daily text messages and interactive gaming elements that promoted the health benefits of physical activity. Compared to control group participants, who received text messages and gaming elements unrelated to health and exercise, those in the intervention group reported significantly more minutes of physical activity at higher intensity levels over the three-month study.

Health psychology is somewhat unique among the subfields of psychology in that it studies a variety of variables as cause and effect. As possible "causes," health psychologists examine internal states (such as optimism and feelings of self-efficacy), overt behaviors (such as exercise and cigarette smoking), and external stimuli (such as a stressful job or a therapeutic program to promote relaxation). As possible "effects," they investigate overt behaviors (such as coping reactions to stressful employment), physiological measurements (such as blood pressure or cholesterol levels), and psychological states (such as anxiety levels). See Figure 2.3 on page 35 for an example of how psychological research methods may be used to assess an issue of interest to health psychologists.

Quasi-Experiments

quasi-experiment A study comparing two groups that differ naturally on a specific variable of interest.

When health psychologists cannot manipulate the variable of interest or randomly assign participants to experimental and control groups, they have another option: quasi-experiments. A quasi-experiment (*quasi* means "resembling") is similar to an experiment in that it involves two or more *comparison* groups. A **quasi-experiment** is not a true experiment, however, because it uses groups that differ from the outset on the variable under study (the *subject variable*). Therefore, no cause-and-effect conclusions can be drawn. (Notice that we refer to a *comparison group* rather than a *control group* because the group naturally differs from the experimental group and no variable is being controlled.)

For example, suppose that researchers wish to investigate the effect of exercise on academic achievement. In a quasi-experiment, the subject variable would be a sedentary lifestyle, with the group consisting of students who by their own admission get little or no exercise. The comparison group would be students who exercise regularly. Health psychologists would collect data on the participants' base levels of daily physical activity over a defined period of time and then identify separate "active" and "sedentary" groups. The researchers would follow these comparison groups for a period of years, regularly reassessing the groups' activity levels and academic achievement. As another example, in one ongoing quasi-experiment, researchers are comparing the diet and health of people living in urban and rural neighborhoods that vary in the local availability of fruits, vegetables, and other healthy foods (Pennsylvania Fresh Food Financing Initiative, 2012).

Subject variables commonly used in quasi-experiments include age, gender, ethnicity, and socioeconomic status—all variables that are either impossible or unethical to manipulate. Researchers also cannot manipulate variables to produce extreme environmental stress, physical abuse, or natural disasters. In such cases, the researcher finds events that have already occurred and studies the variables of interest.

Developmental Studies

cross-sectional study A type of observational study in which data are collected from a population, or representative subset, *at one specific point in time.*

Health psychologists working from the life-span perspective are interested in the ways that people change or remain the same over time. To answer questions about the process of change, researchers use two basic research techniques: *cross-sectional* and *longitudinal studies.*

In a **cross-sectional study,** data are collected on the whole study population (such as comparing groups of people of various ages) at a single point in time. In the YRBS study, for instance, researchers compared six types of risky health behaviors (the dependent variables) among 9th- through 12th-grade students in the United States. A challenge in cross-sectional research is to make sure that the various groups are similar in ways other than different levels of the independent variable—such as socioeconomic status—that might affect the characteristic being investigated. If the groups are similar, then any differences in early patterns among them may be attributed to the variable of interest—in the YRBS example, age-related processes.

Matching different age groups for all subject variables other than age is difficult to do. Another limitation of cross-sectional studies is that they do not reveal information about changes in people over a period of time.

If researchers want to be very sure that age, rather than some other variable, is the reason for differences in the characteristics of different age groups, they may conduct a **longitudinal study,** in which a single group of individuals is observed over a long span of time. This allows information about a person at one age to be compared with information about the same person at another age, revealing how this person changed over time.

> **longitudinal study** A study in which a single group of people is observed over a long span of time.

Suppose that you are interested in studying age-related changes in how people cope with stress. If you choose a cross-sectional approach, you might interview a sample of, say, 25 adults at each of five ages—for example 20, 30, 40, 50, and 60 years—and gather information about the ways in which they handle job stress, family quarrels, financial problems, and so forth. On the other hand, if you choose a longitudinal study to explore the same span of years, you (or, more likely, the researchers who will continue your study 40 years from now) would interview a group of 20-year-olds today and again when they are 30, 40, 50, and 60 years of age. The longitudinal study thus eliminates confounding factors, such as differences in the types of stress encountered.

Longitudinal studies may be the "design of choice" from the life-span perspective, but they have several drawbacks. Such studies are very time consuming and expensive to conduct. More important, over the span of years of longitudinal studies, it is common for some participants to drop out because they move away, die, or simply fail to show up for the next scheduled interview or observation. When the number of dropouts is large, the results of the study may become skewed. Another potential problem is that people who remain in longitudinal studies may change in the characteristic of interest, but for reasons that have little to do with their advancing age. For example, our study of age-related coping responses to stress may show that older people cope more adaptively by not allowing everyday hassles to get to them. But suppose that a large number of the participants dropped out of the study midway (or perhaps died of stress-related illnesses!), and those who remained tended to be those employed in low-stress occupations. Can the researcher conclude that age has produced the results? Despite these drawbacks, longitudinal studies are relatively common in health psychology because they afford a unique opportunity for researchers to observe health changes that occur gradually over long periods of time.

Epidemiological Research: Tracking Disease

When researchers consider the role of psychological and behavioral factors in health, among the first questions asked are: Who contracts which diseases, and what factors determine whether a person gets a particular disease? Such questions are addressed by the field of epidemiology.

Although health recordkeeping can be traced back to ancient Greece and Rome, epidemiology was not formalized as a modern science until the nineteenth century, when epidemic outbreaks of cholera, smallpox, and other infectious diseases created grave

The Granger Collection, New York

DEATH'S DISPENSARY.
OPEN TO THE POOR, GRATIS, BY PERMISSION OF THE PARISH.

The Pump Handle—Symbol of Effective Epidemiology Since John Snow's pioneering efforts to eradicate cholera in nineteenth-century London, the pump handle has remained a symbol of effective epidemiology. Today, the John Snow Pub, located near the site of the once-troublesome pump, boasts of having the original handle. This cartoon was published in 1866 in the London periodical *Fun* with the caption "Death's Dispensary, Open to the Poor, Gratis, By Permission of the Parish."

morbidity As a measure of health, the number of cases of a specific illness, injury, or disability in a given group of people at a given time.

mortality As a measure of health, the number of deaths due to a specific cause in a given group of people at a given time.

incidence The number of new cases of a disease or condition that occur in a specific population within a defined time interval.

prevalence The total number of diagnosed cases of a disease or condition that exist at a given time.

public health threats. As with efforts to pinpoint the cause of more recent conditions, such as the increase in resistant bacterial infections, these diseases were conquered largely as a result of the work of epidemiologists whose painstaking research gradually pinpointed their causes.

The modern era of epidemiology began with the work of John Snow during the 1848 outbreak of cholera in London (Frerichs, 2000). Snow laboriously recorded each death from cholera throughout the city, and he noticed that death rates were nearly 10 times higher in one part of the city than elsewhere. In some instances, residents on one side of a residential street were stricken with the disease far more often than were their neighbors on the opposite side of the street. Like a good detective solving a mystery, Snow kept looking for clues until he found something different in the backgrounds of the high-risk groups: polluted drinking water. Although two separate water companies supplied most of the residents of south London, their boundaries were laid out in patchwork fashion, so residents living on the same street often received their water from different sources. By comparing the death rates with the distribution of customers getting polluted and nonpolluted water, Snow inferred that the cholera came from an as-yet-unidentified "poison" in the polluted water, and thus the field of epidemiology was born.

One incident during this epidemic became legendary. In the neighborhood at the intersection of Cambridge Street and Broad Street, the incidence of cholera cases was so great that the number of deaths reached more than 500 in 10 days. After investigating the site, Snow concluded that the cause was centered on the Broad Street pump. After the doubtful but panicky town officials ordered the pump handle removed, the number of new cases of cholera dropped dramatically. Although the bacterium responsible for transmitting cholera would not be discovered for another 30 years, Snow devised an obvious intervention that broke the citywide epidemic: He simply forced the city to shut down the polluted water main.

Since Snow's time, epidemiologists have described in detail the distribution of many different infectious diseases. In addition, they have identified many of the *risk factors* linked to both favorable and unfavorable health outcomes. In a typical study, epidemiologists measure the occurrence of a particular health outcome in a population and then attempt to discover why it is distributed as it is by relating it to specific characteristics of people and the environments in which they live. For example, some forms of cancer are more prevalent in certain parts of the country than in others. By investigating these geographical areas, epidemiologists have been able to link certain cancers with the toxic chemicals found in these environments.

Epidemiologists record **morbidity,** which is the number of cases of a specific illness, injury, or disability in a given group of people at a given time. They also track **mortality,** which is the number of deaths due to a specific cause, such as heart disease, in a given group at a given time. Morbidity and mortality are outcome measures that are usually reported in terms of *incidence* or *prevalence*. **Incidence** refers to the number of new cases of a disease, infection, or disability, such as whooping cough, that occur in a specific population within a defined period of time. **Prevalence** is defined as the *total* number of diagnosed cases of a disease or condition that exist at a given time. It includes both previously reported cases and new cases at a given moment in time. Thus, if an epidemiologist wished to know how many people overall have hypertension, she would examine prevalence rates. If, however, she sought to determine the frequency with which hypertension is diagnosed, she would look at incidence rates.

To clarify the distinction between incidence and prevalence, consider Figure 2.4, which compares the incidence and prevalence of leading causes of death in the United States between 1980 and 2010. Over this time period, deaths due to accidents and cancer have had a high prevalence and stable incidence, while deaths due to diseases of the heart and stroke have declined.

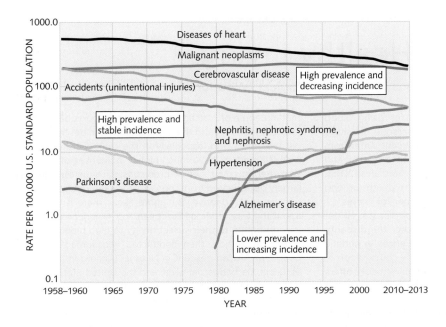

FIGURE 2.4

Age-Adjusted U.S. Death Rates for Leading Causes Between 1980 and 2013, deaths due to malignant neoplasms (cancer) and accidents had a high prevalence and stable incidence, while deaths due to diseases of the heart and cerebrovascular disease (stroke) were highly prevalent but had a decreasing incidence. In contrast, deaths attributed to hypertension, Parkinson's disease, and Alzheimer's disease had a lower prevalence but rising incidence.

Data from Heron, M. (2012). Deaths: Leading causes for 2010. *National Vital Statistics Reports, 61*(7). Hyattsville, MD: National Center for Health Statistics.

Xu, J. Q., Kochanek, K. D., Murphy, S. L., & Tejada-Vera, B. (2007). *National vital statistics reports web release, 58*(19). Hyattsville, MD: National Center for Health Statistics. Released May 2010.

Objectives in Epidemiological Research

Epidemiologists use several research methods to obtain data on the incidence, prevalence, and **etiology** (origins) of disease. Like research methods in psychology, epidemiological research follows the logical progression from description to explanation to prediction and control. Epidemiologists have three fundamental objectives:

etiology The scientific study of the causes or origins of specific diseases.

1. Pinpoint the etiology of a particular disease in order to generate hypotheses.

2. Evaluate the hypotheses.

3. Test the effectiveness of specific preventive health interventions.

Epidemiologists start by counting current cases of an illness (prevalence) or measuring the rate at which new cases appear (incidence) to describe the overall health status of a population. Then they analyze this information to generate hypotheses about which subgroup differences are responsible for the disease, just as John Snow found water source differences that affected cholera prevalence in different groups. A more recent example comes from epidemiologists' efforts to discern the etiology of hypertension in African-Americans (see Diversity and Healthy Living).

Once epidemiologists have identified the origins of a disease or health condition and generated hypotheses about its causes, they evaluate those hypotheses. For example, some doctors have noted that women who smoke are more likely than men who smoke to develop lung cancer. Could hormonal differences, or some other factor linked to gender, allow the cellular damage that cigarette smoking causes to occur more rapidly in women than in men? Indeed, large-scale epidemiological studies have reported this very finding (Iarmarcovai, Bonassi, Botta, Baan, & Orsiere, 2008; Hakim and others, 2012).

Epidemiologists test new hypotheses by attempting to predict the incidence and prevalence of diseases. If the predictions are borne out by the epidemiological data, researchers gain confidence that their understanding of the etiology of the disease is increasing. The emerging science of molecular epidemiology, which relates genetic, metabolic, and biochemical factors to epidemiological data on disease incidence and prevalence, also promises to improve researchers' ability to pinpoint the causes of human disease.

Diversity and Healthy Living

Hypertension in African-Americans: An Epidemiological "Whodunit"

Although one in four Americans experiences rising blood pressure with age, for non-Hispanic black persons, the situation is much more serious: More than 40 percent suffer from hypertension that contributes to heart disease, stroke, and kidney failure (National Center for Health Statistics, 2015). Hypertension accounts for 20 percent of the deaths among blacks in the United States—twice the number for whites.

In their effort to understand and control disease, epidemiologists have sought to determine whether the disparity between blacks and whites is due to differences in genetic susceptibility, environmental factors, or some combination of the two. As discussed in Chapter 1, evolutionary theory offers one perspective on why a certain ethnic or racial group is at greater risk for a particular health outcome. The argument goes as follows: As a result of natural selection, some members of the group in question (and their genes) survived, while others did not. If the survivors primarily mate with members of the same population, their genes are not mixed with those of other groups, and the resulting genetic traits begin to appear with increasing frequency among group members.

Some researchers have suggested that the voyages in slave ships caused exactly the kind of environmental pressure that would select for a predisposition to high blood pressure. During the voyages, many died, often from "salt-wasting conditions" such as diarrhea, dehydration, and infection. Thus, the ability to retain salt might have had a survival value for Africans transported to America against their will. Today, of course, salt retention is *not* adaptive, and it is linked to hypertension.

In 1991, Richard Cooper and his colleagues began a research project that concentrated on the forced migration of West Africans between the sixteenth and nineteenth centuries caused by the slave trade. Knowing that the incidence and prevalence of hypertension in rural West Africa is among the lowest of any place in the world, the researchers compared the prevalence of hypertension in West Africa with that in people of African descent in other parts of the world. The researchers found that people of African descent in other parts of the world, especially in the United States and the United Kingdom, have much higher incidences of hypertension. Perhaps the genes predisposing hypertension have largely disappeared from the West African population, where they are not adaptive. But more likely, there is something about the way of life of European and American blacks that is contributing to their susceptibility to high blood pressure.

The researchers then conducted widespread testing of people of African descent in Nigeria, Cameroon, Zimbabwe, St. Lucia, Barbados, Jamaica, and the United States. In addition to monitoring blood pressure, the researchers focused on high-salt diets, obesity, activity levels, and other common risk factors for hypertension. After several years of investigation, the researchers concentrated on Africans in Nigeria, Jamaica, and Chicago as representative of three key points in the westward movement of Africans from their native lands (see Figure 2.5). The findings were startling: Only 7 percent of those in rural Nigeria had high blood pressure, compared with 26 percent of black Jamaicans and 33 percent of black Americans. In addition, several risk factors for high blood pressure became increasingly prevalent as testing moved westward across the Atlantic. As we saw earlier (see Figure 2.2), body mass index (BMI), a measure of weight relative to height, rose steadily from Africa to Jamaica to the United States, as did the incidence of hypertension. Being overweight, with an associated lack of exercise and poor diet, explained nearly 50 percent of the increased risk for hypertension that African-Americans face, as compared with Nigerians.

The researchers' data suggest that rising blood pressure is not an unavoidable hazard of modern life for people of all skin colors. The human cardiovascular system evolved in a rural African setting in which obesity was uncommon, salt intake was moderate, the diet was low in fat, and high levels of

The final goal of epidemiological research is to determine the effectiveness of intervention programs created as a result of this research. For example, AIDS intervention programs, such as needle-exchange and safer-sex initiatives, tested in large groups of high-risk participants have been determined to be effective in reducing the incidence of new cases of AIDS in targeted groups (see Chapter 12).

Research Methods in Epidemiology

To achieve their purposes, epidemiologists use a variety of research methods, including *retrospective studies, prospective studies,* and *clinical trials.* Like research methods in psychology, each epidemiological method has its strengths and weaknesses.

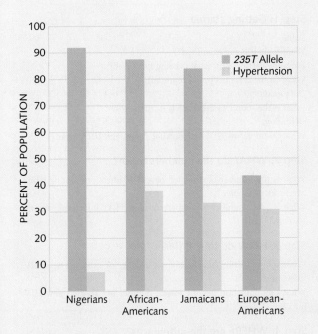

FIGURE 2.5

Incidence of the 235T Gene and Hypertension among Different Ethnic Groups Epidemiologists expected that people who carried the 235T gene would have a higher incidence of hypertension. Surprisingly, 235T is common in certain groups (such as Nigerians), in whom hypertension is exceedingly rare. These findings suggest that both nature and nurture play a role in the development of high blood pressure.

Data from Cooper, R. S., Rotimi, C. N., & Ward, R. (1999). The puzzle of hypertension in African-Americans. *Scientific American, 280*(2), 62.

physical activity were common. The life of subsistence farmers in Nigeria has not changed much, so their blood pressure hardly rises with age, and cardiovascular disease is virtually unknown. This group functions as an epidemiological comparison group against which researchers can test hypotheses about what causes elevated blood pressure in those of African descent.

For instance, blood pressure is higher in the nearby city of Ibadan, Nigeria, than in neighboring rural areas, despite only small differences in the overall level of obesity and salt intake. The researchers suspect that other variables, such as psychological and social stress and lack of physical activity, may help account for the increase. In North America and Europe, those of African descent face a unique kind of stress—racial discrimination. The effect of racism on blood pressure is difficult to establish, of course, but it is worth noting that the average blood pressure of blacks in certain parts of the Caribbean, including Cuba and rural Puerto Rico, is nearly the same as that of other racial groups. Could it be that the relationships among races in these societies impose fewer insults on the cardiovascular system than those in the continental United States do?

The *slavery hypertension hypothesis* remains controversial, and it is important to remember that no single gene or environmental factor can explain why hypertension occurs and why it is so common in African-Americans. Critics of the hypothesis argue that even if a predisposition to salt retention may have advantaged some individual slaves, other factors—such as new selective pressures in North America and mating with non-Africans—would have *increased genetic variability,* rather than reduce today's African-Americans to a single hypertension gene (Kaufman, 2006). They also point to the much larger body of evidence showing that stressful environments raise blood pressure ... and that few things are as consistently stressful as being a member of a marginalized group.

Retrospective studies begin with a group of people who have a certain disease or condition and then look backward in time in an attempt to reconstruct the characteristics that led to their condition and that distinguish them from people who are not affected. For example, retrospective research played an important role in identifying the risk factors that led to AIDS. Initially, researchers observed a sharp increase in the incidence of a rare and deadly form of cancer called Kaposi's sarcoma among gay men and intravenous drug users. By taking extensive medical histories of the men who developed this cancer, epidemiologists were able to pinpoint unprotected anal sex as a common background factor among the first men to die from this deadly form of cancer. This was years before the AIDS virus, the human immunodeficiency virus (HIV), was isolated (see Chapter 12).

retrospective study A longitudinal study that looks back at the history of a group of people, often one suffering from a particular disease or condition.

Interpreting Data...

Tables and Graphs

The ability to interpret information presented in tables and graphs is a key element of statistical literacy. Lacking *graph literacy*, for instance, makes us more likely to rely on the interpretation of others, including those who may present information in carefully chosen ways that support a particular point of view (Gaissmaier and others, 2012). It may be a politician arguing against a policy on climate science, a pharmaceutical company representative presenting evidence for the efficacy of a new drug for the treatment of cancer, or simply a person debating a social problem such as gun control. The information may be presented via printed material in books and journals, during an evening news program or a political speech, on websites, or in survey or opinion-poll data. Whatever the source, learning to scrutinize such information carefully will help you to understand that "all statistics are products of social activity" and should be subject to careful scrutiny (Best, 2002). The following is a *five-step framework* that you can use for interpreting tables and graphs.

Step 1: Getting started

Carefully examine the title; the labels of columns, rows, and graph axes; legends; footnotes; and other details of the table or graph.

Step 2: *What* do the numbers mean?

Make sure that you know what all the numbers represent. Find the largest and smallest values in each category of the graph or table to get an overall impression of the data.

Step 3: *How* do they differ?

Look at the differences in the values of the data in a single row, column, or part of a graph or table. This may involve changes over time, or comparison with a category, such as male and female.

Step 4: *Where* are the differences?

What are the relationships that connect the variables being presented in the table or graph? Use information from step 3 to help you make comparisons across two or more categories.

Step 5: *Why* do they change?

If you see differences in the data, why do you think they are occurring?

Now let's apply the framework to actual data that are illustrated in Figure 2.6. Make sure that you understand the importance of—and answers to—each of the questions listed in column 2.

Step 1: Getting started

Scope
What topic is being examined?
From the vertical axis, what is being measured?
What do the columns (bars) represent?
Data quality
What is the source of the data? Is it trustworthy?
Definitions
What do the terms *HIV, heterosexual, MSM,* and *IDUs* mean?

Step 2: WHAT do the numbers mean?

What is the number of expected new HIV infections among white heterosexual women?
What is the number of expected new HIV infections among Hispanic men?

Step 3: HOW do they differ?

What subpopulation has the highest number of expected new HIV infections?
What subpopulation has the lowest number of expected new HIV infections?

Step 4: WHERE are the differences?

Compare the values for African-American MSM and African-American heterosexual men, which involve individuals of the same gender. Why might these values be different?
Compare the values for white heterosexual women and Hispanic heterosexual women, which also involve individuals of the same gender. Why might these values be different?

Step 5: WHY do they change?

What subpopulations are missing in the figure? Why are they missing?
What other observations can you make about what you see in these data?

Source: Kemp, M., and Kissane, B. (2010). A five-step framework for interpreting tables and graphs in their contexts. In C. Reading (Ed.), *Data and context in statistics education: Towards an evidence-based society. Proceedings of the Eighth International Conference on Teaching Statistics.* Voorburg, The Netherlands: International Statistical Institute.

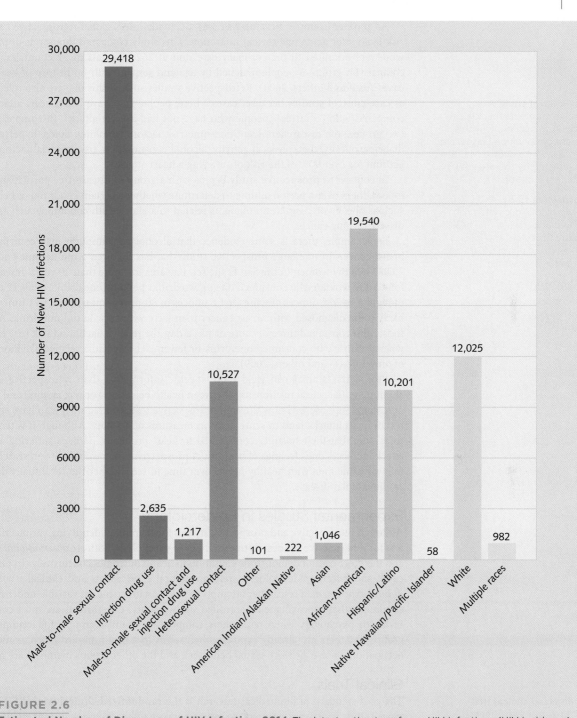

FIGURE 2.6
Estimated Number of Diagnoses of HIV Infection, 2014 The latest estimates of new HIV infections (HIV incidence) in the United States indicate that HIV remains a serious health problem. Certain groups continue to be disproportionately affected by HIV, including men who have sex with men (MSM) and intravenous drug users (IDUs).

Data from Centers for Disease Control and Prevention. (2015). *HIV Surveillance Report, 2014*; vol. 26. http://www.cdc.gov/hiv/library/reports/surveillance/. Retrieved March 30, 2016, from http://www.cdc.gov/hiv/pdf/library/reports/surveillance/cdc-hiv-surveillance-report-us.pdf.

case-control study A retrospective epidemiological study in which people with a disease or condition (cases) are compared with people who are not affected by the disease or condition (controls).

prospective study A forward-looking longitudinal study that begins with a healthy group of subjects and follows the development of a particular disease in that sample.

As another example, INTERHEART was a Canadian-led, global retrospective study of risk factors for acute myocardial infarction. This study compared thousands of patients who were admitted to the coronary care unit at 262 hospitals in 52 countries with a comparison group of people matched by age and sex but with no history of heart disease (Yusuf and others, 2004). Retrospective studies such as this one are also referred to as **case-control studies** because "cases" (here, people who have had a heart attack) are compared with "controls" (people who have not had a heart attack). In comparing the two groups, the researchers identified nine risk factors (smoking, lipids, hypertension, diabetes, obesity, diet, physical activity, alcohol consumption, psychosocial factors) that account for over 90% of the risk of suffering a heart attack.

In contrast, a **prospective study** begins with a group of disease-free participants and follows them over a period of time to determine whether a certain condition or behavior, such as obesity or cigarette smoking, is related to a later health condition, such as heart disease or lung cancer.

For example, there is some evidence that alcohol consumption may contribute to breast cancer. In one large prospective study that has followed a multiethnic cohort of 70,033 healthy women in the San Francisco Bay area for more than 20 years, researchers found that women who consumed one to two drinks per day (one drink equals 12 ounces of regular beer, 5 ounces of wine, or 1.5 ounces of 80-proof liquor) were 1.21 times more likely to be diagnosed with breast cancer than were women who did not drink. Among those who consumed three or more drinks a day, the relative likelihood risk rose to 1.38, whereas those who consumed one drink or fewer each day had a relative likelihood risk of only 1.08 (Li and others, 2009).

Prospective studies can yield more specific information than retrospective studies about potential causal relationships between health behaviors (or risk factors) and health outcomes. Suppose we know through retrospective research that men who have suffered recent heart attacks tend to score high on measures of hostility. Although it is tempting to assume that their hostility contributed to heart problems, perhaps suffering a heart attack increases one's feelings of hostility. A prospective study would allow researchers to follow hostile men with healthy hearts over time to see whether they eventually develop cardiovascular disease.

Experimental Studies in Epidemiology

Although retrospective and prospective studies are helpful in identifying various risk factors for illnesses, like the descriptive methods in psychology, both are *observational studies* and therefore cannot demonstrate causation in health outcomes conclusively. To pinpoint cause and effect, epidemiologists rely on natural experiments and clinical trials. In a *natural experiment*, a researcher attempts to study an independent variable under natural conditions that approximate a controlled study. Natural experiments are most common in health psychology when researchers compare two similar groups; for example, one group's members are already exposing themselves to a health hazard (such as nicotine, occupational noise, or risky sexual behavior), and the other group's members are not.

Clinical Trials

randomized clinical trial (RCT) A true experiment that tests the effects of one independent variable (such as a particular drug or treatment) on individuals or on groups of individuals (community field trials).

The gold standard of biomedical research is the **randomized clinical trial (RCT)**. This type of study is a true experiment, so researchers can safely draw conclusions about cause-and-effect relationships. RCTs test the effects of one or more independent variables on individuals or on groups of individuals.

Although many variations are possible, the most common clinical trial for individuals involves measurement of a *baseline* (starting point) level of a condition, followed by a measure of the effectiveness of a treatment. For example, in testing the effectiveness of an analgesic drug on migraine headaches, the researcher first records each participant's pretrial level of headache pain, perhaps using a self-report pain scale. Once the baseline establishes a pretreatment reference value in the dependent variable (the subject's pain), treatment (the drug), which is the independent variable, is administered, and the dependent element (pain) is assessed once again. If the treatment data show improvement over the baseline data, the researcher concludes that the treatment is likely to be effective in the future. To be sure that the treatment itself, rather than some extraneous factor (such as the mere passage of time), produced the improvement, the researcher removes the medication and then observes whether the baseline condition returns and symptoms reappear. If they do, the researcher can be even more confident in accepting the hypothesis that the drug produces a significant (clinical) improvement.

In the most common type of clinical trial involving groups, baseline measures are taken, and then the participants are randomly assigned to either an experimental group that receives the treatment of interest, such as a new headache medication, or a control group that receives a placebo. If outside variables have been controlled properly, then differences in the groups can be attributed to differences in the treatment.

In the final procedure, a *community field trial*, researchers compare people in one community to those in another. For example, children in one school might receive extensive educational information on the benefits of always wearing a helmet when bicycling, skateboarding, or using inline skates. A control group of children from another school would not receive the educational campaign. Researchers would compare pretrial and posttrial levels of some measure, such as head injuries, in both groups.

Meta-Analysis

Traditionally, when a researcher began investigating a phenomenon, such as the relationship between alcohol consumption and breast cancer, the first step was a thorough review of the relevant research literature. Although the *literature review* has a long and noble history in the annals of science, such reviews are subject to bias in how they are interpreted. No matter how skilled the person reviewing the literature may be, the way that various results are interpreted essentially remains a subjective process, in which the reviewer's own biases, beliefs, overconfidence, and so forth may influence the outcome.

To assist researchers in sifting through the sometimes dozens of research studies that pertain to a particular hypothesis, statisticians have developed **meta-analysis**, a quantitative technique that combines the results of studies examining the same effect or phenomenon. Just as an experiment examines the consistency in the responses of individual participants, a meta-analysis determines the overall consistency of individual studies that address the same topics. A meta-analysis does not replace individual studies; rather, it provides a systematic procedure for summarizing existing evidence about focused research hypotheses that already appear in the health psychology literature.

meta-analysis A quantitative technique that combines the results of many studies examining the same effect or phenomenon.

There are several steps to meta-analysis. First, individual research studies are coded according to specific categories, such as the size and composition of the sample, presence of a control group, use of randomization, and research methodology. The individual study outcomes then are translated into a common unit, called an *effect size*, to allow the results to be compared.

Meta-analysis has a number of advantages. First, by pooling the results of many studies, meta-analysis often reveals significant results simply because combined studies have more participants. Second, demonstrating that a finding holds up across different studies conducted by different researchers at different times and places and with different participants gives researchers greater confidence in the finding's validity. Finally, as with good experiments, meta-analysis is subject to replication. That is, other researchers may repeat the series of statistical steps and should reach the same conclusions. One meta-analysis of 113 separate studies involving 77,539 women who were classified as light drinkers and 44,552 who did not use alcohol concluded that the association between drinking and breast cancer *may* be causal (Seitz, Pelucchi, Bagnardi, & La Vecchia, 2012; Hodgson and others, 2006).

Inferring Causality

No matter which research method they use (see Figure 2.7 for a summary), certain basic conditions must be met before epidemiologists can infer a cause-and-effect relationship between a particular risk factor and a particular disease or other adverse health outcome (Bonita, Beaglehole, & Kjellstrom, 2006):

- *The evidence must be consistent.* Studies that report an association between a risk factor and a health outcome must be replicated. When evidence is not entirely consistent (as is often the case in health research), a convincing majority of the evidence must support the alleged association. If not, causality cannot be inferred.

- *The alleged cause must have been in place before the disease actually appeared.* This may seem obvious, but the importance of this criterion cannot be overstated. For example, if a woman suddenly increases her consumption of alcohol after her breast cancer is diagnosed, drinking alcohol could not have caused the disease. You would be surprised at how often this criterion is overlooked.

- *The relationship must make sense.* This means that the explanation must be consistent with known physiological findings. In the case of the relationship between alcohol and breast cancer, for example, a wealth of other evidence suggests several plausible biological links between alcohol and other forms of cancer, including that alcohol increases hormone levels or that alcohol makes cells more vulnerable to other cancer-causing compounds because of the way it is metabolized in the body.

relative risk A statistical indicator of the likelihood of a causal relationship between a particular health risk factor and a health outcome; computed as the ratio of the incidence (or prevalence) of a health condition in a group exposed to the risk factor to its incidence (or prevalence) in a group not exposed to the risk factor.

- *There must be a dose-response relationship between the risk factor and health outcome.* Dose-response relationships are systematic associations between a particular independent variable, such as cigarette smoking, and a particular dependent variable, such as breast cancer. Such relationships pinpont the relative risk associated with specific levels of an independent variable. Thus, the morbidity rate of breast cancer is higher among women who drink heavily, somewhat less for women who drink moderately, less still for light drinkers, and lowest among women who do not drink.

- *The strength of the association between the alleged cause and the health outcome (relative risk) must suggest causality.* **Relative risk** refers to the ratio of the incidence or preva-

---

FIGURE 2.7

Epidemiological Research Methods Epidemiologists working to help reduce the incidence and prevalence of sexually transmitted infections (STIs) have followed these steps:

1. Measure *prevalence* and *incidence* of STIs in the general population. Determine whether certain subgroups of the population have higher STI levels.

2. Use *retrospective* studies to determine which health behaviors or other factors have affected STI levels in the subgroups with the highest prevalence rates.

3. Generate hypotheses about what causes STIs and how they are spread.

4. Test those hypotheses by using *prospective studies, natural experiments,* and *clinical trials.* Use *meta-analysis* to analyze results.

5. Develop intervention programs to stem the spread of STIs. Continue efforts to understand the etiology of the disease to develop effective treatments.

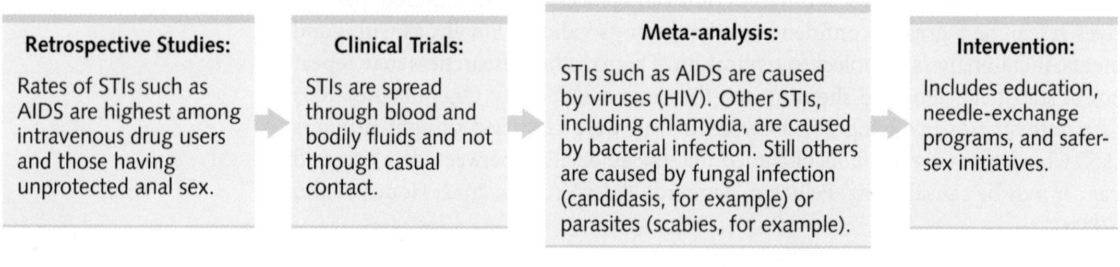

Retrospective Studies:	**Clinical Trials:**	**Meta-analysis:**	**Intervention:**
Rates of STIs such as AIDS are highest among intravenous drug users and those having unprotected anal sex.	STIs are spread through blood and bodily fluids and not through casual contact.	STIs such as AIDS are caused by viruses (HIV). Other STIs, including chlamydia, are caused by bacterial infection. Still others are caused by fungal infection (candidasis, for example) or parasites (scabies, for example).	Includes education, needle-exchange programs, and safer-sex initiatives.

Interpreting Data...

Measuring Risk

Let's look at an actual example of how measures of risk are used to estimate the impact of an actual risk factor on chronic disease. Table 2.2 displays the results of a classic 20-year study of death rates due to lung cancer and heart disease among British physicians. The researchers examined death rates due to both diseases among doctors who smoked at least one pack of cigarettes per day, comparing them to the death rates among those who did not smoke. For smokers, the incidence or absolute risk of developing heart disease during the course of the study (669 per 100,000 people) was much higher than the absolute risk of developing lung cancer (140 per 100,000 people). In contrast, the data demonstrate a very strong *relative* association between smoking and lung cancer (RR = 14.0), and a much smaller association between smoking and heart disease (RR = 1.6).

RR for lung cancer = 5 incidence (smokers)/incidence (nonsmokers) = 140/10 = 14.0
RR for heart disease = 5 incidence (smokers)/incidence (nonsmokers) = 669/413 = 66 = 1.6

Thus, cigarette smoking is a much stronger risk factor for mortality from lung cancer than for heart disease. On the face of it, these data seem to offer powerful support to the idea that smoking causes lung cancer but leave plenty of doubt as to whether there is a causal relationship between smoking and heart disease. Given that there is a large body of evidence that smoking *does* cause both lung cancer and heart disease (see Chapters 10 and 11), how can we make sense of these differences in relative risk?

The explanation is that death from lung cancer is a relatively rare event among nonsmokers, accounting for only 10 deaths per 100,000 people. Because the background rate of lung cancer is very low, a small difference in absolute risk among those who smoke leads to a very high relative risk. In contrast, the annual death rate for heart disease among nonsmokers is much larger (413 per 100,000), so a much larger difference in the *absolute risk* among smokers would be needed before the *relative risk* changed substantially.

It is important to remember that these data are evidence of an *association* between a risk factor (smoking) and two health conditions (lung cancer and heart disease). Assuming that smoking is a causal factor in both diseases, eliminating smoking would prevent far more deaths from chronic heart disease than from lung cancer. A third measure or risk brings this to our attention. **Attributable risk** measures the actual amount of a disease that can be attributed to exposure to a particular risk factor. Attributable risk is determined by subtracting the incidence rate of a disease in people who have been exposed to a risk factor from the incidence rate of the disease in people who have not been exposed to the risk factor.

AR for lung cancer = incidence (smokers) − incidence (nonsmokers) = 140 − 10 = 130

AR for heart disease = incidence (smokers) − incidence (nonsmokers) = 669 − 413 = 256

In this study, differences in attributable risk demonstrate that the actual *public health impact* of smoking is twice as large for heart disease mortality as it is for lung cancer mortality. For every 100,000 people, there are 256 additional deaths from heart disease in smokers, compared to 130 additional deaths over the background rate among nonsmokers from lung cancer.

TABLE 2.2
Relative Risk of Mortality from Lung Cancer among Cigarette Smokers

	Annual Mortality Rate per 100,000	
	Lung Cancer	**Heart Disease**
Cigarette smokers	140	669
Nonsmokers	10	413
Relative risk	14.0	1.6
Attributable risk	130/year	256/year

Data from Doll, R., Peto, R., Boreham, J., & Sutherland, I. (2004). Mortality in relation to smoking: 50 years' observations on British male doctors. *British Medical Journal, 328,* pp. 1519–1528.

attributable risk The actual amount that a disease can be attributed to exposure to a particular risk factor. Attributable risk is determined by subtracting the incidence rate of a disease in people who have been exposed to a risk factor from the incidence rate of the disease in people who have not been exposed to the risk factor.

lence of a disease in a group exposed to a particular risk factor to the incidence or prevalence of that condition in a group not exposed to the risk factor. A relative risk value of 1.0 means there is no difference in risk between the two groups. A relative risk value above 1.0 indicates that there is a positive association between the risk factor and the health condition; that is, the exposed group has a greater risk than the unexposed group. For example, a relative risk of 2.0 indicates that the exposed group is twice as likely to develop a health outcome as an unexposed group is. Conversely, a relative risk of 0.50 means that the incidence or prevalence rate of the condition in the exposed group is only half that of those in the unexposed group; that is, there is a negative association between the risk factor and the condition (see Interpreting Data: Measuring Risk).

■ *The incidence or prevalence of the disease or other adverse health outcome must drop when the alleged causal factor is removed.* Although dose-response and relative risk relationships are necessary to infer causality, they are not sufficient. Before we can infer that drinking causes breast cancer, we must have evidence that women who reduce or eliminate their consumption of alcohol have a reduced risk of this disease. Recent

Criterion	Evidence	Score
1. Problem or Question Studied: *(clearly stated hypothesis, significant or relevant issue, operational definitions included)*		
2. Sampling: *(representative of population, random selection and assignment, sample characteristics identified, group differences controlled, low dropout rate)*		
3. Measurement: *(clearly stated methodology)*		
4. Reliability: *(test yields consistent results, even among multiple raters; questions measure single construct, such as anxiety or degree of disability)*		
5. Validity: *(constructs clearly explained, independent and dependent variable levels clear, generalized to appropriate populations)*		
6. Statistical Significance: *(inferred relationships, accurate and appropriate significance supported by data)*		
7. Justification for Conclusions: *(warranted by data and research design)*		
Total		

FIGURE 2.8

Putting Health Psychology into Practice: Evaluating Scientific Evidence Health psychologists use quality rating forms similar to this to evaluate research studies. For each criterion, they rate the study by assigning a number from 0 (no evidence that the criterion was met) to 3 (strong evidence that the criterion was met). Overall scores on the rating system can range from 0 to 21, with higher scores justifying greater confidence in the study's conclusions.

3 = Good, 2 = Fair, 1 = Poor, 0 = No evidence that the criterion has been met.

Information from Ramons, K. D., Schafer, S., & Tracz, S. M. (2003). Learning in practice: Validation of the Fresno test of competence in evidence based medicine. *British Medical Journal, 326,* 319–321; and Bergstrom, N. (1994). *Treating pressure ulcers: Methodology for guideline development.* U.S. Department of Health and Human Services, Publication No. 96-N014.

research has shown this very thing to be true, in fact, thus meeting our fifth criterion (National Cancer Institute, 2010f). When all conditions are met, epidemiologists are able to infer that a causal relationship has been established, even when a true experiment cannot be conducted.

While working to meet these conditions, health psychologists need to evaluate individual research studies very carefully. Quality rating forms, such as the one in Figure 2.8, are very helpful means of achieving this standard. In medicine, too, there is a new emphasis on the importance of basing patient care on the "best available evidence" for a given health condition. Medical residency programs today are required to train new physicians in evidence-based medicine, which involves virtually all of the principles we have discussed in this chapter, including learning how to appraise research critically for its validity, reliability, and usefulness in clinical practice (Centre for Evidence-Based Medicine, 2010).

In this chapter, we have introduced a variety of research methods for studying biological, psychological, and social factors in health. It is natural to ask, which one is best? Some researchers might answer quickly that the laboratory experiment is most desirable because only in such studies are the variables of interest directly manipulated while all other variables are controlled. But we also have seen that some questions of vital interest to health psychologists do not, for ethical and/or practical reasons, lend themselves to experimentation. Moreover, experiments are often criticized for being artificial and having little relevance to behavior in the real world.

Increasingly, researchers are combining experimental and nonexperimental methods in order to make their investigations more comprehensive. For example, suppose that a researcher is interested in determining whether an educational campaign about safer sex would induce college students to modify their behavior. The researcher might design an experiment in which a randomly assigned group of students who received educational materials related to this issue was compared to a control group that received unrelated materials. The students would be compared on their stated intentions to practice safer sex. However, the researcher surely would want to know whether the educational campaign was equally effective with women, men, members of various ethnic minorities, and so forth. Variables such as these, of course, cannot be manipulated experimentally. Together, however, experimental and nonexperimental methods complement one another, giving health psychologists a larger tool kit with which to study their subjects.

Health psychologists generally have also favored *quantitative research* studies of health phenomena where measurement, prediction, and control are prioritized. However, when data are presented in numbers, some information may be lost. Many health psychologists thus turn to **qualitative research** to complement quantitative data—asking open-ended questions and reporting responses in narrative, rather than numerical, form (Gough & Deatrick, 2015).

For example, a recent study of 18- to 25-year-old New Zealanders used multiple qualitative methods (focus groups, interviews using images from social media, and online materials) to explore the influence of corporate marketing on young people's drinking behavior (Lyons, Goodwin, McCreanor, & Griffin, 2015).

qualitative research Research that focuses on qualities instead of quantities. Participants' expressed ideas are often part of qualitative studies.

Research Ethics and Scientific Misconduct

The most important concern for all scientists, especially for those studying human behavior, is to uphold ethical standards in their research. Responsible researchers ensure that participation is voluntary, harmless, and confidential. Many professional associations, including the American Psychological Association (APA) and National Science Foundation (NSF), have research guidelines to protect the well-being of research participants. The ethics codes of the APA mandate that researchers (1) obtain human participants' **informed consent** beforehand—that is, participants must understand and agree to the research procedures and know what risks are involved, (2) protect participants from harm and discomfort, (3) keep information about individual participants confidential, and

informed consent Permission granted by a client, patient, or research participant with full knowledge of the potential risks involved in a treatment, procedure, or research study.

debrief The process in which research participants are given more details about the study following its completion.

(4) fully **debrief** people (explain the research afterward). Moreover, university ethics committees and *Institutional Review Boards* (IRBs) screen research proposals to make sure safeguards are in place before approving them.

Scientific misconduct is the violation of accepted codes of scholarship and ethical behavior in research. In addition to the mistreatment of research participants, the NSF defines three types of misconduct: *fabrication, falsification,* and *plagiarism.* Fabrication is making up results and recording or reporting them. Falsification is manipulating research materials or changing data and results such that the research is not accurately represented. Plagiarism is appropriating another person's ideas, results, or words without giving appropriate credit.

This type of misconduct has recently been in the news. The University of Connecticut reported that one of its researchers, who studied the link between aging and a substance found in red wine, committed more than 100 acts of data fabrication and falsification, throwing much of this work into doubt (Wood, 2012). Although reports of this type of outright fraud are rare, experts say unethical or sloppy researchers take advantage of a system that sometimes allows them to operate in secrecy and manipulate data to find what they want to find without much fear of being challenged.

Even research that has been conducted under rigorous standards of quality may produce results that are not reproducible. A group called the Reproducibility Project at the Center for Open Science recently conducted replications of 100 experimental and correlational studies published in three psychology journals (Open Science Collaboration, 2015). Despite the use of high-powered study designs and original materials wherever possible, the researchers found that over 60 percent of the studies failed to replicate—that is, the original findings did not hold up the second time around.

Although *reproducibility of results* is a defining feature of the scientific method, some experts say researchers pay too little attention to this issue because the incentives for individual scientists place higher value on novel findings. Journal reviewers and editors may dismiss a study that replicates already published findings for being unoriginal, and therefore unworthy of publication. As the authors of this landmark study concluded, "…there is still more work to do to verify whether we know what we think we know" (p. 950).

This chapter has presented you with the basic tools of the health psychology trade—critical thinking that guards against faulty everyday reasoning and scientific methods that guide researchers in their quest for valid and reliable answers to health-related questions. Armed with this information, you are now ready to begin to address those questions.

Weigh In on Health

Respond to each question below based on what you learned in the chapter. (**Tip:** Use the items in "Summing Up" to take into account related biological, psychological, and social concerns.)

1. Recently, you read about a study that indicated a link between taking a vitamin supplement and lessening the chance of developing Alzheimer's disease in older adulthood. As a health scientist, what kinds of questions would you ask to determine the merits of this study? What kinds of unscientific thinking should you be aware of as you review the study?

2. For each of the following methods of research in health psychology, develop a question that would provide focus for a study: a descriptive study, an experimental study, a quasi-experiment, and a developmental study. Why is the method of research that you chose well suited to each question?

3. In the past, several health psychology professors at your school were involved in epidemiological research to help reduce the severity of the AIDS health crisis. They were involved in retrospective studies, clinical trials, meta-analysis, and intervention. In what way could each of these epidemiological research methods have helped reduce the severity of the AIDS health crisis?

Summing Up

Critical Thinking and Evidence-Based Medicine

1. Our everyday thinking is prone to bias, including making snap judgments and inferring cause and effect inappropriately. Using scientific research methods to search for evidence will help you become a more careful consumer of health psychology reports.

2. An important aspect of critical thinking in health psychology is statistical literacy, the ability to read and interpret statistics and to think critically about arguments that use statistics as evidence.

Health Psychology Research Methods

3. Descriptive studies, which observe and record the behavior of participants, include case studies, interviews and surveys, focus groups, and observation.

4. The strength and direction of a relationship between two sets of scores are revealed visually by scatterplots and statistically by the correlation coefficient. Correlation does not imply causality.

5. In an experiment, a researcher manipulates one or more independent variables while looking for changes in one or more dependent variables. Experiments typically compare an experimental group, which receives a treatment of interest, with a control group, which does not.

6. When health psychologists study variables that cannot be manipulated, they may conduct a quasi-experiment. In this design, participants are assigned to comparison groups on the basis of age, gender, ethnicity, or some other subject variable.

7. Developmental studies focus on the ways people change or remain the same over time. In a cross-sectional study, data are collected on the whole study population (such as comparing groups of people of various ages) at a single point in time.

8. In a longitudinal study, a single group of individuals is followed over a long span of time. To compensate for the problem of subjects dropping out over the lengthy span of years that such studies require, researchers have developed a cross-sectional study, in which different age groups are tested initially and then retested later at various ages.

Epidemiological Research: Tracking Disease

9. Epidemiological research studies measure the distribution of health outcomes, seek to discover the etiology (causes) of those outcomes, and test the effectiveness of specific preventive health interventions. Among the commonly used epidemiological statistics are morbidity, mortality, incidence, and prevalence.

10. Epidemiologists use several basic research designs. In a retrospective study, comparisons are made between a group of people who have a certain disease or condition and a group of people who do not. In contrast, prospective studies look forward in time to determine how a group of people changes or how a relationship between two or more variables changes over time.

11. Epidemiologists use several measures of risk. *Absolute risk* is the number of new cases of a disease or condition that occur in a specific population within a defined time interval. *Relative risk* is the ratio of the incidence (or prevalence) of a health condition in a group exposed to the risk factor to its incidence (or prevalence) in a group not exposed to the risk factor. *Attributable risk* measures the actual amount of a disease that can be attributed to exposure to a particular risk factor.

12. Meta-analysis analyzes data from already published studies, statistically combining the size of the difference between the experimental and control groups to enable researchers to evaluate the consistency of findings.

13. In order to infer causality in epidemiological research, research evidence must be consistent and logically sensible and exhibit a dose-response relationship. In addition, the alleged cause must have been in place before the health outcome in question was observed and must result in a reduced prevalence of the condition when removed.

Key Terms and Concepts to Remember

evidence-based medicine, p. 29
confirmation bias, p. 30
epidemiology, p. 31
descriptive study, p. 31
observational study, p. 32
correlation coefficient, p. 33
scatterplot, p. 33
statistical literacy, p. 34
quasi-experiment, p. 36

cross-sectional study, p. 36
longitudinal study, p. 37
morbidity, p. 38
mortality, p. 38
incidence, p. 38
prevalence, p. 38
etiology, p. 39
retrospective studies, p. 41
case-control studies, p. 44

prospective study, p. 44
randomized clinical trial, p. 44
meta-analysis, p. 45
relative risk, p. 46
attributable risk, p. 47
qualitative research, p. 49
informed consent, p. 49
debrief, p. 50

 **LaunchPad**
macmillan learning

To accompany your textbook, you have access to a number of online resources, including quizzes for every chapter of the book, flashcards, critical thinking exercises, videos, and *Check Your Health* inventories. To access these resources, please visit the Straub *Health Psychology* LaunchPad solo at: **launchpadworks.com**

Biological Foundations of Health and Illness

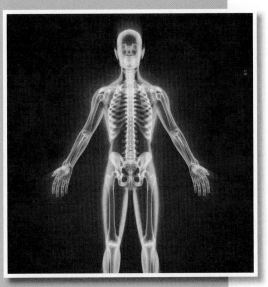

Lakeesha's life story began with a difficult, slow birth that required the use of excessive anesthetics and forceps to pull her roughly into the world. Together, these medical procedures choked off the supply of oxygen to her young brain. Although she survived, Lakeesha's complicated delivery, coupled with her low birth weight and her mother's heavy use of alcohol during her pregnancy, meant that her problems were just beginning. Lakeesha was born with mild spastic cerebral palsy (CP), a movement disorder that results from damage to the brain's motor centers.

This biological condition cast a lifelong shadow over Lakeesha's health, affecting not only her continuing physical development, but her psychological and social development as well. Among the first problems her parents and pediatrician noticed were mild mental retardation, visual and hearing impairment, slight deformities in her teeth and joints, and scoliosis (curvature of the spine). Later, when other children were learning to speak, Lakeesha was having speech difficulties caused by her muscular problems.

Like many children with disabilities, Lakeesha found that everything was harder. From the beginning, she needed extra self-confidence and persistence to master tasks that were routine for other children. During early childhood, when she desperately wanted to be like everyone else, Lakeesha too often found that she couldn't do the same things, look the same way, or keep up with other children. Realizing that her disability was permanent caused Lakeesha to become depressed and angry.

Lakeesha's condition also challenged the members of her family. Her parents experienced grief, guilt, and disappointment. It took more time and effort to raise Lakeesha than it had taken to raise her older sister, and other people were often hurtful in their comments and behavior toward Lakeesha.

Fortunately, interventions were available for Lakeesha and her family. Dental treatments and orthopedic surgery corrected most of Lakeesha's facial and posture problems. Speech and behavior therapy helped Lakeesha improve her muscular control, balance, and speech.

By age 8, Lakeesha's development had progressed far enough that she was able to attend a "normal" elementary school for the first time. In some areas, her skills were poor. Writing with a pencil, for example, was extremely difficult, and continuing vision problems hampered Lakeesha's efforts to learn to read. In other areas, however, her skills were average, or even advanced. She was one of the first in her class, for example, to understand multiplication and division.

Throughout her childhood, Lakeesha had high emotional and psychological needs, but they were met. Her anger, low self-esteem, and perception of herself as damaged or different were corrected with therapy. Similarly, joining a support group and working with a cognitive behavioral therapist helped her parents recognize and cope with their feelings.

Today, Lakeesha is living independently, working part-time in an electronics store, and attending classes at the local community college. She maintains a close, warm relationship with her parents, who live nearby, and she has a small but close-knit circle of friends. Most important, she feels good about herself and has confidence in her ability to overcome life's obstacles. Compared with what she's already managed to conquer, the road ahead seems easy.

Lakeesha's story illustrates the importance of the biopsychosocial perspective. Factors in the realms of biology (difficult birth, alcohol exposure), psychology (dealing with being different), and social relations (struggling to connect with others) all contributed to Lakeesha's health problems, and all three areas were addressed through surgery and therapy as part of her triumphant survival. The biopsychosocial perspective is effective because it advocates thinking of the human body as a system made up of many interconnected subsystems (including, for Lakeesha, the abilities to walk and talk) and externally related to several larger systems, such as society and culture.

Lakeesha's story also makes clear one of health psychology's most fundamental themes: The mind and body are inextricably intertwined. Whether they are focusing on promoting health or treating disease, health psychologists are concerned with the various ways our behaviors, thoughts, and feelings affect and are affected by the functioning of the body.

This chapter lays the groundwork for our investigation into health psychology by reviewing the basic biological processes that affect health. These processes are regulated by the nervous system, the endocrine system, the cardiovascular system, the respiratory system, the digestive system, the immune system, and the reproductive system. For each system, we will consider its basic structure and healthy functioning. In later chapters, you will learn about the major diseases and disorders to which each of these systems is vulnerable.

Because every thought, feeling, and action is also a biological event, the material in this chapter is fundamental to an understanding of the specific aspects of health and illness discussed in later chapters. So study this chapter carefully, and be prepared to refer to it frequently throughout the course.

Cells

All living things are made up of **cells,** which first became known in the mid-1600s when Robert Hooke examined thin slices of cork and other plants with a compound microscope. There are two basic types of cells: *prokaryotic*, which make up bacteria and other single-celled organisms, and *eukaryotic*, which are found in all other living things. Eukaryotic cells contain specialized, membrane-bound internal structures called *organelles*, one of which—the *nucleus*—contains the cell's hereditary material and serves as its control center. Other cellular organelles perform different functions, such as protein synthesis. Prokaryotic cells do not have nuclei or any other organelles. Figure 3.1 illustrates the differences between a prokaryotic and a eukaryotic cell.

The human body contains about 10 trillion cells consisting of 200 specialized types. A group of similar cells that perform the same function is called a **tissue.** Most tissues in humans and other animals are one of two types. *Epithelial tissues* are sheets of closely packed cells covering body organs and other surfaces. They also form *glands* that secrete hormones, breast milk, and other substances. *Connective tissues* are made up of more widely separated cells that function to bind together and support organs and other body tissues. Bone is a type of connective tissue, as is *cartilage*, found in the joints between bones, and *tendons*, which connect bone to muscle. Blood, nerve, and muscle are specialized tissues that do not belong to either the epithelial or connective tissue group.

A group of tissues that work together to perform a specific function, such as the stomach, is an **organ.** Organs have their own blood vessels, nerves, and muscles.

cell The basic unit of structure and function in living things.

tissue A group of similar cells organized into a functional unit.

organ A group of tissues working together to perform a specific function.

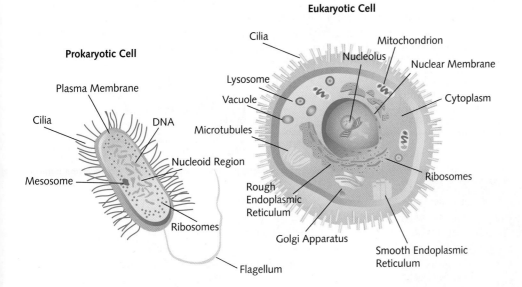

Eukaryotic Cell

Cilia
Nucleolus
Mitochondrion
Nuclear Membrane
Lysosome
Vacuole
Cytoplasm
Microtubules
Ribosomes
Rough Endoplasmic Reticulum
Golgi Apparatus
Smooth Endoplasmic Reticulum

Prokaryotic Cell

Plasma Membrane
Cilia
DNA
Nucleoid Region
Mesosome
Ribosomes
Flagellum

FIGURE 3.1
Prokaryotic versus Eukaryotic Cells Prokaryotic cells do not have nuclei or other organelles. Eukaryotic cells contain nuclei and many other types of organelles.

The Nervous System

Major control over the operation of our body's systems belongs to the nervous system, which is made up of the brain, the spinal cord, and all the peripheral nerves that receive and send messages throughout the body. Without the nervous system, our muscles would not expand or contract, our pancreas would not release insulin, and consciousness would not be possible.

Divisions of the Nervous System

The human nervous system contains billions of *neurons* (nerve cells) that send and receive signals across trillions of *synapses* (communicating connections between neurons), via chemicals called **neurotransmitters.** Traditionally, these neurons (Figure 3.2) are grouped into two major divisions: the *central nervous system* (CNS), which consists of the brain and the spinal cord, and the *peripheral nervous system* (PNS), which contains the remaining nerves of the body.

The PNS is further divided into two subdivisions: the *somatic nervous system,* which includes the nerves that carry messages from the eyes, ears, and other sense organs to the CNS, and from the CNS to the muscles and glands; and the *autonomic nervous system,* the nerves that link the CNS with the heart, intestines, and other internal organs. Because the skeletal muscles that the somatic nerves activate are under voluntary control, the somatic nervous system is often referred to as the *voluntary nervous system.* In contrast, the autonomic, or involuntary, nervous system controls the organs

neurotransmitters Chemical messengers released by a neuron at synapses that communicate across the synaptic gap and alter the electrical state of a receiving neuron.

FIGURE 3.2

The Neuron A neuron may receive messages from other neurons on any of its dendrites, and then it transmits each message down the long axon to other neurons. Nerve impulses travel in one direction only—down the axon of a neuron to the axon terminal. When a nerve impulse reaches the axon terminal, chemical messengers called *neurotransmitters* cross the synapse and bind to receptor sites on the receiving neuron's dendrite—similar to the way that a key fits into a lock. The scanning electron micrograph below shows neurons in the human brain.

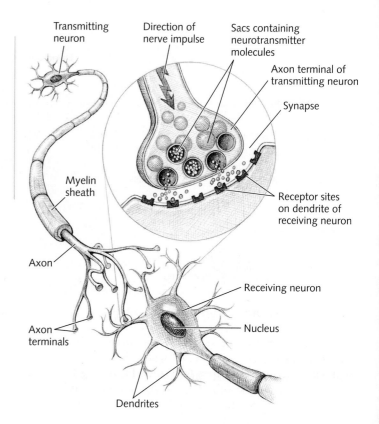

Transmitting neuron

Direction of nerve impulse

Sacs containing neurotransmitter molecules

Axon terminal of transmitting neuron

Synapse

Myelin sheath

Axon

Axon terminals

Receptor sites on dendrite of receiving neuron

Receiving neuron

Nucleus

Dendrites

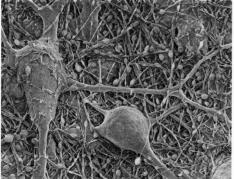

Thomas Deerinck, NCMIR/Science Source

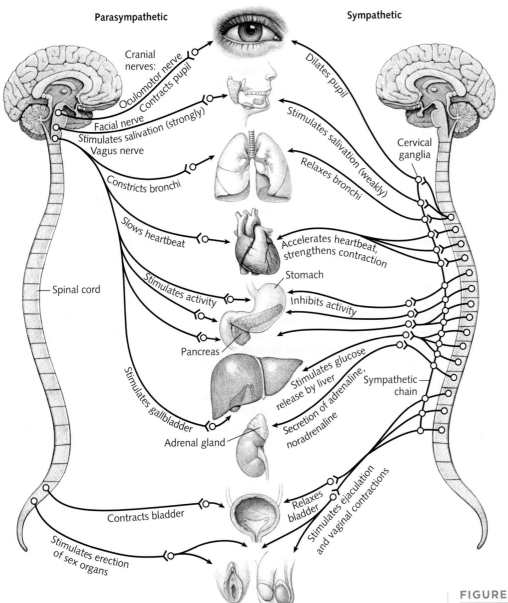

Parasympathetic　Sympathetic

Cranial nerves:
Oculomotor nerve
Contracts pupil
Dilates pupil

Facial nerve
Stimulates salivation (strongly)
Stimulates salivation (weakly)

Vagus nerve

Cervical ganglia

Constricts bronchi
Relaxes bronchi

Slows heartbeat
Accelerates heartbeat, strengthens contraction

Spinal cord

Stimulates activity
Stomach
Inhibits activity

Pancreas

Stimulates glucose release by liver
Sympathetic chain

Stimulates gallbladder

Secretion of adrenaline, noradrenaline

Adrenal gland

Contracts bladder
Relaxes bladder
Stimulates ejaculation and vaginal contractions

Stimulates erection of sex organs

FIGURE 3.3

The Autonomic Nervous System The autonomic nervous system is split into the sympathetic and parasympathetic divisions. The sympathetic division prepares the body for action, accelerating the heartbeat, stimulating the secretion of adrenaline, and triggering other elements of the "fight-or-flight" response. The parasympathetic division calms the body by slowing heartbeat, stimulating digestion, and triggering other restorative activities of the body.

over which we normally have no control. As we'll see in the next chapter, involuntary responses play a critical role in how we react to environmental challenges and stressful situations.

The autonomic nervous system is also composed of two subdivisions (Figure 3.3). The *sympathetic nervous system* consists of groupings of neuron cell bodies called *ganglia* that run along the spinal cord and connect to the body's internal organs. The sympathetic division prepares the body for "fight or flight," a response generated when a person experiences performance stress (preparing for the big football game or an important job interview) or perceives a significant threat (see Chapter 4). It does so by increasing the heart rate and breathing rate, decreasing digestive activity (this is why eating while under stress can lead to a stomachache), increasing blood flow to the skeletal muscles, and releasing energizing sugars and fats from storage deposits. Because all the sympathetic ganglia are closely linked, they tend to act as a single system, or "in sympathy" with one another.

Unlike the ganglia of the sympathetic division, the ganglia of the *parasympathetic nervous system* are not closely linked and therefore tend to act more independently. This system has opposite effects of those of the sympathetic ganglia: it helps the body to recover after arousal by decreasing heart rate, increasing digestive activity, and conserving energy.

The Brain

The human brain weighs about 1400 grams (3 pounds), is thought to consist of perhaps 40 billion individual neurons, and has the consistency of a soft cheese. Yet this mass is the control center of our nervous system and the storage vault for our memories. Without it, we couldn't think, move, speak, or breathe. Let's consider the brain's structure and functions so that we can better understand the role of the brain in achieving good health. We'll be considering the three principal regions of the brain: the brainstem, the cerebellum, and the cerebrum (Figure 3.4).

Lower-Level Structures

Located at the point where the spinal cord swells as it enters the skull, the **brainstem** evolved first in the vertebrate brain. Remarkably similar in animals ranging from fish to humans, the brainstem contains the medulla, the pons, and the reticular formation. Together, they control basic and involuntary life-support functions via the autonomic nervous system. (This is why a blow to the head at the base of the skull is so dangerous.) The brainstem is also the point at which most nerves passing between the spinal cord and the brain cross over, so that the left side of the brain sends and receives messages from the *right* side of the body, and the right side of the brain sends and receives messages from the *left* side of the body.

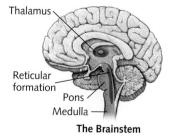

The Brainstem

brainstem The oldest and most central region of the brain; includes the medulla, pons, and reticular formation.

FIGURE 3.4

The Brain This cross-section of the human brain shows its three principal regions: the brainstem, which controls heartbeat and respiration; the cerebellum, which regulates muscular coordination; and the cerebrum, which is the center for information processing. Surrounding the central core of the brain is the limbic system, which includes the amygdala, hippocampus, and hypothalamus. The limbic system plays an important role in emotions, especially those related to sexual arousal, aggression, and pain.

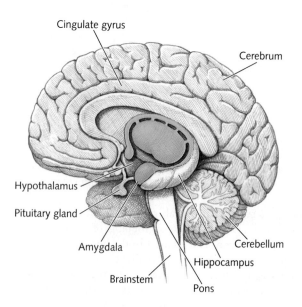

The **medulla** controls several vital reflexes, including breathing, heart rate, salivation, coughing, and sneezing. It also receives sensory information about blood pressure and then, based on this input, varies the constriction or dilation of blood vessels to maintain an optimal state. Damage to the medulla is often fatal. An overdose of an opiate drug such as morphine or heroin may disrupt (or even suppress) breathing because of the drug's effects on the medulla.

Nervous System Connections

See how the nervous system is involved in health psychology issues covered in many later chapters, including coverage of:

+Physiology of Stress (in Chapter 4)
+Coping Interventions for Stress (in Chapter 5)
+Obesity (in Chapter 8)
+Substance Abuse (in Chapter 9)
+The Physiology of Pain (in Chapter 14)

medulla The brainstem region that controls heartbeat and breathing.

reticular formation A network of neurons running through the brainstem involved with alertness and arousal.

thalamus The brain's sensory switchboard; located on top of the brainstem, it routes messages to the cerebral cortex.

cerebellum Located at the rear of the brain, this brain structure coordinates voluntary movement and balance.

limbic system A network of neurons surrounding the central core of the brain; associated with emotions such as fear and aggression; includes the hypothalamus, amygdala, and hippocampus.

amygdala Two clusters of neurons in the limbic system that are linked to emotion, especially aggression.

Located just up from the medulla, the *pons* consists of two pairs of thick stalks that connect to the cerebellum. The pons contains nuclei that help regulate sleep, breathing, swallowing, bladder control, equilibrium, taste, eye movement, facial expressions, and posture.

As the spinal cord's sensory input travels up through the brain, branch fibers stimulate the **reticular formation,** a brainstem circuit that governs arousal and sleep. The reticular formation is also responsible for alerting the brain during moments of danger and for prioritizing all incoming information. When this region is damaged, a person may lapse into a coma and never awaken.

Above the brainstem is the **thalamus.** Consisting of two egg-shaped groups of nuclei, the thalamus sorts sensory information received from the brainstem and routes it to the higher brain regions that deal with vision, hearing, taste, and touch.

Lying at the back of the brain, the **cerebellum,** or "little brain," is shaped like the larger brain. Its main function is to maintain body balance and coordinate voluntary muscle movement. Damage to the cerebellum produces a loss of muscle tone, tremors, and abnormal posture. In addition, some studies suggest that specialized parts of the cerebellum contribute to memory, language, and cognition. Children with *dyslexia* or *attention deficit hyperactivity disorder* (ADHD), for example, often have smaller cerebella or reduced activity in this region of their brains (Kibby, Pavawalla, Fancher, Naillon, & Hynd, 2009; McAlonan and others, 2007).

The Limbic System

Surrounding the central core of the brain is the **limbic system,** which includes the amygdala, hippocampus, hypothalamus, and septal area. The limbic system is believed to play an important role in emotions, especially those related to sexual arousal, aggression, and pain.

In 1939, neurosurgeons Heinrich Kluver and Paul Bucy surgically lesioned (destroyed) the **amygdala** in the brain of an especially aggressive rhesus monkey. The operation transformed the violent creature into a docile one. Other researchers have discovered that electrical stimulation of the amygdala will reliably trigger rage or fear responses in a variety of animals.*

Some scientists believe that a range of behaviors associated with *autism,* such as a reluctance to make eye contact and other deficits in social functioning, may be linked to abnormal size or functioning of the amygdala. Using brain scans, researchers in one study found that among toddlers diagnosed with autism, the amygdala was, on average, 13 percent larger at age 2, compared with control children without autism (Mosconi and others, 2009).

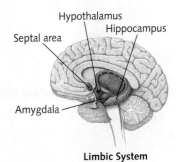

Limbic System

---

*Given that amygdala lesions transform violent animals into docile ones, might the same procedure work with violent humans? Although this type of psychosurgery has been attempted in a few cases involving patients with severe brain abnormalities, the results have been mixed.

hippocampus A structure in the brain's limbic system linked to memory.

hypothalamus Lying just below the thalamus, the region of the brain that influences hunger, thirst, body temperature, and sexual behavior; helps govern the endocrine system via the pituitary gland.

cerebral cortex The thin layer of cells that covers the cerebrum; the seat of conscious sensation and information processing.

The Human Brain The cerebrum, which is covered in a network of blood vessels and made up of extensive folds and convolutions, is divided into two hemispheres.

Another limbic circuit involves areas within the **hippocampus,** which are thought to be involved in spatial orientation, learning, and memory. When the hippocampus is injured, people typically develop *anterograde amnesia,* a form of amnesia in which they are unable to form new memories but retain their memory for previously learned skills. In a famous case, a talented composer and conductor, Clive Wearing (2005), suffered damage to his hippocampus in 1985. He now lives from one moment to the next, always feeling as though he has just awakened and not remembering the moment before, yet he has retained his musical skills.

Lying just below (*hypo*) the thalamus, the **hypothalamus** interconnects with numerous regions of the brain. Neuroscientists have pinpointed hypothalamic nuclei that influence hunger and regulate thirst, body temperature, and sexual behavior. Neuroscientists James Olds and Peter Milner made an intriguing discovery in 1954 about the role of the hypothalamus in the brain's reward system. The researchers were attempting to implant electrodes in the brainstems of laboratory rats when they accidentally stimulated an area in the hypothalamus. Much to the researchers' surprise, the rats kept returning to the precise location in their cages where they had previously been stimulated by the errant electrode. Recognizing that the animals were behaving as if they were seeking more stimulation, Olds and Milner continued to conduct a series of experiments that validated their discovery of the brain's reward circuitry. Indeed, rats have been known to "self-stimulate" their hypothalamic reward centers as many as 7000 times per hour.

As you will see in Chapter 9, some researchers believe that certain addictions—perhaps to food, alcohol, and other drugs—may stem from a genetic *reward deficiency syndrome* in which the brain's reward circuitry malfunctions and leads to powerful cravings.

Geoff Tompkinson/Science Source

The Cerebral Cortex

The *cerebrum,* which represents about 80 percent of the brain's total weight, forms two hemispheres (left and right) that are primarily filled with synaptic connections linking the surface of the brain to its other regions. The thin surface layer of the cerebrum, called the **cerebral cortex,** is what really makes us human. This 3-millimeter-thick sheet of some 20 billion nerve cells contains neural centers that give rise to our sensory capacities, skilled motor responses, language abilities, and aptitude for reasoning.

The cortex in each hemisphere can be divided into four principal regions, or lobes; each lobe carries out many functions, and in some cases, several lobes work together to perform a function (Figure 3.5). The *occipital lobe,* located at the back of the cortex, receives visual information from the retina of each eye. The *parietal lobe,* in the center of the cortex, receives information from the skin and body. Auditory information from the ears projects to the *temporal lobes.* The *frontal*

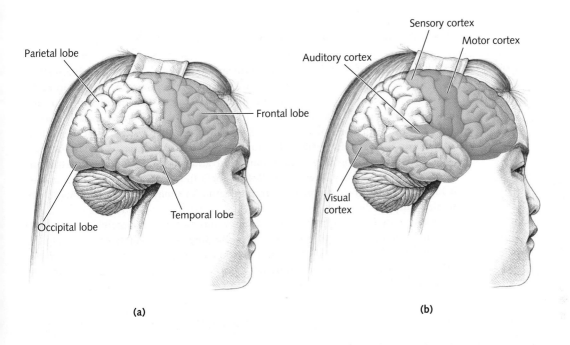

Parietal lobe

Frontal lobe

Occipital lobe

Temporal lobe

(a)

Sensory cortex

Motor cortex

Auditory cortex

Visual cortex

(b)

lobes, lying just behind the forehead, are involved in reasoning, planning, and controlling body movement.

In the parietal lobe, on the edge of the frontal lobe, the **sensory cortex** processes body sensations such as touch. The **motor cortex,** at the back of the frontal lobes, lies just in front of the sensory cortex. Remember Lakeesha from the chapter introduction? Motor cortex damage caused her cerebral palsy.

In 1870, German physicians Gustav Fritsch and Eduard Hitzig discovered that electrical stimulation of the motor cortex triggers movement in the limbs of laboratory animals. Little more than half a century later, neurosurgeon Wilder Penfield (1952) mapped the motor cortex in conscious patients during surgery to remove brain tumors. In addition to mapping the cortex according to the body parts that it controlled, Penfield made the remarkable discovery that the amount of motor cortex devoted to a specific body part is proportional to the degree of control that we have over that body part. The muscles of the face and fingers, for example, have much more representation in the motor cortex than does the thigh muscle. Penfield also mapped the sensory cortex and similarly found that the amount of cortical representation was proportional to the sensitivity of that body part.

The basic functional organization of the primary sensory and motor areas of the cerebral cortex is virtually identical in all mammals, from the rat to the human. However, the sensory and motor areas account for only about one-fourth of the total area of the human cerebral cortex. Researchers are just beginning to understand the functions of the remaining areas, which are called the **association cortex.** These areas are responsible for higher mental functions, such as thinking and speaking. Interestingly, humans do not have the largest brains proportionate to size. Porpoises, whales, and elephants have much larger brains. Yet in ascending the evolutionary scale, it becomes obvious that more intelligent animals have much greater amounts of "uncommitted" association areas.

FIGURE 3.5

The Cerebral Cortex (a) Each of the four lobes, or regions, of the cerebral cortex performs various functions, sometimes separately, but more often in conjunction with another region. (b) Within these regions are the neural centers that give rise to our sensory capacities, skilled motor responses, language ability, and reasoning ability.

sensory cortex Lying at the front of the parietal lobes, the region of the cerebral cortex that processes body sensations such as touch.

motor cortex Lying at the rear of the frontal lobes, the region of the cerebral cortex that controls voluntary movements.

association cortex Areas of the cerebral cortex not directly involved in sensory or motor functions; rather, they integrate multisensory information and higher mental functions such as thinking and speaking.

The Endocrine System

hormones Chemical messengers, released into the bloodstream by endocrine glands, which have an effect on distant organs.

The second of the body's communication systems, the endocrine system (Figure 3.6), is closely connected to the nervous system in regulating many bodily functions. Whereas the nervous system communicates through neurotransmitters, the endocrine system communicates through chemical messengers called **hormones.** Unlike the much speedier nervous system, which is chiefly responsible for fast-acting, short-duration responses, the endocrine system primarily governs slow-acting responses of longer duration. As we'll see in later chapters, these responses play key roles in our health, including our moods and sleep, as well as suggesting why, for some people, stressful situations may promote overweight and obesity.

Endocrine glands secrete hormones directly into the bloodstream, where they travel to various organs and bind to receptor sites. Binding either stimulates or inhibits organs depending on the type of receptor and hormone. In this section, we'll consider the activity of four important endocrine glands—the pituitary, adrenal, and thyroid glands, and the pancreas.

The Pituitary and Adrenal Glands

The **pituitary gland** secretes a number of hormones that influence other glands. These include hormones that influence growth, sexual development, reproduction, kidney functioning, and aging.

FIGURE 3.6

The Endocrine Glands and Feedback Control (a) Under the direction of the brain's hypothalamus, the pituitary releases hormones that, in turn, regulate the secretions of the thyroid, the adrenal glands, and the reproductive organs. (b) A complex negative feedback system regulates the production of many hormones. As the levels of hormones produced in target glands rise in the blood, the hypothalamus and pituitary decrease their production of hormones, and the secretion of hormones by the target glands also slows.

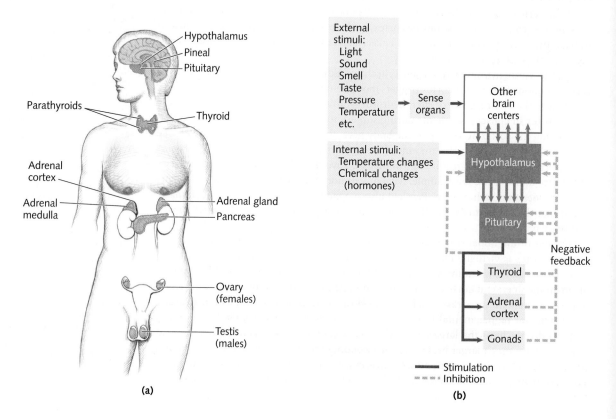

(a)

(b)

Although the pituitary gland is often referred to as the *master gland* of the endocrine system, the brain's hypothalamus more properly deserves this title because it directly (and rigidly) controls pituitary functioning. Together, the hypothalamus and pituitary act as a master control system. For example, during a stressful moment, the hypothalamus secretes the hormone *corticotropin-releasing hormone* (CRH), which travels in the bloodstream to the anterior pituitary, where it stimulates the pituitary to secrete *adrenocorticotropic hormone* (ACTH). ACTH binds to receptor cells on the adrenal cortex, causing this gland to release cortisol into the bloodstream. The increased level of cortisol in the blood acts back on the hypothalamus and pituitary gland to inhibit the release of additional CRH and ACTH (see Figure 3.13 later in this chapter). This example of *feedback control* is similar to the mechanism by which a household thermostat regulates temperature by turning on or off a furnace or air conditioner as needed.

Located atop the kidneys, the **adrenal glands** secrete several important hormones that play a crucial role in the body's response to stress and emergencies. In a moment of danger, for example, the innermost region of the gland (the adrenal medulla) releases *epinephrine* and *norepinephrine* into the bloodstream, which travel to receptor sites on the heart. These hormones increase heart rate, blood pressure, and blood sugar, providing the body with a quick surge of energy. The outermost region of the gland (the adrenal cortex) consists of three regions, each of which produces a different group of steroid hormones: The *gonadocorticoids* include the male androgens and female estrogens. The principal *glucocorticoid* is cortisol, which helps to reduce swelling and inflammation following an injury. The *mineralocorticoids* include aldosterone, which helps maintain normal blood pressure. As the biopsychosocial model notes, each of these hormones represents one way in which our bodies react biologically to the social and psychological events of our lives.

Endocrine System Connections

See how the endocrine system is involved in health psychology issues covered in many later chapters including:

+Mood and Depression (in various chapters)
+Sleep (in Chapter 7),
+Overweight and Obesity (in Chapter 8)
+Diabetes (in Chapter 10)

pituitary gland The master endocrine gland controlled by the hypothalamus; releases a variety of hormones that act on other glands throughout the body.

adrenal glands Lying above the kidneys, the pair of endocrine glands that secrete epinephrine, norepinephrine, and cortisol, which are hormones that arouse the body during moments of stress.

The Thyroid Gland and the Pancreas

Located in the front of the neck, the *thyroid gland* is shaped like a butterfly, with the two wings representing the left and right thyroid lobes, which wrap around the windpipe. The thyroid gland produces the hormone thyroxin, which helps regulate the body's growth and metabolism (energy use). Located just behind the thyroid are four parathyroid glands. The hormones secreted by these glands regulate the level of calcium in the body within a narrow range so that the nervous and muscular systems can function properly.

Overactivity in one or more of these glands (*hyperparathyroidism*) may trigger a host of problems, the symptoms of which have been described as "moans, groans, stones, bones, and psychiatric overtones." "Moans and groans" refers to the aching bones, fatigue, and weakness that patients often experience. "Stones" refers to kidney stones that result when excess calcium circulating in the bloodstream gets caught in the kidneys. "Bones" refers to the possible development of osteoporosis, which occurs when the overactive parathyroid takes calcium from bones, decreasing their density and making them brittle. The "psychiatric overtones" come from the difficulty concentrating and depression that may occur.

Another endocrine gland, the *pancreas,* produces glucagon and insulin, two hormones that act in opposition to regulate the level of the sugar glucose in the blood. Glucagon raises the concentration of glucose in the blood, while insulin controls the conversion of sugar and carbohydrates into energy by promoting the uptake of glucose by the body's cells (see Chapter 8).

The Cardiovascular System

Your heart is about the size of your clenched fist and weighs only about 11 ounces, yet it pumps 5 or more quarts of blood a minute through your circulatory system. Over the course of your life, your heart will beat more than 2.5 *billion* times. The cardiovascular system—the heart, blood vessels, and blood—serves as the body's transportation system. Through the pumping action of the heart, the blood vessels carry blood rich in nutrients and oxygen to our cells and tissues and remove waste products through the lungs, liver, and kidneys.

Blood and Circulation

A blood pressure (BP) level of 120/80 ("120 over 80") mmHg (millimeters of mercury) is considered normal. Systolic BP above 140 mmHg, diastolic BP above 90 mmHg, or both indicate the presence of hypertension.

Human blood is a living tissue; it contains three types of cells that perform different functions. Red blood cells, or *erythrocytes,* carry oxygen from the lungs to the cells of the body. Red blood cells are formed in the bone marrow and contain *hemoglobin,* the iron-rich substance that gives blood its reddish tint. The blood uses hemoglobin to pick up oxygen in the lungs while releasing the carbon dioxide it has carried in from the cells. Blood also carries nutrients from the digestive system to cells and transports cellular waste to the kidneys for excretion in urine.

The white blood cells (*leukocytes*) carried by the blood are part of the immune system, and the *platelets* are small cell fragments that stick together (coagulate) when necessary to form clots along the walls of damaged blood vessels. Without leukocytes, we would have no defenses against infection. Without platelets, we would bleed to death from wounds, even from a small cut.

arteries Blood vessels that carry blood away from the heart to other organs and tissues; a small artery is called an *arteriole.*

veins Blood vessels that carry blood back to the heart from the capillaries.

Blood is transported throughout the body by the *circulatory system,* which consists of several types of blood vessels: **Arteries** carry blood from the heart to the other organs and tissues. The arteries branch into increasingly narrower blood vessels called *arterioles,* which eventually connect with *capillaries.* Capillaries are the smallest of the blood vessels and carry blood directly to the individual cells. **Veins** return blood from the capillaries to the heart.

The vessels of the circulatory system move blood throughout the body by dilating and contracting as needed. When arteries narrow (constrict), resistance to blood flow increases. Blood pressure is a measure of the force exerted by blood against the blood vessel walls. This force is highest during *systole,* when the heart contracts in order to force the blood out. During *diastole,* the heart relaxes as blood flows into the heart and blood pressure drops. Thus, diastolic blood pressure is lower than systolic blood pressure.

Cardiovascular System Connections

See how the cardiovascular system is involved in health psychology issues covered in many later chapters including:

+Coping with Stress (in Chapter 5)
+Overweight and Obesity (in Chapter 8)
+Smoking and Alcohol Use (in Chapter 9)
+Cardiovascular Disease and Diabetes (in Chapter 10)

The Heart

In birds and mammals, the heart is separated into four parts, or chambers: the right and left *atria,* in the upper section of the heart, and the right and left *ventricles,* in the lower section of the heart. These chambers work in coordinated fashion to bring blood into the heart and then to pump it throughout the body (Figure 3.7). Blood returning from the body enters the *right atrium* through two large veins. After expanding to receive the blood, the right atrium contracts, forcing the "used" blood into the *right ventricle.* Depleted of oxygen, this "used" blood is sent into the pulmonary artery (*pulmonary* refers to lungs), then through the capillaries of the lungs, where it picks up oxygen for later distribution to cells and disposes of carbon dioxide (CO_2, which will be exhaled) as waste. The now oxygen-rich blood flows into the pulmonary vein, and the pumping action of cardiac muscles forces that blood into the left atrium and then into the left ventricle. The left ventricle propels the oxygen-rich blood into the aorta, from which it flows into the arterial system, carrying nutrients to all parts of the body. If you listen to your heartbeat, the "lubb-dup, lubb-dup" sound represents the closing of the valves between the atria and ventricles ("lubb"), followed by the closing of the valves between the ventricles and the arteries ("dup").

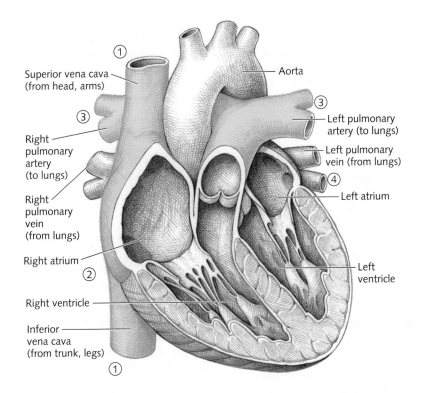

FIGURE 3.7
The Cardiovascular System The heart is separated into four parts, or chambers: the right and left atria, in the upper section of the heart; and the right and left ventricles, in the lower section of the heart.

① Oxygen-depleted blood returns to the heart from the body through the superior and the inferior vena cava. . . .

② This blood is pumped from the right atrium into the right ventricle. . . .

③ And from there, through capillaries of the lungs, where it picks up fresh oxygen and disposes of carbon dioxide. . . .

④ The freshly oxygenated blood is pumped through the pulmonary vein into the left atrium and from there into the left ventricle, from which it flows into the arterial system.

The Respiratory System

bronchi The pair of respiratory tubes that branch into progressively smaller passageways, the bronchioles, culminating in the air sacs within the right and left lungs (the alveoli).

The word *respiration* has two meanings. At the level of the individual cell, it refers to energy-producing chemical reactions that require oxygen. At the level of the whole organism, it refers to the process of taking in oxygen from the environment and ridding the body of carbon dioxide.

The Lungs

The most important organs in the respiratory system, of course, are the lungs (Figure 3.8). After air enters the body through the mouth or nose, it passes to the lungs through the *pharynx* and *trachea,* from which it travels through the **bronchi** that branch into smaller tubes, called *bronchioles.* Each bronchiole ends in a cluster of small, bubblelike sacs called *alveoli.* The membranous wall of each alveolus is thin enough to permit the exchange of gases, allowing oxygen to be exchanged for carbon dioxide. Alveoli are surrounded by millions of capillaries so that gases can be transferred efficiently to and from the bloodstream.

How do the muscles that control lung expansion "know" when it's time to breathe? Sensors in capillaries monitor the chemical composition of the blood. As the level of carbon dioxide rises, this information is relayed to the brain's medulla, which signals the muscles of the *diaphragm* to contract and cause you to inhale. Sensing that the level of carbon dioxide is low, the medulla signals the muscles to slow the rate of breathing until the carbon dioxide level returns to normal.

The respiratory system also has protective mechanisms that eliminate airborne dust particles and other foreign matter from the body. The two reflex mechanisms are sneezing

FIGURE 3.8

The Respiratory System Air enters through the nose and mouth, passes into the pharynx, past the larynx (voice box), and into the trachea, bronchi, and bronchioles to the alveoli. The alveoli are the sites where oxygen and carbon dioxide are exchanged.

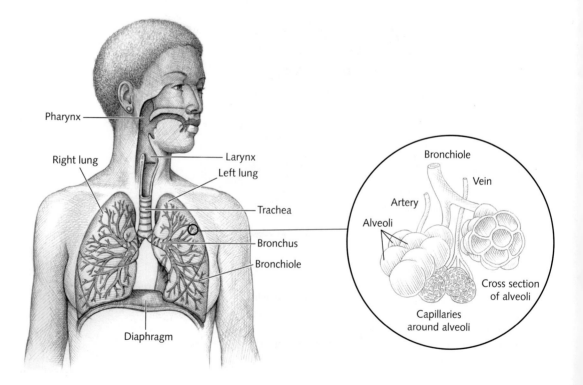

Pharynx

Right lung

Larynx
Left lung

Trachea

Bronchus

Bronchiole

Diaphragm

Bronchiole

Vein

Artery

Alveoli

Cross section of alveoli

Capillaries around alveoli

when the nasal passages are irritated and coughing when the larger airways of the throat are irritated. In addition, the air passages in the nose, mouth, and trachea are lined with tiny hairs called **cilia** that trap germs. Moving in a wavelike fashion, the cilia force the mucus that coats them gradually up toward the mouth, where it is either expelled in a cough or swallowed.

The Diversity and Healthy Living box discusses asthma to give an example of what can happen when the respiratory system malfunctions and of how health psychology contributes to the care and well-being of sufferers.

Science Photo Library/Getty Images

The Digestive System

igestion is the breaking down of food into molecules that can be absorbed by the blood and distributed to individual cells as nutrients for energy, growth, and tissue repair. The digestive system, or **gastrointestinal system,** consists primarily of the *digestive tract*—a long, convoluted tube that extends from the mouth to the anus (Figure 3.9). The digestive system also includes the salivary glands, the pancreas, the liver, and the gallbladder.

Asthma Most childhood cases of asthma are allergic reactions triggered by animal dander, pollen, dust, indoor mold, or damp conditions in homes and buildings.

cilia Tiny hairs; those that line the air passageways in the nose, mouth, and trachea move in wavelike fashion, trapping germs and forcing them out of the respiratory system.

gastrointestinal system The body's system for digesting food; includes the digestive tract, salivary glands, pancreas, liver, and gallbladder.

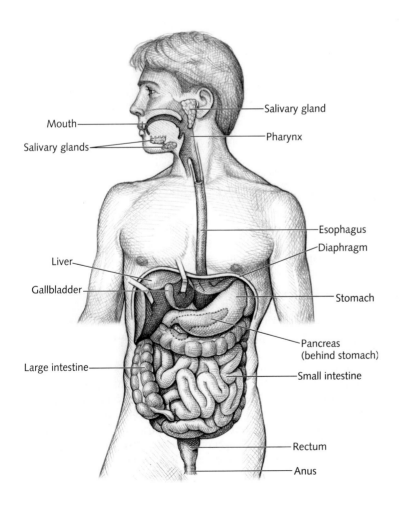

FIGURE 3.9

The Digestive System *Digestion* is the process of breaking food down into simpler chemical compounds to make it absorbable in the digestive tract. The process begins in the mouth, where food is chewed and ground up by the teeth. From the mouth, food passes through the esophagus to the stomach, where it is churned and proteins are chemically digested. From there, food passes into the large and small intestines, where chemical digestion of carbohydrates and proteins is completed. Waste products of food are stored as feces in the rectum and eliminated from the body through the anus.

Mouth
Salivary glands
Salivary gland
Pharynx
Esophagus
Diaphragm
Liver
Gallbladder
Stomach
Pancreas (behind stomach)
Large intestine
Small intestine
Rectum
Anus

Diversity and Healthy Living

Asthma

The rapid rise of chronic **noncommunicable diseases (NCDs)** represents one of the major global challenges to health. By 2020, it is estimated that over 70 percent of the global burden of disease will be caused by NCDs—especially cancer, diabetes, cardiovascular disease, and chronic respiratory diseases such as asthma (World Health Organization, 2015f).

A total of 90 percent of childhood cases of asthma are allergic reactions triggered by animal dander, pollens, dust, indoor mold, or damp conditions in homes and buildings (National Center for Environmental Health, 2006). In the non-allergic form of asthma (which is more likely to affect adults), cold air, viral infections, secondhand smoke, and household chemicals trigger asthma attacks. There are an estimated 6 million chemicals in the environment, and 2800 of these have allergenic properties. Many people with asthma find that strong emotions, stress, or anxiety can make symptoms of asthma worse, especially during a severe attack.

An asthma attack occurs when the immune system produces an antibody that activates the body's defensive cells, causing the muscles surrounding the bronchi in the lungs to constrict and obstruct the flow of air. In addition, the bronchi become inflamed and filled with mucus, further reducing the supply of oxygen. The major symptoms of an asthma attack include wheezing, a whistling sound that may occur throughout the chest or in a local area where the airway has become blocked; coughing as the body attempts to rid itself of any foreign substance (mucus) or irritant (smoke); and shortness of breath caused by fast, shallow breathing as the body attempts to take in sufficient oxygen through narrowed airways.

Although asthma can develop at any age, it usually begins in childhood—it is now the most common chronic childhood disease in the United States—and affects more boys (17 percent) than girls (11 percent), more children in poor families (18 percent) than children in families that are not poor (13 percent), and more non-Hispanic black children (21 percent) than Hispanic children (11 percent) or non-Hispanic white children (13 percent) (Bloom, Cohen, & Freeman, 2009). Asthma was rare in 1900, but now it has grown into an epidemic and is on the rise everywhere: There are more than 20 million people with asthma in the United States (73 per 1000) and 10 times that many around the world (Schiller, Lucas, & Peregoy, 2012). The prevalence of asthma is highest in Western countries, particularly English-speaking ones; the disease is rare in parts of rural South America and Africa. Each year in the United States, there are nearly 2 million visits to the emergency room for asthma, 10 million outpatient visits to private physician offices, 500,000 hospitalizations, and nearly 5000 asthma-related deaths, mostly in

noncommunicable disease (NCD) A chronic disease, such as cardiovascular disease, cancer, or diabetes, that is not passed from person to person.

How Food Is Digested

Digestion begins in the mouth, where chewing and the chemical action of salivary enzymes begin to break food down. Most mammals have teeth that assist in the tearing and grinding of food. As food is chewed, it is moistened by saliva so that it can be swallowed more easily. Saliva contains a digestive enzyme called *amylase* that causes starches to begin to decompose.

Once food is swallowed, it passes into the *esophagus,* a muscular tube about 9.3 inches (25 centimeters) long in the typical adult. The muscles of the esophagus contract rhythmically, propelling the food downward in an involuntary reflexive motion called *peristalsis.* This reflex is so efficient and strong that you are able to swallow food and water even while standing on your head.

In the stomach, the food is mixed with a variety of gastric juices, including hydrochloric acid and *pepsin,* an enzyme that breaks down proteins. At this point, the food has been converted into a semiliquid mass. The secretion of gastric juices (including saliva) is controlled by the autonomic nervous system. Food in the mouth, or even the sight, smell, or thought of food, is sufficient to trigger the flow of gastric juices. Conversely, fear inhibits digestive activity. When you are in danger or under stress, your mouth becomes very dry, and food remains an uncomfortable, undigested lump in your stomach.

older adults. Worldwide, there are more than 180,000 asthma deaths each year (WHO, 2010d).

Although having one parent with asthma—or, worse still, two parents with asthma—increases a child's risk, geographical variations in the prevalence of asthma are probably due to environmental and lifestyle factors rather than genetic ones. Among the candidates for risk factors is the tendency of children to spend more time indoors than did those in earlier generations, thus increasing their exposure to household allergens, including dust mites, animal dander, and indoor pests such as cockroaches. According to another theory, the immune systems of Western children, unlike those in developing countries, are weaker because they are not conditioned to live with parasites, so the children become more vulnerable to asthma and other allergic diseases such as hay fever.

In the United States, both the prevalence and morbidity of asthma are related to ethnicity and socioeconomic status; the disease is particularly prevalent among African-Americans, Hispanic-Americans, and individuals living below the federal poverty threshold (NHIS, 2014). In the largest study of its kind ever conducted, researchers at the National Institute of Allergy and Infectious Diseases studied more than 1500 children, ages 4 to 11, living in inner cities. In a powerful validation of the biopsychosocial model, the researchers found that many factors, rather than a single cause, were responsible for the recent increase in asthma morbidity. Among these factors were environmental toxins, such as indoor allergens and passive smoke; psychological problems of both the children and their caretakers, such as defensiveness and panic disorder; and problems with access to medical care.

Patient education is the most prominent behavioral intervention for asthma, beginning with instruction about basic asthma facts and medications. Most programs instruct patients on avoiding asthma triggers and devising a self-management plan. Some programs also focus on stress management; muscle relaxation techniques that improve breathing; and navigating the health care system, including how to find a doctor, prepare for medical visits, and pay for medical care. Environmental interventions include removing carpeting, draperies, curtains, and upholstered furniture; sealing mattresses and pillows in dustproof enclosures; finding new homes for pets; and installing high-efficiency particle-arresting (HEPA) filters. The goal of these programs is to eliminate or reduce symptoms, minimize the need for emergency interventions, and improve the overall quality of the asthma sufferer's life. Behavioral interventions often result in significant reductions in symptoms and in the need for medical treatment (Clark, Mitchell, & Rand, 2009).

Stomachs vary in capacity. Depending on their success in hunting, carnivores such as hyenas may eat only once every few days. Fortunately, their large-capacity stomachs can hold the equivalent of 30 to 35 percent of their body weight. In contrast, mammals that eat more frequent, smaller meals typically have much smaller stomachs. The capacity of the average college student's stomach is roughly 2 to 4 liters of food—about 2 to 3 percent of the average person's body weight—roughly equal to a burger, fries, and a Coke.

By about four hours after eating, the stomach has emptied its contents into the small and large intestines. Digestive fluids from the pancreas, liver, and gallbladder are secreted into the *small intestine* through a series of ducts. These fluids contain enzymes that break down proteins, fats, and carbohydrates. For example, the *liver* produces a salty substance called *bile* that emulsifies fats almost as effectively as dishwashing liquid, and the pancreas produces the hormone insulin, which assists in transporting glucose from the intestine into body cells.

The breakdown of food that began in the mouth and stomach is completed in the small intestine. The inner lining of the small intestine is composed of gathered circular folds, which greatly increase its surface area. Fully extended, an average adult's small intestine would be almost 20 feet (approximately 6 meters) in length, with a total surface area of 3229 square feet (300 square meters)—roughly the size of a basketball court. This vast area is lined with tiny, fingerlike projections of mucus, called *villi*, through which water and nutrient molecules pass into the bloodstream. Once in the bloodstream, nutrients travel to individual cells.

Food particles that have not been absorbed into the bloodstream then pass into the *large intestine*, or *colon*, where absorption (mainly of water) continues. In the course of digestion, a large volume of water—approximately 7 liters each day—is absorbed. When this process is disrupted, as occurs in diarrhea and other gastric disorders, dehydration becomes a danger. Indeed, dehydration is the reason that diarrhea remains the leading cause of infant death in many developing countries.

The process of digestion is completed when food particles that were not absorbed earlier are converted into feces by colon bacteria such as *Escherichia coli*. (This type of bacteria has gotten a lot of press in recent years for causing sickness in people who eat meat infected with it, but that is actually a different strain than the one that occurs naturally in the colon.) Fecal matter is primarily composed of water, bacteria, cellulose fibers, and other indigestible substances.

The Immune System

At this moment, countless numbers of microorganisms surround you. Most are not dangerous. Indeed, many, such as those that assist in digestion and the decomposition of waste matter, play an important role in health. However, **antigens**—which can be bacteria, viruses, fungi, parasites, or any foreign microorganism—are dangerous to your health, even deadly. Defending your health against these invaders is the job of the immune system.

You may be exposed to antigens through direct bodily contact (handshaking, kissing, or sexual intercourse) or through food, water, insects, and airborne microbes. Antigens may penetrate body tissue through several routes, including the skin, the digestive tract, the respiratory tract, or the urinary tract. Their impact depends on the number and virulence of the microorganisms and the strength of the body's defenses.

Structure of the Immune System

Unlike most other systems, the immune system is spread throughout the body in the form of a network of capillaries, lymph nodes (glands), and ducts that comprise the *lymphatic system,* along with the bone marrow, thymus, and tonsils (Figure 3.10). Lymphatic capillaries carry *lymph,* a colorless bodily fluid formed by water, proteins, microbes, and other foreign substances that are drained from the spaces between body cells. Lymph takes its name from the billions of white blood cells it circulates called **lymphocytes.** These cells, which are produced in the bone marrow, patrol the entire body, searching for bacteria, viruses, cancerous cells, and other antigens.

The lymph nodes contain filters that capture infectious substances and debris; as lymph passes through the lymph nodes, the lymphocytes destroy the foreign particles collected there. During an immune response, the lymphocytes expand, which produces swelling and inflammation. You may have noticed how your lymph nodes swell when you are fighting an infection.

FIGURE 3.10

The Immune System Positioned throughout the body, the organs of the immune system are home to lymphocytes, white blood cells that are the basis of the body's immune defense against foreign agents, or antigens. Other components of the system are the bone marrow, where lymphocytes are produced; lymph nodes, which are glands that help your body fight infection; and the thymus, spleen, and tonsils. The lymph nodes produce the fluid lymph, which travels throughout the body via the lymphatic capillaries and filters impurities.

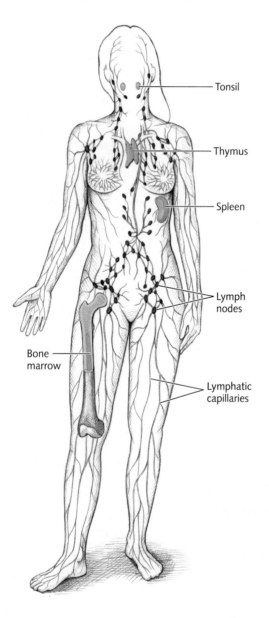

Tonsil

Thymus

Spleen

Lymph nodes

Bone marrow

Lymphatic capillaries

Two structures play a role in the activity of lymphocytes: the thymus and the tonsils. The *thymus,* which also functions as part of the endocrine system, secretes *thymosin,* a hormone that helps control the maturation and development of lymphocytes. Interestingly, the thymus is largest during infancy and childhood and slowly shrinks throughout adulthood, which may partially explain why immune responses are generally more efficient during childhood and aging is associated with reduced immune efficiency. Finally, the *tonsils* are masses of lymphatic tissue that seem to function as a holding station for lymphocytes, as well as a garbage can for worn-out blood cells.

antigen A foreign substance that stimulates an immune response.

lymphocytes Antigen-fighting white blood cells produced in the bone marrow.

The Immune Response

The body's immune reactions can be divided into two broad categories: *nonspecific immunity* and *specific immunity.* Nonspecific immune defenses fight off any foreign substance, including those never before encountered. Specific immune defenses occur only when a particular invader has been encountered before, creating a kind of immunological *memory* for the intruder.

Nonspecific Immune Responses

The body's first line of defense consists of the several layers of tightly knit cells that make up the skin. Chemicals found in perspiration, such as the oily *sebum* secreted by glands beneath the skin, prevent most bacteria and fungi from growing on the skin.

The nose, eyes, and respiratory tract—although they lack the tough, protective barrier of the skin—also provide a first line of defense. The mucous membranes of the nose and respiratory tract are armed with hairlike cilia, which, as noted earlier, catch dust, microbes, and other foreign matter. A powerful enzyme in tears and saliva destroys the cell walls of many bacteria. Similarly, gastric acids are able to destroy most foreign substances that enter the digestive system.

When a foreign substance penetrates the skin cells, it encounters a second line of defense, called *phagocytosis,* in which two specialized lymphocytes called phagocytes and macrophages attack the foreign particles. *Phagocytes* are large scavenger cells that prowl the blood and tissues of the body for invaders, destroying them by engulfing and digesting them. *Macrophages* ("big eaters") are phagocytes found at the site of an infection, as well as in the lymph nodes, spleen, and lungs. These specialized white blood cell "sentries" pass into body tissues, where they hunt antigens and worn-out cells. A single phagocyte can digest 5 to 25 bacteria before it dies from an accumulation of toxic wastes.

Suppose, for instance, that a splinter has punctured your skin. Neighboring cells in the area of the wound immediately release several chemicals, particularly *histamine,* which increases blood flow to the area. Circulating phagocytes and macrophages, attracted by these chemicals, rush to the site of the wound, where they begin to engulf the inevitable bacteria and foreign particles that enter the body through the wound. At the same time, blood clots form, sealing off the wound site, and additional histamine is released, creating a hot environment unfavorable to bacteria.

As a consequence of this sequence of nonspecific immune reactions, collectively referred to as the *inflammatory response,* the injured area becomes swollen, red, and tender to the touch. In addition, some lymphocytes release proteins that produce *systemic effects* (effects throughout the entire body), such as fever, in the most serious cases

The Immune System in Action: A Macrophage Attacks Macrophages ("big eaters") are specialized white blood cell "sentries" that pass into body tissues, where they hunt antigens and worn-out cells. A single macrophage can digest 5 to 25 bacteria before it dies from an accumulation of toxic wastes.

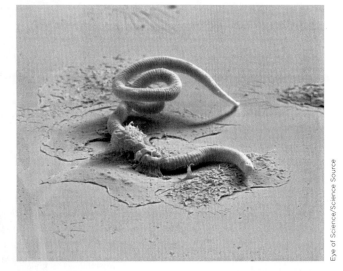

Eye of Science/Science Source

An Inside Story The clever movie *Osmosis Jones* (2001), which takes place both inside and outside a zookeeper named Frank, humorously showcases the immune system. The star is the white blood cell after whom the movie is named, who gallantly fights a fierce, intruding virus to save Frank.

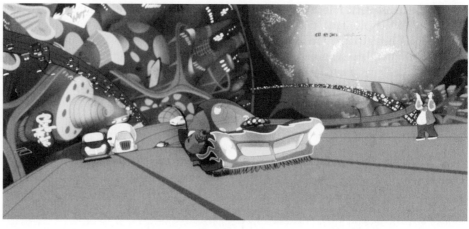

The Kobal Collection at Art Resource

of invasion (for example, food poisoning). In addition to its role in destroying invading microorganisms, inflammation helps restore bodily tissues that have been damaged (Figure 3.11).

In addition to the phagocytes and macrophages, the immune system's nonspecific defenses include smaller lymphocytes called *natural killer* (NK) cells, which patrol the body for diseased cells that have gone awry. Researchers are just now learning how NK cells distinguish normal body cells, or what is *self*, from virus-infected and cancerous cells that are *non-self*. NK cells destroy their targets by injecting them with lethal chemicals. They also secrete various forms of *interferon*, an antimicrobial protein that inhibits the spread of viral infections to healthy cells. Interferons, which differ from species to species, work by preventing viruses from replicating. Interferons are the subject of intensive

FIGURE 3.11

The Inflammatory Response When an infection or, as in this case, an injury breaches the body's first line of defense, histamine and other chemicals are released at the site of the disturbance. These chemicals increase blood flow to the area, attract white blood cells, and cause a clot to form—sealing off the site. Some of the white blood cells engulf foreign particles, while others release a protein that produces fever.

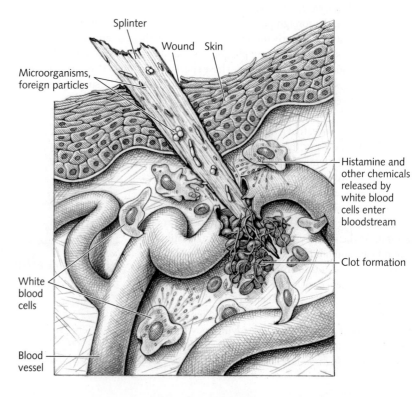

biomedical research and have the potential for treating influenza, the common cold, and other diseases.

Specific Immune Responses

Some invaders either elude the body's nonspecific defenses or are too powerful to be handled by phagocytes, macrophages, and NK cells alone. In such cases, the immune system calls upon its strongest line of defense: specific immune responses. These reactions occur when a particular substance has been encountered before. Some specific immunities are acquired, for example, when a nursing mother passes a specific immunity to her child through breast milk. Others develop when a person successfully weathers a disease such as measles or is *immunized*. As a child, you probably were vaccinated against mumps, chicken pox, whooping cough, polio, and other diseases, making your body artificially resistant to these diseases should you ever be exposed to them. More recently, you may have elected to be immunized against the influenza A virus during the flu season. Your body's ability to develop a "memory" of specific antigens is the basis of acquired immunity. When a child is vaccinated, a killed or nonvirulent form of a specific virus is injected, allowing the body to create a memory of it.

Specific immune responses involve two special lymphocytes, called *B cells* and *T cells*, which recognize and attack specific invading antigens. B cells attack foreign substances by producing specific antibodies, or *immunoglobulins*, which are proteins that chemically suppress the toxic effects of antigens, primarily viruses and bacteria. A particular antibody molecule fits into receptors on an invading antigen as precisely as a key fits a lock. When a B cell is activated by a particular antigen, it divides into two types: a plasma cell capable of making 3000 to 30,000 antibody molecules per second, and an antibody-producing memory cell (Figure 3.12). The rapid response of memory cells,

Although 95 percent of kindergarteners in the United States are immunized (a law in most states), only 40 to 60 percent of preschoolers are—a lower rate than in many developing countries. Prior to health care reform legislation passed in 2010, one in five children went without health insurance.

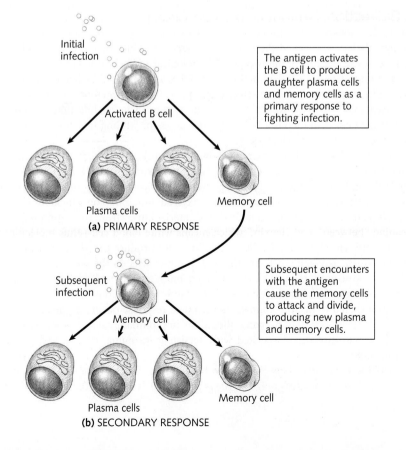

Initial infection

Activated B cell

The antigen activates the B cell to produce daughter plasma cells and memory cells as a primary response to fighting infection.

Plasma cells

Memory cell

(a) PRIMARY RESPONSE

Subsequent infection

Memory cell

Subsequent encounters with the antigen cause the memory cells to attack and divide, producing new plasma and memory cells.

Plasma cells

Memory cell

(b) SECONDARY RESPONSE

FIGURE 3.12

Primary and Secondary Responses of the Immune System (a) When a B cell is activated by an antigen, it divides into plasma cells, which manufacture antibodies, and memory cells. (b) When memory cells encounter the same antigen during a subsequent infection, the secondary immune response occurs. Memory cells release antibodies that attack the antigen and also divide, producing a new generation of plasma cells and memory cells.

called the *primary response,* is the basis of immunity to many infectious diseases, including polio, measles, and smallpox. Unlike the plasma cell, which lives only a few days, memory cells may last a lifetime, producing a stronger, faster antibody reaction should the particular antigen be encountered a second time. When a memory cell encounters the same antigen during a subsequent infection, the *secondary immune response* is triggered.

For many years, scientists believed that circulating antibodies produced by B cells were the sole basis of immunity. They now know that the immune system has a second line of defense, called *cell-mediated immunity,* in which T cells directly attack and kill foreign substances without the aid of antibodies.

There are three major varieties of T cells: *cytotoxic cells, helper cells,* and *suppressor cells.* Cytotoxic T cells, known as "killer cells," are equipped with receptors that match one specific antigen. When that invader is encountered, the killer cell receptor locks onto it and injects it with a lethal toxin. Current estimates suggest that each person is born with enough killer T cells to recognize at least 1 million different kinds of antigens.

Helper T cells and suppressor T cells are the principal mechanisms for regulating the immune system's overall response to infection. They do so by secreting chemical messengers called *lymphokines,* which stimulate or inhibit activity in other immune cells. Helper cells are sentries that travel through the bloodstream hunting antigens. When they find them, they secrete chemical messengers that alert B cells, phagocytes, macrophages, and cytotoxic T cells to attack. Suppressor T cells serve a counter-regulatory function. By producing chemicals that suppress immune responses, these cells ensure that an overzealous immune response doesn't damage healthy cells. Suppressor cells also alert T cells and B cells when an invader has been vanquished successfully.

A Bidirectional Immune-to-Brain Circuit

The body's nonspecific immune response, which is triggered by signals originating in the hypothalamus, is called the *acute phase response* (APR), or more simply, the "sickness" response, because of the sweeping physiological and behavioral changes that occur. In addition to fever and inflammation, the APR is accompanied by reduced activity and food and water intake, increased sensitivity to pain, disrupted memory consolidation, and increased anxiety. The APR, which occurs an hour or two after infection, represents an orchestrated effort to mobilize the body's resources for battling infection by preserving energy through behavior changes.

How does the brain know there is an infection in the first place? The information is conveyed by chemical messengers called **cytokines** (from the Greek prefix *cyto-,* meaning "cell," and the root *kinos,* meaning "movement"). One group of cytokines, called *proinflammatory cytokines*—because they accelerate inflammation—includes the *tumor necrosis factor* (TNF), and interleukin-1 and interleukin-6 (from the Latin prefix *inter-,* meaning "between," and "leukin," which means white blood cell—thus molecules that signal "between white blood cells"). Cytokines are produced in the blood by macrophages, which, as you'll recall, are the first immune cells on the scene of an infection. When cytokine production is blocked with chemical antagonists for their receptor sites, there is no sign of a sickness response *despite* an infection. Conversely, when cytokines are administered to healthy animals, the sickness response occurs in the absence of an infection (Maier, 2003). In humans, alterations in proinflammatory cytokines have also been linked to disorders associated with persistent insomnia, fatigue, and depression (Irwin, 2008).

Cytokine molecules, however, are too big to cross the blood–brain barrier. Instead, they bind to receptor sites along the *vagus nerve,* which is one of the 12 cranial nerves.

cytokines Protein molecules produced by immune cells that act on other cells to regulate immunity (including the interferons, interleukins, and tumor necrosis factors).

The vagus innervates regions of the body in which immune responses occur, including the spleen, thymus gland, and lymph nodes. Picking up the signal, the vagus signals the brain to make its own interleukin-1, which activates immune cells and triggers the APR. Cutting the vagus nerve (in an operation known as a *vagotomy*) prevents the sickness response from occurring (Maier, 2003).

Immune System Connections

See how the immune system is involved in health psychology issues covered in many later chapters including:

+How Does Stress Make You Sick? (in Chapter 4)

+Diabetes (in Chapter 10)

+Immunocompetence in Relation to Cancer (in Chapter 11)

+HIV and AIDS (in Chapter 12)

As shown in Figure 3.13, the brain and immune system form a bidirectional communication network in which cytokines produced by immune cells communicate with the brain and neurotransmitters produced in the brain communicate with immune cells. Viewed in this way, the immune system functions as a *diffuse sense organ* that alerts the brain to infection and injury. As we'll see in the next chapter, health psychologists working within the subfield of *psychoneuroimmunology* are very interested in this circuit because stress also taps into it, suggesting that the neural pathways and chemical signals that underlie some psychological processes and inflammatory diseases are one and the same.

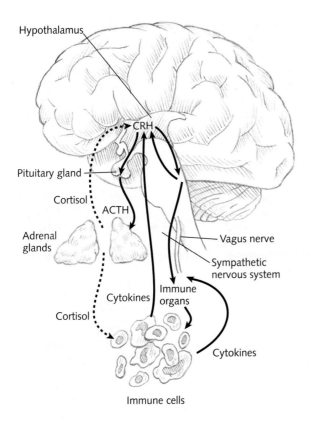

FIGURE 3.13

Bidirectional Immune-to-Brain Circuit We now know that the brain and immune system, once viewed as independent systems, communicate with each other through cytokines, which are produced by immune cells, and neurotransmitters, which are produced by nerve cells in the brain (from Sternberg, 2001, p. 89).

The Reproductive System and Behavior Genetics

The human reproductive system is where life and health begin (see Figure 3.14). The separate development of the female and male reproductive systems begins during prenatal development, when a hormonal signal from the hypothalamus stimulates the pituitary gland to produce the *gonadotropic hormones,* which direct the development of the *gonads,* or sex glands—the ovaries in females and the testes in males. One of these hormones in particular, *GnRH* (gonadotropin-releasing hormone), directs the ovaries and testes to dramatically increase the production of sex hormones, especially *estrogen* in girls and *testosterone* in boys.

Ovaries and Testes

On either side of the female's uterus are two almond-shaped *ovaries,* which produce the hormones estrogen and progesterone. The outer layer of each ovary contains the *oocytes,* from which the *ova* (eggs) develop. The oocytes begin to form during the third month of prenatal development. At birth, an infant girl's two ovaries contain some 2 million oocytes—all that she will ever have. Of these, about 400,000 survive into puberty, and some 300 to 400 reach maturity, generally one at a time, approximately every 28 days from the onset of puberty until menopause, which typically occurs at about age 50. If the released ovum is not fertilized by a sperm, it remains in the uterus for approximately 14 days, after which it is flushed out of the system with the uterine endometrium during menstruation.

The ovaries also produce two important hormones: *estrogen,* which triggers development of secondary sex characteristics, and *progesterone,* which is produced during the second half of the menstrual cycle to prepare the female body for possible pregnancy and declines if pregnancy does not occur.

In males, testosterone produced in the testes stimulates development of secondary sex characteristics and brings about the production of sperm. From puberty until old age, the testes of a human male produce an average of several hundred million sperm

FIGURE 3.14

The Reproductive System In the female, the left and right ovaries make eggs and secrete the sex hormone estrogen. In the male, the testes produce sperm cells and the sex hormone testosterone.

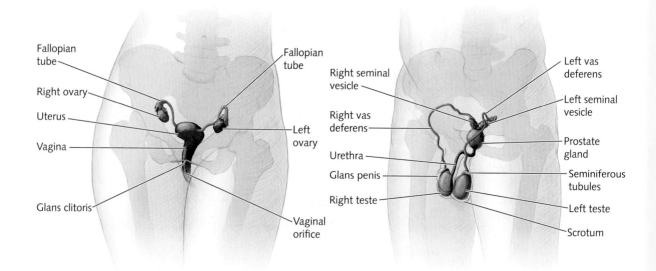

each day. The testes form during prenatal development and are subdivided into some 250 individual compartments, each of which is packed with coiled *seminiferous* ("seed-bearing") *tubules.* Sperm cells form in the tubules.

Fertilization and the Mechanisms of Heredity

Each of us started life as a single fertilized cell, called a zygote. At the moment of conception, a *sperm cell* from the male finds its way upward from the *uterus* into the *fallopian tubes,* where it fertilizes an ovum. Within a few hours, the nuclei of the egg and sperm fuse. Pregnancy is counted from the first day of the woman's last menstrual cycle,

which is also the starting point of gestational (prenatal) age. Full-term pregnancies last 38 weeks, or nine months. Although obstetricians assign a due date based on the woman's last menstrual period, only 5 percent or so of babies are born on that exact date. Babies born between three weeks before and two weeks after that date are considered "full term." Babies born earlier are called *preterm*; babies born later are called *post-term.*

A few hours after fertilization, the single-celled zygote travels down the fallopian tube, where the first cellular divisions take place. The zygote contains inherited information from both parents that will determine the child's characteristics. Each ovum and each sperm contain 23 *chromosomes*, the long, threadlike structures that carry our inheritance. At conception, the 23 chromosomes from the egg and the 23 from the sperm unite, bequeathing to the newly formed zygote a full complement of 46 chromosomes. As the cells of the developing person divide, this genetic material is replicated over and over, so that the nucleus of every cell in the person's body contains the same instructions written at the moment of conception.

The twenty-third pair of chromosomes determines the zygote's sex. The mother always contributes an X chromosome; the father can contribute either an X or a Y chromosome. If the father's sperm also contains an X chromosome, the child will be a girl; a Y chromosome from Dad will produce a boy. Y chromosomes contain a single gene that triggers the *testes* to begin producing testosterone, which in turn initiates the sexual differentiation in appearance and neural differentiation during the fourth and fifth months of prenatal development.

Each chromosome is composed of strings of *genes*—the basic units of heredity that determine our growth and characteristics. Genes are discrete particles of *deoxyribonucleic acid* (DNA). Each cell in the body contains over 20,000 genes that determine everything from the color of your hair to whether you have a tendency toward schizophrenia, a major psychological disorder.

Within the zygote, the 23 pairs of chromosomes carrying the genes from the mother and father duplicate, forming two complete sets of the **genome.** These two sets move toward opposite sides of the zygote, and the cell splits into two cells, each containing the original genetic code. These two cells duplicate and divide, becoming four, which duplicate

Human Chromosomes At conception, 23 gene-carrying chromosomes from each parent unite to form a zygote with a full complement of 46 chromosomes and all the information needed to create a complex new being nine months later.

genome The complete instructions for making an organism, including all the genetic material found in that organism's chromosomes.

Monozygotic Twins About once in every 250 conceptions, one fertilized egg divides into two, producing identical twins: two individuals with the same genetic makeup.

stem cells Early, undifferentiated biological cells with the potential to develop into any other type of specialized cell.

genotype The sum total of all the genes present in an individual.

phenotype A person's observable characteristics; determined by the interaction of the individual's genotype with the environment.

FIGURE 3.15
Epigenetics: Guiding Cells to Their Specialized Roles An organism's genome is a sort of how-to manual for all the tasks individual cells need to perform in order to function. The *epigenome*—a layer of proteins that packages the genome and points cells to specific instructions—is affected by many things, including food, stress, and toxic chemicals. Beginning before birth, life experiences lay down epigenetic marks, which can block the expression of any gene in the DNA segment they affect. So far, more than 100 kinds of epigenetic marks have been found, but researchers are still studying how different parts of the epigenome adjust to the environment.

and divide, becoming eight, and so on—each cell identical to the first. The first cells are **stem cells** and have the potential to develop into many different types of cells in the body. About once in every 250 conceptions, at the two-cell stage, the organism splits and *monozygotic* (identical) twins develop, each of which has the same DNA.

Genes and Environment

Behavior genetics is the study of the relative power and limits of genes and environment on our behavior. Most human characteristics are not determined by genes alone; rather, they are *multifactorial*—influenced by many different factors, including environmental factors. Human traits also tend to be *polygenic*—influenced by many different genes.

The sum total of genes that a person inherits is that person's **genotype.** The observable physical and nonphysical traits that are actually expressed constitute the person's **phenotype.** This distinction is important because each of us inherits many genes in our genotype that are not expressed in our phenotype. In genetic terminology, we are *carriers* of these unexpressed bits of DNA; although we may not manifest them in our own phenotype, they may be passed on to our offspring, who then will have them in their genotype and may or may not express them in their phenotype. Eye color inheritance is among the most straightforward and therefore often is used to help us understand this distinction. For most traits, a person's phenotype is determined by two patterns of genetic interaction: gene–gene and gene–environment.

Gene-Environment Interaction: Epigenetics

As we saw in Chapter 1, the field of *epigenetics* explores the ways in which genes interact with a person's environment. When behavior geneticists refer to "environment," they are referring to everything that can influence a person's genetic makeup from the beginning of prenatal development until the moment of death. Environmental influences include the direct effects of nutrition, climate, and medical care, as well as indirect effects brought on by the particular economic, cultural, and historical context in which the individual develops (see Figure 3.15).

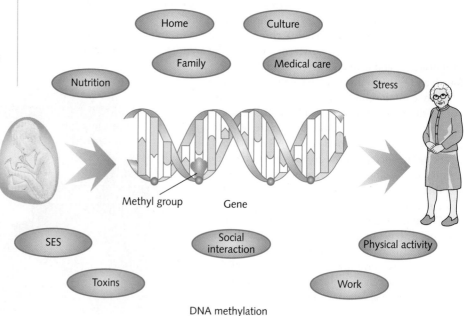

Home   Culture

Family   Medical care

Nutrition   Stress

Methyl group   Gene

SES   Social interaction   Physical activity

Toxins   Work

DNA methylation

Understanding these processes is part of epigenetics. Access to the genes is controlled by the epigenome, a layer of additional DNA, and another molecule, ribonucleic acid (RNA), attached to the genome. In a process called *DNA methylation*, this material transcribes, activates, silences, and in other ways alters the expression of genes and guides cells to their specialized roles. Once considered "junk," this nongenetic material is the subject of intense research as scientists seek to discover exactly what these biological molecules do, and how they respond to stress, pollution, poor diet, and other environmental experiences (Xu and others, 2015).

Methylation begins before birth and continues throughout life, altering how genes are expressed in response to environmental events, even after we are born. Because DNA methylation patterns seem to be set largely during the *perinatal* period (immediately before and after birth), long-term gene expression programming is especially vulnerable to environmental insults that occur early in life. In this way, epigenetics contributes to the development of many multifactorial diseases (Elsing, Datson, van den Maagdenberg, & Ferrari, 2013). For instance, DNA methylation appears to be one of the biological mechanisms responsible for the development of asthma in children who are exposed to air pollution at a young age (Jiang and others, 2012). DNA methylation also may mediate the effect of early stress in increasing an individual's vulnerability to depression by causing a reprogramming of a key neuroendocrine circuit for functioning in a harsh environment (Booij, Wang, Levesque, Tremblay, & Syzf, 2013).

Health psychologists now recognize that most or all health behaviors are influenced by genetic predispositions and physiological states. As the biopsychosocial perspective reminds us, however, health behaviors are also influenced by personality and thinking style and by social and cultural circumstances. In subsequent chapters, you'll see how physical systems combine and interact with psychological and sociocultural factors to determine health behaviors, as well as overall states of wellness or illness.

Weigh In on Health

Respond to each question below based on what you learned in the chapter. (**Tip:** Use the items in "Summing Up" to take into account related biological, psychological, and social concerns.)

1. What would you say to help a classmate distinguish between neurotransmitters and hormones? In your explanation, discuss where and/or how these substances are produced, as well as their functions and the role they play in issues that concern health psychologists.

2. What is a question that researchers in health psychology might want answered about the function of each of the following human systems: the cardiovascular, digestive, and respiratory systems? Explain how these questions and potential research findings might contribute to the biopsychosocial model of health psychology today.

3. Since your childhood, what are three different ways in which your immune system has been able to overcome pathogens that could have harmed your health? As a college student, what are three things (physical, psychological, and/or social) that you might do to keep your immune system as strong as possible?

4. When a friend asks you why it's important to study the human reproductive system and behavior genetics in a course on health psychology, what would you say to your friend in answer to this question?

Summing Up

Cells

1. All living things are made up of cells. There are two types of cells: eukaryotic, which contain nuclei and other organelles, and prokaryotic, which do not. Cells of similar structure and function form a tissue. Tissues working together form an organ.

2. A neuron is a nerve cell that receives signals through its dendrites and cell body and transmits electrical signals down its axon. A neural impulse flows down the axon to the axon terminal and releases chemical neurotransmitters across the synapse.

The Nervous System

3. The central nervous system consists of the brain and the spinal cord. The remaining neurons comprise the peripheral nervous system, which itself has two main divisions: the somatic nervous system, which controls voluntary movements, and the autonomic nervous system, which controls the involuntary muscles and endocrine glands through the sympathetic and parasympathetic nervous systems.

4. As the oldest and most central region of the brain, the brainstem, including the reticular formation, thalamus, and cerebellum, controls basic life-support functions via the autonomic nervous system. The limbic system includes the medulla, which controls heart rate and breathing; the amygdala, which plays an important role in aggression and other emotions; the hippocampus, which is involved in learning and memory; and the hypothalamus, which influences hunger, thirst, body temperature, and sexual behavior.

5. The cerebral cortex is the thin layer of cells that covers the cerebrum. The cortex is the seat of consciousness and includes areas specialized for triggering movement (motor cortex), sensing touch (sensory cortex), speaking and decision making (frontal lobe), vision (occipital lobe), hearing (temporal lobe), and spatial orientation (parietal lobe). The association cortex includes areas that are not directly involved in sensory or motor functions. These areas integrate information and are involved in higher mental functions such as thinking and speaking.

The Endocrine System

6. Operating under the control of the hypothalamus, the pituitary gland secretes hormones that influence growth, sexual development, reproduction, kidney functioning, and aging. Other glands augment the nervous system in regulating the functioning of heart rate and blood pressure (adrenal medulla), reducing inflammation (adrenal cortex), regulating growth and metabolism (thyroid), and regulating blood glucose levels (pancreas).

The Cardiovascular System

7. The heart is separated into four chambers. Oxygen-depleted blood returning from the body is pumped from the right atrium into the right ventricle, and from there through the capillaries of the lungs, where it picks up fresh oxygen and disposes of carbon dioxide. The freshly oxygenated blood is pumped through the pulmonary vein into the left atrium of the heart, and from there into the left ventricle, from which it flows into the arterial system.

The Respiratory System

8. After air enters the body through the mouth or nose, it travels to the lungs via bronchial tubes that branch into the smaller bronchioles and air sacs of the lungs (the alveoli). The thin walls of the alveoli permit the exchange of oxygen and carbon dioxide.

The Digestive System

9. Digestion begins in the mouth, where chewing and salivary enzymes begin to break food down. Once food is swallowed, the rhythmic movements of the esophageal muscles propel food downward to the stomach, where it is mixed with a variety of gastric enzymes under the control of the autonomic nervous system. Digestive fluids from the pancreas, liver, and gallbladder are secreted into the small and large intestines, where—several hours after eating—the breakdown of food is completed.

The Immune System

10. The body's first line of defense against health-threatening pathogens includes the protective barrier provided by the skin, the mucous membranes of the nose and respiratory tract, and gastric enzymes of the digestive system. A pathogen that penetrates these defenses encounters an army of lymphocytes that filter out infectious substances and debris with the passage of fluids through the lymphatic system. Other nonspecific immune defenses include the action of phagocytes, macrophages, and natural killer (NK) cells. NK cells also secrete antimicrobial proteins called interferons and play a role in the body's inflammatory response.

11. The brain and immune system form a complete, bidirectional communication network in which chemical messengers produced by immune cells (cytokines) communicate to the brain, and chemical messengers produced in the nervous system communicate with immune cells.

12. Specific immune reactions occur when B cells and T cells attack specific foreign substances. B cells accomplish this when memory cells produce specific antibodies that kill previously encountered antigens. In cell-mediated immunity,

T cells directly attack and kill antigens by injecting them with lethal toxins. Immune functioning improves throughout childhood and early adolescence and begins to decline as people approach old age.

The Reproductive System and Behavior Genetics

13. The reproductive system, under the control of the hypothalamus and the endocrine system, directs the development of the primary and secondary sex characteristics.

14. The sum total of all the genes that a person inherits is the person's genotype. How those genes are expressed in the person's traits is the phenotype. Human development begins when a sperm cell fertilizes an ovum, resulting in a single-celled zygote that contains the inherited information from the 23 chromosomes inherited from each parent. The twenty-third pair of chromosomes determines the zygote's sex. Genes are segments of DNA that provide the genetic blueprint for our physical and behavioral development. For any given trait, patterns of gene–environment interaction determine the observable phenotype.

15. DNA methylation is a key epigenetic process that may mediate the biological effects of environmental factors by causing a reprogramming of neuroendocrine circuits in the body.

Key Terms and Concepts to Remember

cell, p. 55
tissue, p. 55
organ, p. 55
neurotransmitters, p. 56
brainstem, p. 58
medulla, p. 59
reticular formation, p. 59
thalamus, p. 59
cerebellum, p. 59
limbic system, p. 59
amygdala, p. 59

hippocampus, p. 60
hypothalamus, p. 60
cerebral cortex, p. 60
sensory cortex, p. 61
motor cortex, p. 61
association cortex, p. 61
hormones, p. 62
pituitary gland, p. 62
adrenal glands, p. 63
arteries, p. 64
veins. p. 64

bronchi, p. 66
cilia, p. 67
gastrointestinal system, p. 67
noncommunicable disease (NCD), p. 68
antigen, p. 70
lymphocytes, p. 70
cytokines, p. 74
genome, p. 77
stem cells, p. 78
genotype, p. 78
phenotype, p. 78

LaunchPad
macmillan learning

To accompany your textbook, you have access to a number of online resources, including quizzes for every chapter of the book, flashcards, critical thinking exercises, videos, and *Check Your Health* inventories. To access these resources, please visit the Straub *Health Psychology* LaunchPad solo at: **launchpadworks.com**

PART 2 | Stress and Health

CHAPTER **4**

Stress

Jupiterimages, Brand X Pictures/Getty Images

n 1934, Hungarian-born Hans Selye (1907–1982) was a promising young endocrinologist trying to make a name for himself at Montreal's McGill University by identifying a new hormone. Working with an ovary extract, Selye devised a simple plan: Give daily injections of the extract to a sample of laboratory rats and watch for changes in their behavior and health. Easier said than done! Selye quickly learned that rats, like people, are not fond of being injected. Often, as he was about to insert the needle, a rat would squirm, causing Selye to miss the injection site. Squeezing an uncooperative rat more tightly sometimes caused it to nip at the young experimenter, who then would drop the animal on the floor and be forced to chase it around the laboratory before eventually completing the injection.

After several months of these daily sessions, Selye made an extraordinary discovery: Most of the rats had developed bleeding ulcers, shrunken thymus glands (which produce disease-fighting lymphocytes), and enlarged adrenal glands. His immediate response was elation, for he believed he had discovered the physiological effects of the as-yet-unknown ovarian extract. Being a careful scientist, however, Selye realized that without a control group, this conclusion was premature. So other groups of laboratory rats were given daily injections of extracts of kidneys, spleen, or a saline solution instead of the ovarian extract. Otherwise, these control animals were treated the same: They were often squeezed, dropped, and chased around the lab before receiving their injections! Much to Selye's surprise, at the end of the experiment, these control rats had the same enlarged adrenal glands, shrunken thymus glands, and bleeding ulcers. Because the same changes occurred in both groups of rats, they could not have been caused by the ovarian extract. What, then, could have caused the changes? What else did the two groups have in common? In a moment of insight (and humility), Selye correctly reasoned that his hapless handling of the animals had triggered some sort of nonspecific response. The rats were stressed out!

We now know that Selye had discovered the *stress response*—a breakthrough that helped to forge an entirely new medical field—*stress physiology*. Although not the first to use the term *stress*, Selye is credited with two important new ideas:

- The body has a remarkably similar response to many different stressors.
- Stressors sometimes can make you sick.

That second idea is especially important—that persistent, or *chronic*, stress influences a person's vulnerability to disorders—and it has become a major theme in health psychology. No single topic has generated more research. As we will see in this and later chapters, researchers have established links between stress and many physical and psychological disorders, including cancer, heart disease, diabetes, arthritis, headaches, asthma, digestive disorders, depression, and anxiety. At the same time, stressful experiences that are weathered successfully can ultimately be positive experiences in our lives and leave us with enhanced resources for coping in the future.

Stress: Some Basic Concepts

So, just what is stress? Stress is a part of life. In fact, without some stress, our lives would be dull. But when stress overtaxes our coping resources, it can damage our health. Each of us experiences stress in our everyday lives. Stress can come from many directions, including school, family and friends, interactions with strangers, and work. Stress usually happens in real time, as when you are forced to juggle the ever-changing demands of school, work, family, and friends. Sometimes stress persists for a long time, as when a person loses a loved one or is forced to retire.

Despite the pervasiveness of stress, psychologists have not had an easy time coming up with an acceptable definition of the word. *Stress* is sometimes used to describe a threatening situation or *stimulus,* and at other times to describe a *response* to a situation. Health psychologists have determined that **stressors** are demanding events or situations that trigger coping adjustments in a person and that **stress** is the *process* by which a person both appraises and responds to events that are judged to be challenging or threatening. It's important to recognize that we must judge a challenging event or situation to be threatening or even beyond our ability to cope before we will be stressed by it. Stress arises less from events themselves than from how we appraise them. A significant stressor for one person may be no big deal for another.

In addition, when a stressor is short-lived or perceived as a challenge, it can have positive effects such as mobilizing the immune system to fend off infection and promote healing (Dhabhar and others, 2010). Champion athletes, musicians, actresses, and successful leaders all learn that their best efforts often come when they have been aroused by a challenge. You will hear much more about this very individual appraisal process later in this chapter. In Chapter 5, we will consider effective ways to cope with stress. In this chapter, we will take a *biopsychosocial* approach to understanding stress and its impact on the body, as follows:

- *Biological* processes that occur when we experience stress can differ somewhat according to each individual's unique physiology and levels of physiological reactivity, but the same basic processes affect us all.
- *Psychological* influences affect how we *appraise* challenging situations—either as manageable (not stressful) or unmanageable (stressful)—based on our personalities and individual life experiences. Gender, as we will see, also plays a role in whether we fight or flee, or seek the company of other people when under pressure.

stressor Any event or situation that triggers coping adjustments.

stress The process by which we perceive and respond to events, called *stressors,* that we appraise as threatening or challenging.

■ Our own unique *sociocultural* influences affect how we appraise stress from many different sources, including major life events, daily hassles, work, and family.

Let's turn first to the types of stressors people experience.

Stressors

Everyone experiences stress. How and why we experience stress may change as we journey through life, but none of us escape. Each of us experiences the events of life in a unique way. Research has focused on several types of stressors: significant life events, daily hassles, work, and sociocultural factors.

Significant Life Events

What impact do major life events, such as leaving home, changing jobs, having a child, or losing a loved one, have on the quality of our health? In the late 1950s, psychiatrists Thomas Holmes and Richard Rahe of the University of Washington substantially advanced our understanding of how the events of our lives affect our health. They interviewed more than 5000 people to identify which events forced people to make the most changes in their lives. Then they assigned each event a value in *life change units* (LCUs) to reflect the amount of change that was necessary. For example, a divorce disrupts many more aspects of one's life than does taking a vacation, and thus it would be assigned a larger number of LCUs. The range of events that Holmes and Rahe investigated was broad, even including occasions that called for celebration, such as marriage or a promotion. They then ranked these events and devised the *Social Readjustment Rating Scale* (SRRS), which was the first systematic attempt to quantify the impact of life changes on health. Table 4.1 shows the College Undergraduate Stress Scale, a variation of the original SRRS that is directed specifically at college students.

Holmes and Rahe theorized that the total number of LCUs that a person had accumulated during the previous year could be used to predict the likelihood that he or she would become sick over the next several months. In one study (Rahe, Mahan, & Arthur, 1970), researchers obtained SRRS scores on naval crewmen who were about to depart on a six-month mission. Over the course of the voyage, the researchers found a positive correlation between LCUs and illness rates. Those sailors who reported the highest LCUs were more likely to fall ill than those who reported the lowest LCUs. The message: When life brings many changes at once, the stress that results may make us more vulnerable to health problems.

Although the research of Holmes and Rahe was groundbreaking and influential, the value of the SRRS and other scales for predicting stress and illness has been criticized for several reasons:

■ Many of the items are vague, subjective, and open to interpretation. "Change in living conditions" or "revision of personal habits," for example, can mean almost anything.

■ Assigning specific point values to events fails to take into consideration individual differences in the way events are appraised (and therefore experienced). A divorce, for example, may mean welcome freedom for one person but a crushing loss to another.

■ The SRRS and other scales lump all events together—whether positive or negative, by chance or willfully chosen. Many studies have found that unexpected or uncontrollable negative events, such as the premature death of a family member, are much more stressful than are events that are positive, expected, or under one's control, such as getting married, changing jobs, or taking a vacation.

Significant Stress Catastrophic events, such as the 8.8 magnitude earthquake that struck central Chile in 2010, provide tragic, real-world examples of stress as both a stimulus and a response. The event that triggers coping behavior is the stressor (the stimulus), and the person attempting to flee the event or trying to compensate for the destruction that it causes illustrates the response.

TABLE 4.1
The College Undergraduate Stress Scale

Copy the "stress" rating number into the last column for any item that has happened to you in the last year, then add the numbers.

Event	Stress Ratings	Your Items	Event	Stress Ratings	Your Items
Being raped	100		Change in housing situation (hassles, moves)	69	
Finding out that you are HIV-positive	100		Competing or performing in public	69	
Being accused of rape	98		Getting in a physical fight	66	
Death of a close friend	97		Difficulties with a roommate	66	
Death of a close family member	96		Job changes (applying, new job, work hassles)	69	
Contracting a sexually transmitted disease (other than AIDS)	94		Declaring a major or concerns about future plans	65	
Concerns about being pregnant	91				
Finals week	90		A class you hate	62	
Concerns about your partner being pregnant	90		Drinking or use of drugs	61	
			Confrontations with professors	60	
Oversleeping for an exam	89		Starting a new semester	58	
Flunking a class	89		Going on a first date	57	
Having a boyfriend or girlfriend cheat on you	85		Registration	55	
Ending a steady dating relationship	85		Maintaining a steady dating relationship	55	
Serious illness in a close friend or family member	85		Commuting to campus or work, or both	54	
Financial difficulties	84		Peer pressures	53	
Writing a major term paper	83		Being away from home for the first time	53	
Being caught cheating on a test	83				
Drunk driving	82		Getting sick	52	
Sense of overload in school or work	85		Concerns about your appearance	52	
Two exams in one day	80		Getting straight A's	51	
Cheating on your boyfriend or girlfriend	77		A difficult class that you love	48	
Getting married	76		Making new friends; getting along with friends	47	
Negative consequences of drinking or drug use	75		Fraternity or sorority rush	47	
Depression or crisis in your best friend	73		Falling asleep in class	40	
Difficulties with parents	73		Attending an athletic event (e.g., football game)	20	
Talking in front of a class	72				
Lack of sleep	69		Total		

Note: Of 12,000 U.S. college students who completed this scale, scores ranged from 182 to 2571, with a mean score of 1247. Women reported significantly higher scores than men, perhaps because most of the students used in pretesting items were women. This being the case, items that are stressful for women may be overrepresented in the scale.

Sources: Renner, M. J., & Mackin, R. S. (1998). A life stress instrument for classroom use. *Teaching of Psychology, 25,* 47.

- Many inventories do not differentiate between resolved and unresolved stressful events. There is evidence that stressors that have been resolved successfully have substantially weaker adverse effects on the person's health than events that linger unresolved (Turner & Avison, 1992).

- Life event scales tend to underestimate the stress that African-Americans and other minorities experience (Turner & Avison, 2003).

One measure of a good theory, however, is that it generates research that leads to new understanding, even if it also leads to its own demise. If nothing else, the many studies conducted using the SRRS have revealed that there is no simple, direct connection between life stress and illness: Subjected to the same stressors, one person will get sick, while another will not. The health consequences of stress depend upon our appraisal of the stressors (see the Diversity and Healthy Living: The Stress of Emerging Adulthood box).

Daily Hassles

Significant life changes occur infrequently; everyday hassles happen all the time and thus are the most significant sources of stress. These minor annoyances range from missing a commuter train to work, to not having the required answer booklet for an exam, to losing a wallet, to arguing with a professor, or to living with an aggravating roommate (Repetti, Wang, & Saxbe, 2009).

The impact on health of such hassles depends on their frequency, duration, and intensity. In addition, our reactions to minor hassles are influenced by our personality, our individual style of coping, and how the rest of our day has gone.

The counterpart to daily hassles is daily *uplifts:* mood-lifting experiences such as receiving an approving nod from the boss, hearing your favorite song at just the right moment, or even getting a good night's sleep. Just as hassles may cause physical and emotional stress that may result in illness, uplifts may serve as buffers against the effects of stress.

Richard Lazarus (whose transactional model of stress will be discussed later in the chapter) and his colleagues devised a scale to measure people's experiences with day-to-day annoyances and uplifts (Kanner, Coyne, Schaefer, & Lazarus, 1981). The Hassles and Uplifts Scale consists of 117 events that range from small pleasures to major problems (Kanner and others, 1981). Table 4.2 shows the 10 most frequent hassles and uplifts as reported by this sample of adults, together with the percentage of time each event was checked. An alternative to this scale is the Daily Hassles Microsystem Scale, which was designed for poor, urban, and culturally diverse adolescents (Seidman and others, 1995).

E+/Getty Images

K The expression on this student's face reflects the feeling of dread that can come with receiving an ambiguous text such as this. What does "k" actually mean? Misinterpretation is just one source of anxiety associated with social media use.

Stress may also take a toll on the unborn. Some studies have found that women who reported high levels of stress during pregnancy were more likely to experience a preterm birth (Wadhwa and others, 2011).

TABLE 4.2

Common Hassles and Uplifts

Hassles	Percentage of Times Checked over Nine Months	Uplifts	Percentage of Times Checked over Nine Months
1. Concern about weight	52.4	1. Relating well with your spouse or lover	76.3
2. Health of family member	48.1	2. Relating well with friends	74.4
3. Rising prices of common goods	43.7	3. Completing a task	73.3
4. Home maintenance	42.8	4. Feeling healthy	72.7
5. Too many things to do	38.6	5. Getting enough sleep	69.7
6. Misplacing or losing things	38.1	6. Meeting responsibilities	68.8
7. Yardwork or outside home maintenance	38.1	7. Eating out	68.4
8. Property, investment, or taxes	37.6	8. Visiting, phoning, or writing someone	67.7
9. Crime	37.1	9. Spending time with family	66.7
10. Physical appearance	35.9	10. Home pleasing to you	65.5

Data from Kanner, A. D., Coyne, J. C., Schaefer, C., & Lazarus, R. S. (1981). Comparison of two modes of stress measurement: Daily hassles and uplifts versus major life events. *Journal of Behavioral Medicine, 4,* p. 14.

Diversity and Healthy Living

The Stress of Emerging Adulthood

Until recently, five events generally signified the transition from adolescence to adulthood: completing school, leaving home, becoming financially independent, marrying, and having a child. In 1960, 77 percent of women and 65 percent of men in the United States had reached all five milestones (Henig, 2010). Increasingly, however, millions of young people are postponing these roles. As shown in Figure 4.1, for example, the average age at first marriage in the early 1970s was 21 for women and 23 for men; by 2010, it had climbed to 26 for women and 28 for men; an increase of five years within one generation (U.S. Census Bureau, 2015).

This shift in the timetable for adulthood is so prominent throughout the world that *emerging adulthood*—the period between 18 and 25 years of age—has been called out as a distinct new stage of life, and abundant research is underway aimed at identifying its distinctive features. In 2012, researchers at Clark University began conducting an annual survey of a large, diverse group of emerging adults. The results have revealed that emerging adulthood is a fascinating transitionary period, frequently evoking mixed emotions. Most participants see this time of life as "fun and exciting," as well as a time with "a great deal of freedom." On the other hand, 72% say this time of life is stressful, 56% say they often feel anxious, and 33% report feeling depressed (see Table 4.3).

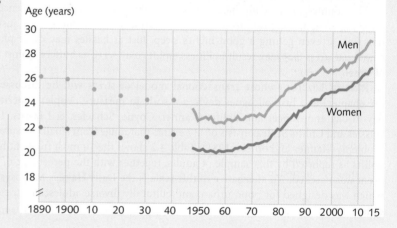

FIGURE 4.1

Average Age at First Marriage, 1890–2015 The average age at first marriage has increased by about five years, for both women and men, within one generation.

Data from U.S. Census Bureau, Decennial Censuses, 1890 to 1940, and Current Population Survey, Annual Social and Economic Supplements, 1947 to 2015.

Hassles seem to be a better predictor of health problems than either major life events or the frequency of daily uplifts. This finding has been confirmed many times. Everyday hassles or mundane irritants and stressors negatively affect physical and mental health to a degree that exceeds the adverse consequences of major life events. Studies have found, for instance, that the revised scale does a better job than the Social Readjustment Rating Scale in predicting headaches, inflammatory bowel disease episodes, and other disorders (Searle & Bennett, 2001). Other studies have shown that daily hassles are associated with a worsening of symptoms in people who are already suffering from illnesses such as lupus (Peralta-Ramirez, Jimenez-Alonzo, Godoy-Garcia, & Perez-Garcia, 2004).

Critics have argued, however, that some of the items listed as hassles may actually be *symptoms of* stress rather than stressors. Items relating to appearance, for example, may tap into lowered feelings of self-esteem that *result from* rather than contribute to stress. In addition, some items refer to alcohol and drug use, sexual difficulties, physical illness, and personal fears—all possible consequences of stress.

TABLE 4.3

% Agreeing (Somewhat or Strongly) with Each Statement

This time of my life is fun and exciting	83%
This time of my life is full of changes	83%
Overall, I am satisfied with my life	81%
At this time of my life, I feel I have a great deal of freedom	73%
This time of my life is stressful	73%
This time of my life is full of uncertainty	64%
I often feel anxious	56%
I often feel depressed	32%
I often feel that my life is not going well	30%

Data from Arnett, J. J., & Schwab, J. (2012). The *Clark University Poll of Emerging Adults: Thriving, Struggling, & Hopeful.* clarku.edu/clarkpoll

Why does an increase in negative emotions take place in emerging adulthood? One reason may be the upheavals that often characterize these years. Emerging adults frequently:

- move (slightly more than 30 percent move *every year*)
- change jobs (averaging seven jobs during their twenties)
- have not made as much progress in their careers as they had hoped to (70 percent)
- move back in with their parents (more than 40 percent do so at least once during their twenties)
- spend time living with a romantic partner (66 percent)

Emerging adulthood is also a time when major life questions are asked, such as: Who am I? What is important to me? Who do I want to have in my life? What do I want to do with my life? All of this can be stressful and take its toll on physical and mental health. Indeed, except for *dementia,* emerging adults experience more of every diagnosed psychological disorder than any older age group—almost double that of adults over age 25 (SAMHSA, 2009). Further, emerging adults have a heightened risk for problems related to alcohol and drug abuse. Because of brain development during emerging adulthood, addiction can be particularly harmful at this time and have long-lasting effects on cognitive development and other aspects of health.

Researchers point to several cultural changes that have led to emerging adulthood. These include the need for more education to survive in today's information-based economy and fewer entry-level jobs even after all that schooling. Emerging adults are the age group most likely to be unemployed. Lacking the steadiness of work and often experiencing rejection after rejection, emerging adults who are still struggling to form an identity can find this time of life to be especially stressful.

In spite of these areas of concern, all is not gloom and doom in this age group. Emerging adults are also more optimistic than at any other time of life. In this respect, the decade of the twenties has been called the "stem cell of human development" (Henig, 2010). It is a time filled with possibilities, when countless outcomes are possible. There is time enough for the obligations of adulthood. Perhaps those who take longer to make their life choices will make fewer mistakes.

In addition, other researchers have suggested that individuals who are high in anxiety to begin with (Kohn, Lafreniere, & Gurevich, 1990), those who have trouble "letting go" of unattainable goals (Miller & Wrosch, 2007), along with people who perceive low levels of social support (Fiksenbaum, Greenglass, & Eaton, 2006), will find daily hassles more stressful. This suggests that an overly anxious or socially isolated person may overreact to daily hassles in a way that magnifies their impact.

Daily hassles also have been demonstrated to interact with *background stressors,* such as job dissatisfaction (Wang, Lesage, Schmitz, & Drapeau, 2008), having a long commute to work or school (Gottholmseder, Nowotny, Pruckner, & Theurl, 2009), and crowded living conditions (Regoeczi, 2003). In impoverished areas—where many people routinely live with inadequate income, unemployment, and the demands of single parenting—such stressors are part of daily life.

For minority populations, daily hassles are compounded by perceived discrimination (Pascoe and Richman, 2009) and racism, which has been linked to hypertension in African-Americans (Mays, Cochran, & Barnes, 2007). Discrimination is also experienced

Purestock/Alamy

Daily hassles and background stressors such as traffic jams seem to be a better predictor of health problems than either major life events or the frequency of daily uplifts.

Work has become such a deeply entrenched ethic in Japanese culture that the Japanese people have created a term, **karoshi,** *to describe death that results from work overload. Under Japanese law, bereaved family members may be entitled to special financial compensation if they are able to prove that the cause of their family member's death was* **karoshi.**

regularly by other ethnic groups (Edwards & Romero, 2008) and by lesbian, gay, bisexual, and transgender people (Wu, 2015; Centers for Disease Control and Prevention, 2015j). A dramatic illustration of the interaction of daily hassles with chronic stress comes from studies of the aftermath of unpredictable large-scale events such as earthquakes, floods, and other catastrophes. In the New York City area, repeated exposure to media images of the September 11, 2001, terrorist attacks, in which two hijacked passenger airliners were crashed into the twin towers of the World Trade Center, turned the event into a *collective trauma.* The research study assessed the mental and physical health of 1,322 participants before and after the 9/11 attacks, along with information about their media exposure. People who watched four or more hours of 9/11-related television per day were significantly more likely to report health problems—even over the next two to three years (Silver and others, 2013). It is suspected that persistent background stress during this difficult period caused many people to overreact to everyday stressors that they would normally have shrugged off.

Work

Because it is true that busy people generally are happier (Hsee, Yang, & Wang, 2010) and that satisfaction with work feeds satisfaction with life (Bowling, Eschleman & Wang, 2010), an extensive amount of research has been devoted to examining the causes and consequences of job-related stress. These studies are important for two reasons. First, almost all people at some time experience stress related to their work. Second, work-related stress may be one of the most preventable health hazards and thereby provides a number of possibilities for intervention

For most of us, job stress is brief in duration and does not pose a serious threat to our health. For some people, however, job stress may be chronic, continuing for years. Data from the massive 2010 Canadian Community Health Survey found that respondents with the highest level of perceived work stress had higher odds of being treated for an emotional or mental-health problem at any point and for being treated in the previous 12 months. These high-stress respondents also had higher odds of being diagnosed for mood and anxiety disorders than their less-stressed counterparts (Szeto & Dobson, 2013).

Changing jobs can be stressful. Between ages 18 and 27, the average worker in the United States holds eight jobs; with those who are college educated changing jobs more often than those with less education (U.S. Bureau of Labor Statistics, 2012). One study found that people who frequently changed jobs before age 36 were more likely to have a variety of health problems by age 42 (Kinnunen, Kaprio, & Pulkkinen, 2005).

For several reasons, the older a worker is, the more stressful a job change becomes (Rix, 2012):

- A loss of job seniority often means a lower salary, a loss of respect, and other disadvantages.

- Older workers may be lacking in newer job skills that didn't even exist when they started working many years earlier. Consequently, many employers are reluctant to hire older workers, so these workers may have trouble even finding a new job in the first place, let alone adjusting to the new situation.

- Although age discrimination is illegal, many older workers believe it is common.

- Having to relocate for a new job is often disruptive to a worker's social network.

Let's take a look at some of the factors that can make certain jobs more stressful than others.

Your Health Assets

The Gallup Employee Engagement Questionnaire

On a scale of 1 to 5, where 1 is "strongly disagree" and 5 is "strongly agree," indicate your agreement with the following statements.

1. I know what is expected from me at work.
2. I have the materials and equipment I need to do my work right.
3. At work, I have the opportunity to do what I do best every day.
4. In the last seven days, I have received recognition or praise for doing good work.
5. My supervisor, or someone at work, seems to care about me as a person.
6. There is someone at work who encourages my development.
7. At work, my opinions seem to count.
8. The mission/purpose of my company makes me feel my job is important.
9. My associates (fellow employees) are committed to doing quality work.
10. I have a best friend at work.
11. In the last six months, someone at work has talked to me about my progress.
12. This last year, I have had opportunities at work to learn and grow.

Scores can range from 12 to 60, with higher scores representing higher levels of employee engagement.

Score	Interpretation
48–60	The employee is highly engaged.
36–47	The employee is neither engaged nor disengaged.
12–35	The employee is disengaged.

Information from Harter, J. K., Schmidt, F. L., & Keyes, C. L. (2003). Well-being in the workplace and its relationship to business outcomes. In C. L. Keyes and J. Haidt (Eds.). *Flourishing: The positive person and the good life.* Washington, DC: American Psychological Association, 205–224.

Social-Evaluative Threat

Even a job environment to which a person is well matched can present momentary stressors. One is the threat of negative evaluations from others. While **social-evaluative threat** is not limited to the workplace and is a central stressor in many models of stress and health (Dickerson, Gruenewald, & Kemeny, 2004), evaluations are a frequent, and explicit, experience in many jobs. Feeling accepted, liked, and included by others is a basic social motive, as are the prospects of achievement, protection of status, and gaining respect (Kenrick, Griskevicius, Neuberg, & Schaller, 2010). Social evaluation poses a threat to these positive health resources and, not surprisingly, has been associated with increased physiological arousal in the workplace, classroom, and other environments (Taylor and others, 2010; Smith, Birmingham, & Uchino, 2012).

A notable example of this fear of negative evaluation is **stereotype threat,** first described by an African-American researcher who called it a "threat in the air." Stereotype threat begins with the thought that other people hold prejudices against one's social group, and then that thought becomes a stressor. In reality, those other people may not hold those stereotypes, but the possibility that they do may be stressful (Inzlicht & Schmader, 2012).

social-evaluative threat A stressor in which people fear negative evaluation by others of their appearance or ability.

stereotype threat The experience of stress in a situation where a person's ability, appearance, or other characteristic has the potential to confirm a negative viewpoint about his or her social group.

Overload

Even a job environment to which a person is well matched can become a stressor if there is *work overload.* People who feel they have to work too long and too hard at too many tasks feel more stressed. They also have poorer health habits, experience more accidents, and suffer more health problems than do other workers (CDC, 2015j). As one example, chronic activation of the part of the neuroendocrine system that controls reactions to stress, which has been linked to overcommitment, increases the risk of cardiovascular disease (Steptoe, Siegrist, Kirschbaum, & Marmot, 2004), as does incomplete rest during weekends and vacations (Kivimaki and others, 2006).

A key factor in the relationship between the number of work hours and worker satisfaction is whether employees can choose their own schedules. Workers who volunteer for paid overtime, for example, are usually more satisfied than workers who are required to work overtime (Klaus, Ekerdt, & Gajewski, 2012).

Combining Work and Family

A related form of stress occurs when people attempt to balance several different jobs at the same time and experience *role overload*. A large study of adult Canadians found that about half of the variation in their self-reported stress was related to employment (working conditions, support at work, occupation, job security), but at least as much was related to family (having children younger than 5 or inadequate amount of support at home) and feeling personally incompetent (Marchand, Durand, & Lupien, 2012).

The problems associated with juggling multiple roles simultaneously have been particularly great for women. Today, most mothers, even those with the youngest children, participate in the labor force (Department for Professional Employees, 2009). Studies have supported two competing hypotheses. One, the *scarcity hypothesis,* maintains that because they have only so much time and energy, women with competing demands suffer from role overload and conflict. The other, the *enhancement hypothesis,* argues that the benefits of meaningful work in enhancing a worker's self-esteem outweigh the costs.

Although some early research seemed to support the scarcity hypothesis, researchers have generally found that the multiple roles of employee, wife, and mother offer health benefits for women (Schnittker, 2007). Moreover, for many working mothers, employment is an important source of self-esteem and life satisfaction. Whether multiple roles are associated with adverse or beneficial health effects depends heavily on the resources people have available to them. Women who are raising children without a partner are especially likely to feel stressed (Livermore & Powers, 2006); they also may be at risk for health problems (Hughes & Waite, 2002). Indeed, researchers have found that those adults—both men and women—who perceive support and are able to balance vocational, marital, and parental roles generally are healthier and happier than adults who function successfully in only one or two of these roles (Hochschild, 1997; Milkie & Peltola, 1999).

From studies such as these, researchers have concluded that what matters most is not the number of roles that a person occupies, but the quality of the experience in those roles. Having control over one's work, a good income, adequate child care, and a supportive family combine to help reduce the likelihood that multiple role demands will be stressful. Similarly, although people often complain that working long hours creates stress, researchers consistently find that stress symptoms, sick days, and overall life satisfaction are more likely to be influenced by other workplace characteristics, such as job autonomy, learning opportunities, supportive supervisors, and scheduling flexibility (Schwartz, 2003). These findings are similar to those related to the

Role Overload The task of managing multiple roles affects both men and women, but the increase in employment of women has triggered more research on role overload and job-related stress in women. Some research findings regarding the stress of role overload have been contradictory; however, the overall conclusion seems to be that what matters most is the quality of a working mother's experiences in her various roles.

E+/Getty Images

potential stress associated with caregiving. The roles may be burdensome, but work and caregiving can also provide satisfaction and a feeling of empowerment (Mitchell, 2011).

Fortunately, partners often adjust to each other's work, which helps them function well as a unit (Abele & Vollmer, 2011). If there are children, partners adjust their work and child-care hours, usually with the mother cutting back on employment, but not always—sometimes the father has fewer outside-the-home work hours and the mother has more. When mothers work full time, fathers often spend far more time with their children, and mothers do less housework (Abele & Vollmer, 2011).

Burnout

Burnout has been defined as a job-related state of physical and psychological exhaustion that can occur among individuals who work with other (often, needy) people in some capacity (Maslach, 2003). Jobs that involve responsibility for other people, rather than responsibility for products, appear to cause high levels of burnout (Sears, Urizar, & Evans, 2000). Health care workers, dentists, paramedics, air traffic controllers, and firefighters are especially susceptible to this type of job stress. A number of studies have demonstrated that as many as one-third of nurses report stress-related symptoms that are severe enough to be considered a warning sign of psychiatric problems (Fasoli, 2010; Tyler & Cushway, 1992). And one study of 185 physicians and 119 nurses found that emotional stress scores among physicians were nearly 50 percent higher than among nurses (Rutledge and others, 2009).

Although burnout customarily develops over a period of years, its warning signs and symptoms may appear early on. These include feelings of mental and physical exhaustion; absenteeism; high job turnover (Schernhammer, 2005); abnormal stress hormone levels (Mommersteeg, Keijsers, Heijnen, Verbraak, & van Doornen, 2006); changes in immune and sympathetic nervous system functioning; an increase in stress-related ailments, such as headaches, backaches, and depression; and shortness of temper (Zanstra, Schellekens, Schaap, & Kooistra, 2006).

Burnout is not, however, an inevitable consequence of employment in certain professions. As the biopsychosocial model reminds us, susceptibility to most health conditions is the product of overlapping factors in every domain of health. For instance, nurses who have high self-esteem, a strong sense of personal control, and a hopeful, optimistic view of life are much less likely to experience burnout than their more pessimistic counterparts on chronic care wards, thereby highlighting the protective function of certain personality styles (Browning, Ryan, Greenberg, & Rolniak, 2006; Sherwin, Elliott, Rybarczyk, & Frank, 1992).

burnout A job-related state of physical and psychological exhaustion.

Job Demands and Lack of Control

Workers feel more stress when they have little or no control over the procedures, pace, and other aspects of their jobs. The relationship between lack of control and illness was clearly revealed in Marianne Frankenhaeuser's (1975) classic study of Scandinavian sawmill workers. Compared with workers who had more say over aspects of their jobs, those working at dull, repetitive, low-control jobs had significantly higher levels of stress hormones, higher blood pressure, more headaches, and more gastrointestinal disorders, including ulcers. Even a little bit of control goes a long way to produce beneficial health effects (Montpetit & Bergeman, 2007).

Other studies have confirmed the relationship between perceived control and work-related stress, especially in Western cultures that emphasize individual autonomy and responsibility. The *demand-control model* for work stress focuses on the balance between job requirements and workers' perception of autonomy (Karasek, 1979). People who experience high demands with little control over their jobs are more likely than other workers to

Burnout Jobs that involve responsibility for other people, rather than responsibility for products, appear to cause high levels of burnout. Physicians have stressful jobs, partly because of their responsibility for other people's lives, which makes them especially susceptible to burnout. Firefighters and other first responders are especially susceptible to this type of job stress.

feel stressed. For example, a barista working in a busy coffee shop is at risk of feeling stressed because he or she must quickly fill orders in the correct way (high demand), while having little or no say about how or when the coffee is made (low control). This type of *job strain* has been linked to increased risk of cardiovascular disease and other health problems (Kivimaki and others, 2012).

Lack of control has also been linked to anger and the development of coronary artery disease (Bosma and others, 1997; Fitzgerald, Haythornthwaite, Suchday, & Ewart, 2003), as well as an increased overall risk of death (Amick and others, 2002).

Secretaries, waitresses, factory workers, and middle managers are among those with the most stressful occupations, marked by repetitive tasks and little control over events. Common to these jobs are complaints of too many demands with too little authority to influence work practices. The sense of powerlessness that results often creates crushing stress. Control issues contribute to the experience of stress among others in our society who have felt powerless, including the impoverished, immigrants, and women.

Other Sources of Job-Related Stress

Several other aspects of jobs increase stress among workers, including these:

- *Role ambiguity or conflict.* Role ambiguity occurs when workers are unsure of their jobs or the standards used to evaluate their performance. Role conflict occurs when a worker receives mixed messages about these issues from different supervisors or coworkers.

- *Shiftwork.* Shiftwork involves continuous staffing of a workplace by groups of employees who work at different times. Off-regular hours shift workers face disruption to their family and domestic lives, as well as to their *biological rhythms.* Most human functions have a rhythm with peaks and valleys that occur over a regular 24- to 25-hour cycle. Shiftwork desynchronizes these rhythms and may lead to a number of health complaints, including headaches, loss of appetite, fatigue, sleep disturbances, gastrointestinal problems, and heart disease (Taylor, 1997; Waterhouse, 1993).

- *Job loss.* Downsizing, layoffs, mergers, and bankruptcies cost thousands of workers their jobs each year. The loss of a job can have a serious impact on a worker's well-being, putting unemployed workers at risk for physical illness, anxiety, depression, and even suicide (Vinokur, Schul, Vuori, & Price, 2000). Job insecurity and the threat of unemployment have been linked to lowered immunity (Cohen, F., and others, 2007) and higher levels of several health-compromising risk factors. One study reported higher blood pressure and serum cholesterol levels among Michigan autoworkers who faced the closing of their factory (Kasl, 1997). Other studies have reported increased smoking, alcohol consumption, use of prescription drugs, body weight, and hospital admissions among laid-off workers (Hammarstrom, 1994; Wanberg, 2012). Adults who can't find employment are 60 percent more likely to die than other people their age, especially if they are younger than 40 (Roelfs, Davidson, & Schwartz, 2011). On the other hand, having job security appears to protect health, and reemployment can reverse the effects of job loss (Cohen, F., and others, 2007).

- *Lack of fairness and inadequate career advancement.* People who feel that they have been promoted too slowly or that they are not getting the recognition they deserve on the job experience more stress and have higher rates of illness (Catalano, Rook, & Dooley, 1986). The sense of fairness is universal and even encoded in the brain

(Hsu, Anen, & Quartz, 2008). This may explain why even though average household income has doubled in the United States over the past half-century, happiness has not increased. While extreme poverty *is* correlated with unhappiness, most people report being mildly happy, and there are people at every income level who suffer from depression (Diener & Biswas-Diener, 2008). This may explain why absolute income matters less to many people than how their income compares with others in the same job or neighborhood, or to their own salary a year or two ago. Workers are more likely to quit if they believe their salary ranking is unfair (Brown, Gardner, Oswald, & Qian, 2008). Workers who have a direct role in setting fair salary levels report higher levels of satisfaction (Choshen-Hillel & Yaniv, 2011). Perceiving fairness in health insurance coverage and other benefits is also very important (Bianchi & Milkie, 2010).

Although job-related stress is difficult to avoid, there are ways to buffer its negative impact. Better ways of responding include knowing what to expect from certain aspects of work (and coworkers), expressing your feelings to increase your perception of control, keeping things in perspective, and avoiding self-defeating thoughts and overreactions. We'll take up the topic of coping with stress much more fully in Chapter 5.

Social Interactions

The health benefits of social support apply throughout the life span, including during the college years (Hale, Hannum, & Espelage, 2005). At work and elsewhere, social relationships are an important factor in how we deal with stress, often serving as a buffer against low control and other work stress (Fitzgerald and others, 2003). The mechanisms for this effect include enhanced immune functioning (Cohen & Herbert, 1996). Loneliness, for example, appears to affect immune functioning adversely, as does relationship stress (Glaser and others, 1992). Immunosuppression has been linked to interpersonal conflict among married couples (Kiecolt-Glaser and others, 1997; Kiecolt-Glaser & Newton, 2001), women recently separated from their husbands (Kiecolt-Glaser and others, 1987), and men whose wives have recently died (Schleifer, Keller, Camerino, Thorton, & Stein, 1983). More recent studies have demonstrated that impaired immunity associated with the loss of a loved one occurs primarily among those people who become depressed in response to their bereavement (Zisook and others, 1994).

The caregiving role, in which one person provides the bulk of care for a loved one with a chronic illness, also can be stressful and adversely affect physical health (Vitaliano, Zhang, & Scanlan, 2003). One recent study of parents who were full-time caregivers of adult children with a serious mental illness found higher self-reported stress levels and abnormalities in the daily production of the hormone cortisol (Barker, Greenberg, Seltzer, & Almeida, 2012). Caregiving stress has also been linked to poor immune functioning. In a series of studies, Janice Kiecolt-Glaser and colleagues demonstrated that family members who provide care for a relative with Alzheimer's disease report more depression and lower life satisfaction than those in the control group (matched family members with no caregiving responsibilities). Caregivers also have lower percentages of T cells and other measures of immunosuppression, as well as concurrent *overproduction* of proinflammatory cytokines (Kiecolt-Glaser and others, 1996, 2003). Overproduction of cytokines has been associated with a broad array of adverse health conditions,

Social Support Social relationships are an important factor in how we deal with stress, often serving as a buffer against low control and other work stress.

Myrleen Pearson/Alamy

including cardiovascular disease, arthritis, Type 2 diabetes, and certain cancers. Ethnic minorities, immigrants, those who are poor, and women often experience the most intense social stress.

The Physiology of Stress

A decade before Hans Selye's discovery that was described in the chapter opening, physiologist Walter Cannon introduced the term *stress* to medicine (Cannon, 1932). Cannon observed that extremes of temperature, lack of oxygen, and emotion-arousing incidents all had a similar arousing effect on the body. He was the first to call this effect *stress,* and he believed that it was a common cause of medical problems.

In one of Cannon's studies, cats were frightened by the sound of a barking dog. Cannon discovered that large amounts of the hormone epinephrine could later be detected in the cats' blood. Cannon called this response to stressful events the body's *fight-or-flight reaction.* An outpouring of epinephrine, along with cortisol and other hormones, helps prepare an organism to defend itself against a threat, either by attacking or by running away.

From an evolutionary perspective, this emergency response system seems highly functional and adaptive. It undoubtedly was essential to our ancestors' survival in a time when human beings faced numerous physical threats and had to either fight or run away. Today, in our modern, highly developed societies, our stressors are apt to be psychological as well as physical, but we still react as though we are facing a standoff with a wild animal. According to neuroscientist Robert Sapolsky, this explains why humans and their primate cousins get more stress-related diseases than any other member of the animal kingdom. All vertebrate animals respond to stressful situations by releasing hormones such as adrenaline and cortisol. Fish, birds, and even reptiles secrete the same hormones as humans, but they do not appear to suffer the same health consequences as humans and other primates. In Sapolsky's words, primates, like humans, "are super smart and organized just enough to devote their free time to being miserable to each other and stressing each other out. We've evolved to be smart enough to make ourselves sick." The result is that even non-life-threatening stressors, such as worrying about money or pleasing the boss, trigger the same hormonal response (Sapolsky, 2004b, 2010).

Many of Sapolsky's insights come from his 30-year field study of wild African baboons, highly social and intelligent primates that, like unhealthy people, often have elevated resting levels of stress hormones despite facing a relatively low level of threat from predators, lack of food, or other life-threatening problems. Baboons who have the lowest rank in the troop and those that are socially isolated are most likely to show stress-induced changes in their physiology. In addition to having elevated resting levels of epinephrine and cortisol, these baboons have reproductive systems that function poorly, blood pressure that is elevated, and wounds that heal more slowly than those of other baboons. High-status baboons that frequently have to defend their dominant position physically are also likely to show these adverse physiological changes (Sapolsky, 2005). What that means, says Sapolsky, is that if you are a baboon living in a troop in the Serengeti, you "only have to work three hours a day for your calories, predators don't mess with you much … and you've got nine hours of free time every day to devote to generating psychological stress toward other animals in your troop" (Shwartz, 2007).

It is important to note, however, that when stressors are short-lived and when they are perceived as challenges rather than threats, they can have positive effects. Momentary stressors mobilize the immune system for fighting off infections and healing wounds

(Segerstrom, 2007). In addition, many experts—from champion athletes to professional entertainers—thrive on challenges and find that their performances improve (Blascovich, Seery, Mugridge, Norris, & Weisbuch, 2004). Selye himself recognized this in his concept of *eustress* (from the Greek prefix *eu-*, meaning "good" or "well"), by which he meant that challenging events can lead to growth if they enhance our functioning, just as working the body by lifting weights ultimately improves a person's muscular strength.

The Role of the Brain and Nervous System

The body's overall reaction to stress is regulated by the central nervous system. Recall from Chapter 3 that the nervous system consists of two parts, the *central nervous system* (the brain and the spinal cord) and the *peripheral nervous system.* The peripheral nervous system is divided into two major branches: the *autonomic nervous system* (ANS) and the *somatic nervous system.* Finally, the ANS is further divided into two branches: the *sympathetic nervous system* (SNS) and the *parasympathetic nervous system* (PNS).

When an external event is first perceived by your sense organs, sensory neurons in the somatic nervous system transmit nerve impulses to lower-level brain regions announcing the impending threat. The *reticular formation,* which runs like a rope through the middle of the brainstem (see Chapter 3), plays a central role in alerting the brain to an impending threat or challenge.

The reticular formation coordinates two neural pathways of brain–body communication. Through the first, it routes information about the existence of a potential stressor to the *thalamus,* which sorts this sensory information and relays it to the *hypothalamus,* the *limbic system,* and higher brain regions in the cerebral cortex that interpret the meaning of the potential stressor. Through the second pathway, the reticular formation carries neural instructions back from the higher brain regions to the various target organs, muscles, and glands controlled by the SNS; as a result of these instructions, the body is mobilized for defensive action.

Under instructions from the SNS, the adrenal glands release hormones that cause the fight-or-flight response, in which heart rate increases, the pupils dilate, stress hormones are secreted, and digestion slows. In addition, SNS activation increases blood flow to the muscles and causes stored energy to be converted to a form that is directly usable by the muscles. The region of the brain that most directly controls the stress response is the hypothalamus. Nearly every region of the brain interacts in some way with the hypothalamus. For this reason, the hypothalamus reacts to a variety of stimuli, from actual threats to memories of stressful moments to imagined stressors. The hypothalamus coordinates the activity of the endocrine system, and, as we will see, the endocrine system's hormones play a key role in how we respond to stress.

The Role of the Endocrine System: The SAM and HPA Axes

As we saw in Chapter 3, the endocrine system is the body's relatively slow-acting communication system consisting of a network of glands that secrete hormones directly into the bloodstream. This communication system is involved in our stress responses in two key ways. First, under stress, the hypothalamus orders the pituitary gland to secrete *adrenocorticotropic hormone* (ACTH), which is taken up by receptors in the *adrenal glands,* a pair of small endocrine glands lying just above the kidneys. Each of these remarkable structures consists of two nearly independent glands: a central region called the *adrenal medulla* and an outer covering called the *adrenal cortex.* Like soldiers following orders from a general to launch a defensive counterattack, when so ordered by the hypothalamus via the pituitary gland, the adrenal medulla secretes *epinephrine* (also called *adrenaline*) and *norepinephrine* (also called *noradrenaline*) into the blood.

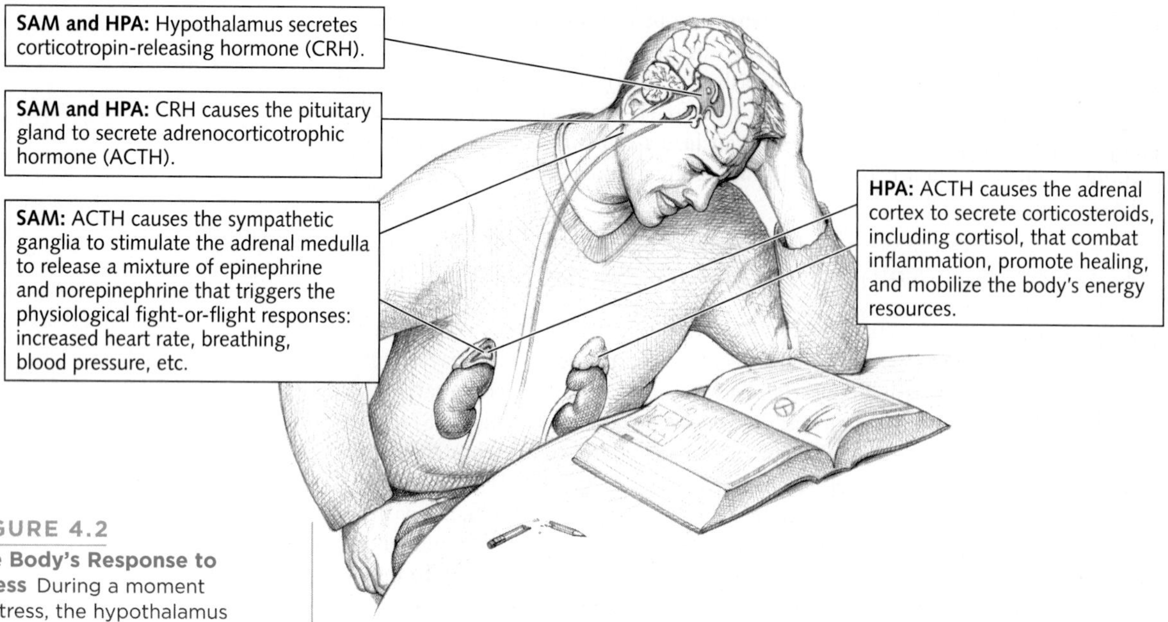

SAM and HPA: Hypothalamus secretes corticotropin-releasing hormone (CRH).

SAM and HPA: CRH causes the pituitary gland to secrete adrenocorticotrophic hormone (ACTH).

SAM: ACTH causes the sympathetic ganglia to stimulate the adrenal medulla to release a mixture of epinephrine and norepinephrine that triggers the physiological fight-or-flight responses: increased heart rate, breathing, blood pressure, etc.

HPA: ACTH causes the adrenal cortex to secrete corticosteroids, including cortisol, that combat inflammation, promote healing, and mobilize the body's energy resources.

FIGURE 4.2

The Body's Response to Stress During a moment of stress, the hypothalamus secretes releasing factors that coordinate the endocrine responses of the pituitary and adrenal glands. As part of the sympatho-adreno-medullary axis (SAM), the adrenal medulla releases the stress hormones epinephrine and norepinephrine as the body's initial, rapid-acting response to stress. Epinephrine and norepinephrine increase heart rate, breathing, and blood pressure; slow digestion; and dilate the pupils. A second, delayed response involves the hypothalamic-pituitary-adrenocortical (HPA) system, which triggers secretion of corticosteroids from the adrenal cortex. These steroid hormones fight inflammation, promote healing, and trigger the release of stored reserves of energy.

sympatho-adreno-medullary (SAM) axis The body's initial, rapid-acting response to stress, involving the release of epinephrine and norepinephrine from the adrenal medulla under the direction of the sympathetic nervous system.

hypothalamic-pituitary-adrenocortical (HPA) axis The body's delayed response to stress, involving the secretion of corticosteroid hormones from the adrenal cortex.

These endocrine reactions, which help trigger the fight-or-flight response, last much longer than those generated directly by the SNS. Taken together, the interaction of the SNS and adrenal medulla is called the **sympatho-adreno-medullary (SAM) axis** (Figure 4.2).

Although *fight-or-flight* characterizes the primary physiological response to stress in both females and males, females may be more likely than males to *tend and befriend*—that is, to seek the company of other people when they are under pressure. Like the fight-or-flight response, tend-and-befriend behaviors depend on underlying physiological mechanisms, in particular the hormone *oxytocin,* which releases rapidly in response to stressful events (Taylor and others, 2006). The tend-and-befriend pattern appears to involve the blunting of SNS responses geared toward aggressing or fleeing. This gender difference was apparent among 634 mothers and fathers who had lost a child within the first months of life (Christiansen, 2015). While the men were more likely to "flee" by sometimes spending hours away from home, the women were more likely to seek social support from other people.

The endocrine system is involved in stress in a second, equally important way. This second way involves the hypothalamus, the pituitary gland, and the adrenal cortex, or what has been called the **hypothalamic-pituitary-adrenocortical (HPA) axis.** While the SAM axis is the body's initial, rapid-acting response to stress, the HPA is a delayed response that functions to restore the body to its baseline state, a process known as **homeostasis.** The HPA axis is activated by messages relayed from the central nervous system to the hypothalamus, which in turn secretes *corticotropin-releasing hormone* (CRH). CRH stimulates the production of ACTH by the pituitary gland, which then activates the adrenal cortex to secrete **corticosteroids,** steroid hormones that reduce inflammation, promote healing, and help mobilize the body's energy resources.

Stressors are normally short-lasting events. Just as the hypothalamus initiates the stress response, it also shuts it down—normally before the body is damaged. The mechanism involves cortisol, a corticosteroid hormone that has a potent effect on all the body's tissues, including raising glucose levels in the blood, stimulating the breakdown of proteins into amino acids, and inhibiting the uptake of glucose by the body tissues but not by the brain (Kemeny, 2003). In a finely tuned *feedback* mechanism, cortisol acts on the hippocampus, which has a high density of cortisol receptors and neurons that project to the hypothalamus, signaling the pituitary to suppress the further release of CRH and ACTH. As the amount of ACTH in the blood decreases, the adrenal cortex shuts down its production of cortisol.

The rate of cortisol secretion, which is remarkably sensitive to psychological factors and peaks about 30 minutes after a stressor occurs, is so closely linked to stress that health psychologists frequently use the level of this hormone circulating in the blood or saliva as a physiological index of stress. For some people, even a seemingly ordinary event such as boarding an airplane can trigger a large increase in cortisol, which means, of course, that CRH has already been released from the hypothalamus and ACTH from the pituitary (Thompson, 2000).

All of these endocrine system actions help the organism deal with stress. When an organism is faced with a threat, its brain needs energy in the form of glucose, which cortisol helps provide. But too much cortisol can have negative consequences, leading to hypertension, a decrease in the body's ability to fight infection, and perhaps psychological problems as well. When Robert Sapolsky studied wild-born vervet monkeys that farmers had trapped and caged in groups to protect their crops, he found that a number of the monkeys became sick and died, especially those that were caged with other monkeys that were especially aggressive. Autopsies of the monkeys showed high rates of bleeding ulcers, enlarged adrenal glands, and something else: pronounced damage to the hippocampal regions of their brains, perhaps as the result of prolonged high cortisol levels triggered by the prolonged stress (Sapolsky, 2004a). Normally regulated by the hippocampus, cortisol levels can spiral upward when, in response to unrelenting stress, more and more cortisol is secreted and the hippocampus is damaged, leaving it unable to signal the hypothalamus to shut off the stress response (Morgan and others, 2001). This condition of *hypercortisolism*, as well as a more prolonged activation of the HPA system, has been linked to the rate of cognitive decline in individuals with Alzheimer's disease (Suhr, Demireva, & Heffner, 2008). It's associated with a disruption in the brain's production of new neurons (Mirescu & Gould, 2006), observed in patients suffering from anorexia nervosa (Haas and others, 2009), and described as evidence of premature aging (Sapolsky, 1990). In a less well understood phenomenon, the HPA axis may become underactive in some individuals in the face of chronic stress, creating a state of adrenal exhaustion and chronically low levels of cortisol (*hypocortisolism*) (Heim, Ehlert, & Hellhammer, 2000). Immune diseases such as fibromyalgia, rheumatoid arthritis, and asthma have all been associated with this state of blunted cortisol production.

Measuring Stress

Health psychologists have used a variety of approaches to measure stress, most of which fall into two categories: self-report inventories and physiological measures. Self-reports such as life events inventories and daily hassle scales are the most common, but as we have seen, they have many limitations in their reliability and validity.

A major disadvantage of self-reports is that information that is recalled long after significant events have occurred is often inaccurate. To overcome this limitation, health psychologists increasingly rely on self-reports made closer in time to the events they are investigating. This approach, called **ecological momentary assessment (EMA)**, involves repeated sampling of people's behaviors and experiences in real time and in their natural environments (Shiffman, Stone, & Hufford, 2008). EMA can take several forms (Wenze and Miller, 2010). One is the collection of information at specified time intervals, such as via daily journal entries. This approach asks research participants to look back, at the end of the day, and report about mood, stressors, social interactions, and other variables. To

homeostasis The tendency to maintain a balanced or constant internal state; the regulation of any aspect of body chemistry, such as the level of glucose in the blood, around a particular set point.

corticosteroids Hormones produced by the adrenal cortex that fight inflammation, promote healing, and trigger the release of stored energy.

ecological momentary assessment (EMA) A method of measuring stress that involves repeated sampling of people's behaviors and experiences in real time and in their natural environments.

reduce the reliance on memory even further, EMA may require the reporting of information several times a day. One example of this type of measurement is *signal-contingent recording* (also called an ambulatory diary record), in which reports are requested in response to a signal from a personal digital assistant, smart phone, or other reminder device that occurs a fixed number of times per day on a random schedule (Smith and others, 2012).

Physiological Measures

Given the limitations of self-report measures, many researchers have relied on physiological and biochemical measures of stress instead. Physiological measures include changes in heart rate, blood pressure, respiration rate, and the electrical conductance of the skin (a measure of sweating). Changes in these measures occur in response to stress- or emotion-induced activation of the sympathetic division of the autonomic nervous system. With advances in technology, many of these measures can be made outside the laboratory with ambulatory monitoring equipment that allows research participants to go about their daily activities. For example, *ambulatory blood pressure* (ABP) is recorded via a cuff worn under the participants' clothing and a small control box (approximately $5.0 \times 3.5 \times 1.5$ inches) attached to their belts (Smith and others, 2012).

More commonly, health psychologists measure stress via its association with hormones such as cortisol, epinephrine, and norepinephrine (Eller, Netterstrom, & Hansen, 2006). Epinephrine and norepinephrine levels are typically measured in either blood or urine samples, and cortisol is measured via a sample of saliva. These measures have several advantages, including being highly reliable and easily quantified. They are not, however, problem-free. Blood levels of hormones decrease quickly (within minutes) after a stressful experience, so researchers must be very quick to obtain accurate measurement. Hormone levels generally persist longer in urine but also are influenced by factors unrelated to stress.

How Does Stress Make You Sick?

Biomedical researchers who study mind–body connections in disease were once ostracized from the scientific community. Harvard University's Herbert Benson notes that when he began doing his research decades earlier, he was told he was jeopardizing his medical career (Sternberg, 2001). Things began to change when two remarkable discoveries were made that would forever change the face of medicine. The first was an accident. Working in a laboratory at the University of Rochester, psychologist Robert Ader had been conducting a classic Pavlovian learning experiment, attempting to condition laboratory rats to avoid saccharin-flavored drinking water. The design of the study was simple. After the rats were given a drink of the artificially sweetened water (a neutral stimulus), they received an injection of a drug (unconditioned stimulus), which made them nauseous (unconditioned response)—sick enough so that a single pairing of the two stimuli should have been sufficient to establish a *conditioned aversion* to the sweetened water.

But Ader discovered a problem. Over the course of several weeks of training and testing, a number of the rats became very sick and died. Puzzled by this development, Ader found that the number of virus- and infection-fighting T lymphocytes was reduced significantly in the bodies of the experimental animals. The nausea-inducing drug apparently had a more serious impact on the rats—it suppressed their immune responses (Figure 4.3).

What was most remarkable in Ader's experiment was that when these same rats were given saccharin-flavored water alone, without the drug, their immune systems responded as if the drug were actually circulating in their bloodstream. Classical conditioning had

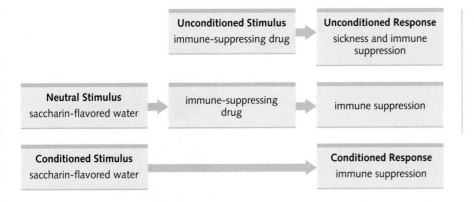

FIGURE 4.3
Conditioning the Immune Response After Robert Ader and Nicholas Cohen paired saccharin-flavored water with an immune-suppressing drug, the taste of the sweetened water alone elicited a conditioned response (immune suppression) in laboratory rats.

created a learned association between the taste of the water as a conditioned stimulus and the suppression of T cells as a conditioned response. Over time, conditioned responding made the animals increasingly susceptible to disease as their immune reserves were weakened with each drink of sweetened water.

Before Ader's study, most biomedical researchers believed that the mind and body were, for the most part, independent systems that had no influence on one another. So entrenched was this belief that Ader himself had difficulty accepting the results of his own research. Good science demands replication of findings, so Ader teamed up with immunologist Nicholas Cohen to see if his initial findings were a fluke. They were not. In a subsequent series of experiments, Ader and Cohen (1985) demonstrated that the immune system could be conditioned, just as Ivan Pavlov had demonstrated that the salivary response could be conditioned in hungry dogs.

The second key discovery that changed medicine was neuroscientist Candace Pert's demonstration that the brain has receptors for immune molecules that enable the brain to monitor, and therefore influence, the activity of the immune system (Pert, 2003). As an example of this communication network (illustrated in Figure 3.13 in Chapter 3), consider that when antigens induce an immune response, cells in the hypothalamus become more active. This may occur when T cells that have been activated by antigens release proinflammatory cytokines.

Recall from Chapter 3 that cytokines are protein molecules produced by immune cells that have a multitude of biological effects, including serving as a means of inter-cellular communication. These chemicals, which attract macrophages and stimulate phagocytosis at wound and infection sites, are similar in structure to neurotransmitters (the chemical messengers in the process of neural communication). Cytokines look enough like neurotransmitters to bind to receptor sites on brain cells and trigger nerve impulses. The apparent interchangeability between neurotransmitters and cytokines suggests that the immune system's lymphocytes may, in effect, act as circulating "language translators," converting information from their direct contact with pathogens into the language of the central nervous system so that the brain can monitor and regulate the immune response.

The work of Ader, Cohen, and Pert gave credibility to George Solomon's landmark article, published a decade earlier, in which he coined the term **psychoneuroimmunology (PNI),** referring to a "speculative theoretical integration" of the links among emotions, immunity, and disease (Solomon & Moos, 1964). This word describes a great deal about its focus: *psycho* for psychological processes, *neuro* for the neuroendocrine system (the nervous and hormonal systems), and *immunology* for the immune system. Focusing on three areas of functioning that at one time were believed to be relatively independent, PNI researchers investigate interactions between the nervous and immune systems, and the relationship

psychoneuroimmunology (PNI) The field of research that emphasizes the interaction of psychological, neural, and immunological processes in stress and illness.

FIGURE 4.4
Research Themes in Psychoneuroimmunology The goal of psychoneuroimmunology research is to reveal the many ways that behaviors and health are interrelated, with a focus on the immunological mechanisms that underlie these interactions.

Information from Irwin, M. R. (2008). Human psychoneuroimmunology: 20 years of discovery. *Brain, Behavior, and Immunity, 22*, 129–139.

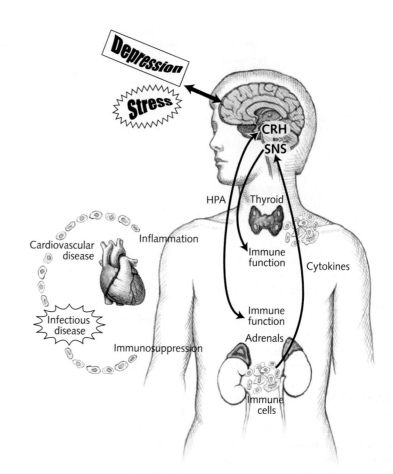

between behavior and health (Figure 4.4). An important goal of PNI is to conduct basic research that can be applied to health care (Psychoneuroimmunology Research Society, 2010).

Since these watershed studies, the evidence for coordinated interactions among the brain, the neuroendocrine system, and the immune system has mounted quickly. There are hundreds of published studies examining the relationship between stress and immune functioning in humans (Segerstrom & Miller, 2004). Taken together, these studies demonstrate that short-term stressors, such as loud noises and electric shocks in the laboratory (or, in the real world, being called on by a professor in class), can have a positive effect by triggering an increase, or *up-regulation,* of natural immunity. Longer-lasting, chronic stressors, however, can have damaging effects by suppressing immunity.

Reduced immune functioning (*immunosuppression*) has been demonstrated following a divorce, bereavement, unemployment, and stressful bouts of exercise or military training; during exam periods; and when one is experiencing occupational stress. Among the changes observed are reduced numbers of natural killer cells, T cells, and total lymphocytes. And there seems to be a "dose–response" relationship between stress and immunosuppression. College students with the highest levels of overall life stress or the tendency to overreact to stressful events, for instance, show the greatest deficit in their immune response during exam weeks (Segerstrom & Miller, 2004).

Stress is also linked to lowered immune resistance to viral infections. In one study, 47 percent of participants living stress-filled lives developed colds after being inoculated with a rhinovirus, compared to only 27 percent of those inoculated who reported relatively stress-free lives (Cohen, Alper, Doyle, Treanor, & Turner, 2006). Other studies demonstrate that both children and adults, when subjected to chronic stress, suffer more bouts of flu, herpes virus infections (cold sores and genital lesions), chickenpox, mononucleosis, and Epstein-Barr virus (Cohen & Herbert, 1996; Cohen, Doyle, Turner, Alper, & Skoner, 2003). Psychological stress has been linked with autoimmune disorders such as rheumatoid arthritis (Rabin, 1999; Straub & Kalden, 2009), as well as coronary artery disease with accelerated progress. This connection occurs as the immune system reacts to stressful events by releasing cytokines that promote inflammation (Rozanski, Blumenthal, & Kaplan, 1999; Steptoe, Hamer, & Chida, 2007).

In addition, stress delays the healing of wounds (Walburn, Vedhara, Hankins, Rixon, & Weinman, 2009). In one study, married couples who received standardized punch biopsy wounds just prior to a 30-minute argument took a day or two longer to heal than did un-stressed couples (Kiecolt-Glaser and others, 2005). In another study, 47 adults were given a standard questionnaire assessing psychological stress before undergoing hernia surgery. Patients who reported higher levels of preoperative stress had significantly slower rates of healing and reported a slower, more painful recovery (Broadbent, Petrie, Alley, & Booth, 2003).

Pathways from Stress to Disease

How stress influences the immune system is the subject of a great deal of ongoing research. Two hypotheses have been suggested. According to the *direct effect hypothesis,* stress directly influences the nervous, endocrine, and immune systems, each of which can lead to disease. Alternatively, the *indirect effect hypothesis* suggests that immunosuppression is an aftereffect of the stress response (Segerstrom & Miller, 2004).

The Direct Effect Hypothesis

Stress may directly affect immune efficiency through the activation of the HPA and SAM axes. T cells and B cells have receptors for corticosteroid "stress" hormones (which produce immunosuppression), and lymphocytes have catecholamine (epinephrine and norepinephrine) receptors. Stress activates these systems; the hormones released attach to the receptors of T cells, B cells, and lymphocytes, suppressing the immune response.

A growing body of research supports the direct effect hypothesis. In a recent study, Timothy Smith and his colleagues at the University of Utah (Smith, Birmingham, & Uchino, 2012) explored the direct cardiovascular effects of social stress in daily experience in 94 married, working couples (mean age 29.2 years). The participants completed a daily protocol from 8 A.M. to 10 P.M. that included the working hours and an evening at home with their spouse on the same day. During the 14-hour period of the protocol, each participant wore an ambulatory blood pressure (ABP) monitor that took a reading at random, averaging once every 30 minutes. After each ABP assessment, participants completed an *ambulatory diary record* (ADR) on a smart phone consisting of a battery of questions. The ADR questions were divided into two sections. The first assessed the participants' posture (sitting, standing, lying down); recent consumption of nicotine, caffeine, alcohol, or a meal (no, yes); temperature (too cold, comfortable, too hot); and other factors that might influence their ABP. The second section included items related to negative affect ("sad," "frustrated," "upset"); social-evaluative threat ("Worried about what others think about me" and "Concerned about the impression I am making"); appearance concerns ("Pleased about my appearance right now," "Feel satisfied with the way my body looks right now"); and ability perceptions ("Confident about my abilities" and "Feel as smart as others").

In both women and men, momentary reports of social-evaluative threat were associated with higher systolic blood pressure (SBP). This effect was mediated by negative affect. In other words, SBP increased when participants were worried about how their appearance or abilities were being perceived, but only if they also were frustrated or upset. Social-evaluative threat was also associated with higher diastolic blood pressure, but only in women, suggesting that gender may play a role in the extent to which evaluative threat has specific physiological effects that might have an adverse effect on health. Other studies have shown that ABP is linked to the development of future cardiovascular problems (Chida & Steptoe, 2010).

As another example of the direct effects of stress, consider the mounting evidence that family conflict early in life is associated with a variety of later health problems (Miller, Chen, & Parker, 2011). In a recent study, Richard Slatcher and Theodore Robles (2012) investigated the associations between conflict in family environments and daily cortisol levels in preschool children. Each child participant wore an ambulatory assessment device called the Child EAR for one full weekend day. The EAR records ambient sounds while participants go about their daily lives, allowing the researchers to note examples of interpersonal conflict (e.g., Child: "No! I don't want to!" Parent: "You are going to shut your mouth and be quiet!"). Parents also collected saliva samples from their children at six specified times each day.

The results showed that greater conflict at home was associated with children having a lower *cortisol awakening response* and flatter cortisol responses throughout the day, both of which have been linked to negative health consequences in adulthood, including earlier mortality (Kumari, Shipley, Stafford, & Kivimaki, 2011). Flatter cortisol levels are also a marker of the cumulative long-term effects of the body's physiological response to stress (McEwen, 2007).

Stress and Blood Clotting In addition to increasing blood pressure, SAM and HPA activation can also influence blood clotting. When you cut yourself, proteins and platelets in your blood stick together (*coagulate*) to stop the bleeding and start the healing process. However, blood shouldn't clot when it's just circulating through the body. When blood clots too much, it is referred to as being in a *hypercoagulable state* (blood clotting disorder). In this state, people have an increased risk for blood clots developing in their arteries and veins, which, in turn, can increase the risk of heart disease and stroke.

Overcommitment, overload, and other forms of job stress have been linked to hypercoagulable states (Austin, Wissman, & von Känel, 2013). Blood clotting disorders have also been reported among caregivers (von Känel and others, 2006) and teachers (von Känel, Bellingrath, & Kudielka, 2009) who feel high levels of stress. Researchers at the University of Bonn (2008) found increased coagulation among 31 patients with anxiety disorders, which may explain why such patients are 3 to 4 times more likely to die from heart disease.

The Indirect Effect Hypothesis

According to the indirect effect hypothesis, stress-induced delays in healing and other adverse health outcomes may occur because stress alters immune processes *indirectly* by encouraging maladaptive behaviors. Among the behavioral risk factors that could delay wound healing through their effects on the immune system are smoking, alcohol and drug abuse, fragmented sleep, not enough exercise, and poor nutrition, each of which has been associated with increased stress (Krueger & Chang, 2008; Steptoe, Wardle, Pollard, & Canaan, 1996). Smoking, for instance, slows healing by weakening the normal proliferation of macrophages at wound sites and by reducing the flow of blood through vasoconstriction (McMaster and others, 2008; Silverstein, 1992). In addition to healing more slowly, smokers are more likely to develop infections following surgical procedures, perhaps because nicotine and other toxins in cigarette smoke suppress both primary and secondary immune responses by reducing the activities of white blood cells.

As another example of how stress indirectly alters immune processes, consider that deep sleep is associated with the secretion of growth hormone (GH), which facilitates wound healing by activating macrophages to kill bacteria at the wound site (see Chapter 3). Loss of sleep, or fragmented sleep, results in reduced GH secretion and delayed healing (Leproult, Copinschi, Buxton, & Van Cauter, 1997; Sander, 2009).

Duration of Stress

Acute stressors that last half an hour or less (for example, in laboratory studies of stress) produce transient immune changes, with most immune cell parameters returning to prestress levels within an hour or so. Longer-lasting but nevertheless acute stressors, such as stress associated with upcoming exams, also produce temporary changes in cellular immune response. For example, a 10-year series of studies of medical students' responses to examinations demonstrated that stressed students' bodies mounted weaker antibody responses to hepatitis B vaccinations than did students who received the vaccination during vacation periods (Glaser and others, 1992). Other studies have confirmed this effect of academic stress; even 5-year-old kindergarteners show elevated cortisol levels on the first day of school (Boyce, Alkon, Tschann, Cesney, & Alpert, 1995; Cohen, Marshall, Cheng, Agarwal, & Wei, 2000). The fact that a stressor as predictable, benign, and transient as an upcoming exam reliably produces immunosuppression suggests that other, everyday stressors probably do so as well.

The ability to recover after a stressful experience strongly influences the total burden that the experience has on an individual. The neuroendocrine system plays an important role in the concept of **allostatic load** (or **allostasis**), which refers to the cumulative long-term effects of the body's physiological response to stress (McEwen, 1998, 2011). Stressors that are unpredictable, uncontrollable, of longer duration, and difficult to cope with cause a buildup of allostatic load, which manifests in many ways, including decreased immunity, elevated epinephrine levels, increased abdominal fat, decreased hippocampal size and functioning (leading to problems with thinking and memory), and the overproduction of interleukin-6 and other proinflammatory cytokines. Interestingly, many of these changes also occur with aging, leading some researchers to characterize a high allostatic load as a form of accelerated aging in response to stress. Unchecked, allostatic overload is associated with increased risk of illness and even death (Karlamangla, Singer, & Seeman, 2006). These adverse responses have been observed, for example, among those with lower socioeconomic status (Dowd, Simanek, & Aiello, 2009), prisoners of war (Dekaris and others, 1993), immigrant workers (Kaestner, Pearson, Keene, & Geronimus, 2009), unemployed adults (Arnetz and others, 1991), and earthquake and hurricane survivors (Solomon, Segerstrom, Grohr, Kemeny, & Fahey, 1997).

allostatic load (allostasis) The cumulative long-term effects of the body's physiological response to stress.

Stress, Inflammation, and Disease

Investigations of the direct and indirect effect hypotheses have given rise to an immunosuppression model of the relationships among stress, immunity, and disease, which nicely summarizes what we've discussed thus far. According to this model, stress suppresses the immune system, which leaves the individual vulnerable to opportunistic infection and disease (Miller, Cohen, & Ritchey, 2002) (Figure 4.5).

The immunosuppression model offers a plausible explanation for how stress influences wound healing, infectious diseases, and some forms of cancer (see Chapter 11). But it does not explain how stress might influence diseases whose central feature is excessive inflammation. These include many allergic, autoimmune, rheumatologic, neurologic, and cardiovascular diseases—all of which are exacerbated by stress (Rozanski and others, 1999). Parkinson's disease, for instance—a neurodegenerative disease that affects more than 1 million Americans—involves a loss of brain neurons that produce dopamine and serotonin (Parkinson's Disease Foundation, 2010). Victims of Parkinson's suffer muscular tremors, rigidity of movement, and a slow, 10- to 20-year deterioration in overall health. Inflammation accelerates the development of Parkinson's, which is why ibuprofen and other nonprescription anti-inflammatory drugs may lower the risk of developing the disease.

To account for the impact of stress on inflammatory diseases, researchers have proposed a **glucocorticoid receptor (GCR) resistance model,** the basic premise of which is that chronic stress interferes with the body's ability to regulate the inflammatory response.

glucocorticoid receptor (GCR) resistance model The idea that chronic stress promotes the development and progression of disease by reducing the sensitivity of immune system receptors to glucocorticoid hormones such as cortisol, thereby interfering with the body's ability to regulate the inflammatory response.

Stress reduces immunity by:

(a) Activating autonomic nervous system fibers that descend from the brain to immune tissue.

(b) Triggering the secretion of hormones that bind to white blood cells and alter their functioning.

(c) Inducing immunosuppressive coping behaviors, such as poor diet and substance abuse.

FIGURE 4.5

Summary of the Physiology of Stress: Immunosuppression Model These conditions compromise the immune system's capacity to mount an effective response to infection or injury.

Runaway inflammation, in turn, can promote the development and progression of many diseases (Cohen and others, 2012). Specifically, chronic stress disrupts the sensitivity of immune system receptors to glucocorticoid hormones such as cortisol, which normally terminate the inflammatory response. In a test of the model, Gregory Miller and his colleagues measured the perceived stress and immune responsiveness of 25 healthy parents of children undergoing active treatment for cancer, in comparison to 25 healthy parents of medically healthy children. Parents of cancer patients reported higher levels of psychological stress than parents of healthy children *and* were found to have diminished sensitivity to a synthetic glucocorticoid hormone, as revealed by higher levels of cytokine production. Remember that glucocorticoid hormones function as *anti-inflammatory* signals by suppressing the production of *proinflammatory cytokines* by immune cells. Parents of cancer patients showed significantly *less suppression* of cytokine production in response to an administered glucocorticoid compared with parents of healthy children (Miller and others, 2002). These findings are significant because overproduction of cytokines has been linked with a spectrum of chronic inflammatory diseases and adverse conditions, including cardiovascular disease (discussed in Chapter 10), osteoporosis, arthritis, Type 2 diabetes, Alzheimer's disease, periodontal disease, and age-related frailty (Kiecolt-Glaser and others, 2003).

More recently, Sheldon Cohen and his colleagues administered a comprehensive stress interview to 276 healthy adults who were then exposed to the rhinovirus that causes the common cold. The participants were held in quarantine for five days and monitored for signs of infection and illness. The results demonstrated that those who had recently experienced a prolonged stressful event were more likely to have immune cells that were unable to respond to hormonal signals that normally regulate inflammation. They were also more likely to develop colds when exposed to the virus. "When under stress, cells of the immune system are unable to respond to hormonal control, and consequently, produce levels of inflammation that promote disease," Cohen said. "Because inflammation plays a role in many diseases such as cardiovascular, asthma and autoimmune disorders, this model suggests why stress impacts them as well" (Cohen and others, 2012).

To sum up, a growing body of psychoneuroimmunological research evidence demonstrates that the immune system does not work in isolation. Rather, it functions as part of a coordinated system involving the brain and the hormone-secreting endocrine system. The brain regulates the production of stress hormones, which in turn influence the body's immune defenses both directly and indirectly.

Other Models of Stress and Illness

The immune suppression and glucocorticoid resistance models of stress and illness developed from many years of research and from other important models, including Selye's general adaptation syndrome, the transactional model, and the diathesis–stress model. We will consider Selye's work first.

Selye's General Adaptation Syndrome

Surely the most significant contribution to our understanding of stress and illness came from the research of Hans Selye, whom you met in the chapter-opening story. Selye devised the concept of stress as a "nonspecific response of the body to any demand" (1974, p. 27). The body's reaction to stress was so predictable that Selye called it the **general adaptation syndrome (GAS).**

As Figure 4.6 shows, GAS consists of three stages. Stage 1, the *alarm reaction,* is essentially the same as Cannon's *fight-or-flight* response, which we considered earlier. The strength of the alarm reaction depends on the degree to which the event is perceived as a threat.

When a stressful situation persists, the body's reaction progresses to Stage 2, the *resistance stage.* In this stage, physiological arousal remains high (but not as high as during the alarm reaction), as the body tries to adapt to the emergency by replenishing adrenal hormones. At this time, there is a decrease in the individual's ability to cope with everyday events and hassles. It is at this stage when people often become irritable, impatient, and increasingly vulnerable to health problems.

If the stressful situation persists and resistance is no longer possible, the body enters the final stage of the GAS—the *stage of exhaustion.* At this point, the body's energy

general adaptation syndrome (GAS) Selye's term for the body's reaction to stress, which consists of three stages: alarm, resistance, and exhaustion.

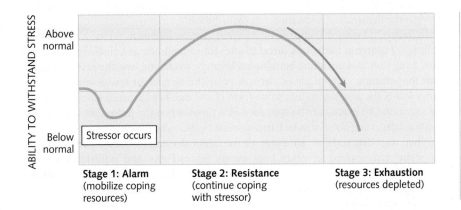

FIGURE 4.6
The General Adaptation Syndrome Under stress, the body enters an alarm phase during which resistance to stress is suppressed temporarily. From this, it rebounds to a phase of increased resistance to stress. The body's resistance can last only so long. In the face of prolonged stress, the stage of exhaustion may be reached. During this final stage, people become more vulnerable to a variety of health problems.

Hans Selye's pioneering animal research more than 80 years ago shed light on how stress can affect the body.

reserves are depleted. Hypocortisolism (depletion of cortisol), for instance, is consistent with this final stage of the syndrome. If stress persists, disease and physical deterioration or even death may occur. For example, one result of exhaustion is increased susceptibility to what Selye referred to as *diseases of adaptation.* Among these are allergic reactions, hypertension, and common colds, as well as more serious illnesses caused by immune deficiencies.

Numerous studies have reinforced Selyes basic point: Prolonged stress exacts a toll on the body. People who have endured the prolonged stress of combat, child abuse, or a chronic disease may suffer enlarged adrenal glands, bleeding ulcers, damage to the brain's hippocampus, and abnormalities in several other cerebral areas. More generally, stress disrupts *neurogenesis,* the brain's production of new neurons (Mirescu & Gould, 2006) and the process by which cells divide. In one study, women who reported high levels of stress as caregivers for children with serious chronic illnesses also displayed a remarkable symptom of premature aging—shorter DNA segments, called *telomeres,* at the ends of chromosomes. Caregivers who reported the highest levels of stress had cells that appeared 10 years older than their true age (Epel and others, 2004). In another study, participants who reported a higher number of ambivalent relationships in their social networks also had shorter telomeres, even after control variables such as age, medication use, and health behaviors were ruled out (Uchino and others, 2012). Telomere shortening, which causes cells to die because they can no longer reproduce, is associated with a wide range of age-related diseases (Starr and others, 2008).

Cognitive Appraisal and Stress

Selye's model has been criticized for largely ignoring how psychological factors contribute to stress. There now is clear evidence that *how* potential stressors are appraised, or perceived, strongly influences their impact on the individual. The most influential model describing the importance of conscious appraisal in stress is the **transactional model,** proposed by Richard Lazarus and Susan Folkman (1984). The fundamental idea behind this model is that we cannot fully understand stress by examining environmental events (stimuli) and people's behaviors (responses) as separate entities; rather, we need to consider them together as a transaction, in which each person must continually adjust to daily challenges.

transactional model Lazarus's theory that the experience of stress depends as much on the individual's cognitive appraisal of a potential stressor's impact as it does on the event or situation itself.

According to the transactional model, the *process* of stress is triggered whenever stressors exceed the personal and social resources that a person is able to mobilize in order to cope. If a person's coping resources are strong enough, there may be no stress, even when—to another person—the situation seems unbearable. On the other hand, if a person's coping resources are weak or ineffective, stress occurs, even when—to another person—the demands of a situation can easily be met.

primary appraisal A person's initial determination of an event's meaning, whether irrelevant, benign-positive, or threatening.

As shown in Figure 4.7, appraising an event as stressful means seeing it as a potential challenge, a source of harm, or a threat to one's future well-being. A *challenge* is perceived when a situation is demanding but ultimately can be overcome, and the person can profit from the situation. Appraisals of harm–loss or threat refer to less positive outcomes. *Harm-loss* is the assessment that some form of damage has occurred already as a result of a situation. An event may be appraised as a *threat* when the person anticipates that a situation may bring about loss or harm at some point *in the future.*

secondary appraisal A person's determination of whether his or her own resources and abilities are sufficient to meet the demands of an event that is appraised as potentially threatening or challenging.

cognitive reappraisal The process by which potentially stressful events are constantly reevaluated.

When the demands of an event or situation do create stress, our response is not static but instead involves continuous interactions and adjustments—called *transactions*—between the environment and our attempts to cope. Each of us is an active agent who can dramatically alter the impact of a potential stressor through our own personal resources.

Lazarus believes that the transactions between people and their environments are driven by our *cognitive appraisal* of potential stressors. Cognitive appraisal involves assessing (1) whether a situation or event threatens our well-being, (2) whether there are sufficient personal resources available for coping with the demand, and (3) whether our strategy for dealing with the situation or event is working.

When we confront a potentially stressful event, such as an unexpected pop quiz, we engage in a **primary appraisal** to determine the event's meaning. In effect, we ask, "Is this situation going to mean trouble for me?" In the primary appraisal, we interpret an event in one of three ways: *irrelevant; benign-positive; threatening* (challenging or harmful) (Figure 4.7). If the event is appraised as irrelevant or benign-positive, no physiological arousal—and no stress—occurs.

Once an event has been appraised as a challenge or threat, **secondary appraisal** addresses the question, "What can I do to cope with this situation?" At this point, we assess our coping abilities to determine whether they will be adequate to meet the challenge or avoid the potential harm, loss, or threat. If these resources are deemed adequate, little or no stress occurs. When a threat or challenge is high and coping resources are low, stress is likely to occur.

Finally, the transactional model emphasizes the ongoing nature of the appraisal process as new information becomes available. Through **cognitive reappraisal,** we constantly update our perception of success or failure in meeting a challenge or threat. New information may allow us to turn a previously stressful appraisal into a benign-positive one, as when we gain confidence in our ability to do well on an unexpected pop quiz after successfully answering the first few questions.

Cognitive reappraisal does not always result in less stress, however; sometimes it increases stress. An event originally appraised as benign or irrelevant can quickly take on a threatening character if a coping response fails or if we begin to see the event differently. For example, a job interview that seems to be going very well may become very stressful when the interviewer casually mentions the large number of well-qualified individuals who have applied for the position.

Lazarus's transactional model has three important implications. First, situations or events are not inherently stressful or unstressful; any given situation or event may be appraised (and experienced) as stressful by one person but not by another. Second, cognitive appraisals are extremely susceptible to changes in mood, health, and motivational state. You may interpret the same event or situation in very different ways on separate occasions. Being forced to wait in traffic may be a minor annoyance on most days; on the day when you are late for an exam, it may seem an insurmountable obstacle. Third, some evidence suggests that the body's stress response is nearly the same whether a situation is actually experienced or merely imagined. This means that even recalled or imagined appraisals of a situation may elicit a stress response.

How might this work? Recall that the HPA axis and homeostasis are central players in the stress response. When the hypothalamus receives signals from its various inputs (including the cerebral cortex) about conditions that deviate from an ideal homeostatic state (such as reliving an emotionally charged event), corticotrophin-releasing hormone is secreted, which in turn causes the pituitary gland to release ACTH. Then ACTH can stimulate the adrenal cortex to release cortisol, and in this way, the stress-response cascade is triggered by an alarming event, whether real or imagined.

FIGURE 4.7

The Transactional Model of Stress The impact of a potential stressor, such as the startling sound of a honking horn, depends on a three-step process of cognitive appraisal. During primary appraisal, events perceived as neutral or benign pose no threat as a source of stress. Events perceived as challenging, harmful, or threatening are subjected to a secondary appraisal, during which the individual determines whether his or her coping resources are sufficient to meet the challenge posed by the stressor. Finally, in the reappraisal process, feedback from new information or ongoing coping efforts is used to check on the accuracy of both primary and secondary appraisals.

The Diathesis–Stress Model

diathesis–stress model The model that proposes that two interacting factors determine an individual's susceptibility to stress and illness: predisposing factors in the person (such as genetic vulnerability) and precipitating factors from the environment (such as traumatic experiences).

Knowing that the stress response varies with how a particular stressor is perceived has led researchers to propose several other models that highlight the interaction of biological and psychosocial factors in health and illness. The **diathesis–stress model** proposes that two continuously interacting factors jointly determine an individual's susceptibility to stress and illness: *predisposing factors* that establish a person's vulnerability and *precipitating factors* from the environment (Steptoe & Ayers, 2004). The predisposition can result from genetic factors or from prior environmental factors, such as chronic exposure to secondhand tobacco smoke. In most cases, the precipitating environmental factors (stress) are not believed to be specific for a given health condition, whereas predisposing genetic factors (diathesis) are.

reactivity Our physiological reaction to stress, which varies by individual and affects our vulnerability to illness.

For instance, some individuals are more vulnerable to illness because their biological systems show greater **reactivity**—they react more strongly to specific environmental triggers. As one example, Jennifer McGrath (2003) found stable individual differences (diathesis) in children's blood pressure and heart rate during a stressful mirror-image tracing test. Interestingly, children who displayed the strongest cardiovascular reactivity were more likely to have a family history of hypertension and cardiovascular disease than less reactive children. Another example involves adolescent girls who inherit a specific variation of a gene related to depression called the 5-HTTLPR serotonin transporter gene (diathesis). Findings indicate that these girls are more vulnerable to depression when they experience bullying (stress) (Benet, Thompson, & Gotlib, 2010). Other studies have shown that cardiac reactivity to stress is linked to the risk of heart attack and stroke. For example, researchers studied the responses of 901 Finnish men on a simple test of memory that was designed to elicit a mild state of mental stress. The men under age 55 who displayed the strongest blood pressure reaction during the test also had the most severe blockages in their carotid arteries. The researchers speculate that, like cholesterol, over time, blood pressure reactions to stress may injure coronary vessels and promote coronary disease (Kamarck & Lichtenstein, 1998).

Post-Traumatic Stress Disorder (PTSD)

post-traumatic stress disorder (PTSD) A psychological disorder triggered by exposure to an extreme traumatic stressor, such as combat or a natural disaster. Symptoms of PTSD include haunting memories and nightmares of the traumatic event, extreme mental distress, and unwanted flashbacks.

The diathesis–stress model highlights the fact that different people have different vulnerabilities, resulting in many possible health consequences due to stress combined with diathesis. An extreme case in point is **post-traumatic stress disorder** (**PTSD**), which historically was diagnosed when a person experienced an overwhelming event so fearful as to be considered *outside the range of normal human experience.* More recently, PTSD has been expanded to include "exposure to an extreme traumatic stressor involving direct personal experience of an event that involves actual or threatened death or serious injury" (American Psychiatric Association, 2000).

Although the traumatic event most often studied is military combat, researchers now also focus on physical attack; diagnosis of a life-threatening illness; or a catastrophic environmental event such as an earthquake, flood, or act of terrorism (Klein & Alexander, 2007). Having a child or adolescent diagnosed with a serious disease such as cancer may put parents at increased risk for PTSD (Dunn and others, 2012). Car accidents are the most frequent cause of trauma in men, and sexual assault is the most frequent source of trauma among women. Children who live in violent neighborhoods or in one of the world's war zones may also show symptoms of PTSD (Garbarino, 1991). In the month following the September 11 terrorist attacks, an estimated 8.5 percent of Manhattan residents experienced symptoms of PTSD (Galea, Nandi, & Vlahov, 2005).

PTSD symptoms include haunting memories and nightmares of the traumatic event, sleep disturbances, excessive guilt, impaired memory, and extreme mental and physical distress. Victims may also suffer flashbacks in which feelings and memories associated with the original event are re-experienced. Other complaints include muscle pains, sensitivity to chemicals and sunlight, and gastrointestinal problems. Those suffering from PTSD also show an increase in inflammatory processes that could promote illness (Shirom, Toker, Berliner, & Shapira, 2008). Their bodies produce increased epinephrine, norepinephrine, testosterone, and thyroxin activity that lasts over an extended period of time, and they respond to audiovisual reminders of their trauma with elevated heart rate, blood pressure, and muscle tension. In terms of glucocorticoid secretions, however, PTSD is often associated with hypocortisolism (unnaturally low levels of cortisol) (Yehuda, 2000).

PTSD has also been associated with poor health behaviors that may play a role in the relationship between PTSD and chronic illnesses such as cardiovascular disease (CVD). Data from the prospective Heart and Soul Study of 1024 adults with CVD found that those with PTSD (9 percent) were more likely to be physically inactive, fail to take medications properly, and to use tobacco (Zen, Whooley, Zhao, & Cohen, 2012).

The concept of vulnerability, or diathesis, is important to keep in mind with PTSD. Several major studies show that, on average, the prevalence of PTSD varies from about 10 percent among soldiers who served in the military but did not see combat in Vietnam, Iraq, or Afghanistan to over 30 percent among those who experienced heavy combat (Dohrenwend and others, 2006; Hoge, Terhakopian, Castro, Messer, & Engel, 2007). Similar prevalence rates have been found among victims of natural disasters, torture, and sexual assault (Stone, 2005).

Biological and familial risk factors have also been implicated in the disorder. For instance, PTSD has been linked to an overly sensitive limbic system, which causes disruptions in the HPA axis, leading to dysregulation of cortisol levels and atrophy of the hippocampus as the traumatic event is "relived" time and time again (Gill, Saligan, Woods, & Page, 2009). In addition, there is a higher prevalence of PTSD among adult children of family members who themselves have PTSD than among children in families without a history of the disorder, even though these adult children, as a group, do not report a greater exposure to traumatic events (Yehuda, 2000). It is difficult to know, of course, to what extent this is due to biological, genetic, or experiential phenomena because of the large degree of shared environment in families.

In summary, the major models of stress and illness just discussed shed light on several key points:

- Prolonged stress has harmful effects in the body (general adaptation syndrome).
- Stress suppresses the immune system, leaving the individual vulnerable to opportunistic infection and disease (*immunosuppression model*).
- Stress interferes with the immune system's sensitivity to the glucocorticoid hormones that normally help control inflammation, which helps explain the role of stress in disorders such as asthma and arthritis (*glucocorticoid resistance model*).
- Women and men respond somewhat differently to stressors, with women displaying more behaviors associated with caring for others and relationship-building (*tend-and-befriend*), and men displaying more behaviors associated with *fight-or-flight*.
- Our cognitive appraisal of challenges determines whether we experience stress. We constantly interact with and adapt to our environment (*transactional model*).
- Both genetic and environmental factors affect our susceptibility to stress and illness (*diathesis–stress model*).

As this chapter concludes, it is worth remembering that although stress is inescapable, it does offer mixed blessings. Some stress arouses and motivates us and, in the process, often brings out our best qualities and stimulates personal growth. A life with no stress whatsoever would be boring and leave us unfulfilled. The price we pay, though, is the toll that stress may take on our physical and psychological health. Too much stress can overtax our coping abilities and leave us vulnerable to stress-related health problems. Fortunately, there are many things we can do to keep stress at a manageable level. It is to this topic that we turn our attention in the next chapter.

Weigh In on Health

Respond to each question below based on what you learned in the chapter. (**Tip:** Use the items in "Summing Up" to take into account related biological, psychological, and social concerns.)

1. Describe a situation or event on your campus that can cause students stress. What are the biological, psychological, and sociocultural influences in that situation that help to create the stress?

2. Provide a hypothetical situation to explain each of the models of stress and illness: GAS, the transactional

model of stress, the diathesis–stress model, and the tend-and-befriend theory. In each situation, what are some biological, psychological, and social or cultural influences?

3. Reconsider the situation or event that you identified in response to the first question. What have you learned in your reading about the psychosocial sources of stress that might help you better understand this situation and advise those who experience stress from it?

Summing Up

Stress: Some Basic Concepts

1. Stress has been defined as both a stimulus and a response. Researchers distinguish among stimulus events that are stressful (stressors), the physical and emotional responses of a person to a stressor, and the overall process by which a person perceives and responds to threatening or challenging events (stress). Stress arises less from events themselves than from how we appraise them.

Stressors

2. Among the sources of stress that have been investigated are significant life events, daily hassles, and job-related stress. Significant life events and daily hassles have been studied in relation to the prevalence of illness. Daily hassles may interact with anxiety and background stressors to influence a person's vulnerability to illness.

3. Work is a potential source of stress for many people. In many parts of the world, the nature of work has been changing, from farming to manufacturing to knowledge work. In addition, people change jobs more often today and more work is being outsourced to temporary employees or being done via telecommuting. Older workers often face age discrimination. Among the factors that make work stressful are work overload, burnout, role conflict or ambiguity, perceived unfairness, inadequate career advancement, lack of control over work, and the challenge of juggling work and family.

4. The threat of negative evaluations from other people is a potential stressor. Social-evaluative threat is not limited to

the workplace and is a central stressor in many models of stress and health.

5. The caregiving role, in which one person provides the bulk of care for a loved one with a chronic illness, also can be stressful and adversely affect physical health.

The Physiology of Stress

6. Modern research on stress began with Walter Cannon's description of the fight-or-flight reaction. During a moment of stress, the hypothalamus secretes releasing factors that coordinate the endocrine response of the pituitary and adrenal glands. The sympatho-adreno-medullary (SAM) axis is the primary or first response to stress. Activation of the SAM axis leads to increased blood flow to the muscles, increased energy, and higher mental alertness.

7. Humans are not the only species in the animal kingdom that suffers stress-related health problems. Baboons, for instance, are highly social and intelligent animals who, like humans, sometimes display elevated resting levels of stress hormones despite the absence of life-threatening stressors.

8. The hypothalamic-pituitary-adrenocortical (HPA) axis is a slower-reacting response to stress that is activated by messages from the central nervous system. HPA activation functions to restore homeostasis to the body. Excessive cortisol production (hypercorticolism) from the adrenal glands, however, may impair immune efficiency.

9. Health psychologists have used a variety of approaches to measure stress, most of which fall into two categories: self-report

inventories and physiological measures. A new approach, called *ecological momentary assessment (EMA),* involves repeated sampling of people's behaviors and experiences in real time and in their natural environments.

10. Ader and Cohen's discovery that the immune system can be conditioned, coupled with Candace Pert's demonstration that the brain has receptors for immune molecules, gave rise to the subfield known as psychoneuroimmunology (PNI), which is a biopsychosocial model. PNI focuses on the interactions among behavior, the nervous system, the endocrine system, and the immune system.

11. According to the direct effect hypothesis, immunosuppression is part of the body's natural response to stress. The indirect effect hypothesis maintains that immunosuppression is an aftereffect of the stress response. Animal and human research studies demonstrate that the brain regulates the production of stress hormones, which in turn influence the body's immune defenses.

12. Stress exacerbates many diseases whose central feature is excessive inflammation, including allergic, autoimmune, rheumatologic, neurologic, and cardiovascular diseases. The glucocorticoid resistance model suggests that this is due to chronic stress interfering with the immune system's sensitivity to glucocorticoid hormones, such as cortisol, which normally terminate the inflammatory response.

Other Models of Stress and Illness

13. Hans Selye outlined the concept of general adaptation syndrome (GAS) to describe the effects of chronic stress. This syndrome consists of an alarm reaction, a stage of resistance, and a stage of exhaustion. Persistent stress may increase a person's susceptibility to a disease of adaptation.

14. According to the transactional model, a key factor in stress is cognitive appraisal. In primary appraisal, we assess whether an event is benign-positive, irrelevant, or a potential threat or challenge. In secondary appraisal, we assess the coping resources available for meeting the challenge. Through reappraisal, we constantly update perceptions of success or failure in meeting a challenge or threat.

15. The diathesis–stress model suggests that some people are more vulnerable to stress-related illnesses because of predisposing factors such as genetic weakness. A good example of how this works is seen in post-traumatic stress disorder (PTSD).

Key Terms and Concepts to Remember

stressor, p. 84
stress, p. 84
social-evaluative threat, p. 91
stereotype threat, p. 91
burnout, p. 93
sympatho-adreno-medullary (SAM) axis, p. 98
hypothalamic-pituitary-adrenocortical (HPA) axis, p. 98
homeostasis, p. 98

corticosteroids, p. 98
ecological momentary assessment (EMA), p. 99
psychoneuroimmunology (PNI), p. 101
allostatic load (allostasis), p. 105
glucocorticoid receptor (GCR) resistance model, p. 105
general adaptation syndrome (GAS), p. 107

transactional model, p. 108
primary appraisal, p. 109
secondary appraisal, p. 109
cognitive reappraisal, p. 109
diathesis–stress model, p. 110
reactivity, p. 110
post-traumatic stress disorder (PTSD), p. 110

LaunchPad
macmillan learning

To accompany your textbook, you have access to a number of online resources, including quizzes for every chapter of the book, flashcards, critical thinking exercises, videos, and *Check Your Health* inventories. To access these resources, please visit the Straub *Health Psychology* LaunchPad solo at: **launchpadworks.com**

Coping with Stress

iStock/Getty Images

As soon as he graduated from high school, Kris Goldsmith fulfilled his childhood dream of serving his country by enlisting in the army. After completing basic training in 2005, he and the rest of his division deployed to Iraq. Trained as a forward observer in charge of detecting artillery, Private Goldsmith was reassigned to document Iraqi-on-Iraqi violence during the army's occupation of Sadr City. "I was a 19-year-old kid taking pictures of mutilated men, women, and boys and little girls," he recalled. "Those are the type of images that never really go away" (Gajilan, 2008).

Returning from Iraq when his tour of duty was finished, Goldsmith found himself a changed man. He began drinking heavily every day, sleeping too little or too much, and displaying an uncontrollable and violent temper with family and friends. Despite a promotion to sergeant and receiving the Army Commendation Medal for his service, Kris looked forward to finishing his army contract and getting his life back to normal. "I just wanted to get out of the army," Kris said, "and I figured all my problems would go away once I got out of the service."

His breaking point came the very week he was supposed to get out of the army. He and his unit received "stop-loss" orders that automatically extended their service past their commitments as volunteers. The orders scheduled an immediate redeployment to Iraq. Before this could take place, however, Kris Goldsmith began experiencing symptoms of what he believed to be a heart attack.

After extensive testing, the doctors at the army hospital at Fort Stewart said Kris most likely had suffered a panic attack, and they ordered him to report to the behavioral health clinic on the base, where he was told he had an "adjustment disorder with disturbance of emotions and conduct." He began seeing a psychiatrist, who further diagnosed chronic severe depression, prescribed group therapy and an antidepressant, and then cleared Kris for duty.

Feeling helpless and out of options, Kris Goldsmith tried to kill himself the night before he was supposed to return to Iraq. "... So I took a black Sharpie magic marker and I wrote across my arms 'Stop-loss killed me. End stop-loss now.' I took my half-bottle of Percocet and ... a liter-and-a-half bottle of vodka and downed the Percocet and I chased it with the vodka and drank until I couldn't drink anymore."

Remarkably, Goldsmith survived his attempted suicide and was discharged from the army. At 23, he moved in with his parents on Long Island, New York, and began to receive $700 in disability each month after his diagnosis was changed to post-traumatic stress disorder (PTSD).

Why was Kris Goldsmith's response to military service so life-disrupting and nearly fatal? As you saw in Chapter 4, appraising a situation or event as stressful does not lead automatically to an adverse physiological and psychological response. In fact, *how* people deal with stressful events is at least as important as the stressors themselves in determining health or illness.

In this chapter, we will take a biopsychosocial approach in considering the factors that affect how people deal with stress. Those factors include biological influences, such as inherited personality traits and our physiological reactivity level, as well as psychological and social influences, such as coping strategies, outlook on life, perception of control, and amount of social support. Through our journey into the biology and psychology of responding to stress, we will see ample evidence supporting the connection between mind and body. At every turn, biological, psychological, and social forces interact in determining our response to stress. We will conclude with a discussion of coping interventions that can help minimize the ill effects of stress.

Responding to Stress

When we talk about how people respond to stress, we generally use the word *cope.* **Coping** refers to the cognitive, behavioral, and emotional ways that people deal with stressful situations and includes any attempt to preserve mental and physical health—even if it has limited value (Moss-Morris & Petrie, 1997; Taylor & Stanton, 2007).

Coping is a dynamic process, not a one-time reaction—it is a series of responses involving our interactions with the environment. For example, when you break up with a romantic partner, you may experience physical and emotional reactions, such as overall sadness, inability to sleep or eat, and even nausea. It is not just the initial incident but also continuing interactions with the environment that affect your responses. For example, friends' sympathetic comments and revisiting special places may trigger a greater response. Together, these responses form our style of coping with stress.

coping The cognitive, behavioral, and emotional ways in which we manage stressful situations.

Problem-Focused and Emotion-Focused Coping

Coping strategies—the ways we deal with stressful situations—are intended to moderate, or buffer, the effects of stressors on our physical and emotional well-being. Not all coping strategies are equally effective, however. Some strategies provide temporary relief but tend to be maladaptive in the long run. For example, although psychological defenses (such as Kris's belief that his problems would go away when he left military service) may allow us to distance ourselves from a stressful situation temporarily by denying its existence, they

DigitalVision/Getty Images

Rooting Out a Problem
Relaxing hobbies such as gardening can be powerful stress busters (and emotion-focused coping strategies).

problem-focused coping A coping strategy for dealing directly with a stressor, in which we either reduce the stressor's demands or increase our resources for meeting its demands.

emotion-focused coping A coping strategy in which we try to control our emotional response to a stressor.

rumination Repetitive focusing on the causes, meanings, and consequences of stressful experiences.

emotional cascade Becoming so focused on an upsetting event that one gets worked into an intense, painful state of negative emotion.

emotional-approach coping (EAC) The process of working through, clarifying, and understanding the emotions triggered by a stressor.

do not eliminate the source of stress. Similarly, alcohol or other drugs push the stress into the background but do nothing to get rid of it. These behaviors are maladaptive because they do not confront the stressor directly and are likely to make the situation worse.

We use **problem-focused coping** to deal directly with the stressful situation, either by reducing its demands or by increasing our capacity to deal with the stressor. For instance, a student who tackles a seemingly overwhelming course load by breaking her assignments into a series of smaller, manageable tasks is using one of these strategies, as is someone recovering from an alcohol problem who joins a support group to share experiences. We use problem-focused coping when we believe our resources and situations are changeable.

When we employ **emotion-focused coping** techniques, we attempt to regulate our emotional reaction to a stressful event. We tend to rely on emotion-focused coping when we believe that little or nothing can be done to alter a stressful situation or when we believe that our coping resources or skills are insufficient to meet the demands of the stressful situation. Examples of emotion-focused coping include keeping yourself busy to take your mind off a stressful event, disclosing your emotions by talking with a friend, or journaling in a gratitude diary. Interestingly, problem-focused coping skills appear to emerge during childhood, while emotion-focused skills develop later, in early adolescence (Compas, Barnez, Malcarne, & Worsham, 1991).

Which is healthier, problem-focused coping or emotion-focused coping? Problem-focused strategies more often are linked with better health outcomes than are emotion-focused strategies. However, in one study, the relationships varied with the duration of the stressor, with problem-focused coping proving more effective with chronic stressors than with acute stressors (Connor-Smith & Flachsbart, 2007).

Which coping strategy is likely to work best also depends on whether the stressor is controllable. With school- or work-related stressors, we are more likely to apply problem-focused coping, while for some health-related problems, distancing oneself through emotional coping may be the better option. Of course, many health-related problems also benefit from the direct action of problem-focused coping, as when, for example, a dietary change or regular exercise regimen improves a person's ability to manage her diabetes. For these reasons, we often use problem-focused and emotion-focused coping together.

Sometimes people overreact in an attempt to control their emotional reactions to a stressor. **Rumination** refers to thinking repetitively about an upsetting situation and how it relates to past and future problems. This may spiral out of control into an **emotional cascade,** a vicious cycle in which intense rumination makes the person more upset, which in turn causes more rumination (Moberly & Watkins, 2008). The end result is a self-amplifying feedback loop of rumination and negative emotion that ultimately may lead to self-destructive behaviors such as binging and purging, self-injury, "self-medicating" with alcohol or drugs, or impulsive shopping (Selby, Franklin, Carson-Wong, & Rizvi, 2013). According to the Emotional Cascade Model, these self-damaging behaviors, which to the outside observer would only seem to make a bad situation worse, are used to distract from rumination through intense physical sensations (Selby, Anestis, Bender, & Joiner, 2009).

Focusing on our emotional reaction to a stressor is not always maladaptive. **Emotional-approach coping (EAC)** is comprised of two emotion-regulating processes: emotional processing and emotional expression. EAC, which involves working through our emotional reactions to a stressful event, is adaptive and healthy (Stanton, 2010).

We may use behavioral strategies, seeking out others who offer encouragement, or keeping ourselves busy to distract attention from the problem. Alternatively, we may try cognitive strategies, such as changing the way that we appraise a stressor or denying unpleasant information.

Coping, Gender, Genes, and Socioeconomic Status

Our coping strategies vary according to the situation but also, researchers have found, according to individual differences in gender, genetics, and socioeconomic status (SES).

Men and women exhibit a number of different physiological reactions to stress depending, in part, on the nature of the stressor. For example, when experiencing acute laboratory stressors, women exhibit lower blood pressure reactivity than men (Arthur, Katkin, & Mezzacappa, 2004). In addition, although men display greater stress-induced secretions of catecholamines (the autonomic nervous system–activating neurotransmitters epinephrine and norepinephrine), women exhibit a stronger glucocorticoid response (terminating immune system response) (Gallucci, Baum, & Laue, 1993).

Several researchers have found that emotional-approach coping is not unequivocally effective for men, particularly for those who display higher levels of masculinity and experience gender role conflict (Hoyt, 2009). For example, many men curb their emotions as a result of being socialized into a restrictive norm of masculinity. This behavior has the disadvantage of making it harder to connect emotionally with others. The loneliness and detachment that may result fosters a gender role conflict. As another example, a diagnosis of a chronic disease such as cancer is inconsistent with the dominant form of socially constructed masculinity (van den Hoonaard, 2009). Common symptoms associated with being treated for prostate cancer, such as erectile dysfunction, as well as feelings of vulnerability and fear, may threaten a man's masculine self-image (Arrington, 2008). One recent study found that men who felt the greatest threat to their masculinity were less likely to process their cancer-related emotions. This decreased emotional processing also predicted greater deterioration in urinary functioning, suggesting that emotion-regulating coping processes constitute one pathway through which gender roles affect recovery from chronic illness (Hoyt, Stanton, Irwin, & Thomas, 2013).

Some research studies have suggested that men are more likely to use problem-focused coping strategies in dealing with stress and that women are more likely to rely on emotion-focused strategies (Marco, 2004). However, gender differences in coping styles may have less to do with being female or male than with the scope of resources available. When researchers compare women and men of similar occupation, education, and income, gender differences in physiological responses to stress and coping strategies often disappear (Persson and others, 2009).

Some research suggests that individual genetic makeup can moderate how people respond to catastrophic events and other stressors. Researchers examined the responses of 755 older adults aged 54 to 74 whose homes were damaged during the earthquake that struck Taiwan in 1999 (Daly & MacLachlan, 2011). They found that many whose homes were damaged felt less in control of their lives one year later and rated their health as poorer than those who were less affected by the earthquake. However, these adverse outcomes occurred only among people who were carriers of a particular allele of the apolipoprotein E gene (APOE), suggesting that when people experience traumatizing events, those who carry risk mutations in their genotype may be more susceptible to unfavorable health outcomes, perhaps because of how they psychologically appraise and cope with stressors.

How people cope with a stressor also is influenced by a number of external factors, including family, friends, education, employment, time, and money. People who have more resources available typically cope with stressful events more successfully. One of the most influential factors with respect to health is socioeconomic status (SES). People who are low in SES have increased risk for chronic disease, disability, and premature mortality (Stowe and others, 2010). It is important to note, though, that access to health care does not completely explain the relationship between SES and health. The association between lower SES and poor health is found even in countries that have universal health care (Cohen, Doyle, & Baum, 2006).

Health disparities increase with each step down the SES ladder (Adler & Rehkopf, 2008). One study found that children with highly reactive emotional styles who grow up in low-SES environments had higher levels of chronic inflammation as adults than did similar children raised in higher-SES environments (Appleton and others, 2012). Chronic inflammation is associated with the risk of a number of age-related diseases, including hypertension, heart disease, and diabetes (Singh & Newman, 2011). Another study found that SES also predicts whether supportive personal relationships confer health benefits. Among women who either were awaiting further evaluation from an abnormal mammogram or newly diagnosed with breast cancer, those with higher SES had a stronger cellular immune response than women with lower SES (Fagundes and others, 2012).

Stressful experiences are especially common among many ethnic minority families, who tend to be overrepresented in groups of low SES. In 2014, for example, 69 percent of African-American children under age 6 live in low-income families (Jiang, Ekono, & Skinner, 2016). Poverty rates for Hispanic children were nearly as high (64 percent), with low-income rates for both groups about twice as high as rates for white (34 percent) and Asian children (30 percent). (See Figure 5.1.) Impoverished families experience more pollution, substandard and overcrowded housing, crime, and dangerous traffic than do more affluent families. They also suffer poor nutrition, limited education, low-paying work, and a lack of health insurance and access to health care (Johnson and others, 1995). Moreover, children from low-SES homes are more likely to experience divorce, frequent school transfers, and harsh and punitive parenting—events that have been linked with a variety of behavioral and emotional difficulties (Aughinbaugh, Robles, & Sun, 2013).

Regardless of ethnicity, people of low SES tend to rely less on problem-focused coping than do people with more education and higher incomes (Billings & Moos, 1981). Their demeaning social experiences may cause them to develop a feeling of hopelessness and to believe that they have little or no **psychological control** over events in

psychological control The perception that one can determine one's own behavior and influence the environment to bring about desired outcomes.

FIGURE 5.1

Family Income by Race/ Ethnicity African-American, American Indian, and Hispanic children are disproportionately low income and poor.

Data from Jiang, Y., Ekono, M., & Skinner, C. (2016). *Basic facts about low income children: Children under 6 years 2014*. New York: National Center for Children in Poverty, Mailman School of Public Health, Columbia University. Retrieved on March 31, 2016, from http://www.nccp .org/publications/pdf/text_1149.pdf.

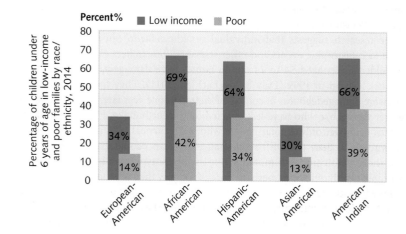

their lives. So, with repeated exposure to stress and no way to break the cycle, their only recourse is to try to control their emotional responses to stress—because they've learned that they can't control the situation itself. This is important because people who believe that they can determine their own behavior and influence the environment to bring about desired outcomes cope more effectively with stressful events (Wrosch, Schulz, Miller, Lupien, & Dunne, 2007). A strong perception of control has also been associated with a healthier lifestyle, a stronger immune response to allergens (Chen, Fisher, Bacharier, & Strunk, 2003), and a lower overall risk of death (Surtees, Wainwright, Luben, Khas, & Dy, 2006). No wonder, then, that psychological control may be especially important for people who are vulnerable to health problems, including children, the elderly, and those who are already being treated for medical conditions (Wrosch and others, 2007).

Judith Stein and Adeline Nyamathi (1999) demonstrated not only that impoverished people have more difficulty coping with stress, but also that women in this situation have more problems than men do. The researchers examined a sample of 486 impoverished men and women of African-American, Latino, and European descent who were recruited to participate in a community-based acquired immunodeficiency syndrome (AIDS) prevention program. Compared with their male counterparts, the impoverished women reported greater stress and were more likely to resort to *avoidant coping* strategies (withdrawing from, minimizing, or avoiding stressors). The subordinate positions of impoverished women may make them even more vulnerable than men to feelings of hopelessness in the face of chronic stress. This finding points to the need for gender-specific interventions in helping people cope with chronic stress.

Socioeconomic status is also a powerful predictor of both health and health behaviors. One study of health behaviors and outcomes in Pitt County, North Carolina, reported that SES was inversely related, among both African-American women and men, to alcohol consumption, cigarette smoking, and risk of hypertension (James, Van Hoewyk, & Belli, 2006). The same study found that low-SES African-Americans perceived weaker levels of emotional support when under stress than did their higher-SES counterparts (Keenan, Strogatz, James, Ammerman, & Rice, 1992; Strogatz and others, 1997). Compared with those of high SES in both childhood and adulthood, low-SES men were also seven times more likely to suffer from hypertension as adults.

Interestingly, socioeconomic indicators at the level of individual neighborhoods predict the health of residents in relationship to smoking and other harmful health behaviors, even after individual differences in SES, lifestyle behaviors, and other risk factors are taken into consideration (Diez Roux, 2001; Kendzor and others, 2009; Paul, Boutain, Manhart, & Hitti, 2008). Pamela Feldman and Andrew Steptoe (2004) believe that neighborhood SES is linked to health because it strongly influences the social and psychological experiences of residents living in a particular neighborhood. The researchers compared 19 low-SES neighborhoods and 18 high-SES neighborhoods in London on four measures: *social cohesion* (trust and solidarity with neighbors); *social control* (confidence that neighbors would take action to maintain the well-being of the neighborhood); *neighborhood problems* (community-wide stressors such as litter and traffic noise); and *neighborhood vigilance* (a measure of feelings of threat and vulnerability in the neighborhood). Londoners living in lower-SES neighborhoods perceived greater *neighborhood strain* (weaker social cohesion, more neighborhood problems, and greater vigilance) than people living in more affluent neighborhoods, which in turn was associated with poorer individual health, poorer social relationships, and lower levels of perceived control among residents. In other studies, community violence has been linked to increased stress symptoms, depression, and anxiety among inner-city African-American adolescents and to the use of negative coping strategies, such as avoidance and aggression (Dempsey, 2002).

Coping and Ethnicity

Although socioeconomic status is a powerful predictor of stress, coping, and health behaviors among women and men in virtually every group that has been studied, the relationship varies with ethnicity. For instance, while SES is inversely related to self-reported stress levels among most groups, including African-American women, the Pitt County study found SES to be positively related to stress in African-American men. Another study of a culturally diverse group of adolescents reported that Hispanic-, Asian-, and African-Americans reported higher levels of social stress than European-Americans (Choi, Meininger, & Roberts, 2006).

David Williams (2000) has identified three factors that help explain the interactions among socioeconomic status, gender, and ethnicity among African-Americans. First, middle-class African-American men report higher levels of racial discrimination than African-American women (Forman, 2002). Racial discrimination and perceived discrimination are significant stressors that can adversely affect physical and mental health (Luo, Xu, Granberg, & Wentworth, 2012). Significantly, the more years of education that an African-American male has completed, the stronger his perception of racial discrimination. A particularly insidious type of discrimination that people of color experience daily are **microaggressions,** which are insults, indignities, and marginalizing messages sent by well-intentioned people who seem unaware of the hidden messages they are sending (Sue, 2011). *Microaggression fatigue* has been noted among African-American men who live or work in environments that are predominantly white (Smith, Hung, & Franklin, 2011). See Table 5.1.

Second, the attainment of middle-class status may be tenuous and marginal for some African-Americans. For instance, college-educated African-Americans are more likely than European-Americans to experience unemployment and job insecurity, both of which are associated with higher levels of stress, illness, disability, and mortality (U.S. Census Bureau, 2004). African-Americans are also less likely to convert their socioeconomic achievements into more desirable housing and community living conditions (Alba, Logan, & Stults, 2000). And even when they do, the outcome is not necessarily rosy. One study even found that while living in the suburbs predicted lower mortality risk for European-American men, it predicted *higher* mortality risk for African-American men (House and others, 2000).

Third, African-American males may experience a unique source of stress because the educational attainment associated with their higher SES has not been rewarded with equitable increases in income. At every level of education, African-American men have lower incomes than European-American men. Moreover, the pay gap between African-Americans and European-Americans is larger for men than for women (Yang, 2010).

microaggressions Insults, indignities, and marginalizing messages sent by well-intentioned people who seem unaware of the hidden messages that they are sending.

Community Support is Priceless Joy erupts at the Sacramento LGBT Community Center with news of the 2013 Supreme Court decision that struck down a law denying federal benefits to married gay couples in the state of California.

Hector Amezcua/AP Images

The Minority Stress Model

Stigma, prejudice, and discrimination often create a stressful social environment for other minorities, including the lesbian, gay, bisexual, and transgender (LGBT) population. This may come in the form of familial rejection, work discrimination, and even interpersonal violence (Lewis, Derlega, Berndt, Morris, & Rose, 2002). Although researchers have not given the physical health of LGBT individuals the same level of attention as other groups, a growing body of evidence suggests that sexual minorities have heightened risk for many physical health conditions, including cancer, cardiovascular disease, diabetes, allergies, chronic gastrointestinal problems, and more (Lick, Durso, & Johnson, 2013).

TABLE 5.1

Examples of Racial Microaggressions

Theme	Microaggression	Message
Alien in own land When Asian-Americans and Latino-Americans are assumed to be foreign-born	"Where are you from?" "Where were you born?" "You speak good English." A person asking an Asian-American to teach him or her words in the Asian person's native language	You are not American. You are a foreigner.
Ascription of intelligence Assigning intelligence to a person of color on the basis of his or her race	"You are a credit to your race." "You are so articulate." Asking an Asian person to help with a math or science problem	People of color are generally not as intelligent as whites. It is unusual for someone of your race to be intelligent. All Asians are intelligent and good in math/sciences.
Color blindness Statements that indicate that a white person does not want to acknowledge race	"When I look at you, I don't see color." "America is a melting pot." "There is only one race, the human race."	Denying a person of color's racial/ethnic experiences Assimilate/acculturate to the dominant culture. Denying the individual as a racial/cultural being
Criminality/assumption of criminal status A person of color is presumed to be dangerous, criminal, or deviant on the basis of the person's race	A white man or woman clutching purse or checking wallet as a black or Latino approaches or passes A store owner following a customer of color around the store A white person waits to ride the next elevator when a person of color is on it	You are a criminal. You are going to steal/You are poor/You do not belong. You are dangerous.
Denial of individual racism A statement made when whites deny their racial biases	"I'm not racist. I have several black friends." "As a woman, I know what you go through as a racial minority."	I am immune to racism because I have friends of color. Your racial oppression is no different from my gender oppression. I can't be a racist. I'm like you.
Myth of meritocracy Statements that assert that race does not play a role in life successes	"I believe the most qualified person should get the job." "Everyone can succeed in this society, if they work hard enough."	People of color are given extra, unfair benefits because of their race. People of color are lazy and/or incompetent and need to work harder.
Pathologizing cultural values/communication styles The notion that the values and communication styles of the dominant/white culture are ideal	Asking a black person: "Why do you have to be so loud/animated? Just calm down." To an Asian or Latino person: "Why are you so quiet? We want to know what you think. Be more verbal." "Speak up more." Dismissing an individual who brings up race/culture in work/school setting	Assimilate to dominant culture. Leave your cultural baggage outside.
Second-class citizen Occurs when a white person is given preferential treatment as a consumer over a person of color	Person of color mistaken for a service worker Having a taxi cab pass a person of color and pick up a white passenger	People of color are servants to whites. They couldn't possibly occupy high-status positions. You are likely to cause trouble and/or travel to a dangerous neighborhood.

Source: Sue, D. W., Capodilupo, C. M., Torino, G. C., Bucceri, J. M., Holder, A. M. B., Nadal, K. L., & Esquilin, M. (2007). Racial microaggressions in everyday life: Implications for clinical practice. *American Psychologist, 62*(4), 271–286.

minority stress theory The concept that proposes that health disparities among minority individuals are due to chronically high levels of stress experienced by members of stigmatized groups.

Minority stress theory proposes that health disparities among populations such as that of gay men can be explained in large part by stressors induced by a hostile, homophobic culture (Meyer, 2003). These stressors may include the perception of prejudice, stigma, rejection, and the internalized homophobia that can occur when gay and bisexual individuals apply negative attitudes toward themselves. This hostile environment contributes to a greater likelihood than in the general population for a number of risk-taking behaviors, including avoidant coping strategies, cigarette smoking, drug use, and risky sexual behavior (Proxmire, 2015; Cochran, Mays, & Sullivan, 2003). Having multiple minority statuses increases the likelihood of feelings of rejection and isolation, along with heightened risk of substance abuse and other hazardous forms of coping (Dentato, 2012).

Factors Affecting the Ability to Cope

We all know that certain life stresses (such as final exams) tend to give us headaches, queasy stomachs, and other ailments, whereas exhilarating or uplifting experiences (such as a ski weekend or a new intimate relationship) make us feel on top of the world. In this section, we explore several biopsychosocial factors that affect how well we cope with potential stressors and, by extension, how this affects our health. Keep in mind that no one factor, by itself, determines your well-being. Health is always a result of biopsychosocial factors interacting in various ways.

Resilience

resilience The quality that allows some people to bounce back from difficult events that might otherwise disrupt their well-being.

Resilience is the ability to bounce back from stressful experiences and to adapt flexibly to changing environmental demands. In the aftermath of the September 11 terrorist attacks on the United States, for example, Barbara Fredrickson and her colleagues (2003) identified resilient individuals as those who were able to experience positive emotions, such as gratitude, and in doing so actually demonstrated *post-traumatic growth* as time passed.

Psychiatrist Steven Wolin (1993) describes the case of Jacqueline, who at 2 years of age was placed by her birth parents in a foster home. Jacqueline's foster father murdered his wife 18 months later, and Jacqueline was moved to another foster family. After two relatively stable years, Jacqueline's birth mother appeared without explanation, taking her daughter to live with her for the next four years. During those years, Jacqueline's mother had a string of dysfunctional relationships with men who moved in and out of the house; some of these men physically abused Jacqueline. At age 10, Jacqueline was once again displaced, this time to an orphanage, where she stayed until she was 17. Although many theories of psychosocial development would predict that Jacqueline would develop into an antisocial, problem-ridden woman, this did not happen. Throughout her childhood, she excelled in school, was a leader among her peers, and remained optimistic about her future. Jacqueline is now an adult with a stable marriage and family. She finds great joy in being "the parent to my children that I never had."

Where does such resilience come from? Research points to two groups of factors. One group relates to individual traits, the other to positive life experiences and social support. Resilient children have well-developed social, academic, or creative skills; easy temperaments; high self-esteem; self-discipline; and strong feelings of personal control (Werner, 1997). These elements of social cognition foster healthy relationships with others who help such children adjust to adverse conditions. The healthy relationships seem to help these children deflect many of the problems that they face at home (Ackerman, Kogos, Youngstrom, Schoff, & Izard, 1999).

Studies of resilient children point to the importance of at least one consistently supportive person in the life of a child at risk. This person can be an aunt or uncle, older sister or brother, grandparent, family friend, or teacher. This supportive person, often a caring parent, is a model of resilience who plays a significant role in convincing at-risk children that they can and will beat the odds.

Although early studies of resilience implied that there was something remarkable about these children, recent research suggests that resilience is a more common phenomenon that arises from the ordinary resources of children, their relationships, and positive community experiences (Masten, 2001; Ong, Bergeman, Biscponti, & Wallace, 2006). Echoing the theme of the positive psychology movement (see Chapter 1), resilience research now focuses on understanding how these adaptive processes develop, how they operate under adverse conditions, and how they can be protected (or restored).

Until recently, research studies of resilience focused mostly on children (Wagnild, 2013). Today, however, researchers increasingly focus on resilience in their investigations of the well-being of adults. In medicine, for instance, biological resilience refers to various protective factors (genetic, demographic, social-cultural, psychological, gender-linked, and environmental) that contribute to positive outcomes in the elderly (Alfieri, Costanzo, & Borgogni, 2011). Resilience is associated with many specific characteristics among adults, including forgiveness (Broyles, 2005), sense of coherence and purpose in life (Nygren and others, 2005), self-efficacy (Caltabiano & Caltabiano, 2006), as well as lower incidence of depression, anxiety, and perceived stress (Wagnild, 2008). As more studies reveal the positive relationships between resilience and aging well, health psychologists are increasingly interested in recognizing and strengthening the ability to bounce back following challenge and adversity among the growing elderly segment of the population (Prince-Embury & Saklofske, 2013).

Explanatory Style

Your **explanatory style**—whether you tend to attribute outcomes to positive or negative causes—also affects your ability to cope with stress. People who look on the bright side of life—who see a light at the end of the tunnel—have a positive explanatory style and tend to cope well with stress (Peterson & Steen, 2002). Those with a negative explanatory style do not cope as well with stress. They expect failure because they believe that the conditions that lead to failure are all around them, or even within them.

Why are some people more prone to one style or the other? Individual attribution styles—whom or what we blame for our failures—are part of the answer. Martin Seligman and his colleagues (1995) believe that negativity and "epidemic hopelessness" are largely responsible for the prevalence of depression among Western people. When failure and rejection are encountered in life (as inevitably happens), maintains Seligman, the self-focused Westerner is more likely to assume personal responsibility. In non-Western cultures, where individualism is typically subordinate to cooperation and a sense of community, depression is less common, perhaps because it is less likely to be linked with self-blame for failure.

> **explanatory style** Our general propensity to attribute outcomes always to positive causes or always to negative causes, such as personality, luck, or another person's actions.

Pessimism

Those with a negative explanatory style tend to explain failures in terms that are global ("Everything is awful"), stable ("It's always going to be this way"), and internal ("It's my fault, as usual"). Anger, hostility, suppressed emotions, anxiety, depression, and pessimism are all associated with a negative explanatory style and are believed to lead to harmful health-related behaviors (smoking and alcohol and drug abuse, for example) and disease (Scheier & Bridges, 1995).

> *"A recipe for severe depression is preexisting pessimism encountering failure."*
>
> —**Martin Seligman (1995)**

Pessimism is also linked with earlier mortality. In a study of personality data obtained from general medical patients at the Mayo Clinic between 1962 and 1965, Toshihiko Maruta and his colleagues (2000) found that patients who were more pessimistic had significantly higher (19 percent) mortality than more optimistic patients. There are at least four mechanisms by which pessimism might shorten life:

1. Pessimists experience more unpleasant events, which have been linked to shorter lives.
2. Pessimists believe that "nothing I do matters," so they are less likely than optimists to comply with medical regimens or take preventive actions (such as exercising).
3. Pessimists are more likely to be diagnosed with major depressive disorder, which is associated with mortality.
4. Pessimists have weaker immune systems than optimists.

Optimism

People with a positive explanatory style tend to explain failures in terms that are situational ('This *situation* is awful. Others are not.'), temporary ('This won't last.'), and external ('It's the situation, not me.'). They also tend to lead healthier, longer lives than their gloom-and-doom counterparts (Segerstrom, 2006). They also have shorter hospital stays, faster recovery from coronary artery bypass surgery, and greater longevity when battling AIDS. Optimists have lower levels of inflammation, respond to stress with smaller increases in blood pressure, and are much less likely to die from heart attacks (Roy and others, 2010; Everson, Goldberg, Kaplan, & Cohen, 1996). Among college students, optimists—those who agree with statements such as "In uncertain times, I usually expect the best" and "I always look on the bright side of things"—report less fatigue and fewer aches, pains, and minor illnesses (Carver & Scheier, 2002). See Your Health Assets: Measuring Optimism for a quick survey to help you determine *your* level of optimism.

Why is optimism beneficial to health? According to the *broaden-and-build theory*, positive emotions increase our physical, cognitive, and social resources, which in turn help us cope more effectively with stressful experiences and live healthier lives (Frederickson,

Your Health Assets

Measuring Optimism

How optimistic are you? Researchers have developed a scale of dispositional optimism to measure this trait. For each item listed below, answer "True" or "False" as it pertains to your typical style.

1. In uncertain times, I usually expect the best.
2. It's easy for me to relax.
3. If something can go wrong for me, it will.
4. I'm always optimistic about my future.
5. I enjoy my friends a lot.
6. It's important for me to keep busy.
7. I hardly ever expect things to go my way.
8. I don't get upset too easily.
9. I rarely count on good things happening to me.
10. Overall, I expect more good things to happen to me than bad.

To score, add together the number of "Trues" that you indicated for items 1, 4, and 10 and the number of "Falses" that you indicated for items 3, 7, and 9. Higher scores indicate a greater tendency toward optimism.

Source: From Scheier, M. P., Carver, C.S., & Bridges, M. W. (1994). Distinguishing optimism from neuroticism (and trait anxiety, mastery, and self-esteem): A reevaluation of the Life Orientation Test. *Journal of Personality and Social Psychology; 67*, 1063–1078. Copyright © 2016 American Psychological Association. Reproduced with permission. No further reproduction or distribution is permitted without written permission from the American Psychological Association.

2001). For example, by shortening the duration of negative emotional arousal, positive emotions may stave off stress-related elevations in blood pressure, inflammation, immunosuppression, and other disease-promoting processes. Among children, positive emotions experienced during play help build social skills, which in turn may foster lasting social bonds and attachments (Aron, Norman, Aron, McKenna, & Heyman, 2000). In support of this theory, one study found that people who consistently experienced positive emotions with their families as children, and again as adults with their own families, were half as likely to display high levels of cumulative wear and tear on their bodies (Ryff, Singer, Wing, & Love, 2001). Another study of older Hispanic-Americans reported that those who generally reported positive emotions were half as likely as those who were more pessimistic and cynical to become disabled or to have died during the two-year duration of the study (Ostir, Markides, Black, & Goodwin, 2000).

Can *unrealistic optimism* be harmful? If a person thinks good outcomes are bound to happen, he/she may not do anything in the face of illness. **Optimistic bias** is the mistaken belief that one's chances of experiencing a negative event are lower (or a positive event higher) than that of other people. In one study, Neil Weinstein (1982) asked college students to complete a health questionnaire estimating their risk of developing a variety of health problems. The students were asked to estimate on a 7-point scale ranging from "much above average" to "much below average" their risk, for example, of becoming a drug addict or alcoholic; developing heart disease, ulcers, lung cancer, or diabetes; and becoming seriously obese. A majority of students believed that they were *much less likely* than their peers to develop all of the above health problems. The results were not a fluke. Optimistic bias has been demonstrated for a wide variety of health problems, including cancer, HIV infection, and substance abuse (Helweg-Larsen & Shepperd, 2001).

So is it more advantageous to be unrealistically optimistic about your health? The answer is not a simple one. On the one hand, as we have seen, optimism conveys health advantages. On the other hand, people who feel somewhat vulnerable to specific health problems are more likely to practice preventive health behaviors. People who underestimate their risk of experiencing a negative outcome may be less likely to take precautions to prevent that outcome from occurring.

Optimists generally have a more positive mood, which has been shown to improve immunity (Segerstrom & Sephton, 2010) and sustain immune functioning under stress. One study demonstrated that the pressure of first-semester law school took a less negative toll on immune activity in students who were optimistic about their academic success, compared with students who were pessimistic (Segerstrom, Taylor, Kemeny, & Fahey, 1998). As Figure 5.2 shows, the number of CD4 cells in the bloodstream of optimists rose by 13 percent, compared with a 3 percent drop in the number of cells in the bloodstream of pessimists. Similarly, NK cell activity rose by 42 percent in the high-scoring optimists but only by 9 percent in pessimists. (CD4 cells and NK cell activity are immune system factors that help fight infection.) Positive affective states in general are associated with reduced levels of stress hormones such as cortisol and—especially in women—reduced levels of biological markers of inflammation such as *C-reactive protein* (Steptoe, O'Donnell, & Badrick, 2008).

Back to our law students: Why did optimism enhance their immune function under stress? Segerstrom and her colleagues believe that optimists have healthier attitudes and better health habits than pessimists. The optimistic law students may have been more likely to appraise their course work as a challenge (and therefore perceive less stress); to exercise more; and to avoid smoking, alcohol abuse, and other health-compromising behaviors. These health-enhancing behaviors would contribute to stronger immune systems and better functioning under stress.

optimistic bias The belief that other people are more likely than oneself to develop a disease, be injured, or experience other negative events.

FIGURE 5.2

Optimism and Immune Function Two months after beginning law school, optimistic law students showed a 13 percent increase in the blood level (estimated total number) of CD4 cells in the bloodstream, compared with a 3 percent drop in the number of cells in the bloodstream of pessimists. Similarly, natural killer (NK) cell cytotoxicity, a measure of cell activity level, rose by 42 percent in the optimists, but only by 9 percent in pessimists.

Data from Segerstrom, S. C., Taylor, S. E., Kemeny, M. E., & Fahey, J. (1998). Optimism is associated with mood, coping, and immune change in response to stress. *Journal of Personality and Social Psychology*, 74(6), 1646–1655. Copyright 1998 by the American Psychological Association. Adapted with permission.

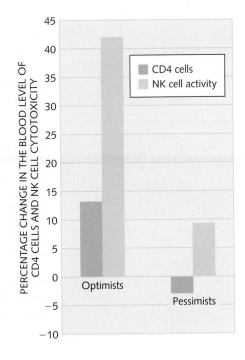

Optimists and pessimists have different physical reactions to stress but also differ in how they cope with stress. Whereas optimists are more likely to try to alter stressful situations or to *actively engage* in direct problem-focused action against a stressor, pessimists are more likely to *passively disengage* and to ruminate—to obsess and be overwhelmed by persistent thoughts about stressors (Carver & Connor-Smith, 2010). This tendency has been linked to self-criticism, a history of past depression, and excessive dependency on others (Spasojevic & Alloy, 2001). Optimists also perceive more control over stressors, which in turn leads to more effective coping responses, including seeking treatment when illness strikes (Segerstrom, 2006; Tromp and others, 2005). In contrast, pessimists are more likely to perceive the world—and their health—as being uncontrollable (Keltner, Ellsworth, & Edwards, 1993).

Fortunately, pessimism is identifiable early in life and can be changed into learned optimism (Seligman & Csikszentmihalyi, 2000). Seligman recommends learning the "ABC's" of optimism. Let's consider how this might work to help Kris Goldsmith, whom we met in our opening vignette, develop a more positive explanatory style.

■ Adversity: Kris should learn to interpret difficulties in terms that are *external* ("It was the military's policies, not me, that caused my troubles."), *temporary* ("This will be a difficult year, but I will get through this."), and *specific* ("My career and family plans are still on hold, but I know other parts of my life have been positive and will continue to go well.").

■ Beliefs: Practicing such optimistic explanations mindfully will lead Kris to healthier, more upbeat beliefs.

■ Consequences: Healthier, more optimistic beliefs will prompt more positive health consequences for Kris.

Martin Bolt (2004, p. 176) explains, "Learning to counterargue, to offer alternative causes for the disappointment, to recognize that you are overreacting, and even to show that the belief is factually incorrect undermine the pessimistic explanation and enable you to cope with setbacks more effectively."

Personal Control and Choice

personal control The belief that we make our own decisions and determine what we do and what others do to us.

Personal control is the belief that we make our own decisions and determine what we do or what others do to us (Rodin, 1986). Healthy children gradually develop a sense of control over their surroundings. Albert Bandura and other researchers have called this *self-efficacy*, which is a belief in our ability to deal with potentially stressful situations (Bandura, 1997). Personal control and self-efficacy both help people cope more effectively with stressful events (Wrosch and others, 2007).

When faced with repeated, uncontrollable stress, people sometimes learn that they cannot affect what happens to them. Low perceived control may be one reason racial and ethnic minorities are high-risk groups when it comes to health. Among minority men, for instance, the word *crisis* has been used to describe the elevated prevalence of disease, disability, and premature death (Williams, 2003). Particularly in Western cultures—where men are socialized under norms emphasizing achievement and competence—discrimination, economic marginalization, and an absence of employment opportunities can have a devastating impact on self-efficacy and on the way that men appraise and respond to potentially stressful situations.

Racism, for instance, can affect the cognitive appraisals of African-Americans dramatically. When it does, the stress response can escalate. When African-American college students in one study overheard European-American classmates negatively evaluating their performance on a task, those who attributed their poor evaluation to racism and discrimination displayed the strongest stress reactions (King, 2005).

Personal Control and Coping Strategies

People with a strong sense of personal control tend to engage in adaptive, problem-focused coping, such as exercising direct control over health-related behaviors. Niall Pender and colleagues (Pender, Walker, Sechrist, & Frank-Stromborg, 1990) studied 589 employees enrolled in six employer-sponsored health-promotion programs. Employees who believed that they exerted greater control over their health were far more likely to stick with wellness programs than were employees who felt less responsible for their well-being. Results such as these indicate that feeling in control of aversive events plays a crucial role in determining our response to stressful situations. Small wonder, then, that a sense of control has been linked to a lower risk of mortality, primarily due to lower levels of risk factors for cardiovascular disease (Paquet, Dube, Gauvin, Kestens, & Daniel, 2010).

Think back to our opening story: What happened to Kris Goldsmith's feelings of personal control when his service contract was extended? What impact did this have on his ability to cope with the stress of his service in Iraq?

Regulatory Control

Have you ever been so angry with a rude driver that you felt like exploding, yet you didn't? Or perhaps you've been at a religious service when you found something hysterically funny, but you needed to stifle your laughter? In such situations, we strive to control which emotions are merely experienced and which are actually expressed. **Regulatory control,** which refers to our capacity to modulate thoughts, emotions, and behaviors, is a part of everyday life. In fact, 9 out of 10 college students report making an effort to control their emotions at least once a day (Gross, 1998).

Controlling your responses and emotions has broad implications for your health (de Ridder, Bertha, & de Wit, 2006). Self-regulation is associated with success in dieting, quitting smoking, and maintaining good interpersonal relationships. In addition, children who have good self-control are calmer, more resistant to frustration, better able to delay gratification (an important factor later in resisting substance abuse), and less aggressive (Muraven, Tice, & Baumeister, 1998). Conversely, undercontrolled people are more likely to become aggressive (Brookings, DeRoo, & Grimone, 2008) and experience depression as they dwell obsessively on self-defeating thoughts (Verstraeten, Vasey, Raes, & Bijttebier, 2009).

Individual differences in regulatory control are related to how people cope with stressful events and experiences. People with good self-control are less likely to resort to maladaptive coping responses such as angry venting of emotions or avoidant coping (Aronoff, Stollak, & Woike, 1994). Similarly, children and adults with good self-control are likely to use constructive, problem-focused coping responses and unlikely to use avoidant or aggressive coping responses in stressful situations (Fabes, Eisenberg, Karbon, Troyer, & Switzer, 1994; Mann & Ward, 2007). Interestingly, some data suggest men expend less effort than women when attempting to control negative emotions. This gender difference is reflected in different patterns of neural activity in the brain's amygdala and prefrontal cortex (McRae, Ochsner, Mauss, Gabrieli, & Gross, 2008).

regulatory control The various ways in which we modulate our thinking, emotions, and behavior over time and across changing circumstances.

Cardiovascular Reactivity

Because of the relationship between self-control and physical arousal, researchers are exploring the use of heart rate and other physiological markers to identify individual differences in how people cope with stress (Quigley, Barrett, & Weinstein, 2002). Physiologically, our reactivity to psychological stress seems to be quite stable. In one study, researchers measured participants' blood pressure while they completed stressful tasks. Years later, follow-up studies demonstrated that those whose blood pressure had increased most during the initial phase of the study were most likely to have chronic hypertension (Matthews, Raikkonen, Sutton-Tyrrell, & Kuller, 2004).

cardiovascular reactivity (CVR) Changes in cardiovascular activity that are related to psychological stress.

reactivity hypothesis The hypothesis that individuals who show large changes in blood pressure and vascular resistance to stress have increased risk of developing heart disease.

Situations that are appraised as threatening may be associated with a different pattern of **cardiovascular reactivity (CVR)** than situations that are appraised as challenging. Threat appraisals have been linked with enhanced *vascular* responses, as reflected by increases in diastolic blood pressure and *total peripheral resistance* (the cumulative resistance of all the body's blood vessels), whereas challenge appraisals have been linked with increased *myocardial* reactivity, as reflected by increases in heart rate and cardiac output (Maier, Waldstein, & Synowski, 2003).

Cardiovascular reactivity to psychological stressors, if exaggerated or prolonged, may be harmful. According to the **reactivity hypothesis,** individuals who are "hyperreactors" (those who show large changes in blood pressure and vascular resistance to stress) have increased risk of developing heart disease (Phillips & Hughes, 2011). In one illuminating study, Karen Matthews and her colleagues (Matthews, Woodall, & Allen, 1993) found that children who showed larger CVR to a combination of mental and physical challenges had higher resting blood pressure. Results such as these suggest that CVR to stress may have a role in the development of hypertension. Interestingly, other researchers have reported that CVR is influenced by the quality of our diet, sleep, and other lifestyle factors. One study reported that participants displayed increased CVR during public speaking and other stress tasks following a single high-fat meal in comparison with a low-fat meal (Jakulj and others, 2007).

Despite findings such as these, the reactivity hypothesis remains controversial (Phillips & Hughes, 2011). One question is whether a person's reactivity to acute laboratory stress also reflects his or her reactivity to stress in real life. Another is whether the reactivity hypothesis can be extended to health outcomes other than those directly associated with the heart, as some researchers have suggested (Carroll, 2011).

Most changes in heart rate, such as those that occur in response to challenging physical and emotional demands, are controlled by the tenth cranial nerve, which is the longest in the body, extending into each limb all the way from the brain. This is the vagus nerve (*vagus* means "wandering" in Latin). The vagus plays an important role in the parasympathetic nervous system's calming response; its main function is to lower blood pressure and heart rate. When a healthy person inhales, for instance, the vagus becomes less active, increasing heart rate; when he or she exhales, vagal activity increases, and heart rate decreases. In response to stress, the autonomic nervous system speeds heart rate (to meet the metabolic demands of the body's emergency response system) by decreasing vagal action on the heart.

Vagal tone (heart rate variability) is thus a measure of the relationship between the rhythmic increases and decreases in heart rate associated with breathing in and breathing out. High vagal tone, measured as greater variability in heart rate as a person breathes in and out, reflects greater regulatory control by the vagus nerve. In contrast, low vagal tone (measured as a more stable heart rate pattern) reflects weaker regulatory control.

Richard Fabes and Nancy Eisenberg (1997) investigated the relationship among heart rate variability, daily stress, and coping responses in college students (Figure 5.3). Students with high vagal tone were less likely than students with lower vagal tone to experience high levels of negative emotional arousal in response to everyday hassles and stress. They also were more likely to rely on constructive coping measures (active coping, seeking social support, positive reinterpretation, emotion-focused coping) rather than maladaptive strategies (psychological and physical distancing, venting of emotion, alcohol/drug use).

Cardiovascular reactivity and regulatory control also may partly explain individual and group differences in coronary disease morbidity and mortality rates. Individuals who face repeated threats and challenges in their daily lives and have weaker cardiac autonomic control may be at a substantially greater risk for coronary artery disease than those who have greater regulatory control (Sloan, Bagiella, & Powell, 1999).

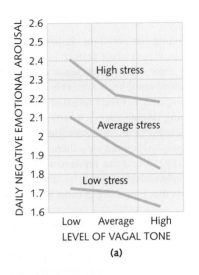

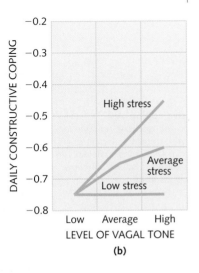

High vagal tone is inversely related to negative emotional arousal and positively related to constructive coping.

Researchers at Harvard University's School of Public Health reported that Caribbean-Americans and African-Americans, two of the largest black ethnic groups in the United States, display different patterns of cardiovascular reactivity to laboratory stressors than European-Americans do (Arthur and others, 2004). In response to a mental arithmetic task, for instance, African-Americans displayed larger decreases in heart period variability (lower vagal tone) than European-Americans, but smaller decreases than their Caribbean-American counterparts.

Choice, Culture, and Control

Psychologists have long argued that choice enhances feelings of personal control (Rotter, 1966). The results of many studies suggest that the positive consequences of choice are apparent even when choice is trivial or illusory. Simply being able to choose the order in which a task is performed appears to reduce anxiety (Glass & Singer, 1972). And in one well-known study, Ellen Langer and Judy Rodin (1976) found that the health of elderly patients in a nursing home improved significantly when they were permitted to choose their own recreational activities and the placement of the furniture in their rooms.

Conversely, situations in which there is no choice or in which choice has been removed have been linked to detrimental effects on motivation, performance, and health. Interestingly, however, several studies have demonstrated that too much choice, in the workplace and elsewhere, may be detrimental to motivation and well-being (Iyengar & Lepper, 2000; Schwartz, 2004) and pointed to cultural differences in the extent to which the perception of choice is associated with well-being. In individualistic cultures, it has been assumed that perceiving oneself as having less choice—as seems to be the case for Asians and Latin Americans—will have negative effects on well-being (Langer & Rodin, 1976). But Sastry and Ross (1998), who examined the impact of people's perceptions of choice and control on psychological distress among participants in 33 different countries, found a much more variable relationship. Among European-Americans, those with a strong sense of freedom of choice and control had lower levels of depression and anxiety than those who perceived less choice and control in their lives. However, this relationship was not observed for Asian-Americans and Asians. Like Asian-Americans, Hispanic-Americans perceived less freedom and control in their lives; however, like European-Americans, Hispanic-Americans also demonstrated the negative association between these perceptions and distress, even after such variables as socioeconomic status were taken into account.

FIGURE 5.3

Vagal Tone and Coping with Stress (a) Students with a high vagal tone were less likely than students with a lower vagal tone to experience high levels of negative emotional arousal in response to everyday hassles and stress. (b) They were also more likely to rely on constructive coping measures.

Data from Fabes, R. A., & Eisenberg, N. (1997). Regulatory control and adults' stress-related responses to daily life events. *Journal of Personality and Social Psychology, 73*(5), 1107–1117. Copyright 1997 by the American Psychological Association. Adapted with permission.

Repression and Negative Affectivity

Sometimes we are not aware that we are controlling our emotions. In laboratory studies of stress, some individuals will report feeling relaxed while performing challenging tasks, but physiologically and behaviorally, they show signs of significant stress, such as slower reaction times, increased muscle tension, and rapid heart rate. This extreme form of regulatory control—in which there is a discrepancy between verbal and physiological measures of stress—is called **repressive coping** (Weinberger, Schwartz, & Davidson, 1979; Myers, 2010). Using this emotion-focused coping style, repressors attempt to inhibit or avoid information and their emotional responses so they can view themselves as emotionally imperturbable. Newton and Contrada (1992) found that repressors displayed the greatest discrepancy between self-reporting and physiological measures of anxiety when their behavior was being observed. This suggests that repression is most likely to occur in a social context.

Is repression healthy? Accumulating evidence suggests not. Emotional suppression activates the sympathetic division of the autonomic nervous system, functioning much like a stressor in elevating blood pressure and triggering the fight-or-flight response (Butler and others, 2003; Myers, 2010). Inhibited emotional expression also has been shown to contribute to greater cortisol reactivity in people with cardiovascular disease, increasing the incidence of adverse cardiac events and cardiac-related death (Whitehead, Perkins-Porras, Strike, Magid, & Steptoe, 2007). It has also been shown that the heart rate variability of repressors, which is the time between two subsequent heartbeats and depends on sympathetic and parasympathetic activity, differs from that of nonrepressors in a way that is associated with cardiac problems (see Chapter 10).

Repressive coping has been associated with the development of cancer, asthma, and diabetes (Myers and others, 2008). Although the empirical evidence for a "cancer personality" is mixed, differences in immunological markers do seem to suggest that repressors are more cancer-prone than nonrepressors.

The same is true for asthma and diabetes, which are both linked to several immune markers. Repressors have a higher number of white blood cells called *eosinophiles*, which become active in allergic diseases and infections. Research on diabetes shows that repressors have an increased level of both insulin and glucose—biomarkers that can signal an emerging resistance to insulin and the development of Type 2 diabetes (Mund and Mitte, 2012).

There is a strong relationship among repression, avoidance coping, and various types of negative affect, including pessimism, depression, and generalized anxiety (Hildebrandt & Hayes, 2012). Like explanatory style, **negative affectivity (NA),** or neuroticism, is considered one of the Big Five global personality traits that reflect an individual's general approach to life. People who score high on measures of NA are extremely tense, anxious, insecure, jealous, hostile, and emotionally unstable.

Social Support

So far, we have focused on a person's internal resources for dealing with stress. These resources—hardiness, optimism, personal control, and disclosure—certainly play important roles in our response to stress. Yet external factors are also important, especially the degree of social support that we receive. Social ties and relationships with other people powerfully influence us, in both positive and negative ways.

Social support is ongoing assistance from and interaction with others that provides emotional concern, material assistance, or honest feedback about a situation. In stressful situations, people who perceive a high level of social support may experience less stress and may cope more effectively. Consider the evidence:

repressive coping An emotion-focused coping style in which we attempt to inhibit our emotional responses, especially in social situations, so we can view ourselves as imperturbable.

negative affectivity (NA) A coping style or personality dimension consisting of chronic negative emotions and distress; also known as neuroticism.

social support Companionship from others that conveys emotional concern, material assistance, or honest feedback about a situation.

- Faster recovery and fewer medical complications: Social support has been associated with better adjustment to and/or faster recovery from coronary artery surgery, rheumatoid arthritis, childhood leukemia, and stroke (Magni, Silvestro, Tamiello, Zanesco, & Carl, 1988; Martin & Brantley, 2004). In addition, women with strong social ties have fewer complications during childbirth (Collins, Dunkel-Schetter, Lobel, & Scrimshaw, 1993), and both women and men with high levels of social support are less likely to suffer heart attacks (Holahan, Holahan, Moos, & Brennan, 1997).

- Lower mortality rates: Having a number of close social relationships is associated with a lower risk of dying at any age. The classic example of this association comes from a survey of 7000 adults in Alameda County, California (Berkman & Syme, 1994). The researchers found that having a large number of social contacts enabled women to live an average of 2.8 years longer and men an average of 2.3 years longer than those who don't have such social contacts (Figure 5.4). These benefits to longevity remained even when health habits such as smoking, alcohol use, physical activity, obesity, and differences in SES and health status at the beginning of the study were taken into account. Similarly, a 15-year prospective study of mortality rates among Swedish men who were 50 years old at the start of the study revealed that social support was inversely related to mortality. Men with a large circle of friends whom they saw regularly were half as likely to develop heart disease or die compared with men who had little social contact or support. The impact of low levels of social support on mortality was comparable in magnitude to that of cigarette smoking (Rosengren, Wilhelmsen, & Orth-Gomer, 2004). Another study showed that cancer patients with the fewest contacts each day were 2.2 times more likely to die of cancer over a 17-year period than were those with greater social support (Spiegel, 1996).

- Less distress in the face of terminal illness: Patients who perceive a strong network of social support experience less depression and hopelessness when undergoing treatment for AIDS, diabetes, and a variety of other chronic illnesses than do patients lacking social support (Kiviruusu, Huurre, & Aro, 2007; Varni, Setoguchi, Rappaport, & Talbot, 1992).

How Social Support Makes a Difference

Clearly, the support of others can benefit our health, but how? According to the **buffering hypothesis,** social support mitigates stress indirectly by helping us cope more effectively (Cohen & McKay, 1984; Cohen & Wills, 1985). For instance, people who perceive strong social support are less likely to ruminate. Rumination tends to lead to more negative interpretations of events, triggering recall of unpleasant memories, interfering

buffering hypothesis A theory that social support produces its stress-busting effects indirectly by helping the individual cope more effectively.

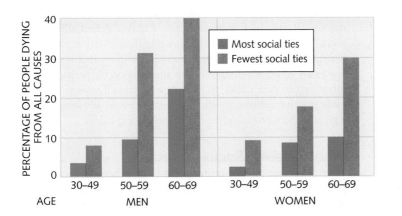

FIGURE 5.4

Social Isolation and Mortality The Alameda County Study was the first to establish a strong connection between social support and long life. Over a nine-year period, women and men with the fewest social ties were two to four times more likely to die than those who were not socially isolated.

Data from Berkman, L. F., & Syme, S. L. (1979). Social networks, host resistance, and mortality: A nine-year follow-up of Alameda County residents. *American Journal of Epidemiology, 109,* p. 190.

direct effect hypothesis
A theory that social support produces its beneficial effects during both stressful and nonstressful times by enhancing the body's physical responses to challenging situations.

with problem solving, and reducing the ruminator's interest in participating in enjoyable activities (Lyubomirsky, Caldwell, & Nolen-Hoeksema, 1998; Spasojevic & Alloy, 2001). As another example, happily married people live longer, healthier lives than those who are unmarried (Kaplan & Kronick, 2006).

According to the **direct effect hypothesis,** social support enhances the body's physical responses to challenging situations (Pilisuk, Boylan, & Acredolo, 1987). Support for the direct effect hypothesis comes from an investigation of the relationships among self-reported stress levels, the availability of social support, and circulating levels of prostate-specific antigen (PSA) in men being screened for prostate cancer (Stone, Mezzacappa, Donatone, & Gonder, 1999). Men with the highest levels of self-reported stress also had significantly higher levels of PSA—a biological marker of prostate malignancy—than their less stressed counterparts. Although stress was positively associated with PSA levels, there was an inverse correlation between PSA levels and the participants' perceived level of social support, as demonstrated by their scores on the six-item Satisfaction with Social Contacts (SSC) scale (see Figure 5.5). The SSC includes items such as "How has the number of people that you feel close to changed in the past six months?" and "How satisfied are you with the amount of social contact you have?" Those low in social support had significantly higher PSA levels than their more socially connected counterparts.

Other research studies have shown that the provision of social support, and especially the perception of supportive personal relationships, can blunt cardiovascular responses to stressful tasks and have other beneficial health outcomes (Uchino, 2009). A recent meta-analysis of 148 studies including over 308,000 participants found that support was even related to an approximately 50 percent lower risk of early mortality (Holt-Lunstad, Smith, & Layton, 2010). Another study found that the quality of one's personal relationships may affect cellular aging. Participants who felt greater ambivalence toward those in their social networks had shorter telomeres (repetitive structures at the end of chromosomes that help promote stability) than those whose relationships were less ambivalent (Uchino and others, 2012). This link was particularly strong among women and remained even after considering control variables such as age, health behaviors, and medication use. Shorter telomeres are strong predictors of mortality from a number of diseases, including cardiovascular disease, cancer, and various infectious illnesses (Willeit and others, 2010).

Remarkably, even the subliminal priming of thoughts about social relationships can have an effect. A study conducted by McKenzie Carlisle and her colleagues (2012) found that activating negative relationships in participants' memories was associated with greater feelings of threat, lower feelings of control, and higher diastolic blood pressure reactivity while they were coping with an acute psychological stressor.

The issue of how social support benefits health continues to be hotly debated. It may be that social support makes potentially stressful events more benign by diffusing or minimizing their initial impact. For example, having a supportive friend may make it less likely that you will interpret a low exam grade as evidence of low intelligence. Or perhaps the belief that other people care about you increases your self-esteem and gives you a more positive outlook on life. The result? Greater resistance to disease and a greater chance of adopting health-enhancing habits.

Who Receives Social Support?

Why are some people more likely than others to receive social support? The answer is predictable: People with better social skills—who relate well to others and who are caring and giving—create stronger

FIGURE 5.5

Stress, Social Support, and Prostate-Specific Antigen (PSA) Level of PSA was positively associated with stress and inversely related to satisfaction with social contacts. Participants who perceived low levels of stress and high satisfaction with social contacts had significantly lower levels of PSA, a biological marker of prostate malignancy.

Data from Stone, A. A., Mezzacappa, E. S., Donatone, B. A., & Gonder, M. (1999). Psychosocial stress and social support are associated with prostate-specific antigen levels in men: Results from a community screening program. *Health Psychology, 18*(5), 485.

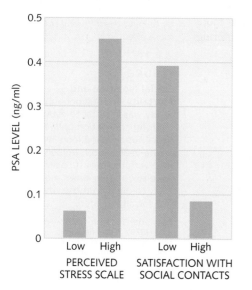

social networks and thus receive more social support. Some evidence comes from a study of college freshmen (Cohen, Sherrod, & Clark, 1986). Researchers categorized incoming students according to their social competence, social anxiety, and self-disclosure skills. Over the course of the study, they discovered that students with greater social skills were the most likely to form strong social networks.

Other researchers have found that angry or hostile people receive less social support than agreeable people do. They also report more negative life events and make people around them feel more stress (Hardy & Smith, 1988; Wager, Fieldman, & Hussey, 2003). One study found that college hostility predicted low social support, risk for depression, achieving less than expected in career and in relationships, being a current smoker, and excessive alcohol consumption at midlife (Siegler and others, 2003). Results such as these suggest an obvious intervention: To help people increase their social support, help them learn to be friendlier and less hostile.

It would seem, then, that the secret to a long, healthy life is to construct a large social network. But can a person be too socially connected? Can some social connections adversely affect our health?

Friends Can Prevent or Eliminate Stress Throughout our lives, friends can be an important stress-busting resource. If we perceive a high level of social support from our friends, we are better able to cope with stress. Social support is also associated with faster recovery and fewer medical complications after surgery, lower mortality rates, and less distress in the face of a terminal illness.

When Social Support Is Not Helpful

Sometimes social support does not reduce stress and benefit health. In fact, it may produce the opposite results. There are several reasons for this surprising fact. First, although support may be offered, a person may not perceive it as beneficial (Wilcox, Kasl, & Berkman, 1994). This may occur because the person does not want the assistance, thinks the assistance offered is inadequate, or is too distracted to notice that help has been offered. For example, in the first hours of coping with the loss of a loved one, a person may want only to be alone with his or her grief.

Second, the type of support offered may not be what is needed at the moment. For example, a single mother who is struggling to complete her college degree may feel stress during exam weeks. Although what she may need most is instrumental social support, such as assistance with child care, all that may be offered is emotional support, such as encouragement to study hard. Instrumental social support is especially valuable for controllable stressors, whereas emotional support is more helpful for uncontrollable stressors, such as a cataclysmic event or the loss of a loved one. In one study of young widows, for example, the stress of losing a spouse was best buffered by emotional support (particularly from their parents). Conversely, among working women with young infants, the only effective buffer for that stress was instrumental support from their spouses (Lieberman, 1982). The role of social support in promoting health, then, is quite specific. It is also subject to social and cultural norms concerning the types of support that are helpful (Abraido-Lanza, 2004).

Third, too much social support may actually increase a person's stress. Perhaps you know someone who is a member of too many organizations or is overwhelmed by intrusive social and family relationships. During periods of stress, this person may feel under siege in the face of all the advice and "support" that is offered (Shumaker & Hill, 1991). The critical factor appears to be having at least one close friend to confide in and share problems with. Having five, six, or even a dozen more may convey no more—and perhaps may give even less—benefit than having one or two (Langner & Michael, 1960). Table 5.2 provides a look at other factors related to effective coping.

TABLE 5.2
Other Factors Related to Effective Coping

Gratitude	People who maintain a grateful outlook on life cope better with stress. In one study, people who kept gratitude journals exercised more regularly, reported fewer physical symptoms, and felt better about their lives, compared with those who recorded hassles or neutral life events (Emmons & McCullough, 2003).
Humor	Laughter and a sense of humor help many people cope with stress. In addition to boosting mood, laughter reduces epinephrine and cortisol secretion, boosts the immune system, reduces the risk of coronary disease, lowers blood pressure, and generally promotes vascular health.
Pets	Pet ownership can reduce loneliness, help lower blood pressure, decrease secretion of cortisol and increase secretion of dopamine, oxytocin, and serotonin—three hormones associated with feelings of well-being.
Spirituality	For many people, spirituality may promote well-being and health. People who are spiritually active tend to eat healthier, exercise more, smoke less frequently, and generally have healthier lifestyles. Because spirituality is often communal, those who are active often benefit from increased social support. Spiritual activity may also promote health by fostering more positive emotions, including optimism, feelings of acceptance, and a sense that life is meaningful.

Coping Interventions

Each of us has coping skills that we have acquired over the years. These include strategies that have worked in the past, techniques that we have read about, and behaviors that we have observed in other people. In most situations, these skills are probably adequate to keep us from experiencing undue stress. Sometimes, however, the demands of a situation may exceed our coping resources. Health psychologists have played a prominent role in developing interventions that help people cope with stress. Some of these techniques, such as biofeedback and meditation, are considered forms of complementary and alternative medicine (Barnes, Bloom, & Nahin, 2008), which is explored in Chapter 15. However, the growing evidence base for the effectiveness of relaxation training, cognitive-behavioral therapy, and emotional disclosure has led to the incorporation of a number of stress management techniques into conventional medicine.

Stress management describes a variety of psychological methods designed to reduce the impact of potentially stressful experiences. These techniques were originally introduced in clinical settings to help patients adapt to chronic illnesses and stressful medical procedures, but now they are used widely. For example, occupational groups (especially health care providers, emergency services personnel, students, and teachers) and people in disadvantaged personal circumstances (such as family caregivers, single parents, the unemployed, and victims of assault or abuse) all benefit from stress-management techniques.

So do students making the transition from high school to college. Consider how stressful the college experience can be. You might be living away from home for the first time, perhaps crammed into a crowded dorm room with people who have very different backgrounds, personalities, and habits. Your professors may seem gruff, and the coursework may be more challenging and accelerated than you expected. You're forced to study more than ever, often under noisy circumstances and with inadequate sleep and campus food that doesn't sit well in your stomach.

To help new students cope with these challenges, many colleges make stress-management programs available. A typical program involves three phases: education, acquiring skills, and practicing skills. In the first phase, participants learn what stress

stress management The various psychological methods designed to reduce the impact of potentially stressful experiences.

According to researchers Gump and Matthews (2000), people who take regular vacations are less likely to die prematurely, especially from heart disease. Bring along your iPad or smartphone, however, and you won't reap the full stress-busting effects of time off—you'll be on guard for potential stress.

is, how it takes a toll on health, and that stress is more a process of their own cognitive appraisal than a characteristic of situations themselves. Next, they are trained to monitor stress in their everyday lives using some of the techniques of ecological momentary assessment. For instance, they learn to observe their own behavior closely and to record when, and under what circumstances, they feel stress. Participants are also encouraged to keep track of their emotional, physical, and behavioral reactions to the stressors they've identified. By charting this information, students can learn to recognize, and then focus on, events and people who are stress carriers that seem to be regular "triggers" of their stress. They also may begin to see an unhealthy pattern in their own behavioral responses to these circumstances, such as emotional eating, oversleeping, or using alcohol and other drugs.

The next phase of stress management involves learning new skills to either eliminate potential stressors or to reduce the experience of stress in healthy ways. There are many techniques available to help people manage stress more effectively. We will consider relaxation training first.

Relaxation Therapies

Although relaxation techniques have been used since antiquity, modern use is usually traced to Edmond Jacobson (1938), whose **progressive muscle relaxation** technique forms the cornerstone for many modern relaxation procedures. In progressive relaxation, you first tense a particular muscle (such as the forehead) and hold that tension for about 10 seconds. Then you slowly release the tension, focusing on the soothing feeling as the tension drains away. Then you tense, then relax other major muscle groups, including the mouth, eyes, neck, arms, shoulders, thighs, stomach, calves, feet, and toes. After practicing the relaxation technique for several weeks, you will identify the particular spots in your body that tense up during moments of stress, such as the jaw or fists. As you become more aware of these reactions, you can learn to relax these muscles at will.

progressive muscle relaxation A form of relaxation training that reduces muscle tension through a series of tensing and relaxing exercises involving the body's major muscle groups.

In another training technique, the **relaxation response,** participants assume the meditative state described below, in which metabolism slows and blood pressure lowers. Cardiologist Herbert Benson became intrigued with the possibility that relaxation might be an antidote to stress when he found that experienced meditators could lower their heart rate, blood lactate level (a by-product of physical exercise that creates the "burn" of muscular exertion), blood pressure, and oxygen consumption (1996). Benson identified four requirements for achieving the relaxation response:

relaxation response A meditative state of relaxation in which metabolism slows and blood pressure lowers.

- A quiet place in which distractions and external stimulation are minimized
- A comfortable position, such as sitting in an easy chair
- A mental device, such as focusing your attention on a single thought or word and repeating it over and over
- A passive, nonjudgmental attitude

There is considerable evidence that relaxation training can help patients cope with a variety of stress-related problems, including hypertension, tension headaches, depression, lower back pain, adjustment to chemotherapy, and anxiety (Smith, 2005). Underlying the effectiveness of these techniques is their ability to reduce heart rate, muscle tension, and blood pressure, as well as self-reported tension and anxiety. Moreover, these techniques generally have been found to be more effective than placebos in reducing pain and alleviating stress.

Deep Breathing and Visualization

When we're stressed, our breathing is often short and hurried. Simply slowing it down by taking long, deep breaths can help induce relaxation. You can try this yourself. Inhale slowly, and then exhale slowly. Count slowly to five as you inhale, and then count slowly to five as you exhale. As you exhale, note how your body relaxes. The keys to deep breathing are to breathe with your diaphragm, or abdomen, rather than your chest, and to take at least as long to exhale each breath as you did to inhale. Imagine a spot just below your navel. Breathe into that spot, expanding your abdomen as it fills with air. Let the air fill you from the abdomen up, then let it out, like deflating a balloon. Each long, slow exhalation should make you feel more relaxed.

Breathing techniques are often combined with matching visualization (guided mental imagery)—a form of focused relaxation used to create peaceful images in your mind—a "mental escape." In guided imagery, the participant is directed to recall or create a pleasant, relaxing image, focusing attention on sensory details such as sensations of color, sound, and touch. Visualization is powerful enough to reduce, or even to trigger, stress reactions in the laboratory. In one study, participants spent five minutes imagining scenes typical of their relationships with a romantic partner. Those who had earlier reported being in an unhappy relationship had significantly greater increases in salivary cortisol following the imagery (indicating higher stress) than those in happier relationships (Berry & Worthington, 2001).

To try it for yourself, find a comfortable place where you can close your eyes and begin breathing rhythmically. Breathe deeply, but make sure you do so in a natural rhythm. Now visualize relaxation entering your body as you inhale and tension leaving your body as you exhale. As you breathe, visualize your breath coming into your nostrils, going into your lungs, and expanding your chest and abdomen. Then visualize your breath going out the same way. Continue breathing, but each time you inhale, imagine that you are breathing in more relaxation. Each time you exhale, imagine that you are getting rid of a little more tension.

Finally, breathing techniques and visualization can be combined with positive self-affirmations, or self-talk, as you relax. The goal is to identify negative self-talk and convert it into healthier, positive self-talk. Here are a few positive statements you can practice:

- I am healthy and strong.
- There is nothing that I cannot handle.
- I am safe.

Mindfulness-Based Stress Reduction

mindfulness-based stress reduction (MBSR) A form of therapy that focuses on using structured meditation to promote mindfulness, a moment-to-moment, nonjudgmental awareness.

Is there a link between effective coping and being more consciously present? **Mindfulness-based stress reduction (MBSR)** was developed at the Stress Reduction Clinic at the University of Massachusetts as an adjunct to medical treatment for people with a variety of chronic health problems. Jon Kabat-Zinn, who developed MBSR, has described mindfulness as "falling awake," "coming to our senses," and "knowing what you are doing as you are actually doing it" (2005). A basic premise of mindfulness training is that in most aspects of life, people function on "automatic pilot"—a mode of behavior characterized by habit. Proponents of mindfulness training believe that stress can be reduced, and quality of life improved, by overriding "autopilot" mode and instead focusing on the present moment.

More generally, mindfulness-based cognitive therapy (MBCT) has been used to improve people's ability to self-regulate negative reactions to stress (Brown & Ryan, 2003). Neuroimaging studies have begun to explore the neural mechanisms underlying MBCT with techniques such as functional magnetic resonance imaging (fMRI). Mindfulness training seems to increase activity in the prefrontal cortex of the brain, an area important in regulating activity in the amygdala and other parts of the limbic system related to anxiety and other negative emotions (Creswell, Way, Eisenberger, & Lieberman, 2007). One study found that college students who scored high in measures of dispositional mindfulness had lower resting neural activity in the amygdala (Way, Creswell, Eisenberger, & Lieberman, 2010).

Using fMRI, another study found increased tissue density in the brain's hippocampus among participants who completed an eight-week MBSR course compared with a control group (Holzel and others, 2011). The hippocampus is believed to play a central role in mediating some of the benefits of mindfulness training due to its involvement in regulating cortical arousal and emotion (Milad and others, 2007). Structural changes in the hippocampus therefore may reflect improved function in regulating emotional responses to potential stressors. In contrast to these increases in tissue density, decreased density of the hippocampus has been associated with several pathological conditions, including major depression (Sheline, 2000) and post-traumatic stress disorder (Kasai and others, 2008).

Mindfulness training may also improve immune functioning and reduce the risk of a number of chronic medical conditions (Hofmann, Sawyer, Witt, & Oh, 2010). One prospective study found that hypertension patients who received MBCT had a 30 percent lower cardiovascular death rate over the next two decades compared to members of other treatment groups (Schneider and others, 2005). Other studies have established the efficacy of mindfulness-based interventions in reducing symptoms of generalized anxiety disorder (Roemer, Orsillo, & Salters-Pedneault, 2008), depression (Teasdale and others, 2000), substance abuse (Bowen and others, 2006), eating disorders (Tapper and others, 2009), and chronic pain (Grossman, Niemann, Schmidt, & Walach, 2004). For an easy primer on how MBSR works, see Your Health Assets: Try Mindfulness-Based Stress Reduction for Yourself.

Cognitive Behavioral Therapy

Cognitive behavioral therapy is based on the view that our way of thinking about the environment, rather than the environment itself, determines our stress level. If thinking can be changed and skills acquired to make positive changes in behavior, stress can be reduced. There are a variety of clinical interventions that use cognitive strategies, including distraction, calming self-statements, and cognitive restructuring. In distraction procedures, people learn to direct their attention away from unpleasant or stressful events. Use of pleasant imagery (also called visualization), counting aloud, and focusing attention on relaxing stimuli (such as a favorite drawing, photograph, or song) are examples of distraction.

Individuals can also be taught to silently or softly make calming, relaxing, and reassuring self-talk statements that emphasize the temporary nature of a stressor ("Let it go, that

Markus Boesch/Getty Images

Mindfulness Many people find meditation to be an effective technique for managing stress. According to research by Herbert Benson, experienced meditators can lower their heart rate, blood lactate level, blood pressure, and oxygen consumption, and so reduce or even eliminate the effects of stress. However, other studies have shown that meditation does not achieve these results more reliably than other forms of relaxation.

cognitive behavioral therapy The use of principles from learning theory to change unhealthy patterns of thinking and behavior.

Your Health Assets

Try Mindfulness-Based Stress Reduction for Yourself

Mindfulness-based stress reduction (MBSR) has been shown to have many benefits, including increased attention, an improved immune response to disease, reduced stress hormones, and perhaps even a higher quality of life. Following are a few suggestions for how to try MBSR:

- Next time you are outside, take several deep breaths. What is the air like? Is it warm or cold? How does the air feel on your body? Try to accept that feeling and not resist it.

- Eat your next meal in silence. Don't do anything but focus on your food. Eat slowly, and savor each bite.

- One morning when you can, take time at the beginning of the day to sit alone and think. Focus on your breathing. Gaze out the window and listen to the sounds outdoors.

- At work or school, try to stop for a few moments each hour. Note how your body feels. Let yourself regroup, and allow your mind to settle before you return to what you were doing.

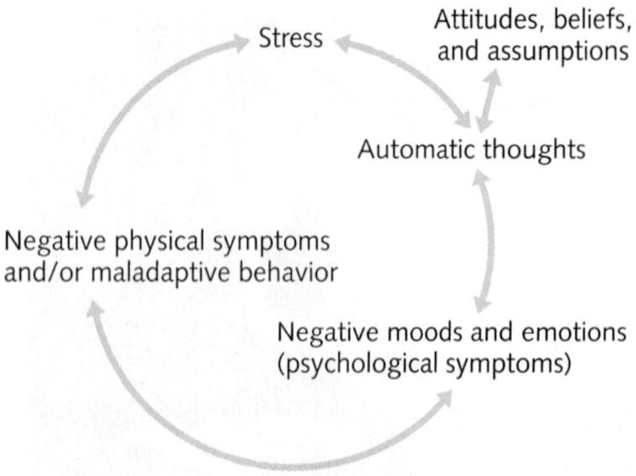

Stress

Attitudes, beliefs, and assumptions

Automatic thoughts

Negative physical symptoms and/or maladaptive behavior

Negative moods and emotions (psychological symptoms)

FIGURE 5.6

The Negative Stress Cycle Stressful events interpreted through a pessimistic, self-defeating style create a negative mood that leads to stress-related physical symptoms and fuels additional stress. Fortunately, this vicious cycle can be interrupted at any point.

stress inoculation training A cognitive behavioral treatment in which people identify stressors in their lives and learn skills for coping with them so that when those stressors occur, they are able to put those skills into effect.

rude driver won't get to me."), are aimed at reducing autonomic arousal ("Stay calm now, breathe deeply, and count to 10."), or are directed at preserving a sense of personal control ("I can handle this."). In our opening story, Kris Goldsmith's therapist might have helped him to learn self-calming techniques and to maintain a sense of self-control.

Cognitive restructuring is a generic term that describes a variety of psychological interventions directed at replacing maladaptive, self-defeating thoughts with healthier adaptive thinking. These interventions aim to break the vicious cycle of negative thinking, which pessimistically distorts perceptions of everyday events and prevents adaptive coping behaviors (Belar & Deardorff, 1996) (Figure 5.6). Therapists teach clients to reinterpret their thoughts in a less negative way and to raise awareness of distorted and maladaptive thinking.

This reciprocal relationship between maladaptive thinking and unhealthy behaviors is well documented. For example, focusing on a negative experience at work can affect your mood and lead to a tension headache. Having a tension headache can sour your mood, which in turn can make your thoughts more pessimistic.

Cognitive Behavioral Stress Management

Cognitive behavioral stress management (CBSM) combines relaxation training, visualization, cognitive restructuring, reinforcement, and other techniques into a multimodal intervention that has helped people cope with a range of stressors. CBSM often begins by teaching people to confront stressful events with a variety of coping strategies that can be used before the events become overwhelming. In this way, individuals are able to "inoculate" themselves against the potentially harmful effects of stress (Antoni, Ironson, & Scheiderman, 2007). Many stress inoculation programs offer an array of techniques so that a client can choose the strategies that work best for him or her.

Stress inoculation training is a three-stage process, with the therapist using a weakened dose of a stressor in an attempt to build immunity against the full-blown stressor (Meichenbaum, 2007). The stages are as follows:

■ Stage 1: Reconceptualization. Patients reconceptualize the source of their stress. Imagine that you are agonizing over an upcoming dental procedure, such as a root canal. During the first stage of stress inoculation training, you would learn that your discomfort is at least partially the result of psychological factors, such as dwelling on how much the procedure is going to hurt. Once you are convinced that some of your pain is psychological in nature, you will be more likely to accept that cognitive behavior therapy can offer some relief.

■ Stage 2: Skills acquisition. Next, you will be taught relaxation and controlled breathing skills. The logic is inescapable: Being relaxed is incompatible with being tense and physically aroused. Therefore, learning to relax at will is a valuable tool in managing pain. Other techniques that you might learn include the use of pleasant mental imagery, dissociation, or humor.

■ Stage 3: Follow-through. Now you will learn to use these coping skills in everyday life. You will be encouraged to increase your physical activity and to take pain medication on a timed daily schedule, rather than whenever you feel pain. Your family members may be taught ways of reinforcing your new healthier behaviors.

CBSM has proved to be effective in helping people cope with a variety of stress-related problems, including job stress (Kawaharada and others, 2009), hypertension (Amigo, Buceta, Becona, & Bueno, 1991), post-traumatic stress disorder (Ponniah & Hollon, 2009), depression associated with breast cancer (Antoni and others, 2009), prostate cancer (Penedo and others, 2004), and AIDS (Antoni and others, 2001). CBSM also has been shown to reduce HPA axis hormones (see Chapter 4) among symptomatic human immunodeficiency virus (HIV)–infected men (Antoni and others, 2001) and reduce postsurgical pain, rehabilitation, and the number of health service visits among competitive athletes (Perna and others, 2003).

Emotional Disclosure

In the 1980s, psychologist James Pennebaker began a fascinating series of studies with college students, most of whom followed this simple protocol: The students were asked to write about an assigned topic for 15 minutes a day for four days. Half of the participants wrote about everyday, ordinary experiences—describing their dorm rooms, for instance. The other students were told to write about their deepest thoughts and feelings regarding a stressful or traumatic experience. Students in the emotional disclosure group took immediately to the task and wrote intimate, gripping stories, sometimes crying and displaying other strong emotional reactions. At the end of the study, most reported that the experience had helped them find new meaning in the traumatic experience. The most striking result, however, came six months later, at the end of the school year, when Pennebaker discovered that those who had written about stressful experiences had visited the university health center far less often than did the students who had written about everyday things (Pennebaker & Susman, 1988).

Over the past 25 years, Pennebaker's finding has been repeated in dozens of settings with scores of people from different walks of life, ethnicities, and cultural backgrounds. The people writing or, alternatively, confiding verbally to a confidante have been prison inmates, crime victims, chronic pain sufferers, Holocaust survivors, college students, bereaved widows and widowers, business executives, and laid-off workers, among others. In almost every instance, emotional disclosure is related to some sort of positive health benefit.

When people write or talk about traumatic events, for instance, skin conductivity, heart rate, and systolic and diastolic blood pressure all decrease (Pennebaker, Hughes, & O'Heeron, 1997). Over time, keeping a daily journal of thoughts and feelings has been associated with decreased absenteeism, fewer medical visits, and even improved immune functioning (Pennebaker & Francis, 1996; Petrie, Booth, & Davison, 1995). In one study, medical students were randomly assigned to write about traumatic events or control topics for four daily sessions. On the fifth day, each received a vaccination for hepatitis B, with boosters administered one and four months later. Before each vaccination, and again six months later, blood samples revealed that participants in the disclosure group had significantly higher antibody levels against the virus.

There are many reasons why **emotional disclosure** may help us cope with stress. Interestingly, people who have been diagnosed with alexithymia, or difficulty in identifying and expressing their own emotions, have been linked to increased cardiovascular mortality (Tolmunen, Lehto, Heliste, Kurl, & Kauhanen, 2010). Writing or talking about stressful experiences may help lower this risk. Confiding in others may allow us to gain helpful advice. It also may provide a source of reinforcement and social support, as well as eliminate the need to ruminate about and inhibit a stressful event, which may reduce the physiological activity linked to the event (Stanton, 2010). Finally, writing or talking about a stressful experience may encourage cognitive reappraisal as we gain a new perspective on the event or develop a plan to deal with a stressful situation (Lestideau &

Photodisc/Getty Images

Expressive Writing Journal writing and other techniques that promote emotional disclosure can have a variety of health benefits.

emotional disclosure A therapeutic activity in which people express their strong, often stress-related emotions by writing or talking about the events that triggered them.

FIGURE 5.7

A Biopsychosocial View of Coping with and Managing Stress

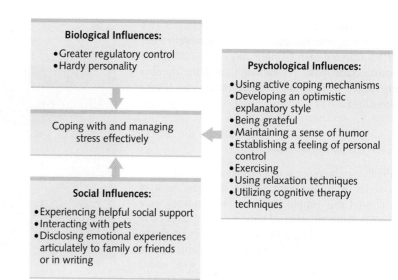

Biological Influences:
- Greater regulatory control
- Hardy personality

Psychological Influences:
- Using active coping mechanisms
- Developing an optimistic explanatory style
- Being grateful
- Maintaining a sense of humor
- Establishing a feeling of personal control
- Exercising
- Using relaxation techniques
- Utilizing cognitive therapy techniques

Coping with and managing stress effectively

Social Influences:
- Experiencing helpful social support
- Interacting with pets
- Disclosing emotional experiences articulately to family or friends or in writing

Lavallee, 2007). In support of this latter idea, Pennebaker has found that people who write the most coherent, persuasive, and well-organized stories tend to experience the greatest health benefits (Niederhoffer & Pennebaker, 2002). Similarly, women who had recently lost a close relative to breast cancer and who were asked to write daily about the death were most likely to demonstrate a bolstered immune response (increased natural killer cell cytotoxicity) when daily written disclosure enabled them to find positive meaning from the loss (Bower, Kemeny, Taylor, & Fahey, 2003). A meta-analysis of studies indicates that emotional disclosure may be more effective in helping people cope with physical rather than psychological challenges (Frisina, Borod, & Lepore, 2004).

We all experience stress, but we don't all cope with it effectively. Our coping resources can best be understood from a biopsychosocial perspective. We cannot control all of the factors. For example, we are affected by our genetic makeup, our personality type, and reactivity, with the most mindful and the least reactive among us coping best. However, the many psychological and social factors affecting our ability to cope with and then manage our stress are well within our control, as shown in Figure 5.7. Pursue these techniques actively, and watch your health improve.

Weigh In on Health

Respond to each question below based on what you learned in the chapter. (Tip: Use the items in "Summing Up" to take into account related biological, psychological, and social concerns.)

1. Imagine that your roommate—a male from a middle-class family and a minority background—learns that he has failed courses in his major, which will put him on academic probation. If he asks your advice about how to cope with the stress he is facing, what strategies would you suggest and why? Would you have any cautionary

data to share with him based on what you've read about stress in relationship to gender, socioeconomic status, or ethnicity?

2. How would you describe yourself in terms of explanatory style, personal control and choice, social support, and any other factors discussed in this chapter? From what you have read, can you list a few ways in which you might improve your stress responses and possibly improve the way in which you cope with stressful situations?

Summing Up

Responding to Stress

1. Coping refers to the various ways—sometimes healthy, sometimes unhealthy—in which people attempt to prevent, eliminate, weaken, or simply tolerate stress.

2. Problem-focused coping refers to efforts to deal directly with a stressor by applying problem-solving skills to anticipate and prevent potential stressors or by directly confronting the source of stress. Emotion-focused coping refers to efforts to control your emotional response to a stressor, either by distancing yourself from it or by changing how you appraise it.

3. Rumination refers to thinking repetitively about an upsetting situation and how it relates to past and future problems associated with a stressor. This may spiral out of control into an emotional cascade, a vicious cycle in which intense rumination makes the person more upset, which in turn causes more rumination.

4. Emotional-approach coping (EAC) is comprised of two emotion-regulating processes: emotional processing and emotional expression. EAC, which involves working through our emotional reactions to a stressful event, is adaptive and healthy.

5. When people experience potentially traumatizing events, those who carry risk mutations in their genotype, such as the APOE allele, may be more susceptible to unfavorable health outcomes, perhaps because of how they psychologically appraise and cope with stressors.

6. How people cope with a stressor is influenced by a number of external resources, including family, friends, education, employment, time, money, and the presence of other stressors. People who have more resources available typically cope with stressful events more successfully because they have more options available to them.

7. One of the most influential resources with respect to health is socioeconomic status (SES). People who are low in SES have increased risk for chronic disease, disability, and premature mortality.

8. Compared to women, men react to stress with larger increases in blood pressure, low-density lipoprotein cholesterol, and certain stress hormones. In general, women report more symptoms of stress and are more emotionally responsive to stressful situations. When women and men of similar SES are compared, gender differences in coping styles disappear. People of higher SES are more likely than those of lower SES to use problem-focused coping strategies in dealing with stress. Low SES is often accompanied by a stressful lifestyle that limits a person's options in coping with stress.

9. Hispanic-, Asian-, and African-Americans often report higher levels of social stress than European-Americans, including discrimination. A particularly insidious type of discrimination that people of color experience daily are microaggressions from well-intentioned people who seem unaware of the hidden messages that they are sending.

Factors Affecting the Ability to Cope

10. People whose explanatory style is negative tend to explain failures in terms that are global, stable, and internal. This, in turn, may increase their sensitivity to challenging events and promote self-blame, pessimism, and depression. In contrast, optimists may be healthier and more resistant to stress. Optimism is also related to greater perceived control and self-efficacy, which in turn are related to more effective coping responses.

11. The opportunity to control aversive events plays a crucial role in determining a person's response to a stressful situation. Biologically, exposure to stressors without the perception of control activates the autonomic nervous system. The perception of control buffers stress-related arousal and enhances immune activity.

12. Cardiovascular reactivity is a biological marker of individual differences in regulatory control during moments of stress. People with high vagal tone experience less negative emotional arousal in response to stress. They are also more likely to rely on constructive coping measures than are people who exercise less regulatory control.

13. According to the reactivity hypothesis, people who have exaggerated cardiovascular responses to stress have increased risk of developing hypertension and heart disease.

14. There is a strong relationship among repression, avoidance coping, and various types of negative affect, including pessimism, depression, and generalized anxiety. People who score high on measures of negativity are extremely tense, anxious, insecure, jealous, hostile, and emotionally unstable.

15. People who perceive a high level of social support may cope with stress more effectively than people who feel alienated. Along with companionship, social ties can provide emotional support, instrumental support, and informational support. Social support produces its beneficial effects indirectly, by helping people cope more effectively (buffering hypothesis), or directly, by enhancing the body's responses to challenging events (direct effect hypothesis).

16. People with better social skills—who relate well to others and who are caring and giving—create stronger social networks and thus receive more social support. Social support does not always reduce stress and benefit health, however. Sometimes, support is perceived as intrusive; other times, the type of support offered is not what is needed.

Coping Interventions

17. Relaxation techniques such as progressive muscle relaxation and the relaxation response (meditation) can help people cope with a variety of stress-related problems, including hypertension, headaches, chronic pain, and anxiety. Mindfulness-based stress reduction focuses on using structured meditation to promote mindfulness, a moment-to-moment, nonjudgmental awareness.

18. Cognitive behavioral therapy is based on the view that our way of thinking about the environment, rather than the environment itself, determines our stress level. If thinking can be changed and skills acquired to make positive changes in behavior, stress can be reduced.

19. Cognitive behavioral stress management is a multimodal form of therapy that helps people to confront stressful events with coping strategies that can be put in place before stressors become overwhelming.

20. Expressive writing and other techniques that promote emotional disclosure have a variety of health benefits.

Key Terms and Concepts to Remember

coping, p. 115
problem-focused coping, p. 116
emotion-focused coping, p. 116
rumination, p. 116
emotional cascade, p. 116
emotional-approach coping (EAC), p. 116
psychological control, p. 118
microaggressions, p. 120
minority stress theory, p. 122

resilience, p. 122
explanatory style, p. 123
optimistic bias, p. 125
personal control, p. 126
regulatory control, p. 127
cardiovascular reactivity (CVR), p. 128
reactivity hypothesis, p. 128
repressive coping, p. 130
negative affectivity (NA), p. 130
social support, p. 130

buffering hypothesis, p. 131
direct effect hypothesis, p. 132
stress management, p. 134
progressive muscle relaxation, p. 135
relaxation response, p. 135
mindfulness-based stress reduction (MBSR), p. 136
cognitive behavioral therapy, p. 137
stress inoculation training, p. 138
emotional disclosure, p. 139

LaunchPad
macmillan learning

To accompany your textbook, you have access to a number of online resources, including quizzes for every chapter of the book, flashcards, critical thinking exercises, videos, and *Check Your Health* inventories. To access these resources, please visit the Straub *Health Psychology* LaunchPad solo at: **launchpadworks.com**

PART  3

Behavior and Health

CHAPTER 6

Staying Healthy: Primary Prevention and Positive Psychology

W hen Sara Snodgrass found a lump in her breast, her first thoughts were of her aunt and mother, both of whom died after battling breast cancer. After her aunt was diagnosed with cancer, she "went home, pulled all the curtains closed, refused to leave the house except for chemotherapy treatments, and allowed very few visitors. She waited for death" (Snodgrass, 1998, p. 3). Sara's biopsy was followed by a lumpectomy (removal of the malignant tumor) and two months of radiation treatments. Although she and her doctor were hopeful that she was through with cancer, less than one year later, metastasized (widely spread) cancer was found in her abdomen. In her words, she has been "submerged in cancer" ever since, having undergone three surgeries, five different courses of chemotherapy, two types of hormone therapy, three months of radiation, a bone marrow transplant, and a stem cell transplant. Throughout her treatment, she also has battled unpredictable, debilitating pain 10 to 14 days per month.

Unlike her aunt, however, Sara continued her work as a university professor throughout her surgery, radiation, and chemotherapy. Determined that cancer would not interfere with her life, she also continued scuba diving, skiing, and other activities that flowed from her natural optimism, sense of self-mastery, and confidence. And she took charge of her health care, learning everything she could about her treatments, making her own decisions, and refusing to work with doctors who did not treat her with respect and honor her desire to maintain a sense of control over her life.

Perhaps most remarkable of all is Sara's conviction that her cancer has led to a reorganization of her self-perception, relationships, and philosophy of life. It has taught her to live more in the present rather than to be concerned about the future. She stopped worrying about whether she would find the right man, whether her students would give her good evaluations, and whether she would have enough money to live comfortably in retirement. She also has learned that relationships with friends and family are the most important part of her life. When thinking about dying, she asserts, "I will not say I wish I had written more articles. However, I might say I wish I had seen or talked to more friends or acquaintances with whom I had lost contact." So that is what she is doing—corresponding, telephoning, and traveling to renew old relationships, and reveling in new ones that have extended her network of social support throughout the country.

Sometimes illness cannot be prevented, as in Sara's case. Yet even in such extreme cases, building our human strengths may allow us the capacity to thrive. In this chapter, we will consider the connection between behavior and health, and then explore how health psychology's biopsychosocial approach to prevention, first, and positive psychology, second, can help build healthy individuals, families, and communities.

Health and Behavior

It is difficult to imagine an activity or behavior that does not influence health in some way. **Health behaviors** are actions that people take to improve or maintain their health. Exercising regularly, using sunscreen, eating a healthy diet, sleeping well, practicing safe sex, and wearing seatbelts are all behaviors that help "immunize" you against disease and injury, while activities such as meditation and laughter help many people manage stress and remain upbeat.

Because they occur on a continuum, some health behaviors can have both a positive and a negative impact on health. For example, exercise and dieting are often beneficial, but if carried to the extreme, they can actually be hazardous to health. Other behaviors influence health indirectly, through their association with behaviors that have a direct impact on health. Many people who drink coffee excessively, for example, also smoke and engage in other risky behaviors that increase the risk of heart disease (Cornelis, El-Sohemy, Kabagambe, & Campos, 2006).

As part of its *Youth Risk Behavior Surveillance* project, the Centers for Disease Control and Prevention identified six health-risk behaviors—often begun while young—that put people at risk for premature death, disability, and chronic illness (YRBSS, 2013):

1. Smoking and other forms of tobacco use

2. Eating high-fat and low-fiber foods

3. Not engaging in enough physical activity

4. Abusing alcohol or other drugs (including prescription drugs)

5. Not using proven medical methods for preventing or diagnosing disease early (e.g., flu shots, practicing healthy sexual behaviors, Pap smears, colonoscopies, mammograms)

6. Engaging in violent behavior or behavior that may cause unintentional injuries (e.g., driving while intoxicated)

health behavior A health-enhancing behavior or habit.

FIGURE 6.1

Health Behaviors and Death Rate Nine and a half years into the famous Alameda Health Study, the mortality of men who regularly practiced all seven health habits (sleeping seven to eight hours daily, never smoking, being at or near a healthy body weight, moderate use of alcohol, regular physical exercise, eating breakfast, and avoiding between-meal snacking) was 28 percent of the mortality of those who had practiced three or fewer healthy behaviors.

Data from Housman, J., & Dorman, S. (2005). The Alameda County study: A systematic, chronological review. *American Journal of Health Education*, 33(5), 302–308.

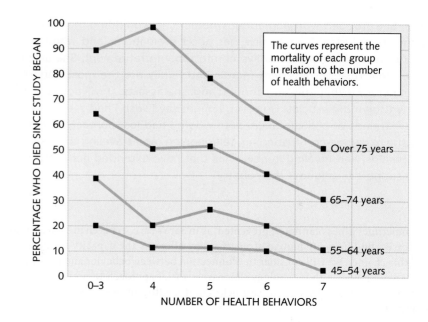

The curves represent the mortality of each group in relation to the number of health behaviors.

Some behaviors (not wearing a seatbelt) affect health immediately, while others (eating a healthy diet) have a long-term effect. Still others (exercising or smoking) have both immediate *and* long-term effects on health. Health behaviors also interact and are often interrelated. The combined interactive effect of smoking, drinking alcohol, and consuming too much coffee, for example, is stronger than that of only one such behavior. Similarly, exercising, eating healthy foods, and drinking a lot of water also tend to come together, but in a positive way.

What is the potential impact of adopting a healthier lifestyle? In one classic epidemiological study begun in 1965, Lester Breslow and Norman Breslow began to track the health and lifestyle habits of male residents of Alameda County, California. Over the many years of this landmark study, the salutary effects of seven healthy habits—sleeping seven to eight hours daily, never smoking, being at or near a healthy body weight, moderate use of alcohol, regular physical exercise, eating breakfast, and avoiding between-meal snacking—have proved striking (Figure 6.1) (1993).

Theories of Health Behavior

Health psychologists have developed a number of theories to explain why people engage (or do not engage) in healthful or unhealthful behaviors. In this section, we discuss several of the most influential theories.

The Health Belief Model (HBM)

health belief model (HBM)
A nonstage theory that identifies four factors that influence decision making regarding health behavior: perceived susceptibility to a health threat, perceived severity of the disease or condition, perceived benefits of and barriers to the behavior, and cues to action.

According to the **health belief model (HBM),** decisions about health behavior are based on four interacting factors that influence our perceptions about health threats (see Figure 6.2) (Strecher & Rosenstock, 1997):

- *Perceived susceptibility.* Some people worry constantly about health threats such as HIV; others believe that they are not in danger. The greater the perceived susceptibility, the stronger the motivation to engage in health-promoting behaviors. Adolescents especially seem to live their lives following an *invincibility fable,* which gives them little motivation to change risky behaviors.

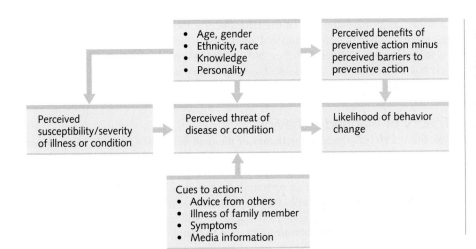

FIGURE 6.2

The Health Belief Model This nonstage theory emphasizes the interacting factors that influence our decision making about health behaviors. If we believe that an available course of action will reduce our susceptibility to or the severity of the condition, then we will engage in that health behavior.

Source: Strecher, V. J., & Rosenstock, I. W. (1997). The health belief model. In A. Baum, S. Newman, J. Weinman, R. West, & C. McManus (Eds.), *Cambridge handbook of psychology, health, and medicine.* Cambridge, UK: Cambridge University Press, 115.

- *Perceived severity of the health threat.* Among the factors considered are whether pain, disability, or death may result, as well as whether the condition will have an impact on family, friends, and coworkers.

- *Perceived benefits of and barriers to treatment.* In evaluating the pros and cons of a particular health behavior, a person decides whether its perceived benefits exceed its barriers. For example, someone may overlook the huge advantages of quitting smoking due to concerns about becoming overweight and unattractive.

- *Cues to action.* Advice from friends, media health campaigns, and factors such as age, socioeconomic status, and gender also will influence the likelihood that the person will act.

In summary, the HBM is a commonsense theory proposing that people will take action to ward off or control illness-inducing conditions if (1) they regard themselves as susceptible, (2) they believe the condition has serious personal consequences, (3) they believe a course of action will reduce either their susceptibility or the severity of the condition, (4) they believe that the benefits of the action outweigh the costs, and (5) environmental influences are encouraging change.

The HBM has been subjected to extensive research. People are more likely to have regular dental checkups, practice safe sex, eat in a healthy way, obtain health screenings for colorectal and other forms of cancer, and engage in other health-protective behaviors if they feel susceptible to the various health problems that might stem from failure to do so (Deshpande, Basil, & Basil, 2009). Importantly, interventions aimed at changing health beliefs increase health-protective behaviors.

Despite these successes, some studies have found that health beliefs only modestly predict health behaviors and that other factors, such as perceived barriers to action, are also important determinants (Chen, Fox, Cantrell, Stockdale, & Kagawa-Singer, 2007). One such barrier occurs when people don't believe they are capable of changing their behavior. *Protection Motivation Theory* (PMT) adds *self-efficacy* as a separate component, focusing not only on how people appraise threats to their health, but also on their ability to manage these threats by acting more healthfully (Rogers, 1975). A large meta-analysis of research on PMT found that increases in self-efficacy worked hand in hand with threat severity in promoting a wide range of health behaviors (Floyd, Prentice-Dunn, & Rogers, 2000).

Cigarette? Health psychologists have developed a number of theories to explain why people smoke and engage (or do not engage) in other unhealthy behaviors.

iStock/Getty Images

Other critics have argued that the HBM focuses too heavily on attitudes about perceived risk rather than on emotional responses, which may more accurately predict behavior (Lawton, Conner, & Parker, 2007). The HBM represents an important perspective, but it is incomplete. Let's look at another theory now that focuses on the role that intentions and self-efficacy play in the practice of health behaviors.

Theory of Planned Behavior

Like the health belief model, the **theory of planned behavior (TPB)** specifies relationships among attitudes and behavior (see Figure 6.3). The theory maintains that the best way to predict whether a health behavior will occur is to measure **behavioral intention—** the decision to either engage in or refrain from a health-related behavior. Behavioral intentions are shaped by three factors: 1) *attitude toward the behavior,* which is determined by the belief that engaging in the behavior will lead to certain outcomes; 2) the **subjective norm,** which reflects our motivation to comply with the views of other people regarding the behavior in question; and 3) *perceived behavioral control,* which refers to our expectation of success in performing the health behavior. So, for instance, we may decide that reducing the amount of sugar in our diet is a good thing to do because 1) we believe that doing so will lead to weight loss; 2) our relatives and friends are following similar diets; and 3) we are confident that we will be able to shop for healthy ingredients, make the time to prepare meals, and still enjoy the flavor of food even though our diet is more restricted.

The specific intention to adopt or change a health behavior (what, when, where) can, indeed, help to bring it about (McEachan and others, 2011). People's self-reported attitudes and intentions predict a variety of health-promoting actions, including genetic testing for diseases, taking medication (Goldring and others, 2002), reducing consumption of soft drinks among teens (Kassem & Lee, 2004), healthy eating (Conner, Norman, & Bell, 2002), condom use (Bogart & Delahanty, 2004), and not smoking (Van de Ven, Engels, Otten, & Van Den Eijnden, 2007), among others.

Given its emphasis on planning, it is not surprising that the TPB is most accurate in predicting intentional behaviors that are goal-oriented and fit within a rational framework (Gibbons, Gerrard, Blanton, & Russell, 1998). In some cases, such as substance abuse (Morojele & Stephenson, 1994), premarital sexual behavior (Cha, Doswell, Kim, Charron-Prochownik, & Patrick, 2007), and drunk driving (Stacy, Bentler, & Flay, 1994), the model has been less successful, perhaps because these behaviors are often reactions to social situations. For example, young people may attend a party where others are smoking marijuana or drinking excessively, or they may agree to the demands of an overzealous girlfriend or boyfriend who wants to have sex.

---

theory of planned behavior (TPB) A theory that predicts health behavior on the basis of three factors: personal attitude toward the behavior, the subjective norm regarding the behavior, and perceived degree of control over the behavior.

behavioral intention In theories of health behavior, the rational decision to engage in a health-related behavior or to refrain from engaging in the behavior.

subjective norm An individual's interpretation of the views of other people regarding a particular health-related behavior.

FIGURE 6.3

Theory of Planned Behavior This theory predicts that a person's decision to engage in a particular health behavior is based on three factors: personal attitude toward the behavior, the subjective norm regarding the behavior, and perceived degree of control over the behavior.

Source: Sutton, S. R. (1997). The theory of planned behavior. In A. Baum, S. Newman, J. Weinman, R. West, & C. McManus (Eds.), *Cambridge handbook of psychology, health, and medicine.* Cambridge, UK: Cambridge University Press, 177.

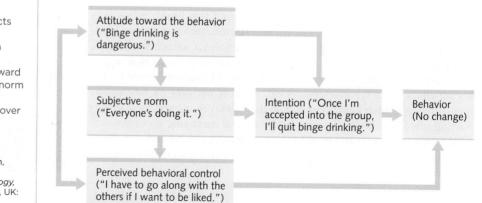

The Transtheoretical Model

The theories of health behavior that we have considered thus far attempt to identify variables that influence health-related attitudes and behaviors and combine them into a formula that predicts the probability that a particular individual will act in a certain way in a given situation. The **transtheoretical model (TTM)** (also called the *stages of change model*), on the other hand, maintains that behavior often changes systematically through distinct stages (Rothman, 2000).

The TTM contends that people progress through five stages in altering health-related behaviors. The stages are defined in terms of past behavior and intentions for future action:

Stage 1: Precontemplation. During this stage, people are not seriously thinking about changing their behavior. They may even refuse to acknowledge that their behavior needs changing.

Stage 2: Contemplation. During this stage, people acknowledge the existence of a problem (such as smoking) and are seriously considering changing their behavior (quitting smoking) in the near future (typically within six months).

Stage 3: Preparation. This stage includes both thoughts and actions. In preparing to quit smoking, for example, a person obtains a prescription for a nicotine patch, joins a support group, enlists family support, and makes other specific plans.

Stage 4: Action. During this stage, people have actually changed their behavior and are trying to sustain their efforts.

Stage 5: Maintenance. People in this stage continue to be successful in their efforts to reach their final goal. Although this stage can last indefinitely, its length is often set arbitrarily at six months.

The TTM recognizes that people move back and forth through the stages in a nonlinear, spiral fashion (Velicer & Prochaska, 2008). Figure 6.4 illustrates a smoker's progression through the five stages of change in quitting smoking. Many recently reformed ex-smokers relapse from *maintenance* to *preparation*, cycling through stages 2 to 5 one or more times until they have completed their behavioral change.

transtheoretical model (TTM) A stage theory that contends that people pass through five stages in altering health-related behavior: precontemplation, contemplation, preparation, action, and maintenance.

FIGURE 6.4
The Transtheoretical Model The transtheoretical, or stages of change, model assesses a person's readiness to act on a new, healthier behavior. The model also identifies strategies and processes to guide the individual through the stages of change to successful action and maintenance. Critics point out that the stages are not mutually exclusive, and people do not always move sequentially through discrete stages as they strive to change health behaviors.

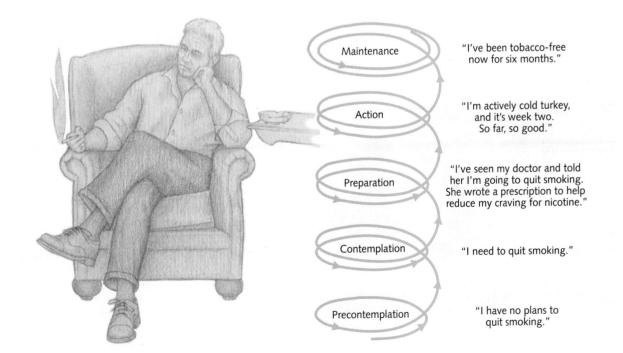

Maintenance — "I've been tobacco-free now for six months."

Action — "I'm actively cold turkey, and it's week two. So far, so good."

Preparation — "I've seen my doctor and told her I'm going to quit smoking. She wrote a prescription to help reduce my craving for nicotine."

Contemplation — "I need to quit smoking."

Precontemplation — "I have no plans to quit smoking."

Although the TTM is more successful in predicting some behaviors than others, research has generally confirmed that people at higher stages are more successful at improving health-related behaviors, such as adopting a healthier diet (Armitage, Sheeran, Conner, & Arden, 2004), exercising regularly (Hellsten, Johansson, Dahlman, Sterner, & Bjartell, 2011), using sunscreen (Adams, Norman, Hovell, Sallis, & Patrick, 2009), and testing for colorectal and breast cancer (Champion and others, 2007; Lauver, Henriques, Settersten, & Bumann, 2003).

Other research has shown that stage theories such as the TTM promote the development of more effective health interventions by providing a "recipe" for ideal behavior change (Sutton, 1996). This enables health psychologists to match an intervention to the specific needs of a person who is "stuck" at a particular stage (Perz, DiClemente, & Carbonari, 1996). The model also acknowledges that different behavioral, cognitive, and social processes may come to the forefront as we struggle to reach our ultimate health goals. These include consciousness raising (for example, seeking more information about a health-compromising behavior), counterconditioning (substituting alternative behaviors for the target behavior), and reinforcement management (rewarding oneself or being rewarded by others for success).

Addressing the Perceived Benefits of High-Risk Behaviors

Although the health belief model, theory of planned behavior, and transtheoretical model include both perceived benefits and risks, the intention of these models was primarily to explain preventive behaviors motivated by the desire to avoid disease or injury. Consequently, these models tend to focus on the risks of unhealthy behaviors rather than on any perceived *benefits* of high-risk behaviors to the individual. Researchers have found, however, that perceived benefits are important predictors of certain behaviors, such as adolescent drinking (Katz, Fromme, & D'Amico, 2000), tobacco use (Pollay, 2000), and unprotected sex (Parsons, Huszti, Crudder, Rich, & Mendoza, 2000).

In a survey of fifth, seventh, and ninth graders, Julie Goldberg and her colleagues (Goldberg, Halpern-Felsher, & Milstein, 2002) gave the participants the following scenario:

> Now imagine that you are at a party. During the party, you have a couple of drinks of alcohol (like two glasses of wine, beer, or hard liquor). Even if this is something you'd never do, please try to imagine it.

The students were then asked several open-ended questions about the good and bad things that can happen if they drink at a party. They were also asked about their actual experiences with and the consequences of drinking. Six months later, the students were asked once again about their drinking behavior.

The researchers learned a great deal by asking about the perceived benefits of drinking. More so than the fifth and seventh graders, the ninth graders perceived the physical and social benefits of alcohol (e.g., "I'll like the buzz I get from drinking"; "I'll have a better time at the party") to be more likely, and the physical and social risks (e.g., "I'll get sick"; "I'll do something that I'll later regret") to be less likely. These results have a profound implication for health education campaigns targeted at teenagers. Although researchers often have concluded that adolescents are irrational in their decision making, these results suggest that teens are in fact weighing the pros and cons of their behaviors. More effective health messages might focus on how adolescents can obtain the perceived benefits of risky health behaviors in safer ways. For example, messages might identify other ways to feel more mature and be more social at parties than by drinking.

The Power of the Social Situation For many teenagers (as well as young adults), health behaviors are often reactions to social situations rather than rationally planned responses. They drink because their friends drink, not because they have made a conscious decision that they enjoy alcohol. Social situations can trigger healthier behaviors, too, such as dancing, exercise, or enjoying another form of recreation.

The Image Bank/Getty Images

Prevention

We usually think of prevention solely in terms of efforts to modify one's risk *before* disease strikes. In fact, researchers have differentiated three types of prevention that are undertaken before, during, and after a disease strikes.

Primary prevention refers to health-promoting actions that are taken to prevent a disease or injury from occurring. Examples of primary prevention include wearing seatbelts, practicing good nutrition, exercising, avoiding smoking, maintaining healthy sleep patterns, and going regularly for health screening tests.

Secondary prevention involves actions taken to identify and treat an illness early in its course. In the case of a person who has high blood pressure, for example, secondary prevention would include regular examinations to monitor symptoms, the use of blood pressure medication, and dietary changes.

Tertiary prevention involves actions taken to contain or retard damage once a disease has progressed beyond its early stages. An example of tertiary prevention is the use of radiation therapy or chemotherapy to destroy a cancerous tumor. Tertiary prevention also strives to rehabilitate people to the fullest extent possible.

Table 6.1 illustrates a comprehensive program of primary, secondary, and tertiary disease prevention for AIDS based on the national health goals established by the U.S. Department of Health and Human Services as part of its *Healthy People Campaign*. As discussed in Chapter 1, these goals are to increase the span of healthy life, to decrease the disparities in health between different segments of the population, and to provide universal access to preventive services.

We are sometimes our own worst enemies in the battle for health. In our teens and twenties, when we are developing health-related habits, we are usually quite healthy.

primary prevention
Health-enhancing efforts to prevent disease or injury from occurring.

secondary prevention Actions taken to identify and treat an illness or disability early in its course.

tertiary prevention Actions taken to contain damage once a disease or disability has progressed beyond its early stages.

Research clearly shows that prevention is by far the best buy in health. For instance, in the United States alone (Office of the Surgeon General, 2011):

- *For every HIV infection prevented, an estimated $335,000 is saved in the cost of providing lifetime HIV treatment.*

- *A 5 percent reduction in the prevalence of hypertension would save $25 billion in 5 years.*

- *A 1 percent reduction in weight, blood pressure, glucose, and cholesterol risk factors would save $83 to $103 annually in medical costs per person.*

- *Programs that prevent diabetes quickly pay for themselves—$1 of every $5 spent on health care goes to caring for people with diabetes.*

- *Tobacco screening results in an estimated lifetime saving of $9800 per person.*

TABLE 6.1
Levels and Timing of Prevention for HIV/AIDS

Level	Primary	Secondary	Tertiary
Individual	Self-instruction guide on HIV prevention for HIV-positive people	Screening and early intervention for an uninfected, lower-risk, HIV-positive person	
	Designing an immune-healthy diet		
Group	Parents gather to gain skills to communicate better with teens about risky behaviors	Needle exchange program for low-SES, high-risk, IV drug users	Rehabilitation programs for groups of AIDS patients
Work site	Work-site educational campaign focusing on how HIV is transmitted	Work-site safer-sex incentive program (e.g., free condoms, confidential screening)	Extending leave benefits so employees can care for HIV-positive relatives
Community	Focused media campaign to promote safe-sex behaviors	Establishing support network for HIV-positive people	Providing better access to recreational facilities for those with AIDS
Society	Enforcing felony laws for knowingly infecting another person with HIV	Enacting antidiscrimination policies for HIV-positive people	Mandating the availability of HIV medications for uninsured AIDS patients

Source: Winett, R. A. (1995). A framework for health promotion and disease prevention programs. *American Psychologist, 50*(5), 341–350.

Smoking cigarettes, eating junk food, and avoiding exercise seem often to have no effect on health at this time, so young people have little immediate incentive for practicing good health behaviors and correcting poor health habits. Many health-enhancing behaviors are either less pleasurable or require more effort than their less healthy alternatives. If engaging in a behavior (such as eating when you are depressed) causes immediate relief or gratification, or if failing to engage in this behavior provides immediate discomfort, the behavior is difficult to eliminate.

High-risk sexual behaviors that may result in HIV or other sexually transmitted infections are a tragic example of this principle. The far-removed *potential* negative consequences of risky behavior too often are overshadowed by the immediate pleasures of the moment.

Compressing Morbidity

The "fountain of youth" myth is present in the histories of nearly every culture and finds its current expression in the allegedly rejuvenating elixirs, creams, and gadgets that are hawked in infomercials, on alternative medicine Web sites, and in drugstore displays. Claims that people will soon live to be 200 years old because of megadoses of antioxidants, vitamins, herbs, or some other "magic bullet" have resulted in confusion about *longevity* (long duration of life). For decades, scientists have investigated systematically people's claims of having vastly exceeded the normal life span, and in every instance, the claims could not be verified. However, even without a magic bullet, people today can expect to live much longer than previous cohorts. The major diseases of our ancestors, such as polio, smallpox, tetanus, diphtheria, and rheumatic fever, have been eradicated almost completely.

In focusing on healthy life expectancy, health psychologists aim to shorten the amount of time older people spend in *morbidity* (disabled, ill, or in pain). To illustrate, consider twin brothers who, although genetically identical and exposed to the same health hazards while growing up, have had very different health experiences since adolescence. The first brother smokes two packs of cigarettes a day, is obese, never exercises, has an angry and pessimistic outlook on life, and eats foods containing excessive amounts of animal fat and sugar. The second brother pursues a much healthier lifestyle, avoiding tobacco and excessive stress, exercising regularly, watching his diet, and enjoying the social support of a close-knit circle of family and friends. As Figure 6.5 shows, although the two brothers have the same genetic vulnerabilities to lung, circulatory, and cardiovascular disease, the unhealthy lifestyle of the first brother dooms him to an extended period of adulthood morbidity, beginning at about age 45. In contrast, the healthier brother's lifestyle postpones disease until much later in life. If he does contract any of the illnesses, they are likely to be less severe, and recovery will be quicker. In some cases, the illness, such as lung cancer, may be "postponed" right out of his life.

Promoting Healthy Families and Communities

The biopsychosocial model of health is not limited to individuals. Preventive health psychology research is increasingly focused on the various external systems that influence an individual's health. Chief among these systems is the family.

FIGURE 6.5

Compression of Morbidity In focusing on the individual's quality-adjusted life years, health psychologists seek to limit the time that a person spends ill or infirm, as illustrated in this diagram of the illnesses and eventual deaths of identical twin brothers. Although the brothers carry the same disease vulnerabilities and life-span-limiting genetic clocks, the healthy lifestyle of one (b) keeps disease and disability at bay until primary aging is well advanced. In contrast, the unhealthy lifestyle of his brother (a) takes its toll at a much younger age.

Data from Fries, J. F. (2001). *Living well: Taking care of your health in the middle and later years.* New York: Perseus Publishing.

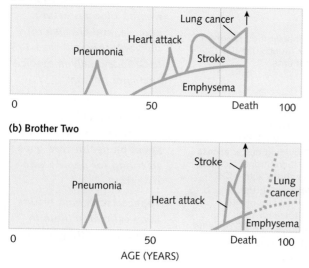

(a) Brother One

Lung cancer
Heart attack
Pneumonia
Stroke
Emphysema
0   50   Death   100

(b) Brother Two

Stroke
Pneumonia
Lung cancer
Heart attack
Emphysema
0   50   Death   100
AGE (YEARS)

Family Barriers

Health habits are typically acquired from parents and others who model health behaviors. When children see others routinely caring for their health, social learning pushes them to follow suit. Establishing good health habits before adolescence is vital for two reasons. First, adolescent egocentrism and rebellion often lead those with chronic illnesses to ignore special diets, medication, and other treatments unless they have already incorporated these habits into daily life (Dean and others, 2010). Second, children who have poor health for whatever reason, including economic and social reasons, are at risk throughout their lives, even if their environmental circumstances improve, because of epigenetic factors in childhood (Blair and Raver, 2012).

Children also acquire expectancies about risky behaviors by observing family members. Older siblings often have an impact on the behavior and attitudes of their younger adolescent siblings. Vicarious learning from an older sibling is one mechanism through which adolescents may form expectancies about risky health-related behaviors. Rena Repetti and her colleagues (Repetti, Taylor, & Seeman, 2002) have argued that certain family characteristics create a "cascade of risk" that begins early in life by "creating vulnerabilities (and exacerbating preexisting biological vulnerabilities) that lay the groundwork for long-term physical and mental health problems" (p. 330). These risky family characteristics fall into two categories: *overt family conflict,* manifested in frequent episodes of anger and aggression, and *deficient nurturing,* including relationships that are unsupportive, cold, and even neglectful. Other family variables linked with risky health-related behaviors among adolescents include absence of parental supervision, absence of the father, homelessness, coercive parent–child relationships, and parental drug and alcohol use (Bracizewski, 2010).

Health System Barriers

Historically, medicine focused on treating conditions that have already developed (secondary and tertiary care), and early warning signs of disease and contributing risk factors often went undetected. People who are not experiencing symptoms of illness see little reason to seek advice regarding potential risk factors, and doctors are oriented toward correcting conditions rather than preventing future problems.

Fortunately, health care has begun to change, and today there is a much greater emphasis on prevention—and even on "thriving." The very cornerstone of the Affordable Care Act (ACA), "strengthening health care," is built around the objective of emphasizing primary and preventive care linked with community prevention services (Calsyn & Rosenthal, 2013). Without successful implementation of the ACA, the number of Americans without health insurance was expected to increase to about 54 million in 2019 (Congressional Budget Office, 2010). The uninsured receive about half of the medical care of people with insurance, which leaves them sicker and likely to die at a younger age. By forgoing regular doctor visits and screening that could catch serious illnesses early, such as cancer and heart disease, many uninsured patients are diagnosed too late to affect the outcome. Although some ethnic groups are at much higher risk of being uninsured, the uninsured don't fit any stereotype. They come from every race and ethnic group, every community, and every walk of life (see Interpreting Data: Who Are the Uninsured and Underinsured?).

Since 2010, when the ACA was passed, the new law has largely succeeded in delivering on its main promises. First, the number of uninsured Americans has continued to

Health System Barriers Not having insurance can have a devastating impact on a person's health and financial security. The uninsured are less likely to have a regular doctor, more likely to rely on emergency room care, and more likely to have chronic health problems.

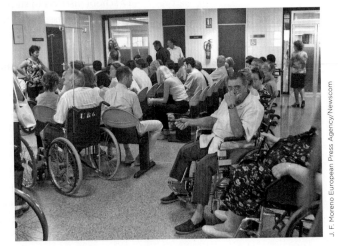

Health Insurance Reform in the United States In Detroit, Michigan, a volunteer "navigator" helps a young man sign up for insurance under the Affordable Care Act.

decline, falling by a third to about 9.2 percent early in 2015 (Cohen & Martinez, 2015). Second, about 85 percent of those who signed up during the ACA enrollment period qualified for federal subsidies, which reduced the cost of their insurance by an average of 76 percent (Sanger-Katz, 2014). Third, the ACA has contributed to a significant slowdown in health care spending. Across most measures, including the cost of hospital care, prescription drugs, and per capita Medicare spending, the national cost of health care has been increasing by smaller margins than it had in the years before the Affordable Care Act was passed (Altarum Institute, 2014).

However, the Affordable Care Act continues to have its detractors, including those who point to the economic consequences of the new law's requirement that insurers provide a wider range of benefits and cover people with pre-existing conditions. This has meant that insurance premiums have actually increased for some people who already had coverage. To keep insurance premiums affordable, enrollment in *high-deductible health plans* (HDHPs) has also increased. HDHPs are of concern because they create their own financial barrier and can result in personal financial hardships when care is needed.

Not having insurance can have a devastating impact on a person's health and financial security. Medical bills can wipe out a family's savings, and fear of high bills is a barrier that prevents many uninsured people from seeking health care. Uninsured adults are four times as likely as those who are insured to report delaying or forgoing needed health services. For example, only 16 percent of uninsured women have mammograms each year, compared with 42 percent of insured women (MMWR, 2012a). Is it any wonder that uninsured women are 40 percent more likely to be diagnosed with late-stage breast cancer and 40 to 50 percent more likely to die from breast cancer than insured women?

Community Barriers

The community can be a powerful force for promoting or discouraging healthy living. People are more likely to adopt health-enhancing behaviors when these behaviors are promoted by community organizations, such as schools, governmental agencies, and the health care system. As one example, psychologists at the University of Minnesota asked 17 school districts to start high school at 8:30 A.M. or later, citing evidence that teen sleep deprivation is associated with poorer cognitive processing, increased anxiety, depression, the use of drugs to stay awake or go to sleep, and driving accidents (Mueller, Bridges, & Goddard, 2011). Three years of data showed that the later start times resulted in increased likelihood of students eating breakfast, improved attendance, less tardiness, greater alertness in class, a calmer school atmosphere, fewer disciplinary referrals to the principal, and fewer student trips to counselors and the school nurse for stress-related and other health problems (National Sleep Foundation, 2013).

Social pressures, however, can be powerful, as evidenced by drug abuse—particularly of alcohol and marijuana—which is more prevalent among college students than among their peers who do not attend college (Johnston, O'Malley, Miech, Bachman, & Schulenberg, 2015). Surveys reveal that binge drinking among college students also is associated with other social risk factors. For some students, the excitement of being together in a largely unsupervised environment seems to trigger such risky behaviors.

Fortunately, most peer-inspired risk taking is a short-lived experiment that is outgrown before irreversible, long-term consequences are felt. Although drinking rates

Interpreting Data...

Who Are the Uninsured and Underinsured?

The percentage of Americans without health insurance has declined sharply since the provision of the Affordable Care Act (ACA, see Chapter 1) requiring most Americans to carry health insurance took effect in 2014 (Goldstein, Clement, & Guo, 2015). Still, nearly 33 million people living in the United States, or 10.4 percent of the population, went without health insurance in 2014. Who were they? Would you guess that most of them belonged to certain groups? Perhaps those who were unemployed, the very young or old, or those living below the poverty level? What does the simple statistic, *10.4 percent,* tell you? As with many statistics, it is easy to misinterpret this information unless you dig deeper. Interpreting data requires thinking critically about it, especially if the information seems incomplete. If you don't, it's too easy to leap to conclusions based on ignorance, political bias, or attitudes about people who are different than you that seem to be confirmed by the statistic.

Here is a more detailed profile of the uninsured people in the United States.

- The majority of the uninsured come from working families. About 70 percent of the uninsured have at least one full-time worker in their family, and another 12 percent have one or more part-time workers. Uninsured workers are more likely to have low-wage or blue-collar jobs and to work for small firms or in service industries.

- People with low incomes are at the highest risk of being uninsured (in 2015, the federal poverty level (FPL) for a family of four was $24,250). More than 80 percent of those without health insurance are in low- to mid-income families (incomes between 100 percent and 400 percent of the FPL).

- Although 45 percent of the uninsured are non-Hispanic whites, people of color have a higher risk of being uninsured than non-Hispanic whites. People of color account for 40 percent of the total population of the United States but for over half of the uninsured. This disparity in coverage is particularly high for Hispanics, who comprise 19 percent of the population but 34 percent of those who are uninsured. Hispanics and non-Hispanic blacks have higher uninsured rates (20.9 percent and 12.7 percent, respectively) than whites (9.1 percent).

- Most of the uninsured (79 percent) are U.S. citizens.

- The likelihood of being uninsured traditionally varies from state to state, with people living in the South and West the most likely to lack coverage.

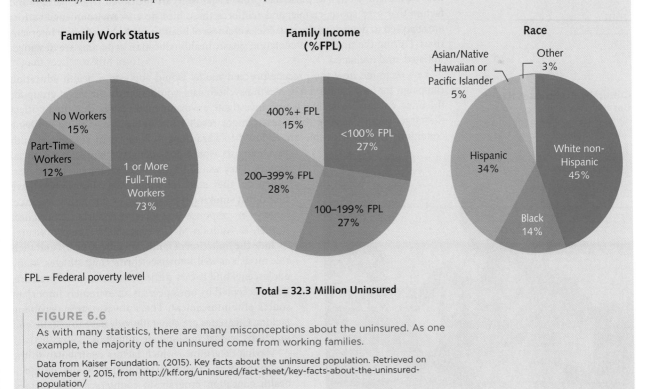

FPL = Federal poverty level

Total = 32.3 Million Uninsured

FIGURE 6.6

As with many statistics, there are many misconceptions about the uninsured. As one example, the majority of the uninsured come from working families.

Data from Kaiser Foundation. (2015). Key facts about the uninsured population. Retrieved on November 9, 2015, from http://kff.org/uninsured/fact-sheet/key-facts-about-the-uninsured-population/

increase significantly in the transition from high school to the college freshman year, heavy drinking declines as students grow older, assume increased responsibilities, and display a pattern called *maturing out* (Bartholow, Sher, & Krull, 2003).

Community Health Education

There is a greater emphasis on health promotion today than at any other time in history. Substantial effort is devoted to shaping the public's views on health issues through educational campaigns in advertisements, on public transportation, in magazines and newspapers, and on television, radio, and Web sites. An excellent example of community health education is embodied in *Promotores de salud* ("promoters of health")—a 2011 initiative of the U.S. Department of Health and Human Services Office of Minority Health (OMH). Under the Affordable Care Act, an estimated 9 million Latinos have or will attain health insurance. *Promotores* are lay health workers, patient navigators, and health advocates who work in Spanish-speaking communities in a culturally competent and linguistically appropriate fashion to promote health care delivery, education and prevention—particularly for groups that have been historically underserved (OMH, 2015).

The importance of campaigns such as this is revealed in research controversies over how information should be presented. (For example, should STI-prevention campaigns concentrate on both safer sex and abstinence?) The most widely used model in health education is the *precede/proceed model* (Yeo, Berzins, & Addington, 2007). According to the model, planning for health education begins by identifying specific health problems in a targeted group. Next, lifestyle and environment elements that contribute to the targeted health problem (as well as those that protect against it) are identified. Then, background factors that predispose, enable, and reinforce these lifestyle and environmental factors are analyzed to determine the possible usefulness of health education and other interventions. During the final implementation phase, health education programs are designed, initiated, and evaluated.

Let's examine how the precede/proceed model would apply to a health education campaign for lung cancer. First, health psychologists would identify the target group for the intervention. Next, they would investigate environmental factors that might affect the target group because the disease might result from unhealthy working or living conditions in which people are exposed to hazardous pollutants. In addition, health psychologists would consider psychological and social factors. They would begin by determining who smokes. When did they start smoking? Why? Researchers have found that smoking typically begins during adolescence, largely in response to social pressures (Rodriguez, Romer, & Audrain-McGovern, 2007). These pressures include the imitation of family members, peers, and such role models as well-known celebrities and athletes. Many adolescents find it very difficult to resist social pressure. Being accepted by one's peers is an extremely important source of reinforcement. There are also strong enabling factors: Cigarettes are generally very easy to obtain, and sanctions against smoking are minimal.

Having determined which factors contributed to the health problem, health psychologists would design a health education program to counteract those factors. For example, if social pressure was found to be a major factor, they might design a health education program that

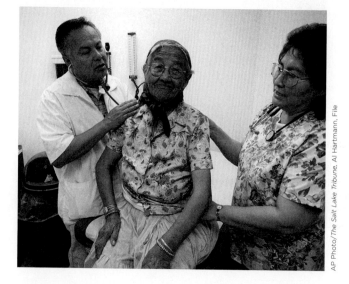

Culturally Competent Health Care A physician assistant and nurse examine a member of the Navajo Nation near Bluff, Utah.

AP Photo/*The Salt Lake Tribune*, Al Hartmann, File

focuses on improving the ability of teens to resist social pressure. Such programs might involve role models urging teens not to smoke, adopting antismoking policies in public buildings, imposing stricter sanctions against the sale of cigarettes, levying higher taxes on cigarettes, or all of the above.

How effective are health education campaigns? Researchers have found that education campaigns that merely inform people of the hazards of health-compromising behaviors are typically ineffective in motivating people to change long-held health habits (Kaiser Foundation, 2010). For example, antismoking messages and other drug education programs by themselves often have little effect—or a negative effect. Simply finding out that one's lifestyle is not as healthy as it could be often is insufficient to provoke change because many people believe they are exempt or invulnerable to the negative consequences of their risky behavior.

Generally speaking, multifaceted community campaigns that present information on several fronts work better than "single-shot" campaigns. For example, two decades of antismoking campaigns combining school intervention programs with communitywide mass media messages resulted in a significant decrease in experimental and regular smoking; a shift in viewing smoking as more addictive and as having more negative social consequences among seventh through eleventh graders in a Midwestern county school system between 1980 and 2001 (Chassin, Presson, Sherman, & Kim, 2003) was also successful. As another example, one skin cancer prevention program focused on the use of sunscreen, wearing hats and sunglasses, and other sun-protection habits by children who were taking swimming lessons at 15 swimming pools in Hawaii and Massachusetts. In addition to targeting the children, the Pool Cool program, which combined education, interactive activities, and environmental changes (providing free sunscreen, portable shade structures, and sun safety posters), was a randomized, controlled trial intervention targeting parents, lifeguards, and swim instructors. Compared with children in a control group at 13 other pools who received a bicycle and inline skating safety intervention, children in the intervention group showed significant positive changes in use of sunscreen and shade, overall sun-protection habits, and the number of sunburns (Glanz and others, 2002). Similarly, other researchers have found that multicomponent sun-protection behavior interventions are particularly effective with adult beachgoers (Pagoto, McChargue, & Fuqua, 2003).

Community programs are on the rise and have several advantages. First, they can promote changes that are difficult for individuals to accomplish, such as creating bike paths and other public exercise facilities or banning smoking in public offices. Second, unlike interventions that concentrate on high-risk individuals, community programs reach out to a broader cross section of the public, potentially reaching those in the lower- to moderate-risk categories earlier in the process of disease. Third, community programs combine information with the social support of friends, neighbors, and family members.

One of the earliest community campaigns was initiated for residents of a rural county in Finland with a very high incidence of coronary heart disease (Puska, 1999). Launched in 1972 by the Finnish government and the World Health Organization, the North Karelia Project had one major goal: to reduce smoking, cholesterol, and blood pressure levels through informational

Antismoking Campaign in China Although the number of smokers in the United States has decreased recently, the reverse seems to be occurring in other countries, such as China. Everyone, no matter what their native language, can understand billboards such as this one.

Michael Reynolds/EPA/Newscom

campaigns. When the program began, the Finns had the highest coronary mortality rates in the world. The initial five-year follow-up study demonstrated a 17.4 percent reduction in these coronary risk factors among men and an 11.5 percent reduction among women. In addition, coronary disability payments had declined by approximately 10 percent, much more than enough to pay for the entire community program. Most significant of all, over three decades, deaths among the working-age population from heart disease have dropped by 82 percent (Templeton, 2004).

Message Framing

An important factor in the effectiveness of health education is how information is worded, or *framed*. Health messages generally are framed in terms of the benefits associated with a particular preventive action or the costs of failing to take preventive action (Salovey, 2011).

gain-framed message A health message that focuses on attaining positive outcomes or avoiding undesirable ones by adopting a health-promoting behavior.

loss-framed message A health message that focuses on a negative outcome from failing to perform a health-promoting behavior.

Gain-framed messages focus on the positive outcome from adopting a health-promoting behavior ("If you exercise regularly, you are likely to look and feel better") or on avoiding an undesirable outcome ("If you exercise regularly, you decrease your risk of obesity and a number of chronic diseases"). **Loss-framed messages** emphasize the negative outcome from failing to take preventive action ("If you don't exercise, you increase the risk of an undetected, potentially life-threatening disease"). Loss-framed messages also may emphasize missing a desirable outcome ("If you don't exercise, you will miss out on the extra energy that physical fitness brings").

Tailored Messaging

A growing body of literature attests to the importance of tailoring health messages and interventions to individual characteristics of participants instead of giving everyone identically framed information. For instance, the effectiveness of gain- or loss-framed messages appears to vary with whether a person tends to be *avoidance oriented* or *approach oriented*. Approach-oriented individuals are highly responsive to rewards and incentives, while avoidance-oriented individuals are highly responsive to punishments or threats. In one study, Traci Mann and her UCLA colleagues (Mann, Sherman, & Updegraff, 2004) found that when college students received loss-framed messages promoting dental flossing, avoidance-oriented students reported taking better care of their teeth, and when given a gain-framed message, approach-oriented students reported flossing more than avoidance-oriented students. These results suggest that tailoring health messages to individuals based on their dispositional motivations is an effective strategy for promoting behavior change.

Loss-Framed Fear Appeals

Are fear-arousing messages effective in promoting attitude and behavior change? To find out, Irving Janis and Seymour Feshbach (1953) compared the effectiveness of messages that aroused various levels of fear in promoting changes in dental hygiene. Messages that aroused moderate levels of fear were more effective than more extreme messages in getting junior high school students to change their dental hygiene habits. In accounting for their results, the researchers suggested that individuals and circumstances differ in the optimal level of fear for triggering a change in attitude or behavior. When this level is exceeded, people may resort to denial or avoidance coping measures.

A key factor in determining the effectiveness of threatening health messages is the recipient's perceived behavioral control. Before they can be persuaded, people must believe that they have the ability to follow through on recommendations. In one study, Carol Self and Ronald Rogers (1990) presented highly threatening messages regarding the dangers of sedentary living with or without information indicating that the subjects could perform the health-enhancing behavior

Message Wording Makes a Difference Educational campaigns may use gain-framed or loss-framed messages. A loss-framed message is shown here, while a gain-framed message regarding healthy sexual behavior might say, "Safe Is Sexy!"

Bill Freeman/PhotoEdit

(such as exercise) and succeed in enhancing their health. What did they the researchers find? Threat appeals worked only if participants were convinced that they could cope with the health threat; attempts to frighten participants without reassuring them were ineffective.

Heike Mahler and her colleagues (Mahler, Kulik, Gibbons, Gerrard, & Harrell, 2003) found college-age beachgoers were particularly responsive to an educational campaign promoting sunscreen use and other sun-protection behaviors when it focused on the dangers of sun exposure to each participant's appearance. The intervention began with a 12-minute slide presentation that included graphic photos of extreme cases of wrinkles and age spots. Afterward, each participant's face was photographed with an ultraviolet (UV) ray–filtered camera that accentuated brown spots, freckling, and other existing skin damage from UV exposure. A one-month follow-up indicated that the intervention resulted in a significant increase in sun-protective behaviors and substantially lower reported sunbathing.

However, scare tactics that arouse tremendous fear, such as photographs of grossly decayed or diseased gums, tend to upset people. As a result, such messages may backfire and actually *decrease* a person's likelihood of changing his or her beliefs and hence his or her behavior (Beck & Frankel, 1981). Such messages increase the person's anxiety to such a level that the only coping avenue that he or she perceives as available is a refusal to face the danger.

In conclusion, research on the framing of health messages reveals a basic pattern: Gain-framed messages are effective in promoting prevention behaviors, while loss-framed ones are effective in promoting illness-detection (screening) behaviors (Salovey, 2011).

Cognitive-Behavioral Interventions

Cognitive-behavioral interventions focus on the conditions that elicit health behaviors and the factors that help to maintain and reinforce them (Dobson, 2010). In a typical intervention, the health psychologist identifies a target behavior to be modified (for example, consumption of soft drinks), measuring the current status of the behavior (including the context in which it occurs and its antecedent cues) and examining its consequences. Many programs use **self-monitoring** as the initial step in promoting behavior change. In our example, doing so might include keeping track of the number of soft drinks consumed each day, the situation and time of day, and any cravings or other feelings that occurred before and after each beverage was consumed. In this way, the individual can get a clearer sense of the target behavior, including its initial *baseline* rate of occurrence. This allows the establishment of specific goals for the intervention—goals that are both objective and realistic. Interestingly, many people find that self-monitoring itself may produce a change in the target behavior (Quinn, Pascoe, Wood, & Neal, 2010).

The next step is to manipulate the antecedents and consequences in an effort to modify the target behavior's rate of occurrence. The key to this process is removing reinforcement for unhealthy behaviors and providing reinforcement for healthy ones.

Two key aspects in the use of operant conditioning to modify health behaviors are *stimulus-control* and *contingency contracting*. Habitual behaviors such as cigarette smoking and overeating are often triggered by environmental stimuli to which they have become associated. For example, the sights and smells of a holiday meal that is being prepared can serve as *discriminative stimuli* for overeating. As another example, the various sights, sounds, and smells a former smoker encounters upon entering a noisy bar can be potent discriminative stimuli that trigger the urge to light up. **Discriminative stimuli** are environmental signals that communicate to the brain that certain behaviors will be followed by reinforcement.

self-monitoring People keeping track of their own target behavior that is to be modified, including the stimuli associated with it and the consequences that follow it.

discriminative stimuli Environmental signals that certain behaviors will be followed by reinforcement.

These young protesters recognize the power of tailored messaging—in this instance, tobacco advertising that targets their demographic group.

Richard B. Levine/Newscom

stimulus-control intervention
A behavioral intervention aimed at modifying the environmental discriminative stimuli that control a target behavior by signaling its reinforcement.

Wal-Mart's My Sustainability Plan *(MSP) is a voluntary, employee-driven program that encourages associates to integrate small projects into their lives to benefit their own health (My Health), care for the planet (My Planet), and get the most out of life (My Life). MSP provides an online space with tools associates can use to create and track goals, and use social networking to connect with others who are on the same path. Since the program was launched in 2010, thousands of Wal-Mart associates have defined MSP goals in each area of focus:*

- *My Health (eating healthy, getting active, quitting tobacco, reducing stress)*

- *My Planet (saving water, reducing waste, saving energy, enjoying nature)*

- *My Life (learning new skills, managing money, making quality time, helping others)*

With 1.4 million workers in the United States and 2.2 million globally, the MSP model has the potential for enormous impact. This impact was dramatically illustrated when Wal-Mart Japan challenged associates to keep track of their daily walking using pedometers. The cooperative endeavor added up to over 637 million combined footsteps (or 10 trips around the globe) (Weinreb, 2013).

One reason self-monitoring is an effective step in modifying behavior is that it points out the various discriminative stimuli that have come to control the target behavior. **Stimulus-control interventions** aimed at modifying a health behavior involve two strategies: removing discriminative stimuli for the behavior from the environment and establishing new discriminative stimuli signaling the availability of reinforcement for healthier response choices. For people who are trying to reduce snacking on calorie-dense, low-nutrient junk foods, a good first step is to eliminate the presence of such foods in their homes and to avoid activities that trigger snacking. One such activity is watching television, particularly since exposure to food advertising is likely. In a fairly recent study, elementary-school children watched a cartoon that contained either food advertising or advertising for other products and received a snack while watching. Children consumed 45 percent more snack foods when exposed to food advertising (Harris, Bargh, & Brownell, 2009). Turning off the television can be an effective step in gaining control over this type of automatic, mindless snacking. Another effective strategy to gain stimulus control over eating behavior is to restrict its occurrence to one location, say, at the dining room table. As we'll see in Chapter 8, researchers have found that many people who struggle to control unhealthy eating behaviors are especially sensitive to food-related discriminative stimuli.

Complete elimination of all discriminative stimuli that have become associated with a target behavior is not always possible. A former professor of mine had successfully quit a 20-year smoking habit until he took a cross-country trip as a passenger on a train. When he returned from his trip, he had resumed smoking, complaining that the urge to smoke while he was aboard the train was irresistible. "The last time I took a train ride," he moaned, "I was still a smoker." To forestall this type of occurrence, many **relapse prevention** programs deliberately bring participants into contact with discriminative stimuli that are likely to evoke the target behavior. Doing so gives participants the opportunity to learn and practice coping skills that increase their feelings of self-efficacy and decrease the likelihood of engaging in old and unhealthy patterns of behavior.

A **contingency contract** is a formal agreement between a person attempting to change a health behavior and another individual, such as a therapist, regarding the consequences of target behaviors. The agreement establishes the specific reinforcements or punishments that will be contingent on the participant's behavior. For example, a person who wants to quit smoking might deposit a sum of money and arrange to receive the price of a pack of (unsmoked) cigarettes as a reward for each successful day of not smoking. A contingency contract might also specify that each occurrence of an unwanted target behavior will result in a monetary fine.

Promoting Healthy Workplaces

Occupational health psychologists are leading the way in designing healthy workplaces. Four dimensions of healthy work have been identified: *stress, work–family relations, violence prevention,* and *relationships at work* (Quick & Quick, 2004). Because job stress is a health epidemic in this country, psychological research and intervention are vital tools for promoting the health of workers. Increasingly, insurers are recognizing that the causes of disabilities in the workplace are shifting from injuries to job stress.

The workplace has a profound psychological effect on all aspects of our lives and on the lives of our family members. For instance, job stressors may result in family social interactions that are less sensitive and supportive and more negative and conflicted, which can adversely affect children's biological responses to stress, emotional regulation, and social competence (e.g., Perry-Jenkins, Repetti, & Crouter, 2000). Two behavioral *crossover effects* have been observed between a worker's experiences of job stress and the well-being of other family members. *Negative emotion spillover* occurs when work-related frustrations contribute to greater irritability, impatience, or other negative behaviors at home. *Social withdrawal* occurs when one or more working adult parents or caregivers withdraw behaviorally and emotionally from family life following especially stressful days at work.

Over the past 20 years, there has been a significant shift in how we think about the relationship between work and family life. Employers and governmental agencies have begun to recognize that all employees face complex challenges in balancing work and family roles. These changing views have triggered an explosion of work–family research. Among the most consistent findings is the fact that in the United States, many employees find little support and have little say in the policies of work that affect them and their families. Consequently, they are left on their own to arrange child care, balance work schedules, stave off work stress, and so forth. The 1993 Family and Medical Leave Act (FMLA) helps some workers by protecting their jobs as they care for new babies and family members who are ill, but many workers are not covered by this legislation. FMLA initially applied only to immediate family—parent, spouse, and children. In March 2015, the U.S. Labor Department expanded the policy so that workers in legal same-sex marriages have the same rights as those in opposite-sex marriages to federally protected leave under FMLA to care for a spouse with a serious health condition.

Workplace violence and campus violence have received considerable media attention in recent years. By some estimates, homicide has become the second-leading cause of occupational injury death, exceeded only by motor vehicle deaths. Most of these deaths occur during robberies, but about 10 percent can be attributed to coworkers or former employees. Nearly 2 million American workers report having been victims of workplace violence each year (U.S. Department of Labor, 2015). A number of factors increase a worker's risk of being a victim of violence, including contact with the public; exchange of money; delivery of passengers, goods, or services; having a mobile workplace; working with unstable or volatile people; and working alone, late at night, and in high-crime areas (Quick & Quick, 2004).

In the area of work relationships, building a healthy work culture requires employees to accept responsibility for their own health and safety and that of their coworkers. More generally, as Dorothy Cantor and her colleagues (Cantor, Boyce, & Repetti, 2004) have noted, building a healthy work culture requires attention to three factors: person (individual differences, education, personality), environment (work conditions, equipment, management systems), and behavior (risk behaviors, procedures, group performance).

In addition to a climbing wall, Google's corporate offices have Ping-Pong tables, nap pods and LEGO stations. Employees can also shower, get massages, and swim at their workplace.

relapse prevention Training in coping skills and other techniques intended to help people resist falling back into old health habits following a successful behavioral intervention.

contingency contract A formal agreement between a person attempting to change a health behavior and another individual, such as a therapist, regarding the consequences of target behaviors.

Hippocampal Volume on Magnetic Resonance Imaging (MRI) in PTSD There is smaller hippocampal volume in this patient with PTSD compared with a control.

Work-Site Wellness Programs

The workplace is an ideal site for promoting health for several reasons. First, workers find such programs convenient to attend. Some employers even permit their employees to participate in prevention programs during the workday. In addition, the workplace offers the greatest opportunity for continuing contact, follow-through, and feedback. Finally, coworkers are available to provide social support and help motivate people during difficult moments. The same is true of wellness programs on university and college campuses.

Work-site programs emerged rapidly with the advent of the wellness movement during the 1980s. In the United States today, more than

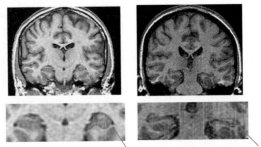

NORMAL   PTSD

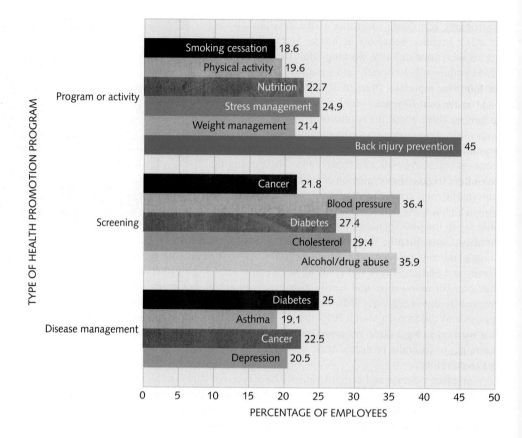

TYPE OF HEALTH PROMOTION PROGRAM

Program or activity
- Smoking cessation 18.6
- Physical activity 19.6
- Nutrition 22.7
- Stress management 24.9
- Weight management 21.4
- Back injury prevention 45

Screening
- Cancer 21.8
- Blood pressure 36.4
- Diabetes 27.4
- Cholesterol 29.4
- Alcohol/drug abuse 35.9

Disease management
- Diabetes 25
- Asthma 19.1
- Cancer 22.5
- Depression 20.5

PERCENTAGE OF EMPLOYEES

FIGURE 6.7

Percentage of Employers Offering Various Types of Health Promotion Programs Workplace wellness programs offer many advantages. They are convenient for workers to attend, follow-through is made easier, and coworkers can provide social support.

Data from Linnan, L., Bowling, M., Childress, J., Lindsay, G., Blakey, C., Pronk, S., Wieker, S., & Royall, P. (2008). Results of the 2004 national worksite health promotion survey. *American Journal of Public Health, 98,* 1503–1508.

80 percent of organizations with 50 or more workers offer some sort of health-promoting program. Work-site wellness programs offer a variety of activities, including weight management, nutrition counseling, smoking cessation, preventive health screenings, educational seminars, stress management, lower back care, fitness centers, immunization programs, and prenatal programs (see Figure 6.7).

At the heart of the wellness movement was the realization that preventing disease is easier, cheaper, and far more desirable than curing disease. Case in point: the H1N1 vaccination campaign on college campuses during the 2009–2010 flu season. World-wide, health care costs have risen from about 3 percent of world gross domestic product (GDP) in 1948 to about 10 percent today (WHO, 2015b). The United States currently spends over 17 percent of its GDP on health care (CMS, 2015i). As noted earlier, an ever-increasing proportion of these costs has been passed along to employers who pay a portion of their employees' health insurance premiums. According to a William B. Mercer study, 97 percent of corporate health benefits costs are spent on treating preventable conditions such as cardiovascular disease, lower back problems, hypertension, stroke, bladder cancer, and alcohol abuse (Arnst, 2009). Employers have realized that work-site programs that are even modestly successful in improving employees' health can result in substantial savings.

Are such programs effective? A large number of careful studies reveals that they are. The cost of the programs is more than offset by reductions in work-related injuries, absenteeism, and worker turnover. The U.S. surgeon general's *National Prevention Strategy* (Office of the Surgeon General, 2011) concluded that medical costs are significantly reduced by $3.27 and worker absenteeism costs by $2.73 for every dollar spent on work-site wellness programs. Clearly, prevention is the best buy when it comes to health.

Positive Psychology and Thriving

n 2001, the American Psychological Association (APA) modified its 60-year-old mission statement to include the word *health* for the first time. Over 95 percent of the organization's membership endorsed the bylaw change, underscoring its awareness that while within each person are physical and psychological elements that contribute to illness and disability, other elements also contribute to health, wellness, and thriving. The bylaw change was part of APA's Healthy World Initiative, which aligned with the **positive psychology** movement described in Chapter 1 to promote a *strength-based, preventive approach* to research and interventions rather than psychology's more traditional approach of attacking problems after they have occurred (Seligman, 2002). As APA President Norine Johnson (2004) stated, "We must bring the building of strength to the forefront in the treatment and prevention of illness, for the promotion of wellness and health" (p. 317).

This new emphasis has generated an upswing in research on such topics as personal growth, positive affect, optimism, meaning, gratitude, and resilience; their relationship to health; and their potential for interventions that promote healing and health (Korb, 2015). No single term has been accepted as the best way to describe the co-occurrence of human strengths in the positive psychology literature, as is the case with *comorbidity* when multiple states of disease occur simultaneously. The terms *flourishing* and *psychological capital* have been used to refer to the combined effects of hope, optimism, self-efficacy, and resilience to predict wellness and success in the workplace (Luthans, Avolio, Avey, & Norman, 2007). Other researchers have recently used the term *covitality* to describe the relations among the positive traits of well-being, self-confidence, and general health among college students (Jones, You, & Furlong, 2013).

A central theme of the positive psychology movement is that the experience of adversity, whether physical or psychological in nature, can sometimes yield benefits, as it did for Sara Snodgrass, whom we met at the beginning of the chapter. As Charles Carver (Carver and others, 2005) noted, when we experience physical or psychological adversity, there are at least four possible outcomes: 1) a continued downward slide, 2) survival with diminished capacity or impairment, 3) a gradual or rapid return to the preadversity level of function, and 4) the emergence of a quality that makes the person somehow better off than before.

Thriving refers to this paradoxical fourth outcome, in which adversity somehow leads people to greater psychological and/or physical well-being (O'Leary & Ickovics, 1995). This is a step beyond *resilience*, the capacity to withstand stress and catastrophe. It is the difference between bouncing back and bounding ahead. How can this be? According to neuroscientist Bruce McEwen (2011), who introduced the concept of *allostatic load*, "Under conditions of stress, one would expect a physically weakened system, but positive physiological changes can occur—often in the context of psychological thriving. In physiological terms, this translates into greater restorative processes than destructive processes at work" (p. 195). Using the analogy of athletes strengthening their muscles by first breaking them down through exercise, allowing recovery, and then repeating this pattern over time to produce muscles that are stronger and capable of doing more work, positive psychologists point to evidence that adversity can similarly trigger "psychological bodybuilding" (Pearsall, 2004).

positive psychology The study of optimal human functioning and the healthy interplay between people and their environments.

thriving A paradoxical outcome in which adversity somehow leads people to greater psychological and/or physical well-being.

Allostasis and Neuroendocrine Health

As we saw in Chapter 4, in response to a stressor, activation of the hypothalamic-pituitary-adrenal (HPA) axis causes a change in the body's overall metabolic state. Most of the time, the cells of the body are occupied with activities that build the body (*anabolism*). When the brain perceives an impending threat or challenge, however, anabolic metabolism is converted into its opposite, *catabolism*, which breaks down tissues to be converted to energy. Catabolic metabolism is characterized by the release of catecholamines, cortisol, and other "fight-or-flight" hormones that help the body quickly mobilize energy. To counteract these neuroendocrine reactions, the parasympathetic nervous system triggers the release of anabolic hormones, including growth hormone, insulin-like growth factor (IGF-1), and sex steroids. Anabolic metabolism counters arousal and promotes relaxation, energy storage, and healing processes such as protein synthesis.

Recall from Chapter 4 that allostasis refers to the body's ability to adapt to stress and other elements of rapidly changing environments (McEwen, 2011). One measure of *physical thriving* is a fluid allostatic system that flexibly shifts from high to low levels of sympathetic nervous system arousal, depending on the demands of the environment. Catabolic hormones, for instance, are essential to health over the short term. However, when people are in a constant state of arousal, prolonged elevations of catabolic hormones can damage the body and promote chronic illness. As an example, repeated stress can strongly affect brain function, especially in the hippocampus, which has large concentrations of cortisol receptors (McEwen, 2011). The consequences of long-term elevations of catabolic hormones, when taken together, look very much like aging. Hypertension, wasted muscles, ulcers, fatigue, and increased risk of chronic disease are common signs of both aging and chronic stress. This state, which has been called **allostatic overload,** is indicated by a predominance of catabolic activity at rest. An elevated resting level of salivary or serum cortisol is one biological indicator of allostatic overload and the general functioning of the HPA system. Conversely, a predominance of anabolic hormones at rest reflects enhanced health and a low allostatic load.

allostatic overload The consequences of long-term elevations of stress-related catabolic hormones, including hypertension, wasted muscles, ulcers, fatigue, and increased risk of chronic disease.

Neurobiology of Resilience

Evolutionary biologists point out that the primary function of all living creatures—from single-celled organisms to humans—is to survive, reproduce, and ensure that genetic material is successfully passed to future generations. In mammals, the *need* to maintain homeostasis is essential for survival and triggers *drives* that range from regulating body temperature to getting adequate food and sleep. Threats to survival engage a host of physiological and behavioral responses meant to defend homeostasis by removing the threat if possible and coping otherwise if not (Karatoreos & McEwen, 2013). As we saw in Chapter 4, in some animals, and especially in humans, internally generated threats, such as ruminating on problems, constant thinking about disappointments, or blaming oneself for mishaps, also threaten homeostasis and health.

Considered in these terms, *resilience* can be thought of as the capacity of the brain and body to withstand challenges to homeostasis. The brain is the central organ of adaptation to a stressor since it determines which behavioral response is needed (for example, fleeing or fighting). The brain also regulates the body's neuroendocrine, autonomic, and metabolic systems. Overuse or *dysregulation* of these systems can lead to allostatic overload and the development and acceleration of many chronic illnesses, from depression to cardiovascular disease.

Positive psychologists are discovering that exposure to certain events early in life may promote the development of resistance to allostatic overload. In recent years, various neural, molecular, and hormonal mechanisms related to this type of resilience have been studied extensively in humans and laboratory animals (Russo, Murrough, Han, Charney, & Nestler, 2012). These mechanisms involve the HPA axis, which regulates the stress response. This work has demonstrated that resilience is mediated by distinct biological adaptations that can blunt stress-induced HPA activation to promote normal functioning, even in the face of adversity.

Much of this research has been conducted with laboratory animals. As with humans, chronic exposure to environmental stressors such as inescapable electric shock leads to the development of depression-like responses in some, but not all, animals. These adverse responses include heightened HPA reactivity, overeating, social avoidance, and shrinkage of the hippocampus (Golden, Covinton, Berton, & Russo, 2011). In any given study, up to one-third of the animals do not display these maladaptive behaviors and metabolic symptoms and have been considered *resilient* (Russo and others, 2012).

One study demonstrated that mice raised in a socially enriched environment (living as members of a group in a communal nest rather than in individual cages) were more resilient later to an acute stressor than were mice that had been raised in a standard, unenriched environment (Branchi, Santarelli, D'Andrea, & Alleva, 2013). Research studies with monkeys have shown that early exposure to *moderate stressors* temporarily activates the HPA axis, which later in life leads to diminished stress-induced arousal, blunted HPA activation, increased curiosity, and prosocial behavior (Parker, 2012). In this way, early experiences may inoculate or immunize the brain and promote resistance to subsequent stressors.

Neuroendocrine adaptations are an important aspect of resilience. For example, the hormone *dehydroepiandrosterone* (DHEA), which is normally released from the adrenal cortex along with cortisol in response to stress, has antioxidant and anti-inflammatory effects. Research studies with soldiers undergoing the extreme stress of military survival training have found that individuals with a higher DHEA-to-cortisol ratio have been shown to have fewer negative symptoms during the extreme stress of military survival training (Rasmusson, Vythilingam, & Morgan, 2003).

The brain also responds to hormonal and neural feedback from neuroendocrine systems as they are engaged as part of the body's effort to maintain homeostasis. This feedback, which has been called **biological embedding,** seems to shape the structure and function of the brain throughout life (McEwen & Gianaros, 2011). For example, animal studies have shown that chronic stress leads to a dramatic shrinkage and loss of connectivity among neurons in one region of the prefrontal cortex (PFC). Often called the "CEO [chief executive officer] of the brain," the PFC is responsible for cognitive analysis, planning, impulse control, and the modulation of intense emotions. Interestingly, neurons in a different region of the PFC often display an *increase* in complexity in response to environmental stress, thus demonstrating how early experiences seem to sculpt the brain (Liston and others, 2006). Four somewhat overlapping periods seem to be especially sensitive to the biological embedding of environmental events. These events include prenatal development, the neonatal period (the first four weeks after birth), the years of early childhood (ages 2 through 6), and adolescence (Karatoreos & McEwen, 2013).

Hormones appear to be the agents of adaptation and change in the brain's response to environmental events. They do so by altering the complexity of dendrites and the turnover of synapses in the PFC, the amygdala, and the hippocampus. For example, research studies have found that the type of maternal care experienced by rat pups affects the expression of glucocorticoid stress hormone receptors in the brain, and ultimately, the adult response of the HPA stress axis. This occurs as a result of changes in the *methylation* (see Chapter 3) of promoter genes for these receptors, ultimately changing the sensitivity of the hippocampus to cortisol and other glucocorticoid hormones (Zhang and others, 2010; Bagot and others, 2012).

Thus, researchers are beginning to understand how changes in early life experiences can alter neural circuits and environmental responses through epigenetic changes (see Figure 6.8). Multiple pathways interact to shape the brain and body's physiological and neurobehavioral responses to early life experiences. Gradually, epigenetic research is building a picture of how the mechanisms of gene–environment interaction can alter the resilience of the brain (Russo and others, 2012).

biological embedding The processes by which the structure and functioning of the brain are shaped by feedback from neuroendocrine systems as they are engaged as part of the body's effort to maintain homeostasis.

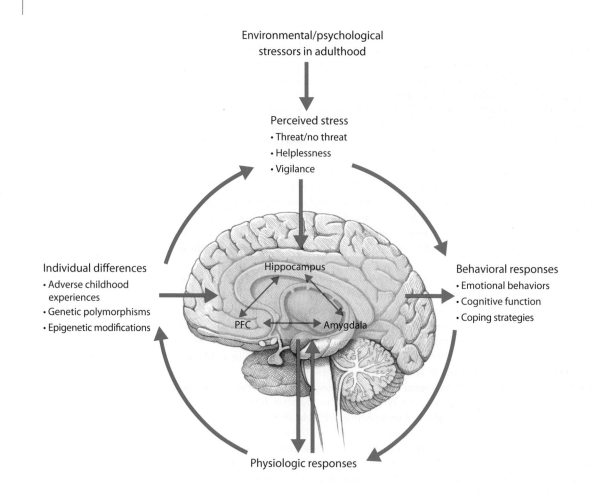

Environmental/psychological
stressors in adulthood

Perceived stress
• Threat/no threat
• Helplessness
• Vigilance

Individual differences
• Adverse childhood
  experiences
• Genetic polymorphisms
• Epigenetic modifications

Hippocampus

PFC   Amygdala

Behavioral responses
• Emotional behaviors
• Cognitive function
• Coping strategies

Physiologic responses

FIGURE 6.8

The Neurobiology of Resilience The interaction of genes and early environmental experiences can induce physiological and neurobehavioral changes that alter the way an individual responds to stressors later in life. These changes alter the structure and function of brain areas involved in cognition and the regulation of emotion, especially the prefrontal cortex (PFC), the amygdala, and the hippocampus.

Information from Karatoreos, I. N., & McEwen, B. S. (2013). Annual research review: The neurobiology of resilience and adaptation across the life course. *Journal of Child Psychology and Psychiatry, 54*(4), 337–347.

Psychosocial Factors and Physiological Thriving

Elsewhere in this book, we have seen how psychosocial factors can modify immune functioning in ways that impair health. In this section, we focus on evidence that psychosocial factors also can have beneficial effects on immune functioning and other bodily systems.

A number of psychological variables have been linked to lowered stress hormones, enhanced immunity, lower levels of inflammation, and healthier patterns of heart rate variability in response to stress. These variables include optimism (Segerstrom & Sephton, 2010), self-esteem and perceptions of personal competence and control over outcomes (O'Donnell, Brydon, Wright, & Steptoe, 2008), self-efficacy (Bandura, Taylor, Williams, Mefford, & Barchas, 1985), and a sense of coherence in one's life (Myrin & Lagerstrom, 2006). These variables also apply to the workplace, and many companies now offer opportunities to promote them. Google, for instance, has a playground area where employees can play basketball, Ping-Pong, and other games when they are feeling overwhelmed.

Self-Enhancement

Until recently, health research has focused almost exclusively on the unhealthy impact of negative emotions such as hostility, stress, and depression. A growing body of evidence demonstrates that people who generally have more positive affect are healthier and even live longer than those with more negative emotions (Pressman & Bowlin, 2014).

Even positive mental states that are unrealistic seem to be linked to healthier physiological functioning. This phenomenon appears to occur in people who lean toward *self-enhancement,* a tendency to recall positive over negative information, to see oneself more positively than do others, and to feel personally responsible for good outcomes. Contrary to early views in psychology, which considered this type of inflated self-perception as evidence of narcissism, self-centeredness, and poor mental health, recent studies have suggested that rather than being associated with maladjustment, self-enhancement is indicative of health, wellness, and the ability to feel good about oneself. Self-enhancement has also been linked to the ability to develop and sustain relationships, to be content, and to thrive in environments that are changing or even threatening (Taylor, Lerner, Sherman, Sage, & McDowell, 2003).

Erroneous but positive views of our medical condition and of the perception of our control over it appear to promote health and longevity. Although these correlational findings do not prove causality, researchers speculate that *self-enhancing cognitions* might blunt physiological and neuroendocrine responses to stress and thus lessen HPA responses to stress (Taylor and others, 2000).

In one study, Shelley Taylor and her colleagues (2003) asked 92 college students to complete the How I See Myself Questionnaire, a measure of self-enhancement on which participants rate themselves in comparison with their peers on academic ability, self-respect, and 19 other positive qualities, as well as on selfishness, pretentiousness, and 19 other negative characteristics. The students also completed personality scales tapping psychological resources such as optimism, extraversion, and happiness. One week later, the participants reported to a UCLA laboratory, where they first provided a saliva sample for cortisol analysis and then performed several standard mental arithmetic tasks that reliably induce stress. As they did so, their heart rates and systolic and diastolic blood pressures were monitored. Following completion of the stress-challenge tasks, a second cortisol measure was taken.

The results showed that self-enhancers had lower baseline cortisol levels at the start of the study *and* lower heart rate and blood pressure responses during the stress-challenge tasks. The baseline cortisol results suggest that self-enhancement is associated with lower resting HPA axis levels, indicating a chronically healthier neuroendocrine state. The blunted heart rate and blood pressure responses suggest that positive self-perceptions help people manage acute stressors. Over time, self-enhancers may experience less stress-related wear and tear on their bodies. Equally interesting were the participants' responses to the psychological resources questionnaire, which suggested that the relationship between self-enhancement and neuroendocrine response was mediated by higher self-esteem, optimism, extraversion, stronger social support, and greater work and community involvement than that found in participants who scored low on measures of self-enhancement.

Because most of the data from such studies comes from research participants in affluent regions of the developed world, Sarah Pressman and her colleagues (Pressman, Gallagher, & Lopez, 2013) wondered if the connection between positive emotions and health was a *First World problem.* In other words, in parts of the world where people might not have adequate food or safety, are emotions still strongly tied to health? To find out, they surveyed over 150,000 people in 142 different countries, asking them about recent emotions, health concerns, as well as about their safety and access to food and shelter. Importantly, the results showed that the relationship between emotions and health not only held true globally, but also was even stronger in poorer countries.

Social Integration

Sara Snodgrass (from the chapter-opening vignette) feels that a key feature of her psychological thriving is the extent to which she has reorganized her life's priorities around her relationships with friends and family. Indeed, the importance of **social integration**—the number of social roles one participates in—has been demonstrated by studies showing that people who maintain strong social ties are more likely to retain better mental and physical health, and to live longer (Berkman, Buxton, Ertel, & Okechukwu, 2010). One recent study

social integration The number of social roles a person participates in.

Social Engagement People who maintain strong social ties are more likely to retain health and live longer.

of over 1000 adults between the ages of 70 and 79 found that the more social roles people engaged in, the better their lung function (Crittenden and others, 2014). Other studies have demonstrated that interventions that include some form of social support have enhancing effects on natural killer (NK) cell cytotoxicity, lymphocyte proliferation, and cell-mediated immunity (Miller & Cohen, 2001).

Relaxation

Wakeful relaxation is also associated with decreases in negative emotions and alterations of neuroendocrine functions (Daruna, 2004). Relaxation can be achieved through methods such as meditation, listening to music, simple breathing exercises, yoga, and a variety of other simple means. For instance, research studies have shown that relaxation promotes decreased leukocyte counts, enhanced natural killer cell activity, and, in the case of students who regularly practice relaxation, improved immune functioning during stressful exam periods (Davidson and others, 2003). The most consistent finding associated with relaxation is an increase in secretory IgA, one of the anabolic hormones discussed earlier in the chapter. Interestingly, hypnosis, which is also thought to induce relaxation, also produces reliable increases in secretory IgA (Johnson, Walker, Heys, Whiting, & Eremin, 1996).

Features of Psychological Thriving

A growing body of research reveals that curiosity and a sense of control over one's life contribute strongly to psychological thriving. Let's examine each of these factors.

Curiosity

Curiosity refers to a person's orientation or attraction to novel stimuli. Research suggests that curiosity in older people is associated with maintaining the health of the aging central nervous system. In examining the relationship between curiosity in older men and women and survival rates, researchers in one classic study found that after 5 years, those with the highest levels of curiosity survived longer than those with lower levels (Swan & Carmelli, 1996). It's important to note, however, that this correlational evidence does not indicate that curiosity automatically increases an older person's chances of survival; it may be simply a sign that his or her central nervous system is operating properly. In some individuals, age-related declines in curiosity reflect declining mental functioning. Because certain brain structures known to be involved in Alzheimer's disease also are involved in directed attention and novelty-seeking behavior, diminished curiosity may be one of the earliest signs of abnormal aging of the central nervous system.

Assuming that the person is a normal, healthy adult, curiosity may enhance healthy aging because it enables older adults to meet daily environmental and physical challenges successfully. Thus, the curious older adult uses active coping strategies (see Chapter 5) to approach potential problems and impediments, and in this way, manages to reduce the strain on his or her physical and mental resources. It seems that such an individual stands a better chance of being physically and mentally healthy in later life.

More recent research does suggest that people with greater curiosity are, in fact, more responsive to healthy opportunities for growth and cognitive stimulation. In one study, for instance, over a 3-week period, people who scored high on a measure of curiosity reported more frequent opportunities to demonstrate persistence at goals in the face of obstacles and to express gratitude to others, along with greater sensitivity to these opportunities for growth (Kashdan & Steger, 2007). Still, more research is needed into the mechanisms linking curiosity to outcomes such as mortality. Several hypotheses have been suggested as to why highly curious people should live longer than their less curious peers (Kashdan & Silvia, 2008). Among these are greater *neurogenesis* from continued novel and cognitive pursuits, greater willingness to try less traditional treatments and health strategies, and the health benefits of responding to stressors as challenges rather than threats (including a less overactive hypothalamic-pituitary-adrenal axis).

Perceived Control and Self-Efficacy

In one major prospective study of personality traits and health, researchers interviewed 8723 late-middle-aged and older persons living independently or in adapted housing for elderly people in the Netherlands (Kempen, Jelicic, & Ormel, 1997). Three measures of personality were investigated: mastery or personal control, general self-efficacy, and neuroticism (emotional instability). *Mastery* concerns the extent to which one regards one's own life changes as being under one's own control, as opposed to being fatalistically ruled. *Self-efficacy* refers to the belief that one can perform specific behaviors successfully. *Neuroticism* is related to a constant preoccupation with things that might go wrong and a strong emotional reaction of anxiety to these thoughts. Research participants with lower levels of neuroticism and higher levels of mastery and self-efficacy perceived significantly higher levels of functioning and well-being.

Why should a sense of control and mastery improve health? Both behavioral and physiological explanations are viable. Those who have a greater sense of control are more likely to take action, to engage in health-promoting behaviors, and to avoid health-damaging behaviors. Because individuals with a high sense of control believe that what they do makes a difference, they behave in healthier ways. In a recent study of 3352 people with type 2 diabetes, patients' mastery and perceived autonomy correlated positively with their self-management skills (Raaijmakers and others, 2014). Findings such as these have significant practice implications for health care providers, since a greater sense of mastery is likely to increase patients' motivation to actively cope with and manage their diseases. In contrast, those who feel helpless and fail to see a relationship between actions and outcomes may be more prone to illness and disease because they fail to engage in health-promoting practices or because they tend toward health-compromising behaviors ("I could get lung cancer no matter what I do, so I might as well smoke").

Having a sense of control also seems to show positive physiological effects. For instance, research has shown that people with a high sense of control have lower cortisol levels and return more quickly to baseline levels after stress (see Hansen and others, 2010, for a review).

Additional evidence comes from research involving people at different socioeconomic levels. Margie Lachman and Suzanne Weaver of Brandeis University (1998) examined three large national samples of various social classes and found that for all income groups, higher perceived control was related to better health, greater life satisfaction, and fewer negative emotions. Although the results showed that, on average, those with lower incomes had lower perceived control as well as poorer health, control beliefs played a moderating role, and participants in the lowest-income group, but with a high sense of control, showed levels of health and well-being comparable to those of the higher-income groups. The results provide some evidence that psychosocial variables such as sense of control may be useful in understanding social-class differences in health.

Beyond Positive Psychology

During the two decades since positive psychology was introduced, there has been a strong push to study various psychological traits, such as those considered in this chapter, that are presumed to be beneficial for well-being. Recently, some critics have suggested that positive psychologists have not paid enough attention to the interpersonal context in which individual traits are displayed (Fincham & Beach, 2010). When the social context is considered, some studies have found that psychological traits are not inherently positive or negative but depend on the context in which they operate.

James McNulty and Frank Fincham (2012) offer the example of a person involved in a physically abusive relationship. There is a large body of research suggesting that people and relationships benefit in the following situations:

- Any negative behaviors in the relationship can be attributed to external causes rather than to dispositional traits in the offending partner.
- Partners in a relationship are optimistic about their future interactions.
- Partners forgive one another.
- Partners remember their positive experiences in the relationship and forget their more negative ones.
- Partners remain committed to one another.

Most of the research studies on which these findings are based involved people who were not involved in abusive relationships. McNulty and Fincham suggest that applying these principles to a woman living in a physically abusive relationship may be unhealthy. Such women may benefit from 1) attributing their partner's abuse to his dispositional qualities rather than to external sources, 2) expecting the abuse to continue, 3) not forgiving the abuse, 4) remembering the abuse, and 5) being less committed to the relationship. In other words, so-called positive traits and processes sometimes can be harmful, whereas traits and processes often thought to be negative can be beneficial for well-being.

Other critics of positive psychology call for researchers to move beyond labeling traits as positive or negative. Doing so, they argue, imposes values on psychological science that influence what researchers choose to study, what they expect to find, and how they interpret results. Although science is never completely value-free, critics argue that positive psychology needs to be thought of as just plain psychology before we can have a fuller understanding of the human condition, and that psychological traits and processes are not inherently positive or negative.

In this chapter, we have explored the connection between behavior and health. We have seen how health psychology's biopsychosocial focus on strength-based approaches to prevention promotes healthier individuals, families, workplaces, and communities. As this healthier, more positive model takes hold, we are also witnessing a tipping point in which health care similarly shifts from its historical emphasis on tertiary prevention to a more balanced delivery system favoring primary prevention.

Weigh In on Health

Respond to each question below based on what you learned in the chapter. (**Tip:** Use the items in "Summing Up" to take into account related biological, psychological, and social concerns.)

1. When Sonia, a student in your health psychology course, moved into off-campus housing, she discovered that many of the residents smoked cigarettes. How would she explain this behavior in terms of the HBM, TPB, and TTM theories of health behavior?

2. Suppose that you were asked by your college or university to design a health campaign to reduce risky health-related behaviors among students. Based on the research discussed in the chapter, what types of interventions are likely to be effective? What types of interventions are likely to be ineffective?

3. What is a health situation that you and other students at your college face that could benefit from greater awareness of positive psychology? How would positive psychology help make your student population healthier? What are some findings that support your response?

Summing Up

Health and Behavior

1. Most behaviors affect health in some way: for better (healthy behaviors) or worse (health-risk behaviors), directly or indirectly, and immediately or over the long term.

2. The health belief model (HBM) assumes that decisions regarding health behavior are based on four interacting factors: perceived susceptibility to a health threat, perceived severity of the threat, perceived benefits of and barriers to treatment, and cues to action.

3. The theory of planned behavior (TPB) maintains that the best way to predict whether a health behavior will occur is to measure a person's decision to engage in a health-related behavior (behavioral intention). The decision to engage in a health behavior is shaped by our attitude toward the behavior, our motivation to comply with the views of others regarding the behavior (subjective norm), and our expectation of success in performing the health behavior (perceived behavioral control).

4. The transtheoretical model (TTM) outlines five stages through which people progress in changing health-related behaviors: precontemplation, contemplation, preparation, action, and maintenance.

Prevention

5. Primary prevention refers to actions to prevent a disease or injury from occurring. Secondary prevention involves actions to treat an illness early in its course. Tertiary prevention involves actions taken to contain damage once a disease has progressed beyond its early stages.

6. In focusing on healthy life expectancy, health psychologists aim to shorten the amount of time that older people spend disabled, ill, or in pain (morbidity).

7. Family connectedness, conflict, and nurturance are powerful influences on the individual's health behavior, as are the health habits and attitudes of other family members. At the community level, people are more likely to adopt health-enhancing behaviors when these behaviors are promoted by community organizations, such as schools, government agencies, and the health care system.

8. Carefully planned health education campaigns that present information on several fronts and are community based often can promote changes that are difficult for individuals to accomplish by themselves.

9. Message framing is a critical factor in the effectiveness of health education. Messages can be framed to emphasize either the positive outcomes from adopting a health-promoting behavior (gain-framed messages) or the negative outcomes from failing to do so (loss-framed messages). Tailoring health messages to individuals is an effective strategy for promoting behavior change. Fear-arousing messages may backfire and actually decrease a person's likelihood of adopting a certain health behavior.

10. Behavioral interventions focus on the conditions that elicit health behaviors and the factors that help to maintain and reinforce them. Many programs use self-monitoring as the initial step in promoting behavior change.

11. Stimulus-control interventions aimed at modifying a health behavior involve two strategies: removing discriminative stimuli for the behavior from the environment and establishing new discriminative stimuli signaling the availability of reinforcement for healthier response choices.

12. Most organizations with 50 or more workers offer some form of work-site wellness program. The cost of such programs has proved to be more than offset by reductions in work-related injuries, absenteeism, and worker turnover.

Positive Psychology and Thriving

13. A central theme of the new positive psychology movement—which promotes a strength-based, preventive approach to research and interventions—is that adversity sometimes actually leads people to greater psychological and/or physical well-being.

14. Although catabolic hormones are essential to our short-term health, when we are in a constant state of arousal (allostatic load), prolonged elevations of catabolic hormones can weaken our immunity and promote illness.

15. Resilience can be thought of as the capacity of the brain and body to withstand challenges to homeostasis. Overuse or dysregulation of the neuroendocrine systems that maintain homeostasis can lead to *allostatic overload* and the development and acceleration of many chronic illnesses, from depression to cardiovascular disease.

16. Neuroendocrine adaptations are an important aspect of resilience. The brain also responds to hormonal and neural feedback from neuroendocrine systems, as they are engaged as part of the body's effort to maintain homeostasis. This feedback (biological embedding) seems to shape the structure and function of the brain throughout life.

17. A number of psychosocial factors have been linked to enhanced immunity in response to stress. These include self-esteem, perceptions of personal competence and control, self-efficacy, and a tendency to recall positive over negative information about ourselves (self-enhancement).

18. Other key features of psychological thriving include curiosity, wakeful relaxation, and social engagement. Curiosity may enhance healthy aging because it helps older adults use active coping strategies to meet daily challenges.

19. Critics have suggested that positive psychologists have not paid enough attention to the interpersonal context in which individual traits are displayed. When the social context is considered, some studies have found that psychological traits are not inherently positive or negative but depend on the context in which they operate.

Key Terms and Concepts to Remember

 LaunchPad
macmillan learning

To accompany your textbook, you have access to a number of online resources, including quizzes for every chapter of the book, flashcards, critical thinking exercises, videos, and *Check Your Health* inventories. To access these resources, please visit the Straub *Health Psychology* LaunchPad solo at: **launchpadworks.com**

Exercise, Sleep, and Injury Control

At 7:00 A.M. on October 9, 2010, I had been treading water in the Pacific Ocean for nearly 20 minutes. I was about 200 meters offshore from Dig Me Beach and the small town of Kailua-Kona, established in the 1800s by King Kamehameha as the capital of his newly unified kingdom of Hawaii. Since 1981, "Kona" has been the seat of the Ironman World Championship, a 140.6-mile triathlon consisting of a 2.4-mile swim, followed by a 112-mile bike ride, and finally a 26.2-mile marathon. I was holding my place at the watery starting line of this incredible event, along with 1500 others who had qualified to be there, amid network news helicopters hovering overhead, race officials floating on paddleboards, a full-size SUV that served as a floating advertisement for the race's major sponsor, and a flotilla of outrigger canoes, pontoon boats, and other small watercraft.

As I waited for the cannon to fire, signaling the start of the race, my mind flashed on several vivid memories along my journey to earn this coveted qualifying spot—one of only 50 for men my age, worldwide. I thought of the day 27 years earlier when I took my first painful, wheezy steps, as a "jogger" and reformed smoker. I had started exercising on the advice of cardiologist and running enthusiast George Sheehan, MD, who'd written that people who want to improve their fitness through exercise should find a form of play—movement that, above all, is fun—so much so that the desire to smoke is pushed aside because it is incompatible with being the "runner" I wanted to be.

My memory reel fast-forwarded several years to the start of the 1987 Boston marathon, a race I'd earned the right to run by running 26.2 miles in under 3 hours at the Detroit marathon. It had taken thousands of miles run in training, dozens of pairs of running shoes, and hundreds of 5K, 10K, and half-marathon road races to earn my entry—a feat of which I was so proud that my dad made the trip with me in celebration.

My hard-won identity as a serious runner came with many benefits, including excellent physical fitness, increased self-esteem, and lower levels of stress. However, the smile that briefly crossed my face at this thought vanished as the next "scene" in my memory movie surfaced—the rather dark period in which my competitiveness as a serious runner took over my life, at times hurting the ones I loved, affecting my work, and ultimately leading to one injury after another as I pushed my running to an average of over 70 miles each week for several years. I remembered the day in 1999, when, 24 hours after partially tearing my right Achilles tendon in the USA Track and Field National Championship 10K, I painfully hobbled a mile in order to keep my four-year streak of daily running intact.

The streak soon ended, however, along with my ability to walk—much less run—without limping, and I began a new, medical journey, intent to find a "cure" for my foot pain. Medicine had three things to offer, only one of which proved the right prescription. It wasn't the various surgical procedures or anti-inflammatory drugs recommended by health care providers who, being specialists in tertiary care, didn't know what to make of the extremely fit, yet obviously unhealthy, guy who sought one referral after another in his quest to continue running.

No, these remedies didn't work at all. What worked was rest and, eventually, embarking on a healthier exercise regimen that was a balance of cross training, swimming, cycling, and moderate amounts of running. I thought of my first days back in the pool, trying to regain the form as a swimmer I'd had as a child ... well, actually, at first it was just trying to make it one length of the pool without stopping! I remembered recapturing the joy and freedom I'd found as a kid riding my Schwinn Stingray around the neighborhood, but this time on a sleek new carbon fiber time-trial bike that was steeply angled to keep my upper body down in an aerodynamic position.

As the cannon boomed, I "found the toes" of the swimmer just ahead of me and wondered if he, and the rest of the 1500 triathletes wearing the gold Ironman Championship wristband, had been "watching" their own memory movies. One thing I was sure of was that this event would surely have a scene in my own movie's sequel.

My journey to the starting line of the Ironman World Championship highlights a number of issues related to the potential benefits and hazards of exercise. Motivation to start exercising can promote more general lifestyle changes, as it did when it helped me quit smoking and, later, take steps to improve my eating habits. And although exercise can enhance physical functioning and reduce anxiety, when taken too far, it poses hazards to physical and psychological health. This chapter explores the role that physical activity plays in people's health, along with two other important lifestyle issues: healthy sleep and injury prevention.

Exercise improves sleep, and sleep improves athletic performance and many other facets of our well-being. Today, however, our sleep patterns are more likely than ever to leave us feeling drained of energy. More than one-quarter of adults in the United States report not getting enough sleep, and about 10 percent experience chronic insomnia (Centers for Disease Control and Prevention, 2015g). Poor sleep undermines health in many ways, including by making people more prone to unintentional injuries, which are the leading causes of death from ages 1 to 44 and a leading cause of disability for all ages, regardless of gender, socioeconomic status, and race/ethnicity. Despite popular belief, most injuries are not "accidents" but instead are predictable and preventable. Promoting increased physical activity, healthier sleep habits, and reducing the prevalence and consequences of injuries are key goals of *Healthy People 2020* and the subject of this chapter.

Physical Activity, Exercise, and Fitness

Physical activity is bodily movement produced by skeletal muscles that requires expenditure of energy. Physical activity includes exercise, as well as other activities that are done as part of working, transportation, household chores, and leisure. Physical activity is natural for humans. Our bodies were designed for it, and staying active is essential for good health. Physical inactivity, on the other hand, is the fourth-leading risk factor for global mortality, each year causing an estimated 3.2 million (6 percent) deaths worldwide. In addition, physical inactivity is a key risk factor for noncommunicable diseases such as cardiovascular disease, cancer, and diabetes (World Health Organization, 2015b).

Physical exercise is physical activity that is planned, repetitive, and purposeful in the sense that it is intended to improve or maintain one or more aspects of physical fitness. Two broad categories of physical exercise are *aerobic* and *nonaerobic*. Often called "cardio," **aerobic exercise** is light- to moderate-intensity exercise performed for an extended period of time. Examples are swimming, cycling, and running. "Aerobic" means "living in air" and refers to the use of oxygen to meet energy demands adequately during this type of exercise. This type of exercise can be contrasted with **anaerobic exercise,** such as strength training and sprinting short distances. This type of exercise is generally performed at a higher intensity than aerobic exercise but for shorter periods of time. Any exercise lasting longer than about two minutes is largely aerobic.

How physically active are you? Do you exercise regularly? How active should you be? About 50 to 70 percent of the total energy that your body burns involves the functioning of cells and vital organs. This is your **basal (resting) metabolic rate (BMR).** Although BMR is not easily determined—because it depends on a number of variables, including your age, gender, current weight, and activity level—a rough estimate of your daily calorie needs to maintain your current weight can be calculated by multiplying your body weight (in pounds) by 13. About 7 to 10 percent of the energy that your body uses serves to break down the food you eat. The rest is the result of physical activity, including the things you have to do every day, such as showering, getting dressed, vacuuming, and leisure activities such as dancing, playing sports, and walking. The more physical activities you choose to do, the more energy you expend.

Energy expenditure is typically measured in **calories,** a measure of food energy equivalent to the amount of energy needed to raise the temperature of 1 gram of water 1 degree Celsius. Table 7.1 lists the calories burned by doing different activities for people of three different weights (Harvard Heart Letter, 2015).

aerobic exercise Light- to moderate-intensity exercise performed for an extended period of time; examples include swimming, cycling, and running.

anaerobic exercise High-intensity exercise performed for short periods of time; examples include weight training and sprinting.

basal metabolic rate (BMR) The minimum number of calories the body needs to maintain bodily functions while at rest.

calorie A measure of food energy equivalent to the amount of energy needed to raise the temperature of 1 gram of water 1 degree Celsius.

For children, exercise means playing and being physically active. Kids exercise when they have gym class at school, during recess, at soccer or swim practice, while playing tag, or when riding bikes.

anatols/Thinkstock/Getty Images

TABLE 7.1

This table lists the calories burned by 30 minutes of the following activities, listed by category (such as gym activities, training and sports activities, home repair, etc.). In each category, activities are listed from least to most calories burned.

	125-pound person	155-pound person	185-pound person
Gym Activities			
Weight lifting: general	90	112	133
Stretching, hatha yoga	120	149	178
Calisthenics: moderate	135	167	200
Stair step machine: general	180	223	266
Circuit training: general	240	298	355
Rowing, stationary: vigorous	255	316	377
Elliptical trainer: general	270	335	400
Aerobics, step: high-impact	300	372	444
Bicycling, stationary: vigorous	315	391	466
Training and Sport Activities			
Bowling	90	112	133
Dancing: slow, waltz, foxtrot	90	112	133
Frisbee	90	112	133
Volleyball: noncompetitive, general play	90	112	133
Golf: using cart	105	130	155
Gymnastics: general	120	149	178
Horseback riding: general	120	149	178
Walking: 3.5 mph (17 min/mi)	120	149	178
Badminton: general	135	167	200
Skateboarding	150	186	222
Walking: 4.5 mph (13 min/mi)	150	186	222
Dancing: disco, ballroom, square	165	205	244
Swimming: general	180	223	266
Rollerblade skating	210	260	311
Soccer: general	210	260	311
Tennis: general	210	260	311
Basketball: playing a game	240	298	355
Bicycling: 12–13.9 mph	240	298	355
Football: touch, flag, general	240	298	355
Running: 5 mph (12 min/mile)	240	298	355
Skiing: cross-country	240	298	355
Running: 5.2 mph (11.5 min/mile)	270	335	400
Running: cross-country	270	335	400
Jumping rope	300	372	444
Running: 6 mph (10 min/mile)	300	372	444
Swimming: laps, vigorous	300	372	444
Running: 6.7 mph (9 min/mile)	330	409	488
Swimming: crawl	330	409	488
Bicycling: 16–19 mph	360	446	533
Running: 7.5 mph (8 min/mile)	375	465	555
Outdoor Activities			
Raking lawn	120	149	178
Gardening: general	135	167	200

	125-pound person	155-pound person	185-pound person
Outdoor Activities (Continued)			
Mowing lawn: push, power	135	167	200
Carrying and stacking wood	150	186	222
Digging, spading dirt	150	186	222
Laying sod/crushed rock	150	186	222
Mowing lawn: push, hand	165	205	244
Chopping and splitting wood	180	223	266
Shoveling snow by hand	180	223	266
Home and Daily Life Activities			
Sleeping	19	23	28
Watching TV	23	28	33
Reading while sitting	34	42	50
Cooking	75	93	111
Child-care: bathing, feeding, etc.	105	130	155
Food shopping with cart	105	130	155
Heavy cleaning: washing car, windows	135	167	200
Playing with kids: vigorous effort	150	186	222
Moving: household furniture	180	223	266
Moving: carrying boxes	210	260	311
Occupational Activities			
Computer work	41	51	61
Light office work	45	56	67
Sitting in meetings	49	60	72
Desk work	53	65	78
Sitting in class	53	65	78
Truck driving	60	74	89
Bartending/server	75	93	111
Operating heavy equipment	75	93	111
Being a police officer	75	93	111
Theater work	90	112	133
Welding	90	112	133
Carpentry work	105	130	155
Coaching sports	120	149	178
Construction, general	165	205	244
Firefighting	360	446	533

Source: Excerpted from the *Harvard Men's Health Watch*, January 2009. © 2009 Harvard University. Updated 2016. www.health.harvard.edu.

NOTE: Harvard Health Publications does not endorse any products or medical procedures.

Benefits from Physical Activity

Regular physical activity is the closest thing we have to a fountain of youth. It becomes even more important as people age, promoting both physical and psychological well-being and possibly helping to slow down or even reverse many of the effects of aging. Regular exercise can reduce the risk of premature disability and many chronic illnesses, including those related to stress. Many of the benefits of physical activity are optimized when people pursue physical fitness.

How physically fit are you? **Physical fitness** has been defined as a set of attributes or characteristics that people have or achieve that relates to the ability to perform physical

physical fitness A set of attributes relating to the ability to perform physical activity that includes muscular strength, endurance, flexibility, and healthy body composition.

cardiorespiratory endurance The ability of the heart, blood vessels, and lungs to supply oxygen to working muscles during physical activity for prolonged periods of time.

activity. The most important attribute is **cardiorespiratory endurance,** or *aerobic fitness,* which refers to the ability of the heart, blood vessels, and lungs to supply oxygen to working muscles during physical activity for prolonged periods of time. The amount of oxygen that your body uses is referred to as *oxygen consumption* or *VO_2,* which stands for "volume of oxygen." As your intensity of exercise increases, VO_2 rises and eventually reaches its peak value, known as VO_2max. VO_2max, also known as *aerobic capacity,* is the measure of cardiorespiratory endurance. The other components of physical fitness include:

- Muscular strength—the amount of force that a muscle or group of muscles can exert against heavy resistance
- Muscular endurance—the ability of a muscle or group of muscles to repeat a movement many times or to hold a particular position for an extended period of time
- Flexibility—the degree to which an individual muscle will lengthen
- Body composition—the amount of fat in the body compared to the amount of *lean mass* (muscle and bones)

Good physical fitness in both men and women delays mortality by two years or more. Research has shown that a person's degree of physical fitness is an excellent predictor of life expectancy and quality of life. Improving physical fitness may also help prevent age-associated diseases. This is true for healthy people, for people with chronic conditions such as cardiovascular disease (Carnethon and others, 2003), and for both women (Gulati and others, 2003) and men (Kurl and others, 2003). Improving one's physical fitness can reduce the risk of death by 44 percent (I.-M. Lee and others, 2013). In addition, improving physical fitness has a favorable influence on self-image and self-esteem, and has been shown to reduce depression, anxiety, and panic syndromes (Kirkcaldy, Shephard, & Siefen, 2002). It has even been reported that while antidepressant medication may produce a more rapid initial response, exercise is just as effective at reducing depression over a period of several months (Harvard Health Publications, 2013).

Appropriately undertaken, physical exercise may be the best means available for delaying and preventing the consequences of aging. Evolutionary biologists define *aging* as an age-progressive decline in intrinsic physiological function, leading to an increase in the age-specific mortality rate (Fabian & Flatt, 2011). Aging can be influenced for the better (delaying it) or worse (accelerating it) by lifestyle factors such as diet and physical activity. This is true regardless of the age, gender, health, or physical condition of the person who undertakes to improve physical fitness. A sedentary lifestyle accelerates aging and its consequences, including physical appearance and risk of disability and disease (Castillo-Garzon, Ruiz, Ortega, & Gutierrez, 2006).

Weight Control

Prevention of weight gain, as well as weight loss, particularly when combined with reduced calorie intake, are notable benefits of regular physical activity. Obesity has been recognized as one of the chief threats to overall health and well-being (see Chapter 8). Sedentary lifestyles are partly to blame—only one in four people in the United States gets the minimum recommended amount of weekly physical activity (Mendes, 2011). Even during their leisure time, many people choose not to engage in any physical activity at all (CDC, 2005).

Broom and colleagues (Broom, Batterham, King, & Stensel, 2009) compared the effects of aerobic and resistance exercise on feelings of hunger and the circulating levels of appetite-regulating hormones. In the study, a group of healthy men completed three trials in a counterbalanced design: 60 minutes of treadmill running at 70 percent maximal oxygen uptake (aerobic exercise), a 90-minute free-weight-lifting session that included 10 different exercises, and a resting control trial in which no exercise was performed. Blood was sampled before, during, and after the exercise sessions to compare levels of three appetite-regulating hormones [ghrelin, peptide tyrosine-tyrosine (PYY), and insulin].

Perceived hunger was assessed using a visual scale in which participants rated their hunger from zero (not hungry) to 15 (very hungry). The results showed that ghrelin (high levels of which stimulate hunger) was lower during both aerobic and resistance exercise than for the control. In contrast, PYY (high levels of which signal satiety) was significantly elevated after aerobic exercise compared to both resistance exercise and the resting control. These hormonal changes were accompanied by reduced feelings of hunger after both aerobic and resistance exercise compared to the control condition, with the response being slightly greater with aerobic exercise.

Although exercise is helpful in maintaining a healthy body weight, a persistent myth is that fat can be targeted for reduction from a specific area of the body (spot reduction). Advertisers exploit this common, yet mistaken, belief when hawking the latest gizmo or pill on late-night infomercials. Most experts do not believe it is possible to reduce fat in one area by exercising that body part alone. Instead, fat is lost from the entire body as a result of diet and regular physical activity.

How much physical activity is needed? The most recent recommendation is that healthy adults between the ages of 18 and 64 years need, at minimum, moderate intensity physical activity for at least 30 minutes, five days each week, or at least 75 minutes of vigorous intensity physical activity throughout the week (WHO, 2015h). For additional health benefits, moderate intensity physical activity should be increased to about 300 minutes per week. In addition, muscle-strengthening activities should be done involving major muscle groups on two or more days each week.

Most important to maintaining vitality is aerobic exercise, in which the heart speeds up in order to pump larger amounts of blood, breathing is deeper and more frequent, and the cells of the body develop the ability to extract increasing amounts of oxygen from the blood, among other benefits (see Table 7.2). In addition, weight-bearing aerobic exercises such as walking, jogging, and racquetball help preserve muscular strength and flexibility, promote healthy body composition, and maintain bone density.

For most people, light daily activities such as shopping, cooking, or doing the laundry do not count toward the guidelines. Examples of moderate-intensity exercise are brisk walking, water aerobics, ballroom dancing, and playing tennis. Examples of vigorous-intensity exercise are race walking, jogging, running, swimming laps, jumping rope, and bicycling 10 miles per hour or faster.

TABLE 7.2
Health Benefits of Aerobic Exercise

- Promotes the growth of new neurons in the brain (*neurogenesis*)
- Decreases resting heart rate and blood pressure
- Improves regulation of blood sugar
- Increases maximum oxygen consumption (VO_2max)
- Increases strength and efficiency of the heart
- Increases slow-wave (deep) sleep
- Increases HDL (good) cholesterol and reduces LDL (bad) cholesterol
- Decreases the risk of cardiovascular disease
- Decreases obesity
- Promotes relaxation
- Decreases menstrual cycle length
- Increases longevity
- Decreases risk of some cancers
- Improves immune system functioning
- Improves mood

Information from Mayo Clinic. (2011). Aerobic exercise: Top 10 reasons to get physical. http://www .mayoclinic.com/health/aerobic-exercise/EP00002

osteoporosis A disease of the bones involving a loss of bone mineral density that leads to an increased risk of fracture.

Protection against Chronic Illness

Physical exercise has been demonstrated to protect against a number of chronic conditions, including **osteoporosis,** a disorder characterized by declining bone density due to calcium loss. This is especially true for those who were active during their youth, when bone minerals were accruing (Hind & Burrows, 2007). Although osteoporosis is most common in postmenopausal women, it also occurs in men, as does the protective effect of exercise. Roughly one woman in four over age 60 has osteoporosis, with white and Asian women being at higher risk than African-American women. Osteoporosis results in more than 1 million bone fractures a year in the United States alone, the most debilitating of which are hip fractures.

In addition to increasing physical strength and maintaining bone density, regular exercise reduces an older person's risk for several of the most common chronic illnesses of adulthood: cardiovascular disease, certain cancers, diabetes, and metabolic syndrome. Exercise helps fight heart disease by strengthening the heart, increasing blood flow, keeping blood vessels open, and lowering both blood pressure and the blood pressure reaction to stress (Ford, 2002). Even moderate exercise, such as gardening and walking, can result in significant increases in HDL—the so-called "good cholesterol"—and decreased total serum cholesterol. Regular exercise is linked to lower triglycerides, which have been implicated in the formation of atherosclerotic plaques, as well as lower levels of LDL, or "bad" cholesterol, and higher levels of HDL (Szapary, Bloedon, & Foster, 2003). Due to these and other benefits, people who exercise suffer half as many heart attacks as do others who are inactive (Visich & Fletcher, 2009).

Several extensive review studies have reported that physical activity also offers protection against cancers of the colon and rectum, breast, endometrium, prostate, and lung (National Cancer Institute, 2015d). Regular physical activity may reduce cancer risk by influencing proinflammatory cytokines (Stewart and others, 2007), which, in turn, have beneficial effects in blocking the development and growth of tumor cells (Rogers, Colbert, Greiner, Perkins, & Hursting, 2008). In addition, physical activity promotes healthy immune functioning by delaying some age-related declines in white blood cells. For example, endurance-trained athletes preserve telomere length in their white blood cells—which otherwise systematically decrease in aging, sedentary adults (LaRocca, Seals, & Pierce, 2010).

Diet and exercise are especially important for people living with diabetes mellitus, as they are the best nonpharmacological means by which patients may improve and manage their blood glucose levels significantly. Sedentary behavior, measured objectively with accelerometers and heart rate monitors, or TV viewing time measured by self-report, has been associated significantly with obesity, waist circumference (Healy and others, 2008), and metabolic syndrome (Thorp and others, 2010). Exercise increases insulin sensitivity (over both the short and long term), lowers blood sugar levels, reduces body fat, and improves cardiovascular function (Zisser, Sueyoshi, Krigstein, Sziglato, & Riddell, 2012).

Metabolic syndrome (MetS) is a cluster of conditions—increased blood pressure, a high blood-sugar level, excess body fat around the waist (abdominal obesity), low HDL cholesterol level, high triglyceride level (a type of fat found in the blood)—that occur together, increasing your risk of heart disease, stroke, and diabetes. The risk of having metabolic syndrome is closely linked to obesity, lack of physical activity, and insulin resistance, a condition in which the body can't use insulin properly. Insulin is a hormone that helps move blood sugar into cells where it's used for energy. Metabolic syndrome is more common in African-American women and Mexican-American women than in men of the same racial/ethnic groups. The condition affects white women and men about equally. Adults who report engaging in regular physical exercise, especially resistance exercise such as lifting weights, push-ups, and sit-ups, have significantly lower prevalence

metabolic syndrome (MetS) A cluster of conditions that includes increased blood pressure, high blood sugar level, abdominal obesity, low HDL ("good") cholesterol level, and high triglyceride level that occur together and increase a person's risk of heart disease, stroke, and diabetes.

estimates of MetS (Churilla, Johnson, Magyari, & Crouter, 2012). Diabetes and metabolic syndrome will be discussed more fully in Chapter 10.

Psychological Well-Being

The benefits from exercise extend to our psychological well-being. Regular exercise is associated with improved mood and elevated well-being just after a workout (Motl and others, 2005). Studies show that over time, exercise may serve as an effective buffer against anxiety and stress (Conn, 2010; Windle, Hughes, Linck, Russell, & Woods, 2010), boost self-esteem and self-efficacy (McAuley, Jerome, Marquez, Elavsky, & Blissmer, 2003), help people feel more vigor and less fatigue (Mead and others, 2010), and offer protection against depression (Daley, 2008) and anxiety (Wipfli, Rethorst, & Landers, 2008). In a massive, 21-country survey of university students, physical exercise was a "strong" and consistent predictor of life satisfaction (Grant, Wardle, & Steptoe, 2009).

The psychological benefits of physical activity are particularly pronounced among older adults who perceive high levels of stress. The four-year Montreal Aging and Health Study of adults over age 60 found that among participants with high baseline levels of perceived stress, those who frequently engaged in physical activities experienced a reduction of perceived stress over two years and fewer increases in physical health symptoms over four years (Rueggeberg, Wrosch, & Miller, 2012).

Regular exercise also predicts better cognitive functioning and reduced risk of dementia and Alzheimer's disease (Kramer & Erickson, 2007). The cognitive benefits can be observed in children as young as 7 years of age. In one study, 171 overweight children between 7 and 11 years of age were randomly assigned to three months of low-dose (20 minutes/day) or high-dose (40 minutes/day) aerobic exercise, or a no-exercise control group. Each day, the participants were transported to an after-school exercise program that included running games, jumping rope, and playing modified basketball and soccer. Neuroimaging data revealed that aerobic exercise was associated with increased prefrontal cortex activity. The prefrontal cortex plays a key role in planning, emotional regulation, and other so-called executive cognitive functions.

Animal studies show that aerobic exercise also increases growth factors in the brain that lead to increased capillary blood supply to the cortex and growth of new neurons and synapses (neurogenesis), resulting in better learning and performance (Dishman and others, 2006; Reynolds, 2009).

Is It Ever Too Late to Begin Exercising?

The answer to the question "Is it ever too late to start exercising?" is no. In one study, frail nursing home residents aged 72 to 98 participated in a 10-week program of muscle-strengthening resistance training three times a week (Raloff, 1996). After the 10 weeks, those in the exercise group more than doubled their muscular strength and increased their stair-climbing power by 28 percent. In another study, Maria Fiatarone and her colleagues (1993) randomly assigned 100 participants, who averaged 87 years of age, to one of four groups. Participants in the first group engaged in regular resistance-training exercises. Participants in the second group took a daily multivitamin supplement. Participants in the third group took the supplement and participated in the resistance training. Participants in the fourth group were permitted to engage in three physical activities of their choice (including aerobic exercise) but could not engage in resistance training. Over the course

Neuroimaging data vividly demonstrate one benefit of aerobic exercise—increased activity in the prefrontal cortex, the part of the brain that plays a key role in planning and emotional regulation.

Figure 2 from Davis, Catherine L.; Tomporowski, Phillip D.; MacDowell, Jennifer E.; Austin, Benjamin P.; Miller, Patricia H.; Yanasak, Nathan E.; Allison, Jerry D.; Naglieri, Jack A. *Health Psychology*, Vol. 30(1), Jan 2011, 91–98. doi: 10.1037/a0021766. Copyright © 2011 by the American Psychological Association. Reproduced with permission.

It's never too late to begin exercising. Physical activity is one of the most important things older adults can do to prevent health problems and to promote healthy aging.

of the study, muscle strength more than doubled in the resistance groups, with an average increase of 113 percent, compared to a minuscule 3 percent increase in subjects in the second group. Interestingly, the group that exercised and took the supplement showed no greater improvement than the groups that exercised but did not take a supplement.

Further evidence that it is never too late to start exercising comes from studies demonstrating that exercise even late in life may still help prevent or reduce the rate of loss in bone density. As compared to a control group of sedentary women, 50- to 70-year-old women who had been sedentary but were assigned to an exercise group showed significantly reduced loss in bone mineral content (Nelson and others, 1994). As an added benefit, women in the exercise group increased their muscle mass and strength. Together, these benefits are associated with lower morbidity and mortality among physically active older adults (Everett, Kinser, & Ramsey, 2007).

Although it's never too late to begin exercising, during late adulthood, the intensity of exercise must be adjusted to reflect declines in cardiovascular and respiratory functioning. For some adults, this means that walking replaces jogging; for others, such as former world-class marathoner Bill Rodgers, now in his sixties, this means training at a 6-minute per mile pace rather than a 5-minute pace.

Why Don't More People Exercise?

Despite the well-documented physical and psychological benefits of lifelong exercise, the percentage of people who exercise regularly declines with age and varies significantly across socioeconomic and ethnic groups (WHO, 2015h). Although some children get regular exercise through school programs, the level of physical activity has declined substantially by adolescence, especially among girls (Davison, Schmalz, & Downs, 2010) and among boys not involved in sports programs (Crosnoe, 2002).

Globally, 1 in 4 adults aged 18 and over are not active enough (WHO, 2015i). An estimated 32 percent of men and 42 percent of women in the United States describe themselves as sedentary. Few people manage to adopt and maintain an exercise habit successfully. Minority group members consistently seem to have lower physical activity levels than majority group members, with minority women being among the least active subgroups in the United States (Cassetta, Boden-Albala, Sciacca, & Giardina, 2007). Why would this be? People choose not to exercise for many reasons, such as lack of time, money, or energy (Ruby, Dunn, Perrino, Gillis, & Viel, 2011). In several large surveys, physical activity was found to be lowest among people with low incomes and lower levels of education.

Some older adults are reluctant—even fearful—of exercising too much due to myths associated with exercise. These myths include the idea that exercise can accelerate the loss of bone density, lead to arthritis, and even increase the risk of dying from a heart attack. In fact, the body is far more likely to rust out than it is to wear out. As the saying goes, "Use it or lose it!"

Exercising behavior also is related to an individual's beliefs regarding its health benefits, confidence in his or her ability to perform certain physical skills correctly (known as *exercise self-efficacy*), and self-motivation. Believing that exercise will help one to live a longer, healthier life is a strong stimulus for initiating exercise. Believing that exercise is difficult, useless, or unsafe, or that declines in health are inevitable and irreversible with increased age, on the other hand, will almost certainly have the opposite effect.

There are several reasons that older adults might lack exercise self-efficacy. For one, they typically have less experience with exercise and have fewer exercising role models than younger people. Older people are also faced with ageist stereotypes about what constitutes appropriate behavior; vigorous exercise, especially for women, is contrary to stereotypes of old age. Finally, many older adults view old age as a time of rest and relaxation and are less likely to initiate and maintain regular exercise.

To explore further why some adults choose to exercise while others do not, Sara Wilcox and Martha Storandt of Washington University (1996) surveyed a random sample of 121 women aged 20 to 85, focusing on three psychological variables: exercise self-efficacy, self-motivation, and attitudes toward exercise. The sample consisted of two groups: exercisers and nonexercisers.

The findings revealed that desire and willingness to exercise had less to do with age than with attitudes about exercise; the belief that exercise would be enjoyable and beneficial decreased with age, but only among nonexercisers. Those who continued to exercise throughout adulthood were significantly more self-motivated, had greater exercise self-efficacy, and had more positive attitudes toward exercise than did nonexercisers. These results suggest that education stressing the benefits and the required frequency, duration, and intensity of exercise needed to reach these benefits must be a key component in exercise interventions with older adults. In addition, *ageist* stereotypes of later adulthood as a time of inevitable decline need to be challenged. Older adults will be less likely to begin an exercise regimen if they believe they are unable to do even basic exercises, so intervention efforts should include some basic instruction. Finally, age-appropriate programs, with exercises such as tai chi, have been shown to reduce older adults' fears of hazards, especially of falling (Zijlstra and others, 2007).

To the list of reasons why people don't exercise, you can add that people fail to appreciate how much they will enjoy it. I'm reminded of chatting with cardiologist George Sheehan many years ago before the start of the Boston Marathon. Sheehan, himself a dedicated runner, said, "People won't do something very long just because it's good for them. They've got to find some activity that, for them, is play." This bias sometimes stems from *forecasting myopia*, in which people contemplating an exercise routine place disproportionate emphasis on the beginning of a workout, which may be unpleasant. (Getting out the door with stiff legs on a cold, winter morning for my daily run comes to mind.)

Another reason that people don't exercise is that environmental barriers make doing so more difficult. The neighborhood environment has emerged as an important area of focus in predicting individual activity levels. Consider, for example, *neighborhood walkability*.

Radius Images/Getty Images

When people feel their neighborhood affords safe opportunities to exercise, such as by having traffic-free bike lanes or well-lit jogging paths, participation levels increase.

A walkable neighborhood allows travel from home to key destinations on foot. Adults who live in low-walkable neighborhoods are less physically active and more likely to be overweight and obese, and to engage in more obesity-related sedentary behaviors than their peers living in more walkable communities (A. C. King and others, 2010; Kozo and others, 2012).

When people feel their neighborhood is safe, when they are not socially isolated, and when they know about exercise facilities that are available to them, they are more likely to be physically active (Hawkley, Thisted, & Cacioppo, 2009). The absence of convenient and easily accessible exercise settings leads to lower rates of participation (Humpel and others, 2004). For example, having few or distant safe playgrounds, traffic-free bike lanes, well-lit jogging paths, and other community resources makes it difficult for urban children and working adults who must fit exercise in around busy schedules. Improving these options increases rates of exercise, and when communities have facilities such as these available, the prevalence of overweight and obesity in the neighborhood is reduced (Dowda, Dishman, Porter, Saunders, & Pate, 2009).

Lack of resources for exercising is a particular barrier for people low in socioeconomic (SES) status (Feldman & Steptoe, 2004). Recent studies have strongly suggested that neighborhood SES influences health, in part because of differences in physical activity (Boone-Heinonen and others, 2011). Neighborhood health disparities are associated with neighborhood SES, which determines the availability of resources for activity such as parks, walking/bike paths, and sports facilities, which in turn are linked to differences in physical activity (Schuz and others, 2012).

Another factor in sedentary lifestyles is the decline in physical education classes in schools due to mounting economic pressure. This means that, for many children, a lifelong habit of healthy physical activity and exercise is hard to establish. The U.S. Department of Health and Human Services recommends that young people between the ages of 6 and 17 participate in at least 60 minutes of physical activity daily. Yet in 2011, only 29 percent of high school students surveyed had participated in at least 60 minutes per day of physical activity on all seven days before the survey, and only 31 percent attended physical education class daily. The percentage of high school students who attended physical education classes daily decreased from 42 percent in 1991 to 25 percent in 1995 and remained stable at that level until 2011 (31 percent). In addition, 14 percent of high school students had not participated in 60 or more minutes of any kind of physical activity on *any* day during the seven days before the survey. To make matters even worse, participation in physical activity declines as young people age.

A 2011 meta-analysis of 50 studies of physical activity and academic performance among schoolchildren conducted by the Centers for Disease Control and Prevention (CDC, 2011b) reached the following conclusions:

- Regular physical activity in childhood and adolescence improves strength and endurance, helps build healthy bones and muscles, helps control weight, reduces anxiety and stress, increases self-esteem, and may improve blood pressure and cholesterol levels.

- Physical activity can help improve academic achievement (including grades and standardized test scores).

- Physical activity can have an impact on cognitive skills, attitudes, and academic behavior, all of which are important components of improved academic performance. These include enhanced concentration and attention, as well as improved classroom behavior.

- Increasing or maintaining time dedicated to physical education may help, and does not appear to adversely affect, academic performance.

Another way to look at the issue of why more people don't exercise is to ask who *is* most likely to exercise. Research suggests that people are most likely to stick with exercise programs if they (Floyd & Moyer, 2010):

- Enjoy exercise
- Have already formed the habit of exercising regularly
- Grew up in families that exercised
- Have social support for exercising from relatives, friends, and coworkers
- Have a favorable attitude and a strong sense of self-efficacy toward exercising
- Perceive themselves as being somewhat athletic
- Believe that people should take responsibility for their health

Exercise Interventions

Health behavior theories identify factors that predict physical activity in the individual. Among these are social cognitive factors, such as attitudes and intentions toward exercise; socioeconomic factors, such as education, which determine the ability to find and understand health-related information; and the financial resources needed to facilitate physical activity. A number of studies have shown that interventions aimed at the individual work best when they are matched to the stage of readiness of the participants (Marshall and others, 2003; Blissmer & McAuley, 2002).

In one recent study of 2790 adults participating in seven hour-long fitness classes, researchers found that participants significantly underestimated how much they would enjoy exercising. Recall from Chapter 6 that the *theory of planned behavior* maintains that attitudes toward a given behavior, along with subjective social norms and perceived behavioral control, shape our behavioral intentions, which in turn guide our behavior. The researchers found that a simple intervention, in which participants were prompted to consider all phases of the workout before starting, increased their expected enjoyment of the exercise routine and boosted their intention to exercise in the future (Ruby and others, 2011).

Also at the level of the individual, interventions that help people develop positive but realistic expectations for a new exercise program (Dunton and Vaughan, 2008) and those that focus on increasing participants' motivation, intentions, and perceptions of behavioral control and exercise self-efficacy can be successful in changing behavior (Conroy, Hyde, Doerksen, & Riebeiro, 2010). Interventions that combine this emphasis on changing social cognitions with behavioral techniques such as teaching self-monitoring skills have been particularly successful (Michie, Abraham, Whittington, McAteer, & Gupta, 2009; van Stralen, De Vries, Mudde, Bolman, & Lechner, 2009).

Many people find it easier to begin an exercise program than to keep it going as part of a permanent lifestyle change. A number of successful interventions incorporate relapse prevention techniques to promote long-term adherence to exercise programs. These include "inoculating" participants against the temptation to skip exercise by increasing their awareness of obstacles such as work and family obligations, stress, and fatigue. For some, simple reminders sent via text messages, phone, or e-mail can help improve adherence (Scholz, Keller, & Perren, 2009; Blanchard and others, 2007).

As we have seen, facilitating and impeding factors for physical activity also can be found in the environment. Neighborhood SES can determine the availability of exercise resources, and urban planning and local policies can facilitate or impede the ability to engage in physical activity (Schuz, Keller, & Perren, 2012).

The most effective interventions designed to promote increased physical activity in a community integrate individual and environmental factors, including demographic, biological, psychological, social/cultural, and public policy. The World Health Organization (2015h) has set a global target of increasing physical activity by at least 10 percent by 2025. To reach this target, WHO's *Global Action Plan* (2013b) promotes policies to ensure that:

- Walking, cycling, and other forms of active transportation are accessible and safe for all
- Labor and workplace policies encourage physical activity
- Schools have safe spaces and facilities for students to spend their free time actively
- Quality physical education supports children to develop behavior patterns that will keep them physically active throughout their lives
- Sports and recreation facilities provide opportunities for everyone to do sports

circadian rhythm A biological clock that operates on a 24-hour cycle.

One in five adults fails to get enough sleep. Changing work schedules, the Internet, and other diversions mean that people today sleep less than their counterparts did a century ago.

Sleep

E+/Getty Images

f exercise is the "fountain of youth," healthy sleep habits may be the "elixir of health" (Grayling, 2009). Unfortunately, about one in five adults fails to get enough sleep and experiences *sleep deprivation* (American Academy of Sleep Medicine, 2010). For some 70 million Americans, a sleep disorder such as insomnia, narcolepsy, sleepwalking, or sleep apnea is the cause. For others, stress or a demanding work or study schedule contributes to their poor sleep habits. Adolescents, who need 9 to 10 hours of sleep each night, now average less than 7 hours—a full 2 hours less than that averaged by their grandparents as teenagers (CDC, 2015g). Nearly a third of high school students responding to a recent survey admitted they routinely fall asleep in class (National Sleep Foundation, 2010).

Our bodies are approximately synchronized with the 24-hour cycle of night and day by an internal biological clock called the **circadian rhythm.** The rhythm is clearly linked to the light–dark cycle because animals, including humans, kept in total darkness for extended periods eventually develop a more free-running rhythm. Daylight and other environmental cues that reset our circadian rhythm when, for instance, we travel across several time zones, are called *zeitgebers* ("timekeepers"). As morning approaches, our body temperature begins to increase, peaking during the day, and then starting to decrease in the evening.

Our thinking and memory are sharpest when we are at our peak in the daily circadian cycle. Try working out a difficult math problem in the middle of the night, and you'll understand this immediately. This is why many people who travel extensively have learned to arrive at their destination a day or two before important meetings or other events where their thinking needs to be sharp. Doing so gives them a chance to use local *zeitgebers* to reset their internal biological clocks. Bright light, which activates light-sensitive proteins in the retinas of our eyes, is the most important factor in setting our 24-hour biological clock. It signals the brain's *suprachiasmatic nucleus* to decrease its production of the sleep-inducing hormone *melatonin*.

Age often alters our circadian rhythm. During adolescence, we are likely to be "night owls," energized during the evening, with cognitive performance improving as the day wears on. After about age 20 (slightly earlier for women), we begin to shift from being owls to being morning-loving "larks" and feel our energy and performance declining through the day (Roenneberg and others, 2004). Women become more lark-like as they have children (Leonhard & Randler, 2009). There is some evidence that people who are at their best in the morning tend to do better in school and to be less vulnerable to depression (Randler & Frech, 2009).

Sleep Stages

Once asleep, the brain operates according to a 90-minute biological rhythm, cycling through four distinct sleep stages (see Figure 7.1). There are two broad types of sleep: non–rapid eye movement (NREM) and **rapid eye movement (REM),** distinguished by different brain wave patterns, changes in breathing and muscle tension, and a few other bodily changes.

rapid eye movement (REM) Rapid eye movement sleep; a sleep stage during which vivid dreams occur.

FIGURE 7.1

The small, fast beta waves of an alert state and the larger alpha waves of a relaxed state differ from the slower, large delta waves of NREM-3 sleep.

Information from Davis, C. L., Tomporowski, P. D., McDowell, J. E., Austin, B. P., Miller, P.H., Yanasak, N. E., Allison, J. D., & Naglieri, J. A. (2011). Exercise improves executive function and achievement and alters brain activation in overweight children: A randomized, controlled trial. *Health Psychology, 30*(1), 91–98. IStockphoto.

(a)

Lokibaho/Getty Images

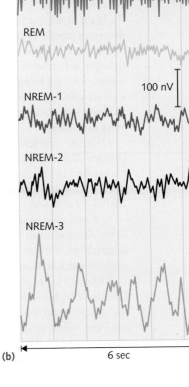
(b)

Waking Beta

Waking Alpha

REM

100 nV

NREM-1

NREM-2

NREM-3

6 sec

When you are awake and alert, the brain generates fast, low-amplitude beta waves. As you begin to relax and your eyes close, your brain begins to generate the slower *alpha waves* of the awake but relaxed state. As you fall asleep, your breathing slows, and your brain generates the irregular waves of non-REM stage 1 sleep (Silber and others, 2008). This is the briefest and lightest stage of sleep, and loud sounds and other stimuli can awaken you easily.

As you relax more deeply, about 20 minutes of NREM-2 occurs, distinguished by periodic bursts of rapid brain waves called *sleep spindles,* which alternate with large K-complex waves. During this stage, breathing and heart rate even out and body temperature drops. You still can be awakened without much difficulty but are clearly asleep. About half of each night's sleep is spent in NREM-2.

Next, you transition to the deep, *slow-wave sleep* of NREM-3, in which your brain emits large (high-amplitude) and very slow (low-frequency) delta waves. During this stage of sleep, you will be much harder to awaken. This stage of deep sleep, marked by delta waves, is most important for restoring energy levels, strengthening the immune system, and stimulating the release of growth hormone.

About one hour after falling asleep, you shift from NREM-3 back to NREM-2 and then enter REM. For 10 minutes or so, your eyes dart back and forth, heart rate and breathing become more irregular, and vivid dreams often occur. REM is also marked by faster beta brain waves and is believed to be important for consolidating memory and other cognitive functions. During REM, the brain's motor cortex is also active, but the brainstem blocks its messages, leaving the muscles relaxed.

The sleep cycle repeats itself about every 90 minutes, but as the night wears on, NREM-3 sleep stages grow shorter and REM and NREM-2 get longer. By the time we awaken, we have spent about 100 minutes (25 percent of sleep) in REM.

Sleep Patterns

Newborns sleep 15 to 17 hours a day, in segments lasting one to three hours, because the brain areas that regulate sleep are immature. The number of hours that babies sleep decreases rapidly as their brains continue to develop—down to a little over 14 hours for the first two months, 13¼ hours for the next three months, and 12¾ hours for the sixth through seventeenth months. Full-term newborns sleep more than low-birth-weight babies, who are hungry every two hours. As every parent learns, the environment has a direct effect on infant sleep behaviors: If parents respond to early morning cries with food and stimulating play, babies wake up early each morning (Sadeh, Mindel, Luedtke, & Wiegand, 2009).

Over the first few months, the amount of time spent in the various stages of sleep changes. About 50 percent of the sleep of full-term newborns is REM sleep, with flickering eyes, rapid brain waves, and dreaming. REM sleep declines over the first few weeks, as does "transitional sleep," the dozing, half-awake NREM-1 stage. At three or four months, NREM-3 (slow-wave sleep) increases, as does time spent alert and wide awake.

Not everyone needs 8 hours of sleep. Newborns and infants sleep nearly two-thirds of the day, and some adults seem to thrive on fewer than 6 hours per night while others regularly get 9 hours or more. On average, adults in North America sleep 6.8 hours a night on weekdays and 7.4 hours a night on weekends (National Sleep Foundation, 2013).

Although genes play an important role in determining our individual sleep patterns (Hor & Tafti, 2009), lightbulbs, work schedules, the Internet, and other diversions mean that people today sleep less than their counterparts did 100 years ago. This phenomenon has been called *social jet lag,* underscoring the fact that it occurs when our body's internal biological clock is out of sync with our social clock, which is set by the demands and distractions of modern life. In one study of 65,000 European adults, 69 percent of participants reported suffering from at least one hour of social jet lag each week, and a third regularly suffered at least two hours (Roenneberg, Allebrandt, Merrow, & Vetter, 2012).

Sleep researchers also have found that insufficient sleep is related to socioeconomic status, race and ethnicity, workplace, neighborhood, and other social factors. A survey of 9714 adults reported a significant *sleep disparity* among participants (Patel, Grandner, Xie, Branas, & Gooneratne, 2010). Overall, minority respondents reported poorer sleep quality than majority group respondents. However, among those with the lowest income levels, majority respondents reported the most sleep problems.

Another study of 500 healthy U.S. adults reported that African-Americans slept an average of only 6.8 hours per night, compared with 7.4 hours, on average, for European-Americans. Asian- and Hispanic-Americans slept an average of 6.9 hours per night (Carnethon and others, 2012). The differences in average sleep time persisted even after the researchers adjusted for weight, high blood pressure, diabetes, and other factors known to interfere with sleep. The authors suggest that social environmental factors such as pollution, noise levels, and crime rates may account for these group differences.

Sleep patterns change as we grow older. Newborns and infants sleep nearly two-thirds of the day, while some adults seem to thrive on fewer than 6 hours per night.

Other researchers have directly investigated the associations among sleep quality, health, and neighborhood conditions. Participants who reported living in neighborhoods with more physical and social disorder also reported having poorer sleep quality, more symptoms of depression, and poorer perceived health (Patel and others, 2010).

People who are coping with stressful events at work or in the home also report poorer sleep (Burgard & Ailshire, 2009), especially when stressors are appraised as uncontrollable (Morin, Rodrigue, & Ivers, 2003). One study of health care workers found that those who had less supportive managers got 29 minutes less sleep daily and were twice as likely as those with more supportive bosses to have several risk factors for cardiovascular disease (Berkman, Buxton, Ertel, & Okechukwu, 2010). People who react to stressful events by focusing on them, or ruminating (see Chapter 5), and people who have high levels of hostility or arousal (Fernandez-Mendoza and others, 2010) are more prone to insomnia than are people who use strategies to blunt the impact of stressors (Zoccola, Dickerson, & Lam, 2009). Interestingly, a growing body of evidence suggests that *long sleepers,* people (other than children and adolescents) who habitually sleep *more* than seven hours night after night are also at risk for health problems such as obesity, diabetes, high blood pressure, and cardiovascular disease (Buxton & Marcelli, 2010).

Pain also can disrupt sleep. Parents of children with chronic arthritis pain rate their children as having significantly more sleep anxiety, night awakenings, and other sleep disturbances (Bromberg, Gil, & Schanberg, 2012). In turn, poor sleep can increase the intensity of pain experienced the next day in adolescents and adults with chronic pain (Lewandowski, Palermo, De la Mott, & Fu, 2010). Other studies have shown that sleep loss leads to exaggerated pain perception, perhaps by increasing blood levels of *interleukin-6,* a signaling cytokine that contributes to inflammation and pain sensitivity (Haack & Mullington, 2007).

Sleep Loss and Sleep Disorders

After a few nights of sleep loss, people have accumulated a *sleep debt* that cannot be repaid by one long sleep (Dement, 1999). College students are among those most likely to be sleep deprived—69 percent in one national survey (Associated Press, 2009). (See Your Health Assets: How Good Is Your Sleep? to determine whether the amount and quality of the sleep that you are getting is adequate.) Students who don't sleep enough also report more conflicts in their friendships and social relationships (Gordon & Chen, 2014).

Sleep loss slows our reaction times and increases errors on visual attention tasks, which may explain why driver fatigue is linked to an estimated 20 percent of traffic accidents (Caldwell, 2012). Remarkably, when the high schools in one Virginia city pushed back their starting times 75 to 80 minutes, over a two-year period, the number of student traffic accidents was 25 percent lower than the number in another city in the same state that kept its earlier starting time (Vorona and others, 2011).

Sleep loss also is a predictor of depression. In one study, students who reported sleeping 5 hours or less a night had a 71 percent higher risk of depression than others who slept 8 hours or more (Gangwisch and others, 2010)! Such findings help explain why pushing back school start times improves mood and alertness among adolescent students (Perkinson-Gloor, Lemola, & Grob, 2013).

Sleep Disorders

insomnia A persistent problem in falling or staying asleep.

About one-third of adults experience sleep problems occasionally, and 10 to 15 percent of adults (1 in 4 older adults) complain of **insomnia**—a persistent problem in falling asleep, staying asleep, or getting restful sleep (Khurshid, 2015).

Poor sleep is enough of a problem that *Healthy People 2020* (2014) established the national goal of increasing the proportion of people who get sufficient sleep. Poor sleep, as noted earlier, takes a toll on both physical and psychological well-being. Although early research focused on the devastating effects of total sleep deprivation, far more common is what researchers today call *partial sleep loss, sleep restriction,* or *short sleep*. Whatever it's called, it refers to routinely cutting one's sleep short by just an hour or two each night (Carpenter, 2013).

cognitive behavioral therapy for insomnia (CBT-I) A structured treatment for insomnia aimed at replacing thoughts and behaviors that cause or worsen sleep problems with habits that promote sound sleep without the use of medication.

Although insomnia can be a serious condition, occasional insomnia may not pose a serious problem. From middle age on, waking occasionally during the night is the norm and does not necessarily signal a problem that needs to be treated with sleeping pills (Vitiello, 2009). Although sleeping pills and other medications can be an effective short-term treatment for insomnia, they may not be the best long-term solution because of bothersome side effects and concerns about developing dependency on drugs. Ironically, the use of sleeping pills, alcohol, and other "quick fixes" often makes the situation worse by suppressing REM sleep and leading to *tolerance,* in which increased doses are needed to produce any sleep-inducing effect.

Poor sleep takes a toll on both physical and psychological well-being.

iStock/Getty Images

Unlike pills, **cognitive behavioral therapy for insomnia (CBT-I)** targets the underlying causes of insomnia instead of its symptoms. CBT-I is a structured intervention that aims to first improve sleep quality and later sleep quantity. CBT-I is a stepwise procedure that helps people identify and replace thoughts and behaviors that cause or aggravate sleep problems with healthier ones that promote restful sleep. This often includes learning how to control or eliminate sleep-interfering thoughts and worries, managing stress, and calming an active mind that won't "shut off" when its owner is trying to fall asleep.

Most people with insomnia have very unpredictable sleep patterns. The behavioral element of CBT-I promotes the development of a 'pro-sleep' routine that establishes a strong connection between the bedroom and restful sleep. Over time, practicing this routine means that falling asleep and staying asleep become more natural and automatic.

CBT-I is typically delivered over the course of 6 to 8 weekly sessions with a trained health psychologist. Treatment is typically tailored to individual needs, and may include:

- *Stimulus control therapy* to remove factors that condition the mind to resist sleep. These include irregular bedtimes and waking times. The therapist might coach a client to set a consistent bedtime and wake time, avoid naps, use the bed only for sleep and sex, and leave the bed if unable to fall asleep within 20 minutes.

- *Relaxation training* to help calm the mind and body. Various approaches are used, including meditation, imagery, and muscle relaxation.

- *Sleep environment improvement.* This focuses on creating a comfortable sleep environment by keeping the bedroom dark, cool, and quiet; not having a television or other devices in the room, and keeping any clocks out of view.

- *Sleep restriction.* Lying in bed when you're awake can quickly become a habit that interferes with restful sleep. This technique reduces the time clients spend in bed, causing partial sleep deprivation designed to make them more tired the next night. As sleep improves, the time in bed is gradually increased.

- *Biofeedback.* This technique, discussed more fully in Chapter 15, enables people to monitor their heart rate, muscle tension, or other physical signs and shows people how to adjust those responses to calm the body.

- *Sleep hygiene* focuses on improving lifestyle behaviors that influence sleep, such as drinking too much alcohol, consuming caffeine late in the day, or not getting regular exercise. It also includes training in ways to wind down before bedtime.

In addition to insomnia, DSM-5 identifies 10 other sleep-wake disorders (see Table 7.3). People with **narcolepsy** don't have difficulty falling asleep. Rather, they experience excessive daytime sleepiness that results in episodes of falling asleep suddenly, typically lasting less than 5 minutes. These sleep attacks may occur during any type of activity and at any time of day. Other symptoms of narcolepsy include abnormal REM sleep, including dreamlike hallucinations and feeling physically weak or even paralyzed for a few seconds.

Narcolepsy, which usually begins between 15 and 25 years of age, is a neurological disease. Researchers have identified genes that appear to trigger the disorder by causing the body's immune system to attack brain cells that signal sleep and awake cycles (De la Herrán-Arita and others, 2013). One promising hypothesis is that narcolepsy may be due to a deficiency of cells in the hypothalamus that produce *hypocretin*, a neurotransmitter that regulates arousal, wakefulness, and appetite (Han and others, 2013).

Narcolepsy is most often treated with drugs, including the use of stimulants that manage sleepiness and antidepressants that relieve the symptoms of abnormal REM sleep. While there is no cure at present for narcolepsy, most patients regain about 80 percent of normal function (Stanford Center for Narcolepsy, 2015).

Sleep apnea is a potentially serious disorder in which breathing repeatedly starts and stops hundreds of times each night, depriving people of slow-wave sleep. Apnea sufferers typically don't recall these waking episodes and so are often unaware of their disorder.

Compared to people with a healthy body mass index, people who are obese have four times the risk of sleep apnea. As the prevalence of obesity has increased, so too this sleep disorder, particularly among men (Keller, Hader, De Zeeuw, & Rasche, 2007). People with thicker necks (17 inches or larger for men, and 15 inches or larger for women) may have narrower airways and have increased risk of sleep apnea. Snoring loudly, morning headache, excessive daytime drowsiness (*hypersomnia*), attention problems, insomnia, and feeling irritable after a full night's sleep are other warning signs for the disorder (Mayo Clinic, 2015).

narcolepsy A sleep disorder characterized by uncontrollable sleep attacks.

sleep apnea A sleep disorder characterized by temporary cessations of breathing.

TABLE 7.3

This table lists the major sleep-wake disorders included in DSM-5. Sleep disorders are often accompanied by anxiety, depression, and other cognitive changes.

Disorder	Symptoms
Insomnia disorder	Persistent difficulty falling asleep or staying asleep
Hypersomnolence disorder	Excessive daytime sleepiness or prolonged nighttime sleep
Narcolepsy	Neurological disorder involving poor control of sleep-wake cycles, excessive daytime sleepiness, and brief, involuntary sleep episodes
Obstructive sleep apnea hypopnea	Brief, involuntary pauses in breathing, or shallow breathing while asleep; caused by an airway that collapses or becomes blocked during sleep
Central sleep apnea	Less common form of apnea (brief pauses in breathing while sleeping) caused by the brain's failure to send correct signals to breathing muscles
Sleep-related hypoventilation	Breathing disorder characterized by abnormal oxygen/carbon dioxide exchange while sleeping
Circadian rhythm sleep-wake disorders	A family of sleep disorders that affects the timing of the sleep-wake cycle
Non-rapid eye movement (NREM) sleep arousal disorder	Episodes of incomplete awakening from sleep; may involve sleepwalking or nightmares
Nightmare disorder	Recurrent dreams that are horrifying or threatening in nature
Rapid eye movement (REM) sleep behavior disorder	Behavioral arousal during rapid-eye movement sleep; dreamer may kick, grab, punch, and in other ways seem to be acting out a dream
Restless legs syndrome	Neurological disorder characterized by a desire to move the legs and uncomfortable sensations such as crawling, tingling, burning, or itching

There are several types of apnea. Most common is *obstructive sleep apnea,* which occurs when throat muscles relax, causing the airway to narrow and preventing the sufferer from getting an adequate breath. As the level of oxygen in the blood drops, the brain briefly rouses the sleeper to reopen the airway, sometimes causing a snorting, choking, or gasping reflex that is repeated 5 to 30 times each hour of the night (Mayo Clinic, 2015).

Mild cases of sleep apnea are often managed through healthy lifestyle changes, including losing weight, quitting smoking, and treating allergies. If these measures aren't effective, a masklike device with an air pump that keeps the airway open often relieves apnea symptoms. For more severe cases, surgery to straighten the partition between the nostrils, remove tissue from the back of the mouth and top of the throat, or reposition the jaw, may be necessary.

Consider some of the findings from research studies on chronic sleep loss:

- Chronic sleep debt promotes increased body weight, increased body mass index (BMI), and obesity. One study reported that healthy men and women who were restricted to just 4 hours of sleep per night over six nights consumed more calories, particularly from fat, than their well-rested counterparts in a control group (St-Onge and others, 2011). Another study found that

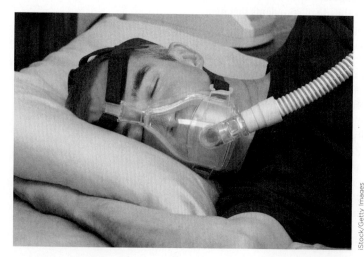

Gentle air pressure administered in the form of a nasal, continuous positive airway pressure device (CPAP) is often effective in the treatment of sleep apnea.

iStock/Getty Images

Your Health Assets

How Good Is Your Sleep?

Cornell University sleep researcher James Maas has reported that 65 percent of people are sleep deprived. To find out if you are in that group, answer the following true-false questions. If you answered "true" to three or more items, you probably are not getting enough sleep.

Please indicate true or false for the following statements:

1. I need an alarm clock in order to wake up at the appropriate time.
2. It's a struggle for me to get out of bed in the morning.
3. Weekday mornings, I hit the snooze button several times to get more sleep.
4. I feel tired, irritable, and stressed out during the week.
5. I have trouble concentrating and remembering.
6. I feel slow when doing critical thinking, problem solving, and being creative.
7. I often fall asleep watching TV.
8. I often fall asleep in boring meetings or lectures or in warm rooms.
9. I often fall asleep after heavy meals or after a low dose of alcohol.
10. I often fall asleep while relaxing after dinner.
11. I often fall asleep within five minutes of getting into bed.
12. I often feel drowsy while driving.
13. I often sleep extra hours on weekend mornings.
14. I often need a nap to get through the day.
15. I have dark circles around my eyes.

Source: Quiz reprinted with permission from Maas, J. B. (2013). *Sleep to Win!* Bloomington, IN: AuthorHouse.

adults who were allowed to sleep only 5.5 hours per night for two weeks ate more snacks than control participants (Nedeltcheva and others, 2009). Sleep complaints such as difficulty falling asleep, difficulty staying asleep, and daytime sleepiness have been linked to increased total calorie intake.

- Children and adults who sleep less have a higher percentage of body fat than those who sleep more. One study reported that as average nightly sleep duration decreased from 8 hours to 5 hours, BMI increased more than 3 percent (from 31.3 to 32.4) (Taheri, Lin, Austin, Young, & Mignot, 2004).

- Poor sleep stimulates an increase in the hunger-triggering hormone *ghrelin* and a decrease in the appetite-suppressing hormone *leptin* (Shlisky and others, 2012). Sleep loss also elevates levels of the stress hormone cortisol, which promotes the storage of calories into body fat (Chen, Beydoun, & Wang, 2008). This effect may help explain why chronically sleep-deprived college students often gain weight.

- Sleep deprivation suppresses immune functioning (Moller-Levet and others, 2013). Immunological signaling molecules such as tumor necrosis factor, interleukin-1, and interleukin-6 play an important role in sleep regulation. Elevated levels of these cytokines, which can occur with poor sleep, also are associated with diabetes, cardiovascular disease, inflammation, pain sensitivity, and a number of chronic illnesses (Motivala & Irwin, 2007).

- Sleep loss also promotes insulin resistance—a key factor in the development of diabetes. Fat cells in people who experience sleep restriction are 30 percent less able to respond to insulin. Fortunately, this biochemical process may be reversible if sleep loss is not chronic. The same study found that when teens who normally got only six hours of sleep per night were allowed just one extra hour of sleep, insulin resistance improved by nearly 10 percent (Matthews, Dahl, Owens, Lee, & Hall, 2012).

- The most recent studies have focused on the role of sleep in promoting *cardiometabolic disease*—a complex of chronic conditions that include obesity, diabetes, and cardiovascular disease. One researcher concluded that sleep restriction leads to "substantial and clinically significant changes in appetite regulation, hunger, food intake, glucose metabolism and blood pressure control" (Carpenter, 2013).

- Sleep loss is linked to chronic inflammation (Motivala & Irwin, 2007) and adversely affects our body's metabolic, neural, and endocrine functioning in ways that mimic accelerated aging (Pawlyck, Ferber, Shah, Pack, & Naidoo, 2007). Older adults who are *not* sleep deprived actually may live longer than people who have trouble falling or staying asleep (Dew and others, 2003).

- Research studies suggest that the brain uses sleep to repair damage, replenish energy stores, and promote *neurogenesis,* or the formation of new nerve cells (Winerman, 2006). Other effects of poor sleep include impaired concentration, memory, and creativity, as well as increased reaction time, errors, and accidents (Lim & Dinges, 2010; Stickgold, 2009). Driver fatigue contributes to an estimated 20 percent of traffic accidents in the United States (Brody, 2002).

The National Sleep Foundation (2015) offers the following tips for improving sleep:

- Go to bed at the same time each night, and rise at the same time each morning.

- Establish a consistent schedule and relaxing bedtime routine (e.g., taking a bath or relaxing with a good book).

- Create a sleep-conducive environment that is dark, quiet, and preferably cool and comfortable.

- Remove all TVs, computers, and other technology from the bedroom.

- Hide the clock face and reassure yourself that occasional, temporary sleep loss causes no great harm.

- Make sure your bed is comfortable and use it only for sleeping and not for other activities, such as reading, watching TV, or listening to music.

- Avoid large meals and caffeine close to bedtime. (This includes coffee, tea, soft drinks, chocolate, and nicotine.)

- Avoid alcohol, which can lead to disrupted sleep.

- Exercise regularly, but complete your workout at least three hours before bedtime.

If you are having sleep problems or regular daytime sleepiness, consider keeping a sleep diary such as the one published by the National Sleep Foundation (2015). In it, record your sleep patterns and the amount of sleep that you get. The diary will help you examine some of your health and sleep habits so that you and your doctor can pinpoint any causes of poor sleep.

Injury Control

One of the many potential consequences of sleep deprivation is an increased risk of human error–related accidents. Sleep deprivation has been shown to produce cognitive, perceptual, and motor impairments equivalent to those caused by alcohol consumption at or above the legal limit. Motor vehicle accidents related to fatigue, drowsy driving, and even falling asleep at the wheel are far too common, and they have a fatality rate and injury severity level similar to alcohol-related crashes (Durmer & Dinges, 2005).

One of health psychology's most important goals is to forestall the development of problems through primary prevention—a much more effective way of improving health than treating disease and disability that has already developed. In 2010, 192, 945 Americans died from injuries, mostly due to motor-vehicles crashes, poisoning, fire-arms, and falling (CDC, 2014a). Most of these fatalities were classified as **unintentional injuries,** or accidents, because the injured person didn't intend for it to happen. Most of the remaining deaths were **intentional injuries,** meaning that the person who caused the injury meant for it to happen. These deaths included suicides, homicides, and fatalities that occurred as part of war or another "legal intervention." In addition to these fatalities, nearly 43 million Americans were treated in hospital emergency departments (CDC, 2014a). One of the major goals of *Healthy People 2020* (2014) is to reduce the overall rate of unintentional injuries to the target of no more than 36 deaths per 100,000 and to reduce motor-vehicle-crash–related deaths to no more than 12.4 per 100,000 Americans.

Although overall injuries are the fifth leading cause of death (after heart disease, can-cer, stroke, and chronic obstructive pulmonary disease), the risk of injury, as well as the likelihood of dying from an injury, varies considerably across the life span (see Figure 7.2). When all people between ages 1 and 44 are considered as a group, unintentional injury is the *leading* cause of death, ahead of cardiovascular disease and cancer (Minino, 2013). Not until age 40 does any specific disease overtake accidents as a cause of mortality.

The five leading causes of death in young people include several *external causes* (accidents, homicide, and suicide), followed by cancer and heart disease. This pattern of external causes accounting for more deaths than *chronic conditions* changes as people get older. In older age groups, chronic conditions account for more deaths than do external

unintentional injury Harm that is accidental, not meant to occur.

intentional injury Harm that results from behaviors designed to hurt oneself or others.

FIGURE 7.2

Leading Causes of Death by Age Group The leading causes of death for those aged 1 to 24 years include a number of external causes (accidents, homicide, and suicide), followed by cancer (malignant neoplasms) and heart disease. This pattern shifts as age increases. In older age groups, chronic conditions account for more deaths than do external causes.

Data from CDC (2016). Ten leading causes of death and injury. Centers for Disease Control and Prevention, National Center for Injury Prevention and Control. Retrieved May 2, 2016 from http://www.cdc.gov/injury/wisqars/leadingcauses.html

10 Leading Causes of Death by Age Group, United States – 2014

Rank	<1	1–4	5–9	10–14	15–24	25–34	35–44	45–54	55–64	65+	Total
1	Congenital Anomalies 4,746	Unintentional Injury 1,216	Unintentional Injury 730	Unintentional Injury 750	Unintentional Injury 11,836	Unintentional Injury 17,357	Unintentional Injury 16,048	Malignant Neoplasms 44, 834	Malignant Neoplasms 115,282	Heart Disease 489,722	Heart Disease 614,348
2	Short Gestation 4,173	Congenital Anomalies 399	Malignant Neoplasms 436	Suicide 425	Suicide 5,079	Suicide 6,569	Malignant Neoplasms 11,267	Heart Disease 34,791	Heart Disease 74,473	Malignant Neoplasms 413,885	Malignant Neoplasms 591,699
3	Maternal Pregnancy Comp. 1,574	Homicide 364	Congenital Anomalies 192	Malignant Neoplasms 416	Homicide 4,144	Homicide 4,159	Heart Disease 10,368	Unintentional Injury 20,610	Unintentional Injury 18,030	Chronic Low. Respiratory Disease 124,693	Chronic Low. Respiratory Disease 147,101
4	SIDS 1,545	Malignant Neoplasms 321	Homicide 123	Congenital Anomalies 156	Malignant Neoplasms 1,569	Malignant Neoplasms 3,624	Suicide 6,706	Suicide 8,767	Chronic Low. Respiratory Disease 16,492	Cerebro-vascular 113,308	Unintentional Injury 136,053
5	Unintentional Injury 1,161	Heart Disease 149	Heart Disease 69	Homicide 156	Heart Disease 953	Heart Disease 3,341	Homicide 2,588	Liver Disease 8,627	Diabetes Mellitus 13,342	Alzheimer's Disease 92,604	Cerebro-vascular 133,103
6	Placenta Cord. Membranes 965	Influenza & Pneumonia 109	Chronic Low. Respiratory Disease 68	Heart Disease 122	Congenital Anomalies 377	Liver Disease 725	Liver Disease 2,582	Diabetes Mellitus 6,062	Liver Disease 12,792	Diabetes Mellitus 54,161	Alzheimer's Disease 93,541
7	Bacterial Sepsis 544	Chronic Low. Respiratory Disease 53	Influenza & Pneumonia 57	Chronic Low. Respiratory Disease 71	Influenza & Pneumonia 199	Diabetes Mellitus 709	Diabetes Mellitus 1,999	Cerebro-vascular 5,349	Cerebro-vascular 11,727	Unintentional Injury 48,295	Diabetes Mellitus 74,488
8	Respiratory Distress 460	Septicemia 53	Cerebro-vascular 45	Cerebro-vascular 43	Diabetes Mellitus 181	HIV 583	Cerebro-vascular 1,745	Chronic Low. Respiratory Disease 4,402	Suicide 7,527	Influenza & Pneumonia 44,836	Influenza & Pneumonia 55,227
9	Circulatory System Disease 444	Benign Neoplasms 38	Benign Neoplasms 36	Influenza & Pneumonia 41	Chronic Low. Respiratory Disease 178	Cerebro-vascular 579	HIV 1,174	Influenza & Pneumonia 2,731	Septicemia 5,709	Nephritis 39,957	Nephritis 48,146
10	Neonatal Hemorrhage 441	Perinatal Period 38	Septicemia 33	Benign Neoplasms 38	Cerebro-vascular 177	Influenza & Pneumonia 549	Influenza & Pneumonia 1,125	Septicemia 2,514	Influenza & Pneumonia 5,390	Septicemia 29,124	Suicide 42,773

causes. For example, accidents account for more than one-third of all deaths among persons aged 1 to 24 years. Accidental deaths are less prevalent in older age groups and do not even rank among the five leading causes of death in people 65 years and older.

Childhood

Compared to other stages of the life span, childhood for most children is uneventful in terms of overall health. In fact, during the school years, children in developed nations are the healthiest people of any age, being least likely to die or become seriously injured or ill (WHO, 2010d). Even so, an estimated 9000 children and teens die each year in the United States as the result of unintentional injury (CDC, 2015a). For children ages 1 to 4, the leading causes of injury-related death are drowning and motor-vehicle accidents. From 5 to 9 years of age, about half of all injury-related deaths occur in motor vehicle crashes, and most of the remainder are caused by fire/burns (just over 14 percent) and drowning (12.6 percent). For children ages 10 to 14, over half of all injury-related deaths occur in motor vehicles (56.6 percent).

Most childhood injuries are predictable and preventable. Adult supervision and the use of safety equipment go a long way in keeping children safe.

(a)

(b)

(c)

lissart/iStock/Getty Images

© Blend Images/Alamy Stock Photo

Crazy80frog | Dreamstime.com

Although most early childhood injuries are not deliberate, public health experts increasingly choose not to call them "accidents," which would imply that they are random and unpredictable. Instead of accident prevention, experts prefer the term **injury control** (or harm reduction). Minor injuries are an inevitable part of any normal, active childhood, but serious injury is unlikely if efforts aimed at prevention are sound.

injury control Systematic efforts to prevent injuries from occurring and to limit the consequences of those that have already occurred.

Adolescence and Emerging Adulthood

Unintentional injury is the leading cause of death for adolescents and young adults, with motor-vehicle accidents far and away the most prevalent type (51.1 percent) of injury resulting in death in these age groups (Hoyert & Xu, 2012). This sobering statistic is true despite the fact that reflexes are faster and vision is better at these ages than at any other point in the life span. What accounts for this seemingly illogical fact? Many experts believe the answer is simple: Adolescents and young adults are prone to thoughtless impulses and poor decisions that lead to risky driving practices, including speeding, driving under the influence of alcohol, and driving while distracted—texting or talking on a cell phone, for instance.

Poor decision making is partly the result of the fact that different parts of the brain grow at different rates. The limbic system, including the amygdala (where fear, excitement, and other intense emotions originate) matures before the prefrontal cortex (where emotional regulation, impulse control, and thoughtful analysis occur). As a result, the emotional areas of the brain develop ahead of the executive, analytic areas. Add to this the fact that the surge of hormones that accompanies puberty strongly affects the amygdala, while the cortex "matures" more as a result of the experiences that accompany aging. For many teens and emerging adults, this is a dangerous time when emotional rushes, unchecked by caution, are common (Blakemore, 2008).

Neurological research finds that during adolescence, brain areas that respond to excitement and pleasure are much more active than brain areas that control inhibition and urge caution (Van Leijenhorst and others, 2010). This is evident in functional magnetic resonance imaging (fMRI) scans of the brains of people in different age groups. When compared with 18- to 23-year-olds, 14- to 15-year-olds show dramatically increased arousal in the brain's limbic areas, making them especially susceptible to excitement and the strong sensations provided by driving fast, participating in extreme sports, and using alcohol and strong drugs (Van Leijenhorst and others, 2010). This may partly explain why younger drivers are more likely to speed than older drivers. As shown in Figure 7.3, the percentage of fatal motor vehicle crashes caused by speeding is highest, for both male and female drivers, between age 16 and age 19 and decreases throughout adulthood (National Highway Traffic Safety Administration, 2014).

A pertinent example of the cautious part of the brain being overwhelmed by the emotions of the moment comes from studies showing how often teens send text messages while they are driving. In one survey, 64 percent of 16- to 17-year-olds said they had been in a car when the driver was texting (Madden & Lenhart, 2009). Other examples of poor impulse control and faulty reasoning while driving abound. Consider the following data from the CDC (2015a):

■ Teens are more likely than older drivers to underestimate dangerous situations and may be unable to recognize hazardous situations.

FIGURE 7.3

Speeding Drivers in Fatal Crashes by Age and Sex For drivers involved in fatal crashes, young males are the most likely to be speeding. The relative proportion of speeding-related crashes to all crashes decreases with driver age.

Data from NHTSA. (2010). *Traffic safety facts: Speeding, 2007 data.* National Highway Traffic Safety Administration. Washington, DC: National Center for Statistics and Analysis.

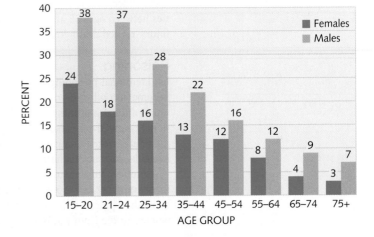

Young adults are prone to poor decisions that lead to risky driving practices, including driving while distracted.

Pawel Gaul/Getty Images

- Teens are more likely than older drivers to speed and to allow shorter headways (the distance between the front of one vehicle to the front of the next). Interestingly, the presence of male passengers increases the likelihood of this risky driving behavior.

- Compared with other age groups, teens have the lowest rate of seatbelt use.

- At all levels of blood-alcohol concentration, the risk of involvement in a motor vehicle crash is greater for teens than for older drivers.

Because the immature brains of young drivers play such a large role in causing motor vehicle accidents, it is not surprising that four preventive measures have saved hundreds of lives: (1) graduated driver licensing (GDL), which requires more time between issuing a learner's permit and granting a full license, (2) restricted driving at night, (3) no teenage passengers, and (4) zero tolerance for driving under the influence of alcohol (Fell, Fisher, Voas, Blackman, & Tippetts, 2011). Consider the impact of GDL, which is designed to delay full licensure while allowing a greater period of time for young drivers with a learner's permit to practice and gain initial driving experience under supervised, low-risk conditions. Research studies demonstrate that comprehensive GDL programs are associated with reductions of 38 percent and 40 percent in fatal and nonfatal injury crashes, respectively, among 16-year-old drivers (Baker, Chen, & Li, 2007).

Adulthood

Injuries remain the leading cause of death in adults ages 35 to 44 but then become less prevalent as chronic illnesses such as cardiovascular disease and cancer begin to cause more deaths in older adults (Hoyert & Xu, 2012). For people who have reached age 65, injuries have dropped to the ninth-leading cause of death.

The types of injuries that people suffer and from which they sometimes die also change as people get older. In adults aged 25 to 34, car accidents are the leading cause of injury-related death, followed by poisoning and homicide. Between ages 35 and 54, poisoning causes the most injury-related fatalities, followed by motor-vehicle crashes and suicides. Car accidents, suicides, and poisoning, in that order, cause the most injury-related fatalities between ages 55 and 64. For those aged 65 and older, falls are the leading cause of injury-related death, followed by car accidents and suicide.

Poisoning

Unintentional poisoning death rates have been increasing steadily since 1992 and have become second only to motor-vehicle crashes as a cause of accidental death. In 2013, unintentional poisonings caused 98,000 deaths worldwide (GBD, 2015). Most unintentional deaths from poisoning (91 percent) are caused by drugs. Prescription painkillers, including hydrocodone, oxycodone, and methadone, are most commonly involved, followed by cocaine and heroin.

Among adults treated in hospital emergency departments for nonfatal poisoning involving drugs, use of pain medications and the central nervous system (CNS)–depressant benzodiazepines (such as Valium) are reported most often. Men are twice as likely as women to die from poisoning, and the prevalence of poison-related deaths varies with ethnicity. In the United States, Native Americans have the highest death rates by poisoning, followed by European-Americans, and then African-Americans (CDC, 2013a).

Homicide

The low rate of chronic illness between ages 18 and 25 is offset by a high rate of severe injuries and violent deaths, with males being more than twice as vulnerable as females. The high rate of violent death is evident particularly among young males. Violent deaths are more common than disease deaths during these years even in nations with rampant infection and malnutrition (Patton and others, 2012).

In 2013, there were 16,121 homicides in the United States, about 5.1 for every 100,000 people. Of these, 11,208 (69.52 percent) involved the use of a firearm (CDC, 2014a). More people are murdered during emerging adulthood than at any other period, with people aged 18 to 24 years consistently having the highest rate of homicide.

The epidemiology of gun violence in the United States reveals the importance of several factors, including gender, ethnicity/race, geographical region, and public policy (NPR, 2013). Briefly put, white people who die by gunfire are much more likely to be male, to live in rural areas, and to commit suicide; black people who die by gunfire are more likely to be male, to live in urban areas, and to be victims of homicide. Males are nearly seven times more likely to die by homicide than females, and African-Americans are twice as likely to die by homicide as whites. Homicide is one reason that African-Americans have a shorter average life expectancy than whites. Stated differently, for every white male shot in a homicide, five shoot themselves; and for every black male who kills himself with a gun, five are killed by homicide. The rates for women are much lower for both homicide and suicide.

These disparities mask underlying issues related to attitudes and access to firearms. Researchers have found that people who suffer homicide among family and friends are more likely to live in cities, have an antigun attitude, and favor gun-control legislation. This is true across all ethnic and racial groups. As one moves from the city to the suburbs and then into rural areas, where firearm fatalities shift to being predominantly suicide, there tends to be a much lower desire for gun control. Consider the differences in gun access and firearm deaths between the states of Wyoming and Massachusetts. The suicide rate in Wyoming, which has very high access to guns, is seven times higher than that in Massachusetts, where it's more difficult to get a gun. Access to guns is especially important when it comes to suicide, which is often impulsive. Teenagers who kill themselves with firearms almost always do it with their family's gun.

Suicide

Homicide is most prevalent in people ages 18 to 24, whereas suicide is most likely among those ages 45 to–54. Nearly 1 million people worldwide commit suicide each year, with prevalence rates varying from country to country (WHO, 2011b). For instance, suicide rates in Britain, Italy, and Spain are little more than half those of the United States, Canada, and Australia. The age-adjusted suicide rate for the total population of the United States is about 11.8 per 100,000 people, with the greatest number occurring between the ages of 45 and 54. Worldwide, women are more likely than men to attempt suicide, but men are four times more likely to actually end their lives and represent nearly 80 percent of all U.S. suicides, probably because they are more likely to use a gun or some other lethal method (WHO, 2011b).

Firearms are the most commonly used method of suicide among males (55.7 percent), while poisoning is the most common method among females (40.2 percent). In the United States, whites and Native Americans commit suicide twice as often as blacks, Hispanics, and Asians (CDC, 2014a). Suicide rates are higher among people who are affluent, single, widowed, divorced, depressed, or alcohol-dependent. Suicidal thoughts also arise when people feel disconnected or that they are a burden to others (Joiner, 2010), when they feel trapped by an inescapable situation (Taylor, Gooding, Wood, & Tarrier, 2011), and when they are driven to reach a goal they believe is unattainable (Chatard & Selimbegovic, 2011). Among gay and lesbian youth, peer rejection and an unsupportive family have been associated with attempted suicide (Haas and others, 2011).

Because suicide is so often an impulsive act, environmental barriers such as preventing access to firearms, which are involved in 57 percent of U.S. suicides, are an important deterrent (Anderson, 2008). People who live in a house where a firearm is kept are five times as likely to die by suicide as people who live in gun-free homes. One massive study examined the association between firearm ownership and suicide across all 50 states (Miller, Lippmann, Azrael, & Hemenway, 2007). After taking into account poverty, unemployment, mental illness, and drug and alcohol abuse, the researchers found that people of all ages and both sexes are more likely to die from suicide when they live in a community in which more households own firearms.

Some people, especially adolescents and young adults, stop short of suicide by turning to *non-suicidal self-injury* (NSSI) behaviors such as cutting the skin, pulling out hair, inserting objects under the skin, and administering their own tattoos (Fikke, Melinder, & Landro, 2011). Although NSSI is a risk factor for future suicide attempts, those who engage in NSSI usually are *suicide gesturers,* not *suicide attempters* (Wilkinson & Goodyer, 2011). They are often extremely self-critical and have poor communication and problem-solving skills (Nock, 2010). Experts also suggest that NSSI behaviors may be an attempt to:

- gain attention and ask others for help;
- get others to stop bullying them;
- use pain to distract persistent negative thoughts and rumination;
- relieve guilt through self-punishment; or
- fit in with a peer group.

Falls

Falls are the second leading cause of unintentional injury deaths worldwide (WHO, 2012). Each year, an estimated 424,000 people globally die as a result of falls, of which over 80 percent are in low- and middle-income countries. Many more suffer nonfatal fall-related injuries. In the United States, falls are the overall leading cause of injury, accounting for twice as many injuries as any other cause (see Figure 7.4).

FIGURE 7.4

Falls Falls are the overall leading cause of injury, accounting for nearly 40 percent of all injuries in the United States each year.

Data from Adams, P. F., Kirzinger, W. K., & Martinez, M. E. (2012). Summary health statistics for the U.S. population: National Health Interview Survey, 2011. National Center for Health Statistics. *Vital Health Stat* 10(255).

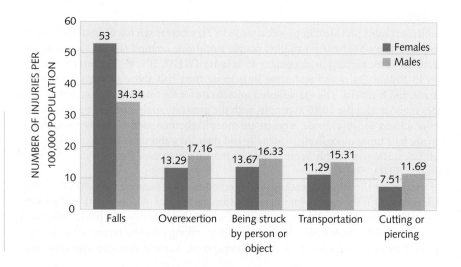

In 2014, 2.5 million nonfatal fall-related injuries among older adults were treated in hospital emergency departments in the United States, resulting in a direct medical cost of $34 billion (CDC, 2015a). One out of every three adults aged 65 and older falls each year. The global result is approximately 37.3 million falls that do not result in death but are serious enough to require medical attention. Nonfatal falls are responsible for the loss of over 17 million *disability-adjusted life years* (DALYs), with the highest rates of morbidity occurring in people 65 and older, followed by young adults aged 15 to 29, and children 15 years and younger.

In addition to the one in every three adults aged 65 and older mentioned above, approximately 2.8 million children are treated in hospital emergency departments for fall-related injuries each year (CDC, 2012a). Among older adults, 20 to 30 percent of falls result in moderate to severe injuries such as bruises, hip fractures, and traumatic brain injuries. This risk level may be in part due to physical, sensory, and cognitive changes associated with aging, in combination with environments that are not optimized for older adults. Many people who fall, even if they are not injured, develop a fear of falling that may cause them to limit their activities. This leads to loss of physical fitness, which in turn increases their future risk of falling.

For children younger than age 2, many of these injuries are the result of falls from cribs and playpens (Yeh, Rochette, McKenzie, & Smith, 2011). Among older children, many nonfatal fall-related injuries are the result of playground accidents that lead to fractures, concussions, and internal injuries. Childhood falls occur largely as a result of children's evolving physical and cognitive development, especially their innate curiosity about their surroundings and increasing levels of independence. Although inadequate adult supervision is often cited as a risk factor, the circumstances are often complex, interacting with poverty, single parenthood, and environments that are particularly hazardous. For instance, several studies have found that playgrounds in low-income areas had more maintenance-related hazards than those in more affluent neighborhoods. These hazards included rusty play equipment, trash, and damaged fall surfaces.

Injury Prevention

Because of the tremendous cost of injuries to individuals and society, health psychologists have an important role to play in developing interventions aimed at prevention. The premise of ecological theory (discussed in Chapter 1) is that an individual does not act or develop in a vacuum, but rather in the presence of people, places, and situations that influence how the person thinks, behaves, and acts. From this perspective, a wide range of contextual factors influences the risk of an injury occurring. These factors vary in their influence across the life span and include societal, neighborhood and community, family, peer, and individual factors. Consistent with this perspective, *Healthy People 2020* identified the following areas as targets for interventions aimed at reducing the risk of unintentional injury and violence (CDC, 2010b):

■ *Individual behaviors.* The choices people make, such as alcohol use, texting while driving, or risk-taking, can increase injuries. As another example, higher levels of activity and injury history are associated with more frequent injuries (Schwebel and others, 2011).

■ *Physical environment.* Features such as lighting, smoke detectors, fences, and so forth can affect the rate of injuries related to falls, fires and burns, drowning, and violence.

■ *Access to services.* Access to health care services, such as systems created for injury-related care, ranging from acute care to rehabilitation, can reduce the consequences of injuries, including death and disability.

- *Social environment.* This area includes adult supervision, peer-group associations, and family interactions, as well as aspects of the school, work, neighborhood, and community environments. During childhood and adolescence, the family environment is a particularly potent factor in the social environment. Higher levels of parental mental distress (Schwebel and others, 2011) and marital conflict (Schwebel and others, 2012) have both been found to predict higher rates of injury in preadolescent children. Conversely, *parental monitoring* can help reduce the risk of young people being injured. Consider gang violence, which accounts for as many as one in five murders in several of the largest cities in the United States. A recent survey of more than 4000 teens between the ages of 14 and 18 living in areas where gang violence is prevalent reported that adolescents who said they were subject to at least moderate supervision from their parents were less likely to get involved in gangs (McDaniel, 2012).

- *Societal-level factors.* This area includes such factors as cultural beliefs, attitudes, incentives and disincentives, and laws and regulations.

The three levels of prevention (discussed in Chapter 6) apply to every health problem, including injuries. Harm reduction and injury control begin with *primary prevention*—changes in laws and other societal policies that are designed to make harm less likely for everyone. *Secondary prevention* is more specific, reducing the chance of injury in high-risk situations or for vulnerable individuals. *Tertiary prevention* begins after an injury has occurred, limiting the damage. Primary prevention is most effective because it begins long before someone does something that is careless, foolish, or neglectful (Cohen & Bloom, 2010).

Consider how the three levels of prevention might apply to childhood drowning, which is a leading cause of unintentional death among 1- to 4-year-olds. Primary prevention would include building codes and local laws requiring that all swimming pools be surrounded completely by a locked fence. Secondary prevention might be the wise parent who puts good life jackets on children before they paddle a canoe on the lake. An example of tertiary prevention is the immediate delivery of cardiopulmonary resuscitation (CPR) to a submerged child who has been pulled from the water.

Other examples of primary prevention through societal changes include state and federal laws that restrict certain behaviors and mandate others. Many states now have laws mandating the use of age-appropriate restraints for children through 6 to 8 years of age, with some states also requiring that children sit in the back seat. As another example, a growing number of communities are banning the use of handheld cell phones and texting while driving. Still other examples of primary prevention are laws regarding alcohol use that are designed to prevent drunk driving; building codes and regulations that require smoke detectors in buildings; local ordinances requiring the wearing of bicycle helmets; and federal laws mandating air bags, the use of seatbelts, and lower speed limits.

Some critics of public health policy say children today are overprotected, with more laws mandating child car seats, cushioned safety surfaces, fewer jungle gyms, and so forth. Consider another example of the effectiveness of primary prevention: accidental poisoning from drugs and household chemicals. In 1970, the U.S. Congress passed the Poison Prevention Packaging Act (PPPA), under which child-resistant packaging was for the first time mandated for 30 categories of medicines and hazardous household products. Since the PPPA became law, the number of childhood deaths from accidental poisoning decreased more than 80 percent, from about 500 that year to an average of about 36 in 2012 (Figure 7.5). Thanks to better awareness and prevention efforts at each of the three levels, when injuries of all types are considered, less than half as many 1- to 4-year-olds in the United States were fatally injured in 2010 as in 1980 (Hoyert, 2012).

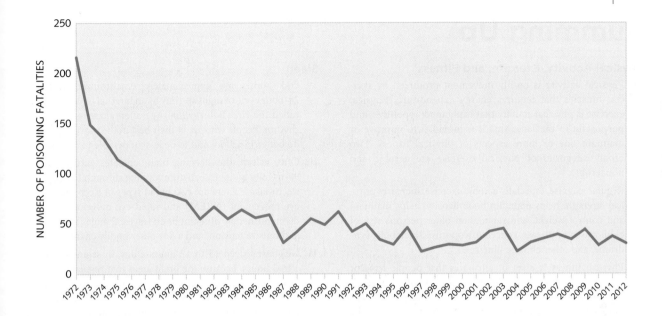

FIGURE 7.5

Childhood Poisoning Fatalities—1972 to 2012 This figure shows the number of poisoning fatalities in the United States for children younger than age 5 from 1972 to 2012.

Data from Qin, A. (2015). Pediatric poisoning fatalities from 1972 through 2012. Consumer Product Safety Commission. Retrieved May 2, 2016 from https://www.cpsc.gov/Global/Research-and-Statistics/Injury-Statistics/Pediatric-Poisonings/PPPAMortality2012.pdf.

Sound laws and policies work hand in hand with secondary prevention in preventing injuries. Even simple and inexpensive efforts such as keeping household chemicals, medications (in child-resistant containers), guns, and other dangerous objects in inaccessible, locked cabinets go a long way in reducing the likelihood of injuries.

Taking a prevention approach to injury control is a recent phenomenon. As recently as the 1980s, injury prevention was not even covered in most textbooks on community psychology. Community health psychologists generally focus on three accepted strategies in injury prevention programs: (1) *education and behavior change,* (2) *legislation and enforcement,* and (3) *engineering and technology.* Education and behavior-change strategies typically are aimed at reducing risk behaviors (anything that increases the likelihood that a person will be injured) and increasing protective behaviors (anything that reduces potential harm from a risk behavior).

Weigh In on Health

1. List as many benefits of physical fitness as you can. Are you getting enough physical activity? If not, what can you do to increase your level of physical fitness? What habits could you adopt to keep physically active throughout your life?

2. You have been asked to deliver a speech about the detrimental effects of sleep deprivation. Using the biopsychosocial model, prepare an outline of an effective speech on this topic. Then fill in the key research findings and other subpoints that support your central ideas.

3. Think about the last time that you suffered an unintentional injury. Was it truly an "accident," or could it have been prevented? How could you have changed the situation, or your own behavior, and avoided injury? What can you do in similar situations in the future to produce a different outcome?

Summing Up

Physical Activity, Exercise, and Fitness

1. Physical activity is bodily movement produced by skeletal muscles that requires energy expenditure. Physical exercise is physical activity that is planned, repetitive, and purposeful in the sense that it is intended to improve or maintain one or more aspects of physical fitness. Two broad categories of physical exercise are aerobic and nonaerobic.

2. Regular exercise, especially aerobic exercise, increases physical strength, helps maintain bone density, helps maintain and control weight, and reduces an older person's risk of cardiovascular disease, cancer, osteoporosis, metabolic syndrome, and other chronic illnesses.

3. Physical fitness is a set of attributes that people have or achieve that relates to the ability to engage in physical activity. The most important attribute is cardiorespiratory endurance, or aerobic fitness, which refers to the ability of the heart, blood vessels, and lungs to supply oxygen to working muscles during physical activity for prolonged periods of time.

4. Over time, exercise may serve as an effective buffer against anxiety and stress, boost self-esteem and self-efficacy, help people feel more vigor and less fatigue, improve cognitive functioning, and offer protection against dementia, depression, and anxiety.

5. Although it is never too late to start exercising, some older adults face several barriers to doing so, including ageist stereotypes, lack of confidence (exercise self-efficacy) and motivation, and myths that exercise can actually undermine their health.

6. Few people manage to adopt and maintain an exercise habit successfully. Minority group members consistently seem to have lower physical activity levels than majority group members, with minority women being among the least active subgroups in the United States. In several large surveys, physical activity was found to be lowest among people with low incomes and lower levels of education.

7. People are most likely to stick with exercise programs if they enjoy exercise; already have formed the habit of exercising regularly; grew up in families that exercised; have social support for exercising from relatives, friends, and coworkers; have a favorable attitude and a strong sense of self-efficacy toward exercising; perceive themselves as being somewhat athletic; and believe that individuals should take responsibility for their own health.

8. Interventions to promote physical activity work best when they are matched to the stage of readiness of individual participants and when they target neighborhood, community, and societal barriers in a comprehensive ecological approach.

Sleep

9. Our bodies are approximately synchronized with the 24-hour cycle of night and day by an internal biological clock called the *circadian rhythm*. Age often alters our circadian rhythm. People who are at their best in the morning tend to do better in school and to be less vulnerable to depression.

10. Once asleep, the sleeping brain operates according to a 90-minute biological rhythm, cycling through four distinct sleep stages. There are two broad types of sleep: non–rapid eye movement (NREM) and rapid eye movement (REM), distinguished by different brain waves, changes in breathing and muscle tension, and a few other bodily changes.

11. Newborns sleep 15 to 17 hours a day, in segments lasting 1 to 3 hours, because the brain areas that regulate sleep are immature. The number of hours that babies sleep decreases rapidly as their brains continue to develop. Not everyone needs eight hours of sleep. Newborns and infants sleep nearly two-thirds of the day, and some adults seem to thrive on fewer than six hours per night, while others regularly get nine hours or more.

12. Sleep researchers have found that insufficient sleep is related to socioeconomic status, race and ethnicity, workplace, neighborhood, and other social factors. People who are coping with stressful events at work or in the home also report poorer sleep, especially when stressors are appraised as uncontrollable. About one-third of adults experience sleep problems occasionally, and 1 in 10 adults (1 in 4 older adults) complains of insomnia.

13. Poor sleep takes a toll on both physical and psychological well-being. Chronic sleep debt promotes increased body weight, suppresses immune functioning, and adversely affects our body's metabolic, neural, and endocrine functioning in ways that mimic accelerated aging. The brain uses sleep to repair damage, replenish energy stores, and promote neurogenesis, or the formation of new nerve cells.

14. DSM-5 classifies 11 categories of sleep disorders. Among these are insomnia, narcolepsy, and sleep apnea.

15. Cognitive behavioral therapy for insomnia (CBT-I) is an effective intervention for improving restful sleep without the use of sleeping pills.

16. Sleep hygiene focuses on improving lifestyle behaviors that influence sleep, such as drinking too much alcohol, consuming caffeine late in the day, or not getting regular exercise. It also includes training in ways to wind down before bedtime.

Injury Control

17. Although, overall, injuries are the fifth-leading cause of death (after heart disease, cancer, stroke, and chronic obstructive pulmonary disease), the risk of injury as well as the likelihood of dying from an injury vary considerably

across the life span. Most injury-related deaths are from unintentional injuries, or accidents, so-called because the injured person didn't intend for it to happen. The remainder are intentional injuries, meaning that the person who caused the injury meant for it to happen.

18. The five leading causes of death in young people include external causes (accidents, homicide, and suicide), followed by cancer and heart disease. This pattern of external causes accounting for more deaths than chronic conditions changes as people get older. In older age groups, chronic conditions account for more deaths than do external causes.

19. Instead of accident prevention, experts prefer the term injury control (or harm reduction). Minor injuries are an inevitable part of any normal, active childhood, but serious injury is unlikely if efforts aimed at prevention are sound.

20. Adolescents and emerging adults are more prone to thoughtless impulses and poor decisions that lead to risky driving practices, including speeding, driving under the influence of alcohol, and driving while distracted—texting or talking on a cell phone, for instance. Poor decision making is partly the result of the fact that different parts of the brain grow at different rates. The limbic system, including the amygdala (where fear, excitement, and other intense emotions originate) matures before the prefrontal cortex (where emotional regulation, impulse control, and thoughtful analysis occur). As a result, the emotional areas of the brain develop ahead of the executive, analytic areas.

21. Unintentional poisoning death rates have been increasing steadily since 1992 and have become second only to motor-vehicle crashes as a cause of accidental death. The epidemiology of gun violence in the United States reveals the importance of several factors, including gender, ethnicity/race, geographical region, and public policy.

22. Homicide is most prevalent in people ages 18 to 24, whereas suicide is most likely among those ages 45 to 54. Because suicide is so often an impulsive act, environmental barriers such as preventing access to firearms, which are involved in 57 percent of U.S. suicides, are an important deterrent.

23. Falls are the second leading cause of unintentional injury deaths worldwide.

24. Injury control begins with primary prevention—changes in laws and other societal policies that are designed to make harm less likely for everyone. Secondary prevention is more specific, reducing the chance of injury in high-risk situations or for vulnerable individuals. Tertiary prevention begins after an injury has occurred, limiting the damage.

Key Terms and Concepts to Remember

aerobic exercise, p. 175
anaerobic exercise, p. 175
basal metabolic rate (BMR), p. 175
calorie, p. 175
physical fitness, p. 177
cardiorespiratory endurance, p. 178

osteoporosis, p. 180
metabolic syndrome (MetS), p. 180
circadian rhythm, p. 186
rapid eye movement (REM), p. 187
insomnia, p. 190

cognitive behavioral therapy for insomnia (CBT-I), p. 190
narcolepsy, p. 191
sleep apnea, p. 191
unintentional injury, p. 195
intentional injury, p. 195
injury control, p. 197

LaunchPad
macmillan learning

To accompany your textbook, you have access to a number of online resources, including quizzes for every chapter of the book, flashcards, critical thinking exercises, videos, and *Check Your Health* inventories. To access these resources, please visit the Straub *Health Psychology* LaunchPad solo at: **launchpadworks.com**

CHAPTER 8

Nutrition, Obesity, and Eating Disorders

Foodcollection/Getty Images

One of my former students (let's call her Jodi) is 26 years old and weighs 78 pounds. She was once a sleek and muscular 800-meter track champion and an academic all-American. She was hospitalized with serious coronary complications that resulted from her 12-year battle with disordered eating. Even at a mere 78 pounds, Jodi saw herself as bloated and obese.

Growing up in an upper-middle-class home, Jodi had a loving family, but she always felt pressure to live up to their high expectations. She found it particularly difficult to follow in the footsteps of her talented and popular sister and felt that she had to be perfect at everything.

Unfortunately, she felt her most significant imperfection was that she did not look like a swimsuit model. Jodi had a short, powerful build that was well suited for running fast. Even though she was the top runner on her high school and college teams, her coaches and trainers believed that she could run faster if she would only shed a few pounds.

Jodi tried her best to lose weight, but her body simply wouldn't cooperate. She tried several diets, all of which made her tired, hungry, and unable to concentrate on her schoolwork, and she never stayed on them very long. Her weight bounced up and down like a yo-yo.

Then one day Jodi found a terrible solution for her "problem": She would eat whatever she wanted and then either throw up or take a large dose of laxatives. She also increased her daily running mileage and added cross-training workouts to her regular routine. She still felt tired but thought it was worth it to gain some control over her weight.

Jodi was able to hide her bingeing and purging throughout high school and college, but once she was living on her own, she started eating less and less, and her weight loss soon became obvious. One holiday, while visiting her family, she fainted while playing basketball with her father. When he picked her up, he realized that she weighed little more than a child.

Jodi's parents insisted that she see a doctor, who quickly placed her into a treatment program in which she was force-fed for a week. Although Jodi's weight increased, the years of disordered eating had taken a severe toll on her body, and her prospects for regaining her health, then and now, are not promising.

Not all ancient cultures valued a stout build. Obesity was stigmatized in medieval Japan because it was viewed as the karmic consequence of a moral failing in Buddhism. In some parts of Europe, obesity was frowned upon as a sign of the Christian sin of gluttony.

Throughout most of history and in developing countries today, a full figure has been considered a sign of prosperity and health. Now that supersized figures are so easy to achieve in our Western cultures, we admire the sleek look instead. We are bombarded with media images of thinness that shape our standards of attractiveness and strongly influence how we feel about our bodies. Several studies have shown that even children as young as 5 years of age have a negative body image and have already engaged in dieting and other weight-loss behaviors (Holmqvist, Frisen, & Anderson-Fye, 2014). As Jodi's heart-wrenching story makes clear, not everyone can have a thin figure. The goal of health psychology is to help people attain and maintain a healthy weight, not necessarily to achieve the cultural ideal. Yet the ease with which we fill out has led more of us to suffer serious health risks from being **overweight** or **obese** (see Figure 8.1). This epidemic has spread worldwide, including Spain, France, Australia, Brazil, Mexico, Denmark, Italy, Russia—where more than half the populations are overweight—and Japan—which now has a national law mandating maximum waistline measurements (33.5 inches for men and 35.4 inches for women) as part of annual physical exams for all adults ages 40 to 74 (Onishi, 2008). A global study of 188 countries revealed that over the last three decades, *no* country has reduced its obesity rate (Ng and others, 2014). The worldwide prevalence of obesity more than doubled between 1980 and 2014, and for the first time in history, the global number of overweight people (1.9 billion) rivals the number of underfed and underweight people (WHO, 2015g). Is it any wonder that the World Health Organization recognizes obesity as one of the top 10 health problems in the world and one of the top five in developed countries?

More people are treated for obesity in the United States than for all other health conditions combined (Carroll, Navaneelan, Bryan, & Ogden, 2015). The global scope of the problem is enormous, sending approximately 3.4 million adults to early graves annually (WHO, 2015g). Each year, the market is flooded with dozens of new weight "solutions," most of which fail to work for any length of time.

The problem became so acute that First Lady Michelle Obama announced a nationwide campaign (dubbed "Let's Move") to eliminate the problem of childhood obesity within one generation (Ferran, 2010). The "Let's Move" program reflects a biopsychosocial solution and emphasizes (1) getting nutrition and exercise information to parents, (2) improving the quality of food in schools, (3) making healthy foods more affordable and accessible, and (4) focusing more on physical education. The new standards for school lunches, which were phased in starting in the 2012–2013 school year, include requirements to double the amounts of vegetables and fruits available, switch all grains to whole grains, and offer milk in only fat-free or low-fat

overweight Body weight that exceeds the desirable weight for a person of a given height, age, and body shape.

obesity Excessive accumulation of body fat.

FIGURE 8.1

Prevalence of Overweight and Obese Americans Data from the National Health and Nutrition Examination Survey (NHANES) reveal that 40 years ago, 47 percent of Americans were classified as overweight or obese (BMI > 25.0); today, 65 percent are overweight or obese. Americans are fatter today than their parents and grandparents ever were, and they are getting fatter every year.

Data from Fryar, C. D., Carroll, M. D., & Ogden, C. L. (2014). Prevalence of overweight, obesity, and extreme obesity among adults: United States, trends 1960-1962 through 2011-2012. Centers for Disease Control and Prevention. National Center for Health Statistics.

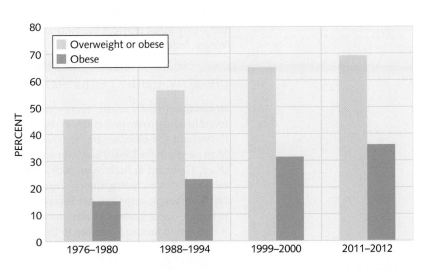

varieties. It is too soon to determine the program's effectiveness; however, the initiative is about generational change, with the goal that children will live in a much healthier food and physical-fitness culture in the near future.

At present, however, the prevalence of obesity among children and adolescents in the United States is three times what it was 30 years ago. In 2015, an estimated 17.5 percent of children and teenagers were obese, and 31.8 percent were either overweight or obese (Robert Wood Johnson Foundation, 2015). Canadians are doing a little better, with an estimated 13 percent of children and adolescents and about 25 percent of adults being obese (Carroll and others, 2015).

U.S. rates for overweight and obesity vary with gender and ethnicity. Among low-income families and certain ethnic groups such as Hispanic boys and African-American girls, the rates are even higher. By 2020, three of four Americans will be overweight or obese (Organization for Economic Co-operation and Development, 2010).

Psychologists have joined forces with molecular biologists, genetic engineers, nutritionists, and other health professionals to find answers to some puzzling questions: Why is obesity becoming more prevalent? Why is it relatively simple to lose weight but nearly impossible to keep it off? Why do some people gain weight more easily than others? Which foods are most healthful to consume, and how can we safely maintain a healthy weight? In this chapter, we will address these and other important questions in our exploration of eating behavior and weight regulation. We begin by examining the components of food and their role in maintaining health.

Nutrition: Eating the Right Foods

In Framingham, Massachusetts, in 1948, a "healthy" breakfast consisted of a plate of fried eggs, a slab of bacon, and several pieces of white toast slathered with margarine. Residents spooned sugar and fatty cream from the top of milk bottles into their coffee. In this town, one in four men age 55 or older developed heart disease, but doctors hadn't yet made the connection to diet and often listed "acute indigestion" as the cause of death.

Researchers descended on the town, and after 50 years and over 1000 scholarly research papers, the Framingham Heart Study has showed that poor nutrition is a leading risk factor for heart disease. We have learned that a diet focused on fruits, vegetables, and lean proteins, while limiting the consumption of saturated fat and entirely avoiding trans-fatty acids, provides the body with the nutrients it needs to protect and repair itself. We are, indeed, what we eat.

Healthy Eating and Adherence to a Healthy Diet

In addition to daily caloric energy, our bodies require 46 *nutrients* (essential substances found in food) to remain healthy. Water is a major source of nutrition, transporting nutrients throughout the bloodstream, removing wastes, and regulating the body's temperature. Most people in the United States do not drink the recommended amount of water each day (Kant, Graubard & Atchinson, 2009). Severe dehydration can lead to serious neurological symptoms, including anxiety, confusion, dementia, seizures, and even coma (Inouye, 2000). Although individual needs vary, most people can stay well hydrated by drinking six to eight 8-ounce glasses of water and other healthy fluids each day—enough so that there is the need to urinate every two to four hours and the urine is a light color.

The remaining nutrients are grouped into five categories: proteins, fats, carbohydrates, minerals, and vitamins. Each of these nutrient groups offers unique contributions to bodily function and health, and in the case of proteins, fats, and carbohydrates, the caloric energy our bodies need to meet the demands of daily living.

The U.S. Department of Agriculture's current nutrition guide, "MyPlate," serves as a quick visual reminder to make healthy choices when choosing your next meal. It depicts a place setting divided into five food groups of approximately 30 percent vegetables, 30 percent grains, 20 percent fruits, and 20 percent protein, accompanied by a small circle representing dairy, such as a glass of skim milk (Figure 8.2). The exact amount that you should eat from each food group depends on your age, gender, and level of physical activity. (For a quick estimate of your needs, see the online calculator at www.choosemyplate.gov.) By mid-2012, MyPlate information began to be displayed on food packaging and restaurant menus and used in nutrition education. Unfortunately, nutritional advice is frequently ignored, and adherence to healthy diets overall tends to be modest at best.

The *glycemic index* (GI) ranks carbohydrates based on how quickly your body converts them to the sugar glucose. The index ranges from 0 to 100, with higher values given to foods that cause the most rapid rise in blood sugar (see Table 8.1). The *glycemic load* (GL) of a food is a measure of how much it will raise a person's blood glucose level. Paying

FIGURE 8.2

A Balanced Diet MyPlate illustrates the five food groups that are the building blocks for a healthy diet. The new guidelines place less emphasis on grains and serving sizes and do not mention fats, oils, and sugars at all.

TABLE 8.1

The Glycemic Index (GI) of Some Common Foods

Low-GI Foods (GI = 55 or less)		
Skim milk	Plums	Slow-cooked oatmeal
Soy beverages	Oranges	Lentils, kidney beans,
Apples	Sweet potatoes	and other legumes

Moderate-GI Foods (GI = 56 − 69)		
Bananas	Brown rice	Whole wheat bread
Pineapple	Basmati rice	Rye bread
Raisins		

High-GI Foods (GI = 70 or more)		
Watermelon	Instant rice	French fries
Dried dates	Sugary breakfast cereals	Table sugar (sucrose)
White potatoes and bread	Bagels	

Not all carbohydrates are created equal! Foods that raise your blood glucose level quickly have a higher GI than foods that raise your blood glucose level more slowly. Choosing low- and moderate-GI foods—which are usually low in calories and fat, while rich in fiber, nutrients, and antioxidants—may help you keep your energy and cholesterol levels balanced, reduce inflammation, and lower your risk of heart disease and Type 2 diabetes.

One factor that has consistently been shown to promote healthy eating is social influence. Social norm messages suggesting that other people are eating healthily may be more effective than messages based solely on the health benefits of foods.

to the GI and GL values of foods is important because your body performs best when blood sugar is relatively constant. When it drops too low, you feel lethargic and hungry; and when it is too high, your pancreas produces more insulin, which brings your blood sugar back down by converting excess sugar to stored fat. High-GI foods tend to cause a surge of energy that is quickly followed by increased fat storage, lethargy—and more hunger! Elevated *postprandial* (after eating) blood glucose levels are considered a global pandemic and a major risk factor for Type II diabetes. Importantly, people's blood sugar rises or falls differently—even when they have eaten the exact same foods—suggesting that diets need to be tailored to our personal characteristics (Zeevi and others, 2015).

The consumption of sugars that have been added to processed and prepared foods has made matters even worse, increasing risk of cardiovascular disease. An estimated 16 percent of U.S. children and adolescents' total caloric intakes come from added sugars, most of which come from foods, not beverages, consumed at home (Ervin, Kit, Carroll, & Ogden, 2012).

Fast-food consumption has become a central part of the diet of many people, with an estimated 11.3 percent of total daily calories coming from fast food among U.S. adults (Fryar & Ervin, 2013). Frequent fast-food consumption has been shown to contribute to weight gain (Anderson, Rafferty, Lyon-Callo, Fussman, & Imes, 2011). Non-Hispanic black adults consume a higher percentage of calories from fast food than non-Hispanic white and Hispanic adults. Among young adults, as income increases, the percentage of calories from fast food decreases. Among adults, the percentage of calories consumed from fast food varies with body weight. In every age group, obese adults consume the highest percentage of their calories from fast food (Figure 8.3).

Equally dangerous is "supersizing." Since the 1970s, portion sizes—of restaurant foods, grocery products, and even the servings suggested in cookbooks—have grown dramatically (Brownell, 2003; Pomeranz & Brownell, 2008). This is significant because of *unit bias*—people eat more when given larger portions (Geier, Roin, & Doros, 2006). In one study, Brian Wansink and his colleagues (Wansink, Van Ittersum, & Painter, 2006) found that even nutrition experts took 31 percent more ice cream when given a big rather than a small bowl, ate 15 percent more when scooping it with a big scoop rather than a small one, and poured 37 percent more liquid when using a short, wide glass compared to a tall, skinny one of the same volume. Businesses such as self-serve frozen yogurt shops, which charge by weight, take full advantage of this phenomenon by offering "small" serving cups that are absurdly large. Most customers tend to fill these cups and ultimately end up consuming far more of this supposedly "healthy" dessert alternative than they ought to.

FIGURE 8.3

Percentage of Calories from Fast Food among Adults by Age and Weight Status Between 2007 and 2010, adults consumed an average 11.3% of their total daily calories from fast food. The percentage of calories consumed from fast food did not differ significantly between men (11.8%) and women (10.9%).

Data from Fryar, C. D., & Ervin, R. B. (2013). Caloric intake from fast food among adults: United States, 2007–2010. *NCHS Data Brief no. 114.* Hyattsville, MD: National Center for Health Statistics.

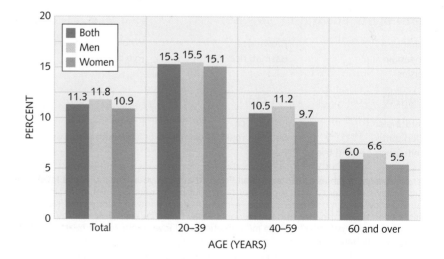

Behavior such as this is an example of *mindless eating,* in which we allow situations to control our eating. Other examples include the tendency to eat more when eating with other people (Hetherington, 2007), to eat more when offered a variety of foods from a buffet (Remick, Polivy, & Pliner, 2009), and mistakenly believing that our stomachs will tell us when they are full and we will stop before overeating. In a remarkable study, Wansink fed participants from a "bottomless bowl" of soup that was pressure-fed under the table and slowly and subtly refilled. The results: Participants with bottomless bowls ate 73 percent more than those with normal bowls, yet when asked, they didn't realize they had eaten more. "The lesson is, don't rely on your stomach to tell you when you're full. It can lie," said Wansink (2011).

Diet and Disease

A food's glycemic load is determined by multiplying the grams of carbohydrate in the food by its glycemic index and then dividing by 100.

About half of all American adults—117 million individuals—have one or more preventable, chronic diseases that are related to poor quality dietary patterns, including cardiovascular disease, hypertension, Type 2 diabetes, and diet-related cancers (Ward, Schiller, & Goodman, 2014). Early dietary habits may set a lifelong pattern that leads to problems in later life. In fact, the foods that we eat are implicated in 5 of the 10 leading causes of death: heart disease, cancer, stroke, diabetes, and atherosclerosis (WHO, 2013c).

Excess dietary fat has been widely acknowledged as a major health hazard. Currently, an unhealthy 40 to 45 percent of the total calories in the average Western diet come from fat. This overconsumption is due in part to our biology. From an evolutionary perspective, we crave fat—a legacy from our prehistoric ancestors, who were much more active and burned far more calories than most modern humans and who lived in a time when regular meals and survival were uncertain. Unfortunately for us, excess dietary fat does not go well with our more sedentary modern lifestyles.

Researchers once thought that all fat was bad, but we now know that they were wrong. Fat is a major source of energy and also helps the body absorb essential vitamins. *Trans fats* are indeed unhealthful and in fact should be avoided altogether. *Saturated fats* should be consumed in moderation, but *monounsaturated fats* and *polyunsaturated fats* (especially *omega-3 fatty acids*) are actually healthful because they help provide satiety, prevent the overeating of other foods, reduce cholesterol levels in the blood, and have a healthy, anti-inflammatory effect on the body (Brownlee, 2006). To help consumers sort through the complexities of choosing food products on the basis of their fat content, beginning in 2006, the FDA required food companies to list a product's total amount of trans fat, saturated fat, and cholesterol on its label. Currently, U.S. children and adolescents consume an unhealthy 11 to 12 percent of their total calories from saturated fat (Ervin & Ogden, 2013).

Coronary Heart Disease

Consumption of saturated fat, and especially trans fat, both of which become dietary cholesterol in the body, is a contributing factor in many adverse health conditions, including coronary heart disease. Cholesterol is a waxy substance essential for strong cell walls, myelination of nerve cells, and the production of hormones. However, the cholesterol that we take in from the fats in our foods is nonessential because the liver manufactures all the cholesterol the body needs. Dietary cholesterol—which comes from animal fats and oils, not from vegetables or plant products—circulates in the blood and therefore is called *serum cholesterol* (serum is the liquid part of the blood).

Serum cholesterol is found in several forms of proteins called *lipoproteins.* There are three types of lipoproteins, distinguished by their density. *Low-density lipoproteins* (LDLs, which carry cholesterol around the body for use by cells) and *triglycerides* (the chemical form in which most fat exists in food) have been linked to the development of heart

In 2006, artificial trans fats were banned from the menus of all 20,000 restaurants in New York City—from fast-food joints to the fanciest bistros. Health psychologists welcomed this promising move.

disease, whereas *high-density lipoproteins* (HDLs) may offer some protection against heart disease. Cholesterol carried by LDL is therefore often called "bad cholesterol," while HDL is referred to as "good cholesterol." Dietary saturated fat (especially trans fat) raises LDL levels, lowers HDL levels, and promotes inflammation.

Nutritionists recommend keeping overall serum cholesterol below 200 milligrams (mg) of cholesterol per deciliter (dl) of blood, with LDL and triglyceride levels below 100 mg/dl and HDL levels above 40 mg/dl. In addition, according to a 2002 National Academy of Science panel, the only safe level of trans fat in a food is "zero." Nutritionists also call for everyone, beginning in their twenties, to obtain a complete serum cholesterol profile (total cholesterol, LDL cholesterol, HDL cholesterol, and triglycerides) every five years (National Heart, Lung, and Blood Institute, 2006), as there is clear evidence linking lipoprotein levels to risk of coronary heart disease (Leon & Bronas, 2009). Just over 13 percent of U.S. adults have high total cholesterol (Carroll, Kit, and Lacher, 2012).

The Framingham Study revealed an important point: The best predictor of heart disease is not total level of serum cholesterol; instead, the culprit is the amount of "bad cholesterol" (LDL and triglycerides) in the body. Even people with lower levels of total serum cholesterol are at increased risk of developing atherosclerosis if their HDL levels are very low. HDL levels below 35 mg/dl are considered unhealthy. Smoking, physical inactivity, and a high dietary intake of cholesterol and saturated fats are linked with increased levels of LDLs and decreased levels of HDLs. Certain types of polyunsaturated and monounsaturated fats, vitamin E, and a low-in-saturated-fat, high-fiber diet may protect against heart disease by elevating HDL levels. Approximately 12 percent of women and 31 percent of men have low HDL cholesterol (Carroll and others, 2012).

Serum cholesterol level is determined partly by heredity. For most people, however, diet and lifestyle play a major role in the amount of serum cholesterol circulating in their bodies. The good news is that this message has been getting out. A fairly recent study found that more than two-thirds of U.S. adults are being screened for cholesterol. The percentage of adults aged 20 and over with adverse concentrations of total cholesterol (15 percent) and LDL cholesterol (25 percent) has declined steadily since 2000. However, screen rates vary from group to group, ranging from 71 percent in non-Hispanic white women to 50 percent in Hispanic men (Carroll and others, 2012).

Cancer

As you will see in Chapter 11, diet is implicated in one-third of all cancer deaths in the United States (American Cancer Society, 2009). Saturated fat, especially that found in red meat and other animal products, is the major dietary culprit. Saturated fat has been linked to several cancers, including breast cancer, prostate cancer, and colorectal cancer. Research published over the last decade suggests that a poor diet can also unleash a persistent, low-level activation of the immune system. One consequence of an immune system that never gets to rest is that it may be "asleep" when it is really needed (Beil, 2015).

Fortunately, there is also evidence that certain foods may protect us against cancer. Vegetables and fruits are rich in *beta-carotene,* which the body processes into vitamin A—a nutrient that helps ensure healthy immune system functioning. Along with beta-carotene, small amounts of selenium, found in fish, whole grains, and certain vegetables, may help prevent some forms of cancer, but only in people with a deficiency in this essential mineral. Selenium taken as a supplement may actually have a toxic effect if no deficiency is present (Rayman, 2012). A diet rich in vitamins C and E may also help prevent cancer by protecting body cells from the damaging effects of *free radicals* (metabolic waste products). Such a diet also may protect against carcinogenic *nitrosamines,* which are produced in the stomach when you eat foods laced with nitrates, nitrites, and other preservatives commonly found in prepared foods.

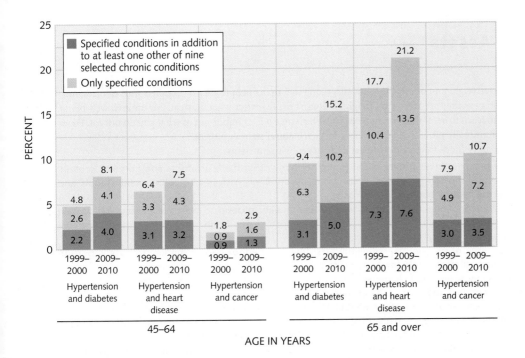

Multiple Chronic Conditions

Heart disease, cancer, and other illnesses sometimes occur together. Between 2000 and 2010, the percentage of American adults aged 45 and older with **multiple chronic conditions (MCC)** increased for men and women, all racial and ethnic groups, and most income groups (Figure 8.4). The most prevalent combinations of chronic conditions are hypertension and diabetes, hypertension and heart disease, and hypertension and cancer. The prevalence of obesity—a clear risk factor for certain types of heart disease and cancer, hypertension, and diabetes—is likely a factor in this trend. The presence of MCC adds a layer of complexity to disease management (Freid, Bernstein, & Bush, 2012).

Weight Determination: Eating the Right Amount of Food

Naturally, it's not only what you eat, but also how much you eat in relation to your body's caloric needs, that determine your weight and your health. Before we discuss obesity—its causes and treatment—you first need to understand the basic mechanisms by which the body determines the type and amount of calories needed.

Basal Metabolic Rate and Caloric Intake

Body weight remains stable when the calories that your body absorbs from the food you eat equal the calories that it expends for basic metabolic functions plus physical activity. How many calories does your body need to maintain bodily functions while at rest?

FIGURE 8.4

Prevalence of the Three Most Common Combinations of Nine Selected Chronic Conditions, by Age and Type of Condition The percentage of adults with the three most common combinations of chronic conditions (hypertension and diabetes, hypertension and heart disease, and hypertension and cancer) increased over the 10-year period between 2000 and 2010 for both men and women, in all racial and ethnic groups, and in most income groups.

Data from Freid, V. M., Bernstein, A. B., & Bush, M. A. (2012). Multiple chronic conditions among adults aged 45 and over: Trends over the past 10 years. *NCHS Data Brief no. 100*. Hyattsville, MD: National Center for Health Statistics.

multiple chronic conditions (MCC) Two or more chronic conditions (lasting a year or more, requiring medical attention, and/or limiting daily activities) that affect a person at the same time.

Your Health Assets

Super Foods for a Super You

Given the pandemic of overweight and obesity, it is not surprising that many people are preoccupied with calories, mistakenly thinking that so long as they aren't gaining weight, it doesn't really matter what they eat. For optimal well-being, however, it is important to learn to eat for health, not weight. What you eat is as important as what you do not eat. Focus on eating foods that are minimally processed and as close to their natural state as possible.

Here are 10 everyday super foods that are easy to eat and packed with nutrients:

- Low-fat or fat-free plain yogurt is higher in calcium than many other dairy products and contains protein, potassium, and other important nutrients. Also, it can be enriched with heart-healthy plant stanols and probiotics to promote healthy bacteria in your gut.
- Eggs are nutritious, economical, and a great way to add quality protein to your diet. They also contain 12 vitamins and minerals, including choline, which is important for brain development and cognitive functioning.
- Nuts are a good source of protein, heart-healthy fats, fiber, and antioxidants. The key to nuts is portion control. In small doses, they can help lower cholesterol levels and promote weight loss.
- The kiwi is one of the most nutritionally dense fruits. Rich in antioxidants, one large kiwi contains a full day's supply of vitamin C and is a good source of potassium, fiber, and vitamins A and E.
- Quinoa (pronounced *keen-wa*) is one of the healthiest grains that you can eat. One cup of cooked quinoa is high in protein (8 grams), fiber (5 grams), and a naturally good source of iron, zinc, vitamin E, and selenium, which can help control weight and lower your risk for diabetes and heart disease.
- Beans are loaded with insoluble fiber, which helps lower cholesterol, as well as soluble fiber, which fills you up and helps the body remove waste. Beans are also an excellent, low-fat source of protein, carbohydrates, magnesium, and potassium. Edamame (whole soybeans) also contain heart-healthy omega-3 fatty acids.
- Salmon is rich in omega-3 fatty acids, protein, and iron, and it is very low in saturated fat. Because of its protective effects on heart health, the American Heart Association recommends eating fatty fish such as salmon twice weekly.
- Broccoli and other cruciferous vegetables (such as kale) are rich sources of vitamin A, vitamin C, and bone-building vitamin K. These super foods are also high in fiber, which helps fill you up and control weight.
- Sweet potatoes are part of the dark orange vegetable family, which lead all foods in their vitamin A content. They are also rich in potassium, which helps reduce bone loss, and low in sodium, which is good for blood pressure.
- Berries are low in calories and high in water and fiber content, which helps to control blood sugar and keep you feeling full longer. In addition, they are loaded with phytonutrients and are some of the best sources of antioxidants around. Especially important is the fact that berries satisfy our cravings for sweets for a fraction of the calories and fat content of baked goods.

Recall from Chapter 7 that this figure, called the *basal metabolic rate* (BMR), is not easily determined, because it depends on a number of variables, including your age, gender, current weight, and activity level.

Individual differences in BMR help explain why it is possible for two people of the same age, height, and apparent activity level to weigh the same, even though one of them has a voracious appetite, while the other merely picks at food. Several factors determine BMR, including, first, heredity. Some people have a naturally higher metabolic rate than others, even when they're asleep. Other people need fewer calories for the same amount and level of physical activity. Second, younger people and those who are active generally have a higher BMR than do older adults and those who are sedentary. Third, fat tissue has a lower metabolic rate (burns fewer calories) than muscle does. Once you add fat to your body, you require less food to maintain your weight than you did to gain the weight in the first place. Finally, because men have proportionately more muscle, their bodies burn 10 to 20 percent more calories at rest than women's bodies do.

The Set-Point Hypothesis

Many people believe that their body weights fluctuate erratically, but in fact our bodies balance energy intake and expenditure quite closely. A typical adult consumes roughly 900,000 to 1 million calories a year. Subtract from this figure the energy costs of BMR, and you'll discover that less than 1 percent of the calories that you eat are stored as fat, a remarkable degree of precision in energy balance (Gibbs, 1996). Because of this precise regulation, experts have used data from national surveys to estimate that affecting energy balance by only 100 calories per day (as little as 15 minutes of walking, or eating just a bit less each meal) could prevent weight gain in most people (Hill, Wyatt, Reed, & Peters, 2003). Evidence of such precision supports the **set-point hypothesis,** the idea that each of us has a body weight "thermostat" that continuously adjusts our metabolism and eating to maintain our weight within a genetically predetermined range, or set point (Keesey & Corbett, 1983).

The set-point concept (today considered by many researchers to be a *settling-point* range of weight rather than a fixed number of pounds) partly explains why it is difficult to bring weight down. As a study by George Bray (1969) showed, with continued dieting, the body defends its precious fat reserves by decreasing its metabolic rate. When obese dieters reduced their daily intake from 3500 to 450 calories for 24 days, their bodies quickly started burning fewer calories until their BMRs had dropped by 15 percent. The result: Although their body weight initially dropped 6 percent, with a lower BMR, they found it difficult to lose any more weight. These findings surely will strike a chord with dieters who suffer the frustrating experience of losing a few pounds relatively quickly but then finding it harder to lose additional weight as their dieting (and reduced metabolism) continues.

If starvation has this effect on metabolism, what effect does overeating have? To find out, researchers in several studies persuaded a group of normal-weight volunteers to eat an additional 1000 calories a day for eight weeks (Levine, Eberhardt, & Jensen, 1999), or until their weights increased by 10 percent (Leibel, Rosenbaum, & Hirsch, 1995). The results mirrored those of the semi-starvation studies. After an initial period of rapid gain, further weight increases came slowly and with great difficulty, even though the participants had access to an abundance of food and kept physical activity to a minimum. The overfed volunteers came to find the experiment unpleasant. Food became repulsive, and they had to force themselves to eat. Some even failed to reach their weight-gain goal, even though they more than doubled the number of calories they consumed each day. At the end of the experiment, however, most lost the weight again quickly.

Interestingly, those who gained the least amount of weight in the overfeeding studies (less than 1 pound) tended to expend their extra caloric energy through greater incidental physical activity, such as fidgeting, sitting up straight, and flexing muscles. This phenomenon has also been found to be true in other studies: Lean people seem to be naturally disposed to move about more than overweight people (Levine and others, 2005). One recent study reported that overweight children engaged in moderate-to-vigorous physical activity for only 17 minutes per day on average, spending the vast majority of their time (86.7 percent) being sedentary (Small, Bonds-McClain, & Gannon, 2013).

Why are our bodies so painfully good at maintaining weight? According to the evolutionary perspective, the capacity to store excess calories as fat was an important survival mechanism for our ancestors. Animals that hibernate and those that must endure periods of nutritional scarcity—as did the human species throughout much of our history—store internal energy reserves when food is plentiful and live off those reserves when food is in short supply. Natural selection favored those human ancestors who developed "thrifty genes," which increased their ability to store fat from each feast to sustain themselves until the next meal. Although those of us who live in well-stocked, developed countries

set-point hypothesis The idea that each person's body weight is genetically set within a given range, or set point, that the body works hard to maintain.

All-you-can-eat-buffets may be inexpensive and tasty, but they can also be unhealthy.

leptin The weight-signaling hormone monitored by the hypothalamus as an index of body fat.

Adipocytes Typically, we each have about 30 billion of these fat cells, or adipocytes. They are like little storage tanks. In a thin person, the fat cells are relatively empty; as the person gains weight, the cells begin to fill up. Each of the cells in this electron photomicrograph is filled by a single lipid droplet, mostly formed by triglycerides. Connective tissue fibers, shown at the upper left, provide support for the fat cells.

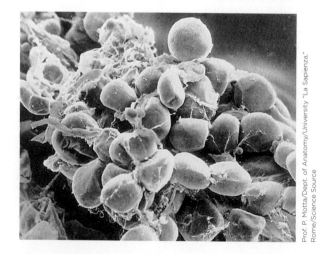

no longer need to store so much fat, many of us continue to do so. For example, obesity is characteristic of the Pima Indians of southern and central Arizona who live a "Western" lifestyle, whereas Pima Indians living a more traditional lifestyle remain leaner and have low levels of the fat hormone **leptin** (Friedman and others, 2003). Similarly, Hispanic-American women have higher rates of obesity than their non-Hispanic white counterparts. This is especially true for Latinas whose families are more strongly *acculturated* to Western dietary norms (Yeh, Viladrich, Bruning, & Roye, 2009).

The Biological Basis of Weight Regulation

Our BMR determines how many calories we need to maintain bodily functioning, but what sets off the initial hunger pangs we all feel? Exactly what triggers hunger and its opposite—*satiety?* Researchers have tackled this question by focusing on where in the brain the signals for hunger and satiety are processed. During the 1960s, researchers located appetite centers in two areas of the hypothalamus: a side region called the *lateral hypothalamus* (LH), which seemed to trigger hunger, and a lower area in the middle called the *ventromedial hypothalamus* (VMH), which seemed to trigger satiety. Animal experiments during the 1960s demonstrated that electrical stimulation of the LH causes an animal that has eaten to the point of fullness to begin eating again; when this area is lesioned, even an animal that has not eaten in days shows no signs of hunger. Conversely, when the VMH is stimulated, animals stop eating; when this area is destroyed, they overeat to the point of extreme obesity (Hoebel & Teitelbaum, 1966). We now know that the lateral hypothalamus secretes the hunger-triggering hormone *orexin* as the time since a last meal increases and blood sugar level drops (Sakurai and others, 1998).

Increased feelings of hunger also have been linked to an increase in the number of fat cells, or **adipocytes,** in the body. When adipocytes reach their maximum storage capacity, they divide—a condition called *fat-cell hyperplasia.* Once the number of fat cells increases in a person's body, it never decreases, even when the person diets (Spalding, 2008). People who are not obese have 25 to 30 billion fat cells. Those who are severely obese may have 200 billion or more (Hirsch, 2003). Recent animal studies show that periods of inactivity can also increase fat stores and the number of fat cells (Roberts, 2007).

Researchers have discussed several other specific mechanisms for regulating how often and how much we eat on a given day and for regulating our body weight over months and years.

Short-Term Appetite Regulation

The pancreas produces the hormone insulin and assists the body in converting glucose into fat. When glucose levels fall, insulin production increases, and we feel hunger. Conversely, when glucose levels rise, hunger and insulin levels decrease. As time passes since the last meal, the level of glucose in the blood drops. In addition to insulin reduction, low blood glucose triggers a release of stored fat from body cells. As fat is depleted, the hypothalamus also arouses hunger, motivating us to replenish our fat and glucose stores by eating.

Researchers have also identified *cholecystokinin* (CCK), a satiety hormone released into the bloodstream by the intestine that signals when we've had enough to eat. CCK suppresses appetite even when injected into starving animals (Thompson, 2000). Two other short-term appetite-regulating hormones that have been identified are *ghrelin*, an appetite stimulant, and *peptide YY* (PYY), an appetite suppressant. The stomach produces ghrelin, which causes the pituitary gland to release growth hormone and stimulates appetite. This discovery helped clear up a mystery in appetite research: why people want to eat at specific times each day. David Cummings and his colleagues (Cummings, Foster-Schubert, & Overduin, 2005) discovered that ghrelin levels rise an hour or two before mealtimes and decrease afterwards, stimulating appetite by activating neurons in the *arcuate nucleus* (ARC) of the hypothalamus. Ghrelin also stimulates receptors on nerve cells in the hippocampus, a brain area involved in learning and memory (Diano and others, 2006). This finding makes evolutionary sense because hungry animals need to remember where they found a food source. Most obese people have lower levels of ghrelin than those who are thinner, and ghrelin production increases in people who are dieting—explaining in part why dieters may find it increasingly difficult to stick to their regimen.

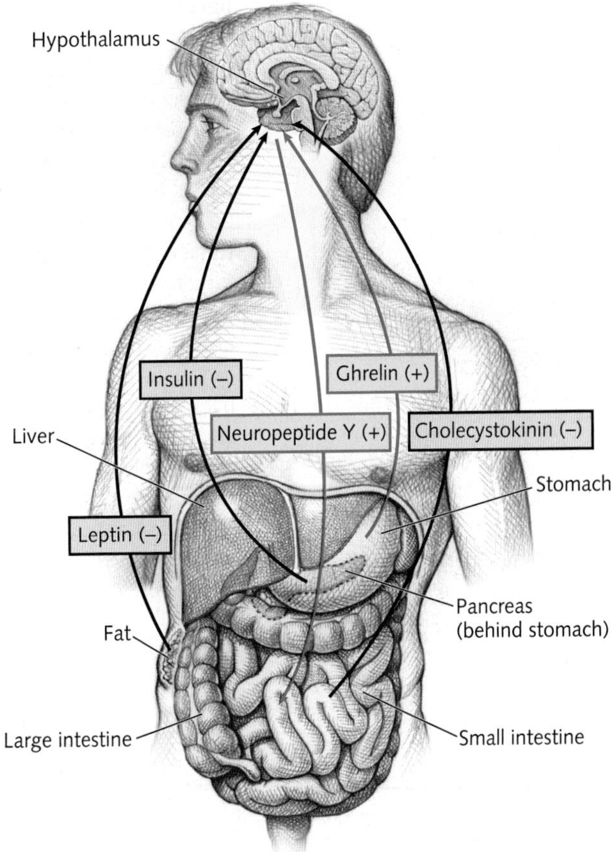

Long-Term Weight Regulation

Why do some people seem to have more potential to become fat? Molecular biologists speculate that genetic disorders may interfere with the body's ability to regulate the number of fat cells, thereby causing people to gain weight. In 1994, researchers discovered that laboratory mice with a defective gene for regulating the hormone leptin could not control their hunger and became obese. Leptin, produced by fat cells, is found at greater levels in people with more body fat and lower levels in those with less body fat. Because they usually have higher body fat content, women generally have higher leptin levels than men do.

As body fat increases, higher levels of leptin signal the normal brain to suppress hunger. Animals with defective leptin genes produce too little leptin and overeat. They become hugely obese and diabetic, and they have a substantially lower BMR than their genetically normal counterparts (Zhang, Proenca, Maffei, & Barone, 1994). When given daily injections of leptin, they eat less, they become more active, and their body weights eventually return to normal (Halaas and others, 1995).

The discovery of leptin renewed support for the set-point theory. According to this line of reasoning, if the body's set point is something like a thermostat, leptin acts as the thermometer (Gibbs, 1996). As a person gains weight, more leptin is produced. This shuts off appetite, increases energy expenditure, and triggers other mechanisms to restore body weight to the set point. Conversely, as a person loses weight (as in dieting), levels of leptin decrease, hunger increases, and metabolism falls until the person's weight returns to its targeted level.

Leptin's signaling ability also may explain why most dieters regain lost weight. After dieting, less leptin is available to signal the brain, possibly increasing hunger and slowing metabolism. In normal mice, leptin levels dropped 40 percent after a three-day fast and 80 percent after a six-day fast (Nakamura and others, 2000). Although the effects of leptin

Hypothalamus
Insulin (−)
Ghrelin (+)
Neuropeptide Y (+)
Cholecystokinin (−)
Liver
Leptin (−)
Stomach
Fat
Pancreas (behind stomach)
Large intestine
Small intestine

FIGURE 8.5

Feedback Loop Involved in Short-Term and Long-Term Appetite Regulation Many different signals interact in regulating appetite and energy expenditure so that body weight remains relatively stable over time. Appetite is stimulated (+) by increased levels of ghrelin and neuropeptide Y. Appetite is suppressed (−) by increased levels of CCK, insulin, and leptin.

adipocytes Collapsible body cells that store fat.

have made researchers enthusiastic about its possible use as a weight-loss drug, so far their efforts have not been successful (Morton, Cummings, Baskin, Barsh, & Schwartz, 2006).

Recent studies have pointed to a different function of this hormone in animals and in people. Although some rare cases of human obesity are caused by defects in leptin production, most obese humans have higher than normal blood levels of the hormone (Marx, 2003). Some believe that the leptin receptors of obese people are simply less sensitive to leptin. Following this line of reasoning leads to the conclusion that leptin's main role may be to protect against weight loss in times of deprivation rather than against weight gain in times of plenty. Obese people simply produce the hormone at a greater rate to compensate for a faulty signaling process (Nakamura and others, 2000).

Although injections of leptin are not effective for treating most cases of obesity in humans, the discovery of the hormone helped pinpoint the neural pathways involved in weight regulation. In particular, this pathway called ARC, which we have seen to be involved in short-term appetite regulation, contains large numbers of receptors for leptin and other hormones involved in long-term weight control. The ARC also contains two major types of neurons with opposing actions. Activation of one type, which produces a neurotransmitter called *neuropeptide Y,* stimulates appetite and reduces metabolism. Activation of the other type causes the release of *melanocyte-stimulating hormone,* which reduces appetite. For these reasons, the ARC has been called the "master center" for both short- and long-term weight regulation (Marx, 2003).

body mass index (BMI) A measure of obesity calculated by dividing body weight by the square of a person's height.

Two Weight Extremes This professional football player has a BMI above 30, which puts him well into the obese category. At the other end of the scale, superthin model Miranda Kerr's very low BMI is also unhealthy.

Obesity: Some Basic Facts

People are concerned about what and how much they eat because of the negative physiological and psychological effects of obesity. Being overweight carries a social stigma in many parts of the world today, indicating the importance that many societies place on physical appearance. In fact, obese people are one of very few disabled groups who regularly endure public criticism. Obese children are frequently teased and, as adults, are often perceived as "ugly" and "sloppy" (Hayden-Wade and others, 2005) and as lacking in willpower (Larkin, 2007).

How our weight affects our psychological well-being depends in great part on our gender. For instance, overweight women are more likely to be depressed, even suicidal, than their thinner counterparts (Carpenter, Hasin, Allison, & Faith, 2000). Interestingly, *underweight* men are more likely to be diagnosed with clinical depression than their heavier counterparts.

How do we define obesity? In recent years, the definition of obesity has been refined to mean the presence of excess body fat. A person with an acceptable weight and figure but too much body fat could be considered obese, and his or her health could be at risk. Thus, at the same weight, you can be healthy or not—it all depends on your individual fat-to-muscle ratio.

The most frequently used measure of obesity today is the **body mass index (BMI),** which is strongly correlated with percentage of body fat. Here's how to determine your

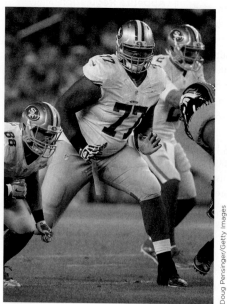

Doug Pensinger/Getty Images

Fairfax Media/Getty Images

BMI: Multiply your weight in pounds (without shoes or clothes) by 705. Divide this product by your height in inches. Then divide it again by your height. Alternatively, you could use the BMI calculator at the National Institutes of Health (NIH) Web site (www.nhlbisupport.com/bmi/). For example, if you weigh 140 pounds and are 5 feet 6 inches tall, your BMI would be 22.66, which is within the normal range (see Table 8.2). A BMI of 40 or greater is considered Class III obesity—the point where the excess body fat begins to interfere with day-to-day movement and even breathing. Class III obesity is equivalent to 294 pounds for a 6-foot man or 247 pounds for a woman 5 feet 6 inches tall.

There is no set ideal amount of body fat for all people because the amount of body fat changes with age. In healthy adults, acceptable levels of body fat range from 25 to 30 percent in women and from 18 to 23 percent in men.

Although the BMI provides a good estimate of body fat, it is an incomplete measure of health as it relates to body fat. For one thing, muscle-bound athletes can have BMIs of 30 or more yet have little body fat. The most significant problem with BMI is that it reflects total body fat without regard to how it is distributed. While the overall amount of body fat is important, evidence indicates that *where* body fat is distributed may be even more significant. The excess *visceral fat* associated with **abdominal obesity** (also called *male-pattern obesity*) has been linked to metabolic syndrome, inflammation, atherosclerosis, hypertension, and diabetes (Despres & Lemieux, 2006), and—pound for pound—it is considered a greater overall health risk than fat that is concentrated on the hips and thighs (sometimes called *female-pattern obesity*). However, the health hazards of a high waist-to-hip ratio apply to both women and men and may even be a more accurate predictor of mortality from all causes than body mass index. To measure your waist-to-hip ratio, perform the following steps:

1. Measure your waist at its slimmest point.

2. Measure your hips at their widest point.

3. Divide your waist measurement by your hip measurement: (waist in inches)/(hips in inches) = _____.

Thus, a woman with a waist of 29 inches and a hip measurement of 37 would have a ratio of 0.78, while a man with a 34-inch waist and a 40-inch hip measurement would have a ratio of 0.85. Both ratios fall within the healthy range. As a rule, the desirable waist-to-hip ratio is less than 0.8 for women and less than 0.95 for men. (See Table 8.3 for instructions on how to measure and interpret waist circumference.) The latest research shows that the chance of suffering a heart attack or stroke increases steadily as a man's ratio rises above 0.95; for women, risk begins to rise when the ratio exceeds 0.85 (*Harvard Health Letter*, 2013).

TABLE 8.2
Body Mass Index (BMI) and Weight

BMI Categories

- Underweight = <18.5
- Normal Weight = 18.5–24.9
- Overweight = 25–29.9
- Class I Obesity = 30–34.9
- Class II Obesity = 35.0–39.9
- Class III Obesity = 40+

Source: Department of Health and Human Services (2015). Centers for Disease Control and Prevention. Retrieved on February 8, 2016, from http:// www.cdc.gov/nccdphp/ dnpa/bmi/index.htm

abdominal obesity Excess fat around the stomach and abdomen; also called *male-pattern obesity.*

TABLE 8.3
Interpreting Your Waist Circumference

An even simpler metric for measuring abdominal fat is waist circumference. To measure your waist circumference, take your shoes off and stand with your feet together. Relax and exhale. Using a cloth measuring tape that can't be stretched, keep the tape parallel to the ground and measure your bare waist at the navel to the nearest one-tenth of an inch.

	Men	Women
Low risk	37 inches and below	31.5 inches and below
Intermediate risk	37.1–39.9 inches	31.6–34.9 inches
High risk	40 inches and above	35 inches and above

Source: Excerpted from Waisted: Abdominal Obesity and Your Health in *Harvard Men's Health Watch*, January 2009. © 2009 Harvard University. Updated 2016. www.health.harvard.edu

NOTE: Harvard Health Publications does not endorse any products or medical procedures.

FIGURE 8.6
Mortality Rates as a Function of Body Mass Index (BMI)
Generally speaking, thinner women and men live longer. At a BMI of 40, a woman's risk of dying is approximately 50 percent higher than that of a person with a BMI of 24; for men with a BMI over 40, the risk of death is about 2.5 times higher. However, very thin people do not have the lowest mortality rates, indicating that the relationship between weight and poor health would actually be U-shaped, were the graph extended to BMIs below 18.

Data from Calle, E. E., Thun, M. J., Petrelli, J. M., Rodriguez, C., & Heath, C. W. (1999). Body-mass index and mortality in a prospective cohort of U.S. adults. *New England Journal of Medicine, 341,* 1097–1105.

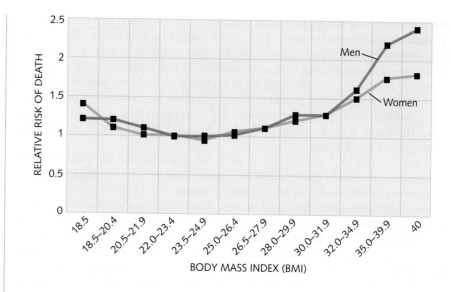

Hazards of Obesity

The NIH cites obesity as second only to cigarette smoking in its importance as a behavioral factor in mortality rates (Figure 8.6; Berrington de Gonzales and others, 2010): As body fat accumulates, it crowds the space occupied by internal organs and contributes to many chronic health problems. Consider:

- The incidence of hypertension in people who are 50 percent or more overweight is three to five times that of normal-weight people.

- The prevalence of *metabolic syndrome,* or MetS (the set of obesity-related factors that increase the risk for coronary artery disease, stroke, inflammation, and diabetes), increases with BMI. Overweight men are 6 times as likely and obese men are 32 times as likely as normal-weight men to meet the criteria for MetS. Overweight women are 5 times as likely and obese women are 17 times as likely to meet the criteria (Ervin, 2009).

- Obese children are more likely to have high blood pressure, high cholesterol, breathing problems such as asthma and sleep apnea, fatty liver disease, and Type 2 diabetes, which historically only affected older adults.

- Obese children as young as 8 years old may have enlarged hearts, a sign that the cardiac muscle is under strain (Beil, 2015).

- During adolescence, obesity and MetS are linked to impairments in brain structure, including reduced hippocampal volumes and reduced white matter (Yau, Castro, Tagani, Tsui, & Convit, 2012).

- Obese children and teens are more likely to have social and psychological problems, such as depression, and are at increased risk of bullying and poor self-esteem (Weir, 2012).

- Obesity promotes *hyperinsulinemia,* an endocrine disorder in which insulin progressively loses its effectiveness in sweeping glucose from the bloodstream into the 60 trillion or so cells of our bodies. For this reason, obesity is a leading cause of Type 2 diabetes.

- The liver manufactures more triglycerides (the most common form of dietary fat in the bloodstream) and cholesterol in those with excess body weight, which increases the risk of arthritis, gout, and gallbladder disease.

- Complications following surgery, including infection, occur more often among the obese.

- There is a strong correlation between obesity and cardiovascular diseases in both men and women, even after statistical adjustments are made for blood pressure, cholesterol, smoking, age, and diabetes.

- Obesity increases the risk of certain cancers.

- Among adults, obesity is associated with lower psychological well-being, especially among women, and with a marked increase in depression (Mendes, 2010). Obese people are mistakenly stereotyped as being slow, lazy, and undisciplined (Puhl & Heuer, 2009). Compared to women of equal intelligence, obese women earn less money, are less likely to be married, and are underrepresented among corporate CEOs (Roehling, Roehling, Vandlen, Bazek, & Guy, 2009).

Given the health hazards that obesity poses, it will come as no surprise that being significantly overweight can cut life short (Adams and others, 2006). A large-scale study following more than 1 million Americans over a 14-year period reported that white men and women with the highest BMI (40 or higher) had two to six times the relative risk of death of their thinner counterparts with a BMI of 24 (Calle, Thun, Petrelli, Rodriguez, & Heath, 1999). Another large prospective study reported that adults who are overweight are likely to die 3 years earlier than their thinner counterparts (Peeters and others, 2003). A more recent examination of BMI and mortality in 1.46 million adults showed that mortality rates for all causes of death were lowest with a BMI of 20 to 24.9 (Berrington de Gonzalez and others, 2010).

However, researchers are still debating whether having a BMI between 25 and 30 is truly hazardous. Some experts suggest that people who are short, elderly, African-, Hispanic-, or Asian-American suffer no ill effects unless they become truly obese (Strawbridge, Wallhagen, & Shema, 2000). For instance, while the lowest mortality rates among European-American women and men occur in those with a BMI of 24 to 25, the lowest mortality rates among African-Americans occur in those with a BMI of 27 (Durazo-Arvizu, McGee, Cooper, Liao, & Luke, 1998).

Another factor that complicates the obesity–health relationship is age. Being overweight increases the risk of death from all causes among young and middle-aged adults (Adams and others, 2006). After about age 65, however, being *underweight* is actually associated with increased risk of dying from all causes (Diehr and others, 1998) because losing weight in late adulthood generally leads to less muscle, thinner bones, and greater risk of accidents and chronic disease.

While being excessively underweight or overweight is hazardous to health, **weight cycling** (also called *yo-yo dieting*)—a pattern of repeated weight gain and loss—is also unhealthy. An ongoing study of Harvard alumni has reported that men who maintained a stable weight had significantly lower death rates from all causes (including cardiovascular disease) than did alumni who had either gained or lost a significant amount of weight over the years (Lee, Manson, Hennekens, & Paffenbarger, 1993). Short-term weight gains and losses, however, are not linked to increased death rates (Maru, van der Schouw, Gimbrere, Grobbeee, & Peeters, 2004).

weight cycling Repeated weight gains and losses through repeated dieting.

The Biopsychosocial Model of Obesity

Although it is tempting to take the view that obesity is simply the result of overeating, research shows that this is an oversimplification. Those who are overweight often do *not* eat more than their thin friends do. Rather, obesity is a complex phenomenon involving biological, social, and psychological factors in both its causes and consequences (Pi-Sunyer, 2003).

Biological Factors

Research on the biological factors that contribute to obesity has focused on the roles of heredity, the brain, and hormones in regulating appetite.

Heredity

Twin studies and adoption studies confirm that genes contribute approximately 50 percent to the likelihood of obesity. This heritability is equal to that of body height and greater than the heritability of many disorders for which a genetic basis is generally accepted. (For a review, see Friedman and others, 2003.) Heredity influences different factors that contribute to obesity, such as basal metabolic rate (BMR). People with a naturally lower BMR burn fewer calories than their thinner counterparts. Given an obese parent, a boy is three times and a girl six times more likely to become obese than a child with normal-weight parents (Carriere, 2003).

The role of heredity in obesity is illustrated by a massive study in which researchers analyzed the weights of more than 3500 adopted Danish children and their biological and adoptive parents (Meyer & Stunkard, 1994). The study found a strong relationship between the body weights of adoptees and their biological parents but little or no relationship between the weights of offspring and their adoptive parents. Additional evidence comes from the strong correlation (0.74) between the body weights and BMIs of identical twins, even when they are raised in separate households (Plomin, DeFries, McClearn, & Rutter, 1997; Schousboe and others, 2004). The much lower correlation between the body weights and BMIs of fraternal twins (0.32) suggests that genes account for approximately two-thirds of individual differences in BMI (Maes, Neale, & Eaves, 1997).

Many different genes influence body weight, most of which, individually, seem to have small effects (Walters and others, 2010). For example, one global study of 40,000 people identified a variant of the FTO gene, which seems to double the risk of becoming obese (Frayling and others, 2007). How might the so-called *fat mass and obesity-associated gene* influence obesity? One possibility is that a variant of the gene might influence BMR, perhaps lowering it and thus promoting weight gain because the body does not burn as many calories. To find out, researchers measured the height, weight, and waist-to-hip ratios of 2700 elementary school kids in Scotland (Cecil, Tavendale, Watt, Hetherington, & Palmer, 2008). They also took saliva samples to check FTO genes. As expected, overweight and obese children were more likely to have the FTO gene variant. The most interesting part of the study involved a subgroup of 76 students who had their metabolism monitored for 10 days while eating special test meals at the school. The researchers weighed the available food before and after each meal to see how much the kids had eaten. The results showed that the FTO variant was not associated with reduced metabolism; rather, it was linked to eating more food, especially high-calorie food. So the FTO variant that confers a predisposition to obesity may be involved in food intake and food choice—especially a preference for energy-dense foods.

A recent study suggests that the FTO gene may also be involved in how the body handles calories, functioning as a "genetic switch" that determines whether people will burn extra calories or store them as body fat. Interestingly, about 42 percent of Southeast Asians, 40 percent of Europeans, but only 5 percent of Africans carry the obesity-risk variant of the FTO gene (Claussnitzer and others, 2015).

Destiny? Genetics versus Environmental Factors

Despite the evidence for the role of biological factors in obesity, it is important to recognize that specific genetic defects are involved in only about 4 percent of cases of human obesity (Clement, Boutin, & Froguel, 2002). Rates of obesity have increased dramatically in recent years, which means that genes can't explain it all. The role of genetic factors in obesity is complex and polygenic (determined by the interaction of several genes), and each of the genes involved may have a relatively small effect. Moreover, heredity alone does not destine a person to be fat. Obesity is a product of genetic vulnerability and environmental factors or maladaptive behaviors (Morrison, 2008). What appears to be inherited is a *tendency* to be overweight; the amount overweight a person becomes is affected by diet and activity level. Regular activity and a healthy diet can limit genetic tendencies toward obesity.

Psychosocial Factors

Hunger and eating behavior are not controlled by physiological factors alone. Psychosocial factors also come into play. One 32-year study of over 12,000 people found that a person is most likely to become obese when a friend is obese (Christakis & Fowler, 2007), and if that friend is a close one, the odds almost triple. As another example, we are conditioned to associate eating with holidays, personal achievements, and most social occasions. And the giving of food is among the first symbols of love between a parent and child. Should we be surprised that people are conditioned to turn to food when they are upset, anxious, or under stress? The idea of *stress–eating* associations is embodied in the familiar concept of *comfort food*. A recent study of college students demonstrated that being provided comfort food during childhood was an important predictor of later stress eating (Brown, Schiraldi, & Wrobleski, 2009).

Neil Grunberg and I (Grunberg & Straub, 1992) asked groups of men and women seated in a comfortable living room to watch either a stressful film about eye surgery or a pleasant travelogue. Within their reach were bowls of snack foods, including M&M candies. The bowls were weighed before and after each session to determine how much of each snack food the subjects ate. All the men and those women who reported little concern about dieting and body weight ate fewer M&Ms when watching a stressful film than did those who watched the nonstressful film. Women who reported being especially conscious of their weight and who had a history of frequent dieting, however, consumed more sweets when stressed.

A growing body of evidence indicates that both acute and chronic stresses are associated with eating in the absence of hunger (Rutters, Nieuwenhuizen, Lemmens, Born, & Westertep-Plantenga, 2009). One study drew on data from the Health and Behavior in Teenagers Study (HABITS) to determine whether long-term stress is associated with unhealthy eating, particularly of fatty foods and snacks (Cartwright and others, 2003). The HABITS sample is a large, socioeconomically and ethnically diverse sample of 4320 schoolchildren (mean age = 12 years) who completed questionnaire measures of stress and dietary practices. Girls and boys who reported the highest levels of stress ate more fatty food and snacks than their less stressed peers and were less likely to consume the recommended five or more daily fruits and vegetables or to eat breakfast.

Studies finding data such as these suggest that stress eating may contribute to long-term disease risk by triggering unhealthy patterns of food consumption. The classic *restraint theory* may help explain why. This theory contends that people who chronically follow a strict diet (restrained eating) will be more likely to eat and possibly overeat (unrestrained eating) when feeling stressed (Herman and Polivy, 1975). Because many obese people diet and attempt to restrain their eating, they may be prone to overeating in stressful situations (Wardle, Parmenter, & Waller, 2000).

Culture, Socioeconomic Status, and Gender

Genes cannot explain why being overweight or obese is more prevalent today than in the past. Today, the average woman in the United States is 5 feet 4 inches tall, weighs between 140 and 150 pounds, has a waist size of 34 to 35 inches, and wears a size 12 to 14 dress. Women 50 years ago averaged the same height, but weighed only about 120 pounds, had a waist of approximately 24 to 25 inches, and wore a size 8 dress (Peeke, 2010). In the late

1980s, 47 percent of Americans were classified as overweight or obese; today this figure has jumped to 65 percent (Freking, 2006). Americans are fatter today than their parents and grandparents ever were, and they are getting fatter every year.

Genes also cannot explain why the increase in weight in our population is not evenly distributed; there has been a disproportionate increase in the number of massively obese people in recent years, especially in certain ethnic groups. Within the United States, obesity is more prevalent among African-Americans, Hispanic-Americans, Native Americans, and other minority groups (Figure 8.7). Socioeconomic factors may be helpful in explaining this relationship. Particularly among women in developed countries, there is an inverse relationship between obesity and socioeconomic status (SES), with people of lower SES more likely to be overweight than those who are more affluent. The fact that members of minority groups are disproportionately represented among lower-SES groups helps explain why they are more likely to be overweight (Sanchez-Vaznaugh, Kawachi, Subramanian, Sanchez, & Acevedo-Garcia, 2009).

Low-income children and adolescents are more likely to be obese than their higher-income counterparts, but the relationship is not consistent across race and ethnicity groups (Ogden, Lamb, Carroll, & Flegal, 2010). Public health researchers commonly use the **poverty income ratio (PIR),** defined as the ratio of household income to the poverty threshold after accounting for inflation and family size. The prevalence of obesity among boys living in households with income at or above 35 percent of the poverty level is 11.9 percent, while 21.1 percent of those who live below 13 percent of the poverty level are obese. Among girls, 12 percent of those with income at or above 35 percent of the poverty level are obese, while 19.3 percent of those with income below 13 percent of the poverty level are obese (Ogden and others, 2010).

The relationship among income, ethnicity, and weight also varies with gender in adulthood. There is a clear income gradient in overweight prevalence among women: Poor women are 1.4 times as likely to be overweight as women with middle incomes and 1.6 times as likely to be overweight as women with high incomes. For men of all races, however, there is little evidence of an income-related gradient in the prevalence of overweight.

Being overweight or obese is also inversely related to education and occupation level. Among all young people between 16 and 24 years of age, those who are overweight tend

poverty income ratio (PIR) The ratio of household income to the poverty threshold after accounting for inflation and family size.

FIGURE 8.7

Percentage of U.S. Women and Men Who Are Overweight and Obese Among adults in the United States, the prevalence of obesity (BMI 30) and of overweight and obesity combined (BMI 25) shows significant variation by racial and ethnic groups.

Data from Ogden, C. L., Carroll, M. D., Fryar, C. D., & Flegal, K. M. (2015). Prevalence of obesity among adults and youth: United States, 2011–2014. *NCHS Data Brief, no. 219.* U.S. Department of Health and Human Services.

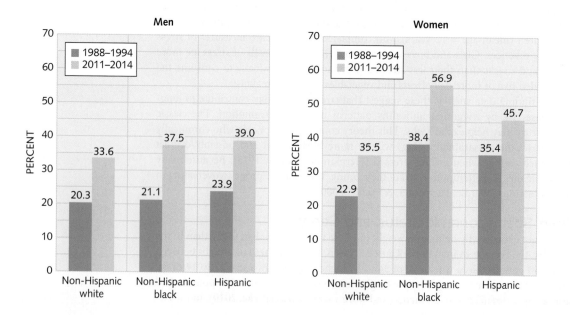

not only to have lower personal incomes but also to have completed fewer years of education and to work in lower occupational categories than their normal-weight counterparts (Martin, Nieto, Ruiz, & Jimenez, 2008). Once again, these socioeconomic variables have a greater predictive value in women than in men. Men and women of all races with a college degree are less likely to be overweight than men and women with fewer than 12 years of education. Since the mid-1970s, however, the prevalence of being overweight or obese among men and women has increased steadily at all education levels (National Center for Health Statistics, 2012).

Why are less educated, lower-SES people at increased risk for obesity? Their risk factors include more limited access to health care services, less knowledge about the importance of a healthy diet and the hazards of obesity, lower perceived self-efficacy in being able to increase their fruit and vegetable intake, and less exercise (Steptoe and others, 2003). Data from the massive Monitoring the Future Study also suggest that social disparities in body weight may occur because African-American women, Hispanic women, and men with lower SES are less likely to practice six important health behaviors regularly: eating breakfast, eating green vegetables, eating fruit, exercising, watching television in moderation, and sleeping seven hours each night (Clarke, O'Malley, & Johnston, 2009). It also has been suggested that the greater daily stress associated with poverty—resulting from prejudice, crowding, and crime, for example—may trigger increased eating as a defensive coping mechanism. Thus, it is not surprising that obesity is less prevalent among minority Americans who live in more affluent neighborhoods than among those living in lower-SES neighborhoods (Hazuda, Mitchell, Haffner, & Stern, 1991). Higher-SES adolescents also display greater awareness of the social ideals of slimness and are more likely to have family and friends who are trying to lose weight (Wardle and others, 2004).

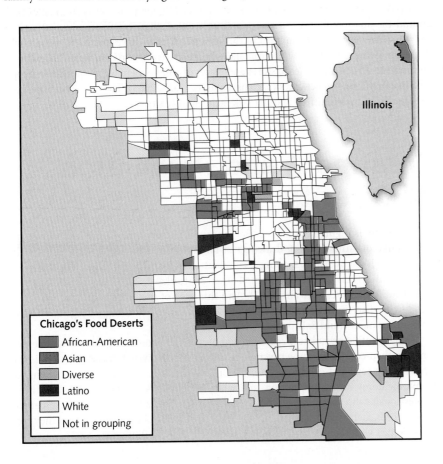

Illinois

Chicago's Food Deserts
- African-American
- Asian
- Diverse
- Latino
- White
- Not in grouping

FIGURE 8.8
Urban Food Deserts Over half a million Chicagoans live in the city's three food deserts, and most of them are African-Americans (Gallagher, 2006).

Accessibility of healthy foods can apparently offset the dietary hazards of low income. A study compared the dietary composition and food attitudes of a large sample of culturally diverse, low- to middle-income middle school students attending two schools. Students who attended a private school where nutritious lunch and snack food choices were available had significantly lower fat in their overall diets and greater awareness of the benefits of a healthy diet than did students attending a public school where food choices were more limited and less nutritious (Frenn & Malin, 2003). This was true despite the fact that, as a group, the private school students came from families with significantly lower incomes than those of students attending the public school.

The issue of access to healthy foods and other barriers to adherence to a healthy-weight lifestyle comes into sharp focus when one considers the plight of residents of cities such as Detroit and Chicago, where a much higher-than-average percentage of citizens are obese. There are hundreds of fast-food restaurants and convenience stores that stock fatty snack foods in these cities but a limited number of supermarkets that sell fruits, vegetables, and other nutritious foods. To make matters worse, these sprawling cities have weak public transportation systems, making it difficult for many Detroiters and Chicagoans to escape the **food deserts** (Figure 8.8 on the previous page) of their neighborhoods in order to purchase healthy foods (Wehunt, 2009). However, more research is needed to determine how access influences the types of foods people actually purchase and consume (CDC, 2012c).

food deserts Geographical areas with little or no access to foods needed to maintain a healthy diet.

In the face of results such as these, health psychologists and legislators are calling for wide-scale public health and policy interventions. Among those being considered are bills that would extend nutrition labeling beyond packaged foods to include foods at fast-food restaurants and the banning of soft drink and snack food machines in schools. Some health psychologists and urban planners are also calling for a shift away from cities built around the automobile toward more "walkable cities" that reengineer physical activity back into daily routines. In support of this idea, researchers have found that people who live in sprawling cities such as Detroit and who must therefore rely more on their cars to commute from distant homes to stores and places of employment weigh more than people who live in more compact cities (Saelens, Sallis, & Frank, 2003). They also are more likely to suffer from hypertension, another risk factor for obesity.

Treatment and Prevention of Obesity

Obesity is highly stigmatized. Beginning in nursery school, children show a dislike of fatness, rating drawings of fat children as having fewer friends, being less liked by parents, doing less well at school, and being lazier, less happy, and less attractive than thinner children (Latner & Stunkard, 2003; Teachman, Gapinski, Brownell, Rawlins, & Jeyaram, 2003). And this type of prejudice continues into adulthood, with discrimination against the obese occurring in housing, college admissions, and employment (Puhl & Brownell, 2001).

Because antifat prejudice is so strong and because fat people are generally held responsible for their condition, some psychologists maintain that weight discrimination is even greater than race and gender discrimination and that it affects every aspect of employment, including hiring, promotion, and salary (Roehling & Winters, 2000). Even health professionals who specialize in obesity hold hidden biases toward their obese patients, using words such as *lazy*, *stupid*, and *worthless* to describe obese people whom they come into contact with (Schwartz, Chambliss, Brownell, Blair, & Billington, 2003).

Attempts to address the serious health implications for the growing number of those who are obese, combined with the social prejudice against obesity, have led to a proliferation of different weight-reduction regimens.

Dieting

A stroll through any bookstore will give you a quick idea of the vast array of dieting strategies—everything from preplanned meals with strict calorie limits to single-food plans to hypnosis. It's easy to be cynical about the number of choices. If any of them were truly effective, there would not be a market for such variety. The main beneficiaries of most of these books are their authors.

Successful weight loss in adults is often defined as at least a 10 percent reduction of initial weight that is maintained for one year (Rich, 2004). Weight losses of this magnitude generally produce significant improvements in health in most overweight adults. However, many people (especially women who are not overweight) are trying to shed pounds for reasons that have little or nothing to do with health. The increasing popularity of dieting has been attributed to the growing cultural pressure to be slim.

How Effective Are Diets?

Dieting alone usually does not work to take weight off and keep it off (Mann and others, 2007). The best way to lose weight and keep it off is to develop sound eating habits *and* to engage in regular physical exercise to raise the BMR. Studies also suggest that daily self-weighing can be an important factor for long-term weight control (LaRose and others, 2014).

Even though most diets fail, Americans spend billions of dollars each year on them. Nearly two-thirds of adults say they are over their ideal weight; 55 percent say they would like to lose weight, yet only 27 percent say they are "seriously trying" to lose weight (Jones, 2009). The gap between the percentage of adults who would like to weigh less and who are actively making the attempt has existed for many years. Overall, 17 percent of teens aged 12 to 19 say they are actively trying to lose weight. This includes only about half of those who are actually overweight, 48 percent of whom say they are trying to lose weight (Saad, 2006).

Why Diets Fail

One reason that diets fail is that many people are not very good at calculating the number of calories their bodies need or the size of the food portions they are eating. Underestimating calorie consumption is a common problem in many failed diets. In one study, for example, obese dieters reported eating an average of 1028 calories per day, but their actual intake averaged 2081 calories, more than twice as many calories as reported.

Diets also fail because many people have unrealistic expectations and find it nearly impossible to comply with dietary restrictions for very long (Wadden, Butryn, & Wilson, 2007). Inconvenience and feelings of deprivation are often cited as factors that undermine adherence (Jeffery, Kelly, Rothman, Sherwood, & Boutelle, 2004). One randomized clinical trial assessed the effectiveness and adherence rates of four popular diets—Atkins, Zone, Weight Watchers, and Ornish. All four diets resulted in "modest, statistically significant weight loss," with no differences in effectiveness among diets. However, only one in four participants was able to sustain that weight loss one year later (Dansinger, Gleason, Griffith, Selker, & Schaefer, 2005).

The most successful diets are clinical interventions that include some form of posttreatment following weight loss, such as social support, exercise programs, or continued contact with the therapist. Commercial group programs like Weight Watchers typically promote social support, self-monitoring in the form of daily food diaries, and discussion

Your Health Assets
Lose Weight the Smart Way

If you are struggling with obesity, you should seek medical guidance. For those who just want to shed a few pounds, here are a few tips:

- *Set a weight loss goal only if you are motivated and self-disciplined.* Losing weight and keeping it off require a lifestyle change combining healthier eating habits with increased exercise.
- *Make healthy food choices.* Choose fresh fruits, vegetables, whole grains, legumes, and healthy fats.
- *Get more exercise.* Exercise burns calories, suppresses appetite, and helps lower your body's weight set point.
- *Keep tempting foods out of sight.* Buy mostly fresh, whole foods like fruits, vegetables, fish and other lean proteins, eggs, and low-fat or nonfat dairy products. Avoid processed packaged foods with long lists of ingredients, especially those that are artificial and hard to pronounce.
- *Manage portion size.* Keep meals simple and modest in size, even when eating healthy foods.
- *Don't starve yourself to eat one big meal.* This eating pattern slows metabolism and causes calories to be stored as fat more readily.
- *Eat slowly and beware of binge eating.* People who eat slowly tend to eat less. Conversely, eating quickly and eating when you drink alcohol or feel anxious can cause you to overeat.

about exercise and nutrition as key components. In one study, two-thirds of the participants who enrolled in a group weight-loss program with friends kept their lost weight off six months after the program ended, compared to only one-fourth of those who attended alone (Wing & Jeffery, 1999).

Behavioral and Cognitive Therapy

Behavior modification, particularly in conjunction with cognitive intervention techniques, has become a mainstay of many contemporary weight-loss programs. Behavior modification programs typically include the following components:

- *Stimulus control* procedures to identify and limit the number of cues that trigger eating (for example, confining eating to one particular place)
- *Self-control* techniques to slow the act of eating (for example, chewing each bite a set number of times or putting down silverware between bites)
- *Aerobic exercise* to boost metabolism, burn calories, and help curb appetite
- *Contingency contracts* in which therapist-delivered or self-controlled reinforcement is made dependent upon reaching weight-loss goals (for example, the client puts up a sum of money to be earned back as goals are attained)
- *Social support* of family members and friends, who are enlisted to provide additional reinforcement for success and compliance
- *Careful self-monitoring* and recordkeeping to increase awareness of what foods are eaten and the circumstances under which eating occurs
- *Relapse prevention therapy* to teach people who are trying to maintain changes in their behavior how to anticipate and cope with urges, cravings, and high-risk situations

Self-monitoring is often sufficient in and of itself to promote and maintain weight loss. In fact, several studies have shown that about 25 percent of weight-control success is due to consistent self-monitoring (Elfhag & Rossner, 2005). Raymond Baker and Daniel Kirschenbaum (1998) examined self-monitoring of eating behaviors during three holiday periods (Thanksgiving, Christmas/Hanukkah, and New Year's Eve). Compared with the controls who gained weight, those participants who were the most thorough in recordkeeping actually lost weight during the holiday weeks. Other researchers have pointed to the effectiveness of another aspect of self-monitoring in weight loss: memory of recent eating. One study examined the effect of being reminded of a recent eating episode on subsequent food intake (Higgs, 2002). Participants ate less at dinner following exposure to a "lunch cue," in which they were simply asked to think about what they had eaten for lunch earlier that day.

Recently, advocates of behavioral treatments have broadened their focus to include a greater concern with the types of foods consumed, the need for exercise and coping skills to aid in overcoming high-risk relapse situations, responses to violating diet and/or binge eating, and primary prevention of obesity during childhood. Consumption of unhealthy food choices can be reduced by increasing the behavioral costs associated with obtaining them—through decreased access, for instance—and by providing healthy alternative foods and enjoyable activities.

Efforts to limit access to unhealthy foods are often controversial, as seen most recently in New York City with the attempted ban on large, sugary sodas (Grynbaum, 2013). However, such efforts can have big payoffs. For example, Daniel Taber and his colleagues (Taber, Chriqui, & Chaloupka, 2012) recently reported the results of a study that tracked more than 6000 students in 40 states. Kids in states with strict laws governing the sale of snacks and sodas in schools gained less weight from fifth grade to eighth grade than kids in states with weaker or fewer school food regulations.

Behavioral methods are most successful when they are combined with cognitive techniques that recognize that overweight people often start treatment with unrealistic expectations and self-defeating thoughts. *Cognitive behavioral therapy* (CBT) focuses on the reciprocal interdependence of feelings, thoughts, behavior, consequences, social context, and physiological processes. The underlying premise of these therapies is that eating habits and attitudes must be modified on a permanent basis for weight loss and the maintenance of that loss to occur.

Rather than attempting to force quick and dramatic weight losses, CBT focuses on the gradual loss of 1 to 2 pounds per week, using a combination of conditioning, self-control, and cognitive restructuring techniques, in which the person learns to control self-defeating thoughts about body weight and dieting. When it comes to weight loss

Spencer Platt/Getty Images

Efforts to limit access to unhealthy foods are often controversial, as seen most recently in New York City with the attempted ban on large sugary sodas.

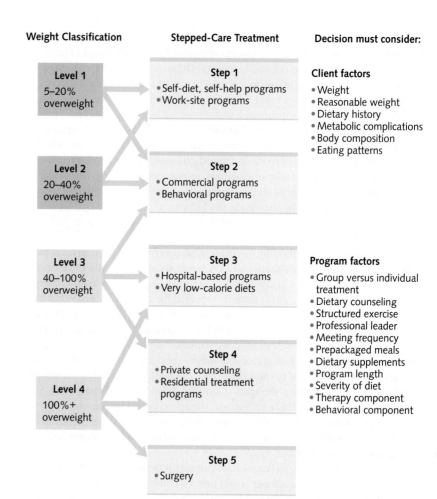

FIGURE 8.9

Stepped Care in the Treatment of Obesity In general, people at levels 1 or 2 should be able to lose weight through steps 1 and 2. At level 3, treatment should begin with step 2 and extend through 4. Those at level 4 who have medical problems may need surgery to solve their weight-loss problems. However, before a health psychologist sets up a program, he or she considers all factors related to both the client and the program (as listed on the right).

Source: Brownell, K.D., & Wadden, T.A. (1991). The heterogeneity of obesity: Fitting individuals to treatments. *Behavior Therapy, 22,* 153–177.

and management in children, CBT generally focuses on prevention, including establishing healthy eating behaviors in the individual and family; reducing television viewing, Internet surfing, and computer-game playing; and promoting positive attitudes toward food. Positive eating messages are critical because studies have shown that dieting during childhood actually may promote weight gain and unhealthy eating behaviors later in life.

Any therapeutic intervention for obesity will be most successful when health psychologists recognize that patients differ in which treatment will be most effective for them. Kelly Brownell and Thomas Wadden (1991) proposed the *stepped-care* process for determining which intervention is most appropriate for a given person (see Figure 8.9). A seriously obese person may require more aggressive and intensive treatment than someone who is moderately obese. After considering relevant factors about the client, including degree of obesity, eating patterns, and medical history, a health psychologist structures the safest, least intensive intervention that will meet that person's needs. Only if this treatment is ineffective is a more intensive intervention warranted.

More than two decades ago, Marlene Schwartz and Kelly Brownell (1995) asked 33 weight-loss experts from several fields (psychology, nutrition, internal medicine, surgery, and neuroendocrinology) to compare 11 popular weight-loss approaches, including self-directed dieting, Weight Watchers, behavioral programs, medication, and surgery. In the ensuing years, they and their Yale University colleagues have continued to investigate the issue of how best to advise people who are trying to lose weight (Brownell and others, 2010). Among their findings:

- Self-directed dieting was recommended for those with mild to moderate obesity, except for people with a history of weight cycling.

- Commercial programs with group support were recommended for an initial weight-loss attempt or for people who had not been able to diet effectively on their own.

- Very-low-calorie diets and surgery were recommended only for those with a medical problem complicated by their obesity.

- Medical supervision was considered necessary for people with diabetes and others with medical conditions that are likely to change with dieting.

- Individual counseling and behavioral weight-loss programs were considered appropriate for those with eating disorders.

Matching individuals to treatment is important because people with different personality styles, levels of obesity, medical histories, and eating practices will respond differently to various treatments (Carels and others, 2005).

Fit Families, Fit Communities

The causes of obesity are as complex as its health hazards. Recall the ecological model that depicts a series of concentric circles, the central one of which is an individual person (see Figure 1.5 in Chapter 1). Moving outward, the circles represent ever-broader influences on a health behavior: the family, the neighborhood, the school, the community, and society at large.

In over 30 years of research, Leonard Epstein and his colleagues (Epstein and others, 2012; Epstein, Lin, Carr, & Fletcher, 2011) have found that the most successful ways to help kids lose weight are *lifestyle interventions* that combine diet, physical activity, and behavioral control *and* that target both parents and children simultaneously. The trick is to help parents engineer healthy home environments by removing TVs from bedrooms, limiting computer time, teaching parents how to find and prepare nutritious foods on a budget, and making physical activity a routine for the entire family. Equally important is *social facilitation maintenance,* extending an intervention across the home, peer, and community environments to build social support and help kids and families keep weight off after they've lost it. The school environment is particularly important since kids consume 35 percent to 50 percent of their total calories at school, many from **competitive foods** purchased from vending machines, school stores, and à la carte cafeteria offerings that typically include cookies, candy, and chips. Fortunately, modifying school environments has become easier since, in 2010, Congress passed the Healthy Hunger-Free Kids Act, which set new school food policies that reduce fat and sugar and increase whole grains, fresh fruits, and vegetables.

Making healthy food choices, self-monitoring, and preventing obesity with other steps that people take on their own to maintain weight may be especially difficult today because too many of us live, work, and attend school in what has been described as an *obesigenic* (obesity-promoting) *environment* (Lowe, 2003). Unhealthy foods are everywhere, and our bodies are genetically programmed to eat when food is available. Consequently, experts are calling for broader community strategies and public health measures in the war on obesity (Khan and others, 2009). These community strategies fall into six categories:

- *Promote the availability of affordable healthy food and beverages.* These include increasing the availability and affordability of healthier food and beverage choices in schools, day-care centers, city and county buildings, and other public service venues; offering incentives for supermarkets to relocate in underserved areas and offer healthier food choices; and providing incentives for the production, distribution, and purchase of food directly from farms.

competitive foods Foods and beverages that are often high in calories, sugar, fat, and sodium that are sold in schools in vending machines, à la carte lines, and student stores.

- *Support healthy food and beverage choices.* These include offering smaller portion-size options in public service venues, limiting advertising of less healthy foods and beverages, and discouraging the consumption of sugar-sweetened beverages.

- *Encourage breast-feeding of infants* (which is linked to decreased pediatric overweight and obesity). These include providing educational interventions, breast-feeding support programs, and increased availability of maternal care in hospitals, workplaces, and public service venues.

- *Encourage physical activity or limit sedentary activity among children and youth.* These include requiring time for physical education in schools, increasing community opportunities for extracurricular physical recreation, and reducing television and other sources of screen time in public service areas.

- *Create safe communities that support physical activity.* These include expanding access to outdoor recreational facilities; enhancing infrastructure to support bicycling and walking by creating safe, well-lit bike lanes, sidewalks, trails, and footpaths; and improving access to public transportation.

- *Encourage communities to organize for change.* These include creating partnerships to address obesity among health care professionals, educational institutions, government, industry, and the media.

Eating Disorders

For some dieters, especially young, overachieving women like Jodi—the young woman we met at the beginning of the chapter—obsession with weight control may turn into a serious eating disorder.

anorexia nervosa An eating disorder characterized by self-starvation; a distorted body image; and, in females, amenorrhea.

Anorexia nervosa is an eating disorder characterized by failure to maintain body weight above a BMI of 18, intense fear of weight gain, and disturbance of body image for at least three months (American Psychiatric Association, 2013). Because a healthy percentage of body fat is necessary for menstruation, post-pubescent women develop amenorrhea if they lose too much weight.

Anorexia can lead to many serious medical complications, including:

- slowed thyroid function
- irregular breathing and heart rhythm
- low blood pressure
- dry and yellowed skin
- brittle bones
- anemia, lightheadedness, and dehydration
- swollen joints and reduced muscle mass
- intolerance to cold temperatures
- starvation

bulimia nervosa An eating disorder characterized by alternating cycles of binge eating and purging through such techniques as vomiting or laxative abuse.

The second major eating disorder is **bulimia nervosa.** Bulimia involves compulsive bingeing followed by purging through self-induced vomiting or large doses of laxatives. Some sufferers purge regularly, others only after a binge. For example, they may consume as many as 5000 to 10,000 calories at one time, eating until they are exhausted, in pain, or out of food. People with bulimia also engage in compulsive exercise to try to control their weight. And, unlike those with anorexia, people with bulimia typically maintain a relatively normal weight (Wonderlich, Joiner, Keel, Williamson, & Crosby, 2007)—as Jodi initially did until she moved out on her own and began reducing her food intake.

People who engage in recurrent binge-eating episodes, followed by feelings of distress or guilt, but without the compensatory behaviors of purging, fasting, or excessive exercise that mark bulimia nervosa, are said to have **binge-eating disorder (BED)**. BED is the most common eating disorder in the United States and Canada, affecting an estimated 3.5 percent of women and 2 percent of men (Swanson and others, 2011). BED is often associated with depression and seems to run in some families. Some people with BED have also experienced emotional or physical abuse, or substance abuse disorders. BED may be treated with medications that reduce the urge to binge and with cognitive behavioral therapy aimed at changing thoughts about eating and understanding what triggers binges (NEDA, 2016).

binge-eating disorder (BED) An eating disorder in which a person frequently consumes unusually large amounts of food.

Although as many as half of all college women report having binged and purged at some time (Fairburn & Wilson, 1993), most would not be considered bulimic. The criteria for a clinical diagnosis include at least one bulimic episode a week for at least three months; lack of control over eating; behavior designed to avoid weight gain; and persistent, exaggerated concern about weight (American Psychiatric Association, 2013).

Unlike anorexia, which has a mortality rate of 2 to 15 percent, bulimia is rarely fatal. But it puts sufferers at risk for many serious health problems, including the following:

- Laxative dependence
- Hypoglycemia (low blood sugar) and lethargy from eating an unbalanced diet (often one high in sweets but lacking sufficient fatty acids)
- Damaged teeth from purging because hydrochloric acid from the stomach erodes tooth enamel (Dentists are often the first health care professionals to suspect bulimia.)
- Bleeding and tearing of the esophagus from vomiting
- Anemia (a condition involving a lack of hemoglobin in the blood) and electrolyte imbalance caused by loss of sodium, potassium, magnesium, and other body minerals from purging

Bulimic episodes are reported by 40 to 50 percent of people with anorexia. It is possible for an individual to meet the criteria for both disorders at the same time.

Demographics

Anorexia and bulimia are unique among psychological disorders in having a strong gender bias (three out of four are females) and in the substantial increase in these disorders during the past century. Before the 1970s, eating disorders generally were found only among upper-middle-class women in Western cultures. Since then, disordered eating has been increasing among other populations, so SES and ethnocultural identity are no longer reliable predictors.

It is estimated that at some point during their lifetimes, 0.6 percent of people in the United States meet the criteria for anorexia, 1 percent for bulimia, and 2.8 percent for binge-eating disorder (Hudson, Hiripi, Pope, & Kessler, 2007). College women are particularly at risk, as are young women between ages 15 and 19 who attend ballet, gymnastics, or modeling academies. Athletes also are at increased risk of eating disorders, even those who participate in sports that do not emphasize appearance or an overly thin body. Until recently, it was thought that only about 10 percent of the diagnosed cases of eating disorders were men. It is now estimated that about one in four of the estimated 8 million Americans with eating disorders are male (Hudson and others, 2007). Of this group, male athletes—especially swimmers, rowers, and wrestlers—are especially vulnerable (Weinberg & Gould, 2015).

Barbie and the Female Body How much blame for girls' plump body image should be placed on the unrealistic body dimensions of Barbie and other popular dolls? By one estimate, to achieve "Barbie doll proportions," a female of average height would have to gain 12 inches in height, lose 5 inches from her waistline, and add 4 inches to her bustline! In recognition of the fact that girls and women don't come in one shape, toy manufacturer Mattel announced that the 2016 line of Barbie dolls would come in four body types, including tall, petite, and curvy, in addition to the original-size doll.

Mattel/Splash News/Newscom

Applying the Biopsychosocial Model

As we have seen, health and illness are best understood in terms of a combination of biological, psychological, and sociocultural factors. Let's take a look at how health psychologists have applied the biopsychosocial model to understand eating disorders.

Biological Factors

A young person's body image at the onset of puberty may foretell healthy or disordered eating behaviors. Girls who perceive the timing of their development to be early tend to feel the least positive about their bodies, whereas girls who perceive their development to be on time feel the most attractive and have the most positive body images (McLaren, Hardy, & Kuh, 2003; Striegel-Moore and others, 2001). Early-maturing girls may feel less comfortable with their bodies because at a time when peer acceptance is crucial to self-esteem, their bodies are different from those of the majority of their peers. On-time development may present the fewest psychological challenges to adolescent girls.

Biochemical abnormalities at all levels of the hypothalamic-pituitary-adrenal axis are associated with both anorexia and bulimia (Gluck, Geliebter, Hung, & Yahav, 2004). These include abnormal levels of norepinephrine and other neurotransmitters that may promote clinical depression (Fava, Copeland, Schweiger, & Herzog, 1989). There is also evidence that bulimia may be caused in part by disturbances in the brain's supply of *endorphins,* the opiatelike neurotransmitters linked to pain control and pleasure. Researchers have found that *opiate antagonists,* which block the action of the endorphins, may be an effective treatment in reducing the frequency of binge–purge episodes. Researchers also have discovered that serum levels of leptin are significantly reduced in people with anorexia (Calandra, Musso, & Musso, 2003).

Might people inherit a predisposition to eating disorders? Studies of eating disorders within families and among twins reveal a possible genetic influence on anorexia and bulimia. Consider:

- Twin and adoption studies both indicate significant genetic influences on eating disorders (Klump, Suisman, Burt, McGue, & Iacono, 2009). When one twin has bulimia, the chances of the other twin's sharing the disorder are substantially greater if they are identical twins rather than fraternal twins (Root and others, 2010).

- Molecular geneticists are currently searching for specific genes that may influence susceptibility to eating disorders. To date, findings indicate some role for genes involving the serotonin, dopamine, and estrogen systems in the development of anorexia nervosa (Klump and others, 2009). These systems have been implicated in anxiety as well as in food intake, and accordingly, may be disrupted in eating disorders.

Psychological Factors

Other theorists argue that the roots of eating disorders can be found in certain psychological situations, such as the competitive, semiclosed social environments of some families, athletic teams, and college sororities.

The families of people with anorexia tend to be high achieving, competitive, overprotective, and characterized by intense interactions and poor conflict resolution (Ma, 2008). The families of people with bulimia have a higher-than-average incidence of alcoholism, drug addiction, obesity, and depression (Depestele, Lemmens, Dierckx, Baetens, & Claes, 2015). Researchers caution, however, against assuming that all children from such homes are alike. Eating disorders are *not,* for example, a telltale sign of an alcohol abuser's home environment (Mintz, Kashubeck, & Tracy, 1995). Young women with anorexia and bulimia rate their relationships with their parents as disengaged, unfriendly, even hostile (Wonderlich, Klein, & Council, 1996). They also feel less accepted by their parents, who are perceived as overly critical, neglectful, and poor communicators (Calam, Waller, Slade, & Newton, 1990). Stated more broadly, eating disorders have been linked to insecure attachments in social relationships (Troisi and others, 2006). Particularly in adolescence, family-based therapy for eating disorders is more successful than therapy focused only on the individual (Couturier, Kimber, & Szatmari, 2013; Bass, 2015).

Despite living in a society that stigmatizes obesity and idealizes thinness, there are many more Americans who are overweight or obese (65 percent) than suffering from eating disorders (0.5–3 percent). As a result of this disparity between the ideal and reality, body image dissatisfaction is so pervasive in the United States that it represents a "normative discontent" among adolescents of all shapes and sizes (Bell and Dittmar, 2010). Judy Rodin (1992) has argued that women too often are brought up to believe that their appearance is not solely their own business. How daughters look, for instance, is an open topic of conversation in many families, making them feel their bodies are fair game for public scrutiny. Sadly, given the common gap between their *actual selves* and *ideal selves,* many come away feeling exposed and shamed. The increased prevalence of eating disorders during the last half-century has coincided with this epidemic of body image dissatisfaction worldwide. Chinese teens express weight gain anxiety similar to that of their peers in the United States and Canada (Chen & Jackson, 2009). A longitudinal study in South Korea found that body image dissatisfaction began at age 10, increasing depression and suicidal ideation (Kim & Kim, 2009). Those most vulnerable to eating disorders are also those who have the greatest body image dissatisfaction and who idealize thinness (Striegel-Moore & Bulik, 2007).

Sociocultural Factors

Sociocultural factors may explain why anorexia and bulimia occur more often in women than in men and more often in weight-conscious Western cultures, and why the prevalence of eating disorders has increased in recent years. According to the sociocultural view, dieting and disordered eating are understandable responses to social roles and to cultural ideals of beauty (Seid, 1994). Binge eating, self-starvation, and thin standards of female beauty have characterized female cohorts who reached adolescence in periods when educational opportunities for women increased but have not characterized cohorts who reached adolescence when educational opportunities remained stable or decreased (Perlick & Silverstein, 1994).

Interestingly, the "thin is beautiful" standard is absent in many developing countries, where a full body means prosperity and thinness can signal poverty or illness (Swami, Kannan, & Furnham, 2011). In Niger, West Africa, for instance, fat is the beauty ideal for women, who often compete to be crowned the heaviest (Onishi, 2001). Among the Calabari of southeastern Nigeria, brides are sent to "fattening farms" before their weddings, where they gorge themselves on food and take steroid drugs to gain bulk and other pills to increase their appetites. At the end of their stay, they are paraded in the village square, where their fullness can be admired.

Anorexia Young girls, as well as an increasing number of boys, who have anorexia look at themselves in the mirror and see not the superthin person that we see, but someone who is overweight and still needs to shed more pounds. If this boy and girl continue to lose weight, their physiological systems will become overburdened with the job of trying to maintain a functioning system with minimal caloric intake. At the extreme, their hearts may stop pumping.

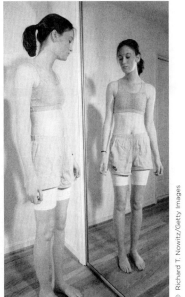

Diversity and Healthy Living

Acculturation and the Latest Nutrition Guidelines

Every five years, the U.S. government issues a new set of dietary guidelines based on the input of a panel of experts who review the latest nutrition studies over a two-year period. The guidelines are important, not only because people look to them for authoritative evidence on how to make healthy food choices, but also because federal law requires that school lunches and other government nutrition programs be based on them. In late 2015, the panel submitted its latest guidelines, which differ significantly from the older guidelines in a number of ways.

- **Cultural Sensitivity and Acculturation**
  The report recognizes the large body of evidence that immigrants, who represent a significant proportion of the U.S. population, "adopt the dietary habits and disease patterns of host cultures."
  A separate subcommittee focused on the equally well-documented finding that immigrants' health tends to go downhill as they shift from traditional diets to the less healthy "typical American diet." For instance, among immigrant adults of Latino/Hispanic national origin—particularly women and persons of Mexican origin—higher acculturation is associated with lower fruit and vegetable intake, and higher intake of fast food. The guidelines recommend increased resources and policy changes for immigrant outreach programs such as the Supplemental Nutrition Assistance

Program (SNAP) to encourage the purchase of healthier foods.

- **Personal Responsibility and Societal Responsibility**
  The panel followed an *ecological-systems approach* (see chapter 1) in establishing the newest dietary guidelines by stating that it isn't enough for individuals to try to eat better; success will come only if attention is paid to the entire environment and context that shapes our food choices. To this end, separate subcommittees focused on the changes that: (a) small groups (such as families) can make on their own; and (b) society can make to support better nutrition. Highlighting the importance of a systems approach, one expert asked, how can we expect people to make half their grains whole until half the grain choices at fast-food restaurants are whole?

- **Importance of Sustainability**
  Along with the dietary emphasis on plants, for the first time, the nutrition panel emphasized the importance of taking sustainability of food production into consideration when choosing what to eat. The panel raised the question, for instance, of whether it's sustainable to recommend 8 to 12 ounces of fish a week. This emphasis on sustainability also underscores the desirability of plant-based foods. The report states that "a diet higher in plant-based foods, such as vegetables....

In recent years, Western cultures have increasingly emphasized the positive attributes of slender bodies, especially for women. As Roberta Seid has noted, "Our culture has elevated the pursuit of a lean, fat-free body into a new religion. It has a creed: 'I eat right, watch my weight, and exercise.' Indeed, anorexia nervosa could be called the paradigm of our age, for our creed encourages us all to adopt the behavior and attitudes of the anorexic" (Seid, 1994, p. 4). Nowhere is this "religion" more apparent than in how women's bodies are represented in the media.

Body Image and the Media

The ideal female weight—represented by actresses, supermodels, and Miss Americas—has progressively decreased to that of the thinnest 5 to 10 percent of American women. Consequently, over three-fourths of normal-weight women think they weigh too much, and body image dissatisfaction is reported by 50 to 70 percent of adolescent girls (Wertheim & Paxton, 2011). When shown images of unnaturally thin models, women often report feeling depressed, ashamed, and dissatisfied with their own bodies—emotions and attitudes linked to increased risk of eating disorders (Grabe, Ward, & Hyde, 2008).

iStock/Getty Images

and lower in calories and animal-based foods is more health promoting and is associated with less environmental impact than is the current U.S. diet."

■ **An Emphasis on Dietary Patterns Rather than Nutrients**

Earlier dietary guidelines put a strong emphasis on nutrients, with recommendations such as "limit intake of saturated fat," and "get more calcium." The new guidelines move from an emphasis on nutrients, which people don't naturally think of as being what they eat, to actual foods. In addition, the new guidelines focus on the ways foods interact with each other based on a person's overall dietary pattern. Healthy dietary patterns such as the Mediterranean and DASH (dietary approach to stop hypertension) diets receive a great deal of attention in the 2015 guidelines.

■ **Special Interests**

The 2015 dietary guidelines quickly sparked criticism among a number of groups. The North American Meat Institute called the recommendations "flawed" and "nonsensical" in failing to recognize the role that nutrient-dense meats can play in a balanced diet. The American Beverage Association was also critical of the report, especially statements such as "sugars should be reduced in the diet and not replaced with low-calorie sweeteners, but rather with healthy options, such as water in place of sugar-sweetened beverages;" and "...some evidence links high caffeine intake in the form of energy drinks to certain adverse outcomes, such as caffeine toxicity and cardiovascular events."

Information from U.S. Department of Health and Human Services and U.S. Department of Agriculture. (2015). *2015–2020 Dietary guidelines for Americans* (8th ed.). Available at http://health.gov/dietaryguidelines/2015/guidelines/.

Society's current emphasis on thinness may be the clearest example of the power of advertising to influence cultural norms and individual behavior. Like clothing styles, body types go in and out of fashion and are promoted by advertising. Media images constantly reinforce the latest ideal, and the impact of the media in establishing role models is undeniable. With increasing Americanization and globalization, body image dissatisfaction is becoming more common among young women throughout the world, as well as among young men. Those who are most vulnerable to eating disorders are also those who idealize thinness and have the greatest body dissatisfaction (Kane, 2010; Stice, Rohde, & Shaw, 2013).

Treatment of Eating Disorders

A number of different therapies have been used to treat anorexia, bulimia, and binge-eating disorder. These include force-feeding, family therapy, interpersonal therapy, dialectical behavior therapy, hypnosis, and psychodynamic approaches (Wilson, Grilo, & Vitousek, 2007). Experts agree that treatment must address both the behavior and the attitudes that perpetuate disordered eating.

family therapy A type of psychotherapy in which individuals within a family learn healthier ways to interact with each other and resolve conflicts.

Restoring body weight is, of course, the first priority in treating anorexia. In extreme cases, inpatient treatment includes force-fed diets that gradually increase from about 1500 to 3500 calories per day. In many cases, a number of secondary biological and psychological disturbances are reduced once body weight is restored. **Family therapy** is the most heavily researched treatment for anorexia nervosa, and in general, the results of a dozen or more clinical trials have been encouraging (Wilson and others, 2007). The best known of these is a form of family therapy called the *Maudsley model,* an intervention applied to adolescent patients involving 10 to 20 family sessions spaced over 6 to 12 months. All family members are seen together, and initially, parents are coached to find effective ways to control their child's eating behavior. In the next phases, this external control gradually fades and—especially with older adolescents—autonomous eating behavior is explicitly linked to long-term resolution of the eating disorder. Because motivational issues surrounding body image and food behavior must be addressed, interventions often must be maintained for long periods of time—one to two years of individual therapy is not uncommon in treating those with very low body weight (Wilson and others, 2007).

Historically, many eating disorder interventions focused on providing information about the unhealthy effects of these conditions, with the hope that this would result in behavioral changes. However, *psychoeducational programs* of this type generally were not very successful (Stice, Shaw, & Marti, 2007). As you will see in subsequent chapters, interventions limited to education alone have also been largely unsuccessful in preventing other problems, including substance abuse, unprotected sex, and depression.

Since the 1970s, cognitive behavioral therapy has become the treatment of choice for bulimia nervosa and binge-eating disorder (Wilson and others, 2007). Treatment focuses on procedures designed to: (a) enhance motivation for change, (b) replace unhealthy dieting with regular and flexible patterns of eating, (c) reduce an unhealthy concern with body weight and shape, and (d) prevent relapse. First, therapists monitor food intake, binge-eating episodes, and stimulus triggers of those episodes. They then use this information to gradually mold the patient's eating into a pattern of three or more meals per day; introduce feared foods into the diet; and change faulty thinking and distorted attitudes about food intake, weight, and body image. Treatment typically includes 16 to 20 sessions of individual therapy over four to five months.

How Effective Are Treatments for Eating Disorders?

Anorexia remains one of the most difficult behavior disorders to treat because many victims see nothing wrong with their eating behavior and resist any attempt to change (Agras and others, 2004). Christopher Fairburn, a leading bulimia researcher, has suggested that the long-term success rate of all eating disorder interventions is a function of two participant variables: self-esteem and body image. Regardless of the type of treatment used, patients with lower self-esteem and persistent body-image distortions tend to be less successful in terms of their long-term recovery (Fairburn, 2005).

Although there are relatively few controlled studies comparing the results of treatments for anorexia, most therapies result in some weight restoration in the short term but a high relapse rate (often in excess of 50 percent) and poor long-term outcome. Longer-term follow-up studies show that the majority of people with anorexia persist in their preoccupation with food and weight and that many continue to show psychological signs of the disorder, have low weight, and exhibit social or mood disturbances. Overall, these follow-up studies indicate that nearly 50 percent of those being treated eventually make a full recovery, 20 to 30 percent continue to show some residual symptoms, 10 to 20 percent remain severely ill, and 5 to 10 percent eventually die (Steinhausen, 2002).

Controlled outcome research on the efficacy of various forms of psychotherapy in treating bulimia nervosa is not extensive. CBT has, however, proved to be fairly effective as a primary prevention for binge eating in high-risk women (Kaminski & McNamara,

The Thin Ideal Over the years, judges have selected increasingly thin women as Miss USA, showing the current Western idealization of the "slim" woman.

AP Photo/Isaac Brekken

1996). The researchers recruited college women with warning signs for eating disorders: low self-esteem, poor body image, perfectionism, and a history of repeated dieting. The students were randomly assigned to either a treatment group or a control group. The treatment group received training in cognitive strategies for increasing self-esteem, challenging self-defeating thinking, improving body image, and combating social pressures for thinness. After 7 weeks, students in the treatment group showed greater improvement in self-esteem and body image than did students in the control group. They also reported significantly fewer disordered eating episodes. Overall, CBT typically eliminates binge eating and purging in about 30 to 50 percent of cases (Wilson and others, 2007).

Controlled studies of treatments for disordered eating show dropout rates ranging from 0 to 34 percent and long-term abstinence from disordered eating ranging from 20 to 76 percent. As Stewart Agras and his colleagues (2004) have noted, out of a treatment group of 100 binge eaters treated with cognitive behavioral therapy (generally the most effective treatment), 16 will probably drop out of treatment, and 40 will be abstinent by the end of treatment. A failure rate of 60 percent suggests that researchers have not yet found the ideal treatment for eating disorders. Even so, a recent meta-analysis of randomized controlled trials found that cognitive behavioral interventions are effective in reducing binge eating (Vocks and others, 2010). Researchers have found that guided self-help (Banasiak, Paxton, & Hay, 2005), and even CBT-based self-help interventions delivered by computer, are effective with some bulimia nervosa and binge-eating patients, particularly if the programs are interactive and focused on girls over age 15 (Schmidt & Grover, 2007).

Cognitive dissonance-based (CD) interventions have emerged as effective eating disorder and body dissatisfaction prevention programs (Halliwell & Diedrichs, 2014). *Cognitive dissonance theory* states that when our behavior is inconsistent with our thoughts, the behavior creates psychological discomfort (dissonance) that motivates us to change either our cognitions or behaviors to restore consistency (Festinger, 1957). CD interventions use techniques such as role-playing, preparing and delivering speeches, and making a public commitment to reduce unhealthy behaviors. CD interventions have proven to be the most effective targeted programs to date for adolescents 14 years and older (Stice, Rohde, Durant, Shaw, & Wade, 2013; Stice and others, 2007).

The Body Project intervention targets the thin-ideal beauty standard. The reasoning is simple: If young women who endorse the "thin is beautiful" standard are given an opportunity to argue against it and the sociocultural forces behind it (e.g., the media, fashion industry, dieting industry), they may experience dissonance that would lead to a change in their attitudes toward this unrealistic ideal, thereby reducing body dissatisfaction and their risk for unhealthy weight control behaviors. A growing body of research supports the effectiveness of dissonance-based interventions for eating disorders. Stice and his colleagues (Stice, Rohde, & Shaw, 2013) also have found that undergraduate peer leaders can effectively deliver a dissonance-based eating disorder prevention program.

There is also good news in the finding that some victims of eating disorders may recover on their own with the passage of time. One longitudinal study followed a cohort of 509 women and 206 men who were teenagers in the late 1970s and early 1980s. The researchers surveyed the participants' eating attitudes and behaviors while in college, and again 10 years later (Heatherton, Mahamedi, Striepe, & Field, 1997). The results showed that body dissatisfaction, chronic dieting, and eating disorder symptoms generally diminished among many of the women in the 10 years following college, with rates of apparent eating disorder dropping by more than half. However, a substantial number of the women, particularly those who were dissatisfied with their body weight or shape in college, continued to have eating problems 10 years after college. More than 1 in 5 of the women who met clinical criteria for an eating disorder in college also did so 10 years later.

These results suggest that some degree of disordered eating may be normative for college women and that diminution of these problems after graduation is also normative.

However, body dissatisfaction and chronic dieting remain problems for a substantial number of women. Changes in maturation and gender role status may partly explain why eating problems diminish after college.

Along with greater awareness of disordered eating, today there is an increased emphasis on healthful eating and diets that are based on nutrient-dense, unprocessed foods rather than on diets that are just low in calories. Sociocultural messages about thinness have changed somewhat as well, again with greater emphasis on health and fitness and less on actual weight.

Health psychologists hope to continue this increased focus on overall good health rather than on attempting to achieve unattainably perfect physiques. This would help many of us avoid the dangers of obesity or eating disorders, as well as the anxiety and dissatisfaction caused by the disparity between our real and longed-for body images.

Weigh In on Health

Respond to each question below based on what you learned in the chapter. (**Tip**: Use the items in "Summing Up" to take into account related biological, psychological, and social concerns.)

1. People typically enjoy eating the kinds of foods they ate as children. Think about the foods you most enjoy eating, as well as your normal daily diet. How have these choices been influenced by your family's diet when you were a child? What changes would be beneficial for your health? Why?

2. In a conference about obesity in the United States—with participants ranging in age (from children to older adults) and experience (from those who struggle with obesity, to those with normal weight and low weight, to experts in the field)—you have been chosen as a college student representative to participate in a panel discussion about obesity hazards, factors, and treatments. What are five points that you want to present to the panel about obesity and college life?

3. Your friend Tony has become a gym rat—so much so that he hardly does anything else. He's constantly thinking about losing weight and building his muscles. You suspect he might have an eating disorder, as well as a problem with body image, and one day Tony confides in you that this is true. What would you advise him to do? Based on what you've read in this chapter, what are some biological, psychological, and social or cultural influences that could be affecting Tony?

Summing Up

Nutrition: Eating the Right Foods

1. Overall, about 65 percent of U.S. adults are overweight and 34 percent are obese, with rates varying with gender, race/ethnicity, income, and education. By 2020, three of four Americans will be overweight or obese.

2. Besides water and daily caloric energy, the body requires 46 nutrients, which are grouped into five categories: proteins, fats, carbohydrates, vitamins, and minerals. "MyPlate" serves as a quick visual reminder to make healthy choices when choosing your next meal. It depicts a place setting divided into five food groups of approximately 30 percent vegetables, 30 percent grains, 20 percent fruits, and 20 percent protein.

3. Fast-food consumption remains a central part of the diet of many people, with an estimated 11.3 percent of total daily calories coming from fast food among U.S. adults. Unit bias is an example of mindless eating, in which we allow situations to control our eating. Other examples include the tendency to eat more when eating with other people, to eat more when offered a variety of foods, and mistakenly believing that our stomachs will tell us when they are full so that we will stop before overeating.

4. Poor nutrition has been implicated in 5 of the 10 leading causes of death: heart disease, cancer, stroke, diabetes, and atherosclerosis. There are three types of lipoproteins: Low-density lipoprotein (LDL) has been linked to heart disease, whereas high-density lipoprotein (HDL) may protect against atherosclerotic plaques. Dietary saturated fat and especially trans fat raise LDL cholesterol levels in the blood. Saturated fat has been implicated as a dietary factor in some forms of cancer. Nutritionists recommend a healthful balance of unprocessed foods, especially those with a low glycemic index (GI).

5. Between 2000 and 2010, the percentage of American adults aged 45 and older with multiple chronic conditions (MCC) increased for men and women, all racial and ethnic groups, and most income groups. The most prevalent combinations of chronic conditions are hypertension and diabetes, hypertension and heart disease, and hypertension and cancer.

Weight Determination: Eating the Right Amount of Food

6. Basal metabolic rate (BMR) depends on a number of variables, including your age, gender, current weight, and activity level. Many people believe that their body weights fluctuate erratically, but in fact their bodies actually balance energy intake and expenditure quite closely. This supports the concept of a body weight set point. Once the number of fat cells in a person's body increases, it never decreases.

7. Researchers have located appetite centers in two areas of the hypothalamus: a side region called the lateral hypothalamus (LH), which may trigger hunger, and a lower area in the middle called the ventromedial hypothalamus (VMH), which may trigger satiety. One region of the hypothalamus, the arcuate nucleus, appears to be the master center for short-term regulation of appetite and long-term regulation of body weight.

8. Two hormones produced by the digestive tract, known as ghrelin and peptide Y (PYY), have been linked to short-term feeding behaviors, whereas leptin (and to a lesser extent, insulin) are key to weight maintenance over months and years.

Obesity: Some Basic Facts

9. Obesity is a risk factor for many diseases. In addition, the obese also have social problems because they are the objects of discrimination. The most frequently used measure of obesity today is the body mass index (BMI), which is strongly correlated with percentage of body fat. Distribution of fat is also important, with abdominal (male pattern) fat being less healthy than lower-body (female pattern) fat. Furthermore, weight cycling may be more hazardous to health than a somewhat high but stable weight.

10. The prevalence of *metabolic syndrome* (the set of obesity-related factors that increase the risk for coronary artery disease, stroke, inflammation, and diabetes) increases with BMI. Overweight men are six times as likely and obese men are 32 times as likely as normal-weight men to meet the criteria for MetS. Overweight women are five times as likely and obese women are 17 times as likely to meet the criteria.

The Biopsychosocial Model of Obesity

11. Obesity is partly hereditary. Researchers have discovered that laboratory mice with a defective gene cannot control their hunger and tend to become obese. The gene appears to regulate the production of leptin, a hormone produced by fat, which the hypothalamus monitors as an index of obesity.

The amount of leptin is generally correlated with how much fat is stored in the body. Another study found that a variant of the FTO gene seems to double the risk of becoming obese.

12. Hunger and eating behavior are not controlled by physiological factors alone. Psychosocial factors, such as stress, socioeconomic status, and culture, also come into play.

13. Being overweight or obese is inversely related to income, education, and occupational level. Those who are at increased risk for obesity often have more limited access to health care services, less knowledge about the importance of a healthy diet and the hazards of obesity, lower perceived self-efficacy in being able to eat a healthy diet, and less commitment to exercise.

Treatment and Prevention of Obesity

14. At all ages, women are twice as likely as men to be dieting, even though there is only a small gender difference in the prevalence of obesity. Dieting is increasingly prevalent among adolescents, which is cause for concern because of the potential hazards to growth and development.

15. The most successful ways to help kids lose weight are lifestyle interventions that combine diet, physical activity, and behavioral control *and* that target both parents and children simultaneously.

16. Today, health psychologists recognize that patients differ in which treatment will be most effective for them. The stepped-care process can be used for determining which intervention is most appropriate for a given person.

17. Many of us live, work, and attend school in an obesigenic (obesity-promoting) environment. Unhealthy foods are everywhere, and our bodies are genetically programmed to eat when food is available. Consequently, experts are calling for broader community strategies and public health measures in the war on obesity.

Eating Disorders

18. Eating disorders are multifactorial—determined by the interaction of biological, psychological, social, and cultural factors. The changes in fat distribution in adolescent girls, particularly those who mature early, may provide the foundations for body image dissatisfaction. A social and family environment in which there is an emphasis on slimness may foster additional frustration with body weight. At the individual level, competitiveness and perfectionism, combined with the stresses of adolescent peer pressure, may promote disordered eating.

19. Anorexia nervosa is an eating disorder characterized by refusal to maintain body weight above a BMI of 18, intense fear of weight gain, and disturbance of body image. Bulimia nervosa involves compulsive bingeing followed by purging through self-induced vomiting or large doses of laxatives. Women with low self-esteem are particularly likely to have a negative body image and to be vulnerable to

eating disorders. The families of people with bulimia have a higher-than-usual incidence of alcoholism, obesity, and depression. People with anorexia often come from families that are competitive, overachieving, and protective.

20. The most prevalent eating disorder in many parts of the world is binge eating disorder, in which sufferers do not purge but feel out of control and distressed about their binge eating episodes.

21. Eating disorders may be partly genetic and linked to abnormal levels of certain neurotransmitters.

22. Cultural factors may explain why anorexia and bulimia occur more often in women than in men and more often in weight-conscious Western cultures, and why the prevalence of eating disorders has increased in recent years. Although eating disorders are more common among women—especially in occupations that emphasize appearance (such as dance)—these disorders also occur in men—especially male athletes in sports such as swimming.

23. A range of therapies has been used to treat anorexia and bulimia, from psychoeducational campaigns to force-feeding to family therapy. Experts agree that treatment must address both the behavior and the attitudes that perpetuate disordered eating. The most widely used therapy for anorexia and bulimia, cognitive behavioral therapy, attacks faulty thinking about food intake, weight, and body image. A growing body of research supports the effectiveness of cognitive dissonance-based interventions.

Key Terms and Concepts to Remember

overweight, p. 207
obesity, p. 207
multiple chronic conditions
  (MCC), p. 213
set-point hypothesis, p. 215
leptin, p. 216

adipocytes, p. 216
body mass index (BMI), p. 218
abdominal obesity, p. 219
weight cycling, p. 221
poverty income ratio (PIR), p. 224
food deserts, p. 226

competitive foods, p. 231
anorexia nervosa, p. 232
bulimia nervosa, p. 232
binge-eating disorder (BED), p. 233
family therapy, p. 238

LaunchPad
macmillan learning

To accompany your textbook, you have access to a number of online resources, including quizzes for every chapter of the book, flashcards, critical thinking exercises, videos, and *Check Your Health* inventories. To access these resources, please visit the Straub *Health Psychology* LaunchPad solo at: **launchpadworks.com**

CHAPTER 9

Substance Use, Abuse, and Addiction

Ryan, who is 24 years old, plays football for a hard-drinking local pub team. One evening, teammates brought him to the emergency room pale, sweating, in obvious pain, and near collapse. "It's my chest," he said to the resident on call and went on to explain that he'd been vomiting profusely for three days. Asked what might have brought this on, a sheepish-looking Ryan explained that his team had made it to the league final the previous weekend and he'd had "a fair bit to drink." Pressed for specifics, he admitted to drinking more than 20 cans of strong lager beer in the course of one evening of celebration.

Upon examination, Ryan had a fever; a rapid pulse of 120 beats per minute, raised white blood cell count, and was dehydrated with abnormal electrolyte levels. A chest X-ray and CT scan showed the presence of free air along the left border of Ryan's heart, apparently caused by a traumatic rupture of his esophagus. Spontaneous rupture of the esophagus is very rare, but it is life threatening and has a survival rate that quickly drops to as low as 11 percent if diagnosis and intervention are delayed by as little as 48 hours. Ryan had been vomiting profusely for three days.

Ryan's perforated esophageal wall was diagnosed as Boerhaave syndrome, the result of forceful vomiting and a sudden increase in pressure within the 12-inch passageway between his stomach and throat. His greatest danger was from extensive sepsis, which occurs when chemicals released into the bloodstream to fight an infection trigger inflammation that spreads throughout the body, potentially causing multiple organs to fail. Fortunately, after surgery and 10 days of hospitalization with broad spectrum antibiotic treatment, Ryan was healthy enough to return home. One month later, he was able to resume playing football, this time swearing that he would never again risk the near-fatal effects that can occur by binge drinking.

Since antiquity, human beings have sought ways to alter their moods, thought processes, and behaviors—often with significantly negative health effects. This chapter examines the different facets of substance abuse—its causes, effects, and prevention, including research pointing to a biopsychosocial common ground in the origins of addiction to many habit-forming substances. We will focus primarily on the two most commonly abused drugs: tobacco and alcohol.

Some Basic Facts

drug abuse The use of a drug to the extent that it impairs the user's biological, psychological, or social well-being.

Drug abuse is the use of a chemical substance to the extent that it impairs the user's well-being in any domain of health: biological, psychological, or social. Tobacco and alcohol, two of the most widely used drugs, both pose significant health dangers. Although tobacco use is decreasing in affluent countries, its use is climbing in low- and middle-income countries. Alcohol is the third-largest risk factor for disease in the world (after lack of food for children and unsafe sex), largely due to injuries, with some 2.5 million deaths each year, including 320,000 among young adults, from alcohol-related causes (WHO, 2010a). Although alcohol consumption has recently declined in many developed countries, its use also has been increasing in developing countries. Moreover, alcohol problems are occurring now in many Asian and Western Pacific countries where they did not previously exist.

The abuse of illegal drugs, alcohol, and tobacco causes more deaths, illnesses, and disabilities than any other preventable health condition (United Nations Office on Drugs and Crime [UNODC], 2015). Alcohol, for instance, is implicated in 40 percent of all traffic deaths. Half of all murders in the United States involve alcohol or some other drug, and 80 percent of all suicide attempts follow the use of alcohol. And each year, tobacco use causes nearly 6 million deaths globally (an estimated 8 million by the year 2030) and results in a net loss of over $300 billion in the United States alone due to medical expenses and lost work time (WHO, 2015i).

Although the use of most drugs has decreased in the United States over the past 30 years, the use of marijuana has recently undergone a resurgence, which I will discuss at the end of this chapter. Further, abuse of synthetic narcotics (so-called *designer drugs*) has also increased. Among the most popular designer drugs are hallucinogens such as NBOMes (pronounced en-bombs), stimulants such as bath salts, and spice—a synthetic drug that mimics the effects of marijuana. When a designer drug first appears for sale—often in convenience stores, gas stations, or online—it is technically not illegal, because its chemical makeup is slightly different from the illicit drug it is modeled after.

The abuse of prescribed medications is also on the rise. Over 2 million people in the United States suffer from substance use disorders related to prescription pain relievers (National Institute on Drug Abuse, 2015). Each year, more than 1 million adults are treated in hospital emergency rooms for overdoses due to "nonmedical" use of over-the-counter or prescription drugs (Raloff, 2010). Figure 9.1 shows the 11 most abused prescription drugs.

Why, despite these enormous financial, health, and social costs, do people continue to abuse drugs? To answer this question, you first need to know how drugs move through and affect the body.

Mechanisms of Drug Action

Drugs are ingested, or administered, in one of five ways: orally, rectally, by injection, by inhalation, or by absorption through the skin or the mucous membranes. The manner in which a drug is administered can alter its physiological effects. For example, because they

FIGURE 9.1

The Most Abused Prescription Drugs In 2010, 7 million Americans reported using a prescription drug for nonmedical reasons in the past month, most commonly a pain reliever, sedative, or stimulant. Symptoms of pain reliever abuse include constricted pupils, nausea and vomiting, and respiratory depressions; symptoms of stimulant abuse include anxiety, delusions, and chest pain with heart palpitations; and symptoms of depressant abuse include slurred speech, dizziness, and respiratory depression.

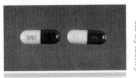

Amphetamine (bennies, black beauties, crosses): Stimulant used to treat ADHD and narcolepsy that mimics effects of adrenaline on body.
Side effects: Irregular heartbeat, panic, heart failure

Methyphenidate (JIF, PMP, R-ball, skippy): Most commonly prescribed central nervous system stimulant used to treat ADHD.
Side effects: Feelings of hostility and paranoia, increased blood pressure, stroke

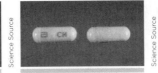

Barbiturates (barbs, block busters): Central nervous system depressants that cause drowsiness and sleepiness.
Side effects: Paranoia, suicidal thoughts, impaired judgment and coordination

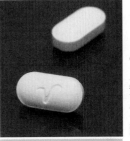

Hydrocodone bitartrate (vike, Watson-387, hydro): Prescription pain reliever often combined with acetaminophen or aspirin to relieve moderate to severe pain.
Side effects: Respiratory arrest, coma, death

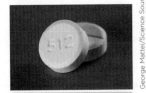

Oxycodone HCL (oxy, O.C., orange crush, Oscar): Prescription pain reliever used to relieve moderate to severe pain.
Side effects: Severe respiratory depression, death

Flunitrazepam (R-2, Mexican Valium, rophies): Drug used to treat insomnia and often given prior to anesthesia. Often called the "date rape drug."
Side effects: Impaired motor coordination, thinking, memory, and judgment

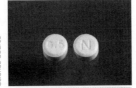

Benzodiazepines (sticks, benZ, footballs, bars): Most commonly prescribed antidepressant drugs used to treat anxiety and tension.
Side effects: Drowsiness, loss of coordination, impaired thinking and memory

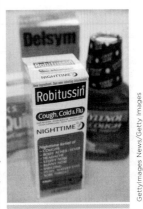

Destromethorphan: Addictive ingredient found in any cold medicines with "DM" or "TUSS" in its name, making it easy and cheap to abuse.
Side effects: Loss of coordination, high blood pressure, seizures, coma, death

Morphine (M, Miss Emma, monkey, white stuff): Highly addictive painkiller used to relieve moderate to severe pain.
Side effects: Sedation, respiratory arrest, coma

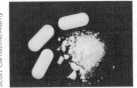

Fentanyl (Apache, China girl, patches, dance fever): Powerful painkiller often used to treat severe pain or post-surgical pain.
Side effects: Confusion, shallow breathing, coma

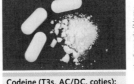

Codeine (T3s, AC/DC, coties): Prescription drug used to relieve moderate pain and suppress coughing.
Side effects: Irregular heartbeat, seizures, difficulty breathing

enter the bloodstream faster, drugs that are injected or inhaled usually have stronger and more immediate effects than those that are swallowed.

Within minutes after a drug is absorbed, it is distributed by the bloodstream to its site of action (receptors). How quickly a drug reaches its target receptors depends on the rate of blood flow and how easily the drug passes through cell membranes and other protective barriers. Blood flow to the brain is greater than to any other part of the body. Therefore, drugs that are able to pass through the network of cells that separates the blood and

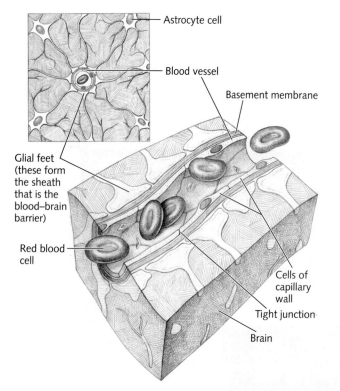

- Astrocyte cell
- Blood vessel
- Basement membrane
- Glial feet (these form the sheath that is the blood–brain barrier)
- Red blood cell
- Cells of capillary wall
- Tight junction
- Brain

FIGURE 9.2

The Blood–Brain Barrier Unlike the porous blood capillaries in most other parts of the body, those in the brain are tightly packed, forming a fatty glial sheath that provides a protective environment for the brain. The glial sheath develops from the nearby astrocyte cells. To reach the brain, a drug first must be absorbed through the capillary wall and then through the fatty sheath.

blood–brain barrier The network of tightly packed capillary cells that separates the blood and the brain.

teratogens Drugs, chemicals, and environmental agents that can damage the developing person during fetal development.

agonist A drug that attaches to a receptor and produces neural actions that mimic or enhance those of a naturally occurring neurotransmitter.

antagonist A drug that blocks the action of a naturally occurring neurotransmitter or agonist.

the brain—the **blood–brain barrier** (Figure 9.2)—move quickly into the central nervous system. The ease with which a drug passes through this barrier depends on its lipid (fat) solubility.

Fat-soluble drugs that cross the blood–brain barrier are usually also able to permeate the *placental barrier,* which separates the blood of a pregnant woman from that of her developing child. For this reason, alcohol, nicotine, or other drugs, as well as chemicals in cosmetics, foods, and the environment absorbed by the mother, can affect her unborn child. Scientists now understand a great deal about **teratogens**—drugs, pollutants, and other substances that cross the placental barrier and damage the developing person. The extent of damaging effects, however, depends on when exposure occurs; the greatest damage occurs during critical periods of development when specific organs and systems are developing most rapidly.

Drugs and Synapses

Once in the brain, drugs affect behavior by influencing the activity of neurons at their synapses. Drugs can achieve their effects in one of three ways: by mimicking or enhancing the action of a naturally occurring neurotransmitter, by blocking its action, or by affecting its reuptake (see Figure 9.3a).

Drugs that produce neural actions that mimic or enhance those of a naturally occurring neurotransmitter are **agonists** (see Figure 9.3b). Recall that synaptic receptors are cellular locks that wait for neurotransmitters with a particular shape to act like a key and trigger activity within the cell. *Partial agonists* are neurotransmitters that bind and activate receptors but elicit a smaller response than true or full agonists (see Figure 9.3c).

Drugs that produce their effects by blocking the action of neurotransmitters or agonist drugs are **antagonists** (see Figure 9.3d). Caffeine, for example, is an antagonist that blocks the effects of *adenosine,* a neurotransmitter that normally inhibits the release of other transmitters that excite (cause to fire) postsynaptic cells. Thus, the excitatory cells continue firing, resulting in the stimulation felt when caffeine is ingested.

Finally, drugs can alter neural transmission by enhancing or inhibiting the reuptake of neurotransmitters in the synapse (that is, the natural breakdown or reabsorption of the neurotransmitter by the presynaptic neuron). One neurotransmitter that plays a major role in addiction is dopamine. As a chemical messenger, dopamine is similar to adrenaline and affects neural processes that control movement, emotions, and the experiences of pleasure and pain. Cocaine, for example, produces its stimulating effect by binding to proteins that normally transport dopamine, thus blocking its reuptake. Because dopamine is not reabsorbed by the sending neuron, it remains in the synapse and continues to excite the receiving neuron. As more dopamine remains to stimulate neurons, the result may be prolonged feelings of pleasure and excitement. Similarly, amphetamine increases dopamine levels and causes overstimulation of the pleasure-pathway nerves in the brain.

Addiction, Dependence, and Tolerance

The American Psychiatric Association's *Diagnostic and Statistical Manual of Mental Disorders* (DSM-5) defines **substance use disorder** as a behavior pattern characterized by impaired control, social impairment, and risky use of a drug.

Dependence is a state in which the body and mind have adjusted to the repeated use of a drug and require its presence in order to maintain "normal" functioning. In this context, *normal* refers to the absence of the withdrawal symptoms that will appear when use of a

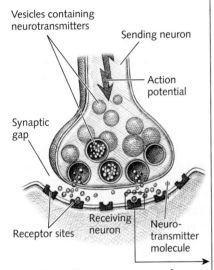

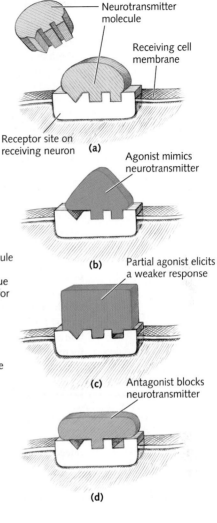

(a) This neurotransmitter molecule has a molecular structure that precisely fits the receptor site on the receiving neuron, much as a key fits a lock.

(b) This agonist molecule excites. It is similar enough in structure to the neurotransmitter molecule that it mimics its effects on the receiving neuron. Morphine, for instance, mimics the action of endorphins by stimulating receptors in brain areas involved in mood and pain sensations.

(c) This partial antagonist molecule also excites, but it elicits a weaker response than does a true or full agonist. Buprenorphine, for instance, is a partial agonist of the receptor activated by morphine. For this reason, the drug is used clinically as an analgesic in pain management and as a treatment for morphine addiction.

(d) This antagonist molecule inhibits. It has a structure similar enough to the neurotransmitter to occupy its receptor site and block its action, but not similar enough to stimulate the receptor. Botulin poisoning paralyzes its victims by blocking acetylcholine (ACh) receptors involved in muscle movement.

Neurotransmitters carry a message from a sending neuron across a synapse to receptor sites on a receiving neuron.

FIGURE 9.3
Agonists, Partial Agonists, and Antagonists

drug is discontinued. Drug **withdrawal** refers to the unpleasant physical and psychological symptoms that occur when a person abruptly ceases using a drug. The symptoms of withdrawal are generally the direct opposite of a drug's primary effects. Amphetamines, for example, create a rush of euphoria, while withdrawal triggers the opposing state of depression, along with vomiting, sleep disturbances, anxiety, and even death.

Consistent with the biopsychosocial model, most drugs give rise to both physical and psychological dependence. For example, alcohol, which produces biochemical changes in the brain (see page 256), also seems to improve mood and allow a person to forget his or her problems. For many former stimulant drug users, memories of the "highs" once experienced fade slowly and are constant triggers for relapse. For people who are dependent, obtaining and using a drug can become the day's focus (see Table 9.1).

The complementary effects of drug use and drug abstinence have led to a general theory—the *hypersensitivity theory*—which proposes that addiction is the result of efforts by the body and brain to counteract the effects of a drug to maintain an optimal internal state. For example, nicotine accelerates heart rate. To compensate, the brain and nervous system respond by stimulating the vagus nerve, which slows the heart rate. Over time,

substance use disorder A pattern of behavior characterized by impaired control, social impairment, and risky use of a drug.

dependence A state in which the use of a drug is required for a person to function normally.

withdrawal The unpleasant physical and psychological symptoms that occur when a person abruptly ceases using certain drugs.

TABLE 9.1

Substance Dependence

According to the *Diagnostic and Statistical Manual of Mental Disorders,* the presence of three or more of the following indicates *dependence* on a substance:

■ Tolerance (with repeated use, a drug must be taken in higher doses to achieve the desired effect)
■ Withdrawal (discomfort and distress when discontinued)
■ Taking the substance longer or in greater amounts than intended
■ Failure to regulate use
■ Much time devoted to obtaining the substance
■ Normal activities abandoned or reduced
■ Continued use despite knowledge that using the substance worsens problems

regular use of nicotine and the associated vagus nerve stimulation seem to create a new, higher "set point" for vagus nerve activity. If the person quits smoking, vagal activity remains high because there is no nicotine in the system to increase the heart rate.

One sign of dependence is the development of *tolerance,* a state of progressively decreasing behavioral and/or physiological responsiveness to a frequently used drug. The drug user's brain chemistry adapts to offset the drug's effect (a process called *neuroadaptation*), and increased dosages are necessary to produce the effect formerly achieved by a smaller dose. With repeated use, some drugs are metabolized at a faster rate by the liver so that more of the drug must be administered simply to maintain a constant level in the body. Also, brain receptors adapt to the continued presence of a particular drug either by increasing the number of receptor sites or by reducing their sensitivity to the drug.

Psychoactive Drugs

psychoactive drugs Drugs that affect mood, behavior, and thought processes by altering the functioning of neurons in the brain; they include stimulants, depressants, and hallucinogens.

Chemical substances that act on the brain to alter mood, behavior, and thought processes are known as **psychoactive drugs.** Psychoactive drugs are grouped into three major categories: hallucinogens, stimulants, and depressants.

Also called *psychedelic drugs, hallucinogens* such as marijuana and LSD alter sensory perception, induce visual and auditory hallucinations as they separate the user from reality, and disrupt thought processes.

Stimulants, including nicotine, caffeine, cocaine, and amphetamines, make people feel more alert and energetic by boosting activity in the central nervous system. At low doses, the moderate stimulants (nicotine and caffeine) reduce fatigue, elevate mood, and decrease appetite. However, in higher doses of the moderate drugs and with the more extreme drugs in any dosage, stimulants may cause irritability, insomnia, and anxiety. Like all psychoactive drugs, stimulants produce their effects by altering the action of neurotransmitters at synapses. They have a dramatic impact on acetylcholine, the catecholamines, dopamine, and, to a lesser extent, norepinephrine. Because of their powerful reward effects, stimulants are widely abused. Dependence and tolerance develop rapidly, forcing the addict to take progressively higher doses. Withdrawal symptoms associated with amphetamines include increased appetite, weight gain, fatigue, sleepiness, and, in some people, symptoms of paranoia.

Depressants (barbiturates, opiates, alcohol, general anesthetics, and antiepileptic drugs) dampen activity in the central nervous system. Low doses reduce responsiveness to sensory stimulation, slow thought processes, and lower physical activity. Higher doses result in drowsiness, lethargy, and amnesia and also can lead to death.

Barbiturates are used to block pain during surgery and to regulate high blood pressure. They are also popular street drugs because they produce a long-lasting sense of euphoria. They are highly addictive and considered particularly dangerous because, when taken in combination with another drug, they increase the effects of that drug, a reaction known as

drug potentiation. In combination with alcohol, for example, a barbiturate may suppress the brain's respiratory centers and cause death.

Another group of depressants, the *opiates* (morphine, heroin, and codeine), derive from the opium poppy. Globally, it is estimated that 16.5 million adults used nonprescribed opiates at least once in 2014, including 12 to 14 million heroin users (UNODC, 2015). Opiates produce their effects by mimicking the body's natural opiates, the *endorphins,* which help regulate our normal experience of pain and pleasure. When the brain is flooded with artificial opiates such as heroin, molecules of these synthetic drugs bind to the receptor sites for the endorphins, and the brain stops producing its own naturally occurring opiates. If the drug is discontinued, withdrawal symptoms soon occur, including rapid breathing, elevated blood pressure, severe muscle cramps, nausea and vomiting, panic, and intense cravings for the drug.

drug potentiation The effect of one drug to increase the effects of another.

Models of Addiction

Theories about how people become addicted to drugs can be grouped into three general categories: biomedical models, reward models, and social learning models.

Biomedical Models: Addiction as Disease

Biomedical models of addiction view physical dependence as a chronic brain disease caused by the biological effects of psychoactive drugs. The simplest model maintains that addicts inherit a biological vulnerability to physical dependence. Researchers point to evidence from studies that compare the **concordance rate,** or rate of agreement, of physical dependence among identical and fraternal twins. However, even though these studies suggest that genes play a role in physical dependence, researchers are cautious in interpreting the results because it is impossible to rule out completely possible confounding effects due to other variables. Moreover, twin studies do not pinpoint the specific gene or genes that might promote physical dependence.

concordance rate The rate of agreement between a pair of twins for a given trait; a pair of twins is concordant for the trait if both of them have it or if neither has it.

Another biomedical model points to altered neurochemistry as the basis for both physical and psychological dependence. According to the *withdrawal-relief hypothesis,* drug use serves to restore abnormally low levels of dopamine, serotonin, and other key neurotransmitters (Robinson & Berridge, 2003). Depression, anxiety, low self-esteem, and other unpleasant emotional states are indeed associated with neurotransmitter deficiencies and with substance use (Kim, Lim, & Kim, 2003). By elevating the release of presynaptic dopamine, drugs such as cocaine and the amphetamines restore neural functioning and produce a sense of psychological well-being.

For most of the twentieth century, the withdrawal-relief model was based primarily on evidence that opiates trigger dependence by suppressing the brain's natural production of endorphins. As the first receptor-based theory of addiction, the opiate model was adopted quickly as the basic biomedical model for addiction to all drugs that induce physical dependence. Nicotine acts on acetylcholine receptors, amphetamine and cocaine act on catecholamine receptors, and barbiturates presumably act on receptors for gamma-aminobutyric acid. In each case, addiction might involve the same sequence of receptor adaptation to an artificial source. One glaring exception to the opiate receptor theory as a general model, however, is alcohol, which does not appear to act on specific receptors.

The withdrawal-relief model was appealing because the idea that addicts need more of their drug to relieve physical distress made their intense determination to obtain drugs seem understandable—a rational response to their withdrawal sickness. However, the model does not explain why addicts begin taking a drug in sufficient dosages and with enough frequency to develop physical dependence in the first place. A second problem with this model is its inability to explain why many users suffer a relapse, even long after withdrawal symptoms have subsided.

Reward Models: Addiction as Pleasure Seeking

Researchers trying to explain the initial motivation for repeated use have focused on the pleasurable effects of psychoactive drugs. Recall from Chapter 3 that some experts believe that certain addictions may stem from a genetic *reward deficiency syndrome* in which the brain's reward circuitry malfunctions and leads to powerful cravings.

The Brain's Reward System

gateway drug A drug that serves as a stepping-stone to the use of other, usually more dangerous, drugs.

All major drugs of abuse overstimulate the brain's reward system, which also becomes active when a person engages in pleasurable behaviors that promote survival, such as eating or having sex. Given the choice between psychoactive drugs that put this reward circuit into overdrive—repeatedly activating the neurons until the drug leaves the body—and other, more mundane pleasures, physically dependent animals and human addicts often will choose the former. Rats that were allowed to press a lever to stimulate their reward systems electrically were observed to do so up to 7000 times per hour (Figure 9.4).

According to the reward models, addiction may best be understood as being motivated by pleasure seeking. Psychoactive drugs may induce physical dependence because they increase the availability of dopamine in the brain, overstimulating the reward system (Thompson, 2000). Evidence for the reward system link comes from the fact that people who develop dependence for one drug are more likely to be addicted to others as well. Use of tobacco, alcohol, and marijuana often plays a pivotal role in the development of other drug dependencies and high-risk behaviors. So these drugs are often referred to as **gateway drugs** because they "open the door" to experimentation with other drugs.

Shortcomings of the Reward Model

FIGURE 9.4

Intracranial Self-Stimulation Whenever the small lamp on the panel is lit, pressing the lever causes an electrical stimulus to be delivered to the reward system of the rat's brain. Using this experimental arrangement, researchers have found that rats press the lever at rates faster than one response per second.

Despite its seeming logic, the reward model does not provide the final answer to the question of what causes addiction. It is true that cocaine, heroin, and other highly addictive drugs evoke the most powerful euphoria, but marijuana and other psychoactive drugs that are not considered physically addictive also produce feelings of well-being. In contrast, tobacco, which is highly addictive and as difficult to abstain from as cocaine or heroin, induces a very mild euphoria that is hardly on the same scale as that elicited by cocaine.

Another shortcoming of the reward model concerns the *gateway hypothesis.* Tobacco and alcohol use, for instance, have historically been considered powerful predictors of marijuana use. However, some newer research indicates that environmental factors may have a stronger influence on subsequent illicit drug use. A 12-year University of Pittsburgh study looked at a group of boys beginning at age 10, 214 of whom eventually used legal or illegal drugs. At 22 years of age, these 214 participants were categorized into three groups: those who had used only tobacco or alcohol, those who first used alcohol or tobacco and later used marijuana (gateway drug use), and those who used marijuana before using alcohol or tobacco. Nearly 25 percent of the participants reported using marijuana first. Three environmental factors differentiated these reverse pattern marijuana users: They were more likely to have lived in economically deprived neighborhood environments, had more exposure to drugs in these neighborhoods, and had less parental

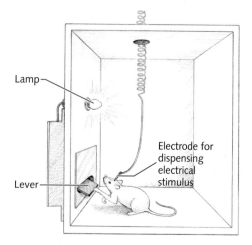

Lamp

Electrode for dispensing electrical stimulus

Lever

involvement when they were young children (Tarter, Vanyukov, Kirisci, Reynolds, & Clark, 2006). These data support what's known as **common liability to addiction,** which states that the likelihood a person will begin using illegal drugs is determined not by the preceding use of other specific legal drugs (gateway hypothesis), but instead by the particular tendencies and environmental circumstances of the drug user (Vanyukov, Tarter, & Ridenour, 2012).

In addition, reward models by themselves are unable to explain why drug use continues even when unpleasant side effects occur. Why don't alcohol abusers abstain, given the nausea and vomiting that they often experience? Terry Robinson and Kent Berridge's (2000) two-stage theory, known as the **wanting-and-liking theory** (also called the *incentive-sensitization theory*), provides a rationale for this. In the first stage, the original good feelings from drug use prevail; in the second stage, drug use becomes an automated behavior. Even though pleasure may not increase (and side effects may even be unpleasant), the reward systems continue to respond to the drug-related cues because they have become conditioned stimuli that evoke dopamine release and craving (Everitt & Heberlein, 2013).

Social Learning Models: Addiction as Behavior

Although psychoactive drugs trigger neurochemical changes and research points to hereditary risk factors in dependence, there is good reason to view addiction as a behavior that is shaped by learning as well as by social-cultural and cognitive factors. For instance, exposure to pro-smoking media, such as point-of-sale displays, magazine advertising, and portrayals of smoking in movies, increases smoking in adolescence (Shadel, Martino, Setodji, & Scharf, 2012). As another example, smokers "learn" to smoke in a variety of situations, such as socializing with friends or after eating a meal. Through conditioning, the pleasurable physiological effects of nicotine, together with other rewarding aspects of social situations, transform these situations into powerful triggers for smoking.

A person's identification with a particular drug also plays a role in both the initiation and the maintenance of addiction. Adolescence is a time of pronounced self-concept development, and self-concept regulation strongly influences health behaviors (Shepperd, Rothman, & Klein, 2011). Adolescents are preoccupied with their public images and the social implications of their behaviors. Drinking and smoking, for example, may lead to the adoption of a certain lifestyle that makes abstinence a monumental task involving a new sense of self. Similarly, research studies have shown that the more adolescents feel that smoking is a defining aspect of who they are, the more likely they are to smoke (Hertel & Mermelstein, 2012). Conversely, adolescents who are encouraged to think about the positive social consequences of abstaining from alcohol use subsequently have lower levels of willingness to drink when opportunities arise (Moeller and others, 2002).

As another example of social influence on drug use, people—especially young people— may be protected by family, school, religion, and other social institutions. According to the *social control theory,* the stronger a young person's attachment to such institutions, the less likely he or she will be to begin using drugs. The University of Michigan's Monitoring the Future Study is an annual survey—ongoing since 1975—of 50,000 eighth-, tenth-, and twelfth-grade students. The data from this study show that adolescents who do well in school are much more likely never to have used alcohol, tobacco, marijuana, or other drugs later in their lives than students who do poorly (MTF, 2015).

The closely related *peer cluster theory* maintains that peer groups are strong enough to overcome the controlling influence of family, school, or religious values. Adolescents tend to change their smoking behavior to that of their friends, and the tendency to select friends based on similar smoking behavior is a strong predictor of smoking behavior (Mercken, Steglich, Sinclair, Holliday, & Moore, 2012). This may be partly because some group settings, such as college campuses, induce false beliefs about social norms

common liability to addiction A model of addiction proposing that the likelihood a person will begin using illegal drugs is determined not by the preceding use of other specific legal drugs (gateway hypothesis), but instead by the particular tendencies and environmental circumstances of the drug user.

wanting-and-liking theory A two-stage theory of drug addiction. In the first stage, the original good feelings from drug use prevail; in the second stage, drug use becomes an automated behavior.

regarding drug use. Research studies have found that when students' illusions about peer drinking are corrected, alcohol use often subsides (Moreira, Smith, & Foxcroft, 2009).

Why Adolescence?

As we have seen, there seems to be a window of vulnerability in adolescence for risky behavior. Both the prevalence and incidence of drug use increase every year from age 10 to 25 and then decrease. One exception to this pattern is the use of *inhalants* from cleaning fluids, aerosol containers, and such, which are used more by younger adolescents, perhaps because they can be acquired more easily. Substance *use* before age 18 is a strong predictor of later substance *abuse*, in part because adolescents are limited in their ability to analyze risks cognitively, partly because brain maturation is incomplete (see Chapter 3). For this reason, health psychologists are concerned with findings from the Monitoring the Future Study showing that 25 percent of high school seniors had five drinks in a row in the past two weeks, 11 percent were daily cigarette smokers, and 5 percent were daily marijuana users (MTF, 2015).

Drug use among adolescents varies markedly from place to place, again suggesting the influence of social-cultural factors. For example, the United States has a drinking age of 21, whereas many European countries have younger minimum drinking ages (as young as 16 in France and Italy and 18 in Ireland, Sweden, and the United Kingdom). Throughout most of Europe, alcohol is widely used, even by children. In much of the Middle East, however, alcohol use is illegal, and adolescents rarely drink. In many Asian countries, smoking is permitted everywhere. In the United States, smoking is widely advertised yet banned in most schools and indoor public places. In Canada, cigarette advertising is banned. Could this be a factor in why fewer Canadian teens smoke?

Throughout the world, adolescent boys generally use more drugs than do girls, and they use them more often. Gender differences in substance use are tied to self-image and self-presentation and are reinforced by social constructions regarding appropriate male and female behavior. That is, they are influenced by teens' efforts to appear sophisticated, cool, or tough in the peer environment (Evans, Powers, Hersey, & Renaud, 2006). In the United States, boys and girls are similar in terms of *which* drugs they use, with two exceptions: boys use more illegal drugs and steroids, while girls use more diet drugs (Johnston, O'Malley, Bachman, & Schulenberg, 2013).

Substance abuse among teens often occurs with other unhealthy behaviors as part of a problem behavior syndrome that also includes intercourse in early adolescence, depressive symptoms, and general delinquency (Donahue, Lichtenstein, Langstrom, & D'Onofrio, 2013). Teens who display one or more of these behaviors often have high levels of family conflict and poor self-control and emotional regulation, which suggests that these behaviors may be emotional coping mechanisms in the face of a stressful environment (Goliath and Pretorius, 2016). For some teens, alcohol and other drugs, for instance, allow for a momentary denial of problems. Too often, however, ignored problems don't go away, a drug is turned to more often, and the teenagers enter a vicious cycle that may lead to addiction.

Findings such as these led some researchers to propose that the stress and strain of adolescence are contributing factors to drug use. In fact, however, prospective studies suggest that drug use *causes* more problems than it solves and often *precedes* depression, rebellion, and anxiety disorders (Meririnne and others, 2010). For example, teenagers who regularly use marijuana may become less motivated to achieve in school and then be more likely to develop other problem behaviors (Ansary & Luthar, 2009).

Fear of addiction may not persuade young adolescents to avoid drug use because, as you may remember from discussions in previous chapters in this book, they often believe that they are invulnerable. They do not know or care that psychoactive drugs excite emotional control centers in the brain's limbic system, while simultaneously interfering with analytical areas in the prefrontal cortex. These neurological effects make drug users more emotional than they otherwise would be, as well as less thoughtful. Every hazard of adolescence—including accidents, unsafe sex, depression, and suicide—is more common among those who are under the influence of a psychoactive drug. For similar reasons, educational campaigns and antidrug advertisements that use scare tactics may backfire and actually increase drug use. Plus, savvy adolescents often recognize exaggerations and other partial truths (Strasburger, Jordan, & Donnerstein, 2009).

An added problem is that many parents and other adult caregivers are unaware of their children's drug use. In one study, less than 1 percent of the parents of U.S. sixth graders thought their children had ever had alcohol, but 22 percent of the children said they had (O'Donnell, Brydon, Wright, & Steptoe, 2008). In addition to parental monitoring, parents influence their children's substance use through their own behavior and the social context that they shape at home. Parents who quit smoking by the time their children reach the third grade have children who are more likely to have negative perceptions of smoking, and, in turn, are less likely to smoke themselves (Wyszynski, Bricker, & Comstock, 2011). When parents forbid smoking in their homes, fewer adolescents smoke (Messer, Trinidad, Al-Delaimy, & Pierce, 2008). When parents are careful with their own drinking, fewer teenagers abuse alcohol (Van Zundert, Van Der Vorst, Vermulst, & Engels, 2006). When parents provide guidance about drinking, teenagers are less likely to get drunk or use other substances (Miller & Plant, 2010). Growing up with two married parents reduces cigarette and alcohol use, even when other influences (such as parental smoking and family income) are taken into account (Brown & Rinelli, 2010).

Changing the broader social context also has an impact. Throughout the United States, higher prices, targeted warnings, and better law enforcement have led to a marked decline in cigarette smoking among younger adolescents. In 2014, only 4 percent of eighth graders had smoked cigarettes in the past month, compared with 21 percent 15 years earlier (MTF, 2015).

Now that you understand more about addiction, let's turn to two of the most common addictions: alcohol and nicotine.

Alcohol Use and Abuse

Alcohol is a depressant that slows the functioning of the central nervous system in a manner similar to tranquilizers. When you drink an alcoholic beverage, approximately 20 percent of the alcohol is rapidly absorbed from the stomach directly into the bloodstream. The remaining 80 percent empties into the upper intestine, where it is absorbed at a pace that depends on whether the stomach is full or empty.

Once alcohol is absorbed, it is evenly distributed throughout body tissues and fluids. It takes a 175-pound man about 1 hour to metabolize the amount of alcohol contained in a 1-ounce glass of 80-proof liquor, a 4-ounce glass of wine, or a 12-ounce bottle of beer (Advokat, Comaty, & Julien, 2014). Drinking at a faster pace results in intoxication because a larger amount of alcohol remains in the bloodstream. Women metabolize alcohol more slowly because they produce less of the enzyme *alcohol dehydrogenase*, which breaks down alcohol in the stomach. Women also tend to weigh less than men. As a result of both of these factors, women have a higher blood alcohol content than men after consuming the same amount of alcohol.

The amount of alcohol in the bloodstream is your **blood alcohol level (BAL).** In most states, a BAL of 0.08 grams per 100 milliliters of blood (*gpercent*) constitutes legal intoxication. It is illegal to attempt to drive an automobile with a BAL at this level or higher. A typical male college student would reach an illegal BAL after consuming one standard drink an hour for every 30 to 35 pounds of body weight. Women would reach an illegal

blood alcohol level (BAL) The amount of alcohol in the blood, measured in grams per 100 milliliters.

BAL sooner. Some people develop a higher tolerance and are able to drink larger amounts of alcohol before becoming visibly impaired. For others, however, obvious intoxication may occur with BALs as low as 0.03 or 0.04 gpercent. Regardless of the visible effects, the damaging internal, physiological effects are comparable for all drinkers.

The short-term effects of alcohol are dose-dependent. At BALs ranging from about 0.01 to 0.05 gpercent, a drinker usually feels relaxed and mildly euphoric. As the level increases to 0.10 gpercent, memory and concentration are dulled, and reaction time and motor functioning are impaired significantly. At 0.10 to 0.15 gpercent, walking and fine motor skills become extremely difficult. By 0.20 to 0.25 gpercent, vision becomes blurry, speech is slurred, walking without staggering is virtually impossible, and the drinker may lose consciousness. Death may occur at a BAL of 0.35 or more.

Prevalence of Alcohol Use

As Figure 9.5 shows, 59.4 percent of full-time college students in the United States ages 18 to 22 drank alcohol in the past month compared with 50.6 percent of other persons the same age. The same year, 39 percent of college students engaged in binge drinking (five or more drinks on one occasion) in the past month compared with 33.4 percent of others the same age. Finally, 12.7 percent engaged in heavy drinking (binge drinking on five or more occasions in the past month) compared with 9.3 percent of other nonstudents the same age (SAMHSA, 2015).

The Institute of Medicine considers **at-risk drinking** as two or more episodes of binge drinking in the past month, or consuming an average of two or more alcoholic drinks per day in the past month. At-risk drinking is a major public health concern because it is linked with poor health, premature death, and a variety of social consequences such as injury, unplanned and unprotected sex, and hostile encounters with police (see Table 9.2). About 1 in 4 college students report academic consequences from their drinking, including missing classes, falling behind, poor exam performance, and getting lower grades overall (National Institute on Alcohol Abuse and Alcoholism, 2015).

The prevalence of the various categories of drinking behavior varies by age, gender, education level, ethnicity, and culture. Adults between 25 and 44 years of age have the highest overall rates of drinking, but the 18 to 24 cohort has the highest rates of binge and heavy drinking (NIAAA, 2015). Alcohol use among adolescents ages 12 to 17 dropped substantially after the legal age for purchasing alcohol was increased to 21 in most states. From the 1980s to 2008, binge drinking among high school students declined by 24 percent (MTF, 2015). Rates of drinking are lowest among older adults (NIAAA, 2015).

at-risk drinking Two or more episodes of binge drinking in the past month, or consuming an average of two or more alcoholic drinks per day in the past month.

FIGURE 9.5

Alcohol Use in the United States A total of 59.4 percent of full-time college students in the United States drank alcohol in the past month compared with 50.6 percent of others the same age. The same year, 39 percent of college students engaged in binge drinking (5 or more drinks on one occasion) in the past month compared with 33.4 percent of others the same age. Finally, 12.7 percent engaged in heavy drinking (binge drinking on 5 or more occasions in the past month) compared with 9.3 percent of other nonstudents the same age.

Data from SAMHSA. (2015). 2014 National Survey on Drug Use and Health (NSDUH). Table 6.88B— Alcohol Use in the Past Month among Persons Aged 18 to 22, by College Enrollment Status and Demographic Characteristics: Percentages, 2013 and 2014. Available at: http://pubs.niaaa.nih.gov/publications/CollegeFactSheet/CollegeFactSheet.pdf

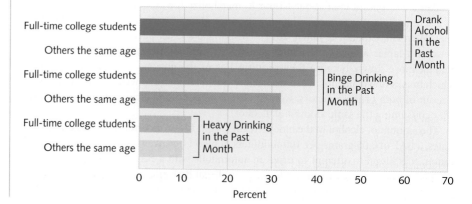

TABLE 9.2
Are You a Problem Drinker?

How will you know if you are drinking too much? Here are some key questions to ask:

- Am I drinking alcohol as a beverage or using it as a drug?
- Do I need alcohol to relax or to relieve stress?
- Do I use alcohol to cope with negative reactions and emotions?
- Do I use alcohol to manage social functions or relationships?
- How does alcohol fit into my life?
- Do I make sure there is always time for alcohol in my schedule?
- Has drinking become an important priority?
- What do I expect from my alcohol consumption? An attitude adjustment? Solace and release from tension?
- Can I honestly say that there are no negative consequences of my drinking? No impact on family or children? No physical effects (hangover, memory loss, loss of control)? No risky behavior (driving after drinking more than two or three drinks)? No family member or friend commenting on my drinking? No impact on my professional responsibilities (lateness, forgetting, poor judgment)?
- Can I drink four or five drinks at a time and not feel negative effects?
- Are there any occasions or circumstances when I feel I have to have a drink?
- Do I have a spouse, friends, or family members who have a drinking problem?

If your answers to one or more of these statements or questions are positive, then you may be engaging either in risky drinking that puts you at risk for alcohol problems or in hazardous drinking that is already producing some negative consequences in your life.

Source: DiClemente, C.C. (2005, September 28). Alcohol and problem drinking. www.apa.org.

Compared with women, significantly more men are current drinkers, binge drinkers, and heavy drinkers (15 or more drinks per week for men or 8 per week for women). Binge drinking is defined as having 5 or more drinks for males and 4 or more drinks for females on one occasion or within a short period of time (Centers for Disease Control and Prevention, 2016a). European-Americans have higher rates of drinking than African-Americans, Asian-Americans, or Hispanic-Americans. African-Americans are less likely to be heavy drinkers than European-Americans and Hispanic-Americans.

Although the specific causes of ethnic and cultural group differences in risk are not known, researchers have pointed to several possibilities. A powerful protective factor in the social-cultural environment is *racial identity* (RI)—an aspect of self-concept and social identity derived from the knowledge and value of group membership. Identifying as part of a group and a sense of belonging and pride are associated with higher levels of psychological well-being and higher self-esteem among minority adolescents and young adults in ethnically diverse settings. Minority adolescents and young adults who have high levels of RI appear to be able to resist or delay substance use initiation, have a more negative attitude toward drugs, and are more likely to perceive substance use as being nonnormative, or atypical, among their racial group than are youths who have low levels of RI (Stock and others, 2013a).

People in certain groups also may be at higher or lower risk because of the way that they metabolize alcohol. One study of Native Americans, for instance, found that they are less sensitive to the intoxicating effects of alcohol (Wall, Garcia-Andrade, Thomasson, Carr, & Ehlers, 1997). People who "hold their liquor" in this way may therefore lack (or can ignore more easily) warning signals that ordinarily make people stop drinking. Asian-Americans, on the other hand, may be less prone to alcohol abuse because they have genetically lower levels of *aldehyde dehydrogenase,* an enzyme used by the body to metabolize alcohol (Asakage and others, 2007). Without this enzyme, toxic substances build up more quickly after a person drinks alcohol, and they cause flushing, dizziness, and nausea.

Several studies suggest that teen drinking is especially damaging to the brain. Although researchers once thought that the brain is fully developed by age 16 or 17, significant neurological development continues at least until age 21. Heavy drinking at a young age may impair that development.

The Physical Effects of Alcohol Consumption

Alcohol affects all parts of the body. At the most basic level, because cell membranes are permeable to alcohol, alcohol enters the cells and disrupts intracellular communication. Alcohol also affects genes that regulate cell functions such as the synthesis of dopamine, norepinephrine, and other important neurotransmitters.

The craving that some people develop for alcohol, the adverse reactions that occur during withdrawal, and the high rate of relapse are all due to biochemical changes in the brain brought on by heavy, long-term use of alcohol. Prolonged heavy drinking can cause the brain to shrink, especially in women (Mayo Clinic, 2006). Binge drinking inhibits *neurogenesis*, the process by which neurons are generated, as well as the formation of new synaptic connections (Crews, He, & Hodge, 2007). In addition, alcohol abuse may interfere with the body's absorption of thiamin, one of the B vitamins. The absence of thiamin may contribute to **Korsakoff's syndrome,** a neurological disorder most often caused by alcohol abuse, and characterized by extreme difficulty with memory.

Alcohol has major effects on the hippocampus, a brain area associated with learning, memory, emotional regulation, sensory processing, appetite, and stress (see Chapter 3). It does so by inhibiting neurotransmitters that are strongly associated with emotional behavior and cravings. Dopamine transmission, in particular, is strongly associated with the rewarding properties of alcohol, nicotine, opiates, and cocaine.

Chronic alcohol abuse weakens the immune system, damages cellular DNA, interferes with normal endocrine system development, and disrupts the secretion of growth hormone, which may cause a problematic variety of other endocrine changes. Alcohol abuse has been linked to decreased testosterone levels in men, leading to impotence and decreased fertility. In women, menstrual disturbances, spontaneous abortions, and miscarriages increase with the level of alcohol consumption. Alcohol also may decrease estrogen levels in women, which may partly explain the association between alcohol use and increased risk of breast cancer (Allen, 2009).

Alcohol promotes the formation of fat deposits on heart muscle, which lowers the efficiency of the heart and contributes to cardiovascular disease. It also increases heart rate and causes blood vessels in the skin to dilate, resulting in a loss of body heat. Chronic abuse may increase blood pressure and serum cholesterol levels and accelerate the development of atherosclerotic lesions in coronary arteries. Although women experience alcohol-related heart damage at lower levels of consumption than men, both men and women who abuse alcohol are equally likely to suffer a fatal heart attack before age 55 (MMWR, 2004).

Excessive use of alcohol contributes to stomach inflammation and the formation of gastrointestinal ulcers. Severe inflammation of the liver (*hepatitis*) and the replacement of normal liver cells by fibrous tissue (*cirrhosis*) are two common chronic diseases caused by alcohol abuse. Chronic liver disease and cirrhosis cause approximately 36,000 deaths each year in the United States (CDC, 2015c).

Alcohol freely crosses the placenta of pregnant women, making alcohol a potent teratogen. Alcohol levels in a developing fetus quickly match those of the drinking mother. Pregnant women who drink during critical stages of fetal development place their infants at risk of developing **fetal alcohol syndrome (FAS).** FAS causes severe birth defects, including low intelligence; microcephaly (small brain); intellectual disability; delayed body growth; facial abnormalities such as malformed eyes, ears, nose, and cheekbones; and congenital heart defects.

The behavioral, psychological, and social effects of alcohol abuse are just as dangerous as its physical effects, as the next section will explain.

Korsakoff's syndrome An alcohol-induced neurological disorder characterized by the inability to store new memories.

fetal alcohol syndrome (FAS) A cluster of birth defects that include facial abnormalities, low intelligence, and delayed body growth caused by the mother's use of alcohol during pregnancy.

Korsakoff's Syndrome These PET scans show brain activity in a normal patient (left) and a patient suffering from Korsakoff's syndrome (right inset). The frontal lobes are seen at the bottom center of each scan; the darker areas represent low metabolic activity. In a PET scan, low metabolic activity in response to thought-provoking questions indicates problems with memory and other cognitive functioning.

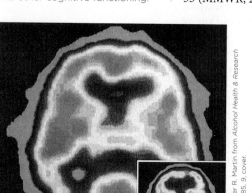

Courtesy Dr. Peter R. Martin from *Alcohol Health & Research World,* Spring 1985, 9, cover.

Psychosocial Consequences of Alcohol Use

As blood alcohol level initially rises, many drinkers feel cheerful, self-confident, and more sexually responsive. As levels continue to rise, however, higher-order cognitive functions are disrupted. Furthermore, alcohol impairs judgment and facilitates urges that otherwise might be resisted (see Chapter 6). This alcohol-induced sense of confidence and freedom from social constraints is known as **behavioral disinhibition,** which often results in increased aggressiveness, risk taking, or other behaviors the individual would normally avoid. When drinking, for example, both women and men are more disposed to casual sex, unprotected sex, and other high-risk behaviors (Ebel-Lam, MacDonald, Zanna, & Fong, 2009).

Alcohol also makes it difficult for drinkers to interpret complex or ambiguous stimuli; that is, they find it harder to attend to multiple cues and easier to focus on only the most salient ones (Chermack & Giancola, 1997). This **alcohol myopia** (nearsightedness) was demonstrated by Antonia Abbey and her colleagues (Abbey, Parkhill, Buck, & Saenz, 2000), who invited unacquainted college students (88 male–female pairs) to converse for 15 minutes after consuming either alcoholic or nonalcoholic drinks.

Both men and women who drank alcohol perceived their partners and themselves as behaving more sexually and in a more disinhibited way than did those who did not drink. However, the effects also depended on the type of cue being evaluated. Intoxicated participants exaggerated the meaning of dating cues and *ignored* more ambiguous signals that were possibly indicating friendliness or sociability, rather than sexual interest. Thus, alcohol seems to make it even easier for people to concentrate on salient cues that fit their current beliefs (or hopes) and disregard more ambiguous cues that do not. Some researchers believe that these cognitive and perceptual changes are the very basis of alcohol's addictive capacity.

These results have implications for college prevention programs. Knowing that intoxication is dangerous does not necessarily keep students from drinking heavily and subsequently engaging in risky behaviors. The challenge of health psychology is to make students take these risks seriously, rather than feeling that they are invulnerable.

Alcohol-induced cognitive impairments are especially destructive during adolescence, perhaps because even low doses can impair the judgment of teens who are already distracted by the ongoing psychological, physiological, and social challenges of puberty. Hundreds of research studies have revealed the link between alcohol and risky sex—in particular, that students who use alcohol tend to have more sexual partners, to be less likely to use condoms, and to have more sexually transmitted infections and unwanted pregnancies than their nondrinking counterparts (Cooper, 2006). Frequent drinkers are also absent from school nearly four times more often than nondrinkers, more likely to ride in a car with a driver who has been drinking, and nearly three times as likely to engage in antisocial behaviors such as stealing and vandalizing property (Lammers, Ireland, Resnick, & Blum, 2000).

Alcohol abuse has been associated with a variety of other social problems, including difficulties in interpersonal relationships and various types of violence, including homicides, assault, robbery, suicides, and spousal abuse (Rogers, Boardman, Pendergast, & Lawrence, 2015; Davis, Norris, George, Martell, & Heiman, 2006). Half of all people convicted of rape or sexual assault were drinking before the commission of their crimes. Drinking also increases the chances of being a victim of crime. Approximately 72 percent of rapes committed on college campuses occur when victims are so intoxicated that they are unable to consent or refuse (Wechsler & Nelson, 2008).

Alcohol contributes to violence not only by loosening restraints due to behavioral disinhibition, but also by increasing a person's sensitivity to pain and frustration. In addition, brain imaging studies show that repeated heavy use of alcohol, stimulants, and

Rick's Photography/Shutterstock

Fetal Alcohol Syndrome If a woman drinks heavily during critical periods of fetal development, she puts her unborn child at risk of having fetal alcohol syndrome (FAS). Besides the specific facial structures seen here (including a thin upper lip and low nasal bridge), the child is also likely to be intellectually disabled.

behavioral disinhibition The false sense of confidence and freedom from social restraints that results from alcohol consumption.

alcohol myopia The tendency of alcohol to increase a person's concentration on immediate events and to reduce awareness of distant events.

other drugs disrupts frontal lobe activity, which impairs decision making and planning and lowers a person's normal threshold for violence.

Alcohol Use Disorder

For most adults, moderate alcohol use—no more than two drinks a day for men and one for women and older people—is relatively harmless. (A "drink" means 1.5 ounces of spirits, 5 ounces of wine, or 12 ounces of beer, all of which contain 0.5 ounces of alcohol.) Moderate use, however, is at one end of a range of drinking, and more than 18 million people in the United States have an **alcohol use disorder (AUD)** (NIAAA, 2013). Under the newest edition of the *Diagnostic and Statistical Manual of Mental Disorders* (DSM-5), a person who meets 2 or more of the 11 problem drinking criteria listed in Table 9.3 would be diagnosed with an AUD.

Various factors have been implicated in explaining why certain people are more likely than others to abuse alcohol. No single factor or influence, however, completely explains the origins of AUD.

Genes and Alcoholism

There is no single gene for alcoholism, but genes and alleles that make alcoholism more likely have been found on every chromosome except the Y (Epps and Holt, 2011). Some people inherit a greater tolerance for the aversive effects of alcohol, as well as a genetically

alcohol use disorder (AUD) A maladaptive drinking pattern in which drinking interferes with role obligations.

As we saw in Chapter 2, heritability refers to the variation in a trait, in a particular population, in a particular environment, that can be attributed to genetic differences among the members of that group. The term heritability also refers to group rather than individual differences in a trait. It does not indicate the degree to which genes determine the likelihood of a trait in a particular person.

TABLE 9.3

Alcohol Use Disorder (based on DSM-5 Criteria)

	In the past year, have you:	
1	Had times when you ended up drinking more, or longer, than you intended?	
2	More than once wanted to cut down or stop drinking, or tried to, but couldn't?	
3	Spent a lot of time drinking? Or being sick or getting over other aftereffects?	The presence of at least 2 of these symptoms indicates an *Alcohol Use Disorder (AUD)*.
4	Wanted a drink so badly you couldn't think of anything else?	
5	Found that drinking—or being sick from drinking—often interfered with taking care of your home or family? Or caused job troubles? Or school problems?	
6	Continued to drink even though it was causing trouble with your family or friends?	The severity of the AUD is defined as:
7	Given up or cut back on activities that were important or interesting to you, or gave you pleasure, in order to drink?	
8	More than once gotten into situations while or after drinking that increased your chances of getting hurt (such as driving, swimming, using machinery, walking in a dangerous area, or having unsafe sex)?	Mild: The presence of 2 to 3 symptoms
9	Continued to drink even though it was making you feel depressed or anxious or adding to another health problem? Or after having had a memory blackout?	Moderate: The presence of 4 to 5 symptoms
10	Had to drink much more than you once did to get the effect you want? Or found that your usual number of drinks had much less effect than before?	Severe: The presence of 6 or more symptoms
11	Found that when the effects of alcohol were wearing off, you had withdrawal symptoms, such as trouble sleeping, shakiness, restlessness, nausea, sweating, a racing heart, or a seizure? Or sensed things that were not there?	

Information from http://pubs.niaaa.nih.gov/publications/dsmfactsheet/dsmfact.htm

greater sensitivity to the pleasurable effects. Both tendencies may be factors in early excessive drinking, leading to dependence. Consider the evidence:

- When either the mother or father of a male child is alcohol-dependent, that child is significantly more likely to later abuse alcohol himself (Ball, 2008). In fact, for males, alcoholism in a first-degree relative is the single best predictor of alcoholism (Plomin, King, Mainous, & Geesey, 2001).

- Identical twins have twice the concordance rate (76 percent) of fraternal twins for AUD. This is true whether the twins were raised together or apart, and whether they grew up in the homes of their biological parents or with adoptive parents (Ball, 2008).

- The personalities of those most likely to abuse alcohol have several common traits, each of which is, at least in part, genetically determined: a quick temper, impulsiveness, intolerance of frustration, vulnerability to depression, and a general attraction to excitement (MacGregor and others, 2009).

Alcohol, Temperament, and Personality

Research studies that link temperament and personality to alcohol dependence provide another clear indication of the interaction of nature and nurture. Researchers no longer attempt to identify a single "alcoholic personality," focusing instead on specific personality traits that appear to be linked to alcohol dependence. One such trait is a temperament that includes attraction to excitement and intolerance of frustration. A second is **behavioral undercontrol,** characterized by aggressiveness, unconventionality, overactivity, and impulsive behavior. A third is **negative emotionality,** which is characterized by depression and anxiety. Marked by such traits, high-delinquent teens show consistently elevated numbers of alcohol-related problems (Allen and Gabbay, 2013).

behavioral undercontrol A general personality syndrome linked to alcohol dependence and characterized by aggressiveness, unconventionality, and impulsiveness; also called *deviance proneness.*

negative emotionality A state of alcohol abuse characterized by depression and anxiety.

Alcohol Expectancy Effects

As is true of all psychoactive drugs, alcohol's impact depends not only on the dose but also on the circumstances under which the drug is taken—the user's personality, mood, and **alcohol expectancy effects.** People who *believe* they have consumed alcohol behave just like those who have imbibed, whether or not they have (Heinz, de Wit, Lilje, & Kassel, 2013).

Several studies have also found that adolescents' and young adults' beliefs about their peers' alcohol use and attitudes predicted their own alcohol use. Those who are certain that many of their friends drink regularly—and enjoy doing so—are themselves more likely to begin using alcohol (Park, Klein, Smith, & Martell, 2009). As another example, people who believe that alcohol promotes sexual arousal become more responsive to sexual stimuli if they believe they have been drinking (Friedman, McCarthy, Förster, & Denzler, 2005).

alcohol expectancy effects The effects of an individual's beliefs about how alcohol affects behavior.

Scott Weiland, former lead singer of Stone Temple Pilots, who overdosed in 2015.

Treatment and Prevention of Alcohol Use Disorders

Although some people with AUDs do recover on their own, some cycle in and out of alcohol problems throughout their lives. Those who seek treatment generally receive outpatient rather than inpatient care. The treatments generally involve the use of drugs or therapy, or some combination of the two.

Factors that influence the willingness of a person to enter treatment for an AUD include gender, age, marital status, and ethnicity. Among women, factors that predict entry into treatment include being older and unmarried and having a lower level of

Getty Images Entertainment/Getty Images

education, employment, and income. For men, factors that predict entry include having experienced alcohol-related social consequences, being older, and belonging to an ethnic minority. Although evaluations of the effectiveness of self-help groups are limited, drinking-related beliefs, readiness and motivation to change, and social support for abstinence are important predictors of the success or failure of treatment.

Drug Treatment

Researchers working to understand the physiological mechanisms by which alcohol affects the brain have uncovered a number of pharmacological treatments for AUDs. Medications include detoxification agents to manage alcohol withdrawal, alcohol-sensitizing agents to deter future drinking, and anticraving agents to reduce the risks of relapse.

As noted, many people with an AUD also suffer from clinical depression. Antidepressants that increase serotonin levels are used sometimes to treat those in the early stages of abstinence from alcohol. The best known of these is *fluoxetine* (Prozac). Some researchers believe that deficiencies of serotonin may cause alcohol craving (Polina, Contini, Hutz, & Bau, 2009). Other researchers have focused instead on drug treatments that block the release of dopamine, which appears to decrease the reward properties of alcohol (Thompson, 2000).

Another approach involves the drug *naltrexone* (Revia), which binds to opiate receptors in the brain, prevents their activation, and also decreases the reward that comes from consuming alcohol. A number of studies have found that patients who received naltrexone as part of their treatment experienced less craving than patients who received a placebo, and they were more successful in maintaining their abstinence (Snyder & Bowers, 2008). For instance, the COMBINE project evaluated the effectiveness of naltrexone versus placebo for over 1383 recently alcohol-abstinent volunteers. Over the 16-week duration of the study, different groups received either naltrexone or the placebo alone, or in combination with CBT. Participants who received naltrexone combined with CBT remained abstinent longer than those who received placebos with or without CBT (Kreibel, 2010).

Researchers generally agree that treatment of AUDs is more successful when drugs are combined with behavioral and psychological therapy. One early technique, **aversion therapy,** associated a nauseating drug such as *disulfiram* (Antabuse) with alcohol. Although the drug does not reduce cravings for alcohol, if the patient takes a single drink within several days of ingesting Antabuse, a variety of unpleasant effects occur, including nausea, sweating, racing heart rate, severe headaches, and dizziness (NIAAA, 2013). Drugs like Antabuse are designed to trigger a *conditioned aversion* to alcohol. When taken daily, Antabuse can result in total abstinence.

But patient adherence to Antabuse is a major problem, so some therapists prefer to conduct aversion therapy in a controlled clinical setting. The client drinks alcohol and then takes an *emetic drug,* which induces vomiting. Because the interval between the drink and the emetic drug is carefully timed, the latter functions as an unconditioned stimulus and becomes associated with the taste, smell, and act of taking a drink of alcohol. These stimuli thus become conditioned stimuli and trigger the unpleasant reaction of nausea.

Relapse Prevention Programs

Because of the unusually high rate of relapse in alcohol dependence (roughly 60 percent a year following treatment), many treatments, while helping the person to remain alcohol-free, focus on enabling the person to deal with situations that tempt relapse. Many relapse prevention programs emphasize gaining control over situations that may precipitate a return to drinking.

One form of relapse prevention is based on the gradual *extinction* of drinking triggers. Treatments have been developed in which drinkers are exposed repeatedly to alcohol-related stimuli, such as the aroma of their favorite drink, but they are not allowed to drink. The patients' initially powerful, conditioned physical and psychological responses diminish with repeated exposure over a number of sessions (Witteman and others, 2015).

aversion therapy A behavioral therapy that pairs an unpleasant stimulus (such as a nauseating drug) with an undesirable behavior (such as drinking or smoking), causing the patient to avoid the behavior.

Many relapse prevention programs also incorporate *coping* and *social-skills* training, which helps "inoculate" drinkers by teaching specific strategies for coping with high-risk situations without the help of alcohol. Inoculation focuses on improving the person's assertiveness, listening skills, and ability to give and receive compliments and criticism, as well as on enhancing close relationships (Foxhall, 2001). In addition, the recovered drinker is taught skills that permit him or her to abstain in drinking situations. *Drink refusal training* entails the modeling and rehearsal of skills needed to turn down offers to drink.

Controlled Drinking

Before 1970, virtually all interventions for alcohol dependency focused on total abstinence. Then several research studies reported that a small percentage of recovered alcoholics were able to drink moderately without relapsing into problem drinking. Since that time, the issue has been highly controversial. It does appear that a small percentage of problem drinkers can become moderate drinkers, particularly those who are young, employed, and live in supportive and stable environments (Dawson and others, 2005). Although many intervention programs continue to insist upon total abstinence, they typically have very high dropout rates. For a small sector of problem drinkers, drinking in moderation may be a more realistic social goal than total abstinence. Some intervention programs teach *controlled drinking* skills to improve the individual's personal control over drinking. One technique, *placebo drinking,* involves consuming nonalcoholic beverages in place of, or in alternation with, alcohol-containing ones. Although controlled drinking treatment programs remain controversial, they have gained more acceptance in Europe than in North America, Japan, and other countries where experts are more likely to promote abstinence (Higuchi, Maesato, Yoshimura, & Matsushita, 2014).

Self-Help Groups

One of the most widely accepted nonmedical efforts to deal with alcohol dependence is Alcoholics Anonymous (AA). Founded in 1935, AA's 12-step approach suggests calling on a (not necessarily religious) higher power to help battle what is viewed as an incurable disease. Its theory is that "once an alcoholic, always an alcoholic," and it opposes "controlled drinking" and disagrees entirely with the belief that alcoholics can be reformed into moderate, responsible drinkers. AA counts more than 2 million members worldwide.

Self-help groups such as AA generally involve group discussions of members' experiences in recovering from alcohol abuse. Members benefit by connecting with a new, nondrinking network and sharing their fears and concerns about relapse. Another self-help group, Rational Recovery, offers a nonspiritual alternative to treating alcohol dependence.

Preventing Alcohol Problems

Alcohol prevention researchers target individual drinkers, as well as the social environments in which drinking occurs. Preventive treatments therefore aim to change attitudes about drinking, strengthen coping skills, and restructure environments to reduce the risk of alcohol-related problems.

Prevention programs are most effective when they target children and adolescents before they have succumbed to the habit. The efforts that have proved at least partly effective include strict enforcement of drunk-driving laws, higher prices of alcohol and cigarettes due to taxes on these items, and harsher punishments for those who sell (or make available) alcohol and cigarettes to minors, as well as classes that inform parents of the hazards of various drugs, help to improve parent–child communication, and/or realistically delineate the potential hazards of drug use.

Several primary prevention programs, including the Alcohol Misuse Prevention Study (AMPS), are based on correcting faulty reasoning about peers' drug use and improving

Ghislain & Marie David de Lossy/Getty Images

Social Support Self-help group meetings such as this one provide members with various types of help in overcoming drug dependence and abuse.

social skills in targeted groups. The AMPS was designed to help preadolescent students resist social pressures that lead toward alcohol consumption. For instance, role-playing exercises allow students to practice declining alcohol, marijuana, and other drug offers in various social situations. Should students actually encounter such situations, they will have developed behavioral and cognitive *scripts* for declining the drug offer.

Realistically, however, health psychologists recognize that so long as drugs are available and are not perceived as serious threats to health, many young people will try them, and many will eventually abuse them. Following this line of reasoning, one strategy is to delay the young person's experimentation as long as possible. Doing so will increase the odds that he or she is informed realistically about the hazards of the drug(s) in question and has the cognitive maturity to avoid the faulty reasoning that often leads to drug abuse. The younger a person is when he or she starts drinking, for example, the more likely that he or she will be to abuse or become dependent on alcohol. One study sponsored by the National Institutes of Health (NIH) found that people who began drinking before they turned 15 were four times more likely to become alcohol abusers than were those who started drinking at the legal age of 21. For every year that drinking alcohol is delayed, the risk of becoming alcohol-dependent decreases by 14 percent.

Tobacco Use and Abuse

Along with caffeine and alcohol, nicotine is one of the three most widely used psychoactive drugs. Native to the New World, the tobacco plant is first represented in history on a Mayan stone carving dated from around 600 to 900 C.E., and tobacco smoking is first mentioned in Christopher Columbus's log books from his legendary voyage of 1492.

Prevalence of Smoking

Cigarette smoking in the United States peaked in the early 1960s, when half of all adult men and one-third of adult women smoked. From the late 1960s until the mid-1990s, the number of U.S. smokers declined steadily—to about 25 percent of all adults (Grunberg, Brown, & Klein, 1997). However, the decline was not evenly distributed, with most of the decrease occurring among upper socioeconomic status (SES) groups and men. Lower-SES individuals continued to smoke, and the prevalence of smoking among women increased sharply. Today, about 17 percent of adults in the United States smoke. Smoking is most prevalent among American Indian/Alaska natives (26.1 percent), followed by white adults 18 to 24 years of age (19.4 percent), African-American adults (18.3 percent), Hispanic-American adults (12.1 percent), and Asian-American adults (9.6 percent) (CDC, 2015b).

Figure 9.6 shows that socioeconomic status also predicts smoking rates (CDC, 2015b). Smoking rates are highest among adults who have a General Education Development (GED) diploma (41.4 percent) and those with 9 to 11 years of education (24.2 percent). Smoking is least prevalent among those who have an undergraduate degree (9.1 percent) or graduate degree (5.6 percent).

Data from the Monitoring the Future study indicate that cigarette smoking among youth in the United States is now at the lowest level recorded in the 40-year history of the survey (MTF, 2015). Overall increases in perceived risk and disapproval of smoking appear to have contributed to the downturn in cigarette use. Despite this good news, use of *electronic cigarettes* (e-cigarettes) has risen sharply worldwide, as I'll discuss later in this chapter.

Although rates continue to decline in some parts of the world, they are skyrocketing in developing countries such as Kenya and Zimbabwe, causing the World Health Organization (WHO) to predict that by the year 2025, 7 out of every 10 tobacco-related deaths will occur in developing countries, where many people are still uninformed about the dangers of smoking (WHO, 2000a).

Physical Effects of Smoking

Cigarette smoking is the single most preventable cause of illness, disability, and premature death in this country and in much of the world. Worldwide, tobacco use causes more than 5 million deaths per year. In the United States, cigarette smoking is responsible for one out of every five deaths—that's more than the combined number of deaths from murders, suicides, AIDS, automobile accidents, alcohol and other drug abuse, and fires (WHO, 2008). Because each cigarette smoked reduces a person's life expectancy by an estimated 14 minutes, an adult who has smoked two packs of cigarettes a day (40 cigarettes) for 20 years can expect to lose about 8 years of life.

Each time a person lights up, 4000 different chemical compounds are released. It is these chemicals that provide pleasure and energy, as well as disease and death. For example, the nicotine in cigarette smoke activates specific neural receptors, which in turn causes an increase in heart rate and blood pressure and the constriction of arteries, all of which contribute to the development of cardiovascular disease. The presence of nicotine also causes serum cholesterol levels to rise, hastening the formation of artery-blocking lesions.

Cigarette smoke leads to bronchial congestion by increasing the production of mucus in the throat and lungs while simultaneously damaging the hairlike cilia that line the respiratory tract. This leads to higher-than-normal incidence rates of bronchitis, emphysema, and respiratory infections.

The link between smoking and cancer is no longer a matter of debate. Benzo[*a*]pyrene (BPDE), a chemical in cigarette smoke, has been identified as a causative agent in lung cancer (Denissenko, Pao, Tang, & Pfeifer, 1996). BPDE damages a cancer suppressor gene, causing a mutation of lung tissue. Smoking is also a significant factor in cancers of the mouth, larynx, stomach, pancreas, esophagus, kidney, bladder, and cervix (CDC, 2008).

Given the same lifetime exposure to tobacco smoke, the risk for developing lung cancer is 20 to 70 percent higher in women than men at every level of exposure, indicating that women are more susceptible to the carcinogens in tobacco. Women who smoke during pregnancy are also more likely to miscarry or to have low-birth-weight infants and infants who die from sudden infant death syndrome (CDC, 2008). Because cigarette smoke reduces the delivery of oxygen to the developing child's brain, the resulting *fetal hypoxia* can cause irreversible intellectual damage. Schoolchildren whose mothers smoked during pregnancy have lower IQs and an increased prevalence of attention deficit hyperactivity disorder (ADHD) (Milberger, Biederman, Faraone, Chen, & Jones, 1996).

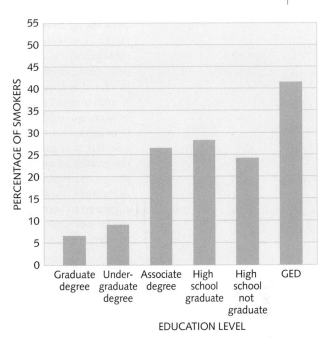

EDUCATION LEVEL

FIGURE 9.6

Who Smokes? Smoking is most prevalent among men and people with less than a high school education. About 17 percent of American adults currently smoke. Clearly, the nation failed to meet the national health goal set by the Healthy People 2000 project of limiting smoking to 15 percent of the population by the year 2000.

Data from Schoenborn, C. A., Adams, P. F., & Perego, J. A. (2013). Health behaviors of adults: United States, 2008–2010. National Center for Health Statistics. *Vital Health Stat 10* (257).

In 2006, a U.S. district judge ruled that major tobacco companies continue to deceive the public by "recruiting new smokers (the majority of whom are under the age of 18), preventing current smokers from quitting, and thereby sustaining the industry."

Smoking Effects Disguised as Aging

Health experts are discovering that a number of disorders once believed to be the normal consequences of aging are, in fact, caused by long-term smoking and other behavioral pathogens. For example, some of the mental decline observed among elderly persons may be caused by tobacco-related bleeding in the brain ("silent strokes") that goes unnoticed. A meta-analysis of four European studies of 9223 people aged 65 and older compared smokers, nonsmokers, and former smokers once, and then again two years later, on short-term memory, attention, and simple mathematical calculations. All three groups showed a decline in cognitive performance over the two-year period, but the decline was by far the greatest among smokers (Launer & Kalmijn, 1998). In another meta-analysis of 19 prospective studies, current smokers had both an increased risk of dementia, including Alzheimer's disease and vascular dementia, and greater declines in mental-state testing compared to participants who had never smoked. These findings suggest that cigarette smoke has neurotoxic effects that are associated with an increased risk of dementia (Anstey, von Sanden, Salim, & O'Kearney, 2007).

Secondhand Smoke

The hazards of smoking extend beyond the direct risks to the smoker. Secondhand smoke contains an even higher concentration of many carcinogens than smoke inhaled directly from a cigarette. According to the Centers for Disease Control and Prevention (CDC), nearly 9 out of 10 nonsmoking Americans are exposed to *environmental tobacco smoke* (ETS). The study reported measurable levels of *cotinine* (a chemical that the body metabolizes from nicotine) in the blood of 88 percent of the nonsmokers.

It is estimated that 49,000 tobacco-related deaths annually in the United States are the result of secondhand smoke exposure (CDC, 2008). Female nonsmokers whose husbands smoke, for instance, stand a 1.32 times greater chance of developing lung cancer than do nonsmoking wives of nonsmoking husbands. Exposure to ETS is also recognized as an independent risk factor for cardiovascular disease (Torpy, Cassio, & Glass, 2005). Children who live with smokers have a significantly higher prevalence of pneumonia, ear and nasal infections, asthma, and the skin disorder eczema. As adults, they also have an increased risk of chronic illness and sickness-related work absences (Eriksen, 2004).

Why Do People Smoke?

To understand why people smoke, we need to consider each of the major stages of smoking behavior: initiation, maintenance, cessation, and relapse (Grunberg, Brown, & Klein, 1997).

Initiation

Initiation of drug use often occurs through social contacts. Initial use of many psychoactive drugs, with the exception of cocaine and amphetamines, is often unpleasant. As a result, a period of experimentation typically precedes the development of regular drug use, thus suggesting that factors other than physical effects are important in the initiation and maintenance of drug use until dependence develops.

Advertising is a powerful influence, and the tobacco industry spends more than $13 billion per year on it in the United States alone. From 1987 to 1997, the R.J. Reynolds company used a cartoon character named Joe Camel to advertise Camel cigarettes. A 1991 study published by the *Journal of the American Medical Association* showed that children as young as 5 and 6 years of age recognized the character (Campaign for Tobacco-Free Kids, 2006).

In a clever twist of this advertising campaign, Sonia Duffy and Dee Burton showed kindergarten through twelfth-grade students two currently used antismoking messages:

A study in the American Journal of Public Health *showed that adolescents who owned a tobacco promotional item and named a cigarette brand whose advertising attracted their attention were twice as likely to become established smokers as those who did neither.*

"Smoking kills" and "Smoking causes lung cancer, heart disease, emphysema, and may complicate pregnancy." The messages were either plain, printed messages or featured a Joe Camel–like cartoon character. All of the cartoon messages received higher ratings of importance and believability than the plain ones (cited in Azar, 1999).

Role modeling and peer influence also lead many teenagers to start smoking. Celebrities who smoke create the image that smoking is linked with success, beauty, and even sexual arousal. Image, smoking among friends, relaxation, and pleasure are most often cited as reasons teens begin smoking (Soldz & Cui, 2002). Having parents, older siblings, and friends who smoke is also predictive of teen smoking (Rodriguez, Romer, & Audrain-McGovern, 2007). In addition, low self-esteem, social isolation, and feelings of anger or depression all increase the likelihood of smoking (Repetto, Caldwell, & Zimmerman, 2005). Among adolescents whose parents and close friends do not smoke, smoking is rare.

The college years are a time when many young adults begin to smoke regularly. A four-year national study identified several personal and environmental factors as important predictors of smoking in college (Choi, Harris, Okuyemi, & Ahluwalia, 2003). Students who were more likely to begin smoking were those who did not like school as much and were more rebellious. High school students who had tried smoking were more likely to become regular smokers if they thought that their college peers approved of smoking and if they believed that experimentation with smoking was not dangerous. Finally, the longer a student avoided smoking, the less likely he or she was to experiment in college. Not surprisingly, students who lived in smoke-free dormitories were less likely to smoke than those who lived where smoking was permitted. The results of this study suggest that interventions that reinforce the message that nonsmoking is the norm and that increase access to smoke-free environments discourage initiation of smoking among college students.

In light of the evidence linking social influences with the initiation of smoking, the U.S. surgeon general has concluded that situational factors are more important than personality factors in explaining why people start smoking. Nevertheless, a number of *vulnerability factors* differentiate teens who are more likely to become dependent on nicotine and other psychoactive drugs. Smoking is especially prevalent among those who feel less competent and less in control of their future and who perceive a lack of social support (Camp, Klesges, & Relyea, 1993). This is particularly true among people of lower SES, who believe that their personal life and health can only be slightly controlled by their own behavior (Droomers, Schrijvers, & Mackenbach, 2002). In addition, rebelliousness, a strong need for independence, and perceptions of benefits such as weight control, increased alertness, and stress management are also linked to smoking initiation. Teenagers who smoke are also more likely to feel alienated from school, engage in antisocial behavior, have poor physical health, and feel depressed (Kandel & Davies, 1996). They also tend to spend more time in passive activities such as watching television and are more likely to be living with a single parent (Soldz & Cui, 2002).

Peer Pressure Psychosocial factors such as peer pressure may contribute to smoking and experimentation with other drugs. The most promising new research takes a systems approach, recognizing that a person's choice to use drugs is the result of many interrelated factors.

Photodisc/Getty Images

Maintenance

Once a person has begun to smoke, a variety of biological, psychological, and social variables contribute to making it difficult for him or her to abstain.

Heavy smokers are physically dependent on nicotine, which has powerful properties as a reinforcer. Nicotine stimulates the sympathetic nervous system and causes the release of catecholamines, serotonin, corticosteroids, and pituitary hormones (Grunberg, Faraday, & Rahman, 2001). In addition, nicotine induces relaxation in the skeletal muscles and stimulates dopamine release in the brain's reward system (Nowak, 1994).

Stanley Schachter and his colleagues (1977) first advanced the idea of the **nicotine-titration model,** suggesting that long-term smokers attempt to maintain a constant level of nicotine in their bloodstream. Schachter discovered that smokers smoke roughly the same amount day after day. When they are unknowingly forced to switch to lower-nicotine brands, they compensate by smoking more cigarettes, inhaling more deeply, and taking more puffs (Schachter, 1978). This *compensatory smoking* behavior has been confirmed in more recent studies and is generally considered to be one of many factors in how nicotine use promotes dependence and contributes to disease (U.S. Department of Health and Human Services [USDHHS], 2010).

Evidence of a genetic component in explaining why people continue to smoke comes from both twin and adoption studies, which estimate heritability for smoking to be as high as 60 percent (Heath & Madden, 1995; Munafo & Johnstone, 2008). Smokers and nonsmokers also appear to differ in a gene for a *dopamine transporter*—a protein that "vacuums up" dopamine after it has been released by a neuron. Caryn Lerman and her colleagues found that people with one form of the gene (the "9-repeat allele") were less likely to be smokers than people with other forms of it. Other studies have linked the 9-repeat allele to increased levels of dopamine, indicating reduced efficiency at removing excess dopamine. In addition, former smokers are more likely than current smokers to have the 9-repeat allele and the same DRD2 dopamine receptor gene implicated in alcohol dependence, indicating that these genes may boost people's ability to quit smoking (Lerman and others, 1999).

Psychosocial factors also contribute to maintenance. Adolescents who smoke often believe that their behavior is only temporary. When asked, they often report they will no longer be smoking in five years and that the long-term consequences of tobacco will not affect them. Adolescents are also oriented toward the present, so warnings of the long-term health hazards of cigarette smoking generally are not sufficient to deter them from smoking.

For many smokers, coping with stress is a key psychological factor in their habit. Schachter (1978) discovered that nicotine metabolism varies with the smoker's level of stress, providing a physiological explanation for why smokers tend to smoke more when anxious. When a smoker feels stressed, more nicotine is cleared from the body unmetabolized, forcing the smoker to smoke more to get his or her usual amount of nicotine.

Closely related to the idea of the nicotine-titration model, the *affect management model* proposes that smokers strive to regulate their emotional states. Accordingly, *positive affect smokers* are trying to increase stimulation, feel relaxed, or create some other positive emotional state. In contrast, *negative affect smokers* are trying to reduce anxiety, guilt, fear, or other negative emotional states. Evidence for this model comes from research showing that nicotine also affects levels of several neuroregulators, including dopamine, acetylcholine, norepinephrine, vasopressin, and endogenous opioids. Because of these effects, smoking may be used to boost mood, lower anxiety, reduce tension, increase concentration and alertness, and enhance memory temporarily.

In support of the affect management model, researchers also have uncovered a link between nicotine use and depression, naturally leading to questions of whether one causes the other or whether some third factor contributes to both (Nauert, 2008). One longitudinal study of high school students suggests that smoking and depression have a reciprocal effect, triggering a vicious cycle of smoking and negative mood (Windle & Windle, 2001). Every six months, students completed questionnaires assessing their emotional state, cigarette smoking, family dynamics, and friends' drug use. Teens who were

nicotine-titration model The theory that smokers who are physically dependent on nicotine regulate their smoking to maintain a steady level of the drug in their bodies.

heavy smokers at the beginning of the 18-month study were more likely than those who smoked less to report symptoms of depression. In addition, students who had persistent symptoms of depression at the start of the study were more likely than other students to increase smoking, even when other factors were taken into consideration.

Prevention Programs

Because it is so difficult for ex-smokers to remain nicotine free, health psychologists have focused a great deal of energy on primary prevention. Their efforts have included educational programs in schools, public health messages, tobacco advertising bans, increasing tobacco taxes, and campaigns to ban smoking in public places. Over the past three decades, these campaigns have changed in ways that reflect the broader social changes in how smoking is viewed. In the 1970s, for instance, school-based prevention programs focused on providing information regarding the hazards of smoking. In the 1980s, programs were increasingly based on social influence models that portrayed smoking as undesirable and taught the necessary skills to resist social pressure to smoke. Most recently, smoking has been portrayed as an addictive disorder as well as a problem behavior. As a result, smoking interventions have increasingly incorporated some form of nicotine replacement therapy (see Chassin, Presson, Sherman, & Kim, 2003, for a review).

Information Campaigns

The most successful antismoking campaigns provide nonsmoking peer role models that change our idea of what behaviors are acceptable and valued (Azar, 1999). Kim Worden and Brian Flynn (1999) followed more than 5000 children in Vermont, New York, and Montana. Half the children participated in a school-based antismoking intervention program and also were exposed to a variety of radio and television commercials featuring nonsmoking role models. The other half only participated in the school program. Instead of focusing on the health hazards of smoking, the commercials featured teens who were enjoying life without smoking, who demonstrated how to refuse a cigarette, and who emphasized that most kids today don't smoke and don't approve of smoking. Four years later, children from the commercial intervention group were less likely to smoke than children who participated only in the school program.

As of September 2012, the U.S. Food and Drug Administration (FDA) mandated that cigarette packages in the United States must carry new graphic warning labels showing cancerous lesions and other impacts of smoking. The warnings cover the upper portion of the cigarette pack, both front and back. In addition, at least 20 percent of most cigarette ads must also include the approved warnings. So far, the tobacco industry has managed to delay implementation of this rule (Cohen, 2016).

Researchers have found that neuroimaging data during antismoking messages can predict behavior change, above and beyond self-reporting (Falk, Berkman, Whalen, & Lieberman, 2011). A group of 31 heavy smokers who intended to quit donned liquid crystal display (LCD) goggles and were shown 16 professionally developed TV commercials designed to help smokers quit smoking while neural activity was recorded using fMRI. The participants rated each ad on a 4-point scale, indicating the extent to which each ad promoted a sense of self-efficacy ("This ad makes me feel that I can quit"), increased intentions to quit ("This ad makes me more determined to quit"), and self-relevance ("I can relate to this ad"). One month later, the participants answered a series of questions regarding their efforts to quit smoking, and a biological verification (exhaled carbon monoxide) of their actual recent smoking. This outcome measure is important because self-reports of smoking behavior are often inaccurate due to poor recall, self-presentation concerns to appear consistent with stated intentions, and other

A proposal to ban smoking in parks and public spaces in London aims at improving the health of people living in the city and setting a better example for children.

Kathy deWitt/Alamy

cognitive biases (Pierce, 2009). The researchers found a positive relationship between neural activity in the medial prefrontal cortex (MPFC) and successful quitting (increased activity in the MPFC was associated with a greater decrease in exhaled CO).

Antismoking Campaigns and Ethnic Minorities

Antismoking campaigns have been less effective with ethnic minorities, perhaps partly because tobacco companies have targeted a disproportionate amount of advertising toward minority communities, especially the African-American and Hispanic-American communities. Non-Hispanic members of multiple races (26.8 percent), American Indian/Alaska natives (26.1 percent), and European-Americans (19.4 percent) have the highest smoking rates. The rate for African-American men is slightly lower than for those others (18.3%; CDC, 2015b) but still on the high side among the major racial/ethnic groups in the United States. African-American men also have the highest rates of death due to lung cancer—six times that of European-American men (see Chapter 11).

Overall, Hispanic men smoke at about the same rate as non-Hispanic men, while Hispanic women smoke somewhat less than non-Hispanic women and Hispanic men (CDC, 2015b). Acculturation partly explains these smoking patterns. Traditional Hispanic culture frowns upon smoking in women but not in men. In an unhealthy twist, the generally less rigid American gender roles have meant that smoking rates among more acculturated Hispanic-American women in the United States are higher than those among less acculturated women. Asian-American women and men are less likely to be current smokers than any other single-race group studied (CDC, 2015b).

Increasing Aversive Consequences

Successful primary prevention programs also strive to increase the aversive consequences of smoking. For example, increasing the tax paid on cigarettes is quite effective. Consider the experience of Canadian smokers, whose cigarette tax has increased more than 700 percent since 1980. When a pack of cigarettes costs more than $5, many teenagers think twice about smoking. The tax impact is the sharpest among teenagers, who have less disposable income and are in the age group most vulnerable to smoking behavior. According to a Health Canada survey, the smoking rate among 15- to 19-year-olds dropped to 18 percent in 2003 from 28 percent in 1999 after the tobacco tax was increased by $2.50 per carton (Canadian Tobacco Use Monitoring Survey, 2004).

The price of a pack of cigarettes in the United States increased 90 percent between 1997 and 2003, which may be part of the reason the CDC reports that the percent of high school students who smoke decreased from 36 percent to 22 percent during the same time period. To counter the arguments of those who object to increasing taxation, it is worth noting that tobacco-caused health care costs increase the average American household's federal tax bill by about $320 each year (Campaign for Tobacco-Free Kids, 2006).

Inoculation

Most effective for deterring smoking in adolescents have been "inoculation" programs that teach practical skills in resisting social pressures to smoke. Because smoking generally begins during the junior high and high school years, prevention programs are typically conducted in schools before children reach their teens.

The most successful programs are based on a *social learning model* that focuses on three variables: social pressure to begin smoking, media information, and anxiety. A program designed by Richard Evans (2003) used films, role-playing, and rehearsal to help young teens improve their social skills and refusal skills. In the films, same-age models were depicted encountering and resisting social pressure to smoke. The students also role-played situations, such as when someone is called "chicken" for not trying a cigarette. The students were instructed to give responses such as "I'd be a real chicken if I smoked just to impress you." After several sessions of "smoking inoculation" during the seventh and eighth grades, these students were only half as likely to start smoking as were those in a control group at another school, even though the parents of both groups had the same rate of smoking.

As noted in Chapter 6, multifaceted community campaigns that intervene on several fronts work better than "single-shot" campaigns. In one Midwestern county school system, two decades of antismoking campaigns have combined school intervention programs with communitywide mass media messages. The results have been gratifying. Between 1980 and 2001, among seventh- through eleventh-grade students, there has been a significant decrease in experimental and regular smoking and a shift in viewing smoking as more addictive and as having more negative social consequences (Chassin and others, 2003).

Cessation Programs

Since 1977, the American Cancer Society has sponsored the annual Great American Smokeout, in which smokers pledge to abstain from smoking for 24 hours. For many smokers, the Smokeout has been a first step in successfully quitting tobacco for good. In existence for over 20 years, "Kick Butts" is a similar program, sponsored by the Campaign for Tobacco-Free Kids, that encourages children and teenagers to avoid tobacco and attacks the image of smoking as being cool (http://kickbuttsday.org/).

Campaigns such as these, along with print and broadcast ads, no-smoking pledge drives, smoking bans, and other programs—many of which have been funded from the $226 billion tobacco settlement in 1998—appear to be working (Pierce & Gilpin, 2004). The settlement originally was between the four largest tobacco companies in the United States and the attorneys general of 46 states. In exchange for exemption from additional, private lawsuits, the tobacco industry agreed to curtail certain tobacco marketing practices and to make annual payments to the states to compensate them for some of the medical costs of caring for persons with smoking-related illnesses.

It is estimated that over 3 million deaths have been prevented as a result of people either quitting smoking or not beginning in the first place. Yet we need to continue these efforts. Each day, more than 4000 kids in the United States try their first cigarette, and 2000 other kids under 18 years of age become new, daily smokers (SAMHSA, 2009).

Smoking cessation programs generally fall into two categories: those based on an addiction model and those with cognitive behavior approaches. Programs based on an addiction model of smoking emphasize the physiological effects and habitual behavior engendered by nicotine (Henningfield, Cohen, & Pickworth, 1993). Cognitive behavior models focus on helping smokers better understand the motivation, conditioning, and other psychological processes that trigger smoking (Lando, 1986). Intervention is aimed at helping smokers develop coping skills to gain control over smoking triggers and to deal with anxiety, stress, and other emotions without smoking.

Addiction Model Treatments

A variety of pharmacological replacement therapy programs have been developed for smokers, including transdermal nicotine patches, nicotine gum, and inhalers. These *nicotine replacement programs* have helped millions of smokers in their efforts to quit smoking. Once available only as expensive prescription drugs, most now are available over the counter.

People who smoke continuously, day in and day out, are good candidates for *transdermal nicotine patches,* which have become the most common pharmacological treatment for smoking. Worn during the day, the bandage-like patches release nicotine through the skin into the bloodstream. Users are able to reduce the daily dose gradually, in a series of steps that minimize withdrawal symptoms and help ensure success in remaining smoke-free (Fiore, Smith, Jorenby, & Baker, 1994; Wetter, Fiore, Baker, & Young, 1995).

However, nicotine patches are only moderately successful as a stand-alone treatment for smoking. After 10 years of research, abstinence rates in patients using the nicotine patch have been found to be about 1.9 times higher than those observed in patients using a placebo (Corelli & Hudmon, 2002). The effectiveness of the patch varies with the user's genotype with respect to the now-familiar dopamine D_2 receptor gene. Oxford University researchers genotyped more than 750 people in 1999 and 2000. All had tried to quit smoking during an earlier clinical trial. At the eight-year mark, 12 percent of women with a particular allele of the dopamine D_2 receptor gene who had received the patch had remained abstinent. Only 5 percent of women without that D_2 receptor gene had maintained their nonsmoking status. Although the same gene variants are found in men, no differences in abstinence based on genotypes were noted (Yudkin and others, 2003).

Like all pharmacological treatments, the effectiveness of nicotine gum varies with the strength of the smoker's dependency on nicotine and his or her particular smoking habits. Nicotine gum appears to be most helpful for smokers who tend to smoke many cigarettes in a short period of time. It may be most effective when used as part of a comprehensive behavioral treatment program. Some researchers believe that the relief of withdrawal symptoms and cravings is largely a *placebo effect,* rather than a pharmacological effect of the actual nicotine in the gum. Although less effective than the nicotine patch, nicotine gum improves cessation rates by about 50 percent compared with control interventions (Davies, Willner, James, & Morgan, 2004).

Another recent intervention is the oral inhaler, a plastic tube filled with 4 milligrams of nicotine that smokers can "puff" on 2 to 10 times a day. Patients who use the nicotine inhaler are 1.7 to 3.6 times more likely to remain abstinent than patients using a placebo inhaler (Rennard and others, 2006).

A treatment option currently being investigated is *bupropion* (Zyban), a powerful antidepressant that may curb nicotine cravings by mimicking tobacco's ability to increase brain levels of dopamine (Lerman and others, 2004). Zyban's efficacy in treating nicotine addiction was discovered by accident. Researchers knew that depression was a common symptom of nicotine withdrawal, so they began experimenting with antidepressants to alleviate addiction rather than depression. Cessation rates in patients who use sustained-release bupropion are generally 2.1 times higher than those observed in patients receiving a placebo (Fiore, 2000). As a partial agonist for nicotine receptors, the newer prescription drug *varenicline* (Chantix) is even more effective than bupropion in reducing cravings for nicotine and in decreasing the pleasurable effects of tobacco use. One study of former smokers found that after one year, the rate of abstinence was 10 percent for participants who received a placebo, 15 percent for those who received bupropion, and 23 percent for those who received varenicline (Jorenby and others, 2006). Most effective is *combination therapy,* in which one intervention (such as the nicotine patch) provides steady levels of nicotine in the body and a second form (such as bupropion or varenicline) is used as needed to control cravings and suppress nicotine withdrawal symptoms (Corelli & Hudman, 2002; Piper and others, 2009).

Cognitive Behavior Treatments for Smoking

Given the importance of modeling, reinforcement, and principles of learning in the development of drug abuse, health experts rely on a number of cognitive and behavioral techniques to help people quit smoking. *Aversion therapy* involves pairing unpleasant consequences with smoking to create an aversion to smoking. In one of the most frequently used techniques, smokers increase their usual smoking rate until the point of **satiation**,

satiation A form of aversion therapy in which a smoker is forced to increase his or her smoking until an unpleasant state of "fullness" is reached.

an unpleasant state of "fullness." One variation involves *rapid smoking,* in which a smoker periodically is asked to smoke a cigarette as fast as he or she can, which often leads to an upset stomach. Both techniques are designed to associate nausea with smoking. Aversion strategies have also used electric shock and nausea-inducing drugs. For many smokers, aversion therapy is an effective way to begin to quit.

Cognitive restructuring of health beliefs and smoking attitudes is also important in successful quitting and avoiding relapse. Research studies demonstrate that those who successfully quit smoking typically change their beliefs to see less psychological benefit and more health threat from smoking, while those who relapse may come to view smoking as having *more* psychological benefits and being less of a personal threat over time (Chassin and others, 2003).

Which Smoking Cessation Programs Are Effective?

There have been relatively few randomly controlled studies examining the effectiveness of smoking cessation programs for adolescents. In general, research studies support the viewpoint that younger smokers, especially those who are heavy tobacco users, are more likely to continue smoking than older smokers (Ferguson, Bauld, Chesterman, & Judge, 2005). A meta-analysis of teen smoking cessation programs revealed that the most effective programs are inexpensive, short-term interventions that include a motivational component, cognitive behavior techniques, and social influence education (Sussman, Sun & Dent, 2006). More specifically, these programs:

- enhanced the intrinsic and extrinsic motivation to quit with rewards and education designed to reduce ambivalence about quitting;

- were tailored to adolescents' developmental needs (rather than adult programs with only superficial changes) and made intervention programs fun;

- provided social support to help teens persevere and avoid relapse; and

- showed teens how to use community resources for remaining nicotine-free.

In contrast, there is an abundance of research on adult smoking cessation efforts. These studies have found that smoking treatment programs are most effective when two or more methods are used together. For example, treatment programs that combine behavioral methods with nicotine replacement are more effective than either approach used alone (Stead, Perera, Bullen, Mant, & Lancaster, 2008). A meta-analysis of over 100 combination therapy studies concluded that smoking treatment programs that include nicotine replacement have significantly higher quit rates than those that include placebos or no nicotine replacement therapy (Silagy, Lancaster, Stead, Mant, & Fowler, 2005).

Whichever combination of techniques is used, Edward Lichtenstein and Russell Glasgow (1997) of the Oregon Research Institute argue that quitting smoking is determined by three interacting factors: motivation to quit, level of physical dependence on nicotine, and barriers to or supports in remaining smoke-free (Figure 9.7). The extent of a smoker's physical dependence, for example, certainly will influence both readiness to quit and persistence. The presence or absence of a smoking spouse, workplace smoking bans, a child pressuring a parent to quit, and other barriers and supports also may influence motivation (Hammond, McDonald, Fong, Brown, & Cameron, 2004).

James Prochaska (1996a) suggests that many smoking cessation programs dilute their effectiveness by targeting multiple

FIGURE 9.7

Factors in Smoking Cessation According to this model, readiness motivation is the primary, proximal causal factor in determining whether a person makes a serious attempt to quit. Social and environmental supports or prompts, such as a workplace no-smoking policy, increases in the price of tobacco, persistent reminders from one's child to stop smoking, or a physician's advice, also can affect readiness motivation.

Information from Lichtenstein, E., & Glasgow, R. E. (1997). A pragmatic framework for smoking cessation. *Psychology of Addictive Behaviors, 11*(2), 142–151 (Figure 1).

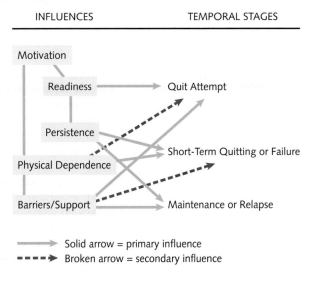

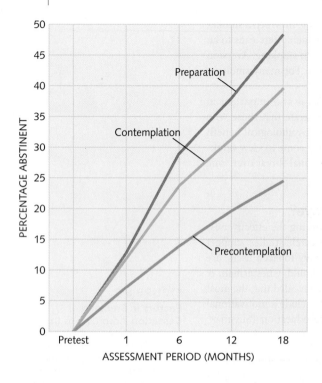

FIGURE 9.8
Percentage of Abstinent Former Smokers by Stage of Quitting The amount of progress that former smokers make in remaining abstinent is directly related to the stage they were in at the start of the intervention. Smokers in the precontemplation phase display the smallest amount of abstinence from smoking over 18 months, whereas those in the preparation stage show the most progress in 6-, 12-, and 18-month follow-ups.

Data from Prochaska, J. O. (1996). Revolution in health promotion: Smoking cessation as a case study. In R. J. Resnick & R. H. Rozensky (Eds.), *Health psychology through the life span: Practice and research opportunities* (pp. 361–375). Washington, DC: American Psychological Association.

behavioral activation A counseling treatment that focuses on increasing engagement in valued life activities through guided goal setting.

behaviors and failing to recognize that different smokers have different needs. Prochaska proposes, instead, that planned interventions be organized according to each smoker's stage of quitting. His transtheoretical model outlines six stages of behavior change: (1) precontemplation, (2) contemplation, (3) preparation, (4) action, (5) maintenance, and (6) termination. Smokers in the precontemplation stage, for example, are often defensive and resistant to action-oriented programs. They often are demoralized by previous failures to quit smoking and consequently are put off by information campaigns condemning their unhealthy behavior. Historically, health experts considered such people as unmotivated or not ready for therapy. Prochaska, however, would suggest that treatment for people at this stage include reassurance that becoming a nonsmoker—like becoming a smoker in the first place—is not something that happens overnight. Rather, there are stages in its development, and many smokers who attempt to quit are not successful the first time.

The stage approach has several advantages over traditional, nonstage interventions. First, it generates a much higher rate of participation. When free smoking clinics are provided by health maintenance organizations (HMOs), only about 1 percent of subscribers participate. Using the stage approach in two home-based interventions involving 5000 smokers each, Prochaska and his colleagues (2006) generated remarkably high participation rates of 82 to 85 percent. A second strength of stage-based interventions is a dramatic improvement in the number of participants who complete the treatment (retention rate). Other researchers have also reported high retention rates when treatment is individualized according to a stage approach (Aveyard, Johnson, Fillingham, Parsons, & Murphy, 2008; Armitage & Arden, 2008).

The third advantage of stage-based approaches is the most important: Progress in remaining smoke-free is directly related to the stage participants were in at the start of the interventions. This *stage effect* is illustrated in Figure 9.8. It shows that smokers in the precontemplation phase displayed the smallest amount of abstinence from smoking over 18 months, whereas those in the preparation stage showed the most progress in 6-, 12-, and 18-month follow-ups. As discussed in Chapter 2, stage-based interventions proceed in a gradual series of steps, with the reasonable goal of helping smokers advance one stage at a time.

Valued Life Activities and Quitting

You may recall from Chapter 7 that I was able to quit smoking largely because it interfered with my desire to run a marathon and be identified as "a runner." Several lines of evidence suggest that the restriction of valued activities affects smoking and other health-compromising behaviors. First, low levels of engagement in valued activities (such as swimming, cycling, and running), restriction of valued activities due to physical condition (such as injuries), and the inability to find replacements for restricted valued activities have been linked to depressed mood (Manos, Kanter, & Busch, 2010). Depressed mood, in turn, is more common among smokers and interferes with efforts to quit. **Behavioral activation,** a counseling treatment that focuses on increasing engagement in valued life activities through guided goal setting, has shown promise as a tool in helping smokers quit (Banducci, Long, & MacPherson, 2014).

Smoking cessation among people with physical disabilities that cause impairment in mobility has been relatively neglected by researchers, despite the fact that cigarette smoking is more common among this group, with rates as high as 40 percent among nonelderly adults (Altman & Bernstein, 2008). Could it be that restriction of valued life activities due to physical limitations is a barrier to quitting in this population? The answer, according to the findings of a recent study of long-term smokers with physical disabilities, is "yes." The study found that participants' readiness to quit smoking was enhanced by an educational intervention that helped identify satisfactory replacements for their most valued restricted activity (Busch & Borrelli, 2012).

Relapse: Back to the Habit

Unfortunately, only a small percentage of people who quit remain smoke-free for very long. Attempts to quit, even within the first weeks of smoking, often fail (DiFranza, 2008). As with other addictions, smokers become *dependent*, and they develop *tolerance*. Quitting triggers withdrawal symptoms, including craving, anxiety, irritability, distractibility, and insomnia (Sayette, Loewenstein, Griffin, & Black, 2008). All it takes to relieve this unpleasant state is the negative reinforcement provided by a cigarette. Within seven seconds, the rush of nicotine causes the brain to release epinephrine, norepinephrine, dopamine, and other neurotransmitters that boost alertness and calm anxiety.

The rewards that nicotine delivers keep people smoking, even among the 8 in 10 smokers who say they'd like to quit. Of these smokers, fewer than 1 in 10 are able to do so, and as many as 80 percent of smokers who quit smoking relapse within 1 year (USDHHS, 2012). Many factors are involved in relapse, the most fundamental being the severity of withdrawal symptoms and craving. In one study of 72 long-term smokers (38 men and 34 women), 48 percent relapsed within the first week of quitting. Participants who relapsed experienced greater distress and withdrawal symptoms during the first 24 hours of nicotine abstinence (al'Absi, Hatsukama, Davis, & Wittmers, 2004). Interestingly, the researchers found that stressful experiences affect men and women who are trying to quit smoking differently. For instance, cortisol responses before and after performing a public-speaking test were stronger in the men than in the women.

Ex-smokers may experience other side effects as well, which are immediately eliminated by a return to smoking. For example, some ex-smokers gain weight (perhaps because of slower metabolism, increased preference for sweet-tasting foods, or substituting eating for smoking), have trouble sleeping, are more irritable, and find it difficult to concentrate. Unfortunately, smoking is even used as a weight-control strategy—particularly by adolescents who are also likely to use other unhealthy strategies, such as diet pills and laxatives (Jenks & Higgs, 2007).

Another factor in relapse is the strength of previously conditioned associations to smoking. Smoking behaviors, as well as nicotine's physiological effects, become conditioned to a variety of environmental stimuli. Many ex-smokers relapse in the face of an irresistible urge (conditioned response) to smoke in certain situations or environments—for example, with that first cup of coffee in the morning or after a meal.

Because of this dismal prognosis for ex-smokers, smoking relapse has received considerable research attention in recent years. A working conference sponsored by the National Institutes of Health (NIH) took a first step in addressing the relapse problem by encouraging health experts to adopt a "stages of change" (see Figure 6.4) model in developing programs to prevent relapse. For example, rather than encouraging ex-smokers to attend an occasional follow-up session reminding them of the hazards of smoking, the NIH group encouraged training in relapse prevention strategies much earlier in the stages of quitting.

Efforts such as these are paying off, and smokers are getting the message that repeated attempts to quit can succeed (see Your Health Assets: You Can Quit Smoking—Here's How), and success is equally likely whether they quit abruptly or gradually (USDHHS, 2012). After a year's abstinence from nicotine, only 1 in 10 will relapse in the next year

Your Health Assets

You Can Quit Smoking—Here's How

Smokers often say, "Don't tell me why I should quit—tell me how." There is no one right way to quit, but four factors are key: *deciding to quit, establishing a plan and setting a day to quit, developing strategies to deal with withdrawal,* and *maintaining your success.*

Prepare the way for quitting:

- Select a specific date to quit.
- Eliminate cigarettes and ashtrays around you.
- Find replacements for cigarettes such as sugarless gum and other oral substitutes.
- Create a plan. Will you use nicotine-replacement therapy?
- Get social support: Find friends or anyone who will be a support person for you.

On your specific quitting day, do the following:

- Avoid any smoking at all!
- Keep active by walking, exercising, or doing other activities you enjoy.
- Drink lots of water and juices—staying hydrated is key.
- Begin using nicotine replacement if you have chosen to do so.
- Stay away from people who are smoking.
- Stay away from places or situations where you may be tempted to smoke.
- Attend a stop-smoking class, or follow your self-help plan.

(Hughes, 2010). Researchers will continue to study all aspects of substance abuse in an effort to help many more of us become "former users"—or, better yet, to avoid altogether the life disruption that substance abuse brings.

The Rise of e-Cigarettes and the Resurgence of Marijuana

n this final section of the chapter, we turn to two recent developments that merit special attention: the rise of electronic cigarettes and the resurgence of marijuana.

Electronic Cigarettes

electronic or e-cigarettes (EC) battery-powered vaporizers that simulate smoking without burning tobacco.

Introduced in 2004, **electronic,** or **e-cigarettes (EC)** are battery-powered vaporizers that simulate smoking without burning tobacco. Consisting of a liquid-filled cartridge (e-juice) and a heating element, e-cigarettes deliver nicotine, along with flavorings and other chemicals, as an aerosol instead of smoke. The user activates the device by taking a puff or pressing a button and inhaling the atomized nicotine (*vaping*).

Manufacturers of e-cigarettes make the devices in many shapes, including some that look like traditional cigarettes and pipes, but also some that look like everyday items such as pens and USB flash drives. E-cigarettes also come in more than 7000 flavors, including some—such as mint, candy, and bubble gum—that likely are targeted to the tastes of younger users (Grana, Ling, Benowitz, & Glantz, 2014). This new industry has become an enormous business: Sales of e-cigarettes were about $3.5 billion in 2015 (Szabo, 2015).

In 2014, 12.6 percent of adults in the United States reported having tried e-cigarettes (see Figure 9.9), and about 3.7 percent are current users (Schoenborn & Gindi, 2015). Most EC users still smoke regular cigarettes, but a 2014 study found that more teens in the United States used e-cigarettes in the past 30 days than any other tobacco product, including traditional cigarettes (MTF, 2015).

There are several reasons e-cigarettes are a cause for concern. First, because they deliver vapor without burning tobacco, e-cigarettes may appear to be safer and less toxic than smoking conventional cigarettes (Drummond & Upson, 2014). Although they do not produce tobacco smoke, e-cigarettes still contain nicotine, which is, as we have seen, a highly addictive drug and has a wide range of harmful effects.

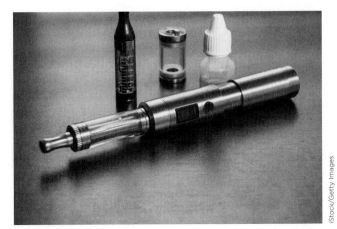

iStock/Getty Images

The Components of an e-Cigarette A battery-powered vaporizer consisting of a liquid-filled cartridge and a heating element.

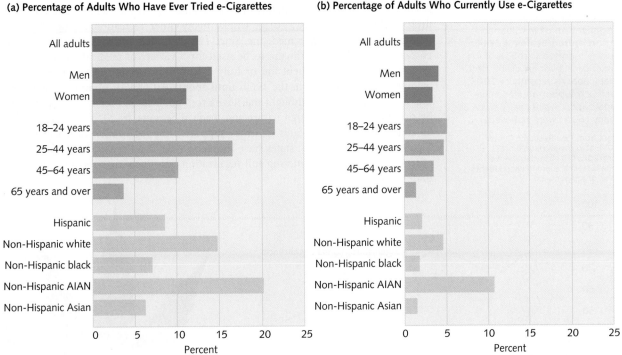

(a) Percentage of Adults Who Have Ever Tried e-Cigarettes

(b) Percentage of Adults Who Currently Use e-Cigarettes

FIGURE 9.9

E-Cigarette Usage Men are more likely than women to have ever tried e-cigarettes but are not more likely to be current users. Younger adults are more likely than older adults to have tried e-cigarettes and to currently use e-cigarettes. Both non-Hispanic AIAN (American Indian or Alaska native) and non-Hispanic white adults are more likely than non-Hispanic black, non-Hispanic Asian, and Hispanic adults to have ever tried e-cigarettes and to be current e-cigarette users

Data from Schoenborn, C. A., & Gindi, R. M. (2015). Electronic cigarette use among adults: United States, 2014. *NCHS Data Brief, No. 217*.

Vaping exposes smokers to harmful substances such as formaldehyde and acetaldehyde—two known carcinogens.

Another worry is that vaping exposes smokers to other harmful substances. E-cigarette vapor may contain formaldehyde and acetaldehyde—two known carcinogens—as well as toxic metal nanoparticles released from the heating element (National Institute on Drug Abuse, 2015). Harvard University researchers recently tested 51 types of flavoring used in e-liquids and found that most of them contained also *diacetyl* and *acetoin,* chemicals that may cause severe lung disease (Allen and others, 2015).

In addition to these issues, several studies suggest that e-cigarette use may encourage the use of other tobacco products (Leventhal and others, 2015). One study showed that students who had used e-cigarettes by the ninth grade were more likely than their non-vaping peers to start smoking traditional cigarettes within one year (Rigotti, 2015). That finding alone should create serious concerns about the rise of electronic cigarettes. Sadly, an even more recent Yale University study of teens who use e-cigarettes cited the low cost of the devices and the promise that vaping can help teens quit smoking as strong predictors of continued use (Barrington-Trimis and others, 2016).

The Resurgence of Marijuana

FIGURE 9.10

Growing Support for Legalization of Marijuana in the United States A 2014 survey reported that 53% of Americans favor legalizing marijuana. As recently as 2006, just 32% supported marijuana legalization, while nearly twice as many (60%) were opposed.

Data from Pew Research Center 2014: http://www.people-press.org/2015/04/14/in-debate-over-legalizing-marijuana-disagreement-over-drugs-dangers/

According to the World Health Organization, cannabis is the most popular recreational drug worldwide (UNODC, 2015). Unlike many other recreational drugs, however, marijuana is also used as a medicine. Since 1996, 23 states and Washington, DC, have passed laws allowing marijuana to be used for a variety of medical conditions, and 17 have reduced punishment for, or fully legalized, possession of small recreational amounts of the drug. From the 1960s until about 2010, public opinion polls showed that a majority of adults thought marijuana (or "pot") should remain illegal. Spurred by rising claims of its benign nature and medical benefits, by 2014 more than half of all adults in the United States said they supported the legalization of marijuana (see Figure 9.10). While many states have loosened older laws regarding marijuana and others are seriously considering full legalization, marijuana use remains an offense under U.S. federal law.

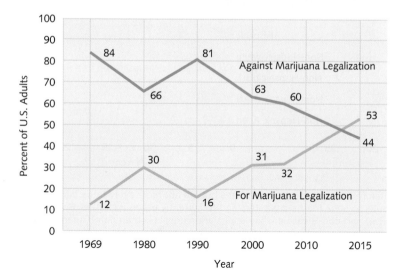

Marijuana: Some Basics about Its Source, How It Is Used, and Its Physical Effects

Marijuana comes from the dried leaves, flowers, stems, and seeds of the hemp plant *Cannabis sativa,* all of which contain the mild hallucinogen THC (*delta-9-tetrahydrocannabinol*). A synthetic form of marijuana, called *K2* or *Spice,* mimics THC. In addition to THC, marijuana contains more than 100 other chemical *cannabinoids.* Marijuana can be smoked in hand-rolled cigarettes (*joints*), water pipes (*bongs*), or emptied cigars refilled with the drug (*blunts*). It can also be inhaled from a vaporizer (*vaping*), added to food (*edibles*), and brewed as a tea. A dangerous new method, *dabbing,* involves smoking or eating THC-rich resins that have been extracted from marijuana using butane (lighter fluid), which can cause serious burns, fires, and explosions.

Marijuana has both short- and long-term effects on the brain (see Figure 9.11). When inhaled, THC quickly passes from the lungs into the bloodstream, which carries the chemical to the brain (in under 10 seconds) and organs throughout the body. THC is absorbed more slowly when eaten, and its effects are typically felt after about 30 minutes to 1 hour. In the brain, THC binds to cannabinoid receptor type 1 (CB1) proteins that ordinarily react to natural THC-like chemicals in the brain. These natural chemicals, called *endocannabinoids,* are involved in pain perception, memory, mood, and appetite regulation, and also play an important role in brain maturation. This brain maturation issue is of special concern to those who question the wisdom of legalizing marijuana, as I'll point out in the next section.

THC has many effects on the brain and behavior, including alterations in mood, time perception, and sensations (for example, seeing brighter colors); and impaired thinking, problem-solving and memory. Like alcohol, marijuana also relaxes, disinhibits, and may produce a euphoric high. Unlike alcohol, which is metabolized and eliminated from the body within hours, THC can remain in the body for more than a week. As a result, regular marijuana users are less likely to experience abrupt withdrawal from the drug and may get high with smaller drug amounts than needed when they first used the drug.

The Debate over Legalization

Some people think pot is nothing less than a gift from nature: a nonaddictive drug that lifts the spirit, is safe at any dose, and has important medical applications. Others portray the drug as dangerous, addictive, and with a high potential for abuse. Who is right? Let's take a look at some of the evidence on both sides of the argument.

Medical marijuana refers to using the plant or its extracts to treat a disease or symptom. Although the FDA has not approved marijuana as medicine, two THC-based drugs, *dronabinol* and *nabilone,* have been approved to relieve the pain and nausea caused by AIDS and

FIGURE 9.11

How Marijuana Affects the Brain Marijuana has both short- and long-term effects on many regions of the brain. Additional research is needed to more fully understand these effects, particularly how marijuana use impacts brain maturation during adolescence.

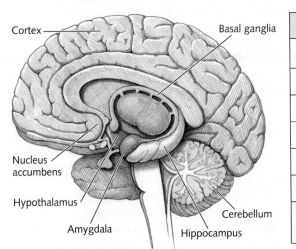

Brain Area	Potential Effects of THC
Amygdala	altered emotions; anxiety and panic in some cases
Basal ganglia	impaired motor skills and learning
Cerebellum	impaired coordination and balance
Cortex	altered consciousness, perceptual distortions
Hippocampus	impaired memory storage recall
Hypothalamus	altered metabolic process such as increased appetite
Nucleus accumbens	euphoria; altered motivation and decision making

cancer, and to increase appetite in patients with AIDS wasting syndrome (Munsey, 2010). THC-based drugs may also help treat seizures and spasticity related to epilepsy and multiple sclerosis, while a related compound called *cannabidiol* (CBD) may be useful in treating auto-immune diseases, inflammation, pain, and substance use disorders (Seppa, 2010).

Advocates for legalizing marijuana (for medical or recreational use) argue that doing so may have important public health benefits, such as reducing the risk of overdoses from other drugs. They point to evidence that death rates from overdoses on prescription painkillers, heroin, and other illicit drugs average 24.8 percent lower in states with medical marijuana laws than in states without similar laws (Bachhuber and others, 2014).

Opponents of legalizing marijuana fear that wider recreational use will adversely affect public health. Case in point: driver safety. Marijuana use has been linked to increased accident risk, likely reflecting marijuana's disruptive effects on motor coordination and time perception. One study estimated that cannabis intoxication doubles a driver's risk of an automobile accident (Asbridge, Hayden, & Cartwright, 2012). Some states have expanded their DUI laws to include cannabis intoxication. Washington and Colorado, where marijuana use was legalized in 2012, have a 5-nanogram limit on the level of THC in a driver's blood. Oregon doesn't use blood testing and instead relies on police officers' observations (Kullgren, 2014).

While most experts agree that marijuana is not nearly as addictive as alcohol, tobacco, and opioids, THC does seem to reduce the number of CB_1 receptors in the brains of people who use marijuana daily. This may explain why about 1 user in 10 struggles to stop using marijuana and does show signs of becoming dependent on the drug (Hirvonen, Goodwin, & Innis, 2012). Among people who begin using pot as teens, the number showing signs of developing dependency seems to increase to about 1 in 6 (Lopez-Quintero and others, 2011). Heavy, regular users also show signs of developing tolerance for THC, as they need to increase their dose over time to experience the same effects. Some users also experience anxiety and irritability—two other features of addiction according to DSM-5—after stopping heavy use of THC (National Institute on Drug Abuse, 2016).

As to the safety of marijuana, critics of the legalization movement argue that while the drug may not be deadly, it is far from harmless. Marijuana smoke irritates the lungs and contributes to the same breathing problems that tobacco smokers experience, including more frequent lung infections and disease. THC also increases the heart rate for several hours after smoking, which may increase the risk of heart attacks. Marijuana use during pregnancy has been linked to increased risk of brain and behavior problems in babies (National Institute on Drug Abuse, 2016).

In Colorado, where marijuana laws have been loosened for both medical and recreational use, emergency room doctors, law enforcement officers, and legalization opponents have pointed to recent problems, such as rising numbers of marijuana-impaired traffic citations, as cautionary lessons for other states considering more lenient cannabis laws. Proponents of legalization note that the overall rate of crime in the state is down by 10 percent since legalization for recreational use went into effect in 2014 and say critics are cherry-picking statistics to undermine a new industry that is flourishing despite intense scrutiny (Healy, 2014).

Opponents of legalization also note that the amount of THC in marijuana has been increasing steadily over the past few decades. Marijuana legally sold in Colorado, for instance, contains three times as much THC as did plants grown 30 years ago (Mole, 2015). This greater potency may help explain the rise in emergency room visits involving marijuana. The growing popularity of edibles also increases the chance of harmful reactions. Because edibles take longer to produce a high, users may consume more to feel the effects faster, leading to dangerous results.

Perhaps the biggest concern is the potential impact on teenagers, a decreasing number of whom believe that marijuana use is risky (Johnston and others, 2014). As we have seen, the adolescent brain is still growing and refining its neural networks—processes regulated in part by the natural endocannabinoid system in the cortex. Marijuana use at this vulnerable time may interfere with healthy brain development. Indeed, research has shown that young adults, ages 18 to 25, who use marijuana at least once a week are more likely than nonusers to have structural differences in two brain areas: the nucleus accumbens and the amygdala (Gilman, Kuster, & Breiter, 2014). Heavy use of THC for 20 years or more may also damage the corpus callosum (Rigucci and others, 2015), lead to a reduced volume of gray matter, and shrinkage of cortical areas that process memory (Filbey and others, 2014). However, other researchers are skeptical of the evidence that THC use harms the brain (Rogeberg, 2013; Weiland and others, 2015).

Marijuana use does seem to affect memory, language proficiency, and motivation—all of which are especially important during adolescence and emerging adulthood. Teens who use marijuana heavily are more likely to perform poorly in school and have other problems (Ansary & Luthar, 2009). One study reported that people who started using marijuana heavily as teenagers and had an ongoing cannabis use disorder lost an average of eight IQ points between ages 13 and 38 (Meier and others, 2012). In addition, the more often marijuana is used, especially during adolescence, the greater the risk of anxiety, depression, or addiction (Hurd, Michaelides, Miller, & Jutras-Aswad, 2014). Heavy cannabis use in early adolescence may even accelerate the onset of schizophrenia (Hill, 2015).

Although laws are changing, the biggest obstacle to truly understanding the potential risks and benefits of cannabis is the fact that research has been stifled by years of prohibition and misconceptions about the plant and its active compounds (Grayson, 2015). Major gaps in knowledge continue to exist. For example, while a recent meta-analysis of cannabinoids for medical use supported their use in treating chronic pain and muscle spasticity, other claims about the benefits of THC and CBD were less well supported (Whiting and others, 2015). Until medical marijuana is made a public health priority and more research funding is made available, these knowledge gaps are unlikely to close. In addition to further research, the effects of the recent legalization of recreational marijuana in Colorado, Washington State, and elsewhere will be instructive. The experience of those states should provide a better sense of the social and public health impacts of this policy change.

Shopping at the Marijuana Store An array of marijuana-infused products beckons, from energy shots and brownies to sour gummies. And if you're 21 or older, it's legal to buy in Colorado.

Denver Post/Getty Images

Weigh In on Health

Respond to each question below based on what you learned in the chapter. (**Tip:** Use the items in "Summing Up" to take into account related biological, psychological, and social concerns.)

1. A classmate questions whether a mutual friend is addicted to cocaine. What would you be able to tell the classmate about what addiction is, and how a psychoactive drug like cocaine might affect your friend?

2. You just found out that your cousin, a senior in high school, started smoking cigarettes when she was a sophomore.

Now she's addicted to smoking but wants to quit before she goes off to college. Based on what you read in this chapter, how would you advise her? What if she asked you whether e-cigarette vaping was a safe alternative to smoking cigarettes?

3. Some states have attempted to criminalize drug use during pregnancy or treat it as grounds for terminating parental rights. Should it be illegal for a pregnant woman to purchase or use alcohol or tobacco products? Why or why not?

Summing Up

Some Basic Facts

1. Drug abuse is the use of a chemical substance to the extent that it impairs the user's well-being in any domain of health: biological, psychological, or social. During pregnancy, many drugs will cross the placenta and act as teratogens to adversely affect fetal development.

2. Drugs affect behavior by influencing the activity of neurons at their synapses. Some (agonists and, to a lesser extent, partial agonists) do so by mimicking natural neurotransmitters, others (antagonists) by blocking their action, and still others by enhancing or inhibiting the reuptake of neurotransmitters in the synapse.

3. Substance use disorder is a behavior pattern characterized by overwhelming involvement with the use of a drug despite its adverse consequences.

4. Psychoactive drugs act on the central nervous system to alter emotional and cognitive functioning. Stimulants, such as caffeine and cocaine, increase activity in the central nervous system and produce feelings of euphoria. Depressants, such as alcohol and the opiates, reduce activity in the central nervous system and produce feelings of relaxation. Hallucinogenic drugs, such as marijuana and LSD, alter perception and distort reality.

Models of Addiction

5. Biomedical models propose that dependence is a chronic disease that produces abnormal physical functioning. One aspect of these models is based on evidence that some people inherit a biological vulnerability toward dependence. The withdrawal-relief hypothesis suggests that drugs deplete dopamine and other key neurotransmitters. Another model proposes that psychoactive drugs are habit-forming because they overstimulate the brain's dopamine reward system.

6. Reward models suggest that the pleasurable effects of psychoactive drugs provide the initial motivation for their repeated use. All major drugs of abuse overstimulate the brain's reward system.

7. Most adolescents experiment with drugs, especially tobacco and alcohol. Age, gender, parental factors, community, and national culture each have a powerful influence on drug use in adolescence.

8. Fear of addiction and antidrug campaigns that use scare tactics may not persuade young adolescents to avoid drug use—they may even backfire.

Alcohol Use and Abuse

9. Alcohol depresses activity in the nervous system, clouds judgment, and is linked to a variety of diseases. Alcohol is also involved in half of all traffic accidents. Genes play a role in alcohol dependence, especially in men. Psychosocial factors such as peer pressure, a difficult home environment, and tension reduction may contribute to problem drinking.

10. The prevalence of drinking varies with ethnic and cultural background. Individuals marked by behavioral undercontrol and negative emotionality are especially prone to alcohol dependence. Alcohol's impact depends in part on the user's personality, mood, past experiences with the drug, and expectations regarding its effects.

11. Alcohol use disorder is defined by several specific behaviors, including the need for daily use of alcohol, the inability to cut down on drinking despite repeated efforts to do so, binge drinking, loss of memory while intoxicated, and continued drinking despite known health problems.

12. Alcohol treatment usually begins with detoxification from alcohol under medical supervision. Counseling, psychotherapy, and support groups such as Alcoholics Anonymous (AA) also may help. Pharmacological treatments for alcohol dependence include aversion therapy, which triggers nausea if alcohol is consumed. Antidepressants such as Prozac may help reduce alcohol cravings.

Tobacco Use and Abuse

13. Cigarette smoking is the single most preventable cause of death in the Western world today. A stimulant that affects virtually every physical system in the body, nicotine induces powerful physical dependence and a withdrawal syndrome. Social pressures most often influence the initiation of smoking.

14. Once a person begins smoking, a variety of psychological, behavioral, social, and biological variables contribute to make it difficult to abstain from nicotine. According to the nicotine-titration model, long-term smokers may smoke to maintain a constant level of nicotine in their bodies. Smoking prevention programs that focus on refusal skills and other inoculation techniques prior to the eighth grade may be the best solution to the public health problems associated with smoking.

15. The most successful antismoking advertisements provide culturally sensitive nonsmoking peer role models that shift people's overall image of what behaviors are "normal" and valuable within one's peer group.

16. No single treatment has proved most effective in helping smokers quit smoking. Most programs have an extremely high relapse rate. Modern treatments for smoking deal with psychological factors through relapse prevention, and physiological factors through nicotine replacement.

The Rise of E-Cigarettes and the Resurgence of Marijuana

17. E-cigarettes are battery-powered vaporizers that simulate smoking without burning tobacco. Because they deliver vapor without burning tobacco, e-cigarettes may appear to be safer and less toxic than smoking conventional cigarettes.

18. Vaping e-cigarettes exposes smokers to other harmful substances, including formaldehyde and acetaldehyde—two known carcinogens—as well as toxic metal nanoparticles released from the heating element.

19. Spurred by rising claims of marijuana's benign nature and new laws loosening restrictions on medical and recreational use, more than half of all adults in the United States now support legalizing the drug.

20. Marijuana comes from the hemp plant *Cannabis sativa*, which contains the mild hallucinogen THC (*delta-9-tetrahydrocannabinol*). THC has many effects on brain and behavior, including alterations in mood, time perception, and sensations; and impaired thinking, problem-solving and memory.

21. While most experts agree that marijuana is not nearly as addictive as many other drugs, THC may reduce the number of CB_1 receptors in the brains of people who use marijuana daily, leading to tolerance and dependence.

22. Marijuana use may adversely affect memory, language proficiency, and motivation—all of which are especially important during adolescence and emerging adulthood. Heavy use of TCH for 20 years or more may also damage the corpus callosum, lead to a reduced volume of gray matter and shrinkage of cortical areas that process memory.

Key Terms and Concepts to Remember

drug abuse, p. 244
blood–brain barrier, p. 246
teratogens, p. 246
agonist, p. 246
antagonist, p. 246
substance use disorder, p. 246
dependence, p. 246
withdrawal, p. 247
psychoactive drugs, p. 248
drug potentiation, p. 249

concordance rate, p. 249
gateway drug, p. 250
common liability to addiction, p. 251
wanting-and-liking theory, p. 251
blood alcohol level (BAL), p. 253
at-risk drinking, p. 254
Korsakoff's syndrome, p. 256
fetal alcohol syndrome (FAS), p. 256
behavioral disinhibition, p. 257
alcohol myopia, p. 257

alcohol use disorder (AUD), p. 258
behavioral undercontrol, p. 259
negative emotionality, p. 259
alcohol expectancy effects, p. 259
aversion therapy, p. 260
nicotine-titration model, p. 266
satiation, p. 270
behavioral activation, p. 272
electronic, or e-cigarettes (EC), p. 274

LaunchPad
macmillan learning

To accompany your textbook, you have access to a number of online resources, including quizzes for every chapter of the book, flashcards, critical thinking exercises, videos, and *Check Your Health* inventories. To access these resources, please visit the Straub *Health Psychology* LaunchPad solo at: **launchpadworks.com**

PART 4 Chronic and Life-Threatening Illnesses

CHAPTER 10

Cardiovascular Disease and Diabetes

B ryan McIver, M.D., a dedicated young endocrinologist at the Mayo Clinic, was driving to his laboratory to check on an experiment. He thought nothing of the mild case of indigestion that he'd been feeling since having a curry dinner with some friends. Mild stomach acidity was something he often experienced, so it seemed like a normal night.

When he arrived at the hospital, he again felt some discomfort in his chest, but he ignored it. When he walked past the emergency room three minutes later, however, things changed dramatically. In his words, "the world went blank ... and I died."

What happened was a sudden and complete blockage of one of his heart's main coronary blood vessels. Within seconds, McIver's heart floundered into a chaotic rhythm, his blood pressure dropped to zero, the oxygen supply to his brain was cut off, and he passed into unconsciousness.

When the brain doesn't have oxygen, it begins to die within about three minutes. After six minutes, brain death occurs, and there is almost no chance for recovery. This would almost certainly have happened to McIver had his heart attack happened a minute earlier, as he strolled through the darkened parking lot, or a minute later, once he'd reached the seclusion of his laboratory. Miraculously, he collapsed in the hospital corridor, just a few feet from the emergency room.

As a 37-year-old nonsmoker with no history of high blood pressure, vascular disease, or diabetes, McIver hardly fit the typical profile of a cardiac patient. Although one grandmother had died of a stroke (in her eighties), his family is generally long lived. McIver did have some risk factors. Although he was not overweight (6 feet 1 inch tall, 197 pounds), he rarely exercised, had a high-stress job, and had unhealthy cholesterol levels. Even so, less than a month before his heart attack, McIver had been given a clean bill of health during a thorough physical exam. He was told only to try to exercise a bit more and lose a pound or two. Yet here he was, being resuscitated from the near-death experience of a massive heart attack.

Although he continues his high-pressure work as a medical researcher, McIver has taken steps to improve his coronary risk factor profile to ensure that he lives a long, healthy life. Many other people, however, are far less fortunate, and cardiovascular disease remains the number one cause of death in the United States and in the developed world.

I n this chapter, we will consider the biological, psychological, and social risk factors in two major chronic illnesses: cardiovascular disease (including high blood pressure, stroke, and heart disease) and diabetes. Although some of the risk factors in these diseases are beyond our control, many reflect lifestyle choices that are modifiable. Because each of these disorders involves the circulatory system, let's first review how the heart and circulatory system should work, and then take a look at what goes wrong when each of these diseases strikes.

The Healthy Heart

A s you'll recall from Chapter 3, the cardiovascular system comprises the blood, the blood vessels of the circulatory system, and the heart. About the size of your clenched fist and weighing on average only about 11 ounces, the heart consists of three layers of tissue: a thin outer layer, called the *epicardium;* a thin inner layer, called the *endocardium;* and a thicker middle layer, the heart muscle itself, or *myocardium* (derived from the Greek roots *myo* [muscle] and *kardia* [heart]). The myocardium is separated into four chambers that work in coordinated fashion to bring blood into the heart and then to pump it throughout the body. Like all muscles in the body, the myocardium needs a steady supply of oxygen and nutrients to remain healthy. And the harder the heart is forced to work to meet the demands of other muscles in the body, the more nutrients and oxygen it needs.

In one of Mother Nature's greatest ironies, the heart's blood supply comes not from the 5 or more quarts of blood pumped each minute through the internal chambers of the heart, but rather from two branches of the aorta (the major artery from the heart) lying on the surface of the epicardium. These left and right *coronary arteries* branch into smaller and smaller blood vessels called *arterioles* until they become the capillaries that supply the myocardium with the blood it needs to function. (See p. 65 in Chapter 3 for a diagram of the heart and the flow of blood through it.)

Cardiovascular Disease

cardiovascular disease (CVD) Disorders of the heart and blood vessel system, including stroke and coronary heart disease (CHD).

W hen the blood supply from the coronary arteries is impeded beyond a critical point, the risk of developing cardiovascular disease increases substantially. About 60 million Americans suffer from some kind of disorder of the heart and blood vessel system, collectively referred to as **cardiovascular disease (CVD).** Leading all diseases in killing nearly one of every 4 people (23.6 percent of all deaths) each year in the United

States, CVD appears in many guises, including stroke and **coronary heart disease (CHD),** a chronic illness in which the arteries that supply the heart become narrowed or clogged and cannot supply enough blood to the heart (Heron, 2015). Before discussing the biological, social, and psychological factors that contribute to the onset of these diseases, we need to describe their underlying physical causes: atherosclerosis and arteriosclerosis.

The Causes: Atherosclerosis and Arteriosclerosis

Most cases of CVD result from **atherosclerosis,** a condition in which the linings of the arteries thicken with an accumulation of cholesterol and other fats. As these **atheromatous plaques** develop, the arterial passageways become narrowed, impeding the flow of blood through the coronary arteries (Figure 10.1). Although plaques tend to develop in most people in their thirties and forties, these plaques will not threaten their health—at least not until age 70 or older. Those not so fortunate, like Bryan McIver, may develop damaging plaques as early as their twenties or thirties—or even younger.

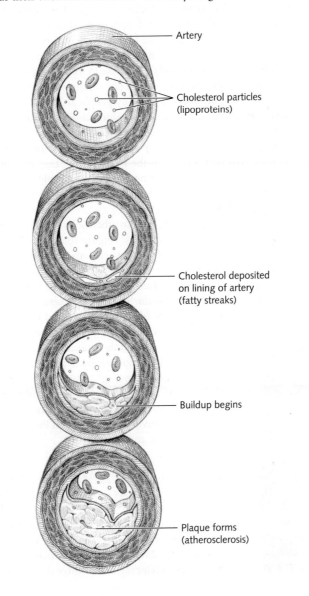

Artery

Cholesterol particles (lipoproteins)

Cholesterol deposited on lining of artery (fatty streaks)

Buildup begins

Plaque forms (atherosclerosis)

coronary heart disease (CHD) A chronic disease in which the arteries that supply the heart become narrowed or clogged; results from either atherosclerosis or arteriosclerosis.

atherosclerosis A chronic disease in which cholesterol and other fats are deposited on the inner walls of the coronary arteries, reducing circulation to heart tissue.

atheromatous plaques Buildups of fatty deposits within the wall of an artery that occur in atherosclerosis.

FIGURE 10.1

Atherosclerosis Atherosclerosis is a common disease in which cholesterol and other fats are deposited on the walls of coronary arteries. As the vessel walls become thick and hardened, they narrow, reducing the circulation to areas normally supplied by the artery. Atherosclerotic plaques cause many disorders of the circulatory system. How atherosclerosis begins is not clear; possibly, injury to the artery causes scavenger macrophages to attack cholesterol deposits.

FIGURE 10.2

Arteriosclerosis In arteriosclerosis, the coronary arteries
lose their elasticity and are unable
to expand and contract as blood
flows through them.

© J & L Weber/Peter Arnold

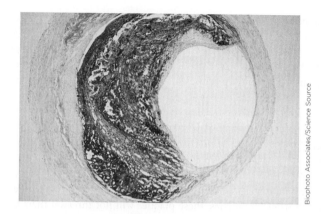

Biophoto Associates/Science Source

atherogenesis The process of
forming atheromatous plaques in
the inner lining of arteries.

arteriosclerosis Also called
"hardening of the arteries," a
disease in which blood vessels
lose their elasticity.

**Egyptian Mummy Being
Scanned by CT** Whole-body
scans of mummies show that
atherosclerosis was common
thousands of years ago.

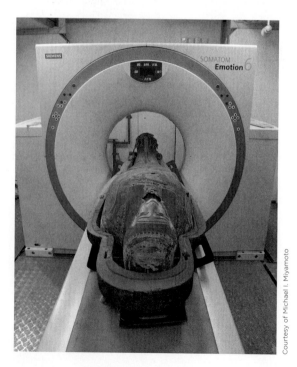

Courtesy of Michael I. Miyamoto

Inflammation in the circulating blood *(systemic inflammation)* can contribute to
atherogenesis—the development of atherosclerosis that can help trigger heart attacks
and strokes. Although the mechanism by which atherogenesis is triggered is unclear,
the process begins with damage to the blood vessel wall that results in the formation of
fatty streaks, which act as a "call for help" from the body's immune system. As we saw in
Chapter 3, inflammation is the body's response to injury, and blood clotting is often part
of that response. Although researchers are not certain what causes the low-grade inflammation that seems to put otherwise healthy people at increased risk for atherosclerosis,
many believe that a chronic bacterial or viral infection might be the underlying cause.

One of the proteins that increase during the inflammatory response, *C-reactive protein*
(CRP), is increasingly being used to assess a person's risk of CVD. CRP is a proinflammatory cytokine that is produced in the liver and released into the bloodstream when
inflammation is present. The risk for heart attack in people with the highest CRP levels
is twice that of people whose CRP levels are at the lowest levels (Abi-Saleh, Iskandar,
Elgharib, & Cohen, 2008).

Closely related to atherosclerosis is **arteriosclerosis,** or "hardening of the arteries" (Figure 10.2). In this condition, the coronary
arteries lose their elasticity, making it difficult for them to expand
and contract. (Imagine trying to stretch a dried-out rubber band.)
This makes it difficult for them to handle the large volumes of
blood needed during physical exertion. In addition, a blood clot
is much more likely to form in and block a coronary artery that
has lost its elasticity due to arteriosclerosis.

Although commonly assumed to be a modern disease, atherosclerosis and arteriosclerosis appear to have been common 4000
years ago among pre-agricultural hunter-gatherers. Whole-body
CT scans of 137 mummies showed evidence of atherosclerosis in
more than one-third of mummies from populations of ancient
Egyptians, Peruvians, and ancestral Puebloans of southwest America (Thompson and others, 2014).

The Diseases: Angina Pectoris, Myocardial Infarction, and Stroke

Left unchecked, atherosclerosis and arteriosclerosis may advance
for years before a person experiences any symptoms. This was the
case with Dr. McIver. Once the process gets underway, however,
the risk of developing one of three diseases increases with time.

The first begins with a gradual narrowing of the blood vessels. Any part of the body that depends on blood flow from an obstructed artery is subject to damage. For example, if the narrowing affects arteries in the legs, a person may experience leg pain while walking. When the arteries that supply the heart are narrowed with plaques, restricting blood flow to the heart—a condition called *ischemia*—the person may experience a sharp, crushing pain in the chest, called **angina pectoris.** Although most angina attacks usually pass within a few minutes without causing permanent damage, ischemia is a significant predictor of future coronary incidents.

Although angina attacks can occur anytime—including while a person is sleeping—they typically occur during moments of unusual exertion, because the body demands that the heart pump more oxygenated blood than it is accustomed to handling—for example, when a casual runner tries to complete a 26.2-mile marathon. Angina may also occur during strong emotional arousal or exposure to extreme cold or heat. Mental stress during daily life, including feelings of tension, frustration, and depression, increases the risk of ischemia (Rosenfeldt and others, 2004).

The second, much more serious cardiac disorder occurs when a plaque ruptures within a blood vessel, releasing a sticky mass that can further reduce blood flow or even obstruct it completely. Within seconds of the complete obstruction of a coronary artery, a heart attack, or **myocardial infarction (MI),** occurs, and a portion of the myocardium begins to die (an *infarct* is an area of dead tissue). Unlike angina, which lasts only a brief time, MI involves a chronic deficiency in the blood supply and thus causes permanent damage to the heart.

The third possible manifestation of cardiovascular malfunction is cerebrovascular disease, or **stroke.** Strokes affect 795,000 Americans annually, claiming more than 130,000 lives each year (one out of every 20 deaths). They are the third leading cause of death, after myocardial infarctions and cancer (CDC, 2015h). The most common type of stroke—*ischemic stroke*—occurs when plaques or a clot obstruct an artery, blocking the flow of blood to an area of the brain (Figure 10.3). *Hemorrhagic stroke* occurs when a blood vessel bursts inside the brain, increasing pressure on the cerebrum and damaging it by pressing it against the skull. Hemorrhagic stroke is associated with high blood pressure, which stresses the artery walls until they break or exposes a weak spot in an artery wall (*aneurysm*), which balloons out because of the pressure of the blood circulating inside.

The effects of stroke may include loss of speech or difficulty understanding speech; numbness, weakness, or paralysis of a limb or in the face; headaches; blurred vision; and dizziness. Strokes usually damage neural tissue on one side of the brain, with a resulting loss of sensation on the opposite side of the body. An estimated 10 percent of adults in the United States have experienced "silent strokes," which damage tiny clusters of cells inside the brain but cause no immediately obvious symptoms. These strokes tend not to be detected until, over time, memory loss, dizziness, slurred speech, and other classic stroke symptoms begin to appear (Das and others, 2008).

angina pectoris A condition of extreme chest pain caused by a restriction of the blood supply to the heart.

myocardial infarction (MI) A heart attack; the permanent death of heart tissue in response to an interruption of blood supply to the myocardium.

stroke A cerebrovascular accident that results in damage to the brain due to lack of oxygen; usually caused by atherosclerosis or arteriosclerosis.

FIGURE 10.3

Stroke Damages the Brain This CT scan of the brain of a 70-year-old stroke victim shows that when blood flow to the brain is blocked, cells in the brain may be destroyed. The darkened area on the right shows where brain tissue has died because of an inadequate blood supply. The lack of blood may be due to an obstruction in a cerebral artery or to the hemorrhaging of a weakened artery wall. The result is paralysis or weakness on the left side of the body (since the tissue destroyed is on the right side of the brain).

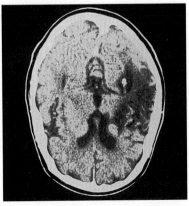

Mehau Kulyk/Science Photo Library/Photo Researchers

Risk Factors for Cardiovascular Disease

What causes plaque to form in the coronary arteries? Why do the coronary arteries of some people escape the buildup of scar tissue while those of others become obstructed at a young age? Research has identified a number of risk factors that are linked to CVD. Much of this knowledge comes from the Framingham Heart Study, one of the most celebrated epidemiological studies in the

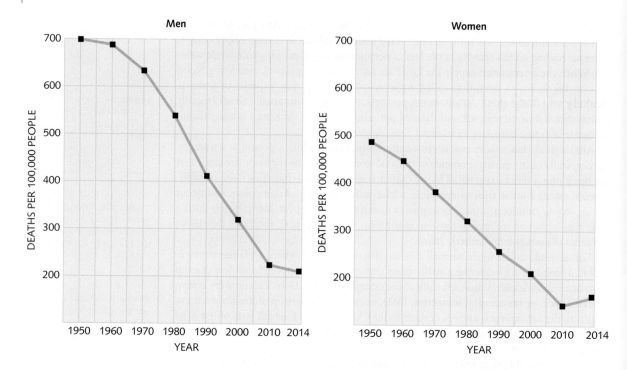

FIGURE 10.4

Annual U.S. Cardiovascular Disease Mortality Although the mortality rate from CVD has decreased for both men and women in the United States and other affluent countries, it has increased in Eastern Europe and the developing world. An estimated 17.5 million people died from CVD in 2014, representing 31 percent of all global deaths. Of these deaths, about 7.4 million were due to coronary heart disease and 6.7 million were due to stroke. Three-fourths of all CVD deaths take place in low- and middle-income countries.

Data from Centers for Disease Control and Prevention, National Center for Health Statistics. (2015i). *Underlying cause of death 1999–2014. CDC WONDER online database.* Retrieved February 13, 2016, from http://wonder. cdc.gov/ucd-icd10.html

World Health Organization (WHO). (2015a). *Cardiovascular disease fact sheet,* no. 317. http://www.who.int/ mediacentre/factsheets/fs317/en/.

history of medicine. When the Framingham study began, in 1948, the mortality rate due to CVD in the United States was nearly 500 cases per 100,000 people. This rate increased to a peak of 586.8 cases per 100,000 in 1950 and has dropped steadily ever since (Figure 10.4). Much of the credit for this dramatic improvement in mortality rates is due to "healthy heart" initiatives that stem from the Framingham study. The results of this remarkable study have undoubtedly extended the lives of millions.

Before Framingham, epidemiologists studied disease by examining medical records and death certificates. Framingham set a new standard for epidemiological research by inaugurating the concept of studying the health of living persons over time with a *prospective design* that included 5209 healthy people in the small town of Framingham, Massachusetts.

Every 2 years, the original participants received a complete physical exam that included an electrocardiogram, blood pressure test, and more than 80 separate medical tests. (Their children have exams every 4 years.) In addition, each participant completed a battery of psychological tests and health questionnaires. The researchers asked questions about the participants' level of anxiety, sleeping habits, nervousness, alcohol and tobacco use, level of education, and their typical response to anger.

Two large-scale studies followed the Framingham study and extended our knowledge of cardiovascular health. Established in 1976, the ongoing Nurses' Health Study (also discussed in Chapter 11) has followed more than 200,000 nurse-participants to assess women's risk factors for CVD, cancer, diabetes, and other conditions (NHS, 2015). The largest case-control study of cardiovascular disease to date is the Canadian-led 52-country INTERHEART Study. This study included nearly 30,000 participants (15,152 cases of people hospitalized for an MI, matched by age and sex with 14,820 control participants with no history of heart disease) (Yusuf and others, 2004).

The findings of these three landmark studies identified two categories of *risk factors* for CVD: those that are largely uncontrollable, such as family history, age, and gender; and those that are more controllable, such as obesity, hypertension, cholesterol level, and tobacco use.

Uncontrollable Risk Factors

A number of risk factors for CVD stem from genetic or biological conditions that are largely beyond our control.

Family History and Age

Family history strongly predicts CVD. This is especially true for those who have a close male relative who suffered a heart attack before age 55 or a close female relative who had a heart attack before age 65. Advancing age is also a risk factor for CVD. Indeed, approximately half of all CVD victims are over the age of 65.

Gender

CVD is the leading killer of both women and men in the United States and most other developed countries (CDC, 2015a). The risk of CVD also rises sharply in men after age 40. Except in women who smoke cigarettes, the risk of CVD remains low until menopause, when, as we will explain, it begins to accelerate. However, the risk is still much higher among men until about age 65. In fact, men have roughly the same rate of CVD as women who are 10 years older (American Heart Association, 2015). Although the gap narrows with advancing age, this gender difference explains in part why women live longer than men. In all developed countries and most developing countries, women outlive men by as many as 10 years. In the United States, life expectancy at birth is currently about 82 years for women and 77 years for men (World Health Organization, 2015d).

Some experts believe that the gender difference in CVD mortality may be caused by differences in the sex hormones testosterone and estrogen. Testosterone has been linked with aggression, competitiveness, and other behaviors that are thought to contribute to heart disease (Morris & Channer, 2012). Coincidentally, testosterone levels increase during early adulthood, just when the difference in mortality between men and women is at its peak.

However, if gender is truly a risk factor for CVD, then the differences between women and men should be similar throughout the world. This does not appear to be the case. Gender differences in CVD mortality are much greater in some countries than in others, especially in Eastern Europe (Mosca and others, 2011). It is likely that lifestyle factors, rather than biology, may be at work. As noted earlier in the text, masculinity norms have been implicated in the so-called crisis in men's health. Men are less likely to visit their general practitioner, more likely to be overweight and drink more alcohol than women, and more likely to make poorer dietary choices than women (Gough, 2013).

Although women may be at lower risk for CVD than men, heart disease takes the lives of more American women than does any other cause, affecting one of about every three women (as opposed to one in eight for breast cancer). Still, many women believe that breast cancer is the biggest threat to their health, despite the fact that CVD takes the lives of five times as many women as breast cancer (Figure 10.5).

Race, Ethnicity, and Socioeconomic Status

The prevalence of CVD also varies across racial and ethnic groups. Compared with Americans of European ancestry, for example, African-Americans are at increased risk while Native Americans, Asian-Americans, and Hispanic-Americans are at lower risk (CDC, 2014d). A key finding from the INTERHEART Study is that the risk factors for CVD are the same in countries throughout the world (Yusuf and others, 2004). Thus, experts believe that social, economic, and behavioral factors contribute to ethnic differences in cardiovascular health.

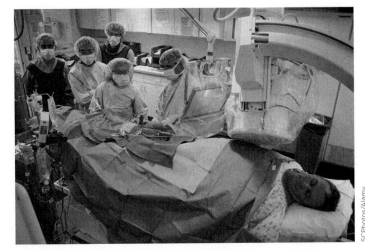

SCPhotos/Alamy

Coronary Angiography In this method of diagnosis, a small cardiac catheter is threaded through an artery into the aorta, then to the coronary artery suspected of blockage. The dye injected through the catheter enables the surgeon to x-ray the artery (see video monitor in the photo) and locate the blockage.

FIGURE 10.5

Mortality Rates for Cardiovascular Disease and Breast Cancer in Women by Age Although women may be at lower risk for CVD than men, heart disease takes the lives of more American women than any other cause, affecting one of about every three women.

Data from National Center for Health Statistics. (2012). *Health, United States, 2011.* Washington, DC: U.S. Government Printing Office.

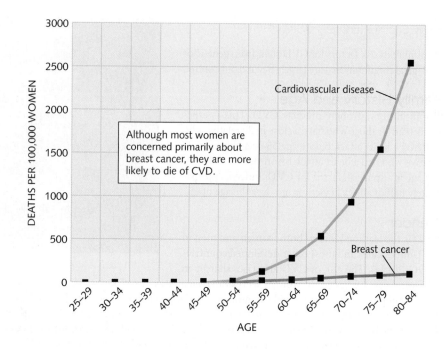

People of low socioeconomic status (SES) tend to have more total risk factors for CVD, including high-fat diets, smoking, and stressful life experiences such as racial discrimination (Huisman and others, 2005), and African-Americans are disproportionately represented among groups with lower SES.

Lack of exercise also may be a factor. People of lower SES tend to exercise less, perhaps because they have less free time, less access to well-equipped public areas such as parks and bike trails, are less able to afford exercise equipment, or may be less informed about the hazards of sedentary living (Onge & Krueger, 2008).

Controllable Risk Factors

Uncontrollable risk factors do not necessarily doom a person to death by heart attack. Knowing one's inherent risk profile is an important step in reducing the risk of CVD, however, because it allows high-risk individuals to minimize their total risk profile by changing those things they *can* control. Even with a family history of heart disease, for example, a person can reduce overall risk by working toward lowering blood pressure, eating a healthy diet, exercising regularly, and maintaining a normal body weight. These efforts can reap huge benefits. For instance, the Chicago Heart Association Detection Project evaluated the health outcomes for men between ages 18 and 39, men between 40 and 59, and women between ages 40 and 59 years. Younger men with the healthiest lifestyles had a life expectancy 9.5 years longer than other men in their age group. For healthy men aged 40 to 59 years, life expectancy was extended by 6 years. For women with the healthiest lifestyles, life was extended by 5.8 years (Yano and others, 2015; Stamler and others, 1999).

Hypertension

hypertension A sustained elevation of diastolic and systolic blood pressure (exceeding 140/90).

Blood pressure is the force exerted by blood as it pushes out against the walls of the arteries. When pressure is too high, it can damage the vessels and lead to atherosclerosis. Blood pressure is considered normal if it is below 120/80 mmHg. Although the condition is not called **hypertension** until it consistently exceeds 140/90, with the increased incidence of hypertension-related mortality, the Centers for Disease Control and Prevention now includes a *prehypertension* category (blood pressure of 120–139/80–89 mmHg) associated with an increased risk of progression to full-blown hypertension.

Most cases of high blood pressure are classified as *primary*, or *essential*, *hypertension*, meaning that the exact cause is unknown. Hypertension is the result of the interaction of biological, psychological, and social factors. Obesity, lack of exercise, dietary salt, and excessive stress can produce hypertension in biologically predisposed people. Hypertension is also related to anxiety and anger, especially in middle-aged men. In a major longitudinal study, researchers measured anxiety, anger, and blood pressure in middle-aged and older men. An 18- to 20-year follow-up revealed that men 45 to 59 who scored high on a standardized measure of anxiety were twice as likely to develop hypertension (Markovitz, Matthews, Kannel, Cobb, & D'Agostino, 1993). Similar findings have been found in children who score high on measures of anxiety and anger (Howell, Rice, Carmon, & Hauber, 2007; Nichols, Rice, & Howell, 2011).

Stress is also linked with hypertension, particularly among people who have poor coping mechanisms or limited coping resources. Exposure to environmental stressors at a young age can be particularly harmful. Adolescents who report experiencing large numbers of chronic, uncontrollable negative family stressors exhibit greater systolic blood pressure throughout the day, regardless of their gender, ethnicity, body mass index, and activity level (Brady & Matthews, 2006). These early experiences may increase their risk of developing hypertension later in life.

Heredity plays a role in hypertension as well, as evidenced by the fact that the prevalence of hypertension varies widely among racial and ethnic groups. For instance, the prevalence of hypertension among African-American women and men in the United States is among the highest in the world. Compared with European-Americans, African-Americans develop hypertension at a younger age, and their average blood pressures are much higher (Flack and others, 2010).

Checking Blood Pressure
Obesity, lack of exercise, dietary salt, and excessive stress can produce hypertension in biologically predisposed people.

Biological Reactivity, Hemostasis, and Inflammation

Although genes may create a biological predisposition to hypertension, heredity alone cannot explain the widespread variation in the prevalence of hypertension among different ethnic and cultural groups. Within the African-American community, for instance, rates of hypertension vary substantially. Those with the highest rates are more likely to be middle-aged or older, overweight or obese, physically inactive, less educated, and to have diabetes (Yoon, Fryar, & Carroll, 2015). A number of researchers have suggested that the prevalence of hypertension among African-Americans might reflect greater **cardiovascular reactivity (CVR)** to social stress—especially the stress of racial discrimination—in the form of larger increases in heart rate and blood pressure and a greater outpouring of epinephrine, cortisol, and other stress hormones.

Researchers have found that acute exposure to stressors such as mental arithmetic tasks (Arthur, Katkin, & Mezzacappa, 2004), racially provocative speeches (Merritt, Bennett, Williams, Edwards, & Sollers, 2006), on-the-job training exercises (Webb and others, 2011), and role-playing scenarios such as being accused of shoplifting (Lepore and others, 2006) are associated with increases in cardiovascular activation (see Huang and others, 2013, for a review). Interestingly, low-SES African-American men tend to display greater CVR to racial stressors than high-SES African-American men *or women*. They also report significantly greater firsthand experience with racial prejudice (Krieger, Sidney, & Coakley, 1998). These findings are important because people who display elevated cardiovascular

cardiovascular reactivity (CVR) An individual's characteristic reaction to stress, including changes in heart rate, blood pressure, and hormones.

Getty Images News/Getty Images

responses to and delayed recovery from psychosocial stressors are at greater risk of cardiovascular disease in the future (Chida & Steptoe, 2010; Panaite, Salomon, Jin, & Rottenberg, 2015). As noted in Chapter 5, however, the impact of a stressor such as racism may depend on the individual's past experience and coping resources. The presence of other factors, including anger, defensiveness, interpersonal skills, and coping style, all are potential mediators and moderators of CVR (Rutledge & Linden, 2003).

Hemostasis

One biological mechanism that may link stress to CHD is **hemostasis**—the process that causes bleeding to stop via the aggregation of *platelets* and the *coagulation* of blood from a liquid to gel state. The hemostatic system requires close regulation to function properly. If the blood does not clot well, it may be due to a bleeding disorder such as *hemophilia.* Overactive clotting can also cause problems, including *thrombosis,* which occurs when blood clots form abnormally and potentially break off to cause *embolisms* that block blood flow in an artery or vein.

Many hemostatic factors are independently associated with coronary heart disease (Folsom, 2001). Elevated concentrations of *fibrinogen*, for instance, are prospectively associated with MI and stroke, independently of other risk factors for cardiovascular disease (von Känel, Malan, Hamer, van der Westhuizen, & Malan, 2014). Fibrinogen is a protein in plasma that plays an important role in determining blood viscosity and platelet aggregation. Elevated fibrinogen levels cause a *hypercoagulable state*—a dangerous situation in which blood clots too easily, increasing the risk of a coronary or cerebrovascular incident. Conversely, low fibrinogen levels have been associated with a low risk of acute coronary events, even when serum cholesterol levels are high (Borissof, Spronk, & ten Cate, 2011).

Remarkably, as part of his "fight-or-flight" research, Walter Cannon noted more than a century ago that activation of the sympathetic nervous system influences hemostasis. Because acute stress is also associated with hypercoagulability (see Chapter 4), stressful events could conceivably trigger a heart attack or stroke (von Känel, 2015).

Inflammation

As you learned in Chapter 3, inflammation is a nonspecific response of the immune system to tissue damage. When damage occurs, white blood cells rush to the injury site and defend against infection and further damage by engulfing bacteria and other potential invaders through the process of phagocytosis. As we've seen, the plaques that can lead to atherogenesis are simply fatty deposits of cholesterol-filled white blood cells.

Chronic inflammation increases the risk of atherosclerosis by affecting the development of plaques. Factors that promote inflammation may increase the likelihood of a stroke or MI by making plaques more likely to rupture into artery-blocking clots (Abi-Saleh and others, 2008). Stress (Miller & Blackwell, 2006), depression (Kop and others, 2010), and metabolic syndrome (Vlachopoulos and others, 2007)—each of which is associated with increased risk of CHD—also seem to promote chronic inflammation.

Obesity

Excess body weight increases a person's risk of hypertension and all CVD, in part because of its association with high cholesterol. The risk of excess fat depends somewhat on how the fat is distributed. *Abdominal obesity* associated with excess fat in the midsection (the "beer belly") promotes the greatest risk of CVD, perhaps because it is often associated with lower levels of HDL cholesterol and higher triglyceride levels. People who carry excess weight in their midsections also have thicker artery walls, increasing blood pressure and the risk of stroke (De Michele and others, 2002). Indeed, waist circumference may be a more accurate predictor of hypertension than body mass index (Gus, Harzheim,

hemostasis The process that causes bleeding to stop via the aggregation of *platelets* and the *coagulation* of blood.

Remember:
CVD = cardiovascular disease (includes heart disease and stroke)
CHD = coronary heart disease

Zaslavsky, Medina, & Gus, 2004). Differences in where body fat is distributed may help to explain why men have higher rates of CVD than women, at least until menopause. Abdominal obesity is more common in men than in women.

Cholesterol Level

Doctors have known for years that people with a genetically high level of cholesterol also have a high rate of CVD, beginning at a young age. Before the Framingham Heart Study, however, there was no prospective evidence that excess dietary cholesterol was a coronary risk factor. The Framingham study found that people with low serum cholesterol rarely developed CVD, whereas those with high levels had a high risk. A blood cholesterol level lower than 200 milligrams per deciliter (mg/dl) is generally associated with a low risk of CVD. A level of 240 or greater doubles the risk.

Total cholesterol is only part of the story, however. As noted in Chapter 3, a more complete picture comes from comparing the relative amounts of *high-density lipoprotein* (HDL), *low-density lipoprotein* (LDL), and *triglycerides*. Men and women who have high total cholesterol levels and low HDL levels have the highest risk of CVD. However, even people with low levels of total cholesterol are at increased risk if these proportions are faulty. The higher a person's HDL cholesterol level is, the better, but a level below 40 mg/dl in adults is considered a risk factor for CVD (American Heart Association, 2015). Control of low-density lipoprotein cholesterol (LDL-C) has also been shown to substantially reduce cardiovascular disease morbidity and mortality (Kuklina, Carroll, Shaw, & Hirsch, 2013).

Research suggests that moderate alcohol consumption may lower total cholesterol and raise HDL levels. Consider the *French paradox:* Mortality rates from CVD are markedly lower in France than in other industrialized countries, despite the fact that the French people eat more rich, fatty foods; exercise less; and smoke more (Ferrieres, 2004). Studies suggest that the French may suffer less CVD because of their regular consumption of natural chemical compounds called *flavonoids*. Flavonoids, found primarily in fruit, vegetables, nuts, and beverages such as tea and wine may lower the risk of CVD in three ways: reducing LDL cholesterol, boosting HDL cholesterol, and slowing platelet aggregation, thereby lessening the chances of a blood clot forming. A seven-year study of nearly 100,000 women and men in their sixties found that flavonoid consumption was associated with lower risk of CVD (McCullough and others, 2012). Despite this interesting possible relationship between moderate wine consumption and a healthy heart, the issue remains controversial. We *do* know that excessive alcohol consumption increases the risk of suffering a myocardial infarction.

Fortunately, an increasing number of people seem to be following recommendations to lower their bad cholesterol. Between 1976 and 2010, the prevalence of high LDL-C among U.S. adults decreased from 59 percent to 27 percent, and the percentage of adults consuming a diet low in saturated fat increased from 25 percent to 41 percent (Kuklina and others, 2013).

Metabolic Syndrome

For an estimated 47 million Americans, obesity, hypertension, and a poor cholesterol profile combine into the **metabolic syndrome,** defined as three or more of the following:

- Waist circumference greater than 40 inches in men and 35 inches in women
- Elevated serum triglyceride level
- HDL cholesterol level less than 40 mg/dl in men and 50 mg/dl in women
- Blood pressure of 130/85 mmHg or higher
- Glucose intolerance (commonly found in those suffering from diabetes, as we will see)

Recall from Chapter 8 that high-density lipoprotein, or HDL, is the so-called good cholesterol, and low-density lipoprotein, or LDL, is the so-called bad cholesterol. Triglycerides, also called very-low-density lipoproteins (VLDL), are especially bad.

metabolic syndrome A cluster of conditions that occur together—including elevated blood pressure and insulin levels, excess body fat, and unhealthy cholesterol ratios—that increase a person's risk for heart disease, stroke, and diabetes.

People with the metabolic syndrome have a significantly higher risk of developing CVD and diabetes (American Heart Association, 2015). In 2012, an estimated 35 percent of all adults in the United States and 50 percent of those 60 years of age and older had metabolic syndrome (Aguilar, Bhuket, Torres, Liu, & Wong, 2015).

Tobacco Use

Smoking more than doubles the chances of having a heart attack and is linked to one of every five deaths due to CHD. Smokers have twice the risk of having a stroke and are less likely to survive an MI than are nonsmokers. On the positive side, one year after a person quits smoking, the risk of CVD decreases by 50 percent. In the United States, adult smoking rates have fallen from about 43 percent in 1965 to about 18 percent today (USDHHS, 2014).

Psychosocial Factors in Cardiovascular Disease

The 52-country INTERHEART Study identified nine risk factors that together accounted for over 90 percent of the variability in cases of myocardial infarction. Behind elevated lipids and smoking, psychosocial factors were the third leading risk factor for CHD (Yusuf and others, 2004). But the first clue that psychosocial factors were strongly related to CHD came decades earlier.

The Type A Personality and Its "Toxic Core"

Type A Friedman and Rosenman's term for competitive, hurried, hostile people who may be at increased risk for developing cardiovascular disease.

Type B Friedman and Rosenman's term for more relaxed people who are not pressured by time considerations and thus tend to be coronary disease-resistant.

In a controversial study, researchers noted a correlation between the estimated hostility scores of U.S. cities and the incidence of CVD. Philadelphia had the highest hostility score and the highest incidence of cardiovascular diseases (Huston, 1997). What other factors might explain this result?

Puzzled by the fact that many coronary patients were *not* obese middle-aged men with elevated cholesterol, researchers decided that they must have been overlooking something. So they broadened their search for risk factors that might offer an explanation. In the late 1950s, cardiologists Meyer Friedman and Ray Rosenman (1959) began to study personality traits that might predict coronary events. They found a coronary-prone behavior pattern that included competitiveness, a strong sense of time urgency, and hostility, which they labeled **Type A.** In contrast, people who are more relaxed and who are not overly pressured by time considerations tend to be coronary disease–resistant. This they called **Type B** behavior.

Hundreds of studies were conducted in the decades that followed, and the published results supported the association between Type A behavior and risk of future CVD in both men and women. Among the findings: Type A people have more rapid blood clotting and higher cholesterol and triglyceride levels under stress than their Type B counterparts (Lovallo & Pishkin, 1980). Type A people display greater autonomic arousal (see Chapter 3), elevated heart rate, and higher blood pressure in response to challenging events (Jorgensen, Johnson, Kolodziej, & Schreer, 1996). In relaxed situations, both types are equally aroused. When challenged or threatened, however, Type A people are less able to remain calm. This pattern of "combat ready" hyperreactivity is most likely to occur in situations in which Type A persons are subjected to some form of feedback evaluation of their performance (Lyness, 1993).

More recently, researchers focused on hostility and anger as the "toxic core" of Type A behavior, especially in men (Player, King, Mainous, & Geesey, 2007). Hostility has been characterized as a chronic negative outlook that encompasses feelings (anger), thoughts (cynicism and mistrust of others), and overt actions (aggression). (See Table 10.1 to find out how you measure up when it comes to hostility.)

TABLE 10.1

Measuring Hostility

For each of the following items, circle the answer that most closely fits how you would respond.

1. A teenager drives by my yard blasting the car stereo.
   a. I begin to understand why teenagers can't hear.
   b. I can feel my blood pressure starting to rise.

2. A boyfriend/girlfriend calls me at the last minute, "too tired to go out tonight." I'm stuck with two $15 tickets.
   a. I find someone else to go with.
   b. I tell my friend how inconsiderate he or she is.

3. I am waiting in a long express checkout line at the supermarket, where a sign says, "No more than 10 items, please."
   a. I pick up a magazine and pass the time.
   b. I glance to see if anyone has more than 10 items.

4. Most homeless people in large cities:
   a. are down and out because they lack ambition.
   b. are victims of illness or some other misfortune.

5. At times when I've been very angry with someone:
   a. I was able to stop short of hitting him or her.
   b. I have, on occasion, hit or shoved him or her.

6. When I am stuck in a traffic jam:
   a. I am usually not particularly upset.
   b. I quickly start to feel irritated and annoyed.

7. When there's a really important job to be done:
   a. I prefer to do it myself.
   b. I am apt to call on my friends to help.

8. The cars ahead of me start to slow and stop as they approach a curve.
   a. I assume that there is a construction site ahead.
   b. I assume that someone ahead had a fender-bender.

9. An elevator stops for a long time at the floor above where I'm waiting.
   a. I soon start to feel irritated and annoyed.
   b. I start planning the rest of my day.

10. When a friend or coworker disagrees with me:
    a. I try to explain my position more clearly.
    b. I am apt to get into an argument with him or her.

11. At times in the past, when I was really angry:
    a. I never threw things or slammed a door.
    b. I sometimes threw things or slammed a door.

12. Someone bumps into me in a store.
    a. I pass it off as an accident.
    b. I feel irritated at their clumsiness.

13. When my significant other is fixing a meal:
    a. I keep a close watch on things to make sure nothing burns.
    b. I talk about my day or read the paper.

14. Someone is hogging the conversation at a party.
    a. I look for an opportunity to put him or her down.
    b. I soon move to another group.

15. In most arguments:

   a. I am the angrier one.

   b. the other person is angrier than I am.

To score your responses, give yourself one point for each of the following answers: **1.** b; **2.** b; **3.** b; **4.** a; **5.** b; **6.** b; **7.** a; **8.** b; **9.** a; **10.** b; **11.** b; **12.** b; **13.** a; **14.** a; **15.** a. Scores of 4 or higher indicate a tendency toward hostility.

Information from Williams, R. B., & Williams, V. (1994). *Anger kills: Seventeen strategies for controlling the hostility that can harm your health.* New York: Harper Perennial, pp. 5–11.

Can a sudden burst of anger lead to a heart attack? It does happen often enough to cause concern. People who experience severe anger outbursts may be more at risk for cardiovascular events in the two hours following the outbursts compared to those who remain calm (Mittleman and others, 1995; Smeijers and others, 2015). In the massive Atherosclerosis Risk in Communities study, 256 of the 13,000 middle-aged participants had heart attacks. Janice Williams and her colleagues (2000) found that people who scored highest on an anger scale were three times more likely to have a heart attack than those with the lowest scores. People who scored in the moderate range on the anger scale were about 35 percent more likely to have a heart attack. This elevated risk was true even after taking into account the presence of other risk factors such as smoking, diabetes, elevated cholesterol, and obesity.

Indeed, strong negative emotions such as anger may be as dangerous to the heart as smoking, a high-fat diet, or obesity (Mittleman & Mostofsky, 2011). In one study, researchers interviewed MI survivors, ages 20 to 92, for information about their emotional state just before their heart attacks. The researchers devised a seven-level anger scale ranging from calm to very angry to enraged. Heart attacks were more than twice as likely to occur in the two hours that followed an episode of anger than at any other time. The largest jump in risk occurred at level 5 anger (enraged), in which the person is very angry and tense, with clenching fists or gritting teeth. Arguments with family members were the most frequent cause of anger, followed by conflicts at work and legal problems (Hilbert, 1994). Other researchers have found that the impact of acute emotional triggers such as anger is greater among individuals with an elevated baseline CVD risk (Edmonson and others, 2013).

Suppressed anger may be as hazardous to health as expressed anger (Jorgensen & Kolodziej, 2007). James Pennebaker's *inhibition theory* is based on the idea that to hold back one's thoughts or feelings requires work that, over time, results in levels of stress that can create or exacerbate illness. In support of this theory, cardiac patients who deny their anger or frustration are 4.5 times more likely to die within five years than are other cardiac patients (Bondi, 1997). Suppressed anger was an even stronger predictor of mortality than elevated cholesterol level or cigarette smoking.

Road Rage Hostility and anger, such as that displayed in extreme cases of aggressive driving, are powerful psychosocial influences on hypertension and cardiovascular disease. Road rage can also lead to assaults and collisions that result in injuries and even deaths.

Chris Rout/Alamy

Taken together, research studies of anger expression and suppression suggest that both too much *and* too little can be hazardous to health. To summarize their review of the literature, Nancy Dorr and her colleagues captured the dilemma faced by those wondering how best to handle situations that trigger anger by applying the familiar expression, "Damned if you do; damned if you don't" (Dorr, Brosschot, Sollers, & Thayer, 2007). In a two-year longitudinal study of over 23,000 male health professionals, researchers found that men with moderate levels of anger expression had a reduced risk of nonfatal MI and stroke compared with those with lower levels of anger expression, even after adjusting for other health behaviors and coronary risk factors (Eng, Fitzmaurice, Kubzansky, Rimm, & Kawachi, 2003).

Depression

Depression is strongly implicated as a risk factor in the development and progression of CVD and metabolic syndrome (Fraser-Smith & Lesperance, 2005; Suls & Bunde, 2005). Even after controlling for other controllable risk factors such as cholesterol and smoking, depression and anxiety predict the development of CVD (Goldston & Baillie, 2008; Shen and others, 2008). It is important to note that depression is not simply an aftereffect of a diagnosis of heart disease; rather, it is an independent risk factor in its own right that likely has both genetic and environmental causes (McCaffery and others, 2006). By some estimates, depression rivals regular exposure to secondhand smoke as a risk factor for CVD (Wulsin & Singal, 2003). Evidence of the relationship between depression and the development and progression of CVD is sufficiently strong that it is now generally recommended that at-risk patients be assessed and, if necessary, treated for depression (Davidson and others, 2006). Unfortunately, depression remains an underdiagnosed and often untreated condition in many people with CVD (Hare, Toukhsati, Johansson, & Jaarsma, 2014). Researchers have reported prevalence rates as high as 27 percent of major depression among patients hospitalized with CVD (Glassman, 2007).

Why Do Hostility, Anger, and Depression Promote Cardiovascular Disease?

An angry, hostile personality predicts an increased risk of CVD, but how do these traits work their damage? The key theoretical models differ in their relative emphasis on biological, psychological, and social factors.

Psychosocial Vulnerability

Some theorists maintain that hostile adults lead more stressful lives and have low levels of social support; this combination, over time, exerts a toxic effect on cardiovascular health. In support of this *psychosocial vulnerability hypothesis,* researchers have found that chronic family conflict, unemployment, social isolation, and job-related stress are all linked to increased risk of CVD (Kop, Gottdiener, & Krantz, 2001).

Education, Income, and the Work Environment

Low socioeconomic status, defined by lower educational level and/or low income, is a risk factor for cardiovascular disease (Huisman and others, 2005). A massive European study that followed 60,000 men and women over a 23-year period reported that those with less education were more likely to smoke, eat an unhealthy diet, and live a sedentary life than those with more education (Laaksonen and others, 2008). Interestingly, the inverse relationship between SES and CVD risk factors is greater in countries with larger class discrepancies in education and income than in countries with smaller social-class divisions (Kim, Kawachi, Vander Hoorn, & Ezzati, 2008). The SES–CVD risk factor connection also can be observed early in life, occurring even in children and adolescents (Karlamangla and others, 2005).

The work environment can be an important source of satisfaction or stress (Mills, Davidson, & Farag, 2004). As we saw in Chapter 5, jobs associated with high productivity demands, excessive overtime work, and conflicting requirements accompanied by little personal control tend to be especially stressful. Data from the 20-year CARDIA study reveal that *job strain,* defined as high job demands and low decision latitude, predicts the incidence of hypertension, even after adjusting for baseline blood pressure, education, body mass index, and age (Markovitz, Matthews, Whooley, Lewis, & Greenlund, 2004). Over time, then, it is not surprising that assembly-line workers, as well as those workers who wait tables and perform similarly stressful jobs, are, in fact, more susceptible to coronary disease (Bosma, Stansfeld, & Marmot, 1998). In addition, workers who feel they have been promoted too quickly or too slowly, those who feel insecure about their jobs, and those who feel that their ambitions are thwarted are more likely to report stress and to show higher rates of illness, especially coronary disease (Taylor, Repetti, & Seeman, 1997).

Social Support

As we saw in Chapter 5, coping with stressful events is especially difficult when an individual feels cut off from others. Considerable prospective research shows that loneliness and the perception of little social support in one's life are risk factors for cardiovascular disease (Caspi, Harrington, Moffitt, Milne, & Poulton, 2006). This risk becomes even more hazardous as we age (Hawkley & Cacioppo, 2007). Interestingly, Julianne Holt-Lunstad and her colleagues (Holt-Lunstad, Uchino, Smith, Olson-Cerny, & Nealey-Moore, 2003) have found that the quality of people's relationships with others actually predicts their blood pressure during everyday social interactions with these people. Interactions with family members and friends for whom the participants reported generally positive, supportive ties were accompanied by lower systolic blood pressure (measuring the force of the heart's contraction), while interactions with people for whom participants reported ambivalent feelings (both positive and negative emotions) were associated with elevations in systolic blood pressure. Low perceived support at work or at home is associated with more rapid development of atheromatous plaques and coronary artery blockage (Wang and others, 2008).

The Health Behavior Explanation

We have seen that hostility, anger, job strain, and social isolation may affect health directly. Some researchers believe that these factors may have an indirect effect on health, as well. For example, people with poor support may not take care of themselves as well as those who have someone to remind them to exercise, eat in moderation, or take their medicine. Similarly, a person with a cynical attitude may perceive health-enhancing behaviors, such as adhering to a healthy diet and active lifestyle, as unimportant and may ignore warnings about smoking and other health-compromising behaviors. Hostility and anger have indeed been linked to excessive alcohol and caffeine consumption, greater fat and caloric intake, elevated LDL cholesterol, lower physical activity, greater body mass, hypertension, sleep problems, and nonadherence to medical regimens (Miller, Smith, Turner, Guijarro, & Hallet, 1996).

Psychophysiological Reactivity Model

Stress, hostility, depression, and anger may act slowly over a period of years to damage the arteries and the heart. When we vent our anger, our pulse quickens, the heart pounds more forcefully, and blood clots more quickly. In addition, blood vessels constrict, blood pressure surges, and blood levels of free fatty acids increase. Our immunity also decreases as adrenaline, cortisol, and other stress hormones suppress the activity of disease-fighting lymphocytes.

To pinpoint the physiological bases of hostility, researchers have studied hostile men and women who were harassed while trying to perform a difficult mental task. The stress caused an unusually strong activation of the fight-or-flight response in these people. When challenged, they displayed significantly greater cardiovascular reactivity (CVR) in the form of larger increases in blood pressure and greater outpourings of epinephrine, cortisol, and other stress hormones (Kop & Krantz, 1997). The Healthy Women Study showed that women who express Type A anger and symptoms of anxiety and depression also have impaired functioning in the endothelial cells lining the internal surface of the coronary arteries. Normally, these cells promote vascular health by releasing substances that cause the blood vessels to relax or contract as needed to promote homeostasis. When these cells do not work properly, this delicate balance is disrupted. Consequently, the coronary arteries may become constricted and inflamed, which facilitates the deposit of lipids and the development of atherosclerotic lesions, thus promoting the development of CHD (Harris, Matthews, Sutton-Tyrrell, & Kuller, 2003).

Interestingly, nighttime cardiac response is normal in hostile people, suggesting the reaction is not innate but rather a direct response to daytime stressors. Hostile people apparently have a lower threshold for triggering their fight-or-flight response than do nonhostile people (Williams, 2001).

However, the association between anger expression and psychophysiological reactivity is far from perfect and varies with such factors as the tendency to dwell on anger-provoking events and a person's tendency to forgive others. Hypertensive women and men who ruminate—that is, agree with such statements as "I think repeatedly about what I really would have liked to have done but did not"—tend to have higher resting blood pressure levels (Gerin and others, 2012; Hogan & Linden, 2004). Conversely, college students who have a generally forgiving personality and are therefore less likely to ruminate have lower blood pressure levels and CVR during interviews about times when they felt betrayed by a parent or friend (Lawler and others, 2003).

Depression may be linked to elevated levels of inflammatory biomarkers such as interleukin-6 and C-reactive protein, which, as we saw earlier, have been implicated in atherogenesis (Matthews and others, 2007; Vaccarino and others, 2007). Depression is also associated with increased heart rate variability, especially following a heart attack, which may be another pathway between the two conditions (Glassman, Bigger, Gaffney, & Van Zyl, 2007).

The Biopsychosocial Model

Health psychologists have combined the insights of these findings to provide a biopsychosocial explanation for how hurriedness, hostility, and anger contribute to cardiovascular disease. This model suggests that for a chronic disease such as CVD to develop, a person first must have a physiological predisposition (Figure 10.6). This is determined by family history of CVD and previous health history (other diseases, poor diet, tobacco use, and so on). Whether CVD develops then depends on a variety of psychosocial factors in the person's life, including the level of stress from the work and home environments and the availability of social support. For example, hostile individuals with a strong sense of time urgency tend to elicit aggressive behaviors from others, producing interpersonal conflict and more hostility. This in turn leads to a reduction in social support, more negative affect, and artery-damaging cardiac reactivity. Thus, hostile attitudes create a self-fulfilling prophecy for the mistrusting, hostile person by producing a hostile environment.

Fortunately, most people can minimize the health-compromising effects of hostility. Although changing one's personality is not easy, hostility can be countered with efforts to control hostile reactions and treat others as you would have them treat you.

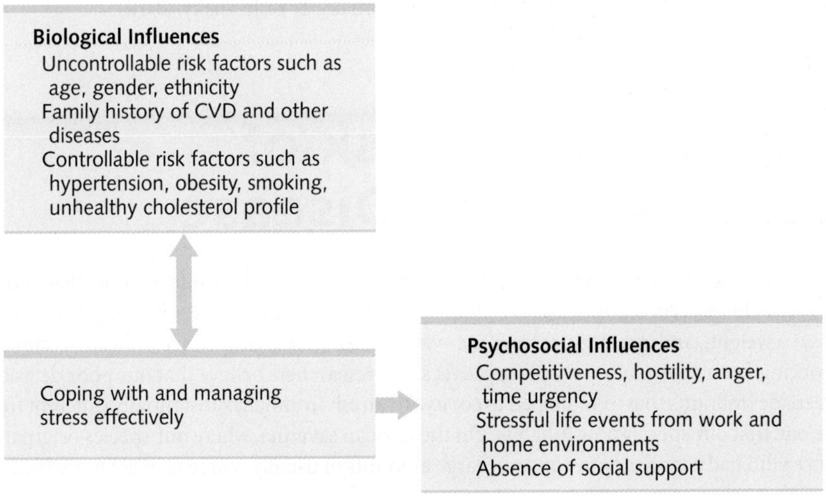

Biological Influences
Uncontrollable risk factors such as age, gender, ethnicity
Family history of CVD and other diseases
Controllable risk factors such as hypertension, obesity, smoking, unhealthy cholesterol profile

Coping with and managing stress effectively

Psychosocial Influences
Competitiveness, hostility, anger, time urgency
Stressful life events from work and home environments
Absence of social support

FIGURE 10.6
A Biopsychosocial Model of CVD For CVD to develop, a hostile person first must have a biological predisposition toward it. Then CVD may be more likely to develop because the hostile person's attitude has chased away social support people and continues to elicit negative responses from others, which leads to more hostility and damaging cardiac reactivity.

Positive Psychological Well-Being and Cardiovascular Disease

Much of the research linking psychological factors with CVD has focused on *psychological ill-being* (pervasive negative feelings and poor functioning in everyday life). In contrast, *psychological well-being* reflects the components of health that characterize people who feel good about life and function well (Keyes & Annas, 2009). Some evidence suggests that positive psychological well-being is associated with cardiovascular health. For example, optimism, emotional vitality, and displays of positive emotions have each been linked with reduced risk of incident CHD (fatal CHD, first nonfatal myocardial infarction, or first definite angina) and reduced cardiovascular mortality (Tindle and others, 2009; Davidson, Mostofsky, & Whang, 2010). Research studies in Japan have reported that *ikigai*—defined as having a life worth living—is associated with lower overall cardiovascular mortality (Tanno and others, 2009).

What accounts for the association between positive psychological well-being and cardiovascular health? Some experts have suggested that well-being may affect CVD indirectly by promoting healthier lifestyle behaviors such as increased physical activity and improved diet (Giltay, Geleijnse, Zitman, Buijsse, & Kromhout, 2007). Others have pointed to possible direct effects via alterations in the neuroendocrine, cardiovascular, and inflammatory systems (Steptoe, Dockray, & Wardle, 2009). Some studies have found effects only in men (Koizumi, Ito, Kaneko, & Motohashi, 2008), or only among certain age groups, such as elderly adults (Giltay, Kamphuis, Kalmijn, Zitman, & Kromhout, 2006).

To shed light on the issue, one study investigated the association between psychological well-being and incident CHD in a prospective cohort of middle-aged women and men from the Whitehall II study. Begun in 1985, the experiment followed 10,308 British civil servants in an effort to understand the relationship between socioeconomic status and health (Marmot and others, 1991). From this initial cohort, the researchers assessed psychological well-being and coronary risk factors between 1991 and 1994 among 7942 individuals without a prior cardiovascular event.

The results showed that both men and women who scored high in emotional vitality—defined as active engagement with the world, effective regulation of emotions, and an overall sense of well-being—and optimism had reduced risk of CHD over a five-year period. This association between well-being and CHD was not explained by differences in biological risk factors (age, gender, ethnicity) or health behaviors (smoking, alcohol consumption, exercise, fruit and vegetable consumption), although individuals with high psychological well-being were also healthier in both categories. Overall, the researchers found that the risk of a coronary event was reduced by 10 to 25 percent with every unit increase in positive psychological well-being (Boehm, Peterson, Kivimaki, & Kubzansky, 2012).

Reducing the Risk of Cardiovascular Disease

Although epidemiological research has provided a wealth of information that should help prevent cardiovascular disease—limit fat intake, quit smoking, lose excess weight, and get regular exercise—we persist in making heart-unhealthy choices. Working from an evolutionary perspective, some researchers believe that our poor decisions are made by brains that were shaped to cope with an environment substantially different from the one that our species now inhabits. On the African savanna, where our species originated, those who had a tendency to consume large amounts of usually scarce fat were more likely to survive famines that killed their thinner companions. Those with a rapid-fire fight-or-flight reaction had a clear advantage in hunting and reacting to hostile threats and were more likely to survive and pass on these traits to their offspring. And we, their descendants, still carry these evolved urges and hostile tendencies.

Health psychology aims to help us overcome these evolved tendencies by establishing heart-healthy habits and modifying behaviors that increase the risk of CVD. Lifelong behaviors such as a poor diet, tobacco use, and a sedentary lifestyle are particularly difficult to modify. Studies of high-risk children (those with elevated cholesterol, obesity, and hypertension) typically reveal that such children remain at increased risk of developing CVD throughout adulthood. Yet perception of control is also a factor. Patients who have experienced an MI or angina and who report the highest levels of *perceived behavioral control* (see Chapter 6) over being able to exercise regularly, give up smoking, and modify other CVD risk behaviors are more likely to report doing so one year later (Johnston, Johnston, Pollard, Kinmouth, & Mant, 2004).

Next, we focus on interventions aimed at controlling hypertension, reducing elevated serum cholesterol, and reversing atherosclerosis. The most serious behavioral risk factor in CVD, cigarette smoking, was discussed in Chapter 9.

Controlling Hypertension

For every 1-point drop in diastolic blood pressure, which measures the pressure between heartbeats, there is an estimated 2 to 3 percent reduction in the risk of an MI (Massey, Hupp, Kreisberg, Alpert, & Hoff, 2000). Interventions aimed at lowering high blood pressure typically begin with pharmacological treatment. However, because hypertension is often symptom free, many patients fail to adhere to prescribed treatment regimens.

Changing behavior also can go a long way toward lowering blood pressure. For example, lowering sodium intake can bring about significant improvement in blood pressure readings. Many people with hypertension are sodium sensitive, meaning that excess sodium raises their blood pressure. Because there is no test for sodium sensitivity, almost everyone with hypertension should restrict dietary sodium to 2000 mg per day.

Numerous studies have shown that even moderate amounts of physical activity can help lower the resting blood pressure of people with hypertension (Ishikawa-Takata, Ohta, & Tanaka, 2003). It also can improve a person's cholesterol profile by increasing HDL cholesterol and by reducing body mass index (Nordstrom, Dwyer, Merz, & Dwyer, 2003). Even when exercise fails to reduce hypertension or improve a person's lipid profile, it conveys a heart-protecting benefit: Physically fit hypertensives with elevated cholesterol actually have a lower overall risk of CVD than unfit individuals who have normal blood pressure and cholesterol. Most impressively, data from the CARDIA study reveal that even after adjustment for age, race, sex, smoking, family history of hypertension, diabetes, and CHD, participants with low fitness levels (below the 20th percentile in performance on a treadmill test) were three to six times more likely to develop hypertension, diabetes, and the metabolic syndrome than participants with high fitness levels (above the 60th percentile) (Carnethon and others, 2003; Seeman and others, 2009). Regular exercise is also associated with significant reductions in the risk of ischemic and hemorrhagic strokes (Lee, Folsom, & Blair, 2003).

Risk Reduction—and Preventing Recurrence Regular exercise and good nutrition are significant factors in preventing CVD and in preventing recurrence of CVD. A former heart attack victim (left, below) saw his illness as a wake-up call and changed his life, beginning with a medically supervised program of aerobic exercise. The person in the photo on the right is improving his cholesterol ratios with a vegetarian diet and a glass of wine.

To be most beneficial, physical exertion should occur in the context of leisure and not work. In a case-control study of 312 patients with stable CHD, researchers found that participants who engaged in regular leisure-time physical activity also had lower levels of C-reactive protein—a protein that we have seen to be linked to the inflammatory response—and interleukin-6, a proinflammatory cytokine linked with immunosuppression (see Chapter 4) (Rothenbacher, Hoffmeister, Brenner, & Koenig, 2003). By contrast, *work-related* physical exertion was strongly associated with *increased* risk of CHD. These results suggest that one mechanism of the heart-protective effects of regular exercise is a beneficial effect on the body's inflammatory response.

Even if a person has had a heart attack, preventive behaviors can play an important role in controlling the negative effects of CVD. For example, exercise improves the heart's ability to pump blood to working muscles, as well as the muscles' ability to extract and use oxygen from the blood. Dozens of research studies involving thousands of heart attack patients demonstrate that patients who participated in cardiac rehabilitation exercise programs are significantly less likely to die from CVD (Stephens, 2009).

Reducing Cholesterol

Reducing serum cholesterol levels requires consuming less saturated fat (no more than 10 percent of your total daily calories). Saturated fats raise serum cholesterol by signaling the body to manufacture fewer LDL receptors, which help the liver to remove cholesterol from the body. The major sources of saturated fats are animal fats, butterfat, some tropical oils, and heavy hydrogenated oils. Even more important is never consuming trans-fatty acids (found in any foods with partially hydrogenated oils), due to the dangerous way that they increase LDL and triglyceride levels.

Monounsaturated and polyunsaturated fats, such as those contained in olive and grape seed oil, are much healthier choices. Although they have just as many calories as saturated fats, they help lower serum cholesterol and improve the HDL/LDL cholesterol ratio. When carbohydrates replace saturated fat, the reduction in LDL cholesterol is often accompanied by an unhealthy increase in triglycerides and reduction in HDL cholesterol. However, when monounsaturated fats are substituted for saturated fats, the same beneficial degree of LDL cholesterol lowering often occurs, with less or no change in triglyceride or HDL levels. A Mediterranean-type diet, rich in fruits and vegetables, whole grains, olive oil and other monounsaturated fats, fish, and moderate consumption of red wine, has been associated with lower heart rates and a reduction in the risk of CVD that is independent of its effect on LDL cholesterol. This is true even after adjustment for differences in physical activity, smoking status, alcohol consumption, and body mass index (Dallongeville and others, 2003). Eating more fiber, fruits, vegetables, and grains also has a cholesterol-lowering effect, perhaps by binding with acids that cause cholesterol to be pulled from the bloodstream.

Regular exercise, too, can improve an individual's lipid profile. How much exercise is needed? In a prospective study, William Kraus and his colleagues (2002) randomly assigned 111 sedentary, overweight men and women with mild-to-moderately-high HDL and triglyceride levels to participate for eight months in either a control group or one of three exercise groups: *high amount–high intensity exercise* (the caloric equivalent of jogging 20 miles per week at 65 to 80 percent of peak oxygen consumption), *low amount–high intensity exercise* (the caloric equivalent of jogging 12 miles per week at 65 to 80 percent of peak oxygen consumption), or *low amount–moderate intensity exercise* (the caloric equivalent of walking 12 miles per week at 40 to 55 percent of peak oxygen consumption). Although the greatest benefit on lipid profiles occurred in the high amount–high intensity group, both lower-amount exercise groups had significantly better lipid profiles than did sedentary participants in the control group. Other researchers have found that the combination of a low-fat, high-fiber diet and daily exercise for 45 to 60 minutes for three weeks can produce a significant decrease in total cholesterol and improved cholesterol ratios (Roberts, Vaziri, & Barnard, 2002).

After CVD: Preventing Recurrence

Most people who survive an MI recover well enough to resume near-normal lives within a few weeks or months. However, they remain high-risk individuals and need to make lifestyle adjustments in order to improve their chances of living a long life and avoiding a recurrence of CHD. Perceived social support, dispositional optimism, low hostility, and religious involvement have all been shown to have beneficial effects in the recovery of heart surgery patients (Mavros and others, 2011).

Patients who participate in *cardiac rehabilitation* (CR) programs generally fare best and have lower morbidity and mortality rates, along with improvements in the control of CHD risk factors, anxiety, stress, hostility, depression, and quality of life (Acevedo and others, 2013; Hsu and others, 2011; Lavie & Milani, 2005). Despite the benefits of CR, only 10 percent to 20 percent of patients who survive an MI enter a CR program (Yohannes, Yalfani, Doherty, & Bundy, 2007). Patients who smoke, those who have been physically inactive, and those with low scores on surveys assessing body pain, social functioning, and general health are less likely to begin or fully adhere to CR programs following a cardiac event (Bustamante and others, 2015).

One recent study of a diverse group of 77 cardiac patients demonstrated that irrational health beliefs also predict adherence to CR programs. Participants completed a 20-item survey that consisted of health-related vignettes such as the following:

> During a routine check-up, your doctor emphasized the importance of exercise and eating right to prevent health problems. You notice that the doctor is quite overweight. You think to yourself, "If good eating habits and exercise were really important, he would lose weight himself" (Christensen, Moran, & Wiebe, 1999).

Those who were most likely to agree with statements such as this one were more likely to drop out of their CR program prematurely (Anderson & Emery, 2014). The results of this study suggest that nonadherence may also be linked with a tendency to rely on beliefs that are not grounded in medical science.

Managing Stress, Anxiety, and Hostility

A heart attack or stroke can cause substantial distress to both the patient and his or her family members. Although many patients make a complete recovery and are able to resume most of their previous activities, some remain psychologically impaired for a long time. A major goal of many intervention programs is to deal with the approximately one-third of the patients who experience significant stress, anxiety, depression, or hostility after their hospitalization (De Jonge & Ormel, 2007). One recent study of 477 acute MI-patients found that those with the most clinical symptoms of anxiety and depression two months after hospitalization had the worst prognosis in terms of recurrent MI and early mortality (Roest, Martens, de Jonge, & Denollet, 2014).

Interventions aimed at reducing hostility are based on two premises:

- Hostile people are more likely to encounter stress, which increases the prevalence of atherosclerosis-promoting experiences involving anger.

- Hostile people are less likely to have stress-busting resources such as social support, partly as a result of their antagonistic behavior.

Intervention studies focus on helping hostile people gain control over their anger. In the typical program, the psychologist first attempts to gain insight into the triggers of anger-inducing incidents by having participants self-monitor their behavior. Next, the participants develop strategies for coping with aggravation—for example, by avoiding especially stressful situations such as rush-hour traffic and controlling their reactions, perhaps by counting to 10 before reacting to a provoking incident. As the participants become increasingly able to cope with problem situations, the psychologist turns to a more cognitive intervention, helping participants learn to challenge cynical attitudes and modify unrealistic beliefs and expectations about life. Dozens of studies have supported the efficacy of these interventions.

Clinical health psychologists have used a variety of other strategies to help individuals cope with anger. One effective strategy is relaxation training, which was discussed in Chapter 5 as an effective means of coping with stress. Another method involves teaching angry persons new social and communication skills in which they learn to be more civilly assertive and to become aware of other people's cues that would normally provoke anger in them. Teaching participants to avoid provocative situations and to take themselves less seriously are also common goals of anger-intervention programs.

Poor lifestyle behaviors and lifestyle-related risk factors are major contributors to cardiovascular disease. Fortunately, lifestyle modifications and comprehensive interventions that combine stress management, exercise, relaxation training, and hostility reduction with nonsmoking and a healthy diet can significantly reduce a person's risk of CVD. We turn our attention now to another major controllable risk factor for CVD: diabetes.

Diabetes

diabetes mellitus A disorder of the endocrine system in which the body is unable to produce insulin (Type 1) or is unable to use this pancreatic hormone properly (Type 2).

One of the most important risk factors for the development of CVD is **diabetes mellitus,** which involves the body's inability to produce or properly use insulin, a hormone that helps convert sugar and starches from food into energy. There is no cure for diabetes, and its cause remains a mystery, although both heredity and lifestyle factors appear to play roles. Diabetes mellitus affects more than 25 million Americans (8.3 percent of the population), is the third most common chronic illness and seventh leading cause of death in the United States, and has an annual cost of more than $174 billion. Overall, the risk of death among people with diabetes is twice that of people of the same age but without diabetes. Adding to the health burden caused by this chronic condition, medical expenses for people with diabetes average more than twice those for people without diabetes (CDC, 2015d).

It is estimated that 86 million Americans aged 20 years and older have *prediabetes,* characterized by blood glucose levels that are higher than normal but have not yet risen to the level that indicates a diagnosis of diabetes. People with prediabetes have an increased risk of developing Type 2 diabetes, heart disease, and stroke (CDC, 2014c).

Prevalence rates for diabetes vary markedly around the world: The disease is absent or rare in some indigenous communities in developing countries in Africa, the Eastern Mediterranean, and the Western Pacific, but prevalence rates rise to as high as 14 to 20 percent in some Arab, Asian Indian, Chinese, and Hispanic-American populations (WHO, 2010b). As with other chronic conditions, Type 2 diabetes is unequally distributed across ethnic groups. The percentage of adults with diagnosed diabetes is highest among American Indians/Alaska Natives (15.9 percent), followed by non-Hispanic blacks (13.2 percent), Hispanics (12.8 percent), Asian-Americans (9.0 percent), and non-Hispanic whites (7.6 percent) (National Diabetes Statistics Report, 2014) (Figure 10.7).

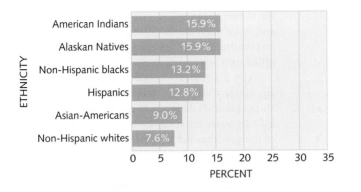

FIGURE 10.7

Estimated Age-Adjusted Prevalence of Diabetes in the United States by Ethnicity, 2014 Diabetes takes a greater toll on some ethnic groups than on others; especially vulnerable are American Indians, Alaska Natives, non-Hispanic blacks, and Hispanic-Americans.

Data from Centers for Disease Control and Prevention (CDC). (2014c). *National diabetes statistics report: Estimates of diabetes and its burden in the United States, 2014.* Atlanta, GA: U.S. Department of Health and Human Services.

Types of Diabetes

There are two basic types of diabetes: *Type 1 diabetes* (previously called *insulin-dependent diabetes mellitus,* or *juvenile diabetes*), and *Type 2 diabetes* (previously called *non-insulin-dependent diabetes mellitus,* or *adult-onset diabetes*) (Table 10.2). Type 1 diabetes, which usually appears in childhood (usually between 5 and 6 years of age) or less frequently during adolescence, is an autoimmune disease in which the person's immune system attacks the insulin- and glucagon-producing *islet cells* of the pancreas. In a healthy person, the opposing actions of these hormones help regulate the blood level of the sugar glucose. Glucagon stimulates the release of glucose, causing blood sugar levels to rise, and insulin decreases blood sugar levels by causing cells to take up glucose more freely from the bloodstream. Without functioning islet cells, the body is unable to regulate blood sugar levels, and the individual becomes dependent on insulin delivered by injections or a pump. The symptoms of Type 1 diabetes, which include excessive

TABLE 10.2

Characteristics and Risk Factors of Type 1 and Type 2 Diabetes

Type 1	Type 2
Autoimmune disorder in which insulin-producing cells of the pancreas are destroyed	Chronic illness in which the body fails to produce enough insulin or to use insulin properly
Peak incidence occurs during puberty, around 10 to 12 years of age in girls and 12 to 14 in boys	Onset occurs after age 30/accounts for 90–95 percent of all cases of diabetes
Accounts for 5–10 percent of all cases of diabetes	Symptoms include any of the Type 1 symptoms and blurred vision, frequent infections, cuts that are slow to heal, tingling or numbness in hands or feet
Symptoms may mimic flu, including excessive thirst, frequent urination, unusual weight loss, extreme fatigue, and irritability	
Requires insulin injections	Requires strict diet and exercise
Who Is at Greater Risk?	**Who Is at Greater Risk?**
Children of parents with Type 1 diabetes	People over age 45 with a family history of diabetes
Siblings of people with Type 1 diabetes	Affects more women than men
Affects women and men equally	People who are overweight
Higher prevalence among European-Americans than other ethnic groups	Women who had gestational diabetes or who had a baby weighing 9 pounds or more at birth
	People who don't exercise regularly
	People with low HDL cholesterol or high triglycerides
	African-Americans, Native Americans, Hispanic-Americans, Asians, and Pacific Islanders/People of low socioeconomic status

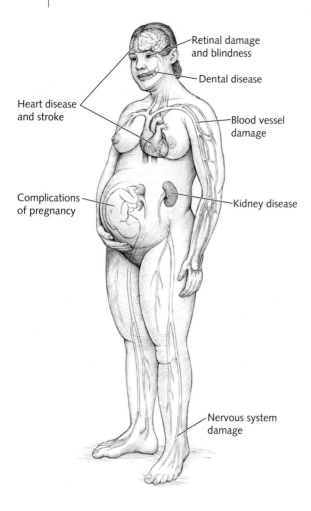

Retinal damage
and blindness

Dental disease

Heart disease
and stroke

Blood vessel
damage

Complications
of pregnancy

Kidney disease

Nervous system
damage

FIGURE 10.8

**Health Complications
Associated with Diabetes** Over
time, consistently high blood
sugar can cause complications
that affect the eyes, teeth and
gums, heart, kidneys, nerves,
feet, and other parts of the body.
Poor blood sugar control during
pregnancy increases the risk of
premature birth, miscarriage, and
birth defects.

Information from Centers for Disease
Control and Prevention (CDC).
(2014c). *National diabetes statistics
report: Estimates of diabetes and its
burden in the United States, 2014.*
Atlanta, GA: U.S. Department of Health
and Human Services.

thirst and urination, craving for sweets, weight loss, fatigue, and irritability, are largely the result of the body's inability to metabolize glucose for energy, which forces it to begin feeding off its own fats and proteins.

Type 2 diabetes—a milder form of the disease, which usually appears after age 30—is found in more than 90 percent of all people with diabetes. It results from *insulin resistance* (also called *glucose intolerance*—a condition in which the islet cells of the pancreas fail to make enough insulin) and/or an insensitivity to insulin caused by a decrease in the number of insulin receptors in target cells. The symptoms of Type 2 diabetes include frequent urination; irregular menstruation in women; fatigue; slow healing of cuts and bruises; dryness of the mouth; and pain or cramps in the legs, feet, and fingers. Type 2 diabetes is more common among women, overweight people, members of certain ethnic groups, and those of low socioeconomic status. If current trends continue, as many as 1 in 3 adults in the United States could have diabetes by 2050 (Boyle and others, 2010).

In both types of diabetes, two types of blood sugar problems can develop: *hypoglycemia* (blood sugar level that is too low) and *hyperglycemia* (blood sugar level that is too high). An estimated 50 to 75 percent of individuals with diabetes develop one or more long-term health complications as a result of their body's inability to regulate blood sugar (CDC, 2009). Figure 10.8 illustrates these health complications. Elevated levels of glucose, for instance, cause the walls of arteries to thicken, accelerating the development of atherosclerosis and CVD. Men and women with diabetes have CHD mortality rates that are up to two times higher than they are for adults without diabetes. Because unregulated glucose levels in the blood can damage the retinas of the eyes, diabetes is also the leading cause of blindness among adults. Diabetes is also the leading cause of end-stage renal (kidney) disease and is associated with cancer of the pancreas, damage to the nervous system that may cause memory impairments (especially among older adults), and loss of sensation or pain in the extremities. In severe cases of poor circulation and loss of sensation in the extremities, amputation of the toes or feet may be required. Overall, the risk of death for people with diabetes is about 1.5 times higher than that of people without diabetes (CDC, 2014c).

Causes of Diabetes

As with other chronic illnesses, diabetes seems to be caused by multiple factors, including viral or bacterial infections that damage the islet cells of the pancreas, an overactive immune system, and genetic vulnerability.

Obesity has been historically known as a major risk factor for Type 2 diabetes. Today, about 30 percent of overweight people have diabetes, and 85 percent of those who have diabetes are overweight (Powell, 2012). Recently, researchers have discovered two critical links between obesity and diabetes. Both are based on the fact that, generally speaking, the more fat tissue a person has, the less sensitive they become to insulin. First, it appears that fat cells release a protein called *pigment epithelium-derived factor* (PEDF) into the bloodstream, which causes muscle cells and the liver to become desensitized to insulin. In response, the pancreas works harder to produce more insulin. As fat accumulates, the pancreas eventually may slow or even stop the release of insulin, thus leading to Type 2 diabetes (Crowe and others, 2009).

A second line of research implicates immune factors in the relationship between obesity and diabetes and suggests that obesity can be uncoupled from insulin resistance. Researchers studied mice that were genetically engineered to lack *T-bet*, a protein that regulates the differentiation and function of immune cells. They found that the mice had improved insulin sensitivity despite being obese. Although the mice had more abdominal fat, that fat contained fewer immune cells and was less inflamed than that of normal mice. The researchers also found that by transferring immune cells lacking T-bet to young, lean mice, they were able to improve insulin-sensitive obesity (Stolarczyk and others, 2013).

Not all diabetes cases are linked to weight. Genetics and environmental factors such as *nutritional Westernization*, which includes a diet high in fat and processed foods as well as total calories, also may be contributing factors in diabetes. Increased television watching associated with reduced physical activity and poor nutrition may also contribute to Type 2 diabetes. One study found that participants with Type 2 diabetes were more likely to watch more than four hours of TV per day compared to control participants (Huffman and others, 2012).

Stress has also been suggested as a precipitating factor in diabetes, especially Type 1 diabetes, among individuals with a strong family history of the disease (Sepa, Wahlberg, Vaarala, Frodi, & Ludvigsson, 2005). People who have already been diagnosed with diabetes, as well as those at high risk for the disease, react to laboratory and environmental stressors with abnormally greater changes in their blood glucose levels than do people not at risk for diabetes (Weisli and others, 2005). Following the *diathesis–stress* model of disease (see Chapter 4), some investigators have suggested that abnormal blood sugar responses to challenging events (a symptom of an overreactive sympathetic nervous system), in conjunction with long-term exposure to high levels of stress, may be a *direct* path to the development of diabetes. Indirectly, stress also may promote the development of diabetes by adversely affecting the individual's diet, level of compliance with treatment regimens, and tendency to exercise.

Prevention of Diabetes

The Diabetes Prevention Program (DPP), a large prevention study of people at high risk for diabetes, showed that lifestyle interventions to lose weight and increase physical activity reduced the development of Type 2 diabetes by 58 percent during a 3-year period (NIDDK, 2008). The reduction was even greater, 71 percent, among adults aged 60 years and older. Prevention or delay with lifestyle intervention was effective in all racial and ethnic groups studied and has been shown to persist for at least 10 years. Research also has found that lifestyle interventions are more cost-effective than medications (NIDDK, 2008).

Diabetes Self-Management

Self-management is a crucial aspect of treatment for diabetes. Fortunately, most people with diabetes can control their disease through lifestyle modifications—by changing their diet, regulating their weight, and exercising regularly, for example—and, in some cases, with daily injections of insulin. The goal of treatment, of course, is tight *glycemic control*—keeping blood sugar at a stable, healthy level—as revealed through a finger prick or venipuncture test measuring *HbA1c* (glycated hemoglobin) levels in the bloodstream, specifically in red blood cells, which contain the molecule hemoglobin. Glucose sticks to hemoglobin, forming HbA1c. The more glucose in the blood, the higher HbA1c levels will be. Because red blood cells live for 8 to 12 weeks before they are replaced, the HbA1c test reveals how high blood glucose has been on average for this period of time.

Diabetes self-management, a prerequisite for tight glycemic control, involves a daily regimen of several behaviors, including healthy eating, physical activity, blood glucose monitoring, foot care, taking medications, problem solving, and active coping (American Diabetes Association, 2010b). Completing these tasks day after day is demanding and often requires significant lifestyle modifications. Doing so, however, pays off. Researchers have consistently found an inverse association between diabetes self-management and HbA1c levels (Fortmann, Gallo, and Philis-Tsimikas, 2011).

Diabetes self-management training programs are especially critical for people who lack access to health care services, which is the case for many ethnic minorities (Anders and others, 2008). For instance, less than 60 percent of Latino adults with Type 2 diabetes receive annual eye and foot exams and participate in daily blood glucose monitoring (CDC, 2011a). To make matters worse, Latinos with Type 2 diabetes perceive self-monitoring of blood glucose as more difficult and have more negative perceptions about their future well-being, than do African-Americans, Asian-Americans, and non-Latino whites with diabetes (Misra and Lager, 2009).

Passage of the Affordable Care Act authorized the creation of the National Diabetes Prevention Program (NDPP) in order to "eliminate the preventable burden of diabetes." Based on the Diabetes Prevention Program discussed earlier, the NDPP is designed to bring evidence-based lifestyle change programs for preventing Type 2 diabetes to communities throughout the country (Burge & Schade, 2014).

Diabetes self-management typically occurs in a social context of family, friends, health care providers, and the community, each of which can influence adherence (Barrera, Toobert, Angell, Glasgow, & MacKinnon, 2006). Individuals with Type 2 diabetes who report receiving greater support resources for their disease management exhibit greater physical activity (measured as caloric expenditure from exercise), better dietary outcomes (fat and fiber intake), greater adherence to blood glucose monitoring, and tighter glycemic control than do people with less support (D. K. King and others, 2010; Brody, Kogan, Mury, Chen, & Brown, 2008).

The medical community is currently debating whether both types of diabetes should be treated in the same way, including medication for precise glucose control, or differently (Tucker, 2002). Type 1 diabetes treatment requires insulin management, but Type 2 diabetes treatment could focus on weight control, exercise, and diet—in particular, reducing sugar and carbohydrate intake and keeping the total number of calories consumed each day within a narrow range. In practice, a combination of treatments is used with Type 1 diabetes, depending on the severity of the individual case and the effectiveness of dietary and exercise modifications. For preventing diabetes, moderate exercise, improved diet, and other lifestyle interventions win hands down over medications (Zepf, 2005).

Health Psychology and Diabetes

The knowledge, beliefs, and behavior of patients strongly affect their ability to manage their diabetes and its impact on every domain of their health. This makes the health psychologist's role in the care and treatment of people with diabetes particularly important, as underscored by the standards of treatment recommended by the American Diabetes Association (ADA). Educational interventions are vitally important, but not sufficient on their own to promote adherence to healthier lifestyle regimens (Garcia-Perez, Alvarez, Dilla, Gil-Guillen, & Orozco-Beltran, 2013; Rutten, 2005). People with diabetes often have deficits in their knowledge about diabetes and their increased risk for heart disease and other chronic conditions (Wagner, Lacey, Abbott, de Groot, & Chyun, 2006). The ADA also emphasizes that *self-management* is the cornerstone of treatment for all people with diabetes. As a result, psychologists are increasingly becoming involved in the primary care of people with diabetes (Gillies and others, 2007).

Diversity and Healthy Living

Cultural Adaptations to Evidence-Based Interventions for Type 2 Diabetes

Women of Hispanic heritage (Latinas) living in the United States have a prevalence of Type 2 diabetes that is almost twice that found for non-Latina white women (National Diabetes Statistics Report, 2014). If current trends continue, over 20 percent of the Latino population overall is expected to have diabetes by 2031.

To delay or prevent the numerous health problems associated with diabetes, people with the chronic condition must maintain tight glycemic control. Latinos with Type 2 diabetes, however, often exhibit poorer glycemic control, and thus, more frequent health complications, greater disease severity, and worse outcomes than non-Latino whites (Fortmann and others, 2011).

One approach to the development of interventions for at-risk ethnic groups such as Latinos is the cultural adaptation of evidence-based interventions that have proven effective with other groups or health conditions (Castro, Barrera, & Holleran Streiker, 2010). A Spanish-language public education campaign called *¡Viva Bien!* was launched in 2005 by the American Diabetes Association, the American Heart Association, and the American Cancer Society. Aimed specifically at Latina women, the campaign was designed to help them make everyday choices that can improve their own health, as well as that of others in their community. The television commercials featured Latino families making healthy lifestyle choices such as taking a walk in the park, planting vegetables with their kids, and buying fruits at the market.

A study conducted fairly recently recruited 280 Latina women, 30 to 75 years of age, living in the Denver, Colorado, area, who had been diagnosed with Type 2 diabetes for at least 6 months. Extending the *¡Viva Bien!* program, health psychologists adapted the *Mediterranean Lifestyle Program,* which has proven effective in promoting diabetes self-management behaviors in non-Latina white women (Osuna and others, 2011). The intervention included a 2½-day retreat that introduced the components of the program and provided time for participants to practice new skills, including (1) following a Mediterranean-style diet adapted for Latino cultures, (2) daily stress-management techniques, (3) 30 minutes of daily physical activity, (4) smoking cessation, and (5) participation in problem-solving–based support groups. Following the retreat, weekly meetings continued for the next 6 months, followed by twice-monthly meetings for an additional 6 months.

Follow-up assessments of body mass index, physical activity, and saturated fat consumption were made at 6 and 12 months. Statistically significant intervention effects were found for each of these outcome variables. Interestingly, the researchers found an interaction between participants' acculturation and several of the dependent variables. Specifically, Latina orientation was associated with both lower saturated fat intake (a protective factor) and less physical activity (a risk factor).

The primary diabetes outcome around which self-management interventions are based is **glycemic control,** as measured by a blood test that indicates average plasma glucose for the previous two to three months. The primary self-care tasks that help to maintain glycemic control, such as monitoring blood glucose levels, injecting insulin, and dosing insulin according to meter results, must be carried out several times per day, often around meals, and in varied contexts such as school, the workplace, home, and restaurants. Given the frequency and nature of these tasks, it is not surprising that adherence rates are often suboptimal (Greening, Stoppelbein, Konishi, Jordan, & Moll, 2007).

Increasingly, smart phones and tablets are being used to sample behaviors and experiences in real time, and as the basis of interventions to promote adherence to self-care behaviors in managing chronic conditions such as diabetes (Mulvaney and others, 2012). This type of *ecological momentary assessment* (EMA) may be particularly effective with adolescents because an estimated 93 percent of 13- to 17-year-olds use cell phones (Lenhart, Purcell, Smith, & Zickuhr, 2010). Diabetes self-care behaviors measured via EMA include completion of blood glucose monitoring, timing of blood glucose monitoring, and timing and dosing of insulin.

glycemic control The action of monitoring glucose levels to keep blood sugar at a stable, healthy level.

Promoting Adjustment to Diabetes

A patient who receives a diagnosis of diabetes may experience a range of emotions, including shock, denial, anger, and depression (Jacobson, 1996). Helping patients accept their diagnoses is the first step in promoting self-management. Consider the case of Beatrice, a 64-year-old woman with a 20-year history of hypertension and a 4-year history of Type 2 diabetes. Beatrice reported feeling anger at her initial diagnosis. Over the next few months, she began exhibiting symptoms of depression and anxiety, and her already poor glucose control got even worse (Feifer & Tansman, 1999). Using *rational-emotive therapy,* psychologists challenged Beatrice's negative perceptions about her disease and helped her to feel better about herself, manage her moods, and deal with her self-care tasks on a day-to-day basis. As her acceptance of the disease and the once seemingly overwhelming tasks of self-management improved, Beatrice ultimately gained much better control over her blood sugar levels.

Even after accepting their diagnoses, many patients with diabetes continue to struggle with **illness intrusiveness,** which refers to the disruptive effect of diabetes on their lives. Illness intrusiveness can affect an individual's well-being adversely in at least two ways: directly, when the condition interferes with valued activities and interests, and indirectly, as a result of perceptions of reduced personal control, self-efficacy, and self-esteem. However, research has shown that having strong social support and good personal coping resources—including high self-esteem, a sense of mastery, and feelings of self-efficacy in the face of adversity—are associated with fewer depressive symptoms in people with diabetes (Rassart and others, 2015).

Psychologists have designed interventions to help people who do not have the support or resources needed to cope with diabetes. They reduce diabetes intrusiveness on daily living by teaching people to redefine personal priorities, increase participation in enjoyable activities, and restructure irrational expectations regarding the intrusiveness of the disease. They also help patients mobilize social support and improve personal coping skills.

illness intrusiveness The extent to which a chronic illness disrupts an individual's life by interfering with valued activities and interests and reducing perceptions of personal control, self-efficacy, and self-esteem.

Blood Glucose Awareness

Diabetes patients often lack proper understanding of their disease and its symptoms. One study found that more than 50 percent of patients with diabetes had inaccurate beliefs about blood glucose levels, including the symptoms of hypoglycemia and hyperglycemia (Gonder-Frederick, Cox, Bobbitt, & Pennebaker, 1989). As a result, the patients often overlooked or missed some potentially serious symptoms and overreacted to other, irrelevant ones. Health psychologists have reported impressive results from *blood glucose awareness training,* in which patients learn to gauge their blood sugar levels from environmental cues (such as time of day or ongoing activity), physical symptoms (such as nausea and mouth dryness), and mood (such as fatigue and irritability). Through such training, which is similar in many ways to biofeedback training, most people with diabetes can learn to reliably recognize various cognitive and behavioral indicators of different blood glucose levels (Gebel, 2013). Compared with untrained control patients, those patients trained in blood glucose awareness have achieved these additional health benefits:

- improved glucose control and fewer long-term health complications
- fewer automobile and other accidents resulting from states of hypoglycemia
- fewer hospitalizations for blood sugar level abnormalities

Treating Diabetes-Related Psychological Disorders

People with diabetes tend toward feelings of depression, especially during the early stages of adjusting to the disease. Psychologists have also found that diagnosable clinical disorders such as major depression, anxiety, and eating disorders are more prevalent among adults with diabetes than they are in the general population (Lustman & Clouse, 2005). Prevalence rates for major depressive disorder, for example, which range from 5 to 25 percent in the general population, have been found to range from 22 to 60 percent among those with diabetes (American Diabetes Association, 2010a). In one study, over 30 percent of Latino participants with diabetes reported depressive symptoms in the moderate to severe range (Gross and others, 2005).

The physical and emotional demands placed on the individual with diabetes, including strict compliance to a complex treatment regimen of daily self-monitoring of blood glucose levels, preparing special meals, and taking medication, can be difficult and frustrating. This regimen is made all the more challenging when the individual suffers from unusual psychosocial distress or a psychological disorder. Many research studies have found an association between depression and the higher hBA1c levels associated with poor glycemic control (e.g., Gross and others, 2005). With depression, for instance, self-care tasks such as daily monitoring of glucose levels or preparation of special foods may seem futile or too difficult to accomplish.

The mechanisms underlying the link between depression and glycemic control are likely to involve a combination of behavioral and physiological factors. Behaviorally, the low energy levels that characterize depression may interfere with a person's ability to follow the self-management regimen. Physiologically, depression is associated with activation of the hypothalamic-pituitary-adrenal axis, sympathetic nervous system, and pro-inflammatory responses, each of which can induce insulin resistance and contribute to poorer diabetes-related health outcomes (Golden, 2007).

Many health professionals have suggested that individuals with diabetes should have psychosocial evaluations at some point during their medical treatment, preferably soon after the time of diagnosis (Gonzalez and others, 2008). Health psychologists who are involved in the primary care of people diagnosed with diabetes are in a good position to refer them to appropriate clinical psychologists, if needed.

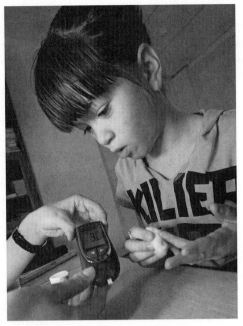

RIA Novosti/Science Source

Self-Management of Diabetes
The goal of diabetes treatment is to keep blood sugar at a stable, healthy level. Here, a health care professional instructs a young child with diabetes on how to draw blood safely, to monitor blood sugar level.

Managing Weight and Stress

Effective weight management is particularly important for patients with diabetes because lower weight improves the body's ability to regulate glucose and thereby reduces the need for medication. Weight-loss programs often produce substantial success among people with diabetes by using a multimodal approach that combines nutrition, education, low-calorie diets, and regular exercise. As with all weight-loss programs, however, the main problem has been in maintaining the loss.

Regular exercise can also help prevent Type 2 diabetes. Several research studies have found that physically active women and men have a much lower incidence of Type 2 diabetes than those who are sedentary (CDC, 2010a). This protective effect remains even after researchers control for other major diabetes risk factors, including obesity, hypertension, and family history of the disease. Interestingly, people with Type 2 diabetes have the greatest difficulty maintaining healthy concentrations of blood sugar in March and April, perhaps because the preceding months of cold weather have promoted inactivity (Doro, Benko, Matuz, & Soos, 2006).

Equally important is stress management. In people with diabetes, reactions to stress strongly influence whether and how well they follow a particular regimen. For example, stress may begin the vicious cycle of overeating, poor control over diabetes, more stress, more overeating, and so on. Relaxation training and other stress-management techniques appear to be beneficial for many individuals with diabetes.

The general topic of why certain people are more likely to delay making healthy lifestyle changes and seeking health care is discussed in Chapter 13.

Increasing Adherence to Diabetes Treatment Regimens

Health psychologists have approached the issue of adherence in two ways: by seeking to identify factors that predict compliance or noncompliance and by developing interventions to improve adherence to different aspects of a treatment regimen. Sociodemographic factors such as age, gender, ethnicity, and personality do not predict adherence to diabetes treatment regimens. Several factors contribute to noncompliance, including the sheer complexity of a lifelong regimen of self-care. Patients with diabetes also may perceive prescribed treatment as recommended and discretionary rather than mandatory, and they fail to comply. Those newly diagnosed with diabetes often feel no ill effects—severe medical complications of diabetes may not arise for a decade or more—and may find their current lifestyle too enjoyable to change. Social and environmental circumstances are also factors in poor adherence. During periods of unusual stress or social pressure to behave in unhealthy ways, for instance, dietary and exercise compliance often decreases among those with diabetes (Cramer, 2004).

Working from the transtheoretical model discussed in Chapter 6, health psychologists might try to get diabetes patients to adhere to treatment regimens by helping them cycle through the stages of precontemplation, contemplation, preparation, action, and maintenance. For example, the psychologist almost certainly would tell an obese woman newly diagnosed with Type 2 diabetes to lose weight. However, since she probably does not feel sick, she sees no reason to change from her delicious high-calorie, high-carbohydrate diet (precontemplation). To move her to the stage of contemplation, the psychologist would try to explain the connection between diet and diabetes. (She perceives a link, but she still isn't ready to give up her favorite foods.) Further education and support for change (family members are enlisted to help her modify her diet, for instance) may nudge the patient into the stage of preparation (she knows she will diet), and then to action (the patient works hard at dieting). Finally, during the maintenance stage (working to avoid relapse to unhealthy eating habits), she is likely to benefit from interventions that focus on how to maintain the treatment regimen in the face of circumstances that undermine it (such as unusual stress or social pressure to eat unhealthy foods). Let's revisit the case of Beatrice, the diagnosed diabetic introduced earlier in this chapter who abandoned her medical regimen each time she encountered a stressful life event. For her, maintenance interventions involved exercises to promote stress management and improve her communication coping skills.

Enhancing Communication and Increasing Social Support

Empowering individuals with diabetes (or any chronic illness) to participate actively in decision making in their treatment regimen produces a variety of benefits. Among these are an increased perception of control, enhanced doctor–patient communication, greater confidence in prescribed treatment regimens, and improved compliance. In one study, diabetes patients who were taught to be more assertive in acquiring knowledge about the disease and in using that information to negotiate treatment decisions with their physicians showed significant increases in their perceived self-efficacy, regulation of blood glucose, and satisfaction with their treatment regimen (Greenfield, Kaplan, Ware, Yano, & Frank, 1988). Beatrice had received from her physician basic information about living with diabetes. She was too intimidated, however, to discuss her fears, self-care needs, and difficulty complying with her treatment regimen. She did, however, discuss these issues with her psychologist, who used assertiveness training to prepare Beatrice to approach her doctor to resolve these issues, which she later did.

The problems of managing diabetes extend beyond the individual to members of the family, who may react in ways that adversely (or favorably) affect the patient. The quality of marital relationships, for example, is an accurate predictor of diabetes regimen adherence (Trief, Ploutz-Snyder, Britton, & Weinstock, 2004). Among adolescents, elevated family conflict and weak parental monitoring are risk factors for poorer glycemic control (Hilliard and others, 2013). Family therapy is often helpful. Therapy often begins with education about diabetes, what must be done to achieve control, and how the behaviors of family members—including parental monitoring—affect the individual's control. This can be particularly important in the management of Type 1 diabetes in children and adolescents. Parents, for example, may become overly protective of a teenager newly diagnosed with diabetes, unnecessarily restricting activities and promoting a sense of helplessness.

Your Health Assets

Benefit Finding

People who have diabetes, cardiovascular disease, or other serious conditions sometimes feel that their experiences have made positive contributions to their lives as well as causing problems. If you have gone through something like this, circle the appropriate number to indicate how often you experienced each of the following benefits. Add your answers. Higher scores indicate higher levels of benefit.

Having had _____ has:	Not at all	A little	Moderately	Quite a Bit	Extremely
shown me that all people need to be loved.	1	2	3	4	5
made me more sensitive to family issues.	1	2	3	4	5
led me to be more accepting of things.	1	2	3	4	5
taught me that everyone has a purpose in life.	1	2	3	4	5
made us more in charge of ourselves as a family.	1	2	3	4	5
made me more aware and concerned for the future of humankind.	1	2	3	4	5
taught me how to adjust to things I cannot change.	1	2	3	4	5
given my family a sense of continuity, a sense of history.	1	2	3	4	5
made me a more responsible person.	1	2	3	4	5
made me realize the importance of planning for my family's future.	1	2	3	4	5
given my life better structure.	1	2	3	4	5
brought my family closer together.	1	2	3	4	5
made me more productive.	1	2	3	4	5
helped me take things as they come.	1	2	3	4	5
helped me to better budget my time.	1	2	3	4	5
made me more grateful for each day.	1	2	3	4	5
taught me to be patient.	1	2	3	4	5
taught me to control my temper.	1	2	3	4	5
renewed my interest in participating in different activities.	1	2	3	4	5
led me to cope better with stress and problems.	1	2	3	4	5

Information from Tomich, P. L., & Helgeson, V. S. (2004). Is finding something good in the bad always good? Benefit finding among women with breast cancer. *Health Psychology, 23*, 16–23; Tran, V. H. (2010). *Benefit finding, negative affect, and daily diabetes management among adolescents with Type 1 diabetes.* Doctoral dissertation. Retrieved from https://repositories.tdl.org/utswmed-ir/bitstream/handle/2152.5/819/tranvincent.pdf?sequence=3.

benefit finding The experience of identifying positive outcomes in the face of adversity.

Another factor that has been associated with better psychosocial well-being and improved adherence in many chronic illnesses is **benefit finding** (see *Your Health Assets* on page 313). Defined as the experience of identifying positive outcomes in the face of adversity, benefit finding is based on the idea that adversity can lead to a new sense of meaning and self-worth. Several recent studies have found that benefit finding is an important resource for adolescents who face heightened stress while dealing with an illness such as diabetes. One study reported that benefit finding was associated with both better adherence to diabetes management behaviors and fewer depressive symptoms among a group of 252 adolescents diagnosed with Type 1 diabetes (Tran, Wiebe, Fortenberry, Butler, & Berg, 2011).

From our biopsychosocial perspective, we have seen that many factors play a role in the development of chronic conditions such as cardiovascular disease and diabetes. Healthy living helps many people avoid or significantly delay the development of chronic conditions. Even those who are already suffering chronic disease still may improve their health by following better health practices, including eating well, exercising, maintaining normal weight, and avoiding tobacco. And physical and psychological coping strategies help many limit the life disruption of chronic conditions.

Weigh In on Health

Respond to each question below based on what you learned in the chapter. (**Tip:** Use the items in "Summing Up" to take into account related biological, psychological, and social concerns.)

1. How does hostility influence biological, psychological, and social or cultural aspects of heart health and cardiovascular disease?

2. A friend, who knows that you are studying health psychology, wants to understand the relationship between practicing health psychology and reducing the risk of diabetes. Based on what you read in this chapter, how will you explain this relationship?

3. Diverse populations have not experienced improvements in health status uniformly. What factors do you think may contribute to health disparities in cardiovascular disease and diabetes among different racial/ethnic, socioeconomic, and cultural groups? What individual actions, programs, or policies could be put in place to reduce these disparities?

Summing Up

The Healthy Heart

1. The cardiovascular system consists of the blood, the blood vessels of the circulatory system, and the heart. The heart consists of three layers of tissue: a thin outer layer, called the *epicardium;* a thin inner layer, called the *endocardium;* and a thicker middle layer, the heart muscle itself, or *myocardium.* The myocardium is separated into four chambers that work in coordinated fashion to bring blood into the heart and then to pump it throughout the body.

Cardiovascular Disease

2. Cardiovascular disease (CVD), which includes coronary heart disease (CHD) and stroke, is the leading cause of death in the United States and most developed countries.

3. CVD results from atherosclerosis, a chronic condition in which coronary arteries are narrowed by fatty deposits and atheromatous plaques that form over microscopic lesions in the walls of blood vessels, and arteriosclerosis, or hardening of the arteries.

4. When the arteries that supply the heart are narrowed with plaques, restricting blood flow to the heart (ischemia), the person may experience chest pain, called angina pectoris. When severe atherosclerosis or a clot causes a coronary artery to become completely obstructed, a heart attack, or myocardial infarction (MI), occurs, and a portion of the myocardium begins to die. A third possible manifestation of cardiovascular malfunction is a stroke, which occurs when a blood clot obstructs an artery in the brain.

Risk Factors for Cardiovascular Disease

5. The Framingham Heart Study, the Nurses' Health Study, and the global INTERHEART Study identified a number of coronary risk factors.

6. The "uncontrollable risk factors" for CVD include family history of heart disease, age, gender, and ethnicity. The risk of CVD increases with age, is much higher among men than among women, and varies across racial and ethnic groups. Economic and social factors may be the actual causes of racial and ethnic variation in CVD.

7. The major "controllable risk factors" for CVD are hypertension, biological reactivity and inflammation, obesity, elevated serum cholesterol, and smoking.

8. Cholesterol levels that are too high promote the development of atherosclerosis. Those with metabolic syndrome are at particularly high risk of developing CVD and diabetes.

Psychosocial Factors in Cardiovascular Disease

9. Characterized by a competitive, hurried, hostile nature, the Type A behavior pattern has been linked to increased risk of CVD. Researchers now point to hostility and anger as the toxic core of Type A behavior.

10. Several theoretical explanations have been proposed to explain the relationship between a hostile, angry personality and cardiovascular disease. The psychosocial vulnerability model maintains that hostile people have more stressful life events and low levels of social support, and that this combination, over time, has a toxic effect.

11. The health behavior model proposes that hostile people are more likely to develop cardiovascular disease because they tend to have poorer health habits than less hostile people.

12. The psychophysiological reactivity model maintains that frequent episodes of anger produce elevated cardiovascular and stress hormone responses that damage arteries and contribute to coronary disease.

13. The biopsychosocial model suggests that, for CVD to develop, a hostile person first must have a biological predisposition toward it. CVD then may be more likely to develop because the hostile person's attitude has chased away social support and continues to elicit negative responses from others, which leads to more hostility and damaging cardiac reactivity.

Reducing the Risk of Cardiovascular Disease

14. Lifestyle modifications can significantly reduce a person's risk of cardiovascular disease. Interventions for hypertension include reducing weight, limiting salt and alcohol intake, increasing exercise, and improving cholesterol ratios. Eating more fiber, fruits, vegetables, grains, and mono- and polyunsaturated fats and less saturated fat can reduce serum cholesterol levels and improve the ratio of HDL cholesterol to LDL cholesterol.

After CVD: Preventing Recurrence

15. Comprehensive interventions that combine stress management, exercise, relaxation training, and low-fat diets may prevent CVD recurrence.

16. Interventions for hostility help people gain control of environmental triggers for their anger and learn to modify their negative emotions and cynical thought processes. Reducing hostility can substantially reduce the risk of future ischemia in cardiac patients.

Diabetes

17. Diabetes mellitus is a chronic disease in which the body is unable to produce or properly use the hormone insulin. Diabetes can develop in either childhood (Type 1) or adulthood (Type 2), with Type 1 diabetes generally involving the need for daily insulin injections. Many individuals with diabetes also benefit from lifestyle modifications that include a strict diet and exercise.

18. Many individuals with diabetes also suffer from psychological disorders, including major depression, anxiety, and eating disorders. Health psychology's role has included studying factors in adjusting to the disease, such as psychological distress, personal coping skills, and social support, as well as factors that affect compliance with treatment regimens.

19. Health psychologists are becoming increasingly involved in the primary care of diabetes by reducing illness intrusiveness, increasing weight control and stress management, enhancing communication, and increasing compliance with complex treatment regimens.

20. The primary diabetes outcome around which self-management interventions are based is glycemic control, as measured by a blood test that indicates average plasma glucose for the previous two to three months. Diabetes self-management, a prerequisite for tight glycemic control, involves a daily regimen of several behaviors, including healthy eating, physical activity, blood glucose monitoring, foot care, taking medications, problem solving, and active coping.

21. Benefit finding is an important resource for people who face heightened stress while dealing with diabetes and other chronic conditions.

Key Terms and Concepts to Remember

cardiovascular disease (CVD), p. 284
coronary heart disease (CHD), p. 285
atherosclerosis, p. 285
atheromatous plaques, p. 285
atherogenesis, p. 286
arteriosclerosis, p. 286
angina pectoris, p. 287

myocardial infarction (MI), p. 287
stroke, p. 287
hypertension, p. 290
cardiovascular reactivity
  (CVR), p. 291
hemostasis, p. 292
metabolic syndrome, p. 293

Type A, p. 294
Type B, p. 294
diabetes mellitus, p. 304
glycemic control, p. 309
illness intrusiveness, p. 310
benefit finding, p. 314

LaunchPad
macmillan learning

To accompany your textbook, you have access to a number of online resources, including quizzes for every chapter of the book, flashcards, critical thinking exercises, videos, and *Check Your Health* inventories. To access these resources, please visit the Straub *Health Psychology* LaunchPad solo at: **launchpadworks.com**

CHAPTER 11

Cancer

"Dad, can we go home now? I don't feel sick, and I don't want to be poked anymore." So said my 6-year-old son, Jeremy, at the end of a very long day in which he was diagnosed with cancer. It was the day my family's world seemed to turn upside down.

It began in a relatively uneventful manner, as childhood health problems often do: soreness and swelling on the left side of Jeremy's neck that seemed to appear overnight and wouldn't go away. An almost-casual visit to the family pediatrician revealed that the discomfort was due to swollen lymph glands, yet it did not seem to be a cause for alarm. Just to be safe, Jeremy was referred to the university's pediatric hospital for a few more tests to rule out any (unlikely) serious health problems. We grew increasingly worried after a morning of blood tests; physical examinations by a stream of nurses, doctors, and interns; and finally magnetic resonance imaging (MRI) of Jeremy's neck. We were ushered into a small waiting room in the pediatric oncology wing of the hospital, where we were stunned by the diagnosis: non-Hodgkin's lymphoma.

Our immediate reaction was disbelief. How? Why? As a health psychologist, I knew that there were probably no simple answers to those questions. There were no warning signs or symptoms. Jeremy had always been a healthy, active kid. He wasn't overweight, ate a nutritious diet, and, to my mind, had no known risk factors for cancer (other than several relatives who'd battled skin cancer). Just as our son's life was beginning, it seemed, inexplicably, to be in danger of ending.

Fortunately, we were not defenseless against this disease, which only a few decades earlier would almost certainly have been fatal. We immediately enacted a full biopsychosocial assault, including state-of-the-art biomedical interventions that arrested the cancer, a healthy diet and exercise program, and relaxation training to ease the discomfort of chemotherapy and promote a positive outlook. Jeremy's family, friends, classmates, primary care physician, and especially nurses, provided extensive social support, and Jeremy himself showed incredible strength of character—especially for a young child. He was stoic throughout his treatment, which was sometimes painful (as in the needle pokes) and included many nausea-inducing

317

bouts of chemotherapy. But his stoicism was not accompanied by withdrawal. He shared his feelings, fears, and determination to beat the disease with us, and we grew stronger because of his strength. At times, he could even laugh at himself and turn adversity into an apparent asset. When chemotherapy caused his hair to fall out, Jeremy—who remains an ardent *Star Trek: The Next Generation* fan—joked that he looked like a young Captain Picard!

Today, many years later, Jeremy is a healthy adult who graduated from college, went on to earn an MBA, and has started a successful company that generates popular mapping software for handheld computers. He travels extensively, pilots his own plane, and credits his survival to early detection, a marvelous health care team, and the powers of mind–body medicine.

While I wouldn't wish this painful chapter of our lives on anyone, our family survived and thrived after bringing Jeremy back to health. We all became more health-conscious . . . and more aware of the interconnections among the physical, psychological, and social aspects of our well-being.

What Is Cancer?

cancer A set of diseases in which abnormal body cells multiply and spread in uncontrolled fashion, often forming a tissue mass called a *tumor*.

Few of us have avoided the life-changing effects of cancer—either in ourselves or in a loved one. Indeed, **cancer** is the second-leading cause of death in the United States, and many more suffer through nonfatal varieties, as Jeremy did. It is not one disease, but a set of more than 100 related diseases in which abnormal body cells multiply and spread in uncontrolled fashion, forming a tissue mass called a *tumor*.

Not all tumors are cancerous. *Benign* (noncancerous) tumors tend to remain localized and usually do not pose a serious threat to health. In contrast, *malignant* (cancerous) tumors consist of renegade cells that do not respond to the body's genetic controls on growth and division. To make matters worse, malignant cells often have the ability to migrate from their site of origin and attack, invade, and destroy surrounding body tissues. If this process of **metastasis** is not stopped, body organs and systems will be damaged, and death may result. Although some malignant cells remain as localized tumors and do not spread automatically, they still pose a threat to health and need to be surgically removed.

metastasis The process by which malignant body cells proliferate in number and spread to surrounding body tissues.

In the next section, we will examine risk factors for cancer, including tobacco and alcohol use, nutrition, obesity, and family history. Throughout the chapter, we will discuss psychosocial risk factors in cancer—especially the significance of stress and negative emotions as both risk factors and consequences of living with cancer. Then we take a look at medical treatments options, including surgery, radiation, and chemotherapy. Finally, we investigate how people adjust to a diagnosis of cancer, including the nature and effectiveness of interventions designed by health psychologists.

Types of Cancer

Most cancers can be classified as one of four types:

carcinoma Cancer of the epithelial cells that line the outer and inner surfaces of the body; includes breast, prostate, lung, and skin cancer.

- **Carcinomas** attack the *epithelial cells* that line the outer and inner surfaces of the body. Carcinomas are the most common type of cancer, accounting for approximately 85 percent of all adult cancers. They include cancer of the breast, prostate, colon, lungs, pancreas, and skin. Affecting one out of every six people in the United States, skin cancer is the most common (and most rapidly increasing) type of cancer in America (National Cancer Institute, 2015a).

- **Sarcomas** are malignancies of cells in muscles, bones, and cartilage. Much rarer than carcinoma, sarcomas account for only about 2 percent of all cancers in adults.

- **Lymphomas** are cancers that form in the lymphatic system. Included in this group are *Hodgkin's disease,* a rare form of lymphoma that spreads from a single lymph node, and Jeremy's *non-Hodgkin's lymphoma,* in which malignant cells are found at several sites. A total of 80,900 people living in the United States were diagnosed with lymphoma in 2015 (9050 cases of Hodgkin's lymphoma and 71,850 cases of non-Hodgkin's lymphoma) (Leukemia & Lymphoma Society, 2016).

- **Leukemias** are cancers that attack the blood and blood-forming tissues, such as the bone marrow. Leukemia leads to a proliferation of white blood cells in the bloodstream and bone marrow, which impairs the immune system. Although often considered a childhood disease, leukemia strikes far more adults (an estimated 23,000 cases per year) than children (about 2600 cases per year) (Leukemia and Lymphoma Society, 2016).

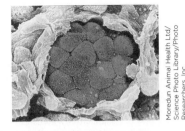

Moredun Animal Health Ltd/ Science Photo Library/Photo Researchers, Inc.

A Malignant Tumor This scanning electron micrograph shows a tiny lung tumor (center) filling an alveolus (one of the air sacs that make up the lungs). The individual cancer cells are coated with microscopic, hairlike structures known as microvilli.

Cancer Susceptibility: Demographic Aspects

Many individual factors, such as gender, age, and ethnic background, affect susceptibility to cancer. For example, although over the course of a lifetime, more men (just under one in two) develop cancer than women (just over one in three), women are more likely to develop any cancer before age 60. Although women are more commonly diagnosed with breast cancer and men with prostate cancer, lung cancer is the top killer of both genders (Figure 11.1) (National Cancer Institute Fast Stats, 2015).

sarcoma Cancer that strikes muscles, bones, and cartilage.

lymphoma Cancer of the body's lymph system; includes Hodgkin's disease and non-Hodgkin's lymphoma.

leukemia Cancer of the blood and blood-producing system.

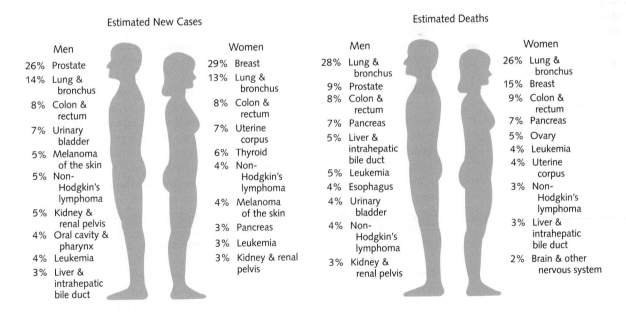

Estimated New Cases

Men
- 26% Prostate
- 14% Lung & bronchus
- 8% Colon & rectum
- 7% Urinary bladder
- 5% Melanoma of the skin
- 5% Non-Hodgkin's lymphoma
- 5% Kidney & renal pelvis
- 4% Oral cavity & pharynx
- 4% Leukemia
- 3% Liver & intrahepatic bile duct

Women
- 29% Breast
- 13% Lung & bronchus
- 8% Colon & rectum
- 7% Uterine corpus
- 6% Thyroid
- 4% Non-Hodgkin's lymphoma
- 4% Melanoma of the skin
- 3% Pancreas
- 3% Leukemia
- 3% Kidney & renal pelvis

Estimated Deaths

Men
- 28% Lung & bronchus
- 9% Prostate
- 8% Colon & rectum
- 7% Pancreas
- 5% Liver & intrahepatic bile duct
- 5% Leukemia
- 4% Esophagus
- 4% Urinary bladder
- 4% Non-Hodgkin's lymphoma
- 3% Kidney & renal pelvis

Women
- 26% Lung & bronchus
- 15% Breast
- 9% Colon & rectum
- 7% Pancreas
- 5% Ovary
- 4% Leukemia
- 4% Uterine corpus
- 3% Non-Hodgkin's lymphoma
- 3% Liver & intrahepatic bile duct
- 2% Brain & other nervous system

FIGURE 11.1

Estimated New Cancer Cases and Deaths by Type and Gender, 2015 Although the breasts in women and the prostate in men are the leading sites of new cases of cancer (left), lung cancer continues to be the leading cause of cancer deaths in both men and women (right).

Data from American Cancer Society (ACS). (2015a). *Cancer facts and figures, 2015.* Atlanta, GA: American Cancer Society. Retrieved on February 27, 2016, from http://www.cancer.org/acs/groups/content/@editorial/documents/document/acspc-044552.pdf.

FIGURE 11.2

The Risk of Cancer Increases with Age Percent of New Cancers by Age Group: All Cancer Sites.

Data from National Cancer Institute. (2015e, April 29). *Surveillance, Epidemiology, and End Results (SEER) program.* Washington, DC: National Institutes of Health. http://www.cancer.gov/about-cancer/causes-prevention/risk/age.

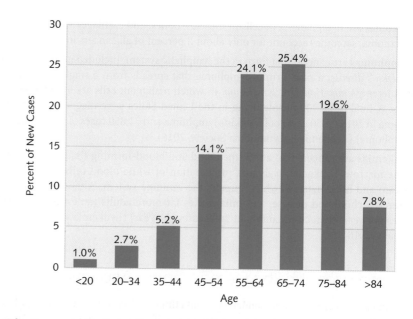

The strongest risk factor for cancer is advancing age (see Figure 11.2). As is true for many other chronic diseases, the older people become, the greater their chances of developing and dying of cancer. But in the United States, cancer is also the second-leading cause of death (after accidents) among children between 1 and 14 years of age.

Variations in the distribution of cancers by race and ethnicity add to the complexity of cancer's epidemiology. Among men, African-Americans have the highest incidence of cancer, followed by European-American, Hispanic-American, Asian/Pacific Islander, and American Indian/Alaska Native men (CDC, 2015b). Among women, European-Americans have the highest rate of cancer incidence, followed by African-American, Hispanic-American, Asian/Pacific Islander, and American Indian/Alaska Native women. African-American men are also more likely to die of cancer than other men, followed by European-American, Hispanic-American, American Indian/Alaska Native, and Asian/Pacific Islander men. Among women, cancer mortality rates are highest for African-Americans, followed by European-American, American Indian/Alaska Native, and Asian/Pacific Islander women. However, Asian Americans have the lowest cancer incidence and death rates when compared to non-Hispanic whites, African Americans, Hispanics, and American Indian/Alaska Natives (American Cancer Society, 2015a).

As noted in Chapter 1, several variables contribute to ethnic disparities in chronic disease incidence and mortality, and cancer is no exception. Among these variables are socioeconomic status (SES), knowledge about cancer and its treatment, and attitudes toward the disease, which may affect access to health care and adherence to medical advice. For example, compared to other ethnic groups, Latino men have lower rates of participation in prostate cancer screening and less knowledge about risk factors for the disease (Glenn and others, 2012). As another example, although white women are more likely to develop breast cancer than African-American women, African-American women are more likely to die of the disease. African-American women historically have been less likely to obtain mammograms, the most effective means of early detection (National Cancer Institute, 2015a). (Table 11.1 highlights key screening tests that have proven effective in reducing deaths from cancer.)

Historically, members of ethnic minorities in the United States have also had less access to health insurance and health care facilities and greater distrust of the medical establishment, which may be perceived as insensitive and even racist. This explains why cancer of all types is generally diagnosed in later (usually more serious) stages in racial and ethnic minorities than it is in European-Americans (American Cancer Society, 2015a).

TABLE 11.1
Screening Tests Shown to Reduce Cancer Deaths

Type of Screening Test	Effectiveness
Colonoscopy, sigmoidoscopy, and high-sensitivity fecal occult blood tests (FOBTs)	These tests reduce deaths from colorectal cancer. Colonoscopy and sigmoidoscopy also help prevent colorectal cancer because they can detect abnormal colon growths (polyps) that can be removed before they develop into cancer. People who are at average risk for colorectal cancer should be screened between 50 and 75 years of age.
Low-dose helical computed tomography (CT)	This test to screen for lung cancer has been shown to reduce lung cancer deaths among heavy smokers.
Mammography	This test reduces mortality from breast cancer disease among women ages 40 to 74, especially those age 50 or older.
Pap test and human papillomavirus (HPV) testing	These tests reduce the incidence of cervical cancer because they allow abnormal cells to be identified and treated before they become cancerous. Testing is recommended to begin at age 21 and to end at age 65, as long as recent results have been normal.
Breast MRI	This imaging test is often used for women who carry a harmful mutation in the *BRCA1* gene or the *BRCA2* gene; such women have a high risk of breast cancer, as well as increased risk for other cancers.

Information from National Cancer Institute. (2016). http://www.cancer.gov/about-cancer/screening/screening-tests#screening-test

African-American cancer patients are also less likely to complete treatment and receive optimal treatment than their European-American counterparts (DeSantis, Naishadham, & Jemal, 2013). This has been partially attributed to the less informative patterns of communication between African-American cancer patients and health care providers (HCPs) (Song, Hamilton, & Moore, 2012). During medical visits, HCPs tend to be more verbally dominant, use less patient-centered communication, and are less likely to understand the cultural values and beliefs of African-American patients. African-American patients are often perceived as less effective communicators and are treated more contentiously than other patients, all of which makes them feel that they are treated unfairly and with disrespect by HCPs (Street & Haidet, 2011).

The issue of culturally competent health care extends to other groups (Lu, Zheng, Young, Kagawa-Singer, & Loh, 2012). Despite the fact that an estimated 18.2 million U.S. residents identify themselves as Asian (Pew Research Center, 2016), their quality of life and overall health during cancer survivorship have largely been overlooked (Yoo, Aviv, Levine, Ewing, & Au, 2010). As another example, the few studies that focus on Latinas have demonstrated that Latinas are less likely to participate in the decision-making process and have higher treatment decision regret, greater dissatisfaction with treatment, and poorer quality of life after treatment (Hawley and others, 2008). In addition to facing language barriers, Latinas often interact with HCPs who have limited understanding of Latino culture and who tend to provide more psychosocial support with patients who are more educated and affluent (Yanez, Stanton, & Maly, 2012).

Finally, ethnic differences in diet, tobacco use, and other risk factors for cancer also play a role. For example, American Indian/Alaska Natives (29.2 percent) and Multiple-Race (non-Hispanics) (27.9 percent) tend to smoke more than African-Americans (17.5 percent) and Asian-Americans (9.5 percent) (CDC, 2015b).

Risk Factors for Cancer

t is interesting to speculate about the number of cancer cases that would arise naturally in a population of otherwise healthy people who completely avoided all environmental carcinogens. By one estimate, epidemiologists suggest that less than 25 percent of all cancers would develop anyway as a result of uncontrollable genetic and biological processes (Lindor, Lindor, & Greene, 2006). In most cases of cancer, controllable factors such as smoking and diet play the most important role.

This section examines a number of risk factors for cancer. Although risk factors increase a person's chance of developing cancer, not every person with those risk factors will develop the disease. Many people with one or more risk factors never develop cancer, whereas others who develop the disease have no known risk factors.

Tobacco Use

As we saw in Chapter 9, smoking is the most preventable cause of death in our society. The American Cancer Society estimates that about one in every five deaths in the United States is caused by tobacco, and most of those tobacco-related deaths were the result of cancer. Tobacco is the single most lethal **carcinogen** (agent that causes cancer) in the United States and Canada (American Cancer Society, 2015a).

Exposure to pro-smoking media, such as to point-of-sale displays, magazine advertising, and portrayals of smoking in movies, is one factor that increases smoking in adolescents and young adults. In a recent study, researchers used ecological momentary assessment (EMA) to examine momentary changes in 135 college students' future smoking risk in response to pro-smoking media. The students, who consisted of *never smokers* (never smoked, even a puff) and *ever smokers* (reported any level of past smoking), carried handheld computers for 21 days and recorded their exposures to all forms of pro-smoking media. They also responded to random control prompts during each day of the assessment period.

After each media exposure event and control prompt, the students answered questions that measured their risk of future smoking. The EMA data showed that all participants reported significantly higher future smoking risk following exposure to pro-smoking messages (Shadel, Martino, Setodji, & Scharf, 2012).

These findings are consistent with other data showing that consideration of immediate consequences may be a more important determinant of health behaviors than **consideration of future consequences,** particularly for young people (Adams, 2012). One study of 160 smokers found that a simple intervention that presented feedback regarding expired-air carbon monoxide levels just before and again just after smoking a cigarette increased perceptions of susceptibility to smoking-related illnesses and was associated with a greater intention to quit smoking (Shahab, West, & McNeill, 2011).

We now know that cancer morbidity and mortality reflects smoking patterns of years earlier. Because North American men have been quitting for decades, lung cancer deaths for 55- to 64-year-old males are about half what they were in 1970 (CDC, 2013e). Because few women smoked at the start of the twentieth century and because their smoking increased later in the century, lung cancer mortality rates for women doubled during this same time period.

Although cancer mortality is decreasing in most developed nations, including the United States, about one-third of adults in

carcinogen A cancer-causing agent such as tobacco, ultraviolet radiation, or an environmental toxin.

consideration of future consequences The extent to which individuals consider and are influenced by the potential future outcomes of their behavior.

Time for a Stiffer Warning? In the 50 years since health warnings were first required on cigarette packs, their effect on smokers has weakened. The warnings are small and often overwhelmed by the designs on cigarette packages.

SURGEON GENERAL'S WARNING: Smoking Causes Lung Cancer, Heart Disease, Emphysema, And May Complicate Pregnancy.

Dan Brandenburg/Getty Images

Japan, Turkey, and the Netherlands still smoke. In India and China, more than half of all men smoke, and rates of smoking and cancer continue to increase, particularly for women. These trends led the World Health Organization in 2010 to call tobacco "the single largest preventable cause of death and chronic disease in the world" (Blas & Kurup, 2010).

Smoking causes cancers of the lungs, mouth, stomach, larynx (voice box), esophagus, pancreas, uterus, cervix, kidney, and bladder (National Cancer Institute, 2010d). Up to 20 percent of lung cancer patients who smoked prior to diagnosis continue to do so (see Schnoll and others, 2003, for a review). Continued use of tobacco after a cancer diagnosis increases the risk of recurrence and the development of additional tumors, reduces the effectiveness of chemotherapy and other cancer treatments, and exacerbates the unpleasant side effects of treatment.

Alcohol Use

Although moderate consumption of alcoholic beverages may reduce the risk of cardio-vascular disease (see Chapter 10), alcohol is a known cause of cancer. Heavy or regular drinking increases the risk of developing cancers of the oral cavity, pharynx (throat), larynx (voice box), esophagus, liver, breast, colon, and rectum (National Cancer Institute, 2015a). The risk of developing cancer increases with the amount of alcohol a person drinks. Women who consume two or more alcohol-containing drinks a day have at least a 25 percent greater risk of developing breast cancer than women who do not use alcohol (Nurses' Health Study, 2010). Alcohol-related cirrhosis is a frequent cause of liver cancer and may place the immune system in "overdrive," even when no threat (other than excessive alcohol) is present. Animal research shows that drinking the equivalent of two to four alcoholic drinks per day also dramatically increases the growth of an existing tumor (Tan, Barger, & Shields, 2006). However, we must be cautious in drawing conclusions about alcohol and immunocompetence. People who abuse alcohol may also suffer from poor nutrition and sleep deprivation and may be exposed to other pathogens that compromise their health.

Nutrition

A great deal of research has investigated the possibility that specific dietary components or nutrients can increase or decrease cancer risk. The cancers that have been most directly linked to foods are those that affect the cells that line bodily tissues, including those in the lungs, colon, bladder, stomach, rectum, and, to a lesser degree, the uterus, prostate, breasts, and kidneys. It should come as no surprise that these cancers are most prevalent in cultures noted for high-fat diets, such as the United States.

Studies of cancer cells in the laboratory and in animals have provided some evidence that some isolated components may be carcinogenic, while others seem to have anti-cancer properties. With few exceptions, however, studies of human populations have not definitively demonstrated that any particularly dietary component causes cancer or, for that matter, prevents cancer.

Some retrospective epidemiological studies that have compared people with and without a certain type of cancer have pointed to dietary differences in the two groups. However, results such as these show only that the dietary component is correlated with a difference in cancer risk, not a causal link. Recall from Chapter 2 that when correlational evidence emerges linking a variable (such as a certain food) with a change in disease risk, a randomized trial is needed to test the possibility of a causal relationship. For ethical reasons, however, randomized trials are generally not conducted when there is evidence that a certain dietary component may be associated with a heightened risk of disease.

Two food products that do appear to cause cancer are meat that has been cooked, or charred, at high temperatures and meat that has been highly processed. Certain chemicals, called *heterocyclic amines* (HCAs) and *polycyclic aromatic hydrocarbons* (PAHs) are formed when beef, pork, fish, or poultry are prepared using high-temperature methods, such as pan frying or grilling over an open flame. In many experiments, animals fed a diet supplemented with HCAs have developed tumors of the colon, liver, lung, prostate, breast, and other organs (National Cancer Institute, 2015b). Rodents fed PAHS also developed cancers, including leukemia and tumors of the gastrointestinal tract and lungs (NCI, 2015b). In addition, a number of prospective epidemiological studies have reported that high consumption of well-done, fried, or barbecued meats is associated with increased risks of colorectal, pancreatic, and prostate cancer (see for example, Cross and others, 2010).

Numerous research studies have also linked processed meat—such as bacon, hot dogs, and salami—to colorectal cancer. Processed meats are altered through salting, curing, fermenting, or smoking. So consistent is the evidence that, after reviewing more than 800 epidemiological studies, the World Health Organization designated processed meats as a *Group 1 carcinogen* (Bouvard and others, 2015). This group of cancer-causing agents also includes asbestos and smoking. The significance of the ranking is that it means that the evidence linking processed meat to colorectal cancer is as strong as the evidence that links smoking to cancer.

The American Institute for Cancer Research (AICR), in conjunction with the World Cancer Research Fund (WCRF), published a comprehensive analysis of the literature on diet and cancer (AICR, 2010). The report identifies five dietary recommendations that people can follow to help reduce their risk of developing cancer: (1) reducing intake of foods and drinks that promote weight gain, namely foods high in saturated fats and sugary drinks; (2) eating mostly plant-based foods; (3) limiting intake of red meat and avoiding processed meat; (4) limiting consumption of alcoholic beverages and salt; and (5) reducing intake of oat-based, corn-based, wheat-based, and rice-based breakfast cereals—such as Cheerios, cornflakes, Total, and Rice Krispies—which may contain *ochratoxin*—a potentially cancer-causing by-product of mold.

What about the possible cancer-inhibiting properties of food? Some studies have found that diets rich in fruits, vegetables, and fiber may offer some protection against colon and rectal cancers, most likely because they promote rapid removal of cancer-causing wastes from the body. Data from the Nurses' Health Study (NHS), one of the most significant studies ever conducted on women's health, reveal that premenopausal women who consumed five or more servings per day of fruits and vegetables were 23 percent less likely to develop breast cancer than those who ate fewer than two servings per day (NHS, 2010). Although this level of protection appears to be modest, we should remember that the link between obesity and breast cancer is very strong (see Chapter 8), and eating a lot of fruits and vegetables also helps to maintain a healthy weight.

Good nutrition is important at all times, including for people who are being treated for cancer. *Nutrition therapy* is used to help cancer patients get the nutrients they need to fight infection and keep up their strength. Good nutrition may benefit people living with cancer in several ways, including providing support for their immune systems, improving tolerance to treatment, and promoting faster recuperation after treatment, all of which may yield a better chance of recovery (National Cancer Institute, 2015a).

Physical Activity

Lack of physical activity may be a risk factor for certain cancers. An early prospective study of men with colon cancer, men with rectal cancer, and healthy men found that the more sedentary a man's job and the longer he had worked at that job, the greater his risk of colon cancer (Vena and others, 1985). More recently, researchers have similarly reported an inverse relationship between overall physical activity levels and the risk of colon cancer in both women and men (Lynch and others, 2010). These results suggest that a sedentary lifestyle is indeed a risk factor for colon cancer, one of the leading causes of cancer mortality.

Regular physical activity—either work-related or recreational—may also protect against breast cancer. For example, Suzanne Shoff and her colleagues (2000) found that physically active women who had lost weight since they were 18 or had gained only minimal amounts of weight were only half as likely as their inactive counterparts to develop breast cancer after menopause. The most compelling evidence comes from the NHS, which reported that women who exercised seven hours or more per week were 20 percent less likely to develop breast cancer than women who exercised less than one hour per week (2010).

Walking, the most frequently reported exercise, was as effective in protecting against cancer as more strenuous forms of exercise. Similarly, data from the massive Women's Health Initiative Cohort Study indicate that women who engaged in the equivalent of as little as an hour and a half of brisk walking each week had an 18 percent decreased risk of breast cancer compared to inactive women (McTiernan and others, 2003). Considering the impact of diet and physical activity together, researchers estimate that up to one-third of breast cancer cases could be prevented if women ate less and exercised more (Cheng, 2010).

Overweight and Obesity

The link between obesity and increased risk of death from cancer and other causes has long been established. Obesity increases the risk of cancers of the endometrium (the lining of the uterus), colon, kidney, esophagus, pancreas, ovaries, and gallbladder (NCI, 2015c). The effect of obesity on the risk of breast cancer depends on a woman's menopausal status. Before menopause, obese women have a lower risk of developing breast cancer than do women who are not obese. However, after menopause, obese women have 1.5 times the risk of developing breast cancer than women who are not obese. The relationship between obesity and breast cancer risk is strongest in women with a large amount of abdominal fat.

Until recently, the relationship between being overweight and increased risk of death remained uncertain. In 2015, an estimated 40 percent of adult men and 30 percent of adult women in the United States were overweight. Almost as many were obese (35 percent of men and 37 percent of women) (Yang & Colditz, 2015).

The massive NIH-AARP Diet and Health Study monitored the health status of over half a million Americans ages 50 to 71 years, from 1995 through 2005, by using mailed questionnaires and surveying death records. Among nonsmokers, the risk of mortality at age 50 among those who were overweight increased by 20 to 40 percent. Mortality risk among obese participants increased twofold to threefold (NCI, 2010d).

The exact mechanisms by which obesity and being overweight increase cancer risk are not known and may be different for different cancers. Possible mechanisms in obese people include alterations in sex hormones (estrogen, progesterone, and testosterone) as well as in insulin and IGF-1 (a hormone similar to insulin) that may cause increased risk for cancers of the breast, endometrium, and colon (NCI, 2010d).

Family History

Across all forms of cancer, an estimated 5 to 10 percent are caused by inherited mutations of genes, with breast, prostate, ovarian, and colorectal cancers being most likely to arise from family history (American Cancer Society, 2015b). Consider breast cancer. Only a small percentage of all breast cancer cases are directly inherited. The vast majority (nearly 95 percent) are linked to a combination of genetic and nongenetic risk factors. Nongenetic risk factors include obesity, younger age at menarche (first menstruation), lack of exercise, smoking, poor diet, use of oral contraceptives, the presence of other diseases of the breast, radiation exposure, and use of alcohol.

Genetic vulnerability can, however, interact with other risk factors to increase an individual's risk. For example, approximately one-third of the 175,000 women diagnosed with breast cancer each year in the United States have a family history of the disease. Evidence again comes from the Nurses' Health Study, which found that the daughters of women diagnosed with breast cancer before age 40 were more than twice as likely to develop breast cancer, as compared to women whose mothers had no history of the disease. The daughters of women with breast cancer after age 70 were one and a half times more likely to develop breast cancer. Participants who had a sister with breast cancer were more than twice as likely to develop this cancer themselves; when both mother *and* sister were diagnosed with breast cancer, the risk increased to two and a half times (NHS, 2010).

Families in which breast cancer is inherited typically demonstrate the following characteristics:

- breast cancer in two or more close relatives, such as a mother and two sisters;
- early onset—often before age 50—of breast cancer in family members;
- history of breast cancer in more than one generation;
- cancer in both breasts in one or more family members;
- frequent occurrence of ovarian cancer; and
- Ashkenazi (Eastern and Central European) Jewish ancestry, with a family history of breast and/or ovarian cancer.

Environmental and Occupational Hazards

The degree of cancer hazard posed by environmental toxins depends on the concentration of the carcinogen and the amount of exposure to the toxin. However, even low-dose exposure can represent a significant public health hazard when a large segment of the population is involved.

Toxic Chemicals

Various chemicals are clearly carcinogenic, including asbestos, vinyl chloride, and arsenic. In addition, some researchers believe that exposure to chlorine-containing compounds found in some household cleaning and pest-control products may increase the risk of breast cancer and, possibly, other hormone-related cancers. Although the popular media have focused on the dangers of pesticides, the very low concentrations found in some foods are generally well within established safety levels and pose minimal risks.

Environmental toxins in the air, soil, and water are estimated to contribute to about 2 percent of fatal cancers, mainly of the bladder and the lungs. Although long-term exposure to high levels of air pollution—especially by smokers—may increase the risk of lung cancer by as much as 50 percent, this pales in comparison to the 2000 percent increased risk caused by heavy smoking itself.

Although a few studies have linked water chlorinating and fluoridation with bladder cancer, most experts believe that the potential health risk is small and is outweighed by the greater danger of the spread of diseases such as cholera and typhoid fever by germs in unchlorinated water. Moreover, fluoride in drinking water is an effective agent in preventing tooth decay (NCI, 2010e).

Radiation

Beginning in the 1960s, a well-tanned complexion became fashionable. However, many people burn rather than tan, and we now know that a serious long-term effect of sunburn is skin cancer. In those days, when skin-protective sunscreens were generally unknown, sunbathing was especially risky. Is it any wonder that one in every five Americans will develop skin cancer (American Cancer Society, 2015c)? An estimated 73,870 new cases of invasive melanoma were diagnosed in 2015 (American Cancer Society, 2015c).

High-frequency radiation, ionizing radiation (IR), and ultraviolet (UV) radiation are proven carcinogens. Ultraviolet B rays, which can damage DNA, cause more than 90 percent of all skin cancers, including **melanoma,** a potentially deadly form of cancer that forms in skin cells. For over 30 years, the incidence rate of melanoma has been increasing in the United States (American Cancer Society, 2015c). A number of researchers believe that the overall frequency of sunburns during childhood is a key factor in melanoma. This explains why people who take longer to develop a sunburn have a lower incidence of melanoma than those who burn quickly. Another factor in the rising trend in skin cancer is the thinning of the earth's ozone layer, which filters skin-damaging UV radiation. A third factor in the rise of melanoma cases is believed to be an increase in suntanning and use of tanning booths, which has exposed people to greater amounts of UV radiation. In 2014, UV tanning devices were reclassified by the FDA from Class 1 (low to moderate risk) to Class II (moderate to high risk) devices (Ogden, 2015).

Given the evidence that the sun's UV rays can cause cancer, why do so many people continue to bask in the sun? In one study, researchers interviewed sunbathers at California beaches to determine the factors that influenced their decision to lie in the sun (Keesling & Friedman, 1987). Those with the deepest tans (who also reported spending the largest amounts of time in the sun) were least knowledgeable about skin cancer. They also were more relaxed, more sensitive to the influence of peers who valued a good tan, more likely to take other risks, and more focused on their appearance. A more recent study of Australian teenagers reported that people with "medium" tans were perceived as healthier and more attractive than people with no tan (Broadstock, Borland, & Gason, 2006). Interestingly, this has not always been so. The tanning business skyrocketed in the 1990s, mostly in Western cultures. In some other parts of the world, fair skin remains the standard of beauty.

Another factor in why people tan appears to be a hopeful belief that their risk of skin cancer is minimal. In one study, 211 sixth-, seventh-, and eighth-grade students were shown pictures of either tanned or fair-skinned models and then responded to a questionnaire that included an assessment of their *comparative optimism* for skin cancer later in life. **Comparative optimism** for a negative event refers to the tendency for people to believe that their personal risk is lower than that of their peers (Harris, Griffin, & Murray, 2008). For some individuals (people who avoid tanning), this belief may be accurate for certain health outcomes (such as skin cancer) because they are in fact at a lower risk than their peers (people who do not avoid tanning). Children as young as 8 years of age demonstrate comparative optimism for health events (Albery & Messer, 2005).

The results of the study showed that the students, as a whole, were comparatively optimistic about their likelihood of developing skin cancer, despite the fact that more than half of

melanoma A potentially deadly form of cancer that strikes the melatonin-containing cells of the skin.

comparative optimism The tendency to think that one will experience more positive and fewer negative events than others.

Suntans Are Unhealthy
Ultraviolet radiation, whether from the sun or tanning booth, injures the skin and ages it prematurely (a 20-year-old who tans frequently may look 10 years older). In addition, frequent tanning may contribute to skin cancer. The only safe tan is a fake one created by a sunless, self-tanning product.

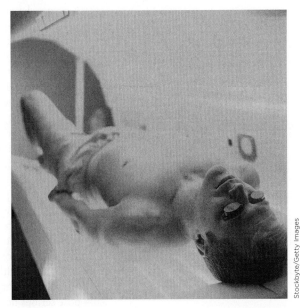

Stockbyte/Getty Images

Your Health Assets

What Is Your Risk of Developing Skin Cancer?

Most experts agree that the following things affect a person's risk of melanoma. Which of them apply to you?

- Older age
- Light or fair physical features
- Childhood sunburns
- Immunosuppressive medications
- Family history

Age As with most cancers, the risk of melanoma goes up with age. However, melanoma tends to develop earlier in life than many other cancers. The average age at diagnosis is 57.

Physical Features People who have fair skin and naturally light-colored hair and eyes have a higher risk of melanoma. This is because people with these features often have lower levels of pigment in their skin and are more likely to get sunburned. Pigment gives skin its color. Higher levels of pigment make skin darker and help protect it from the sun. People with many moles on their skin also have a higher risk of melanoma than do people with fewer moles.

Sunburn People who had repeated, severe sunburns as children have a higher risk of melanoma. Radiation from the sun can cause abnormal changes in skin cells that develop into cancer later in life. Sun damage in adulthood also increases the risk of skin cancer.

Immunosuppressive Medications People who have taken immunosuppressive medication have a higher risk of melanoma. Immunosuppressive medications are very important in the treatment of many medical conditions. However, they can interfere with the body's ability to respond to abnormal cell changes, which increases the risk of abnormal cell growth and cancer.

Family History People who have a mother, father, brother, or sister with melanoma have a higher risk of developing skin cancer. This is because some cases of melanoma are linked to mutations in the DNA of body cells that can be passed from generation to generation.

Information from Siteman Cancer Center. (2015). *Your Disease Risk*. St. Louis, MO: Washington University School of Medicine. http://www.yourdiseaserisk.wustl .edu/YDRDefault.aspx?ScreenControl=YDRGeneral&ScreenName=YDRCancer_Index

them reported intentionally tanning. Among the older students (13- and 14-year-old adolescents), comparative optimism was greatest for those who did not tan but viewed a high-risk (tanned) model. However, although the younger students (11- and 12-year-olds) also demonstrated comparative optimism, their optimism did not vary as a function of their personal tanning behavior or the tanning status of the models that they were shown. These results suggest that the social comparison processes underlying comparative optimism become more complex with age (Roberts, Gibbons, Gerrard, & Alert, 2011).

Nonionizing, or low-frequency, radiation (such as that arising from microwave ovens, radar screens, electricity, and radios) has not been shown to cause cancer. Another common fear—living near a nuclear plant—is largely unfounded. In a 35-year study of over 40 million people, researchers compared the cancer death rates of Americans who lived near nuclear plants with the cancer death rates of people who lived in counties that had no nuclear sites. No differences were found in the two groups (Jablon, Hrubec, & Boice, 1991). A three-year study begun in late 2012 examined cancer risk among people living near six nuclear power plants and one nuclear fuel facility (Ahlers, 2012). The study found no correlation between cancer risk and living near nuclear power plants (Benson, 2015). Similarly, although toxic wastes in dump sites can threaten health through air, water, and soil pollution, most community exposures involve very low-dose levels and do not pose serious health threats.

Occupational Carcinogens and Pollution

People whose work involves exposure to certain chemicals have long been known to be at greater risk of developing cancer than others. *Occupational cancers* mostly affect the lungs, skin, bladder, and blood-forming systems of the body (National Institute for Occupational Safety and Health, 2015). For example, those who work with asbestos, chromium, and chromium compounds are much more likely than other workers to develop lung cancer. Workers exposed to benzene, a solvent used in making varnishes and dyes, are at high risk for developing leukemia.

Other substances now known to be carcinogenic include diesel exhaust and radon. In recent years, however, strict control measures in the workplace (at least in the developed world) have reduced the proportion of cancer deaths caused by job-related carcinogens to less than 5 percent. Unfortunately, such control measures generally lag behind the pace of industrialization in developing countries, where job-related cancers are still likely to increase.

Cancer and Infectious Disease

An estimated 15 to 20 percent of new cancers worldwide each year are attributable to infection (American Cancer Society, 2015a). This percentage is higher in developing countries where certain infections are more prevalent. For example, several types of human papilloma virus (HPV) are the main causes of cervical cancer—the second most common cancer among women living in less developed countries (American Cancer Society, 2015a). HPVs also contribute to some cancers of the mouth and throat. All types of HPV are spread by contact. More than 40 types of HPV can be spread through sexual contact. Hepatitis B virus and hepatitis C virus cause viral hepatitis, which is a type of liver infection that increases a person's chance of developing liver cancer.

Bacterial infections can also cause cancer. For example, long-term infection of the stomach with *helicobacter pylori* (*H. pylori*) can damage the inner layer of the stomach and lead to cancer over time. About two in three adults worldwide are infected with *H. pylori*, with the rate of infection being higher in developing countries and in older age groups. *H. pylori* is spread in several ways, including fecal-oral contact, such as through water contaminated with human waste.

Infections can increase a person's risk of developing cancer in at least three ways:

- Some viruses can insert their own genes into healthy cells, causing them to grow out of control.
- Some infections trigger chronic inflammation in a part of the body, leading to changes in affected cells that can lead to cancer.
- Some infections can suppress the immune system and reduce its ability to protect the body from cancer.

Even though some bacterial and viral infections increase the risk of certain types of cancer, most people with these infections do not develop cancer. Infection with *H. pylori*, for example, may increase your risk of stomach cancer, but whether you smoke, what you eat, and other factors are also important factors.

Stress and Immunocompetence

With advances in *psychoneuroimmunology* (PNI), researchers are paying more attention to psychological risk factors—in particular, the role of stress—in the development of cancer. In Chapter 4, we saw how PNI researchers study the relationships among the

immunocompetence The overall ability of the immune system, at any given time, to defend the body against the harmful effects of foreign agents.

immune surveillance theory The theory that cells of the immune system play a monitoring function in searching for and destroying abnormal cells such as those that form tumors.

mind, the body, and immunity. **Immunocompetence**—our immune system's ability to mount an effective defense against disease and harmful foreign agents—depends on many factors, including our overall health, the nature of the health-threatening disease or foreign agent, and perceived stress.

How might perceived stress promote the development of cancer? According to the **immune surveillance theory,** cancer cells, which develop spontaneously in the body, are prevented from spreading and developing into tumors by natural killer (NK) cells and other agents of the immune system. However, when the immune system is overwhelmed by the number of cancer cells or weakened by stress or some other factor, the immune system's surveillance is suppressed, and cancer may develop.

Perceived stress from exams, work, divorce, bereavement, caring for a terminally ill relative, environmental catastrophes, and unemployment, for example, adversely affects our immune functioning (see Cohen, Miller, & Rabin, 2001, for a review). Based on such findings, one early PNI model, the *global immunosuppression model,* proposed that stress always suppresses immune responses. This type of blunted immunity was assumed to be responsible for the increased incidence of infectious diseases and some cancers found in chronically stressed people.

Although the global immunosuppression model dominated the thinking of PNI researchers for years and continues to be influential, the concept of broad decreases in immunity does not make sense to some researchers as a species' response to all stressors. They reason that if the stress-immune response did indeed evolve, a healthy person should not be adversely affected when it is triggered because this would be maladaptive; natural selection would have selected against this over the course of evolution. Indeed, studies done over the past 40 years, examining the relationship between stress and cancer risk, have produced conflicting results (Segerstrom & Miller, 2004). Some studies have reported an indirect relationship between stress and certain types of virus-related cancers, such as Kaposi's sarcoma and some lymphomas (NCI, 2010c). And although many studies have demonstrated that stress can affect neuroendocrine and immune function adversely, the clinical significance of these changes for cancer patients is not clear (Luecken & Compas, 2002). One reason for the inconsistency in results when examining cancer risk is that it is difficult to separate stress from other factors such as smoking, using alcohol, becoming overweight, and even growing older.

To address this problem, the *biphasic model* proposes that only the most chronic stressors cause global immunosuppression. Short-term stressors that trigger our fight-or-flight response either have no effect on immunity or might actually *enhance* immunity to help prepare us to defend against possible infection or injury (Dhabhar & McEwen, 2001; Segerstrom & Miller, 2004). Examples of acute stressors that enhance natural immunity include challenging computer tasks, mental arithmetic, and loud noises. In contrast, chronic stressors such as bereavement, long-term caregiving, and suffering a traumatic injury produce global suppression of most measures of immune function.

Childhood Adversity

Childhood adversity has been associated with greater emotional and physiological sensitivity to stress (McLaughlin and others, 2010). For example, children who experienced adversity are more likely to report difficulties when they encounter stressors in adulthood than those who did not have these experiences earlier in life (Fagundes, Glaser, Malarkey, & Kiecolt-Glaser, 2013). They also have more pronounced cortisol and autonomic responses to stress (Heim, Newport, Mletzko, Miller, & Nemeroff, 2008). Stressful early life events also may disrupt cellular immune function. One study found that adolescents who were abused or institutionalized had higher antibody responses to the herpes simplex virus, reflecting poorer cellular immune system control compared to those who did not experience these adversities (Shirtcliff, Coe, & Pollak, 2009). Another found that children growing up in poverty had elevated cytomegalovirus (CMV) antibody titers compared to those from higher-income families (Dowd, Palermo, & Aiello, 2012). These studies suggest that childhood adversity may have an impact on whether cancer develops later in life.

Childhood stressors also may promote long-term immune system dysregulation. In addition, childhood adversity seems to heighten the impact of later-life caregiving stress, being associated with elevated inflammation, shorter telomere length, and poorer localized immune response to tumors (Kiecolt-Glaser and others, 2011). A recent study found that breast cancer survivors who experienced more childhood adversities had higher Epstein-Barr virus and CMV antibody titers than those with fewer childhood adversities (Fagundes and others, 2013). They also had more depressive symptoms and poorer sleep quality.

Depression: Both Risk and Result

Depression reduces a person's overall quality of life and subjective well-being, and it can also adversely affect physical health (Wang, Cai, Qian, & Peng, 2014). As such, depression can contribute to an individual's susceptibility to cancer. And receiving a cancer diagnosis and treatments can themselves cause depression. In fact, periodic or long-term clinical depression is relatively common among people adjusting to cancer, with estimated prevalence rates ranging between 13 percent and 40 percent (Walker and others, 2013).

Many of the symptoms of cancer, as well as the side effects of cancer treatment, are similar to those of depression. These include disturbances of sleep and appetite, fatigue, concentration difficulties, and pain, and these may be aggravated by stress hormones such as cortisol (Thornton, Andersen, & Blakely, 2010). People who perceive low levels of social support in their lives and those with a history of high levels of life stress (such as PTSD survivors) may have the most problems (Golden-Kreutz and others, 2005).

Cancer patients who are members of ethnic minorities may also be at increased risk for depression. One meta-analysis of 21 studies reported that Hispanic cancer patients in the United States had significantly higher levels of distress, depressive symptoms, and lower health-related quality of life than European-American cancer patients (Luckett and others, 2011). Similar findings were obtained from a sample of Afro-Caribbean and Latino immigrant cancer patients (Costas and Gany, 2013).

Depression has also been linked to a higher risk of early death among people with cancer. One review of 76 prospective studies reported that a diagnosis of clinical depression and higher levels of depressive symptoms before or after cancer diagnosis were associated with elevated cancer-related mortality (Pinquart and Duberstein, 2010). At least two reasons have been offered for why depression may enhance mortality risk in cancer patients. First, depression may alter neuroendocrine and immunological functions in the hypothalamic-pituitary-adrenal axis, especially those related to daily variation in cortisol (Spiegel & Giese-Davis, 2003). Second, patients who are depressed may be less likely to adhere to recommended preventive screening procedures, cancer treatments, and other recommendations for maintaining their health. For instance, some studies have reported that depressed patients may be less likely to exercise, more likely to smoke or drink alcohol to excess, and may skip medication regimens or miss therapy appointments (see Pinquart & Duberstein, 2010).

Results such as these strongly suggest that screening for depression should be a routine part of cancer treatment. In addition, these findings beg the question of whether effective treatment for depression could not only enhance quality of life, but could also extend survival among cancer patients.

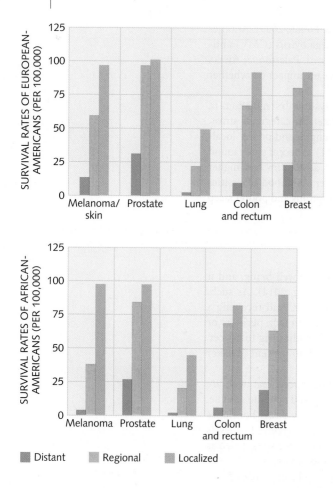

FIGURE 11.3

Five-Year Relative Survival Rates by Race and Stage at Diagnosis Five-Year relative survival rates are commonly used to monitor progress in the early detection and treatment of cancer. This includes all survivors, whether in remission, disease-free, or under treatment. The term *localized* refers to a malignant tumor confined entirely to the organ of origin. *Regional* refers to a malignant tumor that has extended beyond the limits of the organ of origin into the surrounding organs or tissues and/or involves regional lymph nodes by way of the lymphatic system. *Distant* refers to a malignant cancer that has spread to parts of the body remote from the primary tumor either by direct extension or by metastasis, or via the lymphatic system to distant lymph nodes. The earlier the detection, the greater the likelihood that the tumor will be localized; thus, survival increases markedly the earlier the cancer is diagnosed.

Data from National Cancer Institute. (2015e, April 29). *Surveillance, Epidemiology, and End Results (SEER) program.* Washington, DC: National Institutes of Health. http://www.cancer.gov/about-cancer/causes-prevention/risk/age.

Cancer Treatment

When cancer does develop, early detection and treatment can prevent death and perhaps reduce overall treatment time.

Early Diagnosis

A cancer diagnosis may result in months or years of painful or uncomfortable treatment. This is because cancer develops over time, as neoplastic cells grow into tumors that may metastasize to surrounding tissues. Detecting this process early on, before malignant cells have gained a strong foothold, can dramatically improve a person's chances of survival (Figure 11.3). Unfortunately, many people do not follow recommended screening schedules for cancer of the prostate, breasts, colon, rectum, and cervix (Table 11.2). Also, as many as 30 to 50 percent of people with noticeable cancer symptoms delay three or four months before seeking medical attention (Arndt and others, 2002). A growing body of health psychology research demonstrates that the perception of risk and feelings of vulnerability are key factors in whether people follow recommended screening schedules (Fagerlin and others, 2010) and that risk perception can be influenced by tailored educational interventions (Dillard, Ferrer, Ubel, & Fagerlin, 2012).

For those with family histories of cancer, genetic screening has become a useful method of early detection. Nowadays, a simple blood test can detect genetic mutations linked to an increased risk of many types of cancer. Such tests, however, have raised a host of ethical and practical questions. On the practical side, many laboratories administering these tests do not follow the (admittedly vague and inadequate) regulatory controls that help ensure the validity of genetic tests. And some labs market tests to physicians, obstetricians, and primary care providers who lack expertise in medical genetics.

The more significant problem has to do with the ethics of genetic testing and the knowledge that it provides. The ability to predict someone's genetic future also raises a host of psychosocial concerns, both for the individual being tested and for other family members who might be at risk (Cella and others, 2002). If you were fated to develop cancer, would you want to know? What would you do in response? Providing people with a diagnosis of an untreatable disease raises concerns, especially when dealing with children who may not fully understand the implications of the tests. Others fear that children

TABLE 11.2

Prevalence of Cancer Screening among Five Racial and Ethnic Groups

Cancer Screening	European-American	African-American	Hispanic-American	Native American	Asian/Pacific Islander
Prostate test (protoscopy) within the past five years	30.4%	28.2%	22.4%	27.6%	California*: 24.3%; Hawaii*: 40.7%
Colorectal test	18.2%	20.3%	14.2%	12.3%	California*: 2.6%; Hawaii*: 23.8%
Mammogram within the past two years	73.7%	76.1%	63.5%	Alaska*: 93.5% Hawaii*: 80.7%	
Cervical/uterine test within the past three years	84.7%	91.1%	80.9%	90.5%	Hawaii*: 84.2%

*Indicates state-specific prevalence estimates available for the corresponding race/ethnic group

Source: Centers for Disease Control and Prevention (CDC). (2001). Behavioral risk factor surveillance system: Summary data quality report (rev.). National Center for Chronic Disease Prevention and Health Promotion, Centers for Disease Control and Prevention. http://www.cdc.gov/brfss/annual_data/2000/pdf/2000summarydataqualityreport.pdf.

identified as carriers of serious diseases will be discriminated against. A related concern is the real possibility that insurance companies will deny coverage to individuals who have a predisposition toward developing a particular disease. An important goal of the Affordable Care Act has been to prevent this by requiring insurance companies to cover people with preexisting conditions.

Treatment Options

Until recently, the treatment options for most forms of cancer were severely limited, and cancer was often a death sentence. Today, there are many effective treatment options that have reduced death rates from most types of cancer. These options include surgery, chemotherapy, radiation therapy, and combination regimes, such as those involving both bone marrow transplantation and radiation therapy (ASCO, 2015).

Surgery

Surgery is the oldest form of cancer treatment, and it generally offers the greatest chance for cure for most types of cancer. Approximately 60 percent of cancer patients have some form of surgery, which is usually recommended to achieve one or more of the following goals:

- *Diagnostic* surgery is used to obtain a tissue sample for laboratory testing to confirm a diagnosis and identify the specific cancer. A procedure to remove all or part of a tumor for diagnostic tests is called a *biopsy*.

- *Preventive* surgery is performed to remove a growth that is not presently malignant but is likely to become so if left untreated. Sometimes, preventive surgery is used to remove an organ when people have an inherited condition that makes development of a cancer likely.

- *Staging* surgery is used to determine the extent of disease. In *laparoscopy*, for example, a tube is passed through a tiny incision in the abdomen to examine the abdomen's contents and remove tissue samples.

Detecting Skin Cancer Most important in the treatment of cancer is early detection. Here, a health care provider examines a blemish on the arm of a patient. An unusual sore, lump, marking, or change in the way that an area of skin looks or feels may be a sign of skin cancer or a warning that it might occur.

Lauren Shear/Science Source

- *Curative* surgery involves the removal of a tumor when the tumor appears to be localized and there is hope of taking out all of the cancerous tissue.

- *Restorative* (or reconstructive) surgery is used to restore a person's appearance or the function of an organ or body part. Examples include breast reconstruction after mastectomy and the use of bone grafts or *prosthetic* (metal or plastic) bone or joint replacements after surgical treatment of bone cancer.

Chemotherapy

Each year, about 650,000 cancer patients in the United States receive *chemotherapy—* medicines to treat cancer. While surgery and radiation therapy destroy or damage cancer cells in a specific area, chemotherapy can destroy cancer cells that have spread, or metastasized, to parts of the body far from the original, or primary, tumor. These *systemic drugs* travel through the bloodstream to reach all areas of the body.

Depending on the type of cancer and its stage of development, chemotherapy can be used to cure cancer, to keep the cancer from spreading, to slow the cancer's growth, to kill cancer cells that may have spread to other parts of the body from the original tumor, or to relieve symptoms caused by the cancer. In one of the newest forms of chemotherapy, **immunotherapy,** medications are used to enhance the immune system's ability to selectively target cancer cells (Disis, 2005).

Anticancer drugs are made to kill fast-growing cells; however, because these drugs travel throughout the body, they can affect normal, healthy cells as well. The normal cells most likely to be affected are blood cells that form in the bone marrow and cells in the digestive tract, reproductive system, and hair follicles (which is why my son, Jeremy, temporarily lost his hair). Some anticancer drugs also can damage cells of the heart, kidneys, bladder, lungs, and nervous system.

The most common side effects of chemotherapy are nausea and vomiting, hair loss, and fatigue. Less common side effects include bleeding, infections, and anemia. Although side effects are not always as bad as expected, their reputation makes chemotherapy an anxiety-provoking treatment.

Radiation Therapy

All cells, cancerous and healthy, grow and divide. But cancer cells grow and divide more rapidly than many of the normal cells around them. Radiation therapy delivers high doses of x-rays, gamma rays, or alpha and beta particles to cancerous tumors, killing or damaging them so that they cannot grow, multiply, or spread. Although some normal cells may be affected by radiation, most appear to repair themselves and recover fully from the effects of the treatment. Unlike chemotherapy, which exposes the entire body to cancer-fighting chemicals, radiation therapy affects only the tumor and the surrounding area.

An estimated 350,000 cancer patients receive radiation therapy in the United States annually (American Cancer Society, 2013). It is the preferred treatment for cancer in almost any part of the body, including head and neck tumors; early-stage Hodgkin's disease; non-Hodgkin's lymphomas; and cancers of the lungs, breasts, cervix, prostate, testes, bladder, thyroid, and brain. Radiation therapy also can be used to shrink a tumor prior to surgery (so that it can be removed more easily) or after surgery to stop the growth of any cancer cells that remain.

Like chemotherapy, radiation is often associated with side effects, including temporary or permanent loss of hair in the area being treated, fatigue, loss of appetite, skin rashes, and loss of white blood cells. On the positive side, thousands of people have become cancer-free after receiving radiation treatments alone or in combination with surgery or chemotherapy.

immunotherapy Chemotherapy in which medications are used to support or enhance the immune system's ability to selectively target cancer cells.

When child psychologist Elizabeth King was diagnosed with cancer, her son created a story and illustration about a character named "Kemo Shark," who swam around in his mother's body eating cancer cells (and sometimes healthy ones by mistake, which caused her to feel sick). When King completed her treatment, she developed her son's story into a children's comic book and funded the nonprofit organization KIDSCOPE to raise money to distribute the book at no cost.

Courtesy of KIDSCOPE; Concept by Mitchell McGough.

Alternative Treatments

Many cancer patients have tried one or more treatments as alternatives to medical treatments. Among these are aromatherapy, biofeedback, meditation, music therapy, prayer and spiritual practices, yoga, tai chi (an exercise-based form of "moving meditation"), art therapy, massage therapy, and herbal treatments (see Chapter 15). Although alternative therapies are generally unproven and have not been scientifically tested, many *can* be used safely along with standard biomedical treatment to relieve symptoms or side effects, to ease pain, and to improve a patient's overall quality of life.

Alternative treatments for cancer will be discussed more fully in Chapter 15.

Coping with Cancer

Life-threatening chronic diseases such as cancer create unique stresses for both victims and their families. Cancer is a dreaded disease, which most people realize can be intensely painful and lead to disability, disfigurement, or death. An estimated 20 to 40 percent of all cancer patients report elevated levels of affective distress (Holland & Alici, 2010; Hart & Charles, 2013). At diagnosis, during treatment, and even years after treatment, people with a history of cancer often report higher levels of anxiety, anger, hostility, and depression than do their nonaffected same-age peers (Hinz and others, 2010). However, this varies with the age of the individual. Older age generally is associated with less distress among both cancer patients and cancer survivors (Brant and others, 2011). Importantly, although cancer survivors seem to experience similar numbers and types of stressful events as the general population, some studies show that cancer survivors may perceive stressors as somewhat more severe and disruptive, particularly when they involve interpersonal tension (Costanzo, Stawski, Ryff, Coe, & Almeida, 2012).

As patients' expectations of survival have increased, so has the need for psychosocial supports aimed at restoring or maintaining quality of life. Health psychologists are helping focus attention and resources on enabling patients and their families to cope with the adverse effects of cancer treatment. They also are helping health care professionals recognize that the course of adjustment to cancer is not the same for all patients (Helgeson, Snyder, & Seltman, 2004).

Research on the emotional and behavioral responses of cancer patients to surgery consistently shows high levels of anxiety both before and after the operation. Compared with patients who are undergoing surgery for benign conditions, cancer surgery patients have higher overall levels of distress and slower rates of emotional recovery. In one study, breast cancer patients' presurgery expectations were significant predictors of their *postsurgery* pain, fatigue, and nausea (Montgomery, 2004).

Even when cancer treatment is successful and the disease is in remission, the fear, stress, and uncertainty do not go away. The threat of recurrence looms, for some patients for the rest of their lives. In fact, the distress associated with cancer recurrence is often greater than that following the initial diagnosis (Vickberg, 2003). The words of one breast cancer survivor poignantly illustrate this anxiety:

> This is what cancer is about to me, living with possible recurrence. Cancer is not about two months of treatment and a couple of minor surgeries. … I think the hardest thing for women like me who have found their cancers early and kept their breasts is to believe we are going to get away with all this. Am I really going to be OK?

as quoted in Vickberg (2003)

Bettmann/Getty Images

True "Fighting Spirit" Canadian Terry Fox's refusal to be defeated by cancer has inspired several generations. In this photo, Terry, who lost his right leg to cancer, runs along a highway just before reaching the halfway mark in his cross-Canada run. Terry ran coast to coast on an artificial limb—often as far as a 26-mile marathon each day—to raise money to fight the killer disease. The annual "Terry Fox Run," first held shortly after his 1981 death, has grown in size to involve millions of participants in over 60 countries. It is the world's largest one-day fund-raiser for cancer research.

Feelings such as these argue for educating cancer patients about what's normal following treatment and for improving the quality of life of cancer patients. Unfortunately, many health insurance providers do not distinguish between mental illness and psychosocial interventions for cancer patients. As a result, many patients find that psychological healing is not covered by their health insurance.

Emotions, Masculinity, and Ethnicity

Health psychologists are paying increasing attention to the experiences and coping techniques of ethnically diverse samples of people following the diagnosis of cancer, as well as those of men and of people who vary in their ability to regulate emotions.

Emotions and Coping

Although the link between personality traits and the development of cancer is tenuous, some personality factors do predict how well a person copes with cancer. For instance, expression of both positive and negative emotions can be beneficial in adjusting to a diagnosis of cancer (Quartana, Laubmeier, & Zakowski, 2006). In a sense, then, emotion-focused coping and denial of the diagnosis may be *positive* traits for cancer victims.

Other researchers have found that an optimistic disposition at the time the cancer is diagnosed is associated with an active, engaged coping style and less psychological distress over time (Carver and others, 2005). Those breast cancer patients who scored very low on a measure of dispositional optimism at the time of diagnosis reported greater symptoms of anxiety and depression and relied more often on avoidant, emotion-focused coping than did their more optimistic counterparts (Epping-Jordan and others, 1999). At three and six months after diagnosis, symptoms of anxiety and depression tended to occur only in those who continued to be troubled by persistent, intrusive thoughts about their illness. However, the relationship between optimism and long-term outcome in cancer patients remains unclear (Segerstrom, 2007), perhaps because optimists may have more difficulty adjusting to disappointing outcomes than those who are less optimistic but more realistic (Winterling, Glimelius, & Nordin, 2008). Similarly, while research studies have shown that maintaining a "fighting spirit" predicts better adjustment in early-stage cancer (O'Brien & Moorey, 2010), the evidence for its long-term benefits is questionable (Hoffman, 2015; Coyne & Tennen, 2010).

More generally, a growing body of research indicates that emotional regulation is critical to coping with traumatic events such as a diagnosis of cancer (Chuah, 2006). People who possess good skills at identifying and articulating emotions, therefore, might be expected to fare better at coping with traumatic events than people who lack these skills. One dispositional characteristic that psychologists have focused on is *emotional intelligence* (EI), defined as the ability to perceive, understand, express, and regulate emotions accurately (Mayer, Salovey, Caruson, & Sitarenios, 2001).

In one study, John Schmidt and Michael Andrykowski (2004) investigated the relationships among several social and dispositional variables and adjustment to breast cancer among 302 members of five Internet-based breast cancer support groups. In all cases, women who scored higher on a 30-item dispositional measure of EI reported less anxiety, depression, and overall distress than women who scored lower on the dispositional measure for EI. The beneficial effects of EI were especially pronounced among participants who perceived weaker social support and more social constraints that discouraged them from sharing their thoughts and feelings regarding their cancer. The researchers suggest that the presence of social constraints and absence of social support may have caused the women to actively avoid thinking about their cancer experience, thus inhibiting active processing and coping. To make matters worse, women who score low in EI may be less able to identify, communicate, and control their emotions effectively; thus, they "may be seen as irrational, demanding, or aversive" by others around them, who then respond in a manner that further discourages discussion (Schmidt & Andrykowski, 2004, p. 264). Those who have low EI also might be less effective in eliciting social support from others and less capable of recognizing and responding to supportive responses that others may make.

Cancer and Masculinity

As noted in Chapter 5, higher levels of aspects of masculinity, gender role conflict, and gender-linked personality characteristics are related to poorer outcomes in men with cancer. Consider men being treated for prostate cancer. Prostate cancer is the most common cancer in men, accounting for about 26 percent of all new cancer cases among males each year in the United States (American Cancer Society, 2015a). The recorded incidence rate of prostate cancer has increased dramatically in the last 40 years, mainly because of improvements in early detection of the disease (Rachet and others, 2009).

Common symptoms associated with prostate cancer treatment such as erectile dysfunction, loss of libido, pain, fatigue, and feelings of vulnerability and fear are linked to traditional gender role expectations and threatened masculine self-image (Storey and others, 2011). Prostate cancer patients often describe difficulties maintaining social and family role functions and report experiencing bodily changes that cause embarrassment, frustration, and feelings of weakness. Researchers have developed a questionnaire to measure *cancer-related masculine threat* (CMT). Consisting of statements such as "Cancer makes me feel like less of a man," "Cancer makes me feel inferior to other men," and "Cancer is taking away my masculinity," the CMT questionnaire recently was used in a longitudinal study of 66 men who underwent radical prostatectomy and/or radiation therapy for prostate cancer. After controlling for baseline health and age, the researchers found that men who scored high in CMT had poorer prostate-related functioning over time, including sexual, urinary, and bowel functioning. Men with higher CMT were also less likely to process their cancer-related emotions and more likely to engage in rumination and other less constructive forms of emotional processing (Hoyt, Stanton, Irwin, & Thomas, 2013).

Of particular concern to many men who are coping with cancer treatment is how it affects their ability to fulfill work-related roles. One qualitative study of 50 prostate cancer survivors revealed several common themes during a semi-structured interview following completion of their treatment. The first concerned the importance of work to the survivors' self-identity. Consider the following comments from one 52-year-old survivor:

> The only way I know how to live my life is if I work and my work is my life. And therefore when I'm not doing my work my life is obviously, unfortunately not full. My work/life balance is tipped more toward work, than life, I guess. That's just how it is.

> Grunfield, Drudge-Coates, Rixon, Eaton, & Cooper (2013)

Another difficulty for men coping with prostate and other cancers is that role models may not be as readily available as they are to female cancer survivors. This is due to the fact that men are less likely to disclose a cancer diagnosis, and male cancers are underrepresented in the media in comparison to female cancers (Gough, 2006). Fortunately, things are beginning to change. There is a growing amount of literature on masculinity and health, with a move away from a strongly gender-typed view of masculinity toward a more dynamic construct that changes from one context to another (Evans, Frank, Oliffe, & Gregory, 2011).

Once prostate cancer has been diagnosed, masculinities may affect treatment, including men's attitudes toward *active surveillance* (AS). Following the AS protocol, men diagnosed with low-grade, early-stage prostate cancer are monitored, and treatment is deferred until disease markers indicate that active treatment is warranted. During this period of "watchful waiting," no medical treatment—medications, surgery, or radiation—is delivered. The benefits of AS include avoiding comorbidities such as impotence and incontinence, and the reduced quality of life often associated with treatment for prostate cancer (Tosoian and others, 2011). Despite these benefits, some research suggests that less than 10 percent of eligible American men opt for AS, in part because the perception of "doing nothing" is difficult for men to accept (Mroz, Oliffe, & Davison, 2013).

Ethnicity and Coping

Health psychologists are paying increasing attention to the experiences of ethnically diverse samples of people following the diagnosis of cancer. As an example, among breast cancer survivors, African-Americans report more difficulties with physical functioning and activities of daily living than do European-Americans; European-Americans report more sexual difficulties than do African-Americans; Latinas score higher than the other groups on measures of distress; and Filipina patients report the most difficulties with emotional functioning (see Giedzinska, Meyerowitz, Ganz, & Rowland, 2004, for a review).

Other researchers have found that women of lower SES, as well as African-American and Hispanic women, are more likely than European-Americans to perceive *benefits* from a diagnosis of breast cancer, such as a renewed focus on relationships in their lives (Tomich & Helgeson, 2004). The researchers suggest that impoverished and minority women are more likely to face discrimination in their daily lives, which has prepared them to derive benefits from traumatic events. Low-SES and minority persons also are more likely to turn to religion to cope with trauma, which has been characterized as a way of cognitively restructuring events to search for their significance (Harrison, Koenig, Hays, Eme-Akwari, & Pargament, 2001).

Because ethnicity is often linked to other sociodemographic variables, such as income, education, and the nature of the medical treatment received, interpreting differences in coping such as these is difficult. At the very least, however, these findings demonstrate that psychologists and health care providers should not assume that the experiences provided by one ethnic group can be generalized to all others.

The idea that people can overcome challenges to experience a more hardy state is relatively new in health and disease research. Positive change among patients coping with chronic illness has been referred to as **post-traumatic growth (PTG)**, but also as *benefit finding,* or *thriving.* PTG is theorized as occurring when an adverse life event, such as cancer, disrupts a person's view of the world and his or her place in it (Arpawong, Richeimer, Weinstein, Elghamrawy, & Milam, 2013). Disruption in turn may cause cognitive restructuring, a search for meaning, and the rebuilding of a more positive life perspective. Those who experience PTG after being diagnosed and treated for cancer often report several types of benefits, including greater appreciation for life, personal strength, relationships with others, recognition for new possibilities in life, and spiritual understanding (Lelorain, Bonnaud-Antignac, & Florin, 2010; Schroevers, Kraaij, & Garnefski, 2011). A recent cross-sectional study of 114 adult outpatients in active cancer treatment reported that 87 percent of the participants reported at least one positive life change over the course of treatment (Arpawong and others, 2013).

A number of studies have found that the ability to find positive meaning from stressful life events, including a diagnosis of cancer, is associated with improved

post-traumatic growth (PTG) Positive psychological change experienced as the result of struggle with a highly challenging life circumstance. Also referred to as *benefit finding,* or *thriving.*

immune responses. In one study, Julienne Bower and her colleagues (Bower, Kemeny, Taylor, & Fahey, 2003) asked women who had lost a close relative to breast cancer to write about the death (cognitive processing/disclosure group) or about nonemotional topics weekly for four weeks. Women in the cognitive processing/disclosure group who placed greater importance on goals such as cultivating relationships and striving for meaning in their lives following the intervention had stronger measures of immune functioning.

Knowledge, Control, and Social Support

Considering the stress associated with being treated for cancer, most patients display remarkable physical and psychological resilience. Important factors in adjusting to cancer treatment include having access to information, perceiving some degree of control over treatment, and being able to express emotions while feeling supported by others.

Knowledge and Control

Health psychologists have made considerable progress in understanding the psychological reactions of patients to cancer treatment and the types of interventions and information that are effective in assisting their adjustment. They have found, for example, that procedural information (such as how the surgery, radiation, or chemotherapy regimen will be administered, as well as what the patient can expect before and after treatment) has wide-ranging benefits. Among these are fewer negative emotions, reduced pain, and briefer hospitalization (Johnson & Vogele, 1993). Information presented in narrative form, as compared to nonnarrative (usually statistical) form, may be particularly effective (McQueen, Kreuter, Kalesan, & Alcaraz, 2011).

The Internet is an increasingly important source of information for many cancer survivors. Recent data indicate that 81 percent of the U.S. population uses the Internet, and many have gone online to get information about a medical condition (Fox & Duggan, 2013). One study found that using the Internet for as little as 1 hour per week to search for breast health information was associated with greater feelings of social support and less loneliness in women with breast cancer (Fogel, Albert, Schnabel, Ditkoff, & Neugut, 2002). One in five Internet users reported going online in the last year to find others who might share the same health concerns (Fox & Duggan, 2013).

Also beneficial are interventions that focus on preventing patients from feeling helpless during their treatment. Even something as simple as encouraging patients to make choices about the hospital environment can improve a patient's well-being. For this reason, patients often are encouraged to decorate their rooms with pictures, photographs, and other personal items from home. Although the sense of doom and the stigma that once were attached to a diagnosis of cancer have largely disappeared, interventions aimed at *self-presentation* can help patients overcome difficulties in managing social relationships with family, friends, and coworkers that result from changes in their physical appearance (Leary, Tchividjiam, & Kraxberger, 1994; Davies & Batehup, 2010). Such interventions can range from the use of wigs by patients who have lost their hair as a result of chemotherapy to cognitive behavior therapy to improve self-esteem.

Social Comparison

Another source of information that can affect how people cope with cancer is *social comparison* with other cancer patients (Brakel, Dijkstra, Buunk, & Siero, 2012). Listening to testimonials of fellow patients can have a reassuring effect and help patients develop a more positive perspective (Buunk and others, 2009). Whether such information is beneficial for a person coping with cancer depends, first, on how the person perceives the other individual. Is this other individual perceived as doing better (*upward comparison*) or worse (*downward comparison*) than the patient? Second, it depends on the extent to which the person feels similar to the comparison person (*identification*) or feels different, and therefore it represents a state that is not a possible future (*contrast*). *Upward identification* may lead to positive feelings and improved quality of life, while *upward contrast* may lead to negative consequences in which the patient feels inferior. People also differ in their sensitivity to social comparison information. One recent study of 139 Dutch cancer survivors found that those with good health status and a strong social comparison orientation reported a significant improvement in quality of life two months after listening to audio interviews with cancer survivors who talk about the use of active coping strategies, expression of emotion, and seeking social support (Brakel and others, 2012).

Social Support

Key to any effective intervention is providing cancer patients with support and an opportunity to discuss their fears about the disease and its treatment. A great deal of research demonstrates the protective value of social relationships on health in general and cancer-related stress in particular. A spouse or significant other provides an important source of social support for many cancer patients. When this relationship is perceived as solid and supportive, the patient's physical and emotional well-being benefits greatly (Kamen and others, 2015). This is partly because married patients—often because of input from their spouses—generally detect cancer and other diseases at an earlier stage of development, and they are more likely to seek early treatment. Among women with breast cancer, for example, spousal support is associated with lower levels of depression and anxiety, improved psychological adjustment to cancer, greater feelings of intimacy, and improved quality of life (Belcher and others, 2011).

The benefits of social support extend beyond marriage. Women with breast cancer (Nausheen and others, 2009) and men with prostate cancer (Zhou and others, 2010) who have larger social support networks have slower cancer progression than women and men with less social support. However, cancer patients also report unsupportive, negative behaviors that include minimizing the patient's problem, forced cheerfulness, and insensitive comments. Such undesired support may cause cancer patients to view others as insensitive or patronizing and has been associated with poorer adjustment to certain cancers (Gremore and others, 2011).

Other studies have demonstrated that peer support and specific interventions are most effective when delivered individually and at certain times. For example, face-to-face support delivered by one individual can be effective, even over the Internet (Hoey, Ieropoli, White, & Jefford, 2008). In one study, researchers divided breast, colon, lung, and uterine cancer patients into two groups, one that began a group intervention soon after entering the study and the other after 4 months (Edgar, Rossberger, & Nowlis, 1992). At the start of the study, both groups were measured on depression, anxiety, worry about illness, and perceived personal control; follow-up measures were taken at 4-, 8-, and 12-month intervals. The intervention consisted of five one-hour sessions that focused on developing coping skills with such techniques as goal setting, problem solving, cognitive reappraisal, and relaxation training, as well as providing workshops on

Social Support Women and men who feel "socially connected" to a network of caring friends are less likely to die of all types of cancer than their socially isolated counterparts.

Design Pics Inc/Alamy

health care resources. Coping improved for all patients, but the greatest reduction in stress levels occurred in the group whose intervention began 4 months after being diagnosed with cancer. According to the researchers, patients' needs shortly after being diagnosed with cancer are probably quite different from their needs a few months later, after the emotional shock of the situation has been overcome.

A limited number of studies also have suggested that behavioral and psychosocial interventions may lower stress hormone levels and improve immune function in cancer patients and people coping with cancer in a loved one. For instance, among breast cancer patients, biofeedback training, cognitive therapy, relaxation training, guided imagery, and stress management all have been associated with significant decreases in cortisol levels and increases in the number of circulating lymphocytes (for example, Cruess and others, 2000). Although a few studies have even shown lower recurrence rates among cancer patients who participate in psychosocial interventions relative to waiting-list control participants, as noted earlier, the potential effects of such interventions on clinical outcomes remain speculative (see Luecken & Compas, 2002, for a review).

Social animals also fare worse in isolated environments. Researchers at the University of Chicago separated mice, which are highly social and normally live in groups of three or four, into normal and socially isolated groups just a few days after they had been weaned from their mothers' milk. Three weeks later, the researchers found abnormal changes in gene expression in the isolated animals' mammary glands. Gene pathways related to metabolism, known to contribute to increased growth of breast cancer, had been activated. In addition, the isolated mice also released more corticosteroid stress hormones than normally raised mice (Doheny, 2009).

Cognitive-Behavioral Interventions

Health psychologists have made considerable progress in developing cognitive-behavioral interventions in comprehensive cancer care. During and following treatment, a variety of interventions have been used. For adults, the interventions have focused on depression, stress, fatigue, pain, control of aversive reactions to treatment (such as nausea during chemotherapy), and enhancement of emotional well-being (Montgomery and others, 2009). For children, they have focused on increasing adherence to medical advice and reducing suffering. Although the question of whether such interventions can prolong life for people with cancer remains controversial (Coyne, Stefanek, & Palmer, 2007), it is clear that such interventions can be successful in helping cancer patients manage their distress levels (Manne & Andrykowski, 2006). Among the most widely used interventions are hypnosis, progressive muscle relaxation with guided imagery, systematic desensitization, biofeedback, and cognitive distraction. For instance, returning to the chapter-opening story, before Jeremy's attending physician performed a *lumbar puncture* (spinal tap) to sample my son's spinal fluid, the nurse engaged Jeremy in a detailed (and distracting) discussion of the most recent *Star Trek* program. In this section, we describe two of the more common techniques: guided imagery and systematic desensitization.

Many of these interventions stem from the field of psychoneuroimmunology (PNI). PNI researchers believe that the risk for many diseases (including cancer), the course that a particular disease follows, and the remission and recurrence of symptoms are all influenced by the interaction of behavioral, neuroendocrine, and immune responses.

Mindfulness-based stress-reduction interventions are being used with increasing frequency (Bartley, 2012; Gregoire, 2013). In one early study of prostate and breast cancer patients, a mindfulness intervention that focused on cultivating conscious awareness through relaxation, meditation, and yoga resulted in increased quality of life among participants, as well as a healthy shift in neuroendocrine response (Carlson, Speca, Patel, &

Goodey, 2003). A meta-analysis of 22 studies found that mindfulness-based therapies—which included yoga, meditation, breathing exercises, and cognitive training—were associated with significantly reduced symptoms of anxiety and depression in pre- and postcancer treatment (Piet, Wurtzen, & Zachariae, 2012).

Exercise is also increasingly recommended as a general intervention to improve the well-being of cancer patients (Floyd and Moyer, 2010). Several studies have reported that physical exercise improved the physical functioning, quality of life, self-efficacy, and emotional well-being of cancer patients (McAuley, White, Rogers, Motl, & Courneya, 2010; Milne, Wallman, Gordon, & Courneya, 2008). One of the most consistent outcomes of physical activity is self-efficacy, or the individual's belief in his or her personal capabilities. Self-efficacy expectations may well enhance the effects of exercise on depression and fatigue in cancer survivors (McAuley and others, 2010).

Emotional Disclosure and Expressive Writing

Emotional disclosure can have a beneficial effect for people coping with chronic illness. Annette Stanton and her colleagues (2000) examined the importance to patients of being able to actively process and express the emotions involved in coping with breast cancer. The participants were recruited within 20 weeks of completing surgery, chemotherapy, or radiation. Over the next three months, women who expressed their emotions about cancer had fewer medical appointments for cancer-related health problems and reported significantly lower stress levels than their less expressive and less socially receptive counterparts. The researchers suggest that by openly expressing one's fears—for instance, a loss of perceived control—"one may begin to distinguish what one can and cannot control [in order] to channel energy toward attainable goals, and to generate alternate pathways for bolstering control" (Stanton and others, 2000, p. 880). They also suggest that repeated expression of emotions may decrease negative emotions and the physiological arousal that comes with them, leading cancer patients to believe that their situation is not as dire as originally thought and to derive some benefit from their adversity.

In another study, Stanton and her colleagues (Stanton, Thompson, Crespi, Link, & Waisman, 2013) evaluated an intervention to teach patients with cancer how to use blogging to chronicle their experiences and communicate with their social networks via the Internet. Eighty-eight women with breast cancer were randomly assigned to participate in *Project Connect Online* (PCO)—a 3-hour workshop for hands-on creation of personal Web sites—or a control group. Participants in the PCO group developed their own Web sites using a template consisting of six functions:

- a journal (blog) that could contain photos;
- a section for Web site links, to be populated by each participant (for instance, the oncology clinic, National Cancer Institute);
- a How You Can Help page, in which participants could convey actions visitors could undertake (such as meal provision, written cards);
- choice of privacy settings;
- instructions for visitors to post messages and subscribe for automatic notification of Web site updates; and
- an online survey to assess visitors' reactions to PCO.

Over the 6-month period of the research trial, women in the blogging (PCO) group showed significant benefit—relative to control-group women—in symptoms of depression and overall appreciation of life.

Numerous, randomized, controlled trials have arrived at conflicting conclusions regarding the efficacy of *expressive writing* (EW) as a therapeutic intervention for people living with cancer. One meta-analysis of 13 controlled studies reported some positive effects of EW on patients' pain levels, sleep, and general physical and psychological

For many cancer patients, there is a wide gap between optimal care and the care that they actually receive. A report from the Agency for Healthcare Research and Quality, for instance, found that despite the existence of evidence-based clinical practice guidelines, many patients do not receive the recommended care (2012).

symptoms (Merz, Fox, & Malcarne, 2014). However, another meta-analysis of 16 randomized controlled trials found no statistically significant effects of EW on any psychological or physical outcomes in cancer patients (Zachariae & O'Toole, 2015). A third meta-analysis of 11 randomized controlled trials evaluating an EW intervention in breast cancer patients concluded that EW may have a significant positive impact on self-reported physical symptoms, but this benefit may not last very long (Zhou, Wu, An, & Li, 2015).

EW seems to benefit some patients more than others, leading some researchers to conclude that its efficacy may depend more on social support and other factors in the lives of cancer patients than on the intervention itself (Zachariae & O'Toole, 2015). One such factor seems to be the level of social support a patient perceives. To date, until more research is completed, the conclusion that can be most safely drawn is that EW is a simple, low-cost, self-administered intervention that may have a therapeutic effect in some subgroups of patients.

Guided Imagery

Guided imagery draws on patients' psychophysiological reactions to the environment to help them optimize physiological activity in various body systems and thus relieve pain or discomfort. For example, a patient who views an impending surgery as a life-threatening trauma may exhibit hypertension, cardiac arrhythmia, and other health-compromising responses prior to surgery. Conversely, a patient who looks forward to the same operation as a lifesaving event is more likely to remain relaxed before, during, and following treatment.

In guided imagery, the therapist uses one or more external devices to help the patient relax and then form clear, strong, positive images to replace the symptoms. Effective images draw on several sensory modalities, including vision, hearing, touch, and even smell or taste and may be stimulated by taped music, sounds of nature, verbal suggestions, pictures of objects or places, aromas from scented candles, or a variety of other devices.

Guided imagery begins with the patient assuming a comfortable position, either lying down or sitting, with eyes closed or open. After taking several slow, deep breaths, the person begins a process of systematically attending to and then relaxing any areas of bodily tension. A variety of techniques may be used to assist relaxation, including progressive muscle relaxation, biofeedback training, or autogenic training (see Chapter 5).

Once a relaxed state is reached, the person visualizes a safe, peaceful place and strives to make the image as clear and intense as possible by focusing on sights, sounds, smells, and other sensory aspects of the moment. At this point, the patient follows taped suggestions (or a nurse's or therapist's verbal suggestions) and forms a mental image of a symptom, such as pain or nausea. The patient then imagines the symptom changing. For example, the "red" fiery pain changes to a cool shade of blue, or queasiness is expelled from the body with each exhalation.

After a few minutes of focusing on the altered symptom (sometimes describing its changed appearance to the nurse or therapist), the patient is instructed to relax, breathe deeply, and return to the peaceful place. After several sessions, which may last only 5 or 10 minutes, most patients are able to perform imagery without assistance.

Imagery may be beneficial for several reasons (Naparstek, 1994):

- Imagery triggers a state of relaxed concentration that enhances the person's sensitivity to health-promoting images.

- Imagery gives the patient an increased sense of control and a decreased sense of helplessness over stressful aspects of disease or treatment.

- Imagery also may work through the *placebo effect*. In fact, people who believe that imagery and relaxation have the potential to improve their health may experience physiological changes that enhance their ability to fight disease.

guided imagery The use of one or more external devices to assist in relaxation and the formation of clear, strong, positive images.

Systematic Desensitization

After several sessions of chemotherapy, nearly one-third of patients begin to feel nauseated in anticipation of an upcoming treatment session. Many health psychologists consider this *anticipatory nausea* to be a form of classical conditioning, in which events leading up to treatment (such as driving to the hospital and sitting in the waiting room) function as *conditioned stimuli*, becoming linked to the powerful physiological reactions elicited as *unconditioned responses* by the cancer drug.

systematic desensitization
A form of behavior therapy, commonly used for overcoming phobias, in which the person is exposed to a series of increasingly fearful situations while remaining deeply relaxed.

Health psychologists have learned that incorporating guided imagery into **systematic desensitization** effectively counters this classically conditioned side effect of chemotherapy. In this form of behavior therapy, commonly used to help people overcome phobias, the person is gradually exposed to increasingly fearful stimuli or situations, while remaining deeply relaxed. In one study, Gary Morrow and his colleagues (Morrow, Asbury, Hammon, & Dobkin, 1992) trained a group of oncologists and nurses to use desensitization with cancer patients. The patients then were assigned randomly to one of two treatment groups (one conducted by a psychologist and one conducted by a nurse) or to a control group that received no intervention.

In the first stage, cancer patients established a hierarchy of difficult moments related to an approaching chemotherapy session, such as awakening on the morning of treatment, driving to the hospital, and sitting in the treatment room. After instruction in several relaxation-inducing techniques, the patients used guided imagery to visualize each moment in the hierarchy while remaining in a relaxed state. As they gradually worked their way up from the least threatening image to the most threatening image, the patients were *reconditioned* to feel relaxation rather than anxiety and nausea.

Both treatment groups experienced a substantial decline in the duration of their nausea following treatment. In contrast, the control group's nausea actually lasted 15 hours *longer* than before, perhaps as a result of additional classical conditioning. In follow-up studies, Morrow and his colleagues (Morrow, Navari, & Rugo, 2014; Morrow, Hesketh, Schwartzberg, & Ettinger, 2010) have found that the benefits of desensitization often increase over time. Like athletes who gradually improve their visual imagery skills, many patients report much less nausea and vomiting over time as they improve their control over their anxiety in anticipating treatment (Kamen and others, 2014).

The intervention studies that we have discussed in this chapter provide substantial evidence that psychosocial factors can influence a cancer patient's response to treatment and, quite possibly, the course of recovery (or the likelihood of recurrence). Those studies that have reported longer survival for cancer patients are especially vivid demonstrations of the value of such interventions.

Weigh In on Health

Respond to each question below based on what you learned in the chapter. (**Tip:** Use the items in "Summing Up" to take into account related biological, psychological, and social concerns.)

1. As you move forward in your life, what have you learned in this chapter about cancer that helps you better understand your risk, as well as what you can do now to try to prevent an occurrence of cancer in the future?

2. Barring unforeseen difficulties, researchers predict that testing for inherited cancer risk and hundreds of other disease genes soon will be available. For treatable conditions,

genetic testing is rarely controversial. But for untreatable conditions such as Huntington's disease, genetic testing raises many ethical questions. For instance, should all people have equal access to genetic tests? Under what circumstances should the results of genetic tests be shared with others? What other ethical issues does genetic testing raise?

3. Use what you have learned in this chapter to write a checklist about positive ways in which people have learned how to cope with cancer. This checklist could be a valuable resource for someone you know (or even for yourself) one day.

Summing Up

What Is Cancer?

1. Cancer is the second leading cause of death in the United States. It is actually more than 100 different but related diseases. Cancer is the uncontrolled multiplication and spread of body cells that form tumors.

2. There are four general types of cancer: Carcinomas are cancers of the epithelial cells, which line the outer and inner surfaces of the body. Lymphomas are cancers of the lymph system. Sarcomas are cancers that develop from muscle, bone, fat, and other connective tissue. Leukemias are cancers of the blood and blood-forming system.

3. Cancer defies a simple description because its occurrence varies with gender, age, ethnicity, and race.

4. Several variables contribute to ethnic differences in cancer, including socioeconomic status, knowledge about cancer, and attitudes toward the disease, which may affect access to health care and adherence to medical advice. In addition, health care providers do not always provide culturally competent medical care.

Risk Factors for Cancer

5. The leading risk factor for cancer is advancing age. Cancers of the lungs, mouth, pharynx, larynx, esophagus, pancreas, uterus, cervix, kidney, bladder, and breast are linked to all forms of tobacco use. Alcohol use, especially among tobacco users, is a major risk factor for cancer.

6. A person's time perspective, including consideration of future consequences, is another factor in health behaviors.

7. Fatty diets and meat that is either highly processed or cooked at very high temperatures promote cancer of the colon, prostate, testes, uterus, and ovaries. Diets that include plenty of fruits, vegetables, and whole grains may play a protective role against some cancers.

8. Regular exercise may also be a protective factor for certain cancers.

9. Vulnerability to some forms of cancer are inherited. Most cases of breast cancer, however, are caused by nongenetic factors.

10. Research has linked a variety of environmental factors to cancer, including ultraviolet light, toxic chemicals, and occupational carcinogens. A history of frequent sunburns during childhood, the use of tanning booths, and the tendency of people to believe that their personal risk of negative outcomes is lower than that of others (comparative optimism) are factors in the increased prevalence of melanoma.

11. An estimated 15 to 20 percent of new cancers worldwide each year are attributable to infection. HPVs contribute to cervical cancer and some cancers of the mouth and throat.

hepatitis B virus and hepatitis C virus increase a person's chance of developing liver cancer.

12. Periodic or long-term clinical depression is relatively common among people adjusting to cancer. Depression has also been linked to a higher risk of early death among people with cancer.

13. According to the immune surveillance theory, cancer cells are prevented from spreading by agents of the immune system that constantly patrol the body for abnormal cells. Prolonged stress may compromise the immune system and allow malignant cells to spread. Reduced immunocompetence has been demonstrated following exams, divorce, bereavement, unemployment, and occupational stress.

14. Childhood adversity has been associated with greater emotional and physiological sensitivity to stress. Childhood stressors also may promote long-term immune system dysregulation, which influences cancer morbidity.

Cancer Treatment

15. When cancer does develop, its impact on health nearly always can be minimized through early detection and treatment. Advances in genetic screening, mammography, and other detection technologies have dramatically improved the survival rates for many types of cancer. Many people fail to heed early warning signs of cancer, however.

16. Biomedical treatments for cancer include surgery, chemotherapy, and radiation therapy. Surgery generally offers the greatest chance for cure for most types of cancer. Chemotherapy is used to destroy fast-growing cancer cells that have spread to parts of the body far from the primary tumor. Unlike chemotherapy, radiation therapy affects only the tumor and the surrounding area.

17. Many cancer patients try one or more alternative treatments (such as meditation, biofeedback, or herbal treatments) to relieve side effects and to improve their overall quality of life.

Coping with Cancer

18. Cancer and cancer treatment create unique stresses for both patients and their families. Even when treatment is successful, the threat of the disease's recurrence looms. Although cancer survivors seem to experience similar numbers and types of stressful events as the general population, some studies show that cancer survivors may perceive stressors as somewhat more severe and disruptive.

19. Many psychosocial interventions have been used to assist patients in coping with cancer. Effective interventions enhance patients' knowledge about what to expect from treatment, increase the perception of control over their lives,

and offer a supportive social environment in which to share fears and concerns.

20. Expressive writing seems to benefit some cancer patients more than others. Its efficacy may depend more on social support and other factors in the lives of cancer patients than on the intervention itself.

21. Higher levels of masculinity, gender role conflict, and gender-linked personality characteristics are related to poorer outcomes in men with cancer.

22. Interventions that provide health education and teach specific skills for solving problems and managing stress are also beneficial to patients' well-being. Information presented in narrative, as compared to nonnarrative (usually statistical), form may be particularly effective. Another source of information that can affect how people cope with cancer is *social comparison* with other cancer patients. Guided imagery and systematic desensitization effectively help patients control the side effects of chemotherapy and other cancer treatments.

Key Terms and Concepts to Remember

cancer, p. 318
metastasis, p. 318
carcinoma, p. 318
sarcoma, p. 319
lymphoma, p. 319
leukemia, p. 319

carcinogen, p. 322
consideration of future
  consequences, p. 322
melanoma, p. 327
comparative optimism, p. 327
immunocompetence, p. 330

immune surveillance theory, p. 330
immunotherapy, p. 334
post-traumatic growth (PTG), p. 338
guided imagery, p. 343
systematic desensitization, p. 344

LaunchPad
macmillan learning

To accompany your textbook, you have access to a number of online resources, including quizzes for every chapter of the book, flashcards, critical thinking exercises, videos, and *Check Your Health* inventories. To access these resources, please visit the Straub *Health Psychology* LaunchPad solo at: **launchpadworks.com**

CHAPTER 12

HIV/AIDS and Other Communicable Diseases

Six months before the start of the 1988 summer Olympics, 28-year-old diving champion Greg Louganis received an HIV-positive diagnosis, which at that time was widely viewed as a death sentence. Although his first inclination was to "lock myself away in my house and wait to die," he continued to train. He also began taking AZT, the first effective pharmaceutical weapon against the virus—a drug that had been fast-tracked over a mere 25 months of clinical trials and approved by the FDA one year earlier.

His decisions paid off later that summer in Seoul, South Korea. Although Louganis was injured when he struck his head on the board during a preliminary dive, he made a remarkable comeback. Only 30 minutes later and after receiving stitches for his wound, he returned to the 3-meter board competition, won gold for this event, and later gold for the men's 10-meter platform. In doing so, he became the only diver in history to win two gold medals in back-to-back Olympic Games.

Despite this remarkable athletic achievement, Greg didn't expect to live to see age 30. Before the advent of today's carefully calibrated "cocktail" of antiviral drugs, success in stopping the progression of HIV infection into AIDS was rare. In 1989, Louganis officially retired from diving to become a sports commentator and a national speaker on such issues as LGBT rights, HIV/AIDS, domestic violence, and overcoming adversity. In 2011, he returned to diving to help coach the latest generation of U.S. divers. Twenty-eight years after winning his gold medals, 56-year-old Louganis says, "I am still here! I didn't allow my HIV [to] take over as an obsession; it's a mere part of me that I've lived with."

Olympic champion Greg Louganis as he looks today in his 50s—healthy, with HIV under control.

Vivien Killilea/Getty Images

sexually transmitted infections (STIs) Infections that are spread primarily through person-to-person sexual contact.

Louganis, who at 5 feet 9 inches and 175 pounds looks fitter than many people half his age, attributes his health to the ever-evolving combinations of medical treatments that over the past 25 years have transformed the perception of an HIV diagnosis as being an almost certain death sentence into an often manageable, chronic illness. He follows an aggressive program to maintain his overall health: He takes anti-HIV medications each morning and evening, along with nutritional supplements, and alternative medical treatments that include Chinese herbs and acupuncture sessions for immune support. He eats a low-fat, nutrient-dense diet and stays active with daily workouts that include swimming, spin classes, weight lifting, and yoga-based mindful meditation, saying that these aspects of his lifestyle are as important to his well-being as his medication regimen. All of his practices continue to pay off. "The HIV virus may remain in my body," he says, "but it's now undetectable."

[Source of quotes: Louganis, G. (2014, September 20). Living with HIV: New horizons. *Huffington Post.* Retrieved from http://www.huffingtonpost.com/greg-louganis/living-with-hiv-new-horizons_b_5844824.html]

Although AIDS and some other **sexually transmitted infections (STIs)** seem to be recent phenomena, health experts believe that they actually are thousands of years old. AIDS became a global problem because of the dramatic increase in mobility of most of the world's population, which allowed the disease to spread from continent to continent. Although the initial panic created by the outbreak of the HIV virus has subsided in developed countries, where early screening and successful drug treatments have turned AIDS into a survivable, manageable, chronic disease, the picture remains bleak in developing countries.

This chapter focuses on HIV and the AIDS epidemic. We begin by discussing the nature of communicable diseases, including their means of transmission, global burden, and primary measures of control. Next, we'll examine AIDS, including its impact on the body, and how the virus is spread. The chapter concludes with a discussion of health psychology's role in the design and implementation of programs to stop the progress of AIDS, and to provide support for those with HIV and AIDS.

Communicable and Noncommunicable Diseases

noncommunicable disease A noninfectious disease; one that is nontransmissible.

People in much of the world are living longer than ever before. Due to improved infection control and the aging of populations, the global burden of disease has shifted increasingly toward **noncommunicable diseases (NCDs)** such as heart disease, cancer, chronic respiratory disease, and diabetes (Institute for Health Metrics and Evaluation, 2013a). Unlike NCDs, which are noninfectious and nontransmissible, **communicable diseases** are caused by infections, such as tuberculosis (TB), or by parasites, such as hookworm. Communicable diseases can be transmitted from one person to another, from an animal to a person, and from a person to an animal. Transmission can occur directly, such as through respiration, or indirectly through a *vector*, such as a mosquito in the case of malaria or the *Zika virus*.

communicable disease A disease that is transmitted from a human to another human, from a human to an animal, or from an animal to a human.

Examples of communicable diseases and their methods of transmission include:

- *Waterborne*: cholera, rotavirus
- *Sexual or blood-borne*: HIV, hepatitis
- *Food-borne*: salmonella, E coli
- *Traumatic contact*: rabies
- *Inhalation*: meningitis, influenza, tuberculosis
- *Vector-borne*: malaria, Zika virus

Communicable diseases can be controlled in many ways. Vaccination is the primary control measure for infections such as smallpox, meningitis, tetanus, and influenza. Improved treatment and caregiving are primary control measures for respiratory infections, HIV/AIDS, and tuberculosis. Cleaner water, better hygiene, and healthier sanitation measures are the primary control measure for diarrheal diseases. Vector control and containment are primary control measures for malaria, West Nile virus, avian influenza, and the Zika virus. Finally, behavioral change (such as consistent condom use) is a primary control measure for sexually transmitted infections, Ebola virus, and HIV.

The Epidemiological Transition

epidemiological transition A shift in the disease pattern of a population as mortality falls: acute, infectious diseases are reduced, while chronic, noncommunicable diseases increase in prevalence.

The **epidemiological transition** is the fundamental narrative of global health in the twenty-first century (Dye, 2014). This transition occurs as a developing country or region gains increased control over the acute infectious diseases of childhood. As the death rate declines and a higher proportion of children survive into adulthood, parents increasingly choose to have smaller families. Over time, the infectious diseases of childhood are gradually overtaken by the chronic NCDs typical of adulthood. In North America, Western Europe, and other parts of the industrialized world, this transition has occurred over centuries. In some countries, such as Mexico, it has taken place in just a few decades.

In the developing world, where four-fifths of the world's population live, NCDs are fast replacing more traditional enemies such as infectious diseases and malnutrition as the leading causes of disability and mortality. By the year 2020, NCDs are expected to account for seven out of every ten deaths, compared with fewer than half today (WHO, 2016a).

Although the number of deaths caused by pathogens and parasites is falling worldwide, nowhere in the world have communicable diseases become only a negligible cause of mortality and morbidity. Communicable diseases disproportionately impact the poor. Experts once believed that, as countries develop, NCD replaced communicable disease as the main source of ill health. However, there is now evidence that the poorest populations in developing countries face the double burden of high rates of both communicable and noncommunicable disease. In low-income countries, infections still cause the majority of deaths, despite the rise of cardiovascular disease, cancers, injuries and other NCDs (Figure 12.1). In poor countries, the three leading

FIGURE 12.1

Proportion of All Deaths by Cause and Region, 2010 In low-income countries, infections still cause the majority of deaths. In wealthier countries, noncommunicable diseases and injuries cause the majority of deaths.

Data from http://rstb .royalsocietypublishing.org/ content/369/1645/20130426

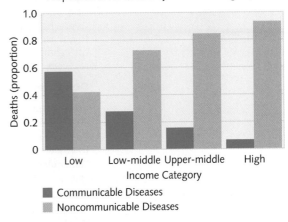

Proportion of All Deaths by Cause and Region, 2010

Income Category

■ Communicable Diseases
■ Noncommunicable Diseases

causes of death are communicable diseases: lower respiratory infections, HIV/AIDs, and diarrheal diseases. In high-income countries, the three leading causes of death are NCDs: stroke, ischemic heart disease, and lung cancer. The fifth-leading and only major communicable cause of death in wealthy countries is lower respiratory infections (mostly due to pneumonia among older people) (Institute for Health Metrics and Evaluation, 2013a). In recent years, medical advances such as oral rehydration salts for diarrheal disease, *antiretroviral therapy* (ART) for AIDS, and vaccines for common infections such as pneumococcal pneumonia have resulted in significant reductions in morbidity and mortality from communicable diseases in middle- and high-income countries. However, low-income countries have had significantly smaller increases in per capita annual health expenditures compared with middle- and high-income countries, and therefore these advances remain out of reach for many of the world's poorest people (HEAL, 2016).

People living in affluent countries are more likely to have the knowledge and ability to protect themselves from diarrhea and parasitic diseases that are often spread by unsafe water. They are less likely to live in overcrowded conditions, which can spread diseases such as tuberculosis, and they are more likely to be able to immunize their children against vaccine-preventable diseases. Although there are safe, effective, and inexpensive treatments for many communicable diseases, those treatments are still underused in low- and middle-income countries (Skolnik, 2016).

Table 12.1 summarizes the leading communicable causes of death for all countries and for low- and middle-income countries. Globally in 2013, the top three were lower respiratory infections, HIV/AIDS, and diarrheal diseases (Institute for Health Metrics and Evaluation, 2013a).

The impact of specific communicable diseases varies by age group. For example, the impact of diarrheal disease, lower respiratory infections, measles, and malaria is greatest on young children, while that of HIV/AIDS and TB is on people between 15 and 59 years of age (Institute for Health Metrics and Evaluation, 2013a). The economic and social costs of communicable disease are also especially high for infants and children, often adversely affecting their schooling and productivity throughout life (Skolnik, 2016). For example, AIDS, which often impacts young adults in low-income countries, can reduce average life expectancy by up to 20 years. As another example, treatment for malaria, which most often impacts children in low-income countries, can easily cost up to 25 percent of a family's income (HEAL, 2016).

TABLE 12.1

Leading Communicable Causes of Death (by number of deaths, in thousands)

The burden of specific communicable diseases varies by region but is overwhelmingly borne by low- and middle-income countries. Globally, lower respiratory infections cause the most deaths, followed by HIV/AIDS and diarrheal diseases, and then by TB and malaria.

Condition	World	Low- and Middle-Income Countries
Lower respiratory conditions	2,814	2,341
HIV/AIDS	1,465	1,370
Diarrheal diseases	1,446	1,413
Tuberculosis	1,196	1,150
Malaria	1,170	1,170
Measles	125	125

Data from Institute for Health Metrics and Evaluation (IHME). (2013c). GBD heat map. Seattle, WA: IHME, University of Washington. Retrieved March 17, 2016, from http://vizhub.heathdata.org/irank/heat.php.

The global burden of communicable disease is generally about the same for females as it is for males. Two exceptions are tuberculosis, which affects more males than females, and HIV/AIDS, which globally now ranks higher as a cause of death for women than for men (Institute for Health Metrics and Evaluation, 2013a).

Emerging and Reemerging Communicable Diseases

Throughout history, new communicable diseases have periodically emerged, sometimes with catastrophic effects. For example, the first major *bubonic plague* that swept through the Mediterranean world in the sixth century was transmitted by black rats that traveled aboard grain ships and transmitted the virus that killed nearly 25 percent of the European population (Horgan, 2014). As another example, since 1976, there have been 26 outbreaks of the Ebola virus in ten African countries, as well as in parts of Europe and the United States. Also believed to originally have been animal-borne, Ebola fatality rates are in the range of 25 percent to 90 percent. The World Health Organization estimates that about 5,000 people died in the most recent outbreak of Ebola in West Africa, which began in 2014 (WHO, 2016b).

HIV, which we'll discuss in detail later in this chapter, emerged in the 1980s. A decade later, *severe acute respiratory syndrome* (SARS) spread to more than two dozen countries in North America, South America, Europe, and Asia before being contained in 2003 (CDC, 2013f). Caused by a respiratory virus, SARS spread from Hong Kong to infect over 8,000 people in 37 countries within a matter of weeks. Of these, 774 died.

Two recently emerging infectious diseases are the avian influenza H5N1, commonly called "bird flu," and the Zika virus. Unlike other types of flu, H5N1, which is deadly to poultry, usually does not spread between people. Zika, which is spread to people primarily through the bite of an infected *Aedes* species mosquito, generally causes only mild symptoms in adults. However, Zika may cause *microcephaly,* a serious birth defect of the brain, as well as other poor birth outcomes in mothers who were infected with the virus while pregnant (CDC, 2016d).

Antimicrobial Resistance

A growing global health concern is the emergence of drug-resistant forms of communicable disease. All microbes have the ability to develop resistance to drugs that are used to kill them and thus become drug-resistant organisms. **Antimicrobial resistance** is the ability of bacteria, viruses, and parasites to change and resist the effect of drugs as a result of mutation or the exchange of genetic material among different strains.

The use of antibiotics is the single most important factor in the development of antimicrobial resistance. Only a few years after penicillin was introduced, for example, strains of bacteria that were resistant to the antibiotic emerged. Similarly, malaria can no longer be treated effectively with the drug *choroquine* because the virus is now resistant to it.

antimicrobial resistance The ability of bacteria, viruses, and other microbes to resist the effect of drugs.

Tuberculosis

Tuberculosis is another case in point. TB is caused by the bacterium *Myocobacterium tuberculosis* and spreads through aerosolized droplets that people inhale from others who are already infected with the disease. An untreated person with active TB may infect 10 to 15 other people each year, about 10 percent of whom will develop the disease themselves. Two-thirds of those who develop the active disease will die if not treated properly (Skolnik, 2016). Among the conditions that increase susceptibility to TB are living in crowded circumstances and having a weakened immune system. Each year, there are about nine million new cases of TB in the world, with Africa having the highest estimated incidence rate (WHO, 2014).

Most people with TB are cured by a strictly followed, six-month treatment regimen with first-line antimicrobial drugs such as isoniazid and rifampicin. *Multidrug-resistant*

TB (MDR-TB) is tuberculosis that does not respond to first-line anti-TB drugs and is then often transmitted from one person to another. Globally, in 2014, an estimated 480,000 developed MDR-TB (WHO, 2015b).

Because the mere use of antibiotics creates resistance, these drugs should be used only to treat infections. However, antibiotics are misused as much as 50 percent of the time, including being prescribed when not needed, dosed incorrectly, or taken for the wrong amount of time (CDC, 2014b). The use of counterfeit or poor quality medicines that do not contain the correct ingredients also contributes to global drug resistance (Skolnik, 2016).

Another important factor in the development of antimicrobial resistance is the spread of resistant strains of bacteria from person to person in crowded settings such as hospitals, nursing homes, schools, and prisons. In such settings, poor sanitation and hygiene and weak infection control often contribute to this danger.

Breakdowns in public health measures can also promote the reemergence of diseases. For example, from the end of World War II until the beginning of the HIV/AIDs pandemic, in many affluent countries, there was a general sense that the most dangerous infectious diseases had been conquered. As a result, many nations loosened their measures to control communicable diseases such as TB. Small wonder that there was a resurgence of TB and MDR-TB in many areas, including New York City in the 1980s (Snowden, 2008).

Figure 12.2 illustrates another way antibiotic resistance can spread. The microbes that contaminate food can also become resistant due to the use of antibiotics. For some germs, such as the bacterium *Salmonella*, antibiotics fed to animals raised for food is the primary factor in increased resistance. Antibiotics that are medically important to treating

FIGURE 12.2
How Antibiotic Resistance Spreads Simply taking antibiotic drugs, or giving them to animals, creates drug resistant-bacteria.

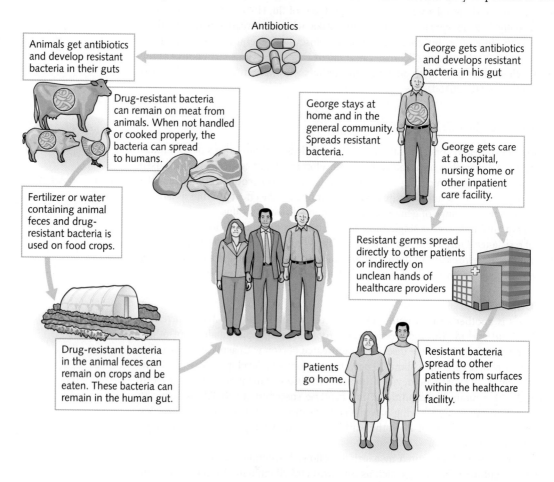

infections in humans should be used in food-producing animals only to treat infectious disease, not to promote growth.

In the last 40 years, no communicable disease has had a greater impact on the human condition than AIDS, the topic we turn to in the next section.

The AIDS Epidemic

cquired immunodeficiency syndrome (AIDS) is a life-threatening communicable disease caused by the **human immunodeficiency virus (HIV)**. The virus attacks the body's immune system and leaves it vulnerable to infection. As HIV infection develops into AIDS, its victims usually struggle with infections that otherwise would be handled with relative ease if their immune systems were not compromised. In this way, AIDS increases its victims' vulnerability to *opportunistic infections,* such as pneumonia and certain cancers, which prey on an individual's weakened immune system.

acquired immunodeficiency syndrome (AIDS) The most advanced stages of HIV infection, defined by a T cell count of less than 200 and the occurrence of opportunistic infections or HIV-related cancers that take advantage of a weakened immune system.

human immunodeficiency virus (HIV) A virus that infects cells of the immune system, destroying or impairing their function.

A Brief History of AIDS

In the late 1970s, unrecognized cases of what we now know to be AIDS began to appear. Although no one knows exactly how the AIDS virus infected the first human, it appears to have originated in west-central Africa, spreading quickly through neighboring countries. HIV is one of a family of primate viruses similar to a harmless virus found in certain subspecies of chimpanzees and green monkeys. Of particular interest in the investigation into the origins of AIDS is the *simian immunodeficiency virus* (SIV), which affects monkeys. This virus is believed to be at least 32,000 years old and closely resembles HIV1 and HIV2, the two types of HIV (Worobey and others, 2010).

Certain viruses can pass between species; the most commonly accepted theory is that SIV was transferred to humans as a result of chimps being killed and eaten or of an infected chimp's blood getting into cuts or wounds on the hunter's body. Normally, the hunter's body would have fought off SIV, but over time, the virus may have adapted to its new human host and become HIV1 (AVERT, 2013).

The disease was first noticed in humans in 1980 when 55 young men were diagnosed with a cluster of similar symptoms with an unknown cause. The symptoms were indicative of **Kaposi's sarcoma,** a rare cancer usually found only among the elderly. Epidemiologists suspected that the cause of the unexpected illness was a weakened immune system. Since most of the first reported victims were gay men and injection drug users, it appeared that the disease was being transmitted sexually or through the exchange of infected blood.

Kaposi's sarcoma A rare cancer of blood vessels serving the skin, mucous membranes, and other glands in the body.

In 1983, the National Institutes of Health (NIH) in the United States and the Pasteur Institute in France concluded that a new virus was the probable cause of the disease. A year later, in the spring of 1984, the U.S. Department of Health announced that it had isolated the new virus—HIV.

The Spread of AIDS

During the second half of the 1980s, AIDS began to threaten the general population. Previously limited mostly to white gay men and injection drug users in the United States, AIDS began surfacing among other demographic groups. In January 1991, AIDS claimed its 100,000th global victim. No cure was in sight as AIDS claimed its 200,000th victim in 1993. The disease continued to grow exponentially, reaching 400,000 cases worldwide by 1994, with increased incidence among women and still no effective drug treatments.

TABLE 12.2
Regional HIV/AIDS Statistics, End of 2010

Region	Adults and Children Living with HIV/AIDS	Adults and Children Newly Infected	Main Mode(s) of Transmission
Sub-Saharan Africa	22.9 million	1.9 million	Hetero
North Africa and Middle East	470,000	59,000	IDU, Hetero
East Asia	790,000	88,000	IDU, Hetero, MSM
South and Southeast Asia	4 million	270,000	IDU, Hetero, MSM
Latin America	1.5 million	100,000	MSM, IDU, Hetero
Caribbean	200,000	12,000	Hetero, MSM
Eastern Europe and Central Asia	1.5 million	160,000	IDU, MSM
Western Europe and Central Europe	840,000	30,000	MSM, IDU
North America	1.3 million	58,000	MSM, IDU, Hetero
Oceania	54,000	3,300	MSM, IDU
Total	34 million	2.7 million	

MSM (sexual transmission among men who have sex with men); IDU (transmission through injection drug use); Hetero (heterosexual transmission)

Data from UNAIDS. (2010). Report on the global AIDS epidemic. http://www.unaids.org/globalreport; UNAIDS. (2011). UNAIDS World AIDS Day Report 2011. http//www.unaids.org.

In 2013, people aged 50 and over accounted for 21 percent (8,395) of the estimated 47,352 HIV diagnoses in the United States (CDC Fast Facts, 2015).

pandemic A worldwide epidemic such as AIDS.

AIDS Awareness On November 7, 1991, NBA superstar Earvin "Magic" Johnson stunned the world by announcing that he was HIV positive. Because of Johnson's fame and the esteem and affection that his fans felt for him, this statement was a major factor in increased AIDS awareness and removal of the stigma associated with the disease, both in the United States and around the world.

Alberto Marquez/AP Images

As the millennium approached, new anti-HIV drugs were finally proving to be effective, and death rates from AIDS declined sharply in the United States (UNAIDS, 2007). However, these drugs weren't available to everyone who needed them, and, worldwide, the AIDS **pandemic** continued to spiral out of control (see Table 12.2). Now, nearly 40 years into the still-emerging pandemic, HIV has reached every corner of the globe, causing more than 34 million deaths from AIDS-related causes so far (WHO, 2015c). Worldwide, 36.9 million people (of whom 2.6 million are children) are living with HIV/AIDS, the vast majority in low- and middle-income countries (Figure 12.3). This number includes 2.0 million people—slightly more than half of them women— who became infected in 2014 (WHO, 2015c). The same year, 1.5 million people died of AIDS-related illnesses, making this disease the sixth-leading cause of death worldwide (WHO, 2015c).

The Epidemiology of AIDS

As you learned in Chapter 2, the first step in fighting and preventing a chronic disease like AIDS is taken by epidemiologists, who investigate the factors that contribute to its prevalence and incidence in a particular population. Keeping track of the distribution of AIDS by demographic traits is a difficult job because of the fluidity of the disease, but it is most prevalent among certain populations. In the United States, the AIDS epidemic has taken the greatest toll on gay, bisexual, and other men who have sex with men (MSM), particularly young African-Americans (Figure 12.4). An estimated 1.2 million people in the United States are living with HIV, and almost 1 in 8 (12.8 percent) are unaware of their infection (CDC, 2015f). In 2010, youth (aged 13 to 24) comprised 17 percent of the population in the United States but accounted for an estimated 26 percent (12,200) of all new HIV infections (CDC, 2015f). This figure may be misleading, however, due to the long incubation period associated with the HIV virus. Many people with AIDS who are now in their twenties undoubtedly were infected while still in their teens.

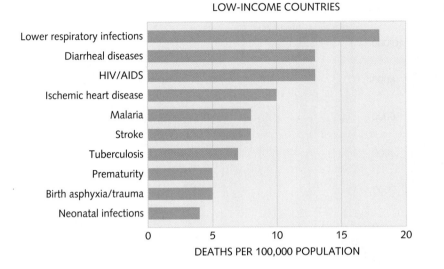

LOW-INCOME COUNTRIES

DEATHS PER 100,000 POPULATION

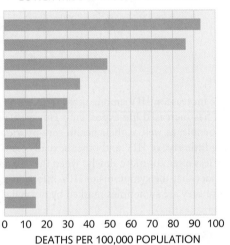

LOWER-MIDDLE-INCOME COUNTRIES

DEATHS PER 100,000 POPULATION

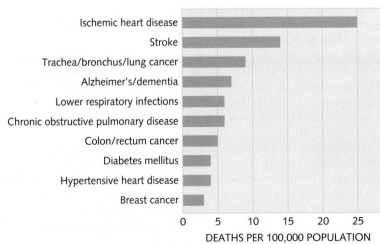

HIGH-INCOME COUNTRIES

DEATHS PER 100,000 POPULATION

FIGURE 12.3

The 10 Leading Causes of Death by Country Income Group Chronic diseases cause increasing numbers of deaths worldwide. HIV deaths decreased slightly from 1.7 million (3.2%) deaths in 2000 to 1.5 million (2.7%) deaths in 2012. High-income countries have the highest proportion of deaths caused by noncommunicable diseases, followed by lower-middle-income countries and low-income countries.

Data from World Health Organization (WHO). (2014, May). The top 10 causes of death, 2012. Fact sheet no. 310, http://www.who.int/mediacentre/factsheets/fs310/en/.

FIGURE 12.4
New HIV Infections in the United States by Risk Group
The estimated incidence of HIV has remained stable in recent years, at about 50,000 new cases each year. Some groups are affected more than others, especially men who have sex with men (MSM), injection drug users (IDUs), and, among races/ethnicities, African-Americans.

Data from Centers for Disease Control and Prevention (CDC). (2013d). *HIV Surveillance Report, 2011, vol. 23.* http://www.cdc.gov/hiv/library/reports/surveillance/index.html.

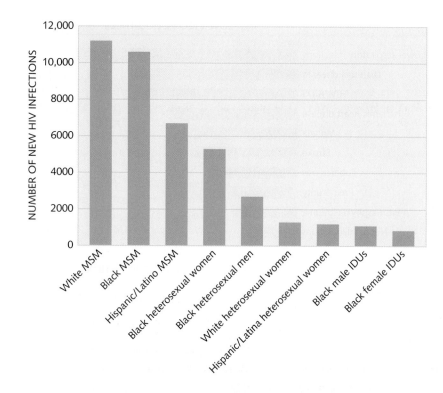

AIDS in Africa Six weeks after she gave birth, 29-year-old Mathato Notsi discovered that both she and her baby were HIV positive. Pediatric doses of antiretroviral drugs are available to only one in four children living in Lesotho, South Africa. Luckily, Mathato's daughter is one of those children receiving this lifesaving treatment.

Gideon Mendel/Getty Images

The increase in HIV among those over age 50 is partly due to advanced HIV therapy, which has increased life expectancy. However, research suggests that it is also because older people, as well as their health care providers, incorrectly perceive older adults as having little risk of HIV and other sexually transmitted infections and therefore recognize it less often (or more slowly) when they do get such diseases. Adding to the problem is the fact that the symptoms of HIV infection are harder to detect among older adults because they are sometimes masked by normal signs of aging.

Gender

Since 1985, the proportion of all AIDS cases in the United States reported among women has more than tripled, with the largest rate of growth occurring among women of color. In 2013, an estimated 9,278 women aged 13 years and older (20 percent) received a diagnosis of HIV infection in the United States (CDC, 2015f). Most of these (84 percent) were from heterosexual contact. African-American women and Latinas are disproportionately affected by HIV compared to women of other races/ethnicities. The rate of new HIV infections among African-American women is 20 times that of white women, and the rate among Hispanic/Latina women is four times that of white women. For more than a decade, AIDS has been the third-leading cause of death among African-American women aged 25 to 44 (CDC, 2013c).

These statistics are sobering, but the situation elsewhere in the world is much worse. Throughout Africa, 12 to 13 women are infected for every 10 men (UNAIDS, 2015). Women in more traditional societies are often less able to protect themselves from HIV because they are typically subordinate to men in intimate relationships (Tigawalana, 2010). Women who use illegal drugs are likely to use a needle only after their male counterparts have used it. They also have less control over whether a condom will be used during sexual intercourse.

More of the virus is found in ejaculate than in vaginal and cervical secretions, so unprotected vaginal sex is much riskier for HIV for women than for men, and unprotected anal sex is even riskier for women than unprotected vaginal sex (CDC, 2013c). After intercourse, the infected lymphocytes in semen may remain in the vagina and cervix for many days, thus giving the virus more time to infect the woman. By contrast, secretions from an HIV-positive (HIV1) vagina and cervix are washed from the penis easily. Male-to-female transmission of HIV through vaginal intercourse is far more common than is female-to-male transmission.

On average, HIV levels in women are about half those of men with similar lymphocyte counts. Women progress to AIDS at a lower overall viral load than men (Farzadegan and others, 1998). These findings suggest the need for gender-based specificity in HIV/AIDS treatment, such as the need for lower HIV level cut-off points for women in determining their drug treatment regimens. Indeed, when women receive treatment when they should, they have the same rate of disease progression as men (Greiger-Zanlungo, 2001).

Demographic Patterns

AIDS has had a devastating effect on minority populations in the United States. For instance, although African-Americans make up around 12 percent of the U.S. population, they account for 44 percent of all new HIV cases. Hispanics/Latinos represent 16 percent of the U.S. population, but they account for about 21 percent of all new cases of HIV infection (CDC, 2015f). The main transmission route for HIV in these groups is high-risk sexual contact (e.g., unprotected sex and sex with multiple partners)—behavior that is made more likely by alcohol and drug use (NIMH Multisite HIV/STD Prevention Trial for African American Couples Group, 2010).

Ethnic and racial differences in rates of HIV transmission are thought to reflect sociocultural differences in drug use. For example, in impoverished minority communities, drug users commonly share needles; of course, when they share with HIV-positive drug users, they almost certainly become infected themselves and expose their sexual partners. Injection drug use (IDU), therefore, is considered a cause of roughly 45 percent of AIDS cases among both African-Americans and Hispanic-Americans, whereas only 17 percent of AIDS cases among whites are linked to shared needles.

The initial spread of the HIV virus among injection drug users and gay men in the United States and other Western countries is believed to have occurred because these are relatively small, closed populations in which an individual is more likely to be exposed to the virus repeatedly. Although rates due to IDU and heterosexual contact are increasing, male-to-male (MTM) sexual contact remains the largest exposure category among AIDS sufferers in the United States. In 2013, gay and bisexual men accounted for 81 percent of HIV diagnoses among males and 65 percent of all new infections (CDC, 2015e). The same year, women made up 19 percent of new HIV diagnoses. Of these, 87 percent were attributable to heterosexual sex and 13 percent due to IDU (CDC, 2016c).

How HIV Is Transmitted

Present in high concentration in the blood and semen of HIV-positive individuals, HIV can enter the body through any tear in the skin or mucous membranes, including those not visible to the human eye. More specifically, HIV can be spread through:

- unprotected sex—primarily vaginal and anal intercourse;
- blood, including by transfusion, accidental needle sticks, or needle sharing;
- mother-to-child transmission—during birth or through breast feeding; and
- transplantation of infected tissue.

hemophilia A genetic disease in which the blood fails to clot quickly enough, causing uncontrollable bleeding from even the smallest cut.

HIV/AIDS is **not** *transmitted by:*

■ *donating blood;*

■ *exposure to airborne particles, contaminated food, or insect bites;*

■ *shaking hands, drinking from the same cup, closed-mouth kissing, hugging, sharing drinking fountains, public telephones, or toilets; or*

■ *sharing a work or home environment.*

genital human papillomavirus (HPV) The most common sexually transmitted infection.

Fortunately, HIV is transmitted less easily than most other less deadly viruses (such as malaria). Without a supportive environment of blood, semen, or the cytoplasm of a host cell, the virus quickly dies, usually within 30 minutes.

A less common route of infection involves a transfusion of infected blood. In the early years of the AIDS epidemic, HIV spread rapidly through transfusions of infected blood to victims of **hemophilia.** Since 1985, however, blood banks have been screening all donor blood for HIV antibodies, and the risk of contracting HIV through transfusion has all but disappeared.

Of the 2.6 million children worldwide living with HIV, most were infected by their HIV-positive mothers during pregnancy, childbirth, or breast feeding. Fortunately, progress is being made in this area. In 2014, 73 percent of the estimated 1.5 million pregnant women living with HIV globally were receiving antiviral therapy to avoid transmission of HIV to their children (UNAIDS, 2015). As a result of such efforts, new HIV infections among children dropped 58 percent between 2000 and 2014.

Sexually Transmitted Infections (STIs) and HIV

People who are infected with other sexually transmitted infections (also called *sexually transmitted diseases*) are up to five times more likely than uninfected people to acquire HIV infection if they are exposed to the virus (CDC Fact Sheet, 2013). HIV-infected individuals also are more likely to transmit HIV to their sexual partners if they are also infected with another STI.

Genital human papillomavirus (HPV) is passed on through genital contact, most often during vaginal and anal sex. HPV also may be passed on through oral sex, even when the infected person has no signs or symptoms. Although the highest prevalence rates for HPV infection have been found among women ages 20 to 24, anyone who is having (or has ever had) sex can get HPV. HPV is so common that nearly all sexually active women and men get it at some point in their lives (CDC, 2013b). Most people with HPV never develop symptoms or health problems and do not even know they have it. HPV can cause serious health problems, however, including genital warts and certain cancers. Most HPV infections are cleared by a person's immune system, making it biologically plausible that the local immune response triggered by HPV infection may put women at increased risk for HIV (Smith-McCune and others, 2010).

STIs increase susceptibility to HIV infection in two other ways (Table 12.3). Genital ulcers such as syphilis, herpes, and chancroid cause lesions or breaks in the lining of the genital tract, which create entry points for HIV and other viruses to attack. In addition, inflammation resulting from genital ulcers or nonulcerative STIs such as chlamydia, gonorrhea, and trichomoniasis increases the concentration of CD4+ and other cells in genital secretions that can serve as targets for HIV.

Fortunately, preventive vaccines exist for many STIs. In 2006, the U.S. Food and Drug Administration (FDA) approved the first vaccine developed to prevent genital warts and cervical cancer caused by several types of HPV. Although HPV vaccines are safe, effective, and recommended for 11- or 12-year-old boys and girls before their first sexual encounter, their use is uneven and controversial. Ten years of vaccinating have cut HPV infections by 64 percent among teenage girls in the United States. Still, only 42 percent of girls and 22 percent of boys between 13 and 17 years of age have received the recommended three doses of the vaccine (Markowitz and others, 2016). Among the barriers to HPV vaccination are beliefs about sexuality; the cost, perceived effectiveness, possible negative health consequences and safety of the vaccine; and lack of information about the timing of vaccination relative to sexual activity (Gerend, Shepherd, & Shepherd, 2013). This may explain why HPV vaccination rates among adolescents and young adults remain lower than rates of vaccination for meningitis (60 percent), tetanus (87.6 percent), and other viruses (MMWR, 2015). In addition, racial disparities exist, including a recent finding that Hispanic-Americans and African-Americans are less likely to be vaccinated than European-Americans (Gelman and others, 2013).

Conversely, several factors have been shown to promote HPV vaccination, including a doctor's recommendation and subjective norms regarding vaccination (Krawczyk and others, 2012). In addition, females who have more positive attitudes toward the vaccine and perceive greater benefits (e.g., prevention of HPV infection and/or cervical cancer) and fewer barriers (e.g., cost, side effects) are more likely to receive the vaccine (Juraskova, Bari, O'Brien, & McCaffery, 2011). Taken together, this body of research suggests that social influence, especially the advice of trusted doctors, friends, and family, are of particular importance in motivating young women to get vaccinated.

TABLE 12.3

About Some STIs

Chlamydia	Symptoms	Complications
Caused by a bacterium that is known to create infections in the throat, genitals, and anus. Spread through contact with infected semen and vaginal fluids during unprotected vaginal sex, anal sex, and oral sex. Treated with antibiotics, although some strains are resistant.	Women usually do not show symptoms. Some may experience pain during sex or urination. Men usually do show symptoms, including a discharge or itchy feeling in the penis, painful urination, or an infection of the throat or anus.	Women: If untreated, the disease may cause infertility, infected cervix, pelvic pain, pelvic inflammatory disease, ectopic pregnancy, or arthritis. Infants can get pneumonia or become blind. Men: If untreated, the disease may cause infertility, arthritis, eye infections, or urinary infections.
Gonorrhea	**Symptoms**	**Complications**
Caused by a bacterium that commonly infects the genitals, anus, and throat. Spread by infected semen and vaginal fluids during unprotected vaginal sex, anal sex, and oral sex. Treated with antibiotics.	Most women show *no* symptoms or some vaginal discharge, or pain on urination. Men usually notice thick yellow-green discharge from the penis, pain on urination, or pain in the penis. If infected in the rectum, men and women have pain, bleeding, and discharge. Sore throats if the throat is infected.	Women: If untreated, the disease may cause sterility or pelvic inflammatory disease. Men: If untreated, the disease may cause sterility, swollen testes, or urinary infections. Women and men: If untreated, may lead to brain, heart, or liver infections, or arthritis.
Trichomoniasis	**Symptoms**	**Complications**
Caused by the parasite *Trichomonas vaginalis*. The vagina is the most common site in women and the urethra in men. Spread through unprotected vaginal sex. Treated with antibiotics.	Abdominal pain; unusual vaginal discharge; vulval or vaginal redness; irritation, itching, or burning inside the penis; and pain during urination or intercourse.	Premature delivery or increased HIV susceptibility.
Genital Herpes	**Symptoms**	**Complications**
Caused by the herpes simplex virus with accompanying blisters on the genitals, in the anal area, and sometimes the mouth. Spread through unprotected vaginal sex, anal sex, oral sex, and direct skin-to-skin touch. Treated with antibiotics. No complete cure.	Fatigue, fever, painful blisters that redden the skin, itch, ulcerate, and may cause scarring.	The virus hides in nerve endings and recurs.

Symptoms and Stages: From HIV to AIDS

HIV infects mostly lymph tissues, where *lymphocytes* develop and are stored. Recall from Chapter 3 that lymphocytes are immune cells that help prevent cancer and other chronic illnesses by controlling cell growth. They also guard against infection by producing antibodies. HIV invades and destroys a type of lymphocyte called the T cell, which is a crucial player in the immune response because it recognizes harmful microbes and triggers the production of antibodies. It also coordinates the release of natural killer (NK) cells.

How HIV Progresses

retrovirus A virus that copies its genetic information onto the DNA of a host cell.

HIV is classified as a **retrovirus** because it works by injecting a copy of its own genetic material, or genome, into the DNA of the T cell (the host cell). Like all viruses, HIV can replicate only inside cells, taking over their machinery to reproduce. However, only HIV and other retroviruses incorporate their own genetic instructions into the host cell's genes.

The infected DNA may remain dormant in the chromosome of the host lymphocyte for a period of time. Eventually, however, the infected lymphocyte is certain to become activated against another virus or some other foreign substance. At that point, it divides, replicating HIV along with itself. As infected cells continue to divide, vast numbers of HIV particles emerge from the infected host and invade other lymphocytes.

Healthy human blood normally contains approximately 1000 T cells per cubic milliliter. Despite the fact that HIV is reproducing in an infected person's body, this level may remain unchanged for years following HIV infection. Then, for reasons that biomedical researchers are still struggling to understand, T cell levels begin to decline, and the immune system grows steadily weaker. Eventually, the victim is left with few functional immune cells and is unable to mount an effective defense against cells harboring HIV, HIV itself, and other invading microorganisms.

The AIDS Virus HIV is classified as a retrovirus because it destroys lymphocytes by injecting a copy of its own genetic material into the host cell's DNA.

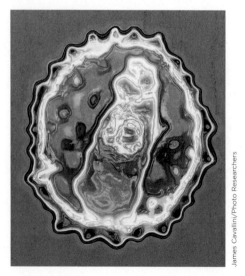

James Cavallini/Photo Researchers

The Four Stages of HIV

HIV progresses through four stages of infection, which vary in length from person to person (see Figure 12.5). During the first stage, which lasts from one to eight weeks, the immune system destroys most HIV, so people experience only mild symptoms that are similar to those of many other illnesses, such as swollen lymph glands, sore throat, fever, chronic diarrhea, skeletal pain, gynecological infection in women, neurological problems, and, in some cases, a skin rash. These symptoms are often so mild that they go unnoticed or unremembered.

The second stage, which may last for months or years, appears to be a period of latency. The person has no obvious symptoms except perhaps for swollen lymph nodes, which may go unnoticed; nevertheless, the HIV infection is far from inactive. In fact, during stage 2, as T cell concentration falls, HIV is constantly replicating. Within five years, 30 percent of infected people move to stage 3, when T cells are further reduced, immune function is impaired, and opportunistic infections occur. Among the most common are Kaposi's sarcoma (a cancer of blood vessels that causes purplish spots in the skin, mouth, and lungs); lymphoma; parasitic gastrointestinal infections; and *pneumocystis carinii pneumonia* (PCP), a bacterial disease that caused

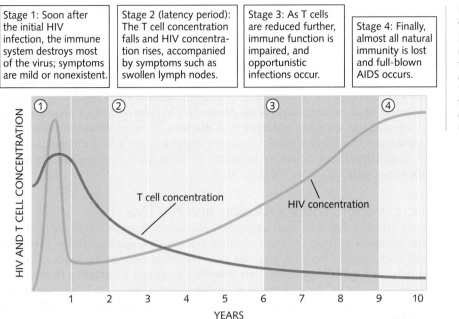

Stage 1: Soon after the initial HIV infection, the immune system destroys most of the virus; symptoms are mild or nonexistent.

Stage 2 (latency period): The T cell concentration falls and HIV concentration rises, accompanied by symptoms such as swollen lymph nodes.

Stage 3: As T cells are reduced further, immune function is impaired, and opportunistic infections occur.

Stage 4: Finally, almost all natural immunity is lost and full-blown AIDS occurs.

FIGURE 12.5

The Course of HIV/AIDS HIV infection may be carried for many years in the unsuspecting victim before symptoms appear. Unfortunately, this long "dormant" period often means that carriers who are unaware of their infection spread HIV unwittingly.

60 percent of all AIDS deaths prior to the development of the effective treatments available today. In populations that do not have access to these treatments, PCP continues to be a major cause of death from AIDS (McLay, 2011).

During stage 4, the number of T cells drops from a healthy count of 1000 to 200 or less per cubic milliliter of blood, and almost all natural immunity is lost. At this point, HIV has developed into AIDS. As T cell levels drop below 100, the balance of power in the immune system shifts to favor the invading virus. HIV levels soar, and microorganisms that the immune system normally would destroy easily begin to proliferate. Without treatment, death generally occurs within a year or two.

Physiological Factors in the Progression of AIDS

The period from diagnosis of full-blown AIDS until death is notoriously unpredictable—as short as several months or as long as five years. Although the average time from HIV infection to AIDS is about 10 years, people with HIV who start treatment with anti-AIDS drugs have life expectancies around 80 percent of that of the general population, provided they start treatment before their CD4 count drops below 200 cells per microliter (Johnson, 2013). Several factors are thought to play a role in the prognosis of AIDS.

One factor is the strength of the initial immune response. HIV progresses much more slowly among patients whose immune systems mount strong lymphocyte activity in the acute stage of HIV sickness (stage 2). This strong defense apparently helps preserve the body's later ability to produce the T cells that target HIV.

Genetic vulnerability also may affect the rate at which AIDS develops. Viruses require collaboration from the body, which in the case of AIDS is the existence of the protein receptor to which HIV particles bind. AIDS researchers suspect that some people have genes that protect against the development of this receptor. Indeed, it appears that 1 percent of people of Northern European descent inherit a gene from both parents that blocks this development, giving them apparent immunity to HIV infection. Another

20 percent inherit the protective gene from only one parent and, while not immune to HIV, display a much slower progression of symptoms (Ring, 2012).

Psychosocial Factors in the Progression of AIDS

After HIV exposure, the pace at which clinical symptoms of AIDS begin to appear and the severity of illness at all stages of the disease vary tremendously. Poor nutrition, drug use, repeated HIV exposure, and other viral infections all can accelerate the progression of the disease. As with other diseases, however, epidemiologists have discovered that even after these physical risk factors are accounted for, there is still a tremendous amount of unexplained variability in the course of AIDS.

Discrimination, Social Exclusion, and HIV Risk

Researchers have begun to focus on psychosocial factors that may contribute to ethnic/racial disparities in HIV risk (Stock, Gibbons, Peterson, & Gerard, 2013b). In particular, racial discrimination has been suggested as an important contributing factor in health-risk behaviors and HIV infection. Data from the Family and Community Health Study (FACHS) have shown that experiences of discrimination at ages 10 to 11 were associated with greater sexual risk-taking at ages 18 to 19, even after controlling for neighborhood risk, SES, gender, age, the absence of a father, and other variables. These data also demonstrate that discrimination is often associated with heightened perceived norms for deviant behavior among peers, which in turn predict higher levels of substance use and risky sex behaviors (Roberts and others, 2012).

Research indicates that there is a profound need for preventive interventions that target substance use and risky sex behaviors in reducing HIV risk, particularly among young black adults, for whom the incidence of HIV/AIDS is 14 times higher than it is for other racial groups in the United States (CDC, 2013d). Interventions that focus on the effects of substance use on sexual risk taking in response to discrimination and other stressors seem especially warranted. In addition, parenting that involves communication, warmth, and discipline (Gibbons and others, 2010), as well as racial identity and socialization (Stock and others, 2013b), may buffer the adverse effects of discrimination on HIV risk taking.

Stress and Negative Emotions

Stress, negative emotions, and social isolation may influence the pace at which AIDS progresses, perhaps by altering hormonal and immune environments that affect the resistance of host cells to the invading virus. One recent study of 117 HIV-positive African-American men found that participants' history of psychosocial trauma predicted levels of stress-related biomarkers in their urine, including cortisol, epinephrine, norepinephrine, and dopamine (Glover, Williams, & Kisler, 2013).

Several researchers have reported that low self-esteem, a pessimistic outlook, chronic depression, and other negative emotions may influence the production of pro-inflammatory cytokines (Pala and others, 2012). They also are linked with a decline in T cells and a more rapid course of illness and the development of opportunistic infections among HIV-infected individuals (Cole, 2008). Patients without depression have significantly healthier immune systems and higher quality of life than depressed patients (Schroecksnadel and others, 2008). Interventions that reduce depression are also valuable in the fight against AIDS because depression increases the severity of many immune-related disorders (Safen, Reisner, Herrick, Mimiaga, & Stall, 2010).

Stress and Social Support

Social support, particularly from peers, is also a critical factor in the progression of HIV sickness and AIDS (Galvan and others, 2008). In one study, patients who tested positive for HIV were followed for five years. Those who reported greater isolation and less emotional support at the start of the study showed a significantly greater decline in T cells over the course of the study than those who reported feeling more socially connected (Theorell and others, 1995). More recently, researchers working with the Veterans Aging Cohort Study reported that social isolation was associated with greater risk of hospitalization and death in HIV-positive veterans (Greysen and others, 2013).

Lack of social support may cause AIDS to develop more quickly, partly because it leaves those who are HIV positive less able to cope effectively with stressful life events (Deichert, Fekete, Boarts, Druley, & Delahanty, 2008). In one prospective study, Jane Leserman and her colleagues (2000) studied 82 HIV-infected gay men every six months. The participants reported the number of stressful events in their lives, their styles of coping, and their satisfaction with the social support available to them. The researchers also measured blood levels of T cells, as well as serum levels of cortisol and other stress hormones.

Although none of the HIV-positive men had any AIDS symptoms at the start of the study, one-third of them have exhibited some symptoms to date. For every increase in the number of stressful life events—equivalent to one severely stressful event or two moderately stressful events—the risk of developing AIDS symptoms doubled. The risk of AIDS has also doubled for every significant *decrease* in the average score on the satisfaction with social support scale, every *increase* in the use of denial as a coping strategy, and every 5 mg/dl increase in the level of serum cortisol.

Given the health benefits of having a strong social network, it is particularly tragic that AIDS is often a stigmatizing condition and that many of its victims also lose friends and companions. A recent study chronicled the isolation, abandonment, betrayal, and discrimination in the interpersonal and social systems of 11 young African-American HIV-infected women. These experiences were identified as key factors in the participants' ability to fully engage in self-care activities (Peltzer, Domian, & Teel, 2016).

Understanding how psychosocial factors affect the course of AIDS may improve a person's chances of surviving HIV infection. The results of these studies also will help us gain a perspective on the interaction of biological, psychological, and social factors in health and disease and thus to refine our understanding of the connections between mind and body.

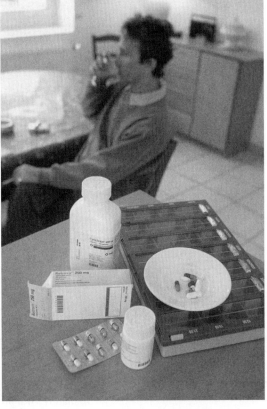

Veronique Burger/Science Source

AIDS Intervention Over the last few years, AIDS patients have been required to take a variety of pills each day on a very strict timetable. However, with research advances, more streamlined pharmacological regimens have been used and have proven equally effective.

In the era of antiretroviral therapy (ART), some groups of people with HIV—especially those who are treated before their CD4 count falls below 350 cells/mm—now have life expectancies equal to or even higher than the U.S. general population (Miller & Hodder, 2014).

Medical Treatments and Psychosocial Interventions

Until the late 1990s, HIV infection was almost always a progressive, fatal disease. Medical interventions focused almost exclusively on treating the opportunistic diseases that resulted from immune failure, not on eliminating (or even controlling) the HIV virus. Today, however, scientists have a much better understanding of how the virus behaves, and treatment advances have transformed AIDS into a manageable chronic condition in which people such as Greg Louganis are living with HIV for longer periods of time.

The Success of Antiretroviral Therapy

Given the capacity of HIV to become integrated into a host cell's DNA, prospects are bleak for a true cure that would detect and destroy every HIV-infected cell in the body. As an alternative, some researchers are looking for a vaccine to minimize and control the impact of HIV on the body. One of the major stumbling blocks is the enormous variability of HIV. In an infected person with replicating HIV, it is estimated that more than 10 billion new viruses are made every day, with new strains constantly appearing. Still, researchers are hopeful of developing a treatment that will block one of the many steps in the HIV life cycle completely. If this is accomplished, the virus may be stopped dead in its tracks.

Today's optimum treatment regimen is *antiretroviral therapy,* or ART, for short. ART involves a combination of antiretroviral drugs that attack different parts of HIV or stop the virus from entering cells. Although the treatment does not get rid of HIV, it slows the pace at which the virus reproduces (WHO, 2015e).

One of the most commonly used drugs in the ART regimen is *zidovudine* (azidothymidine, or AZT), one of a class of drugs called *reverse transcriptase inhibitors,* which block HIV replication by inhibiting production of the enzyme that HIV needs to reproduce itself. AZT reduces AIDS symptoms, increases T cell levels, and may prolong the patient's life. Because AZT's effectiveness wears off as the virus becomes resistant to it, AZT is often combined with anti-HIV drugs called *protease inhibitors,* which block the production of mature viral proteins. This combination of drugs has reduced HIV to undetectable levels in some patients.

ART used to be complicated, requiring patients to take a series of pills at varying times of the day, but a newer, once-a-day regimen has greatly simplified treatment. At a cost of up to $15,000 a year, many AIDS patients simply couldn't afford it. Even in affluent, developed countries, many people lack the income or health insurance coverage necessary to handle such costs. However, as competition among generic manufacturers increases, the cost of treatment continues to fall, which has been especially significant in low-income countries. As of 2015, treatment is now only $100 per patient per year in Equatorial Guinea, Mali, Haiti, and other countries supported by the United Nations Development Programme. These price reductions made it possible to provide ART to 15.8 million people, up from a mere 700,000 people in 2000 (UNDP, 2015).

An Overview of Psychosocial Interventions

Health psychologists play a number of roles in battling AIDS, including both primary and secondary prevention interventions. Primary prevention includes counseling people about being tested for infection and helping individuals modify high-risk behaviors. Secondary prevention includes helping patients cope with treatment regimen, as well as emotional and cognitive disturbances related to infection.

Since the beginning of the AIDS epidemic, many different psychosocial interventions have been implemented. The earliest programs targeted high-risk groups such as gay men or injection drug users, using behavior modification and educational interventions to try to change attitudes and behaviors. Programs at the high school and college level have typically focused on increasing knowledge of AIDS and promoting safe sex. Mass media campaigns have emphasized awareness of how AIDS is transmitted—and they have been quite successful. Despite a slow beginning, AIDS education and other intervention programs skyrocketed during the 1990s, thanks initially to the efforts of the gay community in the United States. As a result, public awareness of AIDS increased, and a corresponding reduction in risk-related behaviors occurred, accompanied by a sharp decline in the number of new cases of HIV infection.

HIV among Older Adults

With more effective HIV treatments and decreasing mortality rates, HIV is increasingly affecting older adults (see Figure 12.6). In 2013, people aged 50 and older accounted for 21 percent (8,395) of the estimated 47,352 HIV diagnoses in the United States (CDC, 2016b). Older adults are more likely than younger people to be diagnosed late in the course of HIV infection, which means they start treatment later and possibly have a poorer prognosis. Aging with HIV also presents special challenges because older people may have an increased risk of cardiovascular disease, certain cancers, and other chronic conditions. Despite numerous studies documenting psychosocial and behavioral differences between older and younger HIV-infected adults, to date there have been few evidence-based behavioral interventions targeting this population (Illa, Echenique, Bustamante-Avellanda, & Sanchez-Martinez, 2014).

In a large sample of persons over 50 with HIV, 39 percent displayed symptoms of major depression, loneliness, and HIV stigma (Grov, Golub, Parsons, Brennan, & Karpiak, 2010). Compared to younger HIV-infected adults, older adults also report greater unhappiness, negative life events, perceived stress, and negative attitudes about aging (Rueda, Law, & Rourke, 2014). Research studies also suggest that lesbian, gay, and bisexual (LGB) adults aged 50 and older may experience higher rates of mental distress than heterosexual older adults (Wallace, Cochran, Durazo, & Ford, 2011). The high rates of depression are of particular importance because of associations between depression and other health-related behaviors, including unprotected sex and nonadherence to HIV medications.

Let's take a look at the theories on which the intervention programs are based and then at some of the interventions that are effective in reducing HIV/AIDS risk-related behavior.

FIGURE 12.6

Estimated Diagnoses of HIV Infection by Age In 2013, people 50 and over accounted for 21 percent of HIV/AIDS diagnoses in the United States.

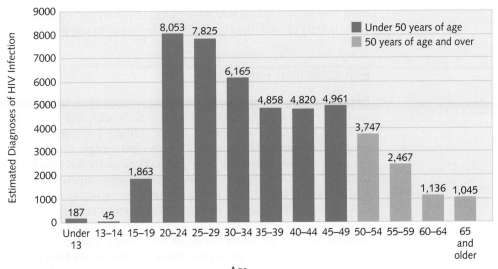

The Basis for Psychosocial Interventions

Many of the theoretical models described in Chapter 6 have been used to predict whether and when people will change a risky health-related behavior, so those models often form the basis for HIV/AIDS intervention programs (Naar-King and others, 2008).

Social-cognitive theory, which focuses on the interaction of environmental events, our internal processes, and our behaviors, has served as the framework for a number of interventions (Kelly & Kalichman, 2002). Three factors addressed by this model appear to be particularly important in successful intervention programs: (1) *perceived social norms* regarding peer acceptance of HIV risk-reducing behaviors; (2) *self-efficacy beliefs* controlling one's own thoughts, emotions, and behaviors in order to avoid unsafe behaviors; and (3) *social skills,* the ability to respond assertively in negotiating risky behaviors. The relevance of the social-cognitive model was demonstrated by Seth Kalichman (2008), who found that gay men who practice high-risk behaviors also score lower on measures of perceived safer-sex norms, safer-sex self-efficacy, and social skills.

The health belief model, which is based on the idea that beliefs predict behavior, has achieved modest success with a variety of high-risk groups in predicting condom use, the number of sexual partners, and knowledge of partners' past sexual history. The theory of planned behavior, which links beliefs and behavior, has achieved greater success, probably due to the influence of social norms on the sexual activity of many at-risk populations, including teenagers (Davis and others, 2016). Researchers have consistently found that people with more favorable attitudes toward condoms, as well as those who believe their friends are supportive of condom use, are more likely to engage in protected sex. The researchers have also found that individuals in high-risk groups, such as young men who have sex with men, often have overly optimistic beliefs about their risk, which does little to deter their risk behaviors (MacKellar and others, 2007). These dangerous beliefs, perhaps fomented by the success of antiretroviral therapy, may create a form of *AIDS optimism:* HIV-negative men who have sex with men are less concerned about contracting HIV, HIV-positive men who have sex with men are less concerned about transmitting it, and both groups are more likely to engage in unsafe sex, resulting in more HIV infection (Pham, 2007).

Support for stage models comes from evidence that certain individuals may profit more than others from a specific intervention. For example, younger, less knowledgeable individuals tend to benefit from educational interventions that close gaps in knowledge about how AIDS is transmitted, while older individuals in certain high-risk groups may be more likely to profit from interventions that stir them into preventive action.

Educational Programs

Educational programs and media campaigns are most likely to be effective when messages are adapted to the target group's sex, nationality, and acculturation (Latkin & Knowlton, 2005). A meta-analysis of over 100,000 participants in HIV-prevention interventions found that groups with higher percentages of Latinos benefited most from interventions delivered by lay community members that included threat-inducing messages, while in samples with low percentages of Latinos, health messages delivered by experts that did not include threat-inducing arguments were more effective (J. Albarracin, Albarracin, & Durantini, 2008). A similar meta-analysis with heterosexual African-Americans found that successful interventions included *cultural tailoring* aimed at modifying social norms regarding safe-sex behavior (Darbes, Crepaz, Lyles, Kennedy, & Rutherford, 2008). Special, targeted interventions were also found to be more effective in cultures where social customs or religious beliefs support male dominance and that tend to have high rates of male-to-female HIV transmission (UNAIDS, 2007).

There are a number of simple precautions that will protect against AIDS and other STIs. Health experts offer the following specific precautions:

- Stay sober. Alcohol and many other drugs lower inhibitions and increase the likelihood of high-risk behaviors.

- Be selective in choosing partners and limit the number of partners in the *sexual network*. Avoid sexual contacts with people who are known to engage in high-risk sexual or drug-use behaviors.

- Use latex condoms during vaginal, anal, and oral sex. These barriers block nearly all sexually transmitted microorganisms, including HIV. Doctor-prescribed and -fitted vaginal diaphragms or cervical caps that block semen and spermicides that paralyze sperm (and lymphocytes) are also advisable.

- Never share hypodermic needles, razors, cuticle scissors, or other implements that may be contaminated with another person's blood or bodily fluids.

- Do not be lulled into a sense of complacency about AIDS and STIs by media reports about treatment breakthroughs. There is still no cure for AIDS.

An important motivational factor in many models of health behavior (see Chapter 6) is *outcome expectancy*, as a person balances the pros and cons of a specific action, such as using a condom. In one study of 410 MSM recruited at different gay venues in Hong Kong, participants completed a costs and benefits of condom use questionnaire that tapped a range of different consequences that could occur if people use condoms with their partners (Table 12.4). The items were rated on a 6-point Likert scale, from (1) *extremely unlikely* to (6) *extremely likely*. The results showed that the perceived benefits of condom use were significantly and most strongly related to condom use intentions, underscoring the importance of emphasizing these issues in STI-prevention campaigns (Teng & Mak, 2011).

All these results suggest that the frequency of unprotected sex can be dramatically reduced with a few steps: Help people to improve their outlook on life, their feelings of self-efficacy, and their sense of personal control, and encourage them to talk more openly about safe sex.

Education Aimed at Prevention In the absence of a vaccine, preventing HIV infection remains our best weapon against AIDS. Throughout the world, educational campaigns are the major means of primary prevention.

TABLE 12.4

Costs and Benefits of Condom Use for MSM

How likely do you think it is that condom use can:
 1. protect both of you against HIV?
 2. show your concern for your partner's well-being?
 3. offend your partner?
 4. provide variety in your sex life?
 5. reduce sexual pleasure?
 6. interrupt foreplay?
 7. reduce the intimacy of sex?
 8. destroy the spontaneity of sex?
 9. reduce trust between you and your partner?

Information from Teng, Y., & Mak, W. W. S. (2011). The role of planning and self-efficacy in condom use among men who have sex with men: An application of the Health Action Process Approach Model. *Health Psychology, 30*(1), 119–128.

Promoting Adherence to Treatment

Another way that health psychologists have become involved in the war on AIDS is by designing interventions to promote adherence to antiretroviral therapy. Poor adherence remains a substantial problem and can lead to significantly decreased life expectancy; it also increases the likelihood of HIV transmission. Poor adherence is particularly problematic among adolescents living in low- and middle-income countries (Hudelson & Cluver, 2015).

One effective intervention is the use of **dynamic tailoring,** which refers to the delivering of individualized health messages over multiple time periods to provide unique feedback based on the individual's status at that moment in time (Johnson, Cummins, & Evers, 2008). In one study, researchers delivered dynamically tailored messages via mobile phones to 52 HIV-positive MSM. For participants who had reported nonadherence to their regimens, as well as those who were just beginning antiretroviral therapy, the reminder messages were delivered one to three times each day (e.g., "Stop, drop, and pop. Take your meds now."). Participants who were adherent received weekly messages that encouraged them to keep taking medications (e.g., "He shoots! He scores! Perfect med adherence. Great job!"). Over the three-month intervention period, participants reported reading and enjoying the text messages, as well as significantly fewer missed days, and researchers found a significant decrease in viral load and increase in CD4 cell counts (Lewis and others, 2013).

dynamic tailoring The delivery of individualized and targeted health messages over multiple periods of time.

Cognitive Behavioral Stress Management (CBSM)

One of the roles of health psychology in helping people cope with HIV and other STIs is helping people live with their infection and illness. Coping with a life-threatening illness is especially challenging for people with the greatest risk for HIV infection, since they are more likely to have a history of trauma and comorbid mental health problems, including anxiety disorders, depression, and substance abuse (Gaynes, Pence, Eron, & Miller, 2008). This is significant because it indicates that they may lack good coping skills (Whetten, Reif, Whetten, & Murphy-McMillan, 2008).

As we have seen, the neuroendocrine consequences of stress may contribute to health problems, including a more rapid course of illness in people with AIDS and an increased likelihood of developing opportunistic infections (Cole, 2008). A growing body of research demonstrates that comprehensive cognitive-behavioral intervention programs focused on increasing positive coping skills are effective in improving the quality of life and emotional and physiological well-being of HIV-positive individuals.

One study evaluated the effectiveness of a 10-week cognitive behavior stress management (CBSM) intervention consisting of both stress-management and relaxation-training components in reducing stress among HIV-positive men (Antoni and others, 2000). The stress-management portion focused on helping the men to identify cognitive distortions in their thinking and to use cognitive restructuring to generate more rational appraisals of everyday stressors. The meetings also taught the men techniques to improve their coping skills, be more assertive, manage their anger, and make greater use of social support. Through group discussions and role-playing exercises, the men also learned to share experiences, disclose their fears, and apply various stress-management concepts. The relaxation portion included progressive muscle relaxation training, meditation, abdominal breathing exercises, and guided imagery.

The results showed that the men who participated in the CBSM intervention reported significantly lower posttreatment levels of anxiety, anger, total mood disturbance, and perceived stress compared to the men who were assigned to an untreated control group

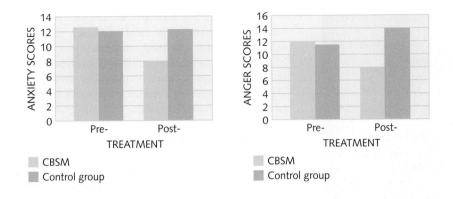

FIGURE 12.7

Pre- and Post-CBSM Treatment Anxiety and Anger in HIV-Positive Men Prior to intervention, the men assigned to CBSM showed mood and anxiety scores similar to those men assigned to the control condition, as measured by scores on the Profile of Mood States. Following the intervention, CBSM participants reported significantly lower posttreatment anxiety and anger than their control group counterparts.

Data from Antoni, M. H., Cruess, D. G., Cruess, S., Lutgendorf, S., Kumar, M., Ironson, G., ... Schneiderman, N. (2000). Cognitive-behavioral stress management intervention effects on anxiety, 24-hour urinary norepinephrine output, and T-cytotoxic/suppressor cells over time among symptomatic HIV-infected gay men. *Journal of Consulting & Clinical Psychology, 68*, 31–45.

(Figure 12.7). Moreover, those in the intervention group also displayed less norepinephrine output and significantly greater numbers of T cells 6 to 12 months later.

Several subsequent CBSM intervention studies have shown similar efficacy. In one, a 10-week group CBSM intervention was associated with reduced life stress and odds of cervical precancer in women with HIV (Antoni and others, 2008). In another study involving racial/ethnic minority women with HIV and HPV, a 10-week CBSM intervention was associated with increased positive affect, positive states of mind, benefit finding, and spiritual well-being (Jensen and others, 2013). In this latter study, women who most increased their confidence in stress management skills showed the largest changes in positive well-being.

CBSM interventions have also been linked with positive physiological changes. One recent clinical trial reported that HIV-positive participants in a 10-week CBSM intervention showed better immune cell functioning and used fewer emotion-focused coping strategies to deal with their distress than control group participants (McCain and others, 2008). A meta-analysis of 35 randomized, controlled trials found that CBSM interventions were successful in reducing anxiety, depression, distress, and fatigue in HIV-positive adults. However, these interventions did not result in improved CD4 cell counts, lower viral load, or other indicators of improved immunity (Scott-Sheldon, Kalichman, Carey, & Fielder, 2008). The shorter (one-week) duration of the post-intervention assessment period in the meta-analysis may have been a factor in the conflicting results. Interestingly, men participating in CBSM also experienced significant increases in testosterone levels.

Because of the biopsychosocial, interactive nature of cognitive, affective, behavioral, and social elements of stress responses, it appears that the most effective way to "package" stress-management interventions for HIV-infected persons may be a multimodal CBSM program (Antoni & Schneiderman, 2001). Those who test positive also may need counseling and other interventions to help them cope with a wide array of issues, including adherence to treatment regimens and adjusting to life with a chronic illness.

Community-Wide Interventions

Intensive, coordinated, community-wide interventions have proved to be the best way to educate people about HIV and to change social norms that influence sexual behavior. The largest AIDS prevention program of this kind to date was implemented in San Francisco in 1982. The *San Francisco Model* involved seven different organizations chosen to reach people at different levels of risk (Coates, Stall, & Hoff, 1990): the mass media, schools, family planning centers, drug abuse clinics, health care organizations, churches, and clubs.

AIDS Awareness In western Africa, a teacher uses storyboards to demonstrate safe sex messages.

Newscom/Eye Ubiquitous/Togo/Lome

Each organization developed an educational program that was appropriate for its clientele. At each site, classes, videos, and models were used to teach safer-sex practices. In addition, mass media motivational messages and social action groups focused on increasing awareness of high-risk behaviors and reducing the social stigma attached to HIV-positive persons.

The program was an immediate success, with reported high-risk behavior among the sample population dropping from 60 percent to 30 percent within five years. The continuing success of the program indicates that HIV/AIDS interventions need to strike on several fronts. Effective interventions are those that

- target high-risk behaviors among at-risk individuals;
- teach specific skills to reduce risk (such as proper condom use and needle cleaning);
- promote interpersonal assertiveness and other communication skills necessary to initiate and maintain lower-risk sexual relationships;
- address social and cultural norms that surround sexual activity;
- focus on improving self-esteem and feelings of self-efficacy regarding how to practice safer sex;
- address faulty, even "magical" thinking regarding HIV transmission and personal vulnerability (see next page); and
- involve coordinated, community-level education.

Psychosocial Barriers to AIDS Intervention

Despite massive efforts to educate the public and discourage high-risk behaviors, condom use remains startlingly low. In the United States, results from the 2013 Youth Risk Behavior Surveillance study indicate that 64 percent of 12th-grade students report having engaged in sexual intercourse, with 23.4 percent having had four or more partners Among students currently sexually active, however, only 59 percent reported that either they or their partner had used a condom during their last sexual intercourse (MMWR, June 13, 2014). Media depictions of sexual encounters, which almost never include the awkward searching for and fumbling with a condom, do little to promote interventions aimed at promoting safe sex. This is particularly damaging for teenagers, who acquire a misleading personal script of how things are supposed to progress and attempt to follow that script during their first intimate experiences. Feeding into this is poor communication between sexual partners. One study of 701 sexually active African-American females ages 14 to 20 found that partner communication was the strongest predictor of condom use (DePadilla, Windle, Wingood, Cooper, & DiClemente, 2011).

A surprisingly common example of faulty reasoning about HIV/AIDS is the belief that the danger of HIV infection depends on the depth of the relationship with the HIV-positive person. This line of thinking causes many people to worry needlessly about casual, nonsexual contact with HIV-positive coworkers and strangers, but to behave recklessly with people they know more intimately. Among college students, for instance, condom use appears to drop off abruptly over the time of a relationship (Pluhar, Frongillo, Stycos, & Dempster-McClain, 2003). Our faulty HIV/AIDS thinking is partly the result of believing that we are somehow less vulnerable to infection than others are. This *optimistic bias* and *perceived invincibility* contribute to our tendency to underestimate the risk that results from high-risk behaviors.

Ironically, a significant impediment to AIDS prevention programs is the success of recent advances in medical treatment, which have brought new hope and optimism for HIV-infected people but at the cost of greater public complacency regarding the dangers of the disease. Those who perceive a reduced threat of HIV/AIDS are more likely to engage in high-risk sexual behaviors, as are people who suppress HIV-related thoughts during intimate encounters (Hoyt, Nemeroff, & Huebner, 2006).

At present, no cure for AIDS exists, and the disease continues to infect people throughout the world. Health psychologists play an important role in battling the HIV pandemic. In the early years, psychologists were key players in designing and implementing primary and secondary prevention efforts to reduce the spread of HIV and to help those who were HIV positive cope with their illness. These efforts included interventions to reduce risky behaviors for AIDS and to help those who were HIV positive adhere to complex treatment regimens. More recently, health psychologists have teamed up with immunologists and other scientists to study how psychosocial factors, such as beliefs about AIDS, perceived social support, coping style, and possible symptoms of anxiety and depression, influence the course of HIV infection and its progression to AIDS. Based on the growing evidence from these investigations, we have seen that psychologists are designing interventions that not only improve the quality of life of HIV-positive persons, but also increase the odds of their long-term survival.

Weigh In on Health

Respond to each question below based on what you learned in the chapter. (**Tip:** Use the items in "Summing Up" to take into account related biological, psychological, and social concerns.)

1. You've been asked to prepare a short talk on the global burden of disease. What are the most important communicable diseases in terms of deaths around the world? What are some of the concerns about drug resistance for these diseases?

2. Among a group of friends, the topic of HIV/AIDS comes up. Anthony says that there's not much to worry about anymore because AIDS is not as prevalent as it used to be and treatments are available. What would you say to him about why it's important for everyone at every life stage to remain vigilant against this disease?

3. Imagine that you and your friends who had the conversation about HIV/AIDS decided that students at your college should be more aware of this disease, plus other STIs. What aspects of intervention and coping with HIV/AIDS or STIs (biological, psychological, and social or cultural) do you think all college students should know about?

Summing Up

Communicable and Noncommunicable Diseases

1. A communicable disease is a disease that is transmitted from a human to another human, from a human to an animal, or from an animal to a human. A communicable disease can be transmitted directly, such as through respiratory means, or indirectly through a *vector,* such as a mosquito in the case of malaria or the Zika virus.

2. The epidemiological transition occurs as the death rate in a country declines and a higher proportion of children survive into adulthood. Over time, the infectious diseases of childhood are gradually replaced by chronic, degenerative noncommunicable diseases.

3. About 30 percent of all deaths in low- and middle-income countries are from communicable diseases. In high-income countries, the three leading causes of death (stroke, ischemic heart disease, and lung cancer) are noncommunicable diseases.

4. All types of microbes have the ability to develop resistance to drugs that are used to kill them. The use of antibiotics is the single most important factor in the development of antimicrobial resistance. Another factor is the spread of resistant strains of bacteria from person to person in crowded settings such as hospitals, nursing homes, schools, and prisons.

5. TB is a bacterial disease that spreads through aerosolized droplets that people breathe in from others who are already infected with the disease.

The AIDS Epidemic

6. The first human cases of AIDS appeared in 1980, when 55 young men (most of whom were gay or injection drug users) were diagnosed with a rare form of cancer. During the last half of the 1980s, AIDS began to threaten the general population.

7. In the United States, the AIDS epidemic has taken the greatest toll on gay, bisexual, and other men who have sex with men (MSM), particularly young African-Americans. For a variety of biological, economic, and sociocultural reasons, women are more vulnerable than men to HIV infection and tend to contract AIDS at a younger age and lower HIV viral load.

8. In other parts of the world, heterosexual sex is the most common mode of transmission. Ethnic and racial differences in rates of HIV transmission are thought to reflect sociocultural differences in drug use and the acceptance of homosexual and bisexual practices.

9. Genital human papillomavirus (HPV), the most common STI, is passed on through genital contact. Anyone who is having (or has ever had) sex can get HPV. HPV can cause serious health problems, but most people who have it never develop symptoms or even know they have it. Most HPV infections are cleared by the immune system, making it biologically plausible that the local immune response triggered by HPV infection may put women at increased risk for HIV.

Symptoms and Stages: From HIV to AIDS

10. HIV is transmitted primarily through the sharing of virus-infected lymphocytes in bodily fluids—blood, semen, vaginal and cervical secretions, and breast milk.

11. High-risk behaviors that promote HIV infection include having unprotected sex with multiple partners, using injection drugs, and sharing needles. HIV also may be transmitted from an infected mother to her unborn child during pregnancy, as well as from mother to child during breast feeding.

12. The chances of casual transmission of AIDS without sexual contact or injection drug use are very low. The best ways to guard against HIV infection are limiting sexual partners, choosing partners carefully, using latex condoms, and avoiding sexual contact with those who are known to engage in high-risk behaviors.

13. HIV is a retrovirus that causes host cells to reproduce the virus's genetic code. In doing so, HIV destroys T cells, progressively reduces immunocompetence, and leaves its victims vulnerable to a host of opportunistic infections.

14. HIV sickness progresses through four stages, which vary in length from person to person. The average time from HIV infection to AIDS is about 10 years, although 5 percent of HIV-positive people live more than 15 years. HIV progresses much more slowly among patients whose immune systems mount strong lymphocyte activity in the acute stage of HIV sickness.

15. Stress, negative emotions, and social isolation may influence the pace at which the disease progresses, perhaps by altering hormonal and immune environments that affect the resistance of host cells to the invading virus. Interventions that reduce depression are valuable in the fight against AIDS because depression increases the severity of many immune-related disorders.

16. Racial discrimination may be a contributing factor to health-risk behaviors and HIV infection. Discrimination often is associated with heightened perceived norms for certain behaviors, which in turn predict reduced feelings of belonging and higher levels of substance use and risky sex behaviors. Findings such as these highlight the potential of preventive interventions that target substance abuse and risky sex behaviors in reducing HIV risk, particularly among young African-American adults.

Medical Treatments and Psychosocial Interventions

17. Until the late 1990s, HIV infection was almost always a progressive, fatal disease. Today, however, antiretroviral therapy (ART) drugs have transformed AIDS into a manageable chronic condition. These drugs include reverse transcriptase inhibitors such as AZT, protease inhibitors, and "cocktail" combinations of these drugs. Researchers continue to work toward developing a vaccine that will minimize the impact of HIV on the body.

18. Health psychologists play a number of roles in the battle against AIDS, including counseling people about being tested for HIV, helping individuals modify high-risk behaviors and helping AIDS patients cope with emotional and cognitive disturbances.

19. Although AIDS prevention programs have had some success, many barriers to prevention remain. Misinformation, feelings of personal invulnerability, cultural norms, and personal resources are all factors in the success (or failure) of AIDS prevention measures.

20. A particularly effective way to package stress-management interventions for HIV-positive patients seems to be a multimodal, cognitive behavioral stress management (CBSM) approach.

Key Terms and Concepts to Remember

sexually transmitted infections (STIs), p. 348
noncommunicable disease, p. 348
communicable disease, p. 349
epidemiological transition, p. 349
antimicrobial resistance, p. 351

acquired immunodeficiency syndrome (AIDS), p. 353
human immunodeficiency virus (HIV), p. 353
Kaposi's sarcoma, p. 353
pandemic, p. 354

hemophilia, p. 358
genital human papillomavirus (HPV), p. 358
retrovirus, p. 360
dynamic tailoring, p. 368

LaunchPad
macmillan learning

To accompany your textbook, you have access to a number of online resources, including quizzes for every chapter of the book, flashcards, critical thinking exercises, videos, and *Check Your Health* inventories. To access these resources, please visit the Straub *Health Psychology* LaunchPad solo at: **launchpadworks.com**

PART 5 | Seeking Treatment

CHAPTER 13

The Role of Health Psychology in Seeking and Obtaining Health Care

ven though the event happened over 30 years ago, it is as vivid in my mind today as it was on that unusually warm afternoon in April when one of my fraternity brothers was nearly blinded. A bunch of us were watching the Detroit Tigers battle the St. Louis Cardinals in a spring training baseball exhibition game. "Anybody want to play handball?" asked Bruce, bounding through the lobby. I declined, as did everyone but Chris. "I'll play," he said, "but only for about half an hour. I've got a chemistry final tomorrow."

The rest of us turned our attention back to the game and thought nothing more about handball until about 45 minutes later, when a worried-looking Chris came through the door with a woozy Bruce leaning heavily on him for support. It was easy to see that Bruce had been hurt—his left eye was discolored and growing puffy.

"Bruce took a handball right in the eye," Chris explained. "I wanted to take him right over to the health center, but he refused."

"It's nothing," Bruce said shakily. "I'll probably have a black eye tomorrow, but I'll be fine. Just get me some ice and a couple of aspirin."

As Bruce stretched out on a couch, somebody ran for the ice and aspirin. The rest of us looked at one another doubtfully. As the minutes passed, Bruce's eye was looking angry and red, and the swelling was starting to force his eyelid closed. He was clearly in pain, wincing with every word he spoke. Vision was not something to mess around with, even if you were trying to keep up a stoic front for a bunch of college buddies and especially if, like Bruce, you were hoping one day to become an airline pilot.

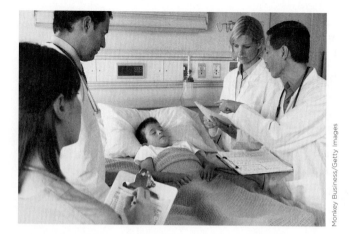

For all of these reasons, I knew what we had to do. In less than five minutes, Glenn, Jack, and I had phoned Campus Safety, the Health Center, and Bruce's parents. Following their instructions, we drove Bruce to the emergency room at County Medical Hospital, paced by a police cruiser with siren blaring and lights flashing. Half an hour after being hit by the handball, Bruce was rushed into the operating room, where a board-certified surgeon sutured his ruptured eyeball and saved his vision.

Collaborative Care Today, the health care system is increasingly focused on collaborative care, the combined efforts of physicians, psychologists, and other health care people, such as this team talking with a patient.

collaborative care A cooperative form of health care in which physicians, psychologists, and other health care providers join forces to improve patient care.

Cancer patients at Delaware County Memorial Hospital in Drexel Hill, Pennsylvania, are offered an integrative approach to care. It includes an eight-week class that teaches mindfulness meditation and cognitive behavior strategies to reduce stress. Patients also can get massages and take a free weekly yoga class. The psychologists may employ hypnosis to help people harness the strengths of the mind over the body's pain.

Why was Bruce reluctant to seek medical care? Why wasn't the severe pain in his eye sufficient to sound the alarm that his health was in jeopardy? In considering why people do or do not seek treatment and how they interact with the health care system, we shift our focus from *primary* prevention to *secondary* prevention—that is, from actions designed to prevent a disease or injury to actions intended to identify and treat an illness early in its course.

This chapter explores the role of health psychology in the relationships between patients and the health care system. Social and psychological factors have both a direct and an indirect impact on those relationships. First, such factors strongly influence when and how people initially decide they are sick. Second, the confidence that people have in their health care providers influences their satisfaction with treatment, as well as how they respond to it. Third, the extent and quality of communication between patients and health care providers indirectly influence almost every aspect of health care, including how patients decide when they need medical attention, why people sometimes choose to ignore health-related symptoms, and why people carefully follow their provider's instructions at some times but not at other times.

As a result of our improved understanding of these psychosocial influences, a significantly increasing number of psychologists now work in general health care settings, and medical school curricula include a greater focus on the behavioral and social sciences (Institute of Medicine, 2006). In addition, a growing number of medical centers are encouraging greater use of **collaborative care** (also called *integrated care* or *primary care behavioral health*), in which physicians, psychologists (sometimes called *behavioral consultants*), and other health care providers join forces to improve patient care (Robinson, Gould, & Strosahl, 2010). Optimum health care is not achieved by defining the separate responsibilities of patients and health care providers, but through their harmonious interaction.

Recognizing and Interpreting Symptoms

How and when do we decide that we are sick? At what point does a nagging headache, upset stomach, or other symptom become serious enough for us to recognize a problem? The criteria that people use to recognize and interpret symptoms vary enormously. However, certain broad psychosocial factors play an important role in the process.

Attentional Focus, Neuroticism, and Self-Rated Health

Attentional focus influences our awareness of physical symptoms (van Laarhoven, Kraaimaat, Wilder-Smith, & Evers, 2010). If we have a strong *internal focus* on our bodies, emotions, and overall well-being, we are more likely to detect and report symptoms than if we are more *externally focused*. People who are socially isolated, are bored with their jobs, and live alone are more likely to be internally focused, whereas people with more active lives are subject to more distractions that keep their minds off their problems.

Attentional focus also determines how we cope with health problems and other stressful events. When threatened with an aversive event, people considered **sensitizers** actively monitor the event and their reactions to it. They cope with health problems by closely scanning their bodies and environments for information. Sensitizers also prefer high levels of information about their health in medical contexts and seem to fare better when it is provided.

In contrast, **repressors** tend to ignore or deny health-related information. They cope with negative events without bother or irritation, often by defending themselves from unwanted thoughts or unpleasant mood states. Repressing may create a powerful reluctance to seek medical screenings, which are typically oriented toward detecting serious illnesses. The distress of thinking about the possibility of disease may create a barrier to noticing symptoms.

Attentional focus highlights the important role that personal factors play in symptom perception and health care utilization. Consider *irritable bowel syndrome* (IBS), a disorder of the lower intestinal tract involving cramping, pain, and abnormal bowel movements. Some people with IBS seek medical services, whereas others do not (Ringstrom, Abrahamsson, Strid, & Simren, 2007). Those who do so are more likely to be sensitizers and anxious about their symptoms. Other research studies have found that people who have strong emotional reactions to ambiguous symptoms and who score high on measures of neuroticism are more likely to perceive such symptoms as signs of an illness and to seek professional care (Rosmalen, Neeleman, Gans, & de Jonge, 2006).

attentional focus A person's characteristic style of monitoring bodily symptoms, emotions, and overall well-being.

sensitizers People who cope with health problems and other aversive events by closely scanning their bodies and environments for information.

repressors People who cope with health problems and other aversive events by ignoring or distancing themselves from stressful information.

Illness Representations

Our personal views of health and illness, called **illness representations,** also affect our health in at least two ways: by influencing our preventive health behaviors and by affecting how we react when symptoms appear. Researchers have studied several components of how we represent illnesses. Each component by itself can affect substantially our motivation to seek medical care. The components are as follows:

illness representation How a person views a particular illness, including its label and symptoms, perceived causes, timeline, consequences, and controllability.

1. *Identity* of the illness—its label and symptoms. There appears to be a symmetrical bond between a disease's label and its symptoms. Thus, a person who has symptoms will seek a diagnostic label for those symptoms; a person who has been diagnosed (labeled) will seek symptoms that are consistent with that label. In a vivid example of this symmetry, Linda Baumann and her colleagues (Baumann, Cameron, Zimmerman, & Leventhal, 1989) found that research participants who were told that they had high blood pressure were more likely than others to report symptoms commonly associated with this illness. This was true regardless of whether or not they really were hypertensive. In this era of direct-to-consumer advertising, many skeptics suspect that pharmaceutical companies capitalize on the human tendency to seek labels for ambiguous symptoms by marketing expensive medications for conditions such as irritable bowel syndrome, fibromyalgia, and restless leg syndrome.

All medical conditions are at least partly *social constructions*, meaning that their identity and diagnosis are shaped by culture, advertising, and other nonbiological forces. German physicians, for example, are far more likely than their counterparts in France, Britain, and the United States to diagnose and treat low blood pressure. Another example is the epidemic of *attention deficit hyperactivity disorder* (ADHD) in the United States. Nowhere in the world are the behaviors associated with this disorder treated with the same intensity as in the United States. The point to remember: People in different places can experience the same biological phenomena in very different ways.

2. *Causes*—attributing symptoms to external factors, such as infection or injury, or internal factors, such as genetic predisposition. A student who interprets her tension headache as a by-product of cramming for an exam will react quite differently from the student who interprets the same symptoms as signs of a brain tumor.

3. *Timeline*—the duration and rate of the disease's development. For example, 4 out of 10 patients being treated for hypertension believe that their condition is *acute* (that is, short in duration, caused by temporary agents, and not a serious threat to long-term health). In contrast, *chronic illnesses* are long in duration, caused by multiple factors, and represent potentially serious threats to long-term health. Patients who believe their illness is acute often drop out of treatment earlier than those who believe it to be chronic.

4. *Consequences*—the physical, social, and economic impact of illness and disease. We are far more likely to ignore symptoms that minimally disrupt our daily lives (such as minor muscle soreness following a strenuous workout) than we are to ignore symptoms that have a serious disruptive effect (such as a severe muscular strain that prevents a laborer from earning a paycheck).

5. *Controllability*—beliefs regarding whether the illness can be prevented, controlled, and/or cured. If we view our disease or condition as incurable, we may skip appointments, neglect treatment, or even behave in self-destructive ways because we feel helpless and lack hope.

Note that the key to these components is our perception of the symptoms rather than the actual facts about the disease. How we initially react to a stomachache, for example, depends not on its actual cause, about which we are unaware, but on what we *believe* is causing the pain.

Explanatory Style and Psychological Disturbances

Explanatory style (optimistic or pessimistic) and psychological health also influence the reporting of symptoms. People who have a more positive outlook on life generally report fewer symptoms than do people who are more negative. Those in a good mood also have higher *self-reported health* and consider themselves less vulnerable to future illness than do people in bad moods (Winter, Lawton, Langston, Ruckdeschel, & Sando, 2007).

People who are anxious and those who score low on tests of emotional stability tend to report more physical symptoms, perhaps because they tend to exaggerate the seriousness of minor complaints that others are more likely to ignore. In addition, symptoms of psychological or emotional disorders sometimes are misattributed to physical problems. Actually, there is substantial **comorbidity** of psychological and physical disorders—physical and psychological symptoms and disorders occurring simultaneously. Psychological disorders such as anxiety or depression can predispose physical disorders through biological, behavioral, cognitive, and social pathways

comorbidity The simultaneous occurrence of two or more physical and/or psychological disorders or symptoms.

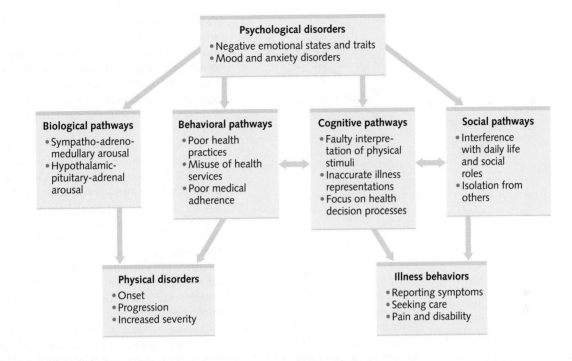

(Figure 13.1). For example, depression might trigger poor health practices, such as alcohol abuse, and a general apathy regarding treatment regimens. Anxiety and depression also can lead to an excessive focus on bodily symptoms.

FIGURE 13.1

Psychological Disorders, Physical Disorders, and Illness Behavior Psychological disorders can predispose physical disorders and illness behavior via a number of biological, behavioral, cognitive, and social pathways.

Source: Cohen, S., & Rodriguez, M. S. (1995). Pathways linking affective disturbances and physical disorders. *Health Psychology, 14,* 374–380.

Seeking Treatment

The presence of symptoms is not always enough to get us into the health care system. Why do some of us keep up our normal activities even in the face of undeniable evidence that something is wrong, while others take time off work in response to the slightest symptom?

We fail to respond to potentially serious medical symptoms for many reasons. We may avoid seeing a doctor because we believe that our symptoms are not serious and that all we need is a day or two of rest, an over-the-counter medication, or some other form of self-care. We may avoid the use of health services because we lack health insurance or are afraid we can't afford it. We may be fearful that our symptoms *are* a sign of a serious condition, and our inaction is a result of denial. Finally, we may avoid medical care because we are suspicious of the health care system and doubt its ability to treat our condition effectively.

Several demographic and sociocultural factors play important roles in determining whether a person will take the next step and seek medical treatment.

Age and Gender

Overall, the very young and the elderly use health services more often than do adolescents and young adults (Schiller, Lucas, & Peregoy, 2012). As any parent knows, children develop many different infectious diseases as their immune systems are developing. They need checkups, vaccinations, and regular health services. In general, however, our younger

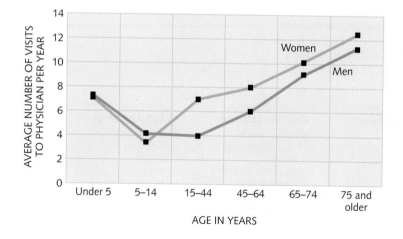

FIGURE 13.2

Age, Gender, and Physician Contact In general, young children and older adults are more likely than adolescents and young adults to use health services. Starting in adolescence, women contact their physicians more than men do.

Data from U.S. Department of Health and Human Services (USDHHS). (1995). *Healthy People 2000 review, 1994.* Washington, DC: U.S. Government Printing Office; and Schiller, J. S., Lucas, J. W., & Peregoy, J. A. (2012). Summary health statistics for U.S. adults: National Health Interview Survey, 2011. *National Center for Health Statistics, Vital Health Stat, 10*(256).

years are among the healthiest of the entire life span. The frequency of illness and the need to visit physicians decline steadily throughout late childhood, adolescence, and young adulthood. Health services begin to increase again in middle age and late adulthood as a result of the increasing prevalence of chronic, age-related diseases (Figure 13.2).

Psychologists long have recognized that every age has its own special way of viewing the world. Childhood concepts of disease often include magical notions about causality. Only at a later age do children begin to understand the concept of contagion and the mechanisms by which infectious diseases are transmitted. Still later, as their concept of self-efficacy continues to mature, they begin to realize that they can take steps to control their health.

During adolescence, thinking is typically distorted by a self-view in which teenagers regard themselves as more significant than they actually are. This manifests itself in many ways, including an *optimistic bias,* in which some young people believe that they will never be harmed seriously by dangerous actions. As a result of this false sense of invulnerability, together with the slow maturation of the brain's cognitive-control system, they are more likely to engage in risky behaviors such as cigarette smoking, substance abuse, unsafe sexual behavior, and dangerous driving. This new, biopsychosocial perspective on adolescent risk taking, which views such behavior from the joint perspectives of brain science and social-behavioral science, explains why many educational interventions designed to change adolescents' attitudes and health behaviors have been largely ineffective (Steinberg, 2007).

During late adulthood, ageist stereotypes can be significant barriers to achieving and maintaining good health. Old age often is viewed as a period of inevitable decline in which elderly people are unable or unwilling to change lifestyle behaviors, adhere to treatment regimens, or gain much benefit from health interventions. This is unfortunate because most people aged 65 years or older suffer from at least one chronic health condition that, in many cases, may be cured or at least controlled. Ageist stereotypes may also prevent older adults from seeking (or receiving) optimal preventive health care, such as cancer screenings, and serve as a barrier to adopting healthier lifestyles aimed at increasing overall health expectancy. Fortunately, research studies indicate that many seniors remain optimistic about their health status—which is a good thing because self-reported health is known to predict mortality and other health outcomes better than objective ratings, and it is the strongest predictor of life satisfaction during old age (Winter and others, 2007).

Gender is another factor in the way that health services are used. Beginning in adolescence and continuing throughout adulthood, women are more likely than men to report symptoms and to use health services (Galdas, Cheater, & Marshall, 2005), due in large part to pregnancy and childbirth. New mothers are staying in the hospital about half a day longer than they did in the mid-1990s, when insurance companies cut childbirth stays to 24 hours, sparking outcries about "drive-by deliveries" (Meara, Kotagal, Atherton, & Lieu, 2004). However, even when medical visits for pregnancy and childbirth are not counted, women still visit their physicians more often than do men.

Historically, women have also paid more for health care than men. The practice of *gender rating*—charging women more for the same coverage—was widespread prior to implementation of the Affordable Care Act (ACA). A large-scale study conducted by the National Women's Law Center found that women "are continuously charged more for health coverage simply because they are women, and individual market health plans often exclude coverage for services that women need, like maternity coverage" (NWLC, 2012). Fortunately, as of 2014, the ACA eliminated gender rating in the insurance market and now requires all insurance plans to provide maternity coverage.

Men, especially low-income young men, more often dodge the doctor, even when faced with potentially serious problems. Large-scale surveys conducted by the National Center for Health Statistics (2006) and Kaiser Family Foundation (2015) revealed that, of those sampled:

- About 72 percent of men report they have a usual source of heath care, compared to 86 percent of women. Only 62 percent of low-income men (those living with less than 200 percent of the federal poverty level) have a regular place to go for care.

- More than one-third of the men wouldn't go to a doctor immediately, even if experiencing severe chest pains (34 percent) or shortness of breath (37 percent).

- In the past two years, 91 percent of women report having seen a health care provider, compared with only 75 percent of men.

- Men are less likely than women to get recommended screening services, including a general checkup, and tests for high blood pressure and cholesterol (see Figure 13.3).

- Gender differences in office visits vary by age, with the largest gap among men and women 18 to 44 years of age, while narrowing among middle-aged adults and disappearing among the oldest age group.

Why are women generally more likely than men to seek health care? It may be because they are exposed to more illness as a result of caring for the elderly and children, who have the highest incidence of being sick. Women also are more likely to be nurses, elementary school teachers, and day-care providers, all of which increase their risk of exposure to infectious agents.

Gender difference in the seeking of health care also may be due in part to social factors. For instance, women visit doctors more than men do because their health care tends to be more fragmented. For a routine physical exam, most men are "one-stop shoppers." That is, they visit a general practitioner or nurse-practitioner who is able to perform most, if not all, of the tests they need. In contrast, a woman may need to visit three or more specialists or clinics for a thorough checkup: an internist for her physical, a gynecologist for a Pap smear, a mammography specialist to screen for breast tumors, and so forth. Some researchers see this fragmentation as an indication that Western medicine is male biased and not well structured to meet women's basic needs.

Socioeconomic Status and Cultural Factors

Socioeconomic status (SES) predicts both symptom reporting and the seeking of health care. High-income people generally report fewer symptoms and better health than do low-income people (Grzywacz, Almeida, Neupert, & Ettner, 2004). However, high-SES people are more likely to seek health care when needed. People in lower-SES groups tend to wait longer before seeking treatment, making it more likely that they will become seriously ill and require

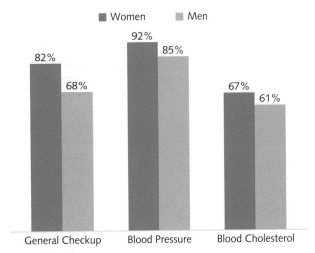

■ Women   ■ Men

General Checkup: Women 82%, Men 68%
Blood Pressure: Women 92%, Men 85%
Blood Cholesterol: Women 67%, Men 61%

FIGURE 13.3

Percentages of Women and Men Receiving Recommended Health Screenings In general, women are more likely than men to get recommended health screening services.

Data from Kaiser Family Foundation. (2015). Gender differences in health care, status, and use: Spotlight on men's health. *Findings from the 2013 Kaiser Men's Health Survey and 2013 Kaiser Women's Health Survey* [slide show]. Retrieved from http://kff.org/womens-health-policy/fact-sheet/gender-differences-in-health-care-status-and-use-spotlight-on-mens-health/

Behavior of Sick Women and the Elderly In general, women are more likely than men to seek health care, and women over 65 are more likely than younger women to seek health care.

lay referral system An informal network of family members, friends, and other nonprofessionals who offer their own impressions, experiences, and recommendations regarding a set of bodily symptoms.

delay behavior The tendency to avoid seeking medical care because symptoms go unnoticed (*appraisal delay*), sickness seems unlikely (*illness delay*), professional help is deemed unnecessary (*behavioral delay*), the individual procrastinates in making an appointment (*scheduling delay*), or the perceived costs of treatment outweigh the perceived benefits (*treatment delay*).

FIGURE 13.4

Stages of Delay in Seeking Medical Attention The Andersen model of patient delay shows that noticing symptoms does not automatically lead to treatment. People have to make a concerted effort to take each step, so it's possible for intervening factors to interrupt the process.

Information from Anderson, B. L., Cacioppo, J. T., & Roberts, D. C. (1995). Delay in seeking a cancer diagnosis: Delay stages and psychophysiological comparison processes. *British Journal of Social Psychology, 34,* 33–52.

hospitalization. In addition, people with lower family incomes are more likely to use outpatient clinics and hospital emergency rooms for medical care because they are less likely to have health insurance and regular physicians than their financially advantaged counterparts (Kaiser Family Foundation, 2015). This helps explain why morbidity and mortality are highest among people at the lowest SES levels.

Cultural factors also influence a person's tendency to seek treatment. People who hold beliefs that conflict with Western medicine are less likely to seek traditional biomedical care and more likely to rely on a **lay referral system**—an informal social network of family, friends, and other nonprofessionals who offer their own impressions and experiences regarding a set of symptoms. A member of the referral system might help interpret a symptom or give advice about seeking treatment.

Several researchers have studied ethnic and cultural variations in the lay referral system. They have found, for example, that ethnic groups differ widely in the degree to which they believe that human intervention in health outcomes is possible or desirable. Some groups attribute disease to nonphysical factors, such as God's will. In such cases, people may be more inclined to employ non-Western practices for treatment (see Chapter 15). This poses an interesting problem for Western health care providers because the closer a patient's cultural or ethnic background is to that of Western physicians, the more the patient's reported symptoms will approximate those that are recognizable as signs of disease.

Upbringing is a related cultural factor in determining the likelihood of a person's seeking treatment for a particular symptom. People whose parents paid close attention to physical symptoms and sought regular health care may be more likely to do the same. Conversely, those whose parents were suspicious of doctors and more likely to rely on self-care or some form of alternative treatment may be more likely to carry that suspicion with them.

Delay Behavior

Clearly, for medical emergencies such as heart attacks, getting help as quickly as possible is of the utmost importance. Although other chronic diseases and conditions may not present this kind of minute-by-minute urgency in survival, seeking timely care when symptoms first appear can make the difference between dying from the disease or condition and discovering it when it still may be treatable. For example, beginning treatment for certain types of cancer while it is still localized and before it has metastasized to other areas of the body often makes the difference between a long, full life and one that is shortened prematurely.

Despite the benefits of seeking care when symptoms first appear, many people, like my friend Bruce whom you met at the beginning of the chapter, ignore their symptoms and do not seek medical help. This is called **delay behavior.** Why do people delay seeking medical attention for such serious conditions? According to one model, there are five stages in the decision-making process for seeking medical care (Walter, Webster, Scott, & Emery, 2012) (see Figure 13.4). The model predicts that people will avoid seeking medical care because symptoms go unnoticed (*appraisal delay*), sickness seems unlikely (*illness delay*), professional help is deemed unnecessary (*behavioral delay*), the individual procrastinates in making an appointment (*scheduling delay*), or the perceived costs of treatment

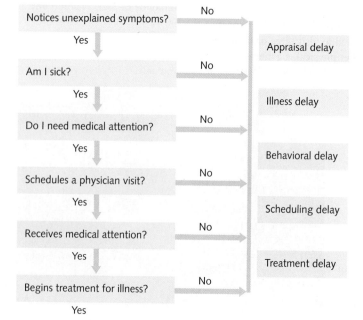

outweigh the perceived benefits (*treatment delay*). At each of these stages, a person can exhibit delay behavior.

During the appraisal delay stage, the sensory prominence of the symptoms is the most important factor in determining the amount of delay. Patients seeking care at hospital clinics indicated delaying less when they were in pain or bleeding. Myocardial infarction patients who stopped to research their symptoms by consulting books and other sources delayed more than five times as long as patients who did not do research. Initial pain led to a short delay, whereas talking with others about one's symptoms resulted in a significantly longer delay (Waller, 2006).

In the illness delay stage, patients who had previously experienced similar symptoms were more likely than those who experienced symptoms for the first time to delay seeking medical attention. For example, with *carpal tunnel syndrome*, a nerve disorder caused by repetitive motion, the symptoms may come and go over a long period of time, so people tend to ignore them. Only when the symptoms become persistent and acute will the person start moving through the stages toward seeking treatment. In addition, patients who spent more time imagining the consequences of being sick were more likely to delay seeking medical attention.

In the last three stages, delay was longest for patients who were more concerned about the cost of treatment, had little pain, and were doubtful that their symptoms could be cured. The association between not feeling pain and delaying medical care is unfortunate because pain is not a major symptom in the early stages of a number of chronic diseases, including cancer, hypertension, and diabetes.

Overusing Health Services

At the opposite extreme are people who misuse health services by seeking care when they do not have a diagnosable health condition. So pervasive is this problem that physicians estimate that as much as two-thirds of their time is taken up by people with problems that are either medically insignificant or the result of emotional disturbances (Franko and others, 2005).

Illness Anxiety Disorder

Some people who visit their physicians when there is no real need suffer from **illness anxiety disorder** (formerly known as *hypochondriasis*), or the false belief that they have a disease. Most people with illness anxiety disorder experience vague or ambiguous symptoms that they exaggerate and misattribute to disease. They also may have an exaggerated fear of contracting a disease, even in the face of evidence that there is no real danger. An underlying factor in many cases of illness anxiety disorder appears to be *neuroticism*, a state of emotional maladjustment that encompasses self-consciousness, the inability to inhibit cravings, vulnerability to stress, and the tendency to experience anxiety, depression, and other negative emotions.

The diagnostic criteria for illness anxiety disorder include, but are not limited to, an absence of somatic (physical) symptoms; chronic, worrisome preoccupation that one has a serious medical condition that has lasted six months or longer; high levels of *health anxiety*, with very low sickness thresholds; constantly checking for signs of illness; and the absence of symptoms of another disorder (American Psychiatric Association, 2013).

Is this official diagnostic explanation of the condition legitimate, or are people who report imaginary symptoms feigning illness, or **malingering**, in order to derive some benefit from their behavior (perhaps sympathy from others or time off from work)? Generally speaking, people suffering from illness anxiety disorder amplify what are, in fact, benign symptoms into excessive worry about their health. People who score high on emotional instability and neuroticism average two to three times as many physical complaints as those who score low on these traits (Goodwin & Friedman, 2006). But does this prove

illness anxiety disorder The condition of experiencing abnormal anxiety over one's health, often including imaginary symptoms.

malingering Making believe that one is ill to benefit from sick role behavior.

Diversity and Healthy Living

Chronic Fatigue Syndrome

Katie Lucas was so exhausted that she could barely get out of bed or perform even the simplest physical or mental task. "I remember on one occasion having to take out a calculator to subtract 12 from 32," she said. "That's pretty bad." In Atlanta, Georgia, Wilhelmina Jenkins was unable to complete her doctoral training in physics due to chronic fatigue that made thinking and writing all but impossible. "All they could recommend to me was changing my lifestyle—getting more rest," she said. "I tried every kind of change I could think of, and nothing helped; I just continued to go downhill."

Lucas and Jenkins suffer from chronic fatigue syndrome (CFS), a puzzling disorder suffered by an estimated 1 million patients in the United States, 80 percent of whom are women (Moss-Morris, Deary, & Castell, 2013). In addition to persistent fatigue that lasts for months or longer, other symptoms of CFS include headaches, infections of unknown origins, and difficulties with concentration and memory. People afflicted with CFS often are so debilitated that they are unable to carry out their normal, everyday activities. Making matters worse is the widespread view that they are not really sick, but merely malingerers whose symptoms are self-induced to gain attention, sympathy, or release from overwhelming responsibilities.

The cause of CFS has been much debated; the majority of patients report that it began with an apparent infection, and a significant number state that they were under considerable stress at the time (Moss-Morris, Deary, & Castell, 2013). Because there is no diagnostic test for CFS and no known treatment, some doctors believe the condition is actually a form of illness anxiety disorder caused by modern culture, or even *hysteria*, which throughout history has served as a physical manifestation of distress. Along with those who have *recovered memories* of childhood trauma and abuse or suffer from *Gulf War syndrome* or *dissociative identity disorder* (formerly called *multiple personality disorder*), CFS "victims," say the critics, are merely manifesting contemporary signs of hysteria.

There is evidence, however, that those who consider CFS to be a form of hysteria or illness anxiety disorder are probably wrong. For example, researchers at Johns Hopkins University have established a link between chronic fatigue and low blood pressure. Strapping CFS patients on a tilt table and then gradually moving them upright to a 70-degree angle, researchers found that at one point, the patients' blood pressure dropped suddenly from about 125 to 45, immediately triggering CFS symptoms. By boosting the CFS patients' water and salt intake and providing pressure-elevating medication, researchers have been able to help about 75 percent of them. Other researchers have found that administering low doses of the stress hormone hydrocortisone, known to be in short supply in many people with CFS, boosts energy, mood, and activity level (Rutz, 1998). The research also indicates that a high percentage of CFS

---

chronic fatigue syndrome (CFS) A puzzling disorder of uncertain causes in which a person experiences headaches, infections of unknown origins, extreme tiredness, and difficulties with concentration and memory.

that neuroticism causes illness anxiety disorder? As we have seen, correlational evidence such as this cannot pinpoint causality. Even if it could, we would be unable to discern the *direction* of causality. It could be that having many aches, pains, and illnesses causes an excessive preoccupation with one's health. Those suffering from **chronic fatigue syndrome (CFS),** for example, have struggled with false assumptions about the causality of their condition (see Diversity and Healthy Living: Chronic Fatigue Syndrome).

Stress and anxiety often create a number of physical symptoms that may resemble the symptoms of a biologically based disorder (Martin & Brantley, 2004). For example, anxiety (perhaps about upcoming exams) may disrupt sleeping and concentration, trigger diarrhea and nausea, suppress appetite, and/or result in a state of general agitation.

Patient Adherence

Surprisingly, even when people seek health care, many simply ignore (or fail to follow closely) the treatment that is prescribed for them. Every health care professional can tell stories about this phenomenon: the patient who cheats on a special diet; the coronary case who, without consulting her doctor, stops taking her hypertension medication; or the accident victim who misuses a prescribed painkiller.

patients suffer from a persistent viral infection and immune system dysfunction and that treatment of these problems can alleviate some of the symptoms (Ablashi and others, 2000; Pall, 2000). Evidence such as this is helpful to frustrated patients, who frequently have been told by doctors who can find nothing wrong with them that they are imagining their symptoms.

The role of psychological factors in CFS, however, continues to be debated. Some experts suggest that CFS and depression have a common cause, while others have pointed to differences between the two disorders. For example, weight loss, suicidal thinking, guilt, and low self-esteem are all less common in CFS than in depression, while flu-like symptoms, muscle weakness and pain, and fatigue are more common.

The course of CFS varies from patient to patient, with some experiencing rapid improvement and full recovery, while others worsen over time or experience repeated cycles of relapse and remission (Moss-Morris, Deary, & Castell, 2013). Because there is no generally accepted drug treatment for CFS, treatment usually involves managing the symptoms and engaging in moderate activity. Cognitive behavioral therapy (CBT) designed to increase tolerance of symptoms and to modify maladaptive illness beliefs also has been effective in some patients (Bazelmans, Prins, & Bleijenberg, 2006). The disorder can be so debilitating, unresponsive to traditional medical regimens, and frustrating that some CFS sufferers turn to various forms of alternative and fringe medicine.

Because the debate appears to be shifting from whether the symptoms of disorders such as CFS are real, some health experts question whether there is any point in continuing the search for specific, organic causes. Simon Wessely, professor of psychological medicine and director of the Chronic Fatigue Syndrome Unit at King's College in London, believes that doing so is a disservice to patients:

> Doctors have been searching for the Holy Grail to explain these syndromes for the last 150 years without success. ... If a patient is told the problem is due to a permanent deficit in the immune system or a persistent virus or chronic disability of the nerves or brain, this just generates helplessness and the patient becomes a victim. And if you say the problem is psychological, this generates anger on the part of patients who don't regard psychological ills as legitimate. Looking for any single cause misses the point. Regardless of how or why they may have started, these syndromes are multifactorial, like heart disease (quoted in Brody, 1999).

This understanding suggests, therefore, that a multifactorial approach to treating CFS would be most effective—certainly better than being turned away from the medical system entirely or told that "it's all in your head."

Adherence is broadly defined as closely following the advice of a health care provider. This includes advice pertaining to medications and lifestyle changes (for example, losing weight or quitting smoking), as well as recommendations about preventive measures (such as avoiding fatty foods or starting an exercise program). Adherence is both an attitude and a behavior. As an attitude, it entails a willingness to follow health advice; as a behavior, it is related to the actual carrying out of specific recommendations.

adherence A patient both agreeing to and then closely following a treatment regimen as advised by his or her health care provider.

When patients do not follow the treatment regimens that their health care providers recommend, the result is **nonadherence,** or noncompliance, which includes refusal to adhere to or the lack of sustained effort in following a treatment regimen. The costs associated with nonadherence are potentially enormous. In patients with organ transplants, for example, failure to adhere to immunosuppressant drug regimens can lead to organ rejection. On a monetary level, it is estimated that nonadherence has an annual economic impact of $100 to $300 billion in avoidable treatment and hospitalization costs (see Iuga and McGuire, 2014, for a review).

nonadherence The condition in which a patient refuses to complete a prescribed therapeutic regimen.

How Widespread Is Nonadherence?

Estimating the prevalence of nonadherence is difficult because the problem takes so many different forms. For example, a patient may not show up for a scheduled appointment, fail to complete the course of an antibiotic, or fail to follow some other treatment regimen.

In other words, there are many degrees of nonadherence. Beyond that, some types of nonadherence, such as not taking every dose of medication, are done by the patient in private, so the doctor has no way of discovering them. In broad terms, a meta-analysis of over 500 studies over a 50-year span indicated that the average rate of nonadherence is about 25 percent—only three out of every four patients follow their treatment regimens closely (DiMatteo, 2004). Here are some specifics:

- Only 20 to 40 percent of participants in treatment programs for smoking, alcohol, and drug abuse continue to comply with treatment after one year.

- In the treatment of obesity, between 10 and 13 percent of participants stop attending program meetings after two to three months, and from 42 to 48 percent after three to four months.

- Only 50 percent of patients comply fully with physician-directed dietary restrictions. Up to 80 percent of patients drop out of programs that prescribe other lifestyle changes (such as fitness programs).

What Factors Predict Adherence?

Are some people more likely than others to comply with treatment? Is adherence more likely for certain kinds of treatment than for others? In their search for answers to these questions, biomedical researchers have examined two broad categories of variables: *patient variables* and *treatment regimen variables*.

Patient and Provider Variables

Although a substantial amount of adherence research has focused on age, gender, ethnicity, education, and income, it is now generally understood that sociodemographic factors are not very accurate predictors of adherence (Dunbar-Jacob & Schlenk, 2001). In general, this is because people are inconsistent in their adherence behaviors. A patient may follow a medication regimen but not necessarily a dietary regimen. Among some patients, alcohol or drug use (Weitzman, Ziemnik, Huang, & Levy, 2015; Sansone and Sansone, 2008) and depression, anxiety, and other mental health problems (Tucker and others, 2004) have been associated with nonadherence. Among other patients, it is memory and cognitive deficits (Stilley, Bender, Dunbar-Jacob, Sereika, & Ryan, 2010) or a disorganized lifestyle (Schreier & Chen, 2010) that contribute to nonadherence.

At the consumer level, what promotes adherence? Being in a good mood, having optimistic expectations, and having trust in one's care provider are important factors (Thom, Hall, & Pawlson, 2004). Having the support of family and friends is also important. For instance, studies have shown that marital support improves adherence to diabetes care regimens that include food purchase and preparation, medication administration, glucose testing, and exercise (Trief, Ploutz-Snyder, Britton, & Weinstock, 2004).

Perceived control and preference for control of treatments also help to explain adherence. Patients who express greater preference for control and involvement in their health care demonstrate better adherence to medical treatments that are largely self-directed and that take place in the home. However, greater preference for control predicts *poorer* adherence when treatments take place in a clinic or hospital (Cvengros, Christensen, & Lawton, 2004).

Provider variables, such as level of job satisfaction, the number of patients seen per week, and communication style, also have a powerful influence on patient adherence. In addition, recent studies have confirmed that the personal characteristics of health care providers are very important to patients. At the top of the list are a provider's display of empathy and confidence, in addition to a forthright and respectful manner (Bendapudi,

Berry, Frey, Parish, & Rayburn, 2006). Perhaps because female physicians spend more time with patients—and ask and encourage more questions—their care promotes higher rates of adherence than that of male physicians (Roter & Hall, 2004).

Treatment Regimen Variables

Patients are more likely to follow recommendations that they believe in and are capable of carrying out. Researchers generally have found that the more complex a treatment regimen, the less the likelihood of complete adherence. Health care providers can take several steps to improve adherence in their patients, including the following:

Promoting Adherence Patients are more likely to follow recommendations that they believe in and that they are capable of carrying out.

- Tailor the treatment to fit the patient's lifestyle. Adherence will increase in response to anything that makes a treatment regimen easier to follow.

- Simplify instructions with clear language to ensure that the patient understands the amount, timing, and duration of the treatment.

- Make sure that the patient understands enough of the treatment rationale to gain confidence in the treatment schedule.

- Involve family members, friends, and other patient supporters in the treatment and the explanation of its rationale.

- Provide feedback about progress.

The Patient–Provider Relationship

The relationship between health care provider and patient is the backbone of all medical treatment. A full 60 to 80 percent of medical diagnoses and treatment decisions are made on the basis of information that arises from the medical consultation process alone. Yet patients and providers do not always share the same view of the effectiveness of the process. Too often, providers overestimate how well a consultation went and how likely it is that the patient will follow through on their advice. The quality of the patient–provider relationship plays an important role in promoting patient adherence to treatment instructions.

Factors Affecting the Patient–Provider Relationship

Research has demonstrated that the central elements of the patient–provider relationship are *continuity of care, communication*, and the overall *quality of consultations*. The same principles apply to this relationship regardless of the provider or the health care system. In a recent investigation of satisfaction with their family doctors, nearly 40 percent of patients cited issues, both positive and negative, concerning interpersonal relationships. Statements concerning competency (12.9 percent) and personal qualities (10.5 percent) of doctors were less common (Marcinowicz, Chlabicz, & Grebowski, 2009). One reason for this decrease in satisfaction is that half of all patients are convinced that treatment decisions are based strictly on what their health insurance will cover. General communication problems may result from a lack of continuity in care, but other factors—from both provider and patient perspectives—also play a role.

Provider Communication Problems

At the heart of the patient–provider relationship are the nature and quality of communication. Health care providers who are good communicators, less businesslike, and meet patient expectations regarding the information that they are entitled to receive tend to have patients who are more likely to adhere to treatment recommendations. In contrast, a lack of information about and poor understanding of medical advice and the recommended treatment tend to leave patients dissatisfied. Ideally, health care providers listen carefully to patients, ask questions to ensure that patients understand their condition and treatment, and fully inform patients about every aspect of their care. Stress levels are particularly high during difficult consultations, making it more challenging for patients to take in everything the doctor says. To improve the situation, communication-skills training is now an integral component of the medical school curriculum (ACGME, 2010).

Many health care providers today have "too little time, and too much to do" and do not spend enough time with patients. Research shows that the more time that physicians spend with patients (even just to chat), the more satisfied the patients are and the more likely they are to follow treatment plans successfully (Dugdale, Epstein, & Pantilat, 1998). Doctors who rush more patients through their practice each day have less-satisfied patients who are also less likely to be up to date on immunizations, mammograms, and other health-enhancing procedures and tests (Chen, 2013).

Some health care providers also have communication issues with patients because they fail to listen carefully or they treat patients either like medical school faculty or children. In one classic study of 74 consultations, researchers reported that in nearly two-thirds of the cases, the physician interrupted the patient's description of symptoms after only 18 seconds (Beckman & Frankel, 1984). Other studies show that far too often, the medical information provided was too detailed or complex for patients to understand or retain, and that patients and doctors frequently interpreted the same information in different ways. To make matters worse, doctors often use a patronizing tone that can leave patients feeling helpless (Castro, Wilson, Wang, & Schillinger, 2007).

The poor communication skills may be explained by the fact that medical training is based on technical expertise, not social skills. Until relatively recently, medical schools placed little emphasis on communication. Few providers were trained to deliver bad news, and many—out of sheer ignorance or in response to time pressures—say things to patients and families that cause unnecessary emotional pain and even may reduce the effectiveness of treatment. And the harm that stems from such poorly delivered bad news can be long-lasting, even permanent. In the worst instances, providers seemed to adopt coping strategies to minimize *their* discomfort with delivering bad news and failed to realize what was needed to minimize the trauma experienced by patients and their loved ones.

Discrimination, Prejudice, and Racism

Discrimination and prejudice adversely affect minority populations and the health care system in general. Discrimination and prejudice may be based on differences due to race, ethnicity, age, ability, gender, religion, sexual orientation, or any other characteristic by

Seeking Social Skills Medical school students now regularly participate in communication-skills training, along with all their technical learning. This will help them establish better patient–provider and other relationships as they move along in their careers.

BSIP SA/Alamy

which people differ. In its landmark report *Unequal Treatment: Confronting Racial and Ethnic Disparities in Health Care*, the Institute of Medicine (IOM) concluded that there is ample evidence of racism within the U.S. health care system (*institutional racism*) and among health care providers (*personally mediated racism*) (Smedley, Stith, & Nelson, 2002). The report went on to say that institutional racism is an important factor in racial/ethnic differences in overall health due to differences in the quality of care members of minority groups receive. Among diabetes patients, for example, African-Americans are less likely to receive influenza vaccinations or have their hemoglobin and cholesterol tested (Peek, Cargill, & Huang, 2007). The IOM found that racial/ethnic differences in health care persisted even after adjusting for other variables such as gender and socio-economic status.

As another example of institutional racism, consider that historically, minorities have been underrepresented in clinical trials (Fisher & Kalbaugh, 2011). This is significant because efforts to address racial and ethnic disparities in health will require physicians, physician assistants, nurses, and other health care professionals to develop new evidence-based approaches to treatment and education for diabetes, cancer, and other diseases that disproportionately affect minorities. It is crucial that the evidence from clinical trials be based on representative populations of study participants.

One impediment to minority participation in clinical trials is a lack of trust in the medical research system stemming from "experiments" such as the infamous Tuskegee Syphilis Study. Conducted by the U.S. Public Health Service from 1932 to 1972, this study aimed to observe the long-term effects of syphilis by withholding treatment from 399 poor African-American men with the sexually transmitted disease. Although penicillin had been widely available since the 1940s and soon thereafter became accepted as the standard of care for syphilis, the participants were never made aware of or given this treatment. Sadly, three-fourths of the men died from complications of the disease, and many of those who survived became blind and crippled. The experiment was conducted without the benefit of the patients' informed consent.

Institutionalized racism does not necessarily entail the personal bias commonly associated with the term *racism*. In contrast, personally mediated racism refers to prejudicial assumptions about people's abilities, motives, and intentions, as well as discriminatory actions toward others according to their race (Jones, 2005). Health care providers may be at increased risk of relying on stereotypes as cognitive short-cuts because of time pressure, limited resources, and other clinical demands. Stereotypes based on patient characteristics (for example, race) may influence the interpretation of symptoms and, consequently, affect clinical decisions (Burgess, van Ryn, Dovidio, & Saha, 2007). For example, one study found that physicians were more likely, after controlling for confounding variables, to rate their African-American patients as less educated, less intelligent, more likely to abuse drugs and alcohol, and less likely to adhere to treatment regimens (van Ryn & Burke, 2000).

Minorities also experience prejudice and discrimination in health care delivery in the form of disrespect and failure to communicate options (Peek and others, 2010). Several studies have reported that physicians provide less information to and are less supportive of African-American and Hispanic patients and patients of lower SES than other patients in the same health care setting (Manfredi, Kaiser, Matthews, & Johnson, 2010). African-American patients are often perceived as less effective communicators and may be treated more contentiously by health care providers (Street, Gordon, & Haidet, 2007). Health care providers are more verbally dominant and engage in less patient-centered communication with African-American patients, and they are less likely to understand the cultural beliefs attached to certain health conditions (Street & Haidet, 2011). In response, minority patients are apt to perceive ineffective communication as a form of disrespect and unfair treatment, which may jeopardize their trust in and strain their relationship with health care providers (Song, Hamilton, & Moore, 2012).

While the issue of how to best measure racism and prejudice in health care remains controversial (Kressin, Raymond, & Manze, 2008), most researchers rely upon patient reports of perceived discrimination. There is growing evidence that such perceptions are associated with adverse outcomes, such as less preventive health care (for example, cancer screening, influenza vaccinations) (Hausmann, Jeong, Bost, & Ibrahim, 2008; Trivedi & Ayanian, 2006), poorer prescription medication adherence, and less medical testing/ treatment (Van Houtven and others, 2005). Among diabetes patients, perceived health care discrimination is also associated with lower-quality physician interactions and worse diabetes care and outcomes (Ryan, Gee, & Griffith, 2008).

There is evidence that many physicians also have negative perceptions of the elderly and those seeking treatment for psychological disorders, and even worse perceptions of older patients who have difficulty communicating. Gender differences are also a factor in the physician–patient relationship. A number of studies have found that female physicians demonstrate more proficient clinical performance than do their male counterparts, conducting longer office visits, asking more questions, and showing significantly more verbal and nonverbal support (Roter & Hall, 2004). Patients often are most comfortable communicating and interacting with health care providers who are of the same gender and similar in other ways to themselves.

Patient Communication Problems

Health care providers are not to blame for all miscommunications. Patients themselves are often the ones who are uninformed and unprepared, at times giving faulty information or discussing symptoms offhandedly for fear that doctors either will not be fully forthcoming about serious conditions or will confirm patients' apprehensions.

The differing educational and social backgrounds of patient and provider also can adversely affect communication. Traditionally, physicians have been upper-middle-class and white, while their patients reflect a much more diverse and heterogeneous group. The provider may think that he or she is explaining a problem clearly, while the patient may get an altogether different (and incorrect) meaning. Research has shown that patients with the most extensive and complicated health care problems are at greatest risk for misunderstanding their diagnoses, medications, and treatment instructions (Parker, 2000). Low-level reading skills among many patients also contribute to this problem. The health care system needs reshaping, including providing nonwritten materials for health education and offering the services of surrogate readers, so that patients with low literacy levels have access to information.

health literacy The capacity to obtain and understand basic health information and services needed to make appropriate health decisions.

Low (or nonexistent) reading levels contribute to low levels of **health literacy,** the ability to understand and use health care information to make decisions and follow instructions for treatment. The Institute of Medicine has said that eradicating low health literacy is the first public health movement of the twenty-first century (Hernandez, 2013). The National Assessment of Adult Literacy conducted by the U.S. Department of Education reported that more than 90 million people in the United States have difficulty reading, with approximately 40 to 44 million being functionally illiterate (National Assessment of Adult Literacy, 2003) and another 50 million being marginally illiterate (Centers for Disease Control and Prevention, 2012b).

One aspect of health literacy is *numeracy,* the ability to think and express oneself effectively in quantitative terms. Numeracy is essential for the understanding of quantitative information about health (Garcia-Retamero & Galesic, 2010a). People with low numeracy skills have less accurate perceptions of the risks and benefits of health screening, are more susceptible to certain errors in judgment, and have greater difficulty following complicated treatment regimens than those with high numeracy skill (Garcia-Retamero & Galesic, 2010b).

Patients with low health literacy are more likely to have difficulty navigating through the health care system, are less likely to seek preventive care and adhere to prescribed treatment and self-care regimens, and are more likely to make medication and treatment errors (Paasche-Orlow, 2011). A large study of patients with inadequate health literacy at two public hospitals (Williams and others, 1995) found that:

- 33 percent were unable to read basic health care materials;
- 42 percent could not comprehend directions to take medication on an empty stomach;
- 26 percent were unable to understand information on an appointment slip;
- 43 percent did not understand the "Rights and Responsibilities" section of a Medicaid application; and
- 60 percent did not understand a standard informed consent form.

Patient difficulties with health literacy also place a huge financial burden on the health care system. Adults with low health literacy average 6 percent more hospital visits, stay in the hospital longer, and have annual health care costs that are four times those of their counterparts with higher health literacy. (See the Your Health Assets feature on Health Literacy near the end of this chapter.)

Improving Patient–Provider Communication

Health care providers increasingly realize that patients who are better informed about the potential consequences of their behaviors are more likely to follow instructions and respond well to treatment. Approximately half of all causes of morbidity and mortality in the United States are linked to behavioral and social factors (MMWR, 2014, October 31; National Center for Health Statistics, 2006), so doctors must treat these risk factors as well as physical symptoms, which requires the patients' active cooperation and good patient–provider communication.

Communication training for health care providers includes a focus on *active listening* skills in which providers echo, restate, and seek to clarify patients' statements to achieve a shared understanding of symptoms, concerns, and treatment expectations. It also includes training in developing good rapport with patients through appropriate eye contact and other responses designed to acknowledge patients' feelings and to help them talk. In addition, providers receive instruction about how to communicate with patients about sensitive or difficult health topics, as well as about how to give bad news.

A number of communication-enhancing interventions also have been directed at patients, especially those about to receive an important consultation. These interventions generally have focused on increasing patients' level of participation, specifically to ensure that their concerns will be heard clearly and that they leave the consultation with a clear understanding of the information that has been provided.

To help overly passive patients, some health psychologists recommend *assertiveness coaching*, beginning with a careful review of each patient's medical record. A psychologist helps patients formulate questions for the doctor and offers tips on entering the doctor's office with a clear sense of one's goals and telling the doctor about feelings, fears, and symptoms without being hindered by embarrassment or anxiety. Assertiveness coaching can pay huge dividends. By establishing a greater degree of control in their office visits, patients who have been coached obtain more information. Follow-up interviews reveal that they also miss fewer workdays, rate their overall health as better, and report fewer symptoms than patients who do not receive assertiveness coaching (T. Y. Lee and others, 2013).

Motivational Interviewing

motivational interviewing (MI)
A widely used counseling method that focuses on strengthening a person's motivation and commitment to change a target health behavior.

Motivational interviewing (MI), is a widely used counseling method that focuses on strengthening a person's motivation and commitment to change a target health behavior (Miller & Rollnick, 2002; 2010). Based on several core principles of social psychology—particularly the concepts of cognitive dissonance and self-efficacy—MI is also closely aligned with the transtheoretical model of behavior change and the concept of readiness to change (see Chapter 6).

MI is based on three principles:

- Collaboration

  MI aims to establish a partnership between patient and provider. This contrasts with older approaches in which clinicians assume the role of "expert," confronting patients and imposing their perspective on the appropriate course of treatment.

- Patient Autonomy

  Unlike treatment models that emphasize the clinician as an authority figure, MI recognizes that it is ultimately up to the individual to follow through with making change happen. This is empowering to patients but also gives them responsibility for their actions. A key assumption underlying motivational interviewing, then, is that it is not the health care professional's job to coerce the patient to change. Rather, it is the patient's responsibility to decide whether to change and how best to go about it. The provider's role is to provide information and support, and offer alternative perspectives on the target behavior.

- Ambivalence

  The concept of ambivalence, feeling two ways about changing a behavior, underscores the fact that people who confront the need to change their behavior often have conflicting feelings. They see benefits and costs associated with both changing their behavior and not doing so. This decisional conflict can leave them stuck in a state in which they are unable to change despite recognizing that there are good reasons to do so.

MI has been extended to a wide range of health behaviors, particularly in medical settings. More than 200 clinical trials and several meta-analyses of MI efficacy have been published. These have largely reported success in motivating change in a variety of target behaviors, including cardiovascular rehabilitation, diabetes management, dietary change, hypertension, infection risk reduction, management of chronic mental disorders, as well as overall adherence to prescribed treatment regimens (see Lundahl and others, 2013).

Not all trials have been positive, however, and null findings for MI have been reported, for example, with eating disorders (Treasure et al., 1998), drug abuse and dependence (Winhusen and others, 2008), smoking (Baker and others, 2006), and problem drinking (Kuchipudi, Hobein, Flinkinger, & Iber, 1990). The efficacy of MI also can vary across populations. One meta-analysis, for instance, reported that MI was significantly more effective when the recipients were predominantly from minority populations, as compared with European-Americans (Hettema, Steele, & Miller, 2005).

The Internet and the Patient–Provider Relationship

In recent years, the Internet has become a major vehicle for health care. Surveys of users indicate that most believe the Internet has made them better consumers of health information. In one survey, nearly half had urged a family member or friend to visit a doctor, changed their exercise or eating habits, or made a treatment decision for themselves as a result of their cyber search (Hughes & Wareham, 2010). Patients who access authoritative medical information also visit emergency rooms and doctors' offices less frequently, cutting health care costs (Landro, 2001).

Telemedicine and *e-health services* are now part of every health care provider's training. With this approach, many physicians use information technologies to provide clinical care at a distance for minor health problems such as common low back pain, upper respiratory infections, and urinary infections (Koutras, Bitsaki, Koutras, Nikolaou, & Heep, 2015). Using patients' test results from reliable home monitoring equipment, uploaded to sites that provide two-way video and audio communication, physicians prescribe and adjust doses of drugs, consult with other health care providers, send laboratory reports, and refer patients to other providers. Increasingly, health care professionals are expected to offer these services, and health insurers will cover them just as they cover medication, surgery, and other medical elements.

Some experts caution, however, that the patient–provider relationship may change for the worse in the wake of enhanced electronic communication, greater access to health and medical information online, and other changes in technology. E-mail or text message exchanges can be impersonal and mechanical and may not communicate emotional tone and context accurately. Nonverbal cues available during a face-to-face consultation may be lost with online care. However, more positive changes from advancing technologies such as VSee—which enables secure, encrypted video conferencing compliant with patient privacy laws—are already being seen in the area of telemedicine, which is especially valuable for people in remote areas (Tsuboi, 2013).

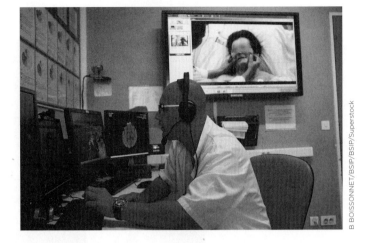

B. BOISSONNET/BSIP/BSIP/Superstock

Telemedicine: Making New Connections In addition to physicians and patients using e-mail for basic communications, advances in technology are providing greater access to health care, especially for people in remote areas. This American cardiologist is using video technology to help a doctor and his patient in Manila, Philippines, where comparable equipment and expertise are not typically available.

The Health Care System

The World Health Organization (WHO) defines a health care system as "all activities whose primary purpose is to promote, restore, or maintain health" (WHO, 2006). Hospitals play an important role in the health care system by offering a range of diagnostic and curative services. How these services are implemented varies considerably from one country to another. In this section, we take a look at the impact of hospitalization on patients, variations in how health care is delivered around the world, and the factors driving the health care reform movement today.

telemedicine The delivery of medical information and clinical services through interactive audiovisual media.

Hospitalization

Although the word *hospital* comes from the same root as the word *hospitality*, many patients don't find hospitals to be very hospitable places. More than 36 million people are admitted each year to the approximately 5700 registered hospitals in the United States (American Hospital Association, 2013), and too many of those people experience problems such as the staff providing them with conflicting information and tests and procedures not being done on time. Furthermore, hospitalization is not as safe as it should be. Globally, millions of people die each year from medical errors and infections linked to health care (Nebehay, 2011). According to the WHO, going to the hospital is far riskier

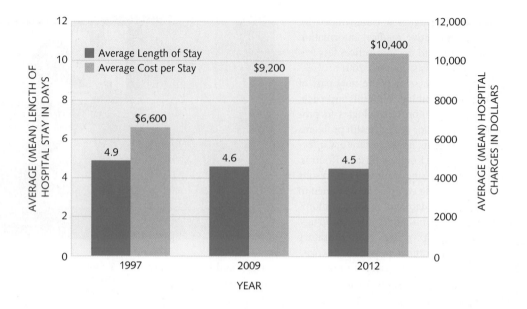

FIGURE 13.5

Average Cost of Hospitalization and Length of Stay Between 1997 and 2012, the average number of days for a hospital stay in the United States decreased slightly, while the average cost per stay increased dramatically. The typical costs of hospitalization include nursing care, medications, diagnostic tests, and food.

Data from Stranges, E., Kowlessar, N., & Elixhauser, A. (2011). Components of growth in inpatient hospital costs, 1997–2009. HCUP Statistical Brief no. 123. Rockville, MD: Agency for Health Care Research and Quality. http://www.hcup-us.ahrq.gov/reports/statbriefs/sb123.pdf; and Weiss, A. J., & Elixhauser, A. (2014). Overview of hospital stays in the United States, 2012. Healthcare Cost and Utilization Project. Statistical Brief No. 180. *Agency for Healthcare Research and Quality.* http://www.hcup-us.ahrq.gov/reports/statbriefs/sb180-Hospitalizations-United-States-2012.pdf.

In 2012, the average hospital stay was 4.5 days, down from 7.3 days in 1980. An increase in same-day surgery, new drug therapies, and cost-management controls account for the shorter average stay.

than flying (Nebehay, 2011). As Figure 13.5 shows, while the cost of a typical hospital stay increased significantly between 1997 and 2012, the average length of stay decreased.

Historically, the psychological well-being of the patient has not been a primary goal of health care. Rather, its goals were to bring together all the necessary medical staff and equipment to cure people who are seriously ill in the most efficient way possible. In fact, surveys from around the world consistently reveal that the single greatest stressor for health care providers is being behind schedule. This need for efficiency has prompted a somewhat one-dimensional, depersonalized view of hospitalized patients.

Loss of Control and Depersonalization

Upon entering the hospital, patients are expected to conform to the rules of the hospital, including its schedule for eating, sleeping, and receiving visitors, and to make their bodies available for examination and treatment whenever necessary. Throughout their hospitalization, patients are expected to remain cooperative, which often leads to passivity and feeling a loss of control.

Patients also often are treated as little more than bodies to be medicated, watched, and managed. Being referred to as "the appendectomy in Room 617" highlights the concept that nearly every aspect of a patient's identity disappears upon entering the hospital. Sometimes this *depersonalization* is so complete that hospital staff converse among themselves about the patient in his or her presence, using medical jargon that excludes the patient. Although medical terminology was designed to allow physicians and nurses to telegraph their conversations to convey a great deal of information quickly, when health providers use it without translation, most patients are left feeling both helpless and anxious (Weitz, 2007).

A need for efficiency is only partly to blame for this depersonalized care. There is also a need to reduce the daily stress of the hospital environment. Hospital staff may attempt to distance themselves emotionally as a way to cope with the pressures of making life-or-death decisions, working in an environment with hazardous chemicals, being exposed to contagious illnesses, and treating patients who may not respond to care or who may die. Excessive waiting, communication problems, and being treated impersonally combine with other aspects of hospitalization to make it a stressful experience for many patients (Weingart and others, 2006).

Preparing for Hospitalization

Facing surgery, chemotherapy, and many other invasive procedures is especially daunting because it means confronting our vulnerability and mortality. Surgeons and anesthesiologists have an old saying: "The way a patient enters anesthesia is the way he or she will come out of it." In other words, patients who approach treatment with an optimistic demeanor, confidence, and a sense of being in control often do better after treatment than do highly anxious people who feel helpless and overwhelmed by the situation. For this reason, psychological interventions are increasingly used to prepare patients for stressful medical procedures, with the most effective interventions being those that increase patients' sense of control over their treatment and recovery. Although interventions often overlap in the types of control that they emphasize, most can be categorized as primarily promoting increased informational, cognitive, or behavioral control.

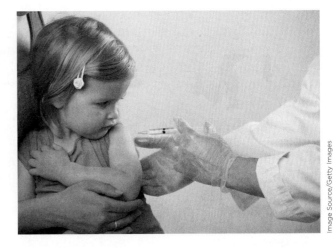

Children and Medical Procedures To get children to undergo difficult or "scary" medical procedures, parents, nurses, and doctors should understand how the child appraises such situations. The parent and nurse shown here are working together to keep the child calm and focused.

Increasing Informational Control **Informational control** interventions focus on the particular procedures and physical sensations that accompany a medical treatment. One of the first psychologists to study the role of informational control in hospitalized patients was Irving Janis, who in 1958 studied fear levels in patients before and after surgery. Following a presurgery intervention, Janis categorized the patients according to the amount of fear, anxiety, and feelings of vulnerability that they reported. After the surgery, Janis reinterviewed the patients to learn how well they had understood and followed the presurgery coping information that they had received and to assess their postoperative emotional mood. The results showed that patients who displayed moderate levels of fear had the fewest postoperative emotional problems, possibly because their concern was appropriate and allowed them to gather information and develop optimal defenses and coping strategies. Patients who were extremely fearful or nonfearful did not ask questions or gather information to prepare for the procedure and thus were poorly equipped to cope with the pain or discomfort that followed the procedure.

informational control Patients' knowledge regarding the particular procedures and physical sensations that accompany a medical treatment.

In a follow-up study, Janis examined the impact of a simple presurgery intervention on the recovery progress of patients. Patients were given information about possible unpleasant symptoms that they might experience following surgery. Compared with a control group of patients who were given little information, the patients in the prepared group requested less pain medication, made fewer demands on the hospital staff, recovered faster, and reported greater satisfaction with their surgeon and the hospital staff than those who were not given the additional information (Janis, 1958).

Since Janis's pioneering studies, many others have conducted research to determine the type of information that is most helpful to patients. Imagine that you are in the hospital for a minor operation that, although not dangerous, is likely to be followed by a painful recovery. What type of information would you want? Would you want a detailed description of the medical steps to be followed before, during, and after the surgery (procedural information); or would you like to know how you can expect to feel before, during, and after surgery (sensory information)? Sensory information allows you to make an accurate attribution for sensations that you actually experience. If you are told, for example, that it is customary to feel nauseated for a few days following a particular medical procedure, you will not be surprised when you actually do feel sick to your stomach. More important, armed with accurate information beforehand, you will not worry when the symptom appears. Unprepared, however, you might fear that your nausea is a sign that something has gone wrong and that you are not recovering properly. Procedural information, on the other hand, may reduce stress by giving patients an increased sense of control over what

BURGER/PHANIE/Science Source

Preparing for Hospitalization
Patients who approach hospitalization with an optimistic demeanor and a sense of being in control often do better after treatment than do people who feel helpless and overwhelmed by the situation.

cognitive control Interventions that direct the patient's attention to the positive aspects of a procedure (such as improved health) rather than to feelings of discomfort.

behavioral control Interventions that teach techniques for controlling pain and speeding recovery during and after a medical procedure.

their bodies are experiencing. When procedures are expected and predictable, many patients develop greater confidence and become more relaxed.

The results of studies comparing the advantages of procedural and sensory information have been mixed, possibly due to differences in the way researchers define improvement. In a large-scale meta-analysis, researchers reported that although procedural information and sensory information are both beneficial, procedural information appears to help the greatest number of patients (Cordasco, 2013; Johnson & Vogele, 1993). In many instances, of course, providing both types of information produces the maximum benefits.

Interestingly, researchers have found that a patient's reaction to procedural or sensory information regarding a stressful medical procedure depends, in part, on his or her style of coping. As might be expected, sensitizers tend to deal with stressful medical procedures with constant vigilance and anxious monitoring of the cues of discomfort, while repressors deny stress, actively suppress stressful thoughts, and do not appear to be anxious. Researchers have also discovered that sensitizers welcome as much detailed information as they can get, while repressors prefer to know as little as possible.

Cognitive-Behavioral Interventions Health psychologists, behavioral consultants, and other collaborative care providers increasingly use cognitive behavioral therapy (CBT) to help patients cope with anxiety and depression, as well as to help them prepare for surgery and other medical procedures. Aimed at improving **cognitive control,** CBT directs the patient's attention to the positive aspects of a procedure (such as improved health) rather than to feelings of discomfort. *Modeling*—learning by watching others—is a widely used intervention for increasing cognitive control. In one study, researchers showed dental patients a videotape of a nervous dental patient who reduced his anxiety by learning to relax and communicate more effectively with the dentist (Law, Logan, and Baron, 1994). Patients with a self-reported need for control, who generally felt helpless during dental treatment, had the most beneficial response to the modeling intervention. Compared with control subjects and those with a lower need for control, these patients reported significantly lower levels of pain, anxiety, and stress.

A number of controversial cognitive control interventions incorporate *guided imagery,* in which patients rehearse instructions for mentally influencing the perception of pain, as well as their blood flow, immune function, and other "involuntary" processes that may influence their recovery. Although traditional Western medicine has considered these processes to be outside voluntary control, the growing body of psychoneuroimmunology research suggests that people can learn to alter them somewhat and thus improve their chances for a speedy recovery (Vedhara & Irwin, 2005; Pert, Dreher, & Ruff, 1998).

CBT interventions encourage patients to redefine their role—from that of an immobile body being operated on to that of an active participant. They also aim at improving patients' **behavioral control** by teaching techniques for controlling pain and speeding recovery during and after a medical procedure. These might include relaxation instructions, breathing exercises, and other techniques to reduce discomfort or speed recovery during or after a stressful medical procedure. Such interventions may provide patients with an even greater sense of control because they focus on actual tools to influence how they are feeling.

In a classic study by anesthesiologist Larry Egbert and his colleagues (Egbert, Battit, Welch, & Bartlett, 1964), 46 patients awaiting abdominal surgery were told that they could relieve their postsurgical pain by relaxing the muscles surrounding the site of their incision. They also were given breathing exercises to reduce pain. Remarkably, these patients requested lower doses of morphine for pain relief during the days after their surgery and were discharged earlier than a control group of patients who did not participate in a behavioral control intervention.

Lamaze training, which is designed to prepare prospective parents for natural childbirth, is perhaps the most widely used intervention aimed at improving behavioral control. At the heart of the Lamaze technique is relaxation training that enhances the prospective mother's behavioral control over breathing and the muscles of the uterus, which push the baby out. Delivering mothers who are afraid tend to counteract the natural, rhythmic contractions of childbirth by tightening their muscles, which lengthens labor and makes it more painful. Cross-cultural research reveals that women in cultures in which childbirth is anticipated with less fear and apprehension generally report shorter, less painful deliveries, indicating that inadequate psychological preparation may play a role in the difficulty that some mothers experience during labor (Wong, 2009).

Interventions aimed at increasing behavioral control are most beneficial for medical procedures in which the patient's participation can assist progress. In delivering a baby, for example, the mother-to-be clearly *can* do something to make things run more smoothly. Conversely, behavioral control interventions may be useless when medical procedures require that the patient remain still and passive. For example, cardiac catheterization and dental surgery both require that patients be inactive. There is little that the patient can do to make the procedures more pleasant or to assist the health care providers.

CBT has been successfully employed with patients waiting for many different medical procedures (Auerbach, Penberthy, & Kiesler, 2004), including coronary artery bypass graft surgery (CABG). In a recent study, a diverse group of 100 patients awaiting CABG were assigned randomly to either a treatment-as-usual (TAU) group or a CBT intervention group. Patients in the intervention group participated in four 60-minute treatment sessions, administered by psychologists and focused on education and enhancing cognitive and behavioral control. Table 13.1 provides an overview of the four sessions of CBT. Measures of both physical and mental health were administered to both groups one week before their surgery and again during a follow-up appointment with their health care team three to four weeks afterward.

The results showed that CBT had beneficial effects on all outcome measures. Patients in the TAU group stayed longer in the hospital than did those in the CBT group (9.2 days

Lamaze training A natural childbirth process designed to prepare prospective parents by enhancing their informational, cognitive, and behavioral control over childbirth.

TABLE 13.1

Overview of Cognitive Behavioral Therapy

Session Number	Duration (minutes)	When	Content
1	60	Before surgery	Overview of intervention Education about cardiovascular disease, surgery, depression, anxiety Overview of patient concerns
2	60	Before surgery	Review behavioral goals Introduce cognitive strategies
3	60	Three days after surgery	Review cognitive strategies Review cognitive distortions Continue to support and encourage
4	60	Five days after surgery	Review strategies Generate plan for continued change Continue to support and encourage

Information from Dao, T. K., Nagy, A. Y., Armsworth, M., Wear, E., Papathopoulos, K. N., & Gopaldas, R. (2011). Randomized controlled trial of brief cognitive behavioral intervention for depression and anxiety symptoms preoperatively in patients undergoing coronary artery bypass graft surgery. Journal of Thoracic and Cardiovascular Surgery, 142(3), e109–e115.

compared to 7.9 days). In addition, symptoms of depression in the TAU group increased at the time of their release from the hospital, whereas patients in the intervention group had decreased symptoms of depression at the time of discharge. Finally, patients in the CBT group had greater improvements in self-reported anxiety and quality of life at the follow-up than did those in the control group (Dao and others, 2011).

Health Care Around the World

Organized health systems barely existed anywhere in the world a century ago. Until well into the nineteenth century, hospitals were little more than homes for the orphaned, crippled, destitute, or insane, but several discoveries made later that same century sparked the development of organized public health measures and eventually led to the creation of the first organized health care delivery systems. Among them was the need to combat and prevent diseases in the workforce. Once it was realized that malaria and yellow fever were transmitted by mosquitoes (as occurred during the construction of the Panama Canal), for instance, control of breeding sites became part of prevention efforts, as did providing clean water and basic living conditions for workers. Another discovery that had an impact was that soldiers who fought in combat (including those who fought in the Civil War) were more likely to be killed by disease than by the enemy.

In both rich and poor countries, health care needs differ greatly from those that existed 100 or even 50 years ago. Expectations of access to some form of health care continue to increase, as do demands for measures to protect individuals against the financial cost of poor health. People today also turn to health care systems for a much more diverse array of problems than ever before—not just pain relief or a specified medical treatment, but also information on nutrition, substance abuse, child-rearing, mental health, and countless other issues.

nurse-practitioner An advanced-practice nurse who, in addition to training in traditional nursing, received training in the delivery of primary health care.

physician assistant (PA) A graduate of a year training program that teaches how to practice medicine under the direction of physicians and surgeons.

Although physicians are the main providers of health care, other professionals are increasingly involved. **Nurse-practitioners** have completed graduate training programs in *advanced-practice nursing*, as well as training in primary care. They often work with physicians in private practice, seeing their own patients and providing all routine medical care, including prescribing treatments for various illnesses and conditions. **Physician assistants (PAs)** perform many of the routine tasks involved in health care, including taking medical histories, conducting physical examinations, ordering and interpreting diagnostic tests, and prescribing medications. PAs often take the same classes as medical students in their first year of training, after which they embark on a second year of training spent in clinical rotations with direct patient contact.

The patient–provider relationship is a crucial factor in how effective and satisfying the care is. It does not matter who provides health care—a nurse, physician, or PA. It also does not matter how the care is financially covered—fee-for-service, health maintenance organization or other forms of managed care, or a national health insurance system, as provided by most European countries, Canada, and Japan.

Global Health Care

Health care delivery systems around the world are modeled to varying degrees on one or more of a few basic designs that emerged and have been refined since the late nineteenth century: *national health service, national health insurance, "pay-as-you-go,"* and *pluralistic* health care (Skolnik, 2016; Reid, 2010; Roemer, 1993). Let's take a brief look at each (Table 13.2).

The national health service model is characterized by universal coverage, tax-based financing, and government ownership. Also called a *single-provider system*, this type of health care is based on the ideas of William Beveridge, a daring social reformer who in 1948 designed the National Health Service in the United Kingdom after the country's health infrastructure was destroyed by war. In this system, health care is provided and financed by the government through tax payments, just like a police force or the public

TABLE 13.2

Characteristics of Health Care Delivery Systems

System Type	Financing	Ownership	Private Insurance?
Single provider (United Kingdom, Italy, Spain, New Zealand, Greece, Portugal, Norway, Sweden, Denmark, Finland, Ireland)	General taxation, central (United Kingdom) or local/regional (Scandinavia) government	Public	Yes
National health insurance/ single-payer (Canada, South Korea, Taiwan)	General taxation, central and/or regional government	Mixed public and private	No
Social insurance (France, Germany, Holland, Switzerland, Belgium, Luxembourg, Japan)	Mandated social insurance, typically funded by payroll taxes	Mixed public and private	Yes
Pay-as-you-go (developing countries)	Out of pocket	Mixed public and private	Yes
Pluralistic (United States, Australia, Singapore)	Mixed	Mixed public and private	Yes

Source: Matthews, R. B., Jenkins, G. K., & Robertson, J. (2012). Health care reform: Why not best practices? *American Journal of Health Sciences, 3*(1), 97–113.

library in a community. This may be done at the national level (as in the United Kingdom) or the regional/local level (as in many Scandinavian countries). Many hospitals and clinics, but not all, are owned by the government, and some doctors are government employees. There is often a private health care option, serviced by private doctors who collect their fees from the government. National health systems have low costs per capita because the government, as the sole payer, controls what doctors can do and what they can charge. Countries that follow a national health service model include Italy, Spain, Norway, Portugal, Greece, the United Kingdom, Ireland, Sweden, Finland, Denmark, and New Zealand. A variant of the single-provider model, called a *single-payer system*, follows the national health insurance model, except that private-sector health care providers are paid directly by a universal, government-run insurance program. Canada, South Korea, and Taiwan have single-payer health care systems.

The national health insurance (NHS) model is characterized by compulsory universal coverage paid for jointly by employers and employees through payroll deductions. This system uses multiple payers (numerous insurance funds that may be government or privately owned) and multiple providers (generally, private doctors and privately owned hospitals). The joint financing of health care by employers and employees and the risk-sharing nature of insurance pools are the advantages of this model. Participants generally have the right to supplement the basic insurance by purchasing policies from private insurers. People do so, for instance, if they prefer not to wait for NHS treatment, or they want to be covered for services they can't get on the NHS (such as specialist treatment for sports-related injuries). In France, for example, which has the most highly ranked health care system in the world, over 99 percent of the population is covered by at least the basic level of insurance. Other countries that follow this model include Canada, Germany, and Japan.

Under the Canada Health Act, the country's health care system is built around the principle that all citizens have access to "medically necessary hospital and physician services on a prepaid basis" (Health Canada, 2016). To accomplish this, each of Canada's 10 provinces and three territories runs its own health insurance plan, all of which share common features and basic standards of coverage.

The pay-as-you-go, or **fee-for-service,** model is characterized by individual purchase of health care at the time of treatment. In most developing countries (approximately

fee-for-service A payment model in which health care services are paid for by patients out of pocket at the time of treatment.

health maintenance organization (HMO) An organization that provides managed care, in which individuals pay a fixed monthly rate and use services as needed.

managed care A system of health care in which health insurance plans contract with providers and medical facilities to provide care for members at reduced rates.

preferred-provider organization (PPO) A managed-care network of physicians, hospitals, and other health care providers that agree to charge preestablished rates for specific services.

patient-centered health care The delivery of health care services that are respectful of and responsive to individual patient preferences, needs, and values.

Japanese Care Japan enjoys high-quality health care, such as the rehabilitation services shown here, for much less than the United States spends. In 2009, Japan spent less than 9 percent of its gross domestic product (GDP) on health care, compared with 17 percent in the United States. Japan has mandatory health insurance coverage for all its citizens. By contrast, recent estimates suggest, over 40 million Americans are completely uninsured.

imagenav/Getty Images

160 countries out of 200), access to a doctor is available if and only if you can pay the bill out of pocket at the time of treatment. The main drawback of this model is its inequitable distribution of resources. In this type of system, it is often only the rich who get medical care. The poor stay sick or die. Only 40 or so of the industrialized, developed countries of the world have established health care systems that fall into the national health service or mandated insurance category. In remote regions of Africa, China, India, and South America, many people go their whole lives without ever seeing a licensed, conventional doctor.

The United States and several other countries (such as Australia and Singapore) are pluralistic systems that combine two or more of these approaches to health care. Until just a few decades ago, most Americans received their health care from private physicians, whom they paid directly at the time of treatment. Today, however, more than 70 million Americans receive their care through a **health maintenance organization (HMO),** a prepaid delivery system in which an employer or employee pays a monthly rate and the individual is allowed to use health services at no additional (or greatly reduced) cost. In a variation of this type of **managed care,** called a **preferred-provider organization (PPO),** a network of health care providers charges fixed rates for specific services.

The health care system of the United States traditionally has been a unique mixture of public, private nonprofit, and private for-profit hospitals, in which most physicians were compensated on a fee-for-service basis. Their compensation has come from a variety of sources—sometimes from insurance companies, sometimes directly from patients, and sometimes from government programs such as Medicare (for the elderly), Medicaid (for the poor), and the Veterans Administration. The health care system in the United States is unlike that of any other country because it maintains so many separate systems for different groups of people and is a combination of several approaches. When it comes to treating Americans over age 65, who are on Medicare, the single-payer system is like that of Canada. For working Americans who have insurance on the job, the system is much like the social insurance system found in Germany. For military veterans, health care in the United States is a single-provider system that is much like that in Cuba or the United Kingdom. Finally, for those who have no health insurance and earn too much to be eligible for Medicaid, American health care is like that in rural India, with access available only to those who can pay out of pocket or who are sick enough to be admitted to the emergency department at a public hospital (R. B. Matthews, Jenkins, & Robertson, 2012).

Patient Dissatisfaction, Patient-Centered Care, and Health Care Reform

Spiraling health care costs, medical errors, and patient dissatisfaction are major factors in why health care in the United States is changing. Most importantly, the role of the physician is changing. New delivery systems under managed care and the increasing number of women in the medical profession have changed the role of the doctor from what was once an authoritarian, paternalistic arrangement to one that is patient-centered and more characterized by shared responsibility.

In **patient-centered health care,** patients become active participants in their own care and receive services designed to focus on their individual needs and preferences. Working with the American Academy of Family Physicians, the Roper and Harris organizations surveyed a large sample of patients, asking them to grade the importance of 40 attributes in physicians. Table 13.3 lists the top 10 things people want from their health care providers (AFP, 2004). These data show that doctors' training and knowledge of new medical treatments are less important to many patients than their ability to center their care

TABLE 13.3

Top 10 Things People Want from Their Health Care Providers

1. To be treated with dignity and respect
2. To listen carefully to their concerns and questions
3. To be easy to talk to
4. To take their concerns seriously
5. To be willing to spend enough time with them
6. To truly care about them and their health
7. To have good medical judgment
8. To ask good questions in order to understand their needs
9. To be up-to-date with the latest research
10. To see them on short notice, if needed

Information from: Hsiao, W. C. (1996). A framework for assessing health financing strategies and the role of health insurance. In D. W. Dunlop & J. M. Martins (Eds.), *An international assessment of health care financing: Lessons for developing countries* (EDI Seminar). Washington, DC: World Bank Publications, pp. 15–29 (Table 2-1, p. 18); and Matthews, R. B., Jenkins, G. K., & Robertson, J. (2012). Health care reform: Why not best practices? *American Journal of Health Sciences, 3*(1), 101.

on patients and their individual needs. So it's not surprising that one of the Institute of Medicine's six aims for twenty-first-century health care—as issued in its landmark report *Crossing the Quality Chasm*—is that it be centered around the patient.

The passage of the Affordable Care Act (ACA) in 2010 brought about significant changes in how health care is paid for and provided in the United States. Supporters of ACA frequently cited a 2000 World Health Organization comparison of global health care delivery systems in which American health care ranked only 37th among 191 member countries in its overall performance. Among the countries with the best overall health care were France, Italy, Japan, Canada, and the United Kingdom—all countries with national health systems. Skeptics of ACA, who generally label the act "Obamacare," express concerns about whether its goals are feasible, whether its reforms represent a step backward instead of forward, and whether a single-payer or single-provider system is desirable or achievable (R. B. Matthews and others, 2012).

A major part of health care reform under the ACA are **accountable care organizations (ACOs),** in which groups of doctors, hospitals, and other health care providers come together to give coordinated, evidence-based care to their patients. The goal of this type of care is to ensure that patients receive high-quality and cost-effective care while avoiding the unnecessary duplication of services that often occurs when health care is not coordinated among primary care doctors, specialists, and other providers. Another key feature of ACOs is *accountability,* which is evaluated by ACOs using quality metrics to measure health care delivery processes. Designed to reduce medical errors, these measurements now include such statistics as the percentage of doctors in an ACO who use electronic prescriptions and patient medical records and the percentage of patients who receive screenings, vaccinations, and counseling about health risks (Meisel & Pines, 2011).

The core principles of ACA include (Kaiser Foundation, 2012):

■ *Individual mandate.* Since the beginning of 2014, people who are not covered by Medicare or Medicaid are required to have health insurance or pay a penalty. In addition, insurance companies no longer are allowed to deny coverage to individuals who have preexisting conditions, to impose lifetime limits on benefits, or to cancel coverage when a person gets sick.

■ *Affordable coverage.* Under the ACA, lower- and some middle-income individuals and families receive financial assistance to help purchase health insurance. In addition, insurance companies are now required to report each year on the number of dollars

accountable care organization (ACO) An organization of health care providers that agrees to be accountable for the quality, cost, and overall care of members.

paid into the system as insurance premiums that were spent on actual medical care and provide rebates to their customers when this number is less than 80 percent.

- *Employer requirements.* There is no employer mandate to provide health care to all workers in the ACA, but those with more than 50 employees will be assessed a fee of $2000 per full-time employee if they do not offer coverage. A new tax credit for employers at smaller-sized companies is designed to encourage them to provide health care to their employees.

- *Coverage for preventive health services.* New group and individual insurance plans are required to pay for certain screenings, immunizations, and other preventive care so that patients can get these services at no cost to themselves.

The research studies that we have discussed in this chapter provide substantial evidence that psychosocial factors strongly influence how people interact with the health care system. This includes how they interpret symptoms, whether they seek treatment (and how well they adhere to it), how they respond to hospitalization, and the quality of their relationships with health care providers. Today, health care around the world is under increasing pressure to become more accessible, accountable, and patient-centered. More than ever, health psychologists are valued members of health care teams.

Your Health Assets

Health Literacy

Health literacy—the ability to read, understand, and act on health information—is critical to good outcomes in health care. Patients with low health literacy may not fully adhere to treatment instructions from physicians and other providers. Identifying people who are at risk for low health literacy allows providers to tailor their communication to promote patients' understanding.

The *Newest Vital Sign* (NVS) is a 3-minute tool administered by health care providers to test patients' literacy skills for information printed on an ice cream label. The ability to read and analyze nutrition labels requires the same analytical and conceptual skills needed to understand and follow medical instructions.

In May 2016, the Food and Drug Administration announced new requirements for nutrition facts labels designed to make it easier for consumers to make better-informed food choices. These new stipulations include increasing the font size for "Calories," "Servings per container," and "Serving size," and boldfacing the number of calories and "Serving size" to highlight this information. In addition, product labels must disclose the actual amount, in addition to percent Daily Value of vitamin D, calcium, iron, and potassium.

Want to test your own literacy? Take a look at the label on the next page, which is on the back of a pint of ice cream. Then answer the questions below.

1. If you eat the entire container, how many calories will you eat?
2. If you are allowed to eat 60 grams of carbohydrates as a snack, how much ice cream could you have?

Is ice cream a healthy food choice? Food labels are an excellent place to test your own health literacy.

iStock/Getty Images

3. Your doctor advises you to reduce the amount of saturated fat in your diet. You usually have 42 grams of saturated fat each day, which includes one serving of ice cream. If you stop eating ice cream, how many grams of saturated fat would you be consuming each day?

4. If you usually eat 2500 calories in a day, what percentage of your daily value of calories will you be eating if you eat one serving?

For questions 5 and 6, pretend that you are allergic to the following substances: penicillin, peanuts, latex gloves, and bee stings.

5. Is it safe for you to eat this ice cream?

6. (Ask only if the patient responds "no" to question 5): Why not?

Correct Answers

1. 1000 is the correct answer.
2. Any of the following are correct: 1 cup (or any amount up to 1 cup); half the container. Note: If patient answers "two servings," ask "How much ice cream would that be if you were to measure it into a bowl?"
3. 33 is the only correct answer.
4. 10 percent is the only correct answer.
5. No.
6. It isn't safe because it has peanut oil.

Scoring

Give yourself 1 point for each correct answer (maximum 6 points).

- Score of 0–1 suggests high likelihood (50% or greater) of limited literacy.
- Score of 2–3 indicates the possibility of limited literacy.
- Score of 4–6 almost always indicates adequate literacy.

Health literacy is so important to good health care outcomes that experts recommend that the patient's NVS score should be entered on his or her medical chart, along with blood pressure, body mass index, and other vital signs.

Information from www.pfizerhealthliteracy.com

Nutrition Facts		
Serving Size		½ cup
Servings per container		4
Amount per serving		
Calories 250	Fat Cal	120
		%DV
Total Fat 13g		20%
Sat Fat 9g		40%
Cholestrerol 28mg		12%
Sodium 55mg		2%
Total Carbohydrate 30g		12%
Dietary Fiber 2g		
Sugars 23g		
Protein 4g		8%

*Percentage Daily Values (DV) are based on a 2,000 calorie diet. Your daily values may be higher or lower depending on your calorie needs.

Ingredients: Cream, Skim Milk, Liquid Sugar, Water, Egg Yolks, Brown Sugar, Milk Fat, Peanut Oil, Sugar, Butter, Salt, Carrageenan, Vanilla Extract.

Weigh In on Health

Respond to each question below based on what you learned in the chapter. (**Tip:** Use the items in "Summing Up" to take into account related biological, psychological, and social concerns.)

1. How have you or someone you know experienced illness? Using this chapter's discussions, explain the experience in terms of how you or the person you're thinking of were influenced psychologically and especially in terms of how symptoms were interpreted and reported.

2. Based on what you've read in this chapter, what are some biological, psychological, and social or cultural influences that affect how illnesses are treated and how people adhere to health care provider advice?

3. Why is communication such an important element in the provider–patient relationship? Support your answer with research discussed in this chapter.

4. Health psychologists participate in health care in a variety of settings, including primary care programs and hospitals, as well as specialized programs for pain management, rehabilitation, and other services. It has been said that no matter what setting they are working in, health psychologists must be experts in human relations. Why do you think this is so, and what kinds of training would be most helpful in preparing for this role?

Summing Up

Recognizing and Interpreting Symptoms

1. Detecting physical symptoms and interpreting their medical significance are influenced strongly by psychological processes, including the individual's personality, culture, gender, and psychological health, as well as by the individual's focus of attention and tendency to either monitor or repress health threats.

2. Sensitizers have a strong internal focus; they detect and report symptoms more quickly than repressors, who are more externally focused. Consequently, repressors are more likely to cope with distressing medical symptoms by distancing themselves from unpleasant information.

3. Illness representations regarding the type of disease, its causes, time frame, consequences, and controllability also influence how people react to and interpret physical symptoms.

Seeking Treatment

4. Social and demographic variables, such as cultural norms, age, gender, and socioeconomic status, influence whether a person seeks treatment.

5. Health services may be underused or overused. Delay behavior may result from a failure to notice symptoms (appraisal delay), refusal to believe that one is actually sick (illness delay) or needs professional help (behavioral delay), procrastination in making an appointment (scheduling delay), or belief that the benefits of seeking treatment are not worth the costs (treatment delay).

6. Some people may use health services when there is no real need because they are feigning illness (malingering) or falsely believe they have a disease when they do not (illness anxiety disorder). In others, bodily symptoms are an expression of emotional stress.

Patient Adherence

7. Adherence means closely following the advice of a health care provider, which less than half of patients do (nonadherence). Patient adherence improves with perceived control (for those who prefer control), optimism, a good mood, trust in the care provider, a strong patient–provider relationship, a simple and clearly explained treatment regimen, and social support.

The Patient–Provider Relationship

8. The central elements of the essential relationship between health care provider and patient are continuity of care, communication, and the overall quality of consultations. Poor communication between health care providers and patients is common, given the time pressures of health care and the fact that providers may lack communication skills. Other factors in miscommunication include the attitudes and beliefs that patients and providers have regarding their roles, as well as gender, cultural, and educational differences between providers and patients.

9. Discrimination and prejudice adversely affect minority populations and the health care system in general. Discrimination and prejudice may be based on differences due to race, ethnicity, age, ability, gender, religion, sexual orientation, or any other characteristic by which people differ.

10. A landmark report stated that institutional racism in the United States is an important factor in racial/ethnic differences in overall health due to differences in the quality of care members of minority groups receive. Historically, minorities have also been underrepresented in clinical trials.

11. During medical visits, health care providers are more verbally dominant and engage in less patient-centered communication with minority patients, and they are less likely to understand the cultural beliefs attached to certain health conditions. In response, minority patients are apt to perceive ineffective communication as a form of disrespect and unfair treatment, which may jeopardize their trust and strain their relationship with health care providers.

12. Patients with low health literacy are more likely to have difficulty navigating through the health care system, less likely to seek preventive care and adhere to prescribed treatment and self-care regimens, and more likely to make medication and treatment errors.

13. Communication-skills training is now a fundamental component of medical and nursing education. Motivational interviewing is a widely used counseling method that focuses on strengthening a person's motivation and commitment to change a target health behavior.

14. The quality of the patient–provider relationship may be challenged by enhanced electronic communication and greater access to Internet health and medical information. The burgeoning field of telemedicine, however, has improved health care greatly in remote locations.

The Health Care System

15. One of the most persistent problems of hospitals is the depersonalization of patients as a result of a need for efficiency and the need of hospital staff to distance themselves emotionally from their stressful daily experiences.

16. Cognitive behavioral therapy (CBT) and other interventions often improve adjustment to hospitalization and to stressful medical procedures. The benefits of preparatory information, relaxation training, modeling, and guided imagery training all have been documented.

17. Although physicians are the main providers of health care, nurse-practitioners, physician assistants, and other professionals are increasingly involved in providing all routine

medical care, including prescribing treatments for various illness and conditions.

18. Health care delivery systems around the world are modeled to varying degrees on one or more of a few basic designs that emerged and have been refined since the late nineteenth century: *single-provider, single-payer, mandated insurance,* and *fee-for-service* health care. The United States and several other countries are pluralistic systems that combine two or more of these approaches to health care.

19. Increasing health care costs, medical errors, and patient dissatisfaction are major factors in why health care in the United States is changing. In patient-centered health care, patients become active participants in their own care and receive services designed to focus on their individual needs and preferences.

20. A major part of health care reform under the Affordable Care Act (ACA) are accountable care organizations (ACOs), in which groups of doctors, hospitals, and other health care providers come together to give coordinated, evidence-based care to their patients.

21. A key feature of ACOs is *accountability,* which is evaluated with quality metrics to measure health care delivery processes.

Key Terms and Concepts to Remember

collaborative care, p. 376
attentional focus, p. 377
sensitizers, p. 377
repressors, p. 377
illness representation, p. 377
comorbidity, p. 378
lay referral system, p. 382
delay behavior, p. 382
illness anxiety disorder, p. 383
malingering, p. 383
chronic fatigue syndrome (CFS),
    p. 384

adherence, p. 385
nonadherence, p. 385
health literacy, p. 390
motivational interviewing (MI),
    p. 392
telemedicine, p. 393
informational control, p. 395
cognitive control, p. 396
behavioral control, p. 396
Lamaze training, p. 397
nurse-practitioner, p. 398
physician assistant (PA), p. 398

fee-for-service, p. 399
health maintenance organization
    (HMO), p. 400
managed care, p. 400
preferred-provider organization
    (PPO), p. 400
patient-centered health care,
    p. 400
accountable care organization
    (ACO), p. 401

LaunchPad
macmillan learning

To accompany your textbook, you have access to a number of online resources, including quizzes for every chapter of the book, flashcards, critical thinking exercises, videos, and *Check Your Health* inventories. To access these resources, please visit the Straub *Health Psychology* LaunchPad solo at: **launchpadworks.com**

E+/Getty Images

CHAPTER 14   Managing Pain

During the 1932 Los Angeles Olympics, the Japanese gymnastics team finished dead last—a humiliating defeat that triggered a national mission to become an international gymnastics power. When the games resumed following World War II, the Japanese gymnasts did improve their performance, and their mission was finally fulfilled, as the Japanese team won the gold medal in four consecutive Olympics: Rome, Tokyo, Mexico City, and Munich. In their attempt at a fifth straight title at the 1976 Montreal Games, however, Shun Fujimoto, their star competitor, broke his kneecap while performing the floor exercise. Remarkably, he didn't disclose the injury to his coaches or teammates. "I did not want to worry my teammates," he recalled. "The competition was so close, I didn't want them to lose their concentration with worry about me."

Blessed with incredible strength and a nearly perfect gymnastics physique, Fujimoto was a fierce competitor and team leader whose buoyant spirit and national pride had rallied his teammates many times in previous competitions. But how could he continue? Although Olympic rules prohibited him from taking a painkiller, Fujimoto decided to stay in the competition and endure the excruciating pain. Fortunately, the next apparatus was the pommel horse—an event in which the knees are mostly locked in place. Unless he fell, the pain might be tolerable. Fujimoto completed a nearly flawless performance, receiving a score of 9.5 out of a possible 10.

The final event, however, would be much more demanding. The high rings test arm strength, but vital points can also be lost during the dismount, when the gymnast descends from a great height after a swinging routine that propels him onto the mat at high velocity. "I knew when I descended from the rings, it would be the most painful moment," Fujimoto remembered. "I also knew that if my posture was not good when I landed, I would not receive a good score. I must try to forget the pain."

After another nearly perfect routine, Fujimoto landed, smiled for the judges, held his position for the required few seconds, and then fell to the mat as his injured leg buckled beneath him. Incredibly, his near-perfect score of 9.7 was enough to propel his team to gold medal victory!

iological, psychological, and social factors contributed to Fujimoto's development as a gymnast, and those same factors played a role in his triumphant Olympic victory. The story also makes clear one of health psychology's most fundamental themes: that the mind and body are inextricably intertwined. Fujimoto's determination not to let his teammates down allowed him to endure a painful injury that in other circumstances most certainly would have been crippling.

The struggle to understand pain—what causes it and how to control it—is a central topic in health psychology. Until recently, however, researchers knew next to nothing about this common, yet extraordinarily complex, phenomenon. Moreover, medical schools did not spend much time covering the topic of pain. Over the past four decades, however, health psychologists have made considerable progress in filling in the gaps about the nature and treatment of pain.

In this chapter, we discuss the components of pain—the ways in which it is experienced; how it is measured; and the biological, psychological, and social factors that influence the experience of pain. Many instances of pain begin with physical injury or a disruption to the normal functioning of human systems, so we will explore technical details about the biology of pain and how it starts from a full biopsychosocial health perspective. And we will take a look at how pain is treated within medicine and at the latest multidimensional interventions introduced by health psychology.

What Is Pain?

ew topics in health psychology are as elusive as pain. Pain is obviously a physical sensation. Yet the pain of losing a loved one or ending a long-term relationship, which is more psychological than physical in nature, often feels just as real. And pain is highly subjective (and sometimes not altogether unpleasant). After a hard workout on the track, for example, I often feel fatigue that is definitely uncomfortable, yet somehow also warm and pleasant.

This chapter focuses on **clinical pain,** which is pain that requires some form of medical treatment. Let's begin by considering how many of us suffer pain and how often.

clinical pain Pain that requires some form of medical treatment.

Components of Pain Pain obviously has a strong physical component, as the face of this soccer player clearly reveals. It also has emotional and psychological components—his pain would probably be more bearable if his injury involved a kick that won the game for his team.

Epidemiology and Components of Pain

Pain is a major public health problem, affecting more than 1.5 billion people worldwide and an estimated 100 million Americans—more than the number affected by heart disease, cancer, and diabetes combined (American Academy of Pain Medicine, 2013). According to a recent report, pain is a significant public health problem that costs the United States around $600 billion annually, or about $2000 for every person living in the United States (Institute of Medicine, 2011b). Chronic pain affects at least 10 percent of the world's population, with prevalence estimates varying considerably in different regions and countries (Jackson, Stabile, & McQueen, 2014). In the United States, 25.3 million adults (11.2 percent) suffer from daily (chronic) pain (Nahin, 2015). Pain is the most common reason that people seek medical treatment and is so pervasive that now it is considered a fifth vital sign, along with blood pressure, pulse, temperature, and respiration. No other class of health problems even approaches this level of impact.

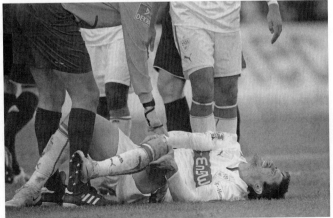

imageBroker/imageBroker/Superstock

Pain clearly illustrates the biopsychosocial model, which distinguishes among the biological mechanisms by which the body processes painful stimuli; the subjective, emotional experience of pain; and the social and behavioral factors that help shape our response to pain. For Shun Fujimoto, the gymnast highlighted at the start of this chapter, the biological mechanisms of his injury sparked an interplay of his emotions with his social perspective, based on principles of Japan's collectivist culture, which resulted in a triumphant performance despite the physical pain of a broken kneecap.

Significance and Types of Pain

Despite the discomfort and stress that it can cause, pain is essential to our survival. It can be bothersome, but it is that bothersome nature that makes it highly adaptive. Pain sounds a warning that something is wrong and alerts you to try to prevent further physical damage. In fact, if you did *not* feel pain, it would be hazardous to your health.

Types of Pain

acute pain Sharp, stinging pain that is short-lived and usually related to tissue damage.

recurrent pain Involves episodes of discomfort interspersed with periods in which the individual is relatively pain-free that recur for more than three months.

chronic pain Dull, burning pain that is long-lasting.

hyperalgesia A condition in which a chronic pain sufferer becomes more sensitive to pain over time.

In general, researchers divide pain into three broad categories: acute, recurrent, and chronic. **Acute pain** is sharp, stinging pain that is usually localized in an injured area of the body. It can last from a few seconds to several months and generally subsides as normal healing occurs. Examples include burns and fractures. **Recurrent pain** involves intermittent periods of discomfort that recur for more than three months (Gatchel & Maddrey, 2004). Periodic migraines and noncardiac chest pain, which is experienced by nearly 10 percent of school-age children (J. L. Lee and others, 2013; Veeram Reddy & Singh, 2010) fall into this category.

Chronic pain, which is traditionally defined as pain that lasts six months or longer—long past the normal healing period—may be continuous or intermittent, moderate or severe, and felt in just about any of the body's tissues (Turk & Okifuji, 2002). Chronic pain lowers overall quality of life and increases vulnerability to infection and thus to a host of diseases. Chronic pain also can take a devastating psychological toll, triggering lowered self-esteem, insomnia, anger, hopelessness, depression, personality disorders, and many other signs of distress.

Hyperalgesia

Those with chronic pain may become even more sensitive to pain, a condition known as **hyperalgesia.** Hyperalgesia also happens during sickness or injury and may facilitate recovery by stimulating recuperative behaviors. For example, the flu makes you weak and achy and drives you back to bed, which is exactly where you need to be to recover.

Painful Struggle Ashlyn Blocker's mother, shown here with Ashlyn (right) and her sister, struggles daily with Ashlyn's inability to sense pain, hot, and cold. "Pain's there for a reason. It lets your body know something's wrong and it needs to be fixed. I'd give anything for her to feel pain" (quoted in Bynum, 2004).

Hundreds of experiments over more than 100 years have confirmed that hyperalgesia often occurs as a normal adaptation during sickness. Most kinds of internal pain are accompanied by increased sensitivity in nearby tissues. In the 1890s, physiologists Henry Head and Mames MacKensie proposed that signals from diseased parts of the body set up an "irritable focus" in the central nervous system that creates areas of enhanced pain sensitivity in nearby, otherwise healthy, body parts, suggesting that the signals originate in the central nervous system. In *opioid-induced hyperalgesia*, long-term use of opioids leads to an increasing sensitivity to noxious stimuli, even to the point at which common sensory stimuli become painful (Angst & Clark, 2006). Researchers believe this sensitization occurs because of a long-lasting enhancement of neural impulses (*long-term potentiation*) among cells in the spinal cord that are involved in relaying pain messages to the brain (Drdla, Gassner, Gingl, & Sandkuhler, 2009).

Stephen Morton/AP Images

Measuring Pain

Because of its multidimensional and subjective nature, pain is not easily measured. Nevertheless, clinicians and researchers have developed a number of ways to assess pain: *physical measures, behavioral measures,* and *self-report measures.*

Physical Measures

There are no objective measures of pain, only subjective ones. It's not that clinicians and researchers haven't tried to find them. In fact, the problem of measuring pain set the stage for the very earliest *psychophysical studies* in the new field of psychology. These studies highlight the familiar *mind–body problem:* How does conscious awareness derive from and affect the physical sensations of the body?

One way to assess pain is to measure the specific physiological changes that accompany pain. For example, *electromyography* (EMG) assesses the amount of muscle tension experienced by patients suffering from headaches or lower back pain. Researchers have also recorded changes in heart rate, breathing rate, blood pressure, skin temperature, and skin conductance—all indicators of the *autonomic arousal* that may accompany pain. But these measures have not demonstrated any consistent differences between those with and those without a specific type of pain. This failure may well be because pain is only one of many factors that contribute to autonomic changes; others include diet, attention, activity level, stress, and the presence of illness.

Behavioral Measures

Another assessment technique measures signs of pain in a patient's behavior. Relatives and friends of the patient or health care professionals can do this in structured clinical sessions. Wilbert Fordyce (1982), a pioneer in pain research, developed a pain behavior-training program in which an observer is asked to monitor 5 to 10 behaviors—the amount of time the patient spends in bed and the number of requests for painkillers, for example—that frequently signal the onset of pain.

In clinical settings, nurses and other health professionals are trained to observe patients' pain behaviors systematically during routine care procedures. One frequently used pain inventory is the Pain Behavior Scale, which consists of a series of target behaviors, including verbal complaints, facial grimaces, awkward postures, and mobility (Feuerstein & Beattie, 1995). Observers rate the occurrence of each target behavior on a three-point scale: "frequent," "occasional," and "none."

More recently, the Pain Response Preference Questionnaire (PRPQ) has been used to assess the degree to which a range of potential pain-related responses are desired from a spouse or partner (McWilliams, Saldanha, Dick, & Watt, 2009). The PRPQ includes items that fall into four separate scales: *solicitude* ("treat me with extra care and concern"; "ask me about my pain"); *management* ("encourage me to rest"; "tell me to take it easy"); *encouragement* ("tell me I can do things despite pain"; "tell me to keep active"); and *suppression* ("help me ignore the pain"; "act like I'm not in pain") (McWilliams, Dick, Bailey, Verrier, & Kowal, 2012).

With children, there is growing consensus that measuring emotional responses to pain is a core outcome measure (McGrath and others, 2008). Fear in children is common and can increase the perception of pain (Mathews, 2011). Needle fears are particularly prevalent. Several scales have been developed to capture the dimensions of pain and fear in children, including the Children's Anxiety and Pain Scales (CAPS) and the Children's Fear Scale (CFS) (McMurtry, Noel, Chambers, & McGrath, 2011).

FIGURE 14.1

Basic Pain Scales A visual analog scale, such as the scale shown in (a), allows people to identify the intensity of their pain at the appropriate point on a continuum. For children ages 3 and over, seniors, and some other adults, using the Wong-Baker FACES Pain Rating Scale, the scale shown in (b), may be more helpful. (Instructions on the use of the latter scale are available from www.wongbakerfaces.org.)

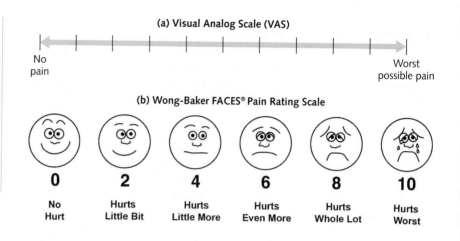

(a) Visual Analog Scale (VAS)

No pain — Worst possible pain

(b) Wong-Baker FACES® Pain Rating Scale

0	2	4	6	8	10
No Hurt	Hurts Little Bit	Hurts Little More	Hurts Even More	Hurts Whole Lot	Hurts Worst

Self-Report Measures

The simplest way to measure pain is to have people use a numeric rating scale (NRS) to assign a number—typically from 1 ("no pain") to 10 ("worst possible pain")—to describe their current discomfort level. Another widely used technique, the *visual analog scale* (VAS), has people locate the level of their pain at a point along a horizontal or vertical line that is about 10 centimeters in length and anchored by two extremes: "no pain," "worst possible pain" (Figure 14.1). The advantage of the VAS is that the scale is continuous and does not take discrete jumps from one level to the next. Patient and research participant reports using the VAS and NRS for assessment of pain intensity agree well and are equally sensitive. Both scales are more powerful in detecting changes in pain intensity than verbal rating scales in which people choose from a list the word that most accurately describes the pain (for example, "none," "mild," "moderate," and "severe") (Hjermstad and others, 2011).

Some years ago, pain research pioneer Ronald Melzack developed a system for categorizing pain along three dimensions (Melzack & Torgerson, 1971). The first dimension, *sensory quality,* highlighted the tremendous variations that occur in the sensation of pain. The second dimension, *affective quality,* focuses on the many different emotional reactions that pain can trigger. The final dimension is *evaluative quality,* which refers to the sufferer's judgment of the severity of the pain, as well as its meaning or significance. From this multidimensional model of pain, Melzack derived the McGill Pain Questionnaire (MPQ), which has become the most widely used pain inventory today (Figure 14.2).

The Physiology of Pain

You slip on an icy sidewalk and fall hard on your elbow. In the instant before you feel the pain, a cascade of biochemical and electrical reactions occurs. The processing of all sensory information begins when *sensory receptors* in your skin convert a physical stimulus into neural impulses. The pressure of striking the ground activates the receptors in your elbow, which stimulates the peripheral nervous system to relay the message to your brain. Only when the brain registers and interprets this neural input is pain experienced. What happens in between the stimulation of sensory receptors and the brain's interpretation has been the subject of a great deal of exciting research.

FIGURE 14.2
The McGill Pain Questionnaire

Part 1. <u>Where Is Your Pain?</u>

Please mark on the drawing below the areas where you feel pain. Put E if external or I if internal near the areas which you mark. Put EI if both external and internal.

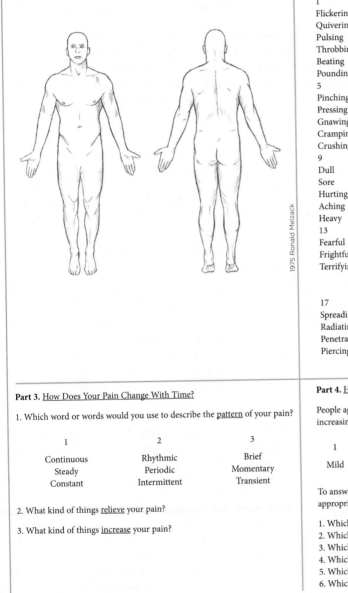

1975 Ronald Melzack

Part 2. <u>What Does Your Pain Feel Like?</u>

Some of the words below describe your <u>present</u> pain. Circle <u>ONLY</u> those words that best describe it. Leave out any category that is not suitable. Use only a single word in each appropriate category—the one that applies best.

1	2	3	4
Flickering	Jumping	Pricking	Sharp
Quivering	Flashing	Boring	Cutting
Pulsing	Shooting	Drilling	Lacerating
Throbbing		Stabbing	
Beating		Lancinating	
Pounding			

5	6	7	8
Pinching	Tugging	Hot	Tingling
Pressing	Pulling	Burning	Itchy
Gnawing	Wrenching	Scalding	Smarting
Cramping		Searing	Stinging
Crushing			

9	10	11	12
Dull	Tender	Tiring	Sickening
Sore	Taut	Exhausting	Suffocating
Hurting	Rasping		
Aching	Splitting		
Heavy			

13	14	15	16
Fearful	Punishing	Wretched	Annoying
Frightful	Grueling	Blinding	Troublesome
Terrifying	Cruel		Miserable
	Vicious		Intense
	Killing		Unbearable

17	18	19	20
Spreading	Tight	Cool	Nagging
Radiating	Numb	Cold	Nauseating
Penetrating	Drawing	Freezing	Agonizing
Piercing	Squeezing		Dreadful
	Tearing		Torturing

Part 3. <u>How Does Your Pain Change With Time?</u>

1. Which word or words would you use to describe the <u>pattern</u> of your pain?

1	2	3
Continuous	Rhythmic	Brief
Steady	Periodic	Momentary
Constant	Intermittent	Transient

2. What kind of things <u>relieve</u> your pain?

3. What kind of things <u>increase</u> your pain?

Part 4. <u>How Strong Is Your Pain?</u>

People agree that the following 5 words represent pain of increasing intensity. They are:

1	2	3	4	5
Mild	Discomforting	Distressing	Horrible	Excruciating

To answer each question below, write the number of the most appropriate word in the space beside the question.

1. Which word describes your pain right now? _____
2. Which word describes it at its worst? _____
3. Which word describes it when it is least? _____
4. Which word describes the worst toothache you ever had? _____
5. Which word describes the worst headache you ever had? _____
6. Which word describes the worst stomachache you ever had? _____

Pain Pathways

Pain is not triggered by only one type of stimulus—nor does it have a single type of receptor. Tissue injury isn't the only thing that will produce pain. The corneas of your eyes, for instance, are exquisitely sensitive. Almost any stimulus, from a speck of dust to the application of a bit too much pressure when inserting a contact lens, will be

free nerve endings Sensory receptors found throughout the body that respond to temperature, pressure, and painful stimuli.

nociceptor A specialized neuron that responds to painful stimuli.

fast nerve fibers Large, myelinated nerve fibers that transmit sharp, stinging pain.

slow nerve fibers Small, unmyelinated nerve fibers that carry dull, aching pain.

substantia gelatinosa The dorsal region of the spinal cord where both fast and slow pain fibers synapse with sensory nerves on their way to the brain.

experienced as pain, even though the cornea suffers no damage. All of these stimuli trigger the pain response in the brain through different receptors.

Pain Receptors

For more than a century, researchers have been on a quest to find the definitive sensory receptors for pain. Among the candidates are **free nerve endings,** which are found throughout the body: in the skin, muscles (cramps), internal organs of the viscera (stomachaches), membranes that surround joints and bones (arthritic pain), and even the pulp of teeth (toothaches).

Free nerve endings are simple, yet they are poorly understood. We know that they respond primarily to temperature change and pressure, and also to certain chemicals secreted in damaged tissues. However they are aroused, it appears that free nerve endings begin a process that ends when the brain registers and interprets the sensation as pain. For this reason, researchers refer to free nerve endings that are activated by *noxious* (painful) stimuli as **nociceptors.**

Fast and Slow Fibers

The pain process begins when neural signals from free nerve endings are routed to the central nervous system via *fast nerve fibers* and *slow nerve fibers.* **Fast nerve fibers** are relatively large, myelinated neurons that conduct neural impulses at about 15 to 30 meters per second. **Slow nerve fibers** are smaller, unmyelinated fibers that conduct electrical impulses at about 0.5 to 2 meters per second.

Fast and slow fibers are the messengers for two pain systems in the brain. The *fast pain system* (involving the fast nerve fibers) appears to serve only the skin and mucous membranes; the *slow pain system* (involving the slow nerve fibers) serves all body tissues except the brain itself, which does not experience pain. The fast pain system carries pain that is perceived as stinging and localized in one area, whereas slow nerve fibers signal dull, aching pain that may be generalized throughout the body.

Strong mechanical pressure or extreme temperatures normally stimulate fast nerve fibers, whereas slow nerve fibers are typically activated by chemical changes in damaged tissues. These chemical changes make both types of nerves more responsive to further stimulation. This is why even the lightest touch on an injured area of skin can be extremely painful.

To get a feeling for the practical differences in the speed of the two pain systems, consider that slow fibers relaying a painful message from your foot could take as long as 2 seconds to reach the brain. In contrast, the faster fibers relay their messages in a fraction of a second. This explains a familiar experience. Sticking your toe in unbearably hot bath water will stimulate the fast pain fibers, producing an immediate sharp pain. The message is carried from the skin to the spinal cord, where it is passed via a single interneuron to motor neurons that cause you to jerk your toe out of the water. But this highly adaptive *spinal reflex* is completed well before you experience the deeper, dull pain that really hurts.

After leaving the skin, the sensory fibers of the fast and slow pain systems group together as nerves to form *sensory tracts* that funnel information up the spinal cord to the brain (Figure 14.3). Both types of pain fibers enter through the back of the spinal cord, where they synapse with neurons in the **substantia gelatinosa.** In the spinal cord, the pain fibers

FIGURE 14.3

Pain Pathways The thinner black line illustrates the pathway for fast, acute pain, which originates with fast nerve fibers in the spinal cord and projects to the somatosensory cortex. The thicker blue line illustrates the pathway for slow, chronic pain, which begins with slow nerve fibers in the spinal cord.

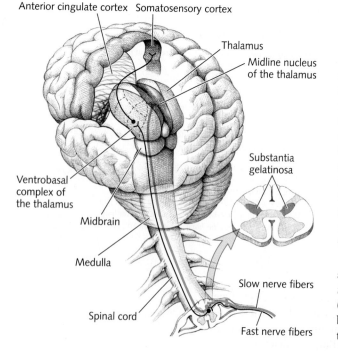

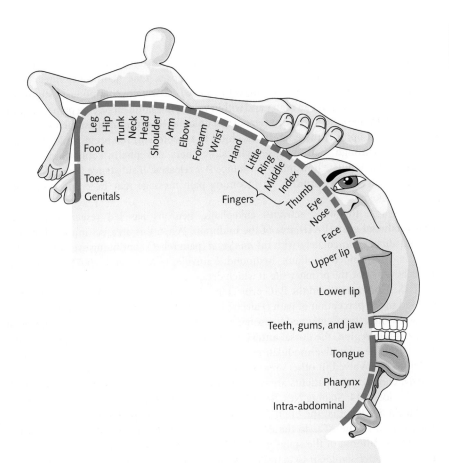

FIGURE 14.4
Mapping the Somatosensory Cortex The brain devotes more cortical tissue to sensitive areas and to areas requiring precise control. For instance, the fingers have a greater representation in the cortex than does the upper arm.

link up with sensory nerves that carry touch, pressure, and limb movement sensations to the thalamus, the brain's sensory switchboard.

On its way to the thalamus, the fast pain pathway triggers neural activity in the reticular formation, which is the brain's mechanism for arousing the cortex in response to important messages and for reducing our awareness of unimportant stimuli. Once in the thalamus, incoming messages are routed to the *somatosensory area* of the cerebral cortex, the area that receives input from all the skin senses.

The amount of somatosensory cortex allotted to various regions of the body determines our sensitivity in that region. For example, even though your face has a much smaller surface area than your back, it has much more somatosensory cortex dedicated to it, making it capable of sensing weaker touch stimuli than your back (see Figure 14.4). The internal organs of the body are not mapped in the cortex in the same way as the skin, making it difficult to pinpoint pain from the body's interior. In fact, visceral (internal) pain often becomes **referred pain,** in that it feels as though it originates on the surface of the body rather than in the organ that produced the pain. So reliable is this phenomenon that referred pain is often used to diagnose serious medical conditions. A patient complaining of pain in the shoulder, for example, is often scheduled for an electrocardiogram (EKG) stress test because that type of pain often accompanies advanced heart disease.

The slow pain system follows roughly the same pathway as the fast system up the spinal cord to the brainstem (see Figure 14.3). In the brainstem, slow pain messages are reprocessed; from there, they travel to the hypothalamus, the rear portion of the thalamus, and then to the amygdala of the limbic system.

referred pain Pain manifested in an area of the body that is sensitive to pain but caused by disease or injury in an area of the body that has few pain receptors.

FIGURE 14.5

The Pain-Inhibiting System
Neural activity resulting from stimulation of the midbrain's periaqueductal gray (PAG) activates inhibitory neurons in the spinal cord. These in turn act directly on incoming slow nerve fibers to block pain signals from being relayed to the brain. The slow nerve fibers contain substance P and glutamate. When the nerve fibers' release of substance P is inhibited, as it is here, the ascending pain signal is aborted (that is, prevented from traveling to the brain).

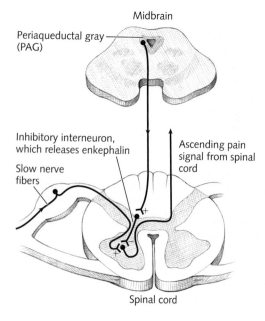

Midbrain

Periaqueductal gray (PAG)

Inhibitory interneuron, which releases enkephalin

Slow nerve fibers

Ascending pain signal from spinal cord

Spinal cord

The Neurochemistry of Pain

Like all neurons, those that carry pain messages depend on several types of chemical neurotransmitters to relay information across synapses. One neurotransmitter, called **substance P,** with another neurotransmitter, called *glutamate,* continuously stimulates nerve endings at the site of an injury and within your spinal cord, increasing pain messages.

A third group of neurotransmitters called **enkephalins** (the smallest member of the brain's natural opiates, the endorphins) bind to receptors in the brain to deaden pain sensations. Through their synapses with slow fibers, enkephalin-containing neurons are believed to regulate how much substance P is released. If substance P is not released or released in small quantities, an incoming pain message may be reduced or completely blocked.

The search for what activates enkephalin neurons has led researchers to the **periaqueductal gray (PAG)** area of the midbrain. When this area is stimulated, pain is reduced almost immediately, with the *analgesia* (pain relief) continuing even after stimulation is discontinued (Goffaux, Redmond, Rainville, & Marchand, 2007). The PAG is also believed to be the primary site at which drugs such as morphine exert their analgesic effects. Sensory neurons in the PAG project into the medulla, a lower brain structure also involved in the perception of pain (Fairhurst, Weich, Dunckley, & Tracey, 2007).

Recent functional magnetic resonance imaging (fMRI) studies have implicated another brain region, the dorsal **anterior cingulate cortex (ACC),** as being specifically involved in the cognitive modulation of pain (Chapin and others, 2013). The ACC is known to be involved in other areas of self-regulation as well (Anderson, 2013). Interestingly, chronic pain patients are often deficient in self-regulatory skills, such as self-control (Flor, 2014; Solberg Nes, Roach, & Segerstrom, 2009).

Thus, it appears that the brain is capable of "turning off" pain through a *descending neural pathway*—the ACC to the PAG down to neurons in the medulla and then to the substantia gelatinosa of the spinal cord. This descending pain control pathway uses the neurotransmitter *serotonin* to activate enkephalin-containing spinal neurons, which, in turn, inhibit pain information coming from substance P fibers (Figure 14.5).

But what turns on the pain-inhibiting cells in the PAG? While still a graduate student, Candace Pert, a pioneer in the field of psychoneuroimmunology, discovered that neural chemicals called **endogenous opiate peptides** function as information messengers that affect the mind, emotions, immune system, and other body systems simultaneously. One of the peptides that she identified was *endorphin,* a natural opioid powerful enough to produce pain relief comparable to that of morphine and other opiates (Julien, Advokat, & Comaty, 2011). It turns out that the PAG has numerous opiate/endorphin receptors.

Research is ongoing, but a variety of events have been demonstrated to increase the level of endorphins. One is stress. **Stress-induced analgesia (SIA)** refers to the pain relief that results from the body's production of endorphins in response to stress. In one study, 14 healthy participants became less sensitive to electrical pain simulation while completing a stressful color word interference test (Stroop task), as indicated by reductions in their heart rate and blood pressure (Fechir and others, 2012). However, participants injected with an endorphin-blocking drug called **naloxone** before the noise did not show the SIA, showing clearly that the pain-relieving effect depends on endorphins.

In addition to endorphins, proteins produced by the immune system called *proinflammatory cytokines* are involved in the experience of pain (Watkins and others, 2007). Recall from Chapter 3 that cytokines trigger a range of sickness responses, including fatigue and increased sensitivity to pain. Cytokines may also be involved in the development of chronic pain by increasing the sensitivity of structures in the spinal cord that affect the message that ascending pain pathways transmit to the brain.

Similar neurochemical effects may account for the *placebo effect* (see Chapter 9) in pain relief. Many research studies have demonstrated that one-quarter to one-third of people suffering pain receive significant relief simply by taking a placebo. A classic field study of dental pain (Levine, Gordon, & Fields, 1978) was the first to suggest that endorphins might mediate SIA and thus produce the placebo effect. Three hours after having a major tooth pulled (ouch!), one-half of a group of dental patients were given a placebo, which they referred to as a "painkiller." The remaining subjects received an injection of naloxone. One hour later, subjects who had received the placebo were injected with naloxone, and those who had received naloxone were injected with the placebo. After each injection, the participants were asked to indicate on a standard pain-rating scale the degree of pain that they were experiencing.

Under the "influence" of the placebo painkiller, patients reported some relief from their pain, which provides additional support for the validity of the placebo effect. Under the influence of naloxone, patients reported feeling increased pain compared to that reported in the placebo condition, indicating that the placebo effect is at least partly the result of the body mustering its own mechanisms of pain relief. Injections of a drug that blocks cholecystokinin, a hormone that inhibits the action of endorphins, enhance the placebo effect in pain relief (Sullivan, Paice, & Benedetti, 2004). Other studies using fMRI have found that when patients expect to feel reduced pain after taking a placebo, their brains also display decreased activity in pain-processing regions (Wager and others, 2004). As we'll see later in the chapter, some other nonmedical techniques for producing analgesia may also work because they trigger the release of endorphins.

Genes and Pain

Chronic pain conditions, as well as sensitivity to pain, have been shown to have a considerable genetic component (Vehof, Zavos, Lachance, Hammond, & Williams, 2014). Several rare but serious pain disorders are caused by mutations in a gene called SCN9A, which encodes instructions for sodium channels that help nerve cells that relay painful sensations in the body's tissues to the central nervous system. In two of the disorders, people have faulty alleles of the gene and suffer intense pain because their sodium channels either open too easily or can't close (Markovic, Jankovic, & Vesilinovic, 2015). In another disorder, which leaves people completely unable to feel pain, SCN9A produces a protein that cannot function (Thompson, Knapp, Feeg, Madden, & Shenkman, 2010).

Studies of twins have reported heritability of about 50 percent for different pain traits, including variation in how people respond to painful stimuli such as skin heating (Norbury, MacGregor, Urwin, Spector, & McMahon, 2007). These studies suggest that genes may exert their influence in at least two ways: by mediating anxiety and depression—both of which have been linked to individual variation in the prevalence and experience of pain—and by affecting individual sensitivity to painful stimuli (Robinson and others, 2013). One study of patients suffering from *fibromyalgia* (FM), a chronic form of generalized musculoskeletal pain, found that those with one variation of the COMT gene displayed the most severe psychological and functional impact scores of FM pain (Desmeules and others, 2012). COMT, or catechol-o-methyl-transferase, is one of several enzymes involved in the metabolism of catecholamine neurotransmitters (dopamine, epinephrine, and norepinephrine). The results of other studies suggest that COMT genetic variations influence the severity of pain reports, as well as the length of physical and psychological recovery from traumatic events such as car accidents that cause the musculoskeletal pain associated with whiplash (McLean and others, 2011).

anterior cingulate cortex (ACC) The front part of the cingulate cortex, which resembles a collar in surrounding the corpus callosum and plays a role in pain processing and many self-regulating functions.

endogenous opiate peptides Opiatelike substances naturally produced by the body.

stress-induced analgesia (SIA) A stress-related increase in tolerance to pain, presumably mediated by the body's endorphin system.

naloxone An opioid antagonist that binds to opioid receptors in the body to block the effects of natural opiates and painkillers.

FIGURE 14.6

The Gate Control Theory of Pain In Melzack and Wall's gate control theory, excitatory signals (pluses) tend to open the gate; inhibitory signals (minuses) tend to close the gate. The drawing on the far left—with a net of +9 excitatory signals—illustrates the conditions that might exist when the pain gate remains open and strong pain is felt. The drawing to the right—with a net of only +1—illustrates the conditions that might exist when the pain gate is closed as a result of strong inhibitory stimulation from the brain and peripheral nerve fibers. In both situations, messages from fast pain fibers tend to close the gate, and messages from slow pain fibers tend to open it.

Information from Melzack, R., & Wall, P. D. (1988). *The challenge of pain.* New York: Basic Books.

gate control theory (GCT) The idea that there is a neural "gate" in the spinal cord that regulates the experience of pain.

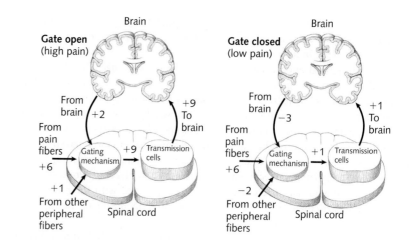

Gate Control Theory

In the past, several theories have been proposed to explain pain perception. Most, however, fell short in accounting for all aspects of pain—biological, psychological, and social. In 1965, Ronald Melzack and Peter Wall outlined a **gate control theory (GCT)** that overcame some of the shortcomings of earlier theories. Although the theory has received its share of criticism, it was the impetus for the biopsychosocial model of pain, which is the dominant theory of pain today (Gatchel, Peng, Peters, Fuchs, & Turk, 2007).

The GCT first introduced the idea that the pain experience is not the result of a straight-through sensory channel that begins with the stimulation of a skin receptor and ends with the brain's perception of pain. Rather, as we have seen, incoming sensations that *potentially* signal pain are modulated in the spinal cord as they are conducted to the brain. They are also subject to modification under the influence of descending pathways from the brain.

The theory proposed the existence of neural structures in the spinal cord and brainstem that function like a gate (see Figure 14.6), swinging open to increase the flow of transmission from nerve fibers or swinging shut to decrease the flow (Melzack & Wall, 1965). With the gate open, signals arriving in the spinal cord stimulate sensory neurons called *transmission cells,* which, in turn, relay the signals upward to reach the brain and trigger pain. With the gate closed, signals are blocked from reaching the brain, and no pain is felt.

Melzack and Wall (1988) suggested that the mechanism for opening and closing the gate is found in the substantia gelatinosa (the "gatekeeper") of the spinal cord, where both small and large pain fibers have synapses (see Figure 14.3). Activity in the fast pain fiber system tends to close the gate, whereas activity in the slow pain fiber system tends to force the gate open.

To account for the influence of thoughts and feelings on the perception of pain, Melzack and Wall also described a *central control mechanism* by which signals from the brain can shut the gate. Through this mechanism, anxiety or fear may amplify the experience of pain, whereas the distraction of other activities, such as athletic competition, can dampen the experience of pain.

Melzack (1990) later proposed that a widely distributed network of brain neurons, which ultimately determine a person's perceptual experience, further processes messages reaching the brain. This network of cells, called the *neuromatrix,* also seems to operate even in the absence of sensory input, placing still greater emphasis on the role of the brain in our experience of pain (as in the phantom limb sensation described in the Diversity and Healthy Living box), as well as in reducing pain.

Factors That Influence the Experience of Pain

The experience of pain is a complex, multidimensional phenomenon involving not only physical events but also psychological factors and social learning (Reimann and others, 2010). All pain patients are unique individuals who are acting (and reacting) members of social groups. In this section, we take a look at how such factors influence the experience of pain.

Age

The National Health and Aging Trends Study (NHATS) investigated pain and other aspects of the health of older adults through in-person interviews of over 7000 Medicare beneficiaries aged 65 years and older (Patel, Guralnik, Dansie, & Turk, 2013). The overall prevalence of bothersome pain among participants was 52.9 percent, with the majority of these (74.9 percent) reporting pain in multiple locations, such as in the back, knees, and hips. Pain reports did not vary after the researchers accounted for differences in cognitive performance, dementia, proxy responses, and residential-care living status. Pain prevalence was higher in women and in people with obesity, musculoskeletal conditions, and depressive symptoms. The NHATS study also found that pain was strongly associated with decreased physical capacity. Older adults with pain, particularly those with pain in multiple locations, had weaker muscle strength, slower walking speed, and poorer overall function than those without pain.

But before we conclude that aging is inevitably accompanied by a world of pain, we would do well to ask ourselves whether other factors, such as overall health, differences in socialization, and coping resources might account for age-related differences in pain experiences. As we have seen, it is very easy for researchers examining differences between groups of people (such as age cohorts) to overlook such factors. For example, older adults who feel a greater sense of overall well-being complain less about pain than others the same age. Pain perceptions are also influenced by social comparisons with people in other reference groups. For example, adults who reported that their parents had experienced frequent severe pain were themselves more likely to report substantial back, muscle, and joint pain. Older people are also generally more vigilant than young people in monitoring their health status, and they see themselves as more vulnerable (Skevington, 1995). This may help explain why there is a progressive increase in reports of pain and a decrease in tolerance to experimentally induced pain as individuals grow older.

Gender

Gender differences in health behavior are already apparent in adolescence, with boys being less likely than girls to seek medical care. As adults, women are more likely to report medical symptoms to a doctor, to experience more frequent episodes of pain, and to report lower pain thresholds and less tolerance to painful stimuli than are men (Bartley & Fillingim, 2013).

Women may also feel pain more intensely than men do. A massive Stanford University study of over 12,000 patients investigated gender differences in reported pain for more than 250 diseases and conditions. For almost every diagnosis, including diabetes, arthritis, respiratory infections, and fibromyalgia, women's pain scores averaged 20 percent higher than men's scores (Ruau, Liu, Clark, Angst, & Butte, 2012).

Diversity and Healthy Living

Phantom Limb Pain

Sometimes people experience pain that has no apparent physical cause. One example is **phantom limb pain,** which is the experience of pain in an amputated body part. Most amputees experience some sort of phantom sensations, but between 65 and 85 percent actually report severe phantom pain (Williams, 1996). The pain may be occasional or continuous and is usually described as "cramping," "shooting," "burning," or "crushing."

Phantom pain develops most often in patients who experienced pain in the limb prior to amputation. In addition, phantom pain often resembles the type of pain that was present before the amputation. Ronald Melzack (1993) describes a patient who continued to report a painful sensation from a splinter in his hand long after he had lost the hand in an industrial accident. Phantom limb sensations are incredibly "real" in their sensory qualities and precise location in space—so real that an amputee may try to step off the bed onto a phantom foot. Even minor sensations, such as a wedding ring on a phantom finger, are felt. Parkinson's patients may even continue to perceive "tremors" like those that occurred prior to amputation.

The Search for a Cause While the underlying cause remains a mystery, recent studies have shed light on a possible mechanism in phantom limb pain—evidence that neurons in the brain rewire themselves to seek input from other sources

An amputee uses a mirror during a therapy session to relieve pain by tricking the brain into "moving" the missing imb, allowing the pain to subside.

phantom limb pain Pain following amputation of a limb; false pain sensations that appear to originate in the missing limb.

Gender differences extend to the types of pain most commonly reported by women and men. Women seem to suffer more than men from migraines and tension headaches, as well as from pelvic pain, facial pain, and lower back pain (Henderson, Gandevia, & Macefield, 2008).

Gender disparities are also apparent in how the medical community treats pain (Leresche, 2011). The Institute of Medicine's report, *Relieving Pain in America,* found not only that women report suffering from more pain than men, but also that women's reports of pain were more likely to be dismissed or treated less aggressively when diagnosed, and women's pain was more likely to be characterized as "emotional" and therefore not real (Institute of Medicine, 2011a).

A number of researchers believe that gender differences in treating pain reflect stereotyped views about women and men rather than specific symptoms (Edwards, 2013). This line of reasoning was explored in a study in which subjects immersed a hand and forearm in icy water for several minutes (Levine & DeSimone, 1991). The results showed that women reported more pain than men did. More interesting was the fact that men reported significantly lower pain ratings to a female experimenter than to a male experimenter. However, there was no difference in the female subjects' self-reports of pain to after a limb is amputated. A team of researchers led by Michael Merzenich amputated the middle fingers from a group of adult owl monkeys. After the monkeys recovered, the researchers electrically stimulated the remaining fingers on each monkey's paw while recording electrical activity from the somatosensory area of the monkeys' brains. Remarkably, Merzenich found that cortical neurons that originally fired in response to stimulation of the amputated fingers responded every time he touched the remaining fingers of the monkeys' paws. The neurons had not responded to stimulation of these fingers before the amputation (cited in Ranadive, 1997).

Vilayanur Ramachandran conducted experiments on people who had lost a finger or a hand (Ramachandran & Rogers-Ramachandran, 2000). Blindfolding his patients, Ramachandran applied pressure to different parts of their bodies and discovered that several subjects reported phantom hand sensations as areas of their faces were touched. Ramachandran suggested that his findings made sense because the cortical areas that once served the missing finger or hand are adjacent to those that serve the face. Perhaps neurons in these adjacent areas invade those areas that are left fallow because sensations are no longer received from the missing limb.

Treatment Phantom limb pain is a condition that often is extremely resistant to conventional pain therapies. Among the treatments that have been tried, with varying degrees of success, are the fitting of prosthetic limbs, ultrasound, trans-cutaneous electrical nerve stimulation (TENS) (see p. 424 of this book), anti-inflammatory and anticonvulsant drugs, and nerve blocks such as injections of local anesthetics into trigger points (Williams, 1996).

More recently, researchers have found that blocking glutamate receptors may prevent abandoned cortical neurons, which are no longer communicating with a missing limb, from forming new synapses with neurons linked to other parts of the body. When the blockage to the spinal cord subsides, the original cortical connections and functions remain intact. Research testing whether blocking glutamate receptors also will prevent neural reorganization in those with amputated limbs (thereby reducing phantom limb pain) is presently underway.

In the meantime, Ramachandran has devised a simpler therapy—a mirror box, which allows a person to "see" the phantom limb. For example, when James Peacock, a security guard whose right arm was amputated, slips his intact left arm into the box, mirrors make it appear as if his missing right arm is there as well. The box has provided the only relief Peacock knows from wrenching spasms in his phantom hand. "When I move my left hand," he says, "I can feel it moving my phantom hand" (quoted in Brownlee, 1995, p. 76).

experimenters of either sex. These and other researchers have suggested that gender differences reflect traditional gender roles, with men responding to female experimenters with a more stoic "macho" image (Fillingim, 2000). Consistent with this view, men who identify more strongly with traditional gender roles are less likely than others of either gender to admit feeling pain (Pool, Schwegler, Theodore, & Fuchs, 2007). Interestingly, a recent study involving the response of 172 women to a similar pain discomfort task found that lesbian and bisexual women reported lower pain intensity ratings and had higher pain threshold and tolerance levels than did heterosexual women (Vigil, Rowell, & Lutz, 2014).

Sociocultural Factors

Why would two patients undergoing the same surgical procedure report vastly different levels of postoperative pain? The answer is that pain is a variable personal experience not closely linked to tissue damage. In this section, we examine social and cultural factors that are the foundation of how pain is conceptualized and experienced.

Socioeconomic Status and Stress

As we have seen, people at lower socioeconomic (SES) levels have greater morbidity and mortality across many diseases when compared with those at higher SES levels (Bacon, Bouchard, Loucks, & Lavoie, 2009). They also experience more stressful life events (Hatch & Dohrenwend, 2007), live in environments that expose them to more chronic stressors (Gee & Payne-Sturges, 2004), and have fewer psychosocial resources for managing stressful experiences (Gallo & Matthews, 2003). Lower SES is also associated with more frequent reports of musculoskeletal pain, pain intensity, and physical disability (Jablonska, Soares, & Sundin, 2006).

The challenges associated with lower SES also make those who suffer chronic pain more vulnerable to the harmful effects of stress on health and physical functioning. A study of 250 women with osteoarthritis, fibromyalgia, or both found that participants with greater levels of economic hardship reported greater pain severity in response to daily financial worries than their counterparts with little or no economic hardship (Rios & Zautra, 2011). Interestingly, the effect of day-to-day financial worry was moderated by employment. Having a job, even a part-time position, was a psychological resource that protected against the adverse effects of day-to-day financial worries on pain.

Culture and Ethnicity

Cultural and ethnic groups differ greatly in their responses to pain, suggesting that different groups establish their own norms for both the degree to which suffering should be expressed openly and the form that pain behaviors should take (Pillay, van Zyl, & Blackbeard, 2014). The sociocultural context also influences how pain is conceptualized, which, in turn, affects the relationship between pain patients and their health care providers. With increased global migration and diversity within most countries, health care providers need to develop increased sensitivity to the influence of culture on pain perceptions and behaviors (Kposowa & Tsunokai, 2002).

The pain responses of patients and research participants are sometimes divided into two culturally related categories: *stoic* and *emotive*. Stoic people tend to "grin and bear" pain. They are less expressive than emotive people and more likely to turn inward and withdraw socially when feeling discomfort, perceiving pain as a private and personal experience. In contrast, emotive people and cultures are more likely to verbalize and in other ways openly express pain. They also prefer to have others around to respond to their discomfort, perhaps to validate it (Carteret, 2012).

Childbirth provides a vivid example of cultural variation in the experience of pain. In some stoic cultures, childbirth is treated as an almost run-of-the-mill activity that brings little pain and is treated with quiet acceptance. When questioned, women who have given birth in such cultures say that they felt pain but that they felt it wrong to openly express it (Callister, 2003). In contrast to this matter-of-fact approach, women in other, expressive cultures view childbirth as a more dangerous and painful process. In these cultures, women are more likely to openly express their pain during their labor and delivery (Wall, 2000).

Over the past few decades, a large number of research studies have compared pain expression in people from various ethnic backgrounds. In one comparative study of people with arthritis, for example, researchers found that work limitation and severe joint pain were higher for non-Hispanic blacks, Hispanics and multiracial participants than for their non-Hispanic white counterparts (Bolen and others, 2010). As another example, researchers comparing Native American Indians, Alaska Natives and Aboriginal people of Canada found that Native American Indians and Alaska Natives reported a higher prevalence of pain symptoms and painful conditions than found in the general North American population (Jimenez, Garroutte, Kundu, Morales, & Buchwald, 2011).

The Spanish word for childbirth labor, dolor, means sorrow or pain.

Research studies have generally reported greater pain sensitivity among African-Americans and Hispanic-Americans compared to European-Americans (for example, Campbell, Edwards, & Fillingim, 2005; Campbell and others, 2008). This difference has been found for both *pain threshold* and *pain tolerance* levels involving a variety of laboratory stimuli, including heat, cold, and pressure (Lavernia, Alcerro, Contreras, & Rossi, 2012). Compared to European-Americans, African-Americans and Latinos also report greater postoperative pain, angina during treadmill exercise, and higher levels of chronic pain related to AIDS, glaucoma, osteoarthritis, and lower back pain (see Belfer, 2013, for a review). Interestingly, researchers have reported that pain sensitivity generally is greater among Hispanic- and African-Americans who express the strongest identification with their ethnic group (Rahim-Williams and others, 2007).

The mechanisms underlying these ethnic differences in pain experiences are unclear. They may reflect environmental factors that disproportionately affect minority populations, such as disparities in socioeconomic status that may lead to undertreated pain, high levels of chronic stress due to discrimination, lower levels of social support, and other possible factors (Belfer, 2013).

Some clinicians and researchers have made the broad generalization that people who are more likely to be expressive than stoic in the face of pain often have Hispanic, Middle Eastern, and Mediterranean backgrounds, while those who are stoic often come from Asian and Northern European backgrounds (Carteret, 2012). It has been suggested that patients from "stoic cultures" may exemplify stoicism as a reflection of cultural values about proper self-conduct. In Asian cultures, for instance, behaving in a dignified manner is generally considered very important. People who openly complain, even when feeling great discomfort, may be perceived as having poor social skills (Callister, 2003). Researchers have also suggested that the underreporting of pain in other stoic groups, such as older Irish adults, might reflect cultural beliefs related to self-blame and guilt (Cornally & McCarthy, 2011).

As with age and gender differences, however, we should be very cautious in interpreting cultural variations in reported pain. For one thing, not all studies have found these group differences in pain expressiveness. Cross-cultural studies are typically correlational in design, making it difficult to rule out differences in socioeconomic pressure, social support, coping resources, education level, and other underlying factors. When variables such as these are controlled for, group differences have sometimes disappeared (McCracken, Matthews, Tang, & Cuba, 2001).

A second reason for caution is that cross-cultural studies often lack ease of comparison. For example, while English has at least four basic words to describe pain—*ache, sore, hurt,* and *pain*—Japanese has three words for pain, and Thai has only two, making it difficult to equate subjective pain reports across groups.

A final reason for caution in generalizing about group differences is that while culture influences behavior, not everyone necessarily conforms to behavioral norms to the same degree. People's experience of pain reflects not only their culture, but also their unique personal history and perceptions (Jarrett, 2011). Researchers are sometimes victims of faulty reasoning that leads them to focus on the relatively few ways in which certain groups differ rather than on the greater number of ways in which they are the same (Campbell & Edwards, 2012). In a striking example of this, one classic study compared the self-reported pain experiences of African-Americans, Irish-Americans, Italian-Americans, Jewish-Americans, and Latin-Americans. Only 34 percent of the participants' responses showed significant intergroup differences, while the remaining 66 percent exhibited similar responses from group to group. In fact, the researchers found much stronger evidence of *intra*-ethnic variation (individual variation within each group) than they did *inter*-ethnic variation (Lipton & Marbach, 1984).

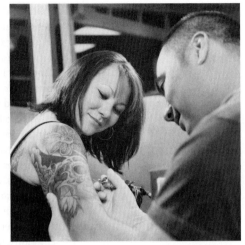

Photodisc/Getty Images

Psychosocial Influences on Pain The experience of pain is shaped by the meanings that we attach to events. In some cultures and religions, tattooing and seemingly excruciating body piercing are perceived as benign and bring great honor. In many Western cultures today, tattooing, body piercing, and "branding" are not only acceptable behaviors but also are desirable in certain age and social groups.

Personality and Mood State

Researchers have used a variety of tests, especially the Minnesota Multiphasic Personality Inventory (MMPI), to determine whether there is such a thing as a *pain-prone personality*. The MMPI contains 10 clinical scales, and acute and chronic pain patients often show elevated scores on two of them: hysteria (the tendency to exaggerate symptoms and behave emotionally) and hypochondriasis (the tendency to be overly concerned about health and to overreport symptoms).

Research also demonstrates that mood disturbances are linked with the experience of pain (Beesdo and others, 2010). People who are anxious, worried, fearful, depressed, and negative in outlook report more pain (Leeuw and others, 2007). In fact, depression is more prevalent among lower back pain patients than among the general population (Williams, Jacka, Pasco, Dodd, & Berk, 2006) and among children coping with certain types of pain (J. L. Lee and others, 2013). However, these results could simply be reflecting the challenges of dealing with pain. Similarly, people who are experiencing pain are more likely to report anxiety and/or depression, with those reporting the highest levels of these emotions also reporting the highest levels of pain (Mok & Lee, 2008).

Because the research linking depression, anxiety, and pain is correlational in nature, it is impossible to conclude that there is a causal relationship between mood state and pain, or if there is, whether depression causes chronic pain or chronic pain causes depression. One study found that patients undergoing dialysis who initially reported symptoms of depression were more likely to develop severe pain during the 2½ year follow-up period (Yamamoto and others, 2010).

Some researchers believe that individual differences in how patients cope with serious health problems are more telling than personality types and that tailoring treatments to match a patient's coping style will achieve better, longer-lasting results. Pain researchers have identified three subtypes of pain patients:

- *Dysfunctional patients* report high levels of pain and psychological distress, feel they have little control over their lives, and are extremely inactive.

- *Interpersonally distressed patients* feel they have little social support and that other people in their lives don't take their pain seriously.

- *Adaptive copers* report significantly lower levels of pain and psychological or social distress than those in the other two groups and continue to function at a high level.

Social Learning

Social and cultural factors can influence people's experience of pain and actually lead to the *social construction* of an illness (Lucire, 2003). But how do they exert their influence? Many health psychologists believe that social learning and social comparison play a critical role in determining future processing of the pain experience, with the family and surrounding culture acting as the earliest models for pain behavior. Observing family members and other people in the reference group helps a person determine what pain behaviors are appropriate in a given situation.

The social environment also shapes an individual's pain experience by way of operant conditioning. The expression of pain serves an adaptive function by capturing the attention of others and triggering caregiving and helping behaviors (Vervoort and others, 2011; Vervoort, Caes, Trost, Notebaert, & Goubert, 2012). Pioneering researcher Wilbert Fordyce's *operant conditioning model of pain* suggests that chronic pain sufferers receive social reinforcement for **pain behaviors** from the attention that they receive from family and friends (Butler, 2010). These *secondary gains* can help maintain these pain behaviors (McClelland & McCubbin, 2008). In some social and cultural groups, a person who grimaces or moans in response to pain is reinforced for that response by receiving attention from others. In other groups, open expressions of pain are either ignored or received with hostility and therefore not reinforced.

pain behaviors Actions that are a response to pain, such as taking drugs, grimacing, or taking time off from school or work.

As with many behaviors, how we learn to respond to pain begins in childhood. Children whose parents disregard their pain behavior may grow up more stoic in their approach to pain than children whose parents pay undue attention to every minor ache and pain (Langer, Romano, Manci, & Levy, 2014; Pennebaker, 1982).

Treating Pain

The treatment of pain is big business. The global market for pain management is predicted to reach $77 billion by 2017, driven mostly by the demand for drugs for pain treatment and the aging of the population (Global Industry Analysts, 2016). There are two broad categories of pain treatment: medical interventions and nonmedical interventions, which include cognitive behavioral treatments such as hypnosis and biofeedback. Although health care professionals once scoffed at most nonmedical treatments, the proven effectiveness of using psychological techniques with pain patients, as well as evidence that some, such as the placebo effect, work partly by mobilizing the body's physical system of analgesia, have increasingly led to the realization that there is no sharp dividing line between physical and nonphysical pain treatments.

In this section, we'll look first at the better-known pharmacological, surgical, and electrical stimulation treatments, then at the cognitive behavioral treatments now widely used in pain control.

Pharmacological Treatments

For most patients, analgesic drugs are a mainstay in pain control. Analgesics fall into two general classes. The first includes *opioid* (centrally acting) drugs such as morphine. The second category consists of *nonopioid* (peripherally acting) chemicals that produce their pain-relieving and anti-inflammatory effects at the actual site of injured tissue.

Opioid Analgesics
Formerly called *narcotics* (from the Greek word *narke,* which means "numbness"), opioids are *agonists* (excitatory chemicals) that act on specific receptors in the spinal cord and brain to reduce either the intensity of pain messages or the brain's response to pain messages.

The most powerful and most widely used opioid for treating severe pain is morphine. After binding to receptors in the PAG, the thalamus, and cells at the back of the spinal cord, morphine produces intense analgesia and indifference to pain, a state of relaxed euphoria, reduced apprehension, and a sense of tranquility. Because of morphine's powerful effects, regular users predictably develop tolerance so quickly that doctor-prescribed doses of morphine sometimes have to be increased to retain their effectiveness—from clinical doses of 50 to 60 milligrams per day to as high as 500 milligrams per day, over as short a period as 10 days (Advokat, Comaty, & Julien, 2014).

There is one drawback to the powerful effects of morphine, however: Its effectiveness makes it highly addictive. Long-term use may eventually lead to opioid-induced hyperalgesia, the condition we noted earlier in the chapter, where the nervous system responds to painful stimuli with increasing sensitivity when opioids are withdrawn. Therefore, many physicians are reluctant to prescribe opioid analgesics and often *undermedicate* pain patients by prescribing doses that are too weak to produce meaningful relief (Reid, Gooberman-Hill, & Hanks, 2008). One solution to the problem of undermedication has been *patient-controlled analgesia*—giving responsibility for administering the painkilling drugs to the patient. Today, some patients with severe, chronic pain have small morphine pumps implanted near sites of localized pain. Patients can activate the pump and deliver a small pain-relieving dose whenever they need it.

A 2001 survey of Australian registered nurses found that there was "a clear knowledge deficit" in the management of pain in the elderly. For example, only 4 out of 10 nurses knew that it is unnecessary to avoid giving potent painkillers to frail elderly patients. Nurses who specialized in palliative care showed the greatest knowledge of treating older patients' pain. Palliative care focuses on providing comfort and improving quality of living in people with chronic, life-threatening illnesses (Brolinson, Price, Ditmyer, & Reis, 2001).

nonsteroidal anti-inflammatory drugs (NSAIDs) Aspirin, ibuprofen, acetaminophen, and other analgesic drugs that relieve pain and reduce inflammation at the site of injured tissue.

prostaglandin The chemical substance responsible for localized pain and inflammation; prostaglandin also causes free nerve endings to become more and more sensitized as time passes.

counterirritation Analgesia in which one pain (for example, a pulled muscle) is relieved by creating another counteracting sensation (such as rubbing near the site of the injury).

transcutaneous electrical nerve stimulation (TENS) A counterirritation form of analgesia involving electrically stimulating spinal nerves near a painful area.

One alternative to the use of prescription opioids stems from the finding that many chronic pain patients have lower-than-normal levels of endorphins in their spinal fluid (Wood, 1983). Clinicians have used synthetic endorphins to boost these stores. Patients have, for example, reported excellent, long-lasting pain relief after receiving injections of a synthetic form of endorphin called *beta-endorphin* (Oyama, Jin, Yamaya, Ling, & Guillemin, 1980).

Nonopioid Analgesics

The nonopioid analgesics include aspirin, acetaminophen, and ibuprofen. Also called **nonsteroidal anti-inflammatory drugs (NSAIDs),** these drugs produce several effects, including pain reduction without sedation, reduction of inflammation, and reduction of body temperature when fever is present.

NSAIDs relieve pain by blocking a chemical chain reaction that is triggered when tissue is injured. Consider sunburn pain. One of the chemicals produced at the site of the burn is called *arachidonic acid,* which the body converts into **prostaglandin,** the substance responsible for sunburn pain (or other localized pain) and inflammation. NSAIDs work their magic by blocking production of the enzyme needed to convert arachidonic acid into prostaglandin.

Surgery, Electrical Stimulation, and Physical Therapy

For centuries, healers have used surgery in their attempts to relieve severe pain. Their reasoning made sense: If pain is a simple *stimulus–response* connection between peripheral pain receptors and the brain, why not simply cut, or lesion, pain fibers so that the messages don't get through?

Sometimes surgery is helpful. For example, destroying thalamic cells of the slow pain system has been demonstrated to alleviate some deep, burning pain without altering the sense of touch or the more acute, stinging pain of the fast pain system. More often, however, surgery has unpredictable results, and its effects are short-lived, perhaps because of the nervous system's remarkable regenerative ability. As a result, some pain patients have endured numerous "hit-or-miss" surgeries that provide only short-term relief. And in some cases, patients actually experience *worse* pain due to the cumulative damage of repeated surgeries. For these reasons, surgery is rarely used to control pain today and only as a last-ditch effort.

More effective than surgery is **counterirritation,** which involves stimulating one area of the body to reduce pain in another. For example, spinal stimulation has proven effective in controlling the lower back pain of many patients (De Andres & Van Buyten, 2006). In **transcutaneous electrical nerve stimulation (TENS),** brief pulses of electricity are applied to nerve endings under the skin near the painful area or where nerve fibers enter the back of the spinal cord, and patients can administer treatment themselves. TENS can produce a feeling of numbness that overcomes the sensation of pain, and it has yielded excellent local pain relief for some chronic pain patients.

TENS Back pain can be relieved with transcutaneous electrical nerve stimulation (TENS). Portable TENS machines help relieve the pain of thousands of sufferers. After the person logistically places the pads shown here on either side of the painful area, he or she can hook the small electrical conduit to a belt and continue with daily activities while pulses are delivered to the body.

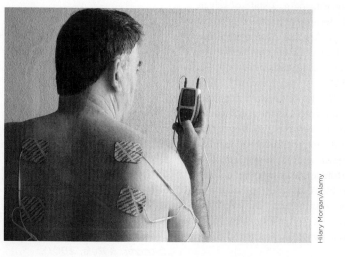

Hilary Morgan/Alamy

For more widespread and severe pain (such as that associated with some advanced cancers), another electrical form of analgesia, called *stimulation-produced analgesia* (SPA), involves delivering mild electrical pulses through electrodes that are surgically implanted in the brain and appears to work by stimulating endorphin neurons. Accordingly, SPA electrodes are implanted in brain sites known to be rich in opioid receptors. Once again, patients self-administer treatment, determining when and how much stimulation is needed. Although

SPA is expensive and risky, many pain patients report that their pain seems to melt away (Kotze & Simpson, 2008).

People who are in pain, as well as those who are suffering disability as a result of disease, injury, or surgery, also may be referred to a physical therapist for assistance. Physical therapists are rehabilitation professionals who promote optimal health and functional independence through their efforts to identify, correct, or prevent movement dysfunction, physical disability, and pain. Physical therapy often begins in the hospital and continues as long as needed.

Cognitive Behavioral Therapy

Because no single pain-control technique has proved to be the most effective in relieving chronic pain, many health care providers today use an eclectic, or "cafeteria," approach to helping their patients manage pain. This means that treatment is tailored to each individual case and that patients are taught several pain-management strategies from which they may choose as needed.

One such program is **cognitive behavioral therapy (CBT),** an umbrella term for a variety of multidisciplinary interventions aimed, in this context, at changing people's experience of pain by changing their thought processes and behaviors and teaching them to employ such strategies as distraction, imagery, meditation, exercising, and deep breathing. CBT has become the dominant model for treating chronic pain (Ehde, Dillworth, & Turner, 2014). Although specific components of CBT vary, most programs include education and goal-setting that focus on the factors influencing pain and that clarify the client's expectations for treatment, cognitive interventions to enhance patients' self-efficacy and sense of control over pain, teaching new skills for responding to pain triggers, and promoting increased exercise and activity levels.

cognitive behavioral therapy (CBT) A multidisciplinary pain-management program that combines cognitive, physical, and emotional interventions.

Education and Goal-Setting

CBT counselors often begin by briefly explaining the differences between acute and chronic pain; the mechanisms of gate control theory; and the contributions of depression, anxiety, lack of activity, and other controllable factors to pain. Patients are encouraged to generate examples from their own pain experiences, perhaps by keeping a daily diary that records pain frequency, duration, and intensity; medication use; and mood and activity levels. The diary almost always gives clients new insights into some of the factors that affect their pain experience, which is invaluable in promoting an increased sense of control over pain.

This phase is most useful for establishing specific goals for the intervention. Goals need to be specific and measurable to prevent miscommunication and the development of unrealistic expectations and also should be phrased in a way that downplays the common tendency to dwell on pain. For example, rather than saying, "I would like to be able to resume my normal activities without feeling pain," a better goal is "I would like to take a brisk, 30-minute walk four times a week."

Cognitive Interventions

Our emotions, attitudes, and beliefs are powerful influences on our health. Faulty reasoning often contributes to poor health outcomes and interferes with treatment. Negative emotions such as anxiety, anger, and depression intensify pain, which in turn intensifies negative emotions (Gilliam and others, 2010). Negative emotions also intensify pain behaviors and complicate treatment (Burns and others, 2008). For this reason, depression and thought processes often need to be targeted along with pain management (Teh, Zasylavsky, Reynolds, & Cleary, 2010). *Cognitive restructuring* challenges maladaptive thought processes and helps pain sufferers to redefine pain as an experience that is more manageable than they once believed. It also helps correct irrational beliefs.

Health psychologists recognize a general pattern of cognitive errors in the thinking of chronic pain patients, including the following:

catastrophizing An error in thinking in which a person believes something, such as pain, is far worse than it actually is.

- **Catastrophizing.** Many pain sufferers overestimate the distress and discomfort caused by an unfortunate experience, such as being injured. They also tend to focus excessively on the negative aspects of pain and use more pain medication than those who think less catastrophically (Wideman and Sullivan, 2011).

- *Overgeneralizing.* Some pain victims believe that their pain will never end and that it will ruin their lives completely, often leading to depression and poorer health outcomes.

- *Victimization.* Some chronic pain patients feel that they have experienced an injustice that consumes them, with many unable to get beyond the "Why me?" stage.

- *Self-blame.* In contrast, some chronic pain patients come to feel worthless and blame themselves for not being able to carry on with their responsibilities.

- *Dwelling on the pain.* Some pain sufferers can't stop thinking about their pain problem, often replaying painful episodes and negative thoughts in their minds.

A growing body of evidence demonstrates that cognitive errors and other individual differences in how people cope with pain are important contributors to variability in the pain experience in part because of neurobiological effects (Edwards, Campbell, Jamison, & Wiech, 2009a). For instance, several fMRI studies using standardized pain stimuli have reported that higher levels of catastrophizing are associated with enhanced neural activity in the anterior cingulate cortex and amygdala (Strigo, Simmons, Matthews, Craig, & Paulhus, 2008); these brain regions are intimately involved in processing the pain experience. Moreover, among healthy subjects exposed to mildly painful electrical stimulation, there was a positive relationship between the degree of catastrophizing about pain and pain-related responses in cortical pain-processing regions of the brain (Seminowicz & Davis, 2006).

Catastrophic thinking also may intensify pain because of its effects on blood pressure reactivity and muscle tension (Shelby and others, 2009; Wolff and others, 2008). Correlational research also links catastrophizing to stronger inflammatory responses to stress and pain (Edwards, Bingham, Bathon, & Haythornthwaite, 2006). This association appears to be specific to catastrophizing. One study of rheumatoid arthritis patients suggested that helplessness (a key component of catastrophizing) was associated with elevated levels of *C-reactive protein* (CRP), a protein produced during the inflammatory response, while anxiety and depression were unrelated to CRP levels (Edwards and others, 2008). Catastrophizing during an acute pain experience also has been associated with elevations in *interleukin-6*, a proinflammatory cytokine that regulates immune functions and inflammation (Edwards and others, 2009a). Catastrophizing and other cognitive errors probably exert their influence through descending, or "top-down," cortical circuits, rather than by directly affecting peripheral pain pathways (Wiech, Ploner, & Tracey, 2008b). Researchers speculate that catastrophizing and other cognitive errors may interfere with activation of opioid-mediated descending pain modulatory systems. Some experts have called for the clinical appraisal of catastrophizing as an indicator of problematic recovery from surgery and other medical treatments, and for the development of routine clinical interventions that target this type of thinking (Wideman & Sullivan, 2011).

In contrast with catastrophizing, victimization, and other cognitive errors, pain-coping strategies such as distraction, efforts to increase the perception of self-control over pain, and reappraising or reinterpreting pain sensations provide potential benefits in terms of reduced pain and improved function (Van Damme, Crombez, & Eccleston, 2008).

Cognitive Distraction

Does *cognitive distraction* have any practical usefulness in pain control? Many CBT therapists think so. Music is frequently used to help burn victims distract their attention from painful treatments, such as having wound dressings changed. In addition, verbal suggestions that distract people with pleasant images ("Think of a warm, comfortable environment") or drawing attention away from painful stimulation ("Count backward by 3s") are especially effective ways to activate pain-inhibiting processes and increase pain tolerance (Edwards and others, 2009a).

One study using spinal fMRI demonstrated that the pain-relieving effects of cognitive distraction are not merely a psychological phenomenon, but also involve the actual inhibition of the central nervous system's response to incoming pain signals. Participants in the study were asked to complete either an easy or a difficult memory task while a painful level of heat was applied to their arms. Participants who were more distracted by the harder of the two memory tasks not only perceived less pain, but their experience was reflected in lower levels of neural activity in their spinal cords (Sprenger and others, 2012).

The pain-relieving effects of cognitive distraction appear to be mediated by the body's production of endogenous opioids. When the study was repeated, this time giving participants an injection of the opioid antagonist naloxone or a saline solution, the amount of pain relief experienced by participants during the distracting memory task dropped by 40 percent (Sprenger and others, 2012).

Diverting attention away from a painful stimulus can diminish self-reported pain intensity by 30 to 40 percent and also seems to reduce activity in pain-processing regions of the cortex (the anterior cingulate cortex) by well over 50 percent (Edwards and others, 2009a)—an amount comparable to the effects of potent analgesic drugs. Distraction from pain also may engage some of the descending pain-inhibitory pathways that catastrophizing seems to disrupt (Wiech and others, 2008b). Some researchers have reported that analgesic medication combined with a virtual-reality video game distractor task can interact to have analgesic effects, illustrating the potential benefits of multimodal interventions in clinical settings (H. G. Hoffman and others, 2007).

Sensory Focus and ACT

Another short-term cognitive technique for coping with acute pain, **sensory focus,** involves attending directly to the sensations of a painful stimulus without necessarily trying to change those reactions. Although it may seem counterintuitive that directing attention *toward* a painful stimulus would increase the ability to cope with it, that is what sometimes seems to occur. For people who score high on measures of health anxiety, sensory focus seems to be more effective than cognitive distraction in coping with acute pain.

In one study, chronic pain patients were instructed to think about their children, relaxing on the beach, the upcoming weekend, or another source of cognitive distraction during their often-painful physical therapy sessions. Other patients were encouraged to focus directly on the concrete sensations they were experiencing as they completed each physical therapy exercise. The results showed that cognitive distraction was the more effective strategy for participants who scored low in measures of overall health anxiety. For those characterized by high health anxiety, however, sensory focus was associated with greater reduction in pain (Hadjistavropoulos, Hadjistavropoulos, & Quine, 2000). Sensory focus has also proven effective in helping patients manage the pain associated with burns, dental procedures, labor and childbirth, and other conditions (Ebert & Kerns, 2010).

Other research studies have shown that being accepting of pain, rather than attempting to suppress it, seems to mitigate its intensity (Masedo & Rosa, 2007). Attempting to suppress pain seems to actually increase pain levels: Ironically, such attempts may actually prolong pain-related thoughts and increase physiological arousal (Burns, 2006).

sensory focus Attending directly to the sensations of a painful stimulus without necessarily trying to change those reactions.

Acceptance and commitment therapy (ACT) is a therapeutic tool that has been applied to many conditions, including chronic pain. As with sensory focus, ACT emphasizes observing thoughts and feelings as they are, without trying to change them, and behaving in ways consistent with valued goals and life directions. The basic premise of ACT as applied to chronic pain is that while pain hurts, it is the struggle with pain that causes suffering. Two aspects of pain acceptance appear to be important: 1) willingness to experience pain and 2) continuing to engage in valued life activities even in the face of pain.

A growing body of evidence demonstrates that acceptance of pain is often associated with lower self-rated pain intensity, less self-rated depression and pain-related anxiety, greater physical and social ability, less pain avoidance, and better work status (McCracken & Vowles, 2014). Laboratory studies with clinical and nonclinical populations have also shown that techniques used in ACT (such as observing and accepting thoughts and feelings as they are) produce greater tolerance of acute pain and discomfort than more traditional techniques of pain control, such as distraction and cognitive restructuring.

Guided Imagery

Guided imagery (GI; see Chapter 11) is a pain-control technique that is designed to promote changes in perception by combining a mental process (as in *imagining*) and a procedure (as in *guided*). GI is actually a form of self-hypnosis because it involves focused concentration and attention. It is incorporated into relaxation techniques that involve suggestions (for example, "Your hands are heavy") and into *mental rehearsal*, which helps patients prepare for an uncomfortable medical treatment and relieves the anxiety, pain, and side effects that are exacerbated by heightened emotional reactions.

GI techniques are based on the concept that our attention and awareness have a limited capacity and that different stimuli compete for our attention. The purpose of the intervention is to teach patients to switch their attention from pain to other stimuli. For example, a pain patient may be taught to construct a vivid, multisensory image, such as strolling through a meadow on a beautiful day, focusing intently on the surrounding sights, sounds, textures, and smells. The elaborated features of the image presumably compete with the painful stimulus and lower its impact.

How effective is GI in controlling pain? One review of randomized clinical trials (RCTs) reported that eight of nine studies provided evidence of the effectiveness of guided imagery as a stand-alone therapy in reducing musculoskeletal pain (lower back pain, tendonitis, and muscle pain) (Posadzki & Ernst, 2012). A separate review of RCTs testing the effectiveness of GI in reducing nonmusculoskeletal pain (that is, pain from the skin, cardiovascular system, and other structures outside the musculoskeletal system) similarly reported that 11 of 15 studies provided evidence of GI's effectiveness (Posadzki and others, 2011). Despite these encouraging results, the researchers concluded that the methodological quality of many of the RCTs was poor. Thus far, it seems that GI works best with low to medium levels of pain intensity. Patients who have been trained in the use of positive imagery may experience benefits such as reduced anxiety and pain during medical procedures, reduced use of pain medication, fewer side effects, and increased pain tolerance (Burhenn and others, 2014).

Cognitive Reappraisal

As noted earlier, chronic pain patients are often deficient in self-regulatory skills such as self-control and the ability to reappraise situations, which may exacerbate their of pain (Solberg Nes, Roach, & Segerstrom, 2009). A key component of CBT is helping individuals *reinterpret* pain-related sensations (for example, labeling a noxious stimulus as "pressure" rather than pain), *restructure* maladaptive thought patterns ("this pain will never get better"), and make *positive self-statements* ("I can handle this"). For example, writing interventions that help pain patients express their emotions and find meaning in

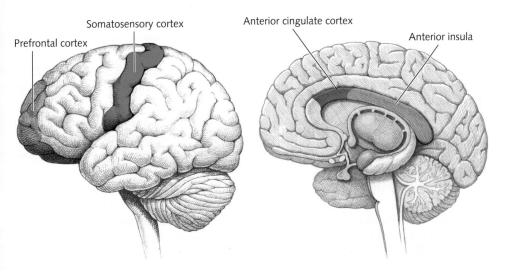

Prefrontal cortex

Somatosensory cortex

Anterior cingulate cortex

Anterior insula

their experience have been effective in reducing both pain and distress (Graham, Lobel, Glass, & Lokshina, 2008).

A growing body of evidence demonstrates that these pain-coping strategies, collectively referred to as **cognitive reappraisal,** are associated with reduced activation of key regions of the pain-processing areas of the brain. For example, *naloxone,* a drug that blocks the binding of endorphins and other opiates to neural receptor sites, disrupts the beneficial effects of cognitive reappraisal, strongly suggesting that these internal biochemical pathways are involved in these effects (Edwards and others, 2009a). These findings dovetail with those on the neurobiology of distraction, suggesting that CBT interventions that enhance these cognitive processes function by activating descending pain-inhibiting systems that originate in the prefrontal cortex (Sprenger and others, 2012).

Meditation

In hundreds of studies, researchers have studied the use of meditation as a treatment for pain, finding meditation often helps relieve pain, sometimes significantly, though it does not cure it (Steiner, 2014). A University of North Carolina study performed MRI scans on the brains of 15 healthy participants while inducing pain. Over the next three days, the participants were taught *mindfulness meditation* (learning to focus on a single sense and breathing, while accepting transient thoughts). On the fourth day, the researchers scanned the participants' brains again, once while not meditating and another time while meditating, with pain induced by an electrical stimulus to the skin during both sessions. The results showed a 40 percent reduction in pain intensity ratings during meditation when compared with nonmeditation (Zeidan, Gordon, Merchant, & Goolkasian, 2009).

Like other aspects of CBT, meditation seems to work best with chronic pain, which, as we have seen, is not the same as the tissue-damaging pain caused by an injury (acute pain). Although it often begins with an injury, chronic pain is perpetuated by stress and environmental and emotional effects long after a reasonable recovery time for physical healing has passed.

Four areas of the brain that are involved in processing pain and regulating emotional and behavioral responses appear to be affected by meditation (see Figure 14.7):

- *primary somatosensory cortex.* This is the brain area directly involved in processing painful stimuli. If a woman burns her hand, this area of the brain figures out where the pain is and an initial pain level.

FIGURE 14.7

Areas of the Brain Involved in Processing Pain and Regulating Emotional and Behavioral Responses The areas of the brain shown here, which are related to processing and responding to pain, are those that seem most affected by meditation.

cognitive reappraisal A key component of CBT that focuses on helping individuals *reinterpret* pain-related sensations, *restructure* maladaptive thought patterns, and make *positive self-statements.*

- *anterior insula.* By monitoring heart rate, blood pressure, and other indicators of arousal, this brain region appraises pain in the body. After a person's hand has been burned, the insula judges how painful the resulting injury is.
- *anterior cingulate cortex.* This area regulates a person's emotional response to a stimulus such as heat. The person who burns her hand may then feel frustrated, scared, or angry as a result of the injury.
- *prefrontal cortex.* As the brain's command center, this area takes information and guides a person's subsequent thoughts and actions. After first feeling angry, the woman who burned her hand may suppress unhelpful thoughts and focus on seeking treatment for her burn.

Research studies have shown that meditation can alter activity in each of these areas of the brain. Decreasing activity in the primary somatosensory cortex and increasing activity in the three other regions can often reduce pain. In the above example, imagine that the woman who burnt her hand meditates regularly. Neuroimaging studies showing the effects of meditation on the brain mean that the burn won't hurt as much from the beginning, the pain won't be judged to be as strong, and the focus will be on regulating the emotional and behavioral reaction to the injury.

Thus, meditation may activate the same descending pain-inhibitory pathways that are involved in distraction and cognitive reappraisal. Interestingly, experienced meditation practitioners have enhanced thickness in regions of the anterior cingulate cortex and about half the activation of pain-processing brain regions compared to nonmeditators. Importantly, similar effects have been observed in new meditation practitioners after only five months of training, suggesting that the benefits are not limited to those who are experts (Orme-Johnson, Schneider, Son, Nidich, & Cho, 2006).

Exercise

Many types of pain are made worse by a lack of flexibility and weak muscles. For this reason, exercise and physical therapy can be effective as pain-management interventions. Both aerobic exercise and resistance (strength) training can help decrease pain. Researchers in one study compared the effectiveness of four common self-management strategies in women with fibromyalgia (Rooks and others, 2007). The participants were randomly assigned to a 16-week program of either aerobic and flexibility training; strength training, aerobic, and flexibility training; a fibromyalgia self-help course; or a combination of strength training and the self-help course. The results showed that women who completed *any* of the types of exercise training reported significantly greater improvements in terms of reduced pain and enhanced functioning than their counterparts who received only the self-help program.

As we discussed in Chapter 7, people who exercise regularly also have lower levels of disability. In another study, researchers randomly assigned fibromyalgia patients to either a 12-week program of 60-minute *tai chi* sessions twice a week or a control group that received wellness education training and participated in light stretching for the same amount of time (Wang and others, 2010). Tai chi is an ancient Chinese form of exercise consisting of graceful and slow movements (see Chapter 15). At the end of the six-month follow-up period, participants in the tai chi group displayed significant clinical improvement in fibromyalgia symptoms, as well as in their quality of life.

The use of technology to promote and motivate increased physical activity among people with chronic pain shows encouraging results. For example, smartphone apps for self-management often include

> *Meditation teaches patients how to react to pain. [If] People are less inclined to have the 'ouch' reaction, then they are able to control the emotional reaction to pain.*
>
> —Fadel Zeidan (2014)

Managing Pain with Your Phone As shown in this example, there are a variety of smartphone apps for monitoring and recording pain. An app such as this can help to promote effective self-management of pain.

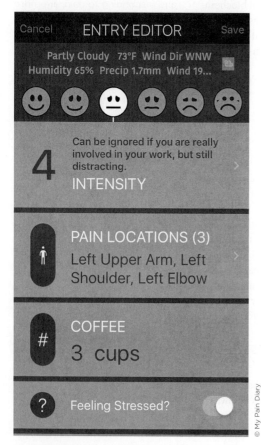

© My Pain Diary

information about pain and how increasing physical activity can reduce pain. Some apps include demonstrations of exercises for increasing strength and promoting relaxation through mindfulness meditation and other techniques. Other apps log data and enable the monitoring of key variables such as mood and pain, and they provide reminders such as for medication, daily mindfulness moments, and other pain-management activities. Movement games using consoles such as the Nintendo Wii and Microsoft Kinect have also been used to promote greater physical activity in older adults, as well as those recovering from strokes and other conditions (Singh and others, 2014).

Apps and games provide multimodal feedback and are inexpensive and accessible, but are they effective in increasing physical activity? In a recent study, 215 adults participated in an evaluation of a smartphone app designed to reduce sedentary time through prompts to interrupt periods of sitting (Kendzor and others, 2016). For seven days, participants carried smartphones and wore accelerometers that measured their movement. Those in the intervention group also received text reminders about the health risks of sitting too much that also encouraged them to get up and move around. Participants in the control group did not receive reminders. Over the course of the week, those who received the reminders were 3 percent more active (about 25 minutes more daily activity) than those in the control group (Kendzor and others, 2016).

Reshaping Pain Behavior

The mainstay of the behavioral aspect of CBT is the targeting of specific pain behaviors that are associated with continued pain and disability for modification. Consider the case of Mrs. Y, a 37-year-old office administrator who entered the University of Washington's pain-management program. For the past eight years, Mrs. Y had experienced constant lower back pain that only allowed her to get out of bed for two hours or less a day. Despite having had four major surgical procedures, her ability to function continued to deteriorate. She was taking several hundred milligrams of highly addictive opiate painkillers per day, even though there was no evidence of any actual organic problem.

Although pain may initially be caused by an injury or underlying organic pathology, its expression over time often is maintained by social and environmental reinforcement. In some cases, treatment may not progress because of the "benefits" (attention, lots of rest, not having to work, and so on) of being a pain patient. Comprehensive treatment programs, therefore, try to modify pain behaviors, such as excessive sleeping and use of pain medication. Stemming from a conditioning model, the intervention begins by identifying the events (stimuli) that precede targeted pain behaviors (responses) as well as the consequences that follow (reinforcers). Treatment then involves changing the *contingencies* between responses and reinforcers to increase the frequency of more adaptive ways of coping with discomfort. In the case of Mrs. Y, reinforcing consequences (hospital staff attention, rest, and so on) were made contingent on desirable behaviors (such as some form of mild exercise) rather than on maladaptive pain behaviors such as complaining and dependence. As a result of the combined efforts of both hospital staff and family members (who participated in the treatment program), Mrs. Y's pain behaviors were quickly extinguished.

Religious/Spiritual Coping

Religious and spiritual coping activities are widely used among chronic pain patients, although their effectiveness is controversial. Some research studies report positive pain-related effects, whereas others have actually found more negative outcomes among spiritual copers, including higher levels of pain. One possible explanation for the inconsistent results is that spiritual coping techniques that encourage passivity may be ineffective, while those that include active coping efforts may engage the same descending pain-inhibiting pathways as do distraction and cognitive reappraisal (Edwards and others, 2009a). One interesting fMRI study found that contemplation of a picture of the Virgin Mary by practicing Catholics was associated with increased activity in the prefrontal cortex and decreased perceived intensity of a painful stimulus (Wiech and others, 2008a). Non-Catholic participants viewing the same image showed no pain reduction or increased prefrontal activity, and Catholics viewing a similar but nonreligious image also showed no beneficial effects. The researchers suggested that Catholics viewing the religious image were able to achieve a calm, distracted state and activate descending pain-inhibitory systems.

Evaluating the Effectiveness of Pain Treatments

Which approach to pain control works best? The most effective pain-management programs are multidisciplinary ones that combine the cognitive, physical, and emotional interventions of CBT therapy with judicious use of analgesic drugs (American Pain Society, 2016). Most important, effective programs encourage patients to develop (and rehearse) a specific, individualized **pain-management program** for coping when the first signs of pain appear and as pain intensifies. In doing so, patients learn to be active and resourceful participants in managing their pain, rather than passive victims. The increased feelings of self-efficacy that follow from these steps are an important element in determining the patient's degree of pain and overall well-being. Individualized CBT programs have proven effective in treating lower back pain (Ostelo and others, 2005), rheumatoid arthritis (Astin, 2004), headaches (Martin, Forsyth, & Reece, 2007), fibromyalgia (Garcia and others, 2006), and pain associated with various types of cancer (Breibart & Payne, 2001).

pain-management program An individualized, multimodal intervention aimed at modifying chronic pain through neurological, cognitive, and behavioral strategies.

With all of these applications, the goals of CBT include reducing pain and psychological distress, identifying and correcting maladaptive thoughts and beliefs, and increasing self-efficacy for pain management (Ehde, Dillworth, & Turner, 2014). Many people with chronic pain also have mood, anxiety, and sleep disorders, and CBT is also used to treat these conditions (Gore, Sadosky, Stacey, Tai, & Leslie, 2012).

A number of meta-analyses have evaluated the efficacy of CBT for treating chronic pain, generally concluding that CBT, compared with treatment-as-usual conditions, has statistically significant but small effects on pain and disability, as well as moderate effects on mood and catastrophizing (Williams, Eccleston, & Morley, 2012). For example, one meta-analysis of 22 randomized controlled trials of chronic back pain management found that CBT had positive effects on pain, pain-related interference with activities, health-related quality of life, and depression (B. M. Hoffman, Papas, Chatkoff, & Kerns, 2007).

Another meta-analysis of headache pain management concluded that CBT-based interventions (relaxation, biofeedback, and cognitive therapy) effectively reduced headaches 30 to 60 percent on average (Andrasik and others, 2007). These benefits surpassed those of control conditions and typically persisted over time, including years after treatment. Biofeedback, in particular, is effective in treating chronic headaches, either as a stand-alone treatment or in conjunction with other CBT techniques (Turk, Swanson, & Tunks, 2008). Meta-analyses provide evidence of significant effects of biofeedback on reducing the frequency and duration of migraine and tension-type headaches, when compared to control conditions (Nestoriuc, Rief, & Martin, 2008).

Other meta-analyses have supported the efficacy of CBT in reducing arthritis pain (Knittle, Maes, & de Gucht, 2010) and fibromyalgia pain (Glombiewski et al., 2010).

The Culture of Childbirth Pain Childbirth is not feared as a painful event in all societies. Prepared childbirth that takes place in a calm and comfortable environment, such as in this home birth, in which loved ones surround the new mother, can greatly reduce both anxiety and the pain that it often causes.

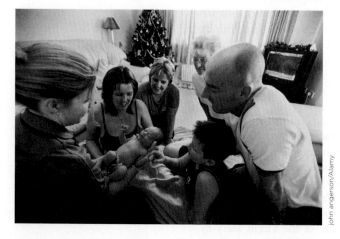

john angerson/Alamy

Taken together, the body of research evidence supports the efficacy of CBT, as compared with control conditions, in treating pain-related problems, with small to medium effects on pain intensity, mood, and cognitive errors such as catastrophizing; and small but beneficial effects on pain-related disability and activity interference. Although average effect sizes are small to moderate across pain outcomes, another benefit of CBT is that it is not associated with the risks of chronic pain medication, surgery, and other medical interventions.

The Joint Commission (2016), which sets standards and accredits nearly 21,000 health care programs in the United States, has underscored the psychological effects of pain by establishing new guidelines for the assessment and management of pain. Under the guidelines, health care facilities (including nursing homes) are required to:

- recognize the right of patients, residents, or clients to appropriate assessment and management of pain;

- screen patients, residents, or clients for pain during their initial assessments and, when clinically required, during ongoing, periodic reassessments; and

- educate patients, residents, or clients suffering from pain, as well as their families, about pain management.

The goals of pain-management programs extend beyond controlling pain to restoring the patient's overall quality of life by decreasing the reliance on medication, restoring activity levels, and enhancing psychological and social well-being.

In Chapter 15, we will consider several alternative treatments for pain, including acupuncture, hypnosis, relaxation, and chiropractic.

Weigh In on Health

Respond to each question below based on what you learned in the chapter. (**Tip:** Use the items in "Summing Up" to take into account related biological, psychological, and social concerns.)

1. Think about a time or an incident that caused you to feel pain. How do you understand that experience differently now that you've read about what pain is and how it is measured? Using what you learned, describe the components of pain you experienced. Also, explain your pain experience according to the gate control theory.

2. Imagine that a friend of your family is going to seek treatment for pain. According to research, what does his gender, age of 65 years, and Latino background suggest about his pain experience?

3. Compare and contrast biomedical and cognitive therapies used to treat pain. Name two kinds of biomedical and cognitive therapies. What pain experiences does each kind of therapy seem to treat best?

Summing Up

What Is Pain?

1. Pain involves our total experience in reacting to a damaging event, including the physical mechanism by which the body reacts; our subjective, emotional response (suffering); and our observable actions (pain behavior).

2. Pain is categorized in terms of its duration as acute, recurrent, or chronic. Chronic pain is experienced by about one-third of the population. The prevalence of chronic pain is slightly higher for females than for males and increases with age.

3. Another challenge faced by people who have chronic pain is that they may become even more sensitive to pain over time (hyperalgesia). In *opioid-induced hyperalgesia*, the long-term use of opioids leads to an increasing sensitivity to noxious stimuli, even to the point to which common sensory stimuli become painful.

Measuring Pain

4. Researchers have tried unsuccessfully to develop objective, physical measures of pain. Because of pain's subjective

nature, however, they have had to rely on behavioral measures, visual and numerical rating scales, and pain inventories such as the McGill Pain Questionnaire (MPQ) and the Pain Response Preference Questionnaire (PRPQ).

5. Fear in children is common, and it can increase the perception of pain. Needle fears are particularly prevalent: Many children consider getting an injection one of the most painful and feared experiences.

The Physiology of Pain

6. Pain typically begins when free nerve endings in the skin called *nociceptors* are stimulated. The nociceptors relay this input to fast nerve fibers that signal sharp, acute pain, or slow nerve fibers that signal slow, burning pain. Pain signals travel from these peripheral nerve fibers to the spinal cord, and from there to the thalamus, a message-sorting station that relays the pain message to your cerebral cortex, the reasoning part of your brain. The cortex assesses the location and severity of damage.

7. Endorphins and enkephalins produced in the brain act as neurotransmitters and inhibit pain by acting on cells in the substantia gelatinosa of the spinal cord and the periaqueductal gray region of the brain. In addition, fMRI studies have implicated another brain region, the dorsal anterior cingulate cortex, as being specifically involved in the cognitive modulation of pain.

8. Chronic pain patients are often deficient in self-regulatory skills, such as self-control.

9. Chronic pain conditions, as well as sensitivity to pain, have a considerable genetic component. Several rare but serious pain disorders are caused by mutations in a gene called SCN9A, which encodes instructions for sodium channels that help nerve cells that relay painful sensations in the body's tissues to the central nervous system.

10. The gate control theory suggests that a pain gate exists in the spinal cord. The pain gate may be closed by stimulation of the fast pain fiber system, whereas activity in the slow pain system tends to open the gate. The gate also may be closed by influences on the brain's descending pathway.

Factors That Influence the Experience of Pain

11. Although older people and women are more likely to report higher levels of pain than younger people and men, the relationships among pain, gender, and aging are complex. In addition, they may reflect faulty reasoning that tends to exaggerate the relatively few ways in which age groups, women, and men differ, while ignoring the greater number of ways in which they are similar.

12. Gender disparities are also apparent in how the medical community treats pain. Women's reports of pain have been more likely to be dismissed, treated less aggressively, or characterized as "emotional," and therefore not real.

13. Low SES is associated with more frequent reports of musculoskeletal pain and pain intensity and physical disability.

The challenges associated with lower SES also makes those who suffer chronic pain more vulnerable to the harmful effects of stress on health and physical functioning.

14. The pain responses of patients and research participants are sometimes divided into two, culturally related categories: *stoic* and *emotive*. People who are more likely to be expressive than stoic in the face of pain often have Hispanic, Middle Eastern, and Mediterranean backgrounds, while those who are stoic often come from Asian and Northern European backgrounds.

15. The mechanisms underlying these ethnic differences in pain experiences are unclear. They may reflect environmental factors that disproportionately affect minority populations. Cross-cultural studies are typically correlational in design, making it difficult to rule out differences in socioeconomic pressure, social support, coping resources, education level, and other underlying factors.

16. Although some researchers have reported ethnic differences in pain, others have found much greater variation among individual members within an ethnic group than variation between ethnic groups.

17. There seems not to be a "pain-prone personality," though certain traits do affect our ability to cope effectively with pain. People who are anxious, worried, fearful, and negative in outlook, in addition to those who score high in depression, also report more pain. In addition, depression is more prevalent among children coping with certain types of pain.

18. Wilbert Fordyce's operant conditioning model of pain suggests that chronic pain sufferers receive social reinforcement for pain behaviors from the attention that they receive from family and friends.

Treating Pain

19. The most common biomedical method of treating pain is the use of analgesic drugs, including opioids such as morphine. These centrally acting drugs stimulate endorphin receptors in the brain and spinal cord. A less addictive class of analgesics, the nonsteroidal anti-inflammatory drugs (NSAIDs), produce their pain-relieving effects by blocking the formation of prostaglandin at the site of injured tissue. Electrical stimulation techniques, such as transcutaneous electrical nerve stimulation (TENS), deliver mild electrical impulses to tissues near the pain-producing area to close the pain gate in the spinal cord.

20. Negative emotions such as anxiety, anger, and depression intensify pain, and pain intensifies these and other negative emotions. For this reason, depression and thought processes often need to be targeted along with the management of pain.

21. Health psychologists recognize a general pattern of cognitive errors in the thinking of chronic pain patients, including catastrophic thinking, overgeneralizing, victimization, self-blame, and dwelling on pain. Cognitive errors are associated with abnormal patterns of neural activity in the

anterior cingulate cortex, greater blood pressure reactivity, and elevations in certain proinflammatory cytokines.

22. Diverting attention away from a painful stimulus can diminish self-reported pain intensity by 30 to 40 percent and also seems to reduce activity in pain-processing regions of the cortex—an amount comparable to the effects of potent analgesic drugs. In addition, guided imagery is an effective strategy for managing pain. The pain-relieving effects of cognitive distraction appear to be mediated by the body's production of endogenous opioids.

23. Another short-term cognitive technique for coping with acute pain, sensory focus, involves attending directly to the sensations of a painful stimulus without necessarily trying to change those reactions. Sensory focus appears to be more effective than cognitive distraction as a coping technique for people who have high health anxiety.

24. The basic premise of ACT as applied to chronic pain is that while pain hurts, it is the struggle with pain that causes suffering. Two aspects of pain acceptance appear to be important: 1) willingness to experience pain and 2) continuing to engage in valued life activities even in the face of pain.

25. A key component of CBT is cognitive reappraisal, which entails helping individuals *reinterpret* pain-related sensations, *restructure* maladaptive thought patterns, and make *positive self-statements*. Cognitive reappraisal and other adaptive pain-coping techniques also have been associated with improved neuroendocrine functioning, especially healthy cortisol rhythms.

26. Meditation may activate the same descending pain-inhibitory pathways that are involved in distraction and cognitive reappraisal. Four areas of the brain that are involved in processing pain appear to be affected by meditation: the primary somatosensory cortex, anterior insula, anterior cingulate cortex, and prefrontal cortex.

27. Many types of pain are made worse by a lack of flexibility and weak muscles. For this reason, exercise and physical therapy can be effective as pain-management interventions. The use of smartphone apps, game consoles, and other technology to promote and motivate increased physical activity among people with chronic pain shows encouraging results.

28. Religious and spiritual coping activities also are widely used among chronic pain patients, although their effectiveness is controversial.

29. The most successful pain treatment programs are multidisciplinary and combine the use of analgesic drugs with eclectic cognitive behavioral programs. These programs use a mix of techniques to develop individualized pain-management programs, including cognitive restructuring of pain beliefs, distraction, imagery, and relaxation training.

30. Behavioral interventions rely on operant procedures to extinguish undesirable pain behaviors while reinforcing more adaptive responses to chronic pain.

Key Terms and Concepts to Remember

clinical pain, p. 407
acute pain, p. 408
recurrent pain, p. 408
chronic pain, p. 408
hyperalgesia, p. 408
free nerve endings, p. 412
nociceptor, p. 412
fast nerve fibers, p. 412
slow nerve fibers, p. 412
substantia gelatinosa, p. 412
referred pain, p. 413
substance P, p. 414

enkephalins, p. 414
periaqueductal gray (PAG), p. 414
anterior cingulate cortex (ACC), p. 414
endogenous opiate peptides, p. 414
stress-induced analgesia (SIA), p. 414
naloxone, p. 414
gate control theory (GCT), p. 416
phantom limb pain, p. 418
pain behaviors, p. 422
nonsteroidal anti-inflammatory drugs (NSAIDs), p. 424

prostaglandin, p. 424
counterirritation, p. 424
transcutaneous electrical nerve stimulation (TENS), p. 424
cognitive behavioral therapy (CBT), p. 425
catastrophizing, p. 426
sensory focus, p. 427
cognitive reappraisal, p. 429
pain-management program, p. 432

Complementary and Alternative Medicine

The Image Bank/Getty Images

I n August 2003, a 53-year-old woman—call her Cynthia—visited an Oregon clinic to undergo chelation therapy. Although she was in good health, Cynthia opted for the unconventional treatment (against the advice of her doctor) because of its reputed health and antiaging effects. Proponents claim that chelation, which involves intravenous infusions of the drug ethylenediaminetetraacetic acid (EDTA), removes heavy metals and other environmental toxins from the body. Although there were no apparent adverse effects from the earlier treatments, about 15 minutes into her fourth infusion, Cynthia lost consciousness. She was rushed to the emergency room of a local hospital, where cardiopulmonary resuscitation was initiated, but it failed, and Cynthia died. The medical examiner determined the cause of death to be cardiac arrhythmia resulting from abnormally low levels of calcium in Cynthia's body (Quackwatch, 2006).

In contrast to Cynthia's tragic story, consider the experience of one patient of alternative medicine guru Andrew Weil, MD. After being diagnosed with bone cancer at age 21, the young man developed feelings of hopelessness and frustration with the treatment offered by conventional doctors, who made his condition seem like a death sentence. Believing he could fight the disease by adopting a healthier lifestyle, the man started an extreme exercise program of biking 500 miles and running 60 miles each week. He also made radical dietary changes by consuming only fresh fruit, whole grains, and juices. He credits this unconventional treatment for returning him to "wholeness" (Weil, 1998).

T he National Institutes of Health (NIH) estimates that less than one-third of the world's health care is delivered by biomedically trained doctors and nurses (National Center for Complementary and Integrative Health, 2015a). The remainder comes from self-care and traditional indigenous approaches. This may mean a trip to the acupuncturist, massage therapist, faith healer, or chiropractor; purchases of aromatherapy ingredients, herbal medicines, or megavitamins; or a daily hour of yoga or meditation.

But do these methods work? Unconventional treatments must be subjected to the same rules of **evidence-based medicine** that traditional biomedical interventions undergo, including rigorous testing and careful evaluation of alleged health benefits. In this chapter, we will consider several alternative treatments, which have varied widely in their tested effectiveness.

evidence-based medicine An approach to health care that promotes the collection, interpretation, and integration of the best research-based evidence in making decisions about the care of individual patients.

What Is Complementary and Alternative Medicine?

Our consideration of alternative approaches to health care prompts the question: What is traditional medicine? The answer to this question depends to a large extent on our belief systems and culture. **Conventional medicine** (also called Western or *allopathic* medicine) is health care as practiced by holders of MD (medical doctor) and DO (doctor of osteopathic medicine) degrees and by allied professionals, including physical therapists, psychologists, and registered nurses.

Osteopathic medicine is a branch of American medicine with a distinct philosophy and approach to patient care. A doctor of osteopathy (DO) receives the same basic four years of medical education as a doctor of medicine (MD), followed by three to eight years of graduate medical education consisting of internships, residencies, and fellowships. DOs practice a "whole-person" approach to health care and receive special training in the musculoskeletal system to understand better how that system influences the condition of all other body systems. In addition, DOs are trained to identify and correct structural problems, which presumably assists the body's natural tendency toward health and self-healing. Both DOs and MDs can practice in any specialty of medicine, such as surgery, pediatrics, or family medicine.

The term **alternative medicine** has been used to identify a broad range of therapeutic approaches and philosophies that are generally defined as health care practices that are not taught widely in medical schools, not generally used in hospitals, and not usually reimbursed by insurance companies. A number of these practices are considered a part of a **holistic medicine** approach, in which the practitioner addresses the physical, mental, emotional, and spiritual needs of the whole client. The boundaries between alternative medicine and conventional medicine are not absolute and may change over time, as specific interventions are subjected to clinical trials and become widely accepted.

In earlier chapters, we discussed several unconventional techniques, including guided imagery, stress management, and cognitive reappraisal. In this chapter, we focus on larger-scale, unconventional therapies that encompass some of these techniques: *acupuncture, mind–body therapies, chiropractic, biofeedback,* and *naturopathy*.

conventional medicine Biomedically based medicine as practiced by holders of the MD (medical doctor) or DO (doctor of osteopathy) degrees and their allied health professionals.

osteopathic medicine A form of medical practice that provides all the benefits of conventional allopathic medicine, including prescription drugs and surgery, and emphasizes the interrelationship between the structure and function of the human body.

alternative medicine A broad range of health care practices that are not taught in medical schools, not generally used in hospitals, and not usually reimbursed by insurance companies.

holistic medicine An approach to medicine that considers not only physical health but also the emotional, spiritual, social, and psychological well-being of the person.

Establishing a Category for Unconventional Medicine

Some "alternative" methods have been around for a very long time; the term *complementary medicine* is actually more appropriate for those methods because it emphasizes that many "alternative medicines" are best used in conjunction with—rather than instead of—regular medicine. For example, the combined effect of drug *and* relaxation-training interventions for hypertension exceeds that of either the drug or relaxation by itself, and relaxation may reduce the doses of the drug needed.

TABLE 15.1

Domains of Complementary and Alternative Medicine

Whole medical systems	Complete health care systems that evolved independently of Western biomedicine. Examples include traditional Chinese medicine, ayurveda, and homeopathy.
Mind and body medicine	Techniques designed to affect the mind's capacity to influence bodily functions and symptoms. Examples include meditation, yoga, acupuncture, deep-breathing exercises, guided imagery, hypnosis, progressive relaxation, qi gong, and tai chi.
Natural products	This area of CAM includes use of a variety of herbal medicines (also known as *botanicals*), vitamins, minerals, and other "natural products." Many are sold over the counter as dietary supplements. CAM natural products also include probiotics—live microorganisms (usually bacteria) that are similar to microorganisms normally found in the human digestive tract and that may have beneficial effects. Probiotics are available in foods (e.g., yogurt) and as dietary supplements.
Manipulative and body-based practices	Techniques that focus primarily on the structures and systems of the body, including the bones and joints, soft tissues, and circulatory and lymphatic systems. Two commonly used therapies fall within this category: ■ Massage therapy ■ Spinal manipulation as practiced by chiropractors, osteopathic physicians, naturopathic physicians, and physical therapists
Other CAM practices	CAM also encompasses *movement therapies*—a broad range of Eastern and Western movement-based approaches such as Pilates, used to promote physical, mental, emotional, and spiritual well-being. *Traditional healers* use methods based on indigenous beliefs and experiences handed down from generation to generation. A familiar example in the United States is the Native American healer/ medicine man/woman. Other CAM practices involve manipulation of various energy fields to affect health (e.g., magnet therapy and light therapy). Practices based on *putative energy fields* (also called biofields) generally reflect the concept that human beings are infused with subtle forms of energy; qi gong, Reiki, and healing touch are examples of such practices.

Information from National Center for Complementary and Integrative Health (2016), https://nccih.nih.gov/health/integrative-health?nav=gsa#types.

complementary and alternative medicine (CAM) The use and practice of therapies or diagnostic techniques that fall outside conventional biomedicine.

In this chapter, we will use the term **complementary and alternative medicine (CAM)** to refer to the use of health-promoting practices and diagnostic therapies that are not generally considered part of conventional medicine together with conventional biomedical interventions. As an example, I used CAM to treat the pain of a running injury by visiting my primary health care provider—an MD who is also a licensed acupuncturist. In addition to several sessions of acupuncture, my treatment consisted of rest (time off from running), daily ice massage, and a moderate course of oral ibuprofen every four to six hours.

The National Center for Complementary and Alternative Medicine (NCCAM), renamed the National Center for Complementary and Integrative Health (NCCIH) in 2014, is part of the U.S. federal government's National Institutes of Health. The NCCIH developed the classification scheme depicted in Table 15.1, which separates CAM practices into five major domains.

Three Ideals of Complementary and Alternative Medicine

Despite the endless variety of alternative therapies, most forms of alternative medicine *do* share several features that distinguish these interventions from traditional medicine. Most work from three fundamental ideals: to provide health treatment that is natural, that is holistic, and that promotes wellness.

Natural Medicine

During most of the twentieth century, the public seemed to have an undying faith in modern technology, science, and biomedicine. Then, in the second half of the twentieth century, evidence increasingly indicated that advances in health-related technology were not always healthy—and things began to change.

The current popularity of CAM seems to indicate a growing desire for more "natural" treatments. Immunization is a powerful example. Although vaccinations are an essential component of pediatric well-child care and are required for entering school, the possibility of adverse side effects and the use of multiple-antigen vaccines are subjects of some controversy (Bonhoeffer, 2007). The antivaccine movement gained traction after an article published by a subsequently discredited UK doctor claimed to find evidence that the measles, mumps, and rubella (MMR) vaccine had caused autism in 12 children (Ziv, 2015). Although the doctor was later stripped of his medical license for ethical violations, the original research article was retracted, and a wealth of authoritative evidence shows no link between the MMR vaccine and autism (Jain and others, 2015), vaccination rates plummeted and a 2014 National Consumers League survey reported that one-third of parents with children under 18 years of age continue to mistakenly believe that vaccinations cause autism (NCL Communications, 2014). Although vaccination rates continue to vary from region to region, MMR vaccination coverage among kindergarten children in the United States during the 2014–15 school year was only 94 percent (MMWR, 2015, August 28).

Although the philosophy of a "natural" medicine inspires many CAM practitioners, it is a mistake to assume that all CAM therapists agree. Herbal therapy and massage certainly are natural, but some other popular alternative treatments are not. Consider the chelation therapy that Cynthia from our chapter opener tried. Some alternative practitioners, controversially, recommend ingesting or injecting into the bloodstream the synthetic chemical EDTA as a treatment for angina and atherosclerosis.

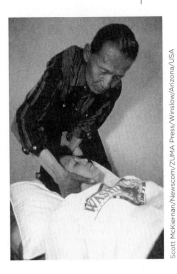

Navajo Healing Complementary and alternative medicine (CAM) includes a wide variety of practices, some more or less accepted in Western civilization. Here, a Navajo medicine man treats a patient.

Holistic Medicine

CAM also aims to avoid the narrow specialization of conventional biomedicine. As physician Patch Adams, a pioneer of holistic medicine, noted, "Treat a disease and you win or lose, treat the person and you win every time" (Adams & Mylander, 1998, p. 22). Many patients seek out alternative care because they prefer to work with practitioners who will see (and treat) them as a whole person. The physician and author Steven Bratman (2007) describes one extreme case of a man whose various symptoms eventually led to treatment by six medical specialists: a neurologist (for cognitive symptoms stemming from a stroke), an orthopedist (for bone degeneration), an ophthalmologist (for eye pain), a dermatologist (for skin lesions), a urologist (for bladder problems), and a cardiologist (for heart valve leakage). Until an elderly neighbor (who happened to be a retired general practitioner) realized that the seemingly independent symptoms were similar to the syphilis cases that he had often seen 40 years earlier, no one suspected that a simple program of penicillin shots was all the man needed.

Specialization and fragmentation are predictable consequences of the analytical nature of biomedicine, which encourages doctors to focus on the fine details of the symptoms that each patient presents. As a backlash against the overspecialization of conventional medicine, many alternative practitioners broaden their analysis of each patient's complaints to examine diet, emotions, and lifestyle as well as the specific symptoms of the disease or condition. This is especially true of traditional Chinese medicine, the ancient system of *ayurveda* from India, and homeopathy. Homeopathy is a largely unproven system of so-called energy medicine developed in the nineteenth century by Samuel Hahnemann, which advocates such ideas as the "law of similars"—that is, the most effective remedy for a particular disease is a minute quantity of the very substance that would trigger the disease's symptoms in a healthy person.

Promoting Wellness

Given Western biomedicine's historical focus on battling disease, it is understandable that the concept of wellness was long considered too vague for medical science to rally around. Instead, biomedicine orbited around disease; in contrast, the primary focus of many alternative treatments is to strengthen the individual, even if the person currently has no serious symptoms. Fortunately, Western medical views are changing, and over the past 25 years, conventional medicine practitioners have increasingly embraced the wellness ideal.

Alternative practitioners believe that medication, surgery, and other mainstream interventions can fight illness but generally cannot produce an optimal state of healthy vitality. Indeed, although most medical interventions eliminate major symptoms, they often leave behind one or more adverse side effects, such as an upset stomach or headache.

Many alternative treatments do make the person "feel like a million bucks," even if only temporarily. Acupuncture, aromatherapy, and massage therapy may produce feelings of relaxation—even symptom relief among cancer patients (Fellowes, Barnes, & Wilkinson, 2004); chiropractic generates a feeling of being energized. Whether these feelings are due to positive suggestion, a placebo effect, the patient's expectations, or an actual physiological effect doesn't matter—the patient still benefits.

CAM is not so rigid that practitioners believe theirs is the only right way; many admit that both disease-focused and wellness-focused approaches are needed, depending on the circumstances. Health care providers who practice **integrative medicine** combine traditional biomedical interventions with CAM therapies for which there is evidence of both effectiveness and safety (NCCIH, 2016b).

For many varieties of CAM, the concept of wellness is closely connected with belief in the existence of a "life energy" or "vital force," known as **vitalism.** In **traditional Chinese medicine,** as you'll recall from Chapter 1, the life force of *qi* (pronounced *chee* in Chinese and *kee* in Japanese) is believed to flow through every cell of the body. Acupuncture, herbal therapy, and other interventions supposedly restore vitality by correcting blockages, deficiencies, and isolated excesses of qi. Ayurveda is one of the world's oldest medical systems. It originated in India more than 3,000 years ago and remains one of that country's traditional health care practices. Ayurveda concepts about health and disease promote the use of herbal compounds, minerals, special diets, and other nonallopathic health treatments.

integrative medicine A multidisciplinary approach to medicine that involves traditional biomedical interventions, as well as complementary and alternative medical practices that have been proven both safe and effective.

vitalism The concept of a general life force, popular in some varieties of complementary and alternative medicine.

traditional Chinese medicine An ancient, integrated herb- and acupuncture-based system of healing founded on the principle that internal harmony is essential for good health.

Ayurvedic Heat Treatments In ayurveda, the practitioner emphasizes treatment of the whole person, including diet, emotions, and lifestyle, as well as the specific symptoms of the disease or disorder. The patient in this photo is receiving ayurvedic oils and massage to improve blood circulation at a clinic in New Delhi, India.

How Widespread Is Complementary and Alternative Medicine?

Health care in the United States remains primarily based on allopathic medicine, yet, according to a recent survey conducted by the National Center for Complementary and Integrative Health, more than 30 percent of adults and 12 percent of children regularly use some form of CAM (NCCIH, 2016b). The most popular uses of CAM are for self-care therapies such as nonvitamin and nonmineral dietary supplements, homeopathic products, and yoga. Some people are more likely than others to use CAM. Overall, CAM is used more by women than by men, by people with higher education levels, and by people who have been hospitalized during the previous year primarily for back problems, anxiety or depression, sleeping problems, and headaches.

The use of unconventional medical therapies is increasing throughout the world. Even more important, the perceived effectiveness of CAM therapies seems to be increasing among

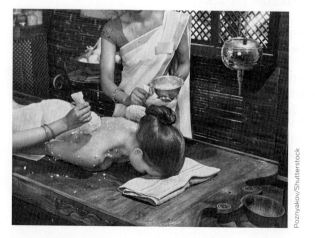

Poznyakov/Shutterstock

TABLE 15.2

Percentage of Physicians Responding to Questions Regarding CAM Treatments

Treatment	Understand treatment but uncomfortable counseling patients	Understand treatment and comfortable counseling patients
Acupuncture	45	21
Biofeedback	48	47
Megavitamin therapy	25	30
Chiropractic	29	38
Massage	27	41
Homeopathy	23	16
Herbal medicine	35	21
Spiritual healing	28	22
Aromatherapy	29	8
Energy healing	12	5
Magnetic therapy	14	12
Naturopathy	12	7
Relaxation	24	38

Data from Wahner-Roedler, D.L., Vincent, A., Elking, P.L., Loehrer, L.L., Cha, S.S., & Bauer, B.A. (2006). Physicians' attitudes toward complementary and alternative medicine and their knowledge of specific therapies: A survey at an academic medical center. *Evidence-Based Complementary and Alternative Medicine, 3*(4), 495–501.

both the general public and traditional allopathic physicians (Table 15.2). A growing number of traditionally trained physicians now practice integrative medicine by incorporating some CAM therapies into their practices (Aratani, 2009). In addition, a 2011 survey of U.S. hospitals by the American Hospital Association (AHA) found that more than 42 percent of responding hospitals indicated they offer one or more alternative medicine therapies, up from 37 percent in 2007 (AHA, 2011).

Medicine or Quackery?

Many of the same trends that led to the emergence of health psychology also have fueled increasing interest in alternative forms of medicine. These trends include increasing public concern about

- the costly and impersonal nature of modern medical care;
- the adverse effects of treatment; and
- the seemingly profit-driven nature of health care and medical research that ignores unpatentable (and unprofitable) treatment options, such as herbal medicines.

Ironically, the surge in popularity of CAM also is due, at least in part, to the success of Western biomedicine. Although people living in developed countries are less likely to die from infectious diseases such as smallpox, as average life expectancy has increased, so have the rates of chronic diseases for which biomedicine has, as of yet, no cure. CAM therapies give people something else to try as they battle such diseases and strive to increase their average health expectancy.

Finally, the "doctor knows best" attitude, which has dominated patient–provider relations, seems to be giving way to a more activist, consumer-oriented view of the patient's role. This, coupled with the growing public distrust of the scientific outlook and a reawakening of interest in mysticism and spiritualism, has given strong impetus to the CAM movement.

What Constitutes Evidence?

CAM advocates and conventional physicians and scientists differ most in their views of what constitutes an acceptable research design and which kinds of evidence are needed to demonstrate effectiveness. Biomedical researchers demand evidence from controlled clinical trials, in which treatments that are effective in eradicating or controlling individual pathogens are isolated. CAM practitioners, whose therapies are based on a more holistic philosophy, claim that treatment variables cannot always be studied independently. Many practitioners of herbal medicine, for example, claim that certain tonics and combinations of plant medicines are effective precisely *because* of the interactions among the various substances. According to this view, any attempt to isolate one ingredient from another would render the treatment useless.

As a result of such differences in perspective, many alternative practitioners are willing to endorse interventions even when the evidence backing their claims is far from convincing based on conventional standards of scientific reasoning. Health food stores, for example, have shelf after shelf of impressive-sounding literature that is largely unsupported. As always, one should keep this in mind when evaluating statements made by alternative practitioners.

Finally, the two groups differ in their focus. Rather than just seeking to remove a pathogen or to "cure" a physical condition, as biomedical practitioners do, CAM therapists emphasize the overall quality of a patient's life, broadening their focus to include important psychological, social, emotional, and spiritual aspects. Consequently, many CAM studies appear unfocused, do not use hypothesis testing or large samples, and tend to rely more on verbal reports from patients as evidence of effectiveness. It is not surprising that the quality of many CAM studies, as judged by Western scientists, is considered poor (National Center for Complementary and Alternative Medicine, 2010).

I've been told to see a chiropractor, to have my liver flushed out, and to drink hydrogen peroxide! My doctor muttered a nasty word when I said I planned to try alternative medicine. She told me it was all garbage. I'd believe her, except for one thing: I'm in pain, and her treatments are not helping me.

—A patient with lower back pain

Participant Selection and Outcome Measures

As noted in Chapter 2, scientists have established specific criteria for the proper design of a clinical trial. Besides the obvious need to use the scientific method, researchers must begin by selecting large, representative samples of research participants, grouped by gender, age, socioeconomic status, and similarity of medical condition. Then these people are assigned randomly to groups so that each has an equal chance of either receiving or not receiving the treatment of interest.

For both practical and ethical reasons, however, randomized clinical trials (RCTs) sometimes present problems for medical researchers, especially for CAM researchers. Many CAM trials include too few people in a group to allow researchers to determine whether results are statistically significant or due to chance alone. Furthermore, CAM practitioners often find it difficult (or morally unacceptable) to persuade volunteers to participate in a study in which they may be "randomized" into a no-treatment control group. For this reason, CAM evidence is often based on informal case studies. This type of *anecdotal evidence,* based as it is on subjective opinions regarding diagnosis and treatment outcomes, does little to advance the credibility of unconventional treatments.

Another weakness in CAM research is the use of incomplete, biased, or invalidated treatment outcome measures. Many CAM studies rely on self-reporting. Although within certain guidelines, self-reporting can yield useful information, skeptics are naturally concerned about the truthfulness of self-report data. Answers can be influenced by the research participants' desire to please the researchers, to appear "normal," and even to persuade themselves that they are experiencing symptom relief. This criticism is made all the more important by the fact that CAM studies too often rely on single-outcome measures rather than on several different measures that might or might not provide converging lines of evidence. Over the years, several NIH panels evaluating research on acupuncture, for example, have concluded that there are too few acceptable studies comparing the effectiveness of acupuncture with either placebo or sham controls, and so these panels encouraged future researchers to provide accurate descriptions of protocols for the types and number of treatments, subject enrollment procedures, and methods of diagnosing outcomes (NCCIH, 2016a; NIH, 1998).

Participant Expectancy and the Placebo Effect

Medical students are often taught the story of "Mr. Wright," a California cancer patient who was given only a few days to live. After hearing that scientists had discovered that a horse serum called *Krebiozen* might be effective against cancer, he begged his doctor to administer it. Reluctantly, the patient's physician gave Mr. Wright an injection. Three days later, the disbelieving doctor found that the patient's golf-ball-sized tumors "had melted like snowballs on a hot stove." Two months later, after reading a medical report that the serum was actually a quack remedy, Mr. Wright suffered an immediate relapse and died.

Although many doctors dismiss this story as an anecdote, researchers have long recognized that part of medicine's power to heal is derived from the expectations that both patients and practitioners bring to therapy. Whenever patients are treated for an illness or health condition, any improvement may be due to one of four explanations:

- The treatment may actually be effective.
- The illness simply improved on its own over time. This is true of most illnesses, including pain, which tend to be cyclical, *self-limiting conditions*. Because most people seek help when they are symptomatic, any intervention that occurs—whether inert or otherwise—is likely to be followed by improvement, often creating a powerful illusory correlation that it is the intervention rather than the passage of time and the body's self-healing, autonomous responses that caused the improvement.
- The patients were misdiagnosed and in fact did not have an illness at all.
- Patients improve on their own because of some nonspecific effect, such as their belief that the treatment will be beneficial (*placebo effect*).

Placebos are physiologically inert substances that have been shown to treat a variety of conditions successfully due to the patient's expectations of healing. Inert substances, however, also can have adverse health effects. When they do, they have been called *nocebos*. A **nocebo** (a word that means in Latin "I will harm," in contrast to *placebo*, which means "I will please") is a harmless substance or treatment that ends up creating a harmful effect. A *nocebo response* occurs, for example, when a participant in a controlled clinical trial of a drug reports uncomfortable side effects after taking a placebo. The same substance or treatment can work as both a placebo and a nocebo. In one study, researchers gave participants who believed they were allergic to various foods an injection that they were told contained the allergen. Although the injection contained only salt water, a number of participants experienced allergic reactions. Then the researchers injected salt water again, this time telling participants it would neutralize the effects of the previous injection. In many cases, it did (Barsky, Saintfort, Rogers, & Borus, 2002).

Why do placebos and nocebos work? According to one explanation, the medical treatments that we receive over the course of our lives are like conditioning trials, and we still may experience a therapeutic benefit as a *conditioned response* to the same medical stimuli. Herbert Benson (1996) has suggested that "remembered wellness" is another conditioned factor in placebo responding. After any therapeutic intervention, he suggests, we have a memory of past events, which helps to trigger a beneficial physical response.

nocebo A harmless substance that nevertheless creates harmful effects in a person who takes it.

FIGURE 15.1

Placebo Analgesia Visible injections of placebos were significantly more effective in reducing pain than hidden injections, suggesting that it was not the placebo itself, but rather knowledge of the placebo that produced analgesia. In addition, injections that blocked endorphin production (naloxone) disrupted placebo-induced analgesia, whereas those that enhanced the activity of endorphins (proglumide) strengthened placebo-induced analgesia.

Data from Benedetti, F. (1996). The opposite effects of the opiate antagonist naloxone and the cholecystokinin antagonist proglumide on placebo analgesia. *Pain, 64*(3), 540.

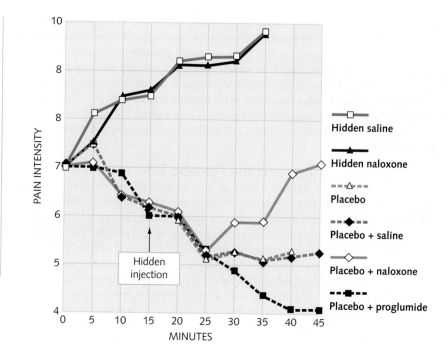

A closely related explanation is that placebos tap into the body's natural "inner pharmacy" of self-healing substances. For instance, placebos may reduce levels of cortisol, norepinephrine, and other stress hormones. Researchers also strongly suspect that at least part of placebo-based pain relief occurs because placebos stimulate the release of *endorphins,* morphine-like neurotransmitters produced by the brain. In one remarkable study, Fabrizio Benedetti (1996) asked 340 healthy people to squeeze hand exercisers repeatedly while tourniquets on their arms limited blood flow, causing pain that increased over time (Figure 15.1). Throughout the ordeal, the participants periodically rated their pain on a 10-point scale that ranged from 1 (no pain) to 10 (unbearable). When participants reached 7 on the scale, one of several drugs or saline solution was administered through an intravenous line, either fully within their view or surreptitiously.

Benedetti's results were important for several reasons. First, because only a *visible* placebo reduced pain, it was clearly not the placebo itself that reduced the pain, but rather the *knowledge* of the placebo that did the trick. Second, placebo-induced analgesia (pain relief) clearly was mediated by the body's autonomous production of endorphins in response to the expectation that a treatment (a visible injection) would be beneficial: Pharmacological interventions that blocked endorphin production (naloxone) disrupted placebo-induced analgesia, while those that enhanced the activity of endorphins (proglumide) strengthened placebo-induced analgesia.

Although any medical procedure—from drugs to surgery—can have a placebo effect, critics contend that CAM is entirely placebo based. When conventional therapies fail to help, the acupuncturist, chiropractor, or herbalist presents a powerful belief system designed to give the suffering patient hope that help is available. It is ironic that biomedicine's insistence on rigorous standards of scientific "proof" of the efficacy of a new drug or alternative therapy actually may have provided the strongest testimony for the prevalence of the placebo effect. "Scientific proof" requires the use of a double-blind RCT (see Chapter 2). The method is based on the premise that if either the patient or the researcher knows which treatment is "supposed to work," it would indeed work. Thus, the working assumption is that the placebo effect occurs routinely.

Does Complementary and Alternative Medicine Work?

How effective is complementary and alternative medicine? What works and what doesn't? In this section, we will try to answer these questions for several of the most widely used alternative treatments: acupuncture, mind–body therapies, chiropractic, and naturopathic medicine.

Acupuncture

Acupuncture was first practiced during the Bronze Age in ancient China as part of an integrated system of healing that was founded on the principle that internal harmony is essential for good health. In the West, it was recognized only 100 years ago or so. Although Asian-Americans have a long history with acupuncture, general interest in acupuncture in the United States did not increase noticeably until 1971, when a *New York Times* reporter underwent an emergency operation in China, was later treated with acupuncture for complications, and then wrote all about it for the newspaper (Reston, 1971). Since then, acupuncture schools have begun springing up, and there are currently about 30,000 licensed acupuncturists in the United States (Council of Colleges of Acupuncture and Oriental Medicine, 2016).

An acupuncture session typically involves inserting thin acupuncture needles superficially or as deep as 1 or more inches, depending on the particular site and the practitioner's style of treatment. Which of the approximately 2000 acupuncture points are selected, along with the angle and depth of the needle insertion, varies with the symptom. Needles are sometimes twirled, heated, or electrically stimulated to maximize their effects. Acupuncturists often also incorporate herbal medicine and dietary recommendations in their treatment regimens—two other common components of traditional Oriental medicine.

acupuncture A component of traditional Oriental medicine in which fine needles are inserted into the skin to relieve pain, treat addiction and illness, and promote health.

How Is Acupuncture Supposed to Work?

The honest answer to this question is that no one really knows. Traditional acupuncturists believe that every part of the body corresponds to the whole, whether it's the ear or the sole of the foot. Classical acupuncture theory identifies 14 "lines of energy" (qi) on the body, called *meridians*. Most acupuncture points, believed to allow for corrections of blockages or deficiencies in qi, lie on these meridians. Treatment typically involves inserting one or more needles at a point at one end of a meridian to produce effects at the other end. Early researchers tried unsuccessfully to match the meridian lines with physical structures in the body.

But many conventional doctors, including those who practice acupuncture, find it hard to accept the concept of an invisible energy path, or qi, preferring instead to explain any treatment success as an example of the placebo effect. Others maintain that the pain of inserting acupuncture needles simply distracts the patient from his or her original pain, or that acupuncture triggers the release of the body's own natural painkillers (endorphins) and anti-inflammatory agents. None of these explanations, however, is widely accepted.

Today, using tools such as functional magnetic resonance imaging (fMRI) and positron emission tomography (PET), researchers are probing the brain in search of specific acupuncture sites and effects. A recent meta-analysis of 34 studies using fMRI to

Acupuncture Acupuncture, originally practiced only in China, has become increasingly popular throughout Western industrialized nations. It has proved most successful in treating pain, although practitioners contend that it rejuvenates the body.

Toronto Star/Getty Images

investigate the effect of acupuncture on the brain reported that acupuncture modulates neural activity in brain regions that are involved not only in somatosensory processing, but also in affective and cognitive processing. Compared to sham acupuncture, needle acupuncture was associated with greater activation in the basal ganglia, brain stem, and cerebellum, and greater deactivation in limbic brain areas such as the amygdala and hippocampus (Huang and others, 2012). These results suggest that acupuncture-induced analgesia may result from activation of descending pain pathways and other brain structures that modulate the perception of pain (see Chapters 3 and 14). Additional evidence that the analgesic effects of acupuncture are reversed by naloxone, which blocks neural receptor sites for endorphins and other opiates, supports the hypothesis that acupuncture triggers the release of opioid peptides (natural painkillers) (Gardea, Gatchel, & Robinson, 2004). In addition, there is some evidence that acupuncture activates the hypothalamic-pituitary-adrenal (HPA) axis (see Chapter 4) and influences the functioning of the immune system (NIH Consensus Conference, 1998).

How Well Does Acupuncture Work?

The only scientific way to determine the effectiveness of interventions such as acupuncture is through controlled studies. But such studies are difficult to perform for several reasons: First, the highly individualized nature of acupuncture does not lend itself well to standardized tests. Acupuncturists themselves disagree about the appropriate acupuncture needle sites for a given medical condition. Also, because some studies allow acupuncturists to choose their own points of stimulation, to control the number of sessions, and to use electrical stimulation if desired, it is very difficult for researchers to isolate independent variables or to compare study results.

Double-blind controls, the mainstay of clinical trials, are even more problematic. Needles can be inserted at points that are inappropriate to a patient's health problem, making the patient blind to treatment, but the acupuncturist has to know whether the points are sham or real, so the study can't be double-blind. In one clever study, one acupuncturist diagnosed the patient's condition and another acupuncturist, who was unaware of the diagnosis, inserted the needles *where the first acupuncturist instructed.* In some patients, the needles were inserted into appropriate points that matched the diagnosis; in others, the needles were inserted into sham sites (Warwick-Evans, Masters, & Redstone, 1991).

Recent fMRI studies indicate that acupuncture modulates neural activity in brain regions that are involved not only in somatosensory processing, but also in affective and cognitive processing.

Information from Huang, W., Pach, D., Napadow, V., Park, K., Long, X, and others (2012). Characterizing acupuncture stimuli using brain imaging with fMRI—A systematic review and meta-analysis of the literature. *PLoS One, 7*(4): e32960: doi:10.1371/journal. pone.0032960.

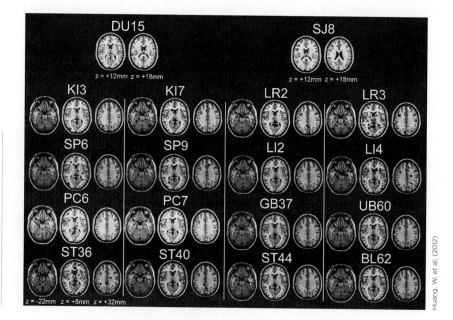

Huang, W. et al. (2012)

Research trials that use sham acupuncture often show that it has some effect—and in some cases, the effect is as strong as genuine acupuncture (Ernst, Pittler, Wider, & Boddy, 2007). Needless to say, the idea that stabbing patients at random points may be nearly as effective as using real acupuncture points is quite disturbing to acupuncturists who spend years memorizing locations.

Yet another difficulty is that operational definitions of successful acupuncture treatments have been inconsistent at best, woefully vague at worst. In the case of addiction research, success has been defined variously as complete abstinence, decreased use, decreased cravings, diminished withdrawal symptoms, improved outlook, and increased productivity. Thus, one study may characterize an intervention as successful because substance use decreased overall even though more than half the participants relapsed, while another may report similar findings as indicating a failed intervention. Such variations make it impossible to compare one study to another.

Acupuncture and Pain

Hundreds of randomized clinical trials testing acupuncture's effectiveness on 10 painful conditions have been conducted. These studies provide evidence, although not statistically conclusive, that acupuncture provides *some* patients with *some* relief from painful conditions such as osteoarthritis, fibromyalgia, neck and lower back pain, pelvic pain during pregnancy, migraine headaches, tennis elbow, and postoperative dental and hemorrhoid pain (Vickers & Linde, 2014).

Despite the evidence that acupuncture holds some promise in treating pain, addiction, and depression, its overall effectiveness remains controversial (NCCIH, 2016a). A 2007 review concluded that while the number of controlled clinical trials had increased for 13 of the 26 conditions studied, the evidence was favorable for only 7 of them. For 6 of the conditions, the evidence was unfavorable (Ernst and others, 2007). Despite the inconsistency of research evidence for acupuncture's effectiveness, acupuncture's success rate is among the highest of all alternative medical interventions, and for some individuals, its effectiveness with some conditions compares favorably with conventional treatments.

Most states and the District of Columbia have established clinical practice standards for acupuncturists. These standards are official statements from professional societies and government agencies that either describe how to care for patients with specific health conditions or illustrate specific techniques. Practitioners who have met these standards are "licensed" or "certified" by the National Certification Commission for Acupuncture and Oriental Medicine.

Acupuncture, Substance Abuse, and Depression

Excluding 12-step programs, acupuncture is the most widely used CAM method for the treatment of substance abuse, especially of nicotine, alcohol, heroin, and cocaine (Carter, Olshan-Perlmutter, Norton, & Smith, 2011). More than 2000 alcohol and drug treatment programs in the United States and 40 other countries have added ear acupuncture to their protocols (Smith, 2012). The goals of acupuncture treatment include reducing the symptoms of withdrawal, including drug craving, keeping abusers in treatment programs, and continued abstinence from drug use.

Research studies of laboratory rats have shown that acupuncture stimulates the release of serotonin in the *nucleus accumbens* (NAC), a brain region that has an important role in pleasure, addiction, the expectation of reward, and the placebo effect (Yoshimoto and others, 2006). Given this effect on the NAC, it may not surprise you to learn that the World Health Organization (WHO) classifies depression as a condition for which acupuncture has been proved through randomized clinical trials to be an effective treatment (WHO, 2013a). In one study, acupuncture was found to be comparable to antidepressant drugs in relieving symptoms of depression (Leo & Ligot, 2007). Another meta-analysis of eight small trials (with a total of 477 patients) concluded that acupuncture "could significantly reduce the severity of depression" (H. Wang and others, 2008). However, a more recent review of studies analyzed data from 30 trials (with a total of 2812 patients) and found "insufficient evidence of a consistent beneficial effect from acupuncture" in treatment of depression (Smith, Hay, & MacPherson, 2010). This latter review, though, included several studies suggesting that acupuncture may have an additive benefit when combined with standard pharmaceutical treatment of depression.

In 1996, the U.S. Food and Drug Administration (FDA) classified acupuncture needles as a type of medical device, boosting the credibility of acupuncturists and increasing the likelihood that an insurance provider will pay for acupuncture treatments. Although the American Medical Association (AMA) does not officially sanction acupuncture, more than 2000 of the 12,000 acupuncturists in the United States are MDs. As another sign of growing recognition, the WHO has identified some 50 diseases for which it considers acupuncture an appropriate treatment (WHO, 2013a).

Mind–Body Therapies

The basic premise of mind–body therapies is that cognitive, emotional, and spiritual factors can have profound effects on one's health (NCCIH, 2016b). In this section, we'll examine three of the most popular mind–body therapies: hypnosis, relaxation and meditation (including tai chi and yoga), and spiritual healing and prayer.

Hypnosis

hypnosis A social interaction in which one person (the hypnotist) suggests to another that certain thoughts, feelings, perceptions, or behaviors will occur.

Hypnosis is a psychological state that results from a social interaction in which one person (the hypnotist) suggests to another (the hypnotized person) that certain thoughts, feelings, perceptions, or behaviors will occur. Hypnosis is most often used to treat pain.

Depending on the hypnotherapist, a variety of cognitive processes may come into play during a session of hypnosis, including focused attention, relaxation, imagery, expectation, and role-playing. The most salient feature of hypnosis is the *hypnotic trance,* which is a waking state of attentive and focused concentration in which the subject becomes detached from his or her surroundings and becomes absorbed by the hypnotist's suggestions.

Hypnosis and Pain A typical hypnosis intervention for pain involves several overlapping stages:

The Power of Suggestion The power of hypnosis resides not in the hypnotist, but in the subject's openness to suggestion.

Superstock/Alamy

- a prehypnotic stage, in which the therapist builds rapport with the subject;
- the use of suggestions and imagery to induce relaxation and the focused attention of the hypnotic trance;
- the treatment stage, which may involve various kinds of suggestions and imagery to reduce the experience of pain;
- a "consolidation phase," which may incorporate *posthypnotic suggestions* to be carried out after the hypnosis session has ended; and
- a posthypnotic stage, in which the patient is awakened, given additional instructions, and released. In addition, the hypnotherapist may train patients in self-hypnosis so they can practice the therapy at home.

Does Hypnosis Work? Physiologically, hypnosis resembles other forms of imagery work and deep relaxation, because it is accompanied by a generalized decrease in sympathetic nervous system activity, a decrease in oxygen consumption and carbon dioxide elimination, a lowering of blood pressure and heart rate, and an increase in certain kinds of brain-wave activity. This suggests that hypnotic phenomena reflect the workings of normal consciousness. We all probably flow naturally in and out of hypnotic-like states all the time—for example, while watching a mind-numbing television program. Many researchers believe that people often move into trancelike states of focused concentration when they are under stress, such as when they are about to experience an uncomfortable treatment. During such moments, when a person in a position of authority issues an instruction, it may have as strong an effect as a posthypnotic suggestion. Those who are most likely to report pain relief from hypnosis also tend to be highly suggestible, fantasy-prone people and to be very responsive to authority figures. Evidence from electroencephalograph (EEG) recordings suggests that there are indeed differences in frontal lobe and temporal lobe activity between individuals who are high and low in hypnotizability.

For highly hypnotizable people, hypnosis does appear to be more powerful than a placebo for coping with pain (Patterson, Jensen, & Montgomery, 2010). For people who are low in hypnotizability, hypnotic suggestions of analgesia are no more effective than drug placebos (Miller, Barabasz, & Barabasz, 1991). For people who are easily hypnotized, however, hypnosis can be an effective intervention for migraine and tension headaches (Milling, 2008), pain associated with the care of burn wounds (Askay, Patterson, Jensen, & Sharar, 2007), pain associated with surgery and other invasive medical procedures, and the pain of childbirth (Cyna, McAuliffe, & Andrew, 2004). Hypnosis seems to be most effective in helping people manage acute pain rather than chronic pain.

A recent meta-analysis of fMRI studies of hypnotic analgesia points to possible neurological mechanisms of pain relief. The study found that hypnotic suggestions are linked to specific changes in activation in several brain areas within the "pain matrix." Compared with control conditions (normal wakefulness or hypnosis with no suggestions of analgesia), hypnotic suggestions of analgesia during experimental pain are associated with increased activation in the right anterior cingulate cortex and insula and with decreased activation in the thalamus. Activation of this bilateral cortical network may result in reductions in pain intensity (Del Casale and others, 2016).

Relaxation and Meditation

As noted in other chapters, relaxation and meditation are related therapies that have proved successful in helping some patients cope with and recover from a number of medical conditions. *Meditation* refers to a variety of techniques or practices intended to focus or control attention (NCCIH, 2016b). Those who practice **mindfulness meditation** learn to pay nonjudgmental, in-the-moment attention to changing perceptions and thoughts. Conversely, in *transcendental meditation,* the person focuses awareness on a single object or on a word or short phrase, called a *mantra.* Proponents of meditation claim that its practice can influence the experience of chronic illness positively and can serve as a primary, secondary, and/or tertiary prevention strategy (Bonadonna, 2003).

In his classic experiment on relaxation, Herbert Benson (1993) fitted experienced practitioners of transcendental meditation with measurement devices to record changes in a number of physiological functions, including oxygen consumption—a reliable indicator of the body's overall metabolic state. After recording the participants' physiological state for a 20-minute baseline period during which they simply sat in a quiet resting position, Benson instructed the participants to begin meditating. The participants were not permitted to change their posture or activity; they simply changed their thoughts to maintain a meditative focus. Following the meditation period, which also lasted 20 minutes, they

In childhood, fantasizers had at least one, but usually many, imaginary companions often drawn from storybook characters, real-life playmates who had moved away, and pets and toys whom they believed could talk. One of my subjects had seen the movie Camelot *as a child and, for two years, imagined being the son of Arthur and Guinevere, commanding the King's court.*

—Deirdre Barrett, hypnotherapist

mindfulness meditation
The practice of paying nonjudgmental, in-the-moment attention to changing perceptions and thoughts.

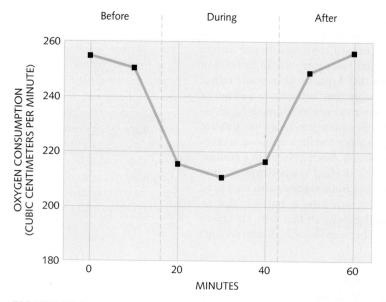

FIGURE 15.2

Oxygen Consumption during Transcendental Meditation The body's metabolic rate, reflected in the amount of oxygen consumed, decreased significantly in experienced meditators when they switched from simply resting (Before) to meditating (During); it rose when they stopped meditating (After).

Data from Benson, H. (1993). The relaxation response. In D. Goleman & J. Gurin (Eds.), *Mind-body medicine* (pp. 233-257). New York: Consumer Reports Books.

were instructed to return to their normal state of thinking. The participants consumed significantly less oxygen while meditating than they did in the premeditation period (Figure 15.2). Other changes occurred during meditation as well: Breathing slowed from a rate of 14 or 15 breaths per minute to approximately 10 or 11 breaths, and brain-wave patterns included more low-frequency alpha, theta, and delta waves—waves associated with rest and relaxation—and significantly fewer high-frequency beta waves associated with higher states of alertness. In addition, during meditation, the level of lactate (a chemical that has been linked to anxiety) in the participants' bloodstream decreased dramatically.

Relaxation, meditation, and other physiological self-regulation techniques are effective in helping to manage a variety of disorders (NCCIH, 2016b). Recall from Chapter 5 that *mindfulness-based stress reduction* (MBSR) and *mindfulness-based cognitive therapy* (MBCT) have been used to improve people's ability to self-regulate negative reactions to stress. MBSR and MBCT have been extensively tested in randomized clinical trials using a standard eight-week instructional format focused on three somatically focused techniques in meditation: body scan, sitting meditation, and mindful yoga (Fjorback, Arendt, Ornbol, Fink, & Walach, 2011). For instance, the first two weeks of the eight-week *standardized mindfulness* (ST-mindfulness) training program involves practice devoted to a meditative body scan of "moving a focused spotlight of attention from one part of the body to another." This exercise presumably enables practitioners to learn to "control the attention spotlight" even when focusing on painful sensations.

Research has shown that the benefits of mindfulness meditation are far-reaching, from minimizing pain sensitivity to helping people regulate their emotions. Indeed, for patients with chronic pain, meditation is effective, according to a National Institutes of Health review (Lebovits, 2007). One study demonstrated the pain-relieving benefits of mindfulness training for people with inflammatory rheumatic joint diseases (Zangl and others, 2011). The study included 73 people with rheumatoid arthritis between ages 20 and 70. Half were randomly assigned to perform mindfulness exercises in 10 group sessions for 15 weeks, as well as another session six months after the 10 sessions were completed. The remaining participants received conventional treatment for the condition, as well as a CD that taught them how to do mindfulness exercises. In this particular study, mindfulness training aimed to help people concentrate on their own thoughts, experiences, and pain in the moment, without actively trying to avoid them or evaluate them. At the end of the study, the people who had the group mindfulness training scored significantly lower in measurements of pain, stress, and fatigue than people who didn't have the training.

Based on multiple RCTs, we find good evidence that mindfulness training is also effective in preventing depression (Piet & Hougaard, 2011) and in improving quality of life in chronic pain conditions such as fibromyalgia (Schmidt and others, 2011) and lower back pain (Morone, Greco, & Weiner, 2008); in chronic functional disorders such as irritable bowel syndrome (IBS) (Gaylord and others, 2011); and in illnesses such as cancer (Speca, Carlson, Goodey, & Angen, 2000) and multiple sclerosis (Grossman and others, 2013). One remarkable study reported that mindfulness meditation also slows the progression of HIV disease, as measured by CD4 T cell count (Creswell, Myers, Cole, & Irwin, 2009). ST-mindfulness also helps people cope with difficult life situations such as caring for a loved one with Alzheimer's disease (Epstein-Lubow, Miller, & McBee, 2006).

Tai Chi and Yoga Sometimes called "moving meditation," **tai chi** originated in China hundreds of years ago and is a component of traditional Oriental medicine. A blend of exercise, dance, and concentration, the movements of tai chi are slow, circular, continuous, smooth, and controlled, and weight is shifted regularly from one foot to another (NCCIH, 2016c). Groups of people concentrating on the rhythmical, dancelike movements of tai chi are a common sight throughout China.

Yoga, a Sanskrit word meaning "union," has strong ties to spiritual and mystical traditions originating in India, where it has been practiced for thousands of years. Yoga encompasses a global lifestyle, consisting of diet, meditation, and physical exercise that is now practiced by more than 20 million people in the United States on a regular basis (Li & Goldsmith, 2012). The two primary forms practiced in the West are *hatha yoga* (physical postures and breathing) and *raja yoga* (relaxation and mental and spiritual mastery).

It is widely believed that yoga and tai chi provide some of the physical and psychological benefits of more strenuous exercise without straining the muscles or the cardiovascular system. Tai chi has been shown to improve balance and stability in older adults and in those with Parkinson's disease, reduce back and knee pain due to osteoarthritis, and generally improve well-being in people with cancer, heart disease, and other chronic diseases (NCCIH, 2016c). Yoga is also used to treat fatigue, chronic pain, and many ailments related to stress and anxiety. Because stress and anxiety contribute to many chronic conditions, yoga and tai chi are nondrug treatment options that many people find improve their quality of life (National Center for Complementary and Alternative Medicine, 2013b).

Although tai chi and yoga may offer no special advantages over other forms of relaxation and exercise, and evidence of their effectiveness may have limited generalizability because most studies failed to use randomized trials with control groups, they are growing in popularity, largely because health benefits *are* often demonstrated when comparing a participant's own pre- and postintervention status (National Center for Complementary and Alternative Medicine, 2013b).

How Might Relaxation and Meditation Promote Health? Just how relaxation or meditation might promote health is the subject of ongoing debate. One suggestion is that the relaxation at the center of these therapies relieves stress, muscle tension, anxiety, and negative emotionality, all of which might exacerbate physical symptoms and increase a person's vulnerability to ill health.

Researchers also have suggested that relaxation and meditation may alter a person's emotional response to symptoms such as pain. "I'm still in constant pain," notes one woman, who joined the pain reduction program at the University of Massachusetts after a bad fall left her with neck and back injuries and fibromyalgia. "Meditation makes the pain more bearable. I have less pain, muscles are more relaxed, and I have much better mobility" (Eisenberg and others, 1998). This makes sense, according to mind–body therapy advocates, because these techniques alter the way that pain sufferers respond to painful sensations and the way that they feel about them. Relaxation interventions often teach pain sufferers to reinterpret painful sensations, regarding them as "warm, even pleasant" rather than "burning and unpleasant" (Eisenberg and others, 1998).

In addition, relaxation and meditation may bolster the immune system. In one randomized trial, 40 adults between the ages of 55 and 85 were divided into two groups. One practiced mindfulness-based stress reduction that involved attending two-hour weekly meetings, meditating at home daily for 30 minutes, and attending a day-long retreat. A control group did not meditate. Researchers took blood samples at the start and end of the study to measure gene expression and levels of inflammation. MBSR participants reported reduced feelings of loneliness, and their blood tests indicated a significant drop in the expression of inflammation-related genes. These included the marker C-reactive

tai chi A form of "moving meditation" that blends exercise, dance, and concentration, and is a component of traditional Oriental medicine.

yoga A movement-based form of relaxation and meditation that combines diet, physical postures, and breathing to promote physical and spiritual well-being.

Mind–Body Interventions Relaxation, meditation, and other physiological self-regulation techniques are effective in helping to manage a variety of disorders.

Radius/Radius/Superstock

protein (CRP), a strong risk factor for heart disease; and a group of genes regulated by the transcription factor NF-κB—a molecular signal that activates inflammation (Creswell and others, 2012).

Other studies have shown that MBSR training significantly reduced levels of a pro-inflammatory cytokine (interleukin-6) (Tomfohr, Pung, Mills, & Edwards, 2015), as well as other markers of inflammation (Rosenkranz and others, 2013). In one randomized clinical trial, a 12-week yoga intervention significantly reduced fatigue and inflammation by altering gene expression in a group of breast cancer survivors (Bower and others, 2014).

Despite the growing body of evidence that mindfulness interventions can improve a broad range of health outcomes, the biological pathways linking mindfulness and health are not well understood. Noting that mindfulness-based health effects seem to most often occur in high-stress populations, some researchers have suggested that mindfulness training produces its effects on health indirectly by altering a person's cognitive appraisal processes when potential stressors are encountered (see Chapter 5). According to this view, mindfulness facilitates a person's capacity to observe stressors as they arise with acceptance and equanimity, which in turn buffers initial threat appraisals and increases secondary appraisals of coping resources. Consequently, mindfulness may decrease the likelihood of rumination about potential stressors and increase the likelihood of using problem-focused, approach-oriented coping strategies (Creswell & Lindsay, 2014).

Using fMRI and other neuroimaging techniques, other research studies have begun to assemble the brain mechanisms by which meditation modulates the experience of pain. These studies indicate that mindfulness meditation engages several brain mechanisms that subjectively influence the pain experience. For instance, mindfulness training may trigger changes in limbic areas involved in emotional regulation. One study reported decreased amygdala activation after mindfulness training in social anxiety patients who were exposed to socially threatening stimuli (Goldin & Gross, 2010).

Other scientists believe that mindfulness practices are accompanied by reduced pain-related activation of areas in the somatosensory cortex and increased activity in the anterior cingulate cortex (ACC), which, as we have seen, are brain areas involved in pain processing. In one study, mindfulness meditation in the presence of painful stimuli reduced pain intensity ratings significantly (by 40 percent) compared to control conditions (Zeidan and others, 2011). Meditation also was associated with *thalamic deactivation,* suggesting a gating effect between incoming sensory signals and executive-order brain areas. In another study, mindfulness practitioners were able to reduce the unpleasantness and anxiety associated with painful stimuli significantly by 22 percent and 29 percent, respectively, compared to controls (Gard and others, 2011). These benefits were associated with decreased activation in the prefrontal cortex during painful stimuli and increased activation in the ACC while anticipating pain.

According to other researchers, mindfulness practice—the ability to observe your thoughts and feelings from an objective distance—works as something of a "volume control" for sensations, giving experienced practitioners better control over how the brain processes pain and emotions. In one study, Brown University scientists observed that when people focused their attention on sensations in the left hand, the corresponding "map" for the hand in the cortex showed a significant decrease in the amplitude of alpha brain waves. When the participants shifted their attention away from the body part, the alpha wave amplitude increased. Subsequent studies showed that participants who received eight weeks of mindfulness training produced quicker and larger changes in alpha wave amplitude during the attention shift than did untrained control participants (Orenstein, 2013).

Perhaps most remarkable of all, scientists have reported that mindfulness meditation is linked to actual physical changes in the brain—beneficial changes that enhance the transmission of neural signals (Tang, Lu, Fan, Yang, & Posner, 2012). Brain imaging researchers from the University of Oregon reported that two weeks after practicing mindfulness meditation, the study participants had an increase in axonal density in their brain's anterior cingulate cortex. After a month, there were even more increases in neural connections, as well as an increase in the myelin coating of axons in the ACC.

Thus, mindful people seem to remain unfazed by potential stressors for two reasons. First, they recruit increased activity in brain regions that aid emotion regulation and show less activity in brain regions such as the amygdala linked to stressful responses (Way, Creswell, Eisenberger, & Lieberman, 2010). Second, their sympatho-adrenal-medullary (SAM) and hypothalamic-pituitary-adrenal (HPA) axes do not go into overdrive when potential stressors are encountered. Mindful people recognize and accept stress, which buffers them from increased heart rate or excessive secretion of cortisol and other stress hormones (Nyklíček, Mommersteeg, Van Beugen, Ramakers, & Van Boxtel, 2013).

Biofeedback

First described by Neal Miller in the late 1960s, **biofeedback** is a technique for converting certain supposedly involuntary physiological responses—such as skin temperature, muscle activity, heart rate, and blood pressure—into electrical signals and providing visual or auditory feedback about them (Miller, 1969). It is based on the principle that we learn to perform a specific response when we receive information (feedback) about the consequences of that response and then make appropriate adjustments.

Using an electronic monitoring device that detects and amplifies internal responses, biofeedback training begins by helping the person gain awareness of a maladaptive response, such as tense forehead muscles. Next, the person focuses attention on a tone, light, or some other signal that identifies desirable changes in the internal response. By attempting to control this biofeedback signal, the patient learns to control his or her physiological state. Finally, the individual learns to transfer control from the laboratory setting to everyday life.

The most common biofeedback technique in clinical use today is *electromyography* (EMG) *feedback*. EMG biofeedback detects skeletal muscle activity by measuring muscle tension via the electrical discharge of muscle fibers. Electrodes are attached to the skin over the muscles to be monitored. The biofeedback machine responds with an auditory signal that reflects the electrical activity (tension) of the muscle being measured. EMG biofeedback to decrease muscle tension has been used to treat facial tics, spasmodic movements, and other muscular disorders. In addition, it has been used to treat headaches and lower back pain.

Another common technique, *thermal biofeedback,* is based on the principle that skin temperature tends to vary in relation to a person's perceived level of stress. The rationale for this technique is that high stress, which often causes blood vessels in the skin to constrict, may be linked to cooler surface skin temperatures. Accordingly, by placing a temperature-sensitive instrument on the skin's surface (most often the fingertips), people sometimes are able to raise their skin temperature by monitoring an auditory or visual feedback signal. Thermal biofeedback is often used to help people cope with stress and pain. It is also frequently used with migraine and tension headache patients (NCCIH, 2016b).

biofeedback A system that provides audible or visible feedback information regarding involuntary physiological states.

A patient undergoes biofeedback monitoring for stress.

Science Source/Getty Images

Heart Rate Variability Biofeedback

Until recently, biofeedback research has focused almost exclusively on calming sympathetic arousal as a by-product of gaining control over visual and aural stimuli that change in response to average heart rate, blood pressure, muscle tension, and the skin's temperature and electrical conductance. As heart rate slows, for instance, and the hands become warm and dry, sympathetic arousal is reduced and relaxation seems to occur. Increasingly, however, researchers are studying the health effects of using feedback to more directly affect parasympathetic activity.

Case in point: heart rate biofeedback. Psychophysiological research studies have shown that the electrical activity of the healthy heart is complex and characterized by considerable variation in the time interval between beats. This beat-to-beat **heart rate variability (HRV)** was not apparent with the simpler measure of average heart rate that was the focus of earlier studies (Billman, 2011). Healthy HRV, which has been described as "chaotic," involves multiple oscillation frequencies controlled by different autonomic feedback loops that work to maintain allostatic balance in response to changing environmental demands (Lehrer & Eddie, 2013).

A good portion of HRV reflects the impact of breathing. Heart rate increases when we inhale and decreases when we exhale. This normal *respiratory sinus arrhythmia* (RSA) is also influenced by external factors, such as exercise and perceived stress, as well as age and fitness levels. RSA is very pronounced in children, but without sufficient cardiovascular exercise, it gradually declines with age. Adults in excellent cardiovascular health, such as endurance runners, swimmers, and cyclists, are likely to have a more pronounced RSA (and HRV). RSA (and HRV) also becomes less prominent in individuals with diabetes, cardiovascular disease, chronic pain, and a variety of other chronic conditions (Lehrer & Gevirtz, 2014).

Because HRV is viewed as a measure of strength and balance in the autonomic nervous system, there is mounting support for the use of *heart rate variability biofeedback* (HRVB) as a treatment for a variety of disorders associated with autonomic dysregulation (Lehrer & Gevirtz, 2014). The procedure consists of displaying autonomic data as participants engage in slow, paced breathing exercises aimed at determining the breathing rate that produces the greatest HRV. Sensors detect beat-to-beat heart rate, breathing, and finger temperature. This feedback is displayed on a computer monitor situated in front of the seated client or study participant, who learns to produce a characteristic heart rate pattern by breathing at a certain rate (for example, six breaths per minute), which over time becomes a very smooth, exaggerated sine wave. The client is then instructed to practice breathing at this rate in daily sessions, often using a smartphone app that provides pacing stimuli and connects to sensors that track heart rate variability. During HRVB, the amplitude of heart rate oscillations typically increases to many times the amplitude at rest.

HRVB interventions have been used with people with many health conditions, including asthma, chronic obstructive pulmonary disease (COPD), IBS, recurrent abdominal pain, fibromyalgia, hypertension, chronic muscle pain, depression, anxiety, and PTSD (see Gevirtz, 2013, for a review). As with other areas of CAM research, the literature on HRVB is dominated by small pilot studies and a few randomized trials. While much more research is needed, HRV biofeedback training appears to offer promise as a health-promoting intervention, especially when combined with cognitive behavioral therapy, acceptance and commitment therapy, or another mindfulness-based intervention (Gevirtz, 2015).

How Effective Is Biofeedback?

Although it can be expensive, biofeedback has proved to be somewhat beneficial in treating stress-related health problems in some people. For example, research support is relatively strong for alleviation of tension headaches (presumed to involve chronic muscle tension in the neck and head) and migraine headaches (Nestoriuc & Martin, 2007). Other disorders for which there is at least some research support to justify the therapeutic use of biofeedback include asthma, fibromyalgia, irritable bowel syndrome, urinary

heart rate variability (HRV) The normal and healthy variation in the rate at which the heart beats.

incontinence, tinnitus, epileptic seizures, and motion sickness (Moss & Gunkelman, 2002).

Despite some promising results, several important questions remain about the medical effectiveness of biofeedback. To date, there have been relatively few well-controlled clinical outcome trials using large numbers of patients who have confirmed medical conditions. Two limitations have emerged in clinical evaluations of biofeedback (Steptoe, 1997). First, people often cannot generalize the training that they receive in clinical settings to everyday situations. Second, research has not confirmed that biofeedback itself enables people to control their internal, involuntary responses. Even when biofeedback is effective, it is not clear why, which raises the possibility that relaxation, suggestion, an enhanced sense of control, or even a placebo effect may be operating (Gatchel, 1997).

The few available studies on the use of biofeedback for maladies such as lower back pain and hypertension have produced mixed results. For instance, although biofeedback alone may be no more effective than simple relaxation training or a drug placebo in treating lower back pain and other conditions, when biofeedback is combined with cognitive behavioral therapy, it may convey some short-term advantages (NCCIH, 2016b). However, because stress is often linked to either momentary or long-term increases in systolic and diastolic blood pressure, biofeedback has been shown to be an effective *complementary* therapy—combined with lifestyle modifications in diet, weight, and exercise—for reducing patients' dependence on medication in managing hypertension (Goebel, Viol, & Orebaugh, 1993).

Other researchers have suggested that relaxation and meditation are no more effective than placebos in modulating physiological responses. Daniel Eisenberg and his colleagues (1993), for instance, performed a meta-analysis of research on the effects of relaxation, meditation, and biofeedback on blood pressure levels in patients with hypertension. As shown in Figure 15.3, compared to patients who received no treatment or were in a wait-list control group, patients receiving the CAM therapies showed a statistically (and clinically) significant reduction in both systolic and diastolic blood pressure. However, compared to a credible placebo intervention (pseudomeditation or sham biofeedback), the CAM therapies showed a smaller blood pressure effect that was neither statistically nor clinically significant. The analysis also showed that no single CAM technique was more effective than any other in reducing blood pressure.

After reviewing a number of studies, Paul Lehrer and his colleagues (Lehrer, Carr, Sargunaraj, & Woolfolk, 1994) concluded that although biofeedback can help reduce autonomic arousal, anxiety, and stress-related disorders in *some* people, it conveys no advantage over other behavioral techniques (such as simple relaxation training) that are easier and less expensive to use. The positive effects of biofeedback are more general than its pioneers had originally believed and may be the result of enhanced relaxation, a placebo effect, the passage of time, or suggestion, rather than direct control of specific targets or the physical underpinnings of stress (Gilbert & Moss, 2003).

The National Center for Complementary and Integrative Health considers biofeedback a mind–body therapy that can offer benefits similar to hypnosis, relaxation training, and meditation. Even though researchers aren't sure exactly how or why biofeedback works, most people who benefit have conditions that appear to be brought on or worsened by stress. Moreover, as with other CAM therapies, some people choose to try biofeedback instead of drugs because of its lack of side effects.

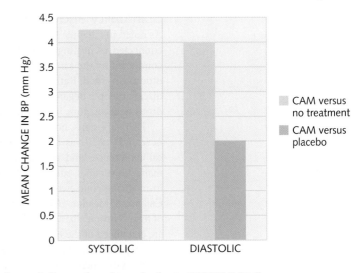

FIGURE 15.3

Relaxation Therapy and Hypertension A meta-analysis of 26 control trials involving 1264 hypertensive patients showed that CAM interventions based on relaxation training, meditation, and biofeedback were significantly more effective than no treatment in reducing systolic and diastolic blood pressure. Compared with credible placebo treatment, however, CAM interventions were much less effective; the difference between the treatments was statistically and clinically insignificant.

Data from Eisenberg, D. M., Delbanco, T. L., Berkey, C. S., Kaptchuk, T. J., Kupelnick, B., Kuhl, J., & Chalmers, T. C. (1993). Cognitive behavioral techniques for hypertension: Are they effective? *Annals of Internal Medicine, 118*, 964–972.

Spirituality and Prayer

As noted in Chapter 1, through much of history, religion and medicine have been closely connected as healing traditions. Indeed, spiritual and physical healing were frequently conducted by the same person. As Western biomedicine matured, however, the two traditions diverged. Rather than consulting a spiritual healer to cure infection and prevent disease, people began turning to vaccines, antibiotics, and the growing number of wondrous new weapons in the modern medical arsenal.

There are signs, however, that the wall between medicine and spiritual healing—which never was nearly as high in some countries as in the United States—is toppling. Medical conferences and centers for research on spirituality and healing are cropping up at many universities, and over 90 percent of U.S. medical schools now offer spirituality-in-medicine coursework, up from only three schools in 1992 (Koenig, Hooten, Lindsay-Calkins, & Meador, 2010). Prayer is being used with increasing frequency in the treatment of many chronic diseases, including cancer (Wachholtz & Sambamoorthi, 2011). And many are convinced of the efficacy of spiritual interventions. Several surveys of family physicians have reported that a majority agree that prayer, meditation, and other spiritual and religious practices can increase the effectiveness of medical treatment (AMA, 2008; Greenberg, 2014).

But is there scientific evidence to support this growing movement? Does spirituality promote health, as four of every five Americans believe (Dembner, 2005)? As is often the case with nontraditional interventions, the evidence is mixed. To be sure, there is evidence that faith and spirituality are correlated with health. A number of studies have reported that devotees of various religions have lower illness and mortality rates than the general population. However, most of those studies were uncontrolled, making them vulnerable to mistaken interpretation and unable to pinpoint causation. For example, ill health may prevent many individuals from attending services in the first place. As another example, if religious people shared other health-promoting traits—say, they exercised as much as they worshipped or avoided smoking or excessive alcohol use—religion might have nothing to do with their improved health.

Although correlation does not prove causality, one study that followed over 5000 Californians over a 28-year period reported that even after ruling out differences due to gender, ethnicity, age, and education, people who were religiously active were 36 percent less likely to die in any given year than their less religious counterparts (Oman, Kurata, Strawbridge, & Cohen, 2002). In another study, which controlled for the age, race, and gender of the participants, researchers reported that those who rarely attended religious services were 1.87 times more likely to die during the 8-year study than were those who attended frequently (Hummer, Rogers, Nam, & Ellison, 1999).

What accounts for the correlation between strong religious practices and longevity? At least three intervening factors remain strong candidates: lifestyle, social support, and positive emotions. First, compared with those in the general population, those who are religiously active tend to smoke less, consume alcohol more moderately, eat less fat, be more active, and be less likely to engage in high-risk sexual behaviors (Masters & Hooker, 2013). Second, because religion tends to be a communal experience, those who are religiously active may benefit from more social ties than those in the general population. Throughout this book, we have seen the beneficial effects of social support on each domain of health (Park and others, 2013). Third, religious activity may promote health by fostering more positive emotions, including an optimistic and hopeful worldview, a feeling of acceptance and personal control, and a sense that life itself is meaningful (Chida, Steptoe, & Powell, 2009).

Chiropractic

chiropractic A complementary and alternative medicine approach to healing that is concerned with the diagnosis, treatment, and prevention of disorders of the neuromusculoskeletal system.

The two most common forms of therapeutic manipulation today—*chiropractic* and *osteopathy*—are the only major forms of CAM originally developed in the United States (osteopathy was described earlier in this chapter). The word **chiropractic** is derived from the Greek roots *cheir* ("hand") and *praktikos* ("done by"). Its actual practice can be traced back to September 1895, when Daniel David Palmer, a magnetic healer in Iowa, supposedly cured a patient's deafness by realigning the man's spine. Two years later, Palmer founded the first school of chiropractic, based on his belief that the human body has an innate self-healing power and seeks a state of *homeostasis,* or balance. Imbalance is believed to be caused by misalignments of bones within joints or abnormal movements that interfere with the flow of nervous impulses. By manipulating the bones, muscles, and joints, particularly in the spine, chiropractors work to improve the function of the neuromusculoskeletal system and restore homeostasis.

According to the National Health Interview Survey (NCHS, 2016b), which included a comprehensive survey of CAM use by Americans, in 2012, about 8 percent of adults and nearly 3 percent of children had received chiropractic manipulation in the previous 12 months.

Today, chiropractors are divided into two major groups, each of which has its own governing body. *Straight chiropractors* are traditionalists who believe that misalignments cause pain and that manipulation is the best form of treatment. *Mixers* combine traditional manipulation with a broad range of other CAM therapies, including massage, physical therapy, and nutritional therapy. Straight chiropractors maintain that chiropractic treatment can be beneficial for a wide range of ailments, from asthma to lower back pain to impotence. Mixers, on the other hand, tend to recognize its effectiveness for a more limited range of conditions, especially acute lower back pain, headaches, and neck pain.

What to Expect during a Chiropractic Examination

Before performing any type of adjustment, the chiropractor will *palpate,* or feel, your vertebrae to detect misalignment of bones or muscular weaknesses. He or she also may test your reflexes to check neural functioning. X-rays may be taken to reveal any underlying joint problems that might interfere with treatment or be worsened by chiropractic adjustment.

During a treatment, the chiropractor will adjust your joints one at a time, using a slight thrusting movement that moves a restricted joint just beyond its limited range of motion. You may be asked to lie on a padded table for a spinal adjustment or to sit or stand for an adjustment of the neck and other joints. Although the treatments are usually painless, it is not uncommon to hear joints crack during an adjustment.

Does Chiropractic Work?

Critics charge that chiropractic treatments are at best useless because misaligned vertebrae are common and harmless, and they usually clear up on their own; and at worst, chiropractic manipulation can cause severe damage to the body if there are fractures or tumors present. Others question the premise that a sound nervous system is the foundation of overall health, pointing to quadriplegics, who often have healthy internal organs despite extensive nerve damage. Some critics accept chiropractic treatment as effective for back pain but argue that it should be restricted to this disorder because there is insufficient evidence to support its efficacy in treating other conditions. Some people use chiropractors as their primary care gatekeepers, which is a cause for concern because not all chiropractors are trained to diagnose all medical conditions.

Despite such criticism, chiropractic remains very popular with the general public; this popularity forced Congress, in 1974, to pass legislation requiring Medicare to pay for chiropractic services. Although still considered a form of alternative medicine by many conventional doctors, chiropractic has achieved mainstream acceptance and is licensed in all 50 states. As another testimonial to the growing acceptability of chiropractic, the services of chiropractors generally are covered not only by Medicare and Medicaid, but also by about 85 percent of major insurance plans.

Evidence for chiropractic's effectiveness in treating back pain has been accumulating since 1952, when a Harvard study reported that this was the most common reason for visiting a chiropractor and that one-fifth of back pain sufferers have used chiropractic successfully (Eisenberg and others, 1993). There have been many controlled clinical trials of *spinal manipulation*, but their results are inconsistent and the studies are often of poor quality (Ernst & Canter, 2006). A 2010 review of evidence on the efficacy of chiropractic concluded that spinal manipulation may be helpful for several conditions, including back pain, migraine headaches, neck pain, upper- and lower-extremity joint conditions, and whiplash-associated disorders. The review also identified a number of conditions for which spinal manipulation appears not to be an effective therapy (including asthma and hypertension), or where the evidence to date is inconclusive (fibromyalgia, premenstrual syndrome, sciatica, and temporomandibular joint disorders) (Bronfort, Haas, Evans, Leininger, & Triano, 2010).

Naturopathic Medicine

naturopathic medicine The system that aims to provide holistic health care by drawing from several traditional healing systems, including homeopathy, herbal remedies, and traditional Oriental medicine.

Naturopathic medicine aims to provide holistic, or whole-body, health care by returning humans to their "natural state." This "back-to-nature" movement has been traced to German doctors such as Vincent Preissnitz (1799–1851), who balked at the harsh treatment used by medical doctors. While medical doctors were "treating" their patients with mercury, bloodletting, and other "modern cures," Preissnitz and other German "nature doctors" were taking patients for walks in the woods and recommending fasting to "detoxify the body," followed by a simple diet and the healing powers of fresh air, sunlight, and bathing in natural hot springs.

At about the same time, a variation of naturopathic medicine called the *hygienic movement* was becoming popular in the United States. This movement, founded by Sylvester Graham (originator of the graham cracker), advocated a strict vegetarian diet, herbal treatments, and an abundance of whole grains. Another dietary mogul who regarded conventional medicine as a fundamentally wrongheaded attempt to improve on nature through artificial means was John Harvey Kellogg, best known as the founder of Kellogg's cereal company.

Benedict Lust (1872–1945), another advocate of natural treatments, coined the word *naturopath*. A German immigrant, Lust also opened the world's first health food store in New York City around 1920. From then until the start of World War II, naturopathic medicine was a popular alternative to conventional medicine. By the 1950s, however, naturopathy was forced out of popularity by the increasingly powerful American Medical Association and by the discovery of penicillin and other potent antibiotics that were effective against many life-threatening diseases.

With the more recent "return-to-nature" movements, naturopathy has regained some of its earlier popularity. Naturopaths follow six basic principles, which are in keeping with the major ideals of CAM: *help nature heal, do no harm, find the underlying cause, treat the whole person, encourage prevention,* and *act as a teacher.* Naturopathic medicine integrates herbal medicine, clinical nutrition, homeopathy, and sometimes other CAM therapies with modern medical methods of diagnosis and treatment.

There are only six accredited naturopathic medical schools in the United States. Elements of naturopathic medicine, therefore, seem destined either to be absorbed into conventional medicine or to become a separate branch of it. Although naturopathic physicians are licensed to practice in only 16 states, the majority of other states allow them to practice in limited ways. Naturopathic practice is regulated by state law, but only a few insurance providers cover naturopathic health care.

Herbs and Other Natural Products

People have used plants to treat physical, mental, and behavioral conditions since the dawn of time, and all known cultures have ancient histories of folk medicine that include the use of herbs. This knowledge was often grouped into a collection called a *pharmacopoeia.* The ancient Greek and Roman cultures developed extensive pharmacopoeias. Until the thirteenth century in Europe, *herbology* was traditionally a woman's profession. When the practice of healing was taken over by male-dominated medical schools as early as the thirteenth century, herbology lost favor, and many women herbalists were persecuted as witches.

In the United States, physicians relied on medicinal plants as primary medicines through the 1930s. In fact, botany was once an important part of the medical school curriculum. But during the second half of the twentieth century, the use of medicinal plants declined due to developments in the ability to produce pharmaceuticals synthetically.

Today, some pharmacists create herbal compounds based on prescriptions written by doctors or naturopaths, but most herbs are marketed as food supplements because it is illegal for doctors to recommend an herb as a treatment for anything. Doing so is considered the same as prescribing an illegal drug. In practice, of course, herbs are widely used as treatments for numerous health conditions, with annual sales reaching into the billions of dollars.

Another natural product that is especially popular today are **probiotics**—live microorganisms (for example, bacteria) that are either the same as or similar to microorganisms found naturally in the human body and that may have health benefits. Also referred to as "good bacteria," probiotics are available in oral products such as capsules, tablets, powders, and yogurts, as well as in other products such as creams. Although some probiotic formulations have shown promise in research (Avadhani & Steefel, 2015) and probiotics usually have few side effects, strong empirical evidence to support specific uses of probiotics for most conditions is lacking, and the U.S. Food and Drug Administration (FDA) has not approved any health claims for probiotics (National Center for Complementary and Alternative Medicine, 2013a).

probiotics Bacteria that help maintain the natural balance of organisms (microflora) in the intestines and help promote a healthy digestive system.

Types of Herbs   Derived from the leaves, stems, roots, bark, flowers, fruits, seeds, and sap of plants, herbs (also called *botanicals*) can be prepared or marketed in different forms—as supplements, medicines, or teas—depending on their intended use. Herbs can be used as tonics and remedies for virtually every known ailment and condition. Herbal teas can be steeped to varying strengths. Roots, bark, and other plant parts can be simmered into potent solutions called *decoctions*. Today, many herbs (in the form of tablets and capsules) are available in health food stores, pharmacies, and even grocery stores. Highly concentrated alcohol-based herb extracts called *tinctures* are also popular.

Herbs play a central role in Chinese medicine, ayurvedic medicine, Native American medicine, and Western herbal medicine. Although many Native Americans prefer to consult an allopathic doctor for health conditions that require antibiotics or surgery, botanical remedies continue to play a major role in the treatment of various ailments. The herbs prescribed by Native American medicine women, medicine men, or **shamans,** vary from tribe to tribe, depending on the condition being treated and what herbs are locally available. Some shamans direct that herbs be eaten; others instruct that they be brewed as a tea. In most healing rites, sage, sweet grass, cedar, or other herbs are burned over the patient, allowing the restorative smoke to drift over the person's body.

shaman A general term used for the practitioner of folk medicine who often uses herbs and a range of rituals to effect cures; also referred to as "medicine man" or "medicine woman."

Western herbs are categorized in several ways. They may be grouped according to their potency. *Tonics,* or normalizers, have a gentle, healing effect on the body, whereas *effectors* have potent actions and are used to treat illness. In addition, herbs are often grouped according to their effects on the body. These categories include anti-inflammatories, diuretics, and laxatives, as well as other, lesser-known classes such as diaphoretics, which promote perspiration and nervousness, allegedly to strengthen the nervous system. Herbs also are often grouped according to which of the body's systems they affect. The cardiovascular system, for example, is said to respond to ginkgo, buckwheat, linden, and other herbs that are touted as being able to strengthen blood vessels.

Herbal Medicines Medicine sellers, like this one in Menghan, Yunan Province, China, set up stalls in the open market to display the many herbs used to treat anything—from a toothache to lower back pain to cancer.

Do Herbs Work? Although roughly 25 percent of our pharmaceutical drugs are derived from herbs, physicians often believe that herbs in general are ineffective and potentially dangerous (McCarthy, 2001). Still, there is at least some evidence that plant-based medicines are effective in treating certain conditions. For example, ginger's proven anti-inflammatory and antirheumatic properties, coming from both human and animal trials, suggest that it may be effective in treating arthritis and perhaps the pain associated with other inflammatory conditions (Rahnama, Montazeri, Fallah Huseini, Kianbakht, & Naseri, 2012). As another example, capsaicin, an extract from the cayenne pepper, is effective in relieving the pain of osteoarthritis. As a third example, aloe vera is a succulent plant that is effective in promoting healing, especially of burns (Maenthaisong, Chaiyakunapruk, Niruntraporn, & Kongkaew, 2007).

On the other hand, the evidence for the effectiveness of some popular herbs is mixed at best. Recently, a panel of experts convened by the National Institutes of Health reported that exercise, a healthy diet, and supplements may help prevent Alzheimer's disease and some other chronic conditions but that there is "insufficient evidence to support the use of pharmaceuticals or dietary supplements to prevent cognitive decline" (NIH Consensus Development Program, 2010).

Results such as these make it impossible to offer a definitive, across-the-board answer to the question, "Do herbs work?" At present, the safest conclusion seems to be that certain herbs may be beneficial for certain conditions. In general, however, there simply is not enough good evidence that herbs work as well as many would like to believe (Gardea and others, 2004). Furthermore, compared to the often-dramatic power of pharmaceutical drugs, herbs usually have fairly subtle effects. *Standardized extracts,* which have long been available in Europe and are increasingly available in the United States, do seem to be more effective, perhaps because the dosages used are generally higher than those found in dried herbs.

Many advocates of herbal medicine claim that the presence of many different active and inactive ingredients in synthetic drugs—known and unknown—means that botanical products are comparatively safer and more effective. This is mostly speculation, however, because there have been few clinical trials directly comparing herbs and pharmaceuticals in their effectiveness in treating specific diseases and conditions. Furthermore, advocates of herbal medicine typically neglect to mention the possible adverse side effects created by the lack of purity and standardization of some herbal products.

Food Supplement Therapy

The use of vitamins and food supplements is a second major emphasis of naturopathy and is perhaps the best known of all CAM treatments. Look through nearly any popular magazine, and you are sure to find a discussion of at least one recommended supplement, such as vitamin E, to deter atherosclerosis and prevent premature aging of the skin, or folic acid, to support the immune system. Although most medical experts have yet to fully endorse nutritional supplementation, over 70 percent of adults in the United States take vitamin supplements, 100 million using them regularly (Bailey and others, 2011).

There is no longer any doubt that food supplements can have important health benefits. A large body of convincing research evidence shows that materials derived from foods can be effective in treating a number of diseases. For example, niacin is effective in lowering cholesterol levels, and glucosamine sulfate is effective in reducing the pain of arthritis. Moreover, food supplements often trigger fewer adverse side effects than do drugs of comparable effectiveness.

Food supplements are generally used in two ways: to correct dietary deficiencies (*nutritional medicine*) or in immense doses to trigger a specific therapeutic effect (*megadose therapy*). As nutritional medicine, they are useful in correcting fairly common deficiencies in many essential nutrients, including deficiencies in calcium, folic acid, iron, magnesium, zinc, and vitamins A, B_6, C, D, and E. Although conventional biomedicine supports eating a balanced diet or, short of that, using nutritional medicine to correct deficiencies in vitamins and minerals, the use of megadose therapy is more controversial. Linus Pauling's famous recommendation to take 4000 to 10,000 milligrams per day of vitamin C is a prime example (Linus Pauling Institute, 2016). According to naturopaths, this huge dose—equivalent to eating 40 to 100 oranges per day, or 10 to 15 times the official recommended daily allowance (RDA)—is needed because the stresses of modern life and the effects of environmental toxins cause nutritional needs to increase beyond what a normal diet can provide. This claim remains controversial among nutritionists.

Dietary Medicine

Naturopaths have always believed that fruits, vegetables, nuts, and whole grains are "natural foods," and that any refinement of these foods reduces their natural vitality and health-promoting properties. In contrast, until quite recently, conventional biomedicine paid little attention to diet. Only in the past three decades have medical researchers begun to take seriously the idea that what people eat has a major impact on their health. As discussed in Chapter 8, the overwhelming evidence from large-scale epidemiological research has shown that diet plays a central role in preventing most of the major chronic diseases, including heart disease, strokes, and cancer of the breast, colon, and prostate.

Despite this agreement, naturopaths typically go well beyond conventional medicine's recommendations regarding diet. In addition to calling for dramatic reductions in the consumption of meat and saturated fat, they decry the use of food preservatives and the artificial fertilizers, pesticides, and hormones used in modern farming. Instead, they recommend eating organic foods that are produced without these adulterations.

Another popular dietary concept in naturopathic medicine has to do with the idea of *food allergy* or, more accurately, *food sensitivity*. Diets based on avoiding "trigger" foods such as sugar, wheat, or dairy products are prescribed for many conditions, from arthritis to irritable bowel syndrome to chronic fatigue (NCCIH, 2016b). When a food sensitivity is suspected, naturopaths typically place the patient on a highly restricted elimination diet of a small number of foods (including rice, sweet potatoes, turkey, and applesauce) known to seldom cause allergic reactions. If symptoms begin to clear up after several weeks on the restricted diet, foods are gradually added back into the diet, one at a time, while the patient keeps a journal of symptoms such as sneezing and headaches.

But even naturopaths disagree about the elements of a healthy diet. Proponents of *raw food theory,* a naturopathic concept dating back more than 100 years, believe that cooking foods destroys the "vital life force" (along with the vitamins, enzymes, and micronutrients) found in food. In contrast, the popular theory of *macrobiotics* condemns raw foods as unhealthy, considering them a cause of multiple sclerosis, rheumatoid arthritis, and other diseases. Macrobiotic nutritionists insist that all foods, including vegetables, should be cooked.

Natural Product Therapies
Supplements and other forms of CAM seem especially effective with cyclical conditions that naturally improve over time, perhaps because people seek out a supplement when symptoms are worst and presume that it worked when they feel better.

Alex Segre/Alamy

Do Dietary Modifications and Food Supplements Work? Epidemiological and experimental studies in animals and humans have provided substantial evidence that diet (in the form of foods or as supplements) can have a major effect on risk factors for certain diseases and the progression of disease. For example, over the past 10 years, plant-based diets, dietary fiber supplementation, and antioxidant supplementation have become increasingly accepted treatments for managing cardiovascular disease. In fact, along with low-fat diets, aerobic exercise, and stress reduction, these treatments, which were considered alternative therapies at one time, are considered today as either complementary or a part of standard medical practice for reducing the risk of cardiovascular disease (NCCIH, 2016b).

Similarly, low-fat, high-fiber, basically vegetarian diets such as the Pritikin diet and the Ornish diet have been demonstrated to be effective in lowering blood glucose levels in people with diabetes. In one study, 60 percent of people with Type 2 diabetes on the Ornish diet no longer required insulin (McGrady & Horner, 1999). A number of epidemiological studies (for example, Ornish and others, 2008) also have suggested a possible decrease in the prevalence of cancer in people who consume higher amounts of fruits and vegetables, perhaps due to their antioxidant effects.

Elimination diets, megavitamin supplementation, and diets that focus on replacing trace elements are popular forms of CAM therapy that have been used to treat *attention deficit hyperactivity disorder* (ADHD). The Feingold diet, for example, eliminates food colorings, artificial flavors, and highly processed foods from the ADHD child's diet, with mixed results in improving symptoms (Millichap & Yee, 2012). Despite the inconsistency in research results, the American Academy of Pediatrics concluded that a low-additive diet is a valid intervention for children with ADHD (American Academy of Pediatrics, 2015).

The value of food supplements, on the other hand, is not so clear. Certain supplements have been proved to be reasonably effective in treating certain conditions—for example, glucosamine sulfate for osteoarthritis and zinc for prostate enlargement. Despite these successes, however, megadose supplements rarely are as powerful as synthetic drugs, and supplement therapy alone usually is inadequate to manage serious health conditions. For instance, a review of clinical trials in the treatment of colds with small and large doses of vitamin C concluded that there is no evidence for the efficacy of this vitamin (Hemila, Chalker, & Douglas, 2010).

Safety Concerns As with herbal medicines, the FDA cautions consumers that some unregulated dietary supplements may contain hazardous substances. For example, in January 1999, the FDA asked dietary supplement manufacturers to recall supplements that contained *gamma butyrolactone* (GBL), which were sold via the Internet and in health food stores and health clubs. Marketed under such brand names as Blue Nitro, GH Revitalizer, and Revivarant, the popular supplement was supposed to build muscles, reduce weight, and improve athletic and sexual performance. In fact, GBL contains a chemical also found in commercial floor strippers that affects the central nervous system, slows breathing and heart rate, and can lead to seizures, unconsciousness, and coma. GBL has been linked to at least six deaths and adverse health effects in hundreds of other people (Casciani, 2009).

The FDA also warns against the use of certain herbs and food supplements by those who are also taking prescription medications. For instance, in a February 2000 public health advisory, the FDA cautioned that St. John's wort had been found to reduce the effectiveness of the AIDS drug indinavir by 57 percent (Piscitelli, Burstein, Chaitt, Alfaro, & Falloon, 2000). The FDA also cited a Zurich, Switzerland, study reporting that this popular herbal remedy for depression reduced levels of a transplant rejection drug (ciclosporin), increasing the odds that a heart transplant patient might reject a donated heart (Fugh-Berman, 2000).

What to Expect from a Visit to a Naturopath

The herbal medicines, food supplements, and dietary medicines discussed in this section are provided by naturopaths, who function as primary, preventive care doctors. A visit to a naturopath generally begins with a standard physical exam, possibly one that includes conventional blood and urine tests, and even radiology. In addition, naturopaths will spend considerable time recording the patient's medical history, focusing on the patient's lifestyle, including diet, exercise level, stress, and even emotional and spiritual issues.

After this initial examination, the patient and naturopath work together to establish a treatment program. Usually, the program emphasizes noninvasive therapies and lifestyle changes such as eliminating unhealthy behaviors. Then the naturopath may prescribe dietary changes, food supplements, and/or herbal medicine for any specific complaints. Depending on where the naturopath practices, conventional drugs, vaccinations, or even surgery may also be recommended.

Does Naturopathy Work?

Diseases that are strongly affected by lifestyle and environment are among those for which naturopathic treatment most often is reported to be effective. For example, it has been used effectively to treat allergies, chronic infections, fatigue, arthritis, asthma, headache, hypertension, and depression, to name only a few conditions (NCCIH, 2015b). In a typical case of hypertension, for example, a naturopathic doctor might prescribe a multifaceted treatment that includes dietary changes, vitamin and mineral supplements, herbal medicine, and lifestyle changes designed to reduce stress. For an arthritis sufferer, the regimen might include dietary modifications, herbal medicine, and massage.

Critics of naturopathic medicine raise several concerns. Chief among these is that unsuspecting consumers are flooded with inaccurate or deceptive information carrying extreme claims about the effectiveness of herbs. In addition, herbal therapy is criticized for being untested according to pharmaceutical standards. Herbalists reply that because herbs are natural products (and therefore cannot be patented), the extremely expensive testing required of pharmaceutical drugs is unlikely to happen. Proponents point out that the modern pharmaceutical industry grew out of herbal medicine and that many drugs—from the digitalis used to treat heart disease (derived from the foxglove plant) to morphine (from the opium poppy)—still are made from plant extracts. Another concern is safety. For this reason, most herbalists recommend purchasing herbs rather than harvesting them in the wild. Plants have natural variations that can be misleading, and this has caused more than one death from a person's ingesting a toxic plant that he or she believed to be a beneficial herb (NCCIH, 2015b).

Looking Ahead: Complementary and Alternative Medicine in Our Future

Growing interest in CAM is viewed by some as one of several indications of a major paradigm shift in medicine and health care in the United States. One of the changes is a shift from the traditional view of the provider–patient relationship, in which patients are willing, passive, and dependent, to one in which patients are activist health consumers. These days, patients are more likely to demand and seek out accurate and timely health information on their own, not likely to blindly accept their doctors' recommendations, and more likely to be critical of traditional medicine and to consider (and use) alternative forms of treatment.

Armed with unprecedented access to health information from the Internet, self-help books, and other media, today's patients are becoming more empowered to manage their own health. Turning to CAM practitioners is a predictable manifestation of this sense of empowerment—choosing your own treatment approach despite what your physician might suggest.

This assessment of changed patient behavior was evident in a published report from 2008 on the growing use of CAM in the United States (NCCAM, 2008). The report indicated that most patients (55 percent) who chose to use CAM did so because they believed that CAM would improve their health when used in combination with conventional medical treatments. Relatively few respondents reported using CAM because they believed that conventional treatments would not help (28 percent) or were too expensive (13 percent). For this reason, it may be more accurate to predict that alternative medicine will become more *complementary*—that is, a supplement to allopathic medicine, rather than an alternative or replacement.

Even the government is jumping on the CAM bandwagon. For example, the NCCIH, part of the NIH, has funded numerous research studies to explore, among other topics, CAM and aging, arthritis, cancer, and cardiovascular disease; chiropractic; botanical supplements and women's health; and acupuncture.

The Best of Both Worlds

In the end, no single approach to health care has all the answers; the search for the best solution to a medical condition often requires a willingness to look beyond one remedy or system of treatment. Already, many insurance companies cover certain alternative methods, including acupuncture. And conventional doctors are incorporating alternative therapies into their treatment regimens. The NIH estimates that more than half of all conventional physicians use some form of CAM themselves or refer their patients to such forms of treatment (NCCAM, 2008). As a result, there is a growing movement to provide CAM instruction as a regular part of the medical school curriculum. A survey of American physicians' knowledge and use of, training in, and acceptance of CAM as legitimate yielded the range of attitudes summarized in Table 15.2. Diet and exercise, biofeedback, and counseling or psychotherapy were used most often.

Thus, health care practitioners in the United States are moving toward a more open-minded view of unconventional medicine. Even the AMA has shifted its views toward greater tolerance. In the mid-1970s, the AMA's official position was that "the fakes, the frauds, and the quackeries need to be identified, exposed, and, if possible, eradicated" (AMA, 1973). By 1995, however, the AMA had substituted "alternative medicine" for "quackery" and passed a resolution encouraging its members to "become better informed regarding the practices and techniques of alternative or complementary medicine" (AMA, 1995). In November 1998, the prestigious *Journal of the American Medical Association* devoted an entire issue to the subject of alternative medicine. And where there once were none, there are now eight peer-reviewed journals devoted to alternative medicine.

Still, "let the buyer beware" is sound advice for consumers considering CAM therapies. Statutory requirements for the practice of CAM differ from state to state. Provider-practice acts for massage exist in 22 states. Licensure is now required in 25 states and the District of Columbia. Naturopathy-practice acts exist in 12 states, although each state defines the scope of such practice differently (American Association of Naturopathic Physicians, 2006).

The Politics of Medicine

The growing acceptability of CAM, however, should not be construed as an indication of its complete acceptance by the biomedical community. One survey of 1150 patients, 333 primary care physicians (PCPs), and 241 CAM practitioners revealed growing acceptance of CAM but differing expectations regarding its use in primary care settings (Ben-Ayre & Frenkel, 2008). Patients expected their family physician to refer them to CAM, to have updated knowledge about CAM, and to offer CAM treatment based on appropriate training. When asked about CAM integration into medical care, more patients expected to receive CAM in a primary care setting (62 percent) compared to PCPs' expectations of prescribing CAM (30 percent).

Both alternative and conventional medicine are guilty of discounting one another's approach to health care, and both conventional medicine and alternative medicine are mixtures of good and bad health practices. The best course is to be an informed consumer and to be skeptical about unsupported claims.

Clearly, the best result would be for patients to have access to the "best of both worlds." Following a conventional medical evaluation and discussion of conventional allopathic options, patients may choose a CAM consultation. But before doing so, the physician (according to Eisenberg, 1997) should

- ensure that the patient recognizes and understands his or her symptoms;
- maintain a record of all symptoms, including the patient's own opinions;
- review any potential for harmful interactions; and
- plan for a follow-up visit to review CAM effectiveness.

This approach is designed to help keep communication channels open between patient and provider so that the patient receives the most effective and safest treatment.

Weigh In on Health

Respond to each question below based on what you learned in the chapter. (**Tip:** Use the items in "Summing Up" to take into account related biological, psychological, and social concerns.)

1. What general opinion did you have about complementary and alternative medicine before you read the chapter? How have the discussions of CAM in this chapter changed your opinion, if at all, on any CAM methods? In particular, what did you read about research on CAM that influenced how you now think about it?

2. Your roommate suffers from chronic headaches, and her medical doctor has not yet been able to diagnose their cause. She is tempted to try hypnosis, acupuncture, a form of meditation and relaxation, or naturopathy. What can you tell her about these methods of CAM from a biopsychosocial perspective? What has research shown about the efficacy of these approaches?

3. Using what you learned about CAM in this chapter, predict a way in which CAM will influence the way that people and providers in the future approach the prevention or treatment of illness, or the maintenance of well-being.

Summing Up

What Is Complementary and Alternative Medicine?

1. Conventional medicine (also called *Western* or *allopathic medicine*) is health care as practiced by holders of MD (medical doctor) and DO (doctor of osteopathic medicine) degrees and by allied professionals, including physical therapists, psychologists, and registered nurses.

2. The term *alternative medicine* refers to a broad range of therapeutic approaches and philosophies that are generally defined as health care practices that are not taught widely in medical schools, not generally used in hospitals, and not usually reimbursed by insurance companies.

3. The term *complementary and alternative medicine* (CAM) refers to the range of health-promoting interventions that fall outside of conventional, Western biomedicine. Most CAM practitioners work from three fundamental ideals: to provide health treatment that is natural, is holistic, and promotes wellness. Various forms of what we now call CAM have been around for thousands of years, but they were eclipsed during most of the twentieth century by the success of biomedicine.

4. Health care in the United States remains primarily based upon allopathic medicine, yet an estimated 30 percent of adults and 12 percent of children regularly use some form of CAM.

5. CAM is used more by women than men, by people with higher education levels, and by people who have been hospitalized during the past year primarily for back problems, anxiety or depression, sleeping problems, and headaches.

Medicine or Quackery?

6. Skeptics of CAM raise several concerns about unconventional treatments. Foremost among these is that many CAM therapies never have been subjected to rigorous empirical scrutiny regarding their effectiveness or safety. When CAM studies are conducted, critics contend, the methods often are poor and the conclusions questionable. Another concern is that people who rely on CAM therapies instead of conventional medicine may delay or lose the opportunity to benefit from scientifically based treatment.

7. Alternative practitioners counter that it is often impossible to conduct the kinds of formal experiments that mainstream medical researchers are most comfortable with. For example, because many CAM therapies are based on a more holistic philosophy, its advocates claim that treatment variables cannot always be studied independently.

8. CAM skeptics also contend that when conventional therapies fail to help, the acupuncturist, chiropractor, or naturopath presents a powerful belief system, and the CAM techniques then seem to work due to the placebo effect. Inert substances can also have adverse health effects. When they do, they have been called *nocebos*.

Does Complementary and Alternative Medicine Work?

9. Acupuncture was originally practiced as part of an integrated system of healing. Today, its use is sanctioned in the United States primarily for the treatment of pain and addiction. Brain imaging studies suggest that acupuncture modulates neural activity in brain regions involved not only in somatosensory processing, but also in affective and cognitive processing.

10. Acupuncture-induced analgesia may result from the activation of descending pain pathways that influence the perception of pain. Acupuncture is widely used to treat pain, substance abuse, and depression.

11. The basic premise of mind–body therapies is that cognitive, emotional, and spiritual factors can have profound effects on one's health. Among the mind–body therapies are hypnosis, relaxation training and meditation (including tai chi and yoga), and spiritual healing.

12. Although hypnosis does not involve a unique state of consciousness, it may be effective in relieving pain in some patients. Hypnotic suggestions of analgesia during experimental pain are associated with increased activation of certain brain areas that may result in reductions in pain intensity.

13. Relaxation and meditation also may promote health by bolstering the immune system, reducing pain, and lowering stress hormones. Some researchers have suggested that mindfulness training produces its effects on health indirectly by altering a person's cognitive appraisal processes when potential stressors are encountered.

14. Research has shown that the benefits of mindfulness meditation are far-reaching, from minimizing pain sensitivity to preventing depression to helping people regulate their emotions. Mindfulness training may trigger changes in limbic areas involved in emotional regulation, as well as reduced pain-related activation of areas in the somatosensory cortex and increased activity and axonal density in the anterior cingulate cortex (ACC).

15. Biofeedback is a technique for converting certain supposedly involuntary physiological responses, such as skin temperature, muscle activity, heart rate, and blood pressure, into electrical signals and providing visual or auditory feedback about them. Although results from studies of biofeedback effectiveness are mixed, the method is a viable means of treating some stress-related disorders when combined with other, more conventional treatments. There is mounting

support for the use of heart rate variability biofeedback as a treatment for a variety of disorders associated with autonomic dysregulation.

16. Several studies have found that people who are religiously active are healthier and live longer lives than their less spiritual or religious counterparts, perhaps due to differences in lifestyle, social support, and positive emotions.

17. The two most common forms of therapeutic manipulation today—chiropractic and osteopathy—are the only major forms of CAM originally developed in the United States. Spinal manipulation may be helpful for several conditions, including back pain, migraine headaches, neck pain, upper- and lower-extremity joint conditions, and whiplash-associated disorders.

18. Naturopathic medicine aims to provide holistic, or whole-body, health care by returning us to our "natural state." Modern naturopathy draws from several CAM traditions, especially herbal medicine, food supplement therapy, and dietary modification.

19. Roughly 25 percent of our modern-day pharmaceutical drugs are derived from herbs. Certain herbs may be beneficial for certain conditions, but caution must be exercised because many herbs remain untested and may have harmful effects.

20. There is substantial evidence from epidemiological and experimental studies on animals and humans that diet (in the form of foods or as supplements) can have a major effect on risk factors for certain diseases and the progression of disease.

Looking Ahead: Complementary and Alternative Medicine in Our Future

21. Growing interest in CAM is viewed by some as one of several indications of a major paradigm shift in medicine and health care in the United States. Even so, a large survey of patients, primary care physicians, and CAM practitioners revealed a growing acceptance of CAM but differing expectations regarding its use in primary care settings.

Key Terms and Concepts to Remember

evidence-based medicine, p. 437
conventional medicine, p. 437
osteopathic medicine, p. 437
alternative medicine, p. 437
holistic medicine, p. 437
complementary and alternative medicine (CAM), p. 438
integrative medicine, p. 440

vitalism, p. 440
traditional Chinese medicine, p. 440
nocebo, p. 443
acupuncture, p. 445
hypnosis, p. 448
mindfulness meditation, p. 449
tai chi, p. 451
yoga, p. 451

biofeedback, p. 453
heart rate variability (HRV), p. 454
chiropractic, p. 456
naturopathic medicine, p. 458
probiotics, p. 459
shaman, p. 459

LaunchPad
macmillan learning

To accompany your textbook, you have access to a number of online resources, including quizzes for every chapter of the book, flashcards, critical thinking exercises, videos, and *Check Your Health* inventories. To access these resources, please visit the Straub *Health Psychology* LaunchPad solo at: **launchpadworks.com**

EPILOGUE

Health Psychology Today and Tomorrow

Christopher Futcher/Getty Images

wasn't always interested in health. Like many students, when I enrolled at Columbia University in the fall of 1975, I was blessed with a sound mind and body that I took for granted. I rarely exercised, ate too much fast food, slept too little, and even began smoking cigarettes—to "cope" with the stress of grad school, I rationalized. Nor was I interested in what psychology might contribute to our understanding of health. My schedule of classes and research focused on learning theory, neurobiology, and cognition.

Things began to change, however, when I decided to branch out and study applied social psychology with Professor Stanley Schachter. His distinctive approach to research was breaking new ground in the study of emotions, obesity, and addiction. Unlike most of his peers, Schachter always focused on the broader context in which social behaviors were embedded. Nowhere is this more evident than in his effort to understand the biological processes involved in seemingly social phenomena, such as increased cigarette smoking at parties or in response to stress. Much of the emerging field of health psychology was rooted in Schachter's work. I began to see a clearer path toward the contributions to humanity that I was hoping to make. Psychology for me became a tool to promote health.

As my professional interests shifted, my personal interests followed. I recall one seminar when Stan, who himself was struggling to quit smoking, asked me when I was going to take up the battle against nicotine addiction. "Why don't you apply what you've learned here to your own life?" he asked. So I began to do so, and I've tried to be faithful to Schachter's challenge ever since. It was tough, but I did quit smoking many years ago. I also exercise, eat a more nutritious diet, and follow a healthier sleep schedule. As new research findings have come along, I've tried to incorporate them into how I cope with stress; the efforts I make to keep strong, positive, social connections with others; and how I appraise the events around me.

My hope is that this book has sparked your interest in the field of health psychology—for some of you as a profession, and for all of you as a tool in promoting your own better health and the health of those in your life whom you care about!

Health psychology has traveled a long way since the American Psychological Association first recognized it in 1978. My goal in this Epilogue is to look back—to review what has been accomplished along the way—and to look ahead to the most pressing challenges of the future. Although I will focus on health psychologists' contributions to various health-related goals, it is important to remember that those psychologists are not working alone. The medical profession and others involved in delivering health care all work together to achieve these ends.

Health Psychology's Most Important Lessons

The science of health psychology remains in its infancy, and its contributions are still unfolding. Thus, much work remains to be done. Yet virtually all health psychologists agree that lessons have been learned during the past four decades of research that all of us should heed.

Lesson 1: Psychological and Social Factors Interact with Biology in Health

As we have seen, for many diseases, heredity plays a role, but not every person with the same genetic vulnerability to a disease eventually gets it. Bacteria, viruses, and other microorganisms cause some diseases, but being exposed doesn't guarantee that a person will become ill. Stress, negative emotions, coping resources, healthy behaviors, and a number of other factors affect our susceptibility to disease, the progression of disease, and how quickly we recover (if at all).

Behavior, mental processes, social influences, and health are intimately connected. This is the fundamental message of the biopsychosocial model of health. Even those among us with "hardy" genes and healthy immune systems can become ill if we engage in risky health behaviors, live in unhealthy social and physical environments, and develop a negative emotional style and poor stress-management techniques.

Unhealthy Behaviors and Social Alienation

Nearly nine out of ten college students report that their health is good, very good, or excellent (American College Health Association, 2015). Morbidity and mortality data confirm this perception. As we learned in Chapter 6, young adults have a lower prevalence of chronic disease and premature death than older adults (Centers for Disease Control and Prevention, 2013g). Although feeling good about your health can be beneficial, we have also seen than it can be hazardous if it causes people to be unrealistically optimistic that their good health will continue in spite of their lifestyle behaviors. And as we discussed in Chapter 6, this illusion is dangerous and may increase the risk of unintentional injury (accidents) and exposure to other serious health hazards.

The evidence is clear: Unhealthy behaviors such as smoking, alcohol and drug use, poor nutrition, high-risk sexual behavior, and physical inactivity lead to or at least accelerate the occurrence of illness, injury, and other adverse chronic conditions. For example, extensive research has eliminated any doubt that smoking is causally related to lung cancer and that alcohol use is related both to diseases of the liver and to traffic fatalities. Similarly, a low-fiber, high-fat diet increases a person's risk of developing cardiovascular disease and some forms of cancer. And, of course, a sedentary life increases the risk of cardiovascular disease and certain kinds of cancer and results in poorer immune functioning.

Numerous studies suggest that psychosocial factors can also affect the development and progression of diseases ranging from a simple cold to chronic conditions such as cardiovascular disease, cancer, and AIDS. Among the psychosocial factors that affect cardiovascular health are socioeconomic status (SES), gender, race, employment, acute and chronic stress, social support versus isolation, anger, and depression (Khayyam-Nekouei, Neshatdoost, Yousefy, Sadeghi, & Manshaee, 2013).

Life expectancy in the United States reached an all-time high of 78.8 years in 2013 (Xu, Murphy, Kochanek, & Bastian, 2016), and psychosocial factors are linked to life expectancy. As a specific example, prospective studies demonstrate that social support reduces the risk of mortality independent of other factors, such as gender and ethnicity (Liao and others, 2015). In a large body of research, Lisa Berkman (2010) has investigated how social networks affect health. In one study of 16,699 French workers, she determined a social integration score for each participant based on marital status, contacts with friends and relatives, church membership, and other group memberships. Over a seven-year follow-up and after adjustment for age, smoking, alcohol consumption, body mass index (BMI), and depressive symptoms, men with low social integration scores had a 2.7 times greater risk of dying than did men with high scores; for women, the rate was 3.64 times greater.

Researchers cannot yet state exactly why social integration protects against chronic disease. So far, the most valid hypotheses proposed include the following: Social support may buffer the effects of stress on the body; social support may influence positively health behaviors associated with disease (such as diet and exercise); and social support may affect directly the underlying physical mechanisms associated with disease (Berkman, 2010). In support of the physical mechanisms hypothesis, researchers have found that social integration is negatively correlated with several inflammatory and immune system markers of cardiovascular disease. In fact, the link between close relationships and immune function is one of the most robust findings in the psychoneuroimmunology literature (Fagundes, Bennett, Derry, & Kiecolt-Glaser, 2011). Relationship conflict and the perception of weak social support in one's life can effectively modulate proinflammatory cytokine secretion both directly (via central nervous system/neural/endocrine/immune biobehavioral pathways) and indirectly by promoting depression, emotional stress responses, and unhealthy behaviors (Kiecolt-Glaser, Gouin, & Hantsoo, 2010). Interestingly, people also expect to live longer when they perceive strong social and emotional support in their lives (Umberson & Montez, 2010). Consequently, many hospitals strongly recommend—and, in some cases, even require—that patients enroll in social support groups during the recovery period following major surgery.

Stress

Since the pioneering stress research of Hans Selye (discussed in Chapter 4), there has been mounting evidence that poor stress management can take a negative toll on health, both directly and indirectly, increasing the risk of many chronic diseases, altering the progression of those diseases, and undermining the effectiveness of treatment (Figure EP.1). Health psychologists have delineated the various possible consequences of how a person responds

STRESS

Indirect health behavior effects

Increased delay in noticing symptoms
Increased delay in seeking care
Decreased likelihood of seeking care
Decreased adherence to treatment
regimens

Indirect behaviorally mediated effects

Increased smoking, alcohol, and other
drug use
Poor nutrition, overeating, undereating
Irregular sleep patterns, insomnia
Obsessive or compulsive behavior

Direct physiological effects

Gastrointestinal: nausea, constipation,
overeating
Endocrine: increased production of
adrenal stress hormones
Cardiovascular: increased heart rate
and blood pressure, inflammation in
the coronary arteries
Musculoskeletal: tense muscles,
tension headaches, migraines
Respiratory: hyperventilation leading
to panic attacks
Reproductive: impaired testosterone
and sperm production in men;
irregular menstrual cycles in women

FIGURE EP.1

**Direct and Indirect Effects
of Stress on the Disease
Process** Stress affects health
directly by elevating blood
pressure and serum cholesterol
levels and by decreasing
immunity. The indirect effects
of stress include reducing
adherence to treatment
instructions, increasing smoking,
and a variety of other unhealthy
behaviors.

An Informed Consumer Each
of us plays a major role in
determining our own well-being,
including knowing the ingredients
of the foods we choose to eat.

to daily hassles, occupational demands, environmental stressors, and other challenging events and situations. We now understand many of the physiological mechanisms by which stress adversely affects health and increases the likelihood of illness. For example, poorly managed stress can result in elevated blood pressure and serum cholesterol levels (Rosenthal & Alter, 2012). In addition, the evidence base for the relationship between stress and inflammatory processes has mounted significantly (Gianaros & Manuck, 2010).

Some of health psychology's most dramatic findings have focused on immune function. For example, temporary psychological stress, including exam taking or daily hassles, can decrease immune function (Goliszek, 2014), especially in people who have poor coping skills and in those who magnify the impact of potential stressors and appraise them as uncontrollable. In addition, chronic stress, such as that arising from natural disasters or caring for a spouse or parent with Alzheimer's disease, can reduce immunocompetence (Haley, Roth, Howard, & Stafford, 2010). These findings are part of the burgeoning field of psychoneuroimmunology. When we have a calm sense of being in control, we tend to have a comparable emotional and physiological reaction. When we become angry or fearful or feel hopeless because we believe a situation is out of our control, we tend to become emotionally

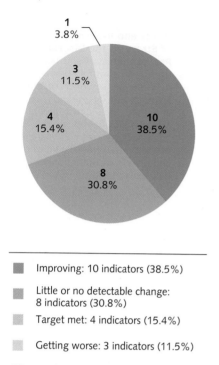

- ■ Improving: 10 indicators (38.5%)

- ■ Little or no detectable change:
  8 indicators (30.8%)

- ■ Target met: 4 indicators (15.4%)

- ■ Getting worse: 3 indicators (11.5%)

- ■ Baseline data only: 1 indicator (3.8%)

FIGURE EP.2

Status of the 26 HP2020 Leading Health Indicators Progress has been generally positive toward achieving *Healthy People 2020* targets. As of 2014, 14 of the 26 indicators (53.9%) either met the target or showed improvement.

Data from Healthy People 2020. (2014). Healthy People 2020 Leading Health Indicators: Progress Update. Washington, DC: U.S. Department of Health and Human Services, Office of Disease Prevention and Health Promotion. Retrieved from https://www.healthypeople.gov/2020/leading-health-indicators/Healthy-People-2020-Leading-Health-Indicators%3A-Progress-Update.

"I used to tell all the campaign staff: 'If you will just let me get sleep and exercise, I can keep going, but if I start cheating on either one of those, then it will have its consequences.'"

—Senator Bill Nelson (D-FL; 2001)

aroused, and consequently, our physiological response is more dramatic. Because we know that reactions such as these, if repeated and chronic, can promote illness, it is important for us to learn to manage our thoughts and emotional reactions.

Lesson 2: It Is Our Own Responsibility to Promote and Maintain Our Health

Our society has become increasingly health conscious. As a result, more of us realize that the responsibility for our health does not rest solely in the hands of health care professionals; rather, we ourselves have a major role to play in determining our overall well-being.

Americans and Canadians have become well informed over recent decades about the hazards of smoking, substance abuse, poor dietary practices, and sedentary living. We know, too, that stress, our emotional temperament, the quality of interpersonal relationships, and coping resources are important factors in health. We have learned about the importance of having regular checkups, adhering to our prescribed treatment, and seeking early detection screening for various chronic illnesses, especially if our age, gender, race, or ethnicity places us in the "high-risk" group for these conditions. And today, people can inquire about health issues and communicate with health providers by tapping into the computer-driven resources of telemedicine.

This awareness does not guarantee that people will follow through on what they know to be the healthiest course of action. As of March 2014, a series of midcourse reviews of progress toward the 26 leading objectives of *Healthy People 2020* demonstrated mixed progress for Americans (Figure EP.2). Progress has been made for a number of objectives. For example,

- ■ fewer adults smoke cigarettes;
- ■ fewer children are exposed to secondhand smoke;
- ■ more adults are meeting targets for physical activity;
- ■ fewer adolescents are using alcohol or illicit drugs;
- ■ more people have medical insurance, access to health services, and a usual primary care provider;
- ■ more people have access to clinical preventive services, including recommended cancer screening and blood pressure control services;
- ■ more children are receiving recommended vaccinations;
- ■ injury deaths and homicides have declined; and
- ■ indices of maternal, infant, and child health have improved, including continued declines in the number of infant deaths and preterm births.

In other areas, however, there has been little or no improvement. For example,

- ■ the percentage of overweight and obese children, adolescents, and adults has increased;
- ■ there are more people with diagnosed diabetes;
- ■ there are worsening trends in the area of mental health, including the number of suicides and adolescents with major depressive episodes;
- ■ there has been little or no change in the status of most objectives for healthier dietary intake;
- ■ the number of people who have regular dental checkups has declined; and
- ■ the number of adults who engage in binge drinking has not declined.

Clearly, Americans have made some gains in improving their health habits. Yet as much as 40 percent of annual deaths from each of the five leading causes (heart disease, cancer, chronic lower respiratory diseases, stroke, and unintentional injuries) are preventable. Taken together, mortality from these causes accounts for about 63 percent of all deaths each year in the United States (Centers for Disease Control and Prevention, 2014d). Many deaths from these causes are avoidable by making changes in personal behaviors and by reducing disparities that result from the social, environmental, and economic attributes of the communities and neighborhoods in which people live and work. If health disparities were eliminated, as called for in *Healthy People 2020* (2014), the country would be much closer to achieving the lowest possible mortality rates for the leading causes of death.

Lesson 3: Unhealthy Lifestyles Are Harder to Change Than to Prevent

Although lifestyle interventions often meet with initial success, too many people "fall off the wagon." Ex-smokers, former heavy drinkers, weight-loss program participants, and those who are new to exercise regimens too often fall back into their old bad habits, a problem that must continue to be a focus for future health psychologists.

Good nutrition, fitness, responsible drinking, and healthy management of body weight, stress, and social relationships are lifelong challenges that are best begun at a young age. Most smokers, for example, take up the habit during adolescence, usually before they graduate from high school. But as we have seen, preventing smoking, like preventing certain risky sexual activities, is a daunting challenge. Many people, especially young people, are more heavily influenced by the immediate "rewards" of smoking—the stimulating "kick" from nicotine, the self-image of doing something that seems mature or perhaps rebellious, wanting to fit in with their peers who are trying smoking—than by worries about long-term health consequences.

Preventing poor health habits from developing in the first place will continue to be a high priority for health psychology. New research will investigate the most effective and efficient interventions for reaching the largest number of people in the workplace, schools and universities, and the community. The use of **behavioral immunization** programs, such as those targeting adolescents most likely to engage in risky sex, smoking, drug abuse, undereating or overeating, and other unhealthy behaviors, also will continue to grow. For some health behaviors, interventions will probably need to target even younger "at-risk" individuals. Among these are pediatric "well-parent/well-child" programs designed to teach new parents how to minimize the risks of accidents in the home and car and how to start their youngsters off on a lifetime of healthy eating and cardiopulmonary fitness.

behavioral immunization Efforts to inoculate people against unhealthy habits by exposing them to mild versions of messages that try to convince them to engage in the adverse behavior.

Lesson 4: Positive Stress Appraisal and Management Are Essential to Good Health

One of health psychology's most important contributions in the area of stress and health has been the resolution of the controversy regarding whether stress is external or internal. Research has clearly revealed that it is both: Stress is a transaction in which each of us must adjust continually to daily challenges. As you learned in Chapters 4 and 5, each of life's stressful events can be appraised as either a motivating challenge or a threatening obstacle. Viewing life's stressors as challenges that we can handle helps us maintain a sense of control and minimizes the impact of stress on our health. Learning to manage the stress that we encounter is crucial to our physical, psychological, and emotional well-being. Research has revealed the benefits of several stress-management strategies: keeping stress at manageable levels; preserving our physical resources by following a balanced diet, exercising, and drinking responsibly; establishing a stress-busting social network; increasing our psychological hardiness; disclosing our feelings when something is bothering us; cultivating a sense of humor; reducing hostile behaviors and negative emotions; and learning to relax.

A Century of Living! One of health psychology's key challenges is helping older adults optimize their well-being later in life.

Health Psychology's Future Challenges

Most of health psychology's challenges stem from two major research agendas. The most recent is the U.S. Department of Health and Human Services report *Healthy People 2020* (2014), which, as we have seen, outlined the nation's highest priorities for promoting health and preventing disease among all Americans. The report was based on the best judgments of a large group of health experts from the scientific community, professional health organizations, and the corporate world. The report's health objectives were organized under four overarching goals:

- attaining high-quality, longer lives free of preventable disease, disability, injury, and premature death;

- achieving health equity, eliminating disparities, and improving the health of all groups;

- creating social and physical environments that promote good health for all; and

- promoting quality of life, healthy development, and healthy behaviors across all life stages.

Inspirational Father–Son Team Dick Hoyt was inspired by his then-teenage son Rick, who has congenital physical disabilities, to train for and compete together in a running race for charity. Rick loved the experience and told his dad that for the first time, while flying along in his specially designed wheelchair, he didn't feel disabled. The pair has gone on to compete in hundreds of athletic competitions—including marathons and Ironman triathlons—over the past 30 years.

The second research agenda, produced more than 20 years ago by the American Psychological Association (1995) in collaboration with the National Institutes of Health (NIH) and 21 other professional societies, focused more specifically on health psychology's role in health care reform. *Doing the Right Thing: A Research Plan for Healthy Living* identified four research tasks, out of which emerge the five challenges that we will discuss in this section.

Challenge 1: To Increase the Span of Healthy Life for All People

The rapid aging of the population draws our attention to a crucial challenge: developing effective interventions that will enable older adults to maintain the highest possible level of functioning, or to improve it, for the greatest number of years.

Healthy life is a combination of average life expectancy and quality of life. The challenge for health psychology is to increase the average number of years that a person can expect to live in full health, along with a **compression of morbidity**—which refers to a shortening of the amount of time that people spend disabled, ill, or in pain. To illustrate, consider twin brothers who, although genetically identical and exposed to the same health hazards while growing up, have had very different health experiences since adolescence. The first brother smokes two packs of cigarettes a day, has an obesity-indicating BMI of 30.2, never exercises, has an angry and pessimistic outlook on life, and eats foods containing excessive amounts of animal fat and sugar. The second brother pursues a much healthier lifestyle, avoiding tobacco and excessive stress, exercising regularly, watching his diet, and enjoying the social support of a close-knit circle of family and friends. As Figure EP.3 shows, although the two brothers have the same genetic vulnerabilities to lung, circulatory, and cardiovascular disease, the unhealthy lifestyle of the first brother dooms him to an extended period of adulthood morbidity beginning at about age 45. In contrast, the healthier brother's lifestyle postpones disease until much later in life. If he does contract any of the illnesses, they are likely to be less severe, and recovery will be quicker. In some cases, the illness, such as lung cancer, may be "postponed" right out of his life.

We have achieved some success, but there is room for much additional improvement. One measure of a nation's health is average life expectancy. The higher the life expectancy, the better the health status of a country. Globally, 71 years is the average life expectancy for people born today. In the United States and Canada, life expectancy currently averages about 80 years; in a middle-income country such as Jordan, life expectancy drops to 74 years; and in a very poor country, such as Sierra Leone, life expectancy is only about 46 years (World Health Organization, 2016c).

Another measure of a nation's health is **health-adjusted life expectancy (HALE)**, the number of healthy, *well years* people can expect to live free from disease and disability. The discrepancy between life expectancy and HALE is quite variable when we compare various socioeconomic groups and countries of the world. Lower SES status is associated with shorter average life expectancy and fewer well years. Around the world, the percentage of life expectancy lost to disability ranges from less than 9 percent in the healthiest regions to more than 14 percent in the least healthy areas (Skolnik, 2016).

compression of morbidity Efforts to limit the time that an older person spends ill or disabled.

health-adjusted life expectancy (HALE) The number of healthy, *well years* a person can expect to live free from disease and disability.

FIGURE EP.3

Compression of Morbidity In focusing on the individual's quality-adjusted life years (QALYs), health psychologists seek to limit the time that a person spends ill or infirm, as illustrated in this diagram of illnesses and eventual deaths of identical twin brothers. Although the brothers carry the same disease vulnerabilities and life-span–limiting genetic clocks, the health lifestyle of one (b) keeps disease and disability at bay until an advanced age. In contrast, the unhealthy lifestyle of his brother (a) takes its toll at a much younger age.

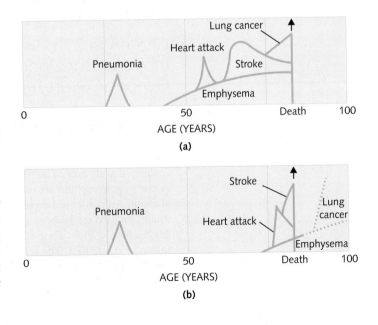

Positive Health

For health psychologists working within the positive psychology movement, an important challenge is to place greater emphasis on a strength-based, preventive approach to research and interventions, rather than use psychology's more traditional approach of tackling problems after they have occurred. Enhancing people's opportunities to not only be well, but also to attain a state of optimal human functioning is a priority for health psychology in the future.

Positive health is the scientific study of *health assets:* behaviors, traits, thoughts, and emotions associated with longer life, reduced morbidity, lower health care expenditure, and greater recuperative power and better prognosis when illness does strike. Martin Seligman and his colleagues (2016) have suggested that the field of positive health generates two broad hypotheses, one modest and one bold. The modest hypothesis is that assets such as positive emotions, self-regulation, cardiorespiratory fitness, and social engagement predict good health. The evidence for the modest proposal is already strong, and for many of these factors, there are evidence-based interventions that pay health dividends.

The second, bolder hypothesis is that there exist health states that have been described as thriving, resilience, or flourishing, that are associated with measurable outcomes such as less frequent and briefer ailments, enhanced recuperative ability when illness does occur, and greater physiological reserves. To date, much of the evidence for this hypothesis comes from anecdotes about people who never miss a day of work, people who stay physically active long after others in their age cohort retire, or people who lead a flourishing life despite serious illness or trauma and people who are off-the-chart with respect to their physiological capabilities.

An ongoing Robert Wood Johnson study seeks to identify biological, psychological, and functional factors that may lead to these states of super health, if indeed they exist. Biological health assets include high heart rate variability, high VO_2 max, greater telomere length, and low BMI. Psychological assets include optimism, personal control, subjective well-being, and curiosity. Functional health assets include such things as indicators of exceptional physical function (such as great strength, endurance, and motor coordination); a good match between a person's abilities and the requirements of his or her chosen roles and lifestyle; and close friends, meaningful work, and integration within a strong social community (Seligman and others, 2016). These assets are desirable in their own right. The challenge for positive health researchers is to expand the evidence base concerning whether and how they contribute to health-related outcomes.

positive health The scientific study of behaviors and traits that are associated with longer life, reduced morbidity, lower health care expenditure, and greater recuperative power.

Challenge 2: To Reduce Health Discrepancies and Increase Our Understanding of the Effects of Race, Gender, Culture, and Socioeconomic Status on Health

Historically, several measures of health have shown substantial differences among various ethnic and sociodemographic groups, as well as between the genders. For example, life expectancy at birth for African-Americans has risen since 1950 but remains noticeably lower than that for European-Americans (National Center for Health Statistics, 2016a). Compared with European-Americans, African-Americans have higher mortality rates in every age group and are more likely to suffer from many chronic health conditions—including heart disease, cancer, and diabetes—as well as fatal on-the-job injuries. Research studies focused on Hispanics/Latinos and Native Americans reveal similar disparities. Asking people about their health reveals even greater differences by ethnic group, as shown in Figure EP.4. The reasons for these discrepancies are undoubtedly complex but may include unequal access to health care, genetic susceptibility to specific diseases, and lifestyle differences.

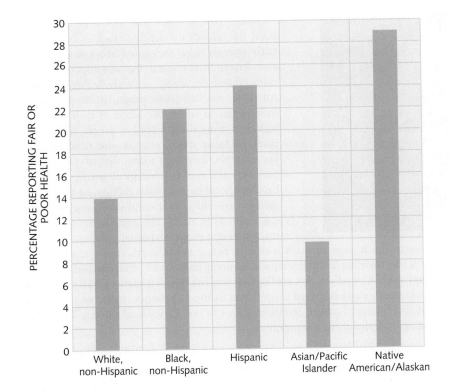

FIGURE EP.4

Quality of Health by Ethnic Group When asked to describe their health, a surprisingly high percentage of all ethnic groups used "fair" or "poor." Especially telling are the differences between ethnic groups, with Asian-Americans and European-Americans having the most positive view of their health and Native Americans being least positive.

Data from Behavioral Risk Factor Surveillance System (BRFSS). (2016). Atlanta, GA: Centers for Disease Control and Prevention. Retrieved from http://www.cdc.gov/brfss/index .html.

The negative effects of ethnicity and poverty on health may be the result of factors such as poor nutrition, crowded and unsanitary environments, inadequate medical care, stressful life events, and subjective perceptions that environmental stressors are beyond one's ability to cope. Another factor is less effective use of health screening among certain groups. For example, African-American women delay longer than white women in seeking care for breast symptoms, and older women, who frequently are at increased risk of breast cancer, are less likely to seek preventive care.

However, ethnic group disparities in health are not completely attributable to the social conditions in which people live. For example, Hispanic-Americans generally fare as well as or better than European-Americans on most measures of health, actually having a lower death rate than European-Americans from heart disease, lung cancer, and stroke. This is paradoxical, given the high rates of hypertension, obesity, and tobacco use among Hispanic-Americans. Some researchers believe that this puzzling fact reflects a lag in acculturation because the same trend can be found in all immigrant groups: As immigrants adopt an American lifestyle, they eventually develop the same patterns of illness and mortality.

Another factor that may be important is education. Regardless of ethnicity, people who have achieved higher levels of education live longer and have better overall health than those with less education, most likely because people with fewer years of education generally are more likely to engage in unhealthy behaviors such as smoking and eating a high-fat diet than those with more years of education. Recognizing the importance of education to health, *Healthy People 2020* (2014) set increasing the number of U.S. students awarded a high school diploma four years after starting the ninth grade as one of its leading social health indicators. A midcourse review showed that while this number has improved to just over 78 percent, there is still room for improvement (National Center for Health Statistics, 2016c).

Molly Riley/Newscom/United Press International (UPI)/ Washington, DC, United States

Education and Health
On average, achieving a higher level of education leads to a longer life and better overall health. Here, graduating students at Howard University listen as President Barack Obama delivers their commencement speech in Washington, D.C., May 7, 2016.

Health psychologists have not been able to pinpoint the reasons for the discrepancies because, until fairly recently, what they knew about health and disease derived from research that was disproportionately concentrated on young, relatively healthy, European-American research participants. Health psychologists have begun to widen the scope of their research to include a more diverse pool of people and, in many cases, to focus specifically on understudied groups. For example, they have found that women and men have very different psychological, social, and biological characteristics and vulnerabilities, so they differ in their susceptibility to various diseases and in their coping reactions to stress. The same seems to be true of many different ethnic and racial groups.

Clearly, much more research is needed before health psychologists can confidently explain why there are health discrepancies among traditionally understudied groups. One attempt to fill the void was provided by the Women's Health Initiative (WHI), a long-term national health study launched in 1991 that focused on the prevention of heart disease, breast and colorectal cancer, and osteoporosis in postmenopausal women. The prospective study included three components:

- a randomized, controlled clinical trial of 64,500 women, testing the impact of a low-fat diet, hormone replacement therapy, and calcium–vitamin D supplementation;

- an observational study of another 100,000 women, examining the biological and psychological determinants of these chronic diseases in women; and

- a massive study evaluating eight different model education/prevention programs in communities throughout the United States.

In 2002, the WHI released findings that hormone replacement therapy—at the time prescribed to 15 million postmenopausal women in the United States to alleviate symptoms of menopause and to prevent osteoporosis and heart attacks—significantly increased the risk of heart disease, stroke, and breast cancer (Rossouw, 2002). Since then, women's use of hormone therapy has plunged in the United States and many other countries, and this reduction has been followed by measurable decreases in breast cancer in several countries and, in the United States, decreases in heart attack and stroke. Here are some of the WHI's other findings as of 2015:

- Low-fat diets may reduce the risk of ovarian cancer and breast cancer in women.

- Women who exercise regularly and keep their weight within a normal range have lower levels of circulating estrogens—suggesting they may be at lower risk for breast cancer.

- Taking calcium and vitamin D supplements increases bone mineral density and may reduce the risk of hip fractures and death.

Globally, the need to focus on the predictors of women's health continues. As Neil Grunberg, my friend and former classmate, and a renowned NIH researcher, noted 25 years ago:

Research on health and behavior should consider men and women—not because it is discriminatory not to do so—but because it is good science. The study of women and men, of young, and old, of African Americans and Caucasians, Asians, Latinos, and American Indians will all help to reveal psychosocial and biological mechanisms that are critical to understanding mortality, morbidity, and quality of life (quoted in Baum & Grunberg, 1991).

Challenge 3: To Achieve Equal Access to Preventive Health Care Services for All People

As we have seen throughout this book, many minorities and impoverished Americans of every ethnicity and race have historically had limited access to preventive health care. And there is a disproportionate concentration of certain minority groups in unhealthy neighborhoods. These are some of the reasons why minorities and the poor tend to suffer more health problems and have a higher mortality rate. Health psychology faces the continuing challenge of understanding barriers that limit access to health care and assisting in their removal.

Health care costs have risen sharply in the past 50 years. In 1960, health care costs represented only 5.1 percent of the gross domestic product (GDP) of the United States. By 2013, the amount spent on health care had more than tripled to 17.1 percent (about $8,508 per person). Although this amount is much more than that of most developed nations in the world, the United States has a lower average life expectancy than that in other affluent countries, fewer physicians, and fewer hospital beds per person. In fact, the United States was, for the fifth time, ranked as worst among 11 industrialized nations as measured by such factors as efficiency, equity, and outcomes, according to the 2014 Commonwealth Fund Survey (see Figure EP.5). The United Kingdom ranked best in this survey, followed by Switzerland (Davis, Stremikis, Squires, & Schoen, 2014).

As we have seen, one reason for these low rankings is the tremendous disparity in the environmental conditions in which Americans live. Underscoring the impact of this disparity in environmental conditions, the Children's Defense Fund's 2011 report, *The State of America's Children*, outlined the following threats: poverty, lack of health care, substance abuse, crime and dangers in the environment, abuse and neglect at home, inadequate child care, poor schools, teen pregnancy, and absent parents. It is obvious that each of these threats, either directly or indirectly, can have a powerful impact on children's health.

FIGURE EP.5

Health Care Rankings of 11 Developed Countries Among the 11 nations compared, the U.S. health care system ranks last, as it did in 2010, 2007, 2006, and 2004. Most troubling, the U.S. system is last or near last on dimensions of access, efficiency, and equity.

Information from Davis, K., Stremikis, K., Squires, D., & Schoen, C. (2014). Mirror, mirror on the wall: How the performance of the U.S. health care system compares internationally. New York: The Commonwealth Fund. Retrieved April 6, 2016, from http://www.commonwealthfund.org/publications/fund-reports/2014/jun/mirror-mirror.

COUNTRY RANKINGS

	AUS	CAN	FRA	GER	NETH	NZ	NOR	SWE	SWIZ	UK	US
OVERALL RANKING (2013)	4	10	9	5	5	7	7	3	2	1	11
Quality Care	2	9	8	7	5	4	11	10	3	1	5
Effective Care	4	7	9	6	5	2	11	10	8	1	3
Safe Care	3	10	2	6	7	9	11	5	4	1	7
Coordinated Care	4	8	9	10	5	2	7	11	3	1	6
Patient-Centered Care	5	8	10	7	3	6	11	9	2	1	4
Access	8	9	11	2	4	7	6	4	2	1	9
Cost-Related Problem	9	5	10	4	8	6	3	1	7	1	11
Timeliness of Care	6	11	10	4	2	7	8	9	1	3	5
Efficiency	4	10	8	9	7	3	4	2	6	1	11
Equity	5	9	7	4	8	10	6	1	2	2	11
Healthy Lives	4	8	1	7	5	9	6	2	3	10	11
Health Expenditures/Capita, 2011**	$3,800	$4,522	$4,118	$4,495	$5,099	$3,182	$5,669	$3,925	$5,643	$3,405	$8,508

Country Rankings legend: Top 2* / Middle / Bottom 2*

Notes: *Includes ties. **Expenditures shown in $US PPP (purchasing power parity); Australian $ data are from 2010.
Source: Calculated by The Commonwealth Fund based on 2011 International Health Policy Survey of Sicker Adults; 2012 International Health Policy Care Physicians; 2013 International Health Policy Survey; Commonwealth Fund *National Scorecard 2011*; World Health Organization; and Organization for Economic Cooperation and Development, *OECD Health Data, 2013* (Paris OECD, Nov. 2013).

So long as some people have access to quality health care while others have no access, we will have a two-tiered health care system in this country: state-of-the-art, high-tech care for those who have managed to get health insurance and substandard care (or no care) for everyone else. Health care reform remains a continuing challenge—for health psychology as well as for the national political agenda.

On March 23, 2010, President Barack Obama signed into law the Patient Protection and Affordable Care Act (PPACA). the most significant overhaul of U.S. health care in nearly 50 years. The primary goals of the law are to decrease the number of people who do not have health insurance and to lower the costs of health care. Additional reforms are aimed at improving health care outcomes and streamlining the delivery of health care. In addition, insurers are required to cover certain types of preventive care at no cost to the consumer, including blood pressure and cholesterol tests, mammograms, colonoscopies, and screenings for osteoporosis.

Challenge 4: To Adjust the Focus of Research and Intervention to Maximize Health Promotion with Evidence-Based Approaches

In the past, health psychology followed biomedicine's lead in focusing on mortality rather than on morbidity. Even when prevention was stressed, health psychologists tended to focus on those chronic diseases that were the leading causes of death. Although reducing mortality will continue to be a priority, health psychology also must devote greater attention to conditions such as arthritis, which have a minimal impact on mortality rates but a dramatic impact on wellness among the elderly.

A related challenge is to place more emphasis on health-enhancing behaviors and factors that may delay mortality and reduce morbidity. In the past, health psychologists focused more of their research on studying risk factors for chronic disease and less of their research on learning about health-promoting behaviors that help prevent people from developing illnesses. The positive psychology movement is working to address this imbalance as researchers pay greater attention to promoting healthy individuals, healthy families and communities, and healthy workplaces.

A continuing challenge for health psychology is to employ evidence-based approaches through documentation of the effectiveness of various interventions. This issue comes into sharp relief as the debate continues over the extent to which psychological interventions should be covered by managed health insurance. Even the most exciting new intervention—if backed only by weak or poorly conducted research studies—is likely to meet with the same skeptical reaction from health care professionals that many complementary and alternative therapies have faced (see Chapter 15). Complicating the research picture is the fact that true primary prevention studies often take decades to complete, and they require expensive, long-term funding. Fortunately, the Centers for Disease Control and Prevention (CDC) has shown considerable interest in continuing behavioral intervention research.

Despite health psychology's successes, much remains to be done before the goals of *Healthy People 2020* are fully met. Although health psychologists continue to focus on eliminating health disparities among various sociocultural groups, greater emphasis is also being placed on improving the health of all Americans.

Challenge 5: To Assist in Health Care Reform

Historically, health care in the United States has faced three fundamental problems: It has been far too expensive, not all citizens have had equal access to high-quality health care, and its services often have been used inappropriately. For many years, researchers therefore predicted a major revolution in the U.S. health care system. Among the issues needing to be addressed has been universal access to health care, comprehensive mandated health benefits, cost containment, quality, accountability, and a shift in emphasis from secondary prevention to primary prevention. Although the PPACA addresses many of these issues, unfortunately health care in this country continues to focus much more on expensive inpatient care (and other efforts at secondary prevention) than on cost-effective primary prevention and health promotion.

To improve health care while cutting costs is among the most pressing of needs. One of health psychology's most fundamental messages is that prevention and health promotion or maintenance must be made as important in the health care system as disease treatment is now. As the Institute of Medicine (2011a) itself has noted, health promotion needs to become a standard part of medical practice, and mounting evidence demonstrates the importance of shifting from a model of tertiary care to primary care. Health care also must be defined more broadly so that it doesn't focus solely on the services provided by doctors, nurses, clinicians, and hospitals. Many health psychologists emphasize the importance of patients taking responsibility for their own well-being, while also recognizing the significant roles played by the individual's family, friends, and community. More effective health care will recognize that schools, places of worship, and workplaces are major sites for promoting health and should become part of the network of interconnected services in the nation's health care system.

The role that psychologists play in improving physical health through enhancing treatment outcomes now has been firmly established (Clay, 2016). This has led to a significant increase in the number of psychologists working in general health care settings. One way to estimate the benefits of preventive actions is with combined measures of life expectancy and **quality-adjusted life years (QALY).** One QALY equates to one year in perfect health. QALYs can be used to calculate the cost-effectiveness of various primary and secondary prevention efforts. For example, a pharmaceutical treatment, medical screening procedure, or behavior intervention that improves the quality of life by half (0.5) for two people will result in the equivalent of 1 QALY over a period of one year. In one early study of the cost-effectiveness of health interventions, researchers estimated that the small benefit of regular mammography among women 40 to 49 years of age (increasing life expectancy by only 2.5 days at a cost of $676 per woman) amounts to a cost of $100,000 for 1 full QALY (Salzmann, Kerlikowske, & Phillips, 1997). As a comparison, researchers have found that regular exercise produces 1 QALY for 2000 to 15,000 euros ($2500–$19,500)—a much more modest expenditure relative to many biomedical secondary prevention interventions (Wu and others, 2011; Annemans, Lamotte, Clarys, & Van den Abeele, 2007). As another example, it is very cost-effective to reduce distracted driving by getting people to stop texting, eating, and in other ways multitasking, but much less cost-effective to save the lives of people who have had car accidents. It is cost-effective to promote the health of children by ensuring their access to healthy food. It is much less cost-effective to provide care for the additional morbidity that may occur from pneumonia, measles, and other diseases that may occur in children who are deficient in vitamin A and other key nutrients (Skolnik, 2016).

Health care policy is not solely to blame. Several studies argue that health psychologists have not always adapted well to new integrated-care models (Clay, 2016). Although health psychologists and primary care providers generally share goals and wish to collaborate, they too often are held back from greater collaboration because of differences in their educations, clinical styles, and reimbursement systems.

quality-adjusted life year (QALY) One year of good health, free from disease and disability.

Psychosocial Interventions

Health psychologists perform a wide range of activities, including training future doctors and nurses on the importance of psychosocial factors in patient adherence and recovery and directly intervening to assist patients who are facing difficult procedures and adjusting to chronic illness (Table EP.1). Treatment interventions cover every domain of health.

TABLE EP.1

Examples of Health Psychology's Treatment Interventions

Interventions for Chronic Illness

- *Pain management*—training in techniques for conditions such as back pain, cancer pain, severe burns, and migraine headaches
- *Symptom management*—interventions to control symptoms associated with medical treatment, such as nausea from chemotherapy, or desensitization to fears resulting from medical procedures such as magnetic resonance imaging (MRI), needles/injections, and cardiac catheterization
- *Stress management*—interventions for patients with illnesses that are made worse by stress, such as hypertension, cardiovascular disease, and ulcers
- *Presurgical patients*—anxiety-reduction interventions for patients about to undergo surgery and other invasive medical procedures
- *Treatment adherence*—cognitive behavioral interventions for dietary and medical regimen adherence for diseases such as diabetes
- *Assessment*—assessing a suspected dementia process, such as Alzheimer's disease, and developing interventions to manage behavioral and functional problems associated with such a disease
- *Adjustment to illness*—individual and group psychological interventions for depression, anxiety, and adjustment issues surrounding chronic illness, all of which affect quality of life
- *Improving patient communication*—interventions designed to improve the patient's ability to communicate effectively with health care providers about medical procedures
- *Family intervention/problem solving*—supportive and problem-solving interventions for family members of patients suffering from chronic illness

Interventions in Disease Prevention and Health Promotion

- *Smoking*—development of smoking cessation programs, including cognitive behavioral skill-building programs and preventive interventions
- *High-risk sexual behavior*—development of preventive and intervention programs aimed at high-risk sexual behavior associated with HIV and other sexually transmitted infections
- *Substance abuse*—development of programs to address such problems as binge drinking
- *Diet and lifestyle*—development of programs to address poor diet and/or sedentary lifestyle, which are often associated with heart disease and other health problems
- *Accidents and injuries*—development of programs to prevent accidents and avoid post-traumatic stress disorder (PTSD) if serious injuries occur

Information from Belar, C. E., & Deardorff, W. W. (2008). *Clinical health psychology in medical settings: A practitioner's guidebook.* Washington, DC: American Psychological Association; Anderson, N. B. (2003). Psychology as a health profession. Washington, DC: American Psychological Association. Retrieved from http://www.apa.org/monitor/mar03/rc.aspx.

In the biological domain, treatment is designed to directly change specific physiological responses involved in the illness. Examples include relaxation to reduce hypertension, hypnosis to alleviate pain, and systematic desensitization to reduce the nausea that often occurs in anticipation of chemotherapy. In the psychological domain, health psychologists have applied both cognitive and behavioral interventions. Cognitive interventions include stress inoculation to decrease anxiety about an upcoming medical procedure, cognitive behavioral treatment for depression, and anger management for hostile cardiovascular disease patients. Behavioral interventions include teaching skills to improve patient–provider communication, to develop a behavioral-change program to modify unhealthy habits, and to help train patients in self-management skills such as daily injections of insulin. Social interventions include establishing support groups for those suffering from chronic illness, providing counseling for families of the terminally ill, and conducting role-playing exercises with young children to socially "inoculate" them against being pressured by peers into risky behaviors.

Such psychosocial interventions actually can yield significant cost savings, particularly when used to prepare patients for surgery and other anxiety-producing medical procedures (Novotney, 2010b). Patients who are overly anxious when facing hospitalization and invasive procedures such as surgery often experience a disintegration of normal coping skills. Relaxation training, postsurgical exercises, distraction techniques, and control-enhancing techniques can reduce the length of hospitalization and the need for pain-relieving medication and help prevent disruptive patient behavior. In addition, psychosocial interventions are perceived as effective and desirable by both patients and their families (Clay, 2016).

The challenge of cost containment is likely to continue because cardiovascular disease and cancer—chronic, age-related diseases that are extraordinarily costly to treat—probably will remain the leading causes of death for some time to come. Health psychology's emphasis on prevention, if widely employed, would help contain overall expenses despite the initial cost of additional health personnel. One of the best ways to contain these costs is to help people improve their health behaviors to avoid getting sick and to help those who become sick to recover as quickly as possible.

Integrated Primary Care When interdisciplinary treatment teams approach diseases from biological, psychological, and sociocultural perspectives, treatment is often improved and costs are reduced.

Integrated Primary Care

As further testimony to health psychology's future role in helping the health care system's efforts to contain costs, the Human Capital Initiative has called for greater use of integrated care (also called collaborative care or blended care; see Chapter 13). This interdisciplinary model, in which treatment teams approach diseases from biological, psychological, and sociocultural perspectives, shows great promise in improving treatment while simultaneously cutting costs (Table EP.2).

One medical trend that affects health psychology is the use of **integrated primary care** in treating chronic conditions. IPC combines medical and behavioral health services by bringing all available treatments together into an individualized intervention plan for a patient. A good example of this approach is the coordinated care available to dying patients in hospice settings. This includes palliative care for pain control; symptom management for comfort; and counseling, bereavement, and education for patients and families. IPC allows patients to feel that for any problem they have, they are in the right place.

integrated primary care
Care that combines medical and behavioral health services by bringing together all available treatments into an individualized intervention plan for a patient.

As we have seen, the potential benefits of integrating health psychology into primary care include better patient retention, higher treatment adherence rates, improved outcomes, and cost. However, challenges remain. There is a pressing need for more research focused on health psychology interventions in real-world treatment settings. And, as with any research study that attempts to study one variable while controlling others,

TABLE EP.2
Reduction in Treatment Frequency with Integrated Care

Total ambulatory care visits	–17%
Visits for minor illnesses	–35%
Pediatric acute illness visits	–25%
Office visits for acute asthma	–49%
Office visits by arthritis patients	–40%
Average length of stay in hospital for surgical patients	–1.5 days
Cesarean sections	–56%
Epidural anesthesia during labor and delivery	–85%

Source: American Psychological Association, Science Directorate. (1995). *Doing the right thing: A research plan for healthy living—A Human Capital Initiative strategy report.* Washington, DC: American Psychological Association. Human Capital Initiative Coordinating Committee.

determining the degree of penetration of health psychology into primary care settings and clarifying the specific roles of health psychologists in integrated care are key issues (Thielke, Thompson, & Stuart, 2011).

The success of integrated care reflects health psychology's growing acceptance by traditional biomedicine over the past 30 years—a trend that is likely to continue (Clay, 2016). One sign of its acceptance is the increase in the number of psychologists working in medical schools and academic health centers—the single largest area of placement of psychologists in recent years (Association of Psychologists in Academic Health Centers, 2016). Increasingly, medical schools recognize that a complete medical education must include, alongside the biological and physical sciences, the perspectives and research findings that have emerged from behavioral and social sciences. Psychologists have become key members of multidisciplinary clinical and research teams in many medical specialties, including family practice, pediatrics, rehabilitation, cardiology, oncology, and anesthesiology. Another sign is the growing role of nurses in delivering psychological services. An increasing number of nurses are obtaining advanced degrees in psychology, and the nursing profession has established the National Institute for Nursing Research (NINR), which focuses on controlled studies of psychological variables in nursing.

Paradoxically, as medical care has grown more specialized and more complex, it also has begun to broaden its scope, incorporating more complementary and alternative aspects of healing. Relaxation training, imagery, and some of the spiritual aspects of non-Western healing traditions are beginning to be accepted by some managed-care programs because these methods are typically inexpensive and yet often effective in helping patients cope with a variety of stress-related symptoms. With ever-rising medical costs, the cost-effectiveness ratio of such interventions can't be ignored.

International Reform

As we have seen, there is great variability in the prevalence of specific diseases throughout the world. Poverty, lack of health care, and ignorance generally contribute to a higher incidence of infectious diseases in developing countries than in developed countries. Non-infectious diseases also follow this trend: For example, as smoking continues to decline in Canada and the United States, its prevalence is increasing in developing parts of the world, resulting in rising rates of lung cancer, cardiovascular disease, and emphysema.

Health psychology can take the lead in carrying the messages of the thousands of research studies from developed nations to other parts of the world in which similar health problems are just beginning to emerge. But the transmission of information can flow in both directions. Health psychologists can help reform the U.S. health care system by helping policymakers understand those things that other countries do better than we do. As an example, consider one aspect of the Australian system: well-woman/well-man clinics. The aim of these clinics is to promote the health of the total woman and man, focusing on wellness rather than only on disease. These free clinics, staffed by nurse-practitioners, are found throughout the country and focus on education, assessment, and nonmedical management of personal and family stress problems (Well Men and Women Too, 2016).

Conclusion

ealth psychology's outlook as a profession is bright. The field has made impressive advances in its brief history, though there is much more to learn. Future health psychologists will face many challenges as they work to improve individual and community health and to help reform the health care system. I hope that your increasing understanding of health psychology will be as motivating to you—both personally and professionally—as it has been to me.

Weigh In on Health

Respond to each question below based on what you learned in the Epilogue and the entire text

1. After having read this textbook, identify some ways that you think you could improve your health related to its biological, psychological, and social or cultural components.

2. Some friends of yours know that you have taken a class in health psychology. They want you to share your insight into the future of health care, especially how it will be influenced by the work of health psychologists. What will you tell them? What research did you read about that supports your thinking?

3. After finishing this course in health psychology, you decide to pursue health psychology as your career. What subfield of health psychology will you choose: teacher, research scientist, or clinician (see Chapter 1)? Identify a goal that you would hope to accomplish in your chosen career.

Summing Up

Health Psychology's Most Important Lessons

Lesson 1: Psychological and Social Factors Interact with Biology in Health

Lesson 2: It Is Our Own Responsibility to Promote and Maintain Our Health

Lesson 3: Unhealthy Lifestyles Are Harder to Change Than to Prevent

Lesson 4: Positive Stress Appraisal and Management Are Essential to Good Health

Health Psychology's Future Challenges

Challenge 1: To Increase the Span of Healthy Life for All People

Challenge 2: To Reduce Health Discrepancies and Increase Our Understanding of the Effects of Race, Gender, Culture, and Socioeconomic Status on Health

Challenge 3: To Achieve Equal Access to Preventive Health Care Services for All People

Challenge 4: To Adjust the Focus of Research and Intervention to Maximize Health Promotion with Evidence-Based Approaches

Challenge 5: To Assist in Health Care Reform

Key Terms and Concepts to Remember

behavioral immunization, p. 473
compression of morbidity, p. 475

health-adjusted life expectancy (HALE), p. 475
positive health, p. 476

quality-adjusted life years (QALY), p. 481
integrated primary care, p. 483

Glossary

abdominal obesity. Excess fat around the stomach and abdomen; also called *male-pattern obesity*.

accountable care organization (ACO). An organization of health care providers that agrees to be accountable for the quality, cost, and overall care of members.

acquired immunodeficiency syndrome (AIDS). The most advanced stages of HIV infection, defined by a T cell count of less than 200 and the occurrence of opportunistic infections or HIV-related cancers that take advantage of a weakened immune system.

acupuncture. A component of traditional Oriental medicine in which fine needles are inserted into the skin to relieve pain, treat addiction and illness, and promote health.

acute pain. Sharp, stinging pain that is short-lived and usually related to tissue damage.

adherence. A patient both agreeing to and then closely following a treatment regimen as advised by his or her health care provider.

adipocytes. Collapsible body cells that store fat.

adrenal glands. Lying above the kidneys, the pair of endocrine glands that secrete epinephrine, norepinephrine, and cortisol, which are hormones that arouse the body during moments of stress.

aerobic exercise. Light- to moderate-intensity exercise performed for an extended period of time; examples include swimming, cycling, and running.

agonist. A drug that attaches to a receptor and produces neural actions that mimic or enhance those of a naturally occurring neurotransmitter.

alcohol expectancy effects. The effects of an individual's beliefs about how alcohol affects behavior.

alcohol myopia. The tendency of alcohol to increase a person's concentration on immediate events and to reduce awareness of distant events.

alcohol use disorder (AUD). A maladaptive drinking pattern in which drinking interferes with role obligations.

allostatic load (allostasis). The cumulative long-term effects of the body's physiological response to stress.

allostatic overload. The consequences of long-term elevations of stress-related catabolic hormones, including hypertension, wasted muscles, ulcers, fatigue, and increased risk of chronic disease.

alternative medicine. A broad range of health care practices that are not taught in medical schools, not generally used in hospitals, and not usually reimbursed by insurance companies.

amygdala. Two clusters of neurons in the limbic system that are linked to emotion, especially aggression.

anaerobic exercise. High-intensity exercise performed for short periods of time; examples include weight training and sprinting.

angina pectoris. A condition of extreme chest pain caused by a restriction of the blood supply to the heart.

anorexia nervosa. An eating disorder characterized by self-starvation; a distorted body image; and, in females, amenorrhea.

antagonist. A drug that blocks the action of a naturally occurring neurotransmitter or agonist.

anterior cingulate cortex (ACC). The front part of the cingulate cortex, which resembles a collar in surrounding the corpus callosum and plays a role in pain processing and many self-regulating functions.

antigen. A foreign substance that stimulates an immune response.

antimicrobial resistance. The ability of bacteria, viruses, and other microbes to resist the effect of drugs.

arteries. Blood vessels that carry blood away from the heart to other organs and tissues; a small artery is called an *arteriole*.

arteriosclerosis. Also called "hardening of the arteries," a disease in which blood vessels lose their elasticity.

association cortex. Areas of the cerebral cortex not directly involved in sensory or motor functions; rather, they integrate multisensory information and higher mental functions such as thinking and speaking.

atherogenesis. The process of forming atheromatous plaques in the inner lining of arteries.

atheromatous plaques. Buildups of fatty deposits within the wall of an artery that occur in atherosclerosis.

atherosclerosis. A chronic disease in which cholesterol and other fats are deposited on the inner walls of the coronary arteries, reducing circulation to heart tissue.

at-risk drinking. Two or more episodes of binge drinking in the past month, or consuming an average of two or more alcoholic drinks per day in the past month.

attentional focus. A person's characteristic style of monitoring bodily symptoms, emotions, and overall well-being.

attributable risk. The actual amount that a disease can be attributed to exposure to a particular risk factor. Attributable risk is determined by subtracting the incidence rate of a disease in people who have been exposed to a risk factor from the incidence rate of the disease in people who have not been exposed to the risk factor.

aversion therapy. A behavioral therapy that pairs an unpleasant stimulus (such as a nauseating drug) with an undesirable behavior (such as drinking or smoking), causing the patient to avoid the behavior.

basal metabolic rate (BMR). The minimum number of calories the body needs to maintain bodily functions while at rest.

behavioral activation. A counseling treatment that focuses on increasing engagement in valued life activities through guided goal setting.

behavioral control. Interventions that teach techniques for controlling pain and speeding recovery during and after a medical procedure.

behavioral disinhibition. The false sense of confidence and freedom from social restraints that results from alcohol consumption.

behavioral immunization. Efforts to inoculate people against unhealthy habits by exposing them to mild versions of messages that try to convince them to engage in the adverse behavior.

behavioral intention. In theories of health behavior, the rational decision to engage in a health-related behavior or to refrain from engaging in the behavior.

behavioral undercontrol. A general personality syndrome linked to alcohol dependence and characterized by aggressiveness, unconventionality, and impulsiveness; also called *deviance proneness.*

benefit finding. The experience of identifying positive outcomes in the face of adversity.

binge-eating disorder (BED). An eating disorder in which a person frequently consumes unusually large amounts of food.

biofeedback. A system that provides audible or visible feedback information regarding involuntary physiological states.

biological embedding. The processes by which the structure and functioning of the brain are shaped by feedback from neuroendocrine systems as they are engaged as part of the body's effort to maintain homeostasis.

biomedical model. The dominant view of twentieth-century medicine that maintains that illness always has a physical cause.

biopsychosocial perspective. The viewpoint that health and other behaviors are determined by the interaction of biological mechanisms, psychological processes, and social influences.

birth cohort. A group of people who, because they were born at about the same time, experience similar historical and social conditions.

blood alcohol level (BAL). The amount of alcohol in the blood, measured in grams per 100 milliliters.

blood–brain barrier. The network of tightly packed capillary cells that separates the blood and the brain.

body mass index (BMI). A measure of obesity calculated by dividing body weight by the square of a person's height.

brainstem. The oldest and most central region of the brain; includes the medulla, pons, and reticular formation.

bronchi. The pair of respiratory tubes that branch into progressively smaller passageways, the bronchioles, culminating in the air sacs within the right and left lungs (he alveoli).

buffering hypothesis. A theory that social support produces its stress-busting effects indirectly by helping the individual cope more effectively.

bulimia nervosa. An eating disorder characterized by alternating cycles of binge eating and purging through such techniques as vomiting or laxative abuse.

burnout. A job-related state of physical and psychological exhaustion.

calorie. A measure of food energy equivalent to the amount of energy needed to raise the temperature of 1 gram of water 1 degree Celsius.

cancer. A set of diseases in which abnormal body cells multiply and spread in uncontrolled fashion, often forming a tissue mass called a *tumor.*

carcinogen. A cancer-causing agent such as tobacco, ultraviolet radiation, or an environmental toxin.

carcinoma. Cancer of the epithelial cells that line the outer and inner surfaces of the body; includes breast, prostate, lung, and skin cancer.

cardiorespiratory endurance. The ability of the heart, blood vessels, and lungs to supply oxygen to working muscles during physical activity for prolonged periods of time.

cardiovascular disease (CVD). Disorders of the heart and blood vessel system, including stroke and coronary heart disease (CHD).

cardiovascular reactivity (CVR). An individual's characteristic reaction to stress, including changes in heart rate, blood pressure, and hormones.

case-control study. A retrospective epidemiological study in which people with a disease or condition (cases) are compared with people who are not affected by the disease or condition (controls).

catastrophizing. An error in thinking in which a person believes something, such as pain, is far worse than it actually is.

cell. The basic unit of structure and function in living things.

cerebellum. Located at the rear of the brain, this brain structure coordinates voluntary movement and balance.

cerebral cortex. The thin layer of cells that covers the cerebrum; the seat of conscious sensation and information processing.

chiropractic. A complementary and alternative medicine approach to healing that is concerned with the diagnosis, treatment, and prevention of disorders of the neuromusculoskeletal system.

chronic fatigue syndrome (CFS). A puzzling disorder of uncertain causes in which a person experiences headaches, infections of unknown origins, extreme tiredness, and difficulties with concentration and memory.

chronic pain. Dull, burning pain that is long-lasting.

cilia. Tiny hairs; those that line the air passageways in the nose, mouth, and trachea move in wavelike fashion, trapping germs and forcing them out of the respiratory system.

circadian rhythm. A biological clock that operates on a 24-hour cycle.

clinical pain. Pain that requires some form of medical treatment.

cognitive behavioral therapy (CBT). The use of principles from learning theory to change unhealthy patterns of thinking and behavior.

cognitive behavioral therapy for insomnia (CBT-I). A structured treatment for insomnia aimed at replacing thoughts and behaviors that cause or worsen sleep problems with habits that promote sound sleep without the use of medication.

cognitive control. Interventions that direct the patient's attention to the positive aspects of a procedure (such as improved health) rather than to feelings of discomfort.

cognitive reappraisal. A key component of CBT that focuses on helping individuals *reinterpret* pain-related sensations, *restructure* maladaptive thought patterns, and make *positive self-statements*.

collaborative care. A cooperative form of health care in which physicians, psychologists, and other health care providers join forces to improve patient care.

common liability to addiction. A model of addiction proposing that the likelihood a person will begin using illegal drugs is determined not by the preceding use of other specific legal drugs (gateway hypothesis), but instead by the particular tendencies and environmental circumstances of the drug user.

communicable disease. A disease that is transmitted from a human to another human, from a human to an animal, or from an animal to a human.

comorbidity. The simultaneous occurrence of two or more physical and/or psychological disorders or symptoms.

comparative optimism. The tendency to think that one will experience more positive and fewer negative events than others.

competitive foods. Foods and beverages that are often high in calories, sugar, fat, and sodium that are sold in schools in vending machines, à la carte lines, and student stores.

complementary and alternative medicine (CAM). The use and practice of therapies or diagnostic techniques that fall outside conventional biomedicine.

compression of morbidity. Efforts to limit the time that an older person spends ill or disabled.

concordance rate. The rate of agreement between a pair of twins for a given trait; a pair of twins is concordant for the trait if both of them have it or if neither has it.

confirmation bias. A form of faulty reasoning in which our expectations prevent us from seeing alternative explanations for our observations.

consideration of future consequences. The extent to which individuals consider and are influenced by the potential future outcomes of their behavior.

contingency contract. A formal agreement between a person attempting to change a health behavior and another individual, such as a therapist, regarding the consequences of target behaviors.

conventional medicine. Biomedically based medicine as practiced by holders of the MD (medical doctor) or DO (doctor of osteopathy) degrees and their allied health professionals.

coping. The cognitive, behavioral, and emotional ways in which we manage stressful situations.

coronary heart disease (CHD). A chronic disease in which the arteries that supply the heart become narrowed or clogged; results from either atherosclerosis or arteriosclerosis.

correlation coefficient. A statistical measure of the strength and direction of the relationship between two variables, and thus of how well one predicts the other.

corticosteroids. Hormones produced by the adrenal cortex that fight inflammation, promote healing, and trigger the release of stored energy.

counterirritation. Analgesia in which one pain (for example, a pulled muscle) is relieved by creating another counteracting sensation (such as rubbing near the site of the injur).

cross-sectional study. A type of observational study in which data are collected from a population, or representative subset, *at one specific point in time.*

cytokines. Protein molecules produced by immune cells that act on other cells to regulate immunity (including the interferons, interleukins, and tumor necrosis factors).

debrief. The process in which research participants are given more details about the study following its completion.

delay behavior. The tendency to avoid seeking medical care because symptoms go unnoticed (*appraisal delay*), sickness seems unlikely (*illness delay*), professional help is deemed unnecessary (*behavioral delay*), the individual procrastinates in making an appointment (*scheduling delay*), or the perceived costs of treatment outweigh the perceived benefits (*treatment delay*).

dependence. A state in which the use of a drug is required for a person to function normally.

descriptive study. A research method in which researchers observe and record participants' behaviors, often forming hypotheses that are later tested more systematically; includes case studies, interviews and surveys, focus groups, and observational studies.

diabetes mellitus. A disorder of the endocrine system in which the body is unable to produce insulin (Type 1) or is unable to use this pancreatic hormone properly (Type 2).

diathesis–stress model. The model that proposes that two interacting factors determine an individual's susceptibility to stress and illness: predisposing factors in the person (such as genetic vulnerability) and precipitating factors from the environment (such as traumatic experiences).

direct effect hypothesis. A theory that social support produces its beneficial effects during both stressful and nonstressful times by enhancing the body's physical responses to challenging situations.

discriminative stimuli. Environmental signals that certain behaviors will be followed by reinforcement.

drug abuse. The use of a drug to the extent that it impairs the user's biological, psychological, or social well-being.

drug potentiation. The effect of one drug to increase the effects of another.

dynamic tailoring. The delivery of individualized and targeted health messages over multiple periods of time.

ecological momentary assessment (EMA). A method of measuring stress that involves repeated sampling of people's behaviors and experiences in real time and in their natural environments.

ecological-systems approach. The viewpoint that nature is best understood as a hierarchy of systems, in which each system is simultaneously composed of smaller subsystems and larger, interrelated systems.

electronic or e-cigarettes (EC). Battery-powered vaporizers that simulate smoking without burning tobacco.

emotional-approach coping (EAC). The process of working through, clarifying, and understanding the emotions triggered by a stressor.

emotional cascade. Becoming so focused on an upsetting event that one gets worked into an intense, painful state of negative emotion.

emotional disclosure. A therapeutic activity in which people express their strong, often stress-related emotions by writing or talking about the events that triggered them.

emotion-focused coping. A coping strategy in which we try to control our emotional response to a stressor.

endogenous opiate peptides. Opiatelike substances naturally produced by the body.

enkephalins. Endogenous (naturally occurring) opioids found in nerve endings of cells in the brain and spinal cord that bind to opioid receptors.

epidemic. Literally, *among the people*; an epidemic disease is one that spreads rapidly among many individuals in a community at the same time.

epidemiological transition. A shift in the disease pattern of a population as mortality falls: acute, infectious diseases are reduced, while chronic, noncommunicable diseases increase in prevalence.

epidemiology. The scientific study of the frequency, distribution, and causes of a particular disease or other health outcome in a population.

epigenetic. The effects of environmental forces on how genes are expressed.

etiology. The scientific study of the causes or origins of specific diseases.

evidence-based medicine. The use of current best evidence in making decisions about the care of individual patients or the delivery of health services.

explanatory style. Our general propensity to attribute outcomes always to positive causes or always to negative causes, such as personality, luck, or another person's actions.

family therapy. A type of psychotherapy in which individuals within a family learn healthier ways to interact with each other and resolve conflicts.

fast nerve fibers. Large, myelinated nerve fibers that transmit sharp, stinging pain.

fee-for-service. A payment model in which health care services are paid for by patients out of pocket at the time of treatment.

fetal alcohol syndrome (FAS). A cluster of birth defects that include facial abnormalities, low intelligence, and delayed body growth caused by the mother's use of alcohol during pregnancy.

food deserts. Geographical areas with little or no access to foods needed to maintain a healthy diet.

free nerve endings. Sensory receptors found throughout the body that respond to temperature, pressure, and painful stimuli.

gain-framed message. A health message that focuses on attaining positive outcomes or avoiding undesirable ones by adopting a health-promoting behavior.

gastrointestinal system. The body's system for digesting food; includes the digestive tract, salivary glands, pancreas, liver, and gallbladder.

gate control theory (GCT). The idea that there is a neural "gate" in the spinal cord that regulates the experience of pain.

gateway drug. A drug that serves as a stepping-stone to the use of other, usually more dangerous, drugs.

general adaptation syndrome (GAS). Selye's term for the body's reaction to stress, which consists of three stages: alarm, resistance, and exhaustion.

genital human papillomavirus (HPV). The most common sexually transmitted infection.

genome. The complete instructions for making an organism, including all the genetic material found in that organism's chromosomes.

genomics. The study of the structure, function, and mapping of the genetic material of organisms.

genotype. The sum total of all the genes present in an individual.

glucocorticoid receptor (GCR) resistance model. The idea that chronic stress promotes the development and progression of disease by reducing the sensitivity of immune system receptors to glucocorticoid hormones such as cortisol, thereby interfering with the body's ability to regulate the inflammatory response.

glycemic control. The action of monitoring glucose levels to keep blood sugar at a stable, healthy level.

guided imagery. The use of one or more external devices to assist in relaxation and the formation of clear, strong, positive images.

health. A state of complete physical, mental, and social well-being.

health-adjusted life expectancy (HALE). The number of healthy, well years a person can expect to live free from disease and disability.

health behavior. A health-enhancing behavior or habit.

health belief model (HBM). A nonstage theory that identifies four factors that influence decision making regarding health behavior: perceived susceptibility to a health threat, perceived severity of the disease or condition, perceived benefits of and barriers to the behavior, and cues to action.

health disparities. Preventable differences in the burden of disease, injury, violence, or opportunities to achieve optimal health that are experienced by socially disadvantaged populations.

health literacy. The capacity to obtain and understand basic health information and services needed to make appropriate health decisions.

health maintenance organization (HMO). An organization that provides managed care, in which individuals pay a fixed monthly rate and use services as needed.

health psychology. The application of psychological principles and research to the enhancement of health and the prevention and treatment of illness.

heart rate variability (HRV). The normal and healthy variation in the rate at which the heart beats.

hemophilia. A genetic disease in which the blood fails to clot quickly enough, causing uncontrollable bleeding from even the smallest cut.

hemostasis. The process that causes bleeding to stop via the aggregation of *platelets* and the *coagulation* of blood.

hippocampus. A structure in the brain's limbic system linked to memory.

holistic medicine. An approach to medicine that considers not only physical health but also the emotional, spiritual, social, and psychological well-being of the person.

homeostasis. The tendency to maintain a balanced or constant internal state; the regulation of any aspect of body chemistry, such as the level of glucose in the blood, around a particular set point.

hormones. Chemical messengers, released into the bloodstream by endocrine glands, which have an effect on distant organs.

human immunodeficiency virus (HIV). A virus that infects cells of the immune system, destroying or impairing their function.

humoral theory. A concept of health proposed by Hippocrates that considered wellness a state of perfect equilibrium among four basic body fluids, called *humors*. Sickness was believed to be the result of disturbances in the balance of humors.

hyperalgesia. A condition in which a chronic pain sufferer becomes more sensitive to pain over time.

hypertension. A sustained elevation of diastolic and systolic blood pressure (exceeding 140/90).

hypnosis. A social interaction in which one person (the hypnotist) suggests to another that certain thoughts, feelings, perceptions, or behaviors will occur.

hypothalamic-pituitary-adrenocortical (HPA) axis. The body's delayed response to stress, involving the secretion of corticosteroid hormones from the adrenal cortex.

hypothalamus. Lying just below the thalamus, the region of the brain that influences hunger, thirst, body temperature, and sexual behavior; helps govern the endocrine system via the pituitary gland.

illness anxiety disorder. The condition of experiencing abnormal anxiety over one's health, often including imaginary symptoms.

illness intrusiveness. The extent to which a chronic illness disrupts an individual's life by interfering with valued activities and interests and reducing perceptions of personal control, self-efficacy, and self-esteem.

illness representation. How a person views a particular illness, including its label and symptoms, perceived causes, timeline, consequences, and controllability.

immigrant paradox. The finding that, although low socioeconomic status usually predicts poor health, this is not true for some ethnic groups, such as Hispanics, in the United States.

immune surveillance theory. The theory that cells of the immune system play a monitoring function in searching for and destroying abnormal cells such as those that form tumors.

immunocompetence. The overall ability of the immune system, at any given time, to defend the body against the harmful effects of foreign agents.

immunotherapy. Chemotherapy in which medications are used to support or enhance the immune system's ability to selectively target cancer cells.

incidence. The number of new cases of a disease or condition that occur in a specific population within a defined time interval.

informational control. Patients' knowledge regarding the particular procedures and physical sensations that accompany a medical treatment.

informed consent. Permission granted by a client, patient, or research participant with full knowledge of the potential risks involved in a treatment, procedure, or research study.

injury control. Systematic efforts to prevent injuries from occurring and to limit the consequences of those that have already occurred.

insomnia. A persistent problem in falling or staying asleep.

integrated primary care. Care that combines medical and behavioral health services by bringing together all available treatments into an individualized intervention plan for a patient.

integrative medicine. A multidisciplinary approach to medicine that involves traditional biomedical interventions, as well as complementary and alternative medical practices that have been proven both safe and effective.

intentional injury. Harm that results from behaviors designed to hurt oneself or others.

Kaposi's sarcoma. A rare cancer of blood vessels serving the skin, mucous membranes, and other glands in the body.

Korsakoff's syndrome. An alcohol-induced neurological disorder characterized by the inability to store new memories.

Lamaze training. A natural childbirth process designed to prepare prospective parents by enhancing their informational, cognitive, and behavioral control over childbirth.

lay referral system. An informal network of family members, friends, and other nonprofessionals who offer their own impressions, experiences, and recommendations regarding a set of bodily symptoms.

leptin. The weight-signaling hormone monitored by the hypothalamus as an index of body fat.

leukemia. Cancer of the blood and blood-producing system.

limbic system. A network of neurons surrounding the central core of the brain; associated with emotions such as fear and aggression; includes the hypothalamus, amygdala, and hippocampus.

longitudinal study. A study in which a single group of people is observed over a long span of time.

loss-framed message. A health message that focuses on a negative outcome from failing to perform a health-promoting behavior.

lymphocytes. Antigen-fighting white blood cells produced in the bone marrow.

lymphoma. Cancer of the body's lymph system; includes Hodgkin's disease and non-Hodgkin's lymphoma.

malingering. Making believe that one is ill to benefit from sick role behavior.

managed care. A system of health care in which health insurance plans contract with providers and medical facilities to provide care for members at reduced rates.

massification. The transformation of a product or service that was once only available to the wealthy such that it becomes accessible to everyone. Applied to education and health, it is the idea that college can benefit everyone.

medulla. The brainstem region that controls heartbeat and breathing.

melanoma. A potentially deadly form of cancer that strikes the melatonin-containing cells of the skin.

meta-analysis. A quantitative technique that combines the results of many studies examining the same effect or phenomenon.

metabolic syndrome (MetS). A cluster of conditions that includes increased blood pressure, high blood sugar level, abdominal obesity, low HDL ("good") cholesterol level, and high triglyceride level that occur together and increase a person's risk of heart disease, stroke, and diabetes.

metastasis. The process by which malignant body cells proliferate in number and spread to surrounding body tissues.

microaggressions. Insults, indignities, and marginalizing messages sent by well-intentioned people who seem unaware of the hidden messages that they are sending.

mindfulness-based stress reduction (MBSR). A form of therapy that focuses on using structured meditation to promote mindfulness, a moment-to-moment, nonjudgmental awareness.

mindfulness meditation. The practice of paying nonjudgmental, in-the-moment attention to changing perceptions and thoughts.

minority stress theory. The concept that proposes that health disparities among minority individuals are due to chronically high levels of stress experienced by members of stigmatized groups.

morbidity. As a measure of health, the number of cases of a specific illness, injury, or disability in a given group of people at a given time.

mortality. As a measure of health, the number of deaths due to a specific cause in a given group of people at a given time.

motivational interviewing (MI). A widely used counseling method that focuses on strengthening a person's motivation and commitment to change a target health behavior.

motor cortex. Lying at the rear of the frontal lobes, the region of the cerebral cortex that controls voluntary movements.

multiple chronic conditions (MCC). Two or more chronic conditions (lasting a year or more, requiring medical attention, and/or limiting daily activities) that affect a person at the same time.

myocardial infarction (MI). A heart attack; the permanent death of heart tissue in response to an interruption of blood supply to the myocardium.

naloxone. An opioid antagonist that binds to opioid receptors in the body to block the effects of natural opiates and painkillers.

narcolepsy. A sleep disorder characterized by uncontrollable sleep attacks.

naturopathic medicine. The system that aims to provide holistic health care by drawing from several traditional healing systems, including homeopathy, herbal remedies, and traditional Oriental medicine.

negative affectivity (NA). A coping style or personality dimension consisting of chronic negative emotions and distress; also known as neuroticism.

negative emotionality. A state of alcohol abuse characterized by depression and anxiety.

neurotransmitters. Chemical messengers released by a neuron at synapses that communicate across the synaptic gap and alter the electrical state of a receiving neuron.

nicotine-titration model. The theory that smokers who are physically dependent on nicotine regulate their smoking to maintain a steady level of the drug in their bodies.

nocebo. A harmless substance that nevertheless creates harmful effects in a person who takes it.

nociceptor. A specialized neuron that responds to painful stimuli.

nonadherence. The condition in which a patient refuses to complete a prescribed therapeutic regimen.

noncommunicable disease (NCD). A chronic disease, such as cardiovascular disease, cancer, or diabetes, that is not passed from person to person.

nonsteroidal anti-inflammatory drugs (NSAIDs). Aspirin, ibuprofen, acetaminophen, and other analgesic drugs that relieve pain and reduce inflammation at the site of injured tissue.

nurse-practitioner. An advanced-practice nurse who, in addition to training in traditional nursing, received training in the delivery of primary health care.

obesity. Excessive accumulation of body fat.

observational study. A nonexperimental research method in which a researcher observes and records the behavior of a research participant.

optimistic bias. The belief that other people are more likely than oneself to develop a disease, be injured, or experience other negative events.

organ. A group of tissues working together to perform a specific function.

osteopathic medicine. A form of medical practice that provides all the benefits of conventional allopathic medicine, including prescription drugs and surgery, and emphasizes the interrelationship between the structure and function of the human body.

osteoporosis. A disease of the bones involving a loss of bone mineral density that leads to an increased risk of fracture.

overweight. Body weight that exceeds the desirable weight for a person of a given height, age, and body shape.

pain behaviors. Actions that are a response to pain, such as taking drugs, grimacing, or taking time off from school or work.

pain-management program. An individualized, multimodal intervention aimed at modifying chronic pain through neurological, cognitive, and behavioral strategies.

pandemic. A worldwide epidemic such as AIDS.

pathogen. A virus, bacterium, or some other microorganism that causes a particular disease.

patient-centered health care. The delivery of health care services that are respectful of and responsive to individual patient preferences, needs, and values.

Patient Protection and Affordable Care Act (PPACA). A federal law aimed at reducing the number of people in the United States who do not have health insurance, as well as lowering the costs of health care.

periaqueductal gray (PAG). A region of the midbrain that plays an important role in the perception of pain; electrical stimulation in this region activates a descending neural pathway that produces analgesia by "closing the pain gate."

personal control. The belief that we make our own decisions and determine what we do and what others do to us.

phantom limb pain. Pain following amputation of a limb; false pain sensations that appear to originate in the missing limb.

phenotype. A person's observable characteristics; determined by the interaction of the individual's genotype with the environment.

physical fitness. A set of attributes relating to the ability to perform physical activity that includes muscular strength, endurance, flexibility, and healthy body composition.

physician assistant (PA). A graduate of a two-year, postcollege training program that teaches how to practice medicine under the direction of physicians and surgeons.

pituitary gland. The master endocrine gland controlled by the hypothalamus; releases a variety of hormones that act on other glands throughout the body.

positive health. The scientific study of health assets, which are factors that produce longer life, reduce illness, and increase overall well-being.

positive psychology. The study of optimal human functioning and the healthy interplay between people and their environments.

post-traumatic growth (PTG). Positive psychological change experienced as the result of struggle with a highly challenging life circumstance. Also referred to as *benefit finding*, or *thriving*.

post-traumatic stress disorder (PTSD). A psychological disorder triggered by exposure to an extreme traumatic stressor, such as combat or a natural disaster. Symptoms of PTSD include haunting memories and nightmares of the traumatic event, extreme mental distress, and unwanted flashbacks.

poverty income ratio (PIR). The ratio of household income to the poverty threshold after accounting for inflation and family size.

preferred-provider organization (PPO). A managed-care network of physicians, hospitals, and other health care providers that agree to charge preestablished rates for specific services.

prevalence. The total number of diagnosed cases of a disease or condition that exist at a given time.

primary appraisal. A person's initial determination of an event's meaning, whether irrelevant, benign-positive, or threatening.

primary prevention. Health-enhancing efforts to prevent disease or injury from occurring.

probiotics. Bacteria that help maintain the natural balance of organisms (microflora) in the intestines and help promote a healthy digestive system.

problem-focused coping. A coping strategy for dealing directly with a stressor, in which we either reduce the stressor's demands or increase our resources for meeting its demands.

progressive muscle relaxation. A form of relaxation training that reduces muscle tension through a series of tensing and relaxing exercises involving the body's major muscle groups.

prospective study. A forward-looking longitudinal study that begins with a healthy group of subjects and follows the development of a particular disease in that sample.

prostaglandin. The chemical substance responsible for localized pain and inflammation; prostaglandin also causes free nerve endings to become more and more sensitized as time passes.

psychoactive drugs. Drugs that affect mood, behavior, and thought processes by altering the functioning of neurons in the brain; they include stimulants, depressants, and hallucinogens.

psychological control. The perception that one can determine one's own behavior and influence the environment to bring about desired outcomes.

psychoneuroimmunology (PNI). The field of research that emphasizes the interaction of psychological, neural, and immunological processes in stress and illness.

psychosomatic medicine. A branch of psychiatry that developed in the 1900s and focused on the diagnosis and treatment of certain diseases believed to be caused by emotional conflicts.

qualitative research. Research that focuses on qualities instead of quantities. Participants' expressed ideas are often part of qualitative studies.

quality-adjusted life year (QALY). One year of good health, free from disease and disability.

quasi-experiment. A study comparing two groups that differ naturally on a specific variable of interest.

randomized clinical trial (RCT). A true experiment that tests the effects of one independent variable (such as a particular drug or treatment) on individuals or on groups of individuals (community field trials).

rapid eye movement (REM). Rapid eye movement sleep; a sleep stage during which vivid dreams occur.

reactivity. Our physiological reaction to stress, which varies by individual and affects our vulnerability to illness.

reactivity hypothesis. The hypothesis that individuals who show large changes in blood pressure and vascular resistance to stress have increased risk of developing heart disease.

recurrent pain. Involves episodes of discomfort interspersed with periods in which the individual is relatively pain-free that recur for more than three months.

referred pain. Pain manifested in an area of the body that is sensitive to pain but caused by disease or injury in an area of the body that has few pain receptors.

regulatory control. The various ways in which we modulate our thinking, emotions, and behavior over time and across changing circumstances.

relapse prevention. Training in coping skills and other techniques intended to help people resist falling back into old health habits following a successful behavioral intervention.

relative risk. A statistical indicator of the likelihood of a causal relationship between a particular health risk factor and a health outcome; computed as the ratio of the incidence (or prevalence) of a health condition in a group exposed to the risk factor to its incidence (or prevalence) in a group not exposed to the risk factor.

relaxation response. A meditative state of relaxation in which metabolism slows and blood pressure lowers.

repressive coping. An emotion-focused coping style in which we attempt to inhibit our emotional responses, especially in social situations, so we can view ourselves as imperturbable.

repressors. People who cope with health problems and other aversive events by ignoring or distancing themselves from stressful information.

resilience. The quality that allows some people to bounce back from difficult events that might otherwise disrupt their well-being.

reticular formation. A network of neurons running through the brainstem involved with alertness and arousal.

retrospective study. A longitudinal study that looks back at the history of a group of people, often one suffering from a particular disease or condition.

retrovirus. A virus that copies its genetic information onto the DNA of a host cell.

rumination. Repetitive focusing on the causes, meanings, and consequences of stressful experiences.

sarcoma. Cancer that strikes muscles, bones, and cartilage.

satiation. A form of aversion therapy in which a smoker is forced to increase his or her smoking until an unpleasant state of "fullness" is reached.

scatterplot. A graphed cluster of data points, each of which represents the values of two variables in a descriptive study.

secondary appraisal. A person's determination of whether his or her own resources and abilities are sufficient to meet the demands of an event that is appraised as potentially threatening or challenging.

secondary prevention. Actions taken to identify and treat an illness or disability early in its course.

self-monitoring. People keeping track of their own target behavior that is to be modified, including the stimuli associated with it and the consequences that follow it.

sensitizers. People who cope with health problems and other aversive events by closely scanning their bodies and environments for information.

sensory cortex. Lying at the front of the parietal lobes, the region of the cerebral cortex that processes body sensations such as touch.

sensory focus. Attending directly to the sensations of a painful stimulus without necessarily trying to change those reactions.

set-point hypothesis. The idea that each person's body weight is genetically set within a given range, or set point, that the body works hard to maintain.

sexually transmitted infections (STIs). Infections that are spread primarily through person-to-person sexual contact.

shaman. A general term used for the practitioner of folk medicine who often uses herbs and a range of rituals to effect cures; also referred to as "medicine man" or "medicine woman."

sleep apnea. A sleep disorder characterized by temporary cessations of breathing.

slow nerve fibers. Small, unmyelinated nerve fibers that carry dull, aching pain.

social-evaluative threat. A stressor in which people fear negative evaluation by others of their appearance or ability.

social integration. The number of social roles a person participates in.

social support. Companionship from others that conveys emotional concern, material assistance, or honest feedback about a situation.

statistical literacy. The ability to read and interpret statistics and to think critically about arguments that use statistics as evidence.

stem cells. Early, undifferentiated biological cells with the potential to develop into any other type of specialized cell.

stereotype threat. The experience of stress in a situation where a person's ability, appearance, or other characteristic has the potential to confirm a negative viewpoint about his or her social group.

stimulus-control intervention. A behavioral intervention aimed at modifying the environmental discriminative stimuli that control a target behavior by signaling its reinforcement.

stress. The process by which we perceive and respond to events, called *stressors*, that we appraise as threatening or challenging.

stress-induced analgesia (SIA). A stress-related increase in tolerance to pain, presumably mediated by the body's endorphin system.

stress inoculation training. A cognitive behavioral treatment in which people identify stressors in their lives and learn skills for coping with them so that when those stressors occur, they are able to put those skills into effect.

stress management. The various psychological methods designed to reduce the impact of potentially stressful experiences.

stressor. Any event or situation that triggers coping adjustments.

stroke. A cerebrovascular accident that results in damage to the brain due to lack of oxygen; usually caused by atherosclerosis or arteriosclerosis.

subjective norm. An individual's interpretation of the views of other people regarding a particular health-related behavior.

subjective well-being. The cognitive and emotional evaluations of a person's life.

substance P. A neurotransmitter secreted by pain fibers in the spinal cord that stimulates the transmission cells to send pain signals to the brain.

substance use disorder. A pattern of behavior characterized by impaired control, social impairment, and risky use of a drug.

substantia gelatinosa. The dorsal region of the spinal cord where both fast and slow pain fibers synapse with sensory nerves on their way to the brain.

sympatho-adreno-medullary (SAM) axis. The body's initial, rapid-acting response to stress, involving the release of epinephrine and norepinephrine from the adrenal medulla under the direction of the sympathetic nervous system.

systematic desensitization. A form of behavior therapy, commonly used for overcoming phobias, in which the person is exposed to a series of increasingly fearful situations while remaining deeply relaxed.

tai chi. A form of "moving meditation" that blends exercise, dance, and concentration, and is a component of traditional Oriental medicine.

telemedicine. The delivery of medical information and clinical services through interactive audiovisual media.

teratogens. Drugs, chemicals, and environmental agents that can damage the developing person during fetal development.

tertiary prevention. Actions taken to contain damage once a disease or disability has progressed beyond its early stages.

thalamus. The brain's sensory switchboard; located on top of the brainstem, it routes messages to the cerebral cortex.

theory of planned behavior (TPB). A theory that predicts health behavior on the basis of three factors: personal attitude toward the behavior, the subjective norm regarding the behavior, and perceived degree of control over the behavior.

thriving. A paradoxical outcome in which adversity somehow leads people to greater psychological and/or physical well-being.

tissue. A group of similar cells organized into a functional unit.

traditional Chinese medicine. An ancient, integrated herb- and acupuncture-based system of healing founded on the principle that internal harmony is essential for good health.

transactional model. Lazarus's theory that the experience of stress depends as much on the individual's cognitive appraisal of a potential stressor's impact as it does on the event or situation itself.

transcutaneous electrical nerve stimulation (TENS). A counterirritation form of analgesia involving electrically stimulating spinal nerves near a painful area.

transtheoretical model (TTM). A stage theory that contends that people pass through five stages in altering health-related behavior: precontemplation, contemplation, preparation, action, and maintenance.

Type A. Friedman and Rosenman's term for competitive, hurried, hostile people who may be at increased risk for developing cardiovascular disease.

Type B. Friedman and Rosenman's term for more relaxed people who are not pressured by time considerations and thus tend to be coronary disease-resistant.

unintentional injury. Harm that is accidental, not meant to occur.

veins. Blood vessels that carry blood back to the heart from the capillaries.

vitalism. The concept of a general life force, popular in some varieties of complementary and alternative medicine.

wanting-and-liking theory. A two-stage theory of drug addiction. In the first stage, the original good feelings from drug use prevail; in the second stage, drug use becomes an automated behavior.

weight cycling. Repeated weight gains and losses through repeated dieting.

withdrawal. The unpleasant physical and psychological symptoms that occur when a person abruptly ceases using certain drugs.

yoga. A movement-based form of relaxation and meditation that combines diet, physical postures, and breathing to promote physical and spiritual well-being

References

Abbey, A., Parkhill, M. R., Buck, P. O., & Saenz, C. (2007). Condom use with a sexual partner: What distinguishes college students' use when intoxicated? *Psychology of Addictive Behaviors, 21*(1), 76–83.

Abele, A. E., & Vollmer, J. (2011). Dual-career couples: Specific challenges for work-life integration. In S. Kaiser, M. J. Ringlstetter, D. R. Eikhof, & M. Pina e Cunha (Eds.), *Creating balance: International perspectives on the work-life integration of professionals* (pp. 173–192). Berlin: Springer-Verlag.

Abi-Saleh, B., Iskandar, S. B., Elgharib, N., & Cohen, M. V. (2008). C-reactive protein: The harbinger of cardiovascular diseases. *Southern Medical Journal, 101*, 525–533.

Ablashi, D. V., Eastman, H. B., Owen, C. B., Roman, M. M., Friedman, J., Zabriskie, J. B., Peterson, D. L., Pearson, G. R., & Whitman, J. E. (2000). Frequent HHV-6 reactivation in multiple sclerosis (MS) and chronic fatigue syndrome (CFS) patients. *Journal of Clinical Virology, 16*, 179–191.

Abraido-Lanza, A. F. (2004). Social support and psychological adjustment among Latinas with arthritis: A test of a theoretical model. *Annals of Behavioral Medicine, 27*(3), 162–171.

Acevedo, M., Kramer, V., Bustamante, M. J., Yanez, F., Guidi, D., Corbalan, R., ... Fernandez, M, (2013). Exercise and cardiac rehabilitation in secondary cardiovascular prevention. *Revista Medica de Chile, 141*(10), 1307–1314.

ACGME. (2010). *Accreditation council for graduate medical education.* Retrieved from http://www.acgme.org/acgmeweb

Ackerman, B. P., Kogos, J., Youngstrom, E., Schoff, K., & Izard, C. (1999). Family instability and the problem behaviors of children from economically disadvantaged families. *Developmental Psychology, 35*, 258–268.

Adams, J. (2012). Consideration of immediate and future consequences, smoking status, and body mass index. *Health Psychology, 31*(2), 260–263.

Adams, K. F., Schatzkin, A., Harris, T. B., Kipnis, V., Mouw, T., & Ballard-Barbash, R. (2006). Overweight, obesity, and mortality in a large prospective cohort of persons 50 to 71 years old. *The New England Journal of Medicine, 355*, 763–778.

Adams, M. A., Norman, G. J., Hovell, M. F., Sallis, J. F., & Patrick, K. (2009). Reconceptualizing decisional balance in an adolescent sun protection intervention: Mediating effects and theoretical interpretations. *Health Psychology, 28*(2), 217–225.

Adams, P., & Mylander, M. (1998). *Gesundheit! Bringing good health to you, the medical system, and society through physician service, contemporary therapies, humor, and joy.* Rochester, NY: Inner Traditions International.

Adams, P. F., Kirzinger, W. K., & Martinez, M. E. (2012). Summary health statistics for the U.S. population: National Health Interview Survey, 2011. Hyattsville, MD: National Center for Health Statistics. *Vital Health Statistics, 10*(255). Retrieved from http://www.cdc.gov/nchs/data/series/sr_10/sr10_255.pdf

Ader, R., & Cohen, N. (1985). CNS-immune system interactions: Conditioning phenomena. *Behavioral and Brain Sciences, 8,* 379–394.

Adler, N. E., & Rehkopf, D. H. (2008). U.S. Disparities in health: Descriptions, causes, and mechanisms. *Annual Review of Public Health, 29*, 235–252.

Advokat, R. M., Comaty, J. E., & Julien, R. M. (2014). *Julien's primer of drug action.* New York: Worth Publishers.

Agency for Healthcare Research and Quality (AHRQ). (2012). *National healthcare disparities report.* U.S. Department of Health and Human Services. Publication No. 12-0006. Rockville, MD. Retrieved from http://www.ahrq.gov/qual/qrdr11.htm

Agras, W. S., Brandt, H. A., Bulik, C. M., Dolan-Sewell, R., Fairburn, C. G., & Halmi, K. A. (2004). Report of the National Institutes of Health workshop on overcoming barriers to treatment research in anorexia nervosa. *International Journal of Eating Disorders, 35*, 506–521.

Aguilar, M., Bhuket, T., Torres, S., Liu, B., & Wong, R. J. (2015). Prevalence of the metabolic syndrome in the United States, 2003–2012. *Journal of the American Medical Association, 313*(19), 1973–1974.

Ahlers, M. M. (2012). Do you live near a nuclear power plant? Study will assess cancer risks. *CNN Health.* Retrieved from http://www.cnn.com/2012/10/23/health/study-nuclear-plants

al'Absi, M., Hatsukama, D., Davis, G. L., & Wittmers, L. E. (2004). Prospective examination of effects of smoking abstinence on cortisol and withdrawal symptoms as predictors of early smoking relapse. *Drug and Alcohol Dependence, 73*(3), 267–278.

Alashwal, H., Dosunmu, R., & Zawia, N. H. (2012). Integration of genome-wide expression and methylation data: Relevance to aging and Alzheimer's disease. *Neurotoxicology, 33*(6), 1450–1453.

Alba, R. D., Logan, J. R., & Stults, B. J. (2000). How segregated are middle-class African Americans? *Social Problems, 47*(4), 543–558.

Albarracin, J., Albarracin, D., & Durantini, M. (2008). Effects of HIV-prevention interventions for samples with higher and lower percents of Latinos and Latin Americans: A meta-analysis of change in condom use and knowledge. *AIDS and Behavior, 12*(4), 521–543.

Albery, I. P., & Messer, D. (2005). Comparative optimism about health and nonhealth events in 8- and 9-year-old children. *Health Psychology, 24*, 316–320.

Alexander, E. (1950). *Psychosomatic medicine.* New York: Norton.

Alfieri, D. W., Costanzo, S., & Borgogni, T. (2011). Biological resilience of older adults against frailty. *Medical Hypotheses, 76*(2), 304–305.

Allen, J. G., Flanigan, S. S., LeBlanc, M., Vallarino, J., MacNaughton, P., Stewart, J. H., & Christiani, D. C. (2015). Flavoring chemicals in e-cigarettes: Diacetyl, 2,3-pentanedione, and acetoin in a sample of 51 products, including fruit-, candy-, and cocktail-flavored e-cigarettes. *Environmental Health Perspectives.* Retrieved from http://ehp.niehs.nih.gov/wp-content/uploads/advpub/2015/12/ehp.1510185.acco.pdf

Allen, K. J. D., & Gabbay, F. H. (2013). The amphetamine response moderates the relationship between negative emotionality and alcohol use. *Alcoholism: Clinical and Experimental Research, 37*(2), 348–360.

Allen, N. E. (2009). Moderate alcohol intake and cancer incidence in women. *Journal of the National Cancer Institute, 101*(5), 296–305.

Altarum Institute. (2014, September 18). Clarifying feasible procedures for reinvesting health care cost savings. Retrieved February 25, 2016, from http://altarum.org/publications/

clarifying-feasible-procedures-for-reinvesting-health-care-cost-savings

Altbach, P. G. (2010). The realities of mass higher education in a globalized world. In D. B. Johnstone, M. B. d'Ambrosio, & P. J. Yakoboski (Eds.), *Higher education in a global society* (pp. 25–41). Cheltenham, UK: Edward Elgar.

Altman, B., & Bernstein, A. (2008) *Disability and health in the United States, 2001–2005*. Hyattsville, MD: National Center for Health Statistics.

American Academy of Pain Medicine (AAPM). (2013). AAPM facts and figures. Retrieved from http://www.painmed.org/patientcenter/facts_on_pain.aspx#refer

American Academy of Pediatrics (AAP). (2015). AAP recommends whole diet approach to children's nutrition. Retrieved March 2, 2016, from https://www.aap.org/en-us/about-the-aap/aap-press-room/Pages/AAP-Recommends-Whole-Diet-Approach-to-Children's-Nutrition.aspx

American Academy of Sleep Medicine (AASM). (2010). Sleep deprivation. Retrieved March 1, 2010, from http://www.aasmnet.org/Search.aspx?SearchTerm=sleep%20deprivation

American Association of Naturopathic Physicians (AANP). (2006). Naturopathic medicine: How it works. Retrieved from http://naturopathic.lv0.net/DesktopDefault.aspx

American Cancer Society. (2009). Diet and physical activity: What's the cancer connection? Retrieved March 4, 2010, from http://www.cancer.org/cancer/cancercauses/dietandphysicalactivity/diet-and-physical-activity

American Cancer Society. (2012). Cancer treatment and survivorship: Facts and figures 2012–2013. Retrieved May 23, 2016, from http://www.cancer.org/acs/groups/content/@epidemiologysurveilance/documents/document/acspc-033876.pdf

American Cancer Society (ACS). (2015a). *Cancer facts and figures 2015*. Atlanta, GA: Author. Retrieved February 27, 2016, from http://www.cancer.org/acs/groups/content/@editorial/documents/document/acspc-044552.pdf

American Cancer Society (ACS). (2015b). Family cancer syndromes. Retrieved from http://www.cancer.org/cancer/cancercauses/geneticsandcancer/heredity-and-cancer

American Cancer Society (ACS). (2015c). Skin cancer. Retrieved from http://www.cancer.org/cancer/skincancer/index

American College Health Association (ACHA). (2015). *National College Health Assessment II: Undergraduate Student Reference Group Executive Summary*. Hanover, MD: Author.American Diabetes Association (ADA). (2010a). Living with diabetes: Depression. Retrieved April 5, 2010, from http://www.diabetes.org/living-with-diabetes/women/depression.html

American Diabetes Association (ADA). (2010b). Standards of medical care in diabetes—2010. *Diabetes Care, 33* (Supplement 1), S11–S61.

American Family Physician (AFP). (2004). What people want from their family physician. *American Family Physician, 69*(10). Retrieved from http://www.aafp.org/afp/2004/0515/p2310.html

American Heart Association (AHA). (2015). Heart disease and stroke statistics—2015 update. Dallas, TX: Author. Retrieved from https://www.heart.org/idc/groups/ahamah-public/@wcm/@sop/@smd/documents/downloadable/ucm_470707.pdf

American Hospital Association (AHA). (2011, September 7). More hospitals offering complementary and alternative medicine services. Retrieved March 2, 2016, from http://www.aha.org/presscenter/pressrel/2011/110907-pr-camsurvey.pdf

American Hospital Association (AHA). (2013). Fast facts on U.S. hospitals. Retrieved from http://www.aha.org/research/rc/stat-studies/fast-facts.shtml

American Institute for Cancer Research (AICR). (2010). Diet: What we eat. Retrieved from http://www.aicr.org/reduce-your-cancer-risk/diet/

American Medical Association (AMA). (1973). *Proceedings of the House of Delegates*. New York: Author.

American Medical Association (AMA). (1995). *Proceedings of the House of Delegates*. Chicago: Author.

American Medical Association (AMA). (2008, March 10). More schools teaching spirituality in medicine. Retrieved from Amednews.com/article/20080310/profession/303109968/7/

American Pain Society. (2016). *Interdisciplinary pain management*. Retrieved March 1, 2016, from http://americanpainsociety.org/uploads/about/position-statements/interdisciplinary-white-paper.pdf

American Psychiatric Association. (1994). *Doing the right thing: The human capital initiative strategy*. Washington, DC: American Psychological Association.

American Psychiatric Association. (2000). *Diagnostic and statistical manual of mental disorders—DSM-IV-TR* (Text revision). Washington, DC: American Psychiatric Association.

American Psychiatric Association. (2010). American Psychological Association section on positive psychology, Division 17. Retrieved September 24, 2010, from http://www.div17pospsych.com

American Psychiatric Association. (2013). *Diagnostic and statistical manual of mental disorders—DSM-V (5th ed.)*. Arlington, VA: American Psychiatric Association.

American Psychological Association (APA). (2009). 2009 doctoral psychology workforce fast facts. Washington, DC: Author. Retrieved December 14, 2010, from http://www.apa.org/workforce/snapshots/2009/fast-facts.pdf

American Psychological Association (APA). (2010, November 9). Stress in America findings. Washington, DC: American Psychological Association.

American Psychological Association (APA). (2013). Psychology is a behavioral and mental health profession. Washington, DC: American Psychological Association. Retrieved from http://www.apa.org/about/gr/issues/health-care/profession.aspx

American Psychological Association, Science Directorate. (1995). *Doing the right thing: A research plan for healthy living—A Human Capital Initiative strategy report*. Washington, DC: American Psychological Association Human Capital Initiative Coordinating Committeee.

Amick, B. C., McDonough, P., Chang, H., Rodgers, W. H., Pieper, C. F., & Duncan, G. (2002). Relationship between all-cause mortality and cumulative working life course psychosocial and physical exposure in the United States labor market from 1968 to 1992. *Psychosomatic Medicine, 64*, 370–381.

Amigo, I., Buceta, J. M., Becona, E., & Bueno, A. M. (1991). Cognitive behavioral treatment for essential hypertension: A controlled study. *Stress Medicine, 7*, 103–108.

Anders, R. L., Olson, T., Wiebe, J., Bean, N. H., DiGregorio, R., Guillermina, M., & Ortiz, M. (2008). Diabetes prevalence and treatment adherence in residents living in a colonia located on the West Texas, USA/Mexico border. *Nursing and Health Sciences, 10*, 195–202.

Anderson, B., Rafferty, A. P., Lyon-Callo, S., Fussman, C., & Imes, G. (2011). Fast-food consumption and obesity among Michigan adults. *Preventing Chronic Disease, 8*(4), A71.

Anderson, B. L., Cacioppo, J. T., & Roberts, D. C. (1995). Delay in seeking a cancer diagnosis: Delay stages and psychophysiological comparison processes. *British Journal of Social Psychology, 34*, 33–52.

Anderson, D. R., & Emery, C. F. (2014). Irrational health beliefs predict adherence to cardiac rehabilitation. *Health Psychology, 33,* 1614–1617.

Anderson, N. B. (2003). Psychology as a health profession. Washington, DC: American Psychological Association. Retrieved from http://www.apa.org/monitor/mar03/rc.aspx

Anderson, P. (2013). Where is pain in the brain? *Medscape Medical News,* April 18. Retrieved from http://www.medscape.com/viewarticle/782732

Anderson, S. (2008, July 8). The urge to end it. *The New York Times.* Retrieved from http://www.nytimes.com

Andrasik, F., Grazzi, L., Usai, S., D'Amico, D., Kass, S., & Bussone, G. (2007). Disability in chronic migraine with medication overuse: Treatment effects at 3 years. *Headache, 47*(9), 1277–1281.

Angel, R., Angel, J., & Hill, T. (2008). A comparison of the health of older Hispanics in the United States and Mexico. *Journal of Aging and Health, 20,* 1, 3–31.

Angst, M. S., & Clark, D. J. (2006). Opioid-induced hyperalgesia: A qualitative systematic review. *Anesthesiology, 104,* 570–587.

Annemans, L., Lamotte, M., Clarys, P., & Van den Abeele, E. (2007). Health economic evaluation of controlled and maintained physical exercise in the prevention of cardiovascular and other prosperity diseases. *European Journal of Cardiovascular Prevention and Rehabilitation, 14*(6), 815–824.

Annual Editions. (2010/2011). *Drugs, society, and behavior.* Boston: McGraw-Hill Higher Education.

Ansary, N. S., & Luthar, S. S. (2009). Distress and academic achievement among adolescents of affluence: A study of externalizing and internalizing problem behaviors and school performance. *Development and Psychopathology, 21*(1), 319–341.

Anstey, K. J., von Sanden, C., Salim, A., & O'Kearney, R. (2007). Smoking as a risk factor for dementia and cognitive decline: A meta-analysis of prospective studies. *American Journal of Epidemiology, 166,* 367–378.

Antoni, M. H., Cruess, D. G., Cruess, S., Lutgendorf, S., Kumar, M., Ironson, G., … Schneiderman, N. (2000). Cognitive-behavioral stress management intervention effects on anxiety, 24-hour urinary norepinephrine output, and T-cytotoxic/suppressor cells over time among symptomatic HIV-infected gay men. *Journal of Consulting & Clinical Psychology, 68,* 31–45.

Antoni, M. H., Ironson, G., & Scheiderman, N. (2007). *Cognitive-behavioral stress management workbook.* New York: Oxford University Press.

Antoni, M. H., Lechner, S., Diaz, A., Vargas, S., Holley, H., Phillips, K., McGregor, B. A., Carver, C. S., & Blomberg, B. (2009). Cognitive behavioral stress management effects on psychosocial and physiological adaptation in women undergoing treatment for breast cancer. *Brain, Behavior and Immunity, 23,* 580–591.

Antoni, M. H., Lehman, J. M., Kilbourn, K. M., Boyers, A. E., Culver, J. L., Alferi, S. M., … Carver, C. S. (2001). Cognitive-behavioral stress management intervention decreases the prevalence of depression and enhances benefit finding among women under treatment for early-stage breast cancer. *Health Psychology, 20*(1), 20–32.

Antoni, M. H., Pereira, D. B., Marion, I., Ennis, N., Andrasik, P., Rose, R., & O'Sullivan, M. J. (2008). Stress management effects on perceived stress and cervical neoplasia in low-income HIV-infected women. *Journal of Psychosomatic Research, 65,* 389–401.

Antoni, M. H., & Schneiderman, N. (2001). HIV and AIDS. In D. W. Johnston & M. Johnston (Eds.), *Health psychology: Comprehensive clinical psychology* (Vol. 8, pp. 237–275). Amsterdam: Elsevier.

Appleton, A. A., Buka, S. L., McCormick, M. C., Koenen, K. C., Loucks, E. B., & Kubzansky, L. D. (2012). The association between childhood emotional functioning and adulthood inflammation is modified by early-life socioeconomic status. *Health Psychology, 31*(4), 413–422.

Aratani, L. (2009, June 9). Mainstream physicians give alternatives a try. *The Washington Post.* Retrieved April 29, 2010, from http://www.washingtonpost.com/wp-dyn/content/article/2009/06/08/AR2009060802368.html

Armitage, C. J., & Arden, M. A. (2008). How useful are the stages of change for targeting interventions? Randomized test of a brief intervention to reduce smoking. *Health Psychology, 27*(6), 789–798.

Armitage, C. J., Sheeran, P., Conner, M., & Arden, M. A. (2004). Stages of change or changes of stage? Predicting transitions in transtheoretical model stages in relation to healthy food choice. *Journal of Consulting and Clinical Psychology, 72,* 491–499.

Arndt, V., Sturmer, T., Stegmaier, C., Ziegler, H., Dhom, G., & Brenner, H. (2002). Patient delay and stage of diagnosis among breast cancer patients in Germany: A population-based study. *British Journal of Cancer, 86,* 1034–1040.

Arnett, J. J., & Schwab, J. (2012). *The Clark University poll of emerging adults, 2012: Thriving, struggling, & hopeful.* Retrieved from clarku.edu/clarkpoll

Arnetz, B. B., Brenner, S. O., Levi, L., Hjelm, R., Petterson, I. L., Wasserman, J., Petrini, B., Eneroth, P., Kallner, A., & Kvetnansky, R. (1991). Neuroendocrine and immunologic effects of unemployment and job insecurity. *Psychotherapy and Psychosomatics, 55*(2–4), 76–80.

Arnst, C. (2009). 10 ways to cut health-care costs right now. *Bloomberg Business Week.* Retrieved April 8, 2016, from http://www.bloomberg.com/news/articles/2009-11-12/10-ways-to-cut-health-care-costs-right-now

Aron, A., Norman, C. C., Aron, E. N., McKenna, C., & Heyman, R. E. (2000). Couples' shared participation in novel and arousing activities and experienced relationship quality. *Journal of Personality and Social Psychology, 78,* 273–284.

Aronoff, J., Stollak, G. E., & Woike, B. A. (1994). Affect regulation and the breadth of interpersonal engagement. *Journal of Personality and Social Psychology, 67,* 105–114.

Arpawong, T. E., Richeimer, S. H., Weinstein, F., Elghamrawy, A., & Milam, J. E. (2013). Posttraumatic growth, quality of life, and treatment symptoms among cancer chemotherapy outpatients. *Health Psychology, 32*(4), 397–408.

Arrington, M. I. (2008). Prostate cancer and the social construction of masculine sexual identity. *International Journal of Men's Health, 7,* 299–306.

Arthur, C. M., Katkin, E. S., & Mezzacappa, E. S. (2004). Cardiovascular reactivity to mental arithmetic and cold pressor in African Americans, Caribbean Americans, and white Americans. *Annals of Behavioral Medicine, 27*(1), 31–37.

Asbridge, M., Hayden, J. A., & Cartwright, J. L. (2012). Acute cannabis consumption and motor vehicle collision risk: Systematic review of observational studies and meta-analysis. *British Medical Journal, 344.* Retrieved from http://www.bmj.com/content/344/bmj.e536

ASCO. (2015). Clinical cancer advances, 2015. *Journal of Clinical Oncology.* Retrieved February 27, 2016, from http://cancerprogress.net/sites/cancerprogress.net/files/cca2015_fnl_web_012515.pdf

Askay, S. W., Patterson, D. R., Jensen, M. P., & Sharar, S. R. (2007). A randomized controlled trial of hypnosis for burn wound care. *Rehabilitation Psychology, 52*, 247–253.

Aslund, C., Nordquist, N., Comasco, E., Leppert, J., Oreland, L., & Nilsson, K. W. (2011). Maltreatment, MAOA, and delinquency: Sex differences in gene-environment interaction in a large population-based cohort of adolescents. *Behavior Genetics, 41*, 262–272.

Associated Press (AP). (2009). AP-mtvU poll: Financial worries, stress, and depression on college campuses. Retrieved from http://www.hosted.ap.org

Association of Psychologists in Academic Health Centers (APAHC). (2016). APAHC task force on behavioral and social science foundations for physicians. Retrieved April 7, 2016, from http://www.div12.org/section8/index.html

Astin, J. A. (2004). Mind-body therapies for the management of pain. *Clinical Journal of Pain, 20*, 27–32.

Auerbach, S. M., Penberthy, A. R., & Kiesler, D. J. (2004). Opportunity for control, interpersonal impacts, and adjustment to a long-term invasive health care procedure. *Journal of Behavioral Medicine, 27*, 11–29.

Aughinbaugh, A., Robles, O., & Sun, H. (2013, October) Marriage and divorce: Patterns by gender, race, and educational attainment. *Monthly Labor Review*. Washington, DC: Bureau of Labor Statistics. Retrieved March 31, 2016, from http://www.bls.gov/opub/mlr/2013/article/marriage-and-divorce-patterns-by-gender-race-and-educational-attainment.htm#

Austin, A. W., Wissman, T., & Von Känel, R. (2013). Stress and hemostasis: An update. *Seminars in Thrombosis and Hemostasis, 39*(9), 902–912.

Avadhani, A., & Steefel, L. (2015). Probiotics: A review for NPs. *Nurse Practitioner, 40*(8), 50–54.

AVERT. (2013). The origin of HIV and AIDS. Retrieved from http://www.avert.org/origin-aids-hiv.htm

Aveyard, P., Johnson, C., Fillingham, S., Parsons, A., & Murphy, M. (2008). Nortriptyline plus nicotine replacement versus placebo plus nicotine replacement for smoking cessation: pragmatic randomised controlled trial. *British Medical Journal, 336*(7655), 1223–1227.

Azar, B. (1999). Antismoking ads that curb teen smoking. *American Psychological Association Monitor, 30*, 14.

Bachhuber, M. A., Saloner, B., Cunningham, C. O., & Barry, C. L. (2014). Medical cannabis laws and opioid analgesic overdose mortality in the United States, 1999–2010. *Journal of the American Medical Association Internal Medicine, 174*(10), 1668–1673.

Bacon, S. L., Bouchard, A., Loucks, E. B., & Lavoie, K. L. (2009). Individual-level socioeconomic status is associated with worse asthma morbidity in patients with asthma. *Respiratory Research*. Retrieved March 4, 2016, from http://respiratory-research.biomedcentral.com/articles/10.1186/1465-9921-10-125

Bagot, R. C., Zhang, T. Y., Wen, X., Nguyen, T. T., Nguyen, H. B., Diorio, J., Meaney, M. J. (2012). Variations in postnatal maternal care and the epigenetic regulation of metabotropic glutamate receptor 1 expression and hippocampal function in the rat. *Proceedings of the National Academy of Sciences of the United States of America, 109*(Supplement 2), 17200–17207.

Baicorissoff, J. I., Spronk, H. M. H., & ten Cate, H. (2011). The hemostatic system as a modulator of atherosclerosis. *The New England Journal of Medicine, 364*(18), 1746–1760.

Bailey, R. L., Gahche, J. J, Lentino, C. V., Dwyer, J. T., Engel, J. S., Thomas, P. R., … Picciano, M. F. (2011). Dietary supplement use in the United States: 2003–2006. *Journal of Nutrition, 141*, 261–266.

Baker, A., Richmond, R., Haile, M., Lewin, T. J., Carr, V. J., Taylor, R. L., Jansons, S., & Wilhelm, K. (2006). A randomized controlled trial of a smoking cessation intervention among people with a psychotic disorder. *American Journal of Psychiatry, 63*, 1934–1942.

Baker, R., & Kirschenbaum, D. S. (1998). Weight control during the holidays: Highly consistent self-monitoring as a potentially useful coping mechanism. *Health Psychology, 17*, 367–370.

Baker, S. P., Chen, L., & Li, G. (2007). *Nationwide review of graduated driver licensing*. Washington, DC: AAA Foundation for Traffic Safety. Retrieved from http://www.aaafoundation.org/pdf/NationwideReviewOfGDL.pdf

Ball, D. (2008). Addiction science and its genetics. *Addiction, 103*, 360–367.

Banasiak, S. J., Paxton, S. J., & Hay, P. (2005). Guided self-help for bulimia nervosa in primary care: A randomized controlled trial. *Psychological Medicine, 35*, 1283–1294.

Banducci, A. N., Long, K. E., & MacPherson, L. (2014). A case series of a behavioral activation-enhanced smoking cessation program for inpatient substance users with elevated depressive symptoms. *Clinical Case Studies, 14*(1), 61–77.

Bandura, A. (1997). *Self-efficacy: The exercise of control*. New York: Freeman.

Bandura, A., Taylor, C. B., Williams, S. L., Mefford, I. N., & Barchas, J. D. (1985). Catecholamine secretion as a function of perceived coping self-efficacy. *Journal of Consulting and Clinical Psychology, 53*(3), 406–414.

Barger, S. D., & Gallo, L. C. (2008). Ability of ethnic self-identification to partition modifiable health risk among U.S. residents of Mexican ancestry. *American Journal of Public Health, 98*(11), 1971–1978.

Barker, E. T., Greenberg, J. S., Seltzer, M. M., & Almeida, D. M. (2012). Daily stress and cortisol patterns in parents of adult children with a serious mental illness. *Health Psychology, 31*(1), 130–134.

Barnes, P. M., Bloom, B., & Nahin, R. (2008). Complementary and alternative medicine use among adults and children: United States, 2007. *National Health Statistics Reports* (12). Hyattsville, MD: National Center for Health Statistics.

Barrera, M., Toobert, D. J., Angell, K. L., Glasgow, R. E., & MacKinnon, D. P. (2006). Social support and social-ecological resources as mediators of lifestyle intervention effects for type 2 diabetes. *Journal of Health Psychology, 11*, 483–495.

Barrington-Trimis, J. L., Urman, R., Leventhal, A. M., Gauderman, J., Cruz, T. B., Gilreath, T. D., … McConnell, R. (2016, August 8). E-cigarettes, cigarettes, and the prevalence of adolescent tobacco use. *Pediatrics, 138*(2). Retrieved from http://pediatrics.aappublications.org/content/pediatrics/138/2/e20153983.full.pdf

Barsky, A. J., Saintfort, R., Rogers, M. P., & Borus, J. F. (2002). Nonspecific medication side effects and the nocebo phenomenon. *Journal of the American Medical Association, 287*(5), 622–627.

Bartholow, B. D., Sher, K. J., & Krull, J. L. (2003). Changes in heavy drinking over the third decade of life as a function of collegiate fraternity and sorority involvement: A prospective, multilevel analysis. *Health Psychology, 22*(6), 616–625.

Bartley, E. J., & Fillingim, R. B. (2013). Sex differences in pain: A brief review of clinical and experimental findings. *Medicine and Health, 111*(1), 52–58.

Bartley, T. (2012). *Mindfulness-based cognitive therapy for cancer*. West Sussex, UK: John Wiley.

Bass, P. F. (2015). Family-based therapy for eating disorders. *Contemporary Pediatrics*. Retrieved from http://

contemporarypediatrics.modernmedicine
.com/contemporary-pediatrics/news/
family-based-therapy-eating-disorders?page=full

Batty, G. D., Shipley, M. J., Mortensen, L. H., Galef, C. R., & Deary, I. J. (2008). IQ in late adolescence/early adulthood, risk factors in middle-age and later coronary heart disease mortality in men: The Vietnam experience study. *European Journal of Cardiovascular Prevention and rehabilitation, 15*(3), 359–361.

Baum, A., & Grunberg, N. E. (1991). Gender, stress, and health. *Health Psychology, 10,* 80–85.

Baumann, L. J., Cameron, L. D., Zimmerman, R. S., & Leventhal, H. (1989). Illness representations and matching labels with symptoms. *Health Psychology, 8,* 449–469.

Bazelmans, E., Prins, J., & Bleijenberg, G. (2006). Cognitive behaviour therapy for relatively active and for passive chronic fatigue syndrome patients. *Cognitive Behaviour Practice, 13,* 157–166.

Bech, P. (2004). Measuring the dimensions of psychological general well-being by the WHO-5. *Quality of Life Newsletter, 32,* 15–16.

Beck, K. H., & Frankel, A. (1981). A conceptualization of threat communications and protective health behavior. *Social Psychology Quarterly, 44,* 204–217.

Beckman, H. B., & Frankel, R. M. (1984). The effect of physician behavior on the collection of data. *Annals of Internal Medicine, 101,* 692–696.

Beesdo, K., Hoyer, J., Jacobi, F., Low, N. C. P., Hofler, M., & Wittchen, H. U. (2010). Association between generalized anxiety levels and pain in a community sample: Evidence for diagnostic specificity. *Journal of Anxiety Disorders, 24*(2), 290–291.

Behavioral Risk Factor Surveillance System (BRFSS). (2016). Atlanta, GA: Centers for Disease Control and Prevention. Retrieved from http://www.cdc.gov/brfss/index.html

Beil, L. (2015). Typical American diet can damage immune system. *Science News, 187*(11). Retrieved from https://www.sciencenews.org/article/typical-american-diet-can-damage-immune-system

Belar, C. D., & Deardorff, W. W. (1996). *Clinical health psychology in medical settings: A practitioner's guidebook.* Washington, DC: American Psychological Association.

Belar, C. D., & Deardorff, W. W. (2008). *Clinical health psychology in medical settings: A practitioner's guidebook* (2nd ed.). Washington, DC: American Psychological Association.

Belcher, A. J., Laurenceau, J. P., Graber, E. C., Cohen, L. H., Dasch, K. B., & Siegel, S. D. (2011). Daily support in couples coping with early stage breast cancer: Maintaining intimacy during adversity. *Health Psychology, 30*(6), 665–673.

Belfer, I. (2013). Nature and nurture of human pain. *Scientifica, 2013,* article ID 415279. Retrieved from http://dx.doi.org/10.1155/2013/415279

Bell, B., & Dittmar, H. (2010). Does media type matter? The role of identification in adolescent girls' media consumption and the impact of different thin-ideal media on body image. *Sex Roles, 65*(7/8), 478–490.

Ben-Ayre, E., & Frenkel, M. (2008). Referring to complementary and alternative medicine: A possible tool for implementation. *Complementary Therapies in Medicine, 16,* 325–330.

Bendapudi, N. M., Berry, L. L., Frey, K. A., Parish, J. T., & Rayburn, W. L. (2006). Patients' perspectives on ideal physician behaviors. *Mayo Clinic Proceedings, 81,* 338–344.

Benedetti, F. (1996). The opposite effects opiate antagonist naloxone and the cholecystokinin antagonist proglumide on placebo analgesia. *Pain, 64*(3), 540.

Benet, C., Thompson, R. J., & Gotlib, I. H. (2010). 5-HTTLPR moderates the effect of relational peer victimization on depressive symptoms in adolescent girls. *Journal of Child Psychology and Psychiatry, 51*(2), 173–179.

Benson, H. (1993). The relaxation response. In D. Goleman & J. Gurin (Eds.), *Mind-body medicine: How to use your mind for better health* (pp. 233–257). New York: Consumer Reports Books.

Benson, H. (1996). *Timeless healing: The power and biology of belief.* New York: Scribner.

Benson, J. (2015, September 8). NRC cancels study of cancer risk in communities near power plants. *The Day.* Retrieved from http://www.theday.com/article/20150908/NWS01/150909423

Bergstrom, N. (1994). *Treating pressure ulcers: Methodology for guideline development.* U.S. Department of Health and Human Services, Publication No. 96-N014.

Berkman, L. F. (2010). Social networks and health. Presented at *Ageing and health: From evidence to policy.* Meeting of the Study on global AGEing and adult health (SAGE), June 10. Geneva: World Health Organization. Retrieved from http://www.who.int/healthinfo/systems/sage/en/index3.html

Berkman, L. F., Buxton, O., Ertel, K., & Okechukwu, C. (2010). Managers' practices related to work-family balance predict employee cardiovascular risk and sleep duration in extended care settings. *Journal of Occupational Health Psychology, 15*(3), 316–329.

Berkman, L. F., Melchior, M., Chastang, J., Niedhammer, I., Leclerc, A., & Goldberg, M. (2004). Social integration and mortality: A prospective study of French employees of electricity of France-Gas of France. *American Journal of Epidemiology, 159*(2), 167–174.

Berkman, L. F., & Syme, S. L. (1979). Social networks, host resistance, and mortality: A nine-year follow-up of Alameda County residents. *American Journal of Epidemiology, 109,* 190.

Berkman, L. F., & Syme, L. S. (1994). Social networks, host resistance, and mortality: A nine-year follow-up study of Alameda County residents. In A. Steptoe & J. Wardle (Eds.), *Psychosocial processes and health: A reader* (pp. 43–67). Cambridge, UK: Cambridge University Press.

Berrington de Gonzales, A. G., Hartge, P., Cerhan, J. R., Flint, A. J., Hannan, L., MacInnis, R. J. … Thun, M. J. (2010). Body-mass index and mortality among 1.46 million white adults. *New England Journal of Medicine, 363,* 2211–2219.

Berry, J. W., & Worthington, E. L. (2001). Forgiveness, relationship quality, stress while imagining relationship events, and physical and mental health. *Journal of Counseling Psychology, 48*(4), 447–455.

Best, J. (2002). *Damned lies and statistics: Untangling numbers from the media, politicians, and activists.* Berkeley: University of California Press.

Bianchi, S. M., & Milkie, M. A. (2010). Work and family research in the first decade of the 21st century. *Journal of Marriage and Family, 72*(3), 705–725.

Billings, A. G., & Moos, R. H. (1981). The role of coping responses and social resources in attenuating the stress of life events. *Journal of Behavioral Medicine, 4,* 139–157.

Billman, G. E. (2011). Heart rate variability—A historical perspective. *Frontiers in Physiology.* Retrieved March 2, 2016, from http://journal.frontiersin.org/article/10.3389/fphys.2011.00086/abstract

Blair, C., & Raver, C. C. (2012). Child development in the context of adversity: Experiential canalization of brain and behavior. *American Psychologist, 67*(4), 309–318.

Blakemore, S.-J. (2008). Development of the social brain during adolescence. *Quarterly Journal of Experimental Psychology, 61,* 40–49.

Blanchard, C. M., Fortier, M., Sweet, S., O'Sullivan, T., Hogg, W., Reid, R. D., & Sigal, R. J. (2007). Explaining physical activity levels from a self-efficacy perspective: The physical activity counseling trial. *Annals of Behavioral Medicine, 34,* 323–328.

Blas, E., & Kurup, A. S. (Eds.). (2010). *Equity, social determinants, and public health programmes.* Geneva, Switzerland: World Health Organization.

Blascovich, J., Seery, M. D., Mugridge, C. A., Norris, R. K., & Weisbuch, M. (2004). Predicting athletic performance from cardiovascular indexes of challenge and threat. *Journal of Experimental Social Psychology, 40,* 683–688.

Blissmer, B., & McAuley, E. (2002). Testing the requirements of stages of physical activity among adults: The comparative effectiveness offstage-matched, mismatched, standard care, and control interventions. *Annals of Behavioral Medicine, 24,* 181–189.

Bloor, L. E., Uchino, B. N., Hicks, A., & Smith, T. W. (2004). Social relationships and physiological function: The effects of recalling social relationships on cardiovascular reactivity. *Annals of Behavioral Medicine, 28*(1), 29–38.

Boehm, J. K., Peterson, C., Kivimaki, M., & Kubzansky, L. (2011). A prospective study of positive psychological well-being and coronary heart disease. *Health Psychology, 30*(3), 259–267.

Bogart, L. M., & Delahanty, D. L. (2004). Psychosocial models. In T. J. Boll, R. G. Frank, A. Baum, & J. L. Wallander (Eds.), *Handbook of clinical health psychology: Models and perspectives in health psychology* (Vol. 3, pp. 201–248). Washington, DC: American Psychological Association.

Bolen, J., Schieb, L., Hootman, J. M., Helmick, C. G., Theis, K., Murphy, L. B., & Langmaid, G. (2010). Differences in the prevalence and impact of arthritis among racial/ethnic groups in the United States, National Health Interview Survey, 2002, 2003, and 2006. *Preventing Chronic Disease, 7*(3), A64–A68.

Bolt, M. (2004). *Pursuing human strengths: A positive psychology guide.* New York: W. H. Freeman.

Bonadonna, R. (2003). Meditation's impact on chronic illness. *Holistic Nursing Practice, 17*(6), 309–319.

Bondi, N. (1997, March 19). Stressed out? Holding it in may be deadly. *The Detroit News,* p. A1.

Bonhoeffer, H. J. (2007). Adverse events following immunization: Perception and evidence. *Current Opinions Infectious Disease, 20*(3), 237–246.

Bonita, R., Beaglehole, R., & Kjellstrom, T. (2006). *Basic epidemiology* (2nd ed.). Geneva, Switzerland: World Health Organization.

Booij, L., Wang, D., Levesque, M. L., Tremblay, R. E., & Szf, M. (2013). Looking beyond the DNA sequence: The relevance of DNA methylation processes for the stress-diathesis model of depression. *Philosophical Transactions of the Royal Society of Biological Sciences, 368*(1615). Retrieved from http://rstb.royalsocietypublishing.org/content/current

Boone-Heinonen, J., Diez Roux, A. V., Kiefe, C. I., Lewis, C. E., Guilkey, D. K., & Gordon-Larsen, P. (2011). Neighborhood socioeconomic status predictors of physical activity through young to middle adulthood: The CARDIA study. *Social Science & Medicine, 72*(5), 641–649.

Borissoff, J. I., Spronk, H. M. H., & ten Cate, H. (2011). The hemostatic system as a modulator of atherosclerosis. *The New England Journal of Medicine, 364*(18), 1746–1760.

Bosma, H., Marmot, M. G., Hemingway, H., Nicholson, A. C., Brunner, E., & Stanfeld, S. A. (1997). Low job control and risk of coronary heart disease in Whitehall II (prospective cohort) study. *British Medical Journal, 314,* 285.

Bosma, H., Stansfeld, S. A., & Marmot, M. G. (1998). Job control personal characteristics, and heart disease. *Journal of Occupational Health Psychology, 3*(4), 402–409.

Bouvard, V., Loomis, D., Guyton, K. Z., Grosse, Y., Ghissassi, F. E., Benbrahim-Tallaa, L., … Straif, K. (2015). Carcinogenicity of red and processed meat. *The Lancet Oncology, 16*(16), 1599–1600.

Bowen, S., Witkiewitz, K., Dillworth, T. M., Chawla, N., Simpson, T. L., Ostafin, B. D., Larimer, M. E., Blume, A. W., Parks, G. A., & Marlatt, G. A. (2006). Mindfulness meditation and substance use in an incarcerated population. *Psychology of Addictive Behaviors, 20*(3), 343–347.

Bower, J. E., Greendale, G., Crosswell, A. D., Garet, D., Sternlieb, B., Ganz, P. A., … Cole, S. W. (2014). Yoga reduces inflammatory signaling in fatigued breast cancer survivors: A randomized controlled trial. *Psychoneuroendocrinology, 43,* 20–29.

Bower, J. E., Kemeny, M. E., Taylor, S. E., & Fahey, J. L. (2003). Finding positive meaning and its association with natural killer cell cytotoxicity among participants in a bereavement-related disclosure intervention. *Annals of Behavioral Medicine, 25*(2), 146–155.

Bowling, N. A., Eschleman, K. J., & Wang, Q. (2010). A meta-analytic examination of the relationship between job satisfaction and subjective well-being. *Journal of Occupational and Organizational Psychology, 83,* 915–934.

Boyce, W. T., Alkon, A., Tschann, J. M., Cesney, M. A., & Alpert, B. S. (1995). Dimensions of psychobiologic reactivity: Cardiovascular responses to laboratory stressors in preschool children. *Annals of Behavioral Medicine, 17,* 315–323.

Boyle, J. P., Thompson, T. J., Gregg, E. W., Barker, L. E., & Williamson, D. F. (2010). Projection of the year 2050 burden of diabetes in the US adult population: Dynamic modeling of incidence, mortality, and prediabetes prevalence. *Population Health Metrics.* Retrieved February 26, 2016, from http://pophealthmetrics.biomedcentral.com/articles/10.1186/1478-7954-8-29

Braciewski, J. M. (2010). *Family environment and psychological distress: A longitudinal study of at-risk youth.* WorldCat Dissertations and Theses. Udini by ProQuest. Retrieved from http://udini.proquest.com/view/family-environment-and-goid:305231554/

Brady, S. S., & Matthews, K. A. (2006). Chronic stress influences ambulatory blood pressure in adolescents. *Annals of Behavioral Medicine, 31*(1), 80–88.

Brakel, T. M., Dijkstra, A., Buunk, A. P, & Siero, F. W. (2012). Impact of social comparison on cancer survivors' quality of life: An experimental field study. *Health Psychology, 31*(5), 660–670.

Branchi, I., Santarelli, S., D'Andrea, I., & Alleva, E. (2013). Not all stressors are equal: Early social enrichment favors resilience to social but not physical stress in male mice. *Hormones and Behavior, 63,* 503–509.

Brant, J. M., Beck, S., Dudley, W. N., Cobb, P., Pepper, G., & Miaskowski, C. (2011). Symptom trajectories in posttreatment cancer survivors. *Cancer Nursing, 34,* 67–77.

Bratman, S. (2007). *Complementary and alternative health: The scientific verdict on what really works.* New York: Harper Collins.

Bray, G. A. (1969). Effect of caloric restriction on energy expenditure in obese patients. *The Lancet, 2,* 397–398.

Breibart, W., & Payne, D. (2001). Psychiatric aspects of pain management in patients with advanced cancer. In H. Chochinov & W. Breibart (Eds.), *Handbook of psychiatry in palliative medicine* (pp. 131–199). New York: Oxford University Press.

Breslow, L., & Breslow, N. (1993). Health practices and disability: Some evidence from Alameda County. *Preventive Medicine, 22,* 86–95.

Broadbent, E., Petrie, K. J., Alley, P. G., & Booth, R. J. (2003). Psychological stress impairs early wound repair following surgery. *Psychosomatic Medicine, 65*(5), 865–869.

Broadstock, M., Borland, R., & Gason, R. (2006). Effects of suntan on judgments of healthiness and attractiveness by adolescents. *Journal of Applied Social Psychology, 22*(2), 157–172.

Brody, G. H., Kogan, S. M., Mury, V. M., Chen, Y. F., & Brown, A. C. (2008). Psychological functioning, support for self-management, and glycemic control among rural African American adults with diabetes mellitus type 2. *Health Psychology, 27*(Supplement 1), S83–S90.

Brody J. E. (1999, March 16). When illness is real, but symptoms are unseen. *The New York Times.* Retrieved December 14, 2010, from http://www.nytimes.com

Brody, J. E. (2002, November 26). When the eyelids snap shut at 65 miles an hour. *The New York Times.* Retrieved from http://www.nytimes.com

Brolinson, P., Price, J., Ditmyer, M., & Reis, D. (2001). Nurses' perceptions of complementary and alternative medical therapies. *Journal of Community Health, 26*(3), 175–189.

Bromberg, M. H., Gil, K. M., & Schanberg, L. E. (2012). Daily sleep quality and mood as predictors of pain in children with juvenile polyarticular arthritis. *Health Psychology, 31*(2), 202–209.

Bronfort, G., Haas, M., Evans, R., Leininger, B., & Triano, J. (2010). Effectiveness of manual therapies: The UK evidence report. *Chiropractic and Osteopathy, 18*(3). Retrieved March 2, 2016, from http://chiromt.biomedcentral.com/articles/10.1186/1746-1340-18-3

Brookings, J. B., DeRoo, H., & Grimone, J. (2008). Predicting driving anger from trait aggression and self-control. *Psychological Reports, 103*(2), 622–624.

Broom, D. R., Batterham, R. L., King, J. A., & Stensel, D. J. (2009). Influence of resistance and aerobic exercise on hunger, circulating levels of acylated ghrelin, and peptide YY in healthy males. *American Journal of Physiology. Regulatory, Integrative, and Comparative Physiology. 296*(1), R29–R35.

Brown, G. D. A., Gardner, J., Oswald A. J., & Qian, J. (2008). Does wage rank affect employees' well-being? *Industrial Relations, 47,* 355–389.

Brown, K. W., & Ryan, R. M. (2003). The benefits of being present: Mindfulness and its role in psychological well-being. *Journal of Personality and Social Psychology, 84*(4), 822–848.

Brown, S. L., & Rinelli, L. N. (2010). Family structure, family processes, and adolescent smoking and drinking. *Journal of Research on Adolescence, 20*(2), 259–273.

Brown, S. L., Schiraldi, G. R., & Wrobleski, P. P. (2009). Association of eating behaviors and obesity with psychosocial and familial influences. *American Journal of Health Education, 40*(2), 80–89.

Brownell, K. D. (2003). *Food fight: The inside story of the food industry, America's obesity crisis and what we can do about it.* New York: McGraw-Hill.

Brownell, K. D., Ludwig, K. R., Post, R. C., Puhl, R. M., Schwartz, M. B., & Willett, W. C. (2010). Personal responsibility and obesity: A constructive approach to a controversial issue. *Health Affairs, 29*(3), 379–387.

Brownell, K. D., & Wadden, T. A. (1991). The heterogeneity of obesity: Fitting treatments to individuals. *Behavior Therapy, 22,* 153–177.

Browning, L., Ryan, C. S., Greenberg, M. S., & Rolniak, S. (2006). Effects of cognitive adaptation on the expectation-burnout relationship among nurses. *Journal of Behavioral Medicine, 29,* 139–150.

Brownlee, C. (2006). Eat smart. Foods may affect the brain as well as the body. *Science News, 169,* 136–137.

Brownlee, S. (1995). The route of phantom pain. *U.S. News & World Report, 119,* 76.

Broyles, L. C. (2005). *Resilience: Its relationship to forgiveness in older adults* (Doctoral dissertation). Retrieved from gradworks.umi.com

Burgard, S. A., & Ailshire, J. A. (2009). Putting work to bed: Stressful experiences on the job and sleep quality. *Journal of Health and Social Behavior, 50,* 476–492.

Burge, M. R., & Schade, D. S. (2014). Diabetes and the Affordable Care Act. *Diabetes Technology and Therapeutics, 16*(7), 399–413.

Burgess, D., van Ryn, M., Dovidio, J., & Saha, S. (2007). Reducing racial bias among health care providers: Lessons from social-cognitive psychology. *Journal of General Internal Medicine, 22*(6), 882–887.

Burhenn, P., Olausson, J., Vilegas, G., & Kravits, K. (2014). Guided imagery for pain control. *Clinical Journal of Oncology Nursing, 18*(5), 501–503.

Burns, J. W. (2006). The role of attentional strategies in moderating links between acute pain induction and subsequent psychological stress: Evidence for symptom-specific reactivity among patients with chronic pain versus healthy nonpatients. *Emotion, 6*(2), 180–192.

Burns, J. W., Holly, A., Quartana, P., Wolff, M. S., Gray, E., & Bruehl, S. (2008). Trait anger management style moderates effects of actual ("state") anger regulation on symptom-specific reactivity and recovery among chronic low back pain patient. *Psychosomatic Medicine, 70*(8), 898–905.

Busch, A. M., & Borrelli, B. (2012). Valued life activities and readiness to quit smoking among mobility-impaired smokers. *Health Psychology, 31*(1), 122–125.

Bustamante, M. J., Valentino, G., Kramer, V., Adasme, M., Guidi, D., Ibara, I., ... Acevedo, M. (2015). Patient adherence to a cardiovascular rehabilitation program: What factors are involved? *International Journal of Clinical Medicine, 6,* 605–614.

Butler, E. A., Egloff, B., Wilhelm, F. H., Smith, N. C., Erickson, E. A., & Gross, J. J. (2003). The social consequences of expressive suppression. *Emotion, 3*(1), 48–67.

Butler, S. (2010). A personal experience learning from two pain pioneers, J. J. Bonica and W. Fordyce: Lessons surviving four decades of pain practice. *Scandinavian Journal of Pain, 1*(1), 34–37.

Buunk, A. P., Brakel, T. M., Bennenbroek, F. T. C., Stiegelis, H., Sanderman, R., Van den Bergh, A. C. M., & Hagedoorn, M. (2009). Neuroticism and responses to social comparison among cancer patients. *European Journal of Personality, 23,* 475–487.

Buxton, O. M., & Marcell, E. (2010). Short and long sleep are positively associated with obesity, diabetes, hypertension, and cardiovascular disease among adults in the United States. *Social Science and Medicine, 71*(5), 1027–1036.

Bynum, R. (2004, November 1). Rare disease makes girl unable to feel pain. *NBCNEWS.com*. Retrieved June 15, 2016, from http://www.nbcnews.com/id/6379795/ns/health-childrens_health/t/rare-disease-makes-girl-unable-feel-pain/#.V2FYt1fzglI

Calam, R., Waller, G., Slade, P. D., & Newton, T. (1990). Eating disorders and perceived relationships with parents. *International Journal of Eating Disorders, 9*, 479–485.

Calandra, C., Musso, F., & Musso, R. (2003). The role of leptin in the etiopathogenesis of anorexia nervosa and bulimia. *Eating and Weight Disorders, 8*(2), 130–137.

Caldwell, J. A. (2012). Crew schedules, sleep deprivation, and aviation performance. *Current Directions in Psychological Science, 21*(2), 85–89.

Calle, E. E., Thun, M. J., Petrelli, J. M., Rodriguez, C., & Heath, C. W. (1999). Body-mass index and mortality in a prospective cohort of U.S. adults. *New England Journal of Medicine, 341*(15), 1097–1105.

Callister, L. C. (2003). Cultural influences on pain perceptions and behaviors. *Home Health Care Management and Practice, 15*(3), 207–211.

Calsyn, M., & Rosenthal, L. (2013, May 20). How the Affordable Care Act helps young adults. *Center for American Progress*. Retrieved February 25, 2016, from http://www.americanprogress.org/issues/healthcare

Caltabiano, M. L., & Caltabiano, N. J. (2006). Resilience and health outcomes in the elderly. *Proceedings of the 39th Annual Conference of the Australian Association of Gerontology*, Sydney, Australia.

Camp, D. E., Klesges, R. C., & Relyea, G. (1993). The relationship between body weight concerns and adolescent smoking. *Health Psychology, 12*, 24–32.

Campaign for Tobacco-Free Kids. (2006). Federal tax burdens on U.S. households caused by tobacco use. Retrieved from http://www.tobaccofreekids.org

Campbell, C. M., & Edwards, R. R. (2012). Ethnic differences in pain and pain management. *Pain Management, 2*(3), 219–230.

Campbell, C. M., Edwards, R. R., & Fillingim, R. B. (2005). Ethnic differences in responses to multiple experimental pain stimuli. *Pain, 113*, 20–26.

Campbell, C. M., France, C. R., Robinson, M. E., Logan, H. L., Geffken, G. R., & Fillingim, R. B. (2008). Ethnic differences in the nociceptive flexion reflex (NFR). *Pain, 134*, 91–96.

Canadian Tobacco Use Monitoring Survey (CTUMS). (2004). *Health Canada*. Retrieved from http://www.hc-sc.gc.ca/hl-vs/tobac-tabac/research-recherche/stat/ctums-esutc/2004/index_e.html

Cannon, W. (1932). *The wisdom of the body*. New York: Norton.

Cantor, D. W., Boyce, T. E., & Repetti, R. L. (2004). Ensuring healthy working lives. In R. H. Rozensky, N. G. Johnson, C. D. Goodheart, & W. R. Hammond (Eds.), *Psychology builds a healthy world*. Washington, DC: American Psychological Association.

Carels, R. A., Darby, L., Cacciapaglia, H., Douglass, O. M., Harper, J., Kaplar, M. E. … Tonkin, K. (2005). Applying a stepped-care approach to the treatment of obesity. *Journal of Psychosomatic Research, 59*(6), 375–383.

Carlisle, M., Uchino, B, Sanbonmatsu, D. M., Smith, T. W., Cribbet, M. R., Birmingham, W., … Vaughn, A. A. (2012). Subliminal activation of social ties moderates cardiovascular reactivity during acute stress. *Health Psychology 31*(2), 217–225.

Carlson, L. E., Speca, M., Patel, K. D., & Goodey, E. (2003). Mindfulness-based stress reduction in relation to quality of life, mood, symptoms of stress, and immune parameters in breast and prostate cancer outpatients. *Psychosomatic Medicine, 65*, 571–581.

Carnethon, M., Knutson, K. L., Kim, K., de Chavez, P. J., Goldberger, J. J., Ng, J., Liu, K., & Zee, P. (2012). Racial/ethnic differences in sleep duration and quality in a population sample. Presented at the annual meeting of the Associated Professional Sleep Societies. *Journal of Sleep and Sleep Disorders Research, 35*, abstract supplement, A342.

Carnethon, M. R., Gidding, S. S., Nehgme, R., Sidney, S., Jacobs, D. R. Jr., & Liu, K. (2003). Cardiorespiratory fitness in young adulthood and the development of cardiovascular disease risk factors. *Journal of the American Medical Association, 290*(23), 3092–3100.

Carpenter, K. M., Hasin, D. S., Allison, D. B., & Faith, M. S. (2000). Relationships between obesity and DSM-IV major depressive disorder, suicide ideation, and suicide attempts: Results from a general population study. *American Journal of Public Health, 90*, 251–257.

Carpenter, S. (2013). Awakening to sleep. *Monitor on Psychology, 44*(1), 40–45.

Carriere, G. (2003). Parent and child factors associated with youth obesity. *Statistics Canada, Catalogue 82-003*, Supplement to Health Reports, 2003.

Carroll, D. (2011). A brief commentary on cardiovascular reactivity at a crossroads. *Biological Psychology, 86*(2), 149–151.

Carroll, M. D., Kit, B. K., & Lacher, D. A. (2012). Total and high-density lipoprotein cholesterol in adults: National Health and Nutrition Examination Survey, 2009–2010. *NCHS data brief, no. 92*. Hyattsville, MD: National Center for Health Statistics.

Carroll, M. D., Navaneelan, T., Bryan, S., & Ogden, C. L. (2015). Prevalence of obesity among children and adolescents in the United States and Canada. *NCHS data brief, no. 211*. Hyattsville, MD: National Center for Health Statistics.

Carter, K. O., Olshan-Perlmutter, M., Norton, H. J., & Smith, M. O. (2011). NADA acupuncture prospective trial in patients with substance use disorders and seven common health symptoms. *Journal of Medical Acupuncture, 23*(3), 131–135.

Carteret, M. (2012). Cultural aspects of pain management. *Dimensions of Culture*. Retrieved March 4, 2016, from http://www.dimensionsofculture.com/2010/11/cultural-aspects-of-pain-management/

Cartwright, M., Wardle, J., Steggles, N., Simon, A. E., Croker, H., & Jarvis, M. J. (2003). Stress and dietary practices in adolescents. *Health Psychology, 22*(4), 362–369.

Carver, C. S., & Connor-Smith, J. (2010). Personality and coping. *Annual Review of Psychology, 61*, 679–704.

Carver, C. S., & Scheier, M. F. (2002). Optimism. In C. R. Snyder & S. J. Lopez (Eds.), *Handbook of positive psychology* (pp. 231–243). New York: Oxford University Press.

Carver, C. S., Smith, R. G., Antoni, M. H., Petronis, V. M., Weiss, S., & Derhagopian, R. P. (2005). Optimistic personality and psychosocial well-being during treatment predict psychosocial well-being among long-term survivors of breast cancer. *Health Psychology, 24*(5), 508–515.

Casciani, D. (2009). GBL drug death identified by UK doctors. *BBC News*. Retrieved March 2, 2016, from http://news.bbc.co.uk/2/hi/uk_news/8428802.stm

Caspi, A., Harrington, H., Moffitt, T. E., Milne, B. J., & Poulton, R. (2006). Socially isolated children 20 years later. *Archives of Pediatric Adolescent Medicine, 160*, 805–811.

Cassetta, J. A., Boden-Albala, B., Sciacca, R. R., & Giardina, E.-G. (2007). Association of education and race/ethnicity with physical activity in insured urban women. *Journal of Women's Health, 16*(6), 902–908.

Castillo-Garzon, M. J., Ruiz, J. R., Ortega, F. B., & Gutierrez, A. (2006). Anti-aging therapy through fitness enhancement. *Journal of Clinical Interventions in Aging, 1*(3), 213–220.

Castro, C. M., Wilson, C., Wang, F., & Schillinger, D. (2007). Babel babble: Physicians' use of unclarified medical jargon with patients. *American Journal of Health Behavior, 31*, S85–S95.

Castro, F. G., Barrera, M., Jr., & Holleran Streiker, L. K. (2010). Issues and challenges in the design of culturally adapted evidence-based interventions. *Annual Review of Clinical Psychology, 6*, 213–239.

Catalano, R. A., Rook, K., & Dooley, D. (1986). Labor markets and help-seeking: A test of the employment security hypothesis. *Journal of Health and Social Behavior, 27*, 277–287.

CDC Fact Sheet. (2013). HIV in the United States: At a glance. Centers for Disease Control and Prevention. Retrieved from http://www.cdc.gov/hiv/pdf/statistics_basics_factsheet.pdf

CDC Fast Facts. (2015). HIV among people aged 50 and over. Centers for Disease Control and Prevention. Retrieved March 16, 2016, from http://www.cdc.gov/hiv/group/age/olderamericans/index.html

CDC/NCHS. (2014). *Health, United States, 2014: With special feature on adults aged 55–64.* Hyattsville, MD: National Center for Health Statistics.

Cecil, J. E., Tavendale, R., Watt, P., Hetherington, M. M., & Palmer, C. N. A. (2008). An obesity-associated FTO gene variant and increased energy intake in children. *New England Journal of Medicine, 359*, 2558–2566.

Cella, D., Hughes, C., Peterman, A., Chang, C., Peshkin, B. N., Schwartz, M. D. ... Lerman, C. (2002). A brief assessment of concerns associated with genetic testing for cancer: The Multidimensional Impact of Cancer Risk Assessment (MICRA) questionnaire. *Health Psychology, 21*(6), 564–572.

Centers for Disease Control and Prevention (CDC). (2001). Behavioral risk factor surveillance system: *Summary data quality report* (rev.). National Center for Chronic Disease Prevention and Health Promotion, Centers for Disease Control and Prevention. Retrieved from http://www.cdc.gov/brfss/annual_data/2000/pdf/2000summarydataquality report.pdf

Centers for Disease Control and Prevention (CDC). (2002). Physical activity levels among children aged 9–13 years—United States, 2002. *Morbidity and Mortality Weekly Report, 52*(33), 785–788.

Centers for Disease Control and Prevention (CDC). (2005). *National diabetes fact sheet*, United States, 2005. Atlanta, GA: U.S. Department of Health and Human Services.

Centers for Disease Control and Prevention (CDC). (2008). Cigarette smoking among adults—United States, 2007. *Morbidity and Mortality Weekly Report, 57*(45), 1221–1226.

Centers for Disease Control and Prevention (CDC). (2009). *Diabetes: Successes and opportunities for population-based prevention and control.* Atlanta, GA: National Center for Disease Prevention and Health Promotion.

Centers for Disease Control and Prevention (CDC). (2010a). Diabetes public health resource. Centers for Disease Control and Prevention. Retrieved October 29, 2010, from http://www.cdc.gov/diabetes/consumer/beactive.htm

Centers for Disease Control and Prevention (CDC). (2010b). Healthy youth! Retrieved February 24, 2010, from http://www.cdc.gov/HealthyYouth/index.htm

Centers for Disease Control and Prevention (CDC). (2011a). *National diabetes fact sheet: National estimates and general information on diabetes and prediabetes in the United States,* 2011. Atlanta, GA: U.S. Department of Health and Human Services, Centers for Disease Control and Prevention. Retrieved from http://www.cdc.gov/diabetes/pubs/pdf/ndfs_2011.pdf

Centers for Disease Control and Prevention (CDC). (2011b). Youth risk behavior surveillance—United States, 2011. *Morbidity and Mortality Weekly Report, 61*(SS-4).

Centers for Disease Control and Prevention (CDC). (2012a). Falls: The reality. Retrieved April 16, 2016, from http://www.cdc.gov/safechild/Falls/index.html

Centers for Disease Control and Prevention (CDC). (2012b). Health literacy: Accurate, accessible and actionable health information for all. Retrieved from http://www.cdc.gov/healthliteracy/

Centers for Disease Control and Prevention (CDC). (2012c). A look inside food deserts. Retrieved from http://www.cdc.gov/features/FoodDeserts/

Centers for Disease Control and Prevention (CDC). (2013a). FastStats: Accidents or unintentional injuries. Hyattsville, MD: National Center for Health Statistics. Retrieved from http://www.cdc.gov/nchs/fastats/acc-inj.htm

Centers for Disease Control and Prevention (CDC). (2013b). *Genital HPV infection—Fact sheet.* Retrieved from http://www.cdc.gov/std/hpv/stdfact-hpv.htm

Centers for Disease Control and Prevention (CDC). (2013c). HIV among women. Retrieved from http://www.cdc.gov/hiv/pdf/risk_women.pdf

Centers for Disease Control and Prevention (CDC). (2013d). *HIV surveillance report, 2011* (Vol. 23). Retrieved from http://www.cdc.gov/hiv/library/reports/surveillance/index.html

Centers for Disease Control and Prevention (CDC). (2013e). Lung cancer statistics. Retrieved from http://www.cdc.gov/cancer/lung/statistics/index.htm

Centers for Disease Control and Prevention (CDC). (2013f). Severe acute respiratory syndrome (SARS). Retrieved February 28, 2016, from http://www.cdc.gov/sars/index.html

Centers for Disease Control and Prevention (CDC). (2013g). *The state of aging and health in America 2013.* Atlanta, GA: Centers for Disease Control and Prevention, U.S. Department of Health and Human Services.

Centers for Disease Control and Prevention (CDC). (2014a). All injuries. *Centers for Disease Control and Prevention FastStats.* Retrieved from http://www.cdc.gov/nchs/fastats/injury.htm

Centers for Disease Control and Prevention (CDC). (2014b). Antibiotic resistance threats in the United States, 2013. Retrieved May 26, 2016, from http://www.cdc.gov/drugresistance/threat-report-2013/

Centers for Disease Control and Prevention (CDC). (2014c). *National diabetes statistics report: Estimates of diabetes and its burden in the United States, 2014.* Atlanta, GA: U.S. Department of Health and Human Services.

Centers for Disease Control and Prevention (CDC). (2014d) Up to 40 percent of annual deaths from each of five leading US causes are preventable. Retrieved from http://www.cdc.gov/media/releases/2014/p0501-preventable-deaths.html

Centers for Disease Control and Prevention (CDC). (2015a). Accidents or unintentional injuries. Centers for Disease Control and Prevention FastStats. Retrieved from http://www.cdc.gov/nchs/fastats/accidental-injury.htm

Centers for Disease Control and Prevention (CDC). (2015b). *Cancer prevention and control: Racial or ethnic variations.* Centers for Disease Control and Prevention. Retrieved from http://www.cdc.gov/cancer/dcpc/data/ethnic.htm

Centers for Disease Control and Prevention (CDC). (2015c). Chronic liver disease and cirrhosis. *Center for Disease Control and Prevention FastStats.* Retrieved from http://www.cdc.gov/nchs/fastats/liver-disease.htm

Centers for Disease Control and Prevention (CDC). (2015d). *Diabetes report card 2014.* Atlanta, GA: Centers for Disease Control and Prevention, U.S. Department of Health and Human Services.

Centers for Disease Control and Prevention (CDC). (2015e). HIV among gay and bisexual men. Retrieved March 16, 2016, from http://www.cdc.gov/hiv/group/msm/index.html

Centers for Disease Control and Prevention (CDC). (2015f). HIV in the United States. Retrieved from http://www.cdc.gov/hiv/statistics/overview/ataglance.html

Centers for Disease Control and Prevention (CDC). (2015g). Sleep and sleep disorders. Retrieved from http://www.cdc.gov/sleep/index.html

Centers for Disease Control and Prevention (CDC). (2015h). Stroke facts. Retrieved from http://www.cdc.gov/stroke/facts.htm

Centers for Disease Control and Prevention (CDC). (2015i). Underlying cause of death 1999–2014. *CDC WONDER online database.* Retrieved February 13, 2016, from http://wonder.cdc.gov/ucd-icd10.html

Centers for Disease Control and Prevention (CDC). (2015j). Work, stress, and health: Help us plan the next 25 years. Retrieved February 24, 2016, from http://blogs.cdc.gov/niosh-science-blog/2015/07/01/workplace-stress/

Centers for Disease Control and Prevention (CDC). (2016a). *Fact sheet—Alcohol use and your health.* Retrieved from http://www.cdc.gov/alcohol/pdfs/alcoholyourhealth.pdf

Centers for Disease Control and Prevention (CDC). (2016b). HIV among people aged 50 and over. Retrieved from http://www.cdc.gov/hiv/group/age/olderamericans/index.html

Centers for Disease Control and Prevention (CDC). (2016c). HIV among women. Retrieved March 16, 2016, from http://www.cdc.gov/hiv/group/gender/women/index.html

Centers for Disease Control and Prevention (CDC). (2016d). Zika virus. Retrieved March 16, 2016, from http://www.cdc.gov/zika/index.html

Centre for Evidence-Based Medicine (CEBM). (2010). The five steps of evidence-based practice. Retrieved January 29, 2010, from www.cebm.net

Cha, F. S., Doswell, W. M., Kim, K. H., Charron-Prochownik, D., & Patrick, T. E. (2007). Evaluating the Theory of Planned Behavior to explain intention to engage in premarital sex amongst Korean college students: A questionnaire survey. *International Journal of Nursing Studies, 4,* 1147–1157.

Champion, V., Skinner, C. S., Hui, S., Monahan, P., Julian, B., & Daggy. (2007). The effect of telephone versus print tailoring for mammography adherence. *Patient Education and Counseling, 65,* 416–423.

Chapin, H., Bagarinao, E., Hubbard, E. K., Dixon, E. A., Glover, G. H., & Mackey, S. (2013). *Neural correlates of effective cognitive modulation of pain.* Poster presented at the Meetings of the American Academy of Pain Medicine.

Chassin, L., Presson, C. C., Sherman, S. J., & Kim, K. (2003). Historical changes in cigarette smoking and smoking-related beliefs after 2 decades in a midwestern community. *Health Psychology, 22*(4), 347–353.

Chatard, A., & Selimbegovic, L. (2011). When self-destructive thoughts flash through the mind: Failure to meet standards affects the accessibility of suicide-related thoughts. *Journal of Personality and Social Psychology, 100,* 587–605.

Chen, E., Fisher, E. B., Bacharier, L. B., & Strunk, R. C. (2003). Socioeconomic status, stress, and immune markers in adolescents with asthma. *Psychosomatic Medicine, 65,* 984–992.

Chen, H., & Jackson, T. (2009). Predictors of changes in weight esteem among mainland Chinese adolescents: A longitudinal analysis. *Developmental Psychology, 45*(6), 1618–1629.

Chen, J. Y., Fox, S. A., Cntrell, C. H., Stockdale, S. E., Kagawa-Singer, M. (2007). Health disparities and prevention: Racial/ethnic barriers to flu vaccinations. *Journal of Community Health 32,* 5–20.

Chen, P. W. (2013, May 30). For new doctors, 8 minutes per patient. *The New York Times.* Retrieved from http://well.blogs.nytimes.com/2013/05/30/for-new-doctors-8-minutes-per-patient/?_r=0

Chen, X., Beydoun, M. A., & Wang, Y. (2008). Is sleep duration associated with childhood obesity? A systematic review and meta-analysis. *Obesity, 16,* 265–274.

Cheng, M. (2010). Experts: Up to a third of breast cancer cases could be avoided with diet, exercise. Associated Press. Retrieved April 8, 2010, from http://apdigitalnews.com

Chermack, S. T., & Giancola, P. R. (1997). The relation between alcohol and aggression: An integrated biopsychosocial conceptualization. *Clinical Psychology Review, 17,* 621–649.

Chiaramonte, G. R., & Friend, R. (2006). Medical students' and residents' gender bias in the diagnosis, treatment, and interpretation of coronary heart disease symptoms. *Health Psychology, 25*(3), 255–266.

Chida, Y., & Steptoe, A. (2010). Greater cardiovascular responses to laboratory mental stress are associated with poor subsequent cardiovascular risk status. *Hypertension, 55,* 1026–1032.

Chida, Y., Steptoe, A., & Powell, L. H. (2009). Religiosity/spirituality and mortality: A systematic quantitative review. *Psychotherapy and Psychosomatics, 78*(2), 81–90.

Children's Defense Fund. (2011). *The state of America's children.* Washington, DC: Author. Retrieved from http://www.childrensdefense.org/child-research-data-publications/data/state-of-americas-2011.pdf

Choi, H., Meininger, J. C., & Roberts, R. E. (2006). Ethnic differences in adolescents' mental distress, social stress, and resources. *Adolescence, 41,* 263–283.

Choi, W. S., Harris, K. J., Okuyemi, K., & Ahluwalia, J. S. (2003). Predictors of smoking initiation among college-bound high school students. *Annals of Behavioral Medicine, 26*(1), 69–74.

Choshen-Hillel, S., & Yaniv, I. (2011). Agency and the construction of social preference: Between inequality aversion and prosocial behavior. *Journal of Personality and Social Psychology, 101*(6), 1253–1261.

Christakis, N. A., & Fowler, J. H. (2007). The spread of obesity in a large social network over 32 years. *New England Journal of Medicine, 357,* 370–379.

Christensen, A. J., Moran, P. J., & Wiebe, J. S. (1999). Assessment of irrational health beliefs: Relation to health practices and medical regimen adherence. *Health Psychology, 18*(2), 169–176.

Christiansen, D. M. (2015). Sex differences in PTSD: Mediation and moderation effects. *Comprehensive Guide to Post-Traumatic Stress Disorder,* 1–15. Retrieved from http://link.springer.com/referenceworkentry/10.1007/978-3-319-08613-2_4-1

Chuah, B. L. P. (2006). *The influence of coping and emotional intelligence on psychological adjustment to cancer: A longitudinal study of patients calling a cancer helpline.* Melbourne, Australia: University of Melbourne.

Churilla, J. R., Johnson, T. M., Magyari, P. M., & Crouter, S. E. (2012). Descriptive analysis of resistance exercise and metabolic syndrome. *Diabetes and Metabolic Syndrome: Clinical Research and Reviews, 6*(1), 42–47.

Clark, N. M., Mitchell, H. E., & Rand, C. S. (2009). Effectiveness of educational and behavioral asthma interventions. *Pediatrics, 123*(3), S185–S192.

Clarke, P. J., O'Malley, P. M., & Johnston, L. D. (2009). Differential trends in weight-related health behaviors among American young adults by gender, race/ethnicity, and socioeconomic status: 1984–2006. *American Journal of Public Health, 99*(10), 1893–1901.

Claussnitzer, M., Dankel, S. N., Kim, K-H., Quon, G., Meuleman, W., Haugen, C., ... Kellis, M. (2015). FTO variant circuitry and adipocyte browning in humans. *The New England Journal of Medicine, 373*(10), 895–907.

Clay, R. A. (2016, February). Adventures in integrated care. *Monitor on Psychology, 47*(2), 32–35.

Clement, K., Boutin, P., & Froguel, P. (2002). Genetics of obesity. *American Journal of Pharmacogenomics, 2*(3), 177–187.

CMS. (2015). *NHE fact sheet.* Centers for Medicare and Medicaid Services. Retrieved February 25, 2016, from https://www.cms.gov/research-statistics-data-and-systems/statistics-trends-and-reports/nationalhealthexpenddata/nhe-fact-sheet.html

Coates, T. J., Stall, R. D., & Hoff, C. C. (1990). Changes in sexual behavior among gay and bisexual men since the beginning of the AIDS epidemic. In L. Temoshok & A. Baum (Eds.), *Psychosocial perspectives on AIDS: Etiology, prevention, and treatment* (pp. 103–137). Hillsdale, NJ: Erlbaum.

Cochran, S. D., Mays, V. M., & Sullivan, J. G. (2003). Prevalence of mental disorders, psychological distress, and mental health services use among lesbian, gay, and bisexual adults in the United States. *Journal of Consulting and Clinical Psychology, 71*(1), 53–61.

Cohen, F., Kemeny, M. E., Zegans, L. S., Johnson, P. Kearney, K. A., & Stites, D. P. (2007). Immune function declines with unemployment and recovers after stressor termination. *Psychosomatic Medicine, 69*, 225–234.

Cohen, J. (2006). Infectious disease. At International AIDS Conference, big names emphasize big gaps. *Science, 313*, 1030–1031.

Cohen, J. (2016, June 3). Let smokers see the warning they need. *The New York Times.* Retrieved from http://www.nytimes.com/2016/06/03/opinion/let-smokers-see-the-warning-they-need.html?_r=1

Cohen, L., Marshall, G. D., Cheng, L., Agarwal, S. K., & Wei, Q. (2000). DNA repair capacity in healthy medical students during and after exam stress. *Journal of Behavioral Medicine, 23*, 531–544.

Cohen, R. A., & Martinez, M. E. (2015). Health insurance coverage: Early release of estimates from the National Health Interview Survey, 2014. *National Center for Health Statistics.* Retrieved February 25, 2016, from http://www.cdc.gov/nchs/data/nhis/earlyrelease/insur201506.pdf

Cohen, S. (2004). Social relationships and health. *American Psychologist, 59*, 676–684.

Cohen, S., Alper, C. M., Doyle, W. J., Treanor, J. J., & Turner, R. B. (2006). Positive emotional style predicts resistance to illness after experimental exposure to rhinovirus or influenza A virus. *Psychosomatic Medicine, 68*, 809–815.

Cohen, S., Doyle, W., & Baum, A. (2006). Socioeconomic status is associated with stress hormones. *Psychosomatic Medicine, 68*, 414–420.

Cohen, S., Doyle, W. J., Turner, R., Alper, C. M., & Skoner, D. P. (2003). Sociability and susceptibility to the common cold. *Journal of the American Medical Association, 277*, 1940–1944.

Cohen, S., & Herbert, T. B. (1996). Health psychology: Psychological factors and physical disease from the perspective of human psychoneuroimmunology. *Annual Review of Psychology, 47*, 113–132.

Cohen, S., Janicki-Deverts, D., Doyle, W. J., Miller, G. E., Frank, E., Rabin, B. S., & Turner, R. B. (2012). Chronic stress, glucocorticoid receptor resistance, inflammation, and disease risk. *Proceedings of the National Academy of Sciences, 109*(16), 5995–5999. Retrieved from http://www.pnas.org/content/early/2012/03/26/1118355109.abstract

Cohen, S., & McKay, G. (1984). Social support, stress and the buffering hypothesis: A theoretical analysis. In A. Baum, S. E. Taylor, & J. E. Singer (Eds.), *Handbook of psychology and health* (pp. 253–268). Hillsdale, NJ: Erlbaum.

Cohen, S., Miller, G. E., & Rabin, B. S. (2001). Psychological stress and antibody response to immunization: A critical review of the human literature. *Psychosomatic Medicine, 63*, 7–18.

Cohen, S., & Rodriguez, M. S. (1995). Pathways linking affective disturbances and physical disorders. *Health Psychology, 14*, 374–380.

Cohen, S., Sherrod, D. R., & Clark, M. S. (1986). Social skills and the stress-protective role of social support. *Journal of Personality and Social Psychology, 50*, 963–973.

Cohen, S., & Wills, T. A. (1985). Stress, social support, and the buffering hypothesis. *Psychological Bulletin, 93*, 310–357.

Cole, S. W. (2008). Psychosocial influences on HIV-1 disease progression: Neural, endocrine, and virologic mechanisms. *Psychosomatic Medicine, 70*, 562–568.

Collins, N. L., Dunkel-Schetter, C., Lobel, M., & Scrimshaw, S. C. (1993). Social support in pregnancy: Psychosocial correlates of birth outcomes and postpartum depression. *Journal of Personality and Social Psychology, 65*, 1243–1258.

Commonwealth Fund. (2014). U.S. Health system ranks last among eleven countries on measures of access, equity, quality, efficiency, and healthy lives. Retrieved February 23, 2016, from http://www.commonwealthfund.org/publications/press-releases/2014/jun/us-health-system-ranks-last

Compas, B. E., Barnez, G. A., Malcarne, V., & Worsham, N. (1991). Perceived control and coping with stress: A developmental perspective. *Journal of Social Issues, 47*, 23–34.

Congressional Budget Office (CBO). (2010). Patient protection and the Affordable Care Act. Retrieved February 26, 2010, from http://www.cbo.gov

Conn, V. S. (2010). Depressive symptom outcomes of physical activity interventions. Meta-analysis findings. *Annals of Behavioral Medicine, 39*, 128–138.

Conner, M., Norman, P., & Bell, R. (2002). The theory of planned behavior and healthy eating. *Health Psychology, 21*(2), 194–201.

Connor-Smith, J. K., & Flachsbart, C. (2007). Relations between personality and coping: A meta-analysis. *Journal of Personality and Social Psychology, 93*, 1080–1107.

Conroy, D. E., Hyde, A. L., Doerksen, S. E., & Riebeiro, N. F. (2010). Implicit attitudes and explicit motivation prospectively predict physical activity. *Annals of Behavioral Medicine, 39*, 112–118.

Cooper, M. L. (2006). Does drinking promote risky sexual behavior? A complex answer to a simple question. *Current Directions in Psychological Science, 15*, 19–23.

Cooper, R. S., Rotimi, C. N., & Ward, R. (1999). The puzzle of hypertension in African-Americans. *Scientific American, 280*(2), 56–63.

Cordasco, K. M. (2013). Obtaining informed consent from patients: Brief update. In *Making health care safer II: An updated critical analysis of the evidence for patient safety practices.* Evidence Reports/Technology Assessments, No. 211. Rockville, MD: Agency for Healthcare Research and Quality.

Corelli, R. L., & Hudmon, K. S. (2002). Medications for smoking cessation. *Western Journal of Medicine, 176*(2), 131–135.

Cornally, N., & McCarthy, G. (2011). Chronic pain: The help-seeking behavior, attitudes, and beliefs of older adults living in the community. *Pain Management Nursing, 12*(4), 206–217.

Cornelis, M. C., El-Sohemy, A., Kabagambe, E. K., & Campos, H. (2006). Coffee, CYP1A2 genotype, and risk of myocardial infarction. *Journal of the American Medical Association, 295*(1), 1135–1141.

Costanzo, E. S., Stawski, R. S., Ryff, C. D., Coe, C. L., & Almeida, D. M. (2012). Cancer survivors' responses to daily stressors: Implications for quality of life. *Health Psychology, 31*(3), 360–370.

Costas, R., & Gany, F. (2013). Depressive symptoms in a sample of Afro-Caribbean and Latino immigrant cancer patients: A comparative analysis. *Supportive Care in Cancer, 21*(9), 2461–2468.

Council of Colleges of Acupuncture and Oriental Medicine (CCAOM). (2016). Acupuncture: Frequently asked questions. Retrieved March 2, 2016, from http://www.ccaom.org/faqs.asp

Couturier, J., Kimber, M., & Szatmari, P. (2013). Efficacy of family-based treatment for adolescents with eating disorders: A systematic review and meta-analysis. *International Journal of Eating Disorders, 46*(1), 3–11.

Coyne, J. C., Stefanek, M., & Palmer, S. C. (2007). Psychotherapy and survival in cancer: The conflict between hope and evidence. *Psychological Bulletin, 133*, 367–394.

Coyne, J. C., & Tennen, H. (2010). Positive psychology in cancer care: Bad science, exaggerated claims, and unproven medicine. *Annals of Behavioral Medicine, 39*, 16–26.

Cramer, J. A. (2004). A systematic review of adherence with medications for diabetes. *Diabetes Care, 27*, 1218–1224.

Creswell, J. D., Irwin, M. R., Burklund, L. J., Lieberman, M. D., Arevalo, J. M. G., Ma, J., Breen, E. C., & Cole, S. W. (2012). Mindfulness-based stress reduction training reduces loneliness and pro-inflammatory gene expression in older adults: A small randomized controlled trial. *Brain, Behavior, and Immunity, 26*, 1095–1101.

Creswell, J. D., & Lindsay, E. K. (2014). How does mindfulness training affect health? A mindfulness stress buffering account. *Current Directions in Psychological Science, 23*(6), 401–407.

Creswell, J. D., Myers, H. F., Cole, S. W., & Irwin, M. R. (2009). Mindfulness meditation training effects on CD4+ T lymphocytes in HIV-1 infected adults: A small randomized controlled trial. *Brain, Behavior, & Immunology, 23*(2), 184–188.

Creswell, J. D., Way, B. M., Eisenberger, N. I., & Lieberman, M. D. (2007). Neural correlates of dispositional mindfulness during affect labeling. *Psychosomatic Medicine, 69*, 560–565.

Crews, F., He, J., & Hodge, C. (2007). Adolescent cortical development: A critical period of vulnerability for addiction. *Pharmacology, Biochemistry and Behavior, 86*, 189–199.

Crittenden, C. N., Pressman, S., Cohen, S., Janicki-Deverts, D., Smith, B. W., & Seeman, T. E. (2014). Social integration and pulmonary function in the elderly. *Health Psychology, 33*(6), 535–543.

Crosnoe, R. (2002). Academic and health-related trajectories in adolescence: The intersection of gender and athletics. *Journal of Health and Social Behavior, 43*, 317–335.

Cross, A. J., Ferrucci, L. M., Risch, A., Graubard, B. I., Ward, M. H., Park, Y., … Sinha, R. (2010). A large prospective study of meat consumption and colorectal cancer risk: An investigation of potential mechanisms underlying this association. *Cancer Research, 70*(6), 2406–2414.

Crowe, S., Wu, L. E., Economou, C., Turpin, S. M., Matzaris, M., Hoehn, K. L., Hevener, A. L., James, D. E., Duh, E. J., & Watt, M. J. (2009). Pigment epithelium-derived factor contributes to insulin resistance in obesity. *Cell Metabolism, 10*(1), 40–47.

Cruess, D. G., Antoni, M. H., McGreagor, B. A., Kilbourn, K. M., Boyers, A. E., Alferi, S. M., … Kumar, M. (2000). Cognitive-behavioral stress management reduces serum cortisol by enhancing benefit finding among women being treated for early stage breast cancer. *Psychosomatic Medicine, 62*(3), 304–308.

Cummings, D. E., Foster-Schubert, K. E., & Overduin, J. (2005). Ghrelin and energy balance: Focus on current controversies. *Current Drug Targets, 6*(2), 153–169.

Cvengros, J. A., Christensen, A. J., & Lawton, W. J. (2004). The role of perceived control and preference for control in adherence to a chronic medical regimen. *Annals of Behavioral Medicine, 27*(3), 155–161.

Cyna, A. M., McAuliffe, G. L., & Andrew, M. I. (2004). Hypnosis for pain relief in labour and childbirth: A systematic review. *British Journal of Anaesthesia, 93*(4), 505–511.

Daley, A. (2008). Exercise and depression: A review of reviews. *Journal of Clinical Psychology in Medical Settings, 15*(2), 140–147.

Dallongeville, J., Yarnell, J., Ducimetiere, P., Arveiler, D., Ferrieres, J., Montaye, M., … Amouyel, P. (2003). Fish consumption is associated with lower heart rates. *Circulation, 108*(7), 820–825.

Daly, M., & MacLachlan, M. (2011). Heredity links natural hazards and human health: Apolipoprotein E gene moderates the health of earthquake survivors. *Health Psychology, 30*, 228–235.

Dansinger, M. L., Gleason, J. A., Griffith, J. L., Selker, H. P., & Schaefer, E. J. (2005). Comparison of the Atkins, Ornish, Weight Watchers, and Zone diets for weight loss and heart disease risk reduction. *Journal of the American Medical Association, 293*(1), 43–53.

Dao, T. K., Nagy, A. Y., Armsworth, M., Wear, E., Papathopoulos, K. N., & Gopaldas, R. (2011). Randomized controlled trial of brief cognitive behavioral intervention for depression and anxiety symptoms preoperatively in patients undergoing coronary artery bypass graft surgery. *Journal of Thoracic and Cardiovascular Surgery, 142*(3), e109–e115.

Darbes, L., Crepaz, N., Lyles, C., Kennedy, G., & Rutherford, G. (2008). The efficacy of behavioral interventions in reducing HIV risk behaviors and incident sexually transmitted diseases in heterosexual African Americans. *AIDS* [London, England], *22*(10), 1177–1194.

Daruna, J. H. (2004). *Introduction to psychoneuroimmunology.* Burlington, MA: Elsevier Academic Press.

Das, R. R., Seshadri, S., Beiser, A. S., Kelly-Hayes, M., Au, R., Himali, J. J., … Wolf, P. A. (2008). Prevalence and correlates of silent cerebral infarcts in the Framingham offspring study. *Stroke, 39*, 2929–2935.

Davidson, K. W., Kupfer, D. J., Biggeer, T., Califf, R. M., Carney, R. M., Coyne, J. C., … Suis, J. M. (2006). Assessment and treatment of depression in patients with cardiovascular disease: National Heart, Lung, and Blood Institute working group report. *Psychosomatic Medicine, 68*, 645–650.

Davidson, K. W., Mostofsky, E., & Whang, W. (2010). Don't worry, be happy: Positive affect and reduced 10-year incident coronary heart disease: The Canadian Nova Scotia Health Survey. *European Heart Journal, 31*, 1065–1070.

Davidson, R. J., Kabat-Zinn, J., Schumacher, J., Rosenkranz, M., Muller, D., Santorelli, S. F., … Sheridan, J. F. (2003). Alterations in brain and immune function produced by mindfulness meditation. *Psychosomatic Medicine, 65*(4), 564–570.

Davies, G. M., Willner, P., James, D. L., & Morgan, M. J. (2004). Influence of nicotine gum on acute cravings for cigarettes. *Journal of Psychopharmacology, 18*(1), 83–87.

Davies, N. J., & Batehup, L. (2010). Self-management support for cancer survivors: Guidance for developing interventions. An update of the evidence. *National Cancer Survivorship Initiative.* Retrieved February 27, 2016, from http://www.ncsi.org.uk/wp-content/uploads/Guidance-for-Developing-Cancer-Specific-Self-Management-Programmes.pdf

Davis, C. D., & Uthus, E. O. (2004). DNA methylation, cancer susceptibility, and nutrient interactions. *Experimental Biology and Medicine, 229*(10), 988–995.

Davis, C. L., Temporowski, P. D., McDowell, J. E., Austin, B. P., Miller, P. H., Yanasak, N. E., Allison, J. D., & Nagilieri, J. A. (2011). Exercise improves executive function and achievement and alters brain activation in overweight children: A randomized, controlled trial. *Health Psychology, 30*(1), 91–93.

Davis, K., Stremikis, K., Squires, D., & Schoen, C. (2014). *Mirror, mirror on the wall: How the performance of the U.S. health care system compares internationally.* New York: The Commonwealth Fund. Retrieved April 6, 2016, from http://www.commonwealthfund.org/~/media/files/publications/fund-report/2014/jun/1755_davis_mirror_mirror_2014.pdf

Davis, K. C., Jacques-Tiura, A. J., Stappenbeck, C. A., Danube, C. L., Morrison, D. M., Norris, J., & George, W. H. (2016). Men's condom use resistance: Alcohol effects on Theory of Planned Behavior constructs. *Health Psychology, 35*(2), 178–186.

Davis, K. C., Norris, J., George, W. H., Martell, J., & Heiman, J. R. (2006). Men's likelihood of sexual aggression: The influence of alcohol, sexual arousal, and violent pornography. *Aggressive Behavior, 32*, 581–589.

Davison, K. K., Schmalz, D., & Downs, D. S. (2010). Hop, skip … no! Explaining adolescent girls' disinclination for physical activity. *Annals of Behavioral Medicine, 29*, 290–302.

Dawson, D. A., Grant, B. F., Stinson, F. S., Chou, P. S., Huang, B., & Ruan, W. J. (2005). Recovery from DSM-IV alcohol dependence: United States, 2001–2002. *Addiction, 100*, 281–292.

Dean, A. J., Walters, J., & Hall, A. (2010). A systematic review of interventions to enhance medication adherence in children and adolescents with chronic illness. *Archives of Disease in Childhood, 95*, 717–723.

De Andres, J., & Van Buyten, J. P. (2006). Neural modulation by stimulation. *Pain Practice, 6*, 39–45.

Deichert, N., Fekete, E., Boarts, J., Druley, J., & Delahanty, D. (2008). Emotional support and affect: Associations with health behaviors and active coping efforts in men living with HIV. *AIDS and Behavior, 12*(1), 139–145.

De Jonge, P., & Ormel. J. (2007). Depression and anxiety after myocardial infarction. *British Journal of Psychiatry, 190*, 272–273.

Dekaris, D., Sabioncello, A., Mazuran, R., Rabatic, S., Svoboda-Beusan, I., Racunica, N. L., & Tomasic, J. (1993). Multiple changes of immunologic parameters in prisoners of war. *Journal of the American Medical Association, 270*(5), 595–599.

De la Herrán-Arita, A. K., Kornum, B. R., Mahlios, J., Jiang, W., Lin, L., Hou, T., … Mignot, E. (2013). CD4+ T cell autoimmunity to hypocretin/orexin and cross-reactivity to a 2009 H1N1 influenza A epitope in narcolepsy. *Science Translational Medicine, 5*(216). Retrieved February 25, 2016, from http://stm.sciencemag.org/content/5/216/216ra176

Del Casale, A., Ferracuti, S., Rapinesi, C., De Rossi, P., Angeletti, G., Sani, G., Kotsalidis, G. D., & Girardi, P. (2016). Hypnosis and pain perception: An activation likelihood estimation (ALE) meta-analysis of functional neuroimaging studies. *Journal of Physiology.* Retrieved March 2, 2016, from http://www.sciencedirect.com/science/article/pii/S0928425716300018

Dembner, A. (2005, July 25). A prayer for health: Scientists attempt to measure what religions accept on faith. *The Boston Globe.* Retrieved April 29, 2010, from http://www.boston.com/news/globe/health_science/articles/2005/07/25/a_prayer_for_health

Dement, W. C. (1999). *The promise of sleep.* New York: Delacorte Press.

De Michele, M., Panico, S., Iannuzzi, A., Celentano, E., Ciardullo, A. V., Galasso, R., … Rubba, P. (2002). Association of obesity and central fat distribution with carotid artery wall thickening in middle-aged women. *Stroke, 33*(12), 2923–2928.

Dempsey, M. (2002). Negative coping as mediator in the relation between violence and outcomes: Inner-city African American youth. *American Journal of Orthopsychiatry, 72*(1), 102–109.

Denissenko, M. F., Pao, A., Tang, M., & Pfeifer, G. P. (1996). Preferential formation of benzoapyrene adducts at lung cancer mutational hotspots in P53. *Science, 274*, 430–432.

Dentato, M. P. (2012). The minority stress perspective. *Psychology and AIDS Exchange Newsletter.* Retrieved February 24, 2016, from http://www.apa.org/pi/aids/resources/exchange/2012/04/minority-stress.aspx

DePadilla, L., Windle, M., Wingood, G., Cooper, H., & DiClemente, R. (2011). Condom use among young women: Modeling the theory of gender and power. *Health Psychology, 30*(3), 310–319.

Department for Professional Employees (DPE). (2009). *Fact sheet 2009, Professional women: Vital statistics.* Retrieved February 11, 2010, from http://www.dpeaflcio.org/programs/factsheets/fs_2009_Professional_Women.htm

Department of Health and Human Services. (2015). Body mass index (BMI). Centers for Disease Control and Prevention. Retrieved February 8, 2016, from http://www.cdc.gov/nccdphp/dnpa/bmi/index.htm

Depestele, L., Lemmens, G. M. D., Dierckx, E., Baetens, I., & Claes, L. (2015). The role of non-suicidal self-injury and binge-eating/purging is in the caregiving experience among mothers and fathers of adolescents with eating disorders. *European Eating Disorders Review, 24*(3), 257–260. Retrieved from http://onlinelibrary.wiley.com/doi/10.1002/erv.2428/abstract

de Ridder, D. T. D., Bertha, J., & de Wit, F. (2006). *Self-regulation in health behavior.* Hoboken, NJ: John Wiley.

DeSantis, C., Naishadham, D., & Jemal, A. (2013). Cancer statistics for African Americans, 2013. *CA: A Cancer Journal for Clinicians, 63*(3), 151–166.

Deshpande, S., Basil, M. D., & Basil, D. Z. (2009). Factors influencing healthy eating habits among college students: An application of the health belief model. *Health Marketing Quarterly, 26*(2), 145–164.

Desmeules, J., Piguet, V., Besson, M., Chabert, J., Rapiti, E., Rebsamen, M., … Cedraschi, C. (2012). Psychological distress in fibromyalgia patients: A role for catechol-O-methyl-transferase Va1158Met polymorphism. *Health Psychology, 31*(2), 242–249.

Despres, J.-P., & Lemieux, I. (2006). Abdominal obesity and metabolic syndrome. *Nature, 444*, 881–887.

Dew, M. A., Hoch, C. C., Busse, D. J., Monk, T. H., Begley, A. E., Houck, P. R., Hall, M., Kupfer, D. J., & Reynolds, C. F. (2003). Healthy older adults' sleep predicts all-cause mortality at 4 to 19 years of follow-up. *Psychosomatic Medicine, 65*, 63–73.

Dhabhar, F. S., & McEwen, B. S. (2001). Bidirectional effects of stress and glucocorticoid hormones on immune function: Possible explanations for paradoxical observations. In R. Ader, D. L. Felten, & N. Cohen (Eds.). *Psychoneuroimmunology* (3rd ed.). San Diego: Academic Press.

Dhabhar, F. S., Saul, A. N., Daugherty, C., Holmes, T. H., Bouley, D. M., & Oberysyzn, T. M. (2010). Short-term stress enhances cellular immunity and increases early resistance to squamous cell carcinoma. *Brain, Behavior, and Immunity, 24*(1), 127–137.

Diano, S., Farr, S. A., Benoit, S. C., McNay, E. C., da Silva, I., Horvath, B. ... Horvath, T. L.. (2006). Ghrelin controls hippocampal spine synapse density and memory performance. *Nature Neuroscience, 9*(3), 381–388.

Dickerson, S. S., Gruenewald, T. L., & Kemeny, M. E. (2004). When the social self is threatened: Shame, physiology, and health. *Journal of Personality, 72*(6), 1192–1216.

DiClemente, C. C. (2005, September 28). Alcohol and problem drinking. Retrieved from http://www.apapracticecentral.org/ce/self-care/drinking.aspx

Diehr, P., Bild, D. E., Harris, T. B., Duxbury, A., Siscovick, D., & Rossi, M. (1998). Body mass index and mortality in nonsmoking older adults: The Cardiovascular Health Study. American Journal of Public Health, 88, 623–629.

Diener, E., & Biswas-Diener, R. (2008). The science of optimal happiness. Boston: Blackwell Publishing.

Diener, E., & Chan, M. Y. (2011). Happy people live longer: Subjective well-being contributes to health and longevity. *Applied Psychology: Health and Well-Being, 3*(1), 1–43.

Diez Roux, A. (2001). Investigating area and neighborhood effects on health. *American Journal of Public Health, 91*(11), 1783–1789.

DiFranza, J. R. (2008, May). Hooked from the first cigarette. *Scientific American*, 82–87.

Dillard, A. J., Ferrer, R. A., Ubel, P. A., & Fagerlin, A. (2012). Risk perception measures' associations with behiavor intentions, affect, and cognition following colon cancer screening measures. *Health Psychology, 31*(1), 106–113.

DiMatteo, M. R. (2004). Variations in patients' adherence to medical recommendations: A quantitative review of 50 years of research. *Medical Care, 42*, 200–209.

Dishman, R. K., Berthoud, H-R., Booth, F. W., Cotman, C. W., Edgerton, R., ... & Zigmond, M. J. (2006). Neurobiology of exercise. *Obesity, 14*, 345–356.

Dishman, R. K., Hales, D. P., Pfeifer, K. A., Felton, G., Saunders, R., & Ward, D. S. (2006). Physical self-concept and self-esteem mediate cross-sectional relations of physical activity and sport participation with depression symptoms among adolescent girls. *Health Psychology, 25*, 396–407.

Disis, M. L. (2005). *Immunotherapy of cancer*. New York: Humana Press.

Dobson, K. S. (Ed.). (2010). *Handbook of cognitive behavioral therapies*. New York: Guilford.

Doheny, K. (2009, September 29). Social isolation adversely affects breast cancer. *HealthDay*. Retrieved April 12, 2010, from http://www.mentalhelp.net/poc/view_doc.php?type=news&id=122467&cn=117

Dohrenwend, B. P., Turner, J. B., Turse, N. A., Adams, B. G., Koenen, K. C., & Marshall, R. (2006). The psychological risks of Vietnam for U.S. veterans: A revisit with new data and methods. *Science, 255*, 946–956.

Doll, R., Peto, R., Boreham, J., & Sutherland, I. (2004). Mortality in relation to smoking: 50 years' observations on British male doctors. *British Medical Journal, 328*, 1519–1528.

Donahue, K. L., Lichtenstein, P., Langstrom, N., & D'Onofrio, B. M. (2013). Why does early sexual intercourse predict subsequent maladjustment? Exploring potential familial confounds. *Health Psychology, 32*(2), 180–189.

Doro, P., Benko, R., Matuz, M., & Soos, G. (2006). Seasonality in the incidence of type 2 diabetes: A population-based study. *Diabetes Care, 29*(1), 173–184.

Dorr, N., Brosschot, J. F., Sollers, J. J., & Thayer, J. F. (2007). "Damned if you do, damned if you don't": The differential effect of expression and inhibition of anger on cardiovascular recovery in Black and White males. *International Journal of Psychophysiology, 66*, 125–134.

Dowd, J. B., Palermo, T. M., & Aiello, A. E. (2012). Family poverty is associated with cytomegalovirus antibody titers in U.S. children. *Health Psychology, 31*, 5–10.

Dowd, J. B., Simanek, A. M., & Aiello, A. E. (2009). Socioeconomic status, cortisol and allostatic load: A review of the literature. *International Journal of Epidemiology, 38*(5), 1297–1309.

Dowda, M., Dishman, R. K., Porter, D., Saunders, R. P., & Pate, R. R. (2009). Commercial facilties, social cognitive variables, and physical activity of 12th-grade girls. *Annals of Behavioral Medicine, 37*, 70–87.

Drdla, R., Gassner, M., Gingl, E., & Sandkuhler, J. (2009). Induction of synaptic long-term potentiation after opioid withdrawal. *Science, 325*(5937), 207–210.

Droomers, M., Schrijvers, C. T., & Mackenbach, J. P. (2002). Why do lower educated people continue smoking? Explanations from the longitudinal GLOBE study. *Health Psychology, 21*(3), 263–272.

Drummond, M. B., & Upson, D. (2014). Electronic cigarettes: Potential harms and benefits. *Annals of the American Thoracic Society, 11*(2), 236–242.

Dugdale, D. C., Epstein, R., & Pantilat, S. Z. (1998). Time and patient–physician relationship. *Journal of General Internal Medicine, 14*(Supplement 1), S34–S40.

Dunbar-Jacob, J., & Schlenk, E. A. (2001). Treatment adherence in chronic disease. *Journal of Clinical Epidemiology, 54*, S57–S60.

Dunn, M. J., Rodriguez, E. M., Barnwell, A. S., Grossenbacher, J. C., Vannatta, K., Cerhardt, C. A., & Compas, B. (2012). Posttraumatic stress symptoms in parents of children with cancer within six months of diagnosis. *Health Psychology, 31*(2), 176–185.

Dunton, G. F., & Vaughan, E. (2008). Anticipated affective consequences of physical activity adoption and maintenance. *Health Psychology, 27*, 703–710.

Durazo-Arvizu, R. A., McGee, D. L., Cooper, R. S., Liao, Y., & Luke, A. (1998). Mortality and optimal body mass index in a sample of the U.S. population. *American Journal of Epidemiology, 147*, 739–749.

Durmer, J. S., & Dinges, D. F. (2005). Neurocognitive consequences of sleep deprivation. *Seminars in Neurology, 25*(1), 117–129.

Dye, C. (2014). After 2015: Infectious diseases in a new era of health and development. *Philosophical Transactions of the Royal Society, 369*(1645). Retrieved February 28, 2016, from http://rstb.royalsocietypublishing.org/content/369/1645/20130426

Eaton, D. K., Kann, L., Kinchen, S., Shanklin, S., Ross, J., & Hawkins, J. (2008). Youth risk behavior surveillance—United States,

2007. *Morbidity and Mortality Weekly Report, 57*(SS–4), 1–130.

Ebel-Lam, A. P., MacDonald, T. K., Zanna, M. P., & Fong, G. T. (2009). An experimental investigation of the interactive effects of alcohol and sexual arousal on intentions to have unprotected sex. *Basic and Applied Social Psychology, 31*, 226–233.

Ebert, M. H., & Kerns, R. D. (Eds.). (2010). *Behavioral and psychopharmacologic pain management.* Cambridge, UK: Cambridge University Press.

Edgar, L., Rossberger, Z., & Nowlis, D. (1992). Coping with cancer during the first year after diagnosis: Assessment and intervention. *Cancer, Diagnosis, Treatment, Research, 69*, 817–828.

Edmondson, D., & Cohen, B. E. (2013). Posttraumatic stress disorder and cardiovascular disease. *Progress in Cardiovascular Disease, 55*(6), 548–556.

Edwards, L. (2013, March 16). The gender gap in pain. *The New York Times.* Retrieved March 1, 2016, from http://www.nytimes.com/2013/03/17/opinion/sunday/women-and-the-treatment-of-pain.html?_r=0

Edwards, L. M., & Romero, A. J. (2008). Coping with discrimination among Mexican-descent adolescents. *Hispanic Journal of Behavioral Sciences, 30*, 24–39.

Edwards, R. R., Bingham, C. O., Bathon, J., & Haythornthwaite, J. A. (2006). Catastrophizing and pain in arthritis, fibromyalgia, and other rheumatic diseases. *Arthritis & Rheumatism, 55*(2), 325–332.

Edwards, R. R., Campbell, C., Jamison, R. N., & Wiech, K. (2009a). The neurobiological underpinnings of coping with pain. *Current Directions in Psychological Science, 18*, 237–241.

Edwards, R. R., Grace, E., Peterson, S., Klick, B., Haythornthwaite, J. A., & Smith, M. T. (2009b). Sleep continuity and architecture: Associations with pain-inhibitory processes in patients with temporomandibular joint disorder. *European Journal of Pain, 10*, 1043–1047.

Edwards, R. R., Kronfli, T., Haythornthwaite, J. A., Smith, M. T., McGuire, L., & Page, G. G. (2008) Association of catastrophizing with interleukin-6 responses to acute pain. *Pain, 140*(1), 135–144.

Egbert, L. D., Battit, C. E., Welch, C. E., & Bartlett, M. K. (1964). Reduction of postoperative pain by encouragement and instruction of patients. A study of doctor-patient rapport. *New England Journal of Medicine, 75*, 1008–1023.

Ehde, D. M., Dillworth, T. M., & Turner, J. A. (2014). Cognitive-behavioral therapy for individuals with chronic pain. *American Psychologist, 69*(2), 153–166.

Eisenberg, D. M. (1997). Advising patients who use alternative medical therapies. *Annals of Internal Medicine, 127*, 61–69.

Eisenberg, D. M., Davis, R. B., Ettner, S. L., Appel, S., Wilkey, S., Van Rompay, M., & Kessler, R. C. (1998). Trends in alternative medicine use in the United States, 1990–1997: Results of a follow-up national survey. *Journal of the American Medical Association, 280*, 1569–1575.

Eisenberg, D. M., Delbanco, T. L., Berkey, C. S., Kaptchuk, T. J., Kupelnick, B., Kuhl, J., & Chalmers, T. C. (1993). Cognitive behavioral techniques for hypertension: Are they effective? *Annals of Internal Medicine, 118*(12), 964–972.

Elfhag, K., & Rossner, S. (2005). Who succeeds in maintaining weight loss? A conceptual review of factors associated with weight loss maintenance and weight regain. *Obesity Review, 6*(1), 67–85.

Eller, N. H., Netterstrom, B., & Hansen, A. M. (2006). Psychosocial factors at home and at work and levels of salivary cortisol. *Biological Psychology, 73*, 280–287.

Emmons, R. A., & McCullough, M. E. (2003). Personality processes and individual differences—counting blessings versus burdens: An experimental investigation of gratitude and subjective well-being in daily life. *Journal of Personality & Social Psychology, 84*(2), 377–389.

Eng, P. M., Fitzmaurice, G., Kubzansky, L. D., Rimm, E. B., & Kawachi, I. (2003). Anger expression and risk of stroke and coronary heart disease among male health professionals. *Psychosomatic Medicine, 65*(1), 100–110.

Epel, E. S., Blackburn, E. H., Lin, J., Dhabhar, F. S., Adler, N. E., Morrow, J. D., & Cawtho, R. M. (2004). Accelerated telomere shortening in response to life stress. *Proceedings of the National Academy of Sciences, 101*(49), 17312–17315.

Epping-Jordan, J. E., Compas, B. E., Osowiecki, D. M., Oppedisano, G., Gerhardt, C., Primo, K., & Krag, D. N. (1999). Psychological adjustment in breast cancer: Processes of emotional distress. *Health Psychology, 18*, 315–326.

Epps, C., & Holt, L. (2011). The genetic basis of addiction and relevant cellular mechanisms. *International Anesthesiology Clinics, 49*(1), 3–14.

Epstein, L. H., Jankowiak, N., Nederkoorn, C., Raynor, H. A., French, S. A., & Finkelstein, E. (2012). Experimental research on the relation between food price changes and food-purchasing patterns: A targeted review. *American Journal of Clinical Nutrition, 95*(4), 789–809.

Epstein, L. H., Lin, H., Carr, K. A., & Fletcher, K. D. (2011). Food reinforcement and obesity: Psychological moderators. *Appetite, 58*, 157–162.

Epstein-Lubow, G. P., Miller, I. W., & McBee, L. (2006). Mindfulness training for caregivers. *Psychiatric Services, 57*(3), 421.

Eriksen, W. (2004). Do people who were passive smokers during childhood have increased risk of long-term work disability? A 15-month prospective study of nurses' aides. *European Journal of Public Health, 14*(3), 296–300.

Ernst, E., & Canter, P. H. (2006). A systematic review of systematic reviews of spinal manipulation. *Journal of the Royal Society of Medicine, 99*(4), 192–196.

Ernst, K. K., Pittler, E. E., Wider, B., & Boddy, K. (2007). Acupuncture: Its evidence-base is changing. *American Journal of Chinese Medicine, 35*(1), 21–25.

Ervin, R. B. (2009). Prevalence of metabolic syndrome among adults 20 years of age and over, by sex, age, race and ethnicity, and body mass index: United States, 2003–2006. *National Health Statistics Reports, 5*(13) 1–7.

Ervin, R. B., Kit, B. K., Carroll, M. D., & Ogden, C. L. (2012). Consumption of added sugar among U.S. children and adolescents, 2005–2008. *NCHS data brief, no. 87.* Hyattsville, MD: National Center for Health Statistics.

Ervin, R. B., & Ogden, C. L. (2013). Trends in intake of energy and macronutrients in children and adolescents from 1999–2000 through 2009–2010. *NCHS data brief, no. 113.* Hyattsville, MD: National Center for Health Statistics.

Evans, J., Frank, B., Oliffe, J. L., & Gregory, D. (2011, March). Health, illness, men and masculinities (HIMM): A theoretical framework for understanding men and their health. *American Journal of Men's Health, 8*(1), 7–15.

Evans, R. I. (2003). Some theoretical models and constructs generic to substance abuse prevention programs for adolescents: Possible relevance and limitations for problem gambling. *Journal of Gambling Studies, 19*(3), 287–302.

Evans, W. D., Powers, A., Hersey, J., & Renaud, J. (2006). The influence of social environment and social image on adolescent smoking. *Health Psychology, 25*, 26–33.

Everett, M. D., Kinser, A. M., & Ramsey, M. W. (2007). Training for old age: Production functions for the aerobic exercise inputs. *Medicine and Science in Sports and Exercise, 39,* 2226–2233.

Everitt, B. J., & Heberlein, U. (2013). Addiction. *Current Opinion in Neurobiology. 4,* 463–466.

Everson, S. A., Goldberg, D. E., Kaplan, G. A., & Cohen, R. D. (1996). Hopelessness and risk of mortality and incidence of myocardial infarction and cancer. *Psychosomatic Medicine, 58,* 113–121.

Fabes, R. A., & Eisenberg, N. (1997). Regulatory control and adults' stress-related responses to daily life events. *Journal of Personality and Social Psychology, 73*(5), 1107–1117.

Fabes, R. A., Eisenberg, N., Karbon, M., Troyer, D., & Switzer, J. (1994). The relations of children's emotion regulation to their vicarious emotional responses and comforting behaviors. *Child Development, 65,* 1678–1693.

Fabian D., & Flatt T. (2011). The evolution of aging. *Nature Education Knowledge, 2,* 9.

Fagerlin, A., Zikmund-Fisher, B. J., Nair, V., Derry, H. A., McClure, J. B., Greene, S., & Ubel, P. A. (2010). Women's decisions regarding tamoxifen for breast cancer prevention: Responses to a tailored decision aid. *Breast Cancer Research & Treatment, 119,* 613–620.

Fagundes, C. P., Bennett, J. M., Alfano, C. M, Glaser, R., Povoski, S. P., Lipari, A. M., … Kiecolt-Glaser, J. K. (2012). Social support and socioeconomic status interact to predict Epstein-Barr virus latency in women awaiting diagnosis or newly diagnosed with breast cancer. *Health Psychology, 31*(1), 11–19.

Fagundes, C. P., Bennett, J. M., Derry, H. M., & Kiecolt-Glaser, J. K. (2011). Relationships and inflammation across the lifespan: Social developmental pathways to disease. *Social and Personality Psychology Compass, 5*(11), 891–903.

Fagundes, C. P., Glaser, R., Malarkey, W. B., & Kiecolt-Glaser, J. K. (2013). Childhood adversity and Herpesvirus latency in breast cancer survivors. *Health Psychology, 32*(3), 337–344.

Fairburn, C. G. (2005). Evidence-based treatment of anorexia nervosa. *International Journal of Eating Disorders, 37*(Suppl.), S26–S30.

Fairburn, C. G., & Wilson, G. T. (1993). Binge eating: Definition and classification. In C. G. Fairburn & G. T. Wilson (Eds.), *Binge eating: Nature, assessment, and treatment* (pp. 3–14). New York: Guilford.

Fairhurst, M., Weich, K., Dunckley, P., & Tracey, I. (2007). Anticipatory brainstem activity predicts neural processing of pain in humans. *Pain, 128,* 101–110.

Falk, E. B., Berkman, E. T., Whalen, D., & Lieberman, M. D. (2011). Neural activity during health messaging predicts reductions in smoking above and beyond self-report. *Health Psychology, 30*(2), 177–185.

Farzadegan, H., Hoover, D. R., Astemborski, J., Lyles, C. M., Margolick, J. B., Markham, R. B., … Vlahov, D. (1998). Sex differences in HIV-1 viral load and progression to AIDS. *The Lancet, 352,* 1510–1514.

Fasce, N. (2008). Depression and social support among men and women living with HIV. *Journal of Applied Biobehavioral Research, 12*(3), 221–236.

Fasoli, D. R. (2010). The culture of nursing engagement: A historical perspective. *Nursing Administration Quarterly, 34*(1), 18–29.

Fava, M., Copeland, P. M., Schweiger, U., & Herzog, D. B. (1989). Neurochemical abnormalities of anorexia nervosa and bulimia nervosa. *American Journal of Psychiatry, 146,* 963–971.

Fechir, M., Breimhorst, M., Kritzmann, S., Geber, C., Schlereth, T., Baier, B., & Birklein, F. (2012). Naloxone inhibits not only stress-induced analgesia but also sympathetic activation and baroreceptor-reflex sensitivity. *European Journal of Pain, 16*(1), 82–92.

Feifer, C., & Tansman, M. (1999). Promoting psychology in diabetes primary care. *Professional Psychology: Research and Practice, 30,* 14–21.

Feldman, P. J., & Steptoe, A. (2004). How neighborhoods and physical functioning are related: The roles of neighborhood socioeconomic status, perceived neighborhood strain, and individual health risk factors. *Annals of Behavioral Medicine, 27*(2), 91–99.

Fell, J. C., Fisher, D. A., Voas, R. B., Blackman, K., & Tippetts, A. S. (2011). The relationship of underage drinking laws to reductions in drinking drivers in fatal crashes in the United States. *Accident Analysis & Prevention, 40,* 1430–1440.

Fellowes, D., Barnes, K., & Wilkinson, S. (2004). Aromatherapy and massage for symptom relief in patients with cancer. *Cochrane Database of Systematic Reviews (Online), 2004*(2): CD002287.

Ferguson, J., Bauld, L., Chesterman, J., & Judge, K. (2005). The English smoking treatment services: One-year outcomes. *Addiction, 100*(Supplement 2), 59–69.

Fernandez-Mendoza, J., Vela-Bueno, A., Vgontzas, A. N., Ramos-Platon, M. J., Olavarrieta-Bernardono, S., Bixler, E. O., & de la Cruz-Troca, J. J. (2010). Cognitive-emotional hyperarousal as a premorbid characteristic of individuals vulnerable to insomnia. *Psychosomatic Medicine, 72,* 397–403.

Ferran, L. (2010, February 9). Michelle Obama: "Let's Move" initiative battles childhood obesity. Retrieved from http://abcnews.go.com/GMA/Health/michelle-obama-chldhood-obesity;initiative/story?id=9781473

Ferrieres, J. (2004). The French paradox: Lessons for other countries. *Heart, 90*(1), 107–111.

Ferris, P. A., Kline, T. J. B., & Bourdage, J. S. (2012). He said, she said: Work, biopsychosocial, and lifestyle contributions to coronary heart disease risk. *Health Psychology, 31*(4), 503–511.

Festinger, L. (1957). *A theory of cognitive dissonance.* Stanford, CA: Stanford University Press.

Feuerstein, M., & Beattie, P. (1995). Biobehavioral factors affecting pain and disability in low back pain: Mechanisms and assessment. *Physical Therapy, 75,* 267–280.

Fiatarone, M. A., O'Neill, E. F., Doyle, N., Clements, K. M., Roberts, S. B., Kehayias, J. J., Lipsitz, L. A., & Evans, W. J. (1993). The Boston FICSIT study: The effects of resistance training and nutritional supplementation on physical frailty in the oldest old. *Journal of the American Geriatrics Society, 41,* 333–337.

Fikke, L. T., Melinder, A., & Landro, N. I. (2011). Executive functions are impaired in adolescents engaging in non-suicidal self-injury. *Psychological Medicine, 41,* 601–610.

Fiksenbaum, L., Greenglass, E., & Eaton, J. (2006). Perceived social support, hassles, and coping among the elderly. *Journal of Applied Gerontology, 25*(1), 17–30.

Filbey, F. M., Aslan, S., Calhoun, V. D., Spence, J. S., Damaraju, E., Caprihan, A., & Segall, J. (2014). *Proceedings of the National Academy of Sciences, 111*(47), 16913–16918.

Fillingim, R. B. (2000). Sex, gender, and pain: Women and men really are different. *Current Review of Pain, 4,* 24–30.

Fincham, F. D., & Beach, S. R. H. (2010). Marriage in the new millennium: A decade in review. *Journal of Marriage and Family, 72,* 630–649.

Fiore, M. C. (2000). A clinical practice guideline for treating tobacco use and dependence. *Journal of the American Medical Association, 283*(24), 3244–3254.

Fiore, M. C., Smith, S. S., Jorenby, D. E., & Baker, T. B. (1994). The effectiveness of the nicotine patch for smoking cessation: A meta-analysis. *Journal of the American Medical Association, 271*, 1940–1947.

Fisher, J. A., & Kalbaugh, C. A. (2011). Challenging assumptions about minority participation in U.S. clinical research. *American Journal of Public Health, 101*(12), 2217–2222.

Fitzgerald, S. T., Haythornthwaite, J. A., Suchday, S., & Ewart, C. K. (2003). Anger in young black and white workers: Effects of job control, dissatisfaction, and support. *Journal of Behavioral Medicine, 26*, 283–296.

Fjorback, L. O., Arendt, M., Ornbol, E., Fink, P., & Walach, H. (2011). Mindfulness-based stress reduction and mindfulness-based cognitive therapy: A systematic review of randomized controlled trials. *Acta Psychiatrica Scandinavica, 124*, 102–119.

Flack, J. M., Sica, D. A., Bakris, G., Brown, A. L., Ferdinand, K. C., Grimm, R. H., ... Jamerson, K. A. (2010). Management of high blood pressure in blacks: An update of the International Society on Hypertension in Blacks Consensus Statement. *Hypertension, 56*, 780–800.

Flor, H. (2014). Psychological pain interventions and neurophysiology. *American Psychologist, 69*(2), 188–196.

Floyd, A., & Moyer, A. (2010). Group versus individual exercise interventions for women with breast cancer: A meta-analysis. *Health Psychology Review, 4*, 22–41.

Floyd, D. L., Prentice-Dunn, S., & Rogers, R. W. (2000), A meta-analysis of research on protection motivation theory. *Journal of Applied Social Psychology, 30*, 407–429.

Fogel, J., Albert, S. M., Schnabel, F., Ditkoff, B. A., & Neugut, A. I. (2002). Internet use and social support in women with breast cancer. *Health Psychology, 21*(4), 398–404.

Folsom, A. R. (2001). Hemostatic risk factors for atherothrombotic disease: An epidemiologic view. *Thrombosis and Haemostasis, 86*(1), 366–373.

Ford, E. S. (2002). Does exercise reduce inflammation? Physical activity and C-reactive protein among U.S. adults. *Epidemiology, 13*, 561–569.

Fordyce, W. E. (1982). A behavioural perspective on chronic pain. *British Journal of Clinical Psychology, 21*, 313–320.

Forman, T. A. (2002). The social psychological costs of racial segmentation in the workplace: A study of African Americans' well-being. *Journal of Health and Social Behavior, 44*(3), 332–352.

Fortmann, A. L., Gallo, L. C., & Philis-Tsimikas, A. (2011). Glycemic control among Latinos with Type 2 diabetes: The role of social-environmental support resources. *Health Psychology, 30*(3), 251–258.

Fox, S., & Duggan, M. (2013, January 15). Health online 2013. *Pew Internet and American Life Project*. Retrieved from http://www.pewinternet.org/Reports/2013/Health-online/Summary-of-Findings.aspx

Foxhall, K. (2001). Preventing relapse. *Monitor on Psychology, 32*(special issue on substance abuse), 46–47.

Frankenhaeuser, M. (1975). Sympathetic-adreno-medullary activity behavior and the psychosocial environment. In P. H. Venables & M. J. Christie (Eds.), *Research in psychophysiology* (pp. 71–94). New York: Wiley.

Frankenhaeuser, M. (1991). The psychophysiology of workload, stress, and health: Comparison between the sexes. *Annals of Behavioral Medicine, 13*, 197–204.

Franko, D. L., Striegel-Moore, R. H., Bean, J., Tamer, R., Kraemer, H. C., Dohm, F. A., ... Daniels, S. R. (2005). Psychosocial and health consequences of adolescent depression in black and white young adult women. *Health Psychology, 24*, 586–593.

Fraser-Smith, N., & Lesperance, F. (2005). Reflections on depression as a cardiac risk factor. *Psychosomatic Medicine, 67*(Supplement 1), S19–S25.

Frayling, T. M., Timpson, N. J., Weedon, M. N., Zeggini, E., Freathy, R. M., Lindgren, C. M., ... McCarthy, M. I. (2007). A common variant in the FTO gene is associated with body mass index and predisposes to childhood and adult obesity. *Science, 316*, 889–894.

Frederickson, B. L. (2001). The role of positive emotions in positive psychology: The broaden-and-build theory of positive emotions. *American Psychologist, 56*, 218–226.

Fredrickson, B. L., Tugade, M. M., Waugh, C. E., & Larkin, G. R. (2003). What good are positive emotions in crises? A prospective study of resilience and emotions following the terrorist attacks on the United States on September 11, 2001. *Journal of Personality and Social Psychology, 84*, 365–376.

Freid, V. M., Bernstein, A. B., & Bush, M. A. (2012). Multiple chronic conditions among adults aged 45 and over: Trends over the past 10 years. *NCHS data brief, no. 100.* Hyattsville, MD: National Center for Health Statistics.

Freking, K. (2006, August 30). Rise in obesity weighs on health care experts. *The Detroit News*. Retrieved from http://www.detroitnews.com

Frenn, M., & Malin, S. (2003, October 24). Obesity risk factor: Access to low-fat foods increases health eating among adolescents. *Drug Week*, 273.

Frerichs, R. R. (2000). *John Snow: A portrait*. UCLA Department of Epidemiology. Retrieved from http://www.ph.ucla.edu/epi/snow.html

Friedman, M., Camoin, L., Faltin, Z., Rosenblum, C. I., Kallouta, V., Eshdat, Y., & Strosberg, A. D. (2003). Serum leptin activity in obese and lean patients. *Regulatory Peptides, 11*(1), 77–82.

Friedman, M., & Rosenman, R. H. (1959). Association of specific overt pattern with blood and cardiovascular findings. *Journal of the American Medical Association, 169*, 1286–1296.

Friedman, R., McCarthy, D., Förster, J., & Denzler, M. (2005). Automatic effects of alcohol cues on sexual attraction. *Addiction, 100*(5), 672–681.

Fries, J. F. (2001). *Living well: Taking care of your health in the middle and later years*. New York: Perseus Publishing.

Frisina, P. G., Borod, J. C., & Lepore, S. J. (2004). A meta-analysis of the effects of written emotional disclosure on the health outcomes of clinical populations. *Journal of Nervous and Mental Disease, 192*, 629–634.

Fritsch, G., & Hitzig, E. (1870). On the electrical excitability of the cerebrum. Translation in Von Bonin, G. (1960). *Some papers on the cerebral cortex*. Springfield, IL: Charles C Thomas.

Fryar, C. D., Carroll, M. D., & Ogden, C. L. (2014). *Prevalence of overweight, obesity, and extreme obesity among adults: United States, trends 1960-1962 through 2011-2012*. Hyattsville, MD: Centers for Disease Control and Prevention. National Center for Health Statistics.

Fryar, C. D., & Ervin, R. B. (2013). Caloric intake from fast food among adults: United States, 2007–2010. *NCHS data brief, no. 114.* Hyattsville, MD: National Center for Health Statistics.

Fryar, C. D., Hirsch, R., Eberhardt, M. S., Yoon, S. S., & Wright, J. D. (2010). Hypertension, high serum total cholesterol, and diabetes: Racial and ethnic prevalence differences in U.S. adults, 1999–2006. *NCHS data brief, no. 36.* Hyattsville, MD: National Center for Health Statistics.

Fugh-Berman, A. (2000). Herb-drug interactions. *The Lancet, 355*(9198), 134–138.

Gaissmaier, W., Wegwarth, O., Skopec, E., Muller, A., Broschinski, S., & Politi, M. C. (2012). Numbers can be worth a thousand pictures: Individual differences in understanding graphical and numerical representations of health-related information. *Health Psychology, 31*(3), 286–296.

Gajilan, A. C. (2008). Iraq vets and post-traumatic stress: No easy answers. *The Utah Veteran*. Retrieved October 19, 2010, from http://www.utvet.com/IraqVet&PTSD.htm

Galdas, P. M., Cheater, F., & Marshall, P. (2005). Men and health help-seeking behavior: Literature review. *Journal of Advanced Nursing, 49*, 616–623.

Galea, S., Nandi, A., & Vlahov, D. (2005). The epidemiology of post-traumatic stress disorder after disasters. *Epidemiologic Reviews, 27*(1), 78–91.

Gallagher, M. (2006). Examining the impact of food deserts on public health in Chicago. Retrieved April 25, 2016, from http://www.marigallagher.com/site_media/dynamic/project_files/Chicago_Food_Desert_Report.pdf

Gallo, L. C., & Matthews, K. A. (2003). Understanding the association between socioeconomic status and physical health: Do negative emotions play a role? *Psychological Bulletin, 129*, 10–51.

Gallucci, W. T., Baum, A., & Laue, L. (1993). Sex differences in sensitivity of the hypothalamic-pituitary-adrenal axis. *Health Psychology, 12*, 420–425.

Galvan, F., Davis, E., Banks, D., & Bing, E. (2008). HIV stigma and social support among African Americans. *AIDS Patient Care and Standards, 22*(5), 423–436.

Gangwisch, J. E., Babiss, L. A., Malaspina, D., Turner, J. B., Zammit, G. K., & Posner, K. (2010). Earlier parental set bedtimes as a protective factor against depression and suicidal ideation. *Sleep, 33*(1), 97–106.

Garbarino, J. (1991). The context of child abuse and neglect assessment. In J. C. Westman (Ed.), *Who speaks for the children? The handbook of individual and class child advocacy* (pp. 183–203). Sarasota, FL: Professional Resource Exchange.

Garcia, J., Simon, M. A., Duran, M., Canceller, J., & Aneiros, F. J. (2006). Differential efficacy of a cognitive-behavioral intervention versus pharmacological treatment in the management of fibromyalgic syndrome. *Psychology, Health, and Medicine, 11*, 498–506.

García Coll, C., & Marks, A. K. (2012). *The immigrant paradox in children and adolescents: Is becoming American a developmental risk?* Washington, DC: American Psychological Association.

Garcia-Perez, L. E., Alvarez, M., Dilla, T., Gil-Guillen, V., & Orozco-Beltran, D. (2013). Adherence to therapies in patients with type 2 diabetes. *Diabetes Therapy, 4*(2), 175–194.

Garcia-Retamero, R., & Galesic, M. (2010a). How to reduce the effects of framing on messages about health. *Journal of General Internal Medicine, 25*, 1323–1329.

Garcia-Retamero, R., & Galesic, M. (2010b). Statistical numeracy for health: A cross-cultural comparison with probabilistic national samples. *Archives of Internal Medicine, 170*, 462–468.

Gard, T., Holzel, B. K., Sack, A. T., Hempel, H., Lazar, S. W., Vaitl, D., & Ott, U. (2011). Pain attenuation through mindfulness is associated with decreased cognitive control and increased sensory processing in the brain. *Cerebral Cortex*. Retrieved from http://cercor.oxfordjournals.org/content/early/2011/12/14/cercor.bhr352.full.pdf+html

Gardea, M. A., Gatchel, R. J., & Robinson, R. C. (2004). Complementary health care. In T. J. Boll, R. G. Frank, A. Baum, & J. L. Wallander (Eds.), *Handbook of clinical health psychology, Volume 3: Models and perspectives in health psychology* (pp. 341–375). Washington, DC: American Psychological Association.

Gatchel, R. J. (1997). Biofeedback. In A. Baum, S. Newman, J. Weinman, R. West, & C. McManus (Eds.), *Cambridge handbook of psychology, health, and medicine* (pp. 197–199). Cambridge, UK: Cambridge University Press.

Gatchel, R. J., & Maddrey, A. M. (2004). The biopsychosocial perspective of pain. In J. M. Raczynski & L. C. Leviton. *Handbook of clinical health psychology, Volume 2: Disorders of behavior and health* (pp. 357–378). Washington, DC: American Psychological Association.

Gatchel, R. J., Peng, Y. B., Peters, M. L., Fuchs, P. N., & Turk, D. C. (2007). The biopsychosocial approach to chronic pain: Scientific advances and future directions. *Psychological Bulletin, 133*, 581–624.

Gaylord, S. A., Palsson, O. S., Garland, E. L., Faurot, K. R., Coble, R. S., Mann, J. D., … Whitehead, W. E. (2011). Mindfulness training reduces the severity of irritable bowel syndrome in women: A randomized controlled trial. *American Journal of Gastroenterology, 106*, 1678–1688.

Gaynes, B. N., Pence, B. W., Eron, J. J., & Miller, W. C. (2008). Prevalence and comorbidity of psychiatric diagnoses based on reference standard in an HIV+ patient population. *Psychosomatic Medicine, 70*, 505–511.

GBD. (2015). Global burden of disease. *Institute for Health Metrics and Evaluation*. Retrieved from http://www.healthdata.org/sites/default/files/files/Projects/GBD/GBDcause_list.pdf

Gebel, E. (2013). Diabetes distress. *Diabetes forecast*. American Diabetes Association. Retrieved February 26, 2016, from http://www.diabetes.org/living-with-diabetes/complications/mental-health/diabetes-distress.html

Gee, G. C., & Payne-Sturges, D. C. (2004). Environmental health disparities: A framework integrating psychosocial and environmental concepts. *Environmental Health Perspectives, 112*, 1645–1653.

Geier, A. B., Roin, P., & Doros, G. (2006). Unit bias: A new heuristic that helps explain the effects of portion size on food intake. *Psychological Science, 17*, 521–525.

Gelman, A., Miller, E., Schwarz, E. B., Akers, A. Y., Jeong, K., & Borrero, S. (2013). Racial disparities in human papillomavirus vaccination: Does access matter? *Journal of Adolescent Health, 53*(6), 756–762.

Gerend, M. A., Shepherd, M. A., & Shepherd, J. E. (2013). The multidimensional nature of perceived barriers: Global versus practical barriers to HPV vaccination. *Health Psychology, 32*(4), 361–369.

Gerin, W., Zawadzki, M. J., Brosschot, J. F., Thayer, J. F., Christenfeld, N. J. S., Campbell, T. S., & Smyth, J. M. (2012). Rumination as a mediator of chronic stress effects on hypertension: A causal model. *International Journal of Hypertension*. Retrieved February 26, 2016, from http://www.ncbi.nlm.nih.gov/pmc/articles/PMC3296188/

Gevirtz, R. (2013). The promise of heart rate variability biofeedback: Evidence-based applications. *Biofeedback, 41*(3), 110–120.

Gevirtz, R. (2015). Integrating heart rate variability biofeedback into mindfulness-based therapies. *Association for Applied Psychophysiology & Biofeedback, 43*(3), 129–132.

Gianaros, P. J., & Manuck, S. B. (2010). Neurobiological pathways linking socioeconomic position and health. *Psychosomatic Medicine, 72*, 450–461.

Gibbons, F. X., Etcheverry, P. E., Stock, M. L., Gerrard, M., Weng, C., & O'Hara, R. (2010). Exploring the link between racial discrimination and substance use: What mediates and what buffers? *Journal of Personality and Social Psychology, 99*, 785–801.

Gibbons, F. X., Gerrard, M., Blanton, H., & Russell, D. W. (1998). Reasoned action and social reaction: Willingness and intention as independent predictors of health risk. *Journal of Personality and Social Psychology, 74*, 1164–1180.

Gibbs, W. W. (1996). Gaining on fat. *Scientific American, 275*, 88–95.

Giedzinska, A. S., Meyerowitz, B. E., Ganz, P. A., & Rowland, J. H. (2004). Health-related quality of life in a multiethnic sample of breast cancer survivors. *Annals of Behavioral Medicine, 28*(1), 39–51.

Gilbert, C., & Moss, D. (2003). Biofeedback and biological monitoring. In D. Moss, A. McGrady, T. Davies, & I. Wickramasekera (Eds), *Handbook of mind-body medicine for primary care* (pp. 109–122). Thousand Oaks, CA: Sage Publications.

Gill, J. M., Saligan, K., Woods, S., & Page, G. (2009). PTSD is associated with an excess of inflammatory immune activities. *Perspectives in Psychiatric Care, 45*(4), 262–277.

Gilliam, W., Burns, J. W., Quartana, P., Matsuura, J., Nappi, C., & Wolff, B. (2010). Interactive effects of catastrophizing and suppression on responses to acute pain: A test of an appraisal x emotion regulation model. *Journal of Behavioral Medicine, 33*, 191–199.

Gillies, C. L., Abrams, K. R., Lambert, P. C., Cooper, N. J., Sutton, A. J., & Hsu, R. T. (2007). Pharmacological and lifestyle interventions to prevent or delay Type 2 diabetes in people with impaired glucose tolerance: Systematic review and meta-analysis. *British Medical Journal, 334*, 299–302.

Gilman, J. M., Kuster, J. K., & Breiter, H. C. (2014). Cannabis use is quantitatively associated with nucleus accumbens and amygdala abnormalities in young adult recreational users. *Journal of Neuroscience, 34*(16), 5529–5538.

Giltay, E. J., Geleijnse, J. M., Zitman, F. G., Buijsse, B., & Kromhout, D. (2007). Lifestyle and dietary correlates of dispositional optimism: The Zutphen Elderly Study. *Journal of Psychosomatic Research, 63*, 483–490.

Giltay, E. J., Kamphuis, M. H., Kalmijn, S., Zitman, F. G., & Kromhout, D. (2006). Dispositional optimism and the risk of cardiovascular death: The Zutphen Elderly Study. *Archives of Internal Medicine, 166*, 431–436.

Glanz, K., Geller, A. C., Shigaki, D., Maddock, J. E., & Isnec, M. R. (2002). A randomized trial of skin cancer prevention in aquatic settings: The PoolCool program. *Health Psychology, 21*(6), 579–587.

Glaser, R., Kiecolt-Glaser, J. K., Bonneau, R. H., Malarkey, W., Kennedy, S., & Hughes, J. (1992). Stress-induced modulation of the immune response to recombinant hepatitis B vaccine. *Psychosomatic Medicine, 54*(1), 22–29.

Glass, D. C., & Singer, J. E. (1972). *Urban stress: Experiments on noise and social stressors.* New York: Academic Press.

Glassman, A. H. (2007). Depression and cardiovascular comorbidity. *Dialogues in Clinical Neuroscience, 9*(1), 9–17.

Glassman, A. H., Bigger, J. T., Gaffney, M., & Van Zyl, L. T. (2007). Heart rate variability in acute coronary syndrome patients with major depression, influence of sertraline and mood improvement. *Archives of General Psychiatry, 64*(9), 1025–1031.

Glenn, B. A., Bastani, R., Maxwell, A. E., Mojica, C. M., Herrmann, A. K., Gallardo, N. V., Swanson, K. A., & Change, L. C. (2012). *Health Psychology, 31*(5), 562–570.

Global Industry Analysts. (2016). *Pain management: A global strategic business report.* Retrieved March 1, 2016, from http://www.strategyr.com/Pain_Management_Market_Report.asp

Glombiewski, J. A., Sawyer, A. T., Gutermann, J., Koenig, K., Rief, W., & Hoffmann, S. G. (2010). Psychological treatments for fibromyalgia: A meta-analysis. *Pain, 151*(2), 280–295.

Glover, D. A., Williams, J. K., & Kisler, K. A. (2013). Using novel methods to examine stress among HIV-positive African American men who have sex with men and women. *Journal of Behavioral Medicine, 36*, 283–294.

Gluck, M. E., Geliebter, A., Hung, J., & Yahav, E. (2004). Cortisol, hunger, and desire to binge eat following a cold stress test in obese women with binge eating disorder. *Psychosomatic Medicine, 66*, 876–881.

Goebel, M., Viol, G. W., & Orebaugh, C. (1993). An incremental model to isolate specific effects of behavioral treatments in essential hypertension. *Biofeedback and Self-Regulation, 18*(4), 255–280.

Goffaux, P., Redmond, W. J., Rainville, P., & Marchand, S. (2007). Descending analgesia: When the spine echoes what the brain expects. *Pain, 130*, 137–143.

Goldberg, J., Halpern-Felsher, B. L., & Milstein, S. G. (2002). Beyond invulnerability: The importance of benefits in adolescents' decision to drink alcohol. *Health Psychology, 21*(5), 477–484.

Golden, S. A., Covinton, H. E., Berton, O., & Russo, S. J. (2011). A standardized protocol for repeated social defeat stress in mice. *Nature Protocols, 6*, 1183–1191.

Golden, S. H. (2007). A review of the evidence for a neuroendocrine link between stress, depression, and diabetes mellitus. *Current Diabetes Review, 3*, 252–259.

Golden-Kreutz, D. M., Thornton, L. M., Wells-Di Gregorio, S., Frierson, G. M., Jim, H. S., Carpenter, K. M., Shelby, R. A., & Andersen, B. L. (2005). Traumatic stress, perceived global stress, and life events: Prospectively predicting quality of life in breast cancer patients. *Health Psychology, 24*(3), 288–296.

Goldin, P. R., & Gross, J. J. (2010). Effects of mindfulness-based stress reduction (MBSR) on emotion regulation in social anxiety disorder. *Emotion, 10*(1), 83–91.

Goldring, A. B., Taylor, S. E., Kemeny, M. E., & Anton, P. A.. (2002). Impact of health beliefs, quality of life, and the physician-patient relationship on the treatment intentions of inflammatory bowel disease patients. *Health Psychology, 21*(3), 219–228.

Goldstein, A., Clement, S., & Guo, J. (2015, September 17). Proportion of Americans without health insurance dropped in 2014. *The Washington Post.* Retrieved February 25, 2016, from https://www.washingtonpost.com/national/health-science/proportion-of-americans-without-health-insurance-dropped-in-2014/2015/09/16/60915d4c-5be5-11e5-9757-e49273f05f65_story.html

Goldston, K., & Baillie, A. J. (2008). Depression and coronary heart disease: A review of the epidemiological evidence, explanatory mechanisms, and management approaches. *Clinical Psychology Review, 28*, 289–307.

Goliath, V., & Pretorius, B. (2016). Peer risk and protective factors in adolescence: Implications for drug use prevention. *Social Work, 52*(1), 113–129.

Goliszek, A. (2014, November 12). How stress affects the immune system. *Psychology Today.* Retrieved March 24, 2016, from https://www.psychologytoday.com/blog/how-the-mind-heals-the-body/201411/how-stress-affects-the-immune-system

Gonder-Frederick, L. A., Cox, D. J., Bobbitt, S. A., & Pennebaker, J. W. (1989). Mood changes associated with blood glucose fluctuations in insulin-dependent diabetes mellitus. *Health Psychology, 8*, 45–59.

Gonzalez, J. S., Safren, S. A., Delanhanty, L. M., Cagliero, E., Wexler, D. J., Meigs, J. B., & Grant, R. W. (2008). Symptoms of depression prospectively predict poorer self-care in patients with Type 2 diabetes. *Diabetes Medicine, 9*, 1102–1107.

Goodwin, R., & Friedman, H. (2006). Health status and the five-factor personality traits in a nationally representative sample. *Health Psychology, 11*(5), 643–654.

Gordon, A. M., & Chen, S. (2014). The role of sleep in interpersonal conflict: Do sleepless nights mean worse fights? *Social Psychological and Personality Science, 5*, 168–175.

Gore, M., Sadosky, A., Stacey, B., Tai, K.-S., & Leslie, D. (2012). The burden of chronic low back pain: Clinical comorbidities, treatment patterns, and health care costs in usual care settings. *Spine, 37*(11), E668–E677.

Gottholmseder, G., Nowotny, K., Pruckner, G. J., & Theurl, E. (2009). Stress perception and commuting. *Health Economics, 18*(5), 559–576.

Gough, B. (2006). Try to be healthy, but don't forgo your masculinity: Deconstructing men's health discourse in the media. *Social Science and Medicine, 63*, 2476–2488.

Gough, B. (2013). The psychology of men's health: Maximizing masculine capital. *Health Psychology, 32*(1), 1–4.

Gough, B., & Deatrick, J. A. (2015). Qualitative health psychology research: Diversity, power, and impact. *Health Psychology, 34*(4), 289–292.

Grabe, S., Ward, L. M., & Hyde, J. S. (2008). The role of the media in body image concerns among women: A meta-analysis of experimental and correlational studies. *Psychological Bulletin, 134*, 460–476.

Graham, J. E., Lobel, M., Glass, P., & Lokshina, I. (2008). Effects of written anger expression in chronic pain patients: Making meaning from pain. *Journal of Behavioral Medicine, 31*, 201–212.

Grana, R. A., Benowitz, N., & Glantz, S. (2014). Electronic cigarettes. *Circulation, 129*(19), e490–e492.

Grant, N., Wardle, J., & Steptoe, A. (2009). The relationship between life satisfaction and health behavior: A cross-cultural analysis of young adults. *International Journal of Behavioral Medicine, 16*, 259–268.

Grayling, A. C. (2009). Sleep, the elixir of health? *New Scientist, 201*, 44.

Grayson, M. (2015). Cannabis. *Nature, 525*, S1. Retrieved June 7, 2016, from http://www.nature.com/nature/journal/v525/n7570_supp/full/525S1a.html

Greenberg, R. (2014, March). More than a diagnosis: Medical schools and teaching hospitals address patients' spiritual needs. *AAMC Reporter* [Association of American Medical Colleges]. Retrieved April 2, 2016, from https://www.aamc.org/newsroom/reporter/march2014/374624/spiritual.html

Greenfield, S., Kaplan, S. H., Ware, J. E., Yano, E. M., & Frank, H. J. (1988). Patients' participation in medical care: Effects on blood sugar control and quality of life in diabetes. *Journal of General Internal Medicine, 3*, 448–457.

Greening, L., Stoppelbein, L., Konishi, C., Jordan, S. S., & Moll, G. (2007). Child routines and youths' adherence to treatment for Type 1 diabetes. *Journal of Pediatric Psychology, 32*, 437–447.

Gregoire, C. (2013, April 17). Mindfulness-based therapies may help ease stress of cancer treatment. *The Huffington Post*. Retrieved from http://www.huffingtonpost.com/2013/04/17/mindfulness-cancer-treatment-therapies-stress_n_3095435.html

Greiger-Zanlungo, P. (2001). HIV and women: An update. *Female Patient, 26*, 12–16.

Gremore, T. M., Baucom, D. H., Porter, L. S., Kirby, J. S., Atkins, D. C., & Keefe, F. J. (2011). Stress buffering effects of daily spousal support on women's daily emotional and physical experiences in the context of breast cancer concerns. *Health Psychology, 30*(1), 20–30.

Greysen, S. R., Horwitz, L. I., Covinsky, K. E., Gordon, K., Ohl, M. E., & Justice, A. C. (2013). Does social isolation predict hospitalization and mortality among HIV+ and uninfected older veterans? *The American Geriatrics Society, 61*, 1456–1463.

Gross, J. J. (1998). The emerging field of emotion regulation: An integrative review. *Review of General Psychology, 2*, 271–299.

Gross, R., Olfson, M., Gameroff, M. J., Carasquillo, O., Shea, S., Feder, A., & Weissman, M. M. (2005). Depression and glycemic control in Hispanic primary care patients with diabetes. *Journal of General Internal Medicine, 20*, 460–466.

Grossman, P., Kappos, L, Gensicke, H., D'Souza, M., Mohr, D. C., Penner, I. K., Hu, A., Lai, M., Wei, J., Wang, L., Mao, H., Zhou, W., & Liu, S. (2013). The effect of electroacupuncture on extinction responding of heroin-seeking behavior and FosB expression in the nucleus accumbens core. *Neuroscience Letters, 534*(8), 252–257.

Grossman, P., Niemann, L., Schmidt, S., & Walach, H. (2004). Mindfulness-based stress reduction and health benefits: A meta-analysis. *Journal of Psychosomatic Research, 57*, 35–43.

Grov, C., Golub, S. A., Parsons, J. T., Brennan, M., & Karpiak, S. E. (2010). Loneliness and HIV-related stigma explain depression among older HIV-positive adults. *AIDS Care, 22*(5), 630–639.

Grunberg, N. E., Brown, K. J., & Klein, L. C. (1997). Tobacco smoking. In A. Baum, S. Newman, J. Weinman, R. West, & C. McManus (Eds.), *Cambridge handbook of psychology, health, and medicine* (pp. 606–611). Cambridge, UK: Cambridge University Press.

Grunberg, N. E., Faraday, M. M., & Rahman, M. A. (2001). The psychobiology of nicotine self-administration. In A. Baum, T. A. Revenson, & J. E. Singer (Eds.), *Handbook of health psychology* (pp. 249–261). Mahwah, NJ: Erlbaum.

Grunberg, N. E., & Straub, R. O. (1992). The role of gender and taste class in the effects of stress on eating. *Health Psychology, 11*, 97–100.

Grunfield, E. A., Drudge-Coates, L., Rixon, L., Eaton, E., & Cooper, A. F. (2013). "The only way I know how to live is to work": A qualitative study of work following treatment for prostate cancer. *Health Psychology, 32*(1), 75–82.

Grynbaum, M. M. (2013, March 11). Judge blocks New York City's limits on big sugary drinks. *The New York Times*. Retrieved from http://www.nytimes.com/2013/03/12/nyregion/judge-invalidates-bloombergs-soda-ban.html?pagewanted=all&_r=0

Grzywacz, J. G., Almeida, D. M., Neupert, S. D., & Ettner, S. L. (2004). Socioeconomic status and health: A micro-level analysis of exposure and vulnerability to daily stressors. *Journal of Health and Social Behavior, 45*(1), 1–16.

Gulati, M., Pandey, D. K., Arnsdorf, M. F., Lauderdale, D. S., Thisted, R. A., Wicklund, R. H., … Black, H. R. (2003). Exercise capacity and the risk of death in women: The St. James Women Take Heart Project. *Circulation, 108*(13), 1554–1559.

Gump, B. B., & Matthews, K. A. (2000). Are vacations good for your health? The 9-year mortality experience after the multiple risk factor intervention trial. *Pscyhosomatic Medicine, 62*, 608–612.

Gus, I., Harzheim, E., Zaslavsky, C., Medina, C., & Gus, M. (2004). Prevalence, awareness, and control of systemic arterial hypertension in the state of Rio Grande do Sul. *Arquivos Brasileiros de Cardiologia, 83*(5), 429–433.

Gwatkin, D. R., Rutstein, S., Johnson, K., Suliman, E., Wagstaff, A., & Amouzou, A. (2007). Socio-economic differences in health, nutrition, and population within developing countries: An overview. *World Bank*. Retrieved February 23, 2016, from http://siteresources.worldbank.org/INTPAH/Resources/IndicatorsOverview.pdf

Haack, M., & Mullington, J. M. (2007). Shorter habitual sleep duration is associated with higher increase in subjective estimation of pain in response to a total sleep deprivation (TSD) challenge. *Sleep, 129*, A133.

Haas, A., Eliason, M., Mays, V., Mathy, R., Cochran, S., D'Angelli, A., & Clayton, P. (2011). Suicide and suicide risk in lesbian, gay, bisexual, and transgender populations: Review and recommendations. *Journal of Homosexuality, 58*(1), 10–51.

Haas, V. K., Kohn, M. R., Clarke, S. D., Allen, J. R., Madden, S., Muller, J. J., & Gaski, K. J. (2009). Body composition changes in female adolescents with anorexia nervosa. *American Journal of Clinical Nutrition, 89*(4), 1005–1010.

Hadjistavropoulos, H. D., Hadjistavropoulos, T., & Quine, A. (2000). Health anxiety moderates the effects of distraction versus attention to pain. *Behaviour Research and Therapy, 38*(5), 425–438.

Hakim, I. A., Harris, R. B., Garland, L. L., Cordova, C., Mikhael, D. M., & Sherry Crow, H. H. (2012). Gender difference in systematic oxidative stress and antioxidant capacity in current and former heavy smokers. *Cancer Epidemiology, Biomarkers & Prevention, 21*(12), 2193–2200.

Halaas, J. L., Gajiwala, K. S., Maffei, M., Cohen, S. L., Chait, B. T., Rabinowitz, D., Lallone, R. L., Burley, S. K., & Friedman, J. M. (1995). Weight-reducing effects of the plasma protein encoded by the obese gene. *Science, 269*, 543–545.

Hale, C. J., Hannum, J. W., & Espelage, D. L. (2005). Social support and physical health: The importance of social support. *Journal of American College Health, 53*, 276–284.

Haley, W. E., Roth, D. L., Howard, G., & Stafford, M. M. (2010). Caregiving strain and estimated risk for stroke and coronary heart disease among spouse caregivers: Differential effects by race and sex. *Stroke, 41*, 331–336.

Halliwell, E., & Diedrichs, P. C. (2014). Brief report: Testing a dissonance body image intervention among young girls. *Health Psychology, 33*, 201–204.

Hammarstrom, A. (1994). Health consequences of youth unemployment—review from a gender perspective. *Social Science and Medicine, 38*, 699–709.

Hammond, D., McDonald, P. W., Fong, G. T., Brown, K. S., & Cameron, R. (2004). The impact of cigarette warning labels and smoke-free bylaws on smoking cessation: Evidence from former smokers. *Canadian Journal of Public Health, 95*(3), 201–204.

Han, F., Faraco, J., Dong, X. S., Ollila, H. M., Lin, L., Li, J., … Mignot, E. (2013). Genome wide analysis of narcolepsy in China implicates novel immune loci and reveals changes in association prior to versus after the 2009 H1N1 influenza pandemic. *PLOS Genetics*. Retrieved February 25, 2016, from http://journals.plos.org/plosgenetics/article?id=10.1371/journal.pgen.1003880

Hansen, A. M., Blangsted, A. K., Hansen, E. A., Sogaard, K., & Sjogaard, G. (2010). Physical activity, job demand-control, perceived stress energy, and salivary cortisol in white-collar workers. *International Archives of Occupational and Environmental Health, 83*(2), 143–153.

Hardy, J. D., & Smith, T. W. (1988). Cynical hostility and vulnerability to disease: Social support, life stress, and physiological response to conflict. *Health Psychology, 7*, 447–459.

Hare, D. L., Toukhsati, S. R., Johansson, P., & Jaarsma, T. (2014). Depression and cardiovascular disease: A clinical review. *European Heart Journal, 35*(21), 1365–1372.

Harris, J. L., Bargh, J. A., & Brownell, K. D. (2009). Priming effects of television food advertising on eating behavior. *Health Psychology, 28*(4), 404–413.

Harris, K. F., Matthews, K. A., Sutton-Tyrrell, K., & Kuller, L. H. (2003). Associations between psychological traits and endothelial function in postmenopausal women. *Psychosomatic Medicine, 65*(3), 402–409.

Harris, P. R., Griffin, D. W., & Murray, S. (2008). Testing the limits of optimistic bias: Event and person moderators in a multilevel framework. *Journal of Personality and Social Psychology, 95*, 1225–1237.

Harrison, M. O., Koenig, H. G., Hays, J. C., Eme-Akwari, A. G., & Pargament, K. I. (2001). The epidemiology of religious coping: A review of recent literature. *International Review of Psychiatry, 13*(2), 86–93.

Hart, S. L., & Charles, S. T. (2013). Age-related patterns in negative affect and appraisals about colorectal cancer over time. *Health Psychology, 32*(3), 302–310.

Harter, J. K., Schmidt, F. L., & Keyes, C. L. (2003). Well-being in the workplace and its relationship to business outcomes. In C. L. Keyes and J. Haidt (Eds.), *Flourishing: Positive psychology and the life well-lived*. Washington, DC: American Psychological Association.

Harvard Health Letter. (2013). Abdominal obesity and your health. Retrieved from http://www.health.harvard.edu/fhg/updates/abdominal-obesity-and-your-health.shtml

Harvard Health Publications. (2013). Exercise and depression. Retrieved from http://www.health.harvard.edu/newsweek/Exercise-and-Depression-report-excerpt.htm

Harvard Heart Letter. (2004). Calories burned in 30 minutes for people of three different weights. Retrieved from http://www.health.harvard.edu/newsweek/Calories-burned-in-30-minutes-of-leisure-and-routine-activities.htm

Harvard Heart Letter. (2015). Exercise-free activities that work your muscles and heart. Retrieved from http://www.health.harvard.edu/heart-health/exercise-free-activities-that-work-your-muscles-and-heart

Harvard Medical School. (2010). Options for mild or moderate depression: Exercise, psychotherapy, and relaxation techniques are good first choices. *Harvard Mental Health Letter. 26*(10), 5.

Hatch, S. L., & Dohrenwend, B. P. (2007). Distribution of traumatic and other stressful life events by race/ethnicity, gender, SES, and age: A review of the research. *American Journal of Community Psychology, 40*, 313–332.

Hausmann, L. R. M., Jeong, K., Bost, J. E., & Ibrahim, S. A. (2008). Perceived racial discrimination in health care: A comparison of veterans affairs and other patients. *American Journal of Public Health, 99*(Supplement 3), S718–S724.

Hawkley, L. C., & Cacioppo, J. T. (2007). Aging and loneliness: Downhill quickly? *Current Directions in Psychological Science, 16*, 187–191.

Hawkley, L. C., Thisted., R. A., & Cacioppo, J. T. (2009). Loneliness predicts reduced physical activity: Cross-sectional and longitudinal analyses. *Health Psychology, 28*, 354–363.

Hawley, S. T., Janz, N. K., Hamilton, A., Griggs, J. J., Alderman, A. K., Mujahid, M., & Katz, S. J. (2008). Latina patient perspectives about informed treatment decision making for breast cancer. *Patient Education and Counseling, 73*, 363–370.

Hayden-Wade, H. A., Stein, R. I., Ghaderi, A., Saelens, B. E., Zabinski, M. F., & Wilfley, D. E. (2005). Prevalence, characteristics, and correlates of teasing experiences among overweight children vs. non-overweight peers. *Obesity Research, 13,* 1381–1392.

Hazuda, H. P., Mitchell, B. D., Haffner, S. M., & Stern, M. P. (1991). Obesity in Mexican-American subgroups: Findings from the San Antonio Heart Study. *The American Journal of Clinical Nutrition, 53,* 1529S–1534S.

HEAL. (2016). *Communicable diseases.* Bronx, NY: Health & Ecosystems: Analysis of Linkages. Retrieved February 28, 2016, from http://www.wcs-heal.org/global-challenges/public-health-issues-and-costs/communicable-diseases

Health Canada. (2016). *Canada Health Act—frequently asked questions.* Retrieved February 29, 2016, from http://www.hc-sc.gc.ca/hcs-sss/medi-assur/faq-eng.php

Healthy People 2020. (2013). Washington, DC: U.S. Department of Health and Human Services, Office of Disease Prevention and Health Promotion. Retrieved April 16, 2016, from https://www.healthypeople.gov

Healthy People 2020. (2014). *Healthy People 2020 leading health indicators: Progress update.* Washington, DC: U.S. Department of Health and Human Services, Office of Disease Prevention and Health Promotion. Retrieved from https://www.healthypeople.gov/2020/leading-health-indicators/Healthy-People-2020-Leading-Health-Indicators%3A-Progress-Update

Healy, G. N., Dunstan, D. W., Salmon, J., Cerin, E., Shaw, J. E., Zimmet, P. Z., & Owen, N. (2008). Breaks in sedentary time: Beneficial associations with metabolic risk. *Diabetes Care, 31*(4), 661–666.

Healy, J. (2014, May 31). After 5 months of sales, Colorado sees the downside of a legal high. *The New York Times.* Retrieved from http://nyti.ms/1kjtwf8

Heath, A. C., & Madden, P. A. (1995). Genetic influences on smoking behavior. In J. R. Turner & L. R. Cardon (Eds.), *Behavior genetic approaches in behavioral medicine* (pp. 45–66). New York: Plenum Press.

Heatherton, T. F., Mahamedi, F., Striepe, M., & Field, A. E. (1997). A 10-year longitudinal study of body weight, dieting, and eating disorder symptoms. *Journal of Abnormal Psychology, 106,* 117–125.

Heim, C., Ehlert, U., & Hellhammer, D. H. (2000). The potential role of hypocortisolism in the pathophysiology of stress-related bodily disorders. *Psychoneuroendocrinology, 25*(1), 1–24.

Heim, C., Newport, D. J., Mletzko, T., Miller, A. H., & Nemeroff, C. B. (2008). The link between childhood trauma and depression: Insights from HPA axis studies in humans. *Psychoneuroendocrinology, 33,* 693–710.

Heinz, A. J., de Wit, H., Lilje, T. C., & Kassel, J. D. (2013). The combined effects of alcohol, caffeine, and expectancies on subjective experience, impulsivity, and risk-taking. *Experimental and Clinical Psychopharmacology, 21*(3), 222–234.

Helgeson, V. S., Snyder, P., & Seltman, H. (2004). Psychological and physical adjustment to breast cancer over 4 years: Identifying distinct trajectories of change. *Health Psychology, 23*(1), 3–15.

Hellsten, R., Johansson, M., Dahlman, A., Sterner, O., & Bjartell, A. (2011). Galiellalactone inhibits stem cell-like ALDH-positive prostate cancer cells. *PLOS ONE, 6*(7), e22118; doi:10.1371/journal.pone.0022118.

Helweg-Larsen, M., & Shepperd, J. A. (2001). Do moderators of the optimistic bias affect personal or target risk estimates? A review of the literature. *Personality and Social Psychology Review, 5*(1), 74–95.

Hemila, H., Chalker, E., & Douglas, B. (2010). Vitamin C for preventing and treating the common cold. *Cochrane Database of Systematic Reviews.* Retrieved April 29, 2010, from http://mrw.interscience.wiley.com/cochrane/clsysrev/articles/CD000980/frame.html

Henderson, L. A., Gandevia, S. C., & Macefield, V. G. (2008). Gender differences in brain activity evoked by muscle and cutaneous pain: A retrospective study of single-trial fMRI data. *NeuroImage, 39,* 1867–1876.

Henig, R. M. (2010, August 18). What is it about 20-somethings? *The New York Times Magazine.* Retrieved February 24, 2016, from http://www.nytimes.com/2010/08/22/magazine/22Adulthood-t.html?pagewanted=all

Henningfield, J. E., Cohen, C., & Pickworth, W. B. (1993). Psychopharmacology of nicotine. In C. T. Orleans & J. D. Slade (Eds.), *Nicotine addiction: Principles and management* (pp. 24–45). New York: Oxford University Press.

Herman, C. P., & Polivy, J. (1975). Anxiety, restraint, and eating behavior. *Journal of Abnormal Psychology, 84,* 208–225.

Hernandez, L. M. (2013). *Health literacy: Improving, health, health systems, and health policy around the world.* Washington, DC: National Academies Press.

Heron, M. (2012). Deaths: Leading causes for 2010. *National Vital Statistics Reports, 61*(7). Hyattsville, MD: National Center for Health Statistics.

Heron, M. (2015). Deaths: Leading causes for 2012. *National Vital Statistics Reports, 64*(10). Hyattsville, MD: National Center for Health Statistics.

Hertel, A. W., & Mermelstein, R. J. (2012). Smoker identity and smoking escalation among adolescents. *Health Psychology, 31*(4), 467–475.

Hetherington, M. M. (2007). Cues to overeat: Psychological factors influencing overconsumption. *Proceedings—Nutrition Society of London, 66*(1), 113.

Hettema, J., Steele, J., & Miller, W. R. (2005). Motivational interviewing. *Annual Review of Clinical Psychology, 1,* 91–111.

Hjermstad, M. J., Fayers, P. M., Haugen, D. F., Caraceni, A., Hanks, G. W., Loge, J. H., Fainsinger, R., Aass, N., & Kaasa, S. (2011). Studies comparing numerical rating scales, verbal ratings scales, and visual analogue scales for assessment of pain intensity in adults: A systematic literature review. *Journal of Pain and Symptom Management, 41*(6), 1073–1093.

Higgs, S. (2002). Memory for recent eating and its influence on subsequent food intake. *Appetite, 39*(2), 139–166.

Higuchi, S., Maesato, H., Yoshimura, A., & Matsushita, S. (2014). Acceptance of controlled drinking among treatment specialists of alcohol dependence in Japan. *Alcohol and Alcoholism, 49*(4), 447–452.

Hilbert, G. A. (1994). Cardiac patients and spouses: Family functioning and emotions. *Clinical Nursing Research, 3,* 243–252.

Hill, J. O., Wyatt, H. R., Reed, G. W., & Peters, J. C. (2003). Obesity and the environment: Where do we go from here? *Science, 299*(5608), 853–855.

Hill, K. (2015). Medical marijuana does not increase adolescent marijuana use. *The Lancet Psychiatry, 2*(7), 572–573.

Hildebrandt, M. J., & Hayes, S. C. (2012). The contributing role of negative affectivity and experiential avoidance to increased cardiovascular risk. *Social and Personality Psychology Compass, 6*(8), 551–565.

Hilliard, M. E., Holmes, C. S., Chen, R., Maher, K., Robinson, E., & Streisand, R. (2013). Disentangling the roles of parental monitoring and family conflict in adolescents' management of Type 1 diabetes. *Health Psychology, 32*(4), 388–396.

Hind, K., & Burrows, M. (2007). Weight-bearing exercise and bone mineral accrual in children and adolescents: A review of controlled trials. *Bone, 40*(1), 14–27.

Hinz, A., Krauss, O., Hauss, J. P., Hockel, M., Kortmann, R. D., Stolzenburg, J. U., & Schwartz, R. (2010). Anxiety and depression in cancer patients compared with the general population. *European Journal of Cancer Care, 19*, 522–529.

Hirsch, J. (2003). Obesity: Matter over mind? *Cerebrum: The Dana Forum on Brain Science, 5*(1), 16.

Hirvonen, J., Goodwin, R. S., & Innis, R. B. (2012). Reversible and regionally selective downregulation of brain cannabinoid CB1 receptors in chronic daily cannabis smokers. *Molecular Psychiatry, 17*(6), 642–649.

Hochschild, A. R. (1997). *The time bind: When work becomes home, and home becomes work.* New York: Metropolitan Books.

Hodgson, S., Omar, R. Z., Jensen, T. K., Thompson, S. G., Boobis, A. R., Davies, D. S., & Elliott, P. (2006). Meta-analysis of studies of alcohol and breast cancer with consideration of the methodological issues. *Cancer Causes and Control, 17*(6), 759–770.

Hoebel, B. G., & Teitelbaum, P. (1966). Effects of forcefeeding and starvation on food intake and body weight in a rat with ventromedial hypothalamic lesions. *Journal of Comparative and Physiological Psychology, 61*, 189–193.

Hoey, L. M., Ieropoli, S. C., White, V. M., & Jefford, M. (2008). Systematic review of peer-support programs for people with cancer. *Patient Education and Counseling, 70*, 315–337.

Hoffman, B. M., Papas, R. K., Chatkoff, D. K., & Kerns, R. D. (2007). Meta-analysis of psychological interventions for chronic low back pain. *Health Psychology, 26*, 1–9.

Hoffman, H. G., Richards, T. L., Van Oostrom, T., Coda, B. A., Jensen, M. P., Blough, D. K., & Sharar, S. R. (2007). The analgesic effects of opioids and immersive virtual reality distraction: Evidence from subjective and functional brain imaging assessments. *Anesthesia & Analgesia, 105*, 1776–1783.

Hoffman, K. (2015). Positivity and cancer—myth or reality? *Medivizor.* Retrieved from https://medivizor.com/blog/2015/04/30/positive-thinking-and-cancer/

Hofmann, S. G., Sawyer, A. T., Witt, A. A., & Oh, D. (2010). The effect of mindfulness-based therapy on anxiety and depression: A meta-analytic review. *Journal of Consulting and Clinical Psychology, 78*(2), 169–183.

Hogan, B. E., & Linden, W. (2004). Anger response styles and blood pressure: At least don't ruminate about it! *Annals of Behavioral Medicine, 27*(1), 38–49.

Hoge, C. W., Terhakopian, A., Castro, C. A., Messer, S. C., & Engel, C. C. (2007). Association of posttraumatic stress disorder with somatic symptoms, health care visits, and absenteeism among Iraq War veterans. *American Journal of Psychiatry, 164*, 150–153.

Holahan, C. J., Holahan, C. K., Moos, R. H., & Brennan, P. L. (1997). Psychosocial adjustment in patients reporting cardiac illness. *Psychology and Health, 12*, 345–359.

Holland, J. C., & Alici, Y. (2010). Management of distress in cancer patients. *Journal of Supportive Oncology, 8*, 4–12.

Holmqvist, K., Frisén, A., & Anderson-Fye, E. (2014). Body image and child well-being. In A. Ben Arieh, F. Casas, I. Frønes, & J. E. Korbin (Eds.), *Handbook of child well-being* (pp. 2409–2436). New York: Springer Reference.

Holt-Lunstad, J., Smith, T. B., & Layton, J. B. (2010). Social relationships and mortality risk: A meta-analytic review. *PLOS Medicine, 7*(7). Retrieved from http://www.plosmedicine.org/article/info%3Adoi%2F10.1371%2Fjournal.pmed.1000316

Holt-Lunstad, J., Uchino, B. N., Smith, T. W., Olson-Cerny, C., & Nealey-Moore, J. B. (2003). Social relationships and ambulatory blood pressure: Structural and qualitative predictors of cardiovascular function during everyday social interactions. *Health Psychology, 22*(4), 388–397.

Holzel, B. K., Carmody, J., Vangel, M., Congleton, C., Yerramsetti, T. G., & Lazar, S. W. (2011). Mindfulness practice leads to increases in regional bray gray matter density. *Psychiatry Research: Neuroimaging, 91*(1), 36–43.

Hor, H., & Tafti, M. (2009). How much sleep do we need? *Science, 325*, 825–826.

Horgan, J. (2014). Justinian's plague. *Ancient history encyclopedia.* Retrieved February 28, 2016, from http://www.ancient.eu/article/782/

House, J. S., Lepkowski, K. D., Williams, R., Mero, R. P., Lantz, P. M., Robert, S. A., & Chen, J. (2000). Excess mortality among urban residents: How much, for whom, and why? *American Journal of Public Health, 90*(12), 1898–1904. Retrieved from http://www.ncbi.nlm.nih.gov/pubmed/11111263

Housman, J., & Dorman, S. (2005). The Alameda County study: A systematic, chronological review. *American Journal of Health Education, 33*(5), 302–308.

Howell, C., Rice, M., Carmon, M., & Hauber, R. (2007). The relationships among anxiety, anger, and BP in children. *Applied Nursing Research, 20*, 17–23.

Hoyert, D. L. (2012). 75 years of mortality in the United States, 1935–2010. *NCHS data brief, no. 88.* Hyattsville, MD: National Center for Health Statistics.

Hoyert, D. L., & Xu, J. (2012, October 12). Deaths: Preliminary data for 2011. *National Vital Statistics Reports, 61*(6). Hyattsville, MD: National Center for Health Statistics.

Hoyt, M. A. (2009). Gender role conflict and emotional approach coping in men with cancer. *Psychology and Health, 24*(8), 981–996.

Hoyt, M. A., Nemeroff, C. J., & Huebner, D. M. (2006). The effects of HIV-related thought suppression on risk behavior: Cognitive escape in men who have sex with men. *Health Psychology, 25*(4), 455–461.

Hoyt, M. A., Stanton, A. L., Irwin, M. R., & Thomas, K. S. (2013). Cancer-related masculine threat, emotional approach coping, and physical functioning following treatment for prostate cancer. *Health Psychology, 32*(1), 66–74.

Hsee, C. K., Yang, A. X., & Wang. L. (2010). Idleness aversion and the need for justifiable busyness. *Psychological Science, 21*, 926–930.

Hsiao, W. C. (1996). A framework for assessing health financing strategies and the role of health insurance. In D. W. Dunlop & J. M. Martins (Eds.), *An international assessment of health care financing: Lessons for developing countries* (EDI Seminar). Washington, DC: World Bank Publications.

Hsu, C. J., Chen, S. Y., Su, S., Yang, M. C., Lan, C., Chou, N. K., Hsu, R. B., Lai, J. S., & Wang, S. S. (2011). The effect of early cardiac rehabilitation on health-related quality of life among heart transplant recipients and patients with coronary artery bypass graft surgery. *Transplantation Proceedings, 43*(7), 2714–2717.

Hsu, M., Anen, C., & Quartz, S. R. (2008). The right and good: Distributive justice and neural encoding of equity and efficiency. *Science, 320*(5879), 1092–1095.

Huang, C. J., Webb, H. E., Zourdos, M. C., & Acevedo, E. O. (2013). Cardiovascular reactivity, stress, and physical activity. *Frontiers in Physiology, 4.* Retrieved February 26, 2016, from http://journal.frontiersin.org/article/10.3389/fphys.2013.00314/full

Huang, W., Pach, D., Napadow, V., Park, K., Long, X., Neumann, J., … Witt, C. M. (2012). Characterizing acupuncture stimuli using brain imaging with fMRI—A systematic review and meta-analysis of the literature. *PLOS ONE, 7*(4).

Hudelson, C., & Cluver, L. (2015). Factors associated with adherence to antiretroviral therapy among adolescents living with HIV/AIDS in low- and middle-income countries: A systematic review. *AIDS Care, 27*(7), 805–816.

Hudson, J. I., Hiripi, E., Pope, H. G., & Kessler, R. C. (2007). The prevalence and correlates of eating disorders in the National Comorbidity Survey replication. *Biological Psychiatry, 61,* 348–358.

Huffman, F. G., Vaccaro, J. A., Exebio, J. C., Zarini, G. G., Katz, T., & Dixon, Z. (2012). Television watching, diet quality, and physical activity and diabetes among three ethnicities in the United States. *Journal of Environmental and Public Health, 2012.* Retrieved February 26, 2016, from http://www.hindawi.com/journals/jeph/2012/191465/

Hughes, B., & Wareham, J. (2010). Knowledge arbitrage in global pharma: A synthetic view of absorptive capacity and open innovation. *R & D Management Special Issue: The Future of Open Innovation, 40*(3), 324–343.

Hughes, J. R. (2010). Craving among long-abstinent smokers: An Internet survey. *Nicotine & Tobacco Research, 12,* 459–462.

Hughes, M. E., & Waite, L. J. (2002). Health in household context: Living arrangements and health in late middle age. *Journal of Health and Social Behavior, 43,* 1–21.

Huisman, M., Kunst, A. E., Bopp, M., Borgan, J-K., Borrell, C., Costa, G., … Mackenbach, J. P. (2005). Educational inequalities in cause-specific mortality in middle-aged and older men and women in eight western European populations. *The Lancet, 365,* 493–500.

Hummer, R. A., Rogers, R. G., Nam, C. B., & Ellison, C. G. (1999). Religious involvement and U.S. adult mortality. *Demography, 36,* 273–285.

Humpel, N., Marshall, A. L., Leslie, E., Bauman, A., & Own, N. (2004). Changes in neighborhood walking are related to changes in perceptions of environmental attributes. *Annals of Behavioral Medicine, 27,* 60–67.

Hurd, Y. L., Michaelides, M., Miller, M. L., & Jutras-Aswad, D. (2014). Trajectory of adolescent cannabis use on addiction vulnerability. *Neuropharmacology, 76,* 416–424.

Hustad, J. T. P., Carey, K. B., Carey, M. P., & Maisto, S. A. (2009). Self-regulation, alcohol consumption, and consequences in college heavy drinkers: A simultaneous latent growth analysis. *Journal of Studies on Alcohol and Drugs, 70*(3), 373–382.

Huston, P. (1997). Cardiovascular disease burden shifts. *The Lancet, 350,* 121.

Iarmarcovai, G., Bonassi, S., Botta, A., Baan, R. A., & Orsiere, T. (2008). Genetic polymorphisms and micronucleus formation: A review of the literature. *Mutation Research, 658*(3), 215–233.

Illa, L., Echenique, M., Bustamante-Avellanda, V., & Sanchez-Martinez, M. (2014). Review of recent behavioral interventions targeting older adults living with HIV/AIDS. *Current HIV/AIDS Reports, 11,* 413–422.

Inouye, S. K. (2000). Prevention of delirium in hospitalized older patients: Risk factors and targeted intervention strategies. *Annals of Medicine, 32*(4), 257–263.

Institute for Health Metrics and Evaluation (IHME). (2013a). The emerging global health crisis of non-communicable diseases. Seattle, WA: IHME, University of Washington. Retrieved from http://www.healthdata.org/events/launch/emerging-global-health-crisis-non-communicable-diseases

Institute for Health Metrics and Evaluation (IHME). (2013b). GBD compare. Seattle, WA: IHME, University of Washington. Retrieved February 23, 2016, from http://vizhub.healthdata.org/gbd-compare/

Institute for Health Metrics and Evaluation (IHME). (2013c). GBD heat map. Seattle, WA: IHME, University of Washington. Retrieved March 17, 2016, from http://vizhub.healthdata.org/irank/heat.php

Institute of Medicine (IOM). (2006). *Preventing medication errors: Quality Chasm Series.* Washington, DC: The National Academies Press. Retrieved from http://www.iom.edu/CMS/3809/22526/35939.aspx

Institute of Medicine (IOM). (2011a). *Informing the future: Critical issues in health* (6th ed.). Washington, DC: The National Academies Press.

Institute of Medicine (IOM). (2011b). *Relieving pain in America: A blueprint for transforming prevention, care, education, and research.* Washington, DC: The National Academies Press.

Inzlicht, M., & Schmader, T. (2012). *Stereotype threat: Theory, process, and application.* New York: Oxford University Press.

Irwin, M. R. (2008). Human psychoneuroimmunology: 20 years of discovery. *Brain, Behavior, and Immunity, 22,* 129–139.

Ishikawa-Takata, K., Ohta, T., & Tanaka, H. (2003). How much exercise is required to reduce blood pressure in essential hypertensives: A dose-response study. *American Journal of Hypertension, 16*(8), 629–633.

Iuga, A. O., & McGuire, M. J. (2014). Adherence and health care costs. *Risk Management and Healthcare Policy, 7,* 35–44.

Iyengar, S. S., & Lepper, M. R. (2000). Personality processes and individual differences—When choice is demotivating: Can one desire too much of a good thing? *Journal of Personality & Social Psychology, 79*(6), 995–1005.

Jablon, S., Hrubec, Z., & Boice, J. D. (1991). Cancer in populations living near nuclear facilities. A survey of mortality nationwide and incidence in two states. *Journal of the American Medical Association, 265,* 1403–1408.

Jablonska, B., Soares, J. J. F., & Sundin, O. (2006). Pain among women: Associations with socioeconomic status and work conditions. *European Journal of Pain, 10,* 435–447.

Jackson, T. P., Stabile, V. S., & McQueen, K. A. (2014). The global burden of chronic pain. *American Society of Anesthesiologists Newsletter, 78*(6), 24–27.

Jacobson, A. M. (1996). The psychological care of patients with insulin-dependent diabetes mellitus. *New England Journal of Medicine, 334,* 1249–1253.

Jacobson, E. (1938). *Progressive relaxation.* Chicago: University of Chicago Press.

Jain, A., Marshall, J., Buikema, A., Bancroft, T., Kelly, J. P., & Newachaffer, C. J. (2015). Autism occurrence by MMR vaccine status among US children with older siblings with and without autism. *Journal of the American Medical Association, 313*(15), 1534–1540.

Jakulj, F., Zernicke, K., Bacon, S. L., van Wielingen, L. E., Key, B. L., West, S. G., & Campbell, T. S. (2007). A high-fat meal increases cardiovascular reactivity to psychological stress in healthy young adults. *The Journal of Nutrition, 137*(4), 935–939.

James, S. A., Van Hoewyk, J., & Belli, R. F. (2006). Life-course socioeconomic position and hypertension in African American men: The Pitt County Study. *American Journal of Public Health, 96*(5), 812–817.

Janis, I. L. (1958). *Psychological stress.* New York: Wiley.

Janis, I. L., & Feshbach, S. (1953). Effects of fear-arousing communications. *Journal of Abnormal and Social Psychology, 48,* 78–92.

Jarrett, C. (2011). Ouch! The different ways people experience pain. *The British Psychological Society, 24*, 416–420.

Jeffery, R. W., Kelly, K. M., Rothman, A. J., Sherwood, N. E., & Boutelle, K. N. (2004). The weight loss experience: A descriptive analysis. *Annals of Behavioral Medicine, 27*(2), 100–106.

Jenks, R. A., & Higgs, S. (2007). Associations between dieting and smoking-related behaviors in young women. *Drug and Alcohol Dependence, 88*, 291–299.

Jensen, S., Pereira, D. B., Whitehead, N., Buscher, I., McCalla, J., Andrasik, M., Rose, R., & Antoni, M. H. (2013). Cognitive-behavioral stress management and psychological well-being in HIV+ racial/ethnic minority women with human papillomavirus. *Health Psychology, 32*(2), 227–230.

Jiang, H., Kuriakose, J. S., Miller, R. L., Moors, K., Niedzwiecki, M. M., & Perera, F. F. (2012). Reproducibility and intraindividual variation over days in buccal cell DNA methylation of two asthma genes, interferon [gamma] (IFN[gamma]) and inducible nitric oxide synthase (iNOS). *Clinical Epigenetics, 4*, 3.

Jiang, Y., Ekono, M., & Skinner, C. (2016). Basic facts about low-income children. *National Center for Children in Poverty.* Retrieved February 24, 2016, from http://www.nccp.org/publications/pub_1099.html

Jimenez, N., Garroutte, E., Kundu, A., Morales, L., & Buchwald, D. (2011). A review of the experience, epidemiology, and management of pain among American Indian, Alaska Native, and Aboriginal Canadian peoples. *Journal of Pain, 12*(5), 511–522.

Johnson, K. W., Anderson, N. B., Bastida, E., Kramer, B. J., Williams, D., & Wong, M. (1995). Panel III: Macrosocial and environmental influences on minority health. *Health Psychology, 14*, 601–612.

Johnson, L. F. (2013). Treatment timing tied to longer life expectancy in HIV patients. *PLOS Medicine.* Retrieved from http://www.healio.com/infectious-disease/hiv-aids/news/online/%7Bc6ea4748-efe3-4e3b-bdf4-32c029327601%7D/treatment-timing-tied-to-longer-life-expectancy-in-hiv-patients

Johnson, M., & Vogele, C. (1993). Benefits of psychological preparation for surgery: A meta-analysis. *Annals of Behavioral Medicine, 15*, 245–256.

Johnson, N. G. (2004). Future directions for psychology and health. In R. H. Rozensky, N. G. Johnson, C. D. Goodheart, & W. R. Hammond (Eds.), *Psychology builds a healthy world: Opportunities for research and practice.* Washington, DC: American Psychological Association.

Johnson, S., Cummins, C., & Evers, K. (2008). The impact of Transtheoretical Model–based multiple behavior interventions on nutrition. In N. E. Bernhardt & A. M. Kasko (Eds.), *Nutrition for the middle aged and elderly* (pp. 195–212). New York: Nova Science Publishers.

Johnson, V. C., Walker, L. G., Heys, S. D., Whiting, P. H., & Eremin, O. (1996). Can relaxation training and hypnotherapy modify the immune response to stress, and is hypnotizability relevant? *Contemporary Hypnosis, 13*(2), 100–108.

Johnston, D. W., Johnston, M., Pollard, B., Kinmouth, A. L., & Mant, D. (2004). Motivation is not enough: Prediction of risk behavior following diagnosis of coronary heart disease from the theory of planned behavior. *Health Psychology, 23*(5), 533–538.

Johnston, L. D., O'Malley, P. M., Bachman, J. G., & Schulenberg, J. E. (2013). *Monitoring the future: National results on drug use: 2012 overview: Key findings on adolescent drug use.* Ann Arbor, MI: Institute for Social Research, University of Michigan.

Johnston, L. D., O'Malley, P. M., Miech, R. A., Bachman, J. G., & Schulenberg, J. E. (2014). *Monitoring the Future National Survey Results on drug use: 1975–2014. 2014 overview: Key findings on adolescent drug use.* Ann Arbor: Institute for Social Research. The University of Michigan.

Johnston, L. D., O'Malley, P. M., Miech, R. A., Bachman, J. G., & Schulenberg, J. E. (2015). *Monitoring the future National survey results on drug use: 1975–2015: 2015 overview: Key findings on adolescent drug use.* Ann Arbor: Institute for Social Research, The University of Michigan.

Joiner, T. E., Jr. (2010). *Myths about suicide.* Cambridge, MA: Harvard University Press.

Joint Commission. (2016). Hospital national patient safety goals. Retrieved June 15, 2016, from https://www.jointcommission.org/assets/1/6/2016_NPSG_HAP_ER.pdf

Jones, C. N., You, S., & Furlong, M. J. (2013). A preliminary examination of covitality as integrated well-being in college students. *Social Indicators Research, 111*(2), 511–526.

Jones, C. P. (2005). Naming racism as a threat to the health and well-being of the nation. *Program and abstracts of the 26th annual meeting of the Society of Behavioral Medicine.* April 13–16, 2005. Boston, Massachusetts.

Jones, J. M. (2009, November 20). In U.S., more would like to lose weight than are trying to. *Gallup News Service.* Retrieved March 8, 2010, from http://www.gallup.com/poll/124448/In-U.S.-More-Lose-Weight-Than-Trying-To.aspx

Jorenby, D. E., Hays, J. T., Rigotti, N. A., Azoulay, S., Watsky, E. J., Williams, K. E., … Reeves, K. R. (2006). Efficacy of varenicline, an alpha4beta2 nicotinic acetylcholine receptor partial agonist, vs. placebo or sustained-release buproprion for smoking cessation: A randomized controlled trial. *Journal of the American Medical Association, 296*(1), 56–63.

Jorgensen, R. S., Johnson, B. T., Kolodziej, M. E., & Schreer, G. E. (1996). Elevated blood pressure and personality: A meta-analytic review. *Psychological Bulletin, 120*, 293–320.

Jorgensen, R. S., & Kolodziej, M. E. (2007). Suppressed anger, evaluative threat, and cardiovascular reactivity: A tripartite profile approach. *International Journal of Psychophysiology, 66*, 102–108.

Julien, R. M., Advokat, C. D., & Comaty, J. E. (2011). *Primer of drug action* (12th ed.). New York: Worth Publishers.

Juraskova, I., Bari, R. A., O'Brien, M. T., & McCaffery, K. J. (2011). HPV vaccine promotion: Does referring to both cervical cancer and genital warts affect intended and actual vaccination behavior? *Women's Health Issues, 21*, 71–79.

Kabat-Zinn, J. (2005). *Coming to our senses.* New York: Hyperion.

Kaiser Family Foundation. (2015). Gender differences in health care, status, and use: Spotlight on men's health. Findings from the 2013 Kaiser Men's Health Survey and 2013 Kaiser Women's Health Survey. Retrieved from http://kff.org/womens-health-policy/fact-sheet/gender-differences-in-health-care-status-and-use-spotlight-on-mens-health/

Kaiser Foundation. (2010). Assessing the effectiveness of public education campaigns. Retrieved February 26, 2010, from http://www.kff.org/entmedia/entmedia042706pkg.cfm

Kaiser Foundation. (2012). Summary of coverage provisions in the Affordable Care Act. Retrieved from http://kaiserfamilyfoundation.files.wordpress.com/2013/01/8023-r.pdf

Kaiser Foundation. (2015). Key facts about the uninsured population. Retrieved November 9, 2015, from http://kff.org/uninsured/fact-sheet/key-facts-about-the-uninsured-population/

Kalichman, S. C. (2008). Co-occurrence of treatment nonadherence and continued HIV transmission risk behaviors: Implications for positive prevention interventions. *Psychosomatic Medicine, 70*(5), 593.

Kamarck, T. W., & Lichtenstein, E. (1998). Program adherence and coping strategies as predictors of success in a smoking treatment program. *Health Psychology, 7,* 557–574.

Kamen, C., Mustian, K. M., Heckler, C., Janelsins, M. C., Peppone, L. J., Mohile, S., … Morrow, G. R. (2015). The association between partner support and psychological distress among prostate cancer survivors in a nationwide study. *Journal of Cancer Survivorship: Research and Practice, 9*(3), 492–499.

Kamen, C., Tejani, M. A., Chandwani, K., Janelsins, M., Peoples, A. R., Roscoe, J. A., & Morrow, G. R. (2014, January 5). Anticipatory nausea and vomiting due to chemotherapy. *European Journal of Pharmacology, 722,* 172–179.

Kaminski, P. L., & McNamara, K. (1996). A treatment for college women at risk for bulimia: A controlled evaluation. *Journal of Counseling and Development, 74,* 288–374.

Kandel, D. B., & Davies, M. (1996). High school students who use crack and other drugs. *Archives of General Psychiatry, 53,* 71–80.

Kane, G. D. (2010). Revisiting gay men's body image issues: Exposing the fault lines. *Review of General Psychology, 14,* 311–317.

Kanner, A. D., Coyne, J. C., Schaefer, C., & Lazarus, R. S. (1981). Comparison of two modes of stress measurement: Daily hassles and uplifts versus major life events. *Journal of Behavioral Medicine, 4,* 1–39.

Kant, A. K., Graubard, B. I., & Atchinson, E. A. (2009). Intakes of plain water, moisture in foods and beverages, and total water in the adult US population—nutritional, meal pattern, and body weight correlates: National Health and Nutrition Examination Surveys 1999–2006. *American Journal of Clinical Nutrition, 90*(3), 655–663.

Kaplan, R. M., & Kronick, R. G. (2006). Marital status and longevity in the United States population. *Journal of Epidemiology and Community Health, 60,* 760–765.

Karasek, R. A. (1979). Job demands, job decision latitude, and mental strain: Implications for job re-design. *Administrative Science Quarterly, 24,* 285–306.

Karatoreos, I. N., & McEwen, B. S. (2013). Annual research review: The neurobiology and physiology of resilience and adaptation across the life course. *Journal of Child Psychology and Psychiatry, 54*(4), 337–347.

Karlamangla, A. S., Singer, B. H., & Seeman, T. E. (2006). Reduction in allostatic load in older adults is associated with lower all-cause mortality risk: MacArthur studies of successful aging. *Psychosomatic Medicine, 68,* 662–668.

Karlamangla, A. S., Singer, B. H., Williams, D. R., Schwartz, J. E., Matthews, K. A., Kiefe, C. I., & Seeman, T. E. (2005). Impact of socioeconomic status on longitudinal accumulation of cardiovascular risk in young adults: The CARDIA Study (USA). *Social Science & Medicine, 60*(5), 999–1015.

Kasai, K., Yamasue, H., Gilbertson, M. W., Shenton, M. E., Rauch, S. L., & Pitman, R. K. (2008). Evidence for acquired pregenual anterior cingulate gray matter loss from a twin study of combat-related posttraumatic stress disorder. *Biological Psychiatry 63,* 550–556.

Kashdan, T. B., & Kane, J. Q. (2011). Post-traumatic distress and the presence of post-traumatic growth and meaning in life: Experiential avoidance as a moderator. *Personality and Individual Differences, 50,* 84–89.

Kashdan, T. B., & Silvia, P. J. (2008). Curiosity and interest: The benefits of thriving on novelty and change. In C. R. Snyder &

S. J. Lopez (Eds.), *Oxford handbook of positive psychology* (2nd ed., pp. 367–375). New York: University of Oxford Press.

Kashdan, T. B., & Steger, M. F. (2007). Curiosity and pathways to well-being and meaning in life: Traits, states, and everyday behaviors. *Motivation & Emotion, 31,* 159–173.

Kasl, S. V. (1997). Unemployment and health. In A. Baum, S. Newman, J. Weinman, R. West, & C. McManus (Eds.), *Cambridge handbook of psychology, health, and medicine* (pp. 186–189). Cambridge, UK: Cambridge University Press.

Kassem, N. O., & Lee, J. (2004). Understanding soft drink consumption among male adolescents using the theory of planned behavior. *Journal of Behavioral Medicine, 27,* 273–296.

Katz, E. C., Fromme, K., & D'Amico, E. J. (2000). Effects of outcome expectancies and personality on young adults' illicit drug use, heavy drinking, and risky sexual behavior. *Cognitive Therapy and Research, 24*(1), 1–22.

Kaufman, J. (2006). The anatomy of a medical myth. *Social Sciences Research Council.* Retrieved March 10, 2016, from http://raceandgenomics.ssrc.org/Kaufman/

Kawaharada, M., Yoshioka, E., Saijo, Y., Fukui, T., Ueno, T., & Kishi, R. (2009). The effects of a stress inoculation training program for civil servants in Japan: A pilot study of a non-randomized controlled trial. *Industrial Health, 47*(2), 173–182.

Kazak, A. E., Bosch, J., & Klonoff, E. A. (2012). Editorial: Health Psychology special series on health disparities. *Health Psychology, 31*(1), 1–4.

Keenan, K., Hipwell, A., & Stepp, S. (2012). Race and sexual behavior predict uptake of the human papillomavirus vaccine. *Health Psychology, 31*(1), 31–34.

Keenan, N. L., Strogatz, D. S., James, S. A., Ammerman, A. S., & Rice, B. L. (1992). Distribution and correlates of waist-to-hip ratio in black adults: The Pitt County study. *American Journal of Epidemiology, 135*(6), 678–684.

Keesey, R. E., & Corbett, S. W. (1983). Metabolic defense of the body weight set-point. In A. J. Stunkard & E. Stellar (Eds.), *Eating and its disorders* (pp. 327–331). New York: Raven Press.

Keesling, B., & Friedman, H. S. (1987). Psychosocial factors in sunbathing and sunscreen use. *Health Psychology, 6,* 477–493.

Keller, T., Hader, C., De Zeeuw, J., & Rasche, K. (2007). Obstructive sleep apnea syndrome: The effect of diabetes and autonomic neuropathy. *Journal of Physiology and Pharmacology, 58*(S5), 313–318.

Kelly, J. A., & Kalichman, S. C. (2002). Behavioral research in HIV/AIDS primary and secondary prevention: Recent advances and future directions. *Journal of Consulting and Clinical Psychology, 70,* 626–639.

Keltner, D., Ellsworth, P. C., & Edwards, K. (1993). Beyond simple pessimism: Effects of sadness and anger on social perception. *Journal of Personality and Social Psychology, 64,* 740–752.

Kemeny, M. (2003). The psychobiology of stress. *Current Directions in Psychological Science, 12,* 124–129.

Kemp, M., & Kissane, B. (2010). A five-step framework for interpreting tables and graphs in their contexts. In C. Reading (Ed.), *Data and context in statistics education: Towards an evidence-based society. Proceedings of the Eighth International Conference on Teaching Statistics.* Voorburg, The Netherlands: International Statistical Institute.

Kempen, G. I., Jelicic, M., & Ormel, J. (1997). Personality, chronic medical morbidity, and health-related quality of life among older persons. *Health Psychology, 16,* 539–546.

Kendzor, D., Businelle, M. S., Mazas, C. A., Cofta-Woerpel, L. M., Reitzel, L. R., Vidrine, J. I., Costello, T. J., Cinciripini, P. M., Ahluwalia, J. S., & Wetter, D. W. (2009). Pathways between socioeconomic status and modifiable risk factors among

African American smokers. *Journal of Behavioral Medicine, 32*(6), 545–557.

Kendzor, D. E., Shuval, K., Gabriel, K. P., Businelle, M. S., Ma, P., High, R. R., … Wetter, D. W. (2016). Impact of a mobile phone intervention to reduce sedentary behavior in a community sample of adults: A quasi-experimental evaluation. *Journal of Medical Internet Research, 18*(1). Retrieved from http://www .jmir.org/2016/1/e19/

Kenrick, D. T., Griskevicius, V., Neuberg, S. L., & Schaller, M. (2010). Renovating the pyramid of needs: Contemporary extensions built upon ancient foundations. *Perspectives on Psychological Science, 5,* 292–314.

Keyes, C. L. M., & Annas, J. (2009). Feeling good and functioning well: Distinctive concepts in ancient philosophy and contemporary science. *Journal of Positive Psychology, 4,* 197–201.

Khan, L. K., Sobush, K., Keener, Goodman, D., Lowry, K., Kakietek, J., & Zaro, S. (2009). Recommended community strategies and measurements to prevent obesity in the United States. *Morbidity and Mortality Weekly Report, 58*(RR07), 1–26.

Khayyam-Nekouei, Z., Neshatdoost, H., Yousefy, A., Sadeghi, M., & Manshaee, G. (2013). Psychological factors and coronary heart disease. *Atherosclerosis, 9*(1), 102–111.

Khurshid, K. A. (2015). A review of changes in DSM-5 sleep-wake disorders. *Psychiatric Times.* Retrieved from https://psychiatry .ufl.edu/files/2015/10/Psychiatric_Times_Khurshid.pdf

Kibby, M., Pavawalla, S., Fancher, J., Naillon, A., & Hynd, G. (2009). The relationship between cerebral hemisphere volume and receptive language functioning in dyslexia and attention-deficit hyperactivity disorder (ADHD). *Journal of Child Neurology, 24*(4), 438–448.

Kiecolt-Glaser, J. K., Fisher, L., Ogrocki, P., Stout, J. C., Speicher, C. E., & Glasser, R. (1987). Marital quality, marital disruption, and immune function. *Psychosomatic Medicine, 49,* 13–34.

Kiecolt-Glaser, J. K., Garner, W., Speicher, C. E., Penn, G. M., Holliday, J. E., & Glaser, R. (1984). Psychosocial modifiers of immunocompetence in medical students. *Psychosomatic Medicine, 46,* 7–14.

Kiecolt-Glaser, J. K., Glaser, R., Gravenstein, S., Malarkey, W. B., & Sheridan, J. (1996). Chronic stress alters the immune response to influenza virus vaccine in older adults. *Proceedings of the National Academy of Sciences, 93,* 3043–3047.

Kiecolt-Glaser, J. K., Gouin, J.-P., & Hantsoo, L. (2010). Close relationships, inflammation, and health. *Neuroscience and Biobehavioral Reviews, 35*(1), 33–38.

Kiecolt-Glaser, J. K., Gouin, J., Weng, N., Malarkey, W., Beversdorf, D., & Glaser, R. (2011). Childhood adversity heightens the impact of later-life caregiving stress on telomere length and inflammation. *Psychosomatic Medicine, 73,* 16–22.

Kiecolt-Glaser, J. K., Loving, T. J., Stowell, J. R., Malarkey, W. B., Lemeshow, S., Dickinson, S. L., & Glaser, R. (2005). Hostile marital interactions, proinflammatory cytokine production, and wound healing. *Archives of General Psychiatry, 62,* 1377–1384.

Kiecolt-Glaser, J. K., & Newton, T. L. (2001). Marriage and health: His and hers. *Psychological Bulletin, 127,* 472–503.

Kiecolt-Glaser, J. K., Newton, T., Cacioppo, J. T., MacCallum, R. C., Glaser, R., & Malarkey, W. B. (1997). Marital conflict and endocrine function: Are men really more physiologically affected than women? *Journal of Consulting and Clinical Psychology, 64,* 324–332.

Kiecolt-Glaser, J. K., Preacher, K. J., MacCallum, R. C., Atkinson, C., Malarkey, W. B., & Glaser, R. (2003). Chronic stress and

age-related increases in the proinflammatory cytokine IL-6. *Proceedings of the National Academy of Sciences, 100*(15), 9090–9095.

Kim, D., Kawachi, I., Vander Hoorn, S., & Ezzati, M. (2008). Is inequality at the heart of it? Cross-country associations of income inequality with cardiovascular diseases and risk factors. *Social Science & Medicine, 66,* 1719–1732.

Kim, D. K., Lim, S. W., & Kim, H. (2003). Serotonin transporter gene polymorphisms in depression. *European Neuropsychopharmacology, 13*(4), S239.

Kim, D. S., & Kim, H. S. (2009). Body-image dissatisfaction as a predictor of suicidal ideation among Korean boys and girls in different stages of adolescence: A two-year longitudinal study. *Journal of Adolescent Health, 45*(1), 47–54.

King, A. C., Goldberg, J. H., Salmon, J., Owen, N., Dunstan, D., Weber, D., … Robinson, T. N. (2010). Identifying subgroups of U.S. adults at risk for prolonged television viewing to inform program development. *American Journal of Preventive Medicine, 38*(1), 17–26.

King, D. K., Glasgow, R. E., Toobert, D. J., Strycker, L. A., Estabrooks, P. A., Osuna, D., & Faber, A. J. (2010). Self-efficacy, problem solving, and social-environmental support are associated with diabetes self-management behaviors. *Diabetes Care, 33,* 751–753.

King, K. R. (2005). Why is discrimination stressful? The mediating role of cognitive appraisal. *Cultural Diversity & Ethnic Minority Psychology, 11*(3), 202–212.

Kinnunen, M.-L., Kaprio, J., & Pulkkinen, L. (2005). Allostatic load of men and women in early middle age. *Journal of Individual Differences, 26*(1), 20–28.

Kirkcaldy, B. D., Shephard, R. J., & Siefen, R. (2002). The relationship between physical activity and self-image and problem behavior among adolescents. *Social Psychiatry and Psychiatric Epidemiology, 37*(11), 544–550.

Kivimaki, M., Head, J., Ferried, J. E., Brunner, E., Marmot, M. G., Vahtera, J., & Shipley, M. J. (2006). Why is evidence on job strain and coronary heart disease mixed? An illustration of measurement challenges in the Whitehall II study. *Psychosomatic Medicine, 68,* 398–401.

Kivimaki, M., Nyberg, S. T., Batty, G. D., Fransson, E., Heikkila, K., Alfredsson, L., … Theorell, T. (2012). Job strain as a risk factor for coronary heart disease: A collaborative meta-analysis of individual participant data. *The Lancet, 380*(9852), 1491–1497.

Kiviruusu, O., Huurre, T., & Aro, H. (2007). Psychosocial resources and depression among chronically ill young adults: Are males more vulnerable? *Social Science & Medicine, 65*(2), 173–186.

Klaus, S. F., Ekerdt, D. J., & Gajewski, B. (2012). Job satisfaction in birth cohorts of nurses. *Journal of Nursing Management, 20*(4), 461–471.

Klein, S., & Alexander, D. A. (2007). Trauma and stress-related disorders. *Psychiatry, 5*(7), 225–227.

Klump, K. L., Suisman, J. L., Burt, S. A., McGue, M., & Iacono, W. G. (2009). Genetic and environmental influences on disordered eating: An adoption study. *Journal of Abnormal Psychology, 118*(4), 797–805.

Kluver, H., & Bucy, P. C. (1939). Preliminary analysis of functions of the temporal lobes in monkeys. *Archives of Neurology and Psychiatry, 42,* 979–1000.

Knittle, K., Maes, S., & de Gucht, V. (2010). Psychological interventions for rheumatoid arthritis: Examining the role of self-regulation with a systematic review and meta-analysis of randomized controlled trials. *Arthritis Care and Research, 62*(10), 1460–1472.

Kochanek, K. D., Murphy, S. L., & Xu, J. (2015). Deaths: Final data for 2011. *National Vital Statistics Reports; 63*(3). Hyattsville, MD: National Center for Health Statistics.

Kochanek, K. D., Murphy, S. L., Xu, J., & Arias, E. (2014). Mortality in the United States, 2013. *NCHS data brief, no. 178.* Hyattsville, MD: National Center for Health Statistics.

Koenig, H. G., Hooten, E. G., Lindsay-Calkins, E., & Meador, K. G. (2010). Spirituality in medical school curricula: Findings from a national survey. *International Journal of Psychiatry in Medicine, 40*(4), 391–398.

Kohn, P. M., Lafreniere, K., & Gurevich, M. (1990). The inventory of college students' recent life experiences: A decontaminated hassles scale for a special population. *Journal of Behavioral Medicine, 13,* 619–630.

Koizumi, M., Ito, H., Kaneko, Y., & Motohashi, Y. (2008). Effect of having a sense of purpose in life on the risk of death from cardiovascular disease. *Journal of Epidemiology, 18,* 191–196.

Kop, W. J., Gottdiener, J. S., & Krantz, D. S. (2001). Stress and silent ischemia. In A. Baum, T. A. Revenson, & J. E. Singer (Eds.), *Handbook of health psychology* (pp. 669–682). Mahwah, NJ: Erlbaum.

Kop, W. J., & Krantz, D. S. (1997). Type A behaviour, hostility and coronary artery disease. In A. Baum, S. Newman, J. Weinman, R. West, & C. McManus (Eds.), *Cambridge handbook of psychology, health, and medicine* (pp. 183–186). Cambridge, UK: Cambridge University Press.

Kop, W. J., Stein, P. K., Tracy, R. P., Barzilay, J. I., Shulz, R., & Gottdiener, J. S. (2010). Autonomic nervous system dysfunction and inflammation contribute to the increased cardiovascular mortality risk associated with depression. *Psychosomatic Medicine, 72,* 626–635.

Korb, A. (2015). *The upward spiral: Using neuroscience to reduce the course of depression, one small change at a time.* Oakland, CA: New Harbinger Publications.

Kotze, A., & Simpson, K. H. (2008). Stimulation-produced analgesia: Acupuncture, TENS, and related techniques. *Anaesthesia and Intensive Care Medicine, 9*(1), 29–32.

Koutras, C., Bitsaki, M., Koutras, G., Nikolaou, C., & Heep, H. (2015, August 17). Socioeconomic impact of e-health services in major joint replacement: A scoping review. *Technology and Health Care, 23*(6), 809–817.

Kozo, J., Sallis, J. F., Conway, T. L., Kerr, J., Cain, K., Saelens, B. E., … Owen, N. (2012). Sedentary behaviors of adults in relation to neighborhood walkability and income. *Health Psychology, 31*(6), 704.

Kposowa, A. J., & Tsunokai, G. T. (2002). Searching for relief: Racial differences in treatment of patients with back pain. *Race and Society, 5*(2), 193–223.

Kramer, A. F., & Erickson, K. I. (2007). Capitalizing on cortical plasticity: Influence of physical activity on cognition and brain function. *Trends in Cognitive Sciences, 11,* 342–348.

Kraus, W. E., Houmard, J. A., Duscha, B. D., Knetzger, K. J., Wharton, M. B., McCartney, J. S., … Slentz, C. A. (2002). Effects of the amount and intensity of exercise on plasma lipoproteins. *New England Journal of Medicine, 347,* 1483–1492.

Krawczyk, A. L., Perez, S., Lau, E., Holcroft, C. A., Amsel, R., Knauper, B., & Rosberger, Z. (2012). Human papillomavirus vaccination intentions and uptake in college women. *Health Psychology, 31*(5), 685–693.

Kreibel, J. (2010, April 30). Behavioral and drug therapy together help treat alcoholism. National Institute on Alcohol Abuse and Alcoholism. Retrieved from http://www.niaaa.nih.gov/research/niaaa-research-highlights/behavioral-and-drug-therapy-together-help-treat-alcoholism

Kressin, N. R., Raymond, K. L., & Manze, M. (2008). Perceptions of race/ethnicity-based discrimination: A review of measures and evaluation of their usefulness for the health care setting. *Journal of Health Care for the Poor and Underserved, 19*(3), 697–730.

Krieger, N., Sidney, S., & Coakley, E. (1998). Racial discrimination and skin color in the CARDIA study: Implications for public health research. *American Journal of Public Health, 88,* 1308–1313.

Krueger, P. M., & Chang, V. W. (2008). Being poor and coping with stress: Health behaviors and the risk of death. *American Journal of Public Health, 98*(5), 889–896.

Kuchipudi, V., Hobein, K., Flinkinger, A., & Iber, F. L. (1990). Failure of a 2-hour motivational intervention to alter recurrent drinking in alcoholics with gastrointestinal disease. *Journal of Studies on Alcohol, 51*(4), 356–360.

Kuklina, E. V., Carroll, M. D., Shaw, K. M., & Hirsch, R. (2013). Trends in high LDL cholesterol, cholesterol-lowering medication use, and dietary saturated-fat intake: United States, 1976–2010. *NCHS data brief, no. 117.* Hyattsville, MD: National Center for Health Statistics.

Kullgren, I. K. (2014, August 29). If Oregon legalizes marijuana, how will it keep roads safe? *The Oregonian.* Retrieved May 4, 2016, from http://www.oregonlive.com/politics/index.ssf/2014/08/if_oregon_legalizes_marijuana.html

Kumari, M., Shipley, M., Stafford, M., & Kivimaki, M. (2011). Association of diurnal patterns in salivary cortisol with all-cause and cardiovascular mortality: Findings from the Whitehall II study. *Journal of Clinical Endocrinology and Metabolism, 96,* 1478–1485.

Kurl, S., Laukkanen, J. A., Rauramaa, R., Lakka, T. A., Sivenius, J., & Salonen, J. T. (2003). Cardiorespiratory fitness and the risk for stroke in men. *Archives of Internal Medicine, 163*(14), 1682–1688.

LaBrie, J. W., Hummer, J. F., & Pedersen, E. R. (2007). Reasons for drinking in the college student context: The differential role and risk of the social motivator. *Journal of Studies on Alcohol, 68*(3), 393–398.

Lachman, M. E., & Weaver, S. L. (1998). The sense of control as a moderator of social class differences in health and well-being. *Journal of Personality and Social Psychology, 74,* 763–773.

Lammers, C., Ireland, M., Resnick, M., & Blum, R. (2000). Influences on adolescents' decision to postpone onset of sexual intercourse: A survival analysis of virginity among youths aged 13 to 18 years. *Journal of Adolescent Health, 26,* 42–48.

Lando, H. A. (1986). Long-term modification of chronic smoking behavior: A paradigmatic approach. *Bulletin of the Society of Psychologists in Addictive Behaviors, 5,* 5–17.

Landro, L. (2001, February 2). Health groups push "information therapy" to help treat patients. *The Wall Street Journal,* p. B1.

Langer, E. J., & Rodin, J. (1976). The effects of choice and enhanced personal responsibility for the aged: A field experiment in an institutional setting. *Journal of Personality and Social Psychology, 34,* 191–198.

Langer, S. L, Romano, J. M., Manci, L., & Levy, R. L. (2014). Parental catastrophizing partially mediates the association between parent-reported child pain behavior and parental protective responses. *Pain Research and Treatment.* Retrieved March 1, 2016, from http://www.hindawi.com/journals/prt/2014/751097/

Langner, T., & Michael, S. (1960). *Life stress and mental health.* New York: Free Press.

Larkin, M. (2007, August 30). The limits of willpower. *The New York Times*. Retrieved March 5, 2010, from http://health .nytimes.com/ref/health/healthguide/esn-obesity-qa.html

LaRocca, T. J., Seals, D. R., & Pierce, G. L. (2010). Leukocyte telomere length is preserved with aging in endurance-trained adults and related to maximal aerobic capacity. *Mechanisms of Ageing and Development, 131*(2), 165.

LaRose, J. G., Fava, J. L., Steeves, E. A., Hecht, J., Wing, R. R., & Raynor, H. A. (2014). Daily self-weighing within a lifestyle intervention: Impact on disordered eating symptoms. *Health Psychology, 33*(3), 297–300.

Lasagna, L. (1964). Hippocratic oath, modern version. Retrieved from http://guides.library.jhu.edu/c.php?g=202502&p=1335759

Latkin, C. A., & Knowlton, A. R. (2005). Micro-social structural approaches to HIV prevention: A social ecological perspective. *AIDS Care, 17*(Supplement 1), 102–113.

Latner, J. D., & Stunkard, A. J. (2003). Getting worse: The stigmatization of obese children. *Obesity Research, 11*(3), 452–456.

Launer, L. J., & Kalmijn, S. (1998). Anti-oxidants and cognitive function: A review of clinical and epidemiologic studies. *Journal of Neural Transmission, 53*, 1–8.

Lauver, D. R., Henriques, J. B., Settersten, L., & Bumann, M. C. (2003). Psychosocial variables, external barriers, and stage of mammography adoption. *Health Psychology, 22*(6), 649–653.

Lavernia, C. J., Alcerro, J. C., Contreras, J. S., & Rossi, M. D. (2011). Ethnic and racial factors influencing well-being, perceived pain, and physical function after primary total joint arthroplasty. *Clinical Orthopaedics and Related Research, 469*(7), 1838–1845.

Lavie, C. J., & Milani, R. V. (2005). Prevalence of hostility in young coronary artery disease patients and effects of cardiac rehabilitation and exercise training. *Mayo Clinic Proceedings, 80*(3), 335–342.

Law, A., Logan, H., & Baron, R. S. (1994). Desire for control, felt control, and stress inoculation training through dental treatment. *Journal of Personality and Social Psychology, 67*, 926–936.

Lawler, K. A., Younger, J. W., Piferi, R. L., Billington, E., Jobe, R., Edmondson, K., & Jones, W. H. (2003). A change of heart: Cardiovascular correlates of forgiveness in response to interpersonal threat. *Journal of Behavioral Medicine, 26*(5), 373–393.

Lawton, R., Conner, M., & Parker, D. (2007). Beyond cognition: Predicting health risk behaviors from instrumental and affective beliefs. *Health Psychology, 26*, 259–267.

Lazarus, R. S., & Folkman, S. (1984). *Stress, appraisal, and coping.* New York: Springer.

Leary, M. R., Tchividjiam, L. R., & Kraxberger, B. E. (1994). Self-presentation can be hazardous to your health: Impression management and health risk. *Health Psychology, 13*(6), 461–470.

Lebovits, A. (2007). Cognitive-behavioral approaches to chronic pain. *Primary Psychiatry, 14*(9), 48–50.

Lee, C. D., Folsom, A. R., & Blair, S. N. (2003). Physical activity and stroke risk: A meta–analysis. *Stroke, 34*(1), 2475–2481.

Lee, I. M., Bauman, A. E., Blair, S. N., Heath, G. W., Kohl, H. W., Pratt, M., & Hallal, P. C. (2013). Annual deaths attributable to physical inactivity: Whither the missing 2 million? *The Lancet, 381*(9871), 992–993.

Lee, I. M., Manson, J. E., Hennekens, C. H., & Paffenbarger, R. S. (1993). Body weight and mortality. A 27-year follow-up of middle-aged men. *Journal of the American Medical Association, 270*(23), 2823–2828.

Lee, J. L., Gilleland, J., Campbell, R. M., Simpson, P., Johnson, G. L., Dooley, K. J., & Blount, R. L. (2013). Health care utilization and psychosocial factors in pediatric noncardiac chest pain. *Health Psychology, 32*(3), 320–327.

Lee, T. Y., Chang, S. C., Chu, H., Yang, C. Y., Ou, K. L., Chung, M. H., & Chou, K. R. (2013). The effects of assertiveness training in patients with schizophrenia: A randomized, single-blind, controlled study. *Journal of Advanced Nursing, 69*(11), 2549–2559.

Leeuw, M., Goossens, M. E. J. B., Linton, S. J., Crombez, G., Boersma, K., & Vlaeyen, J. W. S. (2007). The fear-avoidance model of musculoskeletal pain: Current state of scientific evidence. *Journal of Behavioral Medicine, 30*, 77–94.

Lehrer, P. M., Carr, R., Sargunaraj, D., & Woolfolk, R. L. (1994). Stress management techniques: Are they all equivalent, or do they have specific effects? *Biofeedback and Self-Regulation, 19*, 353–401.

Lehrer, P. M., & Eddie, D. (2013). Dynamic processes in regulation and some implications for biofeedback and biobehavioral interventions. *Applied Psychophysiology & Biofeedback, 38*, 143–155.

Lehrer, P. M., & Gevirtz, R. (2014). Heart rate variability biofeedback: How and why does it work? *Frontiers in Psychology*. Retrieved March 2, 2016, from http://journal .frontiersin.org/article/10.3389/fpsyg.2014.00756/abstract

Leibel, R. L., Rosenbaum, M., & Hirsch, J. (1995). Changes in energy expenditure resulting from altered body weight. *New England Journal of Medicine, 332*, 621–629.

Lelorain, S., Bonnaud-Antignac, A., & Florin, A. (2010). Long-term posttraumatic growth after breast cancer: Prevalence, predictors, and relationships with psychological health. *Journal of Clinical Psychology in Medical Settings, 17*, 14–22.

Lenhart, A., Purcell, K., Smith, A., & Zickuhr, K. (2010). *Social media and mobile internet use among teens and young adults.* Washington, DC: Pew Internet & American Life Project.

Leo, R. J., & Ligot, J. S. A. (2007). A systematic review of randomized controlled trials of acupuncture in the treatment of depression. *Journal of Affective Disorders, 97*, 13–22.

Leon, A., & Bronas, U. (2009). Dyslipidemian and risk of coronary heart disease: Role of lifestyle approaches for its management. *American Journal of Lifestyle Medicine, 3*(4), 257–273.

Leonhard, C., & Randler, C. (2009). In sync with the family: Children and partners influence the sleep-wake circadian rhythm and social habits of women. *Chronobiology International, 26*, 510–525.

Lepore, S. J., Revenson, T. A., Weinberger, S. L., Weston, P., Frisina, P. G., Robertson, R., … Cross, W. (2006). Effects of social stressors on cardiovascular reactivity in black and white women. *Annals of Behavioral Medicine, 31*(2), 120–127.

Leproult, R., Copinschi, G., Buxton, O., & Van Cauter, E. (1997). Sleep loss results in an elevation of cortisol levels the next evening. *Sleep, 20*, 865–870.

Leresche, L. (2011). Defining gender disparities in pain management. *Clinical Orthopaedics and Related Research, 7*, 1871–1877.

Lerman, C., Caporaso, N. E., Audrain, J., Main, D., Bowman, E. D., Lockshin, B., Boyd, N. R., & Shields, P. G. (1999). Evidence suggesting the role of specific genetic factors in cigarette smoking. *Health Psychology, 18*(1), 14–20.

Lerman, C., Kaufmann, V., Rukstalis, M., Patterson, F., Perkins, K., Audrain-McGovern, J., & Benowitz, N. (2004). Individualizing nicotine replacement therapy for the treatment. *Annals of Internal Medicine, 140*, 426–433.

Leserman, J., Petitto, J. M., Golden, R. N., Gaynes, B. N., Gu, H., Perkins, D. O., ... Evans, D. L. (2000). Impact of stressful life events, depression, social support, coping, and cortisol on progression to AIDS. *American Journal of Psychiatry, 157,* 1221–1228.

Lestideau, O. T., & Lavallee, L. F. (2007). Structured writing about current stressors: The benefits of developing plans. *Psychology and Health, 22,* 659–676.

Leukemia & Lymphoma Society. (2016). Lymphoma. Retrieved from http://www.lls.org/lymphoma

Leventhal, A. M., Strong, D. R., Kirkpatrick, M. G., Unger, J. B., Sussman, S., Riggs, N. R., Stone, M. D., ... Audrain-McGovern, J. (2015). Association of electronic cigarette use with initiation of combustible tobacco smoking in early adolescence. *Journal of the American Medical Association, 314*(7), 700–707.

Levine, F. M., & DeSimone, L. L. (1991). The effect of experimenter gender on pain report in male and female subjects. *Pain, 44,* 69–72.

Levine, J. A., Eberhardt, N. L., & Jensen, M. D. (1999). Role of nonexercise activity thermogenesis in resistance to fat gain in humans. *Science, 283,* 212–214.

Levine, J. A., Lanningham-Foster, L. M., McCrady, S. K., Krizan, A. C., Olson, L. R., Kane, P. H., Jensen, M. D., & Clark, M. M. (2005). Interindividual variation in posture allocation: Possible role in human obesity. *Science, 307,* 584–586.

Levine, J. D., Gordon, N. C., & Fields, H. L. (1978). The mechanism of placebo analgesia. *The Lancet, 8091,* 654–657.

Lewandowski, A. S., Palermo, T. M., De la Mott, S., & Fu, R. (2010). Temporal daily associations between pain and sleep in adolescents with chronic pain versus healthy adolescents. *Pain, 15,* 220–225.

Lewis, M. A., Uhrig, J. D., Bann, C. M., Harris, J. L., Furberg, R. D., Coomes, C., & Kuhns, L. M. (2013). Tailored text messaging intervention for HIV adherence: A proof-of-concept study. *Health Psychology, 32*(3), 248–253.

Lewis, R. J., Derlega, V. J., Berndt, A., Morris, L. M., & Rose, S. (2002). An empirical analysis of stressors for gay men and lesbians. *Journal of Homosexuality, 42,* 63–88.

Li, A. W., & Goldsmith, C. A. (2012). The effects of yoga on anxiety and stress. *Alternative Medicine Review, 17*(1), 21–35.

Li, T. K., Hewitt, B. G., & Grant, B. F. (2007). The alcohol dependence syndrome, 30 years later: A commentary. *Addiction, 102,* 1522–1530.

Li, Y., Baer, D., Friedman, G. D., Udaltsova, N., Shim, V., & Klatsky, A. L. (2009). Wine, liquor, beer and risk of breast cancer in a large population. *European Journal of Cancer, 45*(5), 843–850.

Liao, C. C., Yeh, C. J., Lee, S. H., Liao, W. C., Liao, M. Y., & Lee, M. C. (2015). Providing instrumental support is more beneficial to reduce mortality risk among the elderly with low educational level in Taiwan: A 12-year follow-up national longitudinal study. *Journal of Nutrition, Health, and Aging, 19*(4), 447–453.

Lichtenstein, E., & Glasgow, R. E. (1997). A pragmatic framework for smoking cessation: Implications for clinical and public health programs. *Psychology of Addictive Behaviors, 11,* 142–151.

Lick, D. J., Durso, L. E., & Johnson, K. L. (2013). Minority stress and physical health among sexual minorities. *Perspectives on Psychological Science, 8,* 521–548.

Lieberman, M. A. (1982). The effects of social supports on responses to stress. In L. Goldberger & L. Breznitz (Eds.), *Handbook of stress.* New York: Free Press.

Lim, J., & Dinges, D. F. (2010). A meta-analysis of the impact of short-term sleep deprivation on cognitive variables. *Psychological Bulletin, 136,* 375–389.

Lindor, N. M., Lindor, C. J., & Greene, M. H. (2006). Hereditary neoplastic syndromes. In D. Schottenfeld & J. F. Fraumeni Jr. (Eds.), *Cancer epidemiology and prevention* (pp. 562–576). New York: Oxford University Press.

Linnan, L., Bowling, M., Childress, J., Lindsay, G., Blakey, C., Pronk, S., Wieker, S., & Royall, P. (2008). Results of the 2004 national worksite health promotion survey. *American Journal of Public Health, 98,* 1503–1509.

Linus Pauling Institute (LPI). (2016). Linus Pauling Institute micronutrient information center. Retrieved June 16, 2016, from http://lpi.oregonstate.edu/mic/vitamins/vitamin-C

Lipton, J. A., & Marbach, J. J. (1984). Ethnicity and the pain experience. *Social Science and Medicine, 19,* 1279–1298.

Liston, C., Miller, M. M., Goldwater, D. S., Radley, J. J., Rocher, A. B., Hof, P. R., Morrison, J. H., & McEwen, B. S. (2006). Stress-induced alterations in prefrontal cortical dendritic morphology predict selective impairments in perceptual attentional set-shifting. *Journal of Neuroscience, 26*(30), 7870–7874.

Livermore, M. M., & Powers, R. S. (2006). Unfulfilled plans and financial stress: Unwed mothers and unemployment. *Journal of Human Behavior in the Social Environment, 13,* 1–7.

Logie, C. H., James, L., Wangari, T., & Loutfy, M. R. (2012). "We don't exist": A qualitative study of marginalization experienced by HIV-positive lesbian, bisexual, queer and transgender women in Toronto, Canada. *Journal of the International AIDS Society.* Retrieved February 23, 2016, from http://www.jiasociety.org/index.php/jias/article/view/17392

Lopez-Quintero, C., Pérez de los Cobos, J., Hasin, D. S, Okuda, M., Wang, S., Grant, B. F., & Blanco, C. (2011). Probability and predictors of transition from first use to dependence on nicotine, alcohol, cannabis, and cocaine: Results of the National Epidemiologic Survey on Alcohol and Related Conditions (NESARC). *Drug and Alcohol Dependence, 115* (1–2), 120–130.

Louganis, G. (2014, September 20). Living with HIV: New horizons. *The Huffington Post.* Retrieved from http://www.huffingtonpost.com/greg-louganis/living-with-hiv-new-horizons_b_5844824.html

Lovallo, W. R., & Pishkin, V. (1980). A psychophysiological comparison of type A and B men exposed to failure and uncontrollable noise. *Psychophysiology, 17,* 29–36.

Lowe, M. R. (2003). Self-regulation of energy intake in the prevention and treatment of obesity: Is it feasible? *Obesity Research, 11*(S10), 44S–59S.

Lu, Q., Zheng, D., Young, L., Kagawa-Singer, M., & Loh, A. (2012). A pilot study of expressive writing intervention among Chinese-speaking breast cancer survivors. *Health Psychology, 31*(5), 548–551.

Lucire, Y. (2003). *Constructing RSI: Belief and desire.* Sydney: University of New South Wales Press.

Luckett, T., Goldstein, D., Butow, P. N., Gebski, V., Aldridge, L. J., McGrane, J., ... King, M. T. (2011). Psychological morbidity and quality of life of ethnic minority patients with cancer: A systematic review and meta-analysis. *The Lancet Oncology, 12,* 1240–1248.

Luecken, L. J., & Compas, B. E. (2002). Stress, coping, and immune function in breast cancer. *Annals of Behavioral Medicine, 24,* 336–344.

Lundahl, B., Moleni, T., Burke, B. L., Butters, R, Tollefson, D., Butler, C., & Rollnick, S. (2013). Motivational interviewing in medical care settings: A systematic review and meta-analysis of randomized controlled trials. *Patient Education and Counseling, 93*(2), 157–168.

Luo, Y., Xu, J., Granberg, E., & Wentworth, W. M. (2012). A longitudinal study of social status, perceived discrimination, and physical and emotional health among older adults. *Research on Aging, 34*(3), 237–301.

Lustman, P. J., & Clouse, R. E. (2005). Depression in diabetic patients: The relationship between mood and glycemic control. *Journal of Diabetes and Its Complications, 19*, 113–122.

Luthans, F., Avolio, B. J., Avey, J. B., & Norman, S. M. (2007). Positive psychological capital: Measurement and relationship with performance and satisfaction. *Personnel Psychology, 60*, 541–572.

Lynch, B. M., Dunstan, D. W., Healy, G. N., Winkler, E., Eakin, E., & Owen, N. (2010). Objectively measured physical activity and sedentary time of breast cancer survivors, and associations with adiposity: Findings from NHANES (2003–2006). *Cancer Causes Control, 21*, 283–288.

Lyness, S. A. (1993). Predictors of differences between type A and B individuals in heart rate and blood pressure reactivity. *Psychological Bulletin, 114*, 266–295.

Lyons, A. C., Goodwin, I., McCreanor, T., & Griffin, C. (2015). Social networking and young adults' drinking practices: Innovative qualitative methods for health behavior research. *Health Psychology, 34*(4), 293–302.

Lyubomirsky, S., Caldwell, N. D., & Nolen-Hoeksema, S. (1998). Effects of ruminative and distracting responses to depressed mood on retrieval of autobiographical memories. *Journal of Personality and Social Psychology, 75*, 166–177.

Ma, J. L. (2008). Eating disorders, parent-child conflicts, and family therapy in Shenzhen, China. *Qualitative Health Research, 18*(6), 803–810.

Maas, J. B. (2013). *Sleep to win!* Bloomington, IN: AuthorHouse.

MacGregor, S., Lind, P. A., Bucholz, K. K., Hansell, N. K., Madden, P. A., Richter, M. M., Montgomery, G. W., Martin, N. G., Heath, A. C., & Whitfield, J. B. (2009). Associations of ADH and ALDH2 gene variation with self-report alcohol reactions, consumption and dependence: An integrated analysis. *Human Molecular Genetics, 18*(3), 580–593.

MacKellar, D. A., Valleroy, L. A., Secura, G. M., Behel, S., Bingham, T., Celentano, D. D., … Torian, L. V. (2007). Perceptions of lifetime risk and actual risk for acquiring HIV among young men who have sex with men. *AIDS and Behavior, 11*, 263–270.

Madden, M., & Lenhart, A. (2009, November 16). Teens and distracted driving. *PewInternet.* Retrieved from http://pewinternet.org/Reports/2009/Teens-and-Distracted-Driving/Overview.aspx

Maenthaisong, R., Chaiyakunapruk, N., Niruntraporn, S., & Kongkaew, C. (2007). The efficacy of aloe vera used for burn wound healing: A systematic review. *Burns, 33*(6), 713–718.

Maes, H. M., Neale, M. C., & Eaves, L. J. (1997). Genetic and environmental factors in relative body weight and human adiposity. *Behavioral Genetics, 27*(special issue: The Genetics of Obesity), 325–351.

Magni, G., Silvestro, A., Tamiello, M., Zanesco, L., & Carl, B. (1988). An integrated approach to the assessment of family adjustment to acute lymphocytic leukemia in children. *Acta Psychiatrica Scandinavica, 78*, 639–642.

Mahler, H. I. M., Kulik, J. A., Gibbons, F. X., Gerrard, J., & Harrell, J. (2003). Effects of appearance-based interventions on sun protection intentions and self-reported behaviors. *Health Psychology, 22*, 99–209.

Maier, K. J., Waldstein, S. R., & Synowski, S. J. (2003). Relation of cognitive appraisal to cardiovascular reactivity, affect, and task engagement. *Annals of Behavioral Medicine, 26*(1), 32–41.

Maier, S. F. (2003). Bi-directional immune-brain communication: Implications for understanding stress, pain, and cognition. *Brain, Behavior, and Immunity, 17*(2), 69–85.

Manfredi, C., Kaiser, K., Matthews, A. K., & Johnson, T. P. (2010). Are racial differences in patient-physician cancer communication and information explained by background, predisposing, and enabling factors? *Journal of Health Communication, 15*, 272–292.

Mann, T., Sherman, D., & Updegraff, J. (2004). Dispositional motivations and message framing: A test of the congruency hypothesis in college students. *Health Psychology, 23*(3), 330–334.

Mann, T., Tomiyama, A. J., Westling, E., Lew, A.-M., Samuels, B., & Chatman, J. (2007). Medicare's search for effective obesity treatments: Diets are not the answer. *American Psychologist, 62*, 220–233.

Mann, T., & Ward, A. (2007). Attention, self-control, and health behaviors. *Current Directions in Psychological Science, 16*(5), 280–283.

Manne, S. L., & Andrykowski, M. A. (2006). Are psychological interventions effective and accepted by cancer patients? Using empirically supported therapy guidelines to decide. *Annals of Behavioral Medicine, 32*, 98–103.

Manos, R. C., Kanter, J. W., & Busch A. M. (2010). Attempts to measure activation as conceptualized within behavioral activation treatments. *Clinical Psychology Review, 30*, 547–561.

Marchand, A., Durand, P., & Lupien, S. (2012, June 9). Work hours and cortisol variation from non-working to working days. *International Archives of Occupational and Environmental Health, 86*(5), 553–559.

Marcinowicz, L., Chlabicz, S., & Grebowski, R. (2009). Patient satisfaction with healthcare by family doctors: Primary dimensions and an attempt at typology. *BMC Health Services Research, 9*, 63–67.

Marco, C. A. (2004). Coping. In A. J. Christensen, R. Martin, & J. M. Smyth (Eds.), *Encyclopedia of health psychology* (pp. 66–70). New York: Kluwer.

Markovic, D., Jankovic, R., & Vesilinovic, I. (2015). Mutations in sodium channel gene SCN9A and the pain perception disorders. *Advances in Anesthesiology.* Retrieved March 1, 2016, from http://www.hindawi.com/journals/aan/2015/562378/

Markovitz, J. H., Matthews, K. A., Kannel, W. B., Cobb, J. L., & D'Agostino, R. B. (1993). Psychological predictors of hypertension in the Framingham Study. Is there tension in hypertension? *Journal of the American Medical Association, 270*, 2439–2443.

Markovitz, J. H., Matthews, K. A., Whooley, M., Lewis, C. E., & Greenlund, K. J. (2004). Increases in job strain are associated with incident hypertension in the CARDIA Study. *Annals of Behavioral Medicine, 28*(1), 4–9.

Markowitz, L. E., Liu, G., Hariri, S., Steinau, M., Dunne, E. F., & Unger, E. R. (2016, February 22). Prevalence of HPV after introduction of the vaccination program in the United States. *Pediatrics Online, 137*(2). Retrieved February 28, 2016, from http://pediatrics.aappublications.org/content/early/2016/02/19/peds.2015-1968

Marmot, M. G., Smith, G. D., Stansfeld, S., Patel, C., North, F., Head, J., & Feeney, A. (1991). Health inequalities among British civil servants: The Whitehall II study. *The Lancet, 337*, 1387–1393.

Marshall, A. L., Bauman, A. E., Owen, N., Booth, M. L., Crawford, D., & Marcus, B. H. (2003). Population-based randomized controlled trial of a stage-targeted physical activity intervention. *Annals of Behavioral Medicine, 25*, 194–202.

Martin, A. R., Nieto, J. M., Ruiz, J. P., & Jimenez, L. E. (2008). Overweight and obesity: The role of education, employment, and income in Spanish adults. *Appetite, 51*(2), 266–272.

Martin, P. D., & Brantley, P. J. (2004). Stress, coping, and social support in health and behavior. In J. M. Raczynsky & L. C. Leviton (Eds.), *Handbook of clinical health psychology* (Vol. 2; pp. 233–267). Washington, DC: American Psychological Association.

Martin, P. R. (1985). *Alcohol Health & Research World, 9* [Cover].

Martin, P. R., Forsyth, M., & Reece, J. E. (2007). Cognitive-behavioral therapy versus temporal pulse amplitude biofeedback training for recurrent headache. *Behavior Therapy, 38*, 350–363.

Maru, S., van der Schouw, Y. T., Gimbrere, C. H., Grobbee, D. E., & Peeters, P. H. (2004). Body mass index and short-term weight change in relation to mortality in Dutch women after age 50. *American Journal of Clinical Nutrition, 80*(1), 231–236.

Maruta, T., Colligan, R. C., Malinchoc, M., & Offord, K. P. (2000). Optimists vs. pessimists: Survival rate among medical patients over a 30-year period. *Mayo Clinic Proceedings, 75*, 140–143.

Marx, J. (2003). Cellular warriors at the battle of the bulge. *Science, 299*(5608), 846–849.

Masedo, A. L., & Rosa, E. M. (2007). Effects of suppression, acceptance, and spontaneous coping on pain tolerance, pain intensity and distress. *Behaviour Research and Therapy, 45*(2), 199–209.

Maslach, C. (2003). Job burnout: New directions in research and intervention. *Current Directions, 12*, 189–192.

Massey, C. V., Hupp, C. H., Kreisberg, M., Alpert, M. A., & Hoff, C. (2000). Estrogen replacement therapy is underutilized among postmenopausal women at high risk for coronary heart disease. *American Journal of the Medical Sciences, 320*, 124–127.

Masten, A. S. (2001). Ordinary magic: Resilience processes in development. *American Psychologist, 56*, 218–226.

Masters, K. S., & Hooker, S. A. (2013). Religiousness/spirituality, cardiovascular disease, and cancer: Cultural integration for health research and intervention. *Journal of Consulting and Clinical Psychology, 81*(2), 206–216.

Matarazzo, J. (1982). Behavioral health's challenge to academic, scientific, and professional psychology. *American Psychologist, 37*(1), 1–14.

Mathews, L. (2011). Pain in children: Neglected, unaddressed and mismanaged. *Indian Journal of Palliative Care, 17*, S70–S73.

Matthews, K. A., Dahl, R. E., Owens, J. F., Lee, L., & Hall, M. (2012). Sleep duration and insulin resistance in healthy black and white adolescents. *Sleep, 35*(10), 1353–1358.

Matthews, K. A., Raikkonen, K., Sutton-Tyrrell, K., & Kuller, L. H. (2004). Optimistic attitudes protect against progression of carotid atherosclerosis in healthy middle-aged women. *Psychosomatic Medicine, 66*(5), 640–644.

Matthews, K. A., Schott, L. L., Bromberger, J. T., Cyranowski, J., Everson-Rose, S., & Sowers, M. F. (2007). Associations between depressive symptoms and inflammatory/hemostatic markers in women during the menopausal transition. *Psychosomatic Medicine, 69*, 124–130.

Matthews, K. A., Woodall, K. L., & Allen, M. T. (1993). Cardiovascular reactivity to stress predicts future blood pressure status. *Hypertension, 22*(4), 479–485.

Matthews, R. B., Jenkins, G. K., & Robertson, J. (2012). Health care reform: Why not best practices? *American Journal of Health Sciences, 3*(1), 97–113.

Matthews, T. J., MacDorman, M. F., & Thoma, M. E. (2015). Infant mortality statistics from the 2013 period linked birth/infant death data set. *National Vital Statistics Reports, 64*(9). Hyattsville, MD: National Center for Health Statistics.

Mavros, M. N., Athanasiou, S., Gkegkes, I. O., Polyzos, K. A., Peppas, G., & Falagas, M. E. (2011). Do psychological variables affect early surgical recovery? *PLOS ONE, 6*(5). Retrieved February 26, 2016, from http://www.ncbi.nlm.nih.gov/pmc/articles/PMC3102096/#__ffn_sectitle

Mayer, J. D., Salovey, P., Caruson, D. R., & Sitarenios, G. (2001). Emotional intelligence as a standard intelligence. *Emotion, 1*(3), 232–242.

Mayo Clinic. (2006). Alcohol: Even a drink a day can adversely affect women's health. Retrieved March 15, 2010, from http://www.mayoclinic.org/news2006-mchi/3271.html

Mayo Clinic. (2011). Aerobic exercise: Top 10 reasons to get physical. Retrieved from http://www.mayoclinic.com/health/aerobic-exercise/EP00002

Mayo Clinic. (2015). Sleep disorders. Retrieved from http://www.mayoclinic.org/diseases-conditions/sleep-disorders/basics/definition/con-20037263

Mays, V. M., Cochran, S. D., & Barnes, N. W. (2007). Race, race-based discrimination, and health outcomes among African Americans. *Annual Review of Psychology, 58*, 201–225.

McAlonan, G. M., Cheung, V., Cheung, C., Chua, S. E., Murphy, D. G., Suckling, J., Tai, K. S., Yip, L. K., Leung, P., & Ho, T. P. (2007). Mapping brain structure in attention-deficit hyperactivity disorder: A voxel-based MRI study of regional grey and white matter volume. *Psychiatry Research, 154*(2), 171–180.

McAuley, E., Jerome, D. X., Marquez, S., Elavsky, S., & Blissmer, B. (2003). Exercise self-efficacy in older adults: Social, affective, and behavioral influences. *Annals of Behavioral Medicine, 25*(1), 1–7.

McAuley, E., White, S. M., Rogers, L. Q., Motl, R. W., & Courneya, K. S. (2010). Physical activity and fatigue in breast cancer and multiple sclerosis: Psychosocial mechanisms. *Psychosomatic Medicine, 72*, 88–96.

McCaffery, J. M., Frasure-Smith, N., Dube, M. P., Theroux, P. Rouleau, G. A., Duan, Q., & Lesperance, F. (2006). Common genetic vulnerability to depressive symptoms and coronary artery disease: A review and development of candidate genes related to inflammation and serotonin. *Psychosomatic Medicine, 68*(2), 187–200.

McCain, N., Gray, D., Elswick, R., Robins, J., Tuck, Il, Walter, J., … Ketchum, J. M. (2008). A randomized clinical trial of alternative stress management interventions in persons with HIV infection. *Journal of Consulting and Clinical Psychology, 76*(3), 431–441.

McCann, I. L., & Holmes, D. S. (1984). Influence of aerobic exercise on depression. *Journal of Personality and Social Psychology, 46*, 1142–1147.

McCarthy, J. (2001). Superfoods or superfrauds? *Shape, 20*, 104–106.

McClelland, L. E., & McCubbin, J. A. (2008). Social influence and pain response in women and men. *Journal of Behavioral Medicine, 31*, 413–420.

McCracken, L. M., Matthews, A. K., Tang, T. S., & Cuba, S. L. (2001). A comparison of blacks and whites seeking treatment for chronic pain. *The Clinical Journal of Pain, 17*(3), 249–255.

McCracken, L. M., & Vowles, K. E. (2014). Acceptance and commitment therapy and mindfulness for chronic pain. *American Psychologist, 69*(2), 178–187.

McCright, A. M., & Dunlap, R. E. (2011). Cool dudes: The denial of climate change among conservative white males in the United States. *Global Environmental Change, 21*(4), 1163–1172.

McCullough, M. L., Peterson, J. J., Patel, R., Jacques, P. F., Shah, R., & Dwyer, J. T. (2012). Flavonoid intake and cardiovascular disease mortality in a prospective cohort of U.S. adults. *American Journal of Clinical Nutrition, 95*(2), 454–464.

McDaniel, D. D. (2012). Risk and protective factors associated with gang affiliation among high-risk youth: A public health approach. *Injury Prevention.* Retrieved from http://injuryprevention.bmj.com/content/early/2012/01/04/injuryprev-2011-040083.full

McEachan, R. R., Lawton, R. J., Jackson, C., Conner, M., Meads, D. M., & West, R. M. (2011). Testing a workplace physical activity intervention: A cluster randomized controlled trial. *International Journal of Behavioral Nutrition and Physical Activity, 8*(29). Retrieved February 25, 2016, from http://www.ncbi.nlm.nih.gov/pmc/articles/PMC3094266/

McEwen, B. S. (1998). Stress, adaptation and disease: Allostasis and allostatic load. *Annals of the New York Academy of Sciences, 840,* 33–44.

McEwen, B. S. (2007). Physiology and neurobiology of stress and adaptation. *Physiological Review, 87,* 873–904.

McEwen, B. S. (2011). Neurobiology of stress and adaptation: Implications for health psychology, behavioral medicine, and beyond. In M. A. Gernsbacher, R. W. Pew, L. M. Hough, & J. R. Pomerantz (Eds.), *Psychology and the real world: Essays illustrating fundamental contributions to society* (pp. 24–30). New York: Worth.

McEwen, B. S., & Gianaros, P. J. (2011). Stress- and allostasis-induced brain plasticity. *Annual Review of Medicine, 62,* 431–445.

McGrady, A., & Horner, J. (1999). Role of mood in outcome of biofeedback assisted relaxation therapy in insulin dependent diabetes mellitus. *Applied Psychophysiology and Biofeedback, 24,* 79–88.

McGrath, J. (2003). Pediatric cardiovascular reactivity: Evidence for stable individual differences and differentiation of higher- and lower-risk children. *Dissertation Abstracts International, 63*(10-B), 4913.

McGrath, P. J., Walco, G. A., Turk, D. C., Dworkin, R. H., Brown, M. T., Davidson, K., … Zeltzer, L. (2008). Core outcome domains and measures for pediatric acute and chronic/recurrent pain clinical trials: PedIMMPACT recommendations. *Journal of Pain, 9,* 771–783.

McLaren, L., Hardy, R., & Kuh, D. (2003). Women's body satisfaction at midlife and lifetime body size: A prospective study. *Health Psychology, 22*(4), 370–377.

McLaughlin, K. A., Green, J. G., Gruber, M. J., Sampson, N. A., Zaslavsky, A. M., & Kessler, R. C. (2010). Childhood adversities and adult psychiatric disorders in the national comorbidity survey replication II: Associations with persistence of DSM-IV disorders. *Archives of General Psychiatry, 67,* 124–132.

McLay, D. (2011). Breathtaking mortality: Bacterial pneumonia and HIV. *HIV Treatment Update, 207.* Retrieved March 16, 2016, from http://www.aidsmap.com/Breathtaking-mortality-bacterial-pneumonia-and-HIV/page/1839297/

McLean, S. A., Diatchenko, L., Lee, Y. M., Swor, R. A., Domeier, R. M., Jones, J. S., … Liberzon, I. (2011). Catechol-o-methyltransferase haplotype predicts immediate musculoskeletal neck pain and psychological symptoms after motor vehicle collision. *Journal of Pain, 12,* 101–107.

McMaster, S. K., Paul-Clark, M. J., Walters, M., Fleet, M., Anandarajah, J., Sriskandan, S., & Mitchell, J. A. (2008). Cigarette smoke inhibits macrophage sensing of gram-negative bacteria and lipopolysaccharide: Relative roles of nicotine and oxidant stress. *British Journal of Pharmacology, 153*(3), 536–543.

McMurtry, C. M., Noel, M., Chambers, C. T., & McGrath, P. J. (2011). Children's fear during procedural pain: Preliminary investigation of the Children's Fear Scale. *Health Psychology, 30*(6), 780–788.

McNulty, J. K., & Fincham, F. D. (2012). Beyond positive psychology? Toward a contextual view of psychological processes and well-being. *American Psychologist, 67*(2), 101–110.

McQueen, A., Kreuter, M. W., Kalesan, B., & Alcaraz, K. (2011). Understanding narrative effects: The impact of breast cancer survivor stories on message processing, attitudes, and beliefs among African American women. *Health Psychology, 30*(6), 674–682.

McRae, K., Ochsner, K., Mauss, I., Gabrieli, J. D., & Gross, J. (2008). Gender differences in emotional regulation: An fMRI study of cognitive reappraisal. *Group Processes and Intergroup Relations, 11*(2), 143–162.

McTiernan, A., Kooperberg, C., White, E., Wilcox, S., Coates, R., Adams-Campbell, L. L., … Ockene, J. (2003). Recreational physical activity and the risk of breast cancer in postmenopausal women. *Journal of the American Medical Association, 290*(10), 1331–1336.

McWilliams, L. A., Dick, B. D., Bailey, K., Verrier, M. J., & Kowal, J. (2012). A psychometric evaluation of the pain response preference questionnaire in a chronic pain patient sample. *Health Psychology, 31*(3), 343–351.

McWilliams, L. A., Saldanha, K. M., Dick, B. D., & Watt, M. C. (2009). Development and psychometric evaluation of a new measure of pain-related support preferences: The Pain Response Preference Questionnaire. *Pain Research Management, 14,* 461–469.

Mead, G. E., Morley, W., Campbell, P., Greig, C. S., McMurdo, M., & Lawlor, D. A. (2010). Exercise for depression. *Cochrane Database of Systematic Reviews, 2010*(1).

Meara, E., Kotagal, U. R., Atherton, H. D., & Lieu, T. A. (2004). Impact of early newborn discharge legislation and early follow-up visits on infant outcomes in a state Medicaid population. *Pediatrics, 113*(6), 1619–1627.

Meichenbaum, D. (2007). Stress inoculation training: A preventative and treatment approach. In P. M. Lehrer, R. L. Woolfolk, W. S. Sime, & D. H. Barlow (Eds.), *Principles and practice of stress management* (3rd ed., pp. 497–516). New York: Guilford Press.

Meier, M. H., Caspi, A., Ambler, A., Harrington, H., Houts, R., Keefe, R. S., McDonald, K., Ward, A., Poulton, R., & Moffitt, T. E. (2012). Persistent cannabis users show neuropsychological decline from childhood to midlife. *Proceedings of the National Academy of Sciences, 109*(40), E2657–E2664.

Meisel, Z., & Pines, J. (2011, May 31). Post-HMO health care: Are ACOs the answer? *Time Medical Insider.* Retrieved from http://www.time.com/time/health/article/0,8599,2074816,00.html

Melzack, R. (1990). Phantom limbs and the concept of a neuromatrix. *Trends in Neurosciences, 13*(3), 88–92.

Melzack, R. (1993). Pain: Past, present, and future. *Canadian Journal of Experimental Psychology, 47*, 615–629.

Melzack, R., & Torgerson, W. S. (1971). On the language of pain. *Anesthesiology, 34*, 50–59.

Melzack, R., & Wall, P. D. (1965). Pain mechanisms: A new theory. *Science, 150*, 971–979.

Melzack, R., & Wall, P. D. (1988). *The challenge of pain.* New York: Basic Books.

Mendes, E. (2010, February 9). Six in 10 overweight or obese in U.S., more in '09 than in '08. *Gallup News Service.*

Mendes, E. (2011, December 8). U.S. health habits continue sharp winter decline. *Gallup News Service.* Retrieved from http://www.gallup.com/poll/151424/health-habits-continue-steep-winter-decline.aspx

Mercken, L., Steglich, C., Sinclair, P., Holliday, J., & Moore, L. (2012). A longitudinal social network analysis of peer influence, peer selection, and smoking behavior among adolescents in British schools. *Health Psychology, 31*(4), 450–459.

Meririnne, E., Kiviruusu, O., Karlsson, L., Pelkonen, M., Ruuttu, T., Tulsku, V., & Marttunen, M. (2010). Brief report: Excessive alcohol use negatively affects the course of adolescent depression: One-year naturalistic follow-up study. *Journal of Adolescence, 33*(1), 221–226.

Merritt, M. M., Bennett, G. G., Williams, R. B., Edwards, C. L., & Sollers, J. J. (2006). Perceived racism and cardiovascular reactivity and recovery to personally relevant stress. *Health Psychology, 25*(3), 364–369.

Merz, E. L., Fox, R. S., & Malcarne, V. L. (2014). Expressive writing interventions in cancer patients: A systematic review. *Health Psychology Review, 8*(3), 339–361.

Messer, K., Trinidad, D. R., Al-Delaimy, W. K., & Pierce, J. P. (2008). Smoking cessation rates in the United States: A comparison of young adult and older smokers. *American Journal of Public Health, 98*(2), 317–322.

Meyer, I. H. (2003). Prejudice, social stress, and mental health in lesbian, gay, and bisexual populations: Conceptual issues and research evidence. *Psychological Bulletin, 129*(5), 674–697.

Meyer, J. M., & Stunkard, A. J. (1994). Twin studies of human obesity. In C. Bouchard (Ed.), *The genetics of obesity* (pp. 63–78). Boca Raton, FL: CRC Press.

Michael, E. S., & Burns, J. W. (2004). Catastrophizing and pain sensitivity among chronic pain patients: Moderating effects of sensory and affect focus. *Annals of Behavioral Medicine, 27*(3), 185–194.

Michie, S., Abraham, C., Whittington, C., McAteer, J., & Gupta, S. (2009). Effective techniques in healthy eating and physical activity interventions: A meta-regression. *Health Psychology, 28*, 690–701.

Milad, M. R., Wright, C. I., Orr, S. P., Pitman, R. K., Quirk, G. J., & Rauch, S. L. (2007). Recall of fear extinction in humans activates the ventromedial prefrontal cortex and hippocampus in concert. *Biological Psychiatry, 62*, 446–454.

Milberger, S., Biederman, J., Faraone, S. V., Chen, L., & Jones, J. (1996). Is maternal smoking during pregnancy a risk factor for attention deficit hyperactivity disorder in children? *American Journal of Psychiatry, 153*, 1138–1142.

Milkie, M. A., & Peltola, P. (1999). Playing all the roles: Gender and the work-family balancing act. *Journal of Marriage and the Family, 61*, 476–490.

Miller, G. E., & Blackwell, E. (2006). Turning up the heat: Inflammation as a mechanism linking chronic stress, depression, and heart disease. *Current Directions in Psychological Science, 15*, 269–272.

Miller, G. E., Chen, E., & Parker, K. J. (2011). Psychological stress in childhood and susceptibility to the chronic diseases of aging: Moving toward a model of behavioral and biological mechanisms. *Psychological Bulletin, 137*(6), 959–997.

Miller, G. E., & Cohen, S. (2001). Psychological interventions and the immune system: A meta-analytic review and critique. *Health Psychology, 20*, 47–63.

Miller, G. E., Cohen, S., & Ritchey, A. K. (2002). Chronic psychological stress and the regulation of pro-inflammatory cytokines: A glucocorticoid-resistance model. *Health Psychology, 21*(6), 531–541.

Miller, G. E., & Wrosch, C. (2007). You've gotta know when to fold 'em. *Psychological Science, 18*, 773–777.

Miller, K., & Miller, P. M. (2001). *Journey of hope: The story of Irish immigration to America.* New York: Chronicle Books.

Miller, M., Lippmann, S. J., Azrael, D., & Hemenway, D. (2007). Household firearm ownership and rates of suicide across the 50 United States. *Journal of Trauma, Injury, Infection, and Critical Care, 62*, 1029–1035.

Miller, M. F., Barabasz, A. F., & Barabasz, M. (1991). Effects of active alert and relaxation hypnotic inductions on cold pressor pain. *Journal of Abnormal Psychology, 100*, 223–226.

Miller, N. E. (1969). Psychosomatic effects of specific types of training. *Annals of the New York Academy of Sciences, 159*(3), 1025–1040.

Miller, P., & Plant, M. (2010). Parental guidance about drinking: Relationship with teenage psychoactive substance use. *Journal of Adolescence, 33*(1): 55–68.

Miller, T. Q., Smith, T. W., Turner, C. W., Guijarro, M. L., & Hallet, A. J. (1996). A meta-analytic review of research on hostility and physical health. *Psychological Bulletin, 119*, 322–348.

Miller, V., & Hodder, S. (2014). Beneficial impact of antiretroviral therapy on non-AIDS mortality. *AIDS, 28*, 273–274.

Miller, W. R., & Rollnick, S. (2002). *Motivational interviewing: Preparing people for change* (2nd ed.). New York: Guilford Press.

Miller, W. R., & Rollnick, S. (2010). *What makes it motivational interviewing?* Presentation at the International Conference on Motivational Interviewing (ICMI). Stockholm, June 7, 2010.

Millichap, J. G., & Yee, M. M. (2012). The diet factor in attention-deficit/hyperactivity disorder. *Pediatrics, 129*(2), 330–337.

Milling, L. (2008). Is high hypnotic suggestibility necessary for successful hypnotic pain intervention? *Current Pain and Headache Reports, 12*(2), 98–102.

Mills, P. J., Davidson, K. W., & Farag, N. H. (2004). Work stress and hypertension: A call from research into intervention. *Annals of Behavioral Medicine, 28*(1), 1–3.

Milne, H. M., Wallman, K. E., Gordon, S., & Courneya, K. S. (2008). Impact of a combined resistance and aerobic exercise program on motivational variables in breast cancer survivors: A randomized-controlled trial. *Annals of Behavioral Medicine, 36*, 158–166.

Minino, A. M. (2013). Death in the United States, 2011. *NCHS data brief, no. 115.* Hyattsville, MD: National Center for Health Statistics.

Mintz, L. B., Kashubeck, S., & Tracy, L. S. (1995). Relations among parental alcoholism, eating disorders, and substance abuse in nonclinical college women: Additional evidence against the uniformity myth. *Journal of Counseling Psychology, 42*, 65–70.

Mirescu, C., & Gould, E. (2006). Stress and adult neurogenesis. *Hippocampus, 16*, 233–238.

Misra, R., & Lager, J. (2009). Ethnic and gender differences in psychosocial factors, glycemic control, and quality of life among adult type 2 diabetic patients. *Journal of Diabetes and Its Complications, 23*, 54–64.

Mitchell, J. (2011). Caregiving for older adults: An annotated bibliography. *The Idaho Librarian.* Retrieved from http://libraries.idaho.gov/files/ArticleCaregivers.pdf

Mittleman, M. A., Maclure, M., Sherwood, J. B., Mulry, R. P., Tofler, G. H., Jacobs, S. C., … Muller, J. E. (1995). Triggering of acute myocardial infarction onset by episodes of anger. Determinants of Myocardial Infarction Onset Study Investigators. *Circulation, 92*(7), 1720–1725.

Mittleman, M. A., & Mostofsky, E. (2011). Physical, psychological, and chemical triggers of acute cardiovascular events: Preventive strategies. *Circulation, 124*(3), 346–354.

MMWR. (2004). Alcohol-attributable deaths and years of potential life lost—United States, 2001. *Morbidity and Mortality Weekly Report, 53*(37), 866–870.

MMWR. (2012a). Youth risk behavior surveillance—United States, 2011. *Morbidity and Mortality Weekly Report, 61*(4). Centers for Disease Control and Prevention. Retrieved from http://www.cdc.gov/mmwr/pdf/ss/ss6104.pdf

MMWR. (2012b). Cancer screening—United States, 2010. *Morbidity and Mortality Weekly Report, 61*(3), 41–45.

MMWR. (2014, June 13). Youth risk behavior surveillance—United States, 2013. *Morbidity and Mortality Weekly Report, 63*(4), 1–47. Retrieved February 28, 2016, from http://www.cdc.gov/mmwr/pdf/ss/ss6304.pdf

MMWR. (2014, October 31). CDC National Health Report: Leading causes of morbidity and mortality and associated behavioral risk and protective factors [Supplement]. *Morbidity and Mortality Weekly Report, 63*(4), 3–27. Retrieved March 19, 2016, from http://www.cdc.gov/mmwr/preview/mmwrhtml/su6304a2.htm

MMWR. (2015, July 31). National, regional, state, and selected local area vaccination coverage among adolescents aged 13–17 years — United States, 2014. *Morbidity and Mortality Weekly Report, 64*(29), 784–792.

MMWR. (2015, August 28). Vaccination coverage among children in kindergarten—United States, 2014–15 school year. *Morbidity and Mortality Weekly Report, 64*(33), 897–904.

Moberly, N. J., & Watkins, E. R. (2008). Ruminative self-focus, negative life events, and negative affect. *Behaviour Research and Therapy, 46*(9), 1034–1039.

Moeller, F. G., Dougherty, D. M. Barratt, E. S., Oderinde, V., Mathias, C. W., Harper, R. A., & Swann, A. C. (2002). Increased impulsivity in cocaine dependent subjects independent of antisocial personality disorder and aggression. *Drug and Alcohol Dependence, 68*(1), 105–112.

Mok, L. C., & Lee, I. (2008). Anxiety, depression, and pain intensity in patients with low back pain who are admitted to acute care hospitals. *Journal of Clinical Nursing, 17*(11), 1471–1480.

Mole, B. (2015, March 24). Today's pot is more potent, less therapeutic. *Science News.* Retrieved May 3, 2016, from https://www.sciencenews.org/blog/science-ticker/today's-pot-more-potent-less-therapeutic?mode=topic&context=45

Moller-Levet, C. S., Archer, S. N., Bucca, G., Laing, E. E., Slak, A., Kabiljo, R., Lo, J., Santhi, N., von Schantz, M., Smith, C. P., & Dijk, D. (2013). Effects of insufficient sleep on circadian rhythmicity and expression amplitude of the human blood transcriptome. *Proceedings of the National Academy of Sciences.* Retrieved from http://www.pnas.org/content/110/12/E1132.full.pdf

Mommersteeg, P. M. C., Keijsers, G. P. J., Heijnen, C. J., Verbraak, M. J. P. M., & van Doornen, L. J. P. (2006). Cortisol deviations in people with burnout before and after psychotherapy: A pilot study. *Health Psychology, 25*, 243–248.

Montgomery, G. H. (2004). Presurgery distress and specific response expectancies predict postsurgery outcomes in surgery patients confronting breast cancer. *Health Psychology, 23*(4), 381–387.

Montgomery, G. H., Kangas, M., David, D., Hallquist, M. N., Green, S., & Bovbjerg, D. H. (2009). Fatigue during breast cancer radiotherapy: An initial randomized study of cognitive-behavioral therapy plus hypnosis. *Health Psychology, 28*, 317–322.

Montpetit, M. A., & Bergeman, C. S. (2007). Dimensions of control: Mediational analyses of the stress-health relationship. *Personality and Individual Differences, 43*, 2237–2248.

Moreira, M. T., Smith, L. A., & Foxcroft, D. (2009). Social norms interventions to reduce alcohol misuse in university or college students. *Cochrane Database of Systematic Reviews, 2009*(3), CD006748.

Morgan, C. A., Wang, S., Rasmusson, A., Hazlett, G., Anderson, G., Charney, D. S. (2001). Relationship among plasma cortisol, catecholamines, neuropeptide Y, and human performance during exposure to uncontrollable stress. *Psychosomatic Medicine, 63*(3), 412–422.

Morin, C. M., Rodrigue, S., & Ivers, H. (2003). Role of stress, arousal, and coping skills in primary insomnia. *Psychosomatic Medicine, 65*, 259–267.

Morojele, N. K., & Stephenson, G. M. (1994). Addictive behaviours: Predictors of abstinence intentions and expectations in the theory of planned behavior. In D. R. Rutter & L. Quine (Eds.), *Social psychology and health: European perspectives* (pp. 47–70). Aldershot, UK: Avebury.

Morone, N. E., Greco, C. M., & Weiner, D. K. (2008). Mindfulness meditation for the treatment of chronic low back pain in older adults: A randomized controlled pilot study. *Pain, 134*, 310–319.

Morris, P. D., & Channer, K. S. (2012). Testosterone and cardiovascular disease in men. *Asian Journal of Andrology, 14*(3), 428–435.

Morrison, C. D. (2008). Leptin resistance and the response to positive energy balance. *Physiology and Behavior, 94*, 660–663.

Morrow, G. R., Asbury, R., Hammon, S., & Dobkin, P. (1992). Comparing the effectiveness of behavioral treatment for chemotherapy-induced nausea and vomiting when administered by oncologists, oncology nurses, and clinical psychologists. *Health Psychology, 11*, 250–256.

Morrow, G. R., Hesketh, P. J., Schwartzberg, L. S., & Ettinger, D. S. (2010). Recent advances in the management of chemotherapy-induced nausea and vomiting: A case study compendium. *Clinical Advances in Hematology and Oncology, 8*(5 Supplement 9), 1–16.

Morrow, G. R., Navari, R. M., & Rugo, H. S. (2014). Clinical roundtable monograph: New data in emerging treatment options for chemotherapy-induced nausea and vomiting. *Clinical Advances in Hematology and Oncology, 12*(3), 1–14.

Morton, G. J., Cummings, D. E., Baskin, D. G., Barsh G. S., & Schwartz, M. W. (2006). Central nervous system control of food intake and body weight. *Nature, 443*, 289–295.

Mosca, L., Barrett-Conner, E., & Wenger, N. K. (2011). Sex/gender differences in cardiovascular disease prevention: What a difference a decade makes. *Circulation, 124*, 2145–2154.

Mosconi, M. W., Cody-Hazlett, H., Poe, M. D., Gerig, G., Gimpel-Smith, R., & Piven, J. (2009). Longitudinal study of amygdala volume and joint attention in 2- to 4-year-old children with autism. *Archives of General Psychiatry, 65*(5), 509–516.

Moss, D., & Gunkelman, J. (2002). Task force report on methodology and empirically supported treatments. *Applied Psychophysiology and Biofeedback, 27*(4), 271–272.

Moss-Morris, R., Deary, V., & Castell, B. (2013). Chronic fatigue syndrome. In M. P. Barnes & D. C. Good (Eds.), *Handbook of clinical neurology* (Vol. 110, pp. 303–314). Amsterdam: Elsevier.

Moss-Morris, R., & Petrie, K. J. (1997). Cognitive distortions of somatic experiences: Revision and validation of a measure. *Journal of Psychosomatic Research, 43*, 293–306.

Motivala, S. J., & Irwin, M. R. (2007). Sleep and immunity: Cytokine pathways linking sleep and health outcomes. *Current Directions in Psychological Science, 16*(1), 21–25.

Motl, R. W., Konopack, J. F., McAuley, E., Elavsky, S., Jerome, G. J., & Marquez, D. X. (2005). Depressive symptoms among older adults: Long-term reduction after a physical activity intervention. *Journal of Behavioral Medicine, 28*, 385–394.

Mroz, L. W., Oliffe, J. L., & Davison, B. J. (2013). Masculinities and patient perspectives of communication about active surveillance for prostate cancer. *Health Psychology, 32*(1), 83–90.

MTF. (2015). *Monitoring the future: National survey results on drug use 1975–2015.* Bethesda, MD: National Institutes of Health. Retrieved from http://www.monitoringthefuture.org/pubs/monographs/mtf-overview2015.pdf

Mueller, C. E., Bridges, S. K., & Goddard, M. S. (2011). Sleep and parent-family connectedness: Links, relationships and implications for adolescent depression. *Journal of Family Studies, 17*(1), 9–23.

Mulvaney, S. A., Rothman, R. L., Dietrich, M. S., Wallston, K. A., Grove, E., Elasy, T. A., & Johnson, K. B. (2012). Using mobile phones to measure adolescent diabetes adherence. *Health Psychology, 31*(1), 43–50.

Munafo, M. R., & Johnstone, E. C. (2008). Genes and cigarette smoking. *Addiction, 103*, 893–904.

Mund, M., & Mitte, K. (2012). The costs of repression: A meta-analysis on the relation between repressive coping and somatic diseases. *Health Psychology, 31*(5), 640–649.

Munsey, C. (2010). Medicine or menace? Psychologists' research can inform the growing debate over legalizing marijuana. *Monitor on Psychology, 41*(6), 50.

Muraven, M., Tice, D. M., & Baumeister, R. F. (1998). Self-control as a limited resource: Regulatory depletion patterns. *Journal of Personality and Social Psychology, 74*, 774–789.

Murphy, S. L., Kochanek, K. D., Xu, J. Q., & Heron, M. (2015). Deaths: Final data for 2012. *National Vital Statistics Reports, 63*(9). Hyattsville, MD: National Center for Health Statistics.

Myers, L. B. (2010). The importance of the repressive coping style: Findings from 30 years of research. *Anxiety, Stress, and Coping, 23*(1), 3–17.

Myers, L. B., Burns, J. W., Derakshan, N., Elfant, E., Eysenck, M. W., & Phipps, S. (2008). Current issues in repressive coping and health. In A. Vingerhoet (Ed.), *Emotion regulation: Conceptual and clinical issues* (pp. 69–86). New York: Springer.

Myrin, B., & Lagerstrom, M. (2006). Health behaviour and sense of coherence among pupils aged 14–15. *Scandinavian Journal of Caring Sciences, 20*(3), 339–346.

Naar-King, S., Rongkavilit, C., Wang, B., Wright, K., Chuenyam, T., Lam, P., & Phanuphak, P. (2008). Transtheoretical model and risky sexual behavior in HIV positive youth in Thailand. *AIDS Care, 20*(2), 205–211.

Nahin, R. L. (2015). Estimates of pain prevalence and severity in adults: United States, 2012. *The Journal of Pain, 16*(8), 769–780.

Nakamura, M., Tanaka, M., Kinukawa, N., Abe, S., Itoh, K., Imai, K., Masuda, T., & Nakao, H. (2000). Association between basal serum and leptin levels and changes in abdominal fat distribution during weight loss. *Journal of Atherosclerosis and Thrombosis, 6*, 28–32.

Naparstek, B. (1994). *Staying well with guided imagery.* New York: Warner Books.

National Assessment of Adult Literacy (NAAL). (2003). What is NAAL? National Center for Education Statistics. Retrieved from http://nces.ed.gov/naal/

National Cancer Institute (NCI). (2010a). Fluoridated water: Questions and answers. Retrieved April 8, 2010, from http://www.cancer.gov/cancertopics/factsheet/Risk/fluoridated-water

National Cancer Institute (NCI). (2010b). Obesity and cancer: Questions and answers. Retrieved April 8, 2010, from http://www.cancer.gov/cancertopics/factsheet/Risk/obesity

National Cancer Institute (NCI). (2010c). Psychological stress and cancer: Questions and answers. Retrieved April 8, 2010, from http://www.cancer.gov/cancertopics/factsheet/Risk/stress

National Cancer Institute (NCI). (2010d). Quitting smoking: Why to quit and how to get help. Retrieved April 8, 2010, from http://www.cancer.gov/cancertopics/factsheet/Tobacco/cessation

National Cancer Institute (NCI). (2015a). *Annual report to the nation on the status of cancer, 1975–2011.* National Institutes of Health. Retrieved from http://www.cancer.gov/research/progress/annual-report-nation

National Cancer Institute (NCI). (2015b). Chemicals in meat cooked at high temperatures and cancer risk. Retrieved from http://www.cancer.gov/about-cancer/causes-prevention/risk/diet/cooked-meats-fact-sheet

National Cancer Institute (NCI). (2015c). Obesity and cancer risk. Retrieved from http://www.cancer.gov/about-cancer/causes-prevention/risk/obesity/obesity-fact-sheet

National Cancer Institute (NCI). (2015d). Physical activity and cancer. Retrieved from http://www.cancer.gov/about-cancer/causes-prevention/risk/obesity/physical-activity-fact-sheet

National Cancer Institute (NCI). (2015e, April 29). Surveillance, Epidemiology, and End Results program. Washington, DC: National Institutes of Health. Retrieved from http://www.cancer.gov/about-cancer/causes-prevention/risk/age

National Cancer Institute (NCI). (2016). Screening tests. Retrieved from http://www.cancer.gov/about-cancer/screening/screening-tests#screening-test

National Cancer Institute Fast Stats. (2015). Compare statistics by sex. National Cancer Institute. Retrieved from http://seer.cancer.gov/faststats/selections.php?series=sex

National Center for Complementary and Alternative Medicine (NCCAM). (2008). What is CAM? Retrieved April 29, 2010, from http://nccam.nih.gov/health/whatiscam/overview.htm

National Center for Complementary and Alternative Medicine (NCCAM). (2013a). Oral probiotics: An introduction. Retrieved from http://nccam.nih.gov/health/probiotics/introduction.htm

National Center for Complementary and Alternative Medicine (NCCAM). (2013b). Yoga for health (CCAM Publication No. D472). Retrieved April 1, 2016, from https://nccih.nih.gov/health/yoga/introduction.htm

National Center for Complementary and Integrative Health (NCCIH). (2015a). Complementary, alternative, or integrative health: What's in a name? National Center for Complementary and Integrative Health. Retrieved June 16, 2016, from https://nccih.nih.gov/health/integrative-health

National Center for Complementary and Integrative Health (NCCIH). (2015b). Naturopathy. Retrieved June 16, 2016, from https://nccih.nih.gov/health/naturopathy

National Center for Complementary and Integrative Health (NCCIH). (2016a). Acupuncture: In depth. Retrieved March 2, 2016, from https://nccih.nih.gov/health/acupuncture/introduction#hed1

National Center for Complementary and Integrative Health (NCCIH). (2016b). Complementary, alternative, or integrative health: What's in a name? Retrieved March 2, 2016, from https://nccih.nih.gov

National Center for Complementary and Integrative Health (NCCIH). (2016c). Tai chi and qi gong (NCCIH Publication No. D322). Retrieved April 1, 2016, from https://nccih.nih.gov/sites/nccam.nih.gov/files/Tai_Chi_and_Qi_Gong_09-11-2015.pdf

National Center for Environmental Health. (2006). Asthma. Centers for Disease Control and Prevention. Retrieved from www.cdc.gov/asthma/basics.htm#facts

National Center for Health Statistics (NCHS). (2006). *Health, United States, 2006.* Hyattsville, MD: U.S. Department of Health and Human Services.

National Center for Health Statistics (NCHS). (2012). *Health, United States, 2011: With special feature on socioeconomic status and health.* Hyattsville, MD: U.S. Department of Health and Human Services.

National Center for Health Statistics (NCHS). (2015). *Health, United States, 2014: With special feature on adults aged 55–64.* Hyattsville, MD: U.S. Department of Health and Human Services.

National Center for Health Statistics (NCHS). (2016a). FastStats: Life expectancy. Retrieved April 6, 2016, from http://www.cdc.gov/nchs/fastats/life-expectancy.htm

National Center for Health Statistics (NCHS). (2016b). Insurance coverage for complementary health approaches among adult users: United States, 2002 and 2012. Retrieved June 16, 2016, from http://www.cdc.gov/nchs/data/databriefs/db235.htm

National Center for Health Statistics (NCHS). (2016c). *Progress reviews for Healthy People 2020.* Retrieved April 19, 2016, from http://www.cdc.gov/nchs/healthy_people/hp2020/hp2020_progress_reviews.htm

National Diabetes Statistics Report. (2014). Centers for Disease Control and Prevention. Retrieved February 26, 2016, from http://www.cdc.gov/diabetes/pubs/statsreport14/national-diabetes-report-web.pdf

National Heart, Lung, and Blood Institute. (2006). *National cholesterol education program.* Washington, DC: Author. Retrieved from http://www.nhlbi.nih.gov/guidelines/cholesterol/index.htm

National Highway Traffic Safety Administration (NHTSA). (2010). *Traffic safety facts: Speeding, 2007 data.* National Highway Traffic Safety Administration. Washington, DC: National Center for Statistics and Analysis.

National Institute for Occupational Safety and Health (NIOSH). (2015). Occupational cancer. Retrieved from http://www.cdc.gov/niosh/topics/cancer/

National Institute on Alcohol Abuse and Alcoholism (NIAAA). (2006). College issues and drinking. National Institute on Alcohol Abuse and Alcoholism. Retrieved from http://pubs.niaaa.nih.gov/publications/aa29.htm

National Institute on Alcohol Abuse and Alcoholism (NIAAA). (2010). Key facts and stats. Retrieved September 24, 2010, from https://www.niaaa.nih.gov/alcohol-health/overview-alcohol-consumption/alcohol-use-disorders/genetics-alcohol-use-disorders

National Institute on Alcohol Abuse and Alcoholism (NIAAA). (2013). Moderate and binge drinking. Retrieved from http://www.niaaa.nih.gov/alcohol-health/overview-alcohol-consumption/moderate-binge-drinking

National Institute on Alcohol Abuse and Alcoholism (NIAAA). (2015). A snapshot of annual high-risk college drinking consequences. Retrieved from http://www.collegedrinkingprevention.gov/statssummaries/snapshot.aspx

National Institute on Drug Abuse (NIDA). (2015). The 2015 prescription drug abuse summit. Retrieved from https://www.drugabuse.gov/about-nida/noras-blog/2015/04/2015-prescription-drug-abuse-summit

National Institute on Drug Abuse (NIDA). (2016). Can marijuana use during and after pregnancy harm the baby? Retrieved May 3, 2016, from https://www.drugabuse.gov/publications/research-reports/marijuana/can-marijuana-use-during-pregnancy-harm-baby

National Institutes of Health (NIH). (1998). Technology assessment statement: Acupuncture. Washington, DC: Author.

National Sleep Foundation. (2010). How sleep works. Retrieved March 1, 2010, from http://www.sleepfoundation.org/primary-links/how-sleep-works

National Sleep Foundation. (2013). Adult sleep habits and styles. Retrieved from http://www.sleepfoundation.org

National Sleep Foundation. (2015). *Healthy sleep tips.* Retrieved April 16, 2016, from https://sleepfoundation.org/sleep-tools-tips/healthy-sleep-tips

Nauert, R. (2008, April 25). Smoking ups risk of depression. *PsychCentral.* Retrieved March 16, 2010, from http://psychcentral.com/news/2008/04/25/smoking-ups-risk-of-depression/2190.html

Nausheen, B., Gidron, Y., Peveler, R., & Moss-Morris, R. (2009). Social support and cancer progression: A systematic review. *Journal of Psychosomatic Research, 67,* 403–415.

NCL Communications. (2014). Survey: One-third of American parents mistakenly link vaccines to autism. National Consumers League. Retrieved March 2, 2016, from http://www.nclnet.org/survey_one_third_of_american_parents_mistakenly_link_vaccines_to_autism

Nebehay, S. (2011, July 21). Going into hospital far riskier than flying: WHO. Retrieved from http://www.reuters.com/article/2011/07/21/us-safety-idUSTRE76K45R20110721

NEDA. (2016). Binge eating disorder. *National Eating Disorders Association.* Retrieved from https://www.nationaleatingdisorders.org/binge-eating-disorder

Nedeltcheva, A. V., Kilkus, J. M., Imperial, J., Kasza, K., Schoeller, D. A., & Penev, D. V. (2009). Sleep curtailment is accompanied by increased intake of calories from snacks. *American Journal of Clinical Nutrition, 89*(1), 126–133.

Nelson, M. E., Fiatarone, M. A., Morganti, C. M., Trice, I., Greenberg, R. A., & Evans, W. J. (1994). Effects of high-intensity strength training on multiple risk factors for osteoporotic fractures. A randomized controlled trial. *Journal of the American Medical Association, 272,* 1909–1914.

Nelson, W. (2001, August 14). Quoted in S. Krupin, Bill Nelson and John Edwards are running mates. *The Palm Beach Post* [West Palm Beach, FL].

Nestoriuc, Y., & Martin, A. (2007). Efficacy of biofeedback for migraine: A meta-analysis. *Pain, 128,* 111–127.

Nestoriuc, Y., Rief, W., & Martin, A. (2008). Meta-analysis of biofeedback for tension-type headache: Efficacy, specificity, and treatment moderators. *Journal of Consulting and Clinical Psychology, 76*(3), 379–396.

Newton, T. L., & Contrada, R. J. (1992). Repressive coping and verbal autonomic response dissociation: The influence of social context. *Journal of Personality and Social Psychology, 62,* 159–167.

Ng, M., Fleming, T., Robinson, M., Thompson, B., Graetz, N., Margono, C., … Gakidou, E. (2014). Global, regional, and national prevalence of overweight and obesity in children and adults during 1980–2013: A systematic analysis for the Global Burden of Disease Study 2013. *The Lancet, 384*(9945), 766–782.

NHIS. (2014). Early release of selected estimates based on data from the January–March 2014 National Health Interview Survey. *Centers for Disease Control and Prevention.* Retrieved February 23, 2016, from http://www.cdc.gov/nchs/nhis/released201409.htm

Nichols, K. H., Rice, M., & Howell, C. (2011). Anger, stress, and blood pressure in overweight children. *Journal of Pediatric Nursing, 26*(5), 446–455.

NIDDK. (2008). *Diabetes prevention program (DPP).* NIH Publication No. 09-5099, October 2008. National Institute of Diabetes and Digestive and Kidney Diseases, U.S. Dept. of Health and Human Services. Retrieved February 26, 2016, from http://www.niddk.nih.gov/about-niddk/research-areas/diabetes/diabetes-prevention-program-dpp/Pages/default.aspx

Niederhoffer, K. G., & Pennebaker, J. W. (2002). Sharing one's story: On the benefits of writing or talking about emotional expression. In Snyder, C. R., & S. J. Lopez (Eds.), *Oxford handbook of positive psychology* (pp. 573–583). New York: Oxford University Press.

NIH Consensus Conference. (1998). Acupuncture. *Journal of the American Medical Association, 280*(17), 1518–1524; retrieved from http://jama.jamanetwork.com/article.aspx?articleid=188113

NIH Consensus Development Program. (2010). Preventing Alzheimer's disease and cognitive decline. Held April 26–28; retrieved April 29, 2010, from http://consensus.nih.gov/2010/docs/alz/alz_stmt.pdf

NIMH Multisite HIV/STD Prevention Trial for African American Couples Group. (2010). The contribution of male and female partners' substance use to sexual risks and STDs among African American HIV serodiscordant couples. *AIDS and Behavior, 14,* 1045–1054.

Nock, M. K. (2010). Self-injury. *Annual Review of Clinical Psychology, 6,* 339–363.

Norbury, T. A., MacGregor, A. J., Urwin, J., Spector, T. D., & McMahon, S. B. (2007). Heritability of responses to painful stimuli in women: A classical twin study. *Brain, 130,* 3041–3049.

Nordstrom, C. K., Dwyer, K. M., Merz, C. N., & Dwyer, S. A. (2003). Leisure time physical activity and early atherosclerosis: The Los Angeles Atherosclerosis Study. *American Journal of Medicine, 115*(1), 19–25.

Novotney, A. (2010a). Integrated care is nothing new for these psychologists. *Monitor on Psychology, 41*(1), 41–45.

Novotney, A. (2010b). A prescription for empathy. *Monitor on Psychology, 41*(1), 47–49.

Nowak, R. (1994). Nicotine research. Key study unveiled—11 years late. *Science, 264,* 196–197.

NPR. (2013, March 26). The epidemiology of gun violence: Race, region and policy. *Talk of the Nation.* National Public Radio. Retrieved from http://www.wbur.org/npr/175378043/the-epidemiology-of-gun-violence-race-region-and-policy

Nurses' Health Study (NHS). (2010). Retrieved April 8, 2010, from http://www.channing.harvard.edu/nhs

Nurses' Health Study (NHS). (2015). The nurses' health study. Retrieved from http://www.channing.harvard.edu/nhs/

NWLC. (2012). New NWLC report: Discriminatory health insurance practices cost women $1 billion a year. Washington, DC: National Women's Law Center. Retrieved from http://nwlc.org/press-releases/new-nwlc-report-discriminatory-health-insurance-practices-cost-women-1-billion-year/

Nygren, B., Alex, L., Jonsen, E., Gustafson, Y., Norberg, A., & Lundman, B. (2005). Resilience, sense of coherence, purpose in life and transcendence in relation to perceived physical and mental health among the oldest old. *Aging and Mental Health, 9*(4), 354–362.

Nyklíček, I., Mommersteeg, P. M. C., Van Beugen, S., Ramakers, C., & Van Boxtel, G. J. (2013). Mindfulness-based stress reduction and physiological activity during acute stress: A randomized controlled trial. *Health Psychology, 32,* 1110–1113.

O'Brien, C. W., & Moorey, S. (2010). Outlook and adaptation in advanced cancer: A systematic review. *Psycho-Oncology, 19,* 1239–1249.

O'Donnell, K., Brydon, L., Wright, C. E., & Steptoe, A. (2008). Self-esteem levels and cardiovascular and immunity responses to acute stress. *Brain, Behavior, and Immunity, 22*(8), 1241–1247.

Office of the Surgeon General. (2011). *National prevention strategy.* National Prevention, Health Promotion, and Public Health Council. Rockville, MD: Office of the Surgeon General. Retrieved from http://www.surgeongeneral.gov/initiatives/prevention/strategy

Ogden, C. L., Carroll, M. D., Fryar, C. D., & Flegal, K. M. (2015). Prevalence of obesity among adults and youth: United States, 2011–2014. *NCHS data brief, no. 219.* Hyattsville, MD: National Center for Health Statistics.

Ogden, C. L., Lamb, M. M., Carroll, M. D., & Flegal, K. M. (2010). Obesity and socioeconomic status in children and adolescents: United States, 2005–2008. *NCHS data brief, no. 51.* Hyattsville, MD: National Center for Health Statistics.

Ogden, N. (2015). General and plastic surgery devices: Reclassification of ultraviolet lamps for tanning: A rule by the Food and Drug Administration. *Federal Register.* Retrieved from https://www.federalregister.gov/articles/2014/06/02/2014-12546/general-and-plastic-surgery-devices-reclassification-of-ultraviolet-lamps-for-tanning-henceforth-to

Olds, J., & Milner, P. (1954). Positive reinforcement produced by electrical stimulation of the septal area and other regions of rat brain. *Journal of Comparative and Physiological Psychology, 47,* 419–427.

O'Leary, V. E., & Ickovics, J. R. (1995). Resilience and thriving in response to challenge: An opportunity for a paradigm shift in women's health. *Women's Health, 1*(2), 121–142.

Oman, D., Kurata, J. H., Strawbridge, W. J., & Cohen, R. D. (2002). Religious attendance and cause of death over 31 years. *International Journal of Psychiatry in Medicine, 32,* 69–89.

OMH. (2015). HHS promotores de salud initiative. U.S. Department of Health and Human Services Office of Minority Health. Retrieved February 25, 2016, from http://minorityhealth.hhs.gov/omh/content.aspx?ID=8929

Ondeck, D. M. (2003). Impact of culture on pain. *Home Health Care Management and Practice, 15,* 255–257.

Ong, A. D., Bergeman, C. S., Bisconti, T. L., & Wallace, K. A. (2006). Psychological resilience, positive emotions and successful adaptation to stress in later life. *Journal of Personality and Social Psychology, 91,* 730–749.

Onge, J. M. S., & Krueger, P. M. (2008). Education and race/ethnic differences in physical activity profiles in the U.S. Presented at the American Sociological Association annual meeting. July 31, 2008. Boston, MA.

Ornish, D., Magbanua, M. J., Weidner, G., Weinberg, V., Kemp, C., Green, C., … Carroll, P. R. (2008). Changes in prostate gene expression in men undergoing an intensive nutrition and lifestyle intervention. *Proceedings of the National Academy of Sciences, 105*(24), 8369–8374.

Onishi, N. (2001, February 21). In Africa, Rubensesque rules: Women use animal feed, steroids for beauty ideal. *Anchorage Daily News*, pp. A1–A5.

Onishi, N. (2008, June 13). Japan, seeking trim waists, measures millions. *The New York Times*. Retrieved from http://www .nytimes.com

Open Science Collaboration. (2015). Estimating the reproducibility of psychological science. *Science, 349*(6251). Retrieved February 23, 2016, from http://science.sciencemag.org/ content/349/6251/aac4716.full

Orenstein, D. (2013, February 13). A neural basis for benefits of meditation. *News from Brown* [Brown University]. Retrieved from http://news.brown.edu/pressreleases/2013/02/mindfulness

Organisation for Economic Co-operation and Development (OECD). (2010, September 23). *Obesity and the economics of prevention: Fit not fat*. Paris: Organization for Economic Co-operation and Development.

Orme-Johnson, D. W., Schneider, R. H., Son, Y. D., Nidich, S., & Cho, Z. (2006). Neuroimaging of meditation's effect on brain reactivity to pain. *NeuroReport, 17*(12), 1359–1363.

Ostelo, R. W. J. G., van Tulder, M. W., Vlaeyen, J. W. S., Linton, S. J., Morley, S. J., & Assendelft, W. J. J. (2005). Behavioural treatment for chronic low-back pain. *Cochrane Database of Systematic Reviews*, Cochrane AN: CD002014. Retrieved from http://www.ncbi.nlm.nih.gov/pubmed/15674889

Ostir, G. V., Markides, K. S., Black, S. A., & Goodwin, J. S. (2000). Emotional well-being predicts subsequent functional independence and survival. *Journal of the American Geriatrics Society, 48*, 473–478.

Oyama, T., Jin, T., Yamaya, R., Ling, N., & Guillemin, R. (1980). Profound analgesic effects of beta-endorphin in man. *The Lancet, 1*(8160), 122–124.

Paasche-Orlow, M. (2011). Caring for patients with limited health literacy. *Journal of the American Medical Association, 306*(10), 1122–1129.

Pagoto, S., McChargue, D., & Fuqua, R. W. (2003). Effects of a multi-component intervention on motivation and sun protection behaviors among Midwestern beachgoers. *Health Psychology, 22*(4), 429–433.

Pala, A. N., Steca, P., Varani, S., Calza, L, Colangeli, V., & Viale, P. (2012). Emotions may influence the production of pro-inflammatory cytokines in HIV positive individuals. *European Journal of Psychotraumatology, 3*(1), 1.

Pall, M. L. (2000). Elevated, sustained peroxynitrite levels as the cause of chronic fatigue syndrome. *Medical Hypotheses, 54*, 115–125.

Panaite, V., Salomon, K., Jin, A., & Rottenberg, J. (2015). Cardiovascular recovery from psychological and physiological challenge and risk for adverse cardiovascular outcomes and all-cause mortality. *Psychosomatic Medicine, 77*(3), 215–226.

Park, H. S., Klein, K. A., Smith, S., & Martell, D. (2009). Separating subjective norms, university descriptive and injunctive norms, and U.S. descriptive and injunctive norms for drinking behavior intentions. *Health Communication, 24*, 746–751.

Park, J., Kitayama, S., Karasawa, M., Curhan, K. Markus, H., Kawakami, N., Miyamoto, Y., Love, G., Coel, C., & Ryff, C. (2013). Clarifying the links between social support and health: Culture, stress, and neuroticism matter. *Journal of Health Psychology, 18*(2), 226–235.

Parker, K. J. (2012). Early life stress inoculation in monkeys: A pathway to resilience. *European Journal of Psychotraumatology, 3*, 1.

Parker, R. (2000). Health literacy: A challenge for American patients and their health care providers. *Health Promotion International, 15*, 277–283.

Paquet, C., Dube, L., Gauvin, L., Kestens, Y., & Daniel, M. (2010). Sense of mastery and metabolic risk: Moderating role of the local fast-food environment. *Psychosomatic Medicine, 72*, 324–331.

Parkinson's Disease Foundation. (2010). What is Parkinson's disease? Retrieved October 18, 2010, from http://www.pdf.org

Parsons, J. T., Huszti, H. C., Crudder, S. O., Rich, L., & Mendoza, J. (2000). Maintenance of safer sexual behaviours: Evaluation of a theory-based intervention for HIV seropositive men with haemophilia and their female partners. *Haemophilia, 6*(3), 181–190.

Pascoe, E. A., & Richman, L. S. (2009). Perceived discrimination and health: A meta-analytic review. *Psychological Bulletin, 135*, 531–554.

Patel, K. V., Guralnik, J. M., Dansie, E. J., & Turk, D. C. (2013). Prevalence and impact of pain among older adults in the United States: Findings from the 2011 National Health and Aging Trends Study (NHATS). *Pain, 154*(12). Retrieved from http://www.ncbi.nlm.nih.gov/pmc/articles/PMC3843850/

Patel, N. P., Grandner, M. A., Xie, D., Branas, C. C., & Gooneratne, N. (2010). "Sleep disparity" in the population: Poor sleep quality is strongly associated with poverty and ethnicity. *BMC Public Health, 10*(475). Retrieved from http://www.biomedcentral .com/1471-2458/10/475

Patterson, D. R., Jensen, M. P., & Montgomery, G. H. (2010). Hypnosis for pain control. In S. J. Lynn, J. W. Rhue, & I. Kirsch (Eds.), *Handbook of clinical hypnosis* (2nd ed.). Washington, DC: American Psychological Association.

Patton, G. C., Coffey, C., Cappa, C., Currie, D., Riley, L., Gore, F., Degenhardt, L., Richardson, D., Astone, N., Sangowawa, A. O., Mokdad, A., & Ferguson, J. (2012). Health of the world's adolescents: A synthesis of internationally comparable data. *The Lancet, 379*, 1665–1675.

Paul, K., Boutain, D., Manhart, L., & Hitti, J. (2008). Racial disparity in bacterial vaginosis: The role of socioeconomic status, psychosocial stress, and neighborhood characteristics, and possible implications for preterm birth. *Social Science and Medicine, 67*(5), 824–833.

Pawlyck, A. C., Ferber, M., Shah, A., Pack, A., & Naidoo, N. (2007). Proteomic analysis of the effects and interactions of sleep deprivation and aging in mouse cerebral cortex. *Journal of Neurochemistry, 103*(6), 2301–2313.

Pearsall, P. (2004). *The Beethoven factor: The new psychology of hardiness, happiness, healing, and hope*. New York: Hampton Roads Publishing.

Peek, M. E., Cargill, A., & Huang, E. S. (2007). Diabetes health disparities: A systematic review of health care interventions. *Medical Care Research and Review, 64*(5), 101–156.

Peek, M. E., Odoms-Young, A., Quinn, M. T., Gorwara-Bhat, R., Wilson, S. C., & Chin, M. H. (2010). Racism in healthcare: Its relationship to shared decision-making and health disparities: A response to Brady. *Social Science & Medicine, 71*(1), 13–17.

Peeke, P. (2010, January 25). Just what is an average woman's size anymore? *WebMD Everyday Fitness*. Retrieved March 5, 2010, from http://blogs.webmd.com/pamela-peeke-md/2010/01/ just-what-is-average-womans-size.html

Peeters, A., Barendregt, J. J., Willekens, F., Mackenbach, J. P., Mamun, A. A., & Bonneux, L. (2003). Obesity in adulthood and its consequences for life expectancy: A life-table analysis. *Annals of Internal Medicine, 138*, 24–32.

Peltzer, J. N., Domian, E. W., & Teel, C. S. (2016). Infected lives: Experiences of young African American HIV-positive women. *Western Journal of Nursing Research, 38*(2), 216–230.

Pender, N. J., Walker, S. N., Sechrist, K. R., & Frank-Stromborg, M. (1990). Predicting health-promoting lifestyles in the workplace. *Nursing Research, 39*, 326–332.

Penedo, F. J., Dahn, J. R., Molton, I., Gonzalez, J. S., Kinsinger, D., Roos, B. A., … Antoni, M. H. (2004). Cognitive-behavioral stress management improves stress-management skills and quality of life in men recovering from treatment of prostate carcinoma. *Cancer, 100*(1), 192–200.

Penfield, W. (1952). Memory mechanisms. *AMA Archives of Neurology & Psychiatry, 67*, 178–198.

Pennebaker, J. W. (1982). *The psychology of physical symptoms.* New York: Springer-Verlag.

Pennebaker, J. W., & Francis, M. E. (1996). Cognitive, emotional, and language processes in disclosure. *Cognition & Emotion, 10*, 601–626.

Pennebaker, J. W., Hughes, C. F., & O'Heeron, R. C. (1987). The psychophysiology of confession: Linking inhibitory and psychosomatic processes. *Journal of Personality and Social Psychology, 52*, 781–793.

Pennebaker, J. W., & Susman, J. R. (1988). Disclosure of traumas and psychosomatic processes. *Social Science and Medicine, 26*(3), 327–332.

Pennsylvania Fresh Food Financing Initiative. (2012). Encouraging the development of food retail in underserved Pennsylvania communities. Philadelphia, PA: The Food Trust. Retrieved from http://www.thefoodtrust.org/php/programs/fffi.php

Peralta-Ramirez, M. I., Jimenez-Alonzo, J., Godoy-Garcia, J. F., & Perez-Garcia, M. (2004). The effects of daily stress and stressful life events on the clinical symptomology of patients with lupus erythematosus. *Psychosomatic Medicine, 66*, 788–794.

Perkinson-Gloor, N., Lemola, S., & Grob, A. (2013). Sleep duration, positive attitude toward life, and academic achievement: The role of daytime tiredness, behavioral persistence, and school start times. *Journal of Adolescence, 36*(2), 311–318.

Perlick, D., & Silverstein, B. (1994). Faces of female discontent: Depression, disordered eating, and changing gender roles. In P. Fallon & M. A. Katzman (Eds.), *Feminist perspectives on eating disorders* (pp. 77–93). New York: Guilford.

Perna, F. M., Antoni, M. H., Baum, A., Gordon, P., & Schneiderman, N. (2003). Cognitive behavioral stress management effects on injury and illness among competitive athletes: A randomized clinical trial. *Annals of Behavioral Medicine, 25*(1), 66–73.

Perry, W. G. (1999). *Forms of ethical and intellectual development in the college years.* San Francisco: Jossey-Bass.

Perry-Jenkins, M., Repetti, R. L., & Crouter, A. C. (2000). Relationship processes: Work and family in the 1990s. *Journal of Marriage and the Family, 62*(4), 981–997.

Persson, R., Hansen, A.-M, Ohlsson, K., Balogh, I., Nordander, C., & Orbaek, P. (2009). Physiological and psychological reactions to work in men and women with identical job tasks. *European Journal of Applied Physiology, 105*(4), 595–606.

Pert, C. B. (2003). *Molecules of emotion: The science behind mind-body medicine.* New York: Simon & Schuster.

Pert, C. B., Dreher, H. E., & Ruff, M. R. (1998). The psychosomatic network: Foundations of mind–body medicine. *Alternative Therapies in Health and Medicine, 4*, 30–41.

Perz, C. A., DiClemente, C. C., & Carbonari, J. P. (1996). Doing the right thing at the right time? The interaction of stages and processes of change in successful smoking cessation. *Health Psychology, 15*, 462–468.

Peterson, C., & Steen, T. A. (2002). Optimistic explanatory style. In C. R. Snyder & S. J. Lopez (Eds.), *Oxford handbook of positive psychology* (pp. 244–256). New York: Oxford University Press.

Petrie, K. J., Booth, R. J., & Davison, K. P. (1995). Repression, disclosure, and immune function: Recent findings and methodological issues. In J. W. Pennebaker (Ed.), *Emotion, disclosure, and health* (pp. 223–237). Washington, DC: American Psychological Association.

Pew Internet. (2009, October 30). Internet and American Life Project. Retrieved from http://www.pewinternet.org/Trend-Data

Pew Research Center. (2014). In debate over legalizing marijuana, disagreement over drug's dangers. Retrieved from http://www.people-press.org/2015/04/14/in-debate-over-legalizing-marijuana-disagreement-over-drugs-dangers/

Pew Research Center. (2016). *Social and demographic trends: The rise of Asian Americans.* Retrieved from http://www.pewsocialtrends.org/asianamericans-graphics/

Pham, T. (2007). AIDS optimism and condom usage among men who have sex with men in Australia, the Netherlands, and United States. *Independent Study Project (ISP) Collection. Paper 152.* Retrieved from http://digitalcollections.sit.edu/isp_collection/152/?utm_source=digitalcollections.sit.edu%2Fisp_collection%2F152&utm_medium=PDF&utm_campaign=PDFCoverPages

Phillips, A. C., & Hughes, B. M. (2011). Introductory paper: Cardiovascular reactivity at a crossroads: Where are we now? *Biological Psychology, 86*(2), 95–97.

Pierce, J. P. (2009). Electronic recording, self-report, and bias in measuring cigarette consumption. *Health Psychology, 28*, 527–528.

Pierce, J. P., & Gilpin, E. A. (2004). How did the master settlement agreement change tobacco industry expenditures for cigarette advertising and promotions? *Health Promotion Practice, 5*(3), 84–90.

Piet, J., & Hougaard, E. (2011). The effect of mindfulness-based cognitive therapy for prevention of relapse in recurrent major depressive disorder: A systematic review and meta-analysis. *Clinical Psychology Review, 31*, 1032–1040.

Piet, J., Wurtzen, H., & Zachariae, R. (2012). The effect of mindfulness-based therapy on symptoms of anxiety and depression in adult cancer patients and survivors: A systematic review and meta-analysis. *Journal of Consulting and Clinical Psychology, 80*(6), 1007–1020.

Pilisuk, M., Boylan, R., & Acredolo, C. (1987). Social support, life stress, and subsequent medical care utilization. *Health Psychology, 6*, 273–288.

Pillay, T., van Zyl, H. A., & Blackbeard, B. (2014). Chronic pain perception and cultural experience. *Procedia—Social and Behavioral Sciences, 113*(7), 151–160.

Pinquart, M., & Duberstein, P. R. (2010). Depression and cancer mortality: A meta-analysis. *Psychological Medicine, 40*(11), 1797–1810.

Piper, M. E., Smith, S. S., Schlam, T. R., Fiore, M. C., Jorenby, D. E., Fraser, D., & Baker, T. B. (2009). A randomized placebo-controlled clinical trial of 5 smoking cessation pharmacotherapies. *Archives of General Psychiatry, 66*(11), 1253–1262.

Piscitelli, S. C., Burstein, A. H., Chaitt, D., Alfaro, R. M., & Falloon, J. (2000). Indinavir concentrations and St. John's wort. *The Lancet, 355*, 547–548.

Pi-Sunyer, X. (2003). A clinical view of the obesity problem. *Science, 299*(5608), 859–860.

Player, M. S., King, D. E., Mainous, A. G., & Geesey, M. E. (2007). Psychosocial factors and progression from prehypertension to hypertension or coronary heart disease. *Annals of Family Medicine, 5,* 403–411.

Plomin, R., DeFries, J. C., McClearn, G. E., & McGuffin, P. (2001). *Behavioral genetics* (4th ed.). New York: Worth.

Plomin, R., DeFries, J. C., McClearn, G. E., & Rutter, M. (1997). *Behavioral genetics* (3rd ed.). New York: Worth.

Pluhar, E. I., Frongillo, E. A., Stycos, J. M., & Dempster-McClain, D. (2003). Changes over time in college students' family planning knowledge, preference, and behavior and implications for contraceptive education and prevention of sexually transmitted infections. *College Students Journal, 37*(3), 420–434.

Polina, E. R., Contini, V., Hutz, M. H., & Bau, C. H. (2009). The serotonin 2A receptor gene in alcohol dependence and tobacco smoking. *Drug and Alcohol Dependence, 101*(1), 128.

Pollay, R. W. (2000). Targeting youth and concerned smokers: Evidence from Canadian tobacco industry documents. *Tobacco Control, 9*(2), 136–147.

Pomeranz, J. L., & Brownell, K. D. (2008). Legal and public health considerations affecting the success, reach, and impact of menu-labeling laws. *American Journal of Public Health, 98*(9), 1578–1583.

Ponniah, K., & Hollon, S. D. (2009). Empirically supported psychological treatments for acute stress disorder and posttraumatic stress disorder: A review. *Depression and Anxiety, 26*(12), 1086–1090.

Pool, G. J., Schwegler, A. F., Theodore, B. R., & Fuchs, P. N. (2007). Role of gender norms and group identification on hypothetical and experimental pain tolerance. *Pain, 129,* 122–129.

Posadzki, P., & Ernst, E. (2012). Guided imagery for non-musculoskeletal pain: A systematic review of randomized clinical trials. *Journal of Pain and Symptom Management, 44*(1), 95–104.

Posadzki, P., Lewandowski, W., Terry, R., Ernst, E., & Stearns, A. (2011). Guided imagery for musculoskeletal pain: A systematic review. *Clinical Journal of Pain, 27*(7), 648–653.

Posadzki, P., Lewandowski, W., Terry, R., Ernst, E., & Stearns, A. (2012). Guided imagery for non-musculoskeletal pain: A systematic review of randomized clinical trials. *Journal of Pain and Symptom Management, 44*(1), 95–104.

Powell, A. (2012, March 7). Obesity? Diabetes? We've been set up. *Harvard Gazette.* Retrieved from http://news.harvard.edu/gazette/story/2012/03/the-big-setup

Pressman, S. D., & Bowlin, S. (2014). Positive affect: A pathway to better physical health. In J. Gruber & J. Moskowitz (Eds.), *Positive emotion: Integrating the light sides and dark sides.* New York: Oxford University Press.

Pressman, S. D., & Cohen, S. (2012). Positive emotion word use and longevity in famous deceased psychologists. *Health Psychology, 31,* 297–305.

Pressman, S. D., Gallagher, M., & Lopez, S. (2013). Is the emotion-health connection a "First World" problem? *Psychological Science, 24,* 544–549.

Prince-Embury, S., & Saklofske, D. H. (2013). *Resilience in children, adolescents, and adults: Translating research into practice.* New York: Springer.

Prochaska, J. J., Velicer, W. F., Prochaska, J. O., Dlucchi, K., & Hall, S. M. (2006). Comparing intervention outcomes in smokers treated for single versus multiple behavioral risks. *Health Psychology, 25,* 380–388.

Prochaska, J. O. (1996). Revolution in health promotion: Smoking cessation as a case study. In R. J. Resnick & R. H. Rozensky (Eds.), *Health psychology through the life span: Practice and research opportunities* (pp. 361–375). Washington, DC: American Psychological Association.

Proxmire, C. A. (2015). Study: Health risks high for LGBT people. *Between the Lines News.* Retrieved February 24, 2016, from http://www.pridesource.com/article.html?article=63234

PsychoNeuroImmunology Research Society (PNIRS). (2010). Mission statement. Retrieved February 8, 2010, from https://www.pnirs.org

Puhl, R., & Brownell, K. D. (2001). Bias, discrimination, and obesity. *Obesity Research, 9*(12), 788–805.

Puhl, R. M., & Heuer, C. A. (2009). The stigma of obesity: A review and update. *Obesity, 17,* 941–964.

Puska, P. (1999). The North Karelia project: From community intervention to national activity in lowering cholesterol levels and CHD risk. *European Heart Journal Supplements, 1,* S1–S4.

Quackwatch. (2006). Implausibility of EDTA chelation therapy. Retrieved from http://www.quackwatch.org

Quartana, P. J., Laubmeier, K. K., & Zakowski, S. G. (2006). Psychological adjustment following diagnosis and treatment of cancer: An examination of the moderating role of positive and negative emotional expressivity. *Journal of Behavioral Medicine, 29,* 487–498.

Quick, J. C., & Quick, J. D. (2004). *Organizational stress and preventive management.* New York: McGraw-Hill.

Quigley, K. S., Barrett, L. F., & Weinstein, S. (2002). Cardiovascular patterns associated with threat and challenge appraisals: A within-subjects analysis. *Psychophysiology, 39*(3), 292–302.

Quinn, J. M., Pascoe, A., Wood, W., & Neal, D. T. (2010). Can't control yourself? Monitor those bad habits. *Personality and Social Psychology Bulletin, 36,* 499–511.

Raaijmakers, L. G., Martens, M. K., Hesselink, A. E., de Weerdt, I., de Vries, N. K., & Kremens, S. P. (2014). Mastery and perceived autonomy support are correlates of Dutch diabetes patients' self-management and quality of life. *Patient Education and Counseling, 97*(1), 75–81.

Rabin, B. S. (1999). *Stress, immune function, and health: The connection.* New York: John Wiley.

Rachet, B., Maringe, C., Nur, U., Quaresman, M., Shah, A., Woods, L. M., & Coleman, M. P. (2009). Population-based cancer survival trends in England and Wales up to 2007: An assessment of the NHS cancer plan for England. *The Lancet Oncology, 10,* 351–369.

Rahe, R. H., Mahan, J. L., & Arthur, R. J. (1970). Prediction of near-future health changes from subjects' preceding life changes. *Journal of Psychosomatic Research, 14,* 401–406.

Rahim-Williams, F. B., Riley, J. L., Herrera, D., Campbell, C. M., Hastie, B. A., & Fillingim, R. B. (2007). Ethnic identity predicts experimental pain sensitivity in African Americans and Hispanics. *Pain, 129,* 177–184.

Rahnama, P., Montazeri, A., Fallah Huseini, H., Kianbakht, S., & Naseri, M. (2012). Effect of Zingiber officinale R. rhizomes (ginger) on pain relief in primary dysmenorrhea: A placebo randomized trial. *BMC Complementary and Alternative Medicine, 12,* 92. Retrieved from http://www.biomedcentral.com/1472-6882/12/92

Raloff, J. (1996). Vanishing flesh: Muscle loss in the elderly finally gets some respect. *Science News, 150,* 90–91.

Raloff, J. (2006). Breakfast trends. *Science News, 169*(15), 238.

Raloff, J. (2010, September 24). Clean out your medicine cabinet: Today! *Science News.* Retrieved from https://www.sciencenews

.org/blog/science-public/clean-out-your-medicine-cabinet-tod
ay?mode=magazine&context=723

Ramachandran, V. S., & Rogers-Ramachandran, D. (2000).
Phantom limbs and neural plasticity. *Archives of Neurology, 57,*
317–320.

Ramons, K. D., Schafer, S., & Tracz, S. M. (2003). Learning in
practice: Validation of the Fresno test of competence in
evidence-based medicine. *British Medical Journal, 326,*
319–321.

Ranadive, U. (1997). Phantom limbs and rewired brains.
Technology Review, 100, 17–18.

Randler, C., & Frech, D. (2009). Young people's time-of-day
preferences affect their school performance. *Journal of Youth
Studies, 12,* 653–667.

Rasmusson, A. M., Vythilingam, M., & Morgan, C. A. (2003). The
neuroendoctrinology of posttraumatic stress disorder: New
directions. *CNS Spectrums. 8,* 651–667.

Rassart, J., Luyckx, K., Berg, C. A., Bijttbier, P., Moons, P., & Weets, I.
(2015). Psychosocial functioning and glycemic control in
emerging adults with type 1 diabetes: A 5-year follow-up
study. *Health Psychology, 34*(11), 1058–1065.

Rayman, M. (2012). Selenium and cancer prevention. *Hereditary
Cancer in Clinical Practice, 10*(Supplement 4), A1.

Regoeczi, W. C. (2003). When context matters: A multilevel
analysis of household and neighbourhood crowding on
aggression and withdrawal. *Journal of Environmental
Psychology, 23,* 457–470.

Reid, C. M., Gooberman-Hill, R., & Hanks, G. W. (2008). Opioid
analgesics for cancer pain: Symptom control for the living or
comfort for the dying? A qualitative study to investigate the
factors influencing the decision to accept morphine for pain
caused by cancer. *Annals of Oncology, 19,* 44.

Reid, T. R. (2010). *The healing of America: A global quest for better,
cheaper, and fairer health care.* London: Penguin.

Reimann, F., Cox, J. J., Belfer, I., Diatchenko, L., Zaykin, D. V.,
McHale, D. P., … Woods, C. G. (2010). Pain perception is
altered by a nucleotide polymorphism in SCN9A. *Proceedings
of the National Academy of Sciences, 107,* 5148–5153.

Remick, A. K., Polivy, J., & Pliner, P. (2009). Internal and
external moderators of the effect of variety on food intake.
Psychological Bulletin, 135, 434–451.

Rennard, S., Glover, E. D., Leischow, S., Daughton, D. M., Glover, P. N.,
Muramoto, M., Franzon, M., Danielsson, T., Landfeldt, B., &
Westin, A. (2006). Efficacy of the nicotine inhaler in smoking
reduction: A double-blind randomized trial. *Nicotine and
Tobacco Research, 8*(4), 555–564.

Repetti, R. L., Taylor, S. E., & Seeman, T. E. (2002). Risky families:
Family social environments and the mental and physical
health of offspring. *Psychological Bulletin, 128*(2), 330–338.

Repetti, R. L., Wang, S.-W., & Saxbe, D. (2009). Bringing it all back
home: How outside stressors shape families' everyday lives.
Current Directions in Psychological Science, 18, 106–111.

Repetto, P. B., Caldwell, C. H., & Zimmerman, M. A. (2005). A
longitudinal study of the relationship between depressive
symptoms and cigarette use among African American
adolescents. *Health Psychology, 24,* 209–219.

Reston, J. (1971, July 26). Now, about my operation in Peking. *The
New York Times,* pp. 1, 6.

Reynolds, G. (2009, September 16). Phys ed: What sort of
exercise can make you smarter? *The New York Times.*
Retrieved from http://well.blogs.nytimes.com/2009/09/16/
what-sort-of-exercise-can-make-you-smarter/

Rich. L. E. (2004). Bringing more effective tools to the weight-loss
table. *Monitor on Psychology, 35*(1), 52–55.

Riddihough, G., & Zahn, L. M. (2010). What is epigenetics?
Science, 330(6004), 611.

Rigotti, N. A. (2015). E-cigarette use and subsequent tobacco
use by adolescents: New evidence about a potential risk of
e-cigarettes. *Journal of the American Medical Association,
314*(7), 673–674.

Rigucci, S., Marques, T. R., Di Forti, M., Taylor, H., Dell'Aqua,
F., Mondell, V. … Dazzan, P. (2016). Effect of high-potency
cannabis on corpus callosum microstructure. *Psychological
Medicine, 46*(4), 841–854.

Ring, T. (2012). Is anyone immune to HIV? *HIV Plus.*
Retrieved March 16, 2016, from http://www.hivplusmag
.com/case-studies/research-breakthroughs/2012/09/07/
anyone-immune-hiv

Ringstrom, G., Abrahamsson, H., Strid, H., & Simren, M.
(2007). Why do subjects with irritable bowel syndrome seek
health care for their symptoms? *Scandinavian Journal of
Gastroenterology, 42,* 1194–1203.

Rios, R., & Zautra, A. J. (2011). Socioeconomic disparities in pain:
The role of economic hardship and daily financial worry.
Health Psychology, 30(1), 58–66.

Rix, S. E. (2012). The employment situation, April 2012: Little
encouraging news for older workers. *AARP Public Policy
Institute, Fact Sheet 257.* Washington, DC: AARP Public Policy
Institute.

Roberts, C. K. (2007). Inactivity and fat cell hyperplasia: Fat
chance? *Journal of Applied Physiology, 102*(4), 1308–1309.

Roberts, C. K., Vaziri, N. D., & Barnard, R. J. (2002). Effect of diet
and exercise intervention on blood pressure, insulin, oxidative
stress, and nitric oxide availability. *Circulation, 106*(20),
2530–2532.

Roberts, M. E., Gibbons, F. X., Gerrard, M., & Alert, M. D. (2011).
Optimism and adolescent perception of skin cancer risk.
Health Psychology, 30(6), 810–813.

Roberts, M. E., Gibbons, F. X., Gerrard, M., Weng, C., Murry, V. M.,
Simons, L. G., & Simons, R. L. (2012). From racial
discrimination to risky sex: Prospective relations involving
peers and parents. *Developmental Psychology, 48,* 89–102.

Robert Wood Johnson Foundation. (2015). New report finds 23
of 25 states with highest rates of obesity are in the South and
Midwest. Retrieved from http://www.rwjf.org/en/library/
articles-and-news/2015/09/State-of-Obesity-Report-2015.html

Robinson, P., Gould, D., & Strosahl, K. (2010). *Real behavior
change in primary care: Improving patient outcomes and
increasing job satisfaction* [professional]. Oakland, CA:
New Harbinger Publications, Inc.

Robinson, R. L., Kroenke, K., Williams, D. A., Mease, P., Chen, Y.,
Faries, D., Penx, X., Hann, D., Wohlreich, M., & McCarberg,
B. (2013). Longitudinal observation of treatment patterns
and outcomes for patients with fibromyalgia: 12-month
findings from the REFLECTIONS Study. *Pain Medicine, 14*(9),
1400–1415.

Robinson, T. E., & Berridge, K. C. (2003). Addiction. *Annual
Review of Psychology, 54,* 25–53.

Rodin, J. (1986). Aging and health: Effects of the sense of control.
Science, 233, 1271–1276.

Rodin, J. (1992). *Body traps* (pp. 76–77). New York: William
Morrow.

Rodriguez, D., Romer, D., & Audrain-McGovern, J. (2007). Beliefs
about the risks of smoking mediate the relationship between
exposure to smoking and smoking. *Psychosomatic Medicine,
69,* 106–113.

Roehling, M. V., & Winters, D. (2000). Job security rights: The
effects of specific policies and practices on the evaluation of

employers. *Employee Responsibilities and Rights Journal, 12,* 25–38.

Roehling, P. V., Roehling, M. V., Vandlen, J. D., Bazek, J., & Guy, W. C. (2009). Weight discrimination and the glass ceiling effect among top US CEOs. *Equal Opportunities International, 28,* 179–196.

Roelfs, D. J., Davidson, K. W., & Schwartz, J. E. (2011). Losing life and livelihood: A systematic review and meta-analysis of unemployment and all-cause mortality. *Social Science and Medicine, 72*(6), 840–854.

Roemer, L., Orsillo, S. M., & Salters-Pedneault, K. (2008). Efficacy of an acceptance-based behavior therapy for generalized anxiety disorder: Evaluation in a randomized controlled trial. *Journal of Consulting and Clinical Psychology, 76*(6), 1083–1089.

Roemer, M. (1993). *National health systems of the world.* London: Oxford University Press.

Roenneberg, T., Allebrandt, K. V., Merrow, M., & Vetter, C. (2012). Social jetlag and obesity. *Current Biology, 22*(10), 939–943.

Roenneberg, T., Kuehnle, T., Pramstaller, P. P., Ricken, J., Havel, M., Guth, A., & Merrow, M. (2004). A marker for the end of adolescence. *Current Biology, 14,* R1038–R1039.

Roest, A. M., Martens, E. J., de Jonge, P., & Denollet, J. (2014). Anxiety and risk of incident coronary heart disease: A meta-analysis. *Journal of the American College of Cardiology, 56*(1), 38–46.

Rogeberg, O. (2013). Correlations between cannabis use and IQ change in the Dunedin cohort are consistent with confounding from socioeconomic status. *Proceedings of the National Academy of Sciences, 110*(11), 4251–4254.

Rogers, C. J., Colbert, L. H., Greiner, J. W., Perkins, S. N., & Hursting, S. D. (2008). Physical activity and cancer prevention: Pathways and targets for intervention. *Sports Medicine, 38,* 271–296.

Rogers, R. G., Boardman, J. D., Pendergast, P. M., & Lawrence, E. M. (2015). Drinking problems and mortality risk in the United States. *Drug and Alcohol Dependence, 151,* 38–46.

Rogers, R. W. (1975). A protection motivation theory of fear appeals and attitude change. *Journal of Psychology, 91,* 93–114.

Rooks, D. S., Gautam, S., Romeling, M., Cross, M. L., Stratigakis, D., Evans, B., Katz, J. N. (2007). Group exercise, education, and combination self-management in women with fibromyalgia: A randomized trial. *Archives of Internal Medicine, 167,* 2192–2200.

Root, T. L., Thornton, L. M., Lindroos, A. K., Stunkard, A. J., Lichtenstein, P., Pedersen, N. L., Rasmussen, F., & Bulik, C. M. (2010). Shared and unique genetic and environmental influences on binge eating and night eating: A Swedish twin study. *Eating Behaviors, 11,* 92–98.

Rosenfeldt, F., Miller, F., Nagley, P., Hadj, A., Marasco, S., Quick, D., … Pepe, S. (2004). Response of the senescent heart to stress: Clinical therapeutic strategies and quest for mitochondrial predictors of biological age. *Annals of the New York Academy of Sciences, 1019,* 78–84.

Rosengren, A., Wilhelmsen, L., & Orth-Gomer, K. (2004). Coronary disease in relation to social support and social class in Swedish men: A 15-year follow-up in the study of men born in 1933. *European Heart Journal, 25*(1), 56–63.

Rosenkranz, M. A., Davidson, R. J., Maccoon, D. G., Sheridan, J. F., Kalin, N. H., & Lutz, A. (2013). A comparison of mindfulness-based stress reduction and an active control in modulation of neurogenic inflammation. *Brain, Behavior, & Immunity, 27*(1), 174–184.

Rosenthal, T., & Alter, A. (2012). Occupational stress and hypertension. *Journal of the American Society of Hypertension, 6*(1), 2–22.

Roshania, R., Narayan, K. M., & Oza-Frank, R. (2008). Age at arrival and risk of obesity among U.S. immigrants. *Obesity, 16*(12), 2669–2675.

Rosmalen, J. G. M., Neeleman, J., Gans, R. O. B., & de Jonge, P. (2006). The association between neuroticism and self-reported common symptoms in a population cohort. *Journal of Psychosomatic Research, 62*(3), 305–311.

Rossouw, J. E., Anderson, G. L., Prentice, R. L., LaCroix, A. Z., Kooperberg, C., Stefanick, M. L., … Writing Group for the Women's Health Initiative Investigators. (2002). Risks and benefits of estrogen plus progestin in healthy postmenopausal women: Principal results from the Women's Health Initiative Randomized Controlled Trial. *Journal of the American Medical Association, 288*(3), 321–333.

Roter, D. L., & Hall, J. A. (2004). Physician gender and patient-centered communication: A critical review of empirical research. *Annual Review of Public Health, 25,* 497–519.

Rothenbacher, D., Hoffmeister, A., Brenner, H., & Koenig, W. (2003). Physical activity, coronary heart disease, and inflammatory response. *Archives of Internal Medicine, 163*(10), 1200–1205.

Rothman, A. J. (2000). Toward a theory-based analysis of behavioral maintenance. *Health Psychology, 19,* 64–69.

Rotter, J. B. (1966). Generalized expectancies for internal versus external control of reinforcement. *Psychological Monographs, 80*(1), 1–28.

Roy, B., Diez-Roux, A. V., Seeman, T., Ranjit, N., Shea, S., & Cushman, M. (2010). Association of optimism and pessimism with inflammation and hemostasis in the multi-ethnic study of atherosclerosis (MESA). *Psychosomatic Medicine, 72,* 134–140.

Rozanski, A., Blumenthal, J. A., & Kaplan, J. (1999). Clinical cardiology: New frontiers—Impact of psychological factors on the pathogenesis of cardiovascular disease and implications for therapy. *Circulation, 99*(16), 2192–2217.

Ruau, D., Liu, L. Y., Clark, J. D., Angst, M. S., & Butte, A. J. (2012). Sex differences in reported pain across 11,000 patients captured in electronic medical records. *The Journal of Pain, 13*(3), 228–234.

Ruby, M. B., Dunn, E. W., Perrino, A., Gillis, R., & Viel, S. (2011). The invisible benefits of exercise. *Health Psychology, 30*(1), 67–74.

Rueda, S., Law, S., & Rourke, S. B. (2014). Psychosocial, mental health, and behavioral issues of aging with HIV. *Current Opinion in HIV and AIDS, 9*(4), 325–331.

Rueggeberg, R., Wrosch, C., & Miler, G. E. (2012). The different roles of perceived stress in the association between older adults' physical activity and physical health. *Health Psychology, 32*(2), 164–171.

Russo, S. J., Murrough, J. W., Han, M.-H., Charney, D. S., & Nestler, E. J. (2012). Neurobiology of resilience. *Nature Neuroscience, 15,* 1475–1484.

Rutledge, T., & Linden, W. (2003). Defensiveness and 3-year blood pressure levels among young adults: The mediating effect of stress reactivity. *Annals of Behavioral Medicine, 25*(1), 34–40.

Rutledge, T., Stucky, E., Dollarhide, A., Shively, M., Jain, S., Wolfson, T., Winger, M., & Dresselhaus, T. (2009). A real-time assessment of work stress in physicians and nurses. *Health Psychology, 28*(2), 194–200.

Rutten, G. (2005). Diabetes patient education: Time for a new era. *Diabetic Medicine, 22,* 671–673.

Rutters, F., Nieuwenhuizen, A. G., Lemmens, S. G., Born, J. M., & Westertep-Plantenga, M. S. (2009). Acute stress-related changes in eating in the absence of hunger. *Obesity, 17*(1), 72–77.

Rutz, D. (1998, September 22). Study tracks causes, treatment of perplexing chronic fatigue syndrome. *CNN.com*. Retrieved from http://www.cnn.com/health

Ryan, A. M., Gee, G. C., & Griffith, D. (2008). The effect of perceived discrimination on diabetes management. *Journal of Health Care for the Poor and Underserved, 19*(1), 149–163.

Ryff, C. D., Singer, B. H., Wing, E., & Love, G. D. (2001). Elective affinities and uninvited agonies: Mapping emotion with significant others onto health. In C. D. Ryff & B. H. Singer (Eds.), *Emotion, social relationships, and health* (pp. 133–175). New York: Oxford University Press.

Saad, L. (2006, February 13). Nearly one in five teens is overweight. *Gallup News Service*. Retrieved March 8, 2010, from http://www.gallup.com/poll/21409/Nearly-One-Five-Teens-Overweight.aspx

Sackett, D. L., Straus, S. E., Richardson, W. S., Rosenberg, W., & Haynes, R. B. (2000). *Evidence based medicine. How to practice and teach EBM* (2nd ed.). Edinburgh: Churchill Livingstone.

Sadeh, A., Mindel, J. A., Luedtke, K., & Wiegand, B. (2009). Sleep and sleep ecology in the first 3 years: A Web-based study. *Journal of Sleep Research, 18*(1), 60–73.

Saelens, B. E., Sallis, J. F., & Frank, L. D. (2003). Environmental correlates of walking and cycling: Findings from the transportation, urban design, and planning literatures. *Annals of Behavioral Medicine, 25*(2), 80–91.

Safen, S. A., Reisner, S. L., Herrick, A., Mimiaga, M. J., & Stall, R. (2010). Mental health and HIV risk in men who have sex with men. *Journal of Acquired Immune Deficiency Syndromes, 55*(Supplement 2), S74–S77.

Sakurai, T., Amemiya, A., Ishii, M., Masuzaki, I., Chemelli, R. M., Tanaka, H., … Yanagisawa, M. (1998). Orexins and orexin receptors: A family of hypothalamic neuropeptides and G protein-coupled receptors that regulate feeding behavior. *Cell, 92*, 573–585.

Salovey, P. (2011). Framing health messages. In M. A. Gernsbacher, R. W. Pew, L. M. Hough, & J. R. Pomerantz (Eds.), *Psychology and the real world* (pp. 214–223). New York: Worth Publishers.

Salzmann, P., Kerlikowske, K., & Phillips, K. (1997). Cost-effectiveness of extending screening mammography guidelines to include women 40 to 49 years of age. *Annals of Internal Medicine, 127*, 955–965.

SAMHSA. (2009). *Results from the 2008 National Survey on Drug Use and Health: National findings*. Rockville, MD.: U.S. Department of Health and Human Services, Office of Applied Studies, NSDUH Series H-36.

SAMHSA. (2015). 2014 National Survey on Drug Use and Health (NSDUH). Table 6.88B—Alcohol use in the past month among persons aged 18 to 22, by college enrollment status and demographic characteristics: Percentages, 2013 and 2014. Retrieved from http://pubs.niaaa.nih.gov/publications/CollegeFactSheet/CollegeFactSheet.pdf

SAMHSA News. (2006). Drugs, alcohol, and HIV/AIDS: A consumer guide. Substance Abuse and Mental Health Services Administration. Retrieved from http://www.samhsa.gov/samhsa_news/volumexiv_5/article18.htm

Sanchez-Vaznaugh, E., Kawachi, I., Subramanian, S. V., Sanchez, B. N., & Acevedo-Garcia, D. (2009). Do socioeconomic gradients in BMI vary by race/ethnicity, gender, and birthplace? *American Journal of Epidemiology, 169*(9), 1102–1112.

Sander, R. (2009) Musical therapy to reduce sleep problems. *Nursing Older People, 21*(7), 13.

Sanger-Katz, M. (2014, October 26). Is the Affordable Care Act working? *The New York Times*. Retrieved February 25, 2016, from http://www.nytimes.com/interactive/2014/10/27/us/is-the-affordable-care-act-working.html?_r=0#/

Sansone, R. A., & Sansone, L. A. (2008). Alcohol/substance misuse and treatment nonadherence: Fatal attraction. *Psychiatry, 5*(9), 43–46.

Sapolsky, R. M. (1990). Glucocorticoids, hippocampal damage, and the glutamatergic synapse. *Progress in Brain Research, 86*, 13–20.

Sapolsky, R. M. (1998). *The trouble with testosterone and other essays on the biology of the human predicament*. New York: Simon & Schuster.

Sapolsky R. M. (2004a). Organismal stress and telomeric aging: An unexpected connection. *Proceedings of the National Academy of Sciences, 101*(50), 17323–17324.

Sapolsky, R. M. (2004b). *Why zebras don't get ulcers* (3rd ed.). New York: Holt.

Sapolsky, R. M. (2005). The influence of social hierarchy on primate health. *Science, 308*, 648–652.

Sapolsky, R. M. (2010, November 14). This is your brain on metaphors. *The New York Times*. Retrieved from http://www.nytimes.com

Sastry, J., & Ross, C. E. (1998). Asian ethnicity and the sense of personal control. *Social Psychological Quarterly, 61*(2), 101–120.

Sayette, M. A., Loewenstein, G., Griffin, K. M., & Black, J. J. (2008). Exploring the cold-to-hot empathy gap in smokers. *Psychological Science, 19*, 926–932.

Schachter, S. (1978). Pharmacological and psychological determinants of smoking. *Annals of Internal Medicine, 88*, 104–114.

Schachter, S., Silverstein, B., Kozlowski, L. T., Perlick, D., Herman, C. P., & Liebling, B. (1977). Studies of the interaction of psychological and pharmacological determinants of smoking. *Journal of Experimental Psychology General, 106*, 3–12.

Scheier, M. F., & Bridges, M. W. (1995). Person variables and health: Personality predispositions and acute psychological states as shared determinants for disease. *Psychosomatic Medicine, 57*, 255–268.

Scheier, M. P., Carver, C. S., & Bridges, M. W. (1994). Distinguishing optimism from neuroticism (and trait anxiety, mastery, and self-esteem): A reevaluation of the Life Orientation Test. *Journal of Personality and Social Psychology, 67*, 1063–1078.

Schernhammer, E. (2005). Taking their own lives—The high rate of physician suicide. *New England Journal of Medicine, 352*, 2473–2476.

Schield, M. (2010). Assessing statistical literacy: Take CARE. In P. Bidgood, N. Hunt, & F. Jolliffe (Eds.), *Assessment methods in statistical education: An international perspective* (pp. 133–152). West Sussex, UK: John Wiley.

Schiller, J. S., Lucas, J. W., & Peregoy, J. A. (2012). *Summary health statistics for U.S. adults: National Health Interview Survey, 2011*. Hyattsville, MD: U.S. Department of Health and Human Services.

Schleifer, S. J., Keller, S. E., Camerino, M., Thorton, J. C., & Stein, M. (1983). Suppression of lymphocyte stimulation following bereavement. *Journal of the American Medical Association, 250*, 374–377.

Schmidt, J. E., & Andrykowski, M. A. (2004). The role of social and dispositional variables associated with emotional processing in adjustment to breast cancer: An Internet-based study. *Health Psychology, 23*(3), 259–266.

Schmidt, S., Grossman, P., Schwarzer, B., Jena, S., Naumann, J., & Walach, H. (2011). Treating fibromyalgia with mindfulness-based stress reduction: Results from a 3-armed randomized controlled trial. *Pain, 152,* 361–369.

Schmidt, U., & Grover, M. (2007). Computer-based intervention for bulimia nervosa and binge eating. In J. Latner & G. T. Wilson (Eds.), *Self-help approaches for obesity and eating disorders: Research and practice* (pp. 166–174). New York: Guilford Press.

Schneider, R. H., Alexander, C. N., Staggers, F., Rianforth, M., Salerno, J. W., Hartz, A., Arndt, S., Barnes, V. A., & Nicich, S. (2005). Long-term effects of stress reduction on mortality in persons > or = 55 years of age with systemic hypertension. *American Journal of Cardiology, 95,* 1060–1064.

Schnittker, J. (2007). Working more and feeling better: Women's health, employment, and family life. *American Sociological Review, 72,* 221–238.

Schnoll, R. A., James, C., Malstrom, M., Rothman, R. L., Wang, H., Babb, J., … Goldberg, M. (2003). Longitudinal predictors of continued tobacco use among patients diagnosed with cancer. *Annals of Behavioral Medicine, 25*(3), 214–221.

Schoenborn, C. A., Adams, P. F., & Peregov, J. A. (2013). Health behaviors of adults: United States, 2008–2010. National Center for Health Statistics. *Vital Health Stat 10*(257), 1–184.

Schoenborn, C. A., & Gindi, R. M. (2015). Electronic cigarette use among adults: United States, 2014. *NCHS data brief, no. 217.* Hyattsville, MD: National Center for Health Statistics.

Scholz, U., Keller, R., & Perren, S. (2009). Predicting behavioral intentions and physical exercise: A test of the health action process approach at the intrapersonal level. *Health Psychology, 28,* 702–708.

Schousboe, K., Visscher, P. M., Erbads, B., Kyvik, K. O., Hopper, J. L., Henriksen, J. E., … Sorensen, T. I. (2004). Twin study of genetic and environmental influences on adult body size, shape, and composition. *International Journal of Obesity, 28,* 39–48.

Schreier, H. M. C., & Chen, E. (2010). Longitudinal relationships between family routines and biological profiles among youth with asthma. *Health Psychology, 29,* 82–90.

Schroecksnadel, K., Sarcletti, M., Winkler, C., Mumelter, B., Weiss, G., Fuchs, D., … Zengerle, R. (2008). Quality of life and immune activation in patients with HIV-infection. *Brain, Behavior, and Immunity.* 22(6), 881–889.

Schroevers, M. J., Kraaij, V., & Garnefski, N. (2011). Cancer patients' experience of positive and negative changes due to the illness: Relationships with psychological well-being, coping, and goal reengagement. *Psycho-Oncology, 20,* 165–172.

Schulman, K. A., Berlin, J., Harless, W., Kerner, J. F., Sistrunk, S. H., Gersh, B. J., … Escarce, J. J. (1999). The effect of race and sex on physicians' recommendations for cardiac catheterization. *New England Journal of Medicine, 340*(8), 618–625.

Schuz, B., Wurm, S., Ziegelmann, J. P., Wolff, J. K., Warner, L. M., Schwarzer, R., & Tesch-Romer, C. (2012). Contextual and individual predictors of physical activity: Interactions between environmental factors and health cognitions. *Health Psychology, 31*(6), 714–723.

Schwartz, B. (2004). *The paradox of choice.* New York: Harper Collins Publishers.

Schwartz, M. (2003). Don't blame stress on long work hours. *Benefits Canada, 33*(3), 31.

Schwartz, M. B., & Brownell, K. D. (1995). Matching individuals to weight loss treatments: A survey of obesity experts. *Journal of Consulting and Clinical Psychology, 63,* 149–153.

Schwartz, M. D., Chambliss, H. O., Brownell, K. D., Blair, S. N., & Billington, C. (2003). Weight bias among health professionals specializing in obesity. *Obesity Research, 11*(9), 1033–1039.

Schwebel, D. C., Roth, D. L., Elliott, M. N., Chien, S. A. T., Mrug, S., Shipp, E., Dittus, P., Zlomke, K., & Schuster, M. A. (2012). Marital conflict and fifth-graders' risk for injury. *Accident Analysis and Prevention, 47,* 30–35.

Schwebel, D. C., Roth, D. L., Elliott, M. N., Windle, M., Grunbaum, J. A., Low, B., Cooper, S. P., & Schuster, M. A. (2011). The association of activity level, parent mental distress, and parental involvement and monitoring with unintentional injury risk in fifth graders. *Accident Analysis and Prevention, 43,* 848–852.

Scott-Sheldon, L. A. J., Kalichman, S. C., Carey, M. P., & Fielder, R. L. (2008). Stress management interventions for HIV positive adults: A meta-analysis of randomized controlled trials, 1989 to 2006. *Health Psychology, 27,* 129–139.

Searle, A., & Bennett, P. (2001). Psychological factors and inflammatory bowel disease: A review of a decade of literature. *Psychology, Health, and Medicine, 6,* 121–135.

Sears, S. F., Urizar, G. G., & Evans, G. D. (2000). Examining a stress-coping model of burnout and depression in extension agents. *Journal of Occupational Health Psychology, 5,* 56–62.

Seeman, T. E., Gruenewald, T., Sidney, S., Liu, K., Schwartz, J., McEwen, B., & Karlamangla, A. S. (2009). Modeling multi-system biological risk in young adults: Coronary Artery Risk Development in Young Adults Study (CARDIA). *American Journal of Human Biology.* December 28, 2009 [Epub ahead of print]. PMID: 20039257.

Segerstrom, S. C. (2006). Optimism and resources: Effects on each other and on health over 10 years. *Journal of Research in Personality, 41,* 772–786.

Segerstrom, S. C. (2007). Stress, energy, and immunity: An ecological view. *Current Directions in Psychological Science, 16,* 326–330.

Segerstrom, S. C., & Miller, G. E. (2004). Psychological stress and the immune system: A meta-analytic study of 30 years of inquiry. *Psychological Bulletin, 130*(4), 601–630.

Segerstrom, S. C., & Sephton, S. E. (2010). Optimistic expectancies and cell-mediated immunity: The role of positive affect. *Psychological Science, 21,* 448–455.

Segerstrom, S. C., Taylor, S. E., Kemeny, M. E., & Fahey, J. (1998). Optimism is associated with mood, coping and immune change in response to stress. *Journal of Personality and Social Psychology, 74*(6), 1646–1655.

Seid, R. (1994). Too "close to the bone": The historical context for women's obsession with slenderness. In P. Fallon & M. A. Katzman (Eds.), *Feminist perspectives on eating disorders* (pp. 3–16). New York: Guilford.

Seidman, E., Allen, L., Aber, J. L., Mitchell, C., Feinman, J., Yoshikawa, H., Comtois, K. A., Golz, J., Miller, R. L., Ortiz-Torres, B., & Roper, G. C. (1995). Development and validation of adolescent-perceived microsystem scales: Social support, daily hassles, and involvement. *American Journal of Community Psychology, 23*(3), 355–388.

Selby, E. A., Anestis, M. D., Bender, T. W., & Joiner, T. E. (2009). An exploration of the emotional cascade model in borderline personality disorder. *Journal of Abnormal Psychology, 118*(2), 375–387.

Selby, E. A., Franklin, J., Carson-Wong, A., & Rizvi, S. L. (2013). Emotional cascades and self-injury: Investigating instability of rumination and negative emotion. *Journal of Clinical Psychology,* February 4, 2013 [Epub ahead of print].

Self, C. A., & Rogers, R. W. (1990). Coping with threats to health: Effects of persuasive appeals on depressed, normal, and antisocial personalities. *Journal of Behavioral Medicine, 13,* 343–358.

Seligman, M. E. P. (1975). *Helplessness: On depression, development, and death.* New York: W. H. Freeman.

Seligman, M. E. P. (2002). Positive psychology, positive prevention, and positive therapy. In C. R. Snyder & S. J. Lopez (Eds.), *Oxford handbook of positive psychology* (pp. 3–9). New York: Oxford University Press.

Seligman, M. E. P., & Csikszentmihalyi, M. (2000). Positive psychology: An introduction. *American Psychologist, 55,* 5–14.

Seligman, M. E. P., & Maier, S. F. (1967). Failure to escape traumatic shock. *Journal of Experimental Psychology, 74,* 1–9.

Seligman, M. E. P., Peterson, C., Barsky, A. J., Boehm, J. K., Kubzansky, L. D., Park, N., & Labarthe, D. (2016). *Positive health and health assets: Re-analysis of longitudinal data sets.* Robert Wood Johnson Foundation. Retrieved April 10, 2016, from http://positivehealthresearch.org/sites/positivehealthresearch.org/files/PH_Whitepaper_Layout_Web.pdf

Seligman, M. E. P., Reivich, K., Jaycox, L., & Gillham, J. (1995). *The optimistic child.* Boston: Houghton Mifflin.

Selye, H. (1974). *The stress of life.* New York: McGraw-Hill.

Seminowicz, D. A., & Davis, K. D. (2006). A re-examination of pain-cognition interactions: Implications for neuroimaging. *Pain, 130*(1), 8–13.

Sepa, A., Wahlberg, J., Vaarala, O., Frodi, A., & Ludvigsson, J. (2005). Psychological stress may induce diabetes-related autoimmunity in infancy. *Diabetes Care, 28,* 290–298.

Seppa, N. (2010). Not just a high. Scientists test medical marijuana against MS, inflammation and cancer. *Science News, 177*(13), 16–19.

Shadel, W. B., Martino, S. C., Setodji, C., & Scharf, D. (2012). Momentary effects of exposure to prosmoking media on college students' future smoking risk. *Health Psychology, 31*(4), 460–466.

Shahab, L., West, R., & McNeill, A. (2011). A randomized, controlled trial of adding expired carbon monoxide feedback to brief stop smoking advice: Evaluation of cognitive and behavioral effects. *Health Psychology, 30*(1), 49–57.

Shelby, R. A., Somers, T. J., Keefe, F. J., Silva, S. G., McKee, D. C., She, L., … Johnson, P. (2009). Pain catastrophizing in patients with noncardiac chest pain: Relationships with pain, anxiety, and disability. *Psychosomatic Medicine, 71,* 816–868.

Sheline, Y. I. (2000). 3D MRI studies of neuroanatomic changes in unipolar major depression: The role of stress and medical comorbidity. *Biological Psychiatry, 48*(8), 791–800.

Shen, B. J., Avivi, Y. E., Todaro, J. F., Spiro, A., Laurenceau, J. P., Ward, K. D., & Niaura, R. (2008). Anxiety characteristics independently and prospectively predict myocardial infarction in men: The unique contribution of anxiety among psychologic factors. *Journal of the American College of Cardiology, 51,* 113–119.

Shepperd, J. A., Rothman, A. J., & Klein, W. M. P. (2011). Using self- and identity-regulation to promote health: Promises and challenges. *Self and Identity, 10,* 407–416.

Sherwin, E. D., Elliott, T. R., Rybarczyk, B. D., & Frank, R. G. (1992). Negotiating the reality of caregiving: Hope, burnout and nursing. *Journal of Social & Clinical Psychology, 11,* 129–139.

Shiffman, S., Stone, A. A., & Hufford, M. R. (2008). Ecological momentary assessment. *Annual Review of Clinical Psychology, 4,* 1–32.

Shirom, A., Toker, S., Berliner, S., & Shapira, I. (2008). The Job Demand-Control-Support model and micro-inflammatory responses among healthy male and female employees: A longitudinal study. *Work and Stress, 22*(2), 138–152.

Shirtcliff, E. A., Coe, C. L., & Pollak, S. D. (2009). Early childhood stress is associated with elevated antibody levels to herpes simplex virus type 1. *Proceedings of the National Academy of Sciences, 106,* 2963–2967.

Shlisky, J. D., Hartman, T. J., Kris-Etherton, P. M., Rogers, C. J., Sharkey, N. A., & Nickols-Richardson, S. M. (2012). Partial sleep deprivation and energy balance in adults: An emerging issue for consideration by dietetics practitioners. *Journal of the Academy of Nutrition and Dietetics, 112*(11), 1785–1797.

Shoff, S. M., Newcomb, P. A., Trentham-Dietz, A., Remington, P. L., Mittendorf, R., Greenberg, E. R., & Willett, W. C. (2000). Early-life physical activity and postmenopausal breast cancer: Effect of body size and weight change. *Cancer Epidemiology, 9,* 591–595.

Shumaker, S. A., & Hill, D. R. (1991). Gender differences in social support and physical health. *Health Psychology: Special Issue: Gender and Health, 10,* 102–111.

Shwartz, M. (2007, March 7). Robert Sapolsky discusses physiological effects of stress. *Stanford News.* Retrieved from http://news.stanford.edu/news/2007/march7/sapolskysr-030707.html

Siegler, I. C., Costa, P. T., Brummett, B. H., Helms, M. J., Barefoot, J. C., Williams, R. B., … Rimer, B. K. (2003). Patterns of change in hostility from college to midlife in the UNC alumni heart study predict high-risk status. *Psychosomatic Medicine, 65*(5), 738–745.

Silagy, C., Lancaster, T., Stead, L., Mant, D., & Fowler, G. (2005). Nicotine replacement therapy for smoking cessation. *Cochrane Database of Systematic Reviews.* Retrieved March 18, 2010, from http://www2.cochrane.org/reviews/en/ab000146.html

Silber, M. H., Ancoli-Israel, S., Bonnet, M. H., Chokroverty, S., Grigg-Damberger, M. M., Hirshkowitz, M., … Iber, C. (2008). The visual scoring of sleep in adults. *Journal of Clinical Sleep Medicine, 3,* 121–131.

Silver, R. C., Holman, E. A., Andersen, J. P., Poulin, M., McIntosh, D. N., & Gil-Rivas, V. (2013). Mental- and physical-health effects of acute exposure to media images of the September 11, 2001, attacks and the Iraq war. *Psychological Science.* Retrieved February 24, 2016, from http://pss.sagepub.com/content/early/2013/08/01/0956797612460406.full.pdf+html

Silverstein, P. (1992). Smoking and wound healing. *American Journal of Medicine, 93,* 1A–22S.

Singh, A., Klapper, A., Jia, J., Fidalgo, A., Tajadura Jimenez, A., Kanakam, N., Bianchi-Berthouze, N., & Williams, N. (2014). Motivating people with chronic pain to do physical activity: Opportunities for technology design. *Proceedings of the SIGCHI Conference on Human Factors in Computing Systems.* Retrieved March 1, 2015, from https://www.researchgate.net/publication/261174870_Motivating_People_with_Chronic_Pain_to_do_Physical_Activity_Opportunities_for_Technology_Design

Singh, T., & Newman, A. B. (2011). Inflammatory markers in population studies of aging. *Aging Research Review, 10,* 319–329.

Siteman Cancer Center. (2015). *Your disease risk.* St. Louis, MO: Washington University School of Medicine. Retrieved from http://www.yourdiseaserisk.wustl.edu/YDRDefault.aspx?ScreenControl=YDRGeneral&ScreenName=YDRCancer_Index

Skevington, S. M. (1995). *Psychology of pain.* Chichester, UK: Wiley.

Skipper, M. (2011). Epigenomics: Epigenetic variation across the generations. *Nature Reviews Genetics, 12,* 740.

Skolnik, R. (2016). *Global health 101* (3rd ed.). Burlington, MA: Jones & Bartlett.

Slatcher, R. B., & Robles, T. F. (2012). Preschoolers' everyday conflict at home and diurnal cortisol patterns. *Health Psychology, 31*(6), 834–838.

Sloan, R. P., Bagiella, E., & Powell, T. (1999). Religion, spirituality, and medicine. *The Lancet, 353*, 664–667.

Small, L., Bonds-McClain, D., & Gannon, A. M. (2013). Physical activity of young overweight and obese children: Parent reports of child activity level compared with objective measures. *Western Journal of Nursing Research, 35*(5), 638–654.

Smedley, B. D., Stith, A. Y., & Nelson, A. R. (2002). *Unequal treatment: Confronting racial and ethnic disparities in health care.* Institute of Medicine. Washington, DC: The National Academies Press.

Smeijers, L., Szabo, B. M., Damman, L. V., Wonnink, W., Jakobs, B. S., & Bosch, J. A. (2015). Emotional, neurohormonal, and hemodynamic responses to mental stress in Tako-Tsubo cardiomyopathy. *The American Journal of Cardiology, 115*(11), 1580–1586.

Smith, C. A., Hay, P. P., & MacPherson, H. (2010). Acupuncture for depression. *Cochrane Database Systematic Review, 20*(1), CD0004046.

Smith, J. C. (2005). *Relaxation, meditation, and mindfulness: A mental health practitioner's guide to new and traditional approaches.* New York: Springer.

Smith, M. O. (2012). The use of acupuncture in addiction treatment programs. *The Huffington Post.* Retrieved from http://www.huffingtonpost.com/dr-michael-o-smith/addiction-acupuncture_b_1665796.html

Smith, T. W., Birmingham, W., & Uchino, B. N. (2012). Evaluative threat and ambulatory blood pressure: Cardiovascular effects of social stress in daily experience. *Health Psychology, 31*(6), 763–766.

Smith, W. A., Hung, M., & Franklin, J. D. (2011). Racial battle fatigue and the miseducation of black men: Racial microaggressions, societal problems, and environmental stress. *Journal of Negro Education, 80*(1), 63–82.

Smith-McCune, K. K., Shiboski, S., Chirenje, M. Z., Magure, T., Tuveson, J., Ma, Y., … Sawaya, G. F. (2010). Type-specific cervico-vaginal human papillomavirus infection increases risk of HIV acquisition independent of other sexually transmitted infections. *PLOS ONE, 5*(4), e10094.

Snodgrass, S. E. (1998). Thriving: Broadening the paradigm beyond illness (personal experience with breast cancer). *Journal of Social Issues, 54* (2), 373–378.

Snowden, F. M. (2008). Emerging and reemerging diseases: A historical perspective. *Immunological Reviews, 225*, 9–26.

Snyder, J. L., & Bowers, T. G. (2008). The efficacy of acamprosate and naltrexone in the treatment of alcohol dependence: A relative benefits analysis of randomized controlled trials. *American Journal of Drug and Alcohol Abuse, 34*, 449–461.

Solberg Nes, L., Roach, A. R., & Segerstrom, S. C. (2009). Executive functions, self-regulation, and chronic pain: A review. *Annals of Behavioral Medicine, 37*(2), 173–183.

Soldz, S., & Cui, X. (2002). Pathways through adolescent smoking: A 7-year longitudinal grouping analysis. *Health Psychology, 21*(5), 495–594.

Solomon, G. F., & Moos, R. H. (1964). Emotions, immunity, and disease: A speculative theoretical integration. *Archives of General Psychiatry, 11*, 657–674.

Solomon, G. F., Segerstrom, S. C., Grohr, P., Kemeny, M., & Fahey, J. (1997). Shaking up immunity: Psychological and immunologic changes after a natural disaster. *Psychosomatic Medicine, 59*, 114–127.

Song, L., Hamilton, J. B., & Moore, A. D. (2012). Patient-healthcare provider communication: Perspectives of African American cancer patients. *Health Psychology, 31*(5), 539–547.

Spalding, K. L. (2008). Dynamics of fat cell turnover in humans. *Nature, 453*, 783–787.

Spasojevic, J., & Alloy, L. B. (2001). Rumination as a common mechanism relating depressive risk factors to depression. *Emotion, 1*, 25–37.

Speca, M., Carlson, L. E., Goodey, E., & Angen, M. (2000). A randomized, wait-list controlled trial: The effect of a mindfulness meditation-based stress reduction program on mood and symptoms of stress in cancer outpatients. *Psychosomatic Medicine, 62*(5), 613–622.

Spiegel, D. (1996). Psychological stress and disease course for women with breast cancer: One answer, many questions. *Journal of the National Cancer Institute, 88*(1), 629–631.

Spiegel, D., & Giese-Davis, J. (2003). Depression and cancer: Mechanisms and disease progression. *Biological Psychiatry, 54*(3), 269–282.

Sprenger, C., Eippert, F., Finsterbusch, J., Bingel, U., Rose, M., & Buchel, C. (2012). Attention modulates spinal cord responses to pain. *Current Biology, 22*(11), 1019–1022.

Stacy, A. W., Bentler, P. M., & Flay, B. R. (1994). Attitudes and health behavior in diverse populations: Drunk driving, alcohol use, binge eating, marijuana use, and cigarette use. *Health Psychology, 13*, 73–85.

Stamler, J., Stamler, R., Neaton, J. D., Wentworth, D., Daviglus, M. L., Garside, D., … Greenland, P. (1999). Low-risk factor profile and long-term cardiovascular and noncardiovascular mortality and life expectancy: Findings for 5 large cohorts of young adult and middle-aged men and women. *Journal of the American Medical Association, 282*, 2012–2018.

Stanford Center for Narcolepsy. (2015). About narcolepsy. Retrieved from http://med.stanford.edu/narcolepsy/symptoms.html

Stanovich, K. E., & West, R. F. (1998). Individual differences in rational thought. *Journal of Experimental Psychology: General, 127*(2), 161–188.

Stanton, A. L. (2010). Regulating emotions during stressful experiences: The adaptive utility of coping through emotional approach. In S. Folkman (Ed.), *Oxford handbook of stress, health and coping* (pp. 369–386). New York: Oxford University Press.

Stanton, A. L., Danoff-Burg, S., Cameron, C. L., Bishop, M., Collins, C. A., Kirk, S. B., … Twillman, R. (2000). Emotionally expressive coping predicts psychological and physical adjustment to breast cancer. *Journal of Consulting and Clinical Psychology, 68*(5), 875–882.

Stanton, A. L., Thompson, E. H., Crespi, C. M., Link, J. S., & Waisman, J. R. (2013). Project Connect Online: Randomized trial of an internet-based program to chronicle the cancer experience and facilitate communication. *American Society of Clinical Oncology, 33*(25), 2763–2771.

Starr, J. M., Shields, P. G., Harris, S. E., Pattie, A., Pearce, M. S., Relton, C. L., & Deary, I. J. (2008). Oxidative stress, telomere length and biomarkers of physical aging in a cohort aged 79 years from the 1932 Scottish Mental Survey. *Mechanisms of Ageing and Development, 129*(12), 745–751.

Stead, L. F., Perera, R., Bullen, C., Mant, D., & Lancaster, T. (2008). Nicotine replacement therapy for smoking cessation. *Cochrane Database of Systematic Reviews*, Cochrane AN: CD000146.

Stein, J., & Nyamathi, A. (1999). Gender differences in behavioural and psychosocial predictors of HIV testing and return for test results in a high-risk population. *AIDS Care Special Issue: AIDS Impact: 4th International Conference on the Biopsychosocial Aspects of HIV Infection, 12,* 343–356.

Steinberg, L. (2007). Risk taking in adolescence: New perspectives from brain and behavioral science. *Current Directions in Psychological Science, 16*(2), 55–59.

Steiner, B. (2014, April 1). Treating chronic pain with meditation. *The Atlantic.* Retrieved March 1, 2016, from http://www.theatlantic.com/health/archive/2014/04/treating-chronic-pain-with-meditation/284182/

Steinhausen, H. C. (2002). The outcome of anorexia nervosa in the 20th century. *American Journal of Psychiatry, 159,* 1284–1293.

Stephens, M. B. (2009). Cardiac rehabilitation. *American Family Physician, 80*(9), 955–959.

Steptoe, A. (1997). Stress and disease. In A. Baum, S. Newman, J. Weinman, R. West, & C. McManus (Eds.), *Cambridge handbook of psychology, health, and medicine* (pp. 174–177). Cambridge, UK: Cambridge University Press.

Steptoe, A., & Ayers, S. (2004). Stress, health and illness. In S. Sutton, A. Baum, & M. Johnston (Eds.), *The Sage handbook of health psychology* (pp. 169–196). Thousand Oaks, CA: Sage Publications.

Steptoe, A., Dockray, S., & Wardle, J. (2009). Positive affect and psychobiological processes relevant to health. *Journal of Personality, 77,* 1747–1776.

Steptoe, A., Hamer, M., & Chida, Y. (2007). The effects of acute psychological stress on circulating inflammatory factors in humans: A review and meta-analysis. *Brain, Behavior, and Immunity, 21,* 901–912.

Steptoe, A., O'Donnell, K., & Badrick, E. (2008). Neuroendocrine and inflammatory markers associated with positive affect in healthy men and women: The Whitehall II study. *American Journal of Epidemiology, 167*(1), 96–102.

Steptoe, A., Perkins-Porras, L., McKay, C., Rink, E., Hilton, S., & Cappuccio, F. P. (2003). Psychological factors associated with fruit and vegetable intake and with biomarkers in adults from a low-income neighborhood. *Health Psychology, 22*(2), 148–155.

Steptoe, A., Siegrist, J., Kirschbaum, C., & Marmot, M. (2004). Effort-reward imbalance, overcommitment, and measures of cortisol and blood pressure over the working day. *Psychosomatic Medicine, 66,* 323–329.

Steptoe, A., Wardle, J., Pollard, T. M., & Canaan, L. (1996). Stress, social support and health-related behavior: A study of smoking, alcohol consumption and physical exercise. *Journal of Psychosomatic Research, 41,* 171–180.

Sternberg, E. M. (2001). *The balance within: The science connecting health and emotions.* New York: W. H. Freeman & Company.

Stewart, D. E., Abbey, S. E., Shnek, Z. M., Irvine, J., & Grace, S. L. (2004). Gender differences in health information needs and decisional preferences in patients recovering from an acute ischemic coronary event. *Psychosomatic Medicine, 66,* 42–48.

Stewart, L. K., Flynn, M. G., Campbell, W. W., Craig, B. A., Robinson, J. P., & Timmerman, K. L. (2007). The influence of exercise training on inflammatory cytokines and C-reactive protein. *Medicine and Science in Sports and Exercise, 39,* 1714–1719.

Stice, E., Rohde, P., Durant, S., Shaw, H., & Wade, E. (2013). Effectiveness of peer-led dissonance-based eating disorder prevention groups: Results from two randomized pilot trials. *Behaviour Research and Therapy, 51*(4–5), 197–206.

Stice, E., Rohde, P., & Shaw, H. (2013). *The Body Project: A dissonance-based eating disorder prevention intervention.* New York: Oxford University Press.

Stice, E., Shaw, H., & Marti, C. N. (2007). A meta-analytic review of eating disorder prevention programs: Encouraging findings. *Annual Review of Clinical Psychology, 3,* 207–231.

Stickgold, R. (2009). The simplest way to reboot your brain. *Harvard Business Review, 87*(10), 36.

Stilley, C. S., Bender, C. M., Dunbar-Jacob, J., Sereika, S., & Ryan, C. M. (2010). The impact of cognitive function on medication management: Three studies. *Health Psychology, 21,* 131–138.

Stock, M. L., Gibbons, F. X., Gerrard, M., Houlihan, A. E., Weng, C.-Y., Lorenz, F. O., & Simons, R. L. (2013a). Racial identification, racial composition, and substance use vulnerability among African American adolescents and young adults. *Health Psychology, 32*(3), 237–247.

Stock, M. L., Gibbons, F. X., Peterson, L. M., & Gerrard, M. (2013b). The effects of racial discrimination on the HIV-risk cognitions and behaviors of black adolescents and young adults. *Health Psychology, 32*(5), 543–550.

St-Onge, M. P., Roberts, A. L., Chen, J., Kellerman, M., O'Keefe, M., RoyChoudhury, A., & Jones, P. J. (2011). Short sleep duration increases energy intakes but does not change energy expenditure in normal-weight individuals. *American Journal of Clinical Nutrition, 94*(2), 410–416.

Stolarczyk, E., Vong, C. T., Perucha, E., Jackson, I., Cawthorne, M. A., Wargent, E. T., Powell, N., Canavan, J. B., Lord, G. M., & Howard, J. K. (2013). Improved insulin sensitivity despite increased visceral adiposity in mice deficient for the immune cell transcription factor T-bet. *Cell Metabolism, 17*(4), 520–533.

Stone, A. A., Mezzacappa, E. S., Donatone, B. A., & Gonder, M. (1999). Psychosocial stress and social support are associated with prostate-specific antigen levels in men: Results from a community screening program. *Health Psychology, 18*(5), 482–486.

Stone, R. (2005). In the wake: Looking for keys to posttraumatic stress. *Science, 310,* 1605.

Storey, D. J., McLaren, D. B., Atkinson, M. A., Butcher, I., Liggatt, S., O'Dea, R., & Sharpe. M. (2011). Clinically relevant fatigue in recurrence-free prostate cancer survivors. *Annals of Oncology, 23,* 65–72.

Stowe, R. P., Peek, M. K., Perez, N. A., Yetman, D. L., Cutchin, M. P., & Goodwin, J. S. (2010). Herpes virus reactivation and socioeconomic position: A community-based study. *Journal of Epidemiology and Community Health, 64*(8), 666–671.

Stranges, E., Kowlessar, N., & Elixhauser, A. (2011). Components of growth in inpatient hospital costs, 1997–2009. *HCUP Statistical Brief Number 123.* Rockville, MD: Agency for Healthcare Research and Quality. Retrieved from http://www.hcup-us.ahrq.gov/reports/statbriefs/sb123.pdf

Strasburger, V. C., Jordan, A. B., & Donnerstein, E. (2009). Health effects of media on children and adolescents. *Pediatrics, 125*(4), 756–767.

Straub, R. H., & Kalden, J. R. (2009). Stress of different types increases the proinflammatory load in rheumatoid arthritis. *Arthritis Research and Therapy, 11*(3), 114–115.

Strawbridge, W. J., Wallhagen, M. I., & Shema, S. J. (2000). New NHLBI clinical guidelines for obesity and overweight: Will they promote health? *American Journal of Public Health, 90,* 340–343.

Strecher, V. J., & Rosenstock, I. M. (1997). The health belief model. In A. Baum, S. Newman, J. Weinman, R. West, & C. McManus (Eds.), *Cambridge handbook of psychology, health, and medicine* (pp. 113–117). Cambridge, UK: Cambridge University Press.

Street, R. L, Jr., Gordon, H., & Haidet, P. (2007). Physicians' communication and perceptions of patients: Is it how they look, how they talk, or is it just the doctor? *Social Science & Medicine, 65,* 586–598.

Street, R. L., Jr., & Haidet, P. (2011). How well do doctors know their patients? Factors affecting physician understanding of patients' health beliefs. *Journal of General Internal Medicine, 26,* 21–27.

Striegel-Moore, R. H., & Bulik, C. M. (2007). Risk factors for eating disorders. *American Psychologist, 62,* 181–198.

Striegel-Moore, R. H., Cachelin, F. M., Dohm, F. A., Pike, K. M., Wilfley, D. E., & Fairburn, C. G. (2001). Comparison of binge eating disorder and bulimia nervosa in a community sample. *International Journal of Eating Disorders, 29*(2), 157–165.

Strigo, I. A., Simmons, A. N., Matthews, S. C., Craig, A. D., & Paulhus, M. P. (2008). Association of major depressive disorder with altered functional brain response during anticipation and processing of heat pain. *Archives of General Psychiatry, 65*(11), 1275–1284.

Strogatz, D. S., Croft, J. B., James, S. A., Keenan, N. L., Browning, S. R., Garrett, J. M., & Curtis, A. B. (1997). Social support, stress, and blood pressure in black adults. *Epidemiology, 8*(5), 482–487.

Sue, D. W. (2011). Microaggressions, marginality, and oppression: An introduction. In D. Sue (Ed.), *Microaggressions and marginality: Manifestation, dynamics, and impact* (pp. 3–22). Hoboken, NJ: John Wiley & Sons.

Sue, D. W., Capodilupo, C. M., Torino, G. C., Bucceri, J. M., Holder, A. M. B., Nadal, K. L., & Esquilin, M. (2007). Racial microaggressions in everyday life: Implications for clinical practice. *American Psychologist, 62*(4), 271–286.

Suhr, J., Demireva, P., & Heffner, K. (2008). The reaction of salivary cortisol to patterns of performance on a word list learning task in healthy older adults. *Psychoneuroimmunology, 33*(9), 1293–1296.

Sullivan, M., Paice, J. A., & Beneditti, F. (2004). Placebos and treatment of pain. *Pain Medicine, 5*(3), 325–328.

Suls, J., & Bunde, J. (2005). Anger, anxiety, and depression as risk factors for cardiovascular disease: The problems and implications of overlapping affective dispositions. *Psychological Bulletin, 131,* 260–300.

Sussman, S., Sun, P., & Dent, C. W. (2006). A meta-analysis of teen cigarette smoking cessation. *Health Psychology, 25,* 549–557.

Sutton, S. R. (1996). Can "stages of change" provide guidance in the treatment of addictions? A critical examination of Prochaska and DiClemente's model. In G. Edwards & C. Dare (Eds.), *Psychotherapy, psychological treatments, and the addictions* (pp. 189–205). Cambridge, UK: Cambridge University Press.

Sutton, S. R. (1997). The theory of planned behavior. In A. Baum, S. Newman, J. Weinman, R. West, & C. McManus (Eds.), *Cambridge handbook of psychology, health, and medicine.* Cambridge, UK: Cambridge University Press.

Swami, V., Kannan, K., & Furnham, A. (2011). Positive body image: Inter-ethnic and rural-urban differences among an indigenous sample from Malaysian Borneo. *International Journal of Social Psychiatry, 58*(6), 568–576.

Swan, G. E., & Carmelli, D. (1996). Curiosity and mortality in aging adults: A 5-year follow-up of the Western Collaborative Group Study. *Psychology and Aging, 11,* 449–453.

Swanson, S. A., Crow, S. J., Le Grange, D., Swendsen, J., & Merikangas, K. R. (2011). Prevalence and correlates of eating disorders in adolescents. Results from the national comorbidity survey replication adolescent supplement. *Archives of General Psychiatry, 68*(7), 714–723.

Szabo, L. (2015, February 7). States racing to regulate e-cigarettes. *USA Today.* Retrieved from http://www.usatoday.com/story/news/2015/02/07/state-e-cigarette-bills/22364765/

Szapary, P. O., Bloedon, L. T., & Foster, B. D. (2003). Physical activity and its effects on lipids. *Current Cardiology Reports, 5,* 488–492.

Szeto, A. C. H., & Dobson, K. S. (2013). Mental disorders and their association with perceived work stress: An investigation of the 2010 Canadian Community Health Survey. *Journal of Occupational Health Psychology, 18*(2), 191–197.

Taber, D. R., Chriqui, J. F., & Chaloupka, F. J. (2012). Differences in nutrient intake associated with state laws regarding fat, sugar, and caloric content of competitive foods. *Pediatrics, 166*(5), 452–458.

Taheri, S., Lin, L., Austin, D., Young, T., & Mignot, E. (2004). Short sleep duration is associated with reduced leptin, elevated ghrelin, and increased body mass index. *PLOS Medicine,* Retrieved from http://www.plosmedicine.org/article/info%3Adoi%2F10.1371%2Fjournal.pmed.0010062

Tan, D., Barger, J. S., & Shields, P. G. (2006). Alcohol drinking and breast cancer. *Breast Cancer Online, 9*(4), 1–11.

Tang, Y.-Y. Lu, Q., Fan, M., Yang, Y., & Posner, M. I. (2012). Mechanisms of white matter changes induced by meditation. *Proceedings of the National Academy of Sciences,* Early Edition. Retrieved from http://www.pnas.org/content/early/2012/06/05/1207817109.abstract?sid=0229e3f4-0b13-4a40-bbfe-67990e8c8468

Tanno, K., Sakata, K., Ohsawa, M., Onoda, T., Itai, K., Yaegashi, Y., & Tamakoshi, A. (2009). Associations of ikigai as a positive psychological factor with all-cause mortality and cause-specific mortality among middle-aged and elderly Japanese people: Findings from the Japan Collaborative Cohort Study. *Journal of Psychosomatic Research, 67,* 67–75.

Tapper, K., Shaw, C., Illsey, J., Hill, A. J., Bond, F. W., & Moore, L. (2009). Exploratory randomized controlled trial of a mindfulness weight loss intervention for women. *Appetite, 52*(2), 396–404.

Tarter, R. E., Vanyukov, M., Kirisci, L., Reynolds, M., & Clark, D. B. (2006). Predictors of marijuana use in adolescents before and after illicit drug use: Examination of the gateway hypothesis. *American Journal of Psychiatry, 163*(12), 2134–2140.

Taylor, E. (1997). Shiftwork and health. In A. Baum, S. Newman, J. Weinman, R. West, & C. McManus (Eds.), *Cambridge handbook of psychology, health, and medicine* (pp. 318–319). Cambridge, UK: Cambridge University Press.

Taylor, P. J., Gooding, P., Wood, A. M., & Tarrier, N. (2011). The role of defeat and entrapment in depression, anxiety, and suicide. *Psychological Bulletin, 137,* 391–420.

Taylor, S. E., Cousino, L., Lewis, B. P., Grunewald, T. L., Gurung, R. A., & Updegraff, J. A. (2000). Biobehavioral responses to stress in females: Tend-and-befriend, not fight-or-flight. *Psychological Review, 107*(3), 411–429.

Taylor, S. E., Gonzaga, G., Klein, L. C., Hu, P., Greendale, G. A., & Seeman, S. E. (2006). Relation of oxytocin to psychological stress responses and hypothalamic-pituitary-adrenocortical axis activity in older women. *Psychosomatic Medicine, 68,* 238–245.

Taylor, S. E., Lerner, J. S., Sherman, D. K., Sage, R. M., & McDowell, N. K. (2003). Are self-enhancing cognitions associated with healthy or unhealthy biological profiles? *Journal of Personality and Social Psychology, 85*(4), 605–615.

Taylor, S. E., Repetti, R. L., & Seeman, T. (1997). Health psychology: What is an unhealthy environment and how does it get under the skin? *Annual Review of Psychology, 48,* 411–447.

Taylor, S. E., Seeman, T. E., Eisenberger, N. I., Kozanian, T. A., Moore, A. N., & Moons, W. G. (2010). Effects of a supportive or unsupportive audience on biological and psychological responses to stress. *Journal of Personality and Social Psychology, 98,* 47–56.

Taylor, S. E., & Stanton, A. (2007). Coping resources, coping processes, and mental health. *Annual Review of Clinical Psychology, 3,* 129–153.

Teachman, B. A., Gapinski, K. D., Brownell, K. D., Rawlins, M., & Jeyaram, S. (2003). Demonstrations of implicit anti-fat bias: The impact of providing causal information and evoking empathy. *Health Psychology, 22*(1), 68–78.

Teasdale, J. D., Segal, Z. V., Williams, J. M. G., Ridgeway, V. A., Soulsby, J. M., & Lau, M. A. (2000). Prevention of relapse/recurrence in major depression by mindfulness-based cognitive therapy. *Journal of Consulting and Clinical Psychology, 68*(4), 615–623.

Teh, C. F., Zasylavsky, A. M., Reynolds, C. F., & Cleary, P. D. (2010). Effect of depression treatment on chronic pain outcomes. *Psychosomatic Medicine, 72,* 61–67.

Templeton, S. (2004). Up in smoke: Our hopes for health. Finland beat heart disease by changing the nation's diet. *The Sunday Herald.* Published January 11, 2004; retrieved October 21, 2010, from http://business.highbeam.com/61222/article-1P2-10000665/up-in-smoke-our-hopes-health-obesity-finland-beat-heart

Teng, Y., & Mak, W. W. S. (2011). The role of planning and self-efficacy in condom use among men who have sex with men: An application of the Health Action Process Approach Model. *Health Psychology, 30*(1), 119–128.

Theorell, T., Blomkvist, V., Jonsson, H., Schulman, S., Berntorp, E., & Stigendal, L. (1995). Social support and the development of immune function in human immunodeficiency virus infection. *Psychosomatic Medicine, 57,* 32–36.

Thielke, S., Thompson, A., & Stuart, R. (2011). Health psychology in primary care: Recent research and future directions. *Journal of Psychology Research and Behavior Management, 4,* 59–68.

Thom, D. H., Hall, M. A., & Pawlson, L. G. (2004). Measuring patients' trust in physicians when assessing quality of care. *Health Affairs, 23*(4), 124–132.

Thompson, L. A., Knapp, C. A., Feeg, V., Madden, V. L., & Shenkman, E. A. (2010). Pediatricians' management practices for chronic pain. *Journal of Palliative Medicine, 13*(2), 171–178.

Thompson, R. (2000). *The brain: A neuroscience primer* (3rd ed.). New York: Worth.

Thompson, R. C., Allam, A. H., Zink, A., Wann, L. S., Lombardi, G. P., Cox, S. L., … Thomas, G. S. (2014). Computed tomographic evidence of atherosclerosis in the mummified remains of humans from around the world. *Global Heart, 9*(2), 187–196.

Thornton, L. M., Andersen, B. L., & Blakely, W. P. (2010). The pain, depression, and fatigue symptom cluster in advanced breast cancer: Covariation with the hypothalamic-pituitary-adrenal axis and the sympathetic nervous system. *Health Psychology, 29*(3), 333–337.

Thorp, A. A., Healy, G. N., Owen, N., Salmon, J., Ball, K., Shaw, J. E., Zimet, P. Z., & Dunstan, D. W. (2010). Deleterious associations of sitting time and television viewing time with cardiometabolic risk biomarkers: Australian diabetes, obesity, and lifestyle (AusDiab) study 2004–2005. *Diabetes Care, 33*(2), 327–334.

Thorsteinsen, K., Vittersø, J., & Svendsen, G. B. (2014). Increasing physical activity efficiently: An experimental pilot study of a website and mobile phone intervention. *International Journal of Telemedicine and Applications.* Retrieved February 23, 2016, from http://www.hindawi.com/journals/ijta/2014/746232/

Tigawalana, D. (2010). Why African women are more vulnerable to HIV/AIDS. *Rwanda News Agency.* Retrieved February 28, 2016, from http://rnanews.com/health/4206-why-african-women-are-more-vulnerable-to-hivaids

Tindle, H. A., Change, Y. F., Kuller, L. H., Manson, J. E., Robinson, J. G., Rosal, M. C., & Matthews, K. A. (2009). Optimism, cynical hostility, and incident coronary heart disease and mortality in the Women's Health Initiative. *Circulation, 120,* 656–662.

Tolmunen, T., Lehto, S. M., Heliste, M., Kurl, S., & Kauhanen, J. (2010). Alexithymia is associated with increased cardiovascular mortality in middle-aged Finnish men. *Psychosomatic Medicine, 72,* 187–191.

Tomaka, J., Blascovich, J., Kelsey, R. M., & Leitten, C. L. (1993). Subjective, physiological, and behavioral effects of threat and challenge appraisal. *Journal of Personality & Social Psychology, 65*(2), 248–260.

Tomfohr, L. M., Pung, M. A., Mills, P. J., & Edwards, K. (2015). Trait mindfulness is associated with blood pressure and interleukin-6: Exploring interactions among subscales of the Five Facet Mindfulness Questionnaire to better understand relationships between mindfulness and health. *Journal of Behavioral Medicine, 38*(1), 28–38.

Tomich, P. L., & Helgeson, V. S. (2004). Is finding something good in the bad always good? Benefit finding among women with breast cancer. *Health Psychology, 23,* 16–23.

Torpy, J. M., Cassio, L., & Glass, R. M. (2005). Smoking and pregnancy. *Journal of the American Medical Association, 293*(1), 1286–1287.

Tosoian, J. J., Trock, B. J., Landis, P., Feng, Z., Epstein, J. I., Partin, A. W., & Carter, H. B. (2011). Active surveillance program for prostate cancer: An update of the Johns Hopkins experience. *Journal of Clinical Oncology, 29,* 2185–2190.

Tran, V. H. (2010). *Benefit finding, negative affect, and daily diabetes, management among adolescents with Type 1 diabetes* (Doctoral dissertation). Retrieved from https://repositories.tdl.org/utswmed-ir/bitstream/handle/2152.5/819/tranvincent.pdf?sequence=3

Tran, V. H., Wiebe, D. J., Fortenberry, K. T., Butler, J. M., & Berg, C. A. (2011). Benefit finding, affective reactions to diabetes stress, and diabetes management among early adolescents. *Health Psychology, 30*(2), 212–219.

Treasure, J. L, Katzman, M., Schmidt, U., Troop, N., Todd, G., & deSilva, P. (1998). Engagement and outcome in the treatment of bulimia nervosa: First phase of a sequential design comparing motivational enhancement therapy and cognitive behavioural therapy. *Behaviour Research and Therapy, 37,* 405–418.

Trief, P. M., Ploutz-Snyder, R., Britton, K. D., & Weinstock, R. S. (2004). The relationship between marital quality and adherence to the diabetes care regimen. *Annals of Behavioral Medicine, 27*(3), 148–154.

Trivedi, A. N., & Ayanian, J. Z. (2006). Perceived discrimination and use of preventive health services. *Journal of General Internal Medicine, 21*(6), 553–558.

Tromp, D. M., Brouha, X. D. R., Hordijk, G. J., Winnubst, J. A. M., Gebhardt, W. A., van der Doef, M. P., & De Leeuw, J. R. J.

(2005). Medical care-seeking and health-risk behavior in patients with head and neck cancer: The role of health value, control beliefs and psychological distress. *Health Education Research, 20*(6), 665–675.

Tsuboi, K. (2013, March 21). New telemedicine tech maintains patient privacy. *CNet.* Retrieved from http://news.cnet.com/8301-11386_3-57575658-76/new-telemedicine-tech-maintains-patient-privacy

Tucker, J. S., Orlando, M., Burnam, M. A., Sherbourne, C. D., Kung, F.-Y., & Gifford, A. (2004). Psychosocial mediators of antiretroviral nonadherence in HIV-positive adults with substance use and mental health problems. *Health Psychology, 23*(4), 363–370.

Tucker, M. E. (2002). Lifestyle intervention is clear choice for diabetes prevention. *Internal Medicine News, 35*(15), 4.

Turk, D. C., & Okifuji, A. (2002). Chronic pain. In A. J. Christensen & M. H. Antoni (Eds), *Chronic physical disorders: Behavioral medicine's perspective* (pp. 165–190). Malden, MA: Blackwell Publishing.

Turk, D. C., Swanson, K. S., & Tunks, E. R. (2008). Psychological approaches in the treatment of chronic pain patients—when pills, scalpels, and needles are not enough. *Canadian Journal of Psychiatry, 53*(4), 213–223.

Turner, R. J., & Avison, W. R. (1992). Innovations in the measurement of life stress: Crisis theory and the significance of event resolution. *Journal of Health and Social Behavior, 33,* 36–50.

Turner, R. J., & Avison, W. R. (2003). Status variations in stress exposure: Implications for the interpretation of research on race, socioeconomic status, and gender. *Journal of Health and Social Behavior, 44,* 488–505.

Tyler, P., & Cushway, D. (1992). Stress, coping and mental well-being in hospital nurses. *Stress Medicine, 8,* 91–98.

Uchino, B. N. (2009). Understanding the links between social support and physical health. *Perspectives on Psychological Science, 4*(3), 236–255.

Uchino, B. N., Cawthon, F. M., Smith, T. W., Light, K. C., McKenzie, J., Carlisle, M., Gunn, H., Birmingham, W., & Bowen, K. (2012). Social relationships and health: Is feeling positive, negative, or both (ambivalent) about your social ties related to telomeres? *Health Psychology, 31*(6), 789–796.

Umberson, D., & Montez, J. K. (2010). Social relationships and health: A flashpoint for health policy. *Journal of Health and Social Behavior, 51,* S54–S66.

UNAIDS. (2007). *AIDS epidemic update, 2007.* Geneva, Switzerland: Joint United Nations Programme on HIV/AIDS.

UNAIDS. (2010). *Report on the global AIDS epidemic.* Retrieved from http://www.unaids.org/globalreport

UNAIDS. (2011). *UNAIDS World AIDS Day Report 2011.* Retrieved from http//www.unaids.org

UNAIDS. (2015). Treatment 2015. *Joint United Nations Programme on HIV/AIDS.* Retrieved February 28, 2016, from http://www.unaids.org/en/resources/campaigns/treatment2015

UNDP. (2015). World AIDS day: Record drop in cost of HIV treatment. United Nations Development Programme. Retrieved May 27, 2016, from http://www.undp.org/content/undp/en/home/presscenter/articles/2015/11/30/world-aids-day-record-drop-in-cost-of-hiv-treatment.html

United Nations Office on Drugs and Crime (UNODC). (2015). *World drug report.* United Nations Office on Drugs and Crime. Retrieved May 3, 2016, from https://www.unodc.org/documents/wdr2015/World_Drug_Report_2015.pdf

University of Bonn. (2008, March 26). Anxiety linked to blood clots: Fear that freezes the blood in your veins.

ScienceDaily. Retrieved from http://www.sciencedaily.com/releases/2008/03/080325111800.htm

U.S. Bureau of Labor Statistics. (2012). *Labor force statistics from the current population survey.* Washington, DC: U.S. Bureau of Labor Statistics. Retrieved from http://www.bls.gov/cps/tables.htm#charunem

U.S. Bureau of the Census. (1975). *Historical statistics of the United States: Colonial times to 1970.* Washington, DC: U.S. Department of Commerce.

U.S. Census Bureau (USCB). (2000). *Statistical abstract of the United States; 2000.* Washington, DC: U.S. Department of Commerce.

U.S. Census Bureau (USCB). (2004). *Statistical abstract of the United States; 2004.* Washington, DC: U.S. Department of Commerce.

U.S. Census Bureau (USCB). (2011a). *2010 census demographic profile summary file.* Washington, DC: U.S. Department of Commerce. Retrieved from http://www.census.gov/prod/cen2010/doc/dpsf.pdf

U.S. Census Bureau (USCB). (2011b). Infant mortality rates by race—States. *The 2010 statistical abstract.* Washington, DC: U.S. Department of Commerce.

U.S. Census Bureau (USCB). (2012). *Statistical abstract of the United States: 2011* (130th ed.). Washington, DC: U.S. Department of Commerce.

U.S. Census Bureau (UCSB). (2015). *Decennial censuses, 1890 to 1940, and current population. Survey, annual social and economic supplements, 1947 to 2015.* Figure MS-2. Median age at first marriage: 1890 to present. Retrieved February 24, 2016, from https://www.census.gov/hhes/families/files/graphics/MS-2.pdf

U.S. Department of Health and Human Services (USDHHS). (1995). *Healthy People 2000 review, 1994.* Washington, DC: U.S. Government Printing Office.

U.S. Department of Health and Human Services (USDHHS). (2001). NIH policy and guidelines on the inclusion of women and minorities as subjects in clinical research (amended). Retrieved from http://grants.nih.gov/grants/funding/women_min/guidelines_amended_10_2001.htm

U.S. Department of Health and Human Services (USDHHS). (2007). *Healthy People 2010 midcourse review.* Retrieved January 10, 2010, from http://www.healthpeople.gov/Data/midcourse

U.S. Department of Health and Human Services (USDHHS). (2008). *Physical Activity Guidelines Advisory Committee report.* Washington, DC: U.S. Department of Health and Human Services.

U.S. Department of Health and Human Services (USDHHS). (2010). *How tobacco smoke causes disease: The biology and behavioral basis for smoking-attributable disease: A Report of the Surgeon General.* Atlanta, GA: U.S. Department of Health and Human Services, Centers for Disease Control and Prevention, National Center for Chronic Disease Prevention and Health Promotion, Office on Smoking and Health.

U.S. Department of Health and Human Services (USDHHS). (2011). *Presidents Cancer Panel 2009–2010 report: American's demographic and cultural transformation: Implications for cancer.* Bethesda, MD: National Institutes of Health, National Cancer Institute.

U.S. Department of Health and Human Services (USDHHS). (2012). *Preventing tobacco use among youth and young adults. A Report of the Surgeon General.* Atlanta, GA: U.S. Department of Health and Human Services, Centers for Disease Control and Prevention, National Center for Chronic

Disease Prevention and Health Promotion, Office on Smoking and Health.

U.S. Department of Health and Human Services (USDHHS). (2014a). *The health consequences of smoking —50 years of progress. A report of the surgeon general.* Atlanta, GA: U.S. Department of Health and Human Services, Centers for Disease Control and Prevention, National Center for Chronic Disease Prevention and Health Promotion, Office on Smoking and Health.

U.S. Department of Health and Human Services (USDHHS). (2014b). *Healthy People 2020.* Retrieved August 31, 2015, from www.healthypeople.gov

U.S. Department of Health and Human Services and U.S. Department of Agriculture. (2015). *2015–2020 dietary guidelines for Americans* (8th ed.). Retrieved from http://health.gov/dietaryguidelines/2015/guidelines/

U.S. Department of Labor. (2015). *What is workplace violence? OSHA fact sheet.* Retrieved February 25, 2016, from https://www.osha.gov/OshDoc/data_General_Facts/factsheet-workplace-violence.pdf

Vaccarino, V., Johnson, B. D., Sheps, D. S., Reis, S. E., Kelsey, S. F., Bittner, V., … Bairey-Merz, C. N. (2007). Depression, inflammation, and incident cardiovascular disease in women with suspected coronary ischemia: The National Heart, Lung, and Blood Institute-sponsored WISE Study. *Journal of the American College of Cardiology, 50*(21), 2044–2050.

Van Damme, S., Crombez, G., & Eccleston, C. (2008). Coping with pain: A motivational perspective. *Pain, 139,* 1–4.

van den Hoonaard, D. K. (2009). I was the man: The challenges of masculinity in older men. In Z. D. Buchholz & S. K. Boyce (Eds.), *Masculinity: Gender roles, characteristics and coping* (pp. 69–84). New York: Nova Science.

Van De Ven, M. O. M., Engels, R. C. M., Otten, R., & Van Den Eijnden, R. J. J. (2007). A longitudinal test of the theory of planned behavior predicting smoking onset among asthmatic and non-asthmatic adolescents. *Journal of Behavioral Medicine, 30,* 435–445.

Van Houtven, C. H., Voils, C. I, Odone, E. Z., Weinfurt, K. P., Friedman, J. Y., Schulman, K. A., & Bosworth, H. B. (2005). Perceived discrimination and reported delay of pharmacy prescriptions and medical tests. *Journal of General Internal Medicine, 20*(7), 578–583.

Van Laarhoven, A. I., M., Kraaimaat, F. W., Wilder-Smith, O. H., & Evers, A. (2010). Role of attentional focus on bodily sensations in sensitivity to itch and pain. *Acta Derma Venereological, 90*(1), 46–51.

Van Leijenhorst, L., Zanolie, K., Van Meel, C. S., Westenberg, P. M., Rombouts, S. A., & Crone, E. A. (2010). What motivates the adolescent? Brain regions mediating reward sensitivity across adolescence. *Cerebral Cortex, 20*(1), 61–69.

van Ryn, M., & Burke, J. (2000). The effect of patient race and socio-economic status on physicians' perceptions of patients. *Social Science & Medicine, 50*(6), 813–828.

van Ryn, M., & Fu, S. S. (2003). Paved with good intentions: Do public health and human service providers contribute to racial/ethnic disparities in health? *American Journal of Public Health, 93*(2), 248–255.

van Stralen, M. M., De Vries, H., Mudde, A. N., Bolman, C., & Lechner, L. (2009). Determinants of initiation and maintenance of physical activity among older adults: A literature review. *Health Psychology Review, 3,* 147–207.

Vanyukov, M. M., Tarter, R. E., & Ridenour, R. A. (2012). Common liability to addiction and "gateway hypothesis": Theoretical, empirical and evolutionary perspective. *Drug and Alcohol Dependence, 123*(S1), S3–S17.

Van Zundert, R. M. P., Van Der Vorst, H., Vermulst, A. A., & Engels, R. C. (2006). Pathways to alcohol use among Dutch students in regular education and education for adolescents with behavioral problems: The role of parental alcohol use, general parenting practices, and alcohol-specific parenting practices. *Journal of Family Psychology, 20*(3), 456–467.

Varni, J. W., Setoguchi, Y., Rappaport, L. R., & Talbot, D. (1992). Psychological adjustment and perceived social support in children with congenital/acquired limb deficiencies. *Journal of Behavioral Medicine, 15*(1), 31–44.

Vedhara, K., & Irwin, M. R. (2005). *Human psychoneuroimmunology.* Oxford, UK: Oxford University Press.

Veeram Reddy, S. R., & Singh, H. R. (2010). Chest pain in children and adolescents. *Pediatrics in Review, 31,* e1–e9.

Vehof, J., Zavos, H. M., Lachance, G., Hammond, C. J., & Williams, F. M. (2014). Shared genetic factors underlie chronic pain syndromes. *Pain, 155*(8), 1562–1568.

Velicer, W. F., & Prochaska, J. O. (2008). Stages and non-stage theories of behavior and behavior change: A comment on Schwarzer. *Applied Psychology: An International Review, 57,* 75–83.

Vena, J. E., Graham, S., Zielezny, M., Swanson, M. K., Barnes, R. E., & Nolan, J. (1985). Lifetime occupational exercise and colon cancer. *American Journal of Epidemiology, 122,* 357–365.

Verstraeten, K., Vasey, M. W., Raes, F., & Bijttebier, P. (2009). Temperament and risk for depressive symptoms in adolescence: Mediation by rumination and moderation by effortful control. *Journal of Abnormal Child Psychology, 37*(3), 349–361.

Vervoort, T., Caes, L., Crombez, G., Koster, E. H. W., Van Damme, S., De Witte, M., & Goubert, L. (2011). Parental catastrophizing about children's pain and selective attention to varying levels of facial expression of pain in children: A dot-probe study. *Pain, 152,* 1751–1757.

Vervoort, T., Caes, L., Trost, Z., Notebaert, L., & Goubert, L. (2012). Parental attention to their child's pain is modulated by threat-value of pain. *Health Psychology, 31*(5), 623–631.

Vickberg, S. M. (2003). The concerns about recurrence scale (CARS): A systematic measure of women's fears about the possibility of breast cancer recurrence. *Annals of Behavioral Medicine, 25*(1), 16–24.

Vickers, A. J., & Linde, K. (2014). Acupuncture for chronic pain. *Journal of the American Medical Association, 311*(9), 955–956.

Vigil, J. M., Rowell, L. M., & Lutz, C. (2014). Gender expression, sexual orientation and pain sensitivity in women. *Pain Research and Management, 19*(2), 87–92.

Vinokur, A. D., Schul, Y., Vuori, J., & Price, R. H. (2000). Two years after a job loss: Long-term impact of the JOBS program on reemployment and mental health. *Journal of Occupational Health Psychology, 5,* 32–47.

Visich, P. S., & Fletcher, E. (2009). Myocardial infarction. In J. K. Ehrman, P. M., Gordon, P. S. Visich, & S. J. Keleyian (Eds.), *Clinical exercise physiology* (2nd ed., pp. 281–300). Champaign, IL: Human Kinetics.

Vitaliano, P. P., Zhang, J., & Scanlan, J. M. (2003). Is caregiving hazardous to one's physical health? A meta-analysis. *Psychological Bulletin, 129*(6), 946–972.

Vitiello, M. V. (2009). Recent advances in understanding sleep and sleep disturbances in older adults: Growing older does not mean sleeping poorly. *Current Directions in Psychological Science, 18,* 316–320.

Vittinghoff, E., Shlipak, M. G., Varosy, P. D., Furberg, C. D., Ireland, C. C., Khan, S. S., Blumentahl, R., Barrett-Connor, E.,

Hulley, S. (2003). Risk factors and secondary prevention in women with heart disease: The Heart and Estrogen/Progestin Replacement Study. *Annals of Internal Medicine, 13*, 81–89.

Vlachopoulos, C., Rokkas, K., Ioakeimidis, N., & Stefanadis, C. (2007). Inflammation, metabolic syndrome, erectile dysfunction, and coronary artery disease: Common links. *European Urology, 52*, 1590–1600.

Vocks, S., Tuschen-Caffier, B., Pietrowsky, R., Rustenbach, S. J., Kersting A., & Herpertz, S. (2010). Meta-analysis of the effectivenss of psychological and pharmacological treatments for binge eating disorder. *International Journal of Eating Disorder, 43*, 205–217.

von Känel, R. (2015). Acute mental stress and hemostasis: When physiology becomes vascular harm. *Thrombosis Research, 135*(S1), S52–S55.

von Känel, R., Bellingrath, S., & Kudielka, B. M. (2009). Association between longitudinal changes in depressive symptoms and plasma fibrinogen levels in school teachers. *Psychophysiology, 46*(3), 473–480.

von Känel, R., Dimsdale, J. E., Mills, P. J., Ancoli-Israel, S., Patterson, T. L., Mausbach, B. T., & Grant, I. (2006). Effect of Alzheimer caregiving stress and age on frailty markers Interleukin-6, C-reactive protein, and d-dimer. *Journals of Gerontology, Series A: Biological and Medical Sciences, 61A*, 963–969.

von Känel, R., Malan, N. T., Hamer, M., van der Westhuizen, F. H., & Malan, L. (2014). Leukocyte telomere length and hemostatic factors in a South African cohort: The SABPA Study. *Journal of Thrombosis and Haemostasis, 12*(12), 1975–1985.

Vorona, R. D., Szklo-Coxe, M., Wu, A., Dubnik, M., Zhao, Y., & Ware, J. C. (2011). Dissimilar teen crash rates in two neighboring southeastern Virginia cities with different high school start times. *Journal of Clinical Sleep Medicine, 7*(2), 145–151.

Wachholtz, A. B., & Sambamoorthi, U. (2011). National trends in prayer use as a coping mechanism for health concerns: Changes from 2002 to 2007. *Psychology of Religion and Spirituality, 3*(2), 67–77.

Wadden, T. A., Butryn, M. L., & Wilson, C. (2007). Lifestyle modification for the management of obesity. *Gastroenterology, 132*(6), 2226–2238.

Wadhwa, P. D., Entringer, S., Buss, C., & Lu, M. C. (2011). The contribution of maternal stress to preterm birth: Issues and considerations. *Clinics in Perinatology, 38*(3), 351–384.

Wager, N., Fieldman, G., & Hussey, T. (2003). The effect on ambulatory blood pressure of working under favourably and unfavourably perceived supervisors. *Occupational and Environmental Medicine, 60*(7), 468–474.

Wager, T. D., Rilling, J. K., Smith, E. E., Sololik, A., Casey, K. L., Davidson, R. J., … Cohen, J. D. (2004). Placebo-induced changes in fMRI in the anticipation and experience of pain. *Science, 303*, 1162–1167.

Wagner, J., Lacey, K., Abbott, G., de Groot, M., & Chyun, D. (2006). Knowledge of heart disease risk in a multicultural community sample of people with diabetes. *Annals of Behavioral Medicine, 31*(3), 224–230.

Wagnild, G. (2008). Resilience and depression among middle-aged and older adults. *Journal of Psychosocial Nursing and Mental Health Services, 47*(12), 28–33.

Wagnild, G. (2013). Development and use of the Resilience Scale (RS) with middle-aged and older adults. In S. Prince-Embury & D. H. Saklofske (Eds.), *Resilience in children, adolescents, and adults: Translating research into practice.* New York: Springer.

Wahner-Roedler, D. L., Vincent, A., Elking, P. L., Loehrer, L. L., Cha, S. S., & Bauer, B. A. (2006). Physicians' attitudes toward complementary and alternative medicine and their knowledge of specific therapies: A survey at an academic medical center. *Evidence-Based Complementary and Alternative Medicine, 3*(4), 495–501.

Walburn, J., Vedhara, K., Hankins, M., Rixon, L., & Weinman, J. (2009). Psychological stress and wound healing in humans: A systematic review and meta-analysis. *Journal of Psychosomatic Research, 67*(3), 253–271.

Walker, J., Holm Hansen, C., Martin, P., Sawhney, A., Thekkumpurath, P., Beale, C., … Sharpe, M. (2013). Prevalence of depression in adults with cancer: A systematic review. *Annals of Oncology, 24*(4), 895–900.

Wall, P. (2000). *Pain: The science of suffering.* New York: Columbia University Press.

Wall, T. L., Garcia-Andrade, C., Thomasson, H. R., Carr, L. G., & Ehlers, C. L. (1997). Alcohol dehydrogenase polymorphisms in Native Americans: Identification of the ADH2*3 allele. *Alcohol and Alcoholism, 32*, 129–132.

Wallace, S. P., Cochran, S. D., Durazo, E. M., & Ford, C. L. (2011). The health of aging lesbian, gay, and bisexual adults in California. *Policy Brief (UCLA Center for Health Policy Research).* Retrieved February 28, 2016, from http://www.ncbi.nlm.nih.gov/pmc/articles/PMC3698220/

Waller, G. (2006). Understanding prehospital delay behavior in acute myocardial infarction in women. *Critical Pathways in Cardiology, 5*(4), 228–234.

Walter, F., Webster, A., Scott, S., & Emery, J. (2012). The Andersen model of total patient delay: A systematic review of its application in cancer diagnosis. *Journal of Health Services Research and Policy, 17*(2), 110–118.

Walters, R. G., Jacquemont, S., Valsesia, A., de Smith, A. J., Martinet, D., Andersson, J., … Beckmann, J. S. (2010). A novel, highly penetrant form of obesity due to deletions on chromosome 16p11.2. *Nature, 463*, 671–675.

Wanberg, C. R. (2012). The individual experience of unemployment. *Annual Review of Psychology, 63*(1), 369–396.

Wang, C., Schmid, C. H., Rones, R., Kalish, R., Yinh, J., Goldenberg, D. L., Lee, M. S., & McAlindon, T. (2010). A randomized trial of tai chi for fibromyalgia. *New England Journal of Medicine, 363*, 743–754.

Wang, H., Qi, H., Wang, B. S., Cui, Y. Y., Zhu, L., Rong, Z. X., & Chen, H. Z. (2008). Is acupuncture beneficial in depression: A meta-analysis of 8 randomized controlled trials? *Journal of Affective Disorders. 111*(2–3), 125–134.

Wang, H. X., Mittleman, M. A., Leineweber, C., & Orth-Gomer, K. (2008). Depressive symptoms, social isolation, and progression of coronary artery atherosclerosis: The Stockholm Female Coronary Angiography Study. *Psychotherapy and Psychosomatics, 75*, 96–102.

Wang, J. L., Lesage, A., Schmitz, N., & Drapeau, A. (2008). The relationship between work stress and mental disorders in men and women: Findings from a population-based study. *Journal of Epidemiology and Community Health, 62*, 42–47.

Wang, X., Cai, L., Qian, J., & Peng, J. (2014). Social support moderates stress effects on depression. *International Journal of Mental Health Systems, 8*, 41–46.

Wansink, B. (2011). Modifying the food environment: From mindless eating to mindlessly eating better. Washington, DC: *Annual Meeting of the American Psychological Association,* August 5, 2011.

Wansink, B., van Ittersum, K., & Painter, J. E. (2006). Ice cream illusions: Bowls, spoons, and self-served portion sizes. *American Journal of Preventive Medicine, 31*, 240–243.

Ward, B. W., Schiller, J. S., & Goodman, R. A. (2014). Multiple chronic conditions among U.S. adults: A 2012 update. *Preventing Chronic Disease, 11*. Retrieved from http://www.cdc.gov/pcd/issues/2014/pdf/13_0389.pdf

Wardle, J., Parmenter, K., & Waller, J. (2000). Nutrition knowledge and food intake. *Appetite, 34*(3), 269–275.

Wardle, J., Robb, K. A., Johnson, F., Griffith, J., Brunner, E., Power, C., & Tovee, M. (2004). Socioeconomic variation in attitudes to eating and weight in female adolescents. *Health Psychology, 23*(3), 275–282.

Warwick-Evans, L. A., Masters, I. J., & Redstone, S. B. (1991). A double-blind placebo controlled evaluation of acupressure in the treatment of motion sickness. *Aviation, Space, and Environmental Medicine, 62*, 776–778.

Waterhouse, J. (1993). Circadian rhythms. *British Medical Journal, 306*, 448–451.

Watkins, L. R., Hutchinson, M. R., Ledeboer, A., Wieseler-Frank, J., Milligan, E. D., & Maier, S. F. (2007). Glia as the "bad guys": Implications for improving clinical pain control and the clinical utility of opioids. *Brain, Behavior and Immunity, 21*, 131–146.

Way, B. M., Creswell, J. D., Eisenberger, N. I., & Lieberman, M. (2010). Dispositional mindfulness and depressive symptomatology: Correlations with limbic and self-referential neural activity during rest. *Emotion, 10*(1), 12–24.

Wearing, D. (2005, January 12). The man who keeps falling in love with his wife. *The Daily Telegraph*. Retrieved March 19, 2016, from http://www.telegraph.co.uk/news/health/3313452/The-man-who-keeps-falling-in-love-with-his-wife.html

Webb, H. E., Garten, R. S., McMinn, D. R., Beckman, J. L., Kamimori, G. H., & Acevedo, E. O. (2011). Stress hormones and vascular function in firefighters during concurrent challenges. *Biological Psychology, 87*, 152–160.

Wechsler, H., & Nelson, T. F. (2008). What we have learned from the Harvard School of Public Health College Alcohol Study: Focusing attention on college student alcohol consumption and the environmental conditions that promote it. *Journal of Studies on Alcohol and Drugs, 69*(4), 481–490.

Wehunt, J. (2009, July). The "food desert." *Chicago Magazine*. Retrieved March 8, 2010, from http://www.chicagomag.com/Chicago-Magazine/July-2009/The-Food-Desert

Weil, A. (1998). *Eight weeks to optimum health*. New York: Random House.

Weiland, B. J., Thayer, R. E., Depue, B. E., Sabbineni, A., Bryan, A. D., & Hutchinson, K. E. (2015). Daily marijuana use is not associated with brain morphometric measures in adolescents or adults. *The Journal of Neuroscience, 35*(4), 1505–1512.

Weinberg, R. S., & Gould, D. (2015). *Foundations of sport and exercise psychology* (6th ed.). Champaign, IL: Human Kinetics.

Weinberger, D. A., Schwartz, G. E., & Davidson, R. J. (1979). Low-anxious, high-anxious, and repressive coping styles: Psychometric patterns and behavioral and physiological responses to stress. *Journal of Abnormal Psychology, 88*, 369–380.

Weingart, S. N., Pagovich, O., Sands, D. Z., Li, J. M., Aronson, M. D., Davis, R. B., … Bates, D. W. (2006). Patient-reported service quality on a medicine unit. *International Journal for Quality in Health Care, 18*, 95–101.

Weinreb, E. (2013, January 9). How Walmart associations put the "U" and "I" into sustainability. *GreenBiz*. Retrieved February 25, 2016, from https://www.greenbiz.com/blog/2013/01/09/walmart-associates-u-i-sustainability

Weinstein, N. D. (1982). Unrealistic optimism about susceptibility to health problems. *Journal of Behavioral Medicine, 5*(4), 441–460.

Weir, K. (2012). Big kids. *Monitor on Psychology, 43*(11), 58–63.

Weisli, P., Schmid, C., Kerwer, O., Nigg-Koch, C., Klaghofer, R., & Seifert, B. (2005). Acute psychological stress affects glucose concentrations in patients with Type I diabetes following food intake but not in the fasting state. *Diabetes Care, 28*, 1910–1915.

Weiss, A. J., & Elixhauser, A. (2014). Overview of hospital stays in the United States, 2012. *Healthcare Cost and Utilization Project. Statistical Brief No. 180*. Rockville, MD: Agency for Healthcare Research and Quality. Retrieved from http://www.hcup-us.ahrq.gov/reports/statbriefs/sb180-Hospitalizations-United-States-2012.pdf

Weitz, R. (2007). *The sociology of health, illness, and health care: A critical approach* (4th ed.). Belmont, CA: Wadsworth.

Weitzman, E. R., Ziemnik, R. E., Huang, Q., & Levy, S. (2015). Alcohol and marijuana use and treatment nonadherence among medically vulnerable youth. *Pediatrics, 136*(3). Retrieved from http://pediatrics.aappublications.org/content/136/3/450

Well Men and Women Too. (2016). The complete health program. Retrieved April 7, 2016, from http://www.wellmen.com.au/site%20map.htm

Wertheim, E. H., & Paxton, S. J. (2011). Body image development in adolescent girls. In T. F. Cash & T. Pruzinsky (Eds.), *Body image: A handbook of theory, research, and clinical practice* (2nd ed., pp. 76–84). New York: The Guilford Press.

Wenze, S. J., & Miller, I. W. (2010). Use of ecological momentary assessment in mood disorders research. *Clinical Psychology Review, 30*(6), 794–804.

Werner, E. (1997). Endangered childhood in modern times: Protective factors. *Vierteljahresschrift für Heilpädagogik und ihre Nachbargebiete, 66*, 192–203.

Wesley, J. (2003). *Primitive physic: An easy and natural method of curing most diseases*. Eugene, OR: Wipf and Stock Publishers.

Wetter, D. W., Fiore, M. C., Baker, T. B., & Young, T. B. (1995). Tobacco withdrawal and nicotine replacement influence objective measures of sleep. *Journal of Consulting and Clinical Psychology, 63*, 658–667.

Whetten, K., Reif, S., Whetten, R., & Murphy-McMillan, L. K. (2008). Trauma, mental health, distrust, and stigma among HIV-positive persons: Implications for effective care. *Psychosomatic Medicine, 70*, 531–538.

White, H. R., Labouvie, E. W., & Papadaratsakis, V. (2005). Changes in substance use during the transition to adulthood: A comparison of college students and their noncollege-age peers. *Journal of Drug Issues, 35*(2), 281–305.

Whitehead, D. L., Perkins-Porras, L., Strike, P. C., Magid, K., & Steptoe, A. (2007). Cortisol awakening response is elevated in acute coronary syndrome patients with Type D personality. *Journal of Psychosomatic Research, 62*, 419–425.

Whiting, P. F., Wolff, R. F., Deshpande, S., Di Nisio, M., Duffy, S., Hernandez, A. V., … Kleijnen, J. (2015). Cannabinoids for medical use: A systematic review and meta-analysis. *Journal of the American Medical Association, 313*(24), 2456–2473.

Wideman, T. H., & Sullivan, M. J. (2011). Reducing catastrophic thinking associated with pain. *Pain Management, 1*(3), 249–256.

Wiech, K., Farias, M., Kahane, G., Shackel, N., Tiede, W., & Tracey, I. (2008a). An fMRI study measuring analgesia enhanced by religion as a belief system. *Pain, 139*, 467–476.

Wiech, K., Ploner, M., & Tracey, I. (2008b). Neurocognitive aspects of pain perception. *Trends in Cognitive Sciences, 12*, 306–313.

Wilcox, S., & Storandt, M. (1996). Relations among age, exercise, and psychological variables in a community sample of women. *Health Psychology, 15*(2), 110–113.

Wilcox, V. L., Kasl, S. V., & Berkman, L. F. (1994). Social support and physical disability in older people after hospitalization: A prospective study. *Health Psychology, 13*, 170–179.

Wilkinson, P., & Goodyer, I. (2011). Non-suicidal self-injury. *European Child and Adolescent Psychiatry, 20*, 103–108.

Willeit, P., Willeit, J., Brandstatter, A., Ehrlenbach, S., Mayr, A., Gasperi, A., … Kiechl, S. (2010). Cellular aging reflected by leukocyte telomere length predicts advanced atherosclerosis and cardiovascular disease risk. *Arteriosclerosis, Thrombosis, and Vascular Biology, 30*, 1649–1656.

Williams, A. C., Eccleston, C., & Morley, S. (2012). Psychological therapies for the management of chronic pain (excluding headache) in adults. *The Cochrane Database of Systematic Reviews.*

Williams, D. A. (1996). Acute pain management. In R. Gatchel & D. C. Turk (Eds.), *Psychological approaches to pain management: A practitioner's handbook* (pp. 55–77). New York: Guilford.

Williams, D. R. (2003). The health of men: Structured inequalities and opportunities. *American Journal of Public Health, 93*(5), 7.

Williams, D. S. (2000). Racism and mental health: The African American experience. *Ethnicity & Health, 5*(3–4), 243–268.

Williams, J. E., Paton, C. C., Siegler, I. C., Eigenbrot, M. L., Nieto, F. J., & Tyroler, H. A. (2000). Clinical investigation and reports: Anger proneness predicts coronary heart disease risk: Prospective analysis from the Atherosclerosis Risk in Communities (ARIC) Study. *Circulation, 101*, 2034–2039.

Williams, L. J., Jacka, F. N., Pasco, J. A., Dodd, S., & Berk, M. (2006). Depression and pain: An overview. *Acta Neuropsychiatrica, 18*, 79–87.

Williams, M. V., Parker, R. M., Baker, D. W., Parikh, N. S., Pitkin, K., Coates, W. C., & Nurss, J. R. (1995). Inadequate functional health literacy among patients at two public hospitals. *Journal of the American Medical Association, 21*, 1677–1682.

Williams, R. B. (2001). Hostility (and other psychosocial risk factors): Effects on health and the potential for successful behavioral approaches to prevention and treatment. In A. Baum, T. A. Revenson, & J. E. Singer (Eds.), *Handbook of health psychology* (pp. 661–668). Mahwah, NJ: Erlbaum.

Williams, R. B., & Williams, V. (1994). *Anger kills: Seventeen strategies for controlling the hostility that can harm your health* (pp. 5–11). New York: Harper Perennial.

Wilson, G. T., Grilo, C. M., & Vitousek, K. M. (2007). Psychological treatment of eating disorders. *American Psychologist, 62*(3), 199–216.

Windle, G., Hughes, D., Linck., P., Russell, I., & Woods, B. (2010). Is exercise effective in promoting mental well-being in older age? A systematic review. *Aging and Mental Health, 14*, 652–669.

Windle, M., & Windle, R. C. (2001). Depressive symptoms and cigarette smoking among middle adolescents: Prospective associations and intrapersonal and interpersonal influences. *Journal of Consulting and Clinical Psychology, 69*, 215–226.

Winerman, L. (2006). Brain, heal thyself. *Monitor on Psychology, 37*(1), 56–57.

Winett, R. A. (1995). A framework for health promotion and disease prevention programs. *American Psychology, 50*(5), 341–350.

Wing, R. R., & Jeffery, R. W. (1999). Benefits of recruiting participants with friends and increasing social support for weight loss and maintenance. *Journal of Consulting and Clinical Psychology, 67*(1), 132–138.

Winhusen, T., Kropp, F., Babcock, D., Hague, D., Erickson, S. J., Renz, C., Rau, L., Lewis, D., Leimberger, J., & Somoza, E. (2008). Motivational enhancement therapy to improve treatment utilization and outcome in pregnant substance users. *Journal of Substance Abuse Treatment, 35*, 161–173.

Winter, L., Lawton, M., Langston, C., Ruckdeschel, K., & Sando, R. (2007). Symptoms, affects, and self-rated health. *Journal of Aging and Health, 19*(3), 453–569.

Winterling, J., Glimelius, B., & Nordin, K. (2008). The importance of expectations on the recovery period after cancer treatment. *Psycho-Oncology, 17*, 190–198.

Wipfli, B. M., Rethorst, C. D., & Landers, D. M. (2008). The anxiolytic effects of exercise: A meta-analysis of randomized trials and dose-response analysis. *Journal of Sport and Exercise Psychology, 30*(4), 392–410.

Witteman, J., Post, H., Tarvainen, M., de Bruijn, A., Perna, E., Ramaekers, J. G., & Weirs, R. W. (2015). Cue reactivity and its relation to craving and relapse in alcohol dependence: A combined laboratory and field study. *Psychopharmacology, 232*(20), 3685–3696.

Wolff, B., Burns, J. W., Quartana, P. J., Lofland, K., Bruehl, S., & Chung, O. Y. (2008). Pain catastrophizing, physiological indexes, and chronic pain severity: Tests of mediation and moderation models. *Journal of Behavioral Medicine, 31*, 105–114.

Wolin, S. (1993). *The resilient self: How survivors of troubled families rise above adversity*. New York: Villard Books.

Women's Health Initiative (WHI). (2010). Women's health initiative update. Retrieved from http://www.nhlbi.nih.gov/whi/update.htm

Women's Health Initiative (WHI). (2015). Publications overview. Retrieved June 28, 2016, from https://www.whi.org/researchers/bibliography/SitePages/Home.aspx

Wonderlich, S. A., Joiner, Jr., T. E., Keel, P. K., Williamson, D. A., & Crosby, R. D. (2007). Eating disorder diagnoses: Empirical approaches to classification. *American Psychologist, 62*, 167–180.

Wonderlich, S. A., Klein, M. H., & Council, J. R. (1996). Relationship of social perceptions and self-concept in bulimia nervosa. *Journal of Consulting and Clinical Psychology, 64*, 1231–1237.

Wong, C. A. (2009). Advances in labor analgesia. *International Journal of Women's Health, 1*, 139–154.

Wong, L. P. (2008). Focus group discussion: A tool for health and medical research. *Singapore Medical Journal, 49*(3), 256–260.

Wood, J. H. (1983). *Neurobiology of cerebrospinal fluid 2*. New York: Plenum Press.

Wood, S. (2012). Resveratrol scientists react to fraud scandal. *Medscape*. Retrieved February 23, 2016, from http://www.medscape.com/viewarticle/756905

Worden, J., & Flynn, B. (1999). Multimedia-TV: Shock to stop? *British Medical Journal, 318*, 64.

World Bank. (2015). Life expectancy at birth, total (years). Retrieved February 23, 2016, from http://data.worldbank.org/indicator/SP.DYN.LE00.IN

World Health Organization (WHO). (2000a). *The world health report, 2000*. Geneva, Switzerland: Author.

World Health Organization (WHO). (2000b). *The world health report. Health systems: Improving performance*. Geneva, Switzerland: Author.

World Health Organization (WHO). (2006). *The world health report 2006: Working together for health*. Geneva, Switzerland: Author.

World Health Organization (WHO). (2008). *WHO report on the global tobacco epidemic, 2008*. Geneva, Switzerland: Author.

World Health Organization (WHO). (2010a). *ATLAS on substance abuse: Resources for the prevention and treatment of substance abuse disorders*. Geneva, Switzerland: Author.

World Health Organization (WHO). (2010b). *Diabetes programme*. Geneva, Switzerland: Author.

World Health Organization (WHO). (2010c). *The global burden of chronic disease*. Geneva, Switzerland: Author. Retrieved February 2, 2010, from http://www.who.int/nutrition/topics/2_background/en/index.html

World Health Organization (WHO). (2010d). *Global recommendations on physical activity for health*. Geneva, Switzerland: Author.

World Health Organization (WHO). (2011a, May). The 10 leading causes of death by broad income group, 2008. *Fact sheet no. 310*. Retrieved from http://www.who.int/mediacentre/factsheets/fs310_2008.pdf

World Health Organization (WHO). (2011b). *Suicide prevention*. Geneva, Switzerland: Author. Retrieved from http://www.who.int/mental_health/prevention/suicide/suicideprevent/en

World Health Organization (WHO). (2012). *Violence and injury prevention fact sheets*. Geneva, Switzerland: Author. Retrieved from http://www.who.int/violence_injury_prevention/violence/world_report/factsheets/en/index.html

World Health Organization (WHO). (2013a). *Acupuncture: Review and analysis of reports on controlled clinical trials*. Retrieved from http://apps.who.int/medicinedocs/pdf/s4926e/s4926e.pdf

World Health Organization (WHO). (2013b). *Global action plan for the prevention and control of noncommunicable diseases 2013–2020*. Geneva, Switzerland: Author. Retrieved April 16, 2016, from http://apps.who.int/iris/bitstream/10665/94384/1/9789241506236_eng.pdf

World Health Organization (WHO). (2013c). The top 10 causes of death. *Fact sheet no. 310*. Retrieved from http://www.who.int/mediacentre/factsheets/fs310/en

World Health Organization (WHO). (2014). *Global tuberculosis report 2014*. Geneva, Switzerland: Author. Retrieved February 28, 2016, from http://apps.who.int/iris/bitstream/10665/137094/1/9789241564809_eng.pdf

World Health Organization (WHO). (2014, May). The top 10 causes of death, 2012. *Fact sheet no. 310*. Retrieved from http://www.who.int/mediacentre/factsheets/fs310/en/

World Health Organization (WHO). (2015a). Cardiovascular disease. *Fact sheet no. 317*. Retrieved from http://www.who.int/mediacentre/factsheets/fs317/en/

World Health Organization (WHO). (2015b). *Deaths from NCDs*. Geneva, Switzerland: Author. Retrieved February 28, 2016, from http://www.who.int/gho/ncd/mortality_morbidity/ncd_total_text/en/

World Health Organization (WHO). (2015c). HIV/AIDS. *Fact sheet no. 360*. Retrieved from http://www.who.int/mediacentre/factsheets/fs360/en/#

World Health Organization (WHO). (2015d). *Life expectancy*. Geneva, Switzerland: Author. Retrieved from http://www.who.int/gho/mortality_burden_disease/life_tables/situation_trends/en/

World Health Organization (WHO). (2015e). *Maximizing the treatment and prevention potential of antiretroviral drugs: Early country experiences towards implementing a treat-all policy*. Geneva, Switzerland: Author. Retrieved from http://www.who.int/hiv/en/

World Health Organization (WHO). (2015f). Noncommunicable diseases. *Fact sheet no. 355*. World Health Organization Media Centre. Retrieved February 23, 2016, from http://www.who.int/mediacentre/factsheets/fs355/en/

World Health Organization (WHO). (2015g). Obesity and overweight. *Fact sheet no. 311*. Retrieved from http://www.who.int/mediacentre/factsheets/fs311/en/

World Health Organization (WHO). (2015h). Physical activity. *Fact sheet no. 385*. World Health Organization Media Centre. Retrieved from http://www.who.int/mediacentre/factsheets/fs385/en/

World Health Organization (WHO). (2015i). *World health statistics, 2015*. Geneva, Switzerland: Author. Retrieved February 26, 2015, from http://www.who.int/gho/publications/world_health_statistics/2015/en/

World Health Organization (WHO). (2016a). 10 facts on HIV/AIDS. Retrieved February 28, 2016, from http://www.who.int/features/factfiles/hiv/en/#

World Health Organization (WHO). (2016b). Ebola virus disease. *Fact sheet no. 103*. Retrieved from http://www.who.int/mediacentre/factsheets/fs103/en/

World Health Organization (WHO). (2016c). Global Health Observatory data repository: Life expectancy. Retrieved April 16, 2016, from http://apps.who.int/gho/data/node.main.688

Worobey, M., Telfer, P., Souquiere, S., Hunter, M., Coleman, C. A., Metzger, M. J., … Marx, P. A. (2010). Island biogeography reveals the deep history of SIV. *Science, 329*, 1487.

Wrosch, C., Schulz, R., Miller, G. E., Lupien, S., & Dunne, E. (2007). Physical health problems, depressive mood, and cortisol secretion in old age: Buffer effects of health engagement control strategies. *Health Psychology, 26*, 341–349.

Wu, J. (2015, July 6). Dignity declared, yet still denied. *The Huffington Post*. Retrieved February 24, 2016, from http://www.huffingtonpost.com/janson-wu/dignity-declared-yet-stil-denied_b_7701954.html

Wu, S., Cohen, D., Shi, Y., Pearson, M., & Sturm, R. (2011). Economic analysis of physical activity interventions. *American Journal of Preventive Medicine, 40*(2), 149–158.

Wulsin, L. R., & Singal, B. M. (2003). Do depressive symptoms increase the risk for the onset of coronary disease? A systematic quantitative review. *Psychosomatic Medicine, 65*, 201–210.

Wyszynski, C. M., Bricker, J. B., & Comstock, B. A. (2011). Parental smoking cessation and child daily smoking: A 9-year longitudinal study of mediation by child cognitions about smoking. *Health Psychology, 30*(2), 171–176.

Xu, H., Xiao, T., Chen, C.-H., Li, W., Meyer, C. A., Wu, Q., … Liu, S. X. (2015). Sequence determinants of improved CRISPR sgRNA design. *Genome Research, 25*(8), 1147–1157.

Xu, J. Q., Kochanek, K. D., Murphy, S. L., & Tejada-Vera, B. (2007). *National vital statistics reports web release*. Hyattsville, MD: National Center for Health Statistics. Released May 2010.

Xu, J. Q., Murphy, S. L., Kochanek, K. D., & Bastian, B. A. (2016). Deaths: Final data for 2013. *National Vital Statistics Reports, 64*(2). Hyattsville, MD: National Center for Health Statistics.

Yamamoto, Y., Hayashino, Y., Akiba, T., Akizawa, T., Akira, S., Kurokawa, K., & Fukuhara, S. (2010). Depressive symptoms predict the subsequent risk of bodily pain in dialysis patients: Japan dialysis outcomes and practice patterns study. *Pain Medicine, 10*(5), 883–889.

Yanez, B., Stanton, A. L., & Maly, R. C. (2012). Breast cancer treatment decision making among Latinas and non-Latina whites: A communication model predicting decisional outcomes and quality of life. *Health Psychology, 31*(5), 552–561.

Yang, L., & Colditz, G. A. (2015). Prevalence of overweight and obesity in the United States, 2007–2012. *Journal of the American Medical Association Internal Medicine, 175*(8), 1412–1413.

Yang, S. (2010). Racial disparities in training, pay-raise attainment, and income. *Research in Social Stratification and Mobility, 25*(4), 323–335.

Yano, Y., Stamler, J., Garside, D. B., Daviglus, M. L., Franklin, S. S., Carnethon, M. R., … Lloyd-Jones, D. M. (2015). Isolated systolic hypertension in young and middle-aged adults and 31-year risk for cardiovascular mortality: The Chicago Heart Association Detection Project in Industry Study. *Journal of the American College of Cardiology, 65*(4), 327–335.

Yau, P. L., Castro, M. G., Tagani, A., Tsui, W. H., & Convit, A. (2012). Obesity and metabolic syndrome and functional and structural brain impairments in adolescence. *Pediatrics, 130*(4), 856–864.

Yeh, E. S., Rochette, L. M., McKenzie, L. B., & Smith, G. A. (2011). Injuries associated with cribs, playpens, and bassinets among young children in the U.S., 1990–2008. *Pediatrics, 127*, 479–486.

Yeh, M.-C., Viladrich, A., Bruning, N., & Roye, C. (2009). Determinants of Latina obesity in the United States. *Journal of Transcultural Nursing, 20*(1), 105–115.

Yehuda, R. (2000). Biology of posttraumatic stress disorder. *Journal of Clinical Psychiatry, 61*(7), 14–21.

Yeo, M., Berzins, S., & Addington, D. (2007). Development of an early psychosis public education program using the precede/proceed model. *Health Education Research, 22*(5), 639–647.

Yohannes, A. M., Yalfani, A., Doherty, P., & Bundy, C. (2007). Predictors of drop-out from an outpatient cardiac rehabilitation programme. *Clinical Rehabilitation, 21*(3), 222–229.

Yoo, G., Aviv, C., Levine, E., Ewing, C., & Au, A. (2010). Emotion work: Disclosing cancer. *Supportive Care in Cancer, 18*(2), 205–213.

Yoon, S. S., Fryar, C. D., & Carroll, M. D. (2015). Hypertension prevalence and control among adults: United States 2011–2014. *NCHS data brief, no. 220.* Hyattsville, MD: National Center for Health Statistics.

Yoshimoto, K., Fukuda, F., Hori, M., Kato, B., Kato, H., Hattori, H., Tokuda, N., Kuriyama, K., Yano, T., & Yasuhara, M. (2006). Acupuncture stimulates the release of serotonin, but not dopamine, in the rat nucleus accumbens. *Tohoku Journal of Experimental Medicine, 208*(4), 321–326.

Youth Risk Behavior Surveillance System (YRBSS). (2013). Adolescent and school health: Youth Risk Behavior Surveillance System. Centers for Disease Control and Prevention. Retrieved from http://www.cdc.gov/HealthyYouth/yrbs/index.htm

Yudkin, P., Hey, K., Roberts, S., Welch, S., Murphy, M., & Walton, R. (2003). Abstinence from smoking eight years after participation in randomized controlled trial of nicotine patch. *British Medical Journal, 327*(7405), 28–29.

Yusuf, S., Hawken, S., Ounpuu, S., Dans, T., Avezum, A., Lanas, F., … INTERHEART Study Investigators. (2004). Effect of potentially modifiable risk factors associated with myocardial infarction in 52 countries (the INTERHEART study): Case-control study. *The Lancet, 364*(9438), 937–952.

Zachariae, R., & O'Toole, M. S. (2015). The effect of expressive writing intervention on psychological and physical health outcomes in cancer patients—A systematic review and meta-analysis. *Psycho-Oncology, 24*(11), 1349–1359.

Zakhari, S. (2006). Overview: How is alcohol metabolized by the body? *Alcohol Research and Health, 29*, 245–255.

Zangl, H. A., Mowinckel, P., Finset, A., Eriksson, L. R., Hoystad, T. O., Lunde, A. K., & Hagen, K. B. (2011). A mindfulness-based group intervention to reduce psychological distress and fatigue in patients with inflammatory rheumatic joint diseases: A randomized controlled trial. *Annals of the Rheumatic Diseases, 71*(6), 911–917.

Zanstra, Y. J., Schellekens, J. M. H., Schaap, C., & Kooistra, L. (2006). Vagal and sympathetic activity burnouts during a mentally demanding workday. *Psychosomatic Medicine, 68*, 583–590.

Zeevi, D., Korem, T., Zmora, N., Israeli, D., Rothschild, D., Weinberger, A., … Segal, E. (2015). Personalized nutrition by prediction of glycemic responses. *Cell, 163*(5), 1079–1094.

Zeidan, F. (2014). Quoted in Steiner, B., Treating chronic pain with meditation. *The Atlantic*, 2014, April 1.

Zeidan, F., Gordon, N. S., Merchant, J., & Goolkasian, P. (2009). The effect of brief mindfulness training on experimentally induced pain. *The Journal of Pain, 11*(3), 199–209.

Zeidan, F., Martucci, K. T., Kraft, R. A., Gordon, N. S., McHaffie, J. G., & Coghill, R. (2011). Brain mechanisms supporting the modulation of pain by mindfulness meditation. *Journal of Neuroscience, 31*(14), 5540–5548.

Zen, A. L., Whooley, M. A., Zhao, S., & Cohen, B. E. (2012). Post-traumatic stress disorder is associated with poor health behaviors: Findings from the Heart and Soul Study. *Health Psychology, 31*(2), 194–201.

Zepf, B. (2005). Lifestyle changes most effective in preventing diabetes. *American Family Physician, 65*(11), 2338–2448.

Zhang, T. Y., Hellstrom, I. C., Bagot, R. C., Wen, X. Z., Diorio, J., & Meaney, M. J. (2010). Maternal care and DNA methylation of a glutamic acid decarboxylase 12 promoter in rat hippocampus. *Journal of Neuroscience, 30*, 13130–13137.

Zhang, Y., Proenca, R., Maffei, M., & Barone, M. (1994). Positional cloning of the mouse obese gene and its human analogue. *Nature, 372*, 425–432.

Zhou, C., Wu, Y., An, S., & Li, X. (2015). Effect of expressive writing intervention on health outcomes in breast cancer patients: A systematic review and meta-analysis of randomized controlled trials. *PLOS ONE, 10*(7). Retrieved from http://journals.plos.org/plosone/article?id=10.1371/journal.pone.0131802

Zhou, E. S., Penedo, F. J., Lewis, J. E., Rasheed, M., Traeger, L., Lechner, S., … Antoni, M. H. (2010). Perceived stress mediates the effects of social support on health-related quality of life among men treated for localized prostate cancer. *Journal of Psychosomatic Research, 69*, 587–590.

Zijlstra, G. A., van Haastregt, J. C., van Rossum, E., van Eijk, J. T., Yardley, L., & Kempen, G. I. (2007). Interventions to reduce fear of falling in community-living older people: A systematic review. *Journal of the American Geriatrics Society, 55*(4), 603–615.

Zisook, S., Shuchter, S. R., Irwin, M., Darko, D. F., Sledge, P., & Resovsky, K. (1994). Bereavement, depression, and immune function. *Psychiatry Research, 52*, 1–10.

Zisser, H., Sueyoshi, M., Krigstein, K., Sziglato, A., & Riddell, M. C. (2012). Advances in exercise, physical activity, and diabetes mellitus. *International Journal of Clinical Practice, 66*(s175), 62–71.

Ziv, S. (2015, February 10). Andrew Wakefield, father of the anti-vaccine movement, responds to the current measles outbreak for the first time. *Newsweek*. Retrieved March 2, 2016, from http://www.newsweek.com/2015/02/20/andrew-wakefield-father-anti-vaccine-movement-sticks-his-story-305836.html

Zoccola, P. M., Dickerson, S. S., & Lam, S. (2009). Rumination predicts longer sleep onset latency after an acute psychosocial stressor. *Psychosomatic Medicine, 71*, 771–775.

Zuger, A. (1998, March 24). At the hospital, a new doctor is in. *The New York Times*, p. B19.

Name Index

Subject Index

Note: Page numbers followed by f indicate figures; those followed by t indicate tables.